LION OF THE LORD

LION OF THE LORD

ESSAYS ON THE LIFE & SERVICE OF BRIGHAM YOUNG

SUSAN EASTON BLACK
& LARRY C. PORTER

DESERET BOOK COMPANY
SALT LAKE CITY, UTAH

Library of Congress Cataloging-in-Publication Data

Lion of the Lord : essays on the life and service of Brigham Young / edited by Susan Easton Black and Larry C. Porter.

p. cm.

Includes bibliographical references and index.

ISBN 1-57345-112-6 (hbk.)

1. Young, Brigham, 1801–1877. 2. Church of Jesus Christ of Latter-day Saints—Presidents—Biography. 3. Mormon Church—Presidents—Biography. I. Black, Susan Easton. II. Porter, Larry C.

BX8695.Y7L56 1996

289.3'092—dc20

[B] 95-42591

CIP

Printed in the United States of America

10 9 8 7 6 5 4 3 2 1

CONTENTS

INTRODUCTION

Few leaders of the nineteenth century match the caliber and dogged determination of Brigham Young, the Lion of the Lord. From humble beginnings in an obscure village in Vermont, he rose to the applause of thinking people, but more important, he grew in favor with God. Although most would contend that the arduous toils of farm labor and unwelcome poverty dominated his early years, it was nevertheless his unwavering search for eternal truth that permeated his thoughts.

Reading the Book of Mormon, listening to missionaries, and baptism brought answers to his search:

> When I saw a man without eloquence, or talents for public speaking, who could only say, "I know, by the power of the Holy Ghost, that the Book of Mormon is true, that Joseph Smith is a Prophet of the Lord," the Holy Ghost proceeding from that individual illuminated my understanding, and light, glory, and immortality were before me.[1]

Anxious to learn more about his new religion, Brigham Young journeyed to Kirtland to meet the Prophet Joseph Smith. "When I went to Kirtland I had not a coat in the world," he wrote, "neither had I a shoe to my feet, and I had to borrow a pair of pants and a pair of boots."[2] Of his initial meeting with Joseph Smith he recalled:

> Here my joy was full at the privilege of shaking the hand of the Prophet of God, and [I received] the sure testimony, by the Spirit of prophecy, that he was all that any man could believe him to be as a true Prophet.[3]

On 14 February 1835 Brigham Young was ordained a member

of the Quorum of the Twelve Apostles. As an Apostle he was zealous in defense of the Prophet. One evening in Kirtland, overhearing a man loudly rail against Joseph Smith, "Woe! woe! unto the inhabitants of this place," Brigham Young reacted:

> [I] put my pants and shoes on, took my cowhide, went out, and laying hold on him, jerked him round, and assured him that if he did not stop his noise and let the people enjoy their sleep without interruption, I would cowhide him on the spot, for we had the Lord's Prophet right here, and we did not want the Devil's prophet yelling round the streets.[4]

To the faithful, Brigham Young was a compassionate friend. As he witnessed Mary Pitt, an Englishwoman who had suffered from crippling arthritis for eleven years, being carried on a litter to her baptism, he pronounced a healing blessing: "[I] rebuked her lameness in the name of the Lord, and commanded her to arise and walk. The lameness left her, and she never afterwards used a staff or crutch."[5] Brigham Young marveled at the miraculous healing and the thousands of converts in the British Isles who embraced the gospel:

> It truly seemed a miracle. . . . We landed in the spring of 1840, as strangers in a strange land and penniless. But through the mercy of God we have gained many friends, established Churches . . . and have left sown in the hearts of many thousands the seeds of eternal truth.[6]

The darkest day of his life was on 27 June 1844, the day of the martyrdom of Joseph Smith:

> Spent the day in Boston with brother Woodruff. . . . In the evening, while sitting in the depot waiting, I felt a heavy depression of Spirit, and so melancholy I could not converse with any degree of pleasure. . . . I could not assign my reasons for my peculiar feelings.[7]

Twelve days later he learned of the tragic deaths of the Prophet Joseph and his brother Hyrum:

> The first thing which I thought of was, whether Joseph had taken the keys of the kingdom with him from the earth. . . . Bringing my hand down on my knee, I said the keys of the kingdom are right here with the Church.[8]

With renewed conviction he returned to Nauvoo and resolutely declared, "The Twelve are appointed by the finger of God . . . an independent body who have the keys of the priesthood—the keys of the kingdom of God to deliver to all the world."[9] The authority of the Twelve was challenged on 8 August 1844 by Sidney Rigdon. Characteristically, Brigham Young met the challenge with unrelenting steadfastness, and as he spoke before an assembled multitude, he seemed to take on the physical stature and speech of the Prophet Joseph Smith. William C. Staines wrote, "I thought it was he and so did thousands who heard it."[10]

Determined to carry forward the plans of Joseph Smith, Brigham Young encouraged the completion of the Nauvoo Temple. "We want to build the Temple in this place," he said, "if we have to build it as the Jews built the walls of the Temple in Jerusalem, with a sword in one hand and the trowel in the other."[11] Yet as the temple neared completion, threatened violence became unrestrained, and a forced exodus was imminent.

In February 1846 Brigham Young cried, "Flee Babylon by land or by sea." Immediately thousands of obedient Saints responded and fled from the comforts of Nauvoo to the rigors of Iowa's wilderness. Their sacrifice and suffering from the loess hills of Iowa to the trek across the barren plains of Nebraska through the rigors of the Rockies marked a historic migration of magnificent proportions.

"This is the right place, drive on," Brigham Young said on 24 July 1847 as he looked over the semiarid desert of the Great Salt Lake Valley.[12] These words were echoed in correspondence to Charles C. Rich: "Let all the brethren and Sisters cheer up their hearts, and know assuredly that God has heard and answered their prayers and ours, and led us to a goodly land."[13]

Intending to guide additional Saints to their new home in the Rockies, Brigham Young returned to the bluffs of the Missouri River. There, in Kanesville, Iowa, he was sustained in December 1847 as prophet and President of The Church of Jesus Christ of Latter-day Saints, fulfilling the prophecy given by Joseph Smith many years before in Kirtland: "The time will come when Brigham Young will preside over this church."[14]

President Young served faithfully for thirty years. His contributions to the church and kingdom of God are immeasurable. As president he faced multiple problems of emigration, settling, and religious persecution. Yet he never swerved in his conviction to the faith. "We have been kicked out of the frying-pan into the fire," he said, "out of the fire into the middle of the floor, and here we are and here we will stay." He knew that God had revealed to him "that this is the spot to locate His people, and here is where they will prosper."[15]

His courageous steadfastness earned for him the title "Lion of the Lord." Even President Abraham Lincoln recognized that the Mormon leader was not someone to offend. "You tell Brigham Young if he will leave me alone, I'll leave him alone," said Lincoln in response to an inquiry.[16] Brigham Young was a man with a mission and a vision of what the future would hold for the Latter-day Saints:

> It has been asked if we intend to settle more valleys. Why certainly we expect to fill the next valley and then the next, and the next, and so on. It has been the cry of late, through the columns of the newspapers, that the "Mormons" are going into Mexico! That is quite right, we calculate to go there. Are we going back to Jackson County? Yes. When? As soon as the way opens up. . . . We intend to hold our own here, and also penetrate the north and the south, the east and the west, there to make others and to raise the ensign of truth. . . . We will continue to grow, to increase and spread abroad, and the powers of earth and hell combined cannot hinder it.[17]

Brigham Young died at 4:00 P.M. on 29 August 1877 in Salt Lake City after calling the words "Joseph, Joseph, Joseph." In life he had been separated from his beloved friend the Prophet Joseph Smith, yet in death they were now united. Like Joseph, he had fulfilled the measure of his creation and advised that at his interment there should be "no crying or mourning with anyone as I have done my work faithfully and in good faith."[18]

We heartily concur. A life so well lived is a life worth remembering. We extend appreciation to the fine scholars who have remembered Brigham Young by studying and writing about his life. Their expertise and meticulous research is conveyed in this volume again and again as they commemorate President Young's life of service.

We also wish to acknowledge the helpful assistance of William W. Slaughter, photograph archivist, and the staff at the LDS Church Historical Department; Scott H. Duvall, Special Collections and Manuscripts Chair of the Harold B. Lee Library at Brigham Young University; Don E. Norton of the BYU English faculty; and Sheri L. Dew and the publishing staff at Deseret Book Company. We appreciate BYU's Department of Church History and Doctrine for permitting the reprinting of portions of a few articles on Brigham Young that appeared in *Regional Studies in Latter-day Saint Church History: New York* and also the *Southern California Quarterly* journal.

NOTES

1. Brigham Young, "March of Mormonism—The Power of God and the Wisdom of Man—Good and Evil Influences—The Law of Increase," *Journal of Discourses*, 26 vols. (Liverpool: Latter-day Saints' Book Depot, 1858), 1: 91.
2. Brigham Young, "Saints Subject to Temptation," *Journal of Discourses*, 2: 128.
3. B. H. Roberts, *A Comprehensive History of The Church of Jesus Christ of Latter-day Saints*, 6 vols. (Salt Lake City: The Church of Jesus Christ of Latter-day Saints, 1930), 1: 289.
4. Elden Jay Watson, comp., *Brigham Young: A Chronology of Known Addresses of the Prophet Brigham Young* (E. Watson, 1979), 17–18.
5. Matthias F. Cowley, *Wilford Woodruff: History of His Life and Labors* (Salt Lake City: Bookcraft, 1964), 120.
6. *A Comprehensive History*, 2: 86.
7. *Journal of Discourses*, 26: 343.
8. *Journal of Discourses*, 26: 359.
9. Joseph Smith, *History of The Church of Jesus Christ of Latter-day Saints*, 7 vols., 2nd ed. rev. (Salt Lake City: The Church of Jesus Christ of Latter-day Saints, 1932–51), 7: 233.
10. William C. Staines as cited in Francis M. Gibbons, *Brigham Young: Modern Moses, Prophet of God* (Salt Lake City: Deseret Book Company, 1981), 104.
11. *History of the Church*, 7: 256.
12. *A Comprehensive History*, 3: 224.
13. Letter of Brigham Young to Charles C. Rich, 2 August 1847, as cited in Leonard J. Arrington, *Charles C. Rich, Mormon General and Western Frontiersman* (Provo, Utah: Brigham Young University Press, 1974), 118.

14. *A Comprehensive History,* 1: 289.
15. James S. Brown, *Life of a Pioneer* (Salt Lake City; George Q. Cannon & Sons, 1900), 121–22.
16. Leonard J. Arrington, *Brigham Young, American Moses* (New York: Alfred A Knopf, 1985), 195.
17. Brigham Young, "The United Order, etc.," in *Journal of Discourse,* 18: 355–56.
18. Preston Nibley, *Brigham Young: The Man and His Work* (Salt Lake City: Deseret News Press, 1936), 536–37.

RECOVERING YOUR STORY

RECOVERING YOUR STORY

PROUST | JOYCE | WOOLF
FAULKNER | MORRISON

Arnold Weinstein

RANDOM HOUSE / NEW YORK

Published in the United States by Random House, an imprint of The Random House
Publishing Group, a division of Random House, Inc., New York.

RANDOM HOUSE and colophon are registered trademarks of Random House, Inc.

Grateful acknowledgment is made to the following for
permission to reprint previously published material:

Harcourt, Inc., and Faber and Faber Ltd.: Excerpt from "East Coker" from *Four Quartets* by T. S. Eliot, copyright © 1940 by T. S. Eliot and renewed 1968 by Esme Valerie Eliot. Reprinted by permission.

Harcourt, Inc., and The Society of Authors as the Literary Representative of the Estate of Virginia Woolf: Excerpt from *A Room of One's Own* by Virginia Woolf, copyright © 1929 by Harcourt, Inc., and renewed 1957 by Leonard Woolf. Excerpt from *To the Lighthouse* by Virginia Woolf, copyright © 1927 by Harcourt, Inc., and renewed 1954 by Leonard Woolf. Excerpt from *Mrs. Dalloway* by Virginia Woolf, copyright © 1925 by Harcourt, Inc., and renewed 1953 by Leonard Woolf. Reprinted by permission.

Indiana University Press: Excerpt from *James Joyce and the Making of Ulysses* by Frank Budgen.

International Creative Management, Inc.: Excerpt from *Sula* by Toni Morrison, copyright © 1973, 2004, and renewed 2002 by Toni Morrison. Excerpt from *Beloved* by Toni Morrison, copyright © 1987, 2004, by Toni Morrison. Reprinted by permission of International Creative Management, Inc.

The Random House Group Ltd.: Excerpt from *Virginia Woolf* by Hermione Lee, published by Chatto & Windus. Reprinted by permission of The Random House Group Ltd.

Random House, Inc., and Curtis Brown Group Ltd.: Excerpt from *Absalom, Absalom!* by William Faulkner, copyright © 1936 by William Faulkner, and renewed 1964 by Estelle Faulkner and Jill Faulkner Summers. Excerpt from *The Sound and the Fury* by William Faulkner, copyright © 1929, and renewed 1957 by William Faulkner. Reprinted by permission of Random House, Inc. and Curtis Brown Group Ltd., London, on behalf of the Estate of William Faulkner.

Random House, Inc., and The Random House Group Ltd.: Excerpts from *Remembrance of Things Past, Vols. 1–3* by Marcel Proust. Vols. 1 and 2 translated by C. K. Scott Moncrieff and Terence Kilmartin, and Vol. 3 translated by C. K. Scott Moncrieff, Terence Kilmartin, and A. Mayor, copyright © 1981 by Random House, Inc., and Chatto & Windus. Reprinted by permission of the publishers, the Estate of Marcel Proust, and the Estate of Terence Kilmartin.

The Society of Authors as the Literary Representative of the Estate of Virginia Woolf: Excerpt from *A Writer's Diary* by Virginia Woolf. Reprinted by permission.

LIBRARY OF CONGRESS CATALOG-IN-PUBLICATION DATA

Weinstein, Arnold L.

Recovering your story: Proust, Joyce, Woolf, Faulkner, Morrison /
Arnold Weinstein.—1st ed.

p. cm.

ISBN 1-4000-6094-X (acid-free paper)

1. English fiction—20th century—History and criticism. 2. Self in literature. 3. Faulkner, William, 1897–1962—Criticism and interpretation. 4. Proust, Marcel, 1871–1922. A la recherche du temps perdu. 5. Woolf, Virginia, 1882–1941—Criticism and interpretation. 6. Psychological fiction—History and criticism. 7. Joyce, James, 1882–1941. Ulysses. 8. Consciousness in literature. 9. Morrison, Toni. Beloved. 10. Fiction—Appreciation. I. Title.

PR888.S427W45 2006

823'.9109384—dc22 2005046468

Printed in the United States of America on acid-free paper

www.atrandom.com

2 4 6 8 9 7 5 3 1

FIRST EDITION

Book design by Casey Hampton

To Ann, again

PREFACE

I am frequently asked by students and friends: Do you ever write novels? I have always taken it as a compliment, as a recognition that what I do with literature has some kinship with fiction itself, rather than being straightforward literary criticism. But I have always answered: No, I don't write novels. And I sometimes add, by way of confession: My relation to art is parasitic—I take from it, I feed on it, but I don't create it. This usually concludes the conversation.

I always said no, because I understood the question in relation to my biography: childhood in Memphis, Tennessee, in the forties and fifties, college and graduate school at Princeton and Harvard, study in France and Germany, marriage to a Swedish woman, career at Brown University, making of a family of children, and now grandchildren, over the long years. Those are the facts of my life. No, I have not elected to write directly, or even indirectly, about that, to transpose that into fiction. I am a professor, not a novelist.

But are things this simple? It occurs to me—very late in the game, reflecting on this book I've written, and close to the end of my career—that perhaps I do write novels, that *Recovering Your Story* is, in ways I neither foresaw nor intended, a novel, my novel, my story. I need great books, have always needed them, for it is in these novels (that I read and teach and write about) that I find my own voice.

In one sense, this has to do with my central argument in the pages ahead. At the center of this long book about long books is a simple truth:

We want to recover our story. The simple part is: our story—the melody of our felt life—is what most eludes us, since it is not to be found in mirrors or scrapbooks or diaries or résumés or even in our immediate thoughts. So, where is it? In novels, I claim, especially in Modernist fiction. These groundbreaking narratives seek to uncover the actual shape and texture of a life: its temporal strata of past and present and conditional, its spatial parameters that chart person and place, but also—crucially—its inside testimony of consciousness, as the inner noise we make while going through the world and processing life.

These matters are, however, no longer simple at all; in fact they can only be transcribed or conveyed or created by a writing that is attuned to both psyche and event, to private landscape and public stage. Such is the writing in Proust, Joyce, Woolf, Faulkner, and Morrison; it stuns and dazzles us with its vistas and purview, with its mixed levels of reality, with its radical break from traditional notation. These five authors reinvent the novel by exploding our sense of what we are. I want my book to send you into theirs.

But my book plays by the rules (which theirs break). It is a guidebook of sorts, a personal tour of these rich and varied fictional worlds, and it is meant to open them up, to make you realize how intimate and hospitable and mirrorlike they are—rather than how daunting or inaccessible they may appear. Needless to say, then, my own prose could hardly be as emancipated and glorious as that of the books we are discussing.

And yet, in looking back at what I have written—that is what prefaces do: They are the author's last word, even if they are your first words—I find that I have indeed limned my own story in this book. In some instances this is quite evident: I do not step back from personal commentary (is there any other kind?), and I occasionally speak of the events of my own life as I first read these authors, or as I now see them. I find myself a player in this book.

Thus, the readings you will encounter are themselves *longitudinal*, and in ways I had not fully anticipated. I have graphed, quite unintentionally, my own four and a half decades of conversance with Proust, Joyce, Woolf, and Faulkner, as well as a briefer but still substantial involvement with Morrison covering close to twenty years. The sheer number of hours I have spent in their company, when I actually go about tallying it, is enough to give me serious pause concerning my priorities. What I never imagined was the human curve and consequences of this literary acquaintanceship.

You will of course see these pages as unfurling commentary, taking place on one plane. But I see them as a history, as an almost lifelong series of relationships, arguably among the deepest and most nuanced relationships that I know how to create and sustain and enjoy. It is not merely that I reflect back on my various readings of these wonderful books, but rather the opposite: These books *send* me back to my earlier engagements with them, to earlier selves, to an entire conversation evolving over time, consisting of thirty-five years of lecturing on these figures, as well as positions I have taken on them, in print, from college essays to my doctoral thesis to articles and books I have written. Not to mention the vast amount of mental and emotional noise about these five writers, still sounding in my brain. Faulkner's Quentin Compson describes himself as a "barracks filled with stubborn . . . ghosts," and I suspect that these books inhabit me along just those vampirish lines.

But this is my novel for other, perhaps deeper reasons. I realize ever more clearly that these novels tell my story as much as I tell theirs. My life and my thinking—as professor, as person, as sentient being—are inextricably, even frighteningly intertwined with their work. Their views about life and death and love and memory and the purposes of art are threaded into my existence, far beyond my capacity to sort it all out. In delving as deeply as I knew how, throughout my adult life as well as during the writing of this book, into the rich work of Proust, Joyce, Woolf, Faulkner, and Morrison, I have been stealing riches for a lifetime, stealing them by dint of internalizing them and furnishing my own mind and heart with their words and visions.

Let me rephrase this: If you ask what is on the *inside*—and the central claim of my study is that these great writers depict our inner life as no one else has ever done—my own answer, at least in part, is *these books*. I grasp life through the prisms and lenses offered by these books (and, yes, others), prisms and lenses that I have quite simply adopted and incorporated into my way of seeing. None of this was done intentionally, but that means it was done even more profoundly and invisibly. Writing about them now has brought the extent of this poaching to visibility. I make no apologies. On the contrary, I am proud to have rifled and pilfered and taken from their work. But I now recognize that they have stocked my house, fed my mind, nourished my heart, etched my vision, and layered my words in ways far more profound than I ever imagined.

A motif that comes up in my discussion of Morrison's *Beloved* is that of an umbilical cord, a vital conduit that connects us to our loved ones, existing well beyond the moment of birth and the apparent severing of the cord; it is clear to me that these five authors live in me in that fashion. How, then, can I be surprised that these writers speak me every bit as much as I speak them? In writing this book, in reflecting consciously on the personal hold these novels have on me, I have wanted to make that special conversation—between them and me, between book and reader—audible. Books live in this way. Better still, writing this book has been my way of continuing the exchange, of perhaps giving back something of my own after having taken so much.

I do read and teach other authors as well, but these are my life companions, the books I hold above all the others, the ones I always find it possible to insert into my courses, the ones I reread. (I reread them to stay honest, and I am frequently surprised by what I find, puzzled by my earlier views, unsure where things "now" stand, aware of how mobile and indeterminate all this is.) So I have attempted, in this book, to put it all together, to distill from all these decades of intimacy with these writers some kind of final statement, saying what I have learned over the years, what I now make of it, and what you might make of it. And I feel a bit like a man called upon to offer some defining image of loved ones: How do you size them up? And who are you ultimately talking about: them or yourself?

Doubtless one never says it all. And if one did, it would be tantamount to a death sentence, since continued living and reading produce new ideas, and lead one to scrap some of the old ideas. Nonetheless, I don't foresee writing about these writers again. I suppose I am finally cutting the cord.

To be sure, there are scholarly industries out there, producing professional commentary on these five authors at a fast and furious pitch. My approach has been different. I have attempted to give "my" plenary account, by asking the basic question that underwrites all teaching, as well as all reading: What claim do these books have on *you*? How will they alter your sense of who you are? For that is what they will do. In them you will encounter, in ways you could not have anticipated, versions of yourself, enactments of your own story.

Proust, Joyce, Woolf, Faulkner, Morrison: a grand quintet whose silhouettes may seem as rugged and unapproachable as the figures carved on Mount Rushmore. But they are also as intimate as a looking glass. I hope my book helps to bring you into them, and them into you. For that is my guiding truth: Great art discovers for us who we are.

CONTENTS

RECOVERING YOUR STORY

INTRODUCTION

OUR UNTOLD STORY

How do you find out who you are? Most of us can come up with the vital statistics: name, age, sex, education, work, and so forth. Even if we were amnesiac, we usually have a résumé handy to remind us of the facts: where we come from and what we've done. We also have photographs to consult, even mirrors, so that there is evidence galore of our surface form. Granted, that form changes over time, yet scrapbooks keep these records. But how much do scrapbooks and résumés and mirrors actually tell us? And how much do they leave out? They may well delineate the outside: body, career, vital statistics. But the inside? All of those soft venerable old unscientific words that resist inventory—heart, soul, spirit, self—never show up on your CV or on camera, yet must have some kind of reality.

We know this because we feel it; at every moment we feel life in the form of sensation, consciousness, incessant testimony of both body and mind. In contrast to any and all docile well-behaved statistics or even photos, it is all swirling on the inside, anarchic, unmapped. And we know there is inside us an internal history as well, a trajectory that eludes calendars and checkups, a sort of longitudinal string or chain of events and memories, of people we've known and people we've been. It is this aggregate, this composite, that gives the measure of one's actual, fuller existence. But, how does one get a fix on this *other* life that eludes both camera and notation? How many people, one wonders, feel locked out of this inner sanctum? How does one get in? Can one get in? Is this realm shareable? Representable? How would it be expressed?

L'INVITATION AU VOYAGE

I have written this book in the belief that the great literary performances of Proust, Joyce, Woolf, Faulkner, and Morrison are bridges toward self-discovery, reflecting mirrors on how we live and how our equipment—our eyes, ears, stomach, genitals, brain, heart—actually works. These novels are windows onto a world of consciousness and perception that has miraculously made it into print, and can now be processed into an understanding of our lives. These books have long been misconstrued as esoteric, elitist, and inaccessible. I think they can be seen as a magic but intimate script whose strangeness testifies to all that is strange, unknown, and unlabeled in ourselves. These books move us into our own selves. One of the French poet Baudelaire's loveliest poems is titled "*L'Invitation au voyage*," and its refrain goes like this: "*Là, tout n'est qu'ordre et beauté / Luxe, calme et volupté*" (There, all is order and beauty/ Richness, peace, and pleasure). The poet is seeking to characterize that magic experience he has yearned for all his life, and he conceives of it as a place, a place you get to, by dint of *travel*.

Those terms—*ordre, beauté, luxe, calme, volupté*—are not the ones usually evoked in order to give the measure of these great novels. In fact, these novels uncover the originary perceptual violence and tempest within us. Nonetheless, at the far side of each one of them, when you've made the trip, arrived at the place—Proust's inwardly recovered past, Joyce's humor and wisdom about flesh and mind, Woolf's resurrection of dead youth and dead love, Faulkner's "overpass to love," even Morrison's dark picture of wounds and bonding—lies an achieved order that both gratifies and enlarges us because we ourselves have had to work toward it, in order to perceive its reality. Yes, these books dispense with authorial guidance, but just because of that, we must plunge in on our own, unaided, but also freed of the customary road marks and blinders.

Hence, these novels proffer a unique reading experience, an invitation to voyage, an unparalleled encounter with the pulsions of heart and mind, from which we emerge enriched. For the final quarry is not so much an understanding of some five writers, but rather a possession of our own strange, vexed, elusive, explosive lives. And that is what you get: an altered, expanded, altogether greater apprehension of what the texture of consciousness is. These writers call their people Marcel, Bloom, Stephen, Clarissa, Mrs. Ramsay, Quentin, Sutpen, Sethe, and Beloved, but your entry into these books is a colonial project of the finest sort: You are expanding your own territory. In contrast with other explorations made possible at our moment—via cruise ship or modem—you need neither money nor electricity for this trip: just mind and heart. And the direction has changed: You're going *in*.

TECHNOLOGY AS THE VOYAGE "OUT"

Marshall McLuhan argued, many decades ago, that the history of evolving media tells us about the externalizing of the human brain, the expansion of its reach. To be sure, horses and cars and trains and planes have played their role in extending our physical whereabouts in space, but the still more dramatic breakthroughs are arguably to be found in the invention of the radio, telegraph, telephone, television, and, of course, today's Internet. Each of these venues explosively aggrandizes the outward reach of the human subject, enabling contact and communication in unheard-of ways, transcending physical proximity, yielding a kind of network that criss-crosses the planet, driven by electricity or digital technology, pushing the frontiers ever further. I think there has never been a comparable moment in history where so many people are able to access so much of the globe, expanding our parameters in a dizzying, revolutionary manner, empowering us to go further and further out. But: What about *inside*? How do we get there? Modern medical imaging can show us the precincts of our somatic corridors and organs in unprecedented fashion, and even though a story can be deduced from these images (sometimes a terrifying story involving cancer or disease), no one is likely to greet these pictures as their secret self.

Doubtless the oldest technology for extending (as well as representing) human reach would be language itself: The very structures of grammar enable us to domesticate, even to colonize, time and space. We make use of verb tenses in order to represent events or projects taking place in the past, in the future, and in the conditional. Is this not time travel? Likewise, the syntactical arrangements involving subjects and objects enable us to incorporate space as well into utterance or writing, and of course adjectives and adverbs add point, nuance, specificity, and coloration to those arrangements. I am not a linguist, and these matters are exponentially more complex than I have indicated, but already it is clear that the institution of language is, in some basic sense, a carrier of the human subject, a means of transportation, a representation of our reach. Language is the instrument for going *in*, for chronicling and choreographing that huge realm of feeling and consciousness, memory and fantasy, that is one's ultimate "real estate." Can it therefore surprise anyone that *stories* are among the oldest means we have for saying who we are, what we are, and where we are? No one better exemplifies this impulse than Rousseau who, in the latter eighteenth century, was so painfully aware that the inner data of his life—the true reasons he did what he did, said what he said—were invisible to his fellows that he wrote his great autobiographical narrative, *Les Confessions*, in order to give his true measure, to bring the opaque inner record to light and language. Whether this was depiction or invention, truth or fantasy, is another matter; what counts is that writing was the great instrument for self-representation.

FICTION AS THE VOYAGE "IN"

The novel is born out of this same need. Narrative is humankind's magical and most precious means of mapping the entire gamut of human deeds—ranging from emotion and thought to words and acts—and it thus retrieves and makes visible the shape of a life. Great novels have always had a profound, even if unaccented, caretaking mission. Behind the stories of adventure and picaresque forays, the narratives of the seventeenth and eighteenth centuries testify to an imperative of *recuperation*. From the most ambitious and self-regarding of the bunch—Cervantes's *Don Quijote*—on to the episodic confections such as Defoe's *Moll Flanders* and the more tightly structured psychological investigations such as we see in Richardson's *Pamela* and *Clarissa* or Prévost's *Manon Lescaut*, the project at hand seems to be one of retrieval, of grasping the shape of a life. How can we be surprised that so many early novels have personal names as titles? Beginning with the sketchy, rudimentary Lazarillo de Tormes, going on to more developed figures such as Robinson Crusoe, Joseph Andrews, Tom Jones, Rousseau's Julie, Goethe's Werther, it seems as though the very institution of fiction is enlisted in endowing life with a shape and a proprietary name via the offices of plot and character.

THE REASON FOR LITERATURE: RECOVERING YOUR STORY

My terms—retrieval, recuperation, possession—have a severe corollary that goes with them: *We cannot perceive or possess our life, on our own; we need stories.* Like grains of sand going through the hourglass, like water that flows through your fingers, experience washes through us from birth to death; life marks us incessantly, yes, but we cannot easily get our heads and hands around it, see its cumulative shape. And we can even less convey it to others. What a magic container a novel is! In the compass of a few hundred pages with printed letters on a page, it can chart an entire life, from birth to death, delivering a plenary mix of thoughts, feelings, words, and deeds. Small wonder that novels gratify, that they answer a deep-seated need.

Nor can we be surprised that so many of these earlier novels revolve around the theme of *recognition,* whether it be the foundling stories used by Fielding or the quest for acknowledgment and legitimacy seen in a figure like Marivaux's Marianne; this impulse lies at the heart of many of Jane Austen's novels as well, since her comedies of alliance and misalliance seem cued to a project of proper measurement, proper evaluation, yielding ever greater definition and self-knowledge at the end. It is as if one of art's great purposes were to give a shape and a grammar to human life, to "package" it in the rich diverse forms of fiction and poetry, painting, and sculpture. I'd argue that the hunger that energizes our encounter with art is the exact opposite of what we may lazily believe—art as escape, art as distraction, art as frills. No, the truth goes the other way: We open books and look at paintings in order to capture life's very form. And we do this, ultimately, as a way of appropriating our own elusive form, our own untold story.

These early fictions of the seventeenth and eighteenth centuries lead us to the great heyday of the genre, the explosion of the novel as serious art form in nineteenth-century Europe and America. By this time, the life-story project has become omnivorous: the unforgettable private destinies and individual trajectories that are charted in the Brontë sisters, Dickens, George Eliot, and on to Hardy and Conrad on the English side, Balzac, Stendhal, Flaubert, and Zola on the French side, not to mention Turgenev, Dostoevsky, and Tolstoy, or Hawthorne, Melville, Twain, and James, or Manzoni or Galdos or many many others as well. These books constitute a form of travel and encounter, a bristling portrait-gallery of individual lives and destinies. Just consider how many of the personal stories we come to know best are, in fact, fictitious, not "real": Heathcliff, Jane Eyre, Oliver Twist, Pip, Rastignac, Julien Sorel, Emma Bovary, Anna Karenina, the Karamazov brothers, Hester Prynne, Ahab, Huck. Through the magic offices of fiction, of print-encoded pages between a front and a back, those lives come to us in their entirety, from birth to death, made coherent and accessible.

THE NOVEL AS "WALKING MIRROR"

Moreover, in the finest of these books the fundamental project of portraiture becomes ever more capacious, moving easily from the social and psychological depiction of the human figures on to the portrayal of an entire class or culture. Stendhal's handsome formula, "*un roman est un miroir qui se promène*" ("the novel is a walking mirror"), captures both the private and public dimensions of narrative performance: a mirror in which we see others and ourselves. A strange and seductive economy, this: The story of the individual becomes part of, inseparable from, the story of the culture. If you produce a "walking mirror," people will flock to it and use it: to see not only themselves but also others, the human story and the sights around them. The great cities of the nineteenth century were changing at a dizzying pace: London, Paris, St. Petersburg. Early capitalism was impacting enormously on the traditional family and class arrangements, as we see so clearly in the French and English novels of the period. Fiction helped a person to see clear, to get his or her bearings, to acquire a sharper sense of how the social game was played, who were its movers and shakers, who were its victims: What happens to people out in the world.

Novels were not too distant from what we can call "wisdom literature." Readers were avid to see what Balzac or Dickens had to say in the next installment, in part because they regarded the novel as a precious form of information as well as insight: about the evolving character of their own society, about the great forces and conflicts of their age, and about the heights and depths of human behavior. Looked at today, these great novels seem to explode with energy and confidence: the confidence that a panoramic view of self-and-society is achievable, and the no less great confidence that the novel form is sufficiently supple, capacious, and reliable to carry out and to pull off these epic projects. Nineteenth-century novelists are mapmakers out to chart the evolving landscapes—social, political, moral—of their readers. Lines are clear, judgments are pronounced, lessons are learned.

To be sure, we can, today, also perceive lines of stress and fissure in any number of these nineteenth-century monuments. Scholars and critics have helped us to question just how secure and intact their various belief systems really were. Read more closely, books like *Le Père Goriot*, *Jane Eyre*, *Bleak House*, and *Madame Bovary* announce a great deal of the ideological debates and issues that were to occupy so much of the twentieth century: the evils of the cash nexus, the repression of women, the diseased and commoditized modern city, the merchandising of desire, and the ennui of modern life. And, yet, these fictions nonetheless have a kind of glorious innocence about them, a quasi-institutional serenity that says: This book is instructive, this story is engaging, these issues (emotional, ethical, ideological) matter, and this whole consort is "tellable." Even Flaubert, the most jaundiced, disbelieving, and (therefore) prophetic of the group, dishes out a story with pizzazz: Emma Bovary's longings, her affairs with Rodolphe and Léon, the fabulous descriptions of the Vaubyssard ball, the trip to Rouen and to the agricultural fair, not to mention the insidiously modern figure of Homais the pharmacist. Such fictions both whet and satisfy our appetite for story, for a full, bristling canvas of people and events, for a great "read." Such fictions deliver rounded characters and measure their historical moment.

THE NOVEL'S METAMORPHOSIS

And then something happens. It is impossible to place a time or single face on it, but the novel-as-genre starts to lose faith in itself. We could claim that this is already present in some of the wilder and more ludic earlier performances of the eighteenth century, such as Sterne's *Tristram Shandy* and Diderot's *Jacques le fataliste*, where plot becomes at once whimsical and embarrassingly highlighted as artifice. But, for the most part at that time, the grand project of the life story wins out, dominates the field, convinces us that such is the mission of fiction. And the baton, as mentioned, is wonderfully passed on and taken up by the huge bevy of talented practitioners of the nineteenth century, yielding an inexhaustible treasure trove of stories to read, some Romantic and Gothic, some more scientific and analytical, all conducted with that same ontological innocence. But trouble is coming.

This is why Conrad and James are such pivotal figures. They do have a story to tell—often a powerful, exciting, instructive story—but they seem almost paralyzed in the telling of it. Conrad's Marlow cannot seem to take himself out of the picture as he seeks to tell the story of Kurtz (in "Heart of Darkness"), so much so that readers have understandably wondered whose story was actually being told; Marlow fares little better when he tackles the adventures of Jim (in *Lord Jim*). And James invented an entire arsenal of marginal figures—*ficelles*, he called them, threads—through whom events were to be refracted and made sense of, leading many a reader to wonder if all of this huffing and puffing, this making out this and speculating that, were really worth it. Just tell it! readers sometimes feel. As for the "late phase" of James's career—*The Ambassadors, The Wings of the Dove, The Golden Bowl*—many readers feel that whatever story is there is virtually smothered by the brooding consciousness that delivers it.

Sometimes the writers themselves took aim at their own work. Flaubert was able, in good faith, to claim that *Madame Bovary*, his epochal story of Romantic love gone sour, was actually "*un livre sur rien*," "a book about nothing." All of Flaubert's books seem, in the light of a second reading, to be falling apart, to be wanting to fall apart, to be showing us that this is the reality of a novel: a structure that (like all structures, particularly perhaps political-moral-emotional structures) falls apart. Or consider Dostoevsky's little anarchic teaser "Notes from Underground," which not only introduces one of the first antiheroes into narrative, but manages to call into question all notions of character and plot as well, now seen as simple-minded constructs of an earlier time. These fictions—and you could add lots to the list, such as bizarre and impudent pieces by Poe or Hoffmann, or Hawthorne's wispy story "Wakefield" or Melville's "modern" classic of undoing, "Bartleby the Scrivener"—seem to be about their own impossibility. Telling a good story is now in bad odor. The walking mirror has disappeared. The writing equipment no longer seems to work. Or, the focus has changed from the story to the equipment itself. *Telling* itself is in trouble. Readers beware.

MODERNISM

If all these skirmishes were preparing the ground for a pending battle, we could say that in 1922 there occurred the grand explosive event, the in-your-face proclamation that traditional, confident, cogent, readable fiction was now a thing of the past: the publication of James Joyce's *Ulysses.* T. S. Eliot, who admired Joyce's novel so much that he used it as inspiration in his own epochal poem of that same year, "The Waste Land," nonetheless conceded that *Ulysses* was the coup de grâce for the future of fiction, that it turned the writing of subsequent novels into something impossible. I think Eliot was right. Joyce's astonishing depiction of consciousness, his erudite yet playful reworking not only of Homer but of virtually every Western cultural authority into his text, his shocking frankness about the antics and needs of the human body, his decision to reconceive the *Odyssey* as an eight-hundred-page representation of a single (uneventful) day in the lives of a few people in Dublin, all this more or less blew traditional fiction to smithereens. The intellectuals, the writers, and the professors were among the few who signed on for Joyce's performance, sharing Eliot's sense that it was a monumental achievement. But the ordinary reader was the great casualty here, no matter how much huffing and puffing might (later) come from the academy. With the advent of Joyce, modern literature, at least highbrow modern literature, was in danger of losing its audience.

For no uninitiated reader could hope to glean from *Ulysses* what had been so prodigally and prodigiously offered by Balzac, Dickens, and company: the rich and exciting depiction of both the life story and the social canvas. Likewise, Proust, whose first volumes in his even more monumental book, *Remembrance of Things Past,* had already appeared before the war, looked like something of a white elephant to common readers, for this swollen account of one somewhat neurotic young man's perception of the world had a strikingly precious cast to it, as if it had utterly turned its back on the Stendhalian premise that a novel was a traveling mirror, showing us the great lineaments of social change. Virginia Woolf's masterpieces, *Mrs. Dalloway* and *To the Lighthouse,* appeared in short order, in the middle of that stunning decade, the 1920s, with their fine-grained yet lyrical (and sometimes even hallucinatory) portrayal of consciousness and sensation, hurling readers into interiors where they might perhaps have little inclination to go. Where, one wondered, was that bigger story, that panoramic yet analytical portrait of society and self, that had heretofore been the great mission of the novel? To cap it off, a fairly uneducated Mississippian published in 1929, to no fanfare whatsoever, a still more unreadable tunnel vision text called *The Sound and the Fury*, which saw fit to recount, from the inside (of course), the perceptions of idiots and suicides. Wisdom literature? Decidedly, the novel as institution was in trouble. One would have been forgiven for thinking even that it was dead. Or hijacked by extremists who, whatever mission they may have had, had no love for the public, had no commitment to that old, unquestioned virtue of readability. What was going on?

Scholars and critics have given a name to this artistic movement: Modernism. And many other writers and artists have been adduced as belonging to this fierce and uncompromising phalange: Ezra Pound, W. H. Auden, Wallace Stevens, Paul Valéry; John Dos Passos, Ernest Hemingway, and painters such as Picasso, musicians such as Stravinsky, different but equally opaque writers such as Kafka and Rilke, Pirandello, Broch and Musil, Bely and Blok. Not that there was a shared platform or manifesto—as there soon would be for the Surrealists when André Breton organized his troops in that same extraordinary decade—but there was a common awareness that the old rules governing the art(s) of the past were dead. Something remarkable was unfurling: vital, emancipated, tossing out the conventions of yesterday, ever eager to "make it new."

With just a tad of hindsight, one can see that the very history of literature and art is composed of such upheavals and renewals. There is probably no period in Western culture when artists were not, at least in some sense, engaged in "making it new." Uccello's painterly experiments with perspective seem to lead us from a "flat" medieval artistic scheme to the great "rounded" works of the Italian Renaissance. For literary historians, there is the famous "*Querelle des anciens et modernes*" that shook the scene in early-eighteenth-century France, enlisting partisans on both sides of the divide. Closer to our time, one remembers the revolutionary "Preface to the *Lyrical Ballads*" written by Coleridge and Wordsworth at the beginning of the nineteenth century, it too an effort to clear the decks and make room for the new. Having said this, I want nonetheless to repeat: The advent of the Modernists came at a very real social and cultural price.

The pact between writer and audience that was broken was more than an affair of new aesthetics or changing taste. It signaled a collapse of institutional and existential proportions, because the very rationale of the novel (in its heyday)—to propose a walking mirror—was scuttled. No author bothered to announce such nefarious intentions, of course, but the result was there, and people voted with their feet and their purses: They found the Modernist fare largely unreadable. Put crudely, those books were not written in such a way as to help readers find out who they were or where they were. It seemed devilishly hard to find a life story in them. Or to use them to find one's own. I think it impossible to overstate the importance of this outcome. People felt (and feel) cheated.

And a writer who makes use of the Modernist legacy, such as Toni Morrison, risks the same fate. Even the bestowing of a Nobel Prize will not alter the fact that *Beloved*—not to mention her later, more convoluted fictions—still seems to many readers enigmatic and inaccessible.

The schools and universities are implicated here. The Modernist giants, after a short time of neglect, have been enshrined in the academy. But this adulation by the professionals has not made these books one whit more readable or enjoyable (even though there is an industry out there producing guidebooks and keys; you may suspect you are reading one). Something of a scandal is at hand. Those books that the intellectuals and the pros tout as the pinnacle of achievement are—when read—treated with suspicion, even anger, by the hungry "common reader" who (naively?) continues to believe that novels are something you could pick up and read at your leisure, and learn something from. I come into this equation as a professor who has been teaching literature for more than three decades, and who finds that only the most motivated of students are prepared to do the work, put in the time, required for reading Proust, Joyce, Woolf, Faulkner, and Morrison.

IS FICTION DEAD?

Not that they don't read novels; they do. People have not stopped reading fiction. They are still hunting for the life story, even if they find it more easily in bestselling biographies of the great and famous. That hunger does not go away. The elemental pulse of fiction—to clothe human life into stories, to give a shape to one's existence over time—is still vital. Readers' desire for fictional nourishment, for tracking life's shape in books, has not waned. Novels are still written, published, and read. So, perhaps T. S. Eliot was wrong when he said that Joyce killed the entire genre of fiction.

The novel is not dead. You need merely glance at people on subways, buses, trains, and planes, on beaches and on cruises, in waiting rooms and in hospitals and in hotels and in airports and in train stations, and you see people reading novels. They are also reading novels in places you cannot see, such as armchairs and sofas and, above all, beds at night. Moreover, English departments at universities give courses on "the novel," and reading groups across the globe meet regularly to discuss novels, and the major newspapers and magazines and journals commit pages, often entire sections, to the review and discussion of novels. Prizes are won (ranging from local recognition all the way to the Nobel Prize), money is spent and made (by consumers, by publishers, sometimes by authors), prestige is acquired (under the rubric of "culture"): all in the name of novels. There would not seem to be any problem at all.

Yet, something has changed in the culture at large. The situation resembles that of the man who, when asked if he believed in baptism, replied that he had seen it performed many times. There are lots of novels out there, but do they command belief? Do they perform the same cultural labor as they did at an earlier time? Do they perform their prior role of wisdom literature? Do they constitute a compass for modern life? These are not idle questions. Today, in the twenty-first century, literature itself seems a far more marginalized artistic or cultural activity than it was a century ago. Film, soon followed by its domestic sibling, television, are the first conspicuous intruders here, the new forms of expression and representation that simply knocked narrative fiction out of its crowning position, somewhere around the 1950s. Here was a new kind of "walking mirror" that required very little decoding. For entertainment and story in our era, film and television are, in some unarguable sense, where folks have been turning for quite some time.

But think what has happened further in the past several decades: video, then the Internet, came upon the scene, with their news of a radically different mode of communication, utilizing a different medium altogether, making the print-based machine of fiction (materially sandwiched between two covers) look decidedly low-tech, even (some would say) a bit like a dinosaur, slated for extinction. And there are media scholars who blithely announce the coming death of print in its entirety, arguing that it had a birth in the sixteenth century, via Gutenberg, and that it will also have a death in a time not too far off, as the casualty of an information and digital technology that no longer needs its services.

How do we reconcile the contradiction between the apparent health of the genre—folks reading novels everywhere—and the announced demise prophesied by earlier poets and later scholars? Perhaps we can start to answer this by looking more closely at the kinds of novels that people are now reading. This is a big arena, one that I cannot pretend to define with any authority, but I feel comfortable claiming that the popular fictions of today (not just the bestsellers but the books you'll see on those trains and buses and planes I mentioned) are reasonably straightforward affairs: written with clarity, moving cleanly from beginning to end, possessed of contoured characters and delineated plots. *Books you can read.* By which I mean: You the reader have few hoops to go through, few puzzles to decipher, few somersaults to make. Of course, detective stories (which make you work) still flourish, but they too are followable, chapter by chapter, as crimes are solved and mysteries are cleared up. Murk and confusion (of the long-term variety), it seems to me, are not much appreciated.

It could be that the immediacy and outright visual stimuli of genres such as film and TV, and their modern descendant, video, have created a hunger for quick and direct relay, and that this "delivery system" works enormously to the discredit of language-based art, with its built-in interpretive labor and incessant translation. Films and videos may require interpretation, but they possess motion, color, sound, and a direct sensual impact that words-on-a-page can scarcely claim. As a professor who often mixes film and literature in his courses, I have had ample opportunity to note how quick, keen, and literate young people are when it comes to film, how sharply they negotiate this packaging of images, stimuli, and data, versus their more stumbling and confused efforts when it comes to literature. (I, of course, work the other way: It takes me three viewings to discern in a film what my best students see at once, whereas the patterns of literature, which puzzle them, jump out at me. Intelligence as such does not alter over time, but its modalities do.)

PROUST, JOYCE, WOOLF, FAULKNER, MORRISON: RECOVERING YOUR STORY

Why, then, would I devote this book to exactly those novels you are *not* likely to see people reading: Proust's *Remembrance of Things Past*, Joyce's *Ulysses*, Woolf's *Mrs. Dalloway* and *To the Lighthouse*,

Faulkner's *The Sound and the Fury* and *Absalom, Absalom!*, and Toni Morrison's *Beloved*? First of all, those are the books that I most love, and I suppose, at some gut level, I am trying to pass that love on to you. I also believe, however, that they are our *great books*, and that even if the scholars are right about the demise of fiction in some future time, these will be the books that survive, that anthropologists will be studying, in order to make out how we worked and played, lived and loved, thought and felt, remembered and forgot, lost and found, in the twentieth century. And beyond. These books will not stale or wither. And, most crucial of all, these fierce and uncompromising Modernist novels do exactly what the best fiction has always done: They tell the life story.

But they do so in ways we are unaccustomed to seeing. The trappings of plot and character are no longer up-front and clear, as in the work of Balzac or Dickens, and the ideological mission of offering social portraiture may seem scanted. I am even willing to admit that their language can appear strange, and their handling of story line can look capricious and jumbled. But, make no mistake about it: They are following Hamlet's injunction to the Players—they are holding a mirror up to nature. It isn't Stendhal's mirror. It is ours. For the greatness of Proust, Joyce, Woolf, Faulkner, and Morrison is this: They enable us to recover our story.

Recover our story. Our story is what we have lost and must find. I am not talking about recovered memories or pop psychology; I am referring to the hidden melody, texture, and form of every life.

I began by saying that none of us can say, with ease or certainty, who we are. I believe we go through life searching for this script, this means of reassembling our pieces, recuperating our form, measuring our estate. And, as Galileo said of the earth itself, it *moves*; seismic, fluid, elusive, our sensed fuller life beckons and wants to be graphed. The novel first came into existence to answer this need, by proposing versions of the life story. The supreme achievements of the Modernists that are at the heart of this book keep faith with that same humanist imperative. But it is crucial that we see them aright, so as to retrieve from them the richness, wonder, and joy that they are holding for us. There is treasure here, treasure that has gone long unseen, simply because these books look so inhospitable, so difficult to access. I have written this study in the belief that today's general reader can not only negotiate Proust, Joyce, Woolf, Faulkner, and Morrison but can discover in them fiction's greatest enduring gift: one's own story, but radically reconceived, seen at last in all its strangeness, shifting shape, and vibrancy.

As I have noted, these ambitious books do not play by the familiar rules. The confident authorial voice that speaks out to us in the nineteenth-century masterpieces is no longer to be heard. That voice is probably what we most remember about those books: Beyond even the plots and characters, it is what stays in our mind if we try to conjure up who the Brontës or Dickens or Balzac or Stendhal or Tolstoy or Dostoevsky or Melville or Twain are: *are,* not were. This all-seeing, all-knowing, all-telling voice constitutes the definitive signature of the traditional novelists we love, and it constitutes, as well, a great part of the charm and meaning of the books they have written. Why would one jettison this? We the readers are going to be the poorer without it.

The Modernists have recognized that life does not come with authorial assistance. Life as we live it does not have an omniscient narrator to offer us his or her persuasive and authoritative interpretation of events and people. We live in the murk. We may hurtle through or muddle through, but there are no signposts for us, no illuminated instructions. We make things out on our own. Hence, the blandishments of an interpretive guide—however delicious and appreciated they may be—may actually block, rather than enable, the true work of fiction: the representation of living experience, the portrayal of (whimsical, flickering, ungovernable) consciousness, the rendering of our perceptual encounter with reality. Living your life is not a guided tour. Modernist literature isn't, either. Some may argue that this is a dubious exchange, that the genial wisdom of our favorite writers is far more gratifying and appealing to readers than having to negotiate the (sometimes benighted) efforts of Modernist characters trying to make their way through life. There is some truth to this claim, inasmuch as a special kind of conversation between author and reader is fated to disappear from the scene.

THE INNER KINGDOM

But let us now consider what is gained (rather than lost) by the Modernist gambit. And the answer is: the depiction—some would say: the creation—of an inner realm that is simply unavailable, unreachable, perhaps unimaginable in traditional fiction. Proust is the grand theorist of these matters, as he goes about the job of mapping this immense new territory of inwardness and subjectivity, and in this regard his imprint is to be found even in the work of still more daring writers, such as Joyce or Faulkner. Mind you: The outside world—the world so cleanly delineated in the traditional novel—does not (cannot) go away in these brave new fictions, and we shall see that it still possesses much of its forbidding authority. We may indeed live in our heads, but if we don't watch out for the external world, we are likely either to bump into trees or to get run over by trucks or to make an ungodly mess of our lives. Even Proust, who is to declare that the inner world is virtually a new kingdom, knows this much, and therefore knows that life consists of an incessant give-and-take between inner and outer, between subjective experience and material objects and circumstances. Joyce, Woolf, Faulkner, and Morrison all find their own unique ways to stage these encounters, this ongoing give-and-take that can become racheted up to full-blown trauma and annihilation.

What they find, what they show, is that there is an immense and never-before-seen drama in exactly this lifelong interplay, even warfare, of private and public, of self and world. To be sure, Moll Flanders and Pip and Emma Bovary and Huck ran into the same obstacles, and one has to say that Don Quijote's entire life is about the conflict, even the confusion, between these two realms. But only in the Modernists do we discover how this conflict feels on the inside: for them, and also for us. And let me tell you: It feels like a roller coaster. In the work of Proust, Joyce, Woolf, Faulkner, and Morrison, the unruliness of life, the sheer vehemence of perception, the onslaught of sensation, the explosive and despotic character of consciousness itself, all these come to the fore, in unheard-of ways. These great writers restore to life—to our life—the innate violence and force and beauty and terror that are the elemental ingredients, the very material, of what we call living and breathing. They recover for us the primal disruptive power of consciousness and perception.

They know what Chicken Little learned—that the sky can fall in, that the sky is always falling in—and they find ways to announce these destabilizing, unhinging tidings. They remove the complacent cover from life, the cover that we have taken to be real, a cover that has much to do with the packaged notions of character and plot that traditional fiction indulges in; and the result is that they recover the originary tempest of forms and colors and forces in which we are bathed at every minute of our existence. This is why they are hard to read. This is why they must be read. They recover our story, but it is an account we've never seen, a rendition far from history books or journalistic notation: a story emerging at ground zero.

I have thus written this book as my own "*invitation au voyage*" (to use Baudelaire's term), as something of a guided tour into these marvelous fictional worlds. You won't find many scholarly references: My sights are on what these books might mean and deliver to the hungry reader, rather than to the expert. I am convinced that they are, to borrow Hemingway's memorable phrase for Paris, "a moveable feast," that they nourish us by making us more present at our own lives, more attuned to our own frequencies, more aware of our own dimensions, more at home in our own recesses, more appreciative of life's grandeur. They do this by taking us brutally *out* of our familiar ruts and orientations, by assaulting us with a kind of writing that jolts us by its freshness, its untamed quality, its shock value. If Proust, Joyce, Woolf, and Faulkner lead us into what may seem faraway places—fin-de-siècle French social circles, Dublin streets and pubs of a century ago, parties and dinners in long-ago London and the Isle of Skye, varieties of Southern doom from the Civil War to Yoknapatawpha County—I have closed with a modern book, Toni Morrison's *Beloved*, which draws brilliantly on the Modernist heritage in order to take us further still: into the dark and twisted moral landscape of slavery and its victims. These writers take us far out before bringing us home, but that is what the great books have always done.

All these books are preeminent depictions of consciousness as the "undiscover'd country," of consciousness as the ultimate place where we live, even where we die. In them we find psychic landscapes and internal voices and fierce pulsions that were unknown to the nineteenth-century novel. In some beautiful if counterintuitive way, their strangeness is our strangeness, now harnessed and captured in the form of fiction. All of them bear witness to that old struggle between self and world, but a struggle we now see from the inside, as an ongoing form of civil war (to salute Faulkner)—skirmishes and engagements at once cerebral, emotional, and visceral—that punctuates our days and nights, waking and dreaming. Do not think of this as a battle: It is the bristling noise that distinguishes the quick from the dead, the living from the inert. It is your pulse you will be taking. Through these trips into books we move more deeply into our story, ourselves.

MARCEL PROUST

REMEMBRANCE OF THINGS PAST

THE WORLD IS THE SELF

Marcel Proust's great classic, *Remembrance of Things Past,* is one of the longest novels ever published, comprising more than three thousand pages in the large-format, three-volume Random House edition. It weighs several pounds. You are not likely to carry it to the beach. When you open it up and start reading, you encounter a dense prose style, with lengthy sentences, ambitious metaphors, and little discernible plot. It appears to describe, in great detail, a bygone world: French society of the early twentieth century. For these reasons, you might well imagine that this book—whatever fame may be ascribed to it—is likely to be an arduous read, a massive project devoted to distant things, an impersonal act of labor.

Nothing could be further from the truth. Proust's epic novel actually resembles those exploration narratives of the Renaissance in which entire new worlds came into view, the accounts of Columbus, Vasco da Gama and Cortés, and others. But the New World coming into view here is you. And the energies that fuel this long book, page after page, are truly colonizing energies: They are out to lay bare the landscape of self, the new cartography of the human interior. Whereas the conquest of the New World was filled with blood and tears and racial conflict, Marcel Proust's grand exploration—larded though it is with scenes of incomprehension or jealousy—offers its readers a profound pleasure: the enlargement of oneself, the discovery of one's actual but never suspected contours and depths. And with this discovery comes a still greater second pleasure: a *recovery*, a *possession* of that which must be counted our very greatest good: our own life. Not some afterlife, but our life itself. There is nothing moralistic or judgmental about Proust's tidings, inasmuch as he does not indict the flesh or material things as such, in the name of some higher spiritual realm. On the contrary, the ringing, even frightening challenge of Proust's work is more insidious, for it says: We do not know ourselves, we do not possess our own estate, we do not grasp our own story. Against this absolute loss, all of our so-called possessions—wealth, career, even relationships—come across as weightless, as mirage-like. *Remembrance of Things Past* is dedicated to the pursuit of ultimate richness and treasure: our own life.

Therefore this long and heavy book is worth its weight in gold. It has an epic scope to it, yes, but, then, so too does your own existence. If you are able to read my prose, then you have been living for many many years already. Can you recall these years? Are they "yours"? And if you do have their outline still clear—dates, events, perhaps snapshots and scattered memories—can you access the pulsing feelings that went into them, that constituted their very life, your very life? If not—and for most of us, I think the answer is negative: We cannot retrieve this living past—where has it all gone? Is life just an hourglass in which all our doings and strivings simply—fatally—disappear into the bottom, sink into oblivion, never to return? If so, then you could say that the condition of living is that of being buried alive: of having the pith and marrow of life stolen from us by time itself, exiling us into a thin and unechoing present from which there is no reprieve.

One of Adrienne Rich's poems is entitled "Diving into the Wreck"; it is a Proustian title inasmuch as everyone's past is a wreck that needs diving into, is a cemetery of past lives that need resurrecting. Proust's utterly secular book is about that resurrection, that act of ultimate retrieval whereby we achieve our longitudinal form, our actual contours, our true measure. Here is a drama as passionate and significant as the great fables of the Bible and Shakespeare. How does Proust do this? In the pages ahead, I want to explore this great novel by bringing us further and further into it. As we penetrate into this fictional world, we shall see that we are also going further and further into the looking glass, and that the reaches and riches coming to light and life are our own.

PROUST UPFRONT

Since I am attempting to map nothing less than a fictional universe, and since explorers need guidebooks, a preview of what is coming may prove of use. The first note struck is Proustian plenitude: a view of self that is not only huge but often despotic. The remarkable *volume* of things in this novel is at once amazing and counterintuitive, since whole worlds can emerge from tiny precincts, as is the case with the famous episode of the madeleine, which leads to the resurrection of the narrator's past, coming out of a teacup. What is despotic is the sheer egocentrism of the book, its principled willingness to explore to the outer limits what the world looks like when we can never get clear of ourselves, when we are always locked into our own perceptual system. It is not hard to imagine the ethical implications of such a philosophy.

Yet this massive project of portraiture turns out to be brazenly subversive, especially when it comes to negotiating Proustian prose; it all *looks* familiar and readable and clear—no narrative high jinks here—but in fact it is devious and riddled with surprises, requiring that readers be wary, but also rewarding them richly for their efforts. I term such writing "false-bottomed" in order to point out how dependent we are on "bottoms," on knowing what the truth is. Our focus on issues of perception and transformation—issues beautifully materialized in Proustian prose with its stunning metaphors and figurative logic—will lead into the more heated and explosive area of sexuality: its peculiar praxis in Proust, as well as its remarkable narrative presentation. Given that all surfaces in Proust end up being coats of many colors, it is not surprising that sexual behavior follows suit. What is surprising is the way in which these matters *open up* the fictional world, making it into something rich and strange; and the unsettling payoff of such a view derives from the challenge it metes out to our fixed assumptions, our complacent sense that we understand what is in front of our eyes. In Proust's work we begin to grasp the insidious effects of *habit*, the ways in which our take on life is pre-scripted and blinding; and we also learn about the kinds of surprises and horrors that can jump out of the box when habit is routed, when familiar things leap out of their skins, when perception gets clear of preconception.

Proust is never merely descriptive, and hence we need to measure the emotional and ethical ramifications of his worldview. Lying will be seen as a central activity, both in public and in private, leading to incessant deceptions, both large and small. But the familiar gambit of social climbing and societal charade pales in color and in vehemence when we ponder the human consequences of lying in the intimate sphere of erotic ties, and Proust emerges as one of the supreme theorists of jealousy: its pain, but also its odd grandeur, its outright novelistic character. The very possibility of love—at least of sustainable and reciprocal love—is on the docket in this long novel, as the narrator's ongoing relationship with Albertine richly illustrates. One often feels that Proustian psychology and Proustian diagnosis are withering and unflinching in their ceaseless exposure of illusion and naive belief, leaving us with a straitened and narrower picture of our affairs.

Yet we shall see that the polar opposite is true: Proust explodes the small notions we have about life—about our own lives—by illuminating our fuller reach and dimensionality, by recovering the longitudinal scale of human existence. To see ourselves and others *in time* is a mighty challenge, for it means transcending the snapshot images that daily life offers us, and it means factoring not only memory but also death into our equation. Nonetheless, this plenary vision is exhilarating rather than morbid, for it restores richness to our affairs, to our own story. Proust shows us what a long shadow we cast, and in doing so, he exposes the "cheat" of ordinary perception, suggesting that our conventional way of going about life constitutes a set of blinders, robs us of our treasure, misconceives the real shape of our fellows, substitutes false coins for true ones. It will surprise no one that Art is called upon to make good on this revolutionary project, but the art in question has little to do with some pantheon of great creators; on the contrary, every human being is embarked on the sole work of art that matters: possessing one's own life. Proust saw his work as a mirror for the reader, an opportunity to discover one's indigenous lines of force, one's untold psychic and emotional history, one's evolving form. Let us begin.

THE MADELEINE

The most radical, magic moment in modern fiction occurs when a tired, middle-aged man dips a pastry, what the French call a "*madeleine*," into his cup of tea, and thereby recovers his past. This justly celebrated passage, recognized by many readers throughout the world (whether or not they have ever read Proust), epitomizes the French novelist's astonishing breakthrough, his revolutionary new conception of what a novel is, and why we might read it. Everything that the realist nineteenth-century novel stands for, is upended here, stood on its head. New vistas, on the order of new planets, are coming into view.

Consider, for a moment, what the great novels of the nineteenth century offer us: a form of historical portraiture. Balzac chronicles the "new" capitalist order in his *Le Père Goriot* of 1835, in which the traditional allegiances of family and love are brutally torn asunder by the cash nexus. Dickens gives us his version of the same story in book after book, perhaps never more perfectly than in the adventures and misadventures of Pip in *Great Expectations*. Of course, such novels have memorable characters, but their mission seems to be one of social illumination, to reveal to a hungry and curious readership the real workings of their contemporary society. Stendhal's accounts of post-Napoleonic France map out with great acuity the new political horizons. Tolstoy tackles nothing less than the great Napoleonic wars themselves, in his saga *War and Peace*, in which individual subject, family, gesture, and fate are inscribed in the convulsions of Europe at war, of Russia under siege. These are all large-souled enterprises, bent on delivering a new kind of map, one that registers the tremors produced (in people and in societies) by changing values, by political upheaval, by social unrest. Readers flocked to these stories, which often appeared in serial form, in order better to grasp their own conditions. The novel was in its prime; you read this "walking mirror" to gauge your own circumstances by understanding the world around you.

Fast-forward to 1912, when Proust publishes *Swann's Way* (*Du Côté de chez Swann*): "What is going on here?" The rules of the game have changed, and the result is a complex, convoluted narrative whose bottom seems to have dropped out. "Where's the beef?" one might legitimately ask. What, where is the story? Capitalism, Napoleon, London and Paris and St. Petersburg have gone up in smoke. Stendhal's moving mirror is still there, but the depiction of society—Realism's central agenda—no longer matters, has disappeared from the page. In its stead, one encounters . . . a piece of pastry dipped in tea. Many readers in 1912, and many readers since 1912, have thought that Proust's book was absurdly narrow in its charge, too limited in its focus, locked into the thoughts and sensations of one (neurotic) figure, and hence locked out of fiction's supposed goal: to paint a picture of the world we live in.

Of course, Proust is doing exactly that, but in new ways: painting the world we live in. But that world is the self. Here is indeed the brave new world. Proust's mission, far from being narrow or solipsistic, is to show you that the self is a world, is the world we live in, the world we can never get out of, and—most provocatively of all—*it is the world we do not know*, the world we can live in and die in without ever knowing. But why a madeleine dipped in tea? Isn't this really too precious, too quaint, to yield anything on the order of this magnitude?

The best way to understand this question is to look at Proust's actual prose. The passage goes like this: The narrator raises to his lips a spoonful of the tea in which the morsel of cake has been soaked, and is suddenly transformed, metamorphosed, via a sense of pleasure so exquisite and overpowering that everything else in his life—his daily cares, his material and emotional circumstances—is eclipsed, annihilated in favor of this ecstatic feeling of deliverance, of salvation. How is this possible? he wonders, and soon enough, logically enough (even if incredibly), he understands that the madeleine has somehow wrought this miracle. But how? Why? A second mouthful of tea repeats the pleasure but yields no answer; a third mouthful yields less still; he then comprehends that the ineffable pleasure may indeed be inseparable from the tea-soaked pastry, but is of a different nature altogether, in short, an elusive something (an elusive "everything," he feels) that is lodged somewhere *inside him*, and to which this flavor-experience points.

But how to retrieve it? A great quandary, this: How to descend into your own depths and emerge with the secrets that are buried there?

Mustering all the concentration he can, the narrator seeks with all his might to bring this tantalizing, beckoning, precious, yet buried feeling to the surface. And fails. As if Proust wanted to show that the most faraway and unknowable planet for human beings to visit is their own inner self, existing an infinity of years from our present moment, yet somehow, miraculously, stirred and brought back to life here, through the senses, but only momentarily, and already fading. It is as if one glimpsed, far away on the inside, locked in the dark interior, a genie in the bottle, a genie who was signaling, a magic genie who wanted out: one's own genie. But the sight starts to blur, to recede, taking one's magic and salvation with it. The narrator tries with all his might to hold on, to bring it up.

And then it happens. "I feel something start within me, something that leaves its resting place and attempts to rise, something that has been embedded like an anchor at a great depth; I do not know yet what it is, but I can feel it mounting slowly; I can measure the resistance, I can hear the echo of great spaces traversed" (I, 49). Balzac had declared, in a famous passage in *Le Père Goriot*, "*Paris est un océan!*" That city-ocean—Paris-London-St. Petersburg—which Balzac and the other realist novelists explored has become in Proust the infinite oceanic self, and the project of diving into it and retrieving his hidden treasures is as arduous as rescuing the *Titanic* from its watery grave. The retrieval of memory is exactly that: titanic. Proust's narrator knows that this ecstatic sensation heralds, almost like a divine annunciation, the emergence of our buried life.

Now the memory comes. It is of Combray, of the sleepy village where the narrator spent his happiest childhood moments. It differs entirely from that other Combray he can recall at will; on the contrary, it is the green, vital, still-living Combray of his past, now reborn in all its immediacy. What is so special? one might demur. All of us can remember our pasts. Not so, according to Proust. To be sure, we are not amnesiac, but the volitional memory on which we all depend—to be able to say where we were this morning, last week, last year; to recall our childhood, our parents or grandparents when they still lived, our grown-up children when they were not grown up—yes, all of us can do this, at least up to a point. But ask yourself: How pulsing, how vibrant, how living is this? Ask yourself further: Just how much can you truly access? "Truly" in the sense of *feeling* it? For many, the austere answer is: "dead leaves." Dead leaves are what we excavate, what we recall. In fact, few of us are capable of coming up with more than a brief list of the countless things we did just a few hours ago (something we rediscover, with irritation, when we have lost an object and try to retrace our most recent steps and fail to do so; the mind is a pit, a black hole).

So, how do things emerge from this hole? How do we get in? What are the conduits? Could a madeleine in tea be enough? Listen to Proust:

> But when from a long-distant past nothing subsists, after the people are dead, after the things are broken and scattered, taste and smell alone, more fragile but more enduring, more unsubstantial, more persistent, more faithful, remain poised a long time, like souls, remembering, waiting, hoping amid the ruins of all the rest; and bear unflinchingly, in the

> tiny and almost impalpable drop of their essence, the vast structure of recollection. (I, 49–50)

This beautiful sequence is still more striking in Proust's original French: The people are not dead but "destroyed," and the suite of adjectives—fragile, enduring, unsubstantial, persistent, faithful—comes first, leads the way, actualizes in our minds the epic labor at hand here, even before we see what those adjectives apply to: "taste and smell." Taste and smell! Has anyone ever before claimed such imperial greatness for taste and smell? The senses, it is they who reverse the entropic work of time; they are the very medium in which our past life refuses to be past. As if to accentuate the grotesque disparity in this equation—the disparity between the whimsical, wispy, capricious puniness of taste and smell on the one hand, and the galactic grandeur of our past life on the other—Proust wants us to realize that the immense edifice of memory (his exact words in French) rests on a "droplet," a *gouttelette*.

How far this is from the nineteenth-century novel, that moving mirror that reflected society's march! The focus here is on the most intimate, fragile, evanescent things. But they are to be the novel's "Open, Sesame," its portal of discovery and route to possession. To assent to Proust requires rethinking who we are, *where* we are (in the sense of where does the inner "I" reside), what do we have, what have we lost, how might we get it back. And this mandates acknowledging a kind of absolute poverty in ourselves—in knowing and *owning* ourselves—that is at complete odds with all our apparent possessions, such as houses, cars, money in the bank, all those things that can be seen in a "walking mirror." Can Proust be right?

The famous passage about the madeleine is situated at the end of the "Overture" to the long novel, as a gateway to the large things—the big story of recovering a self, a lost time—to come. The very final paragraph begins that task, and once again Proust may seem precious in his choice of metaphors. The birth of memory—nothing less than the genesis of the book, the cornerstone of Proust's worldview—is compared to an exotic Japanese custom. Listen again:

> And as in the game where the Japanese amuse themselves by filling a porcelain bowl with water and steeping in it little pieces of paper which

> until then are without character or form, but, the moment they become wet, stretch and twist and take on colour and distinctive shape, become flowers or houses or people, solid and recognisable, so in that moment all the flowers in our garden and in M. Swann's park, and the water-lilies on the Vivonne and the good folk of the village and their little dwellings and the parish church and the whole of Combray and its surroundings, taking shape and solidity, sprang into being, town and gardens alike, from my cup of tea. (I, 51)

With the flourish of a magician pulling all manner of things out of a hat, Proust lifts an entire village—segment by segment, places and people—out of a cup of tea. The pieces of paper that "stretch and twist and take on colour and distinctive shape" stand for literature itself, literature as the page of paper that may look like paper but actually gives birth to life and generates buildings and beings in front of our eyes. I say magicians and magic, because the discrepancy between a cup and a village is enormous. The sheer *volume* on show here (a world coming out of a cup) is Proust's signature, and he shocks us over and over with surprises, jolts us into a discovery of just how unmapped, how dimensional the world, our world—our selves—really might be.

FALSE BOTTOMS AND REVERSALS

To Proust's cup and madeleine, let me add another metaphor to characterize this discovery of new realms: a false-bottomed suitcase. In today's culture of electronic surveillance and security threats, such suitcases—formerly suited for smuggling drugs and other illicit materials through customs—are less likely to be encountered than in the past, but all of us can visualize them. What does it mean when the bottom of the suitcase opens up to reveal a still deeper, concealed new bottom? Might there be still further bottoms? This image appeals to me because it conveys our dependence on "bottoms" to know what things contain, where the baseline is—to get to the "bottom of the story." Proust is interested in removing that conceptual floor that all of us who stand up are standing on. A false-bottomed novel would be a book that starts with an agreed-on reality base, but then undercuts it; such a fiction would constitute an ongoing series of upheavals and jolting discoveries, as we come to realize just how many of the floors and bottoms we believe in are in fact false. Proust's long novel is just that. And it can be quite a roller coaster.

"Combray," the first section after the Overture, and the enticing, idyllic entry into this book, is filled with leisurely notations of village life. These bucolic scenes introduce to us many of the novel's major players—the adored mother, the loving grandmother, Françoise the servant, Swann the family friend, Legrandin the charmer, Vinteuil the rural composer, Aunt Léonie the hypochondriac, the village *curé*, and a host of others just glimpsed such as Gilberte the first love and Charlus the bizarre aristocrat. Combray would seem to denote a calm and reliable place, a place without roller coasters or false bottoms. Indeed, much of Combray's appeal derives from its rock-bottom certitudes, patterns of behavior, and habits of mind. Firm structures abound here: family outings choose between two options, the Guermantes Way and the Méséglise Way (also known as Swann's Way), and these two walks are as distinct and unrelated as left and right, Occident and Orient. Meals are ritualistically served at precise times, and exceptions (such as Saturday's midday meal one full hour later) merely strengthen the rule, add to the feeling of fixity of all living arrangements.

And it goes without saying that nothing surprising or new—such as a person or even a dog that "you don't know"—can ever happen here in Combray. Aunt Léonie, veteran Combray dweller who spends her life gazing at who or what walks past her house, is virtually traumatized by the reckless assertion that an unknown dog was spotted in the street, and soon enough she dispels that silly notion by coming up with name and owner in short order. The Combray grid covers everything: neighbor Swann, son and nephew of barristers and bankers, is mapped forever by these coordinates; Legrandin the freethinker who loves nature and poetry is defined once and for all; Vinteuil's freckled shy daughter with a "mannish" look is a loving child to this modest country composer; Françoise, loyal servant and peerless cook, displays a peasant-like dignity that harks all the way back to *la vieille France*. Proust's narrator and Proust's readers know where they are.

Mais non! Not so at all, as the actual negotiation of Proustian narrative brilliantly conveys to its readers. Nothing is as fixed or evident as it seems. Especially the people or the things we think we know. Swann, it will emerge, is not the delineated bourgeois figure he is thought to be; he hobnobs with the Prince of Wales, with European royalty. Aunt Léonie is not the loving widow she is thought to be, as we learn when the boy discovers her waking up from a dreadful nightmare in which she dreamed, to her horror, that her husband was still alive. Mlle Vinteuil's "mannish" looks turn out to be more prophetic than suspected, as Marcel, the young protagonist, just happens to fall asleep outside her window, wakes up, and then sees—lo and behold—her enacting a sadistic lesbian ritual with her lover, consisting of desecrating the image of her dead father. Proust's book is an unending parade of reversals, of negotiating false bottoms. Françoise, thought by the boy to be a veritable "Michelangelo of the kitchen," suddenly emerges as a darker, more cruel figure, bloodthirsty in her violent slaying of the chicken that will later grace the table, and outright sadistic in her treatment of the pregnant serving girl who has been preparing all those wonderful asparagus dishes for the boy and family.

I have summed up these matters in the explicit language of critical prose, but Proust's own presentation follows the rule of false bottoms, and it lulls us into thinking we understand where we are. Then, sometimes surreptitiously, sometimes dramatically, he turns the tables on us. These reversals have a bite, a punch, that can be very special. And Proust can dish it up to us when we least expect it. He is at his best with the little stuff, the seemingly innocuous and banal details which most readers process lazily, little suspecting there might be serious venom in play. Thus, I return to the asparagus that have been served and eaten all summer. What reader would be suspicious here? With Marcel Proust, however, reading means peeling away the surface, to see what lurks underneath. Here is what asparagus-peeling has actually entailed:

> There is a species of hymenoptera observed by Fabre, the burrowing wasp, which in order to provide a supply of fresh meat for her offspring after her own decease, calls in the science of anatomy to amplify the resources of her instinctive cruelty, and, having made a collection of weevils and spiders, proceeds with marvelous knowledge and skill to pierce the nerve-center on which their power of locomotion (but none of their other vital functions) depends, so that the paralyzed insect, beside which she lays her eggs, will furnish the larvae, when hatched, with a docile, inoffensive quarry, incapable either of flight or resistance, but perfectly fresh for the larder: in the same way Françoise had adopted, to minister to her unfaltering resolution to render the house uninhabitable

> to any other servant, a series of stratagems so cunning and pitiless that, many years later, we discovered that if we had been fed on asparagus day after day throughout that summer, it was because their smell gave the poor kitchen-maid who had to prepare them such violent attacks of asthma that she was finally obliged to leave my aunt's service. (I, 134–135)

What is this? Why invoke wasps and weevils and spiders? With this unflinching scientific description, Proust seems bent not only on turning the tables, but on leaving the human realm altogether, in his revelations about the secret behavior of his creatures. The two lesbians earlier mentioned were characterized as "clucking fowls," as if to signal that sexual pleasure returns its people to bestiary, just as sadism is linked to the insect realm. Is this vision reductive (we are animals) or expansive (we belong in many disparate realms)? To compare the meticulous and sustained cruelty of Françoise with the genetic and instinctive behavior of wasps feeding their young is signature Proust, for it puts us on notice that our customary notions of psychology may play us false, that human motivation may be as lethal and preprogrammed as that of other species, that what we—as eaters of asparagus, as readers of a text—construe to be harmless routine may in fact be calculated torture.

It is, for certain, contrapuntal. The brutal clinical analysis comes after the reader, following Marcel's own innocent vision, has been treated to long paragraphs of lyrical effusions about those asparagus—"these celestial hues indicated the presence of exquisite creatures who had been pleased to assume vegetable form," conveying to the eater the "radiance of earliest dawn," "hinted rainbows," "blue evening shades"—effusions that close with the remark that this delicious fairy-like vegetable, once ingested and then, hours later, excreted, transforms the boy's "chamber pot into a vase of aromatic perfume" (I, 131). For generations of English readers, the earlier Moncrieff translation omitted the word "pot," and countless Anglo-American readers saw only the lyricism, and missed utterly its end result. Such readers were also blinded to Proust's subsequent mention of the "savour" of Françoise's merits or the "proper perfume" of her virtues. Once the wasp and the urine stench are properly factored in, we begin to realize just how cunning Proust's art is, how the rosy-tinted similes are likely to be followed by nastier, earthier, indeed smellier realities.

It is fair to say that Proust is easy to misread along these lines; he was in fact misread by no less than the great novelist André Gide, who advised the publishing house of Gallimard to turn down this manuscript after he had reviewed it. (Gide later termed this the greatest mistake of his editorial career, and told Proust as much.) But one understands how such errors happen, given the flowery lushness of Proustian prose. Yet a careful reading reveals a profoundly slippery world, one of shiny surfaces and romantic effusions covering mudholes and pits and a range of human antics that belong in just such precincts. This little asparagus epic cannot, I think, be successfully paraphrased or translated into its bottom line. Its meaning is inseparable from its style, from its little roller-coaster ride that goes from poetic effusions to insect murder, and the only way to understand Proust—certainly the only way to enjoy him—is to ride with him, to make your own journey from lyricism to poison, from Françoise the magnificent to Françoise the terrible. If you make this trip, if you watch the "perfume" of Françoise's virtues pirouette from flowers to urine, you experience firsthand not only the fun and games but also the wisdom that can be acquired in a false-bottom world.

That is what a careful reading reveals. But how often does either life or literature get a careful reading? Who expects asparagus to pack a wallop or conceal a message? It is fair to say that most of us are a little bit lazy and sleepy about such matters. When Important Things come our way in a text, we observe closely. Not otherwise. Proust can be unhinging along just these lines. He has put his explosives in the details, in the minutiae. In this he is utterly true to life itself, which is deceptive and fuzzy, which does not underline events, which may conceal great acts of morality and immorality under the most benign and innocuous surfaces. There is something tonic and eye-opening in discovering that kitchen dramas can have the reach of Shakespeare. Reading Proust makes you at once warier and more generous, less likely to dismiss trivia, more aware that trivia may explode with significance, may reveal laws you never suspected.

These revelations come in different guises, sometimes overt, sometimes covert, even requiring sleuthing on the part of the reader. One of the most devious "reversals" occurs when Léonie's friend Eulalie is chatting with the *curé* about the stained-glass windows of the church. The *curé*—a minor figure, talkative and boring, perfect candidate for our inattention—is much enamored of both history and etymology, and he suavely explains to Eulalie that the folks depicted in the stained glass are more elusive than she thinks.

He is talking about Saint Hilaire, whom Eulalie has trouble making out (and about whom you the reader may wonder, why the fuss?):

> "Why yes, have you never noticed, in the corner of the window, a lady in a yellow robe? Well, that's Saint Hilaire, who is also known, you will remember, in certain parts of the country as Saint Illiers, Saint Hélier, and even, in the Jura, Saint Ylie. But these various corruptions of *Sanctus Hilarius* are by no means the most curious that have occurred in the names of the blessed. Take, for example, my good Eulalie, the case of your own patron, *Sancta Eulalia;* do you know what she has become in Burgundy? Saint Eloi, nothing more nor less! The lady has become a gentleman. Do you hear that, Eulalie—after you're dead they'll make a man of you!" (I, 113)

Innocuous banter? Or straight-on prophecy? The devil, once again, is in the details, and once you espy him there, you'll relish Proust all the more. This chitchat about stained-glass windows is indeed a window itself, a window onto the book's major activity: sex-change, just as Marcel earlier espied the two lesbians by looking through a window. That first time was easy and direct; this go-around is more devious, but also more titillating, for we begin to realize that Proust is spilling his story of gender-bending all over the map, that he plants it, like the clue to a treasure hunt, in the oddest places, including the stained-glass window of a country church. Maybe he is telling us that the venerable history of the saints is actually hot stuff if you know how to look, if you bring to it your longitudinal lenses, enabling you to see that, iconically and over time, ladies become men. *Ladies become men.* Once you've read more deeply into Proust and have encountered the homosexual theme, then this humble passage starts to shine in the dark. For women do change into men, and men do change into women, all the time in Proust's book. "After you're dead, they'll make a man of you," the *curé* says; but no one waits so long in Proust's world for sexual transformation, and these changes are hardly limited to stained-glass windows, and you needn't be dead or in Burgundy for it to happen, since it is going to be one of the novel's central ongoing spectacles.

A lot of noise about a church window, you might be murmuring. Proustian prose is delicious and savory along just these lines: It plants clues everywhere, it mines the terrain, it is endlessly preparing its reversals and surprises and revelations. This is art with a pattern. It is not clear to most of us that life itself has pattern; you do not usually expect architectural details to spill the beans about sexual behavior going on around you. In Proust, things bubble and bind, suggesting odd linkages and connections, implying a level of cogency we had not suspected. Life itself seems without pattern, I blithely said. But is it? Ask an anthropologist what exactly he or she examines when visiting a strange people or tribe. The answer will not be simply religious services, sanctioned rituals, and moments of high seriousness; on the contrary, the student of culture is especially focused on the little things, the telling details, the odd bites of information, the pieces of the "story" that are spread out in countless little routines. That is how the anthropologist gets a picture. The Proustian tribe will require a comparable approach.

PERCEPTION AND METAMORPHOSIS

When asparagus tells us about sadism, when stained-glass windows tell us about sex change, we are obliged to readjust our perceptual lenses. Straightforward reporting—the facts, ma'am, just the facts—is going out of business. False-bottom literature not only stuns us with surprises (as, say, to the "nightlife" of its daytime denizens), but also teaches us to be better readers, teaches us to recognize how many bottoms might be false, how many facts might be fictions, how many notations might be door-opening rather than descriptive. In Proust things are multiple, kaleidoscopic, changing in front of our eyes. And whereas we might regard such writing as merely playful or cunning, the real impact of such a vision transcends style altogether and moves into our own backyard: Our own lives, experiences, and perceptions are multiple, kaleidoscopic. Here is the payoff: A novel that upends our own complacent certainties, teaches us to make friends with metamorphosis, shows us what a shimmering thing a life is.

Life shimmers. That is Proust's knowledge. It is not a question of a clever style that likes to link things together; on the contrary, it is a more primitive intuition that the world is more fluid and restless than we think, that everyday experience is wilder and less bounded than we think. It is a point of view that whispers: *All* bottoms are false, all bottom lines illusory. We find evidence of this vision everywhere, high and low, in the mirror as well as in the kitchen or bedroom. Consider, as an especially pedestrian example, the experience of a toothache. What ambiguity here? Your whole head aches and throbs, and this (we say) is rock-bottom certainty. Proust serves it up to us in a new key:

> When we have gone to sleep with a raging toothache and are conscious of it only as of a little girl whom we attempt, time after time, to pull out of the water, or a line of Molière which we repeat incessantly to ourselves, it is a great relief to wake up, so that our intelligence can disentangle the idea of toothache from any artificial semblance of heroism or rhythmic cadence. (I, 30)

Much to ponder in this modest aside. Daylight and waking up restore things to their proper boxes, yes—this is a toothache, that is saving a girl, and the other is Molière—but what are we to make of their fusion at night, in sleep or dream? Even the dreamer "knows" they are different, but they nonetheless become one another. Is this what pain does: erases contours, blends things together, recomposes the world? Have you ever taken notes or made journal entries or tried to be coherent when in great pain or under duress? Things can look awfully jumbled then. We know that our dreams obey this fluid, associative logic, but the deeper and more engaging question is: Does our real daytime life stay put in neat definitions and boxes? Moreover, the nighttime world where forms tumble and things merge is a bristling artistic proposition, for it reshuffles our deck, unfixes what seems fixed, makes the so-called known things unknowable.

What if this kaleidoscopic regime spilled over into the day, took over the day? Proust is going to suggest that, at least in moments of crisis involving jealousy and desire, but even in moments of acute perception and discovery, that is precisely what happens. The old familiar world goes out of business, sloughs off its skin, reveals its startling *alterity*, its otherness. Think how your own story would change in this regimc, how thc very shape of your existence would take on new contours, reveal new connections, disclose a strange new logic.

The curtain is often lifting in Proust, revealing a stage behind the stage, and it is easy to misconstrue these revelations as merely an obsession with secrets and concealment. Proust is indeed modern in the sense that he knows all of us have something to conceal—whether it be our cheating on taxes or our spouses, or our furtive picking of the nose or passing gas, or the altogether more disturbing hidden data such as feelings of inappropriate passion (hunger, hatred, itching to kill or bed) for those we live or work with—but his deeper interest is in the blindness itself that stamps our commerce with the world. It is largely the blindness of complacency, of lazy habits of mind, of finding the world orderly because we have constructed our tiny little fence around a tiny little part of it. Art, in Proust, would be the royal way out of this mire, and some of his most memorable pages are devoted to the unsettling, shape-shifting power of art as seen in painting, music, and literature. We are so accustomed to conceiving art as staid and docile artifacts to be properly viewed from afar that Proust's model comes as a shock: Art is the explosion that wrecks your givens, redraws both your setting and your own contours, destabilizes just about everything you thought was standing still.

TRANSFORMATIVE ART

Remembrance of Things Past contains three massive portraits of the artist: Bergotte the writer, Elstir the painter, and Vinteuil the composer. Scholars have long sought to pin a real historical name to each of these figures, but it seems wisest to treat them as exemplary figures, each showing us what kind of new purchase on reality is made possible by the various arts. We might consider each of these figures as a special lens, a window onto the world; through their vision we are helped to a surprising new sense of what had seemed familiar, including the most familiar thing of all: ourselves.

Bergotte is perhaps the most peculiar of the bunch, inasmuch as the young protagonist finds it simply impossible to reconcile the author of divine pages with the flesh-and-blood figure whom he meets at Mme Swann's. Not that the man at dinner is an impostor, rather that the figure across the table is simply unrelatable, incompatible with the books he has written. The narrator is dumbfounded by this cleavage between the testimony of art and the human being in front of his eyes or across the table. Whatever is meaningful about the artist, we begin to understand, may not be even conveyable in his physical person or his actual conversation or indeed his entire social life.

What do we learn from this? How often have you felt that you would give anything to have an hour's intimate conversation with Plato or Sophocles or Leonardo or Shakespeare or Mozart or Dickens or Picasso? Proust suggests that you'd be disappointed and frustrated, that you'd be wasting your time. Why? Because what these great artists have to give (what they have given) is unamenable to conversation, inasmuch as that self you'd be (hungrily) listening to has no connection with that other self that went into the art. The implications of this insight are far-reaching, since they suggest that biographical research is an idle pastime, that the lines of life and art are parallel in the sense that they can never meet. I call this "far-reaching," since our own age has such an avid appetite for biography, cannot ever know enough about the private life of artists and other luminaries. We think we'll find their secret in their libraries or bedrooms, in the liaisons they had or breakdowns they experienced. I suspect there is both prurience and curiosity at work here, a desire to pry into the affairs of the great and to pounce on what made them great.

We need also to turn this insight in the other direction: How much of our own selves comes across in conversation? Is there a "you" deep inside that never makes it across the threshold of verbal exchange? How does what one conveys through talk actually stack up against the complex and unvoiced person that lurks deep inside each of us? And, indeed, how does what others (including loved ones) know of oneself stack up against one's inner being? Have you ever given your real measure? Could you? Has anyone ever taken your full measure? Could they? How? Proust believes that artists do just that, and he locates Bergotte's genius, oddly enough, in his *style*, in his special way of representing things. Style? Isn't this just ornament? How can it conceal the secret we are searching for? Shouldn't the key to great people be lodged in their ideas and thoughts?

Not so, says Proust. Artistic greatness has nothing to do with intellect, but everything to do with the power of transformation. Proust's own marvelous style is on show here, as he proffers, once again, a remarkable scientific metaphor to account for Bergotte's breakthrough: "To mount the skies it is not necessary to have the most powerful of motors, one must have a motor which, instead of continuing to run along the earth's surface, intersecting with a vertical line the horizontal which it began by following, is capable of converting its speed to lifting power" (I, 597). I find this reference to airplanes utterly astonishing at this date (1919). Proust has the last thing we'd suspect: a technological imagination. I will say more about this later, but even here we can see how a new form of power is being transposed from aeronautics to art, so as to show that art is aeronautic, overcomes the laws of gravity, reorganizes that Newtonian deck we are accustomed to. It does so by transforming the givens you have always taken for granted. *Art is vehicular.* It can even be ballistic, as it shatters and reconfigures what we thought we knew.

Such as asparagus and stained-glass windows and toothaches. Such as the hidden lives of Combray dwellers. Such as what lurks under all those false bottoms we have taken for real. The theory of art being put forth is exactly what has been governing this writing for some time now. But we don't fully measure just how revolutionary and far-reaching this model might be until Proust applies it to the visual world. At first one thinks: Wait a minute now, even if concepts and interpretations are tricky business, all of us *see* the same world, all of us agree on what is black and what is white, what is up and what is down. Or what is land and what is sea.

Well, it would seem that the great painter of the novel, Elstir, is not so sure; or, to be more precise, Elstir has elected to *transpose* land and sea in his paintings. Consider, for example, the depiction of the harbor of Carquethuit, where the painter has employed "for the little town, only marine terms, and urban terms for the sea" (I, 894). Realizing that he, Marcel Proust, only has words at his disposal—as opposed to oil colors—the author actually takes up the gauntlet and *writes* this painting. He writes that the beach has no fixed boundary, that "the men who were pushing down their boats into the sea were running as much through the waves as along the sand," that a painted ship, actually at sea but altered by perspective, "seemed to be sailing through the middle of the town," and that the "women gathering shrimps among the rocks had the appearance, because they were surrounded by water . . . of being in a marine grotto overhung by ships and waves, open yet protected in the midst of miraculously parted waters" (I, 895).

Any reader will immediately recognize the style of Impressionist landscapes and seascapes in which objects are rendered as the eye takes them in, not as the mind knows them to be. This simple principle is far more destabilizing than we might suspect. Those "miraculously parted waters" unmistakably send us back to the Old Testament, to the power of God, who can make miracles happen by sovereignly redistributing land and sea. But the god at work here is an artist, and his powers are equally demiurgic. This is precisely what the narrator has understood the very moment he entered Elstir's studio, and this shape-shifting force is strikingly compared to the work of metaphor: "But I was able to discern from these [seascapes] that the charm of each of them lay in a sort of metamorphosis of the objects represented, analogous to what in poetry we call metaphor, and that, if God the Father had created things by naming them, it was by taking away their names or giving them other names that Elstir created them anew" (I, 893).

One might think that this entire discussion of painting and poetry, transposition and metamorphosis, is arcane, is merely an aesthetic discourse with little punch or further reach. Just as one might think that a pastry dipped into a cup of tea is not very momentous. In fact, huge things are in play here, and they constitute much of the Proustian signature, as well as what we stand to learn in reading him. Elstir's paintings are confusing, just as Renoir's paintings were initially confusing and shocking; art critics pointed out, with pious anger, that Renoir seemed to have forgotten that women's shoulders are not blue, that the colors in a painting are expected to correspond to reality. We smile, today, at the naiveté of these early responses to Impressionism, because painters like Renoir and Monet have taught us to rethink what the world looks like, or, more precisely, to discover that the world *does not look like what we think*, because light reconfigures, transposes, mediates all visual perception. In a certain shadow, yes, a woman's shoulders will be blue, just as the cathedral at Rouen will look utterly different at each hour of the day.

IMPRESSIONIST PROSE: FORGETTING WHAT YOU "KNOW"

What would Impressionist prose look like? Probably like this: "A little tap on the window-pane, as though something had struck it, followed by a plentiful light falling sound, as of grains of sand being sprinkled from a window overhead, gradually spreading, intensifying, acquiring a regular rhythm, becoming fluid, sonorous, musical, immeasurable, universal: it was the rain" (I, 110). Here is prose that delivers our sensory experience, and only later puts a label or cognitive tag on it. This kind of writing, like this kind of painting, is not easy, because it entails *forgetting what you know* in order to convey how it actually feels or looks or sounds: "The effort made by Elstir to strip himself, when face to face with reality, of every intellectual notion, was all the more admirable in that this man who made himself deliberately ignorant before sitting down to paint, forgot everything that he knew in his honesty of purpose (for what one knows does not belong to one-self), had in fact an exceptionally cultivated mind" (I, 898).

What can it possibly mean when Proust slips in, parenthetically, "for what one knows does not belong to oneself"? What we "know" is the entire arsenal of so-called facts and data (and received ideas) that we are taught in school and in books. Two times two equals four. My name is Arnold Weinstein. I am composing on a laptop. It is 4:18 P.M. These things are true enough, but they are not *ours*; we may have "read" them, but they are not written in us, engraved in us, there in the dark waiting to be deciphered, translated. Proust seems to be hinting at a vast, utterly unsuspected and unacknowledged fraud whereby humankind has taken the counterfeit for the real, has taken a conventional, agreed-on, conceptual scheme as reality and thereby lost sight altogether of the radically different data that life offers our eyes, our senses, and even our hearts and minds.

Mind you, this notion has been with mankind for some time now: We find it as early as Plato's allegory of the Cave, in which humans mistake shadows for substance, and we find it as recently as in the film *The Matrix*, in which we learn that everyone has been insidiously blinded to the real machinations and even forms of the actual creatures who've taken over the world, blinded precisely in order to see only their conventional scheme of things and confuse it with reality. Proust fits somewhere in between, inasmuch as he is not suggesting a malevolent takeover by beasts or Others, but rather something different: an individual cheat, a loss of the only thing that can actually matter—our own life, our own perceptions, our own selves. We are all deluded by false currency, even though it is called knowledge, because such currency has no truck with our genuine inmost experience of life. Each of us has to recover his or her own story.

For what one knows does not belong to oneself. What does belong to oneself? Proust's deceptively simple answer is: the way life enters and marks you, the unscripted perception of things, the staggering moments when people and places jump out of their definitional skin, when everything agreed on falls apart, to reveal a new constellation altogether. Bergotte, Elstir, and Vinteuil—the artists—toil in exactly that vineyard. Not that they have an agenda or a program, but that their work peels away layers of convention, removes our blinders, stuns us with its findings. Artistic vision, which we usually think of as creative, is perhaps best understood as dissociative or recombinant. The artist is the person who takes apart and dismantles our fixed ideas and received notions; the artist is the fellow who reassembles things in his own way.

Here is how Proust defines Elstir's peculiar gift: "Artistic genius acts in a similar way to those extremely high temperatures which have the power to split up combinations of atoms which they proceed to combine afresh in a diametrically opposite order, corresponding to another type" (I, 920). Once again we encounter the technological Proust, the man fixated on power. In reference to Bergotte, I have already called art "*vehicular*"; let me now go one step further and say that artistic vision resembles *fission*, and with that term I want explicitly to evoke nuclear energy, the explosive energy that dwells in the atom that is liberated precisely via the breaking of the atom's own armature. To destroy the frame/armature of traditional thinking can be an explosive, perilous undertaking. We know this to be true literally in our post-Hiroshima world, but it has its figurative truth as well. Great artists and inventors wreck our received views, smash the protective forms that have corralled things up to now, produce something on the order of an outing, a wilding. Marcel Proust, darling of psychological fiction, is not the precious figure we often take him to be; he knocks down walls.

Art does not describe or reflect the given world; art takes off its cover and rearranges it according to the artist's own vision. We are told of Elstir's portraits that they do not resemble their subjects nearly so much as they resemble themselves. It is a fascinating insight, and it radically overturns the old Aristotelian mission of art as *mimesis*, or "imitation." One is therefore not in the least surprised to find that the society ladies who sat for Elstir were often horrified by the resulting portraits, since Elstir's ultimate fidelity was to his own inner eye. It would be easy to interpret all this as a maniacally private, hermetic enterprise. But Proust's brilliance goes the other way. In being true to his inner vision, in creating a world that explodes the conventional frames, the artist is performing the ultimate public service. He *refigures* life, shows that the shapes we go by just might be altered, scrapped, reimagined, reinvented. Proust's scheme is not all that different from Blake's: "If the doors of perception were cleansed every thing would appear to man as it is, infinite. For man has closed himself up, till he sees all things thro' narrow chinks of his cavern" (Blake, 73). It is *our* vision that is at stake, and it is our vision that will be changed. Our vision has indeed been changed by Monet and Renoir, just as it has by those who came after Proust.

HOW TO WRITE SEXUAL OTHERNESS

And it is not only a question of reconceiving sunsets or seascapes. And it goes further than transposing urban and marine elements in a painting. It has to do with how we look at what we look at. It can have a lot to do with people, for they, too, like the figures in Combray's church window, may well be more dimensional than we suspect, may have sides to them that we cannot see, just as we cannot see the other side of the moon. This is particularly on show when the fission-like vision of Elstir comes into play, as in this early work entitled *Miss Sacripant,* where the viewer cannot determine the sex of the subject; this portrait of a young actress dressed up as a man is "unreadable," largely because Elstir had

> fastened upon this equivocal aspect as on an aesthetic element which deserved to be brought into prominence, and which he had done everything in his power to emphasise. Along the lines of the face, the latent sex seemed to be on the point of confessing itself to be that of a somewhat boyish girl, then vanished, and reappeared further on with a suggestion rather of an effeminate, vicious and pensive youth, then fled once more and remained elusive. (I, 908)

It now jumps out at us that the same artistic vision that delights in transposing land and sea in its depiction of nature is equally disposed to redistribute sex and gender. It is as if the transformation, the metamorphic principle alone, were what most mattered. And if you look more closely at the description of *Miss Sacripant,* you see the makings of a veritable plot, rendered most acutely in the language of a pursuit that is at once epistemological (what sex is this person?) and emotional (what sex are *you*?), so that terms such as "on the point of confessing," "then vanished . . . reappeared further on . . . fled once more . . . remained elusive" delineate a search, perhaps a frantic search. If you are willing to put some oomph into those words, you have the makings of a tragic dilemma: The lover must but cannot know the actual sex/gender of the beloved. False bottoms again. But fireworks as well, because we now begin to realize that the artistic vision, which revels in metamorphosis and transformation, is delightful when it comes to landscapes but can be a source of boundless anxiety and dread when it characterizes one's own love life. Until you arrive at that pass, until you simply have to know where the bottom is, well then, Proust suggests, you are probably living in the dark while thinking everything is clear.

Maybe that is what clear thinking is: comfortable certainties when it doesn't matter (personally), truths about "other" lives, the clarity of the laboratory rather than the bedroom. Each of us will sort this out differently, but I cannot help thinking that Proust reveals the strange uselessness of so many of the truths, laws, axioms, and other guiding principles we are larded with. We are cemeteries of data and inert facts that, as far as human experience is concerned, never pay off or pay their way. So much of what we proclaim to "know" has no bite on life. When I reflect on the abyss between what school has taught me (all those tests I scored 100 on), and what life has taught me, I am ever more firmly convinced that we live in the dark, and that the bright provable facts governing the physical world are not to be found in the experiential realm. Perhaps that is what makes science delectable: Truth is to be had there.

But science is not the only truth provider. As acculturated human beings, we are awash in principles and theses that are said to govern the soft stuff as well: our emotional and moral lives; family, school, church, and state do their bit in this arena. We are (invisibly, incessantly) barraged by theorems and injunctions, by laws and truths, from the moment we draw breath, coming to us indeed in the very air we breathe. There is nothing harmful here, and there is probably no other way to live in culture. We imbibe norms. Nonetheless, Proust's depiction of sexual otherness tackles all routinized perceptions and notions, and it treats them as false bottoms, as facades, as illusory boundaries about human behavior; to use his own favorite term, it *inverts* them, turns them inside out, upside down.

Not that you sense any of this at the outset, but that, bit by bit, ineluctably, virtually every major character in the novel—except, of course, the narrator and his family—will be exposed as homosexual. Critics and readers alike have been struck by the sheer numbers of homosexuals in Proust. Statistically, this would seem a weak case, but Proust is no statistician. Still, in a book of more than three thousand pages, this progressive set of revelations nonetheless takes considerable time. More to the point, Proust achieves some of his greatest effects and most profound observations by focusing on the moment the curtain goes up, on what it takes to move from false bottom to bottom, from straight to inverted; the French term that Proust invokes for homosexuals is *inverti*, a word that bristles with morphological possibilities, suggesting that forms are malleable, that forward may be backward, that shape-shifting is the nature of the human carnival. Now it might well be thought that this entire dimension of Proust's novel would cease to compel our interest, given how common and unshocking it is, today, to speak of sexual preferences and alternate lifestyles. But I'd want to say that Proust shocks us nonetheless, because his real target here is perceptual rather than moral, and that challenge—how do we see things? how well do we know what we think we know?—is not likely to become obsolete or dated, however much our mores may change.

The book's central and unforgettable pederast is M de Charlus; many think this fascinating figure to be Proust's most stunning achievement. How does Proust get this man across? Just as Proustian asparagus, stained-glass windows, and toothaches are more complicated than we thought, Charlus is also going to be a tricky item whose measure is hard to take. It all has to do with what we see in what we see. We first come across him in the background in *Combray*, where he is said to be Mme Swann's lover, but the prose stages something rather strange: Instead of Charlus being seen by the narrator, the current seems to go the other way, with Charlus doing the looking, targeting the narrator himself: "a gentleman in a suit of linen 'ducks,' whom I did not know either, [who] stared at me with eyes which seemed to be starting from his head" (I, 154). There is veiled appetite here—in fact the novel will never, even when Charlus's cover is entirely off, once say straight-out that this older man lusts after our narrator. Like the children's game show-and-tell, Proust is out to show Charlus, while leaving it to us to tell. Later, the narrator is again *told* about a masculine Charlus with countless female conquests, but *sees*

> a man of about forty, very tall and rather stout, with a very black moustache, who, nervously slapping the leg of his trousers with a switch, was staring at me, his eyes dilated with extreme attentiveness. From time to time these eyes were shot through by a look of restless activity such as the sight of a person they do not know excites only in men in whom, for whatever reason, it inspires thoughts that would not occur to anyone else—madmen, for instance, or spies. (I, 807)

Again, the current is on, and Marcel is on the receiving end once more, trying to guess at what strange pulsion is at work in this older man. Several pages later, in prose that still keeps mum about sexuality, we again find these strange, restless, uncontrollable, wildly significant eyes, eyes that "were never fixed on the person to whom he was speaking, strayed perpetually in all directions, like those of certain frightened animals, or those of street hawkers who, while delivering their patter and displaying their illicit merchandise, keep a sharp look-out, though without turning their heads, on the different points of the horizon from which the police may appear at any moment" (I, 815).

Mind you, at no point does the narrator suspect anything untoward about Charlus (including the fact that he himself seems coveted, desired), but the eyes tell their own bizarre story. Here is a final installment: "the eyes were like two crevices, two loop-holes which alone he had failed to stop, and through which, according to one's position in relation to him, one suddenly felt oneself in the path of some hidden weapon which seemed to bode no good, even to him who, without being altogether master of it, carried it within himself in a state of precarious equilibrium and always on the verge of explosion" (I, 817).

Proust keeps Charlus's actual sexual identity secret for more than 1,600 pages. You may well object that this is a secret in full view, inasmuch as any clued-in reader can fill in the blanks and deduce that Charlus's strange, furtive appearance is tied to his homosexual nature. Or can one? We certainly know that something is powerfully off in this man, but do we know what it is? It is easy enough for us to gauge what this writing does not say: Charlus is homosexual. Far more interesting is what it *does* say. We have been given a portrait of a man tortured by his own indwelling needs and equipment (figured as hidden weapon, as ticking bomb, as trapped animal, as illicit wares), and we also realize that this entire internal repertory of forces and wants is ungovernable, is incessantly jerking Charlus to *its* tune, is at every moment straining to pop out through his eyes. No single word or term that I know of—such as "homosexual"—can possibly rival (in expressive power) this rich ongoing description of creatural and cultural bewitchment, of somatic thralldom versus social masquerade, of the misfit between libido and culture. Yes, indeed, the eyes have it, and we can hardly miss the challenge at hand: Do *our* eyes have it? Can we see what is in front of us? One thing is unmistakable: Proust is writing pretty much the way Elstir paints—he depicts what the retina takes in, while refusing to put a label on it.

Reading Proust is an education in seeing, for he puts our own interpretive powers on the line. This is no mean achievement, for it parallels the actual workings of reality, our own reality, where we never—absolutely never—have the services of a guide or interpreter to tell us what things mean, what they conceal, where the actual bottom might be. Instead, we rely on our smarts, on our intuitive critical abilities, to sort things out, to determine where we are and whom we are dealing with. Those restless, frightened, hungry, explosive, illicit eyes constitute an eloquent signal of inavowable appetite, appetite directed at the narrator himself. In real life you'd feel this, yes? Or would you? This novel helps you find out.

BIRDS AND BEES

At some point even Proust is obliged to come out with the secret. You might expect this discovery to be less provocative (from a writerly perspective) than the earlier so-called innocent depictions of Charlus, but we're in for a surprise. The opening pages of the middle volume, *Cities of the Plain,* are as fascinating as anything in the entire novel. The central, audacious conceit that governs the (now) up-front representation of homosexuality in the novel is the motif of botany. Why botany? The narrator is positioned in the Guermantes' courtyard, waiting to see if a very particular miracle of nature is to take place or not: whether a particular rare orchid will—or will not—be visited and fecundated by the hoped-for bee.

Yes, the most astute psychological novelist of the twentieth century is holding forth about the birds and bees, and he is telling us that our sex life is best understood if we drop all humanistic perspectives and examine, instead, how the animals and plants operate. Flowers, Proust tells us, do not simply wait for the bee to come; they curve their stamens and arch their "styles" so as best to be penetrated by the longed-for insect. And these matters are ruled by natural process, so that fertilization will ensure a future; but—and it is a critical but—at given moments a species may in fact become "over-developed" and then require *self-fertilization.* Such a process—nothing less than a botanical version of homosexuality, it will be seen—is hauntingly described as the curb, the brake, that regulates life itself, not just our sexual life but also our moral life:

> . . . then, as an anti-toxin protects us against disease, as the thyroid gland regulates our adiposity, as defeat comes to punish pride, as fatigue follows indulgence, and as sleep in turn brings rest from fatigue, so an exceptional act of self-fertilisation comes at the crucial moment to apply its turn of the screw, its pull on the curb, brings back within the norm the flower that has exaggeratedly overstepped it. (II, 625)

One feels that an entire philosophical tradition—which the French call the *moraliste* tradition, not in the sense of "moralizing" but in the sense of "unpacking" or "plumbing" events for their ethical significance—is alive and well here, nourishing this prose. The suite of analogies at hand, moving from notations about the immune system on to other check-and-balance systems including defeat and pride, a kind of systolic/diastolic that regulates all life's rhythms, signals something of the reach of this passage. And signals as well, I think, the stifling narrowness of our ordinary labels and categories. Proustian similes and metaphors open up the world, thread discrete events into a larger weave, link the natural to the moral. Large things are in play. The rare orchid that can only be fertilized by a particular bee, and the equally rare intervention of nature to mandate self-fertilization, are the necessary "natural" curtain that Proust places in front of us—instructing us as to what is in play, and why it is in play—so that he can then lift this botanical screen in order to illuminate the intensely human activity about to take place on the stage: the coupling, in the Guermantes' courtyard, of Charlus the grand aristocrat with Jupien the modest tailor.

MATING RITUALS AND HIDDEN KINSHIPS

These two men—whom not only routine but every conceivable social category has kept separate from each other until this moment—perform a wondrous mating ritual. Each alters his posture and movements instantaneously and "in perfect symmetry" as they become locked into their dance, leading Jupien to throw back his head, tilt his body, place his hand "with grotesque effrontery on his hip," stick out his behind, strike "poses with the coquetry that the orchid might have adopted on the providential arrival of the bee" (II, 626–627). This scene is stamped, Proust says, "with a strangeness, or if you like a naturalness, the beauty of which steadily increased" (II, 627).

How, Proust asks, can such synchrony, such a pas de deux that "seemed to have been long and carefully rehearsed" (II, 627), emerge out of nowhere? The answer sheds some light on the stunning *depths* of this book: It is nothing less than a *common language* that Charlus and Jupien—who have never laid eyes on each other—share. The linguistic key is fascinating here: Proust alludes to people whom you meet in a foreign country, people who are compatriots and with whom you have a conversation, with whom in fact you share considerable common ground, even though you do not know each other. Shared sexual preference is to be understood as precisely a lingua franca, and we are obliged to rethink what "knowing" is, to rethink commonality itself. What is stunning here is the limning of new social (as well as verbal) contours, the coming into visibility of an unsuspected community, with its very special native speakers, all sharing a common (even if—especially if—unsuspected) culture.

In our modern era of multiculturalism, of (sometimes strident) identity politics, Proust is a surprising forerunner, for he shows us how layered our identities are, how our citizenship in many different communities—sexual, racial, regional, ethnic, professional, linguistic—makes us fellow travelers, gives us bedfellows (as it were) that our lazy habits of mind and category have ignored. To put this in bald terms: Gays sense one another, connect with one another, just as Jews or Muslims or born-agains or lawyers or doctors or English-speakers abroad might. I can still recall a moment when my parents made their first trip to Europe, made the required ritual visit to the Louvre, stood in front of the *Mona Lisa*, remarked (as countless thousands have) how small it was, and then noticed another smiling American couple standing next to them who said, "Oh, you're Jewish, aren't you?" At which point a lengthy conversation ensued. This incident happened forty years ago, and I am still drawn to the non sequiturs on show: Americans in Paris in front of *La Gioconda* sensing what it is that binds them, what they share, and moving unerringly onto it. (They might have discussed Paris or art, but they didn't.) Is this not kinship?

But in Proust's world of more than a century ago, the central kinship in question—homosexuals sensing one of their kind—is a forbidden kinship, an outlawed family. Yet my personal reference to Jews is quite in keeping with Proust's own vision, since Jews are precisely the group whom the novel presents as analogous to gays, groups that were shunned by polite society, groups whose members recognize one another instinctively: Groups to which Marcel Proust (hatefully, helplessly) belonged by dint of both sexual proclivity and family background. No surprise that the prose becomes overheated, pulsing and rhapsodic as it casts about for a way of mapping homosexuality's lines of force:

> . . . like Jews again . . . shunning one another, seeking out those who are most directly their opposite, who do not want their company, forgiving their rebuffs, enraptured by their condescensions; but also brought into the company of their own kind by the ostracism to which they are subjected, the opprobrium into which they have fallen, having finally been invested, by a persecution similar to that of Israel, with the physical and moral characteristics of a race, sometimes beautiful, often hideous, finding . . . a relief in frequenting the society of their kind, and even some support in their existence, so much so that, while steadfastly denying that they are a race (the name of which is the vilest of insults), they readily unmask those who succeed in concealing the fact that they belong to it, with a view less to injuring them, though they have no scruple about that, than to excusing themselves, and seeking out (as a doctor seeks out cases of appendicitis) cases of inversion in history, taking pleasure in recalling that Socrates was one of themselves, as the Jews claim that Jesus was one of them, without reflecting that there were no abnormal people when homosexuality was the norm, no anti-Christians before Christ. (II, 639)

This long, sinuous, breathless passage lays bare both the mechanisms of Proust's social vision and the mix of appetite, contempt, and self-contempt that animates it. Proust takes it as axiomatic that we are all, in one way or another, in drag, citizens of some proscribed group, bent on both denial (for ourselves) and exposure (for others). The cardinal rule here is that all of us have something to hide, concerning our deepest wants or proclivities or allegiances. It is a dark vision—utterly at odds with any kind of openness or self-acceptance or group solidarity—for Proust understands to perfection how prejudice and hatred actually work, how they go insidiously *inside* to produce bottomless self-contempt and endless tactical maneuvers. (Notions such as gay pride or black pride or any other kind of pride would have made no sense to him.) There is a Freudian dimension here inasmuch as unavowable sexual appetite (especially homosexual appetite) must go underground in our daily dealings, but the libidinal appears inseparable from the racial, so that Jewishness comes across as equally shameful, unspeakable, and unshareable.

Yet, that is the rub. Deeper even than the law of secrecy and hidden nature lies its opposite: membership in community, shared heritages, kinships, outright need—sexually and racially—to find and mix with one's own kind. There is a double bind here that accounts for much of the fireworks of this novel, because it tells us that the deepest pulsions in our lives are at once locked up and leaking out, unavowable and on show, damning us to concealment while compelling us to bond and to bondage. Deny it though we might, we are *secret sharers*, with antennae out, sniffing—hatefully—to see who is of the same persuasion. And I say "fireworks" because this vision is immensely theatrical, consisting of roles and masks, of double identities and hidden identities.

But it is more than theatrical. Proust is of our moment because he grasps the complexity of self-definition, the multiple strands of history and religion that are woven into the fabric of identity. But society (as he knew it) will have none of these mixtures and hybrids and multiple allegiances, which is why Proust is an expert on marginalizing; he knows it to be the ground rule of social behavior, the key defining move that produces insiders and outsiders, the tainted and the clean, a move that governs both the salons of the Faubourg Saint-Germain and the underground communities of homosexuals and Jews, some of whom are trying to "pass," all of whom wear (at least on the inside) their particular Star of David. There is something desperate and heartbreaking in this seesaw of attraction and repulsion, of isolation and kinship, of longing and denial. We have here a view of the human subject as an endless tug-of-war, a creature living perpetually undercover, unable to reconcile or affirm what most deeply moves and defines him. Proust references history in order to ground these dynamics—Jews remembering their long, rich history, homosexuals recalling the different sexual mores of ancient Greece—but then goes on to annihilate what he has grounded, by insisting that today's outlawed groups have nothing in common with the constituencies of the past, precisely because Christ was not crucified then, and homosexuality was acceptable then. *Then* you could wear your heart or your badge on your sleeve. *Now* you go underground.

By equating homosexuality with Judaism, at least in terms of the underground practices they seem to produce, Proust doubtless shocks the modern reader. In our own, more liberal culture, with its proclaimed acceptance of diversity, Proust's conflation of religion and sexual preference may even seem benighted. But no society is as clean underneath (at the gut level) as its trumpeted principles suggest, a fact that minorities throughout the world both recognize and live with, since the realities of sexual and religious (and racial) prejudice are disturbingly alive and well all over the globe, whether it be on our campuses or in the hot spots we know all too well, where scapegoating and genocide still happen. No one is murdered in Proust's polite and civilized world, but there is plenty of suspicion, prejudice, and hatred. His book overwhelms us with a sense of misfit between the well-policed culture and the camouflaged, complex self. It is in this sense that Proust challenges our notions of who we are, which constituencies we claim and which we fear. In a time of ethnic cleansing on the one hand and debates about affirmative action, gay rights, and the politics of the Middle East on the other hand—arenas where black versus white, straight versus gay, Christian versus Muslim versus Jewish divide up the world all too neatly—I'd like to say Proust should be required reading.

THE SEXUAL MAP

As I said earlier, in today's intellectual culture, homosexuality carries little stigma (although it is by no means as accepted by the country at large as it is in the academy and the world of the arts), and one might think that Proust's novel, deriving such punch from sexual secrets, would be a dated proposition. But as we've seen from Bergotte and Elstir on, art is transformative, and the "night side" of Proust's characters opens up his book and scrambles our notions as to who is who (as the transposition of land and sea scrambles our received ideas about what is what). The homosexual card is the wild card, the joker that remakes the entire deck. Yes, homosexuals (in Proust) are preternaturally keen on ferreting out one another, but that is of course the exception to the general rule of blindness and habit that governs ordinary perception. Insiders and initiates recognize each other at once; the rest of us, Proust implies, are blind, walk past the whole show, suspecting nothing.

The peculiar unfurling narrative presentation of the Baron de Charlus is a prime exhibit for just this view. He starts, we recall, as a man said to be

Mme Swann's lover, a man with eyes popping out of his head, is later seen either oozing with tenderness or exploding with rage vis-à-vis the narrator, and is only in mid-novel "exposed." Proust is out to chart the ubiquitous fogginess and complacency that dog all customary perception. Once, however, the secret is out, Proust expands on it. An entire community, previously invisible, now begins to come into view, because homosexuals (according to Proust) form

> . . . a freemasonry far more extensive, more effective and less suspected than that of the Lodges, for it rests upon an identity of tastes, needs, habits, dangers, apprenticeship, knowledge, traffic, vocabulary, and one in which even members who do not wish to know one another recognise one another immediately by natural or conventional, involuntary or deliberate signs which indicate one of his kind to the beggar in the person of the nobleman whose carriage door he is shutting, to the father in the person of his daughter's suitor, to the man who has sought healing, absolution or legal defence in the doctor, the priest or the barrister to whom he has had recourse (II, 639–640)

One could conceivably write an entire book on Proust by analyzing this sole passage. We discover here, once again, that the world is false-bottomed, that the lines of relationship and force that we confidently assume we know are, in fact, mirages. The actual universe emerging here is wildly exotic and unpredictable; Proust writes that "the ambassador is a bosom friend of the felon, the prince . . . on leaving the duchess's party goes off to confer in private with the ruffian" (II, 640). What is coming into view here is nothing less than an unsuspected circuitry, a kind of sexual wiring that links together the most improbable people, but a wiring and a circuitry that are always on, always "hot" (as the electricians say), hence yielding a power grid that is underneath/behind the one you think you see. If my claims seem exaggerated, just look again at Proust's examples. The beggar is shutting the door to the nobleman's carriage—that is what you see—but he is opening the door to the nobleman's bedroom: That is what you do not see. Fiercer, more destabilizing still is the extended sequence of father/son-in-law, doctor/patient, priest/communicant, and barrister/client, because the very terms here denote a legitimate and apparent relational scheme that is being torn down in front of our eyes. Each of these links is now sexualized, and something on the order of a system-wide taboo-and-transgression is now visible: The father of the bride is sexually linked to the bridegroom, the doctor and the priest and the lawyer are sexually linked to the person who has sought healing, confession, and legal help. The functional, surface relations we take for granted—now exposed as mere cover—have gone up in smoke.

Food for thought here. Let us assume for a moment that Charlus himself fools no one, no one especially among the readers of Proust's novel, readers who either know what this fellow is or quickly figure it out. It could seem that I am overstating my case by claiming that Proust surprises us, remakes the deck. But consider now the examples just given: Who among us construes the father of the bride as the bridegroom's "partner"? More troubling still, do we—should we—interpret our relations with doctors, lawyers, and priests as sexually motivated? We see doctors and lawyers and priests out of need, seeking (often dire) help or counsel; but what do we get? Sexual interest. Reading Proust on this topic reinforces for us just how insidious the sexual card can be, must be, since it overturns and perhaps poisons relations where it has no place, where its presence transforms everything into a play of power and desire. Proust helps us to see that there are huge areas in life where the sexual is entirely inappropriate (as if we didn't know), but that it is there anyway, running the show, calling the shots. And who is the wiser? Do you know? When do you know? How do you know?

My account of these revelations is intentionally sensationalist, because Proust shocks us by giving us a sort of thermal photograph, a photograph of linked people whose hot linkages cross boundaries and reveal a clandestine nexus that is the real energy system. I said "taboo," because incest works precisely along just these lines; sibling and parental relations are inverted into sexual bonds. But Proust—again like Freud—is as interested in *sublimated* connections as he is in outright sexual contact, since the libidinal network is what he wants to illuminate. This is especially intriguing inasmuch as sublimated relations defy exposure, never come to fruition, indeed may never even come to full consciousness. *Never come to fruition.* Just because rape or touching is absent is no proof that the sexual current is off. Think how such a view disarms us, makes it possible for us to be in sexual scenarios that we cannot see, for us to be playing a role we do not fathom. Thus, he sketches the trajectory of a young homosexual who hears of his cousin's death and from his inconsolable grief learns (only now) that he has desired this man all his life. Proust is unflinching and relentless about these matters, and he takes his measure at a level where actual behavior (i.e., consummated acts) counts for nothing, since desire itself is his target:

> No doubt the life of certain inverts appears at times to change, their vice (as it is called) is no longer apparent in their habits; but nothing is ever lost: a missing jewel turns up again; when the quantity of a sick man's urine decreases, it is because he is perspiring more freely, but the excretion must invariably occur. (II, 648)

Proust the scientist is visible again here, as he links the urgency and necessity of desire to that of our body's mechanisms for excretion, but this is a scientist obsessed with guilt and secrecy, a scientist who seems to be saying that our sexual need is as censored and shameful (and undeniable) as our need to urinate and defecate, activities that are rarely flaunted socially. Desire is content to go underground, even to elude consciousness altogether, as long as it continues to drive our machine. Sexual need is various, can finance nobler ventures such as chaste affection and love based on esteem, because our desires "have been turned by a sort of transfer as, in a budget, without any alteration in the total, certain expenditure is carried under another head" (II, 648–649).

Thus it is rigorously appropriate that we *now* be told of Charlus that certain forms of sexual conjunction could take place with no physical contact at all, that certain persons could be invited to his house, held for an hour or more under the domination of his talk, in order for Charlus's sexual desire, "inflamed by some earlier encounter, to be assuaged" (II, 652). Rigorously appropriate because this is what the reader has (earlier, unwittingly) witnessed: the narrator involved in a quasi-hysterical encounter with the Baron that seemed merely weird and enigmatic, but that now takes on its true (sublimated) sexual coloration, "just as certain flowers, by means of a hidden spring, spray from a distance the disconcerted but unconsciously collaborating insect" (II, 652).

No one who has read Proust's pages on this topic will ever quite regard human exchange as innocently again, since he is adumbrating a relational world that is 100 percent sexualized, but invisibly, indirectly, untrackably. But no less imperiously. Like the proverbial tip of the iceberg, all that shows in human exchange is the innocuous stuff a camera might record: Underneath, far from being a mountain of ice, there is a kind of libidinal miasma, a circuitry that may require no connection at all, opening up your every encounter into something on the order of those electronic maps installed in the Paris métro, on which you press a button to show where you want to go, and—presto—lights indicate all the various routes that would get you there. Communication in Proust activates all these channels, and you may just as easily be at either end of the circuit, the receiver as well as the sender. I don't think there is any conceivable way of proving such a thesis, so I am counting on my reader to measure its validity against what he or she actually feels in all social situations. How much is going on inside of us at all times? Tremors, unwanted thoughts or sensations, responses and reactions beyond our control, libidinal prongs and jabs that defy articulation? The French novelist Nathalie Sarraute, drawing on both Proust and Woolf, termed this "conversation" and "sub-conversation," and her novels go a far piece in illuminating all the miasmic activity that works around the clock, dwarfing (by both its plenitude and its censored, unspeakable nature) actual utterance. It is all happening underneath the false bottom.

HABIT AND PERCEPTION

Just how much of a welcome gift this is—to see a brave new world teeming with traffic we never suspected—remains an open question. As Samuel Beckett put it in his early monograph on Proust, Proustian discovery takes place when the curtain lifts and "the boredom of living is replaced by the suffering of being" (Beckett, 8). What Beckett terms "boredom," Proust calls "habit," and it is one of his most fruitful and surprising notions. "Skillful arranger" he calls Habit early on, "*aménageuse habile*," who goes about, like a secret emissary that we send out as scout or special forces, to domesticate, to "soften" (as they say in the military) our environment, to diminish our awareness of its otherness, its hostility. Proust shares Freud's view of homeostasis, whereby our lifelong project is to keep stimuli out, since we would be overcome, swept away, annihilated, if they ever got in. Ultimately Habit's job is to convert life into the womb where we started out, to remove all alterity from the varied phenomenal world we inhabit.

Although this may sound esoteric, it is utterly basic: Not only do many of us have trouble sleeping in strange places (where habit is routed), but we work around the clock treating the world as if it were an extension of ourselves, instead of the strange thing it actually is. Think for a moment about how habit functions as a blinder in your everyday moves: Do you *see* the door handle you open, the familiar chairs and bed you use, the actual faces you live and work among? Routine erases contours. This is not serendipitous but strategic, an incessant takeover operation. And we are armored tanks pushing our way through, impenetrable, stamping all terrain as our own, as an extension of our skin. But this armor can be pierced. It is well known that people virtually blind or very old and impaired can still manage, if you leave them in the environment they've always lived in; if you move them into new settings, either they are lost or they collide into walls and corners. Or they die.

Proust understands this phenomenon to perfection. In his book, we see the collapse of the protective blinders, written in every way possible. Elstir inverts land and sea, shows they could be inverted, upends our complacent models of what is what; when he fastens his gaze on a real person, the result is that Miss Sacripant turns mobile and slippery under his artistic gaze, eludes all definition. Things refuse to stay the same in Proust; they morph, and thus they wreck our assumptions and expectations. The entire delivery of Charlus and his actual sexual behavior is geared to initiate us into the realm of inverts, of gender-bending, of sexual currents that cross conventional lines, of new constellations. We are to be schooled in the lessons of metamorphosis, of decimated habit. At first, one treats this as bracing, as a tonic reality check to our tired assumptions. Still, it can sometimes appear labored, as when the hypersensitive narrator bewails his fate in having to sleep in a new room, a room where the mirrors and furniture and ceiling are cruelly displaced, are flaunting their robust priority and his alien status as visitor; we are tempted to say, "Get on with it; that's life." But Proust is nothing if not tenacious, and thus the narrator's trip to Balbec with the grandmother is going to repeat the same torture. So, once again, we are told there is no space "for him" in this hotel bedroom, the things there do not "know him," the clock continues "to utter, in an unknown tongue, a series of observations," the bookcases and mirror make it abundantly clear that he is not likely to find rest in their precincts. Then the smells take over:

> And deep down in that region more intimate than that in which we see and hear, in that region where we experience the quality of smells, almost in the very heart of my inmost self, the scent of flowering grasses

> next launched its offensive against my last feeble line of trenches, an offensive against which I opposed, not without exhausting myself still further, the futile and unremitting riposte of an alarmed sniffling. (I, 717)

At first this seems quite neurotic. "Alarmed sniffling"? Moreover, one wants to shout, "Remember the madeleine! Smells are life-enhancing!"

But the next line makes us realize that this attack is decidedly more serious than we thought: "Having no world, no room, no body now that was not menaced by the enemies thronging round me, penetrated to the very bones by fever, I was alone and longed to die" (I, 717–718). It is at this juncture that we can take the measure of the kind of systemic annihilation that is taking place. Proust—often thought to be the greatest egomaniac in world literature—is dishing up a portrait of total erasure, of the self being completely snuffed out, like a candle, by outer reality, by things, indeed by smells.

For me this passage is virtually medical in tone, and it speaks of the same creatural liability, the same somatic capsizing, that we experience in moments of corporeal upheaval such as stroke or heart attack or seizure. A critic once said that Proust was a man with his insides on the outside, and that bizarre notation conveys the awful vulnerability on show here. Skin is our protective coat, the surface that gloves our bones and organs and flesh and blood; open wounds are horrible because our insides are exposed, could leak out, be further injured. In Proust, we encounter a mind-set of exactly this sort, a system where the protective devices (skin, custom) malfunction. When Habit is laid low, when the world rushes in, in all its alterity, "I" collapses and risks dying. How, one asks, can this be stopped?

LOVE, FUSION, AND TRANSPARENCY

Here is Proust's next sentence: "Then my grandmother came in, and to the expansion of my constricted heart there opened at once an infinity of space" (I, 718). If "I" is being extinguished in virtually cardiovascular fashion ("my constricted heart"), love now appears as a miraculous reprieve, a fabulous opening of space to live. Love is indeed a cosmography in Proust, and we will later see just how much torture this formula can contain, but for now it is salvation and bliss. The grandmother's embrace also erases the boundaries of self, but it does so as pure fusion, pure sustenance.

Folded into her arms, the narrator experiences a kind of primal unity, as if they made one flesh and one soul, as if the penal condition of individuation itself (and its horrid corollary: alterity) were transcended:

> . . . and my thoughts were continued and extended in her without undergoing the slightest deflection, since they passed from my mind into hers without any change of atmosphere or of personality. And—like a man who tries to fasten his tie in front of a glass and forgets that the end which he sees reflected is not on the side to which he raises his hand, or like a dog that chases along the ground the dancing shadow of an insect in the air—misled by her appearance in the body as we are apt to be in this world where we have no direct perception of people's souls, I threw myself into the arms of my grandmother and pressed my lips to her face as though I were thus gaining access to that immense heart which she opened to me. And when I felt my mouth glued to her cheeks, to her brow, I drew from them something so beneficial, so nourishing, that I remained as motionless, as solemn, as calmly gluttonous as a babe at the breast. (I, 718)

We see here a moment of serenity and fusion whose great beauty casts a long and painful shadow over this novel. For nothing can ever match this experience of selfless love. This embrace of souls is as bittersweet as it is exquisite. Reminiscent (once again) of Plato's fable of the Cave, in which we are condemned to live as blind people mistaking shadow for substance, Proust's account of the man misled by his image in the mirror and the dog misled by the shadow points to a radiant spiritual world of transparency and connection, a world where the private walls of body and soul are overpassed so that two creatures can become one by dint of love. The grandmother and the mother are emissaries of that world, and this entire novel is fueled by an Edenic longing for the almost prenatal unity that they once offered the narrator. Can we be surprised that life will not replicate them, that this balm is doomed never to be repeated?

A word is in order about these two maternal figures. Selfless, sensitive, loving, generous, they are the novel's only heroic figures. I want also to emphasize that they are utterly truthful, hence "transparent" in that sense as well: They present to the narrator a limitless supply of love, with nothing held back, no private wants of their own; they ground him. Whether such a conception is credible, or whether it represents the protagonist's dearest fiction, is another matter, one the book never explores. And why should it? These are the protagonist's home truths; they are the gauge by which others in his life are to be measured and found wanting. (Could this be what our term "successful parenting" really means: imparting to our children a sense of being loved without reservation? If so, this novel obliges us to consider it also something of a lifelong boomerang, a set of utopian expectations that are neither discardable nor meetable.)

I called the mother and grandmother the novel's only heroic figures because everyone else in this epic fiction is multiple, mendacious, and kaleidoscopic. Charlus is extreme but also exemplary. In some sense, Proust's novel is about the exit from the Garden, the loss of innocence and sustenance that is entailed by the fate of weaning, of being exiled in a self. The narrator's nostalgia for the purity and grace of mother and grandmother is to be understood as the inevitable reaction to the opaqueness and alterity of all other creatures, not only the dazzling performers such as Charlus, but also the impenetrable objects of desire such as Albertine. My own critical language invests these matters with pathos—and that is apt—but Proust is as cunning and curious as he is tragic, and the novel is more than simply a dirge for lost innocence. Leaving the Garden means entering the world of appearances and lies, of never having Truth again. The spiritual and emotional loss is enormous, but might there be gains as well? Is there something to be said *for* lies?

LIES AND CREATIVITY

The novel's greatest liar is the minor character Legrandin. He poses as a freethinking, poetry-quoting country squire, but is in fact a desperate snob who therefore lives as much "in drag" as Charlus does. One of the most hilarious scenes in the novel is when the narrator and his family run into Legrandin after church, but they catch him at a bad time, since he is deep in conversation with a chatelaine. The narrator observes Legrandin's obsequious courting of the lady, conveyed largely through the sheer appetite expressed in the man's body as it performs its bowing and scraping and straightening-up motions: "This rapid straightening-up caused a sort of tense muscular wave to ripple over Legrandin's rump, which I had not supposed to be so fleshy; I cannot say why, but this undulation of pure matter, this wholly carnal fluency devoid of spiritual significance, this wave lashed into a tempest by an obsequious alacrity of the basest sort, awoke my mind suddenly to the possibility of a Legrandin altogether different from the one we knew" (I, 135–136). We seem to be headed for another of Combray's classic reversals. But Proust has tricks up his sleeve as he moves in for the kill. They walk home, remember an errand, return to the church, and end up smack in Legrandin's path. He is still, intently, working the chatelaine. Will he greet them? After all, they are commoners. This is a tight corner. It is, as they say, a moment of truth. Watch Proust:

> [Legrandin] brushed past us, and did not interrupt what he was saying to her, but gave us, out of the corner of his blue eye, a little sign which began and ended, so to speak, inside his eyelids and which, as it did not involve the least movement of his facial muscles, managed to pass quite unperceived by the lady; but, striving to compensate by the intensity of his feelings for the somewhat restricted field in which they had to find expression, he made that blue chink which was set apart for us sparkle with all the zest of an affability that went far beyond mere playfulness, almost touched the border-line of roguery; he subtilised the refinements of good-fellowship into a wink of connivance, a hint, a hidden meaning, a secret understanding, all the mysteries of complicity, and finally elevated his assurances of friendship to the level of protestations of affection, even of a declaration of love, lighting up for us alone, with a secret and languid flame invisible to the chatelaine, an enamoured pupil in a countenance of ice. (I, 136–137)

It is all too easy, I think, to dismiss this kind of (fabulous) writing as something labored and excessive. Why not simply say, straight-out, that Legrandin is lying? (Why not say, straight-out, that Charlus is an invert?) Because "lying" (as word, even as concept) will not begin to take the measure of what is actually on show here. What we have is a pull-out-the-stops performance on the part of Legrandin, as he compresses his epic declaration of love into the chink of an eye. Of course it is bogus. But then, so what? The very layers of this pantomime, the delicious conflict between the intensity of the (specious) emotion and the tiny platform from which it is launched, tell us something quite wonderful about the reaches and dimensionality of lying.

Lying is a creative act; it is arguably among the most common and most unanalyzed creative acts in human life. To lie is to use language (or, in this case, merely one's eyes) to convey information that is false, indeed counterfeit. But consider: The liar is even harder pressed to make the words work, to be persuasive, than the truth-teller is. The liar's utterance is 100 percent word-based (since it is based on nothing else). And even this formulation is too lame. Lying adds to the world (its own creations), whereas truth merely substantiates what already exists. Lying also generates enormous spaces and vistas, since one's lies are so uninhibited (by truth), so unconstrained, hence so empowered to produce grand visions. (Lying can also produce small visions, but that is less exciting.) Truth, on the other hand, is a rather measly proposition—beautiful though it may be morally—because it is precisely powerless to invent, to embroider, to embark on solo flights. Truth is unitary, because it is limited to what is, whereas lying is, well, kaleidoscopic, because it has no allegiances to respect, nothing that ties it down.

Lying is, as I said, doubtless the most widespread form of human creativity on the planet. It is distressingly underestimated, I think, but we all know why: It wreaks havoc in life, it fouls human relations, it makes a mockery (a splendid, creative, high-flying mockery) of true communication, it leads to untold misery. But, can we be surprised that Proust's novel of morphing figures, concealed depths, and stunning reversals is a novel of lies? In the passage about Legrandin's smile, we see an astonishing portrait of health and vitality. After all, it is no easy matter to cargo so much (false) emotion into the compass of an eye. Legrandin prances through this novel, minor figure though he is, and we see him at the end as at last achieving the (manufactured, false, but taken as real) aristocratic name he has ever yearned for.

The liar has, like the proverbial cat, nine lives. The truth-teller has only one. The grandmother is the novel's most appealing truth-teller: decent, loving, generous, transparent. She is a figure of utter rectitude. And the book kills her. We, like the narrator, watch her become systematically undone. She suffers a mild stroke in the Tuileries, but then goes progressively downhill, losing first one sense, then another—speech, sight, hearing—while heroically seeking to "hold on" to her self, finally to finish up as a "beast" upon a bed. This is doubtless the physiological indignity that all somatic creatures—if they live long enough—are slated for. But there seems something outright sadistic in this onslaught, as this valiant, "true" woman is brutally ejected from the ranks of the human. Note the way Proust describes her on her deathbed:

> Bent in a semi-circle on the bed, a creature other than my grandmother, a sort of beast that had put on her hair and crouched among her bedclothes, lay panting, groaning, making the blankets heave with its convulsions. The eyelids were closed, and it was because they did not shut properly rather than because they opened that they disclosed a chink of eyeball, blurred, rheumy, reflecting the dimness of an organic vision and of a hidden, internal pain. All this agitation was not addressed to us, whom she neither saw nor knew. But if it was only a beast that was stirring there, where was my grandmother? (II, 348)

We can hardly miss the fable-like dimensions of this death, as though the big bad wolf had simply done away with the grandmother and taken her shape. I don't think we can miss, either, the shocking parallel with Legrandin and *his* declaration of love through the chink of an eye. Human recognition is at stake here, and the grandmother is too far gone to manage it; Legrandin pulled it off very smartly, thank you.

I am not so perverse as to argue that Proust wants us to lie. Lying produces horrors in this novel. But he is indeed attentive to the bizarre maneuvering room lying produces, a space for engendering rival versions of the world while truth is chained to a preexisting order. We can now perceive the odd economy of this long novel that may appear so diverse and multifaceted: The shifting, morphing picture of life that is Proust's artistic signature turns out, as well, to be a source of unending pain when it comes to our personal lives and needs. Miss Sacripant's elusiveness in the Elstir painting and Charlus's parade of sexual personae are fascinating as long as they are not, as we say, on our plate; but Albertine's multiplicity is unbearable. Unbearable and yet irresistible. The desired Albertine obeys exactly the same laws that every other denizen of this book does—how could she not?—and the narrator is simply obliged to drain the cup. Combray sprang from the madeleine dipped in tea; what comes from this other cup, the one of jealousy and failure to pin down the loved one, has a bitter flavor that no pastrymaker in the world would recognize.

Bitter, but also ironic, sometimes even hysterically funny. The paths open to lying are not only the preferred strategy of humans with secrets, but also the major avenue of social climbing. Proust's swath of people—aristocrats and bourgeois, sometimes even workers and servants—are all engaged in the Great Game of societal maneuvering, of seeing and being seen, of endless strategic gambits. Yet these antics of the ants in the anthill are also the paths of fiction itself. Proust, like all great writers, wants to have it both ways: to get maximum narrative mileage out of lies before finally pulling the plug on them. Marcel must go the full route. Hence, the book plunges in, for hundreds and hundreds of pages, so that the two great "relational" errors of this novel—snobbery and love, or society and passion—can be exhaustively pursued before being finally judged as vain and mendacious, as sources of endless delusion and betrayal. It is as if you had to go all the way through the world before you could exit it.

SOCIETY

The huge amount of social satire in Proust does not always fare well with the modern reader. The mysteries and rituals of the Faubourg Saint-Germain in the last decades of the nineteenth century engage the social historian more than they do the ordinary reader of novels, no doubt, in part, because that world no longer exists for us, can no longer cast its spell on us (as it did for the novelist). And it is not all satire, alas; occasionally, one feels that Proust himself has lost his critical edge, that he is so obsessed with choreographing the behavior of these social animals that he loses sight of how repetitious this material can be, how inert and arcane it might come to appear. To be sure, Proust sometimes intuits just this, and at novel's end, he is virtually referencing his own readers when he speaks of newcomers to Parisian society, for whom it is all unreadable and without resonance, for whom all the extraordinary social moving and shaking, jockeying for position, and sniping that have been incessantly at work in all spheres, all this is now gibberish, flattened out, essentially erased by the movement of time.

Yes, the very wisdom of Proust's novel undermines the social theme, causes us to wonder why so much time is consumed in (depicting) social acrobatics, wheedling invitations, making appearances, looking over one's shoulder and forever aping one's betters. We have in this book a truly enormous cast of characters committed to the social whirl, each delineated with great care and wit, dished up to us in all his hunger and vanity. The Charlus I have presented as the book's preeminent pederast is also preeminent socially, a lion in the *beau monde*, a tyrant forever establishing (for a long while at least, until he is finally, sadistically, cut down) the ultimate aristocratic pecking order. (And Proust is peerless when it comes to chronicling these intrigues, when it comes to illuminating the inexhaustible supplies of vanity, spite, and hunger that can animate social creatures vying for position.) The two cliques that dominate most of the activity are the exclusive Guermantes circle, ruled over by the brilliant, witty Oriane, Duchesse de Guermantes, queen of fashion and repartee, and her husband, Basin, Duc de Guermantes and (straight) brother to Charlus; and the aspiring Verdurin "clan," the bourgeois counterpart to the Guermantes, made up of the unforgettable Mme Verdurin, grand patroness of the arts and indefatigable social climber, and her wealthy husband, fellow traveler and host to the faithful who religiously attend these *soirées*.

There are many others too, in Proust's large fresco, such as Basin's cousin, Gilbert, the most right-wing of the entire bunch, yet the man who will finally concede to Swann (the elegant Jew who moves in all circles, whose Jewishness grows over the course of the novel) that Dreyfus, sacrificial Jewish victim of the right, was probably innocent after all; or Morel the brilliant, cynical, dazzling sexual chameleon who happens to be a great violinist, too; or, of course, Swann, the refined, enigmatic Jew who is the book's aesthete, the border-crosser who is (for a while) at home in all groups, before falling for Odette, the novel's archetypal (and, it still seems, irresistible) coquette and trendsetter; or the finely rendered elderly couple of Norpois (quintessential diplomat, ever eloquent, ever windy, ever elusive) and his love, Mme de Villeparisis, of Guermantes stock but with scandal in her past, yet still going strong, remembering the writers of an earlier generation—Chateaubriand, Balzac, Hugo—and remembering what sorry figures they cut in her parents' aristocratic circle; Saint-Loup, the elegant and generous aristocratic friend whose admiration for the narrator seems endless (until the inevitable sex change is announced); even Bloch, the work's stage Jew, possessed of precocious and pretentious aesthetic views, outfitted with siblings and relations who flaunt the inversion theme, present in our minds as the unavowable yet undeniable double of our narrator. And I am not even touching on the many vivid others in both circles, the countless aristocrats and their middle-class counterparts, all ensconced in the never-stopping musical chairs of snobbery, being seen, "making it."

I mentioned Dreyfus, and his mere name signals what we know must be true: Proust's book is inscribed in history. The Dreyfus Affair hangs over the novel, debated and discussed over and over, making and breaking social connections; yet the reader who hopes to get some kind of bottom line on this key event in French culture is doomed to be frustrated, because there is only rumor and changing opinion, shifting sands, kaleidoscope once again. As *literature*, I have come to the view that the social satire, albeit done beautifully, is what is hardest to breathe life into for today's readers. To be sure, American society is not without its Verdurins (although there are fewer cases of Guermantes), and anyone who has seen up close the social dance of the jet-setters or the high and mighty or the literati (or any other group you care to mention) will recognize the pith and accuracy of Proust's scalpel vision. Nonetheless, as the fine Proustian critic Roger Shattuck has said, "soul error" is the great theme of the book, and we must see the protagonist's (unacknowledged) social quest—to be accepted into the Guermantes' circle, ultimately (never avowedly, of course) to be desired in *all* the drawing rooms—as a mistake of Dantean proportions, a way of losing your soul.

I called the social quest "unacknowledged" because the protagonist is himself relentlessly critical of societal foibles and manias, but the novel seems to speak otherwise, to show us by the very bulk of this theme how much it matters. One reason it may matter is to convey, in choral fashion, just how desirable and winning our narrator must be, since all these groups are clamoring for his presence among them. (Here, too, readers may have their doubts, since Marcel actually displays very little brilliance—or courage—in such settings, functioning more as a fly on the wall.) One feels, almost a century later in America, that this component of his novel—the social carnival—may have contained more sound and fury for Proust than it can possibly have for us.

JEALOUSY

But the jealousy theme does not stale or wither. Legrandin's epic attempts at faking friendship are delicious because they are innocuous, because no one in the novel needs his truth. But Proustian love is a different matter, and lies in this quarter can be devastating. By definition, the loved one lies. No less axiomatic is the maddened sleuthing and decoding activity that such lies trigger. This is not merely some hermeneutic or mystery in which one translates the telling detail (or the telling silence) into proof of mendacity and betrayal, as if it were a kind of rational puzzle where the pieces need to be put together to yield the pattern. There are more legs to it than that. The jealous Marcel is among the most inventive and beleaguered characters in fiction, as he goes about imagining masochist scenarios out of any and all odds and ends he can gather concerning Albertine. Jealousy would be the purest of fictions, its purity deriving from its horrible independence from fact. As Shakespeare demonstrated in the murderous jealousy of Othello, it is a passion that feeds upon itself. One has heard of roaches who, placed in glass jars, can live for weeks without nourishment, as if their internal system supplied all the nutrients necessary. If there is no corrective evidence, well then, the door is wide open for endless invention. The self-flaying that jealousy produces partakes of that same mutable, shape-shifting character that we've seen everywhere else in Proust:

> . . . always retrospective, [jealousy] is like a historian who would have to compose a history for which there are no documents; always too late, it rushes forth like an enraged bull, to the spot where can no longer be found that proud and dazzling creature who torments it with his thrusts, whose magnificence and cunning are admired by the crowd. Jealousy thrashes about in a void, uncertain just as we are in those dreams where we are pained at not finding in his empty house someone whom we have known well in life but who may be someone else here and has merely borrowed the features of another, uncertain as we are, especially, upon waking up and seeking to identify this or that detail of our dream. What was our friend's expression when she told us that? Didn't she seem happy, wasn't she even whistling, something she does only when she is thinking about love-making, and when our presence disturbs and irks her? Didn't she tell us something that is contradicted by what she is saying now, about knowing or not knowing a certain person? We don't know; we'll never know; we persist in chasing the unsubstantial fragments of a dream, and during the whole time our life with our mistress goes on, our life which passes by what may be of real importance, which is attentive to what may have no significance, which is haunted by creatures who have no real relation to us, which is full of lapses of memory, of gaps, futile anxieties, our life which is like a dream. (III, 143–144)

Every conceivable variety of maddened and futile quest seems registered here: the historian who must compose his narrative but has no data; the bull who seeks his matador-torturer, to no avail; finally, and most fatefully, the interpreter of dreams whose materials are endlessly fluid and interchangeable, for whom people and things glide into one another, wear masks, taunt us with their inaccessibility. The false-bottomed world has now opened itself up to infinity. There is simply no believability in Proust's world, no assertion that might not be revealed as false and deceptive. And intimacy ranks highest on the list of deceptions. For many readers, this view of human relations may seem so jaundiced and overdetermined that they close the book. Why, we might ask, are contact and communication so impossible?

STAGES OF LOVING: YOU CAN'T GET THERE FROM HERE

Nothing is more illuminating here than to pass in quick review the stages of the protagonist's relationship with Albertine. Taking the long view, we perceive nothing less than an *éducation sentimentale* that functions like a laboratory experiment to determine whether "love" is possible, and if so, under what conditions. Marcel first sees her with her friends at the seashore at Balbec, and he falls in love with the entire band of adolescent girls, entranced by their beauty, vigor, animation, and mystery; but he settles on Albertine as his final choice. After pages and pages of anxious efforts to meet her, after initiating a friendship with her, he finally seems close to the success he is seeking: She invites him to come to her room at the hotel, telling him they will be alone. In the boy's code, this invitation is unmistakable in its sexual significance. But he is in for a surprise. Approaching her (in bed) with a kind of frenzied, exalted desire that we see little of in this novel, a desire that is cosmic in its scope and intensity—leading him to feel that he and his hunger are greater than the world, that the moment of gratification is nigh—he pounces upon her only to discover that she is ringing the bell for help with all her might.

Yet, this fiasco is to be short-lived, as he is delighted to see, when she later visits him in his Paris apartment, apparently more experienced now, and hence offers him willingly the sexual intimacy that she had earlier withheld, that he had long desired. But is this an offer that can be made good on? Initially things look promising, but watch how they turn out:

> I told myself that I was going to know the taste of this fleshly rose, because I had not stopped to think that man, a creature obviously less rudimentary than the sea-urchin or even the whale, nevertheless lacks a certain number of essential organs, and notably possesses none that will serve for kissing. For this absent organ he substitutes his lips, and thereby arrives perhaps at a slightly more satisfying result than if he were reduced to caressing the beloved with a horny tusk. (II, 377)

With this cautionary remark about faulty equipment and missing organs, we are in place to negotiate one of Proust's most delicious passages, namely the complex, virtually aeronautic maneuvers necessary for one head to kiss another head. Only Proust would give us this slow-motion account of the *approach to the beloved*—utterly parallel to the approach a plane makes as it comes in for a landing—and we get a dizzying picture of shifting perspectives and altering vistas, yielding not one but now "ten Albertines":

> . . . this one girl being like a many-headed goddess, the head I had seen last, when I tried to approach it, gave way to another. At least so long as I had not touched that head, I could still see it, and a faint perfume came to me from it. But alas—for in this matter of kissing our nostrils and eyes are as ill-placed as our lips are ill-made—suddenly my eyes ceased to see, then my nose, crushed by the collision, no longer perceived any odour, and, without thereby gaining any clearer idea of the taste of the rose of my desire, I learned, from these obnoxious signs, that at last I was in the act of kissing Albertine's cheek. (II, 379)

This crash landing goes a long way, I think, toward Proust's view of individuals as worlds unto themselves, closed off from one another, impenetrable. Proust writes about kisses the way an anthropologist or a Martian who had never seen such gestures would write about them, or the way an Elstir might render them. Every time I read this passage aloud to students, they explode with laughter, and it is evidence of Proustian high comedy. But the farcical is underlaid by a darker plaint about inaccessibility as the primary fact of human relations, never more in-our-face than at moments of sexual intimacy, when we want to believe that physical coupling is the corporeal translation of a still deeper union. Will things stay this way—colliding bodies and all—between the boy and the girl?

It evolves further. Later still in the mammoth novel, Albertine will come to live with the narrator in his Paris apartment (much to the dislike of his mother and Françoise), and of course their sexual *entente* will presumably have become a smoother and more satisfying operation. And Proust does indeed describe, with considerable delicacy and feeling, their nighttime arrangements, but we may still be surprised at what we see.

"Sleeping with somebody" is a time-honored euphemism in English, a dodge that allows us not to say "fornication" or "intercourse" or the four-letter word that usually designates what transpires. That phrase acquires considerable resonance when it comes to the narrator and Albertine. *He* waits until *she* sleeps. Then he moves into action, because "her sleep realised to a certain extent the possibility of love" (III, 64), by which he means: The awake and conscious Albertine is both unreachable and distracting, for she disrupts my connection with her; she is, in some remarkable sense, in the way, by being there. Asleep, no longer observing him, she is available for love, and thus enables the actual gambit in question: his ability to move past surfaces, her surface but also his own. Now she exhibits the "unconscious life of plants, of trees," and this too now seems possessable. Comparing her breathing to a sea breeze, to moonlight, he awaits her descent into deep slumber so that he can examine her at leisure, caress her, and finally mount her, thereby embarking "on the tide of Albertine's sleep."

One is stunned by the natural beauty and serenity of these arrangements, but we cannot fail to see that consciousness is the grand enemy here, that measures must be taken to banish it if real intimacy is to occur. At this point we must ask: What kind of intimacy is there without consciousness? I believe we are looking at the bedrock of Proustian relationships here, and no moral assessment seems applicable. In caressing the sleeping, plantlike Albertine, the protagonist achieves something of the release and self-extension made possible by the grandmother's embrace, but how different these unions are: There the souls mingled, here the eyes and consciousness must be banished if "union" is to occur. "I/eye" is ever in the way, is ever flaunting its alterity, its resistance to being possessed or even understood. At some level I feel that Proust is a natural explorer, fearlessly sketching the conditions necessary for intimacy and coupling, and I leave it to the reader to think about issues such as dark rooms and closed eyes and private fantasies in the midst of (necessary to?) sexual intimacy.

But I would also submit that this scene is not all that far from what we call necrophilia, a kind of desire that is triggered by the dead. (Now the body would be truly docile.) Albertine is not dead (yet), but she will soon die, and the narrator will continue to desire her—be assured that no corpses are ever literally caressed in Proust!—in addition to being even more racked by jealousy now than when she was living. Why? Because her past (imagined and real) lesbian betrayals are all the more virulently present in his mind when she can no longer be sequestered and interrogated; he will even send out emissaries to dig up the dirt on her (which they find) in order to construct the narrative of masochism he seems to need. Albertine dies physically, offstage, within the course of a sentence, in an absurd accident, but she dies far more slowly, more protractedly inside the lover's imagination, where the show is still playing. Looking over this crucial erotic sequence, the stages of the Albertine romance—which takes many hundreds of pages in Proust, just as our own love lives play out in time and are not easily graphed, despite anniversaries and the like, occasions when we seek to take their measure—gives a distinctly bad name to romantic love.

I have wanted to sketch the evolution of this love relationship in order that we might contrast it with its beautiful shimmering opposite: the transparency and selfless love between the narrator and his mother and grandmother. Remember: The narrator's embrace of the grandmother is nothing less than fusion, a total blending of souls and bodies, a mutual flowing of love, a rare experience that is even epistemological. He *knows* these nurturing women, knows that they love him infinitely. Infinitely. Is that not exactly the term used to denote the balm which the suffering young man experienced in Balbec when he was on the verge of going under, and the lifesaving miracle occurred? "Then my grandmother came in, and to the expansion of my constricted heart there opened at once an infinity of space." This infinity of space is pure solace, pure nurturance, pure room for living. But the narrator's curse consists in trying to find the same bliss in his relations with Albertine. Proust uses exactly that word, "infinity," to denote the utter alterity of the young girl, the measureless and unpossessable life of the loved one: "I could, if I chose, take Albertine on my knee, hold her head in my hands, I could caress her, run my hands slowly over her, but, just as if I had been handling a stone which encloses the salt of immemorial oceans or the light of a star, I felt that I was touching no more than the sealed envelope of a person who inwardly reached to infinity" (III, 393). Good infinity versus bad infinity, you might say; when it's good (and this is paradise, the paradise we are doomed to lose), this expanse of space is like a blood transfusion, becoming *our* plenitude; but when it's bad, well, then, it becomes a form of spatial torture, a dreaded map of all the places the loved one has been, the people she has known and desired and had sex with. When it's bad, it becomes jealousy; it becomes a novel.

THE INNER CARTOGRAPHY

I say "novel" because that is the familiar literary form given to these maddening efforts at detection. Proust wants us to understand that our emotional life plays by just such rules: lovers going crazy trying to figure out if the beloved is cheating, and with whom (and, in Proust, how). Worse still, our head games, according to Proust—the anxieties and obsessions that stud our lives—have a kind of immediacy that ordinary novels fail to deliver. That will be Proust's job. A traditional erotic whodunit would trace the actual adventures and misadventures of its people, show whom they desire, whom they lie to, whom they bed, how they get away with it, all of which mandates the kind of incessant lying that Proust also recognizes, but which also stages the scenes themselves (taking readers to hidden rendezvous, motels and the like). But the subjectivist rules of *Remembrance of Things Past* dictate that *actualized* betrayal is off-limits, beyond the reach of this fiction. What really matters here is the imagining psyche of the lover. One might assume that this is going to be a narrow stage, something on the order of a torture chamber. Torture it is, but narrow it's not.

As the dead Albertine continues her (imagined) sexual romp, we begin to see that the brain itself seems unaware of elapsed time, seems horribly "online" temporally, especially at moments of terrible discovery. (These are complex even if basic matters. Ask yourself where you are as you read these lines; further, ask yourself when you are, when you go through the motions of everyday life; is anyone truly, continuously in the present? Is it even possible?) Proust is drawn to this issue of our neural circuits, our whereabouts in time and space, because he knows that those are exactly the flowing currents that declare themselves most explosively when trauma and crisis occur. We naively think that crisis is a momentary injury, something on the order of a collision that happens now. Proust suggests that severe emotional pain is distinctively longitudinal, that we hurt because current events are replaying past events, but that only now are we able to measure the damage.

Consider, in this light, the protagonist's reaction to Albertine's announcement, late in the novel, that she is a dear friend of Mlle Vinteuil and her friend. This provokes a veritable explosion, but it is an affair of pulsions and vectors on the inside. The protagonist now knows with certainty that Albertine too is a lesbian—I am counting on you to remember my earlier discussion of the boy's childhood discovery of Mlle Vinteuil and friend as lesbians, as "clucking fowls"; remembering such things is what this passage is about—but the pain itself is figured as a kind of substance with noxious power that has been earlier absorbed (the witnessed scene) and now activated (the current announcement). Life, Proust says, "punctures" us, deposits residues in us, and time brings out their potency, their virulence. It is distressingly parallel to living in a polluted or even radioactive environment, but not learning it until you realize you have cancer. What is fascinating here is the temporal map that is drawn: A word uttered by your lover on the train brings into horrid play events from the murkiest past, events you had every reason to think were over. This passage itself is rich and gesturing, and the memory of the early lesbian exposure is described as "kept in reserve," is compared even to the role of Orestes, whose death the gods had prevented so that he could carry out his fated revenge on Clytemnestra.

It is worth noting, also, that the excruciating pain this occasion triggers is also, strangely, a source of pride, "almost of joy, that of a man whom the shock he has just received has carried at a bound to a point to which no voluntary effort could have brought him" (II, 1153). Proust aptly characterizes trauma as a *journey*, for that is what it is: a return trip to your past that is also a leap beyond what you could have imagined. Your life is being expanded here, and that (unsolicited) implosion/explosion is both horrible and wonderful. Why wonderful? Why joy? Here, as elsewhere in this novel about betrayal and suffering, we are to understand these events as uniquely instructive, as modes of self-discovery. It is not merely that pain teaches, but that the agonizing encounter with the world of lies and betrayal has a weirdly positive cerebral character to it as well, as if to say that such experiences are growth experiences, that such experiences bring to the light aspects of ourselves that are not reachable or knowable any other way. (In this sense, the actual person we love counts for little, exists ultimately, according to Proust, as a way of "plumbing" us, serves as a means of self-realization, of making good on a repertory of selves and experiences otherwise unachievable; the egoism here is limitless.) Nonetheless, betrayal is not fun even if it educates; it also jolts us with a remarkable view of *exposure.* To express this shock of discovery, the author again invokes a technological metaphor:

> The notion of Albertine as the friend of Mlle Vinteuil and of Mlle Vinteuil's friend, a practising and professional Sapphist, was as momentous, compared to what I had imagined when I doubted her most, as are the telephones that soar over streets, cities, fields, seas, linking one country to another, compared to the little acousticon of the 1889 Exhibition which was barely expected to transmit sound from one end of the house to the other. It was a terrible *terra incognita* on which I had just landed, a new phase of undreamed-of sufferings that was opening before me. (II, 1153)

The suffering of jealousy is indeed time and space transformed into feeling. In Proust we rediscover how drastically our world has been altered by technology. McLuhan argued that we are to understand the media—telephone, telegraph, television (and, now, computers, Internet)—as extensions of the central nervous system, as extensions of our whereabouts in time and space. But note the Proustian turn of the screw: This extension is torture. There is food for thought here.

Most of us see the changes brought into our lives by technology, especially by information technology, as beneficent and empowering. Our reach is magically expanded. A click of the button sends our words and thoughts across the globe, ushers images and information from far away into our laps and laptops. What's not to like? But it all depends on what kind of information we're talking about. The narrator's pain derives from the horrendous double jolt to his system: Albertine's sexual infidelity catapults him into distant places (distant beds), but it also storms his own fortress, brings those betrayals right into his own heart. Emotional information of this sort is akin to being stretched on the rack.

Proust's phrase is telling: "I had perilously allowed to open up within me the fatal and inevitably painful road of Knowledge" (II, 1152). This is a retelling of Genesis, but the old fable of a snake persuading Eve to persuade Adam to eat an apple is now modernized, brought into high-tech reality: Emotional knowledge *opens* you up neurally, bombards your system, is a form of sensory and cerebral overload, not too distant from an electrocution, an electrocution understood as a crucifixion. You are yanked out of your "now" and hurled into other locales, locales where they are hurting you (she is cheating on you: That is what you are now tuning in to/imagining). We are obliged to reconsider the innocuous telephone as an instrument of torture, a machine that hooks us up to intolerable news and scenarios, so that we are horribly exposed, vulnerable, flayed by the affective materials that come from afar, "over streets, cities, fields, seas, linking one country to another." If all this sounds esoteric, ask yourself: What is jealousy? It is the journey from your home base into other spheres, but a journey you are pulled into by your frantic need to know, or by your no less uncontrollable penchant to invent. In jealousy, indeed in love, you are on-line.

This journey is, as we saw, a source of pride as well as torture, and Proust deserves to be seen as one of our great explorers and inventors for just this reason. He expands the place (the prison?) where we live. To be sure, this expansion hurls us into a still larger prison, but that is what tragedy has always done. The fate of Oedipus and of Lear work along similar lines: They brutally knock down the protective walls we live behind, and tell us that our knowledge is faulty, our exposure is terrible, our itinerary is drastically different from what we thought or expected. And this is exhilarating as well as horrible. We are *moved*, both figuratively and literally. Later, reflecting again on the pain and knowledge he has received, the narrator once more speaks of a road, "that connecting road which, though private, opens on to the highway along which passes what we learn to know only from the day when it has made us suffer: the life of other people" (III, 394).

Given that Proust is (rightly) seen as the grand solipsist, the epic writer of self, the man who exposes relationship and knowledge of others as something of a mirage (and even a waste of time), these lines are strikingly and insistently *social:* We negotiate a highway all our life, even if that life takes place in a cork-lined room—as Proust's did for many years—because feeling is tentacular, is a network that binds us. I will return to this key issue of isolation and egoism in Proust, but what I want now to emphasize is the invisibility of the network. We do live in relation, but this mesh is utterly hidden, since it is an affair of memories and feelings, of nerve endings and pulsions that are the very currents on which we are carried into others, and others are carried into us. Not being visible, this experience of linkage announces itself via pain; our pain instructs and enlarges. This model bequeaths us an astonishing new map of where we are actually situated in life.

A WORLD OF LINKAGE AND BONDS

I cannot overstate the radical thrust of this new dispensation. It is as if Proust were cashiering the entire Newtonian worldview—a view of objects and people disposed along measurable axes of space and time, a view corroborated by photographs, retinal data, novels, and résumés, with their confident linear tidings—in order to tell us that this familiar model is true enough for the outside, but that it has zero applicability for the inside. In short, our real arrangements, our real story, cannot be represented along these familiar lines. Well, you may ask, just how would it be represented? Consider how the following passage, coming after Albertine's death, illuminates precisely that affective highway system that extends us in time and space:

> I tried at times to take an interest in the newspapers. But I found the act of reading them repellent, and moreover by no means innocuous. The fact is that from each of our ideas, as from a crossroads in a forest, so many paths branch off in different directions that at the moment when I least expected it I found myself faced with a fresh memory. The title of Fauré's melody *le Secret* had led me to the Duc de Broglie's *Secret du Roi,* the name Broglie to that of Chaumont; or else the words "Good Friday" had made me think of Golgotha, Golgotha of the etymology of the word which is, it seems, the equivalent of *Calvus Mons,* Chaumont. But, whatever the path by which I had arrived at Chaumont, at that moment I received so violent a shock that I was far more concerned to ward off pain than to probe for memories. Some moments after the shock, my intelligence, which like the sound of thunder travels less rapidly, produced the reason for it. Chaumont had made me think of the Buttes-Chaumont, where Mme Bontemps had told me that Andrée used often to go with Albertine, whereas Albertine had told me that she had never seen the Buttes-Chaumont. After a certain age our memories are so in-

> tertwined with one another that what we are thinking of, the book we are reading, scarcely matters any more. We have put something of ourselves everywhere, everything is fertile, everything is dangerous, and we can make discoveries no less precious than in Pascal's *Pensées* in an advertisement for soap. (III, 553–554)

The mind seems to work by associative logic. Hence the casual encounter with a musical piece titled *Le Secret* leads the narrator to the Duc de Broglie's *Secret du Roi*, and Broglie is the name of a historical personage who was exiled at Chaumont. But, likewise, the phrase "Good Friday" is linked to the scene on Calvary, which triggers "Calvus Mons" or its modern equivalent, Chaumont. It may seem as if such linkage were somehow volitional and arcane, a writerly conceit, but Proust says the opposite: The mind automatically performs just this kind of bridgework, producing this kind of connective tissue on its own, requiring no command or decision on our part. What really matters here, however, is not the etymological or verbal games, but the emotional current, the affective power system that fuels all this. That system announces, in every key possible, Chaumont. Why? Because Chaumont refers also to Buttes-Chaumont, a pleasure haunt in Paris, a place where Albertine said she'd never been, a place where Mme Bontemps (Albertine's aunt) says she has been many times with her friend Andrée: in short, a place where Albertine and Andrée had sex together. There is the motor, the humming generator: *had sex together.*

Very curious. Just the same old neurosis, the familiar jealousy, you might say. But look harder. Proust's narrator is, yes, consumed by jealousy (even though poor Albertine is long dead now), but he elects, initiates, nothing here; he *follows* the imperious circuit that keeps bringing Chaumont to him (no accident that Golgotha is in play), keeps torturing him with scenes of lesbian betrayal, lesbian pleasure (that he cannot compete with). It is all too easy to dismiss such passages as the endlessly repeating confirmation of the narrator's peculiar problems. But, remove all the indicting particulars here—Chaumont, lesbianism, betrayal—and you begin to see what is actually at work: *We inundate the world with our inside story.* And the grim corollary: *The world sends it all back to us, bombards us with our own garbage, injures us incessantly.* The protagonist has done nothing more than pick up a newspaper, but this innocuous document is transformed into a script, indeed a mirror. Words meant to be informational (names of musical pieces), words that are indeed informational for others, become dreadfully resonant for him, lead him on a vicious treasure hunt, point (however deviously) inward, toward his own obsessions. Public script becomes private torture. And there is no place to hide. And no effort is required to make this happen (and no effort can stop it, either). It is a kind of vicious projection, a broadcasting of our inner horrors onto the environment that resembles the act of graffiti, a graffiti performance that is as natural as breathing. Proust is saying we spray the world with our own inner story.

I am quite prepared to acknowledge that the public world is real. Streets are streets, chairs are chairs, and newspaper articles are impersonal notations. But, in granting this, I ask you to grant Proust his truth, too. We negotiate between public and private every minute of our lives, by which I mean: Everything we see and hear is susceptible of triggering something within us, can be inflected by our personal history, our private wants. My sense is that we have no lights about this whatsoever. I also believe that madness lies in this direction—as we shall have reason to see in Faulkner—because life goes out of business, goes into the pit (or into the Charles River, as Faulkner's Quentin Compson does), when the outside/public world loses its otherness and gets utterly taken over, co-opted by our personal vision. So there is little cause for celebration in this notion of "leaking" into the world. But what a magic (even if overdetermined) place the world becomes! How resonant and murmurous it becomes, if its forms and names and scents are always beckoning to us, jogging our memories, tuning our machine, playing to our associations, connecting with our own past or present.

This is why Proust felt that cinema was a poor art form, because it was obliged to respect the surface world depicted by the camera (and by our retina). But what counts (for him) is the (invisible) private world, a world of endless associations and linkages, driven largely by our inner demons and personal needs and prior experience. Pain runs this system now, but one feels that pleasure and desire could do the job also: to rescript the world, to confer on it our private coordinates, to show how it speaks to us. A topography is coming into view here: The world of phenomena is of interest (to Proust) only insofar as it yields our private markings, our personal drama. Hence, "secret" and "Chaumont" would have either no resonance or a different resonance for anyone other than the narrator; but for him, they write his (tortured) sex life large. I said we "spray" the world; Proust writes that we "put something of ourselves everywhere," as if we were leaking or secreting our own concerns and issues and personal drama into the environment. But the result is amazing: "everything is fertile, everything is dangerous." Anything at all—a word, a sound, a smell, a sight—can send us careening back into our inner muck, our own drama.

No escape is conceivable in these precincts, since, to borrow James Joyce's phrase in *Ulysses*, the longest way around is the shortest way home. We are always meeting ourselves. Montaigne speaks of a man about whom it was said that he had returned from a long trip, but surprisingly unchanged; Montaigne is not surprised, because he points out that the man took himself with him. We not only take ourselves with us, but we spill out as we do so, transforming the public world into our own story at all times; like birds, we spend our lives feathering our nests, metamorphosing outer circumstances (twigs, events, bits and pieces we see and hear) into a little nest of our own, a cocoon. But our nesting efforts—the lifelong imperative of habit—implode, since the desired goal of softening the environment goes amok, and instead the environment assaults us at every turn, no longer with its alterity, but now with our own reflected markers and miseries, out there, waiting to be energized. Sounds sensationalist, doesn't it, to see the outside world as a torture chamber? Yet, is Proust so wrong? What are the private counters of your life? Or every life? Do we know? Is this ever recorded?

On this head, every human being contains a never-ending novel of private associations and occult linkages that utterly escapes detection. It also means that we run the continuous risk of banging into ourselves, since all encounters are secret mirrors, all objects person-coded, all pools reflecting pools, all our gambits those (in some sense) of Narcissus. There is enormous drama here, inasmuch as "external reality" becomes something bristling and threatening, capable of hurtling us into our own interiors at any moment. Moreover, all existing hierarchies of value and prestige as to what things mean or are worth go up in smoke, since an advertisement for soap may be richer in discovery for us, a better key to our own depths, than the vaunted works of the masters, such as the *Pensées* of Pascal. Finally, we must contrast this universe of private linkage and connective tissue to the clumsy forms of retrieval and information gathering made available to us in today's Internet culture. You can log on and surf at will, just as you can scroll a contemporary hypertext and "travel" its various circuits, but how would you come up with these private landscapes of meaning and pattern, this wholly new affective grammar that recasts our lives, actually shows how things fit together inside of us?

For Marcel, the trip involves "secret," "Chaumont," Calvary, and sexual betrayal. But it need hardly be so melodramatic. Each of us is a symphony of private motifs and chords, a symphony that lasts a lifetime, that *is* a lifetime. Sounds and sights from childhood, abandoned toys, posters, the creaking of doors, the rustling of the wind, the smell of wood fires or oven bread or hot chocolate or Gauloises or wildflowers, half-remembered faces or songs or confidences: These are our materials, the secret furniture of our lives, and although we can scarcely recall them with any certainty, they are nonetheless there on the inside, guideposts, markers, far more active than we think, parsing the public world we inhabit with their own stamp, our own stamp. Every teacup contains, if we know how to look and listen, Combray.

THE FOURTH-DIMENSIONAL WORLD

Proust's world is not without parallels to the project of Cubism: to represent phenomena in time. But, instead of using newspapers and guitars and vases, he focuses his beam on the great human adventures of jealousy, desire, grieving, and identity. (Yes, identity is an adventure, arguably the greatest, most kaleidoscopic of all.) His work shocks us, because time is not only invisible, but it seems to be excised, banished from our customary vision of ourselves and others. With reason. To see people "in time" is to pronounce a death sentence. (Susan Sontag, in a striking notation, said the same of photography, that its every frozen image is a *memento mori*.) For just this reason, Proust's great enemy of perception, *habit*, is also said to be our last defense against entropy, decay, alteration, and death. We cling to fixed images—of our bedrooms and of our bedfellows—because any acknowledgment that they might be alterable or mobile, might be replaceable or disappear, would be tantamount to murder. And murder not just of them, but also of us. Here is the radical Proust: The disappearance of others in our lives—and this is an incessant disappearance act, triggered more by forgetting than by actual death—signals an erasure of *us* as well as of them.

Nowhere is this line of reasoning more tragically actualized than in the sickness and death of the grandmother. This death is unmistakably forecast in the remarkable earlier episode where the boy speaks to the ailing lady on the telephone, *hears* her distress (hears it because her physical presence is removed, so that habitual perception is not allowed to script the scene), and rushes off to visit her. But he gets there unannounced, and thus sees her for a brief moment without blinders, sees her out of the box (as we might say today), freed of the distorting, time-erasing lens that we call habit, that we also know as love. It is a devastating sight: He now registers the brutal physiological truth that she is old, half-decrepit, en route to dying. Proust refers to this moment of truth as a moment when the complex machinery of our customary (editing) perception is replaced by a photographic plate, a kind of naked eye that sees the decimations meted out by time:

> We never see the people who are dear to us save in the animated system, the perpetual motion of our incessant love for them, which, before allowing the images that their faces present to reach us, seizes them in its vortex and flings them back upon the idea that we have always had of them, makes them adhere to it, coincide with it. How, since into the forehead and the cheeks of my grandmother I had been accustomed to read all the most delicate, the most permanent qualities of her mind, how, since every habitual glance is an act of necromancy, each face that we love a mirror of the past, how could I have failed to overlook what had become dulled and changed in her . . . (II, 142)

A very stubborn lifelong battle with time is adumbrated here, a battle we fight without knowing it, since it is our organism, not our willpower, that turns every face we love into a mirror of the past. The truth of these lines will be felt by anyone who has ever been shocked by the sudden transformation of a loved one: a child who is no longer a child, especially a parent or grandparent whose face and body (if not seen for a while) now register entropy and aging, a somatic system starting to move into its final phase. Habit tries to keep this news from us, regarding our loved ones, regarding perhaps our most loved one of all. Indeed do we not ourselves experience at certain moments shocking, unwelcome signs of mortality, announced in the white hair, the new wrinkles, the sagging flesh, the aching joints, the slacking strength, those all-too-familiar indices that limn the shadow of death in our own faces and bodies? (My wife was recently shocked at seeing her own grandmother in the mirror as she walked by it.) Hence, the boy's glimpse into the machinery of death puts the *machine infernale* at center stage, leads ineluctably to the sickness and demise of the grandmother, and the book fells her, as I have said, with considerable brutality.

MEMORY

But she is not down for the count, and I come, at long last, to the great theme that has come to be known as Proust's special signature in the history of Western literature: memory. The loveliest and most heartbreaking chapter in Proust's long novel is titled "The Intermittencies of the Heart," and it is devoted to the grandmother's unexpected return. She returns in the same way the dead always return: as memory. But this sequence adds something of immeasurable value to the grisly, entropic story of her dying, a story that climaxed with a beast on a bed. The grandmother's second death now occurs: in the mind and heart of her grandson this time. Which is to say: She now truly dies, in the sense that only now, via *mémoire involontaire,* does she make her final appearance in his life, an appearance of unbearable emotional fullness, so that he can take his final leave of this woman who loved him entirely. The events take place at Balbec, in that hotel room where she offered him the lifesaving balm that prevented his annihilation, but this time he must confront a different annihilation: hers. Things, I have argued, are imbued with our own inner story, and thus the hotel room houses a ghost that no other visitor could perceive. Bending down, in chest pain, the narrator is invaded by a "divine presence," and hence recovers the vital living presence of his grandmother, but with that horrible price tag that is attached to memory: recovers her as gone. Gone, herself, yes, but present in him. So, now he relives all the hurt he may have inflicted on her, relives it as pain that is now self-inflicted, since "he" is where she now lives.

Closed off to the world, locked up in his room—looking very much like the author Marcel Proust must have seemed, in his cork-lined Parisian apartment—the protagonist nonetheless completes a love relationship with another. It is perhaps the most poignant of all relationships: the saying of farewell. One feels that this could not have happened as she actually was dying: Her own sickness was on center stage, as well as the helplessness of those who loved her and the comedy of her tending physicians. But now, later, apart—she dead, he living—this scene can take place, and he can experience the fullness of her death. In dreams he pursues her, seeks to find her in the tiny apartment she (albeit dead) is said to be inhabiting, cannot find his way, wants ever more desperately to make her know how much he loved her, loves her still. This second stint at Balbec completes the first, since he now learns more about how sick she was even then, about her bottomless generosity for him, about what he has—now that he has found it—actually lost. Proust's treatment of the grandmother's reentry into his life as wound and memory is as perfect a version of what mourning actually entails as we are likely to find in literature, and it is significantly more sinuous, looping, surprising, and moving than the patterns articulated by the psychologists who study these matters.

But I'd want especially to emphasize *richness* as the final vista that is achieved here, richness as a complement to what Shakespeare called ripeness, suggesting the full circle and scope of human life and love, suggesting also how truncated and snapshot-like our customary perceptions are likely to be. In saying this, I am arguing that the view of people in time may be a death sentence, but that it also expands and enriches our sense of what love is. Death robs us of those we love, but time clothes them in their true colors, confers on them their real density. There is an ethos at hand here, a moral imperative of sorts, that would urge us to factor time into our perceptions (difficult though that may be), so that the habituated and frozen images we have might be overlaid and underlaid with the coating of time. Looking at a loved one should involve memory as much as sight, and Proust suggests, in a fine, painterly image, that such persons would then appear covered "with the beautiful and inimitable velvety patina of the years, just as in an old park a simple runnel of water comes with the passage of time to be enveloped in a sheath of emerald" (III, 1020).

Shakespeare's phrase "Full fathom five thy father lies; of his bones are coral made" speaks of the sea change that death brings to the living; Proust's sheath of emerald is a bid for such richness and beauty here and now. With or without Proust's help, most of us know that habit can be a vile friend, that it can reduce our friends and loved ones to silhouettes, that our own coldness of heart is conducive to such reductions. All too often we consign the temporal reach of our friends and loved ones (and selves) to scrapbooks and journals, creating a kind of tucked-away record that obscenely replaces the labor of actual perception, a labor that life asks of us if we are to take truer measures. I have no illusions about how easy such things are. It can be unbearable to register the longitudinal scale of loved ones, of seeing (in our mind's eye) what they were, as well as seeing (with our retina) what they are. Habit itself blocks such perceptions, and it does so to spare us this dreadful news. But are these tidings only dreadful? I am filled with emotion when I see photographs of my (now dead) mother in her (then) prime, and I wish I could have retained that double vision during her time of descent and dying; yes, it would have been horrible, but it would have been *just*, inasmuch as it would have restored something of the roundedness and plenitude of her existence to me, would have reminded me that this last chapter belongs in a book that had (has) many chapters. I feel the same tug when I look at photos of my (now grown) children as babies or as youngsters, with everything in front of them, and the mix of pain and pleasure I then feel is no less than the living badge that life confers on parents. Seeing people in time restores at once the dimensionality and the preciousness of human life.

LIFE AS PALIMPSEST

Hence the final installment of the novel, *Time Regained*, conceived and written at the very beginning of the massive project (leading Proust to insist that any assessment of his work that was based on the first volumes was deeply flawed, cyclopic), sets a great seal on all that has come before, and yields a quasi-epic vision of what a time-drenched world would actually look like. We note, at the same time, how arduous such a vision is, how the forces of both habit and ignorance erode this larger, more dimensional view of people and things. We see this writ both large and small, evident in our private lives and in our social awareness. Here again the "societal" Proust is on show; however, his sights are no longer focused on the comedy of social climbing and salon life, but rather the *illegibility* of social change, the routine blindness that impedes our understanding of history itself. There are large lessons here, I think, concerning the concealed drama of historical events versus the dazed sensations that many of us experience when looking at dates and charts and chronologies. It is essentially a matter of translation, a capacity to see the turns, shifts, conflicts, and transformations that are behind seemingly inert data, requiring an ability to decipher, to espy the baroque work of time in every social notation.

Proust approaches these matters via the society page, and he tells us of two surprising marriages—one between Robert de Saint-Loup and Gilberte Swann, the other between Jupien's niece and the young Cambremer—but of course these marriages are only surprising to those with the requisite historical knowledge (including Proust's own readers) to see what a crazy quilt these unions are. Kaleidoscope once again. Like a game of musical chairs, Proust's people continue to morph, change partners and names, yielding something on the order of a *palimpsest,* that form of medieval script in which the surface text covers earlier, subjacent writings. We who know that Saint-Loup derives from the noblest family in France, the Guermantes, also know that Gilberte, now known as Mlle de Forcheville, is in fact a Swann of both bourgeois and Jewish parentage. Likewise, Jupien's niece is now called Mlle d'Oloron and thought to be the natural daughter of the Baron de Charlus, whereas we know (from our knowledge of what Charlus is) how absurd this rumor is.

But to those not in the know, this storied past is invisible, and Proust tellingly speaks of an American woman witnessing these unions who can fathom nothing of what lurks behind the scene; her view of high society, he says, is like that of a Berlitz School: a linguistic system that is closed to outsiders. I am doubtless exposing my own blinders here, but I believe that the Berlitz School metaphor is distressingly accurate for most people's understanding of most historical events. We can read the pages, see the names and dates, but cannot grasp the living chain of motive, causality, and (sometimes) happenstance that brought about these results. Henry James once wrote that the actual web of human relations is so far-reaching that it recedes into infinity, as contrasted to the lines and contours the mind inevitably confers upon them. The history I am thinking of goes beyond the putative origins of this or that event, but gestures toward that fourth-dimensional portraiture that I have already invoked, a kind of "in-time" depiction that sees the present as merely the here-and-now version of a story that is always much larger, reaching both out and back to the there-and-then, casting its net into space and time.

Sigmund Freud once evoked, in a famous passage in *Civilization and Its Discontents,* the sheer impossibility of representing the actual historicity of a city like Rome; how, he asked, could you "see" the longitudinal city, a place where the modern buildings exist often over the ruins of earlier monuments representing the center of the Catholic world, those monuments themselves covering still older (long-gone) pagan structures of the Rome of the Caesars. After all, only one structure can actually exist in one space. Freud was drawn to this challenge precisely because he sensed that it represented to perfection the temporal reach of the individual psyche every bit as much as the past of any great city. Marcel Proust is out to actualize this vision.

What is true socially is equally true politically. Time plays its merry-go-round, and figures who were in exile or disgrace find themselves back in the limelight a decade or so later: and nobody the wiser. One thinks, in this country, of the picaresque career of American political figures such as Richard Nixon, who seemed to rise and fall and rise again, yet to fall again, but finally to finish his life as elder statesman. But, a historical memory is required to see these resurrections as such, whereas the truth is that the public is often amnesiac, remembers nothing, judges things from today's current events. Such amnesia pours a kind of balm over the past, literally embalms it, removing all that would be conflict and stridence from it. The great social event of the last volume is the grand reception at the Princesse de Guermantes', and we are told of a couple there,

> . . . husband and wife, who were respectively nephew and niece of two men, now dead, who had once come to blows and—worse still—one of them, still further to humiliate the other, had sent him as witnesses his concierge and his butler, indicating that in his judgment gentlemen would have been too good for him. But these stories slumbered in the pages of newspapers of thirty years ago and nobody now remembered them. And thus the drawing room of the Princesse de Guermantes—illuminated, oblivious, flowery—was like a peaceful cemetery. (III, 992)

We all know the adage "Time heals." Most of us chalk it up to wisdom and maturation, but Proust seems to me more the biologist here, as if to say that the very brain cells that carried the earlier stories of humiliation and contempt are now dead. This peaceful cemetery contains not only the now forgotten sound and fury of the past, but our own dead selves. Time erases us. It puts out our fires, quenches our thirsts, ministers to our wounds, by a kind of burial or erosion. We may tout this as maturity and wisdom, but entropy may well deserve the real honors.

Rust is the color of the soul. No one expressed this sense of life's incessant undoing better than Emily Dickinson:

Crumbling is not an instant's Act
A fundamental pause
Dilapidation's processes
Are organized Decays.
'Tis first a Cobweb on the Soul
A Cuticle of Dust
A Borer in the Axis
An Elemental Rust—
Ruin is formal—Devil's work
Consecutive and slow—
Fail in an instant, no man did
Slipping—is Crash's law. (Dickinson, No. 997)

It is *against* this natural entropic (but hard-to-see) scheme that Proust has written his novel. And he wants, among other things, to recover the baroque majesty of what time does to human bodies. When he arrives at the reception, the narrator is at first confused, since all the guests seem to be wearing white wigs. Others are unrecognizably transformed: "I was told a name and I was dumbfounded to think that it could be used to describe both the fair-haired girl, the marvellous waltzer, whom I had known in the past, and the massive white-haired lady making her way through the room with elephantine tread" (III, 982). All these figures required "strenuous intellectual effort" if one was to know who they were, since one needed to study them "with one's eyes and with one's memory." It would be easy to turn morbid here, yet Proust presents this final act as something vibrant and magic: "These were puppets bathed in the immaterial colours of the years, puppets which exteriorized Time, Time which by Habit is made invisible and to become visible seeks bodies, which wherever it finds it seizes, to display its magic lantern upon them" (III, 964).

I find Proust tonic and exhilarating in this last volume, especially when we consider the discourses of aging in modern contemporary life. Old age is either a time of endless leisure, wellness, and opportunity for golf and travel, or an affair of actuarial tables, expensive drug prescriptions, and nursing homes. Proust puts some zest into the matter, and even if his descriptions do not make us (if we are old) delirious with pleasure, they do possess a certain mortuary grandeur:

> Some men walked with a limp, and one was aware that this was the result not of a motor accident but of a first stroke: they had already, as the saying is, one foot in the grave. There were women too whose graves were waiting open to receive them: half paralysed, they could not quite disentangle their dress from the tomb-stone in which it had got stuck, so that they were unable to stand up straight but remained bent towards the ground, with their head lowered, in a curve which seemed an apt symbol of their own position on the trajectory from life to death, with the final vertical plunge not far away. Nothing now could check the momentum of this parabola upon which they were launched; they trembled all over if they attempted to straighten themselves, and their fingers let fall whatever they tried to grasp. (III, 980–981)

With a kind of baroque majesty worthy of *King Lear*, Proust rewrites, in a dreadful human code, those laws of gravity that weigh ever more heavily as we move through time. There is something monumental in this group portrait of descent, yet, as we shall soon see, he is no less interested in the heights from which we fall, heights that will be measured.

TAKING OUR MEASURE

Spectacular and sensationalist as this physical carnival can be, Proust's ultimate interest lies more in the spiritual and existential side of time's role in life. If time erases, then the great challenge is that of restoration. If time dismantles, then the work at hand consists of at least remembering the beautiful cloak itself. Here, again, is where perception must become fourth-dimensional, must restore to its objects the long shadow they cast in time. Yes, love dies; nothing can prevent this routine horror, just as nothing can prevent the physical death of those we love. When the aged Marcel encounters at the reception two of his former loves, Gilberte and the Duchesse de Guermantes, the stage is set for disillusionment, for the wry taste of lost dreams. But the gambit is to remember what was once glorious:

> Bored I may have been as I stood talking this afternoon to Gilberte or Mme de Guermantes, but at least as I did so I held within my grasp those of the imaginings of my childhood which I had found most beautiful and thought most inaccessible and, like a shopkeeper who cannot balance his books, I could console myself by forgetting the value of their actual possession and remembering the price which had once been attached to them by my desire. (III, 1024)

I am perhaps an old fool, but I find these thoughts both wise and beautiful. Proust acknowledges that life itself, by dint of constant entropy, erosion, and change, puts us, as it were, in the red, always in the loss column. The great projects of desire are rarely achieved or gratified (or sustainable), and time teaches us how self-deceived we have been, how empty and vain so much of our agenda is and has been. But we move into the black by recalling and honoring the immense price such projects once possessed for us.

Proust is striking a special note in this regard. It is no accident that those two great realist novels of the nineteenth century, Balzac's *Illusions perdues* and Dickens's *Great Expectations*, are about seeing clear, getting free of one's distorting illusions, achieving an unclouded perspective on the bare truth. Balzac and Dickens are not blind to the lure and seduction of the "world," the hunger that animates and drives astray both Lucien and Pip, but their sights are focused on exposure, on waking up, of seeing the error of our ways. Proust is, I think, a higher realist. He too knows that we are driven by desire and appetite, that we spend our lives trying to make good on things such as success and love, and he knows also that the final tally is frequently inadequate, not to say disastrous. Yet he then goes on to prize exactly those fantasies, desires, and illusions that fueled our hunger and energized our lives. (Fitzgerald is America's Proust, in this regard.)

What is rejected in Proust is bottom-line logic, that familiar logic that goes about demystifying life, that never fails to remind us how vain our projects might be, how often things do not add up, how frequently disillusion is the residue of experience. Not that there is no discrediting in Proust; the protagonist understands to perfection that his objects of desire are unworthy. He understands this in part because of the enormous pain such pursuits have bestowed on him. And he has learned that gratification is a mirage.

We are familiar with the biblical injunction that one must lose one's life to save it. Proust, it seems to me, rewrites, in a secular vein, this severe law, but there is nothing soft or escapist in his version of it. The title Balzac gave to one of his masterpieces, *Illusions perdues, Lost Illusions,* is the grisly lesson that all of us learn, and we are never through with learning it. We are doomed to lose our life simply by dint of living it. With or without soul error, human projects are evanescent if not illusory, and aging (with its news of death) adds its bit, relentlessly shrinks our estate, diminishes our enthusiasms, cools our ardor, revises (downward) our numbers. We are made poor in the elemental sense of not being able to possess our lives, however great our material possessions may be. Could this be overturned? Could deficits become credits? How?

But then comes the great quantum leap, the move upward that counterbalances our steady descent. Neither God nor afterlife is required here. Redemption, total redemption, is nigh. At last the kaleidoscope builds rather than dismantles. Errors, mistakes, losses, and deaths are, yes, the materials of each person's calvary; they are also, Proust now sees, the living, pulsing story of who we are and were, and that story is recoverable.

Memory is the great agent of possession here. Disappointments count less than the expectations we had; the value of things and people is what we invested in them, not what they turned out to be worth. I would even say, our illusions are our truths, for they take the measure of what we have believed and sought, and that is always greater than what we have found and kept. Memory not only helps us balance our books, it also resurrects the dead. Here as well, Proust sovereignly goes past the closure that we have thought life imposes on us. The grandmother lives (still, again) in the grieving mind of her grandson. Albertine, dead, is still there.

RECOVERING YOUR STORY

Still more miraculous, memory brings back to life all the people that we ourselves have been. It is especially here, in the personal realm of self, that most of us are most grievously in the red, and this is because we can scarcely avoid living moment by moment, on the surface, locked out of our past, morphing, forgetting. This ongoing, incessant process of amnesia and metamorphosis we call "living." When we reflect on the countless people we are, the even greater number of people we have been, then we better grasp Proust's serial view of self, a self that alters—over a lifetime—its moods, its wants, its jobs, its mates, its loves, its horizons. This is true even in the instantaneous present, since all of us are chameleon-like, perform, on a quotidian basis, roles that are multiple and distinct. But it is truer still when we think back on our astonishingly long lives: the child we were; the friends we had; the relations with family that time has reconfigured as parents die and children age and we become parents and grandparents; the interests and desires and fears and expectations that we had decades ago, years ago, months ago, days ago. What is most shocking is how dead and gone this is for most of us, how disinherited we are from the actual plentitude of our existence. Proust wants to get this back. He wants to raid the peaceful cemetery.

And he understands that art is for exactly this. Bergotte, Vinteuil, and Elstir have led the way in disclosing and sharing their inner vision, but the final work of art we are to consider is of course the huge book we have been reading, Proust's own *Remembrance of Things Past.* There is more than a little irony here. Throughout the novel, the protagonist shirks his task, procrastinates, goes astray in love and society, feels certain that he will never make it as a writer, that he can never quite get started on the grand philosophical treatises he thinks he should be composing. He doesn't measure up; the great themes are not there. Then, in the final volume, comes the radiant epiphany:

> And I understood that all these materials for a work of literature were simply my past life; I understood that they had come to me, in frivolous pleasures, in indolence, in tenderness, in unhappiness, and that I had stored them up without divining the purpose for which they were destined or even their continued existence any more than a seed does when it forms within itself a reserve of all the nutritious substances from which it will feed a plant. Like the seed, I should be able to die once the plant had developed and I began to perceive that I had lived for the sake of the plant without knowing it . . . (III, 935–936)

The language of seed and plant, of our lives being (unwittingly) part of a larger altruism in which we are seeding the future, playing our allotted role, giving our measure, giving ourselves, all this is a far cry from the familiar complaint that Marcel Proust is a narcissist, a subjectivist, an egomaniac who doesn't even apologize for his tunnel vision (and he doesn't).

The tea-soaked madeleine starts to look cosmic in scope, inscribed in the future of the species itself. We don't usually think in terms of socio-biology when we think of Proust, but it is time to reconceive his work. Art does not demand (and perhaps the future does not ask of us) any wisdom, any lessons; it seeks, instead, something much larger: the transcription of our lives, the *qualitative* script of who we were. Each of us—whatever our gender—is big with Life, has an untold story that needs to be birthed.

For many, art seems frills. Yes of course the world needs poets, but, as most folks see it, does it not, far more urgently, need biologists and bankers? Proust turns this issue on its head by positing art as the most serious labor that exists. But his rationale has little to do with notions of beauty or the like, nothing whatsoever of art for art's sake. The imperative he proposes is radically personal, because he asks us the most difficult question of all: What have you to give? To bequeath? It is a question that is more often dodged than faced, head-on, and it has nothing to do with that other question: How much will you make? (Here at the university, where the costs of education are astronomical, young people and their families wrestle incessantly with the issue of career choice; one needn't be a philistine to imagine the horror on many parents' faces if the student says: I will be an artist.) Proust will present artistic vocation as the truest business of life, and he will not hesitate to say that the artist has only one thing of value to offer: his work. He goes on to say that the artist who neglects his work because of other commitments, including the noblest and most urgent ones, such as family and country, is evading his real, assigned task, is choosing counterfeit currency over the real.

This long book seems almost unreadable to some because it locks us into the nonstop perceptions and ruminations of one fairly dubious, seemingly egomaniacal figure, the protagonist. Proust's subjectivism seems equally abhorrent to many readers who may still want to believe in love, in meaningful human relationships, and in some kind of charity and generosity; you won't find much of it in this book. But ask yourself: Can there be an *egotistic book*? Even the most maniacal narcissism of the narrator is offered to Proust's readers as a kind of aesthetic covenant, as a fundamentally social proposition, whereby he shares his life with us. (When you finish reading Proust's long book, ask yourself: How many "real" people do you know as well as you know this author?)

And he tells us some sobering news: that we ourselves are lost and duped, that we have been fooled into thinking that the public, surface story is the whole story.

> We have to rediscover, to reapprehend, to make ourselves fully aware of that reality, remote from our daily preoccupations, from which we separate ourselves by an ever greater gulf as the conventional knowledge which we substitute for it grows thicker and more impermeable, that reality which it is very easy for us to die without ever having known and which is, quite simply, our life. (III, 931)

Repeatedly Proust brings us into the equation: This, he insists, is *our* story, his book is our mirror. Not that we "are" Proust, but that we too have a unique vision of the world, and to express that vision is precisely the business of art:

> But art, if it means awareness of our own life, means also awareness of the lives of other people—for style for the writer, no less than colour for the painter, is a question not of technique but of vision: it is the revelation, which by direct and conscious methods would be impossible, of the qualitative difference, the uniqueness of the fashion in which the world appears to each one of us, a difference which, if there were no art, would remain for ever the secret of every individual. Through art alone are we able to emerge from ourselves, to know what another person sees of a universe which is not the same as our own and of which, without art, the landscapes would remain as unknown to us as those that may exist in the moon. (III, 931–932)

This is the great credo of the novel. We now live at a time when one can see the landscapes of the moon. What is thus revealed? Is this personally enriching? Far from being an esoteric manifesto, Proust's book is understood by its author to be an intimate form of human contact, a fusion of souls even, one that takes place in the only realm where such things can happen: via art.

Thus the book closes like Uraboros, the serpent that bites its own tail. The protagonist discovers his great mission: to write his life in time. This is a bracing but also tragic formula, because the writer is also a creature in time, and the great anxiety at the close of the novel is: Will I have time? The book itself will showcase a man dipping a madeleine into a cup of tea and recovering his past; it will highlight the ups and downs, the comedy and the mania of this man's life, especially the social and erotic fiascoes of his life. It will depict a man who learns increasingly to withdraw from life, who elects to know himself rather than society; this can be rephrased as a man who seeks to know the society within him, the society of self, the selves he is and has been, so that these disparate and scattered figures can be reassembled into the composite self-portrait he is drawing, so that he can finally possess himself in his entirety.

This longitudinal self encompasses a boy whose greatest trauma revolved around his mother's good-night kiss, another who loved, lost, and found his grandmother, another who went through motions of love and desire with Albertine but never got inside or in control, still another who measured the bizarre antics of his fellows such as Charlus, Legrandin, Françoise, and so many others, yet another who loved art, sought out its masters, learned finally to recognize himself and his calling in the mirror they provided. That calling is severe, draconian, even priestly. It entails saying no to the world so that one can say yes to the self. Bringing us full circle back to the novel's beginning, the now sick and dying protagonist remembers the early drama of the good-night kiss, of waiting to hear the garden bell ring so that at last Swann will have left and Maman will be free to give him his precious kiss, and he then realizes—with terror—that this bell has never stopped pealing, has been ringing all his life. But "in order to get nearer to the sound of the bell and to hear it better it was into my own depths that I had to re-descend" (III, 1105).

This is perhaps a truth that the older among us are more likely to take to heart, for we know more sharply the encroachments of time, the insidious processes of erasure that threaten to annihilate or (worse) undo what our years have wrought. For us, the secret melody of our lives, the melody that habit and routine and the long parade of days and years have muffled and obscured, that melody haunts us, urges upon us the desire to possess it at last. T. S. Eliot captured this very beautifully in one of his *Four Quartets:*

Old men ought to be explorers
Here and there does not matter
We must be still and still moving
Into another intensity

For a further union, a deeper communion
Through the dark cold and the empty desolation,
The wave cry, the wind cry, the vast waters
Of the petrel and the porpoise. In my end is my beginning.

The trip in, the descent into the self—to be still and still moving—is the only way to possess time. Here is the directionality of Proust, the brilliant yet austere truth that not only caps his novel, but which has informed all its major issues and crises. What is jealousy if not exactly this relentless desire to know what the loved one has done, with whom, when, how: in short, to come into possession of the loved one's entire inner world? Life has taught the protagonist that this kind of possession—attempted ruthlessly in the Albertine relationship—is doomed to failure, anguish, and self-laceration. The secret life of others cannot be possessed, but the very effort to do so awakens us to the staggering dimensions of time, to the enormity of all lives of which we glimpse only a few contours or snapshots. All those one has merely known and observed warrant, in the last analysis, the fourth-dimensional approach, because it confers on all of us something of our actual estate, our actual reach and resonance. This is most ghastly true when it comes to perceiving the very old, such as the teetering figure of the Duc de Guermantes, who seems so precarious "upon the almost unmanageable summit of his eighty-three years" (III, 1107).

And this rendition of *time as height* is marvelously, unforgettably expressed in the concluding, circus-like metaphor that epitomizes the Proustian vision: "[A]s though men spend their lives perched upon living stilts which never cease to grow until sometimes they become taller than church steeples, making it in the end both difficult and perilous for them to walk and raising them to an eminence from which suddenly they fall" (III, 1107). Proust the cubist is also Proust the tragic poet, the comic satirist, but above all the man who is bent on seeing and recovering the scope, the sheer dimensionality of any human life.

Once again, this passage will resonate differently, depending upon the age of the reader. But there is something sublime in translating the somatic frailty of age into an almost Shakespearean vision of height and depth and volume, of life at last seen in its awesome temporal reach. In the anguish of not knowing if he'll have time to complete his book, if he will fall from his stilts—and Marcel Proust did not have time; he was still writing and correcting proofs on his deathbed—the protagonist compares his labor to that of a miner who is threatened from within: "I knew that my brain was like a mountain landscape rich in minerals, wherein lay vast and varied ores of great price. But should I have time to exploit them? For two reasons I was the only person who could do this: with my death would disappear the one and only engineer who possessed the skill to extract these minerals and—more than that—the geological formation itself" (III, 1094). It seems fair to say that the entire novel is captured in this strange metaphor: Our inner vision of life is the ore we are to mine, so that it can then be shared with others as what is most uniquely ours.

Very early in the novel, when Proust wants us to realize that Swann is a far more fabled and unmapped creature than the folks in Combray realize, he says that Aunt Léonie would be so surprised to learn about this man's hidden life that it would be as if she had invited Ali Baba to dinner without knowing it, and he had taken her into his cave and shown her his treasure. Is that not what Marcel Proust has done? To take us into the cave so that we might discover the treasure? Geologist or miner or Ali Baba, it matters not, for the task is the same. The ore we must mine is our treasure. It does not consist in sacks of gold, but in the true inside story of our life, a story that Proust helps us recover.

JAMES JOYCE

ULYSSES

SONG OF BODY AND MIND

James Joyce spent his entire literary life finding ways to tell his story. We can discern a clear evolution from the spare tales of small coerced existences in *Dubliners* (seen largely from the outside) to the rather swollen account of the young author himself in *Portrait of the Artist as a Young Man* (caught largely from the inside), as if Joyce were trying out different formulas for saying a life, for taking its measure: either lean external notation or the depiction of consciousness as it emerges. But it is his third book, *Ulysses* (1922), that permanently altered the course of modern fiction; this masterpiece is something of a nonstop series of narrative explosions, challenging our habits of reading and thinking, offering us the liveliest and most brilliant rendition of living in the world that we are ever likely to come across.

First and foremost among the things exploded in *Ulysses* are our customary grids for imagining who we are and how we live; the daunting strangeness of Joyce's book is, if we know how to see it right, profoundly intimate and illuminating, enabling us to discover our own daytime and nighttime antics in shockingly fresh ways. *Ulysses* is no less than a self-help manual, not in the ordinary sense of giving us practical advice, but in the more startling sense of reshaping our grasp of self by making us hear, at last, our own strange music, the song of body and mind that plays around the clock and constitutes who we are.

I fully realize that Joyce's *Ulysses* is the proverbial eight-hundred-pound gorilla in the English literary canon. Literate people throughout the world have heard of it, yet—there is no way to measure this—legions of readers, attempting to read it, have likely put it down in fatigue or despair or anger. Professors, on the other hand, have devoted the decades of energy, intelligence, and life necessary to the enterprise (as Joyce speculated they would), with the result that they see this book as the supreme achievement of the English novel. "We are still learning to be Joyce's contemporaries," Richard Ellmann shrewdly and prophetically noted in his fine biography of Joyce published in 1959, and anyone who has ever *taught* this gargantuan fiction knows how uphill this struggle can sometimes be, how confusing this book initially appears; worse still, readers rightly wonder how much "learning" is required to get "in." The devotees derive enormous pleasure from Joyce, savoring his wit, humor, brilliance, and erudition, but the general reader may often feel locked out.

So, what is the case *for* Joyce, for the literate, interested, yet unprofessional reader? What will you get from the many hours needed to read *Ulysses*? (We'll leave *Finnegans Wake* out of the picture entirely.) I sometimes feel that this—what's in it for me?—is the most ducked question in academic and intellectual culture. Partly, no doubt, because it is so hard to answer. But doesn't this no-nonsense principle lurk in all readers' hearts, even if one is loath to articulate it? Highbrow utterances about "edification" are customarily invoked as the rationale for reading; but I have written this book for the general reader, and I am obeying the principle that all reading—whatever the professors say to the contrary—is an affair of gains and losses, of usable or discardable insights, of equipment that does or does not add to one's repertory, one's life. *Ulysses* pays off on precisely this front. It only *seems* difficult because, in writing it, Joyce jettisons the traditional baggage of the novel in order to give us the human creature—live and screaming, mind and body going full blast—up-front on the page, so up-front, so immediate, that we scarcely know (at first) what we're looking at.

Reading Joyce is the most dramatic wake-up call to our own vortex of thoughts and sensations I have ever known, because his writing brings home to us how asleep we habitually are, how lazy our assumptions are. After all, our own habits of mind have been schooled and shaped by traditional thinking and writing, and we therefore come to Joyce with a whole laundry list of preconceptions about what character and plot—and ourselves—look like. Joyce chucks out our laundry list. He startles us with his findings. He makes the page prance and preen and shine. It has nothing whatsoever to do with his erudition or even his personal intelligence as such; rather, it uncovers for us something of our own genius, our own under-the-table running commentary about life and experience, a commentary that pulses through brain and heart all day and all night long, but one we rarely tap into. Reading *Ulysses*, we recover our story.

This will be a weighted reading of Joyce's book, inasmuch as it will highlight certain revolutionary features of the writing—stream of consciousness, contrapuntal arrangement, experiments in voice, loosened language and syntax, play of perspective—and it will go light with other, more traditionalist aspects of the novel, such as its cargo of erudite references, its altercation with the orthodoxies of Irish nationalism and the Catholic Church, its extravagant rendition of Dublin. *Ulysses* must be freed from the web of erudition that entraps all too many readers. You do not need a library or reference book to read and love Joyce. My aim is not so much a user-friendly Joyce as a fertile Joyce, a companionable and frequently galvanizing Joyce who adds something unique to our stock. What does he add?

Those revolutionary elements of *Ulysses* constitute nothing less than our portal of entry, our way of experiencing a new vision of self. Joyce changes the nature of writing so as to bring to language whole precincts of reality that had never before made it into literature. "Stream of consciousness" is the inner current each of us navigates our whole life long, but Joyce makes us hear its strange, quirky, incessant noise. "Contrapuntal arrangement" is my term for the give-and-take, the check-and-balance of Joycean prose, as it goes about knocking down what it has built up (just as our own second thoughts do, just as our own critical judgement does). "Experiments in voice" testify not only to Joyce's astounding gift for ventriloquism, but to a shocking range of tonalities and styles, thereby recasting his story in different "tongues." "Loosened language and syntax" are Joyce's ways of taking words on a holiday, so that his phrase acquires a musicality and a punch, a sense of echo and resonance, ultimately a higher eloquence, much the way our favorite music and songs recast ordinary sounds and words to give us greater pleasure and deeper meaning. "Play of perspective" is Joyce's supreme strategic gambit in his depiction of his players, for he puts them in dramatic circumstances, and he shows them attending to a medley of voices and forces: inside and outside, private and public, subjective and environmental. Just as we ourselves swim, at every moment of our lives, amid sounds and surfaces, subject to endless stimuli coming from both within and without. This book *moves;* and it makes you realize how static and prepackaged the traditional novel is. With *Ulysses*, we at last have a book that is commensurate with the infinitely strange antics of our own doings: musing, walking, eating, speaking, desiring, fearing, loving.

JOYCE UP-FRONT

Travelers deserve to know where they're headed. Reading Joyce's *Ulysses* is, as I intend to show, on the order of an epic journey, turning you the reader into a voyager *extraordinaire*. All of literature may be characterized as a trip, but the trip into this unique, supreme fiction ranks among the most exhilarating and eye-opening experiences available to verbal creatures. Our initial preparation consists in reconnoitering the early Joyce, the author of *Dubliners* and *Portrait of the Artist as a Young Man*, so that we can better measure the quantum leap that takes place in *Ulysses*, the preeminent modern novel in the English language.

The first thing we will discover, as we negotiate this long and playful book, is how Joyce has utterly changed the rules about how novels are to behave. We shall see that Stephen Dedalus—the very serious young man of *Portrait*—is presented to us as a bristling consciousness, as a song and dance, a mix of outer stimuli and inner pulsions and thoughts, a give-and-take. No writer before Joyce had attempted such a feat, and in one fell swoop, Joyce is calling the bluff of ordinary fiction that establishes its protagonists and then follows them as they go through their paces. He is calling our bluff as well, since the *imploded* rendition of Stephen forces us to realize how life jumps out at us every second we're alive, how much ongoing "buzz" there is in our minds and hearts. We might wonder: What happens to plot in this kind of prancing scheme? It will be seen that Stephen is dreadfully coherent, inasmuch as he is forever wrestling with the choking grip of the past; history thus becomes an affair of living ghosts, such as the invading presence of his own dead mother at whose bedside he refused to pray, but seen as well in the more general fate of flesh: Does it merely rot? Or is it transformed into imperishable spirit?

After three chapters devoted to Stephen's negotiations with these matters of body and soul, Joyce introduces us to his astonishing main character, Leopold Bloom, the modern candidate for Ulysses, the adman who goes through a long day facing and dodging the ghosts who are coming at him: his dead father, his dead son; above all, his wife, Molly, who is about to fornicate with her lover that very afternoon. One might think these would be heavy items for a novel to keep afloat, but Joyce stuns us over and over in his depiction of Bloom's consciousness—an unprecedented spectacle of roadblocks and freebies, of looming worries that share the stage with whimsical fantasies. The representation of Bloom's "artful dodging" is one of *Ulysses*'s greatest triumphs, and one of its pithiest gifts for the reader, because Joyce has writ large a map of our own capacity to manage problems, to find maneuvering room—and even delight—in the very midst of trouble. We soon enough realize that Joyce is graphing no less than the antics of the human subject in culture, but even that formulation is far too pat, inasmuch as it seems to posit the subject—you or I—on one side, and "culture" on the other side, whereas the reality is quite different: a kind of soup that we swim in, a kind of air we breathe, a kind of nonstop traffic between inside and outside. I venture to say that none of us has ever quite seen anything just like this before.

One might expect Joyce to stay with this vein, to stick to the narrative of consciousness, but one would be wrong. Joyce flexes his authorial muscles and—presto—the scene changes entirely, as the chapters become ever more experimental and madcap: One graphs Dublin life as a set of vectors, another consists of newspaper headlines, still another charts the birth of a child by displaying the birth of English style, from Anglo-Saxon and Latinate beginnings through Sterne and Dickens on to contemporary argot. And nonetheless, Joyce keeps his eye on the ball, returns to the fates of Stephen and Bloom, shows us Stephen's famous "Hamlet theory" (in which his filial anxieties are on show), along with Bloom's intractable problems of impending cuckoldry, but now (in the "Sirens" chapter) refracted through new lenses, including the dazzling dance of pure sounds. By the time we get this far into *Ulysses*, we realize that this novel invents its own rules; more unhingingly, we also realize that Joycean experiment *heightens* the pathos of its characters' fates by packaging this material in ever stranger forms, by awakening us to the (shocking) possibility that this is also our own dance.

One quarter of *Ulysses* is devoted to the "Circe" chapter, which is written in dramatic form and takes place in a brothel where the fatherly Bloom watches over the inebriated young artist, Stephen. Accordingly, we too will spend some time in these precincts, so as to gauge what Joyce has wrought here: *Consciousness itself is now on trial.* If much of this novel has gloried in exhibiting the remarkable inner life of its protagonists—an inner life where each of us has our little measure of freedom, our little opportunity to talk back to life—this chapter annihilates such freedom by turning everything that had been merely thought or fantasized into public reality, into indictment. Moreover, this is at once the cruelest and "kinkiest" chapter of the book, the one that taps most deeply into what we'd have to call "sadomasochism," as we watch Bloom's imaginings of sexual betrayal (his wife fornicating with her lover, Blazes Boylan) get enacted in front of his eyes, replete with his own (now willing) role as pimp who gets his jollies by seeing his wife plowed by "a real man." How to measure this? One is tempted to say that Joyce's entire gambit is devoted to that question: Just how do we measure the basic (and the extreme) events of our emotional and sexual lives?

The final part of my discussion focuses on measurement itself, as evidenced in the brilliant "Ithaca" chapter, where Bloom's marital dilemma now appears as it might to a Martian: odd indeed. Joyce seems to be asking: How much can it matter if one body has intercourse with another? In fact, how much can anything at all matter, if we take the truly long view (as, say, how our antics might appear, from outer space). If "Ithaca" is invested in galactic distances, the novel's final chapter, "Penelope," comes home to the human body, and allows us, at long last, to enter into the mind of Molly Bloom and to savor her own rich, carnal, shrewd, and genial take on human affairs, including her love affair(s) and her marriage. Joyce's novel—we realize as we conclude our reading—recasts Homer's epic story of Odysseus's trials in returning home to his wife as one day in the life of Stephen, Bloom, and Molly, and it therefore performs the greatest service that art can provide: It awakens us to the color and drama and sheer brilliance of everyday life.

JOYCEAN BEGINNINGS

Before tackling *Ulysses* proper, a few words about *Dubliners* and *Portrait.* The taut prose renditions of small Dublin lives in Joyce's first collection seem, in retrospect, at once meager and annunciatory: meager in their Flaubertian clinical language, annunciatory in their focus on the metropolis, Dublin. The richest piece, "The Dead," is a more complex affair, and this melancholy account of a (stirring, ritualistic) Christmas party and a husband's dawning recognition of his wife's passional history (wherein he plays no role, of which he's had no inkling) closes with some of the most beautiful lines Joyce ever wrote, about snow falling all over Ireland. With majesty the prose evokes a country slowly and softly being blanketed by snow: the plain, the hills, the bogs, the waves. It must follow that it will also cover the "lonely churchyard" where Michael Furey (the dead lover of the past) lies buried. Gabriel's reaction to this burial-by-snow: "His soul swooned slowly as he heard the snow falling faintly through the universe and faintly falling, like the descent of their last end, upon all the living and the dead" (213–214).

Much is on show here: the lyrical bent that Joyce learned increasingly to rein in so as to better exploit, the view of private life as inscribed in (and obliterated by?) the larger field where it is positioned. Joyce seems almost to be stumbling into richer territory here, for each of us is doomed to uncertainty and guesswork about the actual longings and "coordinates" of those we love. Gabriel Conroy is also undergoing the classic Joycean initiation: One's personal wants and contours are eclipsed by the larger stage, a stage that includes—as we see here—the dead as well as the living. These are not happy tidings, but who among us has not, now and then, experienced the extent of his or her great ignorance about loved ones? Who has not felt, now and then, his or her private desires and markings gradually (or suddenly) lose their authority, become erased, eclipsed, buried under the all-covering snow?

Gabriel's soul swoons, and swooning is still alive and well in Joyce's most popular book, *Portrait of the Artist as a Young Man*, which charts the evolution of Stephen Dedalus from infancy to emancipation. *Portrait* is irresistible fare for students and young people, because it closes with a clarion call of rebellion—modeled explicitly on the fallen angel Lucifer's defiant *Non serviam*—through which a gifted young artist will spring clear of the environmental trap in which he's been caught:

> The soul is born, he said vaguely, first in those moments I told you of. It has a slow and dark birth, more mysterious than the birth of the body. When the soul of a man is born in this country there are nets flung at it to hold it back from flight. You talk to me of nationality, language, religion. I shall try to fly by those nets. (220)

How not to applaud here? Stephen Dedalus is enacting one of the most seductive plots of modern culture: to be free, to be independent, to get clear. (In older, traditional societies, the young were acculturated to take their place *within* the system.) Yet it is worth pondering whether those particular nets—nationality, language, religion—are leavable, are fly-overable. Joyce clearly has in mind Daedalus the mythic figure who flew with wings of his own devising, but he no less clearly is thinking about the tragic fall of Daedalus's son, Icarus, who flew too close to the sun, which melted the wax that held the wings, and hence sent the youth to his death.

And I mentioned swooning as prominent in this book because it seems to characterize Stephen's emotional flights, not only his response to beauty but his discovery of his calling as artist. The best instance of this lyrical outpouring is the well-known "bird-girl" sequence:

> Her long slender legs were delicate as a crane's and pure save where an emerald trail of seaweed had fashioned itself as a sign upon the flesh. Her thighs, fuller and softhued as ivory, were bared almost to the hips where the white fringes of her drawers were like featherings of soft white down. . . . Her bosom was as a bird's soft and slight, slight and soft as the breast of some darkplumaged dove. (185–186)

Stephen gazes upon this (highly constructed, rhetorically loaded) scene with growing ardor, and he sees in it a confirmation of his own artistic fate: "To live, to err, to fall, to triumph, to recreate life out of life! A wild angel had appeared to him, the angel of mortal youth and beauty, an envoy from the fair courts of life . . ." (186). Students have loved this ever since Joyce got into the English curriculum. "The fair courts of life" is a lovely medieval image of grandeur that awaits us, of life as a series of beautiful invitations to give our fullest measure, to reach our destined place. Stirring, heady stuff. I said that the young cannot resist this; I suspect that the no longer young also respond to it. Surely there lurks, even in the oldest and most disabused among us, the remnants of a romantic believer in endless possibility and freedom; that residual ghost gets its fill in *Portrait*.

Or does it? Do not forget the last words of Joyce's title: "as a young man." This often lyrical book is nonetheless written in hindsight, and the going may not be as straightforward as it first appears. A second reading of *Portrait* is a more uncertain, uneasy affair. Then we note the peculiar rhythm of this book, a mix of highs and lows that seems virtually punitive. Hence, chapter 2 closes (in high purple) with Stephen's swooning experience of the prostitute's kiss; he closes his eyes, conscious only of the pressure of her lips as they part, leading to something still more ecstatic: "and between them he felt an unknown and timid pressure, darker than the swoon of sin, softer than sound or odour" (108). But chapter 3 opens on a different note altogether: we see the December dusk "come tumbling clownishly after its dull day," and we have a Stephen whose belly craves for food: stew, turnips, carrots, potatoes, mutton, thick sauce. "Stuff it into you, his belly counseled" (109).

Joyce seems to be writing the soaring/falling drama, the Daedalus/ Icarus drama, in several keys at once, so that ecstasy and ethereal swooning are followed by clownish tumbling and gut-stuffing, leading to the feeling that nothing definitive—such as an emancipation, a flying over nets—is likely to happen, for it must of necessity be followed by a fall. One feels also the contrapuntal rhythm that governs Joycean narrative, a kind of music that sovereignly dispenses high notes and low, sees this mix as inevitable and complementary. For all these reasons, the fate of Stephen Dedalus remains a maddeningly open question, because, even in *Portrait*, his efforts to fly and to enter the "fair courts of life" seem checked, inscribed in a system that is larger than he is.

Yes, the book famously closes with his triumphal exit—"Welcome, O life! I go to encounter for the millionth time the reality of experience and to forge in the smithy of my soul the uncreated conscience of my race" (275–276)—but Stephen will then reappear in *Ulysses*, back in Dublin after a stint in Paris, unvictorious, no longer swooning at all. That altered Stephen leads us to the richer book at hand, the reworking of Homer's epic of wiliness and cunning, fathers and sons, of homecoming and recognition, a book that entertains fewer illusions about flying past nets, a book that is wise about precisely "nationality, language and religion" as the very stuff of consciousness. *Portrait* traces Stephen's evolution from infancy to emancipation, but *Ulysses* offers us a far more complex view of human development, suggesting that the mind may be the least free space imaginable, that we are inhabited by others, and that a fuller sense of our actual contours—our story—needs to take the measure of this greater traffic.

THE READER AS ULYSSES

Leopold Bloom, as we will see, is James Joyce's candidate for a modern-day Odysseus or Ulysses. The novel chronicles one long day in the lives of Bloom, Stephen, and Molly, and it famously closes with Bloom's return home to the marital bed, home to Ithaca, followed by the rich musings of his wife, Molly. Yet it is hardly fanciful to say that the truly epic voyage of *Ulysses* is the amazing journey undertaken by the *reader.*

Homer's hero encounters true monsters and perils, literal adventures of every stripe, whereas Bloom goes through the ordinary paces of his marriage, city, and life. But the reader's encounter with this novel is marked by challenges, threats (to understanding), and an incessant need for wit, suppleness, resourcefulness, even wiliness if he or she is to negotiate this bizarre fiction. Those are precisely Odyssean talents. Each chapter of the novel, especially once you have passed the first six (which seem reliably done in the stream-of-consciousness vein), presents a shockingly new landscape, rife with its own Scyllas and Charybdises, demanding that the reader shift gears, reacclimate, renegotiate, find both the high ground and the low ground so as to continue moving forward. No other novel in world literature poses the question of *readerly survival* as sharply, dauntingly, and—I think—rewardingly as this one does.

Since you are to be the Odyssean reader, I will act as Homeric guide and do my part to equip you for the journey ahead. Let's begin with a cardinal fact about our man, Ulysses, the man you yourself are to emulate: He is an upbeat, confident, wily explorer with intelligence and stamina. He is *not* a dour, maniacal, cerebral type; on the contrary, he *enjoys* his trials and tasks, for they bring out the best in him. His central virtue is his quickness of mind, his uncanny ability to *decipher* strange situations and to make the most of them. It seems to me that these are superb *readerly* attributes, and they will not only take you a far piece into this book, but they will make your trek, indeed your efforts, into something exciting and rewarding as well.

The most important bit of resourcefulness you will need is an open-minded curiosity and suppleness when confronting Joycean prose. Whereas traditional fiction lines up its ducks (its plot and characters) fairly straightforwardly, Joyce writes *musically*, enlisting motifs that resonate ever more powerfully, tending toward an utterance that seems hospitable to very different things at once: thought, speech, setting, others. At first glance this can be off-putting, for we want prose to behave. So, why does he break the rules? And what's in it for us?

First of all, Joyce knows that the noise inside our heads differs entirely from the orderly paragraphs of the books we read. Inside, it is mixed up and multileveled, it comes from different sources, it mocks syntax and grammar. Second, and equally important, this prose has a composite, *plenary* character that offers us what most writing does not: a sense of life in the round, self ensconced in setting. Third—most surprising of all—this mixed writing confers on its major issues—pleasure and pain, love and death—an astonishing kind of reach and pungency. This is why one cannot successfully paraphrase *Ulysses;* the wit, pathos, and humor of the novel are inseparable from Joyce's cunning narration, his capacity to spread out his great issues in repeating motifs and echoes, found sandwiched between bits of banality and chitchat.

Need I say that life is like that? Life does not come in capital letters and paragraphs, but is messy, indeterminate, possessed of jewels but also larded with flotsam and jetsam (where, often enough, the jewels are to be found). Reading *Ulysses* consists of collecting the jewels, watching/helping them take shape, and enjoying the rare pleasure of a book that has the vibrancy and quicksilver fluidity of life itself. You, the Odyssean reader, are involved in a treasure hunt of sorts, not so different from panning for gold, the watchful and exciting pursuit of shimmering nuggets and precious ore that are lodged in the flow of existence. And that is the note I want most to sound: There is gold in *Ulysses*, and there is great fun in prospecting it. Reading this rich book enriches its readers. Often enough, in real life, many of us reflect back over our days and weeks and months and years, and we have trouble seeing the gold. Joyce helps us to a vital sense of life's worth, its savor, its keenness, its unholy mix and its holy value. Time to start the hunt.

REWRITING STEPHEN DEDALUS

The beginning of *Ulysses* is devoted to three "Stephen" chapters, and they herald a kind of writing unlike anything in *Portrait.* We open with Buck Mulligan, Stephen's Mephistophelean roommate, briskly performing his mockery of the Catholic mass, referring to his shaving cream as "the genuine Christine: body and soul and blood and ouns" (3). Mulligan then looks out to sea, calls it "a great sweet mother," which leads to Homeric echoes and epithets, but in a new, modern form: "The snotgreen sea. The scrotumtightening sea" (4–5). Joyce is having fun with "snotgreen" and "scrotumtightening," taking Homeric language in quite a new direction, but beneath these learned and mock references there is a drama much closer to home: the death of Stephen's mother, along with Stephen's refusal to pray at her bedside. This is Joyce's target. Stephen dutifully looks out to sea, and Mulligan then moves in for the attack. Why, he asks, didn't Stephen kneel down to pray? Even Mulligan's aunt thinks Stephen effectively killed his mother. He must have something sinister in him.

Mulligan continues to shave, Stephen gazes at his coat sleeve, and Joyce opens the scene wide and deep, showing us how haunted Stephen is, how the outer stage—shaving cream, sea—merges with the inner stage—dreams, ghosts, remorse, religion. Hence, we read of the dead mother appearing to Stephen in a dream, in her grave-clothes, reeking of wax and rosewood and wet ashes, but this notation is followed by Stephen looking out at the sea—that same sea, which Mulligan had called "a great sweet mother"—but a sea now become "a dull green mass of liquid," thus triggering a deathbed memory of excruciating detail: the china bowl, container of the "green sluggish bile" she had vomited up as her liver gave out. We see in these notations the symphonic reaches of Joycean prose, a language devised to bring thought and consciousness to the page. And more still. In calling the bay and skyline "a dull green *mass* of liquid" (my italics), Joyce energizes and "thickens" his prose, since we are to factor in the (mocked) Catholic mass of a page ago, a ceremony of transubstantiation as well as obeisance. To make certain that all the elements come together, Joyce closes the passage by revisiting the dying mother's bedside and focusing on the "green sluggish bile" she has been vomiting up, so that the earlier "snotgreen sea" and the references to "our great sweet mother" fuse horribly together, yielding an amalgam of meanings in which it is simply no longer possible to distinguish between inside and outside, present and past, as if the setting itself were reinforcing Stephen's torment. The readerly gold consists in seeing how these elements cohere, how Joyce has corraled the mass, Homer, the sea into a rich utterance about Stephen's misery.

And about the large issues of this book. The mass that Stephen has rejected stands for a view of the soul's immortality, as well as the transformation of body and blood into wafer and wine. Stephen has said no to this, but the text has its own say, inasmuch as the dead still live via dreams and ghosts, inasmuch as the spectacle of her dying and his refusal lurks on the inside of Stephen's consciousness, plaguing him with questions. One of the more significant of those questions is: To what end human flesh? Does flesh (at death) simply yield to soul? Or does flesh, like all living matter, rot? What exists on the inside of us: spirit or green sluggish bile? None of these questions is formulated as such, but they are given here as musical motifs, as the elements of a language that is, underneath its appearance of scattered details and references, dreadfully on-target in its evocation of Stephen's troubles. Traditional fiction would have sorted all this out into separate entities; James Joyce has woven it together, and, in so doing, has created a new kind of writing, one in which our existential drama seems written everywhere (in shaving cream, in the sea, in bile, in the mass), and in which the world itself (shaving cream, sea, bile, mass) speaks us.

Speaks *us*? Whose story is this? you may wonder. Stephen's? Yours? Mine? How much do the particulars matter? You scarcely need to have refused to pray at your dying mother's bedside in order to recognize yourself in Stephen's quandary. No one is without ghosts or feelings. Joyce has devised a new language for cargoing human feeling onto the page. By spreading out Stephen's thoughts into the setting, Joyce asks us to reconsider the actual form and locus of our own deepest sensations. *Ulysses* is written in such a way that this psychic material is scattered, is packed into musical notes and motifs, is "out there" as well as inside us. This rendition sharply reverses our customary view that deep feelings are lodged in some kind of private inner sanctum, a place tucked away in the recesses of our heart where we go to visit now and then. Joyce explodes that view. He says that our feelings leak out into the world, that they color everything we see or hear. In some shockingly modern fashion, he is perhaps the first truly *ecological* writer, ecological in the sense that he refuses to rope off inside from outside, crucial from banal, remorse from shaving cream. Seeing Stephen's guilt as Joyce has orchestrated it helps us to a new and capacious view of our own inner drama.

It is instructive to contrast Joyce's version of death-of-the-mother with Proust's account of the "intermittencies of the heart," a vital and unstoppable visitation of the dead via memory. The French novelist devoted some thirty dense, lyrical, unbearably intense pages to the ghostly return of the dead grandmother, including the protagonist's doomed pursuit of her, and his equally doomed reminiscences of the pain he had caused her, the love she bestowed on him, the grace that is now forever gone. But this is not the manner of James Joyce. In *Ulysses,* the ghosts of the past live, but their reign is cramped, and they share the scene with much else, including chitchat, random detail, fretting about Irish art and politics, getting dressed, taking a walk, going to work, not to mention the innumerable sorties and entries into the text of other stuff, such as songs, poems, quotations from multiple languages, ditties, limericks, and the like. Not always easy to process, especially when you're on the lookout for plot.

IF LIFE HAS NO PLOT, WHY SHOULD BOOKS?

How to follow a plot when the plot disappears for pages on end? In some sense *Ulysses* is sticking its tongue out at traditional fiction and at our familiar way of understanding *plot.* It is as if he is saying: What a hash we've made of things by always harping on story, story, whereas our actual perceptual and thinking lives are so much more random, kaleidoscopic, unaccented, meandering, and bumping against an outside world that doesn't know anything about us. You may *think* you muse constantly about your love life or your children or dead parents, but is that really the case? Isn't our actual thinking much more haphazard, serendipitous, filled with eddies and flows, with all manner of extraneous material, than we care to admit? How much weight does our life story really carry? Try comparing the version of that story which exists in your résumé or CV with the random noise that is incessantly being produced in your brain, and ask yourself: Is this noise me? Am I this noise? Where are the clean lines (that I see on my résumé)?

Or, try focusing ever so intently on the grand events of your life, and mix this with actual living. You won't get very far; you'll either get run over by a truck, or be accused of not attending to those speaking to you, or be obliged to table the big story (love, desire, death, etc.), because, after all, there's work to do, places to go, trivia to deal with, money to make, laundry to clean, living to accomplish. True enough, literature has, for centuries, graciously dished up stories that dwell lovingly on our moral and emotional lives; but how much space do those aspects of our lives actually take up? If you had to do a spreadsheet of how much time you actually allot to the needs of either heart or soul—as opposed to stomach or purse—what would it look like? There is a moment in Ibsen's play *Little Eyolf* when the protagonist, a man whose son has just drowned, catches himself thinking about what he's going to have for dinner, and is both shocked and ashamed. Joyce is savvy about such matters, but he is neither shocked nor ashamed. And hence he knows traditional fiction to be, often enough, a whopping lie, a house of cards, a pretend scenario where only important things take place, where we are always and ever focused on great issues, where every encounter is life-altering, every word exchanged is meaningful and resonant, every gesture significant. Life is not like that.

JOYCEAN MUSIC

But the important things are nonetheless smuggled into the text, right and left. Stephen's remorse about his mother's death is part of a larger obsession with whether the soul is real, whether life and history have a purpose, and Joyce is very canny in his way of airing these big issues. They are often clothed in allusions to religion and art and literature. Hence, Stephen is walking on the beach and sees a boatman looking out to sea. We hear a reference to five fathoms of water, along with something the tide will bring in; this is followed by mention of a corpse that has been under for nine days. Joyce then visualizes this corpse—we are in Stephen's mind now, but the shift has not been signaled—by referring to a "swollen bundle" that will come to the surface and offer to the sun a "puffy face, saltwhite. Here I am" (18). Gradually the reader starts to hear the resonance of this prose: "Five fathoms" is an echo of Shakespeare's *The Tempest*, and the famous lines "Full fathom five thy father lies; Of his bones are coral made" are waiting in the wings here, to make their (partial) appearance two chapters later, when the corpse finally comes up.

But why the reference at all? Shakespeare's line bespeaks a beautiful alteration of dead flesh into precious stone, a "wondrous seachange"; Stephen is thinking a great deal about just such things: What do the dead become? What is the "end" of flesh? What is the goal of life? Already he has dreamed of his mother's dead face, come back to haunt and to accuse him. Already, as well, he has glanced at himself in the mirror, wondering how he looks to others, how his face was chosen, a face that asks questions, a face Stephen thinks of as "dogsbody to rid of vermin" (6). *Dogsbody to rid of vermin.* I can hardly imagine a stronger phrase for saying: We are just flesh, flesh that decomposes, that has no spiritual future whatsover. This matters to Stephen, and it matters to Joyce, but their interests are quite different. Stephen seems to despise his body, to be ill at ease in it, and would doubtless prefer to be pure intellect. Joyce, as we will see, has a much broader perspective, and in the figures of Bloom and Molly, the other major protagonists of *Ulysses*, flesh looms larger and larger, but presented with a kind of zest and splendor that do us proud. *Ulysses* is going to make room for flesh and its appetites. But not on Stephen Dedalus's watch. You cannot read this book without widening your own views about what it means to live—and to die—in a body.

Meanwhile, Joyce returns to the drowned body. "Here I am," the corpse risen from the sea announces, in unmistakable counterpoint not only to the Catholic *Ecce homo*, but also to that white shaving lather referred to as the "genuine Christine," "body and soul and blood and ouns," to the spiritual view of the soul's victory over decaying flesh. Once again the musical motifs produce their melody, and we understand that this account of a dead body strikes the very chords that gnaw at Stephen. He refused to pray because he cannot assent to the church's view; nature's laws tell us otherwise, tell us that our bodies are not *Godsbody* (imperishable, immortal spirit), but rather *dogsbody* (swollen corpse, rotting flesh). Don't for a minute regard this as esoterica; it is a life being parsed, a moment when low-profile "data" opens up and discloses bigger game. All of us know such moments. Is there anyone who doesn't occasionally reflect on the afterlife? Not merely death and rot, but aging itself whispers its ugly story to us over and over, concerning the perishability of flesh, the nastinesses to come.

James Joyce has wanted to enlist Shakespeare and the church in his project in order to show us that rotting corpses (and their scandal) are what literature and religion have always been dealing with, even if rarely so openly and brazenly as here. Which is to say: The odd detail and bits and pieces of random notation in this big book are often in dazzling synchrony with one another, obliging us to remember the earlier soundings of these same notes and motifs. In Joyce's eyes the material and the spiritual are interwoven, and that is why the tiniest bytes of his prose can resonate, can point beyond. We are used to interpreting music along such echoing lines; now we need to realize that prose can also be written this way. And when it is, our own story (our hopes and fears about what follows death) jumps out at us from amid the details ("here I am") and gets broadcast in a strikingly resonant fashion.

HISTORY AS A NIGHTMARE

We next find Stephen, in chapter 2, teaching in school, conversing with Mr. Deasy the schoolmaster, continuing to reflect on those notions of history and purpose that have already been sounded, and will continue to resonate. It is easy to chalk up such reflections to a kind of abstract philosophical curiosity, but we can hardly fail to see that the young man musing over these matters has a good deal of history behind him—his mother's death at which he refused to pray—that won't go down. Everywhere in the chapter Stephen's guilt and Stephen's obsession with the work of time are on show. He offers the students a riddle that they cannot fathom, but his own answer is telling: The riddle is about a fox that buries a grandmother. A moment later he watches the students playing field hockey while he chats with Deasy, and this conjunction produces from Stephen one of the most famous lines in the novel: History, Stephen says, is a "nightmare," a nightmare from which he must try to awake. Deasy, shocked, proffers the church's view, exclaiming that history has a single goal and moves inexorably toward the manifestation of God, but Stephen, hearing the voices of the students outside ("Hooray! Ay! Whrrwhee!") calls *that* "God." Deasy is confused, so Stephen clarifies: "A shout in the street" (28).

The Joycean pun—"goal" as manifestation of God, but also as ball between the posts—establishes the bizarre parity of this novel, in which the rough and tumble of physical beings in action rivals the injunctions of scripture. No divine plan in sight. Joyce is to generate some remarkable fireworks out of this ever-repeating clash between the antics of real behavior and feeling on the one hand and the prescriptions of church and state and high culture on the other. This is not just irony; it is the contrapuntal rhythm of our lives. We negotiate endlessly between the material and the spiritual, between quotidian matters such as working/eating/sleeping on the one hand and going to church or contemplating religion, art, literature, the "higher things," on the other. Most highbrow literature leaves the physical stuff largely out of the picture in order to focus on the "higher" things. *Ulysses* shocks us by its unruliness, its insistence on giving all that "low life" its day in court. We rarely follow traditional literary characters into the bathroom (or even the kitchen); not so here. We'll see Stephen pick his nose, Bloom take his seat in the privy, and Molly have her period. Moreover, in calling God "a noise in the street," Joyce acknowledges the rowdiness, haphazardness, and authority of sprawling life, in contrast to neat coherence of theological models and the like.

Joyce also displays a more human Stephen. The weak student, Sargent, stays behind, and Stephen's gaze sizes him up mercilessly: scraggy neck, foggy glasses, weak eyes. One remembers the young Stephen of *Portrait,* a small and lonely child with glasses and weak eyes. Stephen, too, remembers, as he ponders over this sad specimen, musing that this weak child had a loving mother who held him dear, but perhaps mother-love alone is true. The personal analogy then comes home: He and Sargent are alike, and each is possessed of a childhood no one sees or can touch. Each is composed of secrets that are hidden in the dark, that want out, that want to be exposed.

Given the frequently dry arrogance of *Portrait*'s Stephen, this kinder, gentler figure is a welcome arrival. Yet it is worth noting that Stephen's sympathy for Sargent remains strictly internalized, does not cross the threshold of utterance. And pity it is, too, as Stephen suggests, for we *want* to express our feelings, are held in tyranny by our secrets. But Joyce is wise about the constraints that govern and censor actual human exchange, and he will not indulge in the kinds of fulsome communications we routinely find in nineteenth-century fiction, the kinds still on show in *Masterpiece Theatre* types of productions, as people eloquently open their hearts with one another. In real life, much, very much, remains unspoken. But, on the inside, in minds and thoughts, the chatter never stops, the meter is always running. And that will be the territory of this novel. Nothing surprising in this formulation—we all know that thought usually dwarfs utterance (unless we are professors)—but we will be continuously surprised at what Joyce finds when he goes inside.

A TEXT THAT TALKS BACK

Often enough, he finds, inside, that conversation continues, but it is unvoiced and unheard. At other times, a spoken comment triggers something on the inside, as in Stephen's response to Deasy's pronouncement concerning the Englishman's proudest boast that he has ever paid his way, never borrowed a shilling; Deasy wants to know if Stephen knows what this means, if he can feel it. The text itself answers, by producing (without commentary) a grocery list of Stephen's debts, trotted out with the factuality of a bank statement (in deficit) or a guilty conscience. The reader must wonder what these items are doing: names of friends (Mulligan, Ryan, Temple, Reynolds, Koehler), name also of landlady, each serenely accompanied by amount of money owed.

Professional criticism has little use for sorties of this stamp. After all, nothing momentous or "underlineable" is happening in this nagging list of Stephen's actual debts, catalyzed by Deasy's pompous words. Yet I would submit that James Joyce is delicious on exactly this front: to depict our actual noise, a running patter that has no truck with grand themes. I want also to underscore the alertness of Joycean writing, his unwavering view that we in fact are conducting a lifelong internal conversation with events coming our way. Stephen is *responding* here. But I know of no other book that trots this kind of stuff out onto the page, giving it equal status with actual speech, helping us to see how surprisingly "dialogic" our daily life really is, how much we actually talk back to the world. One of the delights of *Ulysses* consists in savoring such small talk, and the best way to do this is to read the book aloud. I know, from lecturing on the novel, that readers go right past such notations, since they are on the lookout for large game (as we professors have always urged them to be); life is a game, all right, but it is small game.

WRITING AND METAMORPHOSIS

It is generally agreed that one of the most dazzling Stephen chapters is chapter 3, "Proteus," in which the brilliant young man displays his formidable intellectual wares. A high-wire performance on a beach, mixing philosophical musings about sight and sound, time and space, this chapter gives us, off the bat, a definition of artistic vocation that is as fine as anything I have ever read: "Signatures of all things I am here to read" (31). As Odyssean reader, you are about to find out just how sparkling this Dedalus fellow can be, and whether or not you have any aspirations for becoming an artist yourself, there is a good deal to be said for going through life as someone who reads all the signatures, who carries on an active correspondence with whatever comes his or her way. Joyce is eye-opening and mind-jolting along just these lines: His characters have lightning responses, bounce us out of our torpor, remind us that just living is a bristling proposition, bursting with signs that we might turn into signatures.

Proteus, of course, is the god of incessant shape-shifting, the god you cannot grasp, and Joyce is out to best this divinity by rivaling him in the arena of language. We ordinarily think language is a stable affair of nouns and verbs and adjectives and the like, but our author dismisses that silly notion by turning adverbs into verbs ("almost" becomes "almosting"); another metamorphosis consists of casting the action in five languages at once, so that a woman "trudges, schlepps, trains, drages, trascines" what she is carrying; still a third is produced by devoting two feisty paragraphs to the gambits of a dog in such a way as to produce a veritable menagerie via simile and metaphor, so that the poor dog ends up being figured sequentially like a hare, with a snout, barking at waves that are herds, waves that serpent, while outfitted with a tongue like a wolf and galloping like a calf. This frisky verbal game closes predictably with the dog's discovery of another dog's corpse on the beach, rendered with the same breathtaking agility: the dog stops and sniffs and stalks, as Stephen's voice draws its canine conclusions. This spectacle of "dogskull, dogsniff" is supposed to be a gathering manifestation of God. How can that be, when what we see before us is "poor dogsbody's body" (39)?

As I said, Stephen can dazzle, and part of the fun here is simply to ride the verbal roller coaster. But Joyce never loses sight of his characters' home truths, and, sure enough, all this animal talk inevitably returns to the obsession with death and meaninglessness. We gradually realize that metamorphosis only *appears* to be a form of fun and games, of freedom, of endless transmutation, but that in reality, once you think about it, all metamorphosis is death-inscribed, is governed by the entropic law that produces rot and "poor dogsbody's body." Something profoundly Joycean is in play here, namely that our mental and imaginative sorties, our capacity to see things kaleidoscopically or metaphorically, are in the last analysis tactical, strategic, efforts to get clear of constraints and fixed forms or laws; but sooner or later we will be yoked back into the ambit of gravity and death.

But the show itself can be quite a sight. All things have signatures to be read, and it follows that all activities can be writeable and readable, but delivered now with the freshness of Genesis, of a world being named for the first time. Activities such as peeing at the edge of the water, for that too is speech: "seesoo, hrss, rsseeiss, ooos" (41). Peeing on the beach: becoming part of the flow, adding to the elements, doing your little Protean jig. If you look askance at this kind of prancing prose, and wonder where the "plot" might lie, the answer has to be: This is the plot. This word dance is the living pulse of the book. But watch: It segues right into the continuing meditation on history and purpose, as we see when the awaited corpse finally enters the scene, dragged up onto the beach: not pretty. The body is puffed and gaseous; minnows are seen moving through the trouser fly. Stephen looks at this and sees a world made for Proteus, not Jesus—a world of pure metamorphosis in which one moves from God to fish, where energy drastically changes form and shape, constituting in its dance of death the very air we breathe: "Dead breaths I living breathe, tread dead dust, devour a urinous offal from all dead" (41–42).

An instructive sight, this. "Seachanged" and metamorphosed indeed, this rotted flesh, food now for minnows (who have attacked the genitals), is bad news for any transcendent view put forth by religion. Instead, we are treated to a death-infested view of life, an affair of being poisoned by breathing, as if existence were solely commerce with the dead. It is possible to see this passage in terms of Stephen's guilt over his mother's death, or perhaps in still broader terms, suggesting Joyce's own relation to "tradition," to that massive stock of authorities and quotations and injunctions that civilization has bequeathed to the living, now seen as stench of the dead, as noxious power.

And yet this dark reading won't quite do, because what jumps out at any responsive reader is the energy and vibrancy of these passages, testifying to *life*, life caught in its mercurial fluidity, rendered in almost alchemical prose. And we the readers are, I think, the richer for it. *Dead breaths I living breathe, tread dead dust, devour a urinous offal from all dead.* There is something glorious as well as macabre in this vision that balances death's hold on life with life's unwavering energy. Of course we are surrounded by death, but we are the hungry and the living who breathe, tread, and devour. And among our trumps is human language. At some point we begin to grasp that James Joyce is playing God, as indeed do all artists who create characters and a fictive world, but that Joyce wants to compete, textually, with natural law, with the forces of decomposition and dying, by giving us its noblest opposite number: living thought, virile language, the shape-shifting power of the human imagination.

STEPHEN EXPOSED

As we have now come to expect, intellectual flashes and philosophical nuggets share the stage with notations of a different stripe altogether, and the most endearing feature of "Proteus" is its mischievousness, its willingness to spoof itself, seen most hilariously in Stephen's own salty self-mocking, those confidences whereby he nails his own pretentiousness, ridicules his own performance. Hence, in reflecting on his earlier desire to be a priest—a theme that is treated with oh so much earnestness in *Portrait*—Stephen divulges to us his less pious yearnings as well, noting that he prayed to the Virgin in order not to have a red nose, followed by a prayer to the devil requesting that a woman seen in the street lift her clothes a bit more. These little avowals reach a crescendo with an image of Stephen on the Howth tram yelling out "*Naked women!*" At this point, Stephen's mind becomes a miniature courtroom: prosecution brings out these tidbits from the past, and defense tries to justify them (in this case by asking, why else were women invented?).

I'd want to say there has indeed been a "seachange" in the conception of one Stephen Dedalus, and that the fellow served up to us in *Ulysses* is decidedly better company than his swooning and pontificating double in *Portrait.* I like especially the way this prose answers itself, the way Stephen dialogues with his own memories and puts himself on trial. Not that he then throws in the towel, not at all: A defense is quickly mounted—fantasizing naked women is, uh, really just obeying nature's laws, yes? What else were they invented for? This is prose we *navigate,* and it pulsates with firing neurons and sinuous turns and fiery retorts, as Stephen passes in review his pretensions, mocks them, but still tries to defend himself. It is also a contest we rarely win, since no outsider can possibly possess as much dirt about us as we ourselves possess, giving the mocker the last word. With stunning malice, Joyce has Stephen trot out his most embarrassing aspirations, even zooming in on the holiest of holies, his yearnings as artist. We now learn of a Stephen sampling seven different books (at the rate of two pages each) every night, preening dramatically in front of the mirror, busy planning the

Great Work to come, work that would have letters (yes, letters) as titles—F, Q, W are mentioned—each wonderful, each sought after. Nothing, we realize, is sacred anymore; even *epiphanies* come in for a beating, as Stephen visualizes them "written on green oval leaves, deeply deep," destined for far-flung libraries, indisputable documents of genius guaranteed to last to the end of time. Stephen actually glimpses his immortality, as when a reader in the distant future pours over his golden prose, reading these immortal pages of "one long gone one feels that one is at one with one who once"(34).

MY JOYCE: FALSTAFFIAN

Reading this mouthwatering passage—the splendid send-up of artistic humbug; the mock awe of fantasized masterpieces titled by letter; the spoofing of that most sacroscant article, the epiphany; the final gag with the last line: one . . . one . . . one . . . once, etc.—I want now to put more of my cards on the table. This is *my* Joyce. This Joyce has a Falstaffian side to him, a rich vein of humor that is on duty at all times, that is especially good at pricking bubbles, bubbles the "other" Joyce has spent some time inflating. Let me say further that this low farcical material bristles with wit and intelligence, and that it constitutes for me not the low road but the high road into the novel. To be sure, "Proteus" has tons more things in it than I have analyzed, including further poetic forays on Stephen's part, reflections about Stephen's family, notions about birth and death and sexuality. And it has pathos, too, as seen in Stephen's yearning for touch and tenderness, his lonely isolation, and his hunger to know human love.

Still, what most saddens me in teaching *Ulysses* is the ponderousness, the intellectual weightiness, one ascribes to it. People miss the fun. They go right past it. Of course it is erudite and allusive, larded with notations beyond the casual reader's grasp, filled with lore that only makes sense to the specialists. And, yes, it also has plenty of seriousness that we can all get our teeth into: fathers and sons, husbands and wives, betrayal and recognition. But it is also a plebeian book, a book of pratfalls and carnival, of teasing and playing, of peeing and farting and defecating and fornicating, a book where the serious issues are never allowed to take over entirely. Better still, it is a book that *lives* on the page like none other, and it challenges us, I think, to live as keenly, as alertly, as exuberantly, as self-reflexively as it does. To see Stephen Dedalus harpoon himself, to watch him puncture his own inflated pieties, to follow his splendid self-repartee is tonic and instructive, for we, too, can be pretty puffed up creatures at times, can be fooled by our show. Joyce loves both inflating and deflating, for he understands that they are the two major directionalities of human energy, and there is something deeply honest and fitting about this contrapuntal rhythm, this willingness to prick one's own bubbles, this knowledge that the human animal makes bubbles that need pricking. It is in this sense that *Ulysses* is most Homeric: The writing itself is alert, undeceived, cunning, and resourceful.

THE ADVENT OF BLOOM

With this last sentence, the wily reader will have sensed that I am now leaving Stephen Dedalus in order to approach the remarkable figure whom James Joyce posited as a modern-day Ulysses: Leopold Bloom, man of many turns, *polytropic*, and equipped with the liveliest (not the deepest, the liveliest) intelligence of any character in literature. Joyce intended chapters 4 to 6, the first Bloom chapters, to be a replay of the Stephen-issues we have just considered. "Replay" seems to me a good term to characterize the sheer zest in graphing Bloom's engagement with having breakfast, taking a walk, remembering his dead, facing death. Stephen Dedalus, at his worst, is the impossible fellow that Buck Mulligan sees him as, that Joyce himself saw him as: a figure of dreadful moral earnestness, firmly bounded and unbending ("unchangeable," as Joyce put it to his friend Budgen). At his *best*, Stephen is the teaser we've seen.

Still, what a refreshing surprise Bloom is. This observant, thinking, musing man can and will pay attention to just about anything under the sun, wrecking our sense of all hierarchies (and surprising us, repeatedly, as to what a novel might contain). Thus, on the first page of his entry, he checks out the kitten. A kitten who speaks: "Mkgnao!" Do you know many books where kittens speak? This one does it enough to get Bloom's attention: He is preparing breakfast for his wife. Watching Bloom at work gets the following response: "Mrkgnao!" (Note that the spelling has changed, to signal the ratcheting up of cat-talk, adding urgency to the milk plot.) At this, Bloom reflects over the nature of felines. He senses that kitty understands plenty, even though they have been called stupid, and this line of reasoning eventuates into a little portrait of the species: they can be cruel, they can be vindictive, they do in mice. Wondering all this leads to Bloom's signature move: He ponders what he might look like to kitty. Does he look like a tower? No, he decides, since she can jump him. These meditations are completed by cat-cry number three, adding another "r" this time—"Mrkrgnao!"—and kitty gets her milk.

What have we seen? A curiosity and elasticity and fidelity that will be with us for hundreds of pages, that is keyed to the "Wonder what . . . ?" approach to all things, that is invested in the carnal world, enjoys checking it out. Is this not intelligence on the move? Bloom rejects the truism of cats being stupid, reflects instead about what her life is actually like: what she feels, what she sees, indeed what he must look like to her. This is an *activist* imagination of the first stripe. Bloom is the only character in fiction who would ponder whether fish get seasick; he is the fellow who sees a flock of pigeons flying over parliament and then wonders how they make their choices when it comes to dropping their load. Being Bloom, he imagines it as a little group conversation, each pigeon selecting his target, taking aim, and letting go. This little sortie is capped by a marvelous moment of empathy as Bloom imagines the birds' little pleasure: "Must be thrilling from the air" (133). Reading the exploits of Leopold Bloom entails sidling into the prose (not unlike what cats do with us), simply enjoying the little ride, then discovering that we've moved into strange precincts. *Must be thrilling from the air*: Now, there is food for thought. Thrilling to shit? Thrilling to choose targets? Thrilling to score?

Joyce's novel shocked a good many readers in 1922 because he had followed his protagonist right into the jakes and noted what transpired there, but Joyce's knowledge of input and output, of the small pleasures of defecation or the small drama of choosing to let your fart out when a tram is coming, displays a creatural savvy on the far side of conventional notation. *Ulysses* does not merely confirm the fact that we live in flesh; it startles us again and again with the perkiness, willfulness, zest, and reach of flesh. This book will end with a woman lying in bed, musing about her past (love life) on Gibraltar, thinking of the sea and sunsets and her (now arriving) menstrual flow in the same terms, showing us that the *body* can never be taken out of the picture, reminding all readers of that "great sweet mother," "the winedark sea" signaled in the book's opening chapter.

LIFE'S SMALL PLEASURES; PLOT RETURNS

The book now tracks Bloom as he goes out to buy his breakfast kidney, as he notes the fine summer weather and muses about whether his black clothes will make him especially uncomfortable, characteristically remembering that black either conducts or reflects or refracts the heat. A light suit, however, would be frivolous, would make it seem like a picnic. The mix of conducts/reflects/refracts is pure Bloom, displaying the bric-a-brac of his science education, the little laws of science that all of us have absorbed but never fully understood, now seen as the buzzing static of consciousness. There is fresh information here as well (Bloom is in black clothes because he must attend the funeral of Paddy Dignam later in the morning), and something beyond information in the remark about why a light suit, albeit fine for a picnic, would be wrong. A picnic not only because of the casual attire, but because, as we shall soon see, cemeteries are, in Bloom's mind, picnic grounds.

Where, we wonder, is the plot? Well, it's everywhere you look. Standing behind the next-door servant girl with substantial hips while waiting at the butcher's, that's a nice plot. One that makes Bloom impatient to be served his kidney because the girl is already out the door, ready to walk back. This is cause for alarm, leading Bloom to point quickly to the goods he wants, in hopes that he might be served and done soon enough to walk behind these hips, since, after all, this is a fine thing to start the day with, a fine eyefull, but will he make it in time? At the level where Joyce is taking his data, it would seem there is nothing but plot, nothing but microscopic little sorties and fantasies and scenarios, as libido goes through its little paces. Getting the kidney is taking too long, won't be able to follow those hams, but, hey, no matter, it will be for another, and that's not so bad, that's also imaginable, leading our man to fantasize an ersatz outcome, an off-duty constable enjoying the prize, caressing the girl; those fellows, Bloom knows, like them big—"prime sausage" the text says, tying in sweetly with the breakfast kidney Bloom is in the process of buying—and the fantasy closes with the servant girl demurely playing her role, calling out to the nice Mr. Policeman for help please, help because she's lost her way in the wood. Here is the singsong on the inside—a mix of modest bodily needs and snatches of rhymes and tidbits of fairy tales, and presto: a little storylet to pass the time, a little byte of cogency that takes its place with other small ventures, such as reading the newsprint in which your kidney is wrapped (nothing printed goes unread, in this book), or musing about advertising schemes and shop-windows as you walk down the street. Such is Bloom. It is a busy life.

Joyce alerts us to the fact that every moment we live and breathe is filled with bristling data, is often organized into minuscule plots and scenarios, but that these tiny dramas pass right under the big radar screen reserved for Important Things. *Ulysses* delights in making them visible and audible. I'd go further and say that this novel is a superb remedy against boredom, against thinking that one's life and routines are empty, when, in fact, they are filled to the brim. If we know how to see. But how many of us do know how to see? I would give a great deal to be able to walk down any street with Bloom's eyes and mind, with his quickness of response and openness to stimuli. Instead, I am all too often a blindfolded creature of routines and rituals, a craft that makes its way readily enough through the waters of life but does so without the incessant, tiny but resonant encounters that jump out at us on Joyce's page.

BLOOM THE ARTFUL DODGER

Not that large things are never in play. Creatural Bloom can be downright heliotropic, and the disappearance of the sun behind the clouds triggers apocalyptic thoughts, bringing to his mind the Dead Sea, the cities of the plain, Sodom and Gomorrah, the desert wanderings of the Jews, barrenness everywhere. Fortunately for Bloom, help is nearby, in the shape of his own Ithaca, in the shape, especially, of his wife, Molly: "Be near her ample bedwarmed flesh. Yes, yes" (50). Joycean critics and readers alike will never come to a bottom-line understanding of the marriage between Bloom and Molly—some say it's kaput, she is to cheat on him this very day, they've not had sex since their infant boy, Rudy, died, years ago; others say it's okay, they're still together, they retain a complex, not uncritical, emotional connection—but the wisest course is to recognize the importance of "bedwarmed flesh," to see Molly as the living and sustaining anchor in Bloom's orbiting life.

And, so, home it is. Returning with his kidney, Bloom picks up the mail, consisting of two letters and a card—one of the letters addressed to Mrs Marion Bloom and done in a bold hand—and Joyce conveys this little event (it is an event) in the trickiest fashion: his fingers grasp the letters, but the mention of a beating heart tells us something is stirring. He then hands her the letters, lifts the blind, and—finally, furtively—slips a look backward that catches Molly glancing at the letter, then her placing it under the pillow. Plot at last! By these signs—Mrs Marion Bloom on the envelope, change of heartbeat, bold hand, backward glance, tucking it under the pillow—the reader is introduced to the erotic plot of the novel: the assignation made here (in this letter with the bold hand) by the book's great phallus, Blazes Boylan, with Molly (Mrs Marion) Bloom, to be consummated at 4 P.M. at their apartment, under the guise of a singing lesson, obliging Bloom to be out and about all day long, leaving him with much (much) time for reflection and imagination. But please note: My direct (even dramatic) words are utterly different from Joyce's occulted, glancing, barely hinted-at account. Here, too, I see a kind of narrative wisdom: Of course we go through life desiring and fearing, anticipating and worrying, but these emotions rarely shout out loud (contrary to what novels often tell us), and moreover, they coexist with lots of other stuff. French seventeenth-century writers often referred to a "*Carte du Tendre*," a "Map of the Emotions," which gave you an actual landscape with pleasure here, jealousy there, anticipation in this corner, deception in that, all in capital letters. But they never mentioned bathrooms, kitchens, money, clothes, and so on. James Joyce is drawing for us his own cartography of human emotions, and his map is a busy one, filled with life's bric-a-brac, displaying the ecological bigger picture in which love, hate, and so forth take up a fairly small space.

Hence, Bloom goes on through his paces. Fries his kidney, opens his letter from his sixteen-year-old daughter, Milly, brings up the bread and butter and tea and sugar and cream to Molly in bed, is asked by Molly to explain an esoteric term she's just come across in the porn book she's reading—"metempsychosis"—explains that it means "transmigration of souls," looks over her "smudged pages," reflects on the sadism of such work, adds a bit more about reincarnation, and then rushes down to the kitchen to rescue the burning kidney, whose smell Molly has detected. Once there, he reads Milly's letter (she's away in Mullingar), which mentions a possible young suitor, and then—then—sexual intercourse reenters the book. It starts with his fatalistic rumination about his nubile daughter, thinking: She can take care of herself . . . maybe . . . she's still all right . . . still . . . but soon? . . . then visualizing the rambunctious Milly running up the stairs . . . realizing that destiny is in the wings, and that there can be no stopping it: "Ripening now. Vain: very" (54).

Much is on show. Metempyschosis, however esoteric it may appear as concept, is at the heart of *Ulysses*, for it is the fluid principle of the novel, accounting for much of its incessant traffic: the play of memory, the visiting of ghosts, the interweaving of players, the associative linkages of the mind itself. We also see the family drama writ large: the father's concern for his daughter, his visual sense of her growing up, and his certainty that all this is unstoppable. "Vain: very" suggests not so much the young Milly's vanity as the vain effort to resist nature itself. A paragraph or so later, the evocation of Milly predictably fuses (metempsychosis in action) with that of Molly, evoking her lying in her bed, fingers in her hair, counting and smiling and braiding; this Penelope-like image then triggers something considerably more physiological, a rich notation of sexuality in which the male is passive, done to, engulfed, overwhelmed. Everything becomes soft and fluid: regret is felt, growing, in his backbone, the body is powerless to move or resist, and carnal fusion takes place through the gluing of lips together, light lips of a girl, full lips of a woman. As Milly and Molly fuse into each other, we see what I take to be a signature statement in this book without signature statements: Sex will happen, nature prevails, leaving morality and judgment out of the picture.

It is in this regard that James Joyce is an emblematic figure in modern thinking: On the one hand, he is possessed of endless erudition and learning, hence aware of all the religious, moral, and literary formulas and theorems thought to regulate human life (as seen in the countless allusions to "tradition" in all its forms); yet, on the other hand, he is no less attuned to the rival law of life, an imperious law of carnality and libido, which has no truck whatsoever with the prescriptions of culture. What is modern here is the emerging picture of the human subject as a crossroads, a site where culture and nature intersect and do battle. Mind you, Joyce differs entirely from the high-minded Victorians or their successors, inasmuch as he sees these interactions as comic, not tragic, as a melodic proposition of voices and vectors. But there are—for us who are equally caught within this tug-of-war, us who also negotiate between appetite and law—some fascinating ramifications in the strange human dance that *Ulysses* stages in this regard. For Joyce understands that conflict and collision—the predictable rhythm of tragedy and high seriousness—are at home perhaps in literature but are to be avoided at all costs in life. And that they can be avoided. Our age-old injunction to face up to things is inspected by Joyce and found not only wanting, but inapplicable to real human maneuvering.

LOTUS AND THE TECHNIQUES OF EVASION

Hence, chapter 5, "Lotus Eaters," is a fascinating display of what I'd call "Lotus solutions," involving the various strategies, indeed the narcotics of turning aside, dodging, ducking, and in general buying into fantasies of accommodation (instead of colliding with unbending harsh truths). Joyce manages to show us that the oldest institutions of culture have understood the need for Lotus arrangements—it is not for nothing that Marx called religion "the opiate of the masses"—and that these same tactics of evasion govern most human lives, not merely in moments of great crisis (where dodging can make good sense), but in the quotidian small moments as well (where dodging may make even more sense). As my own parentheses suggest, delivering a moral verdict on Lotus, deciding whether it is better to face the facts or escape into fiction, is no easy matter, however clear we may want such issues to be.

Now, Bloom has a passel of facts that need avoiding: his wife's love affair, of course, but other unseemly matters such as death, a topic that is squarely on his agenda this day because of the coming funeral of Paddy Dignam. How will Lotus help him out? One solution to no marital sex (Bloom's fact) is to have a clandestine affair, but true Lotus suggests that it also be unactualized, that it be just an epistolary romance (Bloom's fiction). Walking down the street with the unread letter from Martha Clifford (his clandestine epistolary romance) in his pocket, Bloom meets M'Coy. Bloom is itching to read his letter, but M'Coy, noting that Bloom is dressed in black, thinks initially there may be a death in Bloom's family, but then realizes it concerns Paddy Dignam. M'Coy himself was shocked to learn of Paddy's death, and he wants to share this with Bloom; Bloom would rather, Lotus-fashion, think about more pleasant things, not merely Martha's unread letter, but the sight across the street (right now, in mid-conversation with M'Coy) of female flesh, namely a woman (haughty, horsy, the type that excites Bloom) getting ready to mount a carriage. I don't know of any other novel that would even consider narrating something as banal as this, but Joyce warms up to just such challenges, because he sees them as bursting with plotlike energy, as well as compositionally rewarding. Hence, the sequence will blithely sandwich together a number of discrete but simultaneous events: M'Coy's palaver about Paddy's death *along with* Bloom's ogling of the woman across the street, all bathed in the flow of Bloom's thoughts. The woman's body and clothes are noted with libidinal acuity: boots, laces, a foot that is well turned, all given as preparation for the expected little climax, which is gathering, gathering, gathering. A Joycean shorthand tells us that Bloom thrives on such sights: "Proud: rich: silk stockings."

But there is this little matter of M'Coy who is chattering away, rehearsing his own little narrative about poor Paddy, about how surprised he was to learn of it from a friend, about how he thought Paddy was still among the living, about being told he's not. Not? Well, what could be the matter? Answer: He's dead. Dead? Can't be; M'Coy had just seen him a day or so ago. Dead he is. Happened on Monday. Gone.

Note that I have recounted this event in two distinct paragraphs: one about Bloom, one about M'Coy. But Joyce delights in interweaving these bytes, and in doing so, he achieves prodigious effects. Because you mustn't forget that, all the while, the woman is preparing to mount the carriage: flesh is about to be seen. Bloom—cornered by M'Coy though he is, moving his head to keep the main event in view—is at once desperate and aroused: "Watch! Watch! Silk flash rich stockings white. Watch!" But, as so often happens in life, gratification is not to be had. A tramcar comes in between, blocking Bloom's view. Bloom feels piqued, senses life is unfair, remembers past incidents of being robbed of pleasure, returns to M'Coy and—sublimely— agrees with him that, yes, it is sad indeed: "Another gone" (60–61).

The textualized seesaw between italicized dialogue and internalized thought carries Joyce's signature: the sauciness of the language, the drawn-out account of how M'Coy learned about Dignam's death, the increasing breathlessness ("Watch! Watch!") of Bloom's perception of stirring and provocative female flesh. Bloom feels cheated out of this morsel of voyeurist pleasure, even suggests that things always happen this way (either a comrade covers up the exposed flesh—*esprit de corps,* indeed, as the text has it—or reality in the shape of a tramcar comes between us and the little freebies that are almost within our reach), but readers of *Ulysses* have reason to be grateful, I think, for the gift at hand, the wide-angled lens that brings talk and desire together in their little *mésalliance*, their dance, their little party got on the cheap. A high-minded criticism on the lookout for grand things will go right past this savory sequence. Is this not what Joyce has to offer us? A sighting, a purchase on the vibrant (even if thwarted) opportunities for pleasure that are available at any moment.

What pleasures? you may ask. The pleasures of an eyeful of flesh, yes, but most especially the pleasures of thought, of bubbling, irrepressible thought, released into the air, turned (here, miraculously) into prose. And it is here, of course, that Lotus comes back into the picture: Pleasure need have nothing to do with narcotics or sleep or evasion; no, it can be the prancing mind that salts and peppers whatever comes its way, delighting in small congruences between inner and outer, so that the removing of Paddy Dignam from this earth and the missed bit of leg or thigh ascending into the carriage are both accorded the same honors: "Another gone." This pitter-patter has gone on forever in the human mind, but it has always been under (way under) the radar screen of fiction; Joyce has not only caught it, but he has scooped it out of the environment and offered it to us as a little gift (not a large gift) that restores to us something of our own daily activity, our small-scale improvisations and disappointments and jollies, now shimmering on the page.

KEEPING GHOSTS AT BAY

And yet, it is not quite this easy. Can the minute little goodies (that every moment offers to the resourceful) obviate or replace the Big Bad Things that are still there, looming? For Stephen, his mother's death—and its indictment of Stephen's pride and coldness of heart—is not likely to fade into the background entirely, not some net you can definitively fly over. Bloom also has his share of bad news, of troubles that no amount of tactical shrewdness will dissolve. His wife is going to fornicate with Blazes Boylan at 4 P.M. today, and he's got two deaths that shadow him permanently: his father's, by suicide, and that of little Rudy, who lived only eleven days. Is there a right way to deal with this? Should you face your dead or trick them by running from them? Can you run from them? Bloom furnishes us, in this chapter and throughout, insights about crisis management. In the matter of his father's suicide, he remembers not going into the bedroom to identify the corpse, and says to himself it was doubtless best not to, best even for his father. In short, better not to think about it. Lotus-evasion. Will he get away with it?

Next paragraph opens with Bloom walking past a hackney, noting the horses with their heads deep into feed, again thinking it wisest "not to think about . . ." but rather to concentrate on feed: "Nosebag time" (63). The dreariness of horse-life is given a little lift at "nosebag time," and as Bloom examines them crunching their oats, he reflects on the price they've paid, a price visible in the piece of "black guttapercha" that he sees wagging between their legs, and then concludes that maybe happiness is purchased in this fashion. This depiction of nosebag and guttapercha as the little bargain life has made with the horses is also a version of Joycean music, since we cannot fail to see that Bloom's arrangements are not so different from the horses'. And more Lotus on the way, as we finally get to see Martha's letter to Bloom, the little love-letter dalliance (conducted by Bloom in the alias of Henry Flower) by mail that is not going to go anywhere, that is patent substitution, ersatz, for the failed romance at home. To make sure we see the sugary, evasive character of this correspondence, Joyce writes it in "flowerese," recasting the *billet doux* from Martha to her "manflower" as an affair of tulips that are angry, cactus that is punished, violets that are longed for, concluding with a "naughty nightstalk" (64). We begin to note, here, that this novel could do anything, anything at all, including the invention of flower doggerel, in order to spin and pirouette its themes. (Can you imagine replaying your own little fantasies in ditties of this stripe? Try it. There is an alert intelligence here that never lets anyone off the hook.)

THE OPIATE OF THE MASSES

But Joyce has more Lotus to check out, located now in its institutional home, the Catholic church. Bloom saunters into church, thinks it a good place to meet some girl, and then observes more closely the performance of the mass. What does he see? He sees the women kneeling with red "halters" circling their necks, depicted in herdlike terms, attended to by a priest with something in his hands, murmuring, elaborately dispensing his "communions": taking them out, shaking them off, inserting them into mouths. Bloom's ignorance of the service may initially fool us, but soon enough we register the shrewd analysis at work here: Those crimson halters and the batch kneeling signal back to us the horses and their nosebags.

With a kind of anthropological acuity, Bloom dissects the ritual, assesses its functionality like the good advertising man he is, on the lookout for strategies of persuasion: He shrewdly notes the combination of closed eyes, open mouth, and Latin formulas. *Corpus,* he realizes, has common cause with body and corpse, along with the added benefit of foreign-language narcotic action. One doesn't know whether to laugh or cry at this, but how not to see its corrosive power? Again, the mockery of the mass, seen in the book's opening, is on the docket, but now seen as admirable in its effectiveness as Lotus-scheme. The service is examined by Bloom as a mix of drug and candy; it gives bliss, makes its "consumers" think they've ingested the kingdom of God, resulting in big-time blessedness: salvation, no pain, sleep all the way to paradise.

Bloom being the curious fellow he is, further aspects of Catholic ritual are presented for inspection. Confession is quickly understood as irresistible, since the itch to tell ("schschschschschshch") is perfectly matched by the itch to hear ("chachachachacha?"); this weekly prurient cleaning system is devised by a church that knows what it is doing, that cashes in major-league on sin, showcasing the public confessions of reformed sinners, all doubtless filling the coffers of the folks in Rome. I think we'd have to be tone-deaf to read this as criticism of the church; rather, it testifies to the strange antics of human behavior and the institutions that "manage" such behavior, delivered with a kind of whimsy and pungency that have a flavor all their own. This man *enjoys* thinking. He has what we might call "street smarts," but whereas that term usually connotes a kind of savvy for getting by unhurt, in *Ulysses* it is a much larger and more ambitious proposition, since Bloom's shrewd mind espies everywhere the great institutions of mankind, reflects on their intimate workings (intimate because they are cued to daily behavior), and shows us how that distant abstract word "culture" is in fact a living mesh that we are all trapped in, is even the air we breathe. What is most pungent about this book is its take on modern life. Reading this chapter, we understand that Lotus, far from being a salute to Homer's epic poem, is operative wherever we look, all around us.

THE ART OF SELF-DEFENSE

In chapter 6, "Hades," Joyce recasts the encounter with the dead that we noted in "Proteus." Stephen obsessed about "godsbody" and "dogsbody";

now, at last, Bloom will get to his funeral. His way there, however, is via a coach that he shares—"shares" is quite misleading, given that the other occupants (Simon Dedalus, Martin Cunningham, and Jack Power) are united in a kind of first-name intimacy and solidarity that make his outsider status as Jew (as they see it) all the more poignant—with three Dubliners. The conversation steers early toward Stephen, and Simon snarls out his disapproval of Mulligan and company, the degenerate outfit Stephen is with; Bloom, listening, thinks, not surprisingly, homeward, comparing Simon's somewhat swollen fatherly demeanor with his own emptiness. Here we see one of the few, but moving, references to little Rudy, the dead child: one would have a successor, one would watch him mature, one would listen to him at home, one would walk together: mother, father, and son. Above all, one would live on, reflected in the child's eyes, *feeling* the kinship, the continuity. Such passages, rare but affecting, applied to the text like a kind of herb or spice Joyce uses sparingly, remind us of the emotional baggage Bloom carries (but tries not to think about). How often have you said to others, or to yourself: Try not to think about that? Can one do it? What does it look like when you do it? Joyce is going to show us.

A few pages later, as the others are conversing and Bloom is musing about Martha's letter, about going to the theater, something strange happens in the text, requiring that we exercise all our Odyssean skills in reading. Out of nowhere the prose announces that "he" will be coming later today: Hmm, we wonder, who? Next comes a mention of a statue presumably sighted; this time the text asks: Who? Who's "he"? Who's the statue? Who's thinking here? This hide-and-seek then segues into recorded chitchat between Cunningham and Power in the coach as each greet a figure who is never named, until Dedalus inquires. Guess who? Blazes Boylan. Dedalus now greets him as well. Aha! Even the uninitiated reader grasps that critical things are in play here: Boylan is doubtless seen by the others en route to Eccles Street, to have intercourse with Mrs. Marion Bloom—and that is how any traditional novelist would have written it, but James Joyce is not a traditional novelist. Instead, Boylan seems to break into the text as an unnamed "he," more or less daring us to identify him.

At this juncture things get curiouser and curiouser. For we now realize that Bloom himself has espied Boylan, his nemesis, which is what started the entire sequence about "him" coming in the first place. As noted, the other three Dubliners in the coach salute Boylan, but for our man Bloom this encounter possesses considerably more heat. But, when this book turns on the heat, it responds with dodges. No Bloom-salute for Boylan, but rather a thorough review, on the part of Bloom the would-be-cuckold, of the fingernails of his left hand. And afterward, the nails of his right hand are examined. Nail-time. (The initiated reader will connect these nails with a recurring motif in the story about crucifixion, about Bloom's misreading of INRI as "iron nails ran in." We begin to wonder: Are dodges working?) Now thrown into the mind of this man examining his nails, we see that he is indeed thinking about Boylan, wondering what "they she sees" in him—Joyce shrewdly links the pronouns to signal that Boylan has made it through Bloom's defenses. This is painful! Quick: back to the nails! Another sentence about nails being reviewed is put forth.

Those nails are described as "well pared." We start now to realize that, with Joyce, it is almost always from the frying pan into the fire. Dodging is marvelous in its own way, but the Joycean text sets out booby traps, derails the exits. well pared? What about: well *paired*? Joyce's prose starts to live and breathe, as we ponder its plenitude, its many tongues. After its maniacal focus on well-pared nails, the text acknowledges Bloom as "thinking alone," thinking alone afterward. This is the dodge again: "I've checked my nails; now I am meditating." Except that it also speaks the temporality, the losses of Bloom's life: "thinking alone" is his fate; a fate that set in "after," after Rudy's death, after the cessation of sex between him and Molly.

No sex hardly means no memory. And so Molly follows Boylan into the text, bringing that "ample bedwarmed flesh" with it, as Bloom inventories his truest loss: shoulders, hips, plump. Here is the body that stays ever present in his thoughts, a body whose shape remains, is always there. Yes, it is: not merely that Molly has not lost her own shape, but that it is *there, still there* in Bloom's consciousness, unbanishable, shaping his thoughts, sabotaging his dodge, bringing him relentlessly home. Much of *Ulysses* functions like a textual boomerang: The harder you throw something away to avoid it, the more fiercely it returns to you. Freud would have had no trouble understanding this dynamic as the modus operandi of the human psyche. Joyce has found a way to write Bloom so that we see all his (fine, pitiful) defenses, and also see that they don't work, that what you send out through the door comes back in through the window. I do not know of any other book in the world that offers a spectacle of this sort. It is an intensely moving spectacle, with its view of both human wisdom (Odyssean cunning, resourcefulness?) and human limits. And it is because this passage is so overdetermined, so rich in poignant meanings, in failed stratagems, so "full" of meaning, that we are downright awed by the way Joyce closes this account of the cornered man reviewing his nails: As a final gesture, Bloom sends out "over" the faces of his acquaintances in the coach a glance that Joyce terms "vacant." *Vacant?* Whatever else we may say of Bloom, the Joycean text teaches us that he is not empty.

This sequence is worth an entire chapter of psychological theory. It does not pontificate, nor does it set forth any laws or theorems about human behavior, but it does something much more interesting and engaging: It displays, in living color, up close, the very antics of a person cornered in a tight place. "Cornered" in the most intimate and quotidian way: by nasty personal facts of life (rather than, say, by a murderer or rapist, as might happen in a simpler novel). It is a mirror held up to nature, to *our* nature, since I can hardly imagine that anyone has failed to do, at some time or another, a version of Bloom's dance. And it is worth volumes and volumes of realist prose, since representations of the sort we've just witnessed are simply out of reach, as well as never imagined, in such writing.

ESCAPING DEATH

Everything said up to now about *Ulysses* suggests that this book is peculiarly alive; it won't surprise us that the dead and dying are also an active group. We've already noted the lively ghosts. Bloom possesses a gallows humor of the first rank, and hence sees the cemetery as something of a processing plant, receiving its quotidian ration of dead bodies: young and old, men and women, bearded and bald, child-bearing and consumptive. Once underground, this population changes shape: Their colors metamorphose, their flesh decomposes, and this last process, Bloom suspects, takes longer with the lean ones, moving from a waxy, cheesy state to black ooze before finally drying up altogether. Ever the optimist, Bloom sees this somatic merry-go-round as a kind of cellular fiesta, as the endless permutation of cells that want only to live, that will feed on each other if nothing else is available. All of us go to funerals, but how many of us go there with Bloomish curiosity? In visualizing the evolution of flesh after death, he is not being morbid but, rather, the opposite, since life never stops, even underground. Here, too, is a variant of metempsychosis, and it is not surprising that Bloom, watching the coffin descend into the earth, wonders, "If we were all somebody else" (91).

With this (unaccented but astonishing) remark, we crash right through realism's gates, since the most policed border in any culture is the bounded self, the individual subject that has distinct contours. And yet, don't the very activities of thinking, feeling, desiring—indeed, living—take us incessantly out of ourselves and into others? Isn't that the nature of exchange, as inevitable as breathing? "Wonder whose thoughts you're chewing" advertises an open fluid universe with a good bit of traffic. It is just that traditional fiction and traditional thinking are blind to this traffic, because they think the world to be composed of bounded, roped-off individuals. Joyce, given his delight in choreographing the individual in consort with the group, given his interest in metempsychosis and human change, offers us a more fluid picture. It is a dance: We are enmeshed with others, and those others can be both living and dead. This may sound a bit macabre, but in Joyce's hands both the dance and the transformations can be hilarious.

Especially that late-stage transformation that we call dying. Ever-curious Bloom imagines how it must feel when you actually get the shove: Rather nasty, Bloom assumes, downright incredible, doubtless a mistake, got the wrong person, try next door, still so much to do. But the trip is irreversible, and these thoughts yield to a vision of the death chamber itself: a dark place with whispering everywhere, being asked if you want a priest, then everything beginning to loosen up and leak out, the dike breached, the delirium you've spent your life hiding now coming into full view. This is not Homer's way of visiting the realm of the dead, but what it loses in stateliness it gains in comic trauma. With stubborn focus, Joyce tracks dying from the initial shock on to the final moments when the gates of self open (because they can no longer be held shut by discipline or decorum), and everything repressed is expressed.

As the earlier scene in the church made clear, Bloom does not buy into "otherworldly" fables, and one of the novel's most hysterical sequences describes Bloom's thoughts in response to Tom Kernan's solemn remark that the grand phrases of the church—*I am the resurrection and the life*—are intensely moving and touch at the very core of one's heart. Yours maybe, Bloom thinks, but what about the chap who is lying six feet under. How do you touch him? And as for this business of an "inmost" heart, why not see it for what it is: a pump. A pump that moves gallons and gallons of blood on a daily basis when the going is good, but a pump that must eventually get "bunged up." Cemeteries, Bloom opines, are a treasure trove of dysfunctional organs that have played out; not much room here to imagine resurrection. The dead, Bloom figures, stay dead. This line of reasoning leads inevitably to the biggest conceit of all: the specter of the last day. For Bloom perceives it as a kind of crazy vaudeville scheme, with bodies being torn out of their graves and hustled back to life, each one of them busily trying to find all those decayed organs and spare parts, so as to be presentable for the big occasion. A rousing event it must be, bringing the dead to life. Wake up, wake up! Lazarus now enters the text: "Come forth, Lazarus! And he came fifth and lost the job" (87).

Joyce is not anticlerical. But he thinks the church's formulas blind us to what is actually going on. It is as if the otherworldly slogans constituted the really cheap shots, because they come at the expense of our membership in this marvelous carnal scheme. After all, a pump that moves thousands of gallons through your body every day is worthy of our consideration. The job of life is living (rather than musing about Heaven); even Lazarus knows that. Of course, Joyce again rewards reading aloud, since if you don't, you might just miss the delicious "come forth . . . and he came fifth and lost the job." And I am impressed by the organs as well. Bloom famously enters this novel as someone who loves to eat inner organs, and his sights remain constant, right on into death. That is what a cemetery is: a storehouse of organs, but independent now, freed of individual ownership, having their day in the sun.

The chapter closes with a final reference to ghosts: visiting spirits, Hamlet's ghost, a place called hell that comes after death. It is here that Bloom rises to the challenge and asserts the rights of the living, for he champions warm-blooded carnal life: people to look at, listen to, touch; bodies close by, sharing your bed (so different from the worm-eaten beds of the dead), giving heat and substance to living. Yes, Bloom concludes, our job (as well as our pleasure) is to be on the side of the living. An ethos is being sketched here, one that is consistent with Bloom's reverence for flesh, for adventures on this side of the grave. All those representatives of duty and guilt and undying blood, are, I think, summoned here, in order to be vanquished. But we have already seen enough of Joyce, especially his handling of memory, to be on our guard: Can you live entirely in the here and now? No matter: One wants to cheer this man leaving a cemetery, intent on the work and play of living.

He wants what he says: live, warm beings near him. But he is in a book plotted by James Joyce, and that afternoon his own bed is going to be occupied by Blazes Boylan. And the one sexual release he will experience will be masturbatory, on a beach, ogling a girl leaning back, showing her wares. Full-blooded life? Maybe, but nothing simple or straightforward about it.

JOYCEAN PYROTECHNICS

We know, from the *Odyssey*, that Homer seemed to delight in putting obstacles in the way of his hero. I also happen to think that Odysseus delighted in tackling them. Joyce has similar plans, and a good bit of the fun of *Ulysses* consists in negotiating this text that seems increasingly to want to jump out of its skin. One shouldn't, I think, press this material too hard (for information about Bloom or Stephen or Molly), but rather go with the flow. For example we have chapter 7, "Aolus," written in newspaper format, devoted to the similarity between words and wind, causing us to realize that bloated rhetoric is called "hot air" for a reason, and that it can smell. Joyce covers the gamut from grandiloquent political speeches to the various merits of Greek versus Latin versus English (when speechifying) to straight-out puns, and finally moving all the way down to the smallest imaginable unit of speech, namely "sllt," which is the noise machines and doors make. Even though we may wonder where the plot went, we can see here Joyce's abiding belief in language as the cardiac principle of his book, as if writing a novel were first and foremost a way of making words sing and dance, of using the "sllt" principle to bring all manner of things to speech.

Or consider chapter 10, "Wandering Rocks," which gives us a spatial rendition of Dubliners going through their paces, more than a dozen of them, most of them unknown to the reader. Where, you may wonder, are our heroes? The answer is: This is city narrative. This is the teeming reality of an urban landscape that dwarfs individual purpose, plot, or itinerary. Joyce is filling out his novel, and to hell with that old-fashioned distinction between major and minor characters. In this ecosystem, all are equal. And they are written equal: as so many pawns on the board, coexisting with other objects, such as posters or reflections in mirrors. Occasionally this parity suggests lines on a graph rather than humans on the move, and readers should take note: This author likes bird's-eye views, likes to map trajectories and lines of motion.

These vector-like renditions of people as ants in an anthill would seem to preclude any narrative possibility of inwardness, but, no, Joyce is as genial as ever, swooping into or hovering over his people with sovereign sport, giving us snippets of thought and fantasy and daydream, larding his map with vibrant bytes of conversation—Dubliners seem unable to speak limp or clichéd English; their every utterance has zip—composing a veritable *tableau vivant.* What is gained here? A view of our comings and goings as it might appear to someone in an airplane, or a Martian, or God. Or to any Odyssean reader who lives in a city. Surely you have occasionally sensed this eerie leveling sensation when walking down a crowded thoroughfare, suddenly aware that all these countless, nameless, faceless others have their own designs, their own secret data, their own appointments and rendezvous. The ecological Joyce is showing his hand.

BIRTHING BABIES, BIRTHING ENGLISH

No chapter of *Ulysses* has more notoriety than the fourteenth, "Oxen of the Sun," which purportedly deals with the sin of murdering human seed (contraception, masturbation, other more figurative curbs on fertility and procreation), but which *performatively* offers a pastiche of English prose from the Latinate and Anglo-Saxon origins on through recognizable moments of high style—saluting Mallory, Sterne, Gibbon, Lamb, De Quincey, Carlyle, Dickens, Newman, Pater, Ruskin, and others en route—to finish with contemporary slang, dialect, and gathering linguistic confusion. The putative metaphoric bridge that connects the evolution of literary styles and the ongoing labor/birth of a child is, I think, a bridge that many will refuse to cross. I feel that Joyce is at his most impudent and Olympian in this chapter, showing us just how wide and deep and spellbinding his bag of tricks is, and—with tongue deeply lodged in cheek—asking us to take this spectacle as thematically important, as advancing his story of Bloom, Stephen, and Molly. If you read Joycean criticism, you will find countless brilliant disquisitions on this chapter, all invested in demonstrating Joycean wit and learning and verbal prowess. Few of them ask the (vulgar) question: Is there a payoff here? Do we have any interest in Mina Purefoy's delivery in the first place? What is this writing *doing*?

These are not simple matters. Is the writer's style subordinate to something larger or not? (Remember "sllt.") Has Joyce so utterly ruptured the older narrative forms of plot and character and language that *we* are at fault, with our old-fashioned questions? Is this what it means to learn to be Joyce's contemporary? Put less abrasively, how *elastic* is style? How far can it go? And if we decide (perhaps out of ignorance) that this chapter does go too far, is over the top, what are we saying? My answer is: We are saying that the old covenant between author and reader has been broken, flouted; that covenant consists of telling a story, and that even if Odyssean readers are willing (under some circumstances) to stretch mightily, they want (after stretching) to have something for their efforts. What do they get?

Joyce the stylistic poacher can achieve memorable effects: We read of the bliss the babe had before it was born, we read of the worship it won within the womb. I cannot espy Bloom or Stephen here, but I love the alliterative medieval prose, the paean to the unborn fetus. And the writing sparkles in new ways, displaying Joyce's brilliance in putting new wine in old bottles. Here is an account of midwives (and the circle of life) worthy of Shakespeare, telling us of the "aged sisters" who bring us into the world for our brief term during which we "wail, batten, sport, clip, clasp, sunder, dwindle, die," after which they come to us yet again. Likewise, the medieval discourse reconceives—that is the word, yes?—Bloom's own sexual dilemma by pointing out that he has a fallow field close to home that wants plowing. A strange eloquence comes into play here. It is, if you wish, costumed language, language borrowed from earlier periods, but it can be remarkably expressive for just those reasons, not unlike the surprising revelations of character that can result from wearing a costume or mask to a party (and realizing that you've "freed" a part of yourself that was otherwise invisible).

But at other moments, Joyce seems to slip into his charade some of the most vital elements of the Bloom marriage, as if to defy us to discern them there. (I say this, having taught the book a dozen times or more, and knowing that students do not pick up the reference, do not perceive the jewel.) In this set piece, the style of Mallory will be enlisted to convey perhaps the book's single most poignant account of the Bloom family tragedy surrounding the death of Rudy and its subsequent impact on both Bloom and Molly. Bloom, now cast as Sir Leopold, is said to have a grave demeanor in the scream-filled house of the women waiting for delivery, for he is reminded of his own personal tragedy: the birth of a boy baby that lived but eleven days, despite all medical art. With this memory comes another: the touching gesture of the afflicted mother (referred to, of course, as Lady Marion), who placed the dead child on a precious bit of lambs wool so that he would not go unprotected into death. The sequence then informs us that Sir Leopold, bereft of a male child, naturally turned his sights toward a nearby ersatz, Stephen Dedalus, young man of great promise, with a mixture of feelings ranging from pain (that he himself had no heir) to dismay that Stephen is carousing with his dissolute companions and doubtless (in keeping with the chapter's motif) wasting his seed with prostitutes. Here then is the elemental emotional history and substance of the Bloom marriage, indeed of the very fate and behavior of both Bloom and Molly, but you won't easily recognize it as such, given the antiquated medieval trappings that Joyce enlists for the telling.

Hence, I read these heartbreaking passages—finally telling us directly about Rudy's demise, Molly's tenderness toward this infant corpse, Bloom's bitterness about his loss and his (crucial for this novel) investment in Stephen as figurative son—and am filled with both wonder and anger. Wonder that Joyce has used the "sllt" principle so brilliantly, casting his story of family grief into the language of medieval romance, where it comes to us with a pathos all the more affecting by dint of the knightly trappings and antiquated discourse. But anger because most of *Ulysses*'s readers will pass right by it as they move, dazed, through this virtuoso chapter, and anger especially because Joyce seems to have been quite willing to have it so. Is he being coy? Tough and unsentimental? Dispatching feeling only under the guise of stylistic masquerade? Something in me wants this passage to be in bold print, put in the center of a chapter where no reader could possibly miss it. That Joyce has not done so tells us how iconoclastic *Ulysses* is, how broad its swath is, how wide-angled our own entry into it should be.

Joyce could not resist the fun and games of "Oxen of the Sun," because it gave him a chance to rival with and outdo the entire English canon. To what end? I have asked. *Because he can do it* is the obvious answer. A more fetching, more tentative answer is this: Joyce is cannibalizing the English corpus in order to do what cannibals have always done—to ingest the power, the *virtu* of their dead rivals. And this power floods his novel, moves into all its interstices, even bathes his characters, reflects and refracts the harsh story of Leopold and Molly and Stephen. Chaucer, Mallory, Sterne, Dickens, and crew are hauled in for that work, because insemination is the cultural game that every writer plays, and Joyce is the fellow who steals the work of others and puts it to his own procreative uses. Hence, it is appropriate that Carlyle's stentorian voice should be borrowed to celebrate the potent achievement of the father of the newborn, one Theodore Purefoy (a.k.a., according to me, James Joyce): Insemination is the name of the game, and Purefoy has performed admirably, emerging as the supreme progenitor of all in this "most farraginous chronicle" (345). Siring a child and siring a book may involve more people than you might think. If metempsychosis announces that our souls visit and interpenetrate, "Oxen of the Sun" tells us something similar (yet surprising) about human utterance: namely, that we do not simply have our *own* voice, but that language itself is layered, echoing, an accretion of recorded styles and effects achieved over the centuries. As these pastiches show, words and styles form a rich and collective historical storehouse; and we ourselves—in cursing, in storytelling, even in speaking our heart—poach from it every time we open our mouths or put pen to paper.

STEPHEN'S HIGH-WIRE ACT

I return now to the Stephen-Bloom plot, and hence to chapter 9, "Scylla and Charybdis," which takes place in a library and is the most bookish chapter in *Ulysses*. But there is nothing stale or antiquarian about it. Joyce takes the prancing Stephen of "Proteus" and puts him, at long last, on center stage with his humongous Hamlet theory, surrounded by literati and intellectuals, and lets him perform. One has the sense of a trained athlete going through his paces, trotting out his stuff, giving his measure. We see the warm-up: Stephen trots out a number of the bons mots and razor-sharp aphorisms he has been culling through the book: keen definitions, prancing principles of logic and argument, bytes of hoary philosophical proclamation. In this intellectual prep work, where we find remnants of earlier thoughts that Stephen has crafted, taking them from Aristotle and (countless) others and making them his own, I think of latter-day barbers honing their blade against a leather strap, putting the edge on their blade, preparing not so much to cut as to thrust and parry.

On to Shakespeare. Asked to deliver, Stephen begins with local color, describing the playhouse, the Elizabethan audience, to bring his listeners in. The basic elements of Stephen's argument, as far as I can tell, are as follows. Hamlet is to be understood as Shakespeare's figurative son, replacing the dead male child Hamnet, inaugurating the notion of artistic creation as a form of engendering. Moreover, Stephen's Shakespeare is a sexually anxious male whose relation to an aggressive, older Ann Hathaway, his wife, has both checked and spurred his drive. Stephen goes into ever higher gear, claiming that the imagination of sexual vulnerability and injury found in *Hamlet*, *Othello*, "The Rape of Lucrece," *Cymbeline*, et al. must needs derive from the author's own emotional past. And cites chapter and verse to prove it.

I will not attempt to take the full measure of this dithyramb on Shakespeare, but do want to emphasize how luxurious, thoroughgoing, and provocative it is, as opposed to the thin schematic account I have just given. Stephen enters into the very marrow of the plays, reinserts them into his ongoing narrative, juggles their metaphors and images for his own purposes, poaches and performs. It is dazzling in its mix of Shakespeare on a couch, the known bits of biography, the vexed and fertile plot turns in the plays, the inimitable language of the Bard (now harnessed and recast by Stephen), the teasing correspondences among life, art, and history. You have to be more than an Odyssean reader to fully appreciate this extravaganza; you need to know your Shakespeare inside out. The veiled references, the inside jokes, the inebriated tone, the sweeping angle of vision, all conspire to give us a feast of learning, inquiry, theorizing, and provocation that we are hard put to evaluate. As indeed all feasts are hard to evaluate. Does the common reader go hungry here? Feel inadequate to the text? Maybe so; but I'd wager that you'll never quite see Shakespeare the same way afterward. And you'd probably think twice before engaging Stephen Dedalus in a debate.

But as intensely focused as the Shakespeare discussion is, its most remarkable insights seem to point outward, gesturing toward a fascinating model of human development and artistic creation. The wounded Shakespeare, according to Stephen, is maniacally self-inventing, spewing visions that he cannot possess, propelled into a future he cannot harness or foresee, *becoming himself* through his art. This same exploratory logic, whereby we move ever unseeingly toward our own shape and identity, is expressed yet again some pages later, where Stephen articulates the stunning *concordance* achieved by the Bard, a shimmering synchronization of inner and outer worlds, yielding a view of daily experience that is anything but haphazard and contingent. On the contrary, life *actualizes* us, makes good on our internal repertory. Stephen cites Maeterlinck on this head, claiming that the Socrates who exits his house in the morning will find the wise man waiting for him on the doorstep upon his return home; Judas is also given in example as the man whose every move, every step, is en route to Judas. So, too, with all our lives: Through every chance encounter we are on a trajectory of self-enactment.

Once again we are surprisingly close to Proust's vision of kaleidoscope and alterity, even though Joyce does not privilege memory as a means of recuperation. It is hard to escape the view that Joyce is describing his own unbounded characters here, and that Stephen and Bloom and Molly are not to be thought of as set and established, but rather as *becoming*. Here is one reason *Ulysses* is so diabolically hard to read: Its main people are evolving, on the move.

But it goes further still, I believe. One *achieves* one's identity, Joyce is saying; it is not innate or preplanned or encoded, but rather a kind of sinuous adventure, astonishingly close in nature to what Borges was to term "a forking path," an identity-trajectory that moves through time and space, that is always gathering, that must be open both to experience and to others, since they (experience and others) "complete" us, "realize" us, make us who we are to be. It is a remarkable notion, inasmuch as it endows life with both mystery and purpose, telling us that the meanest details, the oddest encounters (robbers, ghosts, giants, old men, young men, etc.), are the stations of our own pilgrimage, are forms of self-enactment. I think it also schools us in perception and open-mindedness, for what we may cavalierly dismiss as extraneous or random or haphazard in our lives—chance meetings, accidents—warrants a more thoughtful assessment, because these could be the central threads of our evolving identity, the chief landmarks of who we are en route to becoming, the gathering lineaments of self.

Probably the most famous single pronouncement in "Scylla and Charybdis" concerns the root issue behind the Shakespeare thesis: fatherhood. Stephen pronounces the bold theorem at hand: Fatherhood is unknowable along conscious lines, and must be seen as a condition that is a mystical link from sire to sired. The church understood this paradox perfectly, for it developed a brilliant double strategy: to brandish and flaunt the figure of the Madonna as a carnal certainty for the crowd, while actually founding its true raison d'être on the void, upon the unknowable and unprovable, the perfect mystery. What is paternity then? Nothing but a fiction sanctioned by law. Why then—and here we sense the emotional core of this hifalutin argument—should fathers love sons, or sons love fathers? Why indeed?

Inevitably brought up and saluted in Joycean commentary, this bravura sequence is not easy going. Shakespeare's relation to Hamlet fuses with Bloom's figurative arrangements with Stephen, but we are meant to ponder the paradox in play here. *Amor matris* is the only knowable reality in life—the mother's knowledge/ love of the child, the child's knowledge/ love of the mother—but that rock-bottom truth that flaunts the fictiveness of everything else is seen as an opening to art and imagination. A massive deception is implied, whereby the figure of the Virgin Mother was shrewdly annexed by the church because this was a relationship that was primal, provable, undeniable. But the dynamic that engages Joyce is the other one: the father/son dyad, the empty equation that must be ever forged and filled. In that challenge Joyce saw life, freedom, and art. And the abyss as well, since all must be made if nothing is given.

One sometimes wonders whether the rock-bottom truths of motherhood deeply interest James Joyce, or even if the father-son arrangements engage him all that profoundly either, except at the theoretical level, or indeed as trap. Yes, May Dedalus haunts her son, but we never get the feeling that he knew her or cared to know her. He fared only little better with his father. There is a strange pathos in this dazzling chapter, and it stems from the sharp contrast between Stephen's intellectual endowments and his emotional deficits. To be sure, the Shakespeare performance is inspired and delivered with chutzpah, but given the wide-angled nature of Joycean narrative, we see more than the high-flying literary performance. We also espy, once again, thanks to the interior monologue, the hurting young man who is more than his thesis. Just before the brilliant fatherhood manifesto is unloaded, a reference is made to Simon Dedalus, "the widower." We then read of Stephen encountering Simon on the quay: son come home from Paris to be there for his dying mother. It is a sad encounter, with none of the bravado of the grand pronouncements Stephen has just been making; instead, the young male touches the older male's hand, listens to a voice explaining the new medical arrangements, and then looks into the eyes of the man who is his father. Eyes full of goodwill; eyes empty of knowledge.

In despair, recognizing the hopelessness that stamps both paternity and "sonship," Stephen makes his little truce, terming his father simply—tragically —"a necessary evil" (170).

Ulysses is rich and human because of such moments in the narrative. Yes, the great thesis about fatherhood stands on its own—and is cited as such in the commentaries—but the young man who mouths it is terribly aware of the umbilical cords that bind, whether or not knowledge passes through them. The artist who tried to fly over the nets returned to Dublin by boat, to be with his dying mother, meeting his flesh-and-blood father, charting what is present and what is absent: love but not knowing. These lines are searing in their honesty about the limits of understanding, the pathos of felt orphanhood as the generic condition of sons despite the best of intentions. From this, Stephen launches into his grand aria about fathers. We battle against hopelessness; where blood disappoints, imagination may provide. Yet Shakespearean high ground, even with pathos, is not the only ground of this novel.

RETURN TO BLOOM: WONDER WHOSE THOUGHTS YOU'RE CHEWING

Bloom began this book thinking about food, and he remains on message in chapter 8, "Lestrygonians," one of the novel's most pungent, almost gastric performances. Joyce knows what appetite feels like, knows how our somatic needs are a clanking and noisy operation, demanding our attention several times daily, unconcerned with so-called higher things. Bloom enters a restaurant, and we see what a gut-world looks like: bodies perched everywhere, going at it, shoving it in, swilling, ordering more, eyes popping, moustaches dripping. Bloom's roving eye takes it all in: one fellow using a napkin to polish glass and implements (thereby gaining a fresh installment of germs), another with stained napkin busily at work getting the soup down, still another—returning the favor this time—sending stuff back to his plate: gristle half-chewed, doubtless no teeth to chew it with. Taking in this somatic spectacle of feeding creatures, Bloom has a characteristic moment of self-awareness, wondering if he too looks like this, wondering further how any of us actually look to others.

The camera misses nothing of the eating machinery in gear. Nor does the mind skip a beat, as Bloom sizes up the damage while continuing to take in. Am I like that? How often do we try to see ourselves when the carnal takes over? Have you ever watched yourself eat? Could you? Watch yourself? Eat? Pornography battens on to the erotic side, but our fleshly career is held hostage to urgent drives beyond (before?) the sexual. And a good bit of it is distinctly unattractive, unappetizing. How could things such as revery or imagination find a perch here?

Well they do. "Lestrygonians" gives us the fullest account of the Bloom marriage that we are likely to find in this novel. But it gives it to us grudgingly, on the sly, serendipitously. Bloom crosses the street, thinks back (by happenstance) to his early years of marriage, ending up (as usual) with an image of Molly in a tight-fitting dress that fits her as snug as a glove, emphasizing her shoulders and hips. The memory, including even what they ate that day (rabbit pie), closes with the sneaky (crucial) notation: "Happy. Happier then" (128), followed by more details of the rooms they lived in, the soap they used for Milly's bath, the changing look of Milly's body now, the oddness of Milly and the dead father sharing a taste for photography. What is missing here?

Nothing, you could say. Joyce achieves a peculiar fullness by dwelling only on the material particulars: the room, the dress, the soap, the bath, the body. And the next paragraph stays with these domestic intimacies: Molly in the wind with her skirts blown up, coming home and raking up the fire, eating fried mutton with the Chutney sauce, drinking the mulled rum, unclamping her stays that made a swishing soft noise on the bed, a bed filled with warmth. It is a sweet domestic memory: the wife moving through stages of undress (stays off, hairpins out), the daughter tucked away in bed. And it is capped in the most elemental fashion: "Happy. Happy" (128). Not derived from any pastry in a teacup, utterly without fanfare, this scene nonetheless *is* Bloom's marital past, the domestic life he no longer has.

No longer has. That is the unaccented hard law here. And we have only to consider what this material would look like—what explosions of tragic consciousness or wistful lyricism or striking metaphor or plain old pulse-taking and navel-gazing—in the hands of a Proust or a Woolf or a Faulkner, to gauge what Joyce has done. He has almost entirely refused to interpret this memory, other than in the simplest possible shorthand of "happy . . . happier then." No rage, no tears, not even a moment of reflection itself. In keeping with this chapter's focus on food, I'd say this material is still there all right, but it is never digested as such. And I'd go on to say that it has pathos for just those reasons. This little reminiscence, bare but shimmering with felt life, is just another piece in the mosaic, is indeed fighting for its life textually, requiring that *we* underline it, take it out of its mix, savor its homely poetry, do in short the kind of critical appraisal that Leopold Bloom refrains from doing.

More is to come. Still larger, more savory and ingestible segments of that lost domestic past emerge a few pages later. Bloom wonders if he was happier back then, and if so, *who* is the real Bloom: the chap back then, only twenty-eight, with his young wife only twenty-three, or the fellow now reminiscing? At this point comes a crucial line in the book: "Could never like it again after Rudy"; it refers to the changes that took place in their lives. But *who* could never like it again? Most readers assume it is Molly who gives up on sex with her husband after Rudy's death, but it is equally plausible to posit Bloom here as the figure whose desire died. Yet, overall, Bloom's tone is as philosophical as it is plangent, for he knows time cannot be stopped, that you cannot go back to those more innocent days. And would you if you could? These memories then fuse with a refrain lifted from the letter sent by his pen pal, Martha Clifford, asking if the naughty boy is happy in his little home.

As we see, the question as to whether you'd go back even if you could carries a hint of foolishness as well as impossibility. Not only is time irretrievable, but people who seek to recover it are denying the presentness of their lives. And yet, as Bloom mused about Molly in the coach going to the cemetery, *the shape is still there*. The shape of our past not only remains but also scripts much of our present, so that Bloom's epistolary flirtation with Martha (is the naughty boy unhappy in his home?) has to be seen as ersatz, as substitution for the sexual union of the past. Is that what we are destined for: Passion's time goes, and substitutions are all that is left? And if this is true, is it bitterness or is it wisdom?

The richest moment in this chapter, its pièce de résistance, comes a few pages later still and caps the memories of lost passion by giving us, at last, the thing itself: the recalled sexual splendor. There is nothing else like it in the novel. In quasi-Proustian fashion, triggered by the lingering taste of wine on his palate, the senses lead Bloom into his past. He remembers lying, hidden, with Molly on Howth Head, ferns under them and soundless sky above. It is a moment of scope as well as passion: The world rolls out beneath them—in the sea, in the grass, harboring entire cities. There, her hair spread out on his cape, his hand under her neck, they performed the timeless dance that time has now taken away. Her body is evoked in all its immediacy and power: her hand touched him, her eyes gazed upon him, her mouth—lips open, with warm seedcake half-chewed—were his to kiss and to feed from. This gift of body to body, of seedcake from one mouth to another, is remembered with a lyrical splendor that is unforgettable: by Bloom, by everyone of Joyce's readers. Bloom remembers ingesting the very pulp of life: her pouting lips, lips Joyce calls "soft warm sticky gumjelly," her beckoning eyes, her willing body that he lay wildly upon, her nun's blouse, her full breasts with "fat nipples upright." He tongued her, she kissed him. And how is this parsed? How is it seen now, in retrospect? Joyce tells us, with utmost brevity: "Me. And me now" (144).

This passage, bookended by notations of flies stuck together on a windowpane, moves magnificently beyond its "restaurant" base and offers us the novel's most pagan, awestruck moment of passion. The pungent setting with its cosmic reaches frames a scene of coupling suffused with magic and wonder, suggesting a carnal Eden that can never be repossessed. The passing of the warm and chewed seedcake from mouth to mouth, the overpoweringly delicious woman's body—sticky gumjelly lips, willing eyes, stretched neck, fat nipples upright—are as splendid and rich as anything I have ever read. *And this is what is lost.* Perhaps the severest notation here is Bloom's intuition that such splendor is of necessity located in the past, retrievable only as memory, a buried kingdom of sorts that no one returns to. Please note that my sensationalist language differs entirely from Joyce's. No trumpet blaring whatsoever here, just one dense hedonistic paragraph, bearing the tiniest whiff of tragic regret, "Me. And me now." And that's all you get. It may indeed be paradise lost, but it will cohabit with all the other random notations in the bar-restaurant, as if paradise were merely one item on the menu for James Joyce.

Worse still, some three pages later, Bloom-the-roving-camera perceives a dog on the street whose behavior seems recognizable: It chokes and vomits up a disgusting blob onto the cobblestones, and forthwith laps same blob back up with renewed appetite, like a present received, emptied, digested, and returned. "First sweet then savoury" (147), Bloom concludes. Joycean music once again, and shocking to boot. At first we register only Bloomish wit—the dog spits up something already digested, reingests it, and this comes to us in lovely restaurantese: "first sweet then savoury." And then it dawns on us that we are witnessing a canine retelling of the beautiful seed-cake episode, but pirouetted anew, prismatic, yielding its other colors. I'd want to say that "first sweet then savoury" is the recipe for *Ulysses,* inasmuch as it trains its readers to see its materials as a kind of culinary carnival, a *menu dégustation,* in which the sentimental dish returns, sea-changed, accented and flavored differently, just as "gogsbody" and "dodsbody" require the mere altering of a "g" or a "d" to become each other. There is a plasticity in this novel, a protean shape-shifting energy that wreaks havoc with all fixed categories, including one's love life.

THE SOUND OF LOVE

If "Lestrygonians" is the place where appetite rules, chapter 11, "Sirens," is Joyce's effort to cast his story as *sound.* It should be reasonably obvious by now that each chapter of *Ulysses* is increasingly, dazzlingly on its own, cavorting and displaying whatever strange pyrotechnics Joyce has assigned to it. The unity of style that we are accustomed to in novels is gone for good. What is more surprising is the pathos and heightened meanings that can be gotten out of sound experiments. We know that Joyce loved music, especially opera, and all readers have noted the prominence of songs in *Ulysses,* ranging from the singing practice that is the cover for Boylan's 4 P.M. assignation with Molly on to large chunks of actual librettos and folk songs and ditties of all sorts that make their way into, even take over, the text. And this is rarely innocent: Often enough the words of the lyrics are playing the central story of Bloom, Molly, and Stephen, but in a different key. It is easy to misread "Sirens" as pure virtuosity—this is the great risk the entire novel courts, chapter after chapter—whereas the interesting question is: What happens when sound trumps all other features?

The most immediate effect is a drastic loosening of language. Bloom sitting at the table in the Ormond bar, his fingers toying with an elastic in his pocket as he listens to the throbbing music, is presented as an affair of looping, unlooping, noding, disnoding. Then come the liquids, seemingly called by the music, as fluid language of desire: "warm jamjam lickitup secretness" (226). How would you write tumescence? How would you eavesdrop on a man's thoughts when those thoughts turn on sex, sex between your wife and her lover? "Tipping her tepping her tapping her topping her" (226) is a good start, soon followed by warm sluices and pouring gushes, not to mention a good bit of dilating, to prime you for the finale: "Flood, gush, flow, joygush, tupthrob" (226). Let me say, right off, that such a word feast simply gives (me) pleasure, whatever it may be doing for the plot. We go through our lives being functional creatures, enlisting utilitarian words to say what is necessary to say: hamburger versus cheeseburger, red versus black, you turn right at the next stoplight, the asking price is $200,000. Okay, life requires this, but there's not much fun in it. However, this verbal equipment of ours, this musical instrument that has been gifted to us, has so many other possibilities—much as this laptop I'm composing on, which I use exclusively and reductively as mere typewriter, actually possesses exotic and far-reaching powers that go begging. Joyce brings a verbal carnival into our lives, he shows us that words are explosives, that they can turn abstract concepts into juicy and zaftig utterance. Return to Bloom at the table: the language of love. What is the language of love? Surely, this throbbing, pulsing flow with its mix of tumescence and release, with its rhythms of fornication, conveys something that normal words do not attain: desire, Molly being taken, bodies enthralled, juices flowing, Bloom at once aroused and injured by words and music he hears, by the scene he imagines. It is as if one's entire libidinal circuit were put to music, transformed into a dance of sexuality that enlists body and mind and language, instrumentalizes them all.

Bloom turns with the music. Sometimes the sounds are insistently assertive and phallic, as Bloom, enlisting the help of the well-named pornographer Paul de Kock, imagines Blazes Boylan's entry onto the scene, in terms of rapping, tapping, knocking, knocking with a special knocker, one that is both loud and proud, a "cock carracarracarra cock. Cockcock" (232). Sound dominates everything, but the personal issues do not thereby disappear. Nowhere is the strange new logic of this chapter better on show than in Bloom's reflection that his wife's body is fundamentally a musical instrument, hence attuned to acoustics and the peculiar tinkling sounds produced in a chamber pot. Chamber pot leads to chamber music; Bloom thinks of vessels making noise, of changes of resonance, of the relation between the weight of the water and the falling of the water.

Joyce's signature is on show here, as is Bloom's wisdom. Where traditional fiction would trumpet and fixate on the jealousy note ("cock carracarracarra cock": Boylan's ready endowments), *Ulysses* moves into whimsy and speculation, accords its suffering protagonist time for doodling, has him remember bits of high school physics about acoustics, lets him wonder about the noises emerging when Molly uses the bedpan, includes Liszt's rhapsodies in the purview, delivers the very sound of the peeing/raining body: "Diddleiddle addleaddle ooddlecoodle. Hissss" (232).

But note, please, how it all closes: "Now. Maybe now. Before." It is as if Bloom were able to get clear of his troubles only for a few seconds, were able to free his mind from the impending betrayal only momentarily. But, like a boomerang, the nasty business at hand returns. Very curious, this. What may initially appear to be esoterica and pyrotechnics now shows its richer significance: the very behavior of a mind that is dodging bad news, that seeks to avoid hurt, that "knows" bad things are happening at 4 P.M. but then looks for exits from this knowing. It is in this sense that *Ulysses* is startlingly plot-driven, but the plot is located at the level of neurons and synapses, the little antics that seek to preserve our engine, to keep us out of trouble. Here is an apparatus of self-defense that rarely makes it onto the page, that has no place in the grand realist novels. Yet it delivers the very noise of dodging bullets (dodging bullets is the full-time job that our psyche carries out, in the dark, as if "let's not go there" were the cardinal injunction for staying sane) as we go through our paces. I know of no other writer who has choreographed the strategic gambits of the mind quite like Joyce has.

The masterpiece of artful dodging along these lines is found in the maniacal description of Pat the waiter. Bloom sees him settling napkins, feels trouble approaching (4 P.M. is nigh, Molly and Boylan . . .), wishes they'd do more singing, tries to keep his mind "off," then focuses on Pat. Pat, we learn, is bald and hard of hearing; further, we are edified to learn that he is a waiter, and as such, is a person who will wait as you wait. This is he: a waiter. One who will wait as you wait. As Bloom rehearses these repeating bytes of waiting-information, yielding a songsong, we note that the sequence is cut with one other sound: "hee." Repeated, this sound becomes: "hee hee." And repeated fourfold, it does still more.

Here would be how one keeps one's mind off. The words repeat, roll over, and do somersaults, giving a kind of stuck-record effect that slows down psychological activity. There is a certain Odyssean cunning at work, a kind of verbal boycott, an effort to create a linguistic filibuster, to put up a ludic roadblock. We cannot fail to see, however, that Joyce has once again networked Bloom, displayed Bloom's entrapment in the very midst of his sortie. Because waiting is of the very essence here, not the waiting of Pat but that of Bloom, waiting for Boylan to reach Molly. Hence, to play out waiting in every hue and color, to make it pirouette into singsong, does not so much evade Bloom's predicament as *flaunt* it, spell it out, as it were.

To repeat a word or phrase over and over leads, as everyone knows, to a predictable paradox: The word loses its meaning and becomes an empty shell; but, no less true, the incessant sounding of the word displays its hold on the mind, wildly energizes its signifying power, signals obsession. Finally, we can hardly miss the most obvious ploy of the passage, the sound game it plays: the transformation of "he" into "hee" and then into "hee hee hee hee" delivers unmistakably the sound of laughter. Whose? The text's? Joyce's? Ours? Bloom, as we have noted, has much in his life he cannot afford to think about; in this he resembles all of us. Joyce has succeeded in graphing this little man's brave efforts to slither through, but has, at the same time, shown that such evasion is impossible, that the repressed, as Freud suggested, will return. You can't get clear. There is a virtually sadistic rigor in this huge novel, and it does not let its people off the hook, no matter how much they try (and try they do).

THE "SLLT" PRINCIPLE AT WORK

Yet, given the sound imperative of the chapter, its commitment to the "sllt" principle, Bloom's home truths emerge finally, arguably, as symphonic rather than emotional. Much food for thought here: Could the heaviest issues of our lives—love, sex, pain, death—be ultimately just an arrangement of words and sounds? Bloom hears Ben Dollard singing the popular sentimental song "The Croppy Boy," and reflects on its sad tidings: the death of a family, the end of a name and a race.

He then takes this knowledge "home" in one of the novel's clearest family pictures, as he compares his own fate to that of the Croppy boy: each victimized, each last of the race. Yes, there is Milly the daughter, but no son. And it is too late to alter this. Or, Bloom wonders, is it? Might there still be time? These portentous family matters eventuate into a peculiar Stoic wisdom, but refracted through the technique of "Sirens": Bloom bears no hate. Why? Listen to the sounds. Why? Because "Hate. Love. Those are names. Rudy. Soon I am old" (234). Bloom's life history is given here: dead father, dead son. It is all over, too late; or is it? Could they start again? Produce a child? Here is the material of a gripping story, the key moral and emotional elements of a life. We expect now to see these bristling issues get further unpacked.

But note what happens: The balanced Bloom bears no hate. No hate toward—Molly? Life? At first we see this as Bloom's Odyssean wisdom, his acceptance of fate. But something cuts still deeper. Instead we have the extraordinary notation: "hate" and "love" are *names*. Words, not things. At this point we see just how far the sound principle might go. It empties the world of significance by positing all as just words, letters, shells, sounds, forms. From hate and love, Bloom goes the full route: "Rudy. Soon I am old." The aching truths of his life? The bitter conclusion to be drawn by a man whose marriage is sexless, who has no son? Or just words? I have earlier claimed that *Ulysses* is among the most philosophical books ever written, and it is passages and issues like this that substantiate my claim. "Those are names" is the secret, horrible, corrosive knowledge of all writers, for what is literature if not a rendition of life via the medium of words? The gambit of writing consists in making those words potent, so potent that we go beyond the words themselves on to the *things* they denote. Writers want their words to carry you aloft, to open up vistas. But James Joyce is willing to go in reverse gear, to take the great issues of life—sex, love, children, age—and to *derealize* them, to reduce them to a mere consort of letters and words, no more real and compelling than an entry in a dictionary. Bloom is facing the lingual prison that all of us have lived in, ever since Babel.

I ask: Are you prepared to carry out an injunction of this sort? To see the world as names is both to lose and to gain something. The loss is pretty obvious: If our central life issues are just words, well then, they would appear to lose their bite, their heft, their glory as well as horror. Our projects and our very self become just a house of cards. On the other hand, to see love and hate as just words is also a kind of liberation, a way of getting clear of their awful authority and power. In short, there is something strategic in play here, enabling you to lighten your burden, to manage your issues, by regarding them as *nominal*. Final question: Is such a move wisdom or cowardice? And how long can you get away with it? These are the existential issues that *Ulysses* provokes by its very manner. It is as if literature itself were speaking out to you, saying: Our game consists in conning you with words; do you buy it? If so, great; read on, speak on. But if not, if you see that words are just markings on a page, just lingual constructs, well, then, what do you make of your own life, your name, your values, your beliefs? Could they be just words too?

Yet, as critics have noted, the overall feeling of this chapter is one of gaiety, not despair or even meditation. (Joyce would doubtless convict me of considerable hot air in those sentences you just read.) So let's finish our trip through this sound-chapter by watching, one more time, the body speak. You may even be able to smell it. The chapter closes with a final triumph of sound, as Bloom simultaneously hears the (gaseous) words of a patriotic song (given in italics) and experiences the gaseous effects of the wine he has just drunk. The chauvinistic lyrics (my country will take its place among the nations of the earth and then—and only then—will my epitaph be written) are textually cut by another noise, namely that of the gathering, insistent gas coming from Bloom's lower intestine, a sound that the logic of "Sirens" properly spells out: "Prrprr" . . . "Fff" . . . "Pprrpffrrppffff" (238–239). This bubbling seesaw of gaseous speechifying enters into the realms of Bloomish cunning and Joycean comedy by its strategic interplay—one noise hides another, didn't you know?—with the sounds produced by an arriving tram. An arriving tram? Yes! Our wily hero sees it coming to his rescue noisewise—he will pass wind, but the tram will be his cover—so that the final utterance of the Croppy Boy's poignant legacy ("I have done," he proudly claims) dovetails with the rival utterance from Bloom's colon: "Pprrpffrrppffff."

This book actually farts. It doesn't just say that someone is farting: It makes the noise itself. And it does so with the kind of wit and brio we are now getting accustomed to. I suspect that every human being alive has at some time farted in public, and has very likely sought out the kind of cover ("good oppor") that Bloom finds here, as the coming tram's noise conceals his own. Did I not say that Bloom is surpassingly strategic? But Joyce is still cannier, for he has managed to conflate the flatulence of mawkish patriotism with the intestinal performance of his character, suggesting that smelly hot air is more widespread than we might think.

ONE-EYED VISION

Chapter 12, "Cyclops," manages at once to be the funniest chapter in the novel and also the one where our hero, Bloom, at last shows his mettle. We recall that Homer's Odysseus did battle with the one-eyed giant, Polyphemus the Cyclops, and got the better of him by tricks and cunning. Joyce has decided that giantism could be a way of writing, and that moreover it could be an on-target style for displaying and harpooning the inflated, puffed-up character of Irish nationalism (one of his favorite targets). We end up with music and counterpoint once again, with a presentation that loves to inflate and deflate. *Loves to inflate and deflate.* Yes, "loves" is the right verb, I think, because Joyce has realized that stylistic extravagance—whipped cream followed by vinegar—is *fun,* is also peculiarly expressive, again in the way that costumes or fun houses can be expressive: by twisting and altering familiar things so drastically that, all of a sudden, you see them anew, afresh. Now, none of us is James Joyce, and I am scarcely going to say that this crazy stuff is a secret mirror of you the reader; but, it is not a bad workout for personal use, not a bad perspectival game, for getting a new take on one's own agenda, one's own persona (about which we know so little: Do you know how others see you, what they call you behind your back?).

Let's begin with the carnivalesque. Irish nationalism, like so many nationalisms, taps into big and ugly appetites, blends easily with chauvinism, jingoism, and xenophobia alike, and can be a real hoot as well. James Joyce is a man who relishes excess, and has no qualms about going crazy in his prose, so that the predictable sweeping claims for great venerable heroes of Irish antiquity are backed up by a list of some ninety-three (93) equally venerable proper names, including the following: Christopher Columbus, the Last of the Mohicans, the Man that Broke the Bank at Monte Carlo, Benjamin Franklin, Napoleon Bonaparte, Ludvig Beethoven, Jack the Giantkiller, Gautama Buddha, and still others whose Irishness is only now visible: Patrick W. Shakespeare, Brian Confucius, Murtagh Gutenberg, and so on. Who would have thought they were all Irish?

The narration of familiar figures coming into and out of the bar is conducted in seesaw fashion. The bilious narrator refers to Bloom in his own zippy street lingo, evoking a poor specimen outfitted with "cod's eye" busy sneaking around corners and counting fish guts, but this is followed by the puffed-up, mythicized account that yields a knightly, even Homeric "O'Bloom," dressed in handsome armor, of noble lineage, yet still in character, "he of the prudent soul" (245). Some pages later the narrator learns that Molly's planned singing tour is organized by none other than Blazes Boylan, "the bucko that'll organise her" indeed, all of which produces its inflated counterpart, offering us a "ravenhaired" noble Molly, legendary beauty from the land of loquat and almonds and olive groves, she "of the bountiful bosoms" (262). Half the fun here comes from the contrasting styles, and what we are seeing here is "two-eyed" narrative.

For two-eyed storytelling is fun. Our departed friend Paddy Dignam returns for an appearance here, as folks at the bar dispute whether he's dead or not, but he is now positioned in the great beyond, and offers us his special, now initiated, point of view: As one who no longer sees through a glass darkly, he now has access to all the modern technological creature comforts that go with residence in the spirit realm, including "tālāfānā, ālāvātār, hātākāldā, wātāklāsāt" (248). It may be that my own low character is on show here, but I love this spoof of otherworldly pretensions, beginning with the Pauline murky mirror and concluding with all the *tout confort* to be found in the afterlife (which must be pronounced out loud to be appreciated).

HEROIC BLOOM

The lugubrious emphasis on violence in "Cyclops"—including a vicious and bilious narrator and encompassing themes such as boxing, whipping, tarring and feathering, along with hanging—reaches its conclusion when, in mockery of the Crucifixion, the emblematic Irish nationalist (the Citizen, he is called) sums up, with notable xenophobic vehemence, the way of the (English) world: It is a world given to incessant punishment, as exemplified in the Citizen's account of Jacky Tar whose Calvary consists of being flogged, flayed, and even curried, before finally being resurrected and steered into heaven to await still further commands. This mockery of Christ's resurrection is in keeping with a chapter whose main view of culture is expressed by the word "Syphilization." Joyce's send-up of chauvinistic hatred has, I think, an eerie ring to it in the twenty-first century, where terrorism, ethnic cleansing, and projects at once genocidal and jihadic sprout around the globe like mushrooms. "Cyclops," written quite intentionally under the sign of unrestrained hyperbole and excess, with its strange mix of violence and humor, suggests to me that vehemence in style is never all that far from vehemence in behavior, that anger and hate have common cause with frenzied speech.

This is why Joyce's everyman, his modern Odysseus, is so special, for he possesses a nobler vision of cultures and races living together. Bloom protests to the Citizen's diatribe against English naval custom that discipline is the same everywhere, that Ireland too would be like England if you put force against force. He returns a moment later to the charge, claiming that the history of the world is a history of persecution, of incessant conflict between nations. This leads to some sharp and funny words about nations, about whether Bloom the Jew has a nation, and the tension mounts still higher. Finally Bloom goes still further and defends, with uncommon heat, Judaism itself and most especially the Jews who are a hated race, a race who faces persecution even now, even this moment, all of which leads then to the novel's fullest (if also briefest) articulation of a New Ethos: The long legacy of violence—what Bloom calls "Force, hatred, history"—utterly contradicts life's deepest purposes. Asked what those purposes are, he announces the book's simple but profound wisdom: "Love," which is the "opposite of hatred" (273). And he exits.

Several pages later, the Citizen and his pals at the bar, convinced that Bloom has sneaked out to collect on his winnings at the races (and won't share with them), are ready for real violence, and Bloom, returned, rises still further—incredibly, it may seem to many readers—to the occasion by giving it back full throttle, putting forth his list of illustrious Jews, a list that begins with Mendelssohn, Marx, Mercandante, and Spinoza, and closes with both the Savior and the Savior's father, God himself. This pronouncement is met with such stupor that Bloom elects to reinforce his message, insisting that God and Christ and he, Leopold Bloom, are all Jews (a family resemblance guaranteed to provoke), at which point we are ready for a second crucifixion, gift of the Citizen. The chapter closes, hilariously, with the Citizen hurling a biscuit box at the exiting carriage with Bloom on it, all of which is narrated in both mock-heroic and scientese, yielding a visionary finale of Bloom ascending to Heaven.

No critical discussion of *Ulysses* fails to signal the importance of this episode. We see a truly heroic Bloom here, and only here. And, as mentioned, our current moment is so saturated with intolerance, religious warfare, and tribalism that Joyce's model of peace through love has much indeed to be said for it. "Cyclops," notwithstanding its hilarious send-ups, is also a religious debate of sorts, which closes with Bloom's pronouncement of Truth: *Love*. When folks argue that Joyce's novel is without values, that it has no moral vision, no ethical center, you can be sure that this scene will be hauled out and cited at length. But I myself honor the two-eyed Joyce too much to leave it on this note. "Sweet then savory" is still the rule of the game, and hence it is no surprise that Bloom's famous pronouncement of love as the solution to violence and syphilization is followed by pure satire: Joyce offers us a fulsome paragraph about the New Dispensation of Love, in which nurses love chemists, policemen love commoners, X loves Y, the elephant Jumbo loves the elephant Alice, the deaf old man loves the blind old woman, the King loves the Queen, I love you, you love me, and you-know-who—God—well, he just loves everybody.

Here is love turned into a joke, singsong, a pirouetting cliché, mush. Here is "savory" following "sweet." Democracy rules in this novel, rules despotically (if one can put it that way), inasmuch as statements we are inclined to see in bold print are then parodied and undercut, proving that no single item or pronouncement is upheld with finality, is without threat of being turned upside down. Joyce's integrity seems to lie in a principled unwillingness to let any single affirmation stand. Single affirmations, clear declarations of principle, are, in the nature of things, one-eyed propositions. Joyce cannot be rescued from his contrapuntalism, his two-eyed joy at opening up all utterance, all belief, into an Olympian stylistic game. I leave it to my Odyssean reader to decide whether such a perspective alleviates or complicates living.

ROMANCE: HARLEQUIN-STYLE

Even though "Cyclops" closed with Bloom speaking out and then figuratively ascending the Heavens, one can scarcely ignore the fact that our hero's "authority" is increasingly in trouble. It is as if the book occasionally enjoyed ganging up on him (sometimes getting him through style itself) or at other times weren't listening to him, or as if it (the book) were seeing and hearing more interesting fare elsewhere (as, for example, in the outbreaks of the Citizen). One of the cardinal rules of traditional fiction used to be that you stay with your man (that the author stay with your man), and this is one reason fiction soothes us: It whispers, page after page, its little assurances about the centrality of self, about our own place on stage. Hero may die or be killed at end, but hardly before that. It wouldn't be fair (to readers).

But, has it ever occurred to you that you are also existing in other folks' fictions? Perhaps as major player, more likely as minor player, and quite conceivably as part of the wallpaper. Our eyes and ears are hardly equipped to convey such tidings to us, but via imagination, just maybe, one could try to see oneself "from the other side." Chapter 13, "Nausicaa," is intriguing along just these lines, because the mind-set it seeks to deliver, for over half the chapter, is not that of Bloom or Stephen, but rather of Gerty MacDowell, the girl who is to fantasize about Bloom, the girl Bloom is to fantasize about. Now who, you should be asking, is Gerty MacDowell? She is *a girl on the beach,* and I put it this way to signal her unmistakable origin as the "bird-girl" from *Portrait,* the female form that Stephen gazed at with lyrical (purple) rapture (and with zero interest in *her* thoughts), leading him to an ecstatic discovery of his vocation as artist devoted to "mortal beauty." All of this now returns in the later book, sea-changed, as Joyce moves from object to subject, so that the young girl's own subjectivity is given voice. (This is the pivotal move that feminist criticism rightly demands—presenting women as subjects rather than objects—but Joyce's Gerty is not likely to be a big hit with feminists.)

We shall in fact see, soon enough, that she is still an object of the male gaze—Bloom's, not Stephen's—but what is extraordinary is the consciousness that Joyce has constructed for her. The bird-girl lyricism of *Portrait* is coarsened, cheapened, poked fun at, turned on its head. Gerty sees the world exclusively through the lenses of romantic desire and sentimental longings, the nature of which strikes us as utterly prepackaged, clichéd to the nth degree. What does "prepackaged" desire sound like? Well, it sounds like a slew of choice formulations such as "prince charming," "manly man," "sheltering arms"—all yearning to enfold dearest Gerty into a passionate embrace on this lovely summer evening, to give her divine bliss—replete, needless to say (for Gerty is serious), with the longing to be *wedded* for eternity: poor or rich, sick or well, to be separated only by death, so long as we live.

The language of love has ever been suspect. Both dangerous and prefabricated. As far back as Dante, we see that Paolo and Francesca are ignited by the love poetry they read together. A rather bleaker modern version of these matters is a book Joyce knew as well as he knew his Dante: Flaubert's *Madame Bovary,* saga of romance turned cliché, but no less lethal for that. Emma Bovary's yearnings for emotional-sexual-spiritual gratification have been derived from the romances she read in the convent—just as Don Quijote's longings for a heroic world derived from the courtly romances he ingested—and she is set on a collision course with reality, just as the Don was. One could argue—it has been argued—that the novel's rationale and cultural mission throughout history has been to display the misfit between the paradigms we inherit or subscribe to and the rough world out there that refuses to match our desire. What Joyce saw here is something else as well: There is no such thing as "natural" vision, vision without blinders, since the very fact of being in-culture means that we are equipped with lenses not of our own making, lenses and expectations and appetites formed by institutions such as literature, but also family, church, and state. And marketplace.

Now, you might think such a philosophy to be inhibiting—freedom and maneuvering room, especially in our thoughts, are thrown out—but Joyce doubtless finds it emancipating, since it undergirds precisely his interest in style and voice. Put most brutally, the ideological bottom line here is: *We are constructed.* I do not hesitate to claim that this view is among the central (and darling) tenets of modern thought, and that students of literature and culture are told about it (from clairvoyant, unillusioned professors and critics) from day one. Most young folks react against it in disbelief. At least initially. In part, their reaction stems from an article of faith (for the past two hundred years at least), namely, that each of us is unique, has his or her own originality and soul. For most of us, the idea of being "constructed" sounds like a Frankenstein scenario. I hardly need to say that these are big issues. James Joyce is not a cultural theorist nor a philosopher as such, but his view of human beings is so fluid and porous, composed of so much traffic between setting and self, that *Ulysses* often delights in casting its light on what's inside of us and illuminating where it came from (as if the label were still on it, even though we never knew we were buying anything in the first place). All this may sound abstruse, but give Gerty your attention and you'll quickly see how this works.

Gerty, we saw, has yearned for her gray-flecked manly man to appear, and the gallant James Joyce is delighted to furnish her such a specimen, consisting of the dark stranger on the beach looking her way, our friend Leopold Bloom. Ah, the effusions that follow: The "girlwoman" is smitten with desire for her "dreamhusband," a man who seems to her sharp eyes "more sinned against than sinning." Her love is so powerful that it would overcome all obstacles: were he a sinner, were he wicked, were he even a Protestant or a Methodist, no matter. And this precious balm would not fail of its effect on him either: It would cause him to forget the pains of the past, it would draw him to her, embracing her sweet body gently but passionately, loving her deeply as "his ownest girlie" (293–294).

As always, Joyce gets mileage out of his vehicle. The reference to Protestant or Methodist is a marker traced at the perimeter of how far Gerty-desire can go; Shakespeare's line "more sinned against than sinning," also refracted religiously, doesn't quite turn Bloom into Lear, but leads perfectly to the need to forget the pain of the past, and we must ponder the appropriateness of these clichés, since they actually get Bloom right, not wrong. (He does need to forget the memory of the past.) A bit later, she thinks his face "the saddest she has ever seen," and once again gives us pause. (Maybe she sees his sadness in a way he himself can't.) But "girlwoman," "womanly woman," "his ownest girlie" are the signature moves of this chapter, a kind of ground zero, as it were, of romantic mush and (parodic) gender stereotype, but mouthed by a woman (rather than a man), displaying how deep inside such sappy language can go, as if to say: Clichés are lodged at our core, not at our edges; they hold our emotional life in hostage; they *are* our emotional life.

I mentioned Flaubert's Emma Bovary, and Gerty resembles her in having gotten her notions of beauty, charm, and outright femaleness out of books and advertisements, out of slogans and mottoes designed to sell products, to make money. We learn that she is taking iron jelloids that have done her a world of good, easing the discharges she got in the past, and we are not to forget her eyes either, for they too have benefited from enhancements, such as the "eyebrowleine" championed by no less than "Madame Vera Verity" as the means of acquiring the kind of haunting expression found among the very top people in fashion. And that's not all: Miracle products galore are available, to remedy all of nature's little defects, to cure blushing, to make you taller, to fix your nose.

As we move from eyebrows to blushing, height, and nose, we realize how firmly implanted this discourse of self-beautification is. The advertisers are where they want to be: *inside* Gerty. I think Joyce's rendition of Gerty-fantasy is much more instructive than it may look (it looks like goop), because it presents for *our* inspection the spectacle of someone's feelings being manufactured by the society. The corollary is: We cannot see this in ourselves, we are incapable of eavesdropping on ourselves in this fashion, and we find it hard to believe that our most sincere utterances may come direct from books we've read or films we've seen or music we've heard or advertisements we've absorbed. (It can take a whole lifetime, and often some professional help as well, for many of us to get a handle on these matters.)

Gerty displays all this, helps us to a more critical perspective on how we ourselves are shaped and formed (and deformed).

THE MACHINERY OF ECSTASY

In witnessing Gerty's longings, we also understand better why Joyce has made Bloom an adman: Well-crafted slogans move the human machine, become, as Stephen bemoaned in *Portrait*, "kinetic." And the machines do move in this chapter. Gerty sees Bloom ogling her (Joyce describes him as a snake eying his prey), and her woman's instinct tells her that she has "raised the devil in him." The mating ritual starts: Gerty leans ever further back while swinging her leg in tune to the distant organ (of the nearby church, where Mary is being prayed to and a mass is being performed), and the dark stranger is perceived as worked-up, with his hands in his pockets. Joyce's language fuses the sacred and the profane, the carnal and the spiritual, as he gives the measure of all the distinct raptures now building, yielding a kind of tumescent rhetoric that conflates the adoration of Gerty and of the Virgin, as if these discourses were versions of each other: Hence, his eyes are fixated on her, absorbing every feature, indeed "worshipping at her shrine" (296). She is enraptured by the overt, passionate sensations written all over his face, and she rightly takes it as a direct homage to herself, herself as object of adoration.

It is well to remember Bloom's real curiosity, in "Lotus Eaters," about the *mechanics* of the mass, about the how-to nature of generating belief. There, Bloom focused on the Latin, the solidarity, the ritual, the narcotics of salvation. Here, Bloom himself is a participant in the manufacture of ecstasy, and Joyce tells us that such transcendence derives from intently fantasizing about a body—Gerty's, Mary's, Christ's—to the point of actual release: ejaculation, transubstantiation, or—as the book's recurrent motif has it—metempsychosis. It is, I think, impossible to put a moral bottom line onto these matters: Yes, we usually deem language that causes ejaculation to be obscene or pornographic, but ecstasy is a larger item altogether, and Joyce is bold indeed in linking religious fervor and erotic fervor together here. Readers may initially guffaw when reading this episode—it has been regarded as a triumph of comedy—but it says some disturbing things about what "turns people on."

As Joyce moves into high gear with these various quests for deliverance, we read of "whitehot passion" in the male's face, a man whom Gerty also, in her way, worships, thinking him someone of "inflexible honour to his fingertips" (299). (This is quite a notation, given what Bloom is doing.) It is in this sequence that Joyce rivals Sterne (whose sexual teasing in *Tristram Shandy* finds echoes in "Oxen of the Sun"), as the young girl leans, excitedly, passionately, without shame, ever further back, displaying her legs, her knickers and still more, even the part nobody had ever looked at, while Bloom too reaches his (masturbatory) sexual climax, figured unforgettably, sublimely, in the language of the fireworks that are also going off on the beach (yes indeed, fireworks). This deservedly famous (infamous?) passage tells us of a rocket springing and banging and shooting, followed by a Roman candle going up and finally bursting, causing pure rapture in the crowd, as "a stream of rain gold hair threads" (300) gushes from it, followed by little soft, wet green stars falling from the air. Joycean music. In my view this sequence is so mind-boggling in its fusions of the sexual, the romantic, the religious, and the actual that it hardly matters whether it forwards the plot or not.

Yet it does exactly that. Joyce moves toward the postcoital (post-ejaculatory) as Bloom now sees that Gerty is . . . *lame*, a surprise that may well be one for the reader, too, who has not paid that much attention to her steel buckles, to her isolation. Yet he is grateful for the release obtained, and senses that this act of onanism was nonetheless mutual in its way, that Gerty doubtless felt what he was doing, that this was an *exchange*, even a sort of *language* they shared. I'd want to go further: Joyce has enlisted the "revving-up" language of both cheap romance and religious worship in order to bring this odd couple together, and it affords each of these characters a chance for sexual pleasure and release. And we should not be too churlish in assessing this. Gerty the lame and Bloom the cuckold—each destined for sexual disappointment in general—have both found gratification, and found it, wordlessly, through each other. There is an odd wisdom here, even if it challenges normative thinking, a wisdom about human hydraulics and circuits, about activating and regulating our juices and flows, about strategies for gratification, about the real pleasures of virtual intimacy, about consumerism as a tactical way of assuaging desire (whether it be located on a beach or in a church), about the fireworks of body and mind.

POST-ORGASM MUSING

Nonetheless, the second half of the chapter conveys a spent Bloom, one whose thoughts are ever more fluid, as his mind moves from Gerty on to Molly and Boylan, then musing about the work of time, the memory of passion, the pastness of sexual love between himself and Molly, leading to one of the novel's most Proustian notations. Bloom looks at Howth Hill, remembers they first made love there, and measures his losses: Boylan gets the plums, Bloom gets the plumstones. Even this, he realizes, is a way of continuing the dance: the players may change, but the music is the same. Yet time exacts its toll.

At that point Bloom, feeling drained from his exertions with Gerty, senses that youth is past, that one has it only once, that no amount of revisiting or remembering the sites of passion will bring it back. And yet, we keep bumping into our past nonetheless. Joyce's phrase for these crucial encounters, for the impossibility of either escaping or retrieving your past, is the "Longest way around is the shortest way home." And, so, home it is, for at this point a vignette from the remote past pops into the text, to have its little say: it is a memory of playing charades at a friend's house some seventeen years earlier, in the company of Matt Dillon and all his daughters and Molly as well, Molly with the "Moorish eyes" watching Bloom enact via charades the part of Rip van Winkle, now awake after his twenty-year sleep and coming back. Bloom still remembers how he conveyed the name: *Rip* would be the tear in one of the girl's overcoats; *van* would be a bread van; *Winkle* would be found by cockles and by periwinkles. And Molly looking on. Poor Rip van Winkle: he awoke to a changed world; he was now forgotten; he had been young, but was now old; he had had a gun, but now it was rusty with dew.

Just a party game? "Rip" and "van" and "Winkle" are awful words, and the tragic poetry of time's work is ineluctably given voice: Bloom is the man who has slept through his marriage, who wakes up to change and loss and oblivion, whose gun is rusty from the dew. No charade, this. It is Joycean music, where the motifs come together to yield an almost unbearable eloquence about a life that has been "spent," about the substitutions that are now in play, about the meandering of memory that reminds us of what we have lost.

"Longest way around is the shortest way home" is the secret formula for *Ulysses*, inasmuch as all the discrete details of this plot send us "home," speak volumes about the pathos of Bloom's life, offer a rich form of portraiture. I earlier said that one cannot paraphrase this novel, because its (apparently) random helter-skelter notations actually begin to cohere in front of our eyes, function as musical motifs, provide a strange shorthand for an entire life over time. These are the book's readerly jewels, but they are only possessable after you've ventured deeply into the novel, have had a chance to see how the disparate pieces might fit, form a mosaic. Seeing all this, one might ask: Do I have a comparable sense of pattern in my own life? Do the scattered incidents of my daily experiences also fuse together into a story, a portrait? Are the paths that I walk leading me homeward? How could my story be told? Is a genius like Joyce needed, or could I do it myself?

CIRCE: CIRCUS

Chapter 15, "Circe," taking up roughly a quarter of the text, is the novel's climactic, dreamlike, surreal extravaganza, presented in dramatic form, announcing with utmost impudence that new things are in play, and that the rules of engagement have changed. "Circe" takes place largely in a brothel in "Nighttown," where Bloom follows the drunken Stephen and his friend Lynch, so it seems plausible that things will loosen up even further in these quarters. As illustration, consider the sweet ditty sung by the Prison Gate Girls: "If you see Kay/Tell him he may/See you in tea/Tell him for me" (405); just try saying that one aloud, especially lines 1 and 3. (If you don't get it, read it aloud to a friend.) But the larger shock is literally generic, for who could anticipate that Joyce would actually move out of narrative prose into theatrical notation? What does he achieve?

At first, the question may appear technical, but once you think about it, dramatic form is a very different animal from prose fiction, inasmuch as theater is the place where *everything speaks*. In the hands of Joyce, this translates into talking soap bars, bedsprings, chimes, caps, moths, flybills, fans, hoofs, collective entities such as "sins of the past," yews, waterfalls, paintings, pianolas, gramophones, not to mention all manner of Dubliners encountered during the day, with special guest appearances by the (never distant) ghosts of the past, ranging from Bloom's grandfather, Virag, Molly's father, Tweedy, on to more portentous figures, such as Stephen's dead mother, May Dedalus, and Bloom's dead son, Rudy. Here, then, is the Sorcerer's Apprentice chapter of the book, where anything thought or desired *is actualized and voiced.* It is as if the creative principle were all-powerful, incessantly translating desire into reality, things past into things present, things merely thought into things visible and tangible. An artist's dream, you might say.

CONSCIOUSNESS AS TERRORISM: BLOOM ON TRIAL

Or perhaps a nightmare. The produced world of "Circe" is a hundred-percent *public* realm. I cannot overstate the importance of this. After all, one of the glories of this novel has been its sometimes hilarious, sometimes heartbreaking account of the inside story, the universe of feeling and thought that "passes show" (as Hamlet put it). We know the sensations and perceptions of Stephen and Bloom. In chapter after chapter, Joyce gives us the marvelous seesaw of what is said versus what is thought, enabling us to peer in, to eavesdrop, to be privy to an entire world of interiority that never makes it into actual speech. Stephen's remorse, Bloom's musings, these are the rich fare of *Ulysses*, arguably its greatest reward for readers, given that all of us are locked out of the inner lives of those real people who surround us.

As I have claimed repeatedly, it is this explosive discovery of our story, our consciousness of things, that stamps the great novels under discussion in this book. But that is not all. Consciousness is our sanctuary, our private place, the realm where we are free to agree or disagree, to have our little response. It is the great free space that life makes available even to the most coerced and victimized. It is the trump that those without trumps nonetheless possess. This has everything to do with the invisibility principle. How many times have you been grateful that no one can read your thoughts? God forbid that we should become transparent creatures, or that our inner musings and responses should become visible and audible. Often enough we bemoan the fact that our inner motives and deeper feelings are *invisible* to others. In this harrowing, yet hysterical chapter, James Joyce gives us ample reason to thank our stars that nature has arranged things in this way (for us).

Leopold Bloom is especially memorable and lovable along just these lines of visible action and invisible thoughts. He is the little man who sizes up the puffed-up ones and has his own gentle laugh (on the sly) at their antics. He is the artful dodger, the man who uses thought to get out of tight corners, who thinks about other things when the going gets rough, when his ghosts start to crowd in on him. He is Odyssean in his skill at maneuvering, at avoiding crisis, at savoring the whole spectrum of pleasures that come to us via thought, daydreaming, and fantasy. These inner resources constitute his freedom. *All this is what "Circe" annihilates.* All the prior hiding places—what you did when no one was looking, what you merely thought, what you said to yourself—go up in smoke, because they are brought now into the open, given voice, and *testify against Bloom.* I suppose this is ultimately what the Last Judgment might look like: a gathering chorus of everything we thought we'd hidden, we thought was over and gone, now given full, terrible, indicting speech. Or one might compare this to a nightmarish version of the old TV show *This Is Your Life,* where they used to haul out all your old teachers and friends onto the stage, so that the past ghoulishly came back to life. Very moving, yes? What about: terrifying?

And thus we get a roll call of much that has passed (we thought, Bloom thought). Bloom's early sojourn in the jakes, in which he wiped his behind with the pages of Philip Beaufoy's short story, returns via none other than Philip Beaufoy, who is enraged at Bloom's treatment of his material. Or the splendid reentry of Gerty MacDowell, now leering and limping and displaying: "*coyly her bloodied clout*" (361). We can now begin to measure the stakes of the theatrical-return scheme at work. Page after page of "Nausicaa" was devoted to the fantasies and desires of Gerty, concluding with Bloom's roman-candle masturbation, completing a mating ritual of sorts in which private desire was aroused and assuaged without a word passing from one to the other, since it is all built out of looking and longing. That whole chapter was hard-wired with voyeurist energy (Bloom's, Gerty's), but no voyeurism is conceivable now, since everything is in the open. Hence, this Gerty speaks to Bloom of showing him everything she had, of hating him for it; to which Bloom plays innocent, claims she's dreaming, that he's never seen her. The bawd of the brothel makes to lead Gerty away, but she gets her licks in, nails Bloom for having viewed her private parts, chastises him as both dirty and married, yet closes her little indictment with the avowal that she loves him for doing what he's done to her. How to assess this? The earlier scene of pleasure on the sly has become something else entirely, something more transgressive: Bloom takes the Fifth Amendment, but Gerty has her say, expresses now a twisted desire that would be unimaginable in "realist" terms.

"Circe" is the Kafka chapter of the novel, since it is the one that puts

Bloom on trial. What are his transgressions? Ha! His very life. Beaufoy had it right, by urging an investigation of Bloom's private life, by claiming that Bloom leads "a quadruple existence!" (375). Who among us does not lead a quadruple existence (or quintuple)? Who among us could afford to be *seen*, seen at every single moment? And worse, seen even in our thoughts? Masturbation comes up again later, as the nymph in the bedroom painting indicts Bloom for having profaned her. Bloom is turned inside out by Joyce, so that every possible fantasy or desire—whether or not they were acted on—now has its day in court, rats on its owner. We have already noted that Bloom is turned on by horsy women; well, here they come, out of the stable (as it were), voluptuous, opulent, wrapped in furs and leathers, lambasting Bloom for his indecent overtures. Mrs Elverton Barry notes that Bloom claimed to have gazed upon her at the theater, becoming inflamed by the sight of her "peerless globes" (379); Mrs Bellingham follows suit by noting that Bloom had wildly praised her "nether extremities," while also signaling his intense admiration of her other bodily charms, hidden but imaginable; further, she alleges that Bloom has begged her to desecrate the marriage bed, saying it was his great purpose in life to have intercourse with her as soon as can be possibly arranged. At which point the Honorable Mrs Mervyn Talboys weighs in with her report, claiming that Bloom sent her obscene photographs, representing an almost naked "señorita" having illicit sex with a "muscular torero," urging her further (a) to dirty his letter in a blasphemous way, (b) to punish him as is fully warranted, (c) to straddle and mount him, in order (d) to conclude by bestowing on him a "most vicious horsewhipping" (381).

CIRCE AND SADOMASOCHISM

What exactly is this? Can Bloom actually have sent these missives? Or are these fantasies only? The ontology of "Circe" is unknowable and, perhaps, unimportant, since its precise mission is to turn the world of desire into reality. And hence we must consider that Bloom has likely desired, is likely desiring, *all* of this, including the humiliations and chastisements now heading his way. The lid is off. Joyce, who was heavy into the work of Leopold von Sacher-Masoch, offers us a virtual primer in sadomasochism, with Leopold Bloom as his prime exhibit. The horsy women want at him; Mrs Mervyn Talboys says she's ready to scourge him, to flay him alive. Bloom reacts by closing his eyes and squirming with pleasure, exclaiming that danger excites him. As the coveted whipping nears, he seeks an alibi, noting that the benefits of spanking are many: The body experiences a nice, warm tingle that is good for the circulation. These brief lines are worth pages of Freud, in my view, inasmuch as they depict the creature's incurable need to mask its appetite; the delicious front put forth is that of the scientist Bloom, whose sole interest in being whipped is hygienic, as if it were, merely a sauna, eh, works wonders for the circulation, you know. With hunting crop swishing in the air, Mrs Mervyn Talboys demands that he lower his trousers, and Bloom tremblingly begins to obey, saying "The weather has been so warm" (382). *The weather has been so warm.* Yes, indeed, I am taking down my pants, but the reason, you see, is that the weather has been so warm.

There is simply no measuring stick for these events. Once we consider masochism as the motivation, then we can no longer distinguish whatsoever between pain and pleasure, between humiliation and triumph. To be sure, "Circe" is more than S & M, and some of its most delightful episodes actualize other kinds of Bloomish daydreams, such as his aspirations as a progressive, as Great Reformer who seeks to unite all the religions, who is committed to an entire shopping list of utopian changes. Bloom will rid the world not only of tuberculosis and insanity, but he will also banish war and begging; he will also provide many goodies: Esperanto will be taught as the common brotherly language, and of course all of these benefits will be absolutely free and gratis, yielding a regime of ease and comfort such as never before seen. The rhythm of this chapter is up-and-down, so that each Bloomish accomplishment is followed by an attack, some of which in turn mandate professional defense; Buck Mulligan comes to the rescue here, and he asks leniency of the court, given that his client suffers from numerous maladies, including bisexuality, dementia, epilepsy, elephantiasis, onanism, vice, even metal teeth; as if that were not enough, Mulligan goes on to claim that he has examined Bloom both vaginally and anally, according to the strictest standards, and determined that our hero is also an intact virgin.

I cite this passage to illustrate something of the no-holds-barred, pull-out-all-the-stops treatment of Bloom in this chapter. It would be difficult to refer this kind of authorial roasting exclusively to any deep-seated masochist desire on Bloom's part, but rather, as well, to the limitless theatrics of the actual power game being played here, a game in which Bloom comes to us increasingly as a cipher, as a pawn for the spectacular writerly workout in process.

There would appear to be a kind of Walter Mitty lodged deep inside James Joyce, a wildly creative dreamer who is given free rein to actualize all his fantasies and daydreams. But, it seems to go further still, to set into motion a phantasmagoria that is oddly freewheeling, "liberated," madly producing its libidinal theater. For all the factual ballast of *Ulysses*, what most strikes us in "Circe" is the imperiousness and epic dimensions of desire—whether for pleasure or pain—constituting an engine that cannot be stopped, that is maniacally taking over the entire scene. One feels in the presence of a terrible machine—even if that machine is lodged in our own deepest pulsions—that is churning out its own extravagant scenarios. I hesitate to say that this, too, is what life is all about, since it does appear to be so over the top, but Joyce has his teeth into something quite basic here, at once hilarious and frightening, where "we" are essentially transformed into a target, on the receiving end of the maddest kinds of directives and injunctions coming at us from us without reprieve or mercy. I think that this is the very mechanics of genuine human capsizing, those episodes of nightmare or panic or anxiety or mania that all feeling creatures have encountered now and then.

CHANGING SEX

Is Bloom himself in some indirect way orchestrating this show? (Just as you yourself must be, indirectly, orchestrating your worst nightmares, since who else could be doing it?) Taking pleasure in doing oneself in is the signature move of masochism, and that warped sentiment is lodged deeply in the Bloomian (and, I am sure, Joycean) psyche; it will take us a far piece in evaluating the final sexual humiliations to come. Things heat up still further when Bella Cohen the whoremistress enters the scene. She looks at Bloom with great insistence, her "falcon" eyes glitter, and her large fan—digging up domestic truths, stating that the "missus is master"—carries out the ultimate metamorphosis of the novel: Bloom's transformation from man to woman. Here is (perhaps? can we know?) the up-to-now untold story of Leopold Bloom: his fetishes as young man, his love for dainty women's shoes, his female pantomimes of surrender in the mirror, his clipping off of "backgate" hairs and swooning as other women are taken, his use of the toilet seat by sitting down (this too trumped up as scientific inquiry, in order to do a comparative study of toilet postures). Mind you, none of this is simply confessed; rather it is forced out of Bloom by the brutal coercions of *Bello* Cohen, now become just the kind of vigorous male desired by the womanly Bloom. Bello treats Bloom as sexual slave, threatens nosering, pliers, whipping and hanging, along with possible slaughter and skewering, then squats on Bloom's upturned face and rides him. It is one of the most violent and provocative scenes of the novel: Bello bullies Bloom in every conceivable way: he thrusts his fist and cigar at him, demanding that Bloom kiss them, he straddles Bloom like a horse, presses him with his knees, commands him to "gee up," bends over and squeezes his testicles, rides him cockhorse, singing all the while about the lady going a pace, the coachman going a trot, while the gentleman goes "a gallop a gallop a gallop" (436).

Is this Bloom's deepest wish? To be ridden, to be mounted, to be fucked? Is this a sexualized version of that same curiosity and elasticity that we've observed so often, that talent for seeing and experiencing things from the other side? You can't go further to the other side than changing sex and being serviced the other way.

But Bello's sexual overpowering of Bloom—including thrusting his arm "*elbowdeep in Bloom's vulva*" (440) and then bidding the results to male onlookers—moves unerringly to the main event, the erotic drama at home that Bloom has (seemingly) been trying to avoid thinking about. No more dodging possible. Bello goes right to Bloom's vitals, and sneeringly sizes up what he sees: an organ as limp and unprepossessing as that of a small boy peeing behind a wagon. With equipment of this stamp, Bloom is asked the big question: Can he do "a man's job"? Having now documented Bloom's inadequacy, Bello completes the sexual humiliation (the pleasure?) by recounting, vividly, woundingly, what is going on in his house between Molly and Boylan: A stud is now at work, a fellow of "brawn," a "fullgrown" chap, outfitted with a "weapon" that is endowed with "knobs and lumps and warts," from which he has delivered his load, a load that is "kicking and coughing" in Molly's womb, a load that will be heard from in nine months time. How does that make you feel, he wants to know?

Bloom sees this leering horror show—Bello does not fail to paint a vivid picture of these two fully endowed bodies locked in intercourse—as an indictment of not only his marriage but his life, to which his moving response is: "Moll! I forgot! Forgive me! Moll . . . . We . . . . Still . . . ." (442). Nowhere is Joyce's refusal of sentimentality more evident than here. No flights of self-laceration, no spiraling into anguish or rage; in their stead, a pathetic effort to change things, to stop the clock. Pathetic because the clock is the true enemy here, fiercer and more unyielding, more potent than either Boylan or Bello. "We. . . . Still. . . ." is the poignant theme song of belated recognition, of belatedness itself. No fresh starts in Joyce's scheme. Bello breaks the news, by deriving the final moral of the story: All is over for Leopold Bloom, all is changed, changed ever since he slept his twenty-year sentence in Sleepy Hollow.

And sure enough, Sleepy Hollow enters the book, calls on Rip van Winkle (conjured up already in "Nausicaa" as figure of loss), and Leopold Bloom, outfitted with moccasins and a rusty gun, comes forth, peers through the glass panes, thinks he has magically returned to the past, believes he sees Molly as she once was, the very first night he saw her: Yet, something is wrong, the dress is green, the hair is dyed gold; again Bello breaks the news, pointing out that the figure he sees is his daughter, Milly, not his wife, Molly. With this, Milly Bloom, heretofore unseen in this novel, makes her entry, breaks from the arms of her lover, and announces the simple truth that has been lurking behind the epic dramatization of a single day: yes, she recognizes her father, but he has changed: "O Papli, how old you've grown!" (442). Out of the mouths of babes the law is spoken. Proust, Joyce, Woolf, and Faulkner, unprecedented artists of consciousness and memory that they all are, share the same dirty secret: Time passes, you can't return to the past, each breath puts you closer to the grave.

KINKY

Even this does not quite drain the cup in "Circe." Joyce reserves a final ludic humiliation for the cuckolded Bloom. He will actually get to *watch* the event. It is, I think, the kinkiest moment in the novel, far from the pathos of Bloom begging Molly's forgiveness or hoping to start over. No, this time, Bloom himself is getting his jollies through having his wife be serviced by Boylan. In Joyce's staging, Boylan enters the apartment, hangs his hat on the antlers coming from Bloom's head, is told (by flunkey Bloom) that Molly is in her bath, is invited in by said Molly, is having trouble containing all that is ready to go in his engine. As if that were not enough, Boylan, ever one to help out, suggests that Bloom put his eye to the keyhole and fondle himself while watching him (Boylan) do sport with his wife, to which Bloom replies that, yes indeed, sir, he will do just that, but asks if he might bring two male friends to check out the action as well, and take some pictures, all the while offering Boylan Vaseline and other little necessities. The man and the woman then go to it, and Joyce the ever-reliable sound man delivers the acoustics: Boylan, working away, delivers himself of "Ah! Godblazegrukbrukarchkhrasht!" while Molly, fully engaged as well, responds "O! Weeshwashtkissinapooisthnapoohuck" (462). Bloom's reaction? With dilated eyes and hands on his genitals, he too explodes with passion: "Show! Hide! Show! Plough her! More! Shoot!" (462). This scene is as ecstatic for Bloom as it is for the actual fornicators. I frankly do not know how to reconcile Bloom the wildly aroused pimp with Bloom the long-suffering husband. Joyce has not thought such a reconciliation necessary. Maybe at the libidinal level where Joyce is tapping into his creature, such distinctions are erased. Is this Joyce's deepest meaning?

It is in these fierce episodes that Joyce fractures our sense of human psychology and identity, pointing to reaches of human longing where pleasure and pain—especially where filth and ecstasy, humiliation and jollies—not only coexist but are locked into a crazy dance. Does anyone care to see him- or herself in these garish colors? Who is prepared to say that his or her equipment, at its bottom-most level, functions like this? wants this kind of fare? *Ulysses* turns, to some extent, on such queries. One can always rope off this performance by claiming that it is an exercise in mere farce reserved for the weird Leopold Bloom, but *not* a mirror for self-discovery. It remains an open question how Joyce himself saw it. My own view is that Joyce is out to offer a portrait of the human animal in all its guises, however murky and unlabelable they may be, and that this shocking material is there for our reflection as well as our laughter.

VISIONARY ENCOUNTERS

What is certain is that "Circe" moves, in its final pages, from the Bloom circus to the Stephen trial, and with good vampire logic, the dead May Dedalus returns to the scene, a green rill of bile trickling from her mouth, telling Stephen how she loved him even as he lay in her womb, demanding, with smoldering eyes, that he repent, drawing her face ever nearer, extending her blackened, withered right arm toward her son's breast, which then becomes a red-eyed crab that plunges its claws into Stephen, triggering Stephen's final act of rebellion, his final denial: "*Non serviam!*" (475). Stephen gives his very all to this no, cites Wagner's Siegfried by saying "*Nothung*" ("Fate, Necessity"), lifts his ashplant high, and smashes the chandelier in a final apocalyptic gesture. We cannot fail to be struck by Stephen's last-ditch rigidness, his utter refusal to bend or alter, his heroic pride.

All this is in sharp contrast to the ever-morphing Bloom, the elastic man who ducks and dodges, the man who is in the brothel in the first place in order to keep an eye on this drunken, gifted young poet. Hence, the chapter will close by exiting the brothel, by having Stephen physically decked by the English soldier, by then having Bloom watch over him with tender fatherly solicitude. It is the book's grand moment for fathers seeking sons, and we can hardly fail to see that the kindness bestowed on Stephen adds its measure of plenitude to Bloom's own life. It is as close as the novel is to come to radiance, and it earns Leopold Bloom a vision of his own dead Rudy: a fairy-tale child, a "changeling" attired in the most extraordinary fashion: Eton clothes, shoes of glass, helmet, reading an old text from right to left, with a smile on his face. Right at the edge of kitsch, the spectacle of the Hebrew-reading, Eton-dressed fairy child in glass shoes and bronze helmet, is the warmest moment in *Ulysses*, on the far side of any realist notation, an actualized dream in the most unsentimental novel of the twentieth century.

THERE'S NO PLACE LIKE HOME

One expects the penultimate chapter of *Ulysses*, "Ithaca," to ground the novel. After all, it is a matter of homecoming, and the chapter begins with Bloom leading Stephen home, and it ends with Bloom getting into bed with Molly. But it is a bad day for domesticity. Narrated in a catechism format of authoritarian questions and answers, "Ithaca" positions its characters (and their needs) on a stage that is virtually galactic in scope. When Bloom escorts Stephen out, toward chapter's end, the two of them look upward. What do they see? Joyce writes it first as poetry: "The heaventree of stars hung with humid nightblue fruit" (573). He then, with good contrapuntal logic, expresses Bloom's meditations as a spatial geographer might, measuring the parameters of an expanse that dwarfs all human doing, denoting the stars as eternal travelers crossing through the web of time, against which man's duration of "threescore and ten" is but a tiny parenthesis.

Counterpoint now clocks in once again: As if the mention of life's "infinitesimal brevity" triggered its own rival version of inhuman scale, Joyce proceeds to show how far you might go in the minus direction, getting all the way down to red and white corpuscles, figured as full-scale universes, themselves containing "divisions of redivisible component bodies" subject to still further division, yielding finally a scheme in which "nought nowhere was never reached" (573–574). What kinds of recognitions or reunions could take place in such a realm? And yet, how better to speak to our "homeless" condition, our exiled estate in a galaxy and in a body that we never made, that we can neither measure nor control? Little ground for celebration; much ground for thinking.

CHARACTER AS TOY

I have said that Joyce turns Bloom inside out in "Circe," but in "Ithaca" he seems to go, if possible, a quantum leap farther, transforming his characters and plot into the infinitely malleable, endlessly elastic ciphers of his textual world. After all, when you get right down to it, what is Leopold Bloom? One answer is a series of letters: L-E-O-P-O-L-D B-L-O-O-M. Nothing sacrosanct about that, is there? Why not open it up for other possibilities? Here are the anagrams that Bloom had made in his youth:

Leopold Bloom
Ellpodbomool
Molldopeloob
Bollopedoom
Old Ollebo, M.P. (554)

I love speaking this passage; I relish the sound of these various anagrams coming off my tongue, cavorting, opening up the character the way a hall of mirrors opens up your image. And I invest each of them with psychological possibilities: Ellpodbomool seems a kind of new animal species, Molldopeloob seems to express Bloom's married life, Bollopedoom has a mix of farce and fatalism in it, and Old Ollebo, M.P. is, well, delicious in its conversion of our hero into recognized public servant. It makes me wonder what someone with Joyce's genius might do with A-R-N-O-L-D W-E-I-N-S-T-E-I-N. None of us chose our names. What if we were just the malleable materials of an antic writer-god who enjoyed doodling with those letters that hold us in bondage our entire lives, from learning to spell out our moniker in kindergarten all the way to the inscriptions on our tomb? What's in a name?

For that matter, what's in a relationship? *Ulysses:* a book about fathers and sons? For close to a century, critics have waxed lyrical about the symbolic kinship established between Bloom and Stephen. How close do they really get? Well, we learn that their respective educations separate them; but our friendly author has a cure for that: Why not insert Stephen into Bloom's place? How, you may wonder? Easy: enter "Stoom." This Stoom, you will be happy to know, is now put through the paces of Bloom's schooling, ending with high school. What about his partner, "Blephen"? Now this is more complicated, for Blephen's course is considerably more ambitious, passing through all the grades of the intermediate program, then matriculating at the university so as to complete the various stages of the arts degree course of study. "Blephen and Stoom": that's one way of bringing your folks together. And please note Joyce's shrewd use of the conditional future perfect tense in mapping their fictive trajectories: "would have passed." This is what authorial freedom is about: to remake your deck as a putative, conditional world, to reconfigure your people as the alphabet permits.

Perhaps the finest notation about the gulf between Stephen and Bloom has to do with age, with time. Those of us who have read Proust know how much pathos is possible here. And Joyce himself has already shown us that Bloom, alias Rip Van Winkle Bloom, is time's fool, that Stephen is haunted by his mother's ghost. And do not forget the great Homeric theme, either: "It is a wise child that knows his own father." So, how would you take the measure of the age relationship between father and son? Like this, if you are the arithmetical James Joyce: by concocting a numerical whimsy of cosmic proportions. How? You begin by going back 16 years to 1888, at which point Bloom would be 22 (as Stephen now is) and Stephen would be 6. Then, as balancing move, you go forward 16 years to 1920, at which point Stephen would be 38 (as Bloom now is), and Bloom would be 54. (Please note the crucial "would be" language: it is financing this entire party.) Once, at 1920, you may then jump another 16 years, to arrive at 1936. Why not? But now is when the fun begins, and Joyce moves from simple addition and subtraction to more complex equations. Now—now!—in 1936, the ratios between their respective ages have radically changed: from an original ratio of 16 to 0, to a current one of 17½ to 13½. And that ratio would continue to diminish as the years continued to add up. But—but—what would happen if you maintained the "16-factor" that was valid in 1888, and applied it to subsequent dates? What would you get? Well, using 1904 as your reference date, you'd find that Stephen would be 22, but our man Bloom would now be 374. Yes, 374. So much for 1904, let's check out 1920, at which point Stephen would be 38, the new Bloom would become 646. Time to move further: Fast forward to 1952, at which juncture our friend Stephen would be 70, whereas . . . whereas . . . Bloom would now clock in at 1,190, which would entail his having been born in 714, not to mention his having exceeded by a full 221 years the longest age on record, that of Methusaleh (who had set the earlier record of 969). At this point—you realize that the phrase *at this point* no longer means much—Joyce shows what heroes are made of, for we are now in a position to grant Stephen the same longevity that Bloom has just enjoyed, namely the ripe old age of 1,190, which of course has the consequence of pushing us all the way to the year 3072 (don't forget, Stephen was born in 1882), yet Stephen's venerable lifespan is small beer indeed when we now take the measure of his counterpart, Bloom, who—you haven't forgotten, have you?—has been progressing at a 16 to 1 ratio, entitling him to the majestic age of 83,300 years, which in turn mandates that our man be born quite some time ago, 81,396 B.C. to be exact. Ah, the elegance of numbers!

It is, in my view, one of the most hysterical sequences ever written. Back in *Portrait*, Stephen Dedalus had yearned for absolute freedom, for the power to fly over those nets called "nationality, language and religion." Well, James Joyce has learned now to fly, and in this fantasia of numbers doing their stately dance, compelling the characters to follow along and keep up with them, we see the great craft of fiction lifting off, leaving the earth and its gravity field, moving into outer space. Are you ready to be Joyce's contemporary? If so, buckle up.

BLOOM THE CIPHER

And yet . . . literature is, like it or not, a zero-sum game. Yes, you can toss your people into free flight and you can explode their names into acrostics and their ages into number madness, but there is a price to be paid. They lose the gravity and cogency of old-fashioned, sentient characters; they become tools, ciphers, artistic material. I do not want to overstate this point, since this novel, and indeed this chapter, is so rich in human significance. I love Joycean fun and games, and the spectacle of Bloom/Stephen's malleability is invigorating. But there are no free lunches in art. Joyce anatomizes Bloom in "Ithaca," unpacks his fantasies and daydreams, measures his every move, describes his dwellings (both real and fantasized), inventories his moods and thoughts, views him at once from close up and far away. But in each of these depictions, Bloom comes to us as elastic and commoditized, as sketchpad or carnet that Joyce is flipping through, as the plaything of the text, as a kind of writerly Frisbee that the novelist is hurling about, making him turn and pirouette and somersault and perform moves that few characters have ever been made to do. If you actually persist in seeing Bloom as a flesh-and-blood creature—the classic fantasy that reading seduces us toward—then you've got to wonder at this textual puppet being taken through the author's paces.

At home, preparing for bed, Bloom becomes reflective, muses about desirable and undesirable future scenarios. But, to put it as I have—Bloom reflective, Bloom musing—is to confer on Bloom a kind of agency and authority that he demonstrably, spectacularly lacks. Let me illustrate. Out of nowhere, the text announces: "Reduce Bloom by crossmultiplication of reverses of fortune"; at this juncture, Bloom has been lazily daydreaming about his (real and fantasized) financial holdings, but the text is intent on annihilating this little safety net, and it (the text) intends to do so by going entirely "negative," as if this too were a mathematical game, and all your positives could—presto!—become negatives. (Note that consciousness enjoys these kinds of dirty tricks as well, but the systematic aspect of the punishment meted out here has an authorial character.) There is a kind of narrational terrorism on display here. "Reduce Bloom by crossmultiplication of reverses of fortune" flaunts a kind of authorial and arithmetic bullying that is all the more despotic for being entirely whimsical. As if Joyce were thinking: Bloom is my plaything; let's see what I can do to him.

Now, you could argue that every novelist in history has more or less followed this injunction—creating characters and controlling their destiny is a distinctly godlike endeavor, an assertion of power and control that one rarely has in one's actual life (although dictators and parents sometimes try)—but none of them (as far as I can judge) has ever quite flaunted this power relationship so overtly. None of them has rubbed in our face, quite like Joyce is doing, the marionette-like nature of his people. Maybe ultimately you and I, too, are essentially marionettes, governed by rules and forces we do not see or control or understand, ranging from genetics to economics. But in our day-to-day lives we have the powerful illusion (at least) of being free agents, of making our own choices, of dictating our own moves, of constructing our own plot. In "Ithaca" Joyce is out to smash all such illusions. By the way, would you like to see what the text produces in response to this command to "reduce Bloom by cross-multiplication"? It produces a list of progressively terrible scenarios—as rigorous and automatic as a computer-generated document—and one negotiates (as reader) these descending outcomes as if one were moving through various gears of feared misery, like a vehicle going from first to fourth (fourth being the free fall plunge). Hence, we watch Bloom move from poverty to mendicancy to destitution, with each of these stages richly illustrated by Joyce's vigorous imagination, offering us a kind of "photo-realism" account of just how bad things can become. The list concludes, as it must, at the very bottom of the abyss, bequeathing this appetizing vision of economic and moral ruin: "the aged impotent disfranchised ratesupported moribund lunatic pauper" (596). Here is Joyce's special version of "through a glass darkly": to see yourself on a roller coaster that goes only down, so that each loop carries you deeper into horror.

What kind of a list is this? Bloom's nightmare or Joyce's fun? No way to know. But if you are past a certain age, and if you occasionally have trouble going back to sleep when you wake up at 3 A.M., if you find yourself doing your own little inventory, I'd say that Joyce's list of Bloom's increasingly awful futures will speak to you.

PHILOSOPHY IN THE BEDROOM

Once Bloom has completed his nightly meditations (running the gamut from reveries of being country squire to fears of utter destitution), he makes his way into his bedroom for the final homecoming. And enters—with ever so much prudence, care, concern, and solicitude—the bed. There, in keeping with the geographic and geometric logic of this chapter, his limbs encounter two human forms: one of them, female, physically there, is that of his wife, whereas the other, male, there also but only as "imprint," is termed "not his" (601). Now, if you have read either this book or Joyce's *Ulysses* thus far, you must know that this meeting—which would be a showdown in virtually any other novel—is going to be tricky, tricky. With extraordinary suavity, with philosophical brilliance, Joyce moves once again into the conditional tense: "If he had smiled why would he have smiled?" (601). It is a stunning notation, the last thing on earth you'd expect from a guy collecting solid evidence that his wife has, just hours ago, cheated on him. But then Bloom is a special guy, and hence he *sizes up* this classic dilemma—a sexual dilemma that has been the staple item of comedy and tragedy since the beginning of the human species—in a prodigious fashion. Yes, Bloom reflects, I am entering my conjugal bed, and I am doing so alone, but—but—in reality my entry is part of an endless chain of entries and exits, and we only imagine our trajectory to be unique ("first, last, only and alone" [601] as Joyce states it), whereas in truth we are part of a collective rhythm, no more individualized than a single wave lapping the beach or a single breeze going through the air, for we are always and ever inscribed in a "series" that began at the beginning of time and will continue to its end.

Note: Joyce does not write that Bloom smiled. (And, by the way, would you be smiling at entering a bed with the imprint of your spouse's lover still there?) Joyce writes only: *if* he had smiled. But this opens the door to the book's darkest and lightest truth of all: *The individual is eclipsed.* Dark because it is no fun being erased, finding that your every move is simply impersonal, generic, serial. But light because this discovery soothes, removes all the sound and fury, installs the Olympian perspective that nullifies individual doing. Here is the vista Joyce has been working toward for quite some time now: The dance of the species is alone real. We are thrust into it at birth and exit it at death, but all our efforts to personalize it, to domesticate it into private contour and private meaning, are futile, whimsical. Joyce's genius is to locate that perception at the heart of intimacy, but it is the intimacy of a man entering an already entered bed, aligning himself head to foot with his wife, making his ultimate peace with nature's rule and with the passing of time.

Thus, the modern Ulysses faces his wife's sexual betrayal with four different reactions: envy, jealousy, abnegation, and equanimity. (None of these is very Homeric.) Each of these responses is then anatomized by Joyce, but equanimity strikes the proper "Ithacan" note, inasmuch as Molly's prior sexual behavior (fornicating with Boylan) is not only "natural," but is adjudicated as distinctly less calamitous than a catastrophic destruction of the earth, less blameworthy than robbery or abuse of children or animals, or counterfeiting, or cheating the public or arson or treason or indeed many other things, including premeditated homicide. Hard to disagree with this. Who is prepared to say that a man and a woman having sex—whether or not one of these people is your spouse—is somehow a more grievous offense than the heavyweight list put forth here? But most of us, in such a position, would be hard put to rise to such a distanced Olympian perspective, and that is exactly why *Ulysses* challenges us as it does.

Bloom continues to reflect on these matters, weighing the moral and physiological forces in play here, and he concludes by justifying to himself his equanimity on the grounds that sexual process is essentially automatic, nature-ordained, on the order of a somatic law, and that resistance, therefore, is folly. Why, you may ask, should resistance be folly? (All of traditional literature and morality has been forever at war with such an accepting and permissive view of fornication.) Bloom has an answer here, and it speaks to the final insights of "Ithaca": all is futile, whether it be self-control or resistance or justification; hence, to defend or champion virtue is senseless, given "the lethargy of nescient matter: the apathy of the stars" (604).

We are dead center. All our moral homilies and codes of behavior are deemed futile, pointless, at odds with reality itself. This, "Ithaca" implies, we can learn by widening our perspective sufficiently. Think, for just a moment, of the emotional and ethical grammar that parses and governs so much of your reasoning and doing, that undergirds the values you subscribe to; and then think again: Can it really matter? *The apathy of the stars.* Seen from this extraterrestrial vantage point, yes, all individual doing and misdoing must well appear quaint, harmless, insignificant. "Ithaca" takes us finally to this angle of vision, and we are hard put to know whether such a perspective is to be called wisdom or evasion or cynicism or indifference.

But we do know that most of the acts that count most in our own lives would be emptied of value, would seem weightless and absurd, if ever approached in such a distant, literally otherworldly manner. Most. But perhaps not quite all. One thing remains as meaningful and authoritative as ever. The very life force that underwrites fornication between Molly and Boylan is the same pulsion that brings this husband home to this warm bed. To be sure, his place in that bed (head to toe) and his activities in that bed (kissing the "plump mellow yellow smellow melons" of her behind, kissing them democratically, as it were, on each "melonous hemisphere" and in "their mellow yellow furrow" [604]) are not those of conventional love stories or heroic fables. Nonetheless, *he has arrived:* the "manchild in the womb" now rests in his Ithaca after a long day's adventures, leading Joyce to liken him to the great explorers of yore, ranging from Sinbad the Sailor and Tinbad the Tailor all the way to Darkinbad the Brightdayler. Yet, true to Joyce's deepest beliefs, "the longest way around is the shortest way home." That "ample bedwarmed flesh" that beckoned as far back as chapter 4 is Leopold Bloom's anchor; he is home.

A WOMB WITH A VIEW

The final chapter of the novel, "Penelope," returns us to a mode of writing that is, by *Ulysses*'s standards, surprisingly, gratifyingly manageable: stream of consciousness. In eight very long, uninterrupted sentences, Joyce seeks to deliver a woman's voice and vision. Here is the story this novel owes us, an account that seems long overdue. However, feminist critics have, for some time now, raised questions about this performance (on the author's part), about the gender assumptions that underlie it. Joyce's view of women is, at least arguably, patriarchal, inasmuch as Molly exhibits a decidedly carnal, fleshly take on life, unconcerned with the intellectual, aesthetic, and ideological issues that are front and center in Stephen and more than a little present in Bloom. Molly is a different animal; Joyce was outspoken about this, and referred to his leading lady (reflecting his view of women) in terms that breathe both admiration and misogyny: "sane full amoral fertilisable untrustworthy engaging limited prudent indifferent Weib: 'Ich bin das Fleisch das stets bejaht' " ("I am the flesh that ever affirms") (cited in Budgen, 266). However politically incorrect this model may be—men as spirit, women as flesh—in Joyce's hands it becomes surpassingly eloquent as a final review of the novel's slice of life, as a perspective that challenges and bids to overturn much that has come before.

After all, if Blazes Boylan's assignation with Molly is the repressed, irrepressible "item" in every Bloom chapter of the novel, then it seems both right and overdue to get, at last, a direct account of the rendezvous, this time from a participant's angle of vision. It would appear that studlike Boylan performed according to expectation, in terms both of size ("tremendous big red brute") and endurance (at least three climaxes); Molly confesses to have never felt one this size. A good thing, yes? Well, not entirely. First of all, Boylan was too familiar, too vulgar, slapping Molly on her behind, causing her to reflect that she's after all not a horse. Moreover, even in the performance department, she gives Bloom higher marks, noting that he has "more spunk" than Boylan. Furthermore, a man filling a woman full up has its absurd side to it when you think about it, and Molly wonders why women are made with such a "big hole" inside them. And then, the filling operation itself can be a kind of male power play—Boylan shoving it into her like a stallion—with little tenderness or affection. Not that Molly isn't proud of her conquest or that she isn't already yearning for the next rendezvous some three days off, or that she doesn't long for some kind of a love letter from Boylan, even a simple note with his name on it. At this point you may be wondering, well what *is* her attitude toward Boylan? And the answer is: all of the above. And that is what makes this chapter so fresh and feisty: It exposes, willy-nilly, the quaintness of all positions, all intellectual propositions. Molly Bloom is—attitudinally, gloriously—all over the place.

MERCURIAL MOLLY

All of which means: You cannot pin her down. At some moments she is the book's hedonist, insisting there's nothing wrong with a "bit of fun," asking why otherwise we'd have all these desires, claiming her rights as a creature of flesh and blood, still young. Yet she also sees herself as the Adulteress, and she quite suspects that their daughter Milly has been sent away (by Bloom) to shield her from her mother's love affair. At times she sounds like a card-carrying feminist, remarking that the world would be a lot better off—less killing and slaughtering—if women governed it, but just a few lines later she says it is no surprise men treat women badly, given their bitchlike nature. About the importance of love and sexual passion she once again straddles the issue, remarking how overdone it all is—why all the hocus-pocus devoted to it, she wonders, when in fact only the first time matters, and afterwards it's just routine—yet following this very utterance with its opposite, asserting that absolutely nothing compares to a passionate kiss, the kind that is "long and hot" and goes all the way to the soul.

And it won't quite do to call her contradictory. On the contrary, her mixed, divergent thoughts and feelings seem to tell us that we are, at bottom, unruly creatures propelled by drives and feelings that make a mockery of logic and consistency. Can it then be a surprise that her views about her husband are also mercurial? Poldy is slyboots, plabbery, sneaking in pleasures on the side, easily bamboozled, given to *outré* pronouncements (Christ was the first Socialist, etc.) and to abstract terminology ("metempsychosis" being the chief exhibit here); yet, as mentioned, he has spunk, has wit, knows what a woman feels, knows "how to take a woman," is the person to whom she has famously said Yes.

Joyce himself acknowledged that *Ulysses* was arguably overorganized, overtheorized, overschematized. Molly Bloom is the luminous corrective here, the all-powerful natural force that laughs at latitude and longitude, makes us see that principles and suchlike are capricious constructs, easy to bandy about, with little or no purchase on life itself. Seeing this, we realize how trapped we ourselves are by concepts, by a notional world that has no truck with flesh or feeling. Definitions are at home perhaps in dictionaries, but nowhere else. Could you possibly define your most important relationships? Real human feelings are resistant to language: sprawling, messy, opaque, jumbled; and the deeper they are, the more this is the case. At the level where Joyce is tapping into this character, all is fluid and on the move.

THE WAY OF ALL FLESH

And yet there is pattern in this final chapter. It is not as amorphous or anarchic as it all seems. For the body has a logic of its own, even if it wrecks the mind's categories. One aspect of this corporeal logic is power. For all her complaining that men get all the pleasure, that they are always rushed and too quick when it comes to sex, the chapter nonetheless seems to preen in its celebration of female sexual power. Molly tells us repeatedly of her conquests, her savvy about her own charms—what scents, what colors, what fabrics, what postures most become her—and her no-less-impressive savvy about male response: making Gardner quiver and tremble, arousing Mulvey under the Moorish wall (unbuttoning him, taking it out, drawing back the skin), pulling him off into her handkerchief, and fantasizing most especially about young male bodies as per the statue of the young boy Bloom bought her, equipped with a "lovely young cock" that she could well imagine putting into her mouth, providing no one was watching, not to mention her interactions with Bloom, ranging from the lovely seedcake exchange of the past to current strategic designs in the future, involving Bloom's penchant for kissing her bottom. Yes, she will accommodate him, will open her underwear and shove it up in his face for him to act accordingly, including getting his tongue some seven miles in, if he's up to it; should he have other designs, such as doing it "off on me behind," she will hold up her end, as it were, by tightening her bottom and letting out a few choice words such as "smellrump or lick my shit" (642).

Yes, some of this is male-directed, but a very great deal of it derives from her fascination with her own body: her memory of watching her breasts dance and shake in her blouse, her keen sensation of vaginal pleasure, her conviction that Boylan must have found her a class act, based on her certainty that he'd never seen better thighs than hers, thighs white and smooth and soft and irresistibly appetizing. Molly is, physically, so self-aware, so self-enthralled—she fantasizes changing sex and mounting a nice female body—that there is no mystery whatsoever for her in male desire: of course her full voluptuous curves aroused Boylan, since they excite her too. Not that her body serves only for pleasure. Molly knows childbirth, knows that this big hole in the middle of her fills with blood once a month, as indeed it significantly does in this chapter (provoked by Boylan, given all the "poking" and "rooting" and "ploughing" he delivered himself of), making her wonder, wryly, about Nature's plan: Why do women have all this blood in them? This last plaint, triggered by her beginning period, takes a memorable form: "its pouring out of me like the sea" (633).

Like the sea. Much earlier in the book, Bloom, reflecting on the impossibility of preventing Molly's adultery or Milly's sexual initiation, noted that it was as futile as trying to stop the sea. That sea is the guiding principle of "Penelope." And Molly Bloom performs its sovereign rites. Her body is the medium through which life passes, and all the men she either knows or fantasizes about are just so many vehicles for this indispensable traffic. The chapter is written in such a way as to highlight the interchangeable males who do her service, so that her memory of a wonderful kiss is linked to a "he," a fellow named Gardner, and also her hope that "hell" be coming on Monday, obliging the reader to grasp that three distinct-yet-indistinct males are in play here: Bloom (whose remembered embrace triggers this sequence), then Gardner, and then Boylan ("hell" meaning: he will: meaning: Boylan on Monday). Molly needs men, needs—to put it crassly—fertilizing. When the need comes, a male is wanted, any male, someone that you could stretch out and let yourself go with. Her wants are given as seasonal myth, for she realizes she is always this way in the spring, that nature should ideally follow suit, by granting her a new male to mate with, on a regular annual basis.

So it is fitting that she mixes up her lovers of the past, forgetting their proper names, and that she fantasizes about an endless series of anonymous young men to be summoned to service her, to embrace her "20 times a day" so that she'll look young and be perennially loved and in love. In this she is truly Bloom's mate, Bloom who, if he had smiled upon entering his bed, would have done so because of the same serial scheme, the same anonymous parade of lovers whose individual contours mean nothing, who live by entering the flow. But whereas Bloom is quizzical, Molly is longing.

ENTERING THE WINE-DARK SEA

To be loved incessantly is the supreme gambit for staying young. And it is doomed. Even Molly Bloom cannot stay forever young. She, like her husband and Stephen Dedalus, has a past that can be remembered, but cannot be repossessed or escaped. In that past are lovers, but also her dead child, Rudy, whose first cry was a "deathwatch . . . ticking" and whose death made it clear to her there'd never be another. There is pathos in Joyce's rendition of Molly, especially in some of her sadder moves, such as posting letters to herself out of loneliness. Yet, in her final fantasies about a potential affair with Stephen Dedalus—imagined reeling with pleasure, half-fainting under her, then writing about her as he breaks into fame—we see a paean to desire itself, desire that fights against time, desire that is ever on the side of life.

And in her menstrual flow, imaged by Joyce repeatedly as the sea, the wine-dark sea, we encounter the fertility principle still intact (Boylan has not impregnated her, despite Bello's prediction; she could still conceive). And we also see here, in Molly's rich flow of memory as well as blood, the fullness of consciousness itself, that grand space so beautifully and unforgettably charted in *Ulysses*. Joyce closes this chapter and this book with a truly dazzling rendition of Molly's wayward reminiscences and musings, thinking of her early lovers, thinking of Bloom, whom she was prepared to accept, also thinking of how much he did not know, finally bequeathing to us (in pure Proustian fashion) a vista of her entire Gibraltar past with its physical splendor and its fateful conclusion. There is little in *Ulysses* that matches the outpourings—images, feelings, blood—of Molly's final soliloquy. Again the sea is evoked—crimson, ablaze in the sunset—but we also see fig trees and gardens and streets and houses all awash in color, and flowers, especially flowers: not only jessamine and geraniums, but the young Molly herself, the "Flower of the mountain" who had a rose in her hair and a lover in her arms, and she thought, yes, he'll do as well as another, and her eyes spoke, asking that he ask once more, and he did ask once more, wanting her to say yes, so she enfolded him in her arms and drew him to her, "so he could feel my breasts all perfume yes and his heart was going like mad and yes I said yes I will Yes" (644).

Much has been made of Joyce closing his opus with the word "Yes." It is possible to find Molly Bloom, at times, petulant (as seen in her ever-vigilant concern for people trying to "get around" her), even bitchy (as she herself acknowledges all women are). But for readers of *Ulysses*, Molly's grand soliloquy is the supreme closing gambit, the immensely satisfying final stop in an epic voyage. Here, as elsewhere, our efforts are rewarded with gold, this time in a sensuous, vital, carnal manner that confers on this book the weight and authority of flesh, the final anchor it deserves. The Odyssean reader finds here, more than in the preceding chapter, a true "Ithaca," a homecoming into the rich elements of body and flesh that underlie and give gravity to human life. Hers is, in some sense, the voice of the earth and its primal forces, and that voice—uncensored, shrewd, alert, at one with itself and with the materials of which life is made—adds immeasurably to our own stock, our own story.

She countersigns the book, as Joyce himself said, into eternity. For this final entry into flesh is also an entry into blood, into the flow: out of the book and into the world. I think we exit her chapter, her "womb-vision," transformed, because she is large, vital, and generous, and she, more even than Bloom, is at one with the flowing elements that fuel *Ulysses*, the pulsating stream that animates both consciousness and flesh, that speaks in its various tongues in chapter after chapter. No writer has ever quite matched James Joyce in his rendition of this double flow. Molly Bloom concludes the parade, and that is how we conclude: Consciousness and flesh are voiced in this book with a mix of wit and passion that does honor to our species. Negotiating the Joycean music is not easy or without trials, but it is a properly Odyssean experience, and it awakens its readers to the poetry and vitality—writ large, writ small, writ everywhere—of everyday life, thanks to the magic of art.

VIRGINIA WOOLF

MRS. DALLOWAY

and

TO THE LIGHTHOUSE

YOUR SPREAD-OUT STORY

One of the basic contentions of this book is that each of us has an inner story that eludes ordinary notation. Both Proust and Joyce show us just how enormous this realm of consciousness, memory, and the past might be: a vast space within, housing our prior selves and flowing feelings. Reading, I have argued, constitutes a form of exploration that is tantamount to self-discovery, for we emerge from these books with a heightened sense of our own reaches. Yet, this view of the self as world can seem like a forbiddingly private affair, in which the individual human being comes across as a huge but swollen and isolated figure. Virginia Woolf shares this view of the dimensional self, and it seems fair to say that no writer has ever gone further inward in their depictions of consciousness than she has. But, her enduring greatness as a writer rests, in large part, on a vision of human feeling and human behavior that is shockingly *social.* Going "in," we learn from Woolf's wonderful novels, also means going "out," and hence her grand theme is human relationship: human relationship understood as a collective proposition, as a stunningly public proposition. "Relationship" is ultimately too stifling a term; "interrelationship," however clumsy the word may seem, better characterizes the actual life we lead. The self is spread out. The self is inhabited. The self lives in and through others.

Do not for a minute think that this is some touchy-feely picture of human reality, some sweet scheme in which nice people think about one another. Woolf can be as steely as any writer that ever lived, and her social vision has nothing to do with kindness and caring; it is a structural matter:

We only exist in relation. Thus, in her great novel *Mrs. Dalloway*, we will discover that one's individual contours count for very little. You cannot take the measure of Clarissa Dalloway without bringing London itself into your mesh; you cannot see Clarissa's character without consulting those who know and love or hate her; you cannot understand her most personal longings until you grasp what a *party* signifies. Likewise, the fuller dimensions of Mrs. Ramsay—the unforgettable central figure of *To the Lighthouse*—are located in the astonishing force field she animates: the feelings, thoughts, and desires of husband, children, friends, guests, and all who knew her. This force field not only outreaches her, but outlives her. The ramifications of this vision for you and for me are enormous: Our story is not merely lodged in us, but is also out there, to be found in people and places beyond ourselves, continues its life even after our death. This is the revolutionary Woolf, for she wrecks any view of enclosure that we might entertain: enclosed by body or mind or even class or gender. And yet, her vision is—profoundly and prophetically—a woman's vision, a bold vision that reconfigures how we live and where we live. It does so by showing us that the models we have subscribed to are male models, and that those male lenses have blinded us to the actual traffic and reach of human consciousness. And it is a woman's vision as well, by dint of its unforgettable lyricism, at once tender and fierce, proffering images for our comings and goings and interactions such as few of us have ever before encountered. Identity itself is reconceived in her work.

WOOLF UP-FRONT

Whereas Proust and Joyce have each left us essentially a single monumental achievement—*Remembrance of Things Past* and *Ulysses*—I have elected to pair two of Virginia Woolf's greatest fictions, *Mrs. Dalloway* and *To the Lighthouse*, as joint evidence of her revolutionary achievements in the world of fiction, and in the world of her readers. Here at last we encounter a woman's voice—lyrical, metaphoric, attuned to both flesh and fantasy, bent on voicing the untold story of throbbing consciousness—and the upshot is a new world altogether. Woolf brings to visibility and audibility sensations and vistas that are at once under and above the radar screen of male writers. If one thinks that this is merely domestic, then one is obliged to think again: Woolf is outright Shakespearean in her grandeur, and she shows us that we've been fooled by our own categories, that events such as a party or a dinner among friends can have the resonance, dignity, and metaphysical power that we might ascribe, say, to Lear on the heath.

Mrs. Dalloway is her grand tribute to London, and we will see how magisterial her use of the city frame is, how she orchestrates encounters—both successful and failed—between her players who inhabit the same urban space; but we are also helped to a vision of our own interconnectedness with all those who share our stage, and this recognition goes a long way toward rupturing our fond notions of individual hegemony and private contour. On the contrary, interrelationship would seem to be her great theme: not just physical contact, but rather the dance of others, especially loved ones, in our own minds. No one, not even Joyce, rivals Woolf when it comes to charting the meandering course of human fantasy, of the daydreams and scattershot ruminations that occupy us—occupy us in every sense of the word—on a 24/7 basis, but which narrative literature has rarely taken into account. Woolf is out to choreograph just this.

And she is also Proust's equal regarding the play of time and memory in human affairs. But, unlike the egocentric French writer, Woolf offers us a more generous view of the human dance, of the ways in which others are present within us; hence, the crucial happening in *Mrs. Dalloway* is Clarissa's grand party, what she calls her "offering," as if to show that bringing isolated human beings together were the most essential (and overlooked) requirement of our species. This social injunction has a special heart-tug here, inasmuch as the novel is about fifty-year-olds experiencing the entropic work of time, wondering if they have lived right, if they have kept their souls alive. As someone well over fifty, I do not think that Woolf's query is an idle one, or an easily answered one. But let no one think this novel is keyed merely to social rituals; despite its aura of elegance and refinement, it is as sharp and unflinching an account of horrors—those of society, those of nature—as any book I've ever read, and we shall see that the Great War, with its news of carnage and chaos, punctuates a good bit of this urban tale. But it cuts still deeper even than that, and Woolf stages, in the tragic figure of Septimus Smith, a war survivor who kills himself, an unforgettable rendition of the two greatest terrors Woolf herself faced: incomprehension by others and outright madness itself, madness now seen as the very badge of artistic vision. You close this book with a chastened sense of human vulnerability and ruin, and an appreciation of why gathering the living together matters.

To the Lighthouse, Woolf's masterpiece about her own parents, is at once narrower, deeper, and more tragic in its scope. This beautiful novel has, I think, an aura about it that few other works of fiction possess, and those who love it—I am among them—place it in a category by itself. Its central figure is Mrs. Ramsay, at once earth mother and spiritual goddess, entrancing all who come within her ambit with her beauty and power. All too often, such claims ring empty, but this book has a shocking performative character, so that we *see* Mrs. Ramsay's grace and authority, and we see it from the perspective of those others who are mesmerized, nourished, and altered by it. Woolf's account of her parents has left us with a virtually archetypal depiction of marriage, of marriage as the strangest imaginable ballet between two distinct species, men and women, and I know of no other fiction that brings to the page the humor, poetry, failure, and beauty of love as movingly as this one does. We will nonetheless be struck by the unflinching honesty and brutality of Woolf's novel: Love is at once threatened and undone by a host of brutal forces that no amount of courage or goodwill can vanquish, forces ranging from the innate one of incomprehension to the still more grisly one of death itself.

But Woolf's most astonishing move is to be found in the boundless fluidity that she posits as the elemental core of self, famously defined as a "wedge-shaped core of darkness." With this notation, we realize both the largeness of Woolf's enterprise and the factitiousness of our own categories and concepts, since "identity" is being imploded, turned liquid and strange, in front of our eyes. The gnawing question at the heart of this bottomless book is: How to take the measure of those we love? How to do it when they are living, and how to do it when they are dead? I can think of nothing more solemn yet pedestrian than this injunction; for it is an injunction, a very old one, that says: We owe this to the human family. What it does not quite say, however, is how lax and amnesiac most of us are concerning those we love. Nor does it say how painful, as well as wonderful, it can be to recover our dead, to realize they are not dead. *To the Lighthouse* hallows the small things, such as a dinner party in a secluded summer house, but it meets, head-on, the big things, such as the depradations of war and death as they go about dismantling the family; and, at the end, as we exit, it leaves a unique flavor in our mouths and minds, through its Orpheus-like efforts to bring the dead back to the living, be it through memory or gesture or art.

THE SLIPPERY MRS. WOOLF

In the final pages of her well-nigh definitive biography, *Virginia Woolf* (1996), Hermione Lee remarks on the evolving nature of Woolf's reputation over the course of the past seventy-five years, saying that each generation reformulates her story: "She takes on the shape of difficult modernist preoccupied with questions of form, or comedian of manners, or neurotic highbrow aesthete, or inventive fantasist, or pernicious snob, or Marxist feminist, or historian of women's lives, or victim of abuse, or lesbian heroine, or cultural analyst, depending on who is reading her, and when, and in what context" (Lee, 758). It is, of course, a truism to say that each generation reinvents Shakespeare, but I believe the Woolf phenomenon is virtually unique in Western culture. The other figures in this book—Proust, Joyce, Faulkner, and Morrison—are also rich and multifaceted (and, to be sure, their stock goes up and goes down over time), yet they seem downright stolid and fixed in comparison to the mercurial and chameleonic Woolf, an author who seems to have touched the very nerves of both modern women and modern life, to have been a model and a standard-bearer for her epoch and for ours as well, including many of the folks in between.

This question of identity is all the more gnawing when it comes to an appreciation of her finest novels—*Mrs. Dalloway* and *To the Lighthouse*—written in the 1920s, fluid, kaleidoscopic, judgment-shy, restless, gesturing, hungry, dazzling books that stay with us, disclose only some of their secrets, make the entire project of criticism into something embarrassingly artificial and rigid. How do you package flowing water? Streaming light? The actual pulse of life? As you can see, her two great mid-career novels are where I find her at her most expansive and magical and luminous. It is here that we shall see our own story wondrously refracted and reconceived. It is here that we best make her ours.

Yet, Virginia Woolf was very much a figure of her own historical moment, even of the moment that preceded her, that of the Great Victorians. It is not for nothing that she was the daughter of the prominent author Leslie Stephen, and her lifelong struggle with much of the patriarchal legacy he left her strengthens (rather than weakens) the case that she too was marked by the powerful currents of nineteenth-century Britain. And it seems necessary to add that Virginia Woolf probably has detractors, that some readers may find her fictions self-indulgent, classbound, linked to the manners and mannerisms of a certain Cambridge/Bloomsbury/bluestocking high culture that flowered in the first decades of the twentieth century. Let me go further. The two novels that I propose as her best, as most deserving of our scrutiny or rediscovery in the twenty-first century, have as their central plots either a society party or a gathering at a summer house. Are truly significant things going to happen in precincts like this?

It is instructive to consider Michael Cunningham's successful contemporary novel *The Hours* and its still more popular film version with Meryl Streep, Julianne Moore, and Nicole Kidman, for some illumination here. *The Hours* certainly proves that Woolf is alive and well today, but it does so by cunningly extending the story of Clarissa Dalloway into not only the story of (the quietly imploding) Mrs. Brown in the conformist nineteen-fifties but culminating in a Clarissa of our time, located now in New York, explicitly lesbian but ever loyal to her own Richard, a Septimus-Richard who is dying of AIDS. With considerable savvy, Cunningham has at once tapped into the Woolf reservoir and also shrewdly updated her, helped us to see that her issues and life are still playing. Even here, a skeptic might ask: Where are the grand issues? Woolf's reply would be: "Grand issues" may well lie in places you never suspected.

WOMEN'S TOPICS VERSUS MEN'S TOPICS

Virginia Woolf was acutely aware of the way her work might be seen or categorized. She was, we know, deeply anxious on this front, was wounded by criticism, almost always suspected she had failed; but she was also clairvoyant about the kinds of reasons that would be advanced in rebutting or rejecting her work. Often enough, these reasons testify to biases so deep-seated that we take them as "natural." Our judgments stem all too often from prejudices and blind spots, from uncritical assumptions as to what is important and what is frivolous. Here is how Woolf herself put it:

> Speaking crudely, football and sport are "important"; the worship of fashion, the buying of clothes "trivial." And these values are inevitably

> transferred from life to fiction. This is an important book, the critic assumes, because it deals with war. This is an insignificant book because it deals with the feelings of women in a drawing-room. A scene in a battlefield is more important than a scene in a shop—everywhere and much more subtly the difference of value persists. (*Room*, 74)

The work of Virginia Woolf challenges and complicates this simplistic schema by helping us see that a scene in a drawing room could indeed be as serious as a scene on a battlefield. Better yet, a book such as *Mrs. Dalloway* goes further still, by teaching us that the drawing room is a battlefield, that the reality of war is to be found in shops and at parties, and that we will need an entirely new kind of standard if we are to see and gauge what she has wrought. In this, she is the most iconoclastic figure in this book. She makes us see the male pecking order at work in Proust and Joyce (her contemporaries) and in Faulkner (her successor by a few years): Proust is at great pains to depict social desire as error and self-betrayal, as set against the great artistic calling; Joyce relishes the portrait of the group in Dublin, yet his trio of Stephen, Bloom, and Molly are ultimately loners, working out their fates, mulling over their pasts; Faulkner reveres the social bonds that cohere his "postage stamp of soil" in Mississippi, yet his great art is devoted to the plaint and tragedy of those who cannot fit in, who transgress, who go under. None of this male trio believes much in parties.

Woolf's view of the human enterprise—at times snide or contemptuous, limited in its economic and class range—possesses a strange generosity beyond the reach or imagination of any of the males, because its central given is, as I've said, relationship. This elemental social fact (a fact, again, that lies all too often below the radar screen of male writers) constitutes the field in which individual consciousness (with its own fateful heights and depths) lives (and dies). It is a plenary vision. Finally, in the company of the other writers discussed in this book, Woolf gives up nothing by centralizing human relationship: Her grasp of time and memory (and their pathos) rivals Proust's, her sense of social comedy and of city-art (London lives in *Mrs. Dalloway* as much as Dublin does in *Ulysses*) is as saucy and bold as Joyce's, and her depiction of the outsider's despair and the scapegoat's execution matches anything Faulkner wrote.

MRS. DALLOWAY: PLUNGING INTO LIFE

"Mrs. Dalloway said she would buy the flowers herself" (3). To begin a book on this note is to toss down a gauntlet, it seems to me. Woolf is signaling quite clearly the kind of acts that will matter in this novel, and buying flowers is one of them. The leading (serious) newspaper in the (serious) city where I am writing these lines—Stockholm and its *Dagens Nyheter*—cited just those opening words of *Mrs. Dalloway* in one of its February 2004 quotations of the day, with the explanation that Virginia Woolf's view of flowers and life was one to remember in the dark Swedish winter, as the light slowly comes back. (I was impressed; this woman's vision was lighting my own stage.) Mrs. Dalloway will buy the flowers herself because her servant Lucy has her hands full, with preparations for tonight's party. Moreover, it is such a beautiful summer morning: "fresh as if issued to children on a beach" (3). The goodness of life is handed to us, "issued" as part of nature's carefree contract, and nothing can be more serious than to receive this gift as it deserves, as if we were still children on a beach. "What a lark! What a plunge!" (3) Clarissa feels, and remembers plunging earlier, at Bourton, as a young girl, reverencing the summer-morning air, yet feeling even then "solemn, feeling as she did, standing there at the open window, that something awful was about to happen" (3). It is signature Woolf. Life is so overwhelming in its bounty that we must plunge, yet both the bounty and the plunging are as much fearsome as delightful. Where will the plunge take us? Kierkegaard described the spiritual life as a leap of faith; might it be closer to the mark for secular readers to learn to plunge?

A few pages later, as Clarissa walks through the humming city, remembering her past, thinking about her party, looking at the omnibuses in Piccadilly, Woolf writes: "She sliced like a knife through everything; at the same time was outside, looking on. She had a perpetual sense, as she watched the taxi cabs, of being out, out, far out to sea and alone; she always had the feeling that it was very, very dangerous to live even one day" (8). There is something of a double-edged sword (forgive the cliché) in Woolf's take on things. All is heightened, both inside and outside: the splendor of the scene, the wonder of seeing it, the no less sharp certainty of separation, of being only a witness, of experiencing things "like a knife," of being exile and castaway, of knowing that exactly this intensity of perception might be our undoing. The image of the sea, of being alone and threatened with drowning, haunts Woolf's work and her life; we will see more of it.

LONDON ANTHEM

But one gets this novel wrong if the emphasis is put too squarely on what is foreboding, because you then miss what is so spectacularly alive and celebratory: namely just *being*. Especially, at least here, being in London. Clarissa experiences this pleasure as something so elemental and "prior" that it preexists reasons and explanations, is astonishingly democratic in its workings, affects one and all in the same way that breath and light do: "Heaven only knows why one loves it so, how one sees it so, making it up, building it round one, tumbling it, creating it every moment afresh; but the veriest frumps, the most dejected of miseries sitting on doorsteps (drink their downfall) do the same; can't be dealt with, she felt positive, by Acts of Parliament for that very reason: they love life" (4). Note the give-and-take here, the way in which all creatures swim in life, mesh with it, take it in, and make it up, all in the same rhythm. One shares the stage, one co-breathes the air, one's eyes and ears are filled with others' lives. One's story is public.

Dr. Johnson memorably observed, centuries earlier, that a man tired of London is a man tired of living, and it is a sentiment that Woolf both shares and reproduces. Despite its appearance as a party book, *Mrs. Dalloway* reminds us why cities are special and how their energy is infectious. We have been taught to see certain masterworks of Modernism, such as Joyce's *Ulysses* and Eliot's "The Waste Land" as particularly urban in their form—a vision of the "new" that goes back to Baudelaire—and Woolf very much belongs in this lineup. Not merely that London is present in her book, but that it frames her book, punctuates the chapters via the sounds of Big Ben, and, above all, in ways more giddy and enlivening than anything in Joyce or Eliot, *fuels* her story, breathes vigor, sap, and pith into it much the way a blood transfusion brings life into the human creature. Here is how Woolf writes the carnival: "In people's eyes, in the sing, tramp and trudge; in the bellow and the uproar; the carriages, motor cars, omnibuses, vans, sandwich men shuffling and swinging; brass bands; barrel organs; in the triumph and the jingle and the strange high singing of some aeroplane overhead was what she loved: life; London; this moment of June" (4).

If one were looking for antecedents to this kind of prancing prose, "the sing, tramp and trudge," we'd have to go back to Whitman's magnificent poems about the splendor rough-and-tumble of Brooklyn. But whereas the American poet enclosed his tribute within the visionary lines of poetry, Woolf is out to tap into all this energy as a narrative circuit, as a kinetic stream that flows into the lives of all the inhabitants, leading to a kind of hydra-headed fiction, a city-text that looks at times like a ballet, in which the specific players are all nourished by the same sense of wonder and power. The singing airplane puts the appropriate modernist stamp on this city-portrait, and makes visible Woolf's own project: to break free of the customary bounds of time and space.

Moreover, that plenary vision I referred to has its sights pastward as well as futureward, can see London "as the Romans saw it, lying cloudy, when they landed, and the hills had no names and rivers wound they knew not where" (24), can remember "when the pavement was grass, when it was swamp" and can foresee even a terrible time when "death's enormous sickle" will have struck, turning the earth into "a mere cinder of ice" (81). London sings its "ancient song," its "old bubbling burbling song" in this novel, rising up through the tube station, "soaking through the knotted roots of infinite ages" (81), bathes all human doing and thinking in its murmur and vitality. Later in the novel, Mrs. Dalloway's daughter Elizabeth, out on her own, doing her adolescent version of "lark" and "plunge," walks toward St. Paul's and feels "the geniality, sisterhood, motherhood, brotherhood of this uproar," feels part of an astonishing parade, "as in the rough stream of a glacier the ice holds a splinter of bone, a blue petal, some oak trees, and rolls them on" (138). Step outside your door, Woolf seems to be saying, and realize that you are swimming in history, that civilization is a flowing, wavelike proposition, lapping you, nourishing you, bombarding you with stimuli.

Woolf structures her book according to this pulsing environmental logic. Thus, London is a magnet: It attracts outsiders such as Maisie Johnson, who finds something queer and disturbing in the spectacle of Septimus and Rezia in Regent Park, such as the Morrises from Liverpool, who are much taken with the worldly Peter Walsh, whom they meet at the hotel. And of course it brings back those who have left its precincts, so that Sally Seton and Peter Walsh—the two key players in Clarissa's emotional past—

are seemingly whisked from their far-flung posts in Manchester and India, to be brought, as if by special delivery, to the novel's central event, the party.

Much has been made of the way Big Ben unifies this novel, how its hourly chimes parse the events of the story, and how Woolf's repeated description of this effect—"the leaden circles dissolved in the air"—seems almost like a structural formula for the novel at large. Michael Cunningham rightly uses as epigraph for his novel *The Hours* Woolf's diary entry of August 30, 1923, showing just how resonant and far-reaching these circles might be: "I should say a good deal about The Hours, & my discovery; how I dig out beautiful caves behind my characters . . . The idea is that the caves shall connect, & each comes to daylight at the present moment" (*Diary* 2). There is something quite wonderful in this fusion of the spatial and the temporal, the inside and the outside. Woolf as author claims to dig out the caves, but her image also conveys that each one of us is a cavern, is possessed of underground reaches, reaches that flow into one another, connecting your depth with mine. With the formal aptness of a classical dramatist, Woolf perfectly observes the famous unities of time and space, so that her entire story unfurls in one day, in one place, much the way Joyce's *Ulysses* (which she was reading then) does. As with Joyce (as with Sophocles and Racine, for that matter), this outward frame is illusory, inasmuch as the novel incessantly brings other places and other times into its mix, yet *Mrs. Dalloway* derives great benefits from its fixed stage. Its characters bump into one another, construe and misconstrue what they are witnessing, reappear, come together, separate.

INTERRELATIONSHIP

But whereas the traditional urban story emphasizes encounter, sometimes romantic, sometimes violent, whereby major players intersect or collide with one another, Woolf's great theme is interrelationship; her characters are unbounded, connected, invested, staggeringly mobile, traveling to and from one another at will, sometimes uncontrollably. It is a mistake to think of this as some sort of generosity or sympathy. On the contrary, there is nothing volitional in play; this is the natural state of things in her fluid world. Hence, Clarissa cohabits with other Londoners both inwardly and outwardly, both knowingly and unconsciously. The presumable contours that delineate all of us—making me me, you you; making individual forms visible; conferring on human life the shapes we have always taken for granted—all go up in smoke in Woolf's scheme. As she said in her diary, the caves connect. Here is what Clarissa feels:

> . . . what she loved was this, here, now, in front of her; the fat lady in the cab. Did it matter then, she asked herself, walking toward Bond Street, did it matter that she must inevitably cease completely; all this must go on without her; did she resent it; or did it not become consoling to believe that death ended absolutely? But that somehow in the streets of London, on the ebb and flow of things, here, there, she survived, Peter survived, lived in each other, she being part, she was positive, of the trees at home; of the house there, ugly, rambling all to bits and pieces as it was; part of people she had never met; being laid out like a mist between the people she knew best, who lifted her on their branches as she had seen the trees lift the mist, but it spread ever so far, her life, herself. (9)

It follows, then, that our knowledge of one another must be a peculiarly collective affair, "So that to know her, or anyone, one must seek out the people who completed them; even the places" (152–153).

This view of connection does not, however, rule out the possibility of error, of horrendous error even, as we note when Peter Walsh, seeing Septimus and Rezia in the park, interprets her agony as mere lover's squabble, or when he hears the ambulance carrying the dead Septimus away and then sings the praises of English "efficiency" and "communal spirit." Nonetheless, we become fellow travelers with these characters in an unusual way because they themselves are fellow travelers. Woolf's books portray an incessant human traffic, a nonstop entry-exit scheme in which people think about one another, imagine one another, inhabit one another. Listen inside, she seems to be saying, and you perceive others' sounds, others' lives.

THE OTHER AS MY PORTRAITIST AND SCRIBE

One of the most striking features of *Mrs. Dalloway* is the extent to which its exquisite portraiture is almost always done by others, that so very much of what we are to know of Clarissa and Peter and Septimus does not come from them, but from those who love them, live with them, think about them. Something quite remarkable about human consciousness is on show here: Namely, consciousness is the field where others live inside us. Far from being the egocentric scheme that one might assume—one's own mind as mirror of one's own thoughts and desires—Woolf's view is strikingly other-directed. One is shocked, in this novel, to realize how deeply others are lodged within the self. I actually believe the remarkable corollary to this model is also implied: On our own, we are oddly alien to ourselves, not fully knowable, certainly not as knowable or fleshed out as we are to those who love us. This seems amazing to me, amazingly counterintuitive, inasmuch as one of the guiding principles of this study is that we alone know our inside story. Woolf does not quite say that is untrue (after all, her people are wonderfully aware of themselves as well), but she does show that our lives are richly and fulsomely—sometimes tragically—both etched and played out in the minds of others.

Hence Peter Walsh is the scribe we consult if we are to know Clarissa. He is the one who remembers what she was like at Bourton during the old days, and he remembers because that is when they were so close, when she broke his heart. And of course it goes the other way as well: Who can tell us about Peter Walsh, "dear old Peter," if not Clarissa, who remembers him with fondness and a tug that is more than fondness, who remembers their intimacy, an intimacy so intense that it had to be denied, had to be denied because neither marriage nor happiness could be compatible, she feared, with such closeness? Could Peter himself tell us these things? Each of us is the expert on our inner pulsions, but the patterns we make and break, the *gestalt* of our lives, are off limits to our vision, require the other's care and gaze. In some odd way, our books are kept by others. I quite realize this argument may seem abstruse, but its stakes matter, because Woolf is showing us that the first person is not only a "we," but is also the memorialist, the portraitist, the living screen on which the lives of others take shape and meaning. Let me illustrate this by citing a particularly beautiful evocation of Clarissa, offered (of course) by Peter late in the novel:

> . . . he saw her most often at Bourton, in the late summer, when he stayed there for a week, or fortnight even, as people did in those days. First on top of some hill there she would stand, hands clapped to her hair, her cloak blowing out, pointing, crying to them—she saw the Sev-

> ern beneath. Or in a wood, making the kettle boil—very ineffective with her fingers; the smoke curtseying, blowing in their faces; her little pink face showing through; begging water from an old woman in a cottage, who came to the door to watch them go. They walked always; the others drove. She was bored driving, disliked all animals, except that dog. They tramped miles along roads. She would break off to get her bearings, pilot him back across country; and all the time they argued, discussed poetry, discussed people, discussed politics (she was a Radical then); never noticing a thing except when she stopped, cried out at a view or a tree, and made him look with her; and so on again, through stubble fields, she walking ahead, with a flower for her aunt, never tired of walking for all her delicacy; to drop down on Bourton in the dusk. Then, after dinner, old Breitkopf would open the piano and sing without any voice, and they would lie sunk in arm-chairs, trying not to laugh, but always breaking down and laughing, laughing—laughing at nothing. (154)

One can always claim that Clarissa herself might not even recognize this vivid, impressionist portrait, but my point goes the other way: She is not equipped—none of us is equipped—to make such a portrait of herself. This evocation does honor, I think, to the notion that we are real for others. Clarissa lives and breathes in these lines, is possessed of a life and poignancy that she herself has no access to. Our shape comes through others. Our story is, oddly enough, in their care.

I am happy to acknowledge that biographical truth counts for very little in these matters. For starters, how could there even be such a thing? But surely this is Peter's truth about the woman he loved. Nor do I claim that intimacy results from such thinking; if anything, we sense that our (profound) images of those we love are locked inside us, are largely unsharable. Yet that is the currency of our lives. Consider, in this regard, Richard Dalloway's feelings for his wife. Richard is sketched rather breezily in this novel, but nowhere is he more embodied than in the sequence following his luncheon at Lady Bruton's with Hugh Whitbread; it will be recalled that he follows, almost in torpor (processing that formidable luncheon), Hugh into a jewelry store, is aghast at Hugh's fatuousness, feels the urge to bring some kind of a gift home to Clarissa for her party, realizes ever more forcefully, more unhingingly, how much he loves her, how miraculous his life is, buys flowers, pledges to actually tell her what he feels. But does he? No. She seems distracted, is irritated by having to invite (the dull) Ellie Henderson at the last moment, but of course is happy to receive his flowers, tells him "how lovely" they are. They exchange a few mundane words. He cannot say, "I love you." He must be off. Woolf writes this gentle comedy of spoken/unspoken in the following way:

> He must be off, he said, getting up. But he stood for a moment as if he were about to say something; and she wondered what? Why? There were the roses.
>
> "Some Committee?" she asked, as he opened the door.
>
> "Armenians," he said; or perhaps it was "Albanians."
>
> And there is a dignity in people; a solitude; even between husband and wife a gulf; and that one must respect, thought Clarissa, watching him open the door [. . .] (119–120)

Richard leaves. Clarissa reflects further: "He was already halfway to the House of Commons, to his Armenians, his Albanians, having settled her on the sofa, looking at his roses" (120). Then follows what I take to be evidence—if such were needed—of Woolf's astounding knowledge of human relationships: their imperfections, their stammering quality, their reality. Clarissa cannot help being Clarissa:

> She cared much more for her roses than for the Armenians. Hunted out of existence, maimed, frozen, the victims of cruelty and injustice (she had heard Richard say so over and over again)—no, she could feel nothing for the Albanians, or was it the Armenians? but she loved her roses (didn't that help the Armenians?)—the only flowers she could bear to see cut. (120)

There will be readers who do not much like this passage. Clarissa will stand convicted by them of her superficialness. Large political concerns are ignored, made a hash of. And yet, this fuzzy, static-filled exchange, with its kooky afterthoughts ("didn't that help the Armenians?"), conveys the actual texture of human encounter, of how close together we come and how far apart we remain, how our own ego is invariably in the way, is the filter through which "you" get into "me." And yet, one does get in. This (failed?)

encounter is saturated with tenderness and mutuality, even if we are doomed to playing blindman's bluff all our lives.

YOUR STORY: WHIMSICAL, ELASTIC, FANTASTIC

Woolf can be quite arch in these matters, quite drawn to the fantasy dimensions of our thinking and our intercourse with others. And this is because the mind is as happily engaged in whimsy as it is in truth, that what really counts for it is the voyage of rumination itself. It is a trip one takes by oneself, even if others constitute our itinerary. Peter takes it, standing in Trafalgar Square, after his surprise visit with Clarissa, a visit that closed with tears and a clumsy exit. No one can match Woolf in charting this type of excursion. It begins with Peter's shocked recognition of his own project, his reason for being in London now—to see his lawyers about Daisy's divorce so he can bring her from India and marry her—being just so much twaddle, a house of cards that simply collapses under its own weight (and under the clear light of London day): "What is it? Where am I? And why, after all, does one do it? he thought, the divorce seeming all moonshine. And down his mind went flat as a marsh" (52).

You might expect such a discovery to be painful, unhinging: After all, the man has come across the globe in order to actualize this divorce scheme. For most of us this would be a serious downer. But perhaps our actual story is more elastic, more supple, more open-ended and capricious than we think. Could fixed agendas be actually weightless and discardable, like papier-mâché? Watch Peter: He experiences the collapse of his design as "an irrepressible, exquisite delight; as if inside his brain by another hand strings were pulled, shutters moved, and he, having nothing to do with it, yet stood at the opening of endless avenues, down which if he chose he might wander. He had not felt so young for years" (52).

House of cards collapsed, time now to wander down one of those avenues. Which is precisely what Peter does, in a lovely illustration of the human freedom that bathes us all day long, even in tight corners. He sees a young woman, follows her through the London streets, fantasizes her being what fate has long had in store for him, feels that she is beckoning him, encouraging him, imagines her as kind and tender and witty, thinks of himself as a "buccaneer," and finally sees her enter into a house "of vague impropriety." End of daydream. End of the Woolfian imperative that opens the book: "What a lark, what a plunge." But (we remind ourselves, we pinch ourselves) facts are ultimately real, and we ultimately collide with them. How does Peter react to this (second) collapse? Much of Virginia Woolf's wisdom and scope is displayed here:

> Well, I've had my fun; I've had it, he thought . . . And it was smashed to atoms—his fun, for it was half made up, as he knew very well; invented, this escapade with the girl; made up, as one makes up the better part of life, he thought—making oneself up; making her up; creating an exquisite amusement, and something more. But odd it was, and quite true; all this one could never share—it smashed to atoms. (54)

I'd want to call this an "experimental" attitude toward life. Also, as this passage suggests, there is a strange hedonism at work as well, a gaiety that comes from indulging in fantasy, a gaiety that seems to know, from the beginning, the fictiveness of these arrangements, and is hence unshaken when they dissolve into thin air. Such a mind-set is geared to whimsy and ruminations of considerable vigor and scope, especially good at portraiture and dramatic scenes. Peter's day in London turns out to be corrosive, of course, since a goodly number of his earlier designs "smash to atoms," but they do so in almost theatrical, playable fashion.

Woolf is often thought of as especially gifted at female characters, but the rendition of Peter Walsh is one of the novel's great triumphs. Some critics have thought Peter sentimental—as indeed he can be, when he is purring to himself about the achievements of old England—but what most matters (to us as readers) is the extraordinarily "overheard" consciousness of the man, a buzzing neural activity that Woolf traces to perfection as he mulls over the drawbacks of his arrangements with Daisy. A friend, Mrs. Burgess, has warned him that their great age difference (almost thirty years) will eventually cause problems for Daisy, leaving her a widow with a damaging past. Here is how Peter continues to reflect on these matters:

> But Peter Walsh pooh-poohed all that. He didn't mean to die yet. Anyhow she must settle for herself; judge for herself, he thought, padding about the room in his socks, smoothing out his dress-shirt, for he might go to Clarissa's party, or he might go to one of the Halls, or he might settle in and read an absorbing book written by a man he used to know at

> Oxford. And if he did retire, that's what he'd do—write books. He would go to Oxford and poke about in the Bodleian. Vainly the dark, adorably pretty girl ran to the end of the terrace; vainly waved her hand; vainly cried she didn't care a straw what people said. There he was, the man she thought the world of, the perfect gentleman, the fascinating, the distinguished (and his age made not the least difference to her), padding about a room in an hotel in Bloomsbury, shaving, washing, continuing, as he took up cans, put down razors, to poke about in the Bodleian, and get at the truth about one or two little matters that interested him. And he would have a chat with whoever it might be, and so come to disregard more and more precise hours for lunch, and miss engagements, and when Daisy asked him, as she would, for a kiss, a scene, fail to come up to the scratch (though he was genuinely devoted to her)—in short it might be happier, as Mrs. Burgess said, that she should forget him, or merely remember him as he was in August 1922, like a figure standing at the cross roads at dusk, which grows more and more remote as the dog-cart spins away, carrying her securely fastened to the back seat, though her arms are outstretched, and as she sees the figure dwindle and disappear still she cries out how she would do anything in the world, anything, anything, anything. . . . (157–158)

What a lark! What a plunge! These quite substantial chunks of prose that I am citing in their entirety reveal how elusive and resistant to analysis and hospitable to daydreaming Woolf is, how large a sample you need to take if you want to see exactly what she is doing. This zoom shot into Peter's mind as he mulls over his options, as he pictures both himself and Daisy in their respective roles (himself naturally debonair, charming; Daisy yearning and beseeching), has a Walter Mitty feeling to it, wonderfully conveys the sounds we make to ourselves, the castles in the air that we routinely construct (Peter as dogged intellectual, intent on making his little discoveries, hard-bitten by the intransigent life of the mind; hey, do you believe it for a minute?), delivers the actual beast alive, warts and all. This soap opera appropriately closes in cinematic fashion as life carries Peter away from Daisy.

Life carries. Zeroing in on the mind as she does, Woolf reveals its strange autonomy, its power as driving engine that knows where *it* is going, so that the thinker is really only a passive spectator, watching this melodrama take shape, observing its irresistible conclusion, learning and discovering what he actually thinks. For us as readers, it is no less than a roller coaster. Prose like this jumps out at you, catches you by surprise, makes you realize how strange and unpredictable our thoughts are, our lives are. We do not *lead* our lives, as the cliché would have it; we follow our lives.

Woolf's depictions of consciousness resemble minefields, are larded with booby traps, so that the casual, even cavalier appearance that her work offers is misleading. We scheme and fabulate inwardly at all times, but there is nothing to put your teeth in or even call your own; rather, it all goes in the manner of soap bubbles that take shape, are beautifully iridescent, and then pop. Yes, she is superb at eavesdropping on the small talk that characterizes consciousness, but these mundane matters frequently get out of hand, invert or wreck one's earlier working assumptions, deposit an outright verdict on life. In her books, we go about discovering who we are, where we're going, and how little control we actually have. This model of fiction rejects utterly the traditional plots of earlier novels, largely because every event, every moment (such as buying flowers yourself or sitting in a park) can be an occasion of fireworks and high drama.

THE RETURN OF THE PAST

And yet *Mrs. Dalloway* honors one of the oldest plots in fiction or drama or romance: the return of the past, replete with those players we thought gone. It is as rigorous as Sophocles' story of Oedipus, who, at the end of the play, meets all of the key figures who know his past, who knew him as cast-out infant: the messenger, the shepherd; and only then can the ensuing terrible truth be known for certain. In Woolf's domestic story, there is no abandoned child sent out to die, no parricidal altercation at a crossroads, no riddle of the Sphinx, no crowning of a king, no incestuous marriage. But make no mistake: Her novel is about the significance of the past, about what we were, and what we now are, have become. Freud knew what he was doing when he pounced upon Sophocles' story as emblematic of human behavior: The past shapes us, both visibly and invisibly, in our genes and even in our doings. The cavern-self is deep; its people return.

At the risk of banality, to come down from Sophocles, I now invoke the film *The Big Chill* as a second pertinent analogue to *Mrs. Dalloway*. The film is about a reunion of people in their thirties, occasioned by the suicide of one of their most gifted; the pathos of the story revolves a good bit around the sense of lost promise, of irretrievable youth, as well as the tricks time plays. (Having seen this film when I was in my late forties, I thought these thirty-year-olds—Kevin Kline, Glenn Close, William Hurt, and company—looked awfully fit and trim.) Like the *Oedipus*, this film also sets out to draw our actual contours, to graph the sinuousness of our lifeline, our story line, since today's reality is cued to yesterday's ghosts.

Woolf is considerably more severe in her distribution. Her central characters are, as they note with poignance rather frequently, all in their fifties. They are of course filled with memories of their younger days, and we have already seen how skilled Woolf can be at this type of evocation, as in Peter's memory of Clarissa at Bourton. *Mrs. Dalloway* is orchestrated contrapuntally, interweaving motifs of youth and middle age, and it goes the full route in order to bring this contrast to utmost clarity and urgency: It brings back the two heartthrobs—Peter Walsh and Sally Seton—to London so that they can be at Clarissa's party. It is hard to imagine a more classic showdown: Peter, who loved Clarissa, who inhabits her mind, now walks back into her life in the flesh; still more amazing is the unanticipated reentry of Sally Seton, Clarissa's dearest woman friend, Clarissa's almost-lover, onto the scene as she, too, crashes the party. What better way to dramatize the pulsions of our life story: the clash between past and present, youth and middle age, promise and maturity, desire and reality?

Mrs. Dalloway is no less than a throbbing romance, reveling in its portrayal of stormy passion and emotion, of sexual desire and heartbreak, as located significantly in the past. Here, fueling the plot of lovers' return, is the novel's working chemistry: Clarissa Parry rejected Peter Walsh in order to marry Richard Dalloway; it broke Peter Walsh's heart; Clarissa Parry also had what we'd have to call a passionate crush on Sally Seton, but this too was put behind her in her marriage with Richard Dalloway. Peter and Clarissa, now in their fifties, have never stopped thinking about these crucial might have beens. It would seem we never quite outgrow or jettison our youthful passions.

LOST LOVE: PETER

Clarissa recalls, over and over, Peter's storminess, his vigilant critical attitude toward her ("he could be intolerable; he could be impossible"), yet also their never-to-be-repeated intimacy. He is ever present in her mind: "For they might be parted for hundreds of years, she and Peter; she never wrote a letter and his were dry sticks; but suddenly it would come over her, If he were here with me now what would he say?" (7). Peter examined "people's characters eternally, and the defects of her own soul. How he scolded her! How they argued!" (7). To this day Clarissa is still going over these accounts, this past history, intent on proving to herself (once and for all?) that she had made a wise decision: "So she would still find herself arguing in St. James's Park, still making out that she had been right—and she had been too—not to marry him" (7). Marriage, she says, needs "a little licence, a little independence," and this is what Richard has given her. But the nagging questions remain. Yes, she turned him down—and this was arguably the key event of her life—but the pain hasn't gone away:

> But with Peter everything had to be shared; everything gone into. And it was intolerable, and when it came to that scene in the little garden by the fountain, she had to break with him or they would have been destroyed, both of them ruined, she was convinced; though she had borne about with her for years like an arrow sticking in her heart the grief, the anguish . . . (8)

No reader of this novel can fail to see that Peter Walsh and Clarissa Parry were in love. "In love," this book wisely teaches us, is a poor phrase for capturing the actual nature of human relationships, because our actual linkages with one another are nuanced, multifaceted, and resist simple labels. Nonetheless, what is unmistakable—for us, for Clarissa, for Peter—is that they shared something intimate, intense, turbulent, exciting, and rare. The actual sexual element counts for nothing in this instance. (It will, with Sally.) On the contrary, Peter and Clarissa are, to enlist another cliché, soul mates. They have an *entente*, a closeness, a spontaneity with each other, that makes them natural partners no matter how much they disagree or fight.

That is why Peter's unexpected entry into Clarissa's room on the day of the party is so gripping. Peter, chafing, bursting with things to say about his stint in India, exclaims: " 'I am in love' " (45). Clarissa initially feels that he is a fool, given his age, but this reaction is immediately followed by something fiercer and more painful: "but in her heart she felt, all the same, he is in love. He has that, she felt; he is in love" (45). As Peter then fills in the details—Daisy is young, married to a major in the Indian Army, has two small children; he is here to arrange a divorce—the conversation seems reasonably dispassionate and under control, but then comes, out of nowhere (it seems), the explosion: "and then to his utter surprise, suddenly thrown down by those uncontrollable forces thrown through the air, he burst into tears; wept; wept without the least shame, sitting on the sofa, the tears running down his cheeks" (46).

Here is the primal emotional matter of the novel, of these lives. Something overpowering bursts out of Peter, something elemental, and it is not what we expect in this drawing room with these two composed adults. Woolf writes Clarissa's response in a charged language that combines tenderness and vehemence, joy and regret:

> And Clarissa had leant forward, taken his hand, drawn him close to her, kissed him,—actually had felt his face on hers before she could down the brandishing of silver flashing—plumes like pampas grass in a tropic gale in her breast, which, subsiding, left her holding his hand, patting his knee and, feeling as she sat back extraordinarily at her ease with him and light-hearted, all in a clap it came over her, If I had married him, this gaiety would have been mine all day! (46–47)

It is one of the most moving passages of the novel. One first sees the gentleness and tenderness, as evident in Clarissa's gestures, but soon enough the registers change, as we are informed by the exotic metaphors of silver flashing, plumes like pampas grass, a tropic gale in her breast. With exquisite focus, Woolf maps out this evolving moment, shows us how many pieces it has, how many surprises it has for its own people: The gale subsides, Clarissa feels at ease, and then, exactly like the thunder that soon follows the lightning, "all in a clap it came over her," leading us to the final illumination—"this gaiety would have been mine all day!" What most awes me in this final formulation is the word "gaiety," for I expected something more passionate, perhaps even more somber and unsettling. But, of course, "gaiety" is the right term for naming what is most life-affirming in the intensity of feeling that is brought about here: Being with Peter would have meant living full-throttle and full-pitch all the time (excuse my weak terms here), living at the height of one's feelings, living in a state of continual tempest.

This is life at its keenest. This is what she has said no to. And that is why her final reflections are so appropriate; she realizes she has chosen virginity, stillness, ultimately death: "It was all over for her. The sheet was stretched and the bed narrow. She had gone into the tower alone and left them blackberrying in the sun" (47).

Peter's return makes crystal clear—makes hot and throbbing—what she has lost, what her life might have been like. As for Peter himself, he has always known it. Her refusal of him at Bourton all those years ago haunts him. He returns frequently in his mind to this dire moment in the past when Clarissa turned him down, when Clarissa chose Richard Dalloway. He could see it happening even before the final refusal took place: With preternatural acuity, he knew, from the outset, "she will marry that man." Woolf does not write the full text of their actual break, but what she does write is heartbreaking: "Tell me the truth, tell me the truth," Peter says over and over, but to no avail; Clarissa "was unyielding. She was like iron, like flint, rigid up the backbone" (64). Her only recorded words come at the end: "It's no use. It's no use. This is the end" (64). Peter left that night; he never saw her again. (Until now.) And even now, years later, as he thinks back to that decisive moment when love was lost, all he can say is: "It was awful, he cried, awful, awful!" (64).

LOST LOVE: SALLY

The return to London ushers in these truths, these confirmations, that the choices made many decades ago were fateful, binding, and absolutely present in one's mind even now. The novel's very structure dramatizes these fateful decisions by bringing the lost lovers back for a curtain call. And it is exactly for this reason that Sally Seton must be remembered as the free spirit of the group, the mischievous, unconventional, unpredictable, untrammeled spirit, the one most gloriously alive when young. Sally is (or *was*) all that and more. She was for Clarissa Parry a good bit more: not merely the beautiful, flower-loving, bicycle-riding, cigar-smoking, reckless girl with whom Clarissa was infatuated, but something more sensual, passionate, outright erotic. Among the many turbulent memories of the Bourton past, one especially stands out for Clarissa. It happened when she and Sally were walking together outside:

> Then came the most exquisite moment of her whole life passing a stone urn with flowers in it. Sally stopped; picked a flower; kissed her on the lips. The whole world might have turned upside down! The others disappeared; there she was alone with Sally. And she felt she had been given a present, wrapped up, and told just to keep it, not to look at it—a diamond, something infinitely precious, wrapped up, which, as they walked (up and down, up and down), she uncovered, or the radiance burnt through, the revelation, the religious feeling!—when old Joseph and Peter faced them:
>
> "Star-gazing?" said Peter.
>
> It was like running one's face against a granite wall in the darkness! (35–36)

Here, too, is a smoldering "might have been," a brief taste of something more carnal and more thrilling and more explosive than anything she had previously encountered or ever would again encounter. The metaphor of a present that is wrapped up, that one keeps but does not look at, that is infinitely precious, is hardly a metaphor at all, because we can assume that Clarissa's adult life has followed just this injunction, has kept at arm's length from this sexual memory. And Peter's "star-gazing?" gibe is appropriate as well, inasmuch as the intrinsically lesbian pleasure briefly tasted here will be placed in the outer periphery of Clarissa's universe. Appropriate, too, is the "granite wall" sensation of this pleasure being annihilated, prohibited, for the image reappears like a boomerang when Peter himself later remembers Clarissa's unyielding rejection of himself, "like iron, like flint, rigid up the backbone."

Woolf (whose own sexual experiences, especially her lesbian tryst with Vita Sackville-West, have been the object of furious, virtually prurient scholarly research) is very canny in the way this episode with Sally appears in the novel. It comes a few pages *after* Clarissa has reflected on the coldness and narrowness of her choices and arrangements ("narrower and narrower would her bed be" [31]), leading to a remarkable phrase: "She could not dispel a virginity preserved through childbirth which clung to her like a sheet" (31). That notation of an innate . . . inviolability? . . . untouchability? . . . is followed by obscure references about failing Richard at Cliveden, at Constantinople, leading—the way Woolf always leads, via a process of unfurling and discovery, even self-discovery—to Clarissa's realization that she lacks something essential, "something warm which broke up surfaces and rippled the cold contact of man and woman" (31). I have intentionally cut Woolf's phrase short: It actually concludes with "or of women together," thereby opening still a further door, bringing lesbianism clearly into play. *That,* Clarissa says, she could dimly perceive. It would seem that Clarissa has lesbian leanings but has scruples about them as well "picked up Heaven knows where, or, as she felt, sent by Nature (who is invariably wise)" (31), but leaving her drawn to the intimacy of women (when they confessed to her "some scrape, some folly" [32]). Another teasing sentence about the origins of this interest and desire in her—pity? women's beauty? her own age? the power of scents? of sounds?—comes, almost surprisingly, to its moment of firm truth: "She did undoubtedly then feel what men felt" (32).

There is something remarkably exploratory about this entire sequence, as if one were always uncovering one's own secrets, decoding one's own past and temperament and fate. As if our cave story had depths that we ourselves must descend into, if we are to know what we have become, and why. I have wanted to track this rather insistent exploration of sexual pleasure because I think it is a key ingredient in the small packet of life experiences that Clarissa has said no to. I believe this to be the case because the meditation on (lesbian) desire closes with one of the most exquisite utterances about erotic gratification, erotic *jouissance,* that I have ever read:

> It was a sudden revelation, a tinge like a blush which one tried to check and then, as it spread, one yielded to its expansion, and rushed to the farthest verge and there quivered and felt the world come closer, swollen with some astonishing significance, some pressure of rapture, which split its thin skin and gushed and poured with an extraordinary alleviation over the cracks and sores! Then, for that moment, she had seen an illumination; a match burning in a crocus; an inner meaning almost expressed. But the close withdrew; the hard softened. (32)

Virginia Woolf is in a class by herself when it comes to writing about ecstasy. We will see something very close to this in *To the Lighthouse* as well. The signature style of such writing is its metaphors of rapturous pressure, split skin, gushing, and pouring. Woolf famously wrote, in another context, that language is constitutively unsuited for expressing sensation (as opposed to expressing ideas or even feelings), but passages like this give the lie to her assertion, because they convey (to me) what orgasm feels like, whether it be male or female.

But the passage intrigues for other reasons as well: Note how the description of sheer pleasure is bookended by notations of its brevity, its evanescence, indeed its wilting (as "the hard softened"). We see here a profound awareness of what ecstasy is, and a perhaps still more profound sense of its limits, its rarity, indeed its tiny place within the larger economy of human doings. The match burns in the crocus, the inner meaning is almost expressed, but then life returns in both its immensity and opaqueness; even the cracks and sores, one feels, are permanent, are only momentarily alleviated.

PASSION IN ITS PLACE

The value judgments I have just sketched—pleasure is exquisite but both brief and delimited—are not my own: They are what I take to be the essential meaning and wisdom of *Mrs. Dalloway.* In almost Cubist fashion, this novel is working toward those realizations. This is why the book's plot is so elementary: Bring together a group of sensitive people in their fifties—people with a sharp, almost disabling memory of youthful pleasure, passion, and promise—and watch the fireworks when the two lost lovers miraculously come to the party. Peter returns, Sally returns, yet, oddly enough, their voices are scarcely heard, are simply part of the medley of the party, of the great humming metropolis. (Is it possible that we never have our full say with one another? Never achieve full exchange about the things that matter most?) Still, this does not mean that hard, existential questions about the passing of time are not put. Nor does it mean that these gray-haired figures have no self-doubts about how their lives turned out. One could say that it is their favorite topic of conversation.

We have already noted Clarissa's sense of anguish when Peter comes back, a mix of jealousy about Peter's love life and a rueful sense that she has lost this chance of continual gaiety in her own life. Did she choose wrong? As they were sitting together, a remarkable image came to her of her life taking shape, like a negative being developed, in which shapes and forms change, and we age:

> For she was a child, throwing bread to the ducks, between her parents, and at the same time a grown woman coming to her parents who stood

> by the lake, holding her life in her arms which, as she neared them, grew larger and larger in her arms, until it became a whole life, a complete life, which she put down by them and said, "This is what I have made of it! This!" And what had she made of it? What, indeed? sitting there sewing this morning with Peter. (43)

It is a curious passage. Woolf's mix of registers is on show here: The concrete notation of protected childhood—throwing bread to ducks, between one's parents—is then complicated by the striking image of one's evolving life as something one carries, growing, in one's arms, like a maturing child that must be held and shielded. One is hard put not to think of the children Virginia Woolf never had. She seems to be saying: We birth and nurture our creations, whether children or books or lives; we carry them and sustain their weight forever, yet never quite knowing what they add up to.

WHAT HAVE YOU MADE OF YOUR LIFE?

It is the nagging concern of all these characters: What have I made of it? Is it too much to say that this is what people in their fifties ask themselves? To be sure, the admirable Hugh Whitbread—decent, likable court sycophant—is immune to such queries, but the others are not. Peter knows he has not amounted to much, even though he tries to salvage his conscience: "He had been sent down from Oxford—true. He had been a Socialist, in some sense a failure—true. Still the future of civilisation lies, he thought, in the hands of young men like that; of young men such as he was, thirty years ago" (50). As for the others' opinion of Peter, there is no ambiguity whatsoever: He has come a cropper, has returned to London cadging for a job. Such a verdict comes out very clearly in Lady Bruton's luncheon with Richard and Hugh. But how well has Richard done, for that matter? He never made it into Parliament, that much is certain. Committees are his very life, as Clarissa, Elizabeth, and so many others note; has anything been achieved?

The exchange, late in the novel, between Peter and Sally is cued entirely to questions of this sort. Sometimes it is a cheerful inquiry, such as when Sally, noting that Peter is now "rather shrivelled-looking" (187), but remembering that the Peter of "those days" "was to write," asks the obvious: " 'Have you written?' 'Not a word!' said Peter Walsh, and she laughed"

(187). (Just how funny is this? And how often do we laugh when logically we should weep?) About Clarissa, Sally is more strident in her critique: "How could Clarissa have done it?—married Richard Dalloway? A sportsman, a man who cared only for dogs" (189). Peter loyally defends Richard at this juncture, but has also seen in him Clarissa's downfall throughout the novel. And what about Sally herself, "with her daring, her recklessness"? Clarissa notes at once that "her voice was wrung of its old ravishing richness; her eyes not aglow as they used to be, when she smoked cigars, when she ran down the passage to fetch her sponge bag, without a stitch of clothing on her" (181). Her melodramatic scenes seemed to point to "some awful tragedy; her death; her martyrdom; instead of which she had married, quite unexpectedly, a bald man with a large buttonhole who owned, it was said, cotton mills at Manchester. And she had five boys!" (182).

THE DEATH OF THE SOUL

The passing of time, you might say; what is to be expected? The pathos of the book stems from its worry that the losses are more than just physical. Peter Walsh falls asleep on a park bench, but awakes to the horrid thought that crisscrosses this novel and these people: " 'The death of the soul' " (58). The phrase is initially applied to Clarissa herself, but one sees that it is the nightmare that threatens all Woolf's players. If you have chosen security over passion, distance over intimacy, the social whirl over the spiritual world, you may have lost your soul. If you have been rejected by the one person you loved, if you have squandered your subsequent life with shallow liaisons and have never written a word, you may have lost your soul. If you were the very breath of romance and adventure and feisty independence and are now married to a bald owner of cotton mills at Manchester, you may have lost your soul. These are the questions one asks, the worries one has, at fifty. What are the answers?

To her enormous credit—and to older readers' delight, I suspect—Woolf suggests that age has its virtues, that the passing of time confers as well as removes, that life consists of more than heat, passion, and romance. The soul doesn't die all that easily. Much of the beauty of *Mrs. Dalloway* is ultimately autumnal, on the far side of its fierce memories and its austere reckonings. Yes, tumultuous feelings can be glorious, can be a kind of radiance and—to use Clarissa's word—gaiety, but life is bigger, more capacious than this. Let us revisit the moment when Peter breaks in on Clarissa, causing a pang of regret at how she has lived, at what she has sacrificed (by rejecting Peter, by marrying Richard), leading to her conviction that she has chosen sterility and death: "The sheet was stretched and the bed narrow." This pain reaches its apex when she reflects on the absence of Richard—a distance that seems mutually consented: he with his committees and luncheons, she with her parties—and cries out, in her mind, "Richard, Richard! . . . as a sleeper in the night starts and stretches a hand in the dark for help . . . I am alone for ever, she thought" (47). This sense of anguish and desolation, most keenly expressed in her impulsive desire to go away with Peter "on some great voyage," is nonetheless short-lived, seems, as it were, to burn itself out, yields to a higher clarity about her arrangements. Woolf very consciously chooses the metaphor of *theater* to convey this recognition that incandescent feeling is wondrous yet limited, splendid yet contained within the frames of art, ultimately at odds with real life:

> . . . and then, next moment, it was as if the five acts of a play that have been very exciting and moving were now over and she had lived a lifetime in them and had run away, had lived with Peter, and it was now over.
>
> Now it was time to move, and, as a woman gathers her things together, her cloak, her gloves, her opera-glasses, and gets up to go out of the theatre into the street, she rose from the sofa and went to Peter. (47)

She goes to Peter, yes, but composed, lucid about relative weights and measures, about how much goes to passion versus how much goes to living, wise about the *virtuality* of theater, its way of making a space for the most intense feelings to be indulged and then contained and then gotten past so that one can go on living. One is free to read these lines more critically, of course, to see them as a failure and retreat, as evidence of Clarissa's cowardice and fear of passion. But I prefer to see them as a strange wisdom, as a way of acknowledging the splendor of emotion, of even tasting that emotion, but without taking the next, final, disastrous step of leaping into the maelstrom. Prudence? Maybe. But also a kind of knowledge, not merely about the dangers of feeling, but about what one can manage, what is livable and what is not.

It may be that I have put too fine a face on this. What I am ascribing to personal wisdom might also be seen simply as nature's own resourcefulness, suppleness, flexibility. Clarissa's sense of a missed passional life with Peter as *theater* says a great deal, I think, about the possible factitiousness and unreality of art. Art—literature, theater, opera, the whole shebang—comes, on this head, to be understood as a beautiful, shimmering, extremely useful Never-Never Land, a place where passion rules, where the heart is king, where one is always at one's most intense, most vivid, most exalted. Poems and novels have always sung this siren song to us, have come to us as our yearned-for other homeland, as the realm where glory is possible, where the grayness and constrictions and compromises of life are banished.

Woolf is asking, not only "Is this real?" but also "Could you live there?" And the book suggests that *living* trumps everything, that living puts things into their appropriate places. It is hardly a question of something doctrinal that we might learn in a book or manual. It is, far more profoundly, the secret, unacknowledged, rarely touted lesson that life teaches us every day. Woolf, more than any writer I know, hallows this quotidian wisdom, this shrewd, low-to-the-ground vitality that refuses to take sexual passion or stormy romance all that seriously. Ultimately, Woolf is astonishingly democratic in her take—I claim this in the face of her flagrant cultural and stylistic elitism—because she sees the miracle and majesty of little things; in her work, even the meanest, most inconspicuous elements of life can be conduits of wonder, can be transfigured into something precious and jolting.

To illustrate this point, I return to Peter Walsh in mourning, Peter Walsh suffering (once again) the heartache of having lost Clarissa all those years ago. You remember his words: "It was awful, he cried, awful, awful!" Yet, here is how the next paragraph goes:

> Still, the sun was hot. Still, one got over things. Still, life had a way of adding day to day. Still, he thought, yawning and beginning to take notice—Regent's Park had changed very little since he was a boy, except for the squirrels—still, presumably there were compensations—when little Elise Mitchell, who had been picking up pebbles to add to the pebble collection which she and her brother were making on the nursery mantelpiece, plumped her handful down on the nurse's knee and scudded off again full tilt into a lady's legs. Peter Walsh laughed out. (65)

I hardly want to overdignify this passage by claiming it to be the secret wisdom of the novel. Peter himself deserves little credit here: He is yawning, slack, more or less at half-mast. Moreover, Woolf has orchestrated this sequence according to the book's "city logic," so that the lady whose legs little Elise Mitchell runs full tilt into is no less than Rezia Warren Smith, enabling the author to make now the transition to Rezia and Septimus and their problems. Okay. I can see all that. Still, I want to salute the small series of triumphs that are unfurling here: The warm sun soothes and heals, one *does* get over things, the park and squirrels bear scrutiny, and little Elise Mitchell's machinations and mishaps—while hardly the stuff of great poetry or drama—are worth looking at more closely.

Worth looking at. The worth, the value of things, is the amount of life they either contain or provoke. Peter Walsh's laughter affirms the intrinsic goodness of trivial things; it also goes a fair way toward righting his equilibrium, bringing him out of his slump, easing his path back into life and interest. I don't know how to put a market price on such transactions, but that only proves that our market thinking is itself so impoverished that it cannot affix a value to the infinite little tangibles and intangibles that perk us up or bring us down, that add zest to our arrangements, that keep our little machine going, that help to cure heartache and to reinsert us into the human community. Virginia Woolf is wise about exactly this economy. And she is almost by herself in this arena.

RIPENESS IS ALL: THE GAINS OF AGE

Peter Walsh is the book's philosopher on this score. Admittedly, he has his reasons for seeking compensation in out-of-the-way places, since his record in the high public arena is less than impressive. But "compensation" is exactly the term he uses when mulling over what might be the actual advantages of growing old. Like so much of Woolf's best writing, this series of thoughts has a palpable, delicious kinetic feeling to it, a meandering of the mind that works its way (glides its way) forward toward light and meaning:

> The compensation of growing old, Peter Walsh thought, coming out of Regent's Park, and holding his hat in hand, was simply this; that the pas-

> sions remain as strong as ever, but one has gained—at last!—the power which adds the supreme flavour to existence,—the power of taking hold of experience, of turning it round, slowly, in the light. (79)

Once again, I admit that one could snicker at such a passage, and go on to nail Peter for hypocrisy, delusion, and self-aggrandizement. Maybe I am indulgent because of my own age, but I see here something quite fetching, actually quite provocative: Time *adds* to our estate, adds to our powers. Note the overtly scientific posture in play here: One *holds* one's experiences (what a miraculous notion; holding experience is like holding water), pirouettes them around, examines the various prisms they display, sizes up (at long last) what they mean. No small achievement. And I'd want to add that Woolf's canny prose is playing its part here, as she gives us the embodied Peter Walsh, a man at once thinking and coming out of Regent's Park and holding his hat, as if all these ventures warranted naming, had some fine parity, yielded a ballet of sorts. But the thinking gets (literally) more luminous as it continues, offering one of the novel's clearest distillations of wisdom, on the order of an epiphany:

> A terrible confession it was (he put his hat on again), but now, at the age of fifty-three one scarcely needed people any more. Life itself, every moment of it, every drop of it, here, this instant, now, in the sun, in Regent's Park, was enough. Too much indeed. A whole lifetime was too short to bring out, now that one had acquired the power, the full flavour; to extract every ounce of pleasure, every shade of meaning; which were so much more solid than they used to be, so much less personal. (79)

A great deal is packed into this. One begins with the salty yet fresh confession that the entire business of being with people is overrated, or overrated at least when it comes to folks over fifty. (How many writers are capable of such throwaway wisdom? Especially when it comes from a writer committed to the ethos of human relationships?) This recognition that one doesn't need others does not come because one has aged, has lost the capacity for relationships (thinks Peter), but rather because one has matured, or rather one's powers have now matured, to the point that one is peculiarly independent. But these heightened powers are to be enlisted in savoring life, in hallowing the miracle of each moment, of the sun shining, of just being.

It is as if, in the crucible of older experience, the personal were burning off so that the real matter at hand, nature's bounty, could be savored in its impersonal grandeur. The hedonism expressed here is quite at odds with that cold, narrow bed that Clarissa sees as her fate. Now that one has lived the requisite number of years, life shimmers with beauty, but its spectacle has changed its shape, has become "so much more solid . . . so much less personal." Later, in conversation with Sally, Peter will be even more succinct: "When one was young . . . one was too much excited to know people" (193). It is as if all the heat and splendor of youthful passion are perhaps inaccessible, "unprocessable," to the very people experiencing them, are most fully appropriated only afterward, through memory, through reflection. Woolf is very close to Proust here.

Despite her fear of frigidity, Clarissa seems to have learned the same lesson, learned it from her husband:

> It was due to Richard; she had never been so happy. Nothing could be slow enough; nothing last too long. No pleasure could equal, she thought, straightening the chairs, pushing in one book on the shelf, this having done with the triumphs of youth, lost herself in the process of living, to find it, with a shock of delight, as the sun rose, as the day sank. (185)

If you didn't know better, you'd think you were reading a passage from a handbook on sex. How to go slow enough? How to lengthen pleasure, to make ecstasy last? In some sense, Woolf's answer is in the actual prose, the agile prose that meshes Clarissa's thinking and doing, that integrates consciousness into the round of life (straightening chairs, ranging books), refusing to validate one as higher than the other, sensing that each heightens the other, gives it its integrity. And again we encounter this view of youth as hasty, impetuous, headlong to the point of losing oneself. Where do you recapture not only your fiery past but your own prior self? In the rising sun, in the sinking day.

I mentioned Proust because these reflections in *Mrs. Dalloway* reveal a notion of time, entropy, and recovery every bit as profound as what we saw in his great opus. The flavor is very different. Woolf says yes to very much of what Proust ultimately rejects: secular life. But the challenge of possessing one's self, of coming into one's fuller estate, is central to both of them. And, as in Shakespeare's meditations about ripeness and readiness, Woolf has a rich sense of the bounty that time brings, the way in which time leavens our lives, makes possible harvests that can come only later. One of the most striking passages in the novel focuses on just this sense of process, of how slow, slow, slow it should and must be before we come to knowledge, how much ore is lodged deep within, in the dark, awaiting our ultimate conversion of it into light and meaning:

> There was a mystery about it. You were given a sharp, acute, uncomfortable grain—the actual meeting; horribly painful as often as not; yet, in absence, in the most unlikely places, it would flower out, open, shed its scent, let you touch, taste, look about you, get the whole feel of it and understanding, after years of lying lost. (153)

Clarissa is reflecting here on her thirty-year friendship with Peter, and seems to realize that it takes that long to convert this sensory fact into something closer to understanding. Yet note how sensual and olfactory and outright tactile this process is, as if the visceral plenitude of life's encounters were ineluctably cued to the passing of time, to a process of maturation (both it and us) before release and retrieval are possible. Some might regard this scheme as depressing, since it suggests we are locked out of experiences as they happen, but the upbeat side of the equation has to do with a future that is rich and unpredictable, that will continuously surprise us with its bounty, by converting "lost" into "found."

IT IS CERTAIN WE MUST DIE

Seductive as this model of human repossession is—I certainly find it seductive to think of getting older as a "lark" and a "plunge," as a kind of deep-sea diving that brings up all manner of buried treasure and trophies—it requires a distinct number of givens that are far from assured. One of those givens is that we continue to live, that we do not die. Death is time's big and little secret. Not merely the "death of the soul" that Peter Walsh woke up fearing, but the more banal, vulgar, everyday affair of physical death. Old Mrs. Hilbery, a minor character if ever there was one, nonetheless lets this particular cat out of the bag as she recalls a point that bothered her when she woke up early in the morning: "How it is certain we must die" (175). With beautiful poetic logic, Woolf returns to Mrs. Hilbery again as she is seeking to exit the party, looking for the door, and gives her the most Proustian lines of the novel: "And, she murmured, as the night grew later, as people went, one found old friends; quiet nooks and corners; and the loveliest views. Did they know, she asked, that they were surrounded by an enchanted garden?" (191). It is all there: the certainty that we must die; and the no less certain conviction that, even as night grows later, we are surrounded by an enchanted garden.

What can it mean to be surrounded by an enchanted garden? That we must retain our capacity for wonder, our ability to continue to feel "a shock of delight" as the sun rises, as the day sinks. One may well believe that this requirement is not a very stringent one for the inhabitants of *Mrs. Dalloway.* Clarissa, Peter, even Richard and Elizabeth and Sally stun us over and over with their never-ceasing talent for wonder, for ecstasy. "It is enough!" would seem to be Virginia Woolf's battle cry, the password that anyone who seeks entry into her novels must know and believe and demonstrate. As we have noted, the great bustling metropolis of London is a prime source for these moments of amazed pleasure, whether one sees it longitudinally as it might have appeared to the Romans, or sees the glamour of London "in season," or even the perception of the vibrant, bustling Strand as it comes to a young girl alighting from an omnibus. This London beauty has, Peter thinks, something outright religious about it: "And in the large square where the cabs shot and swerved so quick, there were loitering couples, dallying, embracing, shrunk up under the shower of a tree; that was moving; so silent, so absorbed, that one passed, discreetly, timidly, as if in the presence of some sacred ceremony" (163).

But simpler, only seemingly inanimate things also excite and delight, ranging from flowers to light and heat and water and air. The visionary moments, the explosive moments when the tired phenomenal world sheds its skin, reveals its hidden beauty and mystical aura, would seem to constitute the very pulse of this novel, its bloodstream, its cardiac power.

Such moments, which we mistakenly consider supremely intimate and personal, are in fact moments where subjectivity is eclipsed, where the ego loosens its grip on things, where the world plunges into the human subject—what a lark! what a plunge!—and where the individual realizes his or her kinship with all the others, living and dead. This is the ground for Clarissa's conviction that she will never fully die, that her life is part of the nameless city swirl she both sees and does not see. The roiling energy, the stream of life, the unspoken currents, fuel this novel and point unmistakably to its central formal event: the party. Transmuting the elemental into the social, Clarissa is her world's Prospero, the woman who will compose life's forces into her own willed framework, gather and coerce what is fluid to give it shape and form. This is not easy. And it is subject to hostile and critical fire from every quarter of the novel. Hence, the novel questions her over and over, sometimes downright inquisitorially, "Why the party?"

PARTY GIRL

It is a question Woolf has to have thought long and hard about, since the very word "party" connotes for so many people the trivial, the capricious, the elitist, the reactionary, the unserious. I acknowledged, at the beginning of this chapter, that this dismissive opinion might be still alive and well among many readers. Can it surprise us that all this is foregrounded (rather than obscured or taken for granted) in *Mrs. Dalloway*? Much as Faulkner is to do in his "use" of the Canadian Shreve in *Absalom, Absalom!*, Woolf puts her nastiest indictments up front in her book. Doris Kilman seems virtually conceived as Clarissa's opposite number, not merely the clumsy, turbulent governess who threatens to lead the daughter astray, but the one who savages—mentally: Not a word is said out loud—Clarissa the socialite with pith and vehemence: "Fool! Simpleton! You who have known neither sorrow nor pleasure; who have trifled your life away!" (125). Does Peter not agree essentially with this withering assessment? Marrying Dalloway, he is certain, has been the downfall of Clarissa, has turned her into a social butterfly, awash in costly furnishings, obsessed with parties. "Oh these parties, he thought; Clarissa's parties. Why does she give these parties, he thought" (48). Even the loyal Richard is taken aback by Clarissa's anger at having to invite Ellie Henderson at this late date: "It was a very odd thing how much Clarissa minded about her parties, he thought" (119).

The book goes out of its way, I think, to bring up and then to answer exactly these charges. Clarissa herself knows that Peter and Richard are critical of her. She senses that Peter thinks her snobbish, and Richard thinks her foolish, but that "both were quite wrong. What she liked was simply life"

(121). On the face of it, this seems a bit broad, even a bit lame. Again Clarissa herself takes the lead, imagines Peter pushing her still harder (" 'Yes, yes, but your parties—what's the sense of your parties?' " [121]), and comes up this time with a rather strange answer: "They're an offering" (121). Would any *man* understand this? she wonders. What love is for men, she reckons, her party is for her—"the most important thing in the world" (122)—and neither is comprehensible to the other. "She could not imagine Peter or Richard taking the trouble to give a party for no reason whatsoever" (122), she says to herself rather archly. In typical Woolf fashion, she pursues the issue, digs still deeper. Her parties, she realizes, are about bringing people together. It must be done, and she does it. "And it was an offering; to combine, to create; but to whom?" (122). Note how stubbornly that term "offering" is in play, how Clarissa herself cannot really define it. The best she can manage is to say: "Anyhow, it was her gift" (122).

Offering. Gift. To combine; to create. I believe we have to think anthropologically to start to take the measure of these terms. "Offering" and "gift" are to be understood as elemental, virtually pagan gestures, as rituals needed to stoke the flames, flames needed to warm the human family, to bring it to awareness that it is a family. The apparent reality of life is individualism: We appear to be bounded by our own skin, locked in our own mind, islanded. Not so, says Woolf. We are extended, connected; we flow into one another. I called Clarissa Prospero because she possesses something every character in the novel acknowledges: "that extraordinary gift, that woman's gift, of making a world of her own wherever she happened to be" (76). And there is an ethos here, as Peter himself recognizes: "She hated frumps, fogies, failures, like himself presumably; thought people had no right to slouch about with their hands in their pockets" (76). Clarissa's "genius," Peter understands, is to make "her drawingroom a sort of meeting-place" (77); he is a bit condescending, yet tries to give Clarissa her due. Skeptic, knowing we are all doomed, the Clarissa he portrays is a woman fighting against bad odds: "decorate the dungeon with flowers and air-cushions; be as decent as we possibly can. Those ruffians, the Gods, shan't have it all their own way" (77).

This has its truth, but does not go quite far enough. It misses what is most vital in Clarissa's scheme: the project of overcoming self, of promoting connection, of opening up doors and gates. This is more than being an accomplished Victorian (or Edwardian or Georgian or Bloomsburian) hostess. It is an offer, a gift. It is more akin to a blood transfusion than to a plate with cakes. Clarissa's project is one that women seem fated to carry out, in part because men cannot fathom what it is even about: to bring people together, to create connection. Clarissa stands, I think, for the civilized values, which is one reason she despises Kilman's cult of religion and is even contemptuous of Peter's twaddle about love. Love and religion are the source of much of the world's sufferings and brutalities: "The cruelest things in the world, she thought, seeing them clumsy, hot, domineering, hypocritical, eavesdropping, jealous, infinitely cruel and unscrupulous, dressed in a mackintosh coat, on the landing" (126). A good dose of bile is detectable in this outcry against the barbarous Kilman, but it helps to illuminate the humane, secular ethos that Clarissa Dalloway herself embodies. All of this tells us why the book closes with a thirty-page account of its crowning event, the party.

But it does not tell us what lies deepest under the small talk of parties, under the coming together of men and women. I have said that Peter Walsh and Sally Seton are the surprise guests in London, at the party, come back to their early haunts, bringing with them the (lost) past of romance and passion. But there is another uninvited guest whom I have not mentioned, someone who will crash this party in the same way that Poe's story "The Masque of the Red Death" demonstrates the omnipotence of the plague. Septimus Smith has a rendezvous with Clarissa Dalloway even though neither has ever heard of the other, even though they never meet in the flesh. And I want to remind you here of my earlier cautionary statements: The belief in time as a ripening force requires that we continue to live, and requires as well that we maintain our capacity for wonder. In Septimus Smith—whom I have purposely kept at bay up to now in my discussion of *Mrs. Dalloway*—we see that these two preconditions may not be meetable. Death will enter. The capacity for wonder—the trademark of Virginia Woolf's narrative world—will itself be a death sentence. Welcome to the party.

DAMAGED SEPTIMUS: CLARISSA'S DARK ALTER EGO

Septimus Smith is the black hole at the center of the novel. He is also its contrapuntal figure, the one who is unmistakably Clarissa's *other*, her alter ego of sorts, and Woolf has taken great pains to thread him into the story from beginning to end, so that we find him on the London streets, in Regent's Park, in his flat, and finally—as ghost who cannot be naysaid—at the party itself. He is not easy to get a fix on. Septimus is the precarious poet, the man who is to go mad, the visionary who is prey to his visions. He is also the returnee from the Great War, the damaged one, the young man who has been unhinged by this European calamity, who first seems to be a survivor but becomes increasingly recognized as a kind of delayed-action fatality. And one has to add: He is also the man crucified by doctors, the sacrificial victim of an apparently bluff, but actually inhuman medical ethos of "proportion" and "rest cures" and brutal procedures of "normalization." All these lines of interpretation matter, and Woolf was, I think, drawn to each of them, but they are quite different from one another.

The most obvious, doubtless the most appealing, diagnosis of Septimus is to posit him as destroyed by the war. I say "appealing" inasmuch as this view adds something crucial and otherwise missing from *Mrs. Dalloway:* It enables us to see past the fun and games of the social scheme, to move beyond the upper crust and privileged arena of Clarissa Dalloway and company, to recognize that Woolf is in fact offering a portrait of her moment, of England after World War I. One's story, however personal and private it may seem, is inscribed in history. Much supports this reading: The book's counterpointing of past and present takes on a deeper resonance if we understand that past also to be the experience of 1914–1918.

The book's enduring concern with different generations—from old Miss Parry and Lady Bruton on to the central players in their fifties, but including the young as well, such as Elizabeth, the men and women going through their paces in giddy London, and of course Septimus and Rezia—starts to take on a more serious historical tonality. The war notes are sounded at the very beginning of the novel: Lady Bexborough is pictured "with the telegram in her hand, John her favorite [son], killed; but it was over; thank Heaven—over" (5), leaving us to wonder: Is it over? Can it be over? And we have another pointed reference even if it at first appears veiled: "This late age of the world's experience had bred in them all, all men and women, a well of tears" (9). More echoing still is the bizarre reference to Uncle George, who used to say a lady is known by her shoes and her gloves; the next sentence leaves cliché behind, and is chilling: "He had turned on his bed one morning in the middle of the War. He had said, 'I have had enough' " (11). All these discreet notations signal that the war may not be over, may have left (bred) a legacy yet to be measured, may simply be unsurvivable.

Nowhere is Woolf's logic more sweetly on show than in Richard Dalloway's consciousness as he marches home to Clarissa, flowers in hand, determined to tell her that he loves her, thinking "Why not? Really it was a miracle thinking of the War, and thousands of poor chaps, with all their lives before them, shovelled together, already half forgotten; it was a miracle" (115). All at once we realize that Woolf's signature-issue of "it was a miracle" may seem to be lodged in aesthetic and imaginative enthusiasms of the how-splendid-it-all-is variety, but that very vitality derives its deepest meaning from being juxtaposed against its true grisly opposite: dead young people, all their promise destroyed, shoveled together, forgotten. Human wonder, *plunging* into life, now shows for the elemental virtue it is: Because it is certain we must die, it is imperative that we live and love with utmost intensity.

To see love as the only conceivable counterweight to war is to approach Septimus Smith ever more closely. He has been in war and through it, has been hurt in ways he is still discovering, and had sought, desperately, to save himself by marrying the lovely Italian girl Rezia, the cheerful seamstress living with her mother and sisters; yet he had sensed even then that nothing could save him: "That was the doom pronounced in Milan when he came into the room and saw them cutting out buckram shapes with their scissors; to be alone forever" (145). Life's gay colors and love's great vitality, even together, may not be enough to save you.

SEPTIMUS THE SEER

The war injured Septimus in the most sneaky, surreptitious fashion. Among the first to volunteer, he seemed to have gotten through it unscathed. Yes, the officer whose affection he drew, Evans, was killed just before Armistice, but Septimus appeared undamaged, had congratulated himself for "feeling very little and very reasonably," "had gone through the whole show, friendship, European War, death, had won promotion, was still under thirty and was bound to survive" (86). But the effects came later; he gradually realized that he could no longer feel, and this is what catapulted him into engagement and marriage. But the more Woolf tells us about Septimus's condition, the wider our understanding becomes of the extent of his problems, and we quickly realize that "not feeling" is only part of the trouble. He has also become horribly precarious, waking in the mornings to feel that the bed was falling, that he was falling. Worse still is his postwar suspicion that "it might be possible that the world itself is without meaning" (88). Yet even these impairments are tame and innocuous, merely cerebral, when contrasted to the fiery new apocalyptic truths that Septimus feels he has discovered. He now knows—knows!—how wicked people are, for he "could see them making up lies as they passed in the street" (66), yet lies are the least of it:

> For the truth is . . . that human beings have neither kindness, nor faith, nor charity beyond what serves to increase the pleasure of the moment. They hunt in packs. Their packs scour the desert and vanish screaming into the wilderness. They desert the fallen. They are plastered over with grimaces. (89)

One feels that the battle experiences themselves, along with Evans's death, are being horribly recast in civilian and urban and universal form. But Septimus's poisoned sights are focused on those he sees most, including himself. His employer, Brewer, seems to him an utter hypocrite, proper on the outside, "all coldness and clamminess within" (89), Anna who punctually serves tea at five is really "a leering, sneering, obscene little harpy" (90), and he, Septimus, is as vile as the others, as is evident in his dealings with Rezia, for he "had married his wife without loving her; had lied to her; seduced her; outraged Miss Isabel Pole [the great mentor who introduced him to Shakespeare and Keats], and was so pocked and marked with vice that women shuddered when they saw him in the street" (91). In short, everywhere you look—in the mirror, around you, or on those splendid London streets (that Woolf so loves) whose majesty so moved Clarissa and Peter and Richard—you see a spectacle of horror worthy of Bosch:

> In the street vans roared past him; brutality blared out on placards; men were trapped in mines; women burnt alive; and once a maimed file of lunatics being exercised or displayed for the diversion of the populace (who laughed aloud), ambled and nodded and grinned past him, in the Tottenham Court Road, each half apologetically, yet triumphantly, inflicting his helpless woe. And would *he* go mad? (90)

All this, many have argued, can be chalked up to the impact of the war. And maybe it can, since who is to say how the horrors one either experiences or imagines actually live out their long lives within us, violently reprogram our view of life and self? Do we know? Trauma operates exactly along these lines. Granting all this, I would nonetheless emphasize the Shakespearean dimension of that last line: The text is remembering Lear at this juncture, and the pathos of Septimus's life is not merely what the war may have done to him, but the horrible struggle of trying to keep a lid on, afterward, trying to go on with life. He thinks of himself as the man to whom the Truth has been shown, and he also knows that madness is the last truth. And when it comes in full, it may not be bearable. These are the reasons he is wont to say, much to the horror of his wife and to the disapproval of his doctors, "Now we will kill ourselves" (66).

THE DOCTORS ARRIVE

Very late in the novel, when Sir William Bradshaw, society doctor, apologizes for arriving late at Clarissa's party, he mentions to Richard, in a suitably lowered voice, the need for legislation containing something "about the deferred effects of shell shock" (183). "Shell shock" is itself a shocking term for inclusion in this book, which has taken the psychological high road throughout, and only now proffers an overtly medical diagnosis for the plight of Septimus Smith. One feels—and is meant to feel—the poverty of this medical label versus the complexity and horror of Septimus's actual condition. *Mrs. Dalloway* is not kind to doctors. Thanks to the voluminous critical attention given to Virginia Woolf's various crises and breakdowns (beginning at the time of her mother's death when Woolf was thirteen, flaring up at significant intervals throughout her life, and closing with her suicide in 1941, when she felt the onset of a new and not-to-be-borne bout of madness), we are well informed about her lifelong struggle against "mental illness"; and no less informed about the distressing record of the medical establishment when it came to treating her. She lived at a time prior even to lithium, much less our modern miracle drugs, the psychotropic arsenal that has done so much to alleviate misery in this area, and she was thus subject to protocols ranging from bromides to pulling out teeth, but always in the context of the famous "rest cure" that was the therapy of choice at that time. Those who have read Charlotte Perkins Gilman's unforgettable account of madness and the rest cure in "The Yellow Wallpaper" have, I think, the right perspective for understanding both Septimus's predicament and Woolf's own animus.

Dr. Holmes and Dr. Bradshaw are the book's two monsters. Septimus sees each of them as exemplifying his darkest view of human nature: "the repulsive brute, with the blood-red nostrils" (92). It is as if one took the nastiest elements of Hobbes, mixed in a bit of Lear's crazed visions and Swift's misanthropy, stirred it all up, looked around to see who epitomizes all this, then awarded the palm to the doctors. Septimus's vision is sharp here because he, precarious and down, is on the receiving end of such a doctrine: "Once you fall, Septimus repeated to himself, human nature is on you. Holmes and Bradshaw are on you. They scour the desert. They fly screaming into the wilderness. The rack and the thumbscrew are applied. Human nature is remorseless" (98). One is struck by the savagery of this depiction, and it goes a long way, I think, toward illuminating Woolf's profound suspicion of and contempt for medicine and its pretensions. "Human nature is on you." This is terrifying language, I think, given the breadth and scope of its indictment, and it must reflect Woolf's own hard-earned knowledge about what it feels like to be haunted by demons: those within and those without (the latter wearing the uniforms of polite society's guardians: commonsensical, judgmental, penal).

Woolf would have had no trouble, either, understanding a later book such as Ken Kesey's *One Flew Over the Cuckoo's Nest*, because she regards (what passed for) psychiatry as a form of disguised repression, as a heinous form of societal bullying that can become (as it will here) outright murder, all in the name of norms, or, as Bradshaw likes to say, "proportion." Woolf is doing her own proportions, taking the measure of the price we pay, we the society, we the gifted or ailing or marginalized or simply different, when doctors are sufficiently empowered to impose their will, to lock people away, or to keep them down. How can we not see as well, in the conception and treatment of Septimus, her intimate knowledge of how the world saw *her*, perhaps how she at times saw herself, how in fact the man who loved her most, Leonard, saw her and treated her (insisting on proper rest, proper diet, keeping a vigilant eye out for excess), always—he was certain—in her own best interests? She knew what the rest cure was all about.

This undisguisable revulsion at doctors' treatment of the insane is all the more striking when one takes into account Woolf's conviction that writing must be free of personal animus, personal agenda, indeed personal confession; these matters are wonderfully aired in *A Room of One's Own*, where she rates Jane Austen over Charlotte Brontë (who, she acknowledged, had the more genius) for just this reason: Austen, like Shakespeare, has no ax to grind, no *parti pris*. But ask yourself if the same can be said for this stunning broadside in *Mrs. Dalloway*:

> Worshipping proportion, Sir William Bradshaw not only prospered himself but made England prosper, secluded her lunatics, forbade childbirth, penalised despair, made it impossible for the unfit to propagate their views until they, too, shared his sense of proportion—his, if they were men, Lady Bradshaw's if they were women (she embroidered, knitted, spent four nights out of seven at home with her son), so that not only did his colleagues respect him, his subordinates fear him, but the friends and relations of his patients felt for him the keenest gratitude for insisting that these prophetic Christs and Christesses, who prophesied the end of the world, or the advent of God, should drink milk in bed, as Sir William ordered. (99)

Holmes and Bradshaw are the terrible policemen she feared. I read that line "forbade childbirth" as having its inevitable dosage of home truth, given what we know about Virginia's lifelong envy of her sister, Vanessa Bell's achievements in this area, Virginia's recurrent doubts and remorse about the decision reached (how? according to what criteria?) not to have children. And how can we not see that these two bogeymen are the supreme enemies of art? The most hysterical notation of the novel comes when Bradshaw finds that Septimus, asked about his participation in the war, repeats the word "war" interrogatively: Aha! thinks the doctor: "He was attaching meanings to words of a symbolical kind. A serious symptom, to be noted on the card" (96). Symbols, eh? The alert doctor sees at once how invidious and alarming such behavior can be. One imagines Woolf shuddering as much as laughing when she wrote those lines.

SEPTIMUS WOOLF: A SELF-PORTRAIT

However, should we assess Septimus Smith, finally, as victim of both war and doctors, I believe that we come up short, seriously short, in properly gauging what he means and why he is there. Septimus Smith is, in ways that Woolf only partly intended and controlled, a portrait of the artist as a young man, i.e., a self-portrait. I am not in the least interested in the biography itself here. Certainly the shabby, half-educated, mad young clerk bears little external resemblance to the elegant and poised queenlike figure of Woolf. Yes, some parallels do exist: When the servant girl finds Septimus's writing and falls into a fit of laughing, I suppose we have to see this as a nasty image of what reactions the author must have feared, deep down, concerning her own work. Yet all my best evidence for the Septimus-Woolf link is internal. That is why it is damning. Septimus's vision, his imagination and neurological equipment, testify to all that is truest, richest, and most terrifying about Virginia Woolf's sense of life. I cannot help thinking it was terrifying to her as well.

The ideological, medical, and moral dimensions of his vision—casualty of the war, shell shock, misanthropy, view of behavior as bestial and evil—are appalling, yes, but they pale in importance, I think, when we consider him in still larger terms as the plague that threatened Virginia Woolf all her life: the artistic vision turned explosive, insane, ungovernable, despotic, lethal. Rezia cannot bear to sit next to her deranged husband in Regent's Park when he "stared so and did not see her and made everything terrible: sky and tree, children playing, dragging carts, blowing whistles, falling down; all were terrible" (23). Here is the ultimate toxin: to turn the natural and human world into horror, simply by looking at it, "made everything terrible." One needs to pay heed: sky and tree, children playing. How can this contain terror? We might term this a diseased imagination, or better, imagination as disease, if we bear in mind the etymology of "imagination" as the making of images, the projection of images. That process is in horrible trouble here. Prior to the eighteenth century, people were immensely leery of imagination, suspected it to be a source of error, a dangerous enticement. Ever since the Romantic era, however, we have been told that the splendor of poetry and art lie in the imagination, in the capacity to see (to create) a richer and deeper and more beautiful universe than the sometimes drab objective world that strikes every retina. And how can we not place Virginia Woolf squarely in this post-Romantic tradition?

Thus Septimus is the poison principle. He inverts everything that is hallowed in Woolf's scheme. Clarissa walks the London streets and feels the pulsating splendor of life, feels that her individual death matters not, that she survives nonetheless, lives in others, is part of the trees at home, of the house there, "part of people she had never met." Now consider Septimus. He, too, is connected; death does not exist for him, either; he is inseparable from the myriad spectacle of life. But it is horrible:

> He waited. He listened. A sparrow perched on the railing opposite chirped Septimus, Septimus, four or five times over and went on, drawing its notes out, to sing freshly and piercingly in Greek words how there is no crime and, joined by another sparrow, they sang in voices prolonged and piercing in Greek words, from trees in the meadow of life beyond a river where the dead walk, how there is no death.
>
> There was his hand; there the dead. White things were assembling behind the railings opposite. But he dared not look. Evans was behind the railings! (24–25)

We know that Woolf, during one of her crises, had noted in her diary the Greek singing birds, but the specific details matter little; what counts is that the entire magic spectacle of a world pulsating with life and voice, freed from the contours and boundaries that common sense subscribes to, this spectacle is perceived by Septimus with utmost purity and power. And there is no uplift whatsoever; it is killing him. He sees the airplane with its sign language and knows he is being interpellated:

> Not indeed in actual words; that is, he could not read the language yet; but it was plain enough, this beauty, this exquisite beauty, and tears filled his eyes as he looked at the smoke words languishing and melting in the sky and bestowing upon him in their inexhaustible charity and laughing goodness one shape after another of unimaginable beauty and signalling their intention to provide him, for nothing, for ever, for looking merely, with beauty, more beauty! (21–22)

One can say the man doesn't know how to set limits, to realize that the airplane is *not* addressing him personally. But at issue here is a vision that annihilates limits, a vision in which things jump out of their skins, take on other shapes and forms, metamorphose in front of our eyes and deep in our minds. Septimus feels himself accursed, and the word seems hardly excessive given what he is smitten with (for who among us chooses or regulates the neural and imaginative equipment that operates within us, that *is* us?): "Why could he see through bodies, see into the future, when dogs will become men? . . . His body was macerated until only the nerve fibres were left. It was spread like a veil upon a rock" (68). Those last words have the pith and resonance of Greek myth, make us think of Prometheus on his rock with vultures as company; and they have a biblical ring as well, so that the macerated body with only nerve fibers left in it connotes crucifixion, a modern crucifixion whereby the nerves—seemingly unkillable, perversely powerful and invincible—remain intact to flay us forever.

And the writing itself! Septimus is the true visionary, and little in Woolf's corpus matches the sheer splendor of the prose that delivers his fierce, emancipated, poisoned vision, his calvary of heightened sensations:

> He lay resting, waiting, before he again interpreted, with effort, with agony, to mankind. He lay very high, on the back of the world. The earth thrilled beneath him. Red flowers grew through his flesh; their stiff leaves rustled by his head. Music began clanging against the rocks up here. It is a motor horn down in the street, he muttered; but up here it cannoned from rock to rock, divided, met in shocks of sound which rose in smooth columns (that music should be visible was a discovery) and became an anthem, an anthem twined round now by a shepherd boy's piping (That's an old man playing a penny whistle by the public-house, he muttered) . . . (68)

One is tempted to label such prose surrealist, even drug-induced, and a line like "red flowers grew through his flesh" could have been written by William S. Burroughs in his hallucinatory *Naked Lunch.* But note how the familiar things never quite disappear, so that Septimus both sees a "liberated" world of tumbling forms and knows he is seeing it (the music is really a motor horn, the shepherd's boy is really an old man). This makes things worse, not better, makes the routine, pedestrian, inescapable experience of having open eyes and open ears into a constantly menacing roller-coaster ride, an unchosen trip to a fun house in which anything, at any time, can appear, can take over the shapes you thought you knew.

Words themselves open for him: "The word 'time' split its husk: poured its riches over him; and from his lips fell like shells, like shavings from a plane, without his making them, hard, white, imperishable words . . ." (69). One would have thought, naively, that the spectacle of words opening themselves would be the most gratifying experience a writer could have, the moment when the medium itself miraculously disclosed all its hidden treasures and potentialities. Seeing it here, as part of the incessant barrage of stimuli and visions coming Septimus's way, one is obliged to reconsider. "Ecstasy" itself, the stock in trade of heightened, delicious vision in Virginia Woolf, means "from the place," means being taken from where you are, perhaps taken from who you are. Here, too, conventional thinking says, that's wonderful, but this book spurns conventional thinking by showing just what such stuff looks like, feels like, close up, when it's happening to *you*.

One of the most heartbreaking passages of the novel describes Septimus looking at his wife. The madman looks at his sane (unhappy) wife, and this is how he sees her:

> She held her hands to her head, waiting for him to say did he like the hat or not, and as she sat there, waiting, looking down, he could feel her mind, like a bird, falling from branch to branch, always alighting, quite rightly; he could follow her mind, as she sat there in one of those loose lax poses that came to her naturally and, if he should say anything, at once she smiled, like a bird alighting with all its claws firm upon the bough. (147)

Maybe this is what madness is: to see the miraculous balance and poise of those around you, while knowing that you no longer possess it yourself. To see that others alight rightly, that others' claws firmly grasp the bough they perch on, while knowing that you are doomed to fall. Falling is the sensation Septimus reports on from beginning to end: falling into flames, falling into depths. It is a sensation, it is indeed a voyage, that Virginia Woolf knew much about, seeing it as the twin trajectory of both melancholy and art: "I pitched into my great lake of melancholy. Lord how deep it is! What a born melancholiac I am! The only way I keep afloat is by working. . . . Directly I stop working I feel that I am sinking down, down. And as usual, I feel that if I sink further I shall reach the truth" (*Diary* 3, 225).

It should be clear that I have no interest in putting Woolf on a couch. But I have wanted to show how the madness and fate of Septimus Smith, dark though they are, constitute this novel's and this author's most luminous truths. He replays what is most splendid and lyrical and life-affirming in this novel, but he replays it as tragedy, as unhinging and unbearable, as curse. Septimus commits suicide in order to escape Holmes and Bradshaw. He leaps out the window and impales himself on the wrought-iron fence. And it is the news of this death that the Bradshaws bring to Clarissa's party. Melodramatic though it may sound, Woolf stages the encounter between death and life, between Septimus's houndedness and visions on the one hand and that elemental act of bringing together, that offering, that Clarissa embodies in her party. It is all too easy to say that this is far too schematic, that parties and death (frivolity and tragedy, indeed women's topics and men's topics) do not go together, can only be put together by authorial fiat. Woolf seems to have known the risk she was taking by conflating these two stories, as we can see in the complex series of reactions that Clarissa goes through once she has been told of Septimus's death.

At first there is shock and distaste: How dared the Bradshaws bring death to her party! She then makes her way into the room where the Prime Minister and Lady Bruton were, but finds it empty. It is as if one form of power were being replaced by another, for she now, in this room of her own, processes Septimus's death, seems virtually to experience it somatically, seems to go through it herself: "Her dress flamed, her body burnt. He had thrown himself from a window. Up had flashed the ground; through him, blundering, bruising, went the rusty spikes. There he lay with a thud, thud, thud in his brain, and then a suffocation of blackness. So she saw it" (184). She then contrasts the purity, gravity, and severity of his deed with the "corruption, lies, chatter" of daily life, of memories, of parties. "Death was defiance" (184), she feels, not so much of decorum and cowardice, but of the impenetrable gaps and walls that separate us from others and from ourselves; "There was an embrace in death" (184). These lines can be thought facile, yet I believe they speak to the elemental core of darkness that both grounds and hollows Woolf's view of life and art. Grounds in the sense that the reality of death at once exposes the trivia of our postures and yet underwrites the social ethos that emerges: bring people together, create the flame, attack the isolation. Yet hollows too, for it points to a blankness that precedes all else, that lies prior to talk and touch, and somehow that blankness is what we approach, at our most intense and incandescent. That would be the embrace that Clarissa senses in Septimus's death.

This moment of supreme recognition—that Septimus's death is the unspeakable core of the party—is exquisitely handled by Woolf. Clarissa looks out her window and sees an old woman staring at her, an old woman who is going to bed, who pulls down the blind and puts out the light. It is a mirror scene of sorts, a recognition of the role played by time and night in all their lives (Clarissa too will age and die), and yet it is beautifully counterpointed by the noises and lights of the party, the vital living to whom Clarissa now goes, even as she thinks with wonder and gratitude about Septimus's death:

> She must go back to them. But what an extraordinary night! She felt somehow very like him—the young man who had killed himself. She felt glad he had done it; thrown it away. The clock was striking. The leaden circles dissolved in the air. He made her feel the beauty; made her feel the fun. But she must go back. She must assemble. She must find Sally and Peter. And she came in from the little room. (186)

All the motifs are brought together in musical form. Big Ben strikes, ringing in the heartbeat of London that will never die. But, because death is real for us, it obliges us to embrace life, to leave the dark room and reenter the fray. Above all, I believe that Septimus Smith embodies the terrifying purity of Woolf's own imaginative vision at its most intense and radiant. His death countersigns the novel's bravest perception: The ecstasy of life can annihilate us. We can be wrecked by our visions. This is why he must be brought into the book's culminating embrace. He is the terror that both threatens and parses the bright world of *Mrs. Dalloway;* he is its truth.

But he is not its final word. Peter, whose heart is bursting with things to say to Clarissa, finally espies her at party's end and feels a mix of terror, ecstasy, and extraordinary excitement: " 'It is Clarissa,' he said. For there she was" (194). With perfect tact, Virginia Woolf closes her book by saluting life. "If I sink further I shall reach the truth," she had written in her diary. And she did. Eventually Woolf went down all the way. But we have the books. Clarissa's first words were about plunging, and so, in fact, were mine. But writing itself is a form of rising, not falling, a way of saying and sharing all you've seen and felt—in the mind, in the heart, in the city, in the depths, in the night—a way of turning darkness into light.

UNFOLDING OUR PAST

At the end of *To the Lighthouse*, Woolf's great novel about life, death, memory, and art, Lily Briscoe, trying to re-create via her painting the lost Mrs. Ramsay, affirms that she is not "inventing," but rather "she was only trying to smooth out something she had been given years ago folded up" (295). It is, I think, a very beautiful, very domestic image of what life actually gives us, and how we may go about processing it, years or perhaps decades later. Despite the risk of appearing overly precious and *recherché*, Woolf's image of our past lying enfolded, embedded in some kind of handkerchief or shawl or sweater that we have had forever (but have never gotten around to unfolding it, opening it), is a severe metaphor, because it implies that we have all our treasures within reach, within ourselves, but may nonetheless come to the end of our lives without accessing them. And I think that this haunting novel also suggests that the most beautiful things in our lives are lodged in us in this way, far back and folded up, but that they cannot be possessed when they happen to us, and hence the passing of time (and its messenger of death) is the required price for recovery and possession.

An austere lesson, it might seem, and yet one that makes increasing sense to me as I grow older, as I realize that life's perhaps most arduous challenge is to possess more of one's own estate, of one's own past, both as elusive as quicksilver, as enigmatic as a foreign script, yet no less echoing for all that. How much, one wonders, lies buried and folded up within us, unprocessed and unreachable? How much has never risen to the light of day, so that its fuller colors and human density might at last be seen, measured, and possessed? And there is nothing antiquarian or merely curious here: On the contrary, these are the elemental notes, the fundamental indices to who we are, how we have lived.

A folded handkerchief, a folded shawl: Are these not also texts, surfaces that life has written on, demanding, themselves, to be brought to the surface so they can at last be opened up and read? It scarcely seems metaphoric to suggest that such hidden texts contain our innermost story. Yet, as *To the Lighthouse* will show, this intimate personal script is also wonderfully social and relational, for the lives of others—our parents, our loved ones, our long-ago and faraway exchanges with them—are also woven into this fabric, are also recoverable. In reading Virginia Woolf's work, we enter into a luminous and textured world, as if that infolded handkerchief were akin to the magic handkerchief that Othello gave to Desdemona, a criss-crossing of lives and fates that is rich in feeling, that recasts our story as an affair of intersecting threads and voices.

For these reasons it does not seem amiss for me to start with my own encounter with *To the Lighthouse*, a reading that took place almost half a century ago, constituting the folded experience I want now, in some fashion, to open up. I was a nineteen-year-old (barely literate) sophomore at Princeton taking a course on the British novel given by the legendary Lawrance Thompson—Melville and Faulkner scholar, Frost biographer—known for the acerbic punch of his lectures. Thompson prefaced his lecture by referring to a guest lecture he had recently given on Woolf at one of the women's schools—either Smith or Mount Holyoke, as I recall—a lecture that was interrupted even before he could begin, since a shocked and enraged "girl" (Thompson's term) stood up in the lecture hall and spat out at him, "How can you possibly presume to speak to us about this book!" and promptly walked out of the room. Thompson pronounced these words at Princeton in 1959. I remember nothing whatsoever about the ensuing lecture he gave on *To the Lighthouse*, but the incident with the furious female reader has stayed with me, as a kind of trumpet call about what was so astonishing in the work of Virginia Woolf, about whether men were capable of understanding her or not.

I certainly thought that I did. The story of Mrs. Ramsay—which is all that I saw, which remains (as you will see) what I see most vividly—was the most beautiful thing I had ever read. True enough, I had very little literary background, could hardly pronounce on its artistic merits. But, at nineteen, I was nonetheless prepared for *To the Lighthouse*. I think I was still half in love with my mother, felt that she possessed a kind of radiance that I had seen nowhere else in my life (including in myself), and that her warmth—a warmth that seemed creatural, prior to reasons or motives—was both rare and magic. Certainly the atmosphere at Princeton itself—suave, chilly, overtly driven by intellect and wit, covertly impacted by class and social pulsions—had little in common with the vibrancy and raw vitality that I saw in her. (My move from Tennessee to New Jersey doubtless played its part here as well.) Woolf's depiction of Mrs. Ramsay—a portrait of human generosity without parallel—helped me put some kind of a form and shape on what had been most nurturing in my life, what I knew even then counted most. I had not known that novels could do this. I could not then know how rare Woolf's achievement was. And, of course, there was the heartbreaking pathos of the book, the utterly shocking death of Mrs. Ramsay in the middle of the text (okay, two-thirds in), and the poignant efforts of Lily Briscoe and the surviving Ramsays to come to terms with this loss, to recover this vital woman via memory and art. This last phrase I have written is something I could hardly have articulated at nineteen, but I felt it even then, and I can remember telling friends of mine to read this unbelievable book so they could see for themselves. But I never added: It's also about my mother, about my feeling for what I took to be her gift.

A few years later I met the woman who is still my wife today, and soon enough urged her to read *To the Lighthouse.* She was, and is, a much more voracious reader than I am, and read Woolf's novel with a kind of pleasure and feeling that rivaled my own. I suspect that she saw her own (dead) mother in this book, but I know, too, that she already then had a sharper, more fatalistic sense than I did of human quests, of whether or not, of when and how, one reaches the lighthouse. Do our great desires find gratification? Woolf's first words, " 'Yes, of course, if it's fine tomorrow' " (9), speak Mrs. Ramsay's spirit for nurturance as she assures James that the all-important trip to the lighthouse will indeed take place; yet, as all readers know, on the next page, Mr. Ramsay sounds his note: " 'But,' said his father, stopping in front of the drawing-room window, 'it won't be fine' " (10). To go or not to go is the question the book poses, for its people, for its readers. The novel's answers, and our own answers, are by no means straightforward, and may well hinge on where we are in our own journey. I understood little of this at nineteen, and perhaps not all that much more in my thirties.

And it matters to me as well that my wife's love for this book coincides with the early years of our marriage, when our two children were young, when love and interaction and sustenance had a daily, pragmatic, but no less existential presence in our lives. I think that the portrait of Mrs. Ramsay resonated with my wife's self-image as mother, and I also believe that the parallels are real. The kind of immediacy and richness that one finds in Mrs. Ramsay seemed to both of us then, as it seems within Woolf's own book, cued to a female logic and wisdom that are very old and happen to be much prized in my wife's Swedish family, with a line of strong women who have been thinking back through their mothers for some time now. Given the academic culture in which we were living as a family—at that juncture, I professoring, she mothering—it did not seem terribly far-fetched to see in Woolf's portrait of Mr. and Mrs. Ramsay something of the regnant lines of force that mapped out gender lines and categories of significance in our little world. (I have colleagues who are still pondering how to get from Q to R.) I of course saw myself as a great exception to the rule, but the rules were there nonetheless.

All that was long ago. Now my children are grown up. I have grandchildren. My mother—whom I initially saw as the vibrant living instance of Mrs. Ramsay—is dead, after a painful decline, and I long ago stopped thinking of her in that fashion. My wife still resembles, I think, Woolf's heroine, by dint of her intuitive sense of what life portends, of what values are made of; this parallel will hold. But around her she no longer has growing children to whom her vision might be imparted, even though the grandchildren sense that she is special in this regard. Now, in our sixties, both of us share a knowledge that quests are hard to make good on, and even though we'd hardly use Mr. Ramsay's words, we now silently agree with his conviction that "facts" are "uncompromising," that "our frail barks founder in darkness," and that the "passage to that fabled land" is "one that needs, above all, courage, truth, and the power to endure" (11). What quests are left to grandparents? In what direction should *our* sights be focused? Forward into the future? Backward into the past? What does one make, later, of one's dreams of youth? Of those who nurtured us? Where are the dead?

Lily Briscoe returns to the scene of love, some ten years later, after Mrs. Ramsay and her son Andrew and her daughter Prue have died, and sets her easel up to paint; she looks out over the waters, imagines Mr. Ramsay and Cam and James finally making their way by sail to the lighthouse, and realizes that these waters are

> . . . full to the brim. She seemed to be standing up to the lips in some substance, to move and float and sink in it, yes, for these waters were unfathomably deep. Into them had spilled so many lives. The Ramsays'; the children's; and all sorts of waifs and strays of things besides. A wash-

> erwoman with her basket; a rook; a red-hot poker; the purples and grey-greens of flowers: some common feeling held the whole. (285–286)

The passage is vintage Woolf, and we will return to it at the close of this chapter; but even now we can see the breakthrough that is on show here: The surface of the water invites us to its depths, and in those depths we can recover our own depths, encompassing not only our own dead (loved ones, selves) but all those others, too, with whom we shared the stage, who inhabit us as well.

RECKONING WITH THE DEAD

Let me now turn to the novel itself, to try to unfold it as best I can, attending to its own intricacies and treasures, but cognizant as well of its manifold connections with my life and my past. It is, I believe, the right critical posture for discussing *To the Lighthouse,* since Woolf herself conceived it as a coming to terms with her own past, the mother and father who made her, and whom she is now to make, herself. There is nothing casual or serendipitous about this choice of subject, but rather a kind of reckoning whose time has come, since their dying was inseparable from her birthing, as Woolf noted in her diary on the anniversary of her father's birthday:

> 1928
> Father's birthday. He would have been 1832 96, yes,
> 96
> today; & could have been 96, like other people one has known; but mercifully was not. His life would have entirely ended mine. What would have happened? No writing, no books;—inconceivable. I used to think of him & mother daily; but writing The Lighthouse laid them in my mind. And now he comes back sometimes, but differently. (I believe this to be true—that I was obsessed by them both, unhealthily; & writing of them was a necessary act.) (*Diary* 3, 208)

This passage has not gone unremarked by Woolf critics. One the one hand, it is well known that this is the most autobiographical of her fictions, the book where she consciously portrayed her famous parents, Leslie and Julia Stephen. And given how much is known about both, it is easy enough to read the novel with one eye focused on the biographical data concerning these parents, in order to gauge what Virginia has emphasized or even altered. What is most intriguing in the diary entry, however, is the quasi-therapeutic dimension of writing them *out* of her life, of diminishing their "unhealthy" grip on her mind by dint of constructing them through art. This could only be done, I think, by returning to them in her mind, but returning with maximum feeling and involvement, with minimum personal animus (if possible), so as to get to the very bottom of each of them, to feel each of them from the inside out; only in this way could the cord eventually be cut. That Woolf succeeded in making them extraordinarily lifelike is vouched for by Vanessa's stunned reaction to the book:

> It seemed to me in the first part of the book you have given a portrait of mother which is more like her to me than anything I could ever have conceived possible. It is almost painful to have her so raised from the dead. You have made one feel the extraordinary beauty of her character, which must be the most difficult thing in the world to do. It was like meeting her again with oneself grown up and on equal terms and it seems to me the most astonishing feat of creation to have been able to see her such a way.—You have given father too I think as clearly, but perhaps, I may be wrong, that isn't quite as difficult. There is more to catch hold of. Still it seems to me to be the only thing about him which ever gave a true idea. So you see as far as portrait painting goes you seem to me to be a supreme artist and it is so shattering to find oneself face to face with those two again that I can hardly consider anything else. (quoted in Lee, 474)

I cite Vanessa, not to show that Virginia got it right, but to begin to measure the amplitude of Woolf's actual accomplishment: To alter the corrosive work of time by resurrecting the dead parents so that one might encounter them when oneself is an adult, hence able (only now, I believe) to see them as dimensional living people rather than as parents. It is impossible to overstate the significance of this achievement, because one of the most painful and inevitable lessons that life teaches us is that it is always too late: Loved ones die, and only afterward—sometimes long afterward—are we in a position to understand them, to speak to them as we might have (but did not). Why is this? Because we ourselves must experience the work of time before we grasp these truths? Because—this is the truly grisly view—people must die before they can be understood or appreciated? Vanessa Bell expresses, I think, a sense of the miracle wrought by her sister Virginia: to have another chance; they are, of course, dead, but one at last sees them aright.

Finally, one is struck by the sheer generosity of this book, its Orpheus-like effort to depict parental lives in hindsight, through recollection and creation. I see a lesson as well: Imagination and language are the tools we have for excavating not only our own private story, but, equally crucially, those of our loved ones, so that we may at least now see them in their entirety and—years after their death—take our leave from them. And, of course, there is the beautiful reciprocity of such a venture: In taking the measure of Mother and Father, we give the measure of ourselves.

ENDURING MARRIAGE

I want, however, to add to Vanessa's tribute by saying that the portrait of Mr. and Mrs. Ramsay given to us in *To the Lighthouse* goes beyond the historical Leslie and Julia Stephen, because it makes them into prismatic and resonant figures slated for still wider and more adventurous appropriations, such as I have exemplified in the opening pages of this section, when I spoke of my private sense of Mrs. Ramsay. Woolf herself knew exactly this, as we see in Lily's awareness that this man and woman, together, have a reach that transcends their personal lives: "And suddenly the meaning which, for no reason at all, as perhaps they are stepping out of the Tube or ringing a doorbell, descends on people, making them symbolical, making them representative, came upon them, and made them in the dusk standing, looking, the symbols of marriage, husband and wife" (110–111).

In general, I am terribly suspicious of allegory, of living figures being cast into larger, prescripted roles, but with the Ramsays I believe this to be the case, and it is brought about, as it were, from the inside, from a rendition of this couple that is so richly and finely seen that we feel: This is what relationship portends, this is how relationship lives. *To the Lighthouse* is the greatest marriage text in the English language, as I see it; I say this despite the book's in-house critique of Mrs. Ramsay's maniacal "marry, marry!" philosophy, and I say it despite the obstacles and failures that are unflinchingly observed in this story. Woolf makes us see that marriage is the greatest and most impossible balancing act in the history of our species, and that it has a coloration, humor, pathos, and language all its own. We have spoken much about the project of recovering and telling one's own story. It is now time to widen our lenses and to target something still more elusive and untold, beyond the grasp of any single vision or subjectivity: the story of human connection. How would you map or graph this? Can it be done?

Woolf has no illusions on this score. Her book acknowledges that relationship is—ultimately—doomed. And for many reasons. The distance between you and me is unbridgeable; we live in ourselves. And death is real: The entropic work of time is life's own brutal way of dismantling the human family. No way to alter these givens, and Woolf puts them in the center of her book. Knowing and acknowledging these stark facts, these uncompromising facts (as Mr. Ramsay would say), I may well appear quixotic in sticking to my claim about marriage being the novel's triumph. After all, it goes badly: The idyll at the summer house, in which the beauty of Mrs. Ramsay and the value of human connection are so vividly conveyed, is followed by the chapter "Time Passes," in which war and death and the erosions of time have their dreadful say. And then, almost like a mathematical formula, we have the final chapter, "The Lighthouse," which asks: What is left? There are no evasions or escape routes in this novel. It closes with its peculiar tally, and it is for us to decide what it all means. But we cannot determine what is left until we have fully seen what was there.

MIRACULOUS MRS. RAMSAY

What is, was, and will always be there, at least for readers, is Mrs. Ramsay. The first chapter constitutes a massive yet nuanced portrait of this singular woman, with the emphasis invariably returning to her beauty. Everyone in the book, including (especially) the hard to convince, is convinced of her beauty. And Woolf's strategy is, as always, perspectival: to convey this quality via its impact on others. Here is how the very unsentimental William Bankes has responded:

> ("Nature has but little clay," said Mr. Bankes once, much moved by her voice on the telephone, though she was only telling him a fact about a train, "like that of which she moulded you." He saw her at the end of the line very clearly Greek, straight, blue-eyed. How incongruous it seemed

> to be telephoning to a woman like that. The Graces assembling seemed to have joined hands in meadows of asphodel to compose that face. He would catch the 10:30 at Euston. . . .) (46–47)

Note how the classical Greek references are utterly meshed into a modern urban setting, so that the Graces and meadows of asphodel cohabit with the 10:30 at Euston in this prose. T. S. Eliot worked a comparable counterpoint in "The Waste Land," but Eliot's focus on dissonance and contrast is at complete odds with the gathering harmony of Woolf's notation, as if this woman *cohered* the world, brought into some fusion the ancient and the modern.

A moment later, Bankes muses, "So that if it was her beauty merely that one thought of, one must remember the quivering thing, the living thing (they were carrying bricks up a little plank as he watched them [workmen building a hotel at the back of his house]), and work it into the picture" (47). This may look like disconnected prose, but in it we can see Woolf's classic procedure of fusing—marrying—her materials together in surprising ways, so Mrs. Ramsay's beauty is virtually injected with the pulsing energy shown by the workmen carrying bricks, all of which constitutes precisely that "quivering," "living thing" Bankes noted as necessary. Yes, it is indeed worked into the picture in front of our eyes, producing a kind of fluid dance, so that a remembered face meshes with the sights and sounds around us. Beauty itself is not confined to museums or philosophical treatises; on the contrary, it is adventurous, kinetic, promiscuous, out there on the street. It is as if the clay of nature that Bankes alluded to were being molded and used, fired by Woolf's vision into bricks, and then into buildings, taking shape and heft in the real world.

Mrs. Ramsay's beauty is displayed, over and over, as a profoundly social force, magnetic and invasive, entering all those who see her, stunning them with its authority and intensity. She is literally irresistible, inasmuch as others are swept into her ambit, the way people and things are carried away by flood or tempest. One of my favorite instances of her impact comes early in the book, when she asks the mulish Charles Tansley to accompany her on her errands. As they walk, Tansley (Mr. Ramsay's student) begins to feel a certain male pride in having this woman at his side, yearns to have her see him as a successful academic, but then notices that she is looking at something. At what? he wonders. Watch this prose now go into action:

> At a man pasting a bill. The vast flapping sheet flattened itself out, and each shove of the brush revealed fresh legs, hoops, horses, glistening reds and blues, beautifully smooth, until half the wall was covered with the advertisement of a circus; a hundred horsemen, twenty performing seals, lions, tigers . . . Craning forwards, for she was short-sighted, she read it out . . . "will visit this town," she read. It was terribly dangerous work for a one-armed man, she exclaimed, to stand on top of a ladder like that—his left arm had been cut off in a reaping machine two years ago. (20–21)

This passage is rarely cited by the Woolf scholars, and yet I'd submit that it flaunts exactly the "quivering" life that Bankes ascribed to beauty. *The circus is coming to town.* It enters the fabric of this prose with the most delicious insolence, as we watch the flapping sheet gradually take form (as it takes over the text), give birth to legs, hoops, horses, seals, lions, tigers. This kind of writing is like a roving camera, hungry for life, suspicious of prefabs and ready-mades, registering what comes into its field of vision with a carefree, egalitarian spirit that will accommodate virtually anything, doesn't hesitate to push its characters aside in order to make way for the circus. The crowning touch comes, of course, with Mrs. Ramsay's observation about the dangerousness of this work, since she knows this bill paster's past, knows how he was injured, expresses her sympathy.

And now things begin to simmer. "Let us all go!" cries Mrs. Ramsay. "Let's go" says, weakly, Tansley. And she has her little epiphany about this difficult young man: "Had they not been taken, she asked, to circuses when they were children? Never, he answered, as if she asked the very thing he wanted; had been longing all these days to say, how they did not go to circuses" (21). Upon which Tansley launches into his proud, sad, defensive family history of hard work and no frills and paying his own way (since he was thirteen), with all the deprivations that entails: cannot "return hospitality," smokes cheapest tobacco, works seven days a week, and so forth. Daughter of Leslie Stephen the eminent and prolific Victorian author, all too familiar with the language of the academy, Woolf evokes with great wit and archness the sterile clichés of university culture simply by having Mrs. Ramsay listen to Tansley:

> . . . his subject was now the influence of something upon somebody—they were walking on and Mrs. Ramsay did not quite catch the mean-

> ing, only the words, here and there . . . dissertation . . . fellowship . . . readership . . . lectureship. She could not follow the ugly academic jargon, that rattled itself off so glibly, but said to herself that she saw now why going to the circus had knocked him off his perch, poor little man, and why he came out, instantly, with all that about his father and mother and brothers and sisters, and she would see to it that they didn't laugh at him any more. (22)

I don't know whether to laugh or to cry when I read this passage. Woolf has nailed the world of the academy spot on, exposing the aridity of its rituals and language, and yet, irony of ironies, that is exactly the place where Woolf's own work continues to live and be discussed, perhaps even in terms of the influence of someone on something.

But what moves us in this sequence is the emotional and psychological wisdom it displays, seen here as Mrs. Ramsay's instinctual knowledge of how people work and what they are made of. Later in the book, her native gifts will be described as a "singleness of mind" that "made her drop plumb like a stone, alight exact as a bird" (46), and I think we see this kind of human intelligence in her grasp of Tansley. The two of them continue their walk, arrive at a house where she goes in to comfort someone sick, and, when she exits, he has his realization: "she was the most beautiful person he had ever seen" (250). We are now, I think, dead center: Mrs. Ramsay's impact. On this young man who never went to circuses. Woolf pulls out the stops in writing his surging feelings:

> With stars in her eyes and veils in her hair, with cyclamen and wild violets—what nonsense was he thinking? She was fifty at least; she had eight children. Stepping through fields of flowers and taking to her breast buds that had broken and lambs that had fallen; with the stars in her eyes and the wind in her hair—He took her bag. (25)

It is ecstasy; it is nonsense. She is ravishing; she is fifty at least. They are in a small village; she is stepping through a pastoral landscape with flowers and buds and lambs and stars in her eyes and wind in her hair. This is what the Woolf explosion is all about: those moments when the drab phenomenal world is flooded with feeling and radiance and opens out to become something else altogether. It is as if she has found the secret for making lyricism possible in our mean precincts. The romance—for that is what it is—reaches its perfect conclusion: He took her bag.

He took her bag. Had you been there, watching this little episode, what would you have seen? A woman exiting a house; a man taking her bag. And you would have missed everything. We only think we know what "taking someone's bag" might mean. In this novel, the smallest things are bristling and luminous, mean so much more than any outsider could possibly see. The two of them walk down the street. Tansley feels "an extraordinary pride; a man digging in a drain stopped digging and looked at her; for the first time in his life Charles Tansley felt an extraordinary pride" (25). He feels the wind and the cyclamens and the violets, "for he was walking with a beautiful woman. He had hold of her bag" (25). Irresistible, I said. Even the man digging in the drain offers his tribute.

Mrs. Ramsay is good at receiving homage, is used to it. Gallantry matters; she basks (even though she is not actually vain) in the feelings she arouses, and she feels a touch of insecurity when she fails to arouse them (as with Augustus Carmichael). Her radiance extends democratically to both sexes and all ages: Women and men and children feel her aura, are drawn to her. Lily Briscoe speaks both for herself and, it would seem, for virtually everyone else as well when she imagines saying, "I'm in love with you," and then realizes that her infatuation goes still further, embraces the whole of Mrs. Ramsay's domain: " 'I'm in love with this all,' waving her hand at the hedge, at the house, at the children" (32). I have only begun to take this woman's measure, and I will return to her, but, in keeping with the book's contrapuntal logic, it seems appropriate to leave her for a moment so as to look at the man she is married to.

ANGULAR MR. RAMSAY

Mr. Ramsay, obviously based on Woolf's father, Leslie Stephen, has not fared well in Woolf criticism, or, I suspect, with the general reader. We open the book with his decisive, never-to-be-forgotten put-down, "But it won't be fine," and it seems to go downhill from there. It is hard to see past the notion that he is something of a caricature, and even Vanessa's praise on that score, crediting Virginia with capturing "the only thing about him which ever gave a true idea," is consistent with the view that he is perhaps one-dimensional. The praise he does receive in the book often seems left-handed, as it were. He is called a truth-seeker. Lily remembers, in particular, his son Andrew's advice about how to understand this great man's work; at first she is told that his books are about "subject and object and the nature of reality," but when she, mystified, presses further, he offers a definition that sticks: " 'Think of a kitchen table then,' he told her, 'when you're not there' " (38). This is sly writing, giving us its object (the table), and then removing, three words later, its perceiver (you).

And that is what Lily thinks of when she thinks of Mr. Ramsay's work: a scrubbed kitchen table. With mouthwatering irony, Woolf depicts Lily's apparent admiration for such noble intellectual labor:

> It [the scrubbed kitchen table] lodged now in the fork of a pear tree . . . And with a painful effort of concentration, she focused her mind, not upon the silver-bossed bark of the tree, or upon its fish-shaped leaves, but upon a phantom kitchen table, one of those scrubbed board tables, grained and knotted, whose virtue seems to have been laid bare by years of muscular integrity, which stuck there, its four legs in the air. Naturally, if one's days were passed in this seeing of angular essences, this reducing of lovely evenings, with all their flamingo clouds and blue and silver to a white deal four-legged table (and it was a mark of the finest minds so to do), naturally one could not be judged like an ordinary person. (38)

One smiles at the malice of this put-down. Locating the table in the fork of a pear tree seems hardly necessary from a philosophical point of view, but it is quite useful if one is out to spoof the out-of-it otherworldliness of Mr. Ramsay's pursuits. Hence, the passage makes sure we note the fine sensuous details—"silver-bossed bark" and "fish-shaped leaves" at first, "flamingo clouds and blue and silver" at the end—that the philosopher is blind to, given his (maniacal) focus on that phantom table. Much later, in the aftermath, Lily achieves a more humane perspective on the lofty Mr. Ramsay, and suspects that he "must have had his doubts about that table . . . whether the table was a real table; whether it was worth the time he gave to it; whether he was able after all to find it" (232), but that more mellow perspective is enabled by the passing of time.

QUESTER

The image of Mr. Ramsay that stays in the minds of most readers of *To the Lighthouse* is that of a stick-figure patriarch: a fanatical devotee of truth, a man obsessed by his own self-image and with a quasi-diseased, all-too-visible need for praise. As I have already implied, he represents much of what is most dubious in intellectual culture. The prime example of his excesses would seem to be his unending quest to get from Q to R. Mind you, getting even to Q is quite a feat. "Very few people in the whole of England ever reach Q" (53). But Ramsay wants to go further, and Woolf lays out his program—and his strenuous efforts to make good on it—with fierce irony:

> But after Q? What comes next? After Q there are a number of letters the last of which is scarcely visible to mortal eyes, but glimmers red in the distance. Z is reached once by one man in a generation. Still, if he could reach R it would be something. Here at least was Q. He dug his heels in at Q. Q he was sure of. Q he could demonstrate. If Q then is Q – R—Here he knocked his pipe out, with two or three resonant taps on the handle of the urn, and proceeded. "Then R . . ." He braced himself. He clenched himself. (53–54)

The thinness and brittleness of this venture signal the barrenness of pure philosophy (as I think Woolf conceived it), but once we consider that R must also stand for Ramsay, then the narcissism and the failed self-awareness also come into view. This passage closes with a kind of heroic muscular effort to push thought further than it can go. But Woolf is not content to leave the poor man's exertions alone. Instead, she follows this graph of intellectual exploration with several pages of dripping sentimental notation, casting Ramsay as a kind of swollen epic fool. Ramsay grunts and strains to get to R, but it comes out like this: "Qualities that would have saved a ship's company exposed on a broiling sea with six biscuits and a flask of water—endurance and justice, foresight, devotion, skill, came to his help. R is then—what is R?" (54). A paragraph later, the motif is repeated in slightly altered form, and we are told of "Qualities that in a desolate expedition across the icy solitudes of the Polar region would have made him the leader, the guide, the counselor . . . came to his help again. R—" (54), and thereupon follows still another puffed-up simile of a doomed leader dying on a mist-covered mountaintop, "his eyes fixed on the storm, trying to the end to pierce the darkness" (55).

A good bit of self-pity comes through in these effusions. Ramsay's mix of dryness and puffiness is on show, and his narrow form of excellence looks especially suspicious when contrasted with the richness and vibrancy and authority of his wife. And yet I believe the book as a whole takes a warmer view of this slightly grotesque figure. To be sure, his voracious need for praise and endorsement is singled out for censure, and we know enough of Virginia Woolf's tortured relations with Leslie Stephen, especially in the years after Julia's death, to see these demands for the diseased and suffocating thing they are. But he is more rounded than may appear. He knows he has traded fame for family, and that his greatest achievement may well be his eight children rather than his books. Moreover, there is something lovable in his very oddness, as shown in his bizarre habit of shouting out bits of poetry at unexpected moments, pouncing on others with his tidings, being altogether incorruptible in his judgments. And many of his pronouncements and private thoughts are genuinely provocative, reflective of a mind that moves on its own track, that enjoys the pleasures of thinking. We see him mulling over the question of civilization's progress, asking himself if the average person's lot has improved since the time of the pharaohs, reflecting that the "liftman in the Tube is an eternal necessity" (67), then becoming restless with this pessimistic view, wondering whether art might provide a reprieve, deciding that it probably wouldn't, that it is overrated as boon to mankind, closing this entire line of thought, as "he picked up a leaf sharply from the hedge" (67) with the happy notion that "All this would have to be dished up for the young men at Cardiff next month" (67).

I find nothing caricatural in these ruminations, and they go a long way toward furnishing this novel with its sense of eavesdropping on the actual processes of mind and heart. Even the passages I cited as excessive and sentimental warrant our consideration, for Woolf knows that we *are* sentimental, that we traffic in the most inflated self-images, and that those ready-mades about doomed explorers are as much right as they are wrong, for they do convey the purple excesses of self-indulgent fantasy. In some sense, they are paying their way. These two portraits of mother and father—one poetic and profound, the other a tad satirical—enrich our own portrait gallery, sharpen our sense of how islanded and incommensurate each of us is, how polyphonic the music of human relations must be.

And I am prepared to be more indulgent myself in this matter of Q and R. Those capital letters may seem silly, but the quest imagined here has clear parallels with the other quests of this book: to reach the lighthouse, to reach others, perhaps to reach expression via art. There are moments when Mr. Ramsay sounds a deeper note, and his intuition that his fate is "to come out thus on a spit of land which the sea is slowly eating away, and there to stand, like a desolate sea-bird, alone" (68) is profoundly of a piece with this novel's larger plot and overarching view of the fragility of human doing in a natural scheme that crushes it. He sees himself most resonantly "as a stake driven into the bed of a channel upon which the gulls perch and the waves beat" (69), and one needs little imagination to recognize here the motif of the lighthouse itself, the human marker that is placed in the great elements to help show others the way.

THE VIOLENCE OF MARRIAGE

But no amount of prosing on my part will alter the fact that Mr. and Mrs. Ramsay often seem an odd couple. Her warmth and generosity seem in direct contrast to his angularity and need for praise. Some of the novel's most astonishing images are in the service of conveying how different this man and woman are, how irreconcilable their positions seem to be, even how angry they can make each other. Hence, Mr. Ramsay is furious that his wife has kept alive the children's hope that they might go to the lighthouse tomorrow: "She flew in the face of facts, made his children hope what was utterly out of the question, in effect told lies . . . 'Damn you,' he said" (50). This is brutal, and it is felt as brutal. Woolf writes Mrs. Ramsay's reaction most fulsomely:

> To pursue truth with such astonishing lack of consideration for other people's feelings, to rend the thin veils of civilisation so wantonly, so brutally, was to her so horrible an outrage of human decency that, without replying, dazed and blinded, she bent her head as if to let the pelt of jagged hail, the drench of dirty water, bespatter her unrebuked. There was nothing to be said. (51)

Admittedly, "damn you" is not nice. But you may wonder: Is it commensurate with the extravagant simile that follows? We have here a version of the tempest that Lear experiences on the heath—jagged hail, dirty water, being bespattered—as Woolf's way of conveying the violence and severity of this behavior. We all know the dismissive phrase "a tempest in a teapot," and I think Woolf is interested in such notions; maybe there *are* tempests in teapots, maybe every time we are truly hurt or angry, our little teapot is experiencing its form of tempest. Maybe this is how the grand events of *King Lear* get replayed in a modern marriage. (Certainly *Lear* is as familial and domestic as *To the Lighthouse* is.) Maybe, finally, Woolf is showing us that the most outrageous and melodramatic similes and metaphors are appropriate for expressing human feeling, that there is a lot of thunder and lightning on the inside.

OUR HIDDEN SOUND AND FURY

Yet this metaphor of jagged hail is tame and conventional in comparison to the more ferocious feelings sometimes generated by this couple. Remember once more how this book begins: with a mother saying yes, and a father saying no, to a child's desire for adventure. James's response to his father is rough stuff: "Had there been an axe handy, or a poker, any weapon that would have gashed a hole in his father's breast and killed him, then and there, James would have seized it" (10). No surprise that Oedipal readings exist for this novel. What is surprising is the way this primal scene recurs over and over, and it occasions some of the most splendid language of the novel. Woolf wants to show what it actually feels like when a wife, playing with her child, is then assaulted by her husband's voracious need for sympathy:

> Mrs. Ramsay, who had been sitting loosely, folding her son in her arm, braced herself, and, half turning, seemed to raise herself with an effort, and at once to pour erect into the air a rain of energy, a column of spray, looking at the same time animated and alive as if all her energies were being fused into force, burning and illuminating (quietly though she sat, taking up her stocking again), and into this delicious fecundity, this fountain and spray of life, the fatal sterility of the male plunged itself, like a beak of brass, barren and bare. (58)

How does one even begin to account for language like this? It seems to me that Woolf is creating a new idiom entirely, made up of clear and powerful images—column of spray, fountain, beak of brass—in order to express this fierce intercourse between man and woman. Water imagery is traditional enough for representing femaleness, but the phallic overtones associated with the plunging male beak are reversed here, since the penetrating male is nonetheless coded as sterile and barren. Once again we see the marvelous counterpoint that Woolf is capable of, so that the woman knitting her stocking—what could be more staid?—is actually involved in a dazzling mating ritual of sorts. This sequence makes me think of peacocks and other animals whose dance of desire takes strange and exotic forms. The most mundane activity imaginable—a man approaching his wife, who knits—is turned into something wondrous and primeval, into a myth of fusion and sustenance, an exchange of energies and forces that is outright barbaric. This pagan dance between husband and wife is brutal in its one-way directionality, for the woman gives everything here, makes an entire world for the man: "his barrenness made fertile, and all the rooms of the house made full of life—the drawing-room; behind the drawing-room the kitchen; above the kitchen the bedrooms; and beyond them the nurseries; they must be furnished, they must be filled with life" (59). Almost like in Genesis, we see a universe coming into being, room by room, person by person, and Mrs. Ramsay is the god figure here, the one who is both fertile and potent, who receives and gives, who assures the round of life.

James, standing between his mother's knees, suffers this scene, misses nothing of its voraciousness, knows that his father is taking his mother (body and soul), and taking her from him. He will never forget this ravishing: "James felt all her strength flaring up to be drunk and quenched by the beak of brass, the arid scimitar of the male, which smote mercilessly, again and again, demanding sympathy" (59). You may have noted that I have avoided the word "psychology" for denoting or assessing what is happening in sequences like this, and that is because Virginia Woolf's magnificent, sometimes operatic, wildly metaphoric language makes us realize how lame and inert our customary terms and labels are. But we realize as well that this is what art alone can show us: the tumultuous life behind our innocuous forms and behavior. After all, nothing remotely unseemly or even noteworthy *happens*, in terms of action or movement (they don't even touch each other), and had you been standing there with a camera, you would have found nothing to photograph. And yet, it is wild, fierce, and profoundly sexual. When the male has at last had his fill (like an infant who has suckled enough), he walks off, renewed; but she experiences the exhaustion proper to consummated sexual passion—she is spent:

> Immediately, Mrs. Ramsay seemed to fold herself together, one petal closed in another, and the whole fabric fell in exhaustion upon itself, so that she had only strength enough to move her finger, in exquisite abandonment to exhaustion, across the page of Grimm's fairy story, while there throbbed through her, like the pulse in a spring which has expanded to its full width and now gently ceases to beat, the rapture of successful creation. (60–61)

As is its wont, the composite writing manages to enfold Grimm's fairy story into its story of rapture, reminding us that she is *also* reading a story to her child, as if it were the most natural thing in the world to be stormed by your husband, to respond with oceanic feeling, while at the same time reading a story and knitting a stocking. Not bad. And not some bogus triumph of compartmentalizing, either. Just a richly endowed human being.

FATALISTIC MRS. RAMSAY

It is tempting to view Mrs. Ramsay as some sort of earth mother, a fount of fertility, but this will take us only so far, because the note she strikes is as dark and somber as it is nurturing and loving. To be sure, she "would have liked always to have had a baby" (90), but her tenderness and joy with her children is tinged with melancholy and something darker still, closer to dread. She means it when, touching James's hair with her lips, she thinks "he will never be so happy again" (90), and feels that is true for all eight of them, causing her to wonder: "Why must they grow up and lose it all?" (91). There is nothing trite in this, no rosy sense of childhood as privileged, but rather an unillusioned knowledge that life is deadly and that the odds are against you: "She felt this thing that she called life terrible, hostile, and quick to pounce on you if you gave it a chance" (92). Her view of the world order is harsh and bleak: "With her mind she had always seized the fact that there is no reason, order, justice: but suffering, death, the poor. There was no treachery too base for the world to commit; she knew that. No happiness lasted; she knew that" (98). It is this clear, sober, frighteningly serene certainty about life's harshness that makes her generosity and warmth so very beautiful and haunting. "Marry, marry!" is her vaunted philosophy and theme song, but we must see it as a conscious fiction, a frail structure, standing out against a background of darkness and night and death.

Thus, all that is beautiful in this book is tinged with evanescence and fragility, which leads to scenes of great tenderness. Children are splendidly alive in *To the Lighthouse*—we see each of them in characteristic postures: James between his mother's knees, seething with rage at his father; Cam running like a deer, later being nursed to sleep; Andrew with his great intellectual promise and his embarrassment at seeing Paul and Minta embrace on the beach; Prue with her breathtaking beauty; Jasper and his taste for hunting animals; Roger and Nancy with their wildness; Rose, the sensitive one who will suffer—and they all bathed in the light of mortality and threat. I am always moved by the sequence when Mrs. Ramsay asks Rose and Jasper to select her jewels for the evening, realizing that these matters go very deep for Rose, "divining, through her own past, some deep, some buried, some quite speechless feeling that one had for one's mother at Rose's age" (123). Yes, we have the seeds here of the famous pronouncement about "thinking back through our mothers if we are women" that will appear in *A Room of One's Own*, but, to my taste, this insight possesses an even more special poignance here, when ascribed to the child via the mother's own capacity for empathy and love.

STAMMERING HUMAN CONNECTION: FROM HUSBAND TO WIFE

One's deepest feelings are indeed buried and speechless. Rose goes about choosing the jewelry while her mother intuits the child's need. Nothing is or can be said. Woolf's portrayal of human connection has great pathos because so little can actually be articulated, so little actually shared. No one is at fault here. It is in the nature of things that we are imprisoned in our own minds, and that our efforts at contact and communication are invariably stammering, partial, incomplete. Love, even intense passionate love, can make only modest inroads. Hence, when Mrs. Ramsay and her husband are taking a walk together, we are shown what a complex thing it is for two human beings to talk to each other. One problem is that each has his or her own running interior conversation: She is thinking about needing fifty pounds for the greenhouse; he is concerned with his intellectual standing. But talk occurs: They discuss Jasper's distressing habit of shooting birds, the children's nickname for Charles Tansley. They share a laugh at the possibility of poor Tansley falling in love with Prue. Then they arrive at flowers:

> He did not look at the flowers, which his wife was considering, but at a spot about a foot or so above them. There was no harm in him, he added, and was just about to say that anyhow he was the only young man in England who admired his—when he choked it back. He would not bother her again about his books. These flowers seemed creditable, Mr. Ramsay said, lowering his gaze and noticing something red, something brown. (102)

This passage is never cited by the scholars. And yet it is a heroic passage, graphing the modest but miraculous journey that love makes possible. Mr. Ramsay wants so much to validate Tansley, to reference this young man as admirer, but he squelches this native impulse so that he can join his wife. She is looking at flowers; well, he will, too. Can he help it that he initially misses the target by a foot or so? No matter, he now lowers his gaze so as to meet her. Can he help it that the best he can manage is to call them "creditable"? Is it his fault that his eyes only encounter "something red, something brown"? He goes as far as he knows how to go. He goes in her direction. It is a beautiful passage, for it maps the comedy and the tragedy of human relationships. Our best efforts are only what they are: No amount of goodwill on earth can catapult us out of our own skins and perceptual prison. Such passages tell us something fascinating about our story: namely, that love mandates that we must *leave* it every time we venture into others' space, others' lives; such exits rarely make it into fiction.

A NEW LANGUAGE OF CONNECTION: FROM WIFE TO HUSBAND

Let me now match this notation of the husband with one of the wife. They are still walking, hand in hand, in the garden. She has been thinking about his sometimes erratic behavior, such as shouting out lines of poetry at frightened guests. They reach an incline, and she wants him to slow down a little,

> intimating by a little pressure on his arm that he walked up hill too fast for her, and she must stop for a moment to see whether those were fresh molehills on the bank, then, she thought, stooping down to look, a great mind like his must be different in every way from ours. All the great men she had ever known, she thought, deciding that a rabbit must have got in, were like that, and it was good for young men (though the atmosphere of lecture-rooms was stuffy and depressing to her beyond endurance almost) simply to hear him, simply to look at him. But without shooting rabbits, how was one to keep them down? she wondered. It might be a rabbit; it might be a mole. (108)

Also a sequence that gets under the radar screen of critics. But how sweet it is. The very texture of thinking is rendered here, as moles and great men and rabbits and lecture rooms perform their little dance, all the while with her arm on his. Does this quite rise to the level of irony? After all, to shift immediately from knowing great men to rabbits getting in does have some zing to it, gets our attention, makes us wonder if great men aren't being taken down a few pegs.

But I am reluctant to push this satirical reading, since the true Woolfian note is cohabitation (rather than tension), and Mrs. Ramsay is quite at home thinking of her husband and of rabbits and moles at the same time. And to see it that way is to begin to perceive the sheer zest and openness and freedom of this kind of writing. Nothing is off limits here. The human mind is, whenever you truly listen in, an amazingly agile performer, and it cavorts itself all over the place, into and out of the most surprising precincts, as capricious and uncharted as flowing water or gentle breezes. We frequently admonish people to concentrate and think about one thing at a time, but, in actual fact, thinking is a promiscuous and amphibian affair. Reading Virginia Woolf makes you realize how bizarre and unnatural it is when we actually make sense, how coercive and artificial and reductive and nonbinding our categories and forms are, given the quirkiness of thought and feeling. This kind of writing sticks its tongue out at all our papier-mâché constructs, at those disciplined habits of mind that schooling produces, where we are instructed in logic and coherence. (In the classroom we are taught: either great men or moles, but not both interchangeably.) In Woolf, as we have had occasion to see many times, the circus never stops coming to town.

And yet, for all the playfulness of the passage, it remains credible and even touching as an account of a husband and wife walking in the garden. Our intercourse with one another is a layered performance, consisting of the few words we utter and the countless thoughts and sensations we experience, but it is intercourse all the same. Mrs. Ramsay is fully capable of sitting in the drawing room with her husband, each embarked in reading (she in a poem, he in Scott, she aware of his need to have her tell him she loves him, he hungry and pressing), resulting in nothing but small talk being said and yet everything important being understood: "And as she looked at him she began to smile, for though she had not said a word, he knew, of course he knew, that she loved him" (185). This woman, however sparing or even coy in what she says, is *felt* by everyone in the novel, is, as it were, the single heartbeat that pumps blood throughout the entire family.

LEAVING THE PRISON OF SELF

That is why one is so awed by the famous sequence that follows upon her putting James to bed. It tells us of a different Mrs. Ramsay altogether, a woman whose actual comings and goings go far, far beyond the confines of family, even of flesh. James has been fetched, she is gathering the pictures he has cut out, but alone now, and therefore ready for the great voyage:

> For now she need not think about anybody. She could be herself, by herself. And that was what now she often felt the need of—to think; well, not even to think. To be silent; to be alone. All the being and the doing, expansive, glittering, vocal, evaporated; and one shrunk, with a sense of solemnity, to being oneself, a wedge-shaped core of darkness, something invisible to others. Although she continued to knit, and sat upright, it was thus that she felt herself; and this self having shed its attachments was free for the strangest adventures. When life sank down for a moment, the range of experience seemed limitless. And to everybody there was always this sense of unlimited resources, she supposed; one after another, she, Lily, Augustus Carmichael, must feel, our apparitions, the things you know us by, are simply childish. Beneath it is all dark, it is all spreading, it is unfathomably deep; but now and again we rise to the surface and that is what you see us by. (95–96)

This justly celebrated passage, defining the self as a wedge-shaped core of darkness, challenges not only realist notions of character (all you could capture would just be apparitions, not the real thing), but boldly and provocatively reconceives selfhood as well, opening it up and out by erasing its boundaries and contours. It is an audacious and unhinging vision: The next time you gaze into a mirror or at a friend or loved one, tell yourself that what you *see* is just a shell, a mirage, an illusory frame that we take for real. Ownership disappears here, but instead of the disarray one might expect (how comfortable can it be to lose your markings?), what comes is a mix of adventure and pleasure as one enters the flow, becomes the flow.

On this heading, self is not only a construct but a burden. One thinks of Proust's remark about how miraculous it is that we wake up every morning as ourselves, given the chameleonic lives we lead in our dreams. Faulkner will pick up on the tragic dimensions of this collapse: Quentin Compson's ego dissolves, cannot say "I." Randomness of self is found still earlier in Montaigne's notion of *ondoyant*, "wavelike," as the nature of the subject, and it lurks throughout Shakespeare, most especially in Hamlet's divagations and role playing. But what about the rest of us, those of us who live in flesh rather than literature? (How many times have people told you: You're not yourself today? What do they mean?) How bounded and identifiable are we? How much bookkeeping and caretaking and strings-on-fingers and outright work is necessary to keep us us, to maintain integrity and consistency, so that others might recognize us, so that we might recognize ourselves? Is it possible that *self* could be life's greatest prison, a prison that we make for ourselves (and for others) over time? Isn't this one reason people use alcohol and drugs, change jobs and mates? Not in order to find something or someone new, but in order to make themselves anew, to discard or escape a self that is either damaged or suffocating, so as to launch into something else? Perhaps this would be the best secular meaning of the fundamentalist phrase "born again."

What would the narrative of a wedge-shaped core of darkness look like? Where are the markers of a trajectory that has dispensed with markers? How would you graph the story of this emancipated, fluid spirit travel that knows no boundaries, leaves no prints, acquires no possessions? Woolf asks some rather fierce questions of us, for most of us have, now and then, experienced the sloughing off of outer form that is described in this passage; we experience it in moments of passion, but also in moments of anomie and daydreaming and vacancy, moments when our clothes (as it were) slide off, moments when we fall out of the world. How much do we know of this residual sentient force that has no name or history, but lives inside us in some elemental fashion, prior to all those accoutrements and props that otherwise define our contours?

LOSING SELF AND FINDING ECSTASY

What is certain is that Mrs. Ramsay experiences this dissolution as liberating. Rest can be found only as a core of darkness, not as oneself. Here would be peace and freedom. Here might also be, at last, connection, even fusion. Not so much with others as with the world, with life: "It was odd, she thought, how if one was alone, one leant to inanimate things; trees, streams, flowers; felt they expressed one; felt they became one; felt they knew one, in a sense were one" (97). Mrs. Ramsay's meditation moves ever further outward, and it closes with the novel's most sensual and ecstatic moment, the embrace of the lighthouse:

> . . . she looked at the steady light, the pitiless, the remorseless, which was so much her, yet so little her, which had her at its beck and call (she woke in the night and saw it bent across their bed, stroking the floor), but for all that she thought, watching it with fascination, hypnotised, as if it were stroking with its silver fingers some sealed vessel in her brain whose bursting would flood her with delight, she had known happiness, exquisite happiness, intense happiness, and it silvered the rough waves a little more brightly, as daylight faded, and the blue went out of the sea and it rolled in waves of pure lemon which curved and swelled and broke upon the beach and the ecstasy burst in her eyes and waves of pure delight raced over the floor of her mind and she felt, It is enough! It is enough! (99–100)

Virginia Woolf is a strange bird when it comes to the representation of sex in her books. Her dear friend Lytton Strachey faulted *To the Lighthouse* for not making any room for "copulation." It is not hard to see what he meant. Even when she seems to speak straight-out about this topic as a central ingredient of marriage, often enough Woolf appears either coy or evasive: "Marriage needed—oh, all sorts of qualities (the bill for the greenhouse would be fifty pounds); one—she need not name it—that was essential; the thing she had with her husband. Had they [Paul and Minta] that?" (93). Typical Woolf mix, you might say, conflating greenhouse costs and essential qualities of marriage, yet one still wonders why "she need not name it."

We have already noted the dazzling sequence in which Mrs. Ramsay's fountain and spray receive her husband's beak of brass and male scimitar. All of the metaphors are charged, but sexuality as such seems to get in only between the lines in Woolf. One might feel cheated (as Strachey did). But I raise these objections only in order to return to the passage I cited, where the steady light moves across the floor and then strokes Mrs. Ramsay. This moment is as orgasmic as its counterpart in *Mrs. Dalloway*, when Clarissa is recalling the nature of lesbian desire, that too an affair of quivering and rapture and gushing and pouring. If anything, this sequence is richer still, for it fuses together the human and the natural so that the light itself strokes the floor and the woman and the sea, "silvering" all of them, so that the "waves of pure lemon which curved and swelled and broke upon the beach" are inseparable from the bursting ecstasy and waves of delight inside Mrs. Ramsay herself. Let me go further still. Perhaps Woolf is telling us that the most intense sensations we experience are ultimately impersonal and anonymous, that they come about when our bounded organism bursts out, fuses with not-self, knows ecstasy. Does orgasm have a name and address on it? *Jouissance*, thought of as the self's most extreme pleasure, may signal something else entirely: self's ecstatic eclipse, its triumphant escape from its own bonds.

DINNER AND THE SOCIAL CONTRACT

Knowing, as we now do, how faraway, subterranean, selfless (and close to nihilistic) Mrs. Ramsay can be in her most intense moments, we are all the more moved, I think, by this woman's generosity and capacity for assent. She knows that we live forever in a room of one's own, and she also knows that this room is ultimately not one's own; this is why it is so fine, so right, so unforgettable that the central event of *To the Lighthouse* should be a . . . dinner. How many novels take us to dinner? The French do rather more in this vein than the English, and one remembers the riotous appetites of Rabelais's giants, and the epic repast served at Emma Bovary's wedding feast, as well as some of the more extended culinary extravaganzas in Zola and Proust. Woolf is hardly their rival in terms of gastronomic particulars, of course after course of mouthwatering dishes, replete with sauces and wines. But I do not think anyone has ever surpassed her in showing us what a dinner signifies. By dinner, I mean the sort of thing one has in this novel: a large group of people—both family and guests—seated around a table, sharing food and conversation. If I had to find a parallel for Woolf's achievement, it would doubtless be the delicious and lovable Danish film *Babette's Feast*, drawn from a story by Isak Dinesen.

Dinesen has stacked her deck by framing her account as a kind of marriage between France and Denmark, between the pleasures of the flesh and those of the spirit. Woolf is, I think, more our contemporary, inasmuch as there is no religious ax to grind, no nineteenth-century setting, no exotica at all. Just a dinner party in a summer house. Our contemporary, I said; yet I am acutely aware of the fact that dinner parties are becoming as remote as Dinesen's village parishioners. And there will be those who feel that summer houses are more than a little exotic as well. So, let me put my cards on the table: Dinner parties are not what they were, partly because few people have servants today, partly because both spouses often have jobs (in middle-class marriages), and partly because no one has time for such events. I exaggerate to make a point. And I can only speak out of my own experience. Having said this, I come now to those cards I put out there: The Ramsay dinner gathering—which is not a party, really—stages the most profound conflicts and issues of the novel, and it does so in the most basic and elemental ways. It stages one great question: Why be together? And it stages that question in the dining room, with a real cast of characters, rather than in the bedroom, where we expect to see this issue played out between only two people. Finally, it is mercilessly unflinching, even ferocious, in its critical gaze: *Why, indeed?* What on earth warrants our sitting together around a table to break bread and exchange words? So much effort and trouble, so much mundane chitchat, so much wasted time. And for what? Just hocus-pocus.

That is largely what our heroine feels when she enters that dining room and looks at that table with all those people sitting around it: "But what have I done with my life? thought Mrs. Ramsay, taking her place at the head of the table and looking at all the plates making white circles on it" (125). A bleak notation, that. And one that all of us have known, from time to time, as the nullity of things sinks in. Perhaps, she thinks, her husband will help her out, but a glance in his direction, finding him "all in a heap, frowning" (125), clears up that misconception and opens the door to still worse thoughts. He's frowning; what at? "She did not know. She did not mind. She could not understand how she had ever felt any emotion or affection for him. She had a sense of being past everything, through everything, out of everything" (125). Like a dog with its teeth in your leg, Woolf does not let go of what it actually feels like when you look unblinkingly around you and wonder how on earth you ever invested it—your loved ones, your friends, your life—with meaning and feeling. How often do we die this death?

WOMEN'S WORK, MEN'S WORK

And the people sitting around the table are so many clumps of flesh, inert and unconnected. It is at this juncture that Woolf shows us what heroines are made of. Heroines: female heroes. Males are worthless here, have always been worthless. We witness nothing short of a creation myth:

> Nothing seemed to have merged. They all sat separate. And the whole of the effort of merging and flowing and creating rested on her. Again she felt, as a fact without hostility, the sterility of men, for if she did not do it nobody would do it, and so, giving herself the little shake that one gives a watch that has stopped, the old familiar pulse began beating, as the watch begins ticking—one, two, three, one, two, three. And so on and so on, she repeated, listening to it, sheltering and fostering the still feeble pulse as one might guard a weak flame with a newspaper. (126)

This passage helps us understand how useless our customary labels are for grasping what is living and what is dead, what is men's work and what is women's work. Even our basic term "social" seems thin and abstract when seen in the light of Woolf's notation. Rousseau termed his great political treatise *Le Contrat social,* but he was a Johnny-come-lately, because the real social contract had existed since time immemorial, consisting of the fundamental labor that women have always provided in the service of human gatherings. Likewise, I think of Prometheus stealing fire from the gods, and I say: misgendered. Women got there first, women have always tended the fire and the hearth, have put food on the table for men and children, have tended to, and nurtured, life at its most elemental, just as Mrs. Ramsay shelters the feeble pulse at her table, guards its flame.

Do not think that this battle is won easily, or permanently. It must be fought over and over. William Bankes sits there in mid-meal during a lull, courteous and bored, examining his fingers on the tablecloth, thinking that it is all such a waste of time: "Such are the sacrifices one's friends ask of one. It would have hurt her if he had refused to come. But it was not worth it for him . . . if he had been alone dinner would have been almost over now; he would have been free to work" (133–134). Work: Now, that is a man's thing. Whereas this sitting and pretending to care is . . . ignoble. William, lucid intellectual that he is, goes to the heart of the matter: "The truth was that he did not enjoy family life. It was in this sort of state that one asked oneself, What does one live for? Why, one asked oneself, does one take all these pains for the human race to go on? Is it so very desirable? Are we attractive as a species?" (134). As usual, Woolf has perfect pitch, and one feels she lives as deeply in William as she does in Mrs. Ramsay.

If William is bored, Charles Tansley—ill at ease, insecure, dressed wrong, unconnected—is outright virulent: "For he was not going to talk the sort of rot these people wanted him to talk. He was not going to be condescended to by these silly women. He had been reading in his room, and now he came down and it all seemed to him silly, superficial, flimsy" (129). And so he behaves rudely, boorishly. Lily, in reluctant response to Mrs. Ramsay's (unspoken, unmistakable) plea to please bring this poor man into the conversation, asks him if he is a good sailor. Woolf—who demonstrably writes men as well as she does women—tells us exactly what it feels like to be Charles Tansley on the verge of explosion:

> Mr. Tansley raised a hammer: swung it high in air; but realising, as it descended, that he could not smite that butterfly with an instrument such as this, said only that he had never been sick a day in his life. But in that one sentence lay compact, like gunpowder, that his grandfather was a fisherman; his father a chemist; that he had worked his way up entirely himself; that he was proud of it; that he was Charles Tansley—a fact that nobody here seemed to realise; but one of these days every single person would know it. He scowled ahead of him. He could almost pity these mild cultivated people, who would be blown sky high, like bales of wool

> and barrels of apples, one of these days by the gunpowder that was in him. (138)

One does not think of *To the Lighthouse* as a political novel, but this luminous passage is as wise about class warfare as it is about the peculiar economics of human utterance in tight corners, an economics based on investing innocuous words with all the poison we can muster. What social contract is possible here? How is harmony to be made from these obstinate materials? How to overcome William's boredom, Tansley's rage?

One answer is: Show interest, pose questions, go through the motions, assume the "social manner." Men may well feel exempted from this injunction, which places the burden ever more fully on women. Lily finds herself dragged in. Yet what starts as a reluctant charade may gradually become more authentic. Woolf genially calls such efforts "French"; when people are in strife and can't get together, they should all speak French: "Perhaps it is bad French; French may not contain the words that express the speaker's thoughts; nevertheless speaking French imposes some order, some uniformity" (135–136). Still more order is achieved when the candles are lit, keeping the darkness at bay, bringing the faces nearer, "composing" them "into a party round the table" (146). At this moment, the Ramsay dinner party begins to shimmer, to become something precious and fragile: "order and dry land" as opposed to "outside," where "things wavered and vanished waterily" (147), a tiny island threatened by the sea, frail candlelight threatened by the dark, a group of humans displaying "common cause against that fluidity out there" (147). This dining room with its celebrants speaking French is beginning to show its heroic colors.

A FEAST FOR THE HEART

Another much-valued, immemorial strategy for creating harmony and actualizing the social contract, a strategy so primitive as to seem embarrassing, is *food*. For three days the cook has been working on the main course, *boeuf en daube*, prepared according to an old French recipe of Mrs. Ramsay's grandmother, and Woolf wants us to know that these three days have not been wasted. Mrs. Ramsay peers into the great brown dish, "with its shiny walls and its confusion of savoury brown and yellow meats and its bay leaves and its wine" (151), and a great pagan feeling comes into the novel. Food will be coupled with sex. Two young people are at the table, and their life is poised for momentous change. We know, from Paul's mere use of the pronoun "we," that he (emboldened by his hostess's belief in him) has asked Minta to marry him, and Mrs. Ramsay sees their vows as inseparable from this feast. Her thoughts become quite primitive here, conferring an antic, ritual sense to these happenings, wherein life in all its heat is celebrated, but against the backdrop of death:

> This will celebrate the occasion—a curious sense rising in her, at once freakish and tender, of celebrating a festival, as if two emotions were called up in her, one profound—for what could be more serious than the love of man for woman, what more commanding, more impressive, bearing in its bosom the seeds of death; at the same time these lovers, these people entering into illusion glittering eyed, must be danced round with mockery, decorated with garlands. (151)

Marriage again. Seriousness and mockery, *boeuf en daube* and garlanded lovers, well-behaved dinner guests and Dionysian rites, civilized conversation and passionate lovemaking. Thus, the prose moves unerringly to William Bankes's tribute to the savory dish, a tribute that brings him out of his anomie, that testifies to the flowing of juices, gastric and otherwise: " 'It's a triumph,' said Mr. Bankes, laying his knife down for a moment. He had eaten attentively. It was rich; it was tender. It was perfectly cooked" (151).

The pulse beats, the blood circulates, the words flow. Lily watches, enthralled: Mrs. Ramsay "put a spell on them all" (152). Lily sees her, in her mind's eye, leading "her victims . . . to the altar. It came over her too now—the emotion, the vibration, of love" (153). We are to understand "altar" in both senses here: as site for both marriage and sacrifice. The heat builds still further, as the conversation turns to the brooch that Mina has lost on the shore, a precious heirloom that will never be found, and as Paul speaks of returning to the beach to search for it, Lily becomes almost frantic with the need to be part of this conflagration. So much so that she actually volunteers to accompany him; but he merely laughs. And she realizes that it was as if he had said: "Throw yourself over a cliff if you like, I don't care. He turned on her cheek the heat of love, its horror, its cruelty, its unscrupulosity. It scorched her" (154). There is something wonderfully apt in this evocation of barbaric feeling in the context of meat and wine and talk. Mrs. Ramsay will later think of this as a night that will be remembered "however long they live" (170), but Woolf's finest notation in this regard comes when William Bankes is served another helping of the triumphant *boeuf en daube*. Mrs. Ramsay's rapture at the dinner table, her pleasure in "successful creation," is not all that far from *jouissance:*

> . . . she hovered like a hawk suspended; like a flag floated in an element of joy which filled every nerve of her body fully and sweetly, not noisily, solemnly rather, for it arose, she thought, looking at them all eating there, from husband and children and friends; all of which rising in this profound stillness (she was helping William Bankes to one very small piece more, and peered into the depths of the earthenware pot) seemed now for no special reason to stay there like a smoke, like a fume rising upwards, holding them safe together. Nothing need be said; nothing could be said. There it was, all round them. It partook, she felt, carefully helping Mr. Bankes to a specially tender piece, of eternity. . . . Of such moments, she thought, the thing is made that endures. (158)

Suspended hawk, floating flag, filled nerves, sweet joy, rising smoke: Many are the images that come together here to convey Mrs. Ramsay's well-nigh ecstatic pleasure in being the goddess of the hearth. I suspect that if I had to single out one sentence in all of Woolf for applause, it might well be: "It partook, she felt, carefully helping Mr. Bankes to a specially tender piece, of eternity." If such a thing as the human arts exists, surely we find it in this passage. No other writer on the planet would have conflated a tender piece of meat with a feeling of eternity, but we are collectively the richer for this notation. Of course she does not equate these two things, but her prose marries them, makes us understand that the rich, evanescent pleasures of food and talk are the treasure in front of our eyes, in shining contrast to the brooch that is lost on the shore. Here is our bounty, here is our fragile happiness, here is where death-haunted flesh and time-bound pleasure and civilized human discourse make their beautiful counterargument: They endure.

TIME PASSES, DEATH REIGNS

But, of course, they don't, as the brutal middle chapter of the novel, "Time Passes," informs us with such pith. The magic dinner is over. The summer house is abandoned. The guests are separated; some of them are annihilated. Into what had seemed more than a little idyllic comes now "a downpouring of immense darkness" (180), comes with such force that "Nothing, it seemed, could survive the flood, the profusion of darkness" (189). One remembers the candlelit table with guests, united in "their common cause against that fluidity out there," and one remembers even that "wedge-shaped core of darkness" (which is how Mrs. Ramsay at her most inward saw herself), and one is led to the grim conclusion that these images of fluidity and darkness, now turned lethal and punitive, have completely taken over, have declared war on the fragile human community and its aspirations and visions.

As readers of *To the Lighthouse* know, my term "war" is no metaphor. Woolf wants unmistakably to signal the Great War itself as the actual, historical violence—the mix of darkness and flood—that now emerges on the scene and destroys both peace and life. The writing is figurative, not direct, and the central image that Woolf uses is that of the "airs" that now move freely about, undoing and dismantling what people had lovingly put together; the book asks, perhaps a little coyly, of these airs: "Were they allies? Were they enemies? How long would they endure?" (190–191). It is not hard to see the political ramifications here. Yet even if we initially feel that "certain airs" is too precious a phrase to convey the sheer destructive power of the war, we can scarcely fail to see that the novel's poetic logic requires coding it as a kind of storm, as chaos among the elements themselves. After all, it is the same question Shakespeare posed in *King Lear*: how to represent the outbreak of a violence and terror that are at once familial, political, and metaphysical? Woolf, by staging her own tempest, is following in his lead.

Soon enough, we see that the seemingly diminutive "little airs" are all the more heinous in their destructive work. We see them enter the house: They "crept round corners and ventured indoors" (190), much as a thief might have done; the novel imagines them even "toying with the flap of hanging wall-paper, asking, would it hang much longer, when would it fall?" (190). A systematic translation of politics into domestic imagery is undertaken in this chapter. Woolf wants us to realize that the collapse or dismantling of a house is a more terrifying index of war's fury than any abstract rhetoric might be. First the wallpaper goes, then the "little airs mounted the staircase and nosed around bedroom doors" (191). The text itself protests, as if rape were impending: "But here surely, they must cease. Whatever else may perish and disappear, what lies here is steadfast" (191). But to no avail: Nothing can resist the invasion imaged in these pages. We see the airs make their furtive but unstoppable entry, bending over the bed, extending their reign throughout the house: upstairs bedrooms, attics, dining-room table (where they "blanched the apples," "fumbled the petals of roses"), then trying the picture on the easel, brushing the mat, blowing a little sand on the floor.

With horrid logic, this generalized destruction moves from its material victims to its human prey. Appearing within brackets, almost as footnotes to the dismantling operation at hand, Ramsays in the midst of life begin to die:

> [Mr. Ramsay, stumbling along a passage one dark morning, stretched his arms out, but Mrs. Ramsay having died rather suddenly the night before, his arms, though stretched out, remained empty.] (194)

> [Prue Ramsay, leaning on her father's arm, was given in marriage. What, people said, could have been more fitting? And, they added, how beautiful she looked!] (198)

> [Prue Ramsay died that summer in some illness connected with childbirth, which was indeed a tragedy, people said, everything, they said, had promised so well.] (199)

> [A shell exploded. Twenty or thirty young men were blown up in France, among them Andrew Ramsay, whose death, mercifully, was instantaneous.] (201)

I know of few notations in literature that can match the brutality and shock of these bracketed inserts, brazenly advertising the absurd frailty of human life and love, the unfairness of the contest. Part of the shock lies in Woolf's spectacular rejection of novelistic convention, a convention that promises to keep the main players at the center of the stage, either to keep them alive or, if dead, to focus appropriately—as the event warrants—on their dying.

Not so here. To cite Othello's prophetic line about what love's death would bring: "Chaos is come again." Chaos is come. All fond notions of human dignity and what I called "appropriateness" are blown sky-high. It is as if Mrs. Ramsay's darkest intuitions of truth—that life is merciless, "terrible, hostile"—are now actualized in all their ferocity, so that the wedge-shaped core of darkness that seemed to represent self's liberty reappears now, but no longer a wedge-shaped core, no longer a mode of human freedom, but rather an apocalyptic reign of darkness that annihilates human life.

Yes, this destruction is referrable to the war. Woolf frequently evokes the tempest in language that echoes with military significance: "There came later in the summer ominous sounds like the measured blows of hammers dulled on felt" or "there seemed to drop into this silence, this indifference, this integrity, the thud of something falling" (200, 201). But war is only a partial explanation. Remember again Mrs. Ramsay: *Life* is the enemy. Hence, Prue's death in childbirth is in keeping with her own mother's vision. Life is without pity. It can be riotous and inhuman in its grisly play. Life kills Mrs. Ramsay, leaves her husband's outstretched arms empty. Woolf describes the awful power of the sea as a kind of chaotic spectacle, devoid of human pattern, ceaseless energy without form or meaning:

> . . . as the winds and waves disported themselves like the amorphous bulks of leviathans whose brows are pierced by no light of reason, and mounted one on top of another, and lunged and plunged in the darkness or the daylight (for night and day, month and year ran shapelessly together) in idiot games, until it seemed as if the universe were battling and tumbling, in brute confusion and wanton lust aimlessly by itself. (202–203)

We have no contract with nature. Prue Ramsay dies in childbirth, but life teems with mad energy: "What power could now prevent the fertility, the insensibility of nature?" (207). Woolf knows how to write these convulsions, this scheme gone amok: "There was a purplish stain upon the bland surface of the sea as if something had boiled and bled, invisibly, beneath" (201).

But I'd argue that the ultimate pathos of this novel resides in its domestic frame, its modest but heartbreaking pledge to tell us a story about a wife and husband and children, a dinner, a house. Like *King Lear* yet again, the plot of this novel hurts most when we realize that there is no dividing line between the tempest on the heath or the storm at sea, on the one hand, and our fragile human family on the other. Two of the most resonant images of the novel, from that point of view, are the red-and-brown stocking that Mrs. Ramsay knits throughout the first chapter, and its counterpart, the shawl that she hangs over the boar's skull in the children's room to pacify both Cam and Jasper so that they might go to sleep. The simple question asked is: Will they hold? Will the knitted garment ever be finished or used? Will the shawl remain? Can the beast be covered by our art? What possible authority can our human artifacts have, in the chaotic natural scheme of this book?

Hence, the passages that denote the fate of the shawl seem especially moving to me. As night and violence rupture the house, it begins to give: "One fold of the shawl loosened and swung to and fro" (196); as the lighthouse ray enters the exposed house, "another fold of the shawl loosened" (200); as the "trifling airs . . . seemed to have triumphed," leaving rusted saucepan and decayed mat and toads nosing their way in, "Idly, aimlessly, the swaying shawl swung to and fro" (206–207). Ultimate undoing is nigh: "One feather, and the house, sinking, falling, would have turned and pitched downwards to the depths of darkness" (208). But it does not happen. The chapter closes with the arrival of the witless Mrs. McNab and her associate, Mrs. Bast, commissioned by the family, after a ten-year hiatus, to come to the house and to undertake the heroic labor of cleaning it up, rescuing it from destruction and oblivion. Thus, the door is opened to the splendid last chapter of the book, "The Lighthouse," which asks the terrible final questions. Does the shawl hold? What is left of the human family? Does anything outlast death? Where does love go? Can it die? Is it still possible to go to the lighthouse?

REACHING MRS. RAMSAY

If *Mrs. Dalloway* measures the impact of time on youthful passion, asking "What have we made of our lives?," *To the Lighthouse* takes these issues a momentous and tragic step further: Do the dead still live? If so, where? How? Clearly, Virginia Woolf wrote this book as a way of coming to terms with these matters at once personal and universal. Of course, the novel offers a portrait of Julia and Leslie Stephen; but it offers no less a reflecting mirror for all of us who have dead loved ones somewhere in our lives: in our memories, in our behavior, even in our genes. To carry out this epic project of analysis and—perhaps—retrieval, Woolf now places the shy, virginal, sometimes resistant Lily Briscoe at the center of things. The figurative daughter replaces the dead mother. We need to remember that Lily's love for Mrs. Ramsay was depicted, in the first part of the novel, as a kind of magic medium, an almost palpable substance that bathes the world; likewise, she saw in the entranced feelings of others (such as William Bankes) that same, almost holy reverence, "like the love which mathematicians bear their symbols, or poets their phrases" (73–74). Lily's great hunger was to touch Mrs. Ramsay, to fuse with her, to become one with this radiant woman. In what is one of the most haunting portraits of human desire ever written, Woolf depicted Lily's great need as a quest every bit as arduous and mythic as that of reaching the lighthouse:

> Sitting on the floor with her arms round Mrs. Ramsay's knees, close as she could get, smiling to think that Mrs. Ramsay would never know the reason of that pressure, she imagined how in the chambers of the mind and heart of the woman who was, physically, touching her, were stood, like the treasures in the tombs of kings, tables bearing sacred inscriptions, which if one could spell them out, would teach one everything, but they would never be offered openly, never made public. What art was there, known to love or cunning, by which one pressed through into those secret chambers? What device for becoming, like waters poured into one jar, inextricably the same, one with the object one adored? Could the body achieve, or the mind, subtly mingling in the intricate passages of the brain? or the heart? Could loving, as people called it, make her and Mrs. Ramsay one? for it was not knowledge but unity that she desired, not inscriptions on tablets, nothing that could be written in any language known to men, but intimacy itself, which is knowledge, she had thought, leaning her head on Mrs. Ramsay's knee. (78–79)

Here is prose that has the metaphoric and formal splendor we associate with poetry. We begin and end with Lily leaning against Mrs. Ramsay's knee, but in the middle—like an inner chamber with treasures and inscriptions—lies the unseen world, the realm of desire and longing. Is this shareable?

I know no images anywhere in any book that better convey the urgency and hunger that drive human desire to enter the loved one, to achieve union. It seems, initially, a tribute to *verbal* art that this passage conveys that elemental pulsion as an affair of inscriptions on tablets, of words that bring knowledge. We cannot fail to see that these resonant images stand for the entire institution of literature, of words used as magic instruments for recording what is not on show, what is on the far side of both seeing and touching. Once again, one notes the outright generosity of this book, its view of language as means of seeking intimacy and union; and also its poignant recognition that even the choicest and most heartfelt words will not take us there, will not open the door to the treasure.

But language is hardly the only bridge to the other. The passage seems to pass in review all the modalities available to us—flesh, words—and finds them all lacking: Mrs. Ramsay will never know what the pressure of Lily's embrace says; Lily will never read the inscriptions nor press into the secret chambers. The (male?) sexual imagery of penetration then yields to its female other, a flow of waters that would merge us into one another, that would be intimacy itself. What art was there, known to love or cunning? Lily wondered, touching Mrs. Ramsay's knees. This was desire, burning need, but not consummation. No answers were given. And it was a long time ago. Such were Lily's feelings *then*. But now? Is Mrs. Ramsay, dead, reachable *now*? How?

CAN LOVE DIE?

The final chapter of the book is to explore the basic horrible challenge that time metes out to us: It erases others; and it erases our feelings for others. Perhaps art could be an answer. Not inscriptions as such, not some secret formula or knowledge; but art as the medium of both desire and presence, as the secular equivalent of resurrection. But you have to *want* this, and Lily, returning to the scene ten years later, feels nothing at all. Lily, ineluctably like Virginia herself, is there later, afterward, with only memories, to take measures; and there is nothing to measure. "The house, the place, the morning, all seemed strangers to her. She had no attachment here, she felt, no relations with it. . . . Mrs. Ramsay dead; Andrew killed; Prue dead too—repeat it as she might, it roused no feeling in her" (218–219). Lily, never much for throbbing (even earlier), feels dried out by time, withered.

And she remembers, as terrible object lesson, that the woman she loved may have been destroyed by just that—too much love: "Giving, giving, giving, she had died—and had left all this" (223). Perhaps the high priestess of marriage had it all wrong all along. Among the gifts brought by the passing of time is arguably this: We now see how mistaken people were; we now know how badly they got it wrong. And, moreover, since they are no longer here to bully us—this must be one of the great uncelebrated virtues of surviving others' deaths—well, then, we are now (at long last) in control:

> They [the dead] are at our mercy. Mrs. Ramsay has faded and gone, she thought. We can over-ride her wishes, improve away her limited, old-fashioned ideas. She recedes further and further from us. Mockingly she seemed to see her there at the end of the corridor of years saying, of all incongruous things, "Marry, marry!" (sitting very upright early in the morning with the birds beginning to cheep in the garden outside). And one would have to say to her, It has all gone against your wishes. They're happy like that; I'm happy like this. Life has changed completely. (260)

One remembers Virginia's own gratitude that her parents were dead, that she could never have become who she was had they still been living. Lily now stands up to the great matriarch; she recalls Mrs. Ramsay's fantasy of a marriage between herself and William Bankes. It had not happened. Yes, they were friends who met and talked: about flowers and architecture and furnishings, even about art. But marriage?

Above all, however, Lily informs us about what time has done to the Rayleys, Mrs. Ramsay's prime exhibit in the marriage arcade. Their coming together was among the triumphs celebrated at the dinner ten years before. Yet this is the one that has "gone against your wishes." We are told, in a metaphor that is pregnant with meaning in this book, that "things had worked loose after the first year or so; the marriage had turned out rather badly" (257–258). We are meant, I think, to remember the stocking and the shawl, to reflect that marriage is not time-proof. Lily tells us how separate and bitter the Rayleys' lives have become, how they went through a phase of misery and violence, and are now "excellent friends" but no longer "in love." Standing in front of her easel, having picked up again that painting (of mother and child and place) she never got around to completing ten years ago, Lily is ever more convinced that Mrs. Ramsay's belief in marriage was silly, senseless, a "mania." And just as Lily somewhat gleefully completes this thought, the text explodes:

> (Suddenly, as suddenly as a star slides in the sky, a reddish light seemed to burn in her mind, covering Paul Rayley, issuing from him. It rose like a fire sent up in token of some celebration by savages on a distant beach. She heard the roar and the crackle. The whole sea for miles round ran red and gold. Some winey smell mixed with it and intoxicated her, for she felt again her own headlong desire to throw herself off the cliff and be drowned looking for a pearl brooch on a beach. And the roar and the crackle repelled her with fear and disgust, as if while she saw its splendour and power she saw too how it fed on the treasure of the house, greedily, disgustingly, and she loathed it. But for a sight, for a glory it surpassed everything in her experience, and burnt year after year like a signal fire on a desert island at the edge of the sea, and one had only to say "in love" and instantly, as happened now, up rose Paul's fire again. . . .) (261–262)

Woolf the pagan speaks here. Passion lives now as it did then. Time avails not. The imagery reminds us of the marvelous *boeuf en daube* and the celebration of human heat and warmth that accompanied it. Please note that the Rayleys' marriage may be dead, dead, dead, but the fire on the distant beach rages on, and the whole sea runs red and gold. We are very close to the book's heart in this sequence, even though the Rayleys themselves are minor figures; Woolf seems to be saying—Lily seems to be discovering—that human feeling resists the law of entropy, that it lives like a signal fire on a desert island, even if all the human participants have long disappeared.

HUMAN FEELING: THE MOTOR FORCE OF ART

This sequence is very suggestive from a textual perspective. The vision of searing passion erupts into the text, pushing aside, almost scorching (once again) the demure and crowing Lily Briscoe who had thought herself safe and secure. Now she remembers what a close call it was, ten years ago: "She had only escaped by the skin of her teeth though, she thought. She had been looking at the table-cloth, and it had flashed upon her that she would move the tree to the middle, and need never marry anybody, and she had felt an enormous exultation" (262). For years I read this passage and chuckled at the schoolmarmish Lily, "little Brisk," who countered passion by focusing on her painting and deciding to never marry. Silly Lily, I thought. Yet when I teach this book, I frequently find (to my displeasure) that my students have much more sympathy for Lily than I do, that they in fact may admire her much more than they do Mrs. Ramsay. I, of course, explain to them that they have it wrong—professors always have it right—but a wee bit of light has come my way. There is perhaps no conflict in this sequence, however Lily herself initially sees it. Moving from scorching heat to the composition of the painting is not an escape. The entire logic of the novel goes the other way: The place where the fires still burn and the savages dance is not a desert island at all—it is (to be) Lily's canvas. Art and fire, art and the return of the dead: Those are the ultimate marriages to be envisioned.

Nonetheless, it is all too easy, I believe, to construe *To the Lighthouse* as a book about aesthetics, about art, and to see Lily Briscoe as its spokesperson. Lily's painting is going to matter, but the novel is not interested in aesthetics as such in the least. Things are fiercer than this. Art is recovery. It is the overcoming of time and the capturing—live—of human feeling. Lily is most crucial as a medium, as a conduit, for this is what it finally means, to have one's vision.

There cannot be vision until there is feeling. Lily returns to that house of unrelated passions, and she feels nothing. She scoffs now at the dead priestess. She resists the still-living, still-terrorizing patriarch. But this will all change. One of the most comic yet touching scenes of the novel is Lily's encounter with the still-voracious Mr. Ramsay, as needy for praise as ever, but without a wife to give it to him. Here is the slot poor Lily falls into. He presses closer and closer, she looks at the sea; "Why, thought Mr. Ramsay, should she look at the sea when I am here?" (225–226). The pressure mounts still further: "But Mr. Ramsay, as if he knew that his time ran short, exerted upon her solitary figure the immense pressure of his concentrated woe; his age; his frailty; his desolation" (228). Casting about frantically, Lily manages only to produce a word of praise for his boots. To her amazement, it is enough. Noises are made about boots: how particularly handsome and well made these are, how rare and necessary such artisanal skills are. It is as if a magic lubricant, a salve of immeasurable value, had been bestowed upon a dry world, transforming it entirely: "They had reached, she felt, a sunny island where peace dwelt, sanity reigned, and the sun for ever shone, the blessed island of good boots" (230). He is pleased, she is pleased, he teases her, she is pleased to be teased.

It is gratifying but short-lived. The children, Cam and James, come; they are to accompany their father in undertaking the long-postponed epic voyage of the novel; they will go to the lighthouse. And Lily throbs now. She is now frustrated, sexually frustrated, that she has not fully given this man what he so much wanted, what she now is able to give, what she now wants as well. But she is wrong. Fuel has been given and has been taken. Fuel for both of the final ventures of this novel: the trip of the father and son and daughter to the lighthouse, and the passage of the symbolic daughter, Lily the artist, from conception to execution, from idea to achieved art. These two projects complement each other, draw on the exact same ingredients (all appearances to the contrary), and, in depicting their twin trajectories, Woolf finds the perfect way to complete her book and her vision.

I do not want to minimize the other issues in play here. No one can miss the feminist stakes of Lily's project: Having heard all too often (by Tansley and others, too, one assumes) that "women can't paint," Lily clearly has something to prove as she sets up easel and goes to work. And she does prove it. All this is cleanly argued, and jumps out at us, embarrassingly, almost a century later, partly because we take it for granted today that women can write, women can paint; but we do so as the beneficiaries of Woolf's own pioneering and epochal efforts in this area. The painterly concerns of the novel are also vitally important, and Virginia was much pleased that Vanessa (the painter in the family) was impressed with that dimension of the novel as well. There are conversations between Lily and William Bankes about stylistic choices and the attitudes they imply, but the central aesthetic issues are, ultimately, existential in character. Lily stands in front of the blank canvas with exactly the same fear and trembling that Virginia has doubtless felt in front of the blank page. To make art means, at least initially, to withdraw from human exchange in order to confront the great adversary:

> Here she was again, she thought, stepping back to look at it, drawn out of gossip, out of living, out of community with people into the presence of this formidable ancient enemy of hers—this other thing, this truth, this reality, which suddenly laid hands on her, emerged stark at the back

> of appearances and commanded her attention. She was half unwilling, half reluctant. Why always be drawn out and haled away? . . . Other worshipful objects were content with worship; men, women, God, all let one kneel prostrate; but this form . . . roused one to perpetual combat, challenged one to a fight in which one was bound to be worsted. (236)

The dignity and severity of art come across as daunting. One feels Woolf's own hard-won knowledge about the frightening twin costs of her vocation: Art pulls you out of social intercourse; art is a contest you cannot win. How hard it is to exchange "the fluidity of life for the concentration of painting" (237). Yet, it matters little whether Lily is a genius or not (she is not), whether her painting will be hung in a museum or hidden under a sofa (the latter more likely); what counts is that the calling is an aristocratic one, and that one does not trifle with it. Art is the most serious thing in life, however capricious it may appear on the surface. Hence, Lily's painterly aims are, in the last analysis, exalted: "Beautiful and light it should be on the surface, feathery and evanescent, one colour melting into another like the colours on a butterfly's wing; but beneath the fabric must be clamped together with bolts of iron. It was a thing you could ruffle with your breath; and a thing you could not dislodge with a team of horses" (255). Like the writing of Virginia Woolf: impressionistic if you will, but enduring, made for the long haul, made to last.

ART AND RESURRECTION

The making of art is inscribed in the book's engagement with time and death. And in a crucial double sense. All art, we may say, lives, but Lily Briscoe's art is in the service of bringing the dead Mrs. Ramsay back to life. For Lily's painting is first and foremost a journey outside her narrow self and into the flow of time: "And as she lost consciousness of outer things, and her name and her personality and her appearance, and whether Mr. Carmichael was there or not, her mind kept throwing up from its depths, scenes, and names, and sayings, and memories and ideas, like a fountain spurting over that glaring, hideously difficult white space" (238). Mrs. Ramsay is written everywhere into this. She is the spurting fountain of the past. She and Lily share the same "formidable ancient enemy": not so much a blank canvas as a blank world without human form. Like Mrs. Ramsay, Lily too knows that the meaning of life remains a riddle, but that is the beginning, not the end, of human doing. We knit stockings, we hang shawls over skulls, we bring people together around a table, we bring them back in a painting. Woolf makes the links between mother and artist unmistakable:

> The great revelation perhaps never did come. Instead there were little daily miracles, illuminations, matches struck unexpectedly in the dark; here was one. This, that, and the other; herself and Charles Tansley and the breaking wave; Mrs. Ramsay bringing them together; Mrs. Ramsay saying, "Life stand still here"; Mrs. Ramsay making of the moment something permanent (as in another sphere Lily herself tried to make of the moment something permanent)—this was of the nature of a revelation. In the midst of chaos there was shape; this eternal passing and flowing (she looked at the clouds going and the leaves shaking) was struck into stability. Life stand still here, Mrs. Ramsay said. "Mrs. Ramsay! Mrs. Ramsay!" she repeated. She owed it all to her. (240–241)

This is one of the high epiphanic moments of the novel, where Woolf unfolds her pattern for us, shows us how much common cause there is between the domestic and the artistic, between mother and daughter. Each is at war with time, death, chaos.

But the supreme beauty of this novel resides in the role it grants to human feeling. For it is not enough to pronounce philosophically, even to wax lyrically about the relation between life and art. You have to hurt, want, desire. You have to experience hunger and love. You have to see death as intolerable. Lily is initiated: "And then to want and not to have—to want and want—how that wrung the heart, and wrung it again and again! Oh, Mrs. Ramsay!" (266). Lily looks at her picture, but is surprised that she cannot see it: "Her eyes were full of a hot liquid (she did not think of tears at first) which . . . made the air thick, rolled down her cheeks" (268), and this is followed by the sharp knowledge that we have no immunity, that love punctures our defenses: "What was it then? What did it mean? Could things thrust their hands up and grip one; could the blade cut; the fist grasp? Was there no safety? . . . Could it be, even for elderly people, that this was life?—startling, unexpected, unknown?" (268). There can be no mistake here: We may be wrenched and undone by pain and longing, but such are the wellsprings of art. There is no easy way.

TO THE LIGHTHOUSE

Hence, the final chapter of the book proposes its two beautiful voyages—Lily making the passage to her art; Mr. Ramsay and Cam and James making the trip to the lighthouse—as, in truth, one journey, one quest: retrieving the dead mother, recovering Mrs. Ramsay. Each trip is fueled by love. Each is Orphic in its own way, constituting a journey into death in order to bring her back to life. Each tells us that the past is not past. Thus, Lily paints her way into "a high cathedral-like place, very dark, very solemn" (255). "As Lily dipped into the blue paint, she dipped too into the past there" (256); Lily's painting is a form of "tunneling her way into her picture, into the past" (258). Had you been there, you would have seen nothing, just an older woman in front of an easel, but you would have been wrong: "No one had seen her step off her strip of board into the waters of annihilation" (269).

So, too, do the Ramsays make good on their own trip to the lighthouse, which is little less than a trip to the underworld. Each of the children at first resists the tyrannical father, the incorrigible patriarch who sits in the boat reading poetry, parceling out food, making small talk with Macalister. And the past flushes up: James sullenly remembers being a child with a man standing over his mother, demanding sympathy; Cam, her fingers drifting in the water, recalls "a hanging garden," "a valley, full of birds, and flowers and antelopes" (303), just as her mother had sung to her years ago when putting her to bed. Each wants to maintain solidarity with the other in their struggle against the father, but beyond even this, each desires the patriarch's approval, knows—as Lily Briscoe knows—that his approval is irresistible. They look, with grudging but real admiration, at this man reading in the boat crossing the water. He is nearing the end: "He was reading very quickly, as if he were eager to get to the end. Indeed they were very close to the Lighthouse now" (301). With perfect tact, Woolf again signals how inseparable art and life are, how the book coming to an end is the novel coming to an end, and that the end is the desired goal of the whole story: the lighthouse.

What is a lighthouse? So many things: an outpost, a vista, a silver beam of stroking light. It is a marker in the sea, according to Mr. Ramsay; it is a lonely man with his child, islanded, according to Mrs. Ramsay. She has knitted a stocking as a simple gesture of solidarity. The trip to the lighthouse entails crossing the waters to bring people together, not entirely unlike the crossing necessary to bring people together around a dinner table. *She* is dead now. So, *he* is carrying out her will, moving into the fluid element, those waters of annihilation, with his small parcels of sustenance and solidarity. The marriage theme is alive and well, no matter that Mrs. Ramsay and Prue are dead, that the Rayleys' union has worked loose. They are about to arrive at the lighthouse, but Cam and James are confused by their father's "looking back at the island" (307), at their island. "With his long-sighted eyes perhaps he could see the dwindled leaf-like shape standing on end on a plate of gold quite clearly. What could he see? Cam wondered. It was all a blur to her. What was he thinking now?" (307).

The novel does not answer this question, but the reader knows the answer. Yes, the island with the summer home is now shimmering in gold for this man's vision, and what he is seeing, what he is thinking of, is his dead wife, and the opening gambit of the novel: to go, or not to go, to the lighthouse. He has gone. He is there now, and one is entitled to feel that she too is there, that her vision too is being actualized at last. Both children want nothing more than to give love to their father: "They both wanted to say, Ask us anything and we will give it you" (307–308). They arrive. The children "both rose to follow him as he sprang, lightly like a young man, holding his parcel, on to the rock" (308). I cannot help seeing in that notation "lightly like a young man" a hint that the past has been recaptured, that love conquers time, that he is hallowing his dead wife. And Lily, in front of her easel miles away on that island he had looked back at, knows that he has arrived: " 'He must have reached it,' said Lily Briscoe aloud, feeling suddenly completely tired out" (308). Her fatigue is real, for she too has played her part, has made good on the social contract, has helped to fuel his craft: "Whatever she had wanted to give him, when he left her that morning, she had given him at last" (308–309).

The past lies folded within us. James remembered its "many leaves" (275), and Lily, we recall, "was only trying to smooth out something she had been given many years ago folded up" (295). Lily's painting constitutes this act of unfolding, and it is no less than a journey into death in order to retrieve what one can: "For these waters were unfathomably deep. Into them had spilled so many lives. The Ramsays'; the children's; and all sorts of waifs and strays of things besides" (285–286). That is also the novel we have read, with its cast of characters, its duty to the dead, its transformation of life into art. But every reader of this novel has journeyed as well, has crossed over into these resonant lives and participated in the rhythms of love, life, and death. The book famously ends with Lily drawing a final line "in the centre," thus completing the work: "Yes, she thought, laying down her brush in extreme fatigue, I have had my vision" (310).

Virginia Woolf was entitled to feel that she had done no less than Lily Briscoe. She had traveled into the underworld to bring her dead parents back to life so that they might be at last seen and recognized in their human plenitude, and then let go of. As I said at the beginning of this chapter, life is bitterly unfair in just this fashion: Our loved ones die before we have fully known who they were. We seem doomed by the very cycles of generation to be locked into our separate spheres, to be locked out of true understanding. To have brought them back to life is a miracle. A miracle of art, not of religion. Are they presented as they really were? Who can know? They are created by their daughter the artist, their daughter the writer. It is, as Woolf so often says, enough. The book comes across as a final farewell, an act of creativity and love that makes a second, peaceful, death possible. This, too, is precious.

I write these lines less than a year after my mother's death; many years after that of my father. My memories are faded and gray of the one, and twisted and bitter and mournful of the other. The "plate of gold" that Mr. Ramsay saw when looking back to the island at the invisible figure of his dead wife conveys a preciousness, a transformation into the forms and beauty of art, that are not within my reach. Nor can I believevably (for me) expect to arrive—personally, with my own dead, through my own "unfathomably deep" waters—at the vistas made possible in this novel. Virginia Woolf has not only resurrected her dead parents, she has had the generosity of heart (heart, not imagination) to depict—from the inside as well as the outside—their marriage, their relationship, their mix of beauty and terror and love. She may well have birthed them in art so that they might finally die within her, but for us they are here to stay. She herself is long dead, and they live on the page. And through them, of course, as she also has to have known, she lives too, as their creation and also as their creator. A rare form of justice shines here, through which the child and the parents love and nourish one another reciprocally, evenly, selflessly, creatively. Few of us will achieve so much. For just these reasons *To the Lighthouse* is a moving and unforgettable work of art and soul. One reads it, rereads it, even writes about it, for its gift of life.

WILLIAM FAULKNER

THE SOUND AND THE FURY

and

ABSALOM, ABSALOM!

TRAUMA AND COLLAPSE

One of Faulkner's boldest early novels is titled *As I Lay Dying.* It is a title that could well stand for his entire body of work, inasmuch as his greatest fictions invariably dramatize the ways in which "I" either dies or is murdered. He is our great tragic writer, and no one can match him when it comes to the maelstrom of forces that can destroy us: forces lodged within us, such as desire, sexuality, fear, rage; forces existing in the culture itself, such as racial hatred, cultural straitjackets, community pressure, material greed. Hence, he is the dark star, the death star, of this book, because his magnificent depictions of consciousness, of that fabled inside story that each of us contains, are stories of undoing, of coming apart, of being dismantled and dissolved from both within and without. They are also stories of immense social failure: the family as torture chamber, one's children and parents as either executioners or victims, one's cultural injunctions as life-sapping and homicidal, one's regional and national history as a death sentence.

His unique way of telling our story gives a sometimes unbearable urgency to the issues of this book, for there are no defenses in his work: none of the meditative room or recovery of time we saw in Proust, none of the life-affirming dodging and creatural humor we found in Joyce, none of the lyrical splendor or poignant human connection or reverencing of our dead that were achieved in Woolf. His early novels overwhelm us with the unprecedented violence and despotic power that consciousness exerts over our lives, assailing us from within. His later works move toward the social and the apocalyptic, as he dives into the wreck of American history, seeking to understand the horrors of racism and fear that divide us as a land, that led to the bloodiest war in our history from 1861 to 1865, that still rend our country. Not only does "I" lie dying in his books, but the landscapes he offers us—whether it be the hallucinatory inner world of *The Sound and the Fury*, where all boundaries between private and public are erased, or the broad canvas of Civil War carnage in *Absalom, Absalom!*, where black and white, brother and brother, father and children, all destroy one another—constitute a kind of *huis clos*, a "no exit" that demolishes our fond notions of freedom and maneuvering room. There is nothing negative or pessimistic at work here, but rather an unflinching look at life in crisis. On the contrary, his work is ultimately exhilarating, and he stands, I believe, as our Shakespeare, our Greek tragedian, for he makes us see the stature as well as the depths of our moral and national life. These are the reasons his books are rough going. These are the reasons we must read him.

We must read him because he reconceives the very ground we stand on, the materials of which we are made. Faulkner's signature event is *trauma*. From the moment we draw breath, we are assaulted by life, by the family cocoon into which we are born and where we are formed, by the anarchic urges that well up out of our minds and hearts and bodies, by the existing society that infiltrates us with *its* values and requirements, by the designs that others—those we love, those we hate, those we know, those we've never seen—coercively impose on us. Faulkner's genius as a writer consists in not only showing us what this looks like, but in conveying to us by his very prose what this feels like. Hence *The Sound and the Fury*—his story of a doomed family, doomed by loss of love—is, in my view, the most *immediate* book written in the English language, the book that places us at ground zero in the affairs of the human animal, by immersing us nonstop in the inner tempests and collapses of its people. In *Absalom, Absalom!*, the second Faulkner novel under discussion, we see the richest and most profound effort ever undertaken by an American writer to write war, make us see why it happened, and to show how we are always formed and deformed by our pasts and collective history. If the early book throws us into the cauldron of a dysfunctional family, the later work seeks to comprehend our national fate; each one breaks all the rules of traditional writing in order to bring us—us the readers of another century and probably another place—across the Great Divide that separates now from then, here from there, me from you.

FAULKNER UP-FRONT

To give you a preview of what Faulkner is about goes squarely against the rhythm and logic of his work, since the cardinal fact of his books, for many readers at least, is that they keep you in the dark. If the central theme of his fiction is trauma—the experience of shock, falling into the maelstrom—how much good will lampposts do?

I am a Southerner myself, and Faulkner is dear to my heart in ways that have nothing to do with the academy; having taught him for decades, I am painfully aware of the challenges of his work, yet stubbornly convinced that his is the most rewarding fiction written in America in the past century. It seems appropriate for me to include elements of my own story when sketching that of Faulkner (his evolution as writer, his questionable status today), since my love for his books can scarcely be explained along strictly "literary" lines. In selecting *The Sound and the Fury* and *Absalom, Absalom!* for discussion, I have wanted to present him at his most radical: as the creator of the most poignant stream-of-consciousness narrative in our tradition, and as the architect of the most extravagant and baroque novel we possess. But do not be fooled: Faulknerian *technique* is never merely an aesthetic or narrative issue; on the contrary, it is propulsive and galvanizing, and it is geared to hurtle us into interiors such as we have never known.

The Sound and the Fury is divided into four massive blocks, and that is how I approach it: as a Moses-like figure negotiating a daunting landscape, bent on bringing you through—whether it be scaling the heights or plumbing the depths—so as to see the Promised Land. I have run the risk of invoking Moses for only one reason: The issues in play here are spiritual, not intellectual; these novels are not puzzles. Faulkner challenges us ethically as he throws us into the minds of the three damaged Compson brothers, because he is fundamentally asking: Can you go there? Can you enter into these worlds of pain and hurt? And while this may sound masochistic indeed, the opposite is true: Negotiating the Faulknerian landscape is exhilarating, is an experience filled with beauty as well as pathos, because he makes our blood flow, because he gifts us with something that we cannot have in real life—the tumultuous inner life of others.

Each of the brothers is different, and each of their narratives is different. Benjy the idiot is the most despoiled and naked figure in our literature, and we will see how Faulkner succeeds in conveying the terrible cogency of his life—a cogency he cannot speak, but can only feel—onto the page, thereby making us witnesses to a story of absolute loss: that of his sister, Caddy, who (alone) loved him. We learn to *read* Benjy, to see the horrid shape of his life, and in so doing we register just how privileged *our* optic is—the optic Faulkner has given us—since he is for others just an idiot, a grown man who moans for no reason. Faulkner then takes us into Quentin, who suffers Caddy's loss with as much intensity as Benjy does, but whose injuries are of a different nature. Quentin is the family's great hope, the one they send to Harvard, but he goes there a doomed creature, dying on the inside by dint of wrecked self-image and impossible feelings for his sister, and the burden of the chapter is to make us see ever more clearly the extent of his wounds, the collapse of his defenses. Quentin commits suicide—offstage, it is true—and we come away from this chapter chastened, for we have watched him go under, become a dead man while still living. The rendition of Jason, the surviving brother, is more cued to rage and black humor, and we negotiate this segment devoted to a true son of a bitch with a growing appreciation of Faulknerian range. All three brothers are cursed by the loss of their sister, and in the final chapter, written in the third person and focusing on the Easter sermon in a black church, Faulkner shows us a different kind of love—communal and spiritual, keyed to grace rather than possession—so as to take the final measure of his fierce story. Consciousness itself—the modus operandi of this radical fiction, the modus operandi of your life and mine—is on the docket.

One could assume—Faulkner himself assumed—this rendition of the suffering Compsons to be unsurpassable, and in terms of poignance and sheer moral beauty, that is true. But *Absalom, Absalom!* revisits some of these same figures in order to open up this claustrophobic Southern story and to make it a conduit to a still greater and more tragic Southern catastrophe: the Civil War. It is as if the writer understood that the personal—if truly plumbed—is always something larger: echoing, resonant, inscribed in history. Published in the same year as *Gone with the Wind*, Faulkner's epic story also focuses on a larger-than-life figure—Thomas Sutpen, plantation owner with dynastic ambitions—but that is where the parallels stop. Sutpen's strange saga comes to us as a maddeningly chopped-up narrative, filled with holes and questions, coming to us in driblets, not quite over, yet possessed of a haunting power nonetheless. That power extends into the Harvard dormitory where Quentin is spending the last year of his life, and we watch him collaborate with his Canadian roommate in trying to take the measure of this man Sutpen, as well as trying to understand why Sutpen's son murdered his own best friend (who was engaged to his own sister). How do you know, Faulkner is asking, why people did what they did? Can you know? And if you do not know that, how can you claim to know anything?

All these loose ends frustrate our desire to see the big picture, and the outright conjectural tone and strategy of this novel remind us over and over of the extent of our benightedness. Hence, Faulkner's fractured and groping narrative has one staggering virtue: *It is true to life.* In life no one "knows" our story. In life we are doomed to guessing about the actual motivation and behavior of those we know. And this dilemma becomes exponentially more acute when the people we seek to understand are dead, when the stories we want to grasp are already played out, inaccessible, as cryptic as scratches on a tombstone. Faulkner is facing the central epistemological quandary of living people: to understand the feelings and actions of others. His entire elaborate scaffolding in this novel is geared to bring us further and further into a strange collaborative venture: to make knowledge of the dead. Even this formulation is too tame: Faulkner pairs his Harvard tellers with his Civil War tale because he is seeking to understand *why* the war happened—not what the history books say, but rather the despotic human logic that brought it about—and it will thus be seen that this murder at the gate may be a fratricidal murder, an act of violence that will shed its terrible light on the fratricidal war that fissured our country for four long years.

There is nothing easy here. Just as it is not easy to move from "me" to "you." But that (epic) journey is the one that literature is built out of, and the final part of my Faulkner discussion seeks to measure the ramifications of the extraordinary bridge that human understanding requires, a bridge that Faulkner calls "the overpass to love." By the time you have come through *Absalom, Absalom!*, you will see the astonishing congruences of Faulkner's tale, the insistent parallels it stages between the actions of Sutpen and family in the mid-nineteenth century on the one hand and the rationale of America's founding trauma (as William Faulkner felt it to be, in his bones, head, and heart), the Civil War, on the other; and these parallels open the door to others, leading us to see the fit between the collaborative storytelling of a Southerner and a Northerner at Harvard, and the ethical tragedy they perceive. Such interpretive labor both tests and rewards; it also leads to the dawning (amazing) recognition that William Faulkner could not have told this story, could not have narrated this chapter in our moral history, in any other way.

BEYOND THE SOUTH

You will note that I have not yet spoken overmuch about the South itself. That is because Faulkner is our great universal writer. Poe once said that the horrors he wrote of were not those of Germany (as some critics alleged, thinking of German Romanticism), but those of the soul. This is no less true of William Faulkner. Yes his books focus on what he termed a "postage stamp of soil" to which he gave the name "Yoknapatawpha County," but the ultimate terrain he describes is the blood and soil of the United States of America, and indeed of the fissured world beyond our borders where people are destroying one another as never before because of ethnic, religious, and racial differences. Faulkner knows what hate is, knows why people lynch or murder someone, why they tear an entire country apart to shore up their private beliefs. But he also knows what love is, knows that it, too, can be murderous, but that it might also be generous and looking toward grace rather than possession. This, too, he writes as no one else ever has before or since. Love emerges in his work as the medium of human understanding as well as compassion, even as a writerly proposition; and the loss of love—or its equivalent: the dehumanizing of others—comes across as mortal evil in his scheme, the death principle that erases both "I" and home, self and society.

There is nothing either sentimental or exotic in any of this. Yes, his world may seem strange initially. *The Sound and the Fury* focuses, largely through stream-of-consciousness writing, on the tragedy of the Compson family in early-twentieth-century Mississippi: One segment is devoted to the roller-coaster perceptions of the idiot son, Benjy, another focuses on the tortured consciousness of the suicidal son, Quentin, a third delivers the bile and rage of the only "sane" Compson, Jason, while the final, fourth segment is written in more objective language, but reaching its poetic culmination in an Easter sermon in a black church.

And, yet, despite these odd trappings that many may have trouble identifying with, this story speaks to our most basic and elemental arrangements. Lodged deep in each of us, prior to the cognitive person we became, is the naked and vulnerable Benjy, the prerational, purely emotional creature who craves love, who is destroyed when it disappears, whose unformed mind cannot process time, so that his wounds never heal. This is our story. We also harbor within us the precarious, aching, conflicted, "bleeding" Quentin, the brilliant but damaged youth whose brain never stops and whose defenses fail, the uncompromising purist and idealist whose (impotent) love for his sister is poisoning him, the boy whose skin cannot harden, the child who must die. This is our story. And, at times, we may find that there's a bit of Jason there as well: the boy with his hands in his pockets who grew up to be a cold, angry, sadistic man, bitter about the privileges his siblings enjoyed, furious at the hand he's been dealt, self-righteously torturing those within his reach. Faulkner writes these three tumultuous figures from the inside, so that we as readers are obliged to experience and even endorse their hunger and misery, their enormous needs and paltry resources. Once you've been there, inside these Compsons' heads, you'll know that consciousness is not the leisurely or adventurous or rhapsodic space we may have seen it to be in Proust, Joyce, and Woolf: It is a prisonhouse, it is sound and fury.

Likewise, *Absalom, Absalom!* is not an account of some faraway war way back when. It is about the stranglehold—it never stops choking you—that goes by the name of history. It is about the elusive, changing shape that we confer on the past, about how collective trauma (such as the Civil War) damages everyone in its path, including those born decades later, who are still reckoning the harm done to them. It is about obsessions: the obsessions of dynasty, of revenge, of being haunted by a story that lives in you like a succubus. It is about what it takes to succeed in America, and what it takes to deny someone their humanity, and what happens when humanity is denied. It is about the routine decimations of war and killing in the name of blood or caste or race. It is about recognizing that your story—the story you think began with your birth, the story you think framed by your personal history—in fact started long ago and will not be over until long after your death, connecting you to people you've never seen and to places you've never been. It is about the supreme challenge meted out to a species that possesses only language—the oddest, strangest of tools—to say who it is, where it's been, and what it feels like to be human. It is about the voyage that is further and harder than any of those to Mars or beyond, namely the odyssey required to transform past record into living human experience. It is about why we write books, why we read books.

FAULKNER'S STATURE

There can be little doubt that Faulkner is widely regarded as the greatest novelist America has produced. Not as epic as Melville, not as lovable as Twain, not as barometric as Fitzgerald, not even as influential (on the home front) as Hemingway; nonetheless at the top. More recent figures, such as Ellison, Bellow, Pynchon, Roth, or DeLillo have not yet received comparable canonical status. Toni Morrison is arguably—I plan indeed to argue this in a later chapter—Faulkner's great rival and successor, but even there the jury is still out. About the Mississippian, the verdict is in. Why, then, don't more people read him? And why do so few of even that group read him with pleasure?

Faulkner's great recognition came in 1949, when he received the Nobel Prize, an honor that had everything to do with his exalted international prestige, but which tells us nothing about his neglect in America. When I attended high school in Memphis, Tennessee, in the mid- and late 1950s (close to a decade after the Nobel award), Faulkner was not on our English reading list. I returned to that same school some forty years later to give a lecture, and I chose Faulkner as my topic; I had the feeling he was still not on the reading list, but for other kinds of reasons now (which will be discussed in their place). Moreover, it is a well-known fact of literary history that Faulkner's novels were largely out of print as late as 1946, when Malcolm Cowley edited the (crucial) Viking Portable Faulkner volume, an event that restored him to some kind of visibility for a larger public. These dates are painfully eloquent inasmuch as Faulkner's greatest writing, his incandescent period, had taken place many years earlier, largely between 1928 and 1940. By the time he was granted public attention, he was, in my view, a finished writer, producing books to considerable acclaim (*Life* magazine interviewed him at length in the early fifties, when his monumental failure, *A Fable*, was published), but without the vision, language, or discipline of his finest work. The late books seem often like self-caricatures. And he was finished in other ways too: His drinking problems—always serious—had now escalated into derailing disasters, and I don't think it disrespectful to say that his mind must have been, then (when he was at last in the limelight), somewhat burnt out. One of the last great recognitions—being Writer in Residence at the University of Virginia during 1958 and 1959—displays as well, in the kinds of answers Faulkner gives to undergraduates about his novels, in the kinds of things he can and cannot remember, the insidious corrosive work of time, age, and abuse.

Joyce also drank like a fish all his life, had dreadful eye problems, and did a good bit to wreck his health. Proust suffered from asthma and insomnia as well as neurasthenia, and famously sought refuge in his cork-lined room. Woolf seemed, to her nearest and dearest, a fragile, precarious figure, with a number of significant recorded breakdowns and a history of medical interventions. Hemingway's body seemed, over time, to move from heroic macho exploits to being a ticking bomb—passing through every sort of injury en route—and most critics feel that his suicide was mostly a gesture of closure; he could no longer fight the good fight. And so many others, such as Robert Lowell or Sylvia Plath, stand in our minds as injured spirits. I have known many artists and writers during my own career, and my sense is that they are a hard-living, sometimes demon-haunted breed. But will some image of Faulkner, the town drunk (which is not far from the characterization of him you might have heard on an Oxford, Mississippi, street in the mid-fifties if you were there for a football game), really explain the colossal neglect, for so long, of his work?

HURRAH FOR THE FRENCH

Perhaps it is best to acknowledge that we are lucky to have him (in print) at all. And we owe something to the French! Faulkner was enormously fortunate in having the gifted French scholar Maurice Coindreau (who still taught French literature at Princeton when I was an undergraduate) as reader and translator of his great novels in the 1930s. With remarkable acumen, Coindreau realized the caliber of this Southern writer, and produced highly influential French versions of *Sartoris, The Sound and the Fury, Sanctuary*, and others. Highly influential in that they came to the attention of the most distinguished French writers and intellectuals of the time, leading to brilliant responses and published articles penned by the likes of André Malraux and Jean-Paul Sartre, articles that are still immensely readable three-quarters of a century later. These recognitions contrast rather brutally with the New York reception of much of Faulkner's work, especially as registered in the well-known (hysterically funny) put-down of *Absalom, Absalom!* by Clifton Fadiman in *The New Yorker* in 1937, closing with the view that Faulkner's latest failure constitutes the demise of a once-promising if minor local talent. Yes, the French saved him. They have played their little role in American literature, and have not always gotten the thanks they deserve. Edgar Allan Poe is also to be named as French construct—"Edgarpo," as some critics have it—and they have battened on to the likes of more questionable figures such as Jerry Lewis, always with the same mix of hauteur and enthusiasm and contempt for our American ignorance concerning our most important homegrown products.

FAULKNER AND ME

But, as I said, even this French fanfare did not get Faulkner onto the English curriculum in the 1950s, even down South. Instead, I discovered him at Princeton, in a general literature course that assigned *As I Lay Dying*. As events would have it, I read this novel on a train going from St. Louis to Kansas City at Christmastime, and I can still remember vividly—this was in 1958—my being utterly, explosively, indeed permanently altered by the experience. I knew that I understood nothing, and I knew equally powerfully that this was great literature. What most comes back to me is the actual nonstop experience of finishing the last page of the novel and turning it over and starting again on the first page in one fell swoop, without missing a beat, in a kind of mental and physical hypnotic state that has never entirely disappeared, when it comes to these novels. I had not been much of a reader up to that point, had certainly never encountered anything remotely like Faulkner, and a door opened in my mind, and that door led, I think, to a room that had not existed earlier, and I suppose my birth as thinking reader dates from then.

This love of literature flowered still further during my junior year in Paris, where I discovered French culture, read Baudelaire's and Mallarmé's every poem, discovered I had a voice, realized I wanted to teach and to write. Returning to Princeton in 1961, I took, during my senior year, an unforgettable course on American fiction, taught by the endlessly provocative Laurence Holland, where we tackled Faulkner for real: *The Sound and the Fury*, *Sanctuary*, *Light in August*, *Absalom, Absalom!*, and "The Bear." Once again, the confusion, the goose bumps, the certainty that I was seeing what literature was capable of, but perhaps now through French lenses of a sort, as if the stint with Symbolist poetry and its art of indirection (and Holland's own inimitable style) had prepared me for exactly the kind of narrative art that I encountered in these strange and beautiful novels.

I will soon enough finish with this account of my personal fixation, but I need to add that I went on, a few years later, to write a good chunk of my Ph.D. dissertation on Faulkner (studied in relation to the generation of French novelists who were influenced by him), and thus began my academic career as someone *marked* by Faulkner, someone with a mission to bring Faulkner to others. It is no exaggeration to say that I have been carrying out, for better or for worse (it sounds like wedding vows, maybe it is), that mission for going on forty years now, dishing up this man's novels to generations of Brown University graduates and undergraduates. That experience has opened my eyes still further to the strangeness of the Mississippian's fictional world, a strangeness that speaks to my heart, but that is by no means self-evident or even credible to the students with whom I share my obsessions. And this, too, has been instructive. All of these reflections belong, I think, in this chapter, because they undergird my grasp of just the issues I have been raising: Why is Faulkner great? Why is he neglected? Why does he mean so much to me? Why should he mean this much to you? How will he alter your sense of self, of story? Time now to start with some answers.

THE STRANGE SOUTH

Let me begin with his strangeness. Faulkner writes about a South that many American readers (of whatever age) cannot comprehend. It no longer exists today, and it has not existed for some time now. The "New" South that replaced it—with central bases in heterogeneous, bustling dynamic centers such as contemporary Atlanta and Charlotte, even Memphis, Nashville, and Birmingham—bears little resemblance to the rural culture Faulkner limned: an agrarian universe of often poor but always proud whites, with a few decaying genteel families hanging on to power, with loyal blacks playing their long-defined roles as servants and laborers. The South where Faulkner came of age was already a haunted place, since whatever grandeur it once possessed was definitively a thing of the past, destroyed forever in the Civil War. As historians have pointed out, we cannot understand the attitudes of early-twentieth-century Southern culture unless we realize how much had been wrecked and altered by the collapse of the antebellum system, how much psychic damage was done during Reconstruction. It is not amiss to say (as critics have said) that the South is the only part of the United States to have known military defeat and occupation. Such a perspective helps us to understand the obsession with the past that governs Faulkner's view of both society and psyche. In this he goes profoundly against the grain of many cherished American myths, most notably the dream of an open future and a clean slate, the forward-looking ideal of freedom that still fuels American ideology. Faulkner will gradually elevate this view of an all-powerful past into a grand scheme of Doom and Curse, as he works out the myth of the South.

FAULKNER'S SINS

Jean-Paul Sartre, writing about *The Sound and the Fury* in 1947, memorably defined Faulkner's distinctive outlook by comparing the novelist's vision to that of a man standing in a moving convertible, looking backward: Such a person will see an ever-growing vista *behind* him; such a person is structurally unable to see what is in front of him. For an analogue in American literature, we would have to go back to Nathaniel Hawthorne, who possessed a comparably doom-ridden view of human affairs, a comparably history-drenched picture of both society and psychology (as a classic like *The Scarlet Letter* makes more than clear). If Faulkner's sense of the weight of the past makes his work unpalatable for many readers, what is one to say of his views on both race and gender? Here is, in my opinion, the most strident and passionate objection to his work: His notions about women and blacks are (seen as) dreadfully, embarrassingly reactionary, of another time, dooming him (to use one of his notions) to the ever-growing cemetery of dead white males who have at last been removed from the canon (where they occupied center stage for so long) and put away for good. My analysis of two of his greatest novels, *The Sound and the Fury* and *Absalom, Absalom!*, will tackle these two indictments head-on, but even now a word is in order.

To fault Faulkner on race is, at least in my view, to overlook its central and tragic position in his work. At the beginning of his career, race relations in the South are simply part of the backdrop of the stories he wants to tell. But, certainly from *Light in August* (1932) on, Faulkner increasingly realizes that race is the great fault line of his culture, the condition that he explores ever more painfully and profoundly in the books to come, with the inevitable caveat that he explores them as a white man, indeed as a Southerner. As for gender, the story is trickier, inasmuch as Faulkner's female characters are—with some striking and unforgettable exceptions—all too frequently limited and conventional creatures, derived from stereotypes of Southern womanhood that the male writer could not get clear of. But even where the initial conception seems prefabricated, Faulkner is able to do the most astonishing things with some of these figures—I am thinking of Lena Grove or Rosa Coldfield—and in other cases, as with Caddy Compson, he achieves something of great beauty and pathos.

LITERATURE AND/AS IDEOLOGY?

But let me now go on the offensive. Must we assess the novels we read in terms of their views on race and gender? I firmly believe that English departments throughout the country—especially the most prestigious ones—not infrequently do just that, and hence a very great disservice—not only to literature, but to their own causes—occurs. We are still all too often held hostage to a politically correct critical model that is the result of the vital ideological critical movements of the past half-century that have made the deep-seated race and gender biases of Western culture more and more visible. I find myself telling my students: "If you are only going to read novels you agree with, you won't find much to read, and it won't be very good, either." Needless to say, I have the same ax to grind with much other political criticism as well, the kind that knows in advance that the great villain of every work studied is going to be either Patriarchy or Late Capitalism. Not only should the appreciation of literature and art have nothing to do with litmus tests, but I'd go on to say that you will learn *more* about issues such as race and gender in the works of authors whose views differ from yours than you ever will in pious fables of truth and justice for all. I hope to be able to actualize these convictions of mine in the critical pages ahead.

Having now gotten these ideological concerns off my chest, let me add one final remark: In terms of evaluating the novels of William Faulkner, they (the political critiques) are often an alibi, a front; the unavowed real transgression of Faulkner is more likely his writing itself. His books are too hard to read, but that is something that is too hard to say; much better to claim: "It's his politics I dislike." So, a final word about hard books: The key issue is whether the difficulties of the work *pay off* or not, whether the vistas achieved could have been arrived at, in any other fashion, whether the reading dynamic itself might be where Faulkner challenges and rewards you most. Labor-intensive reading has its place. Faulkner is hard, yes; so is Picasso, so is much modern music, so is life. Now, I have no brief for gratuitous hard work, sweat for sweat's sake, but I do believe in Kierkegaard's beautiful dictum about the difference between what we get in real life (where luck and cheating and much else obtains), and what we get in our souls (where there are no shortcuts, no Cliff's Notes): In that place (our minds and hearts), we have to "work for our bread." End of sermon.

All of this huffing and puffing on my part doubtless makes it quite clear that Faulkner is special to me. I cannot help thinking it is because I see myself as a still-living link between the world he came from and that of the students and readers I address. When I grew up in Memphis, black women from good families worked as maids for white folks for as little as $2 a week, not just cleaning house and preparing meals, but taking care of, indeed raising, children. I know this because it was true for my family, and it changed my life immeasurably for the better. In those days, as well, the word "nigger" was heard on many educated people's lips; I know because I heard it from my teachers in high school, and I suspect that it—and all it stood for—was one of the reasons I left the South in 1958, and have only returned for visits. In the North that I moved to, blacks and whites did not share the same space as they had during my childhood, but the values in the North were different, the opportunities for blacks different, the words said and unsaid, also different. These simple but portentous facts of my life go a long way toward making Faulkner's work cogent for me, while being either exotic or outright evil for many people today, especially outside the South. Thus, the story in *The Sound and the Fury* of the Compson family in 1928—portraying a family of decaying white Southerners with black retainers, a tragic story of the loss of love—makes terrible and immediate sense to me.

THE SOUND AND THE FURY: FAULKNER IS BORN

It is Faulkner's breakthrough novel. He had published three other works earlier, all of which were written in an ambitious third-person narrative form that sought to convey a variety of issues that would stay with him: trauma in *Soldier's Pay*, the art of storytelling in *Mosquitoes*, the doomed romantic legacy of the South in *Sartoris* (now known as *Flags in the Dust*). Nothing, however, could have prepared anyone for *The Sound and the Fury*. It is the book where he both discovered and exhausted, or so he thought, the ecstasy of novel-writing; he thought of its haunting central absent character—Caddy, whose story and whose departure from the family are destiny itself for the remaining three Compson brothers—as his "heart's darling," as a creature terribly dear to him, a female character who stands alone in his work for her feistiness, warmth, and beauty. Yet, despite his unmistakable investment in this work, what most astounds us in *The Sound and the Fury* is the *disappearance* of the author. Faulkner has discovered that this story must be spoken by its own players, that his own voice and values must be removed from the scene. Hence it comes to us as four massive blocks of writing, three of them (two set on Easter weekend 1928, one set in June 1910) in the first person, devoted to capturing the interior monologue of the three Compson brothers: Benjy the idiot, Quentin the suicide, Jason the survivor; the last one, the so-called Dilsey chapter, written in the third person, conveying both the final misadventures of Jason and the magnificent Easter sermon that the black servants and Benjy attend.

For all too many readers, at least at first, it seems largely impenetrable. Thus, it makes good sense to look at the book's actual first page, and to see what is hard and what is easy in this strange writing. On the top of the page we read "April Seventh 1928" and here is what follows:

> Through the fence, between the curling flower spaces, I could see them hitting. They were coming toward where the flag was and I went along the fence. Luster was hunting in the grass by the flower tree. They took the flag out, and they were hitting. Then they put the flag back and they went to the table, and he hit and the other hit. Then they went on, and I went along the fence. Luster came away from the flower tree and we went along the fence and they stopped and we stopped and I looked through the fence while Luster was hunting in the grass.
>
> "Here caddie." He hit. They went away across the pasture. I held to the fence and watched them going away.
>
> "Listen at you, now." Luster said. "Aint you something, thirty three

> years old, going on that way. After I done went all the way to town to buy you that cake. Hush up that moaning. Aint you going to help me find that quarter so I can go to the show tonight." (3)

This is how the world looks to Benjy the idiot. He is incapable of cause-effect logic, even of speech. He cannot tell us he is crying; it must come from Luster: "Listen at you, now." And there is more he cannot say: He notes a flag being taken out and put back, and he registers (five times) the action of "hitting." Yet at no point can he give this scene taking place "between the curling flower spaces" a *name.* You—and every reader who has negotiated this page—know that golf is being described here, yet that label, that cognitive tag, is beyond the reach of the narrator. It is fair to say that a great deal of this page, and of this novel, hinges on the bizarre dialectic, seesaw, of what *you* know versus what *he* knows. You the non-idiot can make all the logical and verbal moves that Benjy cannot. This would be the first thing such prose brings us: a bizarre sense that we see and know more than the speaker does, that something is distinctly wrong here, that this man is damaged goods, and that *we* are obliged to fill in the blanks.

WHAT WE KNOW, WHAT BENJY KNOWS

And, yet, there is a great deal here, squarely on the page, that he knows but that you do not. For example—and it is the key example—*why* is he crying? "Why" is, of course, the timeless question that returns us to motivation and explanation, and we are doubtless free to say: Nobody knows. We might nonetheless ask: Can anyone cry without reason? We see easily enough that the text does not tell us why. (As it would in any traditional narrative, where we'd read: "Benjy felt this or that or the other, and cried.") But, aha! Look again: The text does tell us, in its own way, once we know how to read it properly. The answer is in plain view: "Here caddie." *Whoa,* you might be thinking. "Caddie" is (we know) the person who carries the golf bag or chases the golf balls of the golfers. Yes, indeed. But *he* knows that "Caddy" is the name of his beloved sister, the sister who in 1928 is long, long gone. Now look still more closely: Following "Here caddie," Faulkner has written: "They went away across the pasture." *Pasture?* What pasture? It's a golf course, yes? Here again, *you* know it is a golf course, but he knows it *was* a pasture, his family's pasture, the pasture where he would come daily to the fence to wait for his sister Caddy to come home with love for him, the pasture that has in fact—all this will gradually be disclosed later—been sold to become a golf course to pay the tuition for the brother Quentin at Harvard (where, we are to learn in the next chapter, he only completed his first year, because he jumped into the Charles River to end his life on June 2, 1910, the very day that will be the subject of the next chapter, the next block of narration, done this time by the doomed brother himself).

WRITING THE STORY OF LOSS

Strange writing. Full of words we think we know, but we don't; full of changes and direction signals that don't actually seem signaled. Of which the upshot is: "Here caddie" is extraordinarily—and, for the uninitiated reader, invisibly—charged with meaning, potent in significance, in personal significance for the speaker, Benjy Compson. So potent that it changes the venue from golf course to pasture; i.e., it erases time, and the space becomes once again what it was, what it has never stopped being in Benjy's mind: the pasture he loved. We are now beginning to learn something crucial about Benjy: He does not know time, he cannot separate past from present, it all flows together for him. So that "Here caddie" is still more explosive, since it really (for Benjy) means "Here Caddy," and the reason for the moaning, the key to the tragedy of his life is now coming into horrible focus (for us; he knows or learns it every day of his life): *Caddy is not here.* Faulkner's novel, at least its first chapter, might well have been titled, anticipating Beckett's famous play, "Waiting for Caddy."

While we are at it, I may as well admit there is still more evidence displayed on that first page, evidence that the first-time reader cannot possibly see as such. All this talk about "hitting," hitting golf balls, comes to acquire—later, when the reader comes to the necessary information—a sinister eloquence, when we learn that Benjy is castrated. This fact surfaces several times in the novel, once in this first chapter, when he looks down at himself and starts to cry, but perhaps most indelibly in the third chapter, when Jason (the surviving adult brother) informs us of the situation as follows: "I could hear the Great American Gelding snoring away like a planing mill. . . . Having to wait to do it at all until he broke out and tried to run down a little girl on the street with her own father looking at him. Well, like I say they never started soon enough with their cutting, and they quit too quick" (263). In short, by book's end—if you don't give up but go the full route—the reader understands to perfection why Benjy is moaning. After all, he has lost everything: his sister, his pasture, his genitals.

Faulkner has crafted a weird prose that conveys with great power the damaged Benjy's thoughts and feelings. But what, you may wonder, does this have to do with us, with our story? The answer is: Here is what the world of feeling—exclusively, despotically, tragically, *feeling*—looks like. This is how each of us began life, and at some level in our psyche, tucked away behind doors and buffers and countless layers of protective tissue, it is still there: an elemental world of pure longing, pure pain and pleasure, prior to all the shortcuts and abstractions of logic and language and compromise and the entire, inevitable, bittersweet deadening process that is called *growing up*. Benjy has no dodges, no escapes, no maneuvering room, none of the resources that we the intact and adult possess. He cannot compartmentalize, he cannot forget, he cannot "get past" the loss of his sister. Reading Benjy makes us realize how merciful the passing of time is for the healthy, how it cures our ills and softens our hurts and mends our broken hearts and removes—as a surgeon would remove a cancer—all the intolerable facts that might otherwise kill us: loss of parents or siblings, loss of nurture, loss of love. Benjy's moan recalls Lear's howls on the heath, or the paroxystic figure in Munch's painting *The Scream*, each of them evidence of what bare, forked creatures, creatures denuded and bereft of all defenses, feel. At this level, life is laceration. Reading Benjy offers us a picture of unaccommodated life at its purest and most basic; his calvary has nothing to do with idiocy; it has to do with hurt that cannot go away, and it makes us reappraise (with gratitude) the bargains life offers.

TELESCOPIC WRITING

Faulkner's rendition of Benjy is fourth-dimensional writing in its packaging of time, but there is no balm, no erasure, no healing: just loss. The thirty-three-year-old idiot is still the hurting child. But Faulkner is no less adept at going in the other direction: writing childhood in *telescopic* fashion; hence certain passages are read as simply happening in the past, but we can hardly fail to see how shimmering they also are, with portents for the future. I am thinking of an early passage where the seven-year-old

Caddy has decided to take her dress off and go into the water, leading to the following exchange between her and her older brother Quentin:

> "I bet you won't." Quentin said.
>
> "I bet I will." Caddy said.
>
> "I bet you better not." Quentin said.
>
> Caddy came to Versh [black servant] and me [Benjy] and turned her back.
>
> "Unbutton it, Versh." she said.
>
> "Dont you do it, Versh." Quentin said.
>
> "Taint none of my dress." Versh said.
>
> "You unbutton it, Versh." Caddy said. "Or I'll tell Dilsey what you did yesterday." So Versh unbuttoned it.
>
> "You just take your dress off." Quentin said. Caddy took her dress off and threw it on the bank. Then she didn't have on anything but her bodice and drawers, and Quentin slapped her and she slipped and fell down in the water. . . . (18)

Hard not to see family fate in these limpid words and gestures: Caddy's strong-willed behavior, her flouting of codes (even her disrobing), Quentin's efforts to maintain order and control, his failure to do so. To me, such scenes put Faulkner's genius squarely in front of us: his pitch-perfect notation of childhood games and conflicts, his haunting sense of how much is on show. Here, too, such writing shocks us as a rare form of portraiture, as an account of our actual emotional contours and lines of force and human destiny that elude traditional notation. Can you imagine your own story told in this fashion? Can you see how single gestures might become terrifyingly resonant, secret clues beckoning toward the future, yielding a pattern? There is a terrifying economy on show here, taking what looks limpid and turning it into prophecy. People speak today of genetic testing and the nightmares it may give rise to: giving us, in our childhood, blueprints of what is likely to kill us later. Faulkner has done this: not genetically but morally and emotionally, not through a medical test but via words on a page.

Unquestionably the most famous incident of this sort is the episode of the "muddy drawers," where the child Caddy climbs up the pear tree to look into the room where the grandmother, Damuddy, lies dying. And her brothers watch:

> "Push me up, Versh." Caddy said.
>
> "All right." Versh said. "You the one going to get whipped. I aint." He went and pushed Caddy up into the tree to the first limb. We watched the muddy bottom of her drawers. Then we couldn't see her. We could hear the tree thrashing.
>
> "Mr Jason said if you break that tree he whip you." Versh said.
>
> "I'm going to tell on her too." Jason said.
>
> The tree quit thrashing. We looked up into the still branches.
>
> "What you seeing." Frony whispered.
>
> *I saw them. Then I saw Caddy, with flowers in her hair, and a long veil like shining wind. Caddy Caddy* (39)

Faulkner himself later said that he had not been aware of the symbolism of the muddy drawers, the coming sexual experience, the coming erotic dirtying, when he wrote the passage. But even that will hardly take the measure of the poetry here. The willful little girl goes up the tree and looks over into the great mystery of death, in her grandmother's room. But her brothers gaze at a different mystery: her dirty drawers, and all that they promise and threaten. Everything here is about the fragile evanescence of childhood and innocence. Everything asks to be interpreted, as Frony's whisper makes clear: "What you seeing." And with characteristic brilliance, the final italicized passage transports us to a later moment, that of Benjy's agonized perception of Caddy's marriage, Caddy with flowers in her hair, Caddy leaving his life for good. One could go further still. We have a longitudinal sketch here of female fates: the girlchild with her sexual equipment, the (hastily arranged) marriage, the dead old lady. And all is processed through the fierce, resisting gaze of the male brothers.

LIFE WITHOUT LABELS, FICTION WITHOUT EXPLANATIONS

What I have termed "telescopic" prose really means: prose that is dense with the passage of time. The great paradox of the Benjy chapter consists in the payload that Faulkner achieved by writing through the perspective of the idiot-boy who understood nothing but felt everything. Benjy does not know time, but it is time itself that courses through his story, time as endless, lacerating loss. Time that is nakedly (we now realize) on show in the statement: *Here caddie*. And that's not all. What happens to *us* when we read prose that gives us effects without causes? For that is what Faulkner has been doing: showing us Benjy's moaning, his dreadfully cogent moaning, before handing us the explanation that tells us why.

With this remark I approach the secret of Faulkner's work, and the implicit scandal of all writing. Life itself comes to us, every single minute we live, without explanations or labels. Nobody that I have ever met has their story written on their forehead (or sleeve). Nothing that I have ever seen—in the street, in my classes, in my living room, in my bed—is accompanied by explanation or preparatory instructions. Life does *not* have a user's manual. The minds and intentions and feelings of all the people I know, including those I know and love the most, are ultimately guesswork for me, even if affection and experience have sharpened my interpretive skills. We live in the dark.

But you'd never know it by reading novels. On the contrary, most of the books we love are nonstop exercises in interpretation, shedding light, clarifying, and making sense of the world. Not that you yourself are doing this labor: No, no, that is exactly what the author has done, why you are reading the book, why you bought the book, why the book (maybe) is worth the trouble of reading. And this is not so stupid, after all. Since the world is clothed in darkness, surely one of art's trumps should be to provide a bit of light. To push this still further, what kind of a masochist would actually want a book to provide more darkness? My reply is: Faulkner starts out dark, ends up luminous. And this can only happen because of what we his readers do en route. His would be a body of work that initially approximates the inchoateness of real experience, but that gradually delivers its pattern, its figure in the carpet. But you have to work for your bread.

THE SHAPE OF A LIFE: "HERE CADDIE"

Still, I am hardly saying that the purpose of reading Faulkner is to become a punching bag for emancipated experiences. "Roll with the punches" is indeed what I tell my Faulkner students, but I confess that such a metaphor gives me pause. His work is not so much pugilistic as it is unhinging. But it takes things apart, I think, in order to put them back together. It offers us a kind of affective and physiological realism that bypasses the conventions of ordinary logic, so that we might see the deeper logic at work. Is that not what "Here caddie" ultimately means? "Here caddie" produces an explosion of moaning, and with that notation we realize that the shape of a life is being graphed. The whole chapter is devoted to showing us how unbearably rich and full those two words are. We are meant to see and measure how much Caddy means, so that we can then measure the immeasurable: her loss. Faulkner goes about this with great delicacy, as in this very early scene when Benjy is crying, and Mother, no longer able to bear it, sends him out with Versh and Caddy:

> Caddy took me to Mother's chair and Mother took my face in her hands and then she held me against her.
>
> "My poor baby." she said. She let me go. "You and Versh take good care of him, honey."
>
> "Yessum." Caddy said. We went out. Caddy said,
>
> "You needn't go, Versh. I'll keep him for a while."
>
> "All right." Versh said. "I aint going out in that cold for no fun." He went on and we stopped in the hall and Caddy knelt and put her arms around me and her cold bright face against mine. She smelled like trees.
>
> "You're not a poor baby. Are you. Are you. You've got your Caddy. Haven't you got your Caddy."
>
> *Cant you shut up that moaning and slobbering, Luster said. Aint you shamed of yourself, making all this racket.* (8–9)

Caddy offers Benjy the love he needs. For her he is not a poor baby. And in his homely, lovely idiom, happiness always has the same shape: Caddy smelled like trees. But the beauty of this scene is of course its real horror. "Haven't you got your Caddy," the loving sister says. Any wonder that "Here caddie" provokes weeping? The miracle of this kind of writing is that *we* see Benjy's inner world, his living sense of Caddy's presence as well as his incessant discovery of her absence; Luster cannot possibly have this vision, and he responds accordingly: "*Cant you shut up that moaning and slobbering.*"

Over and over in this chapter Faulkner succeeds in showing us what Benjy has had, and what he has lost. It is always Caddy. His love for her is steadfast, possessive, despotic. He cannot bear her growing up, for he senses that time will lead her out of his life. One of the book's loveliest scenes focuses on Caddy's new adolescent tastes and Benjy's fierce resistance. She is fourteen, wearing what Jason calls a "prissy dress," and Benjy cries, refuses to be comforted. Caddie then goes into the bathroom, but the sequence continues with Benjy listening quite carefully at the bathroom door, hearing the water, hearing the water, then hearing the water stop. Caddy comes out: " 'Why, Benjy.' she said. She looked at me and I went and she put her arms around me. 'Did you find Caddy again.' she said. 'Did you think Caddy had run away.' Caddy smelled like trees" (42). The episode is brought to its conclusion by Caddy's sitting with Benjy in her room, trying again to comfort him:

> "Why, Benjy. What is it." she said. "You mustn't cry. Caddy's not going away. See here." she said. She took up the bottle and took the stopper out and held it to my nose. "Sweet. Smell. Good."
>
> I went away and I didn't hush, and she held the bottle in her hand, looking at me.
>
> "Oh." she said. She put the bottle down and came and put her arms around me. "So that was it. And you were trying to tell Caddy and you couldn't tell her. You wanted to, but you couldn't, could you. Of course Caddy wont. Of course Caddy wont. Just wait till I dress."
>
> Caddy dressed and took up the bottle again and we went down to the kitchen.
>
> "Dilsey." Caddy said. "Benjy's got a present for you." She stooped down and put the bottle in my hand. "Hold it out to Dilsey, now." Caddy held my hand out and Dilsey took the bottle.
>
> "Well I'll declare." Dilsey said. "If my baby aint give Dilsey a bottle of perfume. Just look here, Roskus."
>
> Caddy smelled like trees. "We dont like perfume ourselves." Caddy said. (42–43)

This sequence gestures toward something exquisitely tender and beautiful. With utmost economy, Faulkner has portrayed the struggle within this adolescent girl's heart between her personal wants and her loyalty toward her brother. The final gesture of giving the perfume to Dilsey (via Benjy, no less) is perfect. And heartbreaking, for we know that time cannot be stopped, that Caddy will grow up, that fancy dresses and perfume will ultimately have their say. What most touches me here is, oddly enough, epistemological: Caddy does not merely love Benjy, she seeks to understand him, to decipher him, to create a common language between them. The first words of this novel are "Through the fence," and in the portrayal of Benjy the idiot, Faulkner has created an astonishing depiction of imprisonment and impairment, of being locked into oneself, of an incarceration so powerful and unsayable that moaning seems to be its natural language. It is this that Caddy refuses; he is not a poor baby; he is not incomprehensible; he is trying, forever, to tell her, and she, through love, makes out his meaning, meets his need, sacrifices her own. *This is what he has lost.* This is why "Here caddie" means what it does.

THE INSIDE WORLD AND THE LAW OF INVISIBILITY

We can see in such writing what never reaches visibility in real life: the incessant counterpoint between public event and personal reflection. My terms are far too cerebral, I suspect, since Benjy hardly seems to reflect, but we the readers of this novel possess that fuller picture, that fuller grammar, that enables us to gauge what life has done to him, why he moans. Not that the streets are not full of walking wounded, injured people who go through life moaning; but the law of invisibility is such that we never know why people hurt and are what they are; we are never privy to the past traumas that are still playing out. It is as if every living human being were in fact a book with many chapters, and in those early chapters are located the life-determining events that form and deform their hearts and minds. Yet these origins are shrouded in darkness, unavailable to our sight, with the result that the actual *cogency* of any life—the reason people do what they do—"passes show," is illegible. Poe's brilliant story of urban anonymity, "The Man of the Crowd," is bookended by the German phrase "*es läßt sich nicht lesen,*" "it cannot be read." And this is the brute fact of all social interaction: We see only the current event, the present moment, and we ignore all that has brought it about. Can it be surprising to us that medical inquiry, criminology, and ultimately history itself are keyed to this same conundrum? Only when the disease declares itself, when the crime occurs, when the Bastille is stormed, do the rest of us begin to look back, toward origins, in search of an explanation, an etiology, a theory. Only then. For the most part we are ships passing in the night. Our ignorance and blindness are colossal.

That is why Faulkner satisfies. He offers us that fuller story that neither our eyes nor our lazy habits of mind can comprehend. He makes human fate visible. Benjy Compson's cogency is writ large for readers of *The Sound and the Fury*.

But only for them, the readers outside the novel. Not for the people who live around Benjy. They must judge him exclusively in terms of what they see. They see a golf course, not a pasture; they see a caddie, not Caddy. They see an idiot standing at the fence; T.P., who takes care of him in 1928, knows better: *"He think if he down to the gate, Miss Caddy come back"* (51). And it has become something of a social ritual for the schoolgirls to walk past that gate with the strange man leaning on it, "moaning and slobbering," a man who would run after them to the corner of the fence, but could go no further. But one day he gets out, and here is how Faulkner writes it, from the inside and from the outside:

> It was open when I touched it, and I held to it in the twilight. I wasn't crying, and I tried to stop, watching the girls coming along in the twilight. I wasn't crying.
>
> "There he is."
>
> They stopped.
>
> "He cant get out. He wont hurt anybody, anyway. Come on."
>
> "I'm scared to. I'm scared. I'm going to cross the street."
>
> "He cant get out."
>
> I wasn't crying.
>
> "Don't be a fraid cat. Come on."
>
> They came on in the twilight. I wasn't crying, and I held to the gate. They came slow.
>
> "I'm scared."
>
> "He wont hurt you. I pass here every day. He just runs along the fence."
>
> They came on. I opened the gate and they stopped, turning. I was trying to say, and I caught her, trying to say, and she screamed and I was trying to say and trying and the bright shapes began to stop and I tried to get out. I tried to get it off my face, but the bright shapes were going again. They were going up the hill to where it fell away and I tried to cry.

> But when I breathed in, I couldn't breathe out again to cry, and I tried to keep from falling off the hill and I fell off the hill into the bright, whirling shapes. (52–53)

No passage in literature is better suited to show why art matters. Here is the event that leads to Benjy's castration, and one understands why: He has opened the gate, gotten out, caught the girl. Had we been there as spectators, that is what we would have seen: a man molesting a schoolgirl. But we are not there as spectators. We are there as readers of the Faulkner text, and thus we see something else as well: Benjy's heartbreaking efforts at *trying to say*, and we know what he is trying to say—the overwhelming love he feels (has always felt) for Caddy, Caddy now transformed into the schoolgirls, the girlchild bringing him love. For the public this scene is an attempted rape. For Faulkner's reader it is an attempted expression of love.

And therein lie both the beauty and the horror of the event. For these two interpretations do not rule each other out, they complement each other, complete each other. The double perspective puts us horribly on the inside, makes us understand that all Benjy's moaning—perhaps all the sounds we produce in our lives—is nothing but *trying to say*. And if stammering is the inevitable fate we suffer as lingual creatures—able to speak but not to speak our hearts, to say what truly matters, what we truly are—what can our noises possibly betoken for those who surround us? We have art for these reasons. Faulkner opens up the single most opaque material in existence—others' hearts and minds—and he thereby lays a great burden on his readers, who must contrast their own luminous sense of Benjy Compson with the dark and menacing image that he must be for those around him. Faulkner's presentation of Benjy can be likened to those military special glasses that make night vision possible, for what is otherwise closed to human eyes now becomes, by dint of art, illuminated. For Benjy it all comes to an end, as the desire to say fuses with the memory of the anesthesia—"the bright whirling shapes"—just prior to the castration, an event that forever alters, at least in one crucial sense, this man's capacity to say.

For us as readers it does not quite end so clearly, for it makes us wonder still further about the strange optic of art, about what it should mean to us to see on the inside. How many rapes or murders or other drastic acts might look different, might seem dreadfully cogent, if we had access to the inner world of motive and cause that led to this event? If we could possibly see it as the actor himself or herself saw it. It is, I think, an unsettling question, precisely because such knowledge addles our judgment, complicates our assessment, makes visible the peculiar logic behind even the most horrific acts. And yet, as writing, as perspectival gift of art, it enriches our picture of things, helps us to a view of Benjy Compson that is heart-wrenching in its emotional coherence. Against these hundred pages of prose we are invited to consider what can and might be said of ourselves, of our mix of feelings and acts, of the strange dance between our visible public gestures and our hidden human heart.

Art offers us at least an imagined sense of the inner world, the world of motive and desire and need that is real even if not photographable or provable. That has always been art's special home terrain. Edvard Munch (who was himself an amateur photographer) once said that photography will rival painting only on the day when we can take a camera into either Heaven or Hell. He meant: The business of painting, of art in general, is to depict that inner realm that is our Heaven and Hell, which can never be scientifically documented. The Benjy section of *The Sound and the Fury* is precious because it takes Shakespeare's dark, nihilistic lines from *Macbeth*—"Life is a tale told by an idiot, full of sound and fury, signifying nothing"—and actualizes them with such beauty and pathos that we realize how wrong Shakespeare had it, at least in his last two words, how unbearably full of significance the most maimed life can be.

THE SUICIDE'S STORY

Moving beyond Benjy's story into his brother Quentin's narrative of his "death-day" in Cambridge in June 1910 (eighteen years earlier than the other three sections of the book), we encounter all the earmarks of stream-of-consciousness storytelling; yet it is utterly different from the limpid, sensuous, fluid world of Benjy. Quentin is an intellectual, he is at Harvard, he knows how to think (he doesn't know how to stop thinking); all of which means: His chapter can be hard going. Lots of learned references, quotations, the sort of thing one saw in Joyce's Stephen Dedalus (to whom he has been compared).

If Benjy gives you intimations of the muffled story of the heart that lies deep in all of us, Quentin's mind—which is now spread out before us—looks more like a battleground. Reading him, we sharpen our sense of the cacophony inside us, the incessant negotiations that our psyche conducts to keep us afloat, the pathos of seeking a safe harbor when we are headed for shipwreck. Negotiating this chapter entails finding your way among three distinct levels of narration. On the one hand, there is a bristling account of life at Harvard in 1910, introducing us to Quentin's Canadian roommate, Shreve, to other players, such as Spoade, the sophisticated Southern upperclassman, Gerald Bland, the Lothario of the group, Gerald's impresario mother, and locals such as the Deacon, the shrewd black man who enjoys helping Southern students find their way in this New England community. These people matter, the locales are well sketched, and we get a sense of Quentin's daily routines, as well as the more ominous preparations he's making for the final event: repeatedly trying to kill his shadow, breaking his watch, looking yearningly into the Charles River, thinking of the flatirons that will weight his body down, thinking further of the grottoes of the sea, writing his farewell letters (which we never read) to Shreve and to his family. He also makes a fateful trip into the outskirts of Boston, this too part of the topographical realism of the chapter, but larded with other things as well. One reads all this seemingly innocent material with one's ears as well as eyes, for we soon enough detect the sounds of a ticking bomb, but we don't initially know exactly where it is located.

As I have already hinted, a good bit of the writing depicts Quentin's thoughts. And it is worth distinguishing between his conscious and his unconscious thoughts. Quentin Compson, Mississippian at Harvard, thinks a lot about the South, about his family, about the blacks as well as the whites, about his past, especially the values passed on to him by his father (whose exact words still exist, intact, in the son's mind, filling it up, influencing its moves, legislating much of what is thinkable). All this is, in some sense, volitional recall. Then there is the other stuff, the garbage, the unvolitional stuff, that Quentin has sought to repress, to keep under a lid; this is what I will call the "Caddy material." This is what will kill him, and he seems to know it. It covers everything from Caddy's recent marriage to Herbert Head (brought about by her pregnancy, brought about presumably by her lover, Dalton Ames) on to ever more disturbing facets of his relationship to her, concerning sexuality (his and hers), love (his and hers), and fate (his and hers). It covers all this, but there is the rub: The cover is coming off in the chapter, because it is coming off in Quentin's mind and life. That is the mesmerizing spectacle at hand: not merely the return of the repressed, but the growing, lava-like eruption of an unprocessable past that begins in (italicized) driblets and ends in flood, much like the onset of a hemorrhage, the overflow of a volcano. Quentin will be swept away.

FAILING THE SOCIAL TEST

Quentin's problems, like everyone's problems, may appear to be exclusively personal, but are ineluctably cultural as well. Faulkner would probably have blinked or yawned if someone had pronounced the word "ideology" in front of him, yet the portrait of Quentin Compson is unmistakably that of a tragic misfit between societal expectations and being who you are. The problem, of course, is that you *are*, in some sense, the expectations that have come to you from the outside, which now constitute a good bit of your self-definition and horizons. None of us is free of this; none of us can even see or measure this traffic. Hence, Quentin Compson, as a "good boy" in Mississippi a century ago, subscribes, willy-nilly, to a number of crucial cultural beliefs: It is his job to do well in school (he gets into Harvard, lasts almost a year), to protect the chastity of his younger sister, Caddy (can't be done), and to prevent (somehow) the galloping decline of his family (worsening finances, escalating alcoholism of his father, hypochondria and coldness of his mother, worthless uncle, one idiot brother, one conniving brother).

Some of the items on this list have a very distinct Southern ring to them, an antiquated notion of gallantry and chivalry—the last remembered conversation with his father contains the line "no Compson has ever disappointed a lady"—but it is fair to say that the entire consort of obligations and duties yields a mission-impossible situation for Quentin. (Not for nothing has he also been compared to Hamlet.) If Faulkner were a cultural historian, this portrait would be mildly interesting; but, because he is a great novelist, this depiction of Quentin's problems, his malaise, is something you do not forget. We are, for more than a hundred pages, to see exactly what it looks like when someone comes apart, goes under.

I'd want to compare Faulkner's rendition of these matters with the inert medicalized terms we use every day, such as "stress" or "pressure." All of us know that it is rarely entirely calm and harmonious inside our heads and hearts, that skirmishes and sometimes slaughters can take place in there, that what we lamely call "processing experience" doesn't begin to deliver the actual sights and sounds, the actual landscape within. Faulkner also helps us to understand that the notion of our heads being cameras that blithely make their way through the world—remember Stendhal's definition of the novel as a "walking mirror"—is a fraudulent notion, for these cameras are horribly cued to our emotional history, to our unresolved conflicts, to an entire host of miasmic materials that can gum up our lenses (our eyes) and cause the machinery to short-circuit, or to explode. Reading Quentin sensitizes you to how much you bring to whatever you see.

AMBUSHED FROM THE INSIDE

Our minds, it turns out, are stereophonic, whereas most of our books are single-voiced. I know of no writer who has put this traffic onto the page quite like Faulkner has. This can be tricky reading, but it beautifully renders the actual texture of things. Let's look at a passage where Faulkner cunningly blends together a medley of voices: that of Herbert Head (pregnant Caddy's would-be car-owning husband, on whom she'll be foisted), Mrs. Compson (giddy with happiness that a suitor is on the premises), and of course Quentin, remembering, musing, and parsing and responding to the sounds:

> Going to Harvard. We have sold Benjy's *He lay on the ground under the window, bellowing. We have sold Benjy's pasture so that Quentin may go to Harvard* a brother to you. Your little brother.
>
> You should have a car it's done you no end of good don't you think so Quentin I call him Quentin at once you see I have heard so much about him from Candace.
>
> Why shouldn't you I want my boys to be more than friends yes Candace and Quentin more than friends *Father I have committed* what a pity you had no brother or sister *No sister no sister had no sister* Don't ask Quentin he and Mr Compson both feel a little insulted when I am strong enough to come down to the table I am going on nerve now I'll pay for it after it's all over and you have taken my little daughter away from me *My little sister had no. If I could say Mother. Mother.* (94–95)

What I called Joycean music in another chapter is no less prominently on show here as Faulkner-music: a contrapuntal technique that is almost incantatory as the players' spoken words reverberate inside Quentin, reveal their terrible other meanings, trigger his mental responses. Mother brags to Herbert (also "from" Harvard) that the pasture was sold to pay Quentin's tuition, but Quentin registers the human cost of this transaction, a cost paid by *his* little brother, so that Mother's lines to Herbert—"a brother to you. Your little brother"—are horribly doubled: not Quentin as older Herbert's sibling-to-be, but Benjy as the sacrificed child. Likewise, Herbert's blather about befriending Quentin since he has heard so much about him leads (wonderfully) to Mother's unwitting line "yes Candace and Quentin more than friends," which, of course, detonates the italicized bombshell: "*Father I have committed.*" Committed? Committed what? This must be Quentin thinking, but has he really "committed" something? Has he actually said these words to Father? When the talk moves on to Herbert's lack of siblings, again Quentin gives us the anguished private gloss: *No sister no sister had no sister.* Whoa. What kind of dirge is this? Does it express Quentin's fear or his yearning? Mother finishes her little spiel about "going on nerve" with the expected cliché "and you have taken my little daughter away from me," which catalyzes once again Quentin's feelings of bereftness and pain, this time moving beyond Caddy to Mother herself: "*If I could say Mother. Mother.*"

This superb passage is ultimately symphonic, and it is alchemical as well, transforming the commonplace remarks of both Herbert and Mother into a haunting lyrical refrain about Quentin's misery, his injuries. Alchemical in this odd sense as well: Those casually spoken words (like all words?) turn out to be potent, explosive, triggering devices, cutting right into Quentin's psyche, nailing him. I earlier used the terms "volitional" and "nonvolitional," and I think we can see here what "nonvolitional" means: It means being invaded, it means having no defenses, so that others' words pierce you, script you, rearrange themselves into your own antic dance, provoke confession. Quentin is not choosing any of this; he is not reflecting. Instead, his inner arrangements—which he spends his time trying to keep locked up—are spilling out, are so full and damning that any kind of twaddle whatsoever jolts them into action, into expression. It is not too much to say that Quentin is terrorized by his own emotional history. We know today all too much about terrorism, about ambushes, about being defenseless; William Faulkner's depiction of Quentin Compson intimates, rather heinously, that we don't need to consult the newspapers or our TV screens to find out about such horrors, that our psyche experiences guerrilla warfare every time we're in real trouble.

I quite realize that this description of Quentin's mind-set (to put it very benignly) may seem exaggerated and sensationalist, but I will not back down here. It seems to me that Faulkner is illuminating something very profound about human vulnerability: namely that it is always there on the inside, lurking, waiting to jump out at you, eager to take whatever comes its way and to hurl it back at you, but now as self-script, as wound-language. Our injuries have, as it were, a will of their own, want out, will speak. Such is the distressing spectacle of Quentin Compson, a character often treated harshly by critics, because he seems too self-absorbed, too weak. I think Faulkner knows all this; however, *judging* Quentin is not the issue (just as it is not the issue for Hamlet), because the gambit is to display this dynamic of turning the entire world into a mirror of your own troubles. It is in this sense that Faulkner is radically recasting our grasp of *story*, for nothing could be further from the docile narrative of our accomplishments and life data—that imposing list of degrees, jobs, and achievements that we call our "record," as immovable as scratches on a tombstone—than the weird, volatile, operatic, inside/outside spectacle we find in these pages.

QUENTIN'S HANG-UPS

Caddy's virginity cannot be protected, however much Quentin thinks it should be, and that he should be the one doing it. The first reason is Caddy herself: strong-willed, impulsive, sexually alive. Her virginity seems indeed to matter a great deal more to her brother than to herself. Father tried to tell Quentin this: "Because it means less to women, Father said. He said it was men invented virginity not women" (78). But then he said a few other things too on this topic, and they warrant our attention: "Because women so delicate so mysterious Father said. Delicate equilibrium of periodical filth between two moons balanced" (128). It appears that Father, not Mother, did the honors concerning the birds and the bees with their eldest son, and it is significant that this early instruction remains attributed and intact in Quentin's mind still.

More interesting yet is how this information "plays" inside the young man, triggering a mix of responses including desire, disgust, and outright fear: "With all that inside of them shapes an outward suavity waiting for a touch to. Liquid putrefaction like drowned things floating like pale rubber flabbily filled getting the odor of honeysuckle all mixed up" (128). "Honeysuckle all mixed up" becomes as resonant as "Caddy smelled like trees," inasmuch as each is a private constellation that depicts a level of feeling prior even to thought: in Benjy's case, Caddy's "purity"; in Quentin's case, his panic about sexuality. Yes, that "outward suavity" beckons, seems "waiting for a touch to," but "putrefaction" and "drowning" have the upper hand, and they announce a kind of male terror about female sexuality in general, and female genitalia in particular: You could drown in there.

This malaise (to put it gently) about sex is powerfully underscored in one of Quentin's most striking memories from home:

> Versh told me about a man who mutilated himself. He went into the woods and did it with a razor, sitting in a ditch. A broken razor flinging them backward over his shoulder the same motion complete the jerked skein of blood backward not looping. But that's not it. It's not not having them. It's never to have had them then I could say O That That's Chinese I don't know Chinese. (115–116)

We perceive here something of the infatuation with innocence and purity that seems to lurk in the Faulknerian male psyche. Sexuality can be unmanageable for many of Faulkner's characters: Quentin, Horace Benbow, Joe Christmas, Ike McCaslin. But none of them seems as disabled as Quentin. His anxiety (which triggers this recall) expresses a kind of castration-yearning, an inversion of penis envy. He is still virgin, wishes he had no genitals at all ("O That That's Chinese"). Sex? That's a foreign language. Would that it were so simple.

VERBAL INCEST

Let's try to put some of this together. Quentin is supposed to protect the Compson honor by assuring the chastity of his sister. But Quentin himself is sexually anxious, aroused but fearful. And the final piece: Quentin loves Caddy, loves her with that same Edenic, absolute intensity that Benjy loves her. Which means: He also loves her physically, potentially sexually ("potentially" is a good word here), despite the problems we have just listed. How on earth can these warring impulses be reconciled? There would appear to be no exit from this morass. (The stifling smell of honeysuckle, indeed.) Quentin's solution is startling in its economy and canniness: He will *say* that he has had sex with Caddy! We now see clearly what that earlier tidbit "*Father I have committed*" really means: Father, I have committed incest. Now, this is very cunning (as well as heartbreaking), because saying "I have committed incest" quite wonderfully replaces actually committing incest; better still, in some peculiar way, it repurifies Caddy herself. All, yes all one's ducks line up.

This, then, is the strategic psychic route Quentin goes. The verbal and putative incest with Caddy opens the door *out* of sordid reality (where Caddy is not a virgin, where Quentin still is one) and *into* a "place of one's own": "*If it could just be a hell beyond that: the clean flame the two of us more than dead. Then you will have only me then only me*" (116). But there is a problem: How to convince Caddy to go along? Quentin gives it his best shot, and again Faulkner writes this contrapuntally, lets us hear Quentin's anguished plea and Caddy's gentle, beautiful response:

> *we did how can you not know it if youll just wait Ill tell you how it was it was a crime we did a terrible crime it cannot be hid you think it can but wait* Poor Quentin you've never done that have you *and Ill tell you how it was Ill tell Father then itll have to be because you love Father then well have to go away amid the pointing and the horror the clean flame Ill make you say we did Im stronger than you Ill make you know we did you thought it was them but it was me listen I fooled you all the time it was me you thought I was in the house where that damn honeysuckle trying not to think the swing the cedars the secret urges the breathing locked drinking the wild breath the yes* Yes Yes *yes* (148–149)

Perhaps it is the lost child or anxious man or maladapted adult in me who responds to this passage, but I find it almost unbearably moving in its desperate plea to make reality correspond to need, to alter the facts, to rewrite the givens, to refashion the world so that one can live in it. The number of substitutions in play here is high, since Quentin's gambit at once "innocents" Caddy and "experiences" himself. But the urgent strategy of displacement—"*you thought it was them but it was me*"—starts to pulsate on the page when Quentin imagines the sexual intercourse itself as something overpowering and unhinging, at once undeniable and unassumable: "*the secret urges the breathing locked drinking the wild breath the yes Yes Yes yes.*"

I am willing to concede that Quentin Compson is an extreme case, and that this business of verbal incest may seem over the top. But consider: Is it not entirely possible that our psyche conducts its affairs exactly like this? And on a nonstop basis? Faulkner makes us ponder just how much desperate role playing takes place in our minds: not so much our own performances, but those of others, all those whom we love (or hate) and whom we are internally scripting at every moment. Inside the brain one finds musical chairs, and on those changing chairs we position the key players in our libidinal drama, making them do our bidding. But Faulkner also knows that reality has its little card to play, that those others whom we (internally) push and pull actually have their own wants, their own stubborn integrity, so that our designs must end in failure once they move out of our psyche and into the light of day. In that harsh light of day our schemes collide with the real world.

That is literally what has happened with Quentin, and doubly so. Caddy has refused to play, but, moreover, the remembered exchange is itself located in a very odd context. Quentin has just been fighting with Gerald Bland, while *thinking* he is fighting with Caddy's former lover, Dalton Ames, and has been bloodied considerably in the process. And that's not all, he has narrowly escaped going to jail, and is in the midst of conversation with Shreve, Spoade, Mrs. Bland, and others when this passage explodes into the text and usurps the story. What has been going on here?

THE GHOSTS TAKE OVER

Faulkner is out to graph the spectacle of a young man going under. You may remember my saying there were three levels of narration in the Quentin chapter. Well, they become increasingly entangled with one another, so that it becomes harder and harder for the reader to know exactly where he or she is. But those mixed levels are the levels of his life, and they can't be kept apart by *him.* Nothing can any longer be kept down or locked up. There is something deeply stirring in watching Quentin lose ground, in watching the ground itself become the underground. Sartre remarked that Quentin "falls into his past" in the same way a plane falls into an air pocket.

Thus, Quentin out on a lark, walking about the countryside outside Boston, encountering bucolic scenes consisting of young boys fishing, seems for all the world to be safe. But when he enters a bakery, sees "a dirty little child with eyes like a toy bear's and two patent-leather pigtails," and says to her, "Hello, sister" (125), we know, we know that trouble has arrived, and that it is not going away this time.

The episode with the little girl is the closest Faulkner ever came to Kafka. Foreign, hugging her (very phallic) loaf of bread, never speaking, she sticks close to Quentin (he has given her a bun), becomes effectively his shadow, indeed his shadow-sister that has never left, that cannot leave. In Freudian language, this scene smacks of the *uncanny*, a space that you unwittingly domesticate by projecting your private landscape onto it. Quentin and the girl begin their fateful walk. Not incidentally, they pass by undergarments hanging out to dry, nor does the shape of the bread trying to thrust its nose out of the bag seem innocuous. As if the concert were now officially beginning, so too does Quentin's inner world come to attention, join in the game, send him memories of Father's views on menstruation, open the door to remembrances of adolescent sexual experiment with Natalie, a dalliance undertaken to get Caddy's attention, beautifully evoked in groping children's language:

> It's like dancing sitting down did you ever dance sitting down? We could hear the rain, a rat in the crib, the empty barn vacant with horses. How do you hold to dance do you hold like this
>
> *Oh*
>
> *I used to hold like this you thought I wasn't strong enough didn't you*
>
> *Oh Oh Oh Oh*
>
> *I hold to use like this I mean did you hear what I said I said*
>
> *oh oh oh oh* (135)

These reminiscences—when do you put exclamation marks after each of those breathless "oh"s, "oh"s strong enough to dislocate Quentin's grammar?—punctuate the bizarre promenade of the little immigrant girl (the nose of her loaf now "naked") and the increasingly anxious Harvard student who can't seem to deliver her home. Memories of Natalie lead to those of Caddy, of slapping her, hugging her, smearing mud on her, trying to make her jealous.

But the memories are then interrupted by an intrusion of reality in the form of the raging Julio, the little girl's brother, with his furious tidings: " 'I killa heem,' Julio said. He struggled. Two men held him. The little girl howled steadily, holding the bread. 'You steela my seester,' Julio said" (139). Julio's charge, despite the Italian accent, has a Delphic ring to it. Oracular truths are in the offing. With the timing and tact of a Molière, coupled with the economy of a Sophocles, Faulkner now orchestrates his tragicomedy still further, as Quentin is hauled in for questioning (and falls into a helpless fit of mad laughter "like retching after your stomach is empty" [140]), as Shreve, Spoade, Gerald Bland, and Mrs. Bland (and two shocked squired demoiselles) appear on the scene, asking what is happening, witnessing Quentin's day in court, requiring Spoade's savoir faire to get him out by paying the required bribe.

GOING UNDER

This episode seems so outrageous and absurd that it recalls the satyr play that traditionally followed the three Greek tragedies in Periclean Athens. But Faulkner hasn't shifted genres in the least; his tragic focus is, if anything, all the more intense now. The little-girl episode stages the primal conflict of the entire Quentin chapter, namely the incessant tug-of-war between external life and internal mania, between the public world of streetcars and dormitories and college students and bakeries and little immigrant girls on the one hand and the awful tyranny and sway of one's private ghosts on the other. Quentin has managed to stay alive up to now, just as all of us with ghosts and pulsions gnawing away at us manage to, up to the moment where we stop managing. That is the moment that has come for Quentin. The balancing act between inner voices and social reality can no longer be maintained.

I repeat: This is the balancing act that each of us performs every day of our lives. Madness, breakdown, coming apart, even serious depression: Those are the names we give to the capsizing that happens when our inner world stops being inner, when it triumphantly enters the public arena and takes it over altogether, transforming every single thing it sees into its own ghostly forms. That is exactly the tragedy of both Benjy and Quentin. Quentin's episode with the little girl replays his obsession with Caddy in the same way that Benjy's "embrace" of the schoolgirl is (for him, only for him)

"Caddy here." Each of them has lost—by dint of their overpowering need for their sister, Caddy—the capacity to distinguish between outer reality and inner desire.

There is virtually a ballet-like feeling to both these chapters, trancelike and hypnotic, as we watch the social givens yield to individual fantasy. It is, I think, terrifying. We register the disappearing act of a (hitherto) functional human being. Sartre, who understood Faulkner so well, nonetheless got the Quentin chapter wrong when he criticized Faulkner for failing to divulge more of Quentin's actual thinking concerning the suicide itself. This is wrong because Faulkner has *graphed* the young man's downfall, has shown the triumph of the ghosts. Perhaps we go astray when we seek to account for extreme acts such as suicide (and much else) by invoking some kind of psychological discourse: despair, hopelessness, worthlessness, exhaustion. Might Faulkner be closer to the mark? We die when the outside world vanishes for us, becomes merely a mirror for our own compulsions.

The little-girl episode is followed, of course, by a fall still more precipitous, as Quentin's grasp on externals loosens more and more. Cleared of the charge of stealing Julio's sister, Quentin falls into ever larger and richer and more damning chunks of his past with Caddy, yielding a luminous fifteen-page account of his manifold failures, located at the branch where Caddy tells him of her love for Dalton Ames, where she realizes his innocence and confusion and need. These pages are beautiful reading, and there is nothing elliptic or confusing about them; the past no longer needs to get "in" through driblets and moments of italicized recall or association, because now, in full hemorrhage, its flow—as clear and unstoppable as a death sentence—is unimpeded by censorship or external reality:

> poor Quentin
> she leaned back on her arms her hands locked about her knees
> youve never done that have you
> what done what
> that what I have what I did
> yes yes lots of times with lots of girls
> then I was crying her hand touched me again and I was crying against her damp blouse then she lying on her back looking past my head into the sky I could see a rim of white under her irises I opened my knife

do you remember the day damuddy died when you sat down in the water in your drawers

yes

I held the point of the knife at her throat

it wont take but a second just a second then I can do mine I can do mine then

all right can you do yours by yourself

yes the blades long enough Benjys in bed by now

yes

it wont take but a second Ill try not to hurt

all right

will you close your eyes

no like this youll have to push it harder

touch your hand to it

but she didnt move her eyes were wide open looking past my head at the sky

Caddy do you remember how Dilsey fussed at you because your drawers were muddy

dont cry

Im not crying Caddy

push it are you going to

do you want me to

yes push it

touch your hand to it

dont cry poor Quentin (151–152)

Poignant, ever so clear, bringing the earlier passages into focus and recall, this episode gives the lie to any claim that Faulkner is unreadable or enigmatic. To be sure, you have to make it to page 151 to receive this reward, but then this reward wouldn't be a reward at all without the prior labor. Motivation is crystalline here. Caddy understands Quentin entirely, is ready to die with him if need be, is also (as we learn a few pages later) ready to make love with him if need be. (The repeated references to "pushing" the knife or touching it with Caddy's hands reinforce the sexual aura.) She has just returned from her tryst with Dalton Ames, Quentin still waits by the branch, still tries (as ineffectually as ever) to control her, to send her back home:

are you going in like I told you
I didnt hear anything
Caddy
yes I will if you want me to I will
I sat up she was sitting on the ground her hands clasped about her knee
go on to the house like I told you
yes Ill do anything you want me to anything yes
she didnt even look at me I caught her shoulder and shook her hard
you shut up
I shook her
you shut up you shut up (156–157)

With perfect tact, Faulkner has captured the impossible dilemma of this brother and sister, so impossible that those heavy terms such as "doom" and "curse" don't seem all that misplaced. He wants her innocent, he wants her himself, he can do nothing about either of these wants; she is infatuated with Dalton Ames, she loves her brother endlessly, she will do anything for him, anything at all, including making love with him; he cannot bear this, cannot act, cannot tolerate what she is saying, what she is prepared to do.

One reason for citing these poignant words spoken by Quentin and Caddy is to align Faulkner with the great writers of childhood. Quentin's suicide stems, to be sure, from his own dysfunctional equipment—fear of sexuality, unappeasable desire for Caddy, failure to live up to the Southern code—but it also comes to us as a haunting evocation of the fierce and unyielding drives that reign over our youth. Maturation—the passing of time and the acquisition of experience—teaches us to be more supple, less exigent, less vulnerable, more jaded. Yet we know from the statistics that the young are more apt to commit suicide than their elders; and I think we know, from consulting our own distant memories, that life burned, then, with an intensity and singleness of purpose that (mercifully) fade a bit as we grow older and "wiser." I cannot help feeling that Faulkner understands these phases of human life, and most especially what we crassly term "arrested development," more profoundly than most writers, that he writes his great novels out of a still-living core of vulnerability and naked feeling. We recover something of our own depths and shoals by reading him. I personally experience gratitude: gratitude for the vistas he creates, gratitude that I did not end up there.

Later still, as the chapter approaches its close, Dalton Ames himself appears, virile and Byronic, is asked by Quentin if he ever had a sister, answers "no but theyre all bitches" (160). Quentin tries to hit him, passes out, completes his series of failures, finishes his disappearing act. *Disappearing act.* Hamlet-like Quentin does finally act, but he's on the wrong stage and doesn't know it: Thinking he's finally striking Dalton Ames, he is in fact being pummeled by Gerald Bland. I cannot imagine a more effective way of dramatizing Quentin's exit from reality. All that remains is to take him through his last paces, so that the business of suicide is finally, physically completed. Psychologically, and in terms of the chapter's textual behavior, it has already been carried out.

"I" LIES DYING

Biographies of William Faulkner are frustrating affairs because we never stop feeling the unbridgeable gap between the life and the art. His salad days, his nonchalant stint as "Count No-Count" in Oxford, his marriage to a former sweetheart and his alleged later romances, his chronic excesses with alcohol, his tempestuous relations with Hollywood as scriptwriter, his final persona as courtly country squire, all this seems, somehow, like window dressing when we think of the novels themselves. As if you can't get there from here. The demons and dark forces and sheer genius that live in the great novels live nowhere else. I never met Faulkner personally—and I could have, since he died in 1962, at a time when I was already hooked and was often in Memphis—but I have known many who did have firsthand contact with him: a colleague at Brown who taught at Virginia when Faulkner was writer in residence, an acquaintance whose job it was to ride with Faulkner during the Virginia stint and to pick him up each time he fell off his horse, and, perhaps most mythically for me, a dear friend of my parents' who was among the first psychoanalysts in Memphis and who "treated" Faulkner on a regular basis when he went on drinking binges and came to Memphis to dry out. Yet none of these witnesses seems to have been in on the secret energy sources or wisdom or mania that fuel his novels. It is as if his gift—or his curse, if you see it that way—were expressible only in art. But one thing is obvious: It cannot have been easy to be William Faulkner.

The impossibility of "I." That is also the hard truth that emerges from the Quentin section of *The Sound and the Fury*. I have said that Quentin cannot measure up to the Southern code of manly behavior. But the reality cuts still deeper. Yes, Caddy is the proximate cause of this dissolution, but the sickness goes beyond the sister's doing. The acrobatics on show in this chapter spell out a view of self that is everywhere threatened: by the values of the culture, by the anarchic forces on the inside. And he knows it. He watches over his own undoing:

> Sometimes I could put myself to sleep saying that over and over until after the honeysuckle got all mixed up in it the whole thing came to symbolise night and unrest I seemed to be lying neither asleep nor awake looking down a long corridor of gray halflight where all stable things had become shadowy paradoxical all I had done shadows all I had felt suffered taking visible form antic and perverse mocking without relevance inherent themselves with the denial of the significance they should have affirmed thinking I was I was not who was not was not who. (170)

Faulkner teaches us how to read his books. By page 170, this long sentence without commas or periods should nonetheless be clear enough. The honeysuckle informs us things are coming unstuck, and Quentin now looks upon his life as shadowland, as cardboard props, as hollow forms that mock "the significance they should have affirmed," and he ends up with the single most perfect utterance of imploded self that I have ever seen: "thinking I was I was not who was not was not who."

Like those descriptions of torture whereby a man's stomach is opened, his intestines are tacked to a tree, and he is obliged to walk and slowly disembowel himself, so does Quentin Compson oversee his undoing. This is why his final exit is so moving. He seeks, at the very end, nonetheless, to affirm who he is: He will leave life as the Quentin Compson he has been. My phrase sounds like a tautology—of course he will leave life as the person he has been!—but in Faulkner's swirling universe, such self-affirmation is hard going, perhaps impossible. These issues are central to the final remembered exchange with Father. They talk about and around suicide. It is arguably—I write this as a father—the most painful episode in the book. Quentin conveys (in some four pages of unpunctuated and uncapitalized prose) to his father his misery, his failed strategy of verbal incest, and his impending suicide. Father's eloquent and windy reply is based on one brutal notion: "temporary." No, he explains, you won't kill yourself because you will come to realize that your current misery is . . . temporary. This wisdom comes to us via a dark dialogue in which the father (represented by "he") speaks inside the son's head, and the son ("i") counters as best as he can:

> no man ever does that under the first fury of despair or remorse or bereavement he does it only when he has realised that even the despair or remorse or bereavement is not particularly important to the dark diceman and i temporary and he it is hard believing to think that a love or a sorrow is a bond purchased without design and which matures willynilly and is recalled without warning to be replaced by whatever issue the gods happen to be floating at the time no you will not do that until you come to believe that even she was not quite worth despair perhaps and i i will never do that nobody knows what i know . . . and i temporary (178)

Against this baroque and absurdist picture of human emotions as recallable bonds—you love today, but you're not in control, and tomorrow the gods may "recall" this feeling and replace it with something else—Quentin elects to go the full route and take his life, as a (mad?) form of loyalty: to Caddy, to himself. It is as severe and inevitable and coherent as anything Faulkner ever wrote. And for readers who are enlisting Faulkner as a window onto their own story, the spectacle of a life dissolving in front of our eyes is a sight not easily forgotten. Most of us live, day by day, in the murk, with glimmers now and then of pattern and meaning; we muddle through. Yet this story of an *undoing* shimmers with its own strange beauty, for it shows us the simplest and deepest thing of all: how the heart lives, and how it dies. That is why we have art.

JASON: THE FIRST SANE COMPSON

Faulkner knows how to shift gears, how to pirouette his bleak story of doomed Compsons so as to get actual laughs out of it (as well as a few more tears). I think he wrote the third segment to break a spell, to show that spells can be broken, to make us realize that the difference between tragedy and comedy may be nothing more than perspective. Enter Jason.

Styled "the first sane Compson" in the Appendix that Faulkner wrote some eighteen years after the novel itself, Jason, who has regarded both his brothers, Benjy and Quentin, as loony tunes, may well have a point. His narrative is at least outfitted with the signs and syntax of sanity. (For this, much thanks, many many readers have doubtless felt.) Moreover, his first words, "Once a bitch always a bitch, what I say" (180), denote a world and a point of view that all readers recognize at once. Here, unlike the mysteries and riddles of the first two chapters, is clarity. Jason's account is larded with statements and pronouncements of equal certainty and conviction as his opening salvo. Whether the moral or intellectual or imaginative dimensions of such a voice give us pause is another story. But we know where we are. No more murk. This is true even of the book's grand themes: If we can say that the misery of Benjy and Quentin stems from the loss of Caddy, the loss of love, well, then, Jason again sounds the pragmatic note. He too has lost something: a job. And he has lost it because of Caddy, no less, since her husband-for-a-while, Herbert Head, had promised Jason a job in the bank, but it disappeared when Caddy did, and Jason Compson is a man who never forgets who did him wrong.

Yet Jason sees himself as a man living in the present, and it is surely Faulkner's intention that we perceive him as the Compson who has survived, the one who is (to some extent) a functioning adult (rather than a dead suicide or castrated idiot). As critics have pointed out, a good bit of the novel's pathos lies just here: Jason is the frightening exemplar of what it means to grow up, in this story. The Compsons have lost a lot of ground by now, and I mean more than just a pasture become golf course. Father is now dead, the finances are strained, and Jason is working more or less as a hired hand in a store. He is, as he tirelessly reminds folks, the head of the family, and his obligations are many and mighty: to maintain his mother and his niece and his household of black servants in a proper style. The niece is Caddy's illegitimate daughter named, no less, Quentin. (Here is a stumbling block that generations of readers have tripped over, since *this* Quentin is all over the first, third, and fourth chapters of the novel, but can't be the fellow who kills himself in the second chapter, making readers wonder how many Quentins the novel contains, and wonder also just what kind of a writer would pull a trick like this on them.) The name virtually advertises Caddy's love for her brother, as if their verbal incest had nonetheless produced an offspring.

FULL OF SOUND AND FURY

If you stir all this up properly, then you are in a position to begin to gauge the amount of bile and hatred and rage that are cooking inside Jason. He thinks the servants are "lazy niggers" eating him out of house and home, and he thinks his niece is an award-winning slut, a chip off the old block (given her mother). Being an enterprising man, however, he has taken a few distinct measures to get his revenge. First off, he taunts and tortures the girl Quentin endlessly, cannot bear her flaunting her body on the streets of Jefferson, is sure she is having sex with every "drummer" who comes to town; but along more material lines, he has also set up an elaborate scam whereby he regularly receives checks from Caddy (meant for Quentin's use, sent via Jason because she [Caddy] cannot show herself in Jefferson, given her sins) that he then cashes for himself, gives a pittance of the money to the girl, hoards away the rest, and then joins with his mother, Mrs. Compson, to burn, in ritual fashion, ostensibly these same checks (which he has conveniently forged). Faulkner seems to have an innate genius for imagining tricks, scams, stings, gambling, horse trading, rusing, lying, and the like. There is a low-to-the-ground, shrewd, conniving, sometimes maniacal gamelike streak in his work, poised to win via savvy or to cheat if necessary, and I think it functions as a welcome counterpoise to the Big Things that so easily take over his mind and his books. For all these reasons, Jason Compson—admittedly not the smartest of Faulkner's schemers—strikes me as one of Faulkner's supreme creations, a vitally, often hysterically rotten and funny son of a bitch whom Faulkner seems to know inside out, and who cavorts throughout this novel, giving it a mix of evil, vendetta, humor (and overdue reality check) that are unforgettable.

He can certainly be vicious, as in his signature performance of promising Caddy (who had sneaked into town for Father's burial) a chance to see her child, Quentin, and then putting the baby in Mink's wagon, approaching the pathetically waiting mother, and all of a sudden having Mink whip the horses, thus "going past her like a fire engine" (205). Or his refusal to give Luster a ticket to the carnival: Ever the businessman, he is prepared to sell the ticket for five cents, but Luster doesn't have five cents; Jason explains he needs "the cash" and thus elects to burn the tickets in front of Luster. Much of his bile is focused on the girl Quentin, whose reckless behavior seems to him a constant threat to the family's social standing, whose current escapade with the man from the carnival, the man with a red tie, epitomizes the humiliation/punishment coming his way.

Jason's overt erotic interests stand in stark contrast to the disastrous fate of his two brothers. He has essentially contractual relations with Lorraine, Memphis whore, whom he goes to visit on a regular basis, and with whom he plays the big spender. It is quite understood that she is never to appear in Jefferson. Lorraine expresses her tenderness for Jason in letters like this: "Dear daddy wish you were here. No good parties when daddys out of town I miss my sweet daddy" (193). Jason's secret for managing women, he explains, is to always keep them guessing: "If you cant think of any other way to surprise them, give them a bust in the jaw" (193).

THE LITTLE MAN'S ANGER, THE NOVEL'S HUMOR

I have repeatedly claimed that reading *The Sound and the Fury* gives us a purchase on our own story. But my guess is that most readers are far more likely to see themselves in Benjy and Quentin—idiot and suicide though they are—than in Jason. But his is a personality worth endorsing, I think, because he shows us a side of ourselves we rarely see or acknowledge: the vicious side, the pissed-off side, the avenging side. This little man is furious at the world, furious because of what it has done to him, and most furious of all at those responsible for it. As is signaled by the opening phrase "Once a bitch always a bitch," Jason Compson is a reliable storehouse of stereotypical views about outsiders and "others," groups to which he assigns blacks, women, Northerners, and Jews. A fountainhead of *ressentiment* concerning the exploitation of his region, Jason can be downright barometric as the put-upon common man. Listening to Jason chatting with a drummer, we note Faulkner's ventriloquist genius:

> "There's nothing to it," I says. "Cotton is a speculator's crop. They fill the farmer full of hot air and get him to raise a big crop for them to whipsaw on the market, to trim the suckers with. Do you think the farmer gets anything out of it except a red neck and a hump in his back?

> You think the man that sweats to put it into the ground gets a red cent more than a bare living," I says. "Let him make a big crop and it wont be worth picking; let him make a small crop and he wont have enough to gin. And what for? so a bunch of dam eastern jews I'm not talking about men of the jewish religion," I says. "I've known some jews that were fine citizens. You might be one yourself," I says. (191)

I have made no secret of the fact that the tragic Benjy and Quentin chapters are immensely moving to me. All the more reason, I think, to applaud Faulkner for the dark comedy that Jason brings to a book that badly needs it. Jason's know-it-all view of life is delivered spot on, virtually shimmering in its bilious energy. I especially admire the timing that is registered in this quotation, the way the prose slows down after the first bite about the cotton farmer's travails, in order to zero in on the obvious cause for these sorry matters: "a bunch of dam eastern jews." At this point the speech slows still further, as the speaker begins to realize he just . . . might . . . be speaking to a . . . Jew, all of which ushers in the breezy cover about "fine citizens" with its perfect close, as the camera finishes its 180-degree turn: "You might be one yourself." This little exchange goes a fair way toward planting Jason squarely in front of our eyes, ears, hearts, and brains. His dormant xenophobia, his more active anti-Semitism, his hatred of the North, his wily little performance with the drummer, whereby he feels his way into just how far he can go, all this lives and breathes on the page. It is writing that never misses a beat.

I find myself quoting Jason at length because his voice tells us everything. To reduce him to an ideological proposition is to lose the oomph and vinegar and even wit of his repartee. Yes, "wit," because his presentation of Compson history is a priceless take on the oh so serious materials of the first two chapters. Having lost his promised job in the bank, having stayed at home in Jefferson to pick up the pieces, Jason has had time to reflect on the privileges and performances of his two brothers, along with the fate that came his way in the form of Quentin:

> I says no I never had university advantages because at Harvard they teach you how to go for a swim at night without knowing how to swim and at Sewanee they dont even teach you what water is. I says you [Mother] might send me to the state University; maybe I'll learn how to

> stop my clock with a nose spray and then you can send Ben to the Navy I says or to the cavalry anyway, they use geldings in the cavalry. Then when she sent Quentin home for me to feed too I says I guess that's right too, instead of me having to go way up north for a job they sent the job down here to me and then Mother begun to cry and I says it's not that I have any objection to having it here; if it's any satisfaction to you I'll quit work and nurse it myself and let you and Dilsey keep the flour barrel full, or Ben. Rent him out to a sideshow; there must be folks somewhere that would pay a dime to see him, then she cried more and kept saying my poor afflicted baby and I says yes he'll be quite a help to you when he gets his growth not being more than one and a half times as high as me now. . . . (196)

Jason's vicious perspective is a check and balance on what has come before. Just as the Fool is a crucial ingredient in *King Lear*, Jason adds to the mix in *The Sound and the Fury*, undercuts its pretensions, exaggerates its posturings, makes the whole consort more dimensional, as if Faulkner were intent on subjecting his own pathos to ridicule, as if Faulkner were cannily noting the grotesque nature of his materials.

STRUTTING AND FRETTING HIS HOUR UPON THE STAGE

Jason's story is unquestionably the manic piece of the novel. Filled with anger and a large dose of self-pity to boot, overwound, doing battle with the arrayed forces that threaten his security and self-image, Jason Compson fights his way through life. He displays, willy-nilly, the Compson losses, the hard pass to which this once distinguished family has come. Of all the indignities he must contend with, it would seem that the most humiliating is the decision of his niece to bolt with a carnival man, a man with a red tie. Jason spends fruitless, furious, agonizing hours tracking Quentin and her paramour. This pursuit entails a hurried car trip far beyond Jefferson's city limits, undertaken so hastily that Jason has not had time to take the necessary camphor with him to ward off the inevitable fierce headaches that the smell of gasoline causes him, nor has he had the time to see to it that the spare tire was fixed and put into the car.

A hard day—he has taken a beating in the cotton market, learned that his account closed out, even though he's been paying ten dollars a month extra to prevent just such outcomes—now gets harder still, as Jason responds to the red tie and gives chase. Following them into the country, getting out of his car to sneak up and catch them in the act, crossing a plowed field "with every step like somebody was walking along behind me, hitting me on the head with a club" (remember the gasoline), being waylaid by the sun "getting down just to where it could shine straight into my eyes and my ears ringing so I couldn't hear anything" (240), getting stuck in poison oak, the first sane Compson nonetheless fails to catch his prey but instead watches, helpless, as they make their getaway, blowing their horn.

Returning to his vehicle, getting in, starting off, he then learns that the air has been let out of his tires. The misadventure closes with Jason having to get hold of a pump, make it back into town, and be informed that the cotton market closed forty points down. Back at home, he makes a last stab at winning, at pleasure: He burns the carnival ticket in front of Luster, and he tells his mother and niece at the dinner table that he had loaned his car to someone, "one of those show men . . . It seems his sister's husband was out riding with some town woman, and he was chasing them" (258). This is a day in the life of Jason Compson. It is also a rich portrait of getting even, of getting even as the sole driving force in one's life, if one has been beat up. Faulkner is often characterized as a "determinist" writer, a writer who subjects his people to powerful forces they cannot combat, but what this leaves out is the counterattack of his squeezed people, the manic energies they deploy in order to score a few points of their own. There is something wonderfully democratic in such writing, and, oddly enough, it finds a strange human dignity in the nastiest precincts, because this son of a bitch, Jason Compson, simply refuses to roll over. The book seems therefore to have little choice but to roll over him.

GOING BEYOND THE FIRST PERSON, BEYOND SUBJECTIVITY

Long referred to as the "Dilsey chapter," the last segment of the novel shifts gears radically from the first person to the third, ushering in a vision completely different from those of the three preceding interior monologues. Hence, even along grammatical lines, we are obliged to ask if such "objective" writing can represent the thoughts and feelings of Dilsey, the black matriarchal servant who seems to be keeping this family afloat. But even a casual reading of the chapter tells us that Dilsey's consciousness is not depicted here, that Dilsey herself—selfless, loyal, loving, *enduring*—takes up only a portion of the narration, and that portion has precious little to do with what she either says or thinks. Critics interested in questions of both race and gender have been much exercised by this chapter. Their critique, put most simply and crudely, is that neither women nor blacks have a voice in this novel. Both charges have merit. Dilsey speaks very little, and there is little effort to explore her take on events. As silent (silenced?) woman, she is in good company: Her daughter, Frony, doesn't say much, either, nor actually do the white women of the book, Mrs. Compson and, most especially, Caddy herself. Yes, we hear their voices, but for the most part those voices are recorded via the perceptions of male narrators who occupy center stage. As a silent woman who is black, Dilsey makes a still starker case: Black subjectivity is not central to this novel. Faulkner either does not or will not or cannot write from that angle of vision.

As might be imagined, these liabilities have vexed many of the book's readers, so much so in some cases that Faulkner has been judged glaringly deficient (at best) and complicitous in both patriarchal and racist practices (at worst). My own view is that these are the outer limits of Faulkner's vision (at this point in his career), that he will, in later books, make progress on one of these fronts (writing black subjectivity), but will probably always be vulnerable on the other one (representing women's voices). And, yet, I do not feel that *The Sound and the Fury* is harmed by these limitations. In 1928, Faulkner's view of blacks was indeed paternalistic, but that term is perhaps misleading: It was *pastoral*, as indeed the serene, innocent renditions of Dilsey, Roskus, Frony, T.P., and Luster illustrate. No, Dilsey's subjectivity is not on display, but then Faulkner's true interest in Dilsey is precisely focused on her larger-than-life capacity for love and loyalty. We may easily dismiss such an attitude as racist, patriarchal, elitist, and much else, but one would have to be both tone-deaf and documentably stupid not to see how positively and lovingly Dilsey is portrayed in this novel.

One could delve much much further into these issues. I cannot help thinking—I am doubtless thinking like a privileged white male, so be it—that too much emphasis has been put on issues of both race and gender by the professional scholars. I began this chapter by saying that Faulkner is all too unread. One certain reason for this neglect—a neglect that stares you in the face if you look at the undergraduate offerings in the most prestigious English departments in the country—is to be found in his views on race and gender. I have already hinted that another reason, less often avowed, for avoiding Faulkner is the sheer difficulty of his writing. But I want now to say that the key issue behind representations of both gender and race in *The Sound and the Fury* is something else altogether: subjectivity. It has been taken for granted that the novel offends by its failure to depict the subjectivity of women and blacks. It is time to turn this argument on its head. The novel's deepest meaning and deepest values are lodged in a devastating critique of subjectivity itself. I want to show how this is so, why this is so, and what it means. What it means for the Compson story, but also what it might mean for your story as well. Do you have a story beyond subjectivity?

THIRD-PERSON NARRATIVE: SEEING FROM THE OUTSIDE

In this last chapter, we get to see surfaces. To be sure, the interior monologues that run through the narratives of Benjy, Quentin, and Jason are not without notations of the physical world; each of the brothers certainly tells us what he sees as well as what he feels. But what he cannot tell us, given the inside angle of vision of those chapters, is what he himself looks like. Now, however, we perceive these strange Compsons from the outside. Hence, when a door opens and Luster enters, he is

> followed by a big man who appeared to have been shaped of some substance whose particles would not or did not cohere to one another or to the frame which supported it. His skin was dead looking and hairless; dropsical too, he moved with a shambling gait like a trained bear. His hair was pale and fine. It had been brushed smoothly down upon his brow like that of children in daguerrotypes. His eyes were clear, of the pale sweet blue of cornflowers, his thick mouth hung open, drooling a little. (274)

With this depiction, we realize that one of the purposes of this last chapter is to balance things out a bit, to complement the inside story with the camera vision so as to yield a more multifaceted depiction of the characters.

Does this notation of Benjy change our sense of him? The question is unanswerable, yet I'd say that we are grateful for getting this visual sense of someone whose pain and longings have been known to us for quite some time.

WRITING THE SPIRITUAL

As we already know, the Compson family no longer has the same station as it once did. Jason exercises on the girl Quentin what power he knows he still has, as revenge against Caddy and against life. But there is also a power he and his mother probably don't even fully register cognitively, so natural is it, and that is the power they have over Dilsey and her family. Faulkner is at pains to render this relationship visible, even if he is going to use third-person narrative to do so. Hence, the chapter opens on Easter Sunday, April 8, 1928, and the first words describe a day that is dawning "bleak and chill, a moving wall of gray light out of the northeast" (265); into this steps Dilsey, and this "wall" with its "particles" "needled laterally into her flesh" (265), telling us, in its own way, that the story of the Crucifixion is still playing in Mississippi, and not merely in the coming sermon.

Time has taken its toll on Dilsey, and that same objective narrative that limned Benjy and Jason and Mother is enlisted here, too. But with a difference. Something else is now on show, something we'd have to call "soul":

> She had been a big woman once but now her skeleton rose, draped loosely in unpadded skin that tightened again upon a paunch almost dropsical, as though muscle and tissue had been courage or fortitude which the days or the years had consumed until only the indomitable skeleton was left rising like a ruin or a landmark above the somnolent and impervious guts, and above that the collapsed face that gave the impression of the bones themselves being outside the flesh, lifted into the driving day with an expression at once fatalistic and of a child's astonished disappointment, until she turned and entered the house again and closed the door. (265–266)

No reader can miss Faulkner's emphasis on *rising*—her skeleton, her collapsed face—an emphasis that is to have its special place in the Easter story. The description of Dilsey, third-person though it is, is saturated with spiritual data, as if the material world might actually be a luminous screen for something beyond matter altogether.

Dilsey is, as all Faulkner scholars know, based on Mammie Callie, Caroline Barr, who was the beloved "mammy" of Faulkner's childhood, and her presence in this novel, especially in this final chapter, shimmers with what we'd have to call "grace." All my terms are suspect in today's academy: To suggest that a black mammy is a figure of boundless love (from the angle of the needy white writer) is to invite severe criticism from readers and scholars interested in questions of race; likewise, to speak of "grace" in a secular story is to risk being accused of the worst kind of sentimentality. Still, that is how I see it, and that is how I think Faulkner saw it; whether I can persuade you to see it that way is another matter. But consider the following passage, it too seemingly a descriptive passage, but one where the moral and the spiritual forces are insistently present as well:

> Dilsey prepared to make biscuit. As she ground the sifter steadily above the bread board, she sang, to herself at first, something without particular tune or words, repetitive, mournful and plaintive, austere, as she ground a faint, steady snowing of flour onto the bread board. The stove had begun to heat the room and to fill it with murmurous minors of the fire, and presently she was singing louder, as if her voice too had been thawed out by the growing warmth, and then Mrs Compson called her name again from within the house. Dilsey raised her face as if her eyes could and did penetrate the walls and ceiling and saw the old woman in her quilted dressing gown at the head of the stairs, calling her name with machinelike regularity. (270)

This is the life principle. Later, in the Easter sermon, it will acquire a more doctrinal face. But what we see on the page is the laboring black woman who breathes warmth into that cold house and that cold family this Easter morning (as she has done on countless other mornings). The beautiful evocation of "making biscuit," the lovely synchrony between Dilsey's song and her "snowing of flour," between her voice and her work and the warmth of the fire: All this is what I have called grace-filled. But hardly empowered. The "machinelike regularity" of Mrs. Compson's demands (perfectly, horribly) closes a sentence where again we see Dilsey's spiritual reach, her capacity to see through and beyond the material surface, as if this were Faulkner's counterpoint: warm versus cold, labor versus machine, spirit versus flesh.

How you see Dilsey is probably the crux of the novel, as central to our understanding as the depictions of Benjy and Quentin. Looked at in ideological terms, Dilsey and her labor and her voicelessness cry out the racist sins of the South, of Faulkner's South. Of my South. But there are other ways to look at her, beyond the political. If Faulkner created Dilsey out of his love for Mammie Callie, I know for certain that I read Dilsey out of my love for Vannie Price, the black woman who worked for my family during my entire childhood, and who gave me what Mammie Callie gave Faulkner: "an immeasurable devotion and love" (the epigraph to *Go Down, Moses*). I who write so much about human memory actually have very little of it (which may explain why I am obsessed by it), but much of that very little focuses on the figure of Vannie, a warm, strong, intelligent, gracious, proud, and demanding woman who taught me, wordlessly, about what matters in life. She knew who she was, and she knew what my twin brother and I were supposed to be: decent, caring, upright. It matters little whether I have succeeded in living by her principles, because what counts most for me is that she embodied them herself, made me realize that such things existed. And made me realize as well—in the Memphis I grew up in, in the forties and fifties—that I was given this gift by a black woman whose only power (in our society, in our family) was moral.

The paragraph I just wrote proves, if proof were needed, that I am biased about Faulkner and this particular novel. It is also a paragraph that most scholars of race would find highly inappropriate and objectionable, coming, as it does, from a white male who grew up in the South. But I owe it to this book, and to you, to put these cards on the table, so that you know where I stand, and why my remarks about Dilsey incorporating the life principle belong in this book about literature.

THE COMEUPPANCE OF JASON COMPSON

Faulkner knows that he has to bring his story to closure in this final chapter, but how? The decline of the Compsons cannot be halted, and hence we will see Jason's sorry life of cunning, rage, trials, and vendetta brought to a spectacular nadir. And even the final page of the novel will end with shrieks and howls that are silenced only in the most tenuous fashion. In between, however, this family of black servants will join others in going to church for the Easter service, and there is where Faulkner will offer us whatever of hope there might be for this story of failed love. Let us examine each of these phases.

At the end of Benjy's section occurs a somewhat mysterious passage in italics, stemming from the present day narrative of Saturday, April 7, in which Luster takes Benjy by the arm to look at something unusual: "*Here she come, he said. Be quiet, now. We went to the window and looked out. It came out of Quentin's window and climbed across into the tree, then it came out and we watched it go away across the grass. Then we couldn't see it*" (74). What we have (unwittingly) witnessed is the main event of the novel, at least as Jason would have seen it: the crawling out of the window by Quentin, the climbing "*across into the tree*" (and thence into Jason's bedroom, and thence into his carefully locked safe, where he has been hoarding all the money he has been stealing from Caddy all these years), and finally down the tree, across the grass, and gone forever. We won't learn all this until late in the book, when there has been talk of an unfixed broken window, and Quentin fails to come down to breakfast, and Jason bit by bit puts the pieces together, telling his mother that of course this window was only now broken, " 'Dont you reckon I know the room I live in? Do you reckon I could have lived in it a week with a hole in the window you could stick your hand. . . .' " (280). The long ellipsis is momentous in conveying the horrible thought process happening in Jason. His great stolen treasure—representing all his cunning and skill at repairing life's damages—may itself be stolen. And, as ever in Faulkner, the irreparable has happened, the sanctuary has been invaded, the room broken into, the money stolen. All that is left is to try for justice: to catch Quentin and the carnival man at once, before they can get away or spend the money. Jason acts immediately, phones the sheriff, threatens to call the governor if help is not immediately forthcoming. And it goes downhill from there.

Jason himself descends on the sheriff, is met with suspicions about the provenance of this stolen money, realizes he has no proof who has robbed him, leaves on his own after telling the sheriff that he (the sheriff) will regret this, "This is not Russia, where just because he wears a little badge, a man is immune to the law" (304). The chase is on. Again inhaling copious gasoline fumes, again without camphor, Jason is furiously en route to Mottson, where the carnival now is, closing in on the "bitch of a girl" and the man with the red tie. Arriving at a Pullman car where he is certain they're hiding, breathing "shallowly, so that the blood would not beat so in his skull" (308), espying an "old" man "not as big as I am," Jason acts decisively, enters the car, demands that the man confess where they're hiding. And, at this point, all hell starts to break loose. The little old man becomes increasingly hysterical (especially after Jason started with "Dont lie to me"), shrieks (several times) "You bastard" to Jason, tries to twist out of Jason's grasp so he can get his butcher knife, becomes the very embodiment of fate: "The man's body felt so old, so frail, yet so fatally single-purposed that for the first time Jason saw clear and unshadowed the disaster toward which he rushed" (309–310).

It is the kind of scene Faulkner excels at. The little people are the ones that surprise you, that explode on you. What to do now? How to let go of this man and exit without being destroyed? Jason sees "the little old man leaping awkwardly and furiously from the vestibule, a rusty hatchet high in his hand" (310), comes within an inch of losing his life, and goes down. But a moment later he is hauled to his feet, saved by the carnival owner, informed that he hit his head on the rail, told that the girl and the man with the red tie cleared out. The show is coming to a close. The final humiliation comes when, because of his exploding head, he pays an extortionate price ($4 instead of $1) to a black man to drive him back to Jefferson. He crawls home.

Jason's life is the one most racked by sound and fury. His frenetic chase after the stolen money is a mock pilgrimage of sorts, an inverted quest, a fitting close to an existence that is mad, in every sense of the word. You could argue that all these Compsons are mad, in one way or another; all of them are misfits in life. Their stories are laden with pain. Readers have to wonder: Can there be a remedy for this? What story is there beyond sound and fury?

THE EASTER SERMON

I believe that Faulkner answered, as best he could, just these large questions when he wrote the episode of the Easter sermon. Every reader, even those uninterested in religious symbolism, must feel that some kind of clarification is nigh when Dilsey and her family bring Benjy with them to the church.

At first they are disappointed, since the visiting preacher, Reverend Shegog, hardly seems prepossessing: "The visitor was undersized. . . . He had a wizened black face like a small, aged monkey" (293). But insult is added to injury when the visitor begins to speak, because he talks like a white man (with a "voice level and cold"), and his oratory is compared to that of a "man on a tight rope," displaying a "virtuosity with which he ran and poised and swooped upon the cold inflectionless wire of his voice" (293). Yet this performance nonetheless begins to move its audience, and "the congregation sighed as if it waked from a collective dream" (294). With this last notation, especially that word "collective," we are moving toward the central vision of the chapter itself, because "collective" is precisely what this story has *not* been. The three narratives of Benjy, Quentin, and Jason—whatever their differences are—have been profoundly individual in character. Could that be at the root of the tragedy?

Individual or collective? Could a novel be collective? Could one's own story be—somehow—collective? How would it be told? Who would tell it? Where would you find it? How many of us are capable of seeing our own contours in an Easter sermon in a little black church in Mississippi in 1928?

Reverend Shegog's discourse changes. " 'Brethren and sisteren' " he says. With this, he enfolds not only his congregation but also the pieced-apart Compsons—and indeed us, the individuated readers with our private stories—into his vision. It is a capacious vision, going back to an earlier story of suffering and sacrifice: " 'I got the recollection and the blood of the Lamb!' " (294). This time the preacher's voice is described as wavelike, engulfing, devouring: "He was like a worn small rock whelmed by the successive waves of his voice. With his body he seemed to feed the voice that, succubus like, had fleshed its teeth in him" (294). And again Faulkner registers the impact of these tidings, an impact of immeasurable importance, focusing ever further on human connection: "And the congregation seemed to watch with its own eyes while the voice consumed him, until he was nothing and they were nothing and there was not even a voice but instead their hearts were speaking to one another in chanting measures beyond the need for words" (294). It is all beginning to come together.

The language of the preacher unites this congregation so profoundly that words themselves are no longer necessary, since the desired great aim of utterance—to speak from one heart to another—has been achieved. Faulkner is defining the ultimate credo of his entire work: to write in such a way as to go directly to the human heart, leaving linguistic mediating structures behind, making them disappear. Such is arguably the unstated goal of all writers: to move you—the congregation, the reader—so completely that your heart speaks in chanting measures. The great damning knowledge of the twentieth century, when it comes to literature, is the terrible knowledge that language is forever systemic, a sign system irreparably separated from the things it is trying to denote. It is the word prison that writers are locked in all their lives. Need I go on to say that it is the word prison that we, *Homo sapiens*, the tongued creatures, are also locked in, all our lives? We want to move hearts, but we only have words. Reverend Shegog's sermon, homely though it may first appear, is a dazzling, revolutionary triumph of language itself.

BROTHERS AND SISTERS

But this novel is not about linguistics or language theory. It is about "brethren and sisteren." That is what Dilsey knows, as she "sat bolt upright, her hand on Ben's knee. Two tears slid down her fallen cheeks, in and out of the myriad coruscations of immolation and abnegation and time" (295). And that is what the reader is meant to see, as the reverend focuses ever more on the family story. But now in a different key: " 'Breddren en sistuhn!' " The brothers and sisters of the congregation. The brothers and sister of the Compson family. But that is not all: Could reading this novel do for *us* what the reverend's words are doing for this congregation? Are each of us in some way "brothered and sistered"? The voice now becomes, Faulkner writes, "negroid," as if only that code, that manner of speaking, could go directly to the heart: the heart of the Easter story, the heart of the novel, the heart of the reader. And so the reverend, accompanied by the "Mmmmmmmmmmmmm" of the congregation, delivers his story of sacrifice, a fable of lost love far greater than that of the Compsons:

> "Breddren! Look at dem little chillen settin dar. Jesus wus like dat once. He mammy suffered de glory en de pangs. Sometimes maybe she helt him at de nightfall, whilst de angels singin him to sleep; maybe she look out de do en see de Roman po-lice passin." He tramped back and forth, mopping his face. "Listen, breddren! I sees de day. Ma'y settin in de do

> wid Jesus on her lap, de little Jesus. Like dem chillen dar, de little Jesus. I hears de angels singin de peaceful songs en de glory! I sees de closin eyes; sees Mary jump up, sees de sojer face: We gwine to kill! We gwine to kill! We gwine to kill yo little Jesus! I hears de weepin en de lamentation of de po mammy widout de salvation en de word of God!" (296)

It is the murder of the innocent, the sacrifice of the Lamb, the destruction of love. Faulkner's modern story of a dysfunctional family, of the misery experienced by three brothers and a sister, is unmistakably set against this older story. Can there be any redemption for this? The answers are in the very fabric of the writing, in that collective note sounded ever so insistently: " 'Mmmmmmmmmmmmmmmm! Jesus! Little Jesus!' and another voice, rising: 'I sees, O Jesus, Oh I sees!' and still another, without words, like bubbles rising in water" (296). This novel began with the incomprehensible moaning of an idiot. For every first-time reader, that notation has to have been "full of sound and fury, signifying nothing." But now we are poised to see that moaning has a significance, that it can be collective, that it can be "hearts speaking to one another in chanting measures beyond the need for words." Such connection—and only such connection—produces vision, produces the visionary grasp of the old fable behind everything here: " 'I sees hit, breddren! I sees hit! Sees de blastin, blindin sight! I sees Calvary" (296). Can you see it?

VISION AND WRITING

Faulkner's emphasis on *seeing* is so pronounced, so repeated, that we must grasp its striking relevance for the novel as a whole. Not only is the sermon insistently about "breddren un sistuhn," but it is also celebration of community and collectivity and love as forms of vision. And hence it is horribly eloquent about the *blindness* at the core of the Compson scheme. Faulkner has everywhere underscored this: Quentin takes his broken watch to a man "with a metal tube screwed into his face," Caddy's eyes are described as "running" or "dead," the statue of the Confederate soldier possesses a "blind gaze," and Jason's misadventure in Mottson includes the actual textual production of a huge eye, of the wrong kind of vision: "Keep your eye on Mottson." What to make of all this? I do not for a moment suggest that there is anything narrowly ocular about *The Sound and the Fury*, but I do claim that the book is spectacularly, tragically about vision. About the characters' vision, and about our own.

The Easter sermon shows us what a collective vision might be. Every other chapter in the novel shows us what private vision is like. Let me take this even further. The Easter sermon shows us what *outward* vision might be: a vision that goes back two thousands years, all the way to "de blastin, blindin sight." Every other chapter shows us what *inner* vision is: the psychic landscape we encounter in the stories of Benjy, Quentin, and Jason. My words may sound technical, but my interests are moral and spiritual: Inner vision is the very dynamic of narcissism and self-love, whereas outer vision is the dynamic of community, charity, and grace.

Is this not what Faulkner has wrought? The first three chapters, moving and beautiful as Benjy's and Quentin's dirges are, are also claustrophobic, self-enclosed, penitential, carceral. They are about the awful wants of the self. And what do these three brothers want? Caddy. Each of them desires Caddy, each of them wants, in some dreadful way, to possess Caddy, to stop her growth into womanhood, to freeze her and keep her for himself. To be sure, the tonalities differ: Benjy seeks a creature who will smell like trees, Quentin's desire is mixed up with honeysuckle, Jason's is twisted into revenge for a lost job. But we cannot fail to see that this beautiful, feisty, loving young girl, "my heart's darling," as Faulkner called her, leaves the family in order not to be suffocated, leaves in order to live. Against the three brothers' implacable hunger and need, we are asked to imagine the story of Jesus, the story of a kind of love that is charity, not eros, that is generous not possessive, that sees outward not inward.

Faulkner is interested in vision. Beyond that, he is interested in the moral tragedy of a family, indeed of a culture: not just that of the South, but of all of us. For inner vision is the blight of modern life itself; it is the very modality of consciousness. Now, the rationale for my entire book is that the great works of Proust, Joyce, Woolf, Faulkner, and Morrison are about the explosion of consciousness, about the revolutionary power of Modernist writing to represent our inner landscapes. Thus, there can be no surprise that the great narrative gambit of so much Modernist fiction is the creation of interior monologue or stream of consciousness. Here is where the beauty and pathos of these books lie. But *The Sound and the Fury* is uniquely disturbing in its portrayal of consciousness as voracious hunger, as private vision, as loss of love. This is amazing for several reasons: Faulkner has to have known that interior monologue is his great suit, is the royal road in his own writing, is to be his signature contribution to modern literature. It is the vein he *must* deploy. And yet, somehow, he seems also to have known, at the same time, that this kind of writing—which was capable of a splendor like none other—was simultaneously a symptom of the individual's spiritual death.

Robert Penn Warren, one of Faulkner's greatest admirers, formulated this paradox with great concision. In reflecting on the weight of the past in Faulkner's novels, he said that the characters in these books have an intense consciousness of doom. And one cannot disagree. For our purposes, consider the exemplary thinking of Quentin Compson. Later one finds this same habit of mind in Joe Christmas and Ike McCaslin. But Warren went on, memorably, to alter his phrase, by saying that the true hallmark of Faulkner's work is not consciousness *of* doom, but consciousness *as* doom. I don't think one can improve on this judgment. For it is a judgment, not so much on literature as on life. Because life itself dooms us to the first person. This novel begins with the words "through the fence," and consciousness is the fated fence of our life, the walls within which we live, captive. Yet love entails going beyond. And *The Sound and the Fury* is about exactly this dilemma. Faulkner has written this book in such a way that we the readers are hurled into the prison-like consciousnesses of the Compsons. But that trip into the consciousness of another is itself a strange form of love, an entry into another's life and vision, a bittersweet triumph of art. Nothing in our era of easy electronic travel rivals the arduous vistas made possible by words on a page, for this low-tech journey into the Compson stories, conducted by a reader in search of his or her own story, is—beyond all hunger and pain and rage—an odyssey of the heart.

THE FAULKNER CURVE: FROM PRIVATE STORY TO HISTORICAL TRAGEDY

Faulkner himself felt that he "peaked" with *The Sound and the Fury.* Above all, the sheer pathos of figures such as Benjy and Quentin (and, indeed, Caddy) is not to be found in the no less remarkable fictions that followed. *As I Lay Dying* (1930), another masterpiece, resembles *The Sound and the Fury* by dint of its stunning renditions of consciousness. Its mix of grotesqueness, graveyard humor, and sheer philosophical brilliance makes it one of Faulkner's most vibrant books. In *Light in August* (1932) Faulkner moves, for the first time, frontally, into issues of race, and the figure of Joe Christmas, a man with a mysterious birth who *thinks* he has "a little black blood" in him, shifts from initial conception as minor figure to a powerful, unforgettable central role as ticking bomb of racial and gender violence. The most significant later Faulkner novels explore race ever more torturously, so that *The Sound and the Fury*'s pastoral depiction of Dilsey and family comes to look like a thing of the remote past.

The last great novel that Faulkner published was *Go Down, Moses* (1942), a complex, multivoiced series of stories that come at race and the gathering indictment/defense of the South in remarkable fashion. This autumnal work broods over the tragedy of the South and locates its "curse" in the twin transgressions of ownership: of land and of slaves. Most strikingly of all, this operatic text is magnificently unified by a view of *tracking* that ranges from converting bear prints into a script all the way to a grasp of language itself as markings, scratches on a surface, that demand our translation into human significance. After this, in my view, it is downhill for William Faulkner, even though he continued to write for two more decades.

ABSALOM, ABSALOM!: QUENTIN COMPSON REDUX

One (supremely) great book has been left out of this account, and we now go to *Absalom, Absalom!* (1936) to encounter a different (grander, larger) Faulkner, one who no longer produces the lyrical and tortured interior monologues of the Compson brothers, one who now has taken on the burdens of history and race as the central and tragic ingredients of the story of the South. It is here that Faulkner does something very Balzacian: He retrieves one of his earlier characters and "restories" him. But he goes well beyond Balzac (and any novelist I know) in electing our friend Quentin Compson as his protagonist, Quentin who (we know) is dead, having committed suicide at the end of his segment in *The Sound and the Fury*. Hence, we are returned to that familiar Harvard dormitory, but this time there is no Spoade or Deacon or Gerald Bland or little Italian girl in sight: just Quentin Compson, Mississippian, and Shreve McCannon, Canadian. Just one Southerner and one Northerner, in a cold New

England room, getting ready for sleep, talking, remembering, talking, remembering.

Faulkner returns in this later novel to Quentin Compson with a severe purpose in mind. The young man from *The Sound and the Fury* will be the (obsessed) conduit to the larger historical saga, the unhealed wound, that also obsesses the writer, William Faulkner: the Civil War. Quentin's earlier drama of dysfunction and sickness unto death must now go beyond its private markings and take on the fuller, deeper resonance it deserves. Quentin's earlier manic fixation on a dark shadow and incestuous longings will be exported into the Sutpen family romance. And Quentin's situation as Mississippian speaking to his Canadian roommate about the South, about this man Sutpen, will begin to hum with symbolic meanings, will come to be a weird "retrial" of the fratricidal war, but now played out in a Harvard dormitory forty-five years later, emerging as the ultimate test, the ultimate writerly challenge as to whether war or peace, hate or love, dead words or "hearts speaking to hearts" is possible between the South and the North.

Some may be put off by the portentous machinery of *Absalom, Absalom!*, by its insistence that the personal story—if properly illuminated, if properly interrogated—has historic significance, speaks of region and past, adumbrates something larger than itself. Maybe that is what the passing of time does to the writerly imagination: causes it to see its earlier materials as strangely resonant, insistently murmurous, leading to the view that all private stories are, ultimately, doors that open onto history. Given our interest in how Faulkner impacts on our own personal story, the gambit in *Absalom, Absalom!* couldn't be clearer: We are to learn how inscribed our private markings are, how echoing they are, how they gesture toward the great, sometimes convulsive forces that preceded our birth and will outlast our death.

A STORY WITH ECHOES

Hence the story of Thomas Sutpen, plantation owner, and his children, "who destroyed him or something or he destroyed them or something," is a bristling story, as emblematic and echoing as Faulkner can make it. Faulkner reaches all the way back to Greek tragedy in his rendition of the

House of Sutpen—like, we might say, the House of Atreus—so that we can measure the broader ramifications of these events. Moreover, the Sutpen house is a "house divided," and Faulkner is unquestionably thinking of Lincoln's famous speech in which he spoke of his design to save the Union, and said that a house divided against itself cannot stand. We are to understand that a war about slavery that could pit brother against brother is richly and unmistakably adumbrated by a novel about a family that is torn and divided both racially and sexually.

We are also to realize that Faulkner's title, *Absalom, Absalom!*, signals a still earlier tragically divided House: the story of King David's son Absalom, who killed his brother Amnon because Amnon fornicated with their sister, Tamar; and later Absalom rebelled against David, and was himself killed, leading to a great outpouring of grief on the part of the king: "O my son Absalom, my son, my son Absalom! would God I had died for thee, O Absalom, my son, my son!" Faulkner's interest in these earlier fables has nothing to do with literary ornamentation. The bloody events in the House of David speak long and loud about cyclical tragedy, about family revenge; and David's sorrow and recognition of his transgression as father are to be borne in mind when we come to the fate of Thomas Sutpen and his children, borne in mind as luminous alternative.

One more house warrants mentioning here: "the home of the brave." Faulkner's portrait of Thomas Sutpen speaks also, I think, to issues closer to home, to the kind of concerns a very different sort of writer, F. Scott Fitzgerald, had dealt with in *The Great Gatsby*. Sutpen is, every bit as much as Gatsby, an exemplary American figure, a hero of self-creation, a believer in the American dream of upward mobility. Late in the novel, Faulkner will sketch Sutpen's origins from the hill country in West Virginia down into the Mississippi plantation culture, and in time I shall discuss the young Sutpen's fateful education, the events that led up to *his* "Design." But even now one can see Sutpen as representative figure, as a man who sought to make himself anew, who believed that human volition, if strong and ruthless enough, could have the force of destiny, and that the past could be put behind him and silenced forever.

We can now perceive, I think, something of the ambitiousness and reach of *Absalom, Absalom!* It is not amiss to see it as a Faulknerian summa of sorts, as the book where he put in everything he had learned or imagined about the art of fiction. It is as if he needed the fullest possible arsenal of writerly stratagems and cunning to deliver the huge, heavy, freighted epic story he had in mind. And, perhaps more imperiously still, to deliver himself of the ghosts he lived with. One sympathizes, I think, with poor Quentin Compson, Faulkner's unmistakable surrogate, who has this much baggage on his hands and in his heart.

WRITING HOLOCAUST

In evoking the remarkable scope of *Absalom, Absalom!* and the exemplary fate of Thomas Sutpen, I have mentioned both the Bible and Greek tragedy as key references. Let me now suggest a wildly different analogue, one that occurred after Faulkner's novel was written and published: the Holocaust. Here is the modern apocalyptic scenario par excellence, and it is fair to say that we are still learning to take its measure. The United States Holocaust Memorial Museum in Washington offers one way of understanding the concatenation of historical events that led to the extermination of six million Jews: We actually see photographs and moving-camera footage of those who were living and are now dead—the politicians, the soldiers, the resisters, the victims, the actual places and documents from that bloody chapter in human history. And, yet, do we understand? Is this comprehensible?

I believe that William Faulkner regarded the Civil War in much the same fashion as many of us regard the Holocaust: as a convulsive period of destruction that shaped the lives of millions and altered the course of history. Faulkner was born in 1897, some thirty-two years after the Civil War's close, but this incendiary period in our national life was shockingly alive for him, roiled in his blood, demanded that he eventually give it, via his writing, its due. His situation is not all that different from the offspring of Holocaust survivors: people who did not experience the carnage firsthand, but whose lives had been fatefully haunted and scripted by those events taking place before they were born. A brilliant modern text such as Art Spiegelman's illustrated book *Maus* tells us a great deal about the amount of unprocessed horror that was still a legacy requiring expression, demanding still to be worked through, looking still for the right way to be said. Said in such a way that others who were *not* haunted might finally understand what had truly happened. *Absalom, Absalom!* is written under the sign of a comparable urgency, and its ceaseless narrative experimentation is Faulkner's way of being commensurate with this cataclysmic event: its human causes, its human cost, its continuing human impact.

YOUR STORY: HISTORY'S STAGE

Faulkner has cast this as the story of a family, and that is perhaps its greatest claim on *us*, for we are to see in the Sutpen saga the horrible mesh between individual story and historical event, between the routines of your life and the paroxystic stage on which you've been—willy-nilly, uncomprehendingly, blindly—positioned. We can walk through the Holocaust Museum and we can read through the history books, but we cannot easily grasp what it must have felt like to be alive then, how resistant to both logic and language it has to have been, to see your life swallowed up by disaster, to realize that your personal horizons and expectations were being erased by an unfolding calamity whose contours were immeasurable. And now I raise the question: How can we know these things? How can we know what disaster was like, when those who went through it, those whom it went through, are no longer living? What records are there? What can they convey to us? Can damage of this scope ever be leavened by the passing of time or the rituals of grieving and mourning?

It is clear that such questions concern the basic premises of writing history; but it is no less clear that these matters are every bit as elemental in the creating of art. Faulkner faced a paradox: He knew—in his blood, his heart, and his head—that the Civil War was as alive as ever, yet he also knew that he was writing about it (in the mid-1930s) more than six decades after it was over, and that it was dead for many (if not most) of his readers. His solution for this quandary was simple, elegant, and brilliant. His book would focus on two things at once: the unfurling saga of the Sutpens, who were caught up in the war, but also the strange, compulsive antics of all those who were trying to tell this story, ranging from the living testimony of Rosa Coldfield, who had "been there," to the more distant commentary of Mr. Compson, who had heard much of this from his father, on to the final joint storytelling performed by two students in a Harvard dormitory in 1910. Complicating the picture still further was his conviction that the lives of those Sutpens were themselves rich in testimony about *why* the war happened, so that these people were not simply victims, but were also players whose lives would illuminate the moral stakes of this conflict. Furthermore, he wanted to show that the arduous act of telling this story—which he spread out among distinct speakers, which he took to be emblematic of how narrative art works, what its challenges are, why we have it—might also contain its own truths about the war, especially if he could bring together a Southerner and a Northerner to conduct their peculiar collaborative experiment.

To face and cross the great divide between then and now is to challenge language's own resources. For language is all we have for this purchase, if the living participants are now dead. The language they left about their affairs; the language we devise to tell their story. What is at risk is the death of all we were, for if our lives cannot pass on over to others via words, either spoken or remembered or written, then we simply disappear off the earth, gone for good. For the secular among us, writing is a form of resurrection: not so much a bringing back to life as a recovery of what it was, *what it felt like*, when it existed. In this regard, it is useful to align the fierce narrative antics of *Absalom, Absalom!* with a genre that is much closer to home to most of us: the record left to us by our own parents or grandparents. As I tried to show in my discussion of Virginia Woolf's *To the Lighthouse*, the story of our parents is a profoundly elusive quarry, for we are separated from them by time (and its terrible accomplice: immaturity), so that we never truly share the same adult stage, and all too often they are no longer living when we might at last be able to understand them and speak to them as our hearts urge. Faulkner grew up with stories, stories of colorful and sometimes legendary ancestors, but in this contorted novel of generational divide he shows us how ghostly and silent our own dead are, how much we must furnish on our own—feelings, motivation—through our own devising if we are to hear them still, if they are to be fleshed out as three-dimensional living creatures with their own dreams and fears.

Recovering our story is the unifying thread that goes throughout this book, and no novel goes further than *Absalom, Absalom!* in showing us how rich and daunting and rewarding these matters are. For I am speaking of *our* story, not just Sutpen's story, or Quentin's story, or Faulkner's story, or indeed my own. Let us change registers and move from our parents' story to the story we know best: the inner saga that each of us has been living for some time now. Faulkner asks us to consider how transmittable it is: What words will tell it? How will others come to know it? Here we encounter the *historical* Faulkner, the man who knows that our inner lives not only defy representation (even though they are the dominant fact of our life), but that they disappear when we disappear. So, ask yourself: Will your story live on? Who will tell it? What will they know of it? What form will you have in fifty years? A hundred years?

It is all too easy to dismiss Faulkner's obsession with storytelling from various perspectives and temporal vantage points as the kind of thing writers worry about, but something a bit esoteric and academic for the rest of us. The truth is different: These are the most intimate facts of our lives; these are the issues that determine how long we actually live, how meaningful we are, were, or will be for others. Finally, these issues are as moral and spiritual as they are verbal, because the quality of our investment in others (and their investment in us) is an affair of heart and not just of language. This is why love will emerge as the shimmering final truth in *Absalom, Absalom!*: love as our means of access, love (or its loss) as the ultimate key to all human behavior, ranging from individual acts to Civil War.

QUENTIN COMPSON: HAUNTED

Faulkner begins the action of his book in the fall of 1909, but dates are deceiving. The Quentin Compson whom we now encounter back in Jefferson in September just before going off to Harvard is, in some strange sense, already dead, already a ghost, for he knows "his very body" to be "an empty hall echoing with sonorous defeated names" (7), and he knows himself to be "a commonwealth . . . a barracks filled with stubborn back-looking ghosts" (7). Quentin thinks these thoughts while listening to the crazed words of a little lady from the South, Miss Rosa Coldfield, a lady whose life has been wrecked by a certain Thomas Sutpen, plantation owner, and also by a Civil War, a lady whose hatred for this Sutpen has acted in the way formaldehyde acts: It has preserved her for some forty-three years since the signal insult she received (about which, more, later); it has pickled her. She must tell Quentin the story in Jefferson; he must later tell Shreve the story in Cambridge. With this, we realize, we are a far cry from *The Sound and the Fury*, for this novel is about being haunted—as Faulkner has to have realized that he himself was, always had been—and the urgency of Quentin's situation reminds one of still earlier drastic performances, such as that of the Ancient Mariner, who had a tale to unfold, who battened on to the Wedding Guest because the tale *had to be told*. It is as if everyone touched by this story were contaminated by it, were obliged to empty themselves of it, to pass it on. As readers, we, too, feel cornered and "collared"; even though we don't initially have a clue as to the particulars, or why it should matter to us.

Every time I teach this strange, outrageous, inimitable, magnificent novel to undergraduates, I tell them: It only *looks* exotic and unreadable. It is actually basic meat and potatoes, it is about two roommates (from different parts, yes, different parts) talking, communicating, coming to know each other; it is what you (the students) experience every single day and night at college. They usually look at me in disbelief. But what I do not tell them is: God forbid you should have a Quentin Compson for a roommate, a tortured soul who is not only slated for suicide but who is so obsessed and driven by his cultural past—cultural, *not* personal past—that it is pouring out of him, lava-like, that it is also contagious, that sleep is not going to come, may never come. This part I keep for myself. Why should I tell them? They'll learn soon enough.

GOOD-BYE, SOUTHERN ROMANCE

Absalom, Absalom!, Faulkner's great saga of the Civil War, was published in 1936, the same year that Margaret Mitchell published *Gone with the Wind*, *her* great saga of the Civil War. No two books could be more different, and it can surprise no one that millions of readers and spectators are still enamored of Mitchell's epic rendition of the South, both in print form and on the big screen, whereas Faulkner's book dropped like a piece of lead into the sea, visited only by Faulkner lovers. Mitchell's story is intentionally larger than life, focused on an immortal love story, and it offers for our delectation a stirring account of the fall of the South, a rich chapter from the American past, people with cleanly delineated human figures: Scarlet the irresistible bitch-survivor, Rhett the reckless bold gambling hero, Melanie the heart of gold, Ashley the refined Southerner who is sacrificed.

Faulkner's Civil War book refuses all of this. Whereas Mitchell etches the events and actions of her characters in indelible fashion, Faulkner presents us with overwhelming murk: Neither we nor the players know exactly what is happening, has happened. No problem whatsoever in distinguishing between black and white in Mitchell; for Faulkner, this (crucial, sacred) dividing line is in big trouble, since there is no more certainty here than there is anywhere else in his novel. The tone of the novel is mercilessly conjectural, the chronology is impossible to follow, the very story line is reprised, reconceived, reimagined endlessly. Now, you might take the view that this man Faulkner has made it devilishly hard for us to read his book; you might go still further and ask, just why has this Faulkner presented his stuff in such a punitive, inaccessible way?

For starters, Faulkner believes that history is always playing, that the great events of the past are never entirely past, but that they continue to script our moves and require our reinterpreting even now, in the present. Further, Faulkner knows that history is, among other things, the narrative that is woven by historians, so that we make our histories rather than merely perceive them. Finally, and less obvious, Faulkner intuits that a narrative that acknowledges these obstacles, a narrative that realizes its own potential fictiveness, a narrative that is endlessly groping for its givens and constructing its line, that such a narrative—which might be thought hopelessly esoteric and at several removes from reality—can in fact pack a wallop, can be galvanizing for readers. Why? Because such writing conveys, with great power, its own epistemological honesty, and it also confers a stupendous authority on the very notion of *personal knowledge*. At first blush, such issues may seem arid and academic; as we shall see, they are anything but that: They are passionate, existential, and bloody.

THE SUTPEN STORY: INCOHERENT AND IMPERIOUS

As indicated, the novel starts in Mississippi in September 1909, as Quentin Compson (just before going off to Harvard) visits with Rosa Coldfield. Almost everything in my sentence is wrong: Nothing really starts then, the real Rosa Coldfield died some forty-three years before, and what sits in this dark mausoleum-like room, dressed in black, looking very like a mummy, is a furious creature with a story to tell. And Quentin is not merely visiting; he (being a nice young man in a South where one respects one's elders) is yoked into this room, this presence, this séance, so that the spirits can be released. And thus Quentin both listens and speaks (to himself), thereby giving us the readers our first contact with the actual material of this novel. See what you can make of it:

> *It seems that this demon—his name was Sutpen—(Colonel Sutpen)—Colonel Sutpen. Who came out of nowhere and without warning upon the land with a band of strange niggers and built a plantation—(Tore violently a plantation, Miss Rosa Coldfield says)—tore violently. And married her sister Ellen and begot a son and a daughter which—(Without gentleness begot, Miss Rosa Coldfield says)—without gentleness. Which should have been the jewels of his pride and the shield of his old age, only—(Only they destroyed him or something or he destroyed them or something. And died)—and died. Without regret, Miss Rosa Coldfield says—(Save by her) Yes, save by her. (And by Quentin Compson) Yes. And by Quentin Compson.* (5)

The outline is there. A stranger came into town with strange black servants and built a plantation. He was or became a colonel. He married Rosa's sister Ellen. He had a son and a daughter, but came to a bad end, with someone destroying someone. He is not missed. He is missed. By Rosa Coldfield. And by Quentin Compson. This could be anybody's life, as seen and told years later: a mix of bare facts and gaping holes. Some crucial data is missing: What happened between him and his children? And what exactly is Rosa's involvement? Or, indeed, Quentin's? For we can already see that they are both implicated here, both unfree of this strange figure from the past. Faulkner is tackling the central enigma: a man's shadowy story and the strange impact it has had on others. This could be our fate.

Sutpen, according to Rosa, was a mystery from the very beginning, a man "who rode into town out of no discernible past and acquired his land no one knew how and built his house, his mansion, apparently out of nothing" (7). One wonders: Is this not how we appear to others? As strange figures who simply appear out of nowhere and commit whatever acts they commit? Do those around you have even a clue as to where you come from, or why you have done what you have done? None of this, mind you, diminishes Sutpen's aura, Sutpen's power, which is rendered by Faulkner as primal scene, indeed as creation myth: "Then in the long unamaze Quentin seemed to watch them overrun suddenly the hundred square miles of tranquil and astonished earth and drag house and gardens violently out of the soundless Nothing and clap them down like cards upon a table beneath the up-palm immobile and pontific, creating the Sutpen's Hundred, the *Be Sutpen's Hundred* like the oldentime *Be Light*" (4). The reference to Genesis speaks to the godlike nature of Sutpen's life and deeds: He comes without a past, builds a plantation from nothing, alters both the land and its people, and remains an enigma.

It seems to have happened, in Quentin's inner eye, much like a thunderbolt coming from the heavens. Again: That is how we perceive grand events. Who bothers to do research, to delve into causes or origins? For many of us, history proceeds along just these lines: Vesuvius explodes, the Bastille is stormed, D-Day arrives, Dresden burns, Kennedy is shot, a man walks on the moon, the Berlin Wall crumbles, the World Trade Center falls. Our private inner sanctum is stocked with frozen images of this variety. It comes to us as paintings, as film clips, as visual bites. Just so, with Sutpen, who sprang, full-blown, upon that Mississippi stage, to do what he was to do.

UNRELIABLE ROSA?

In the book's first chapter, Rosa tells Quentin (and us) a good bit more about Sutpen: his ruthlessness, his cunning, his strategic plan to establish himself via marrying Ellen Coldfield, Rosa's (much older) sister, his dynastic ambitions. And, in rapid-fire, telescopic fashion, she offers an outline of the entire story:

> I saw Judith's marriage forbidden without rhyme or reason or shadow of excuse; I saw Ellen die with only me, a child, to turn to and ask to protect her remaining child; I saw Henry repudiate his home and birthright and then return and practically fling the bloody corpse of his sister's sweetheart at the hem of her wedding gown; I saw that man return—the evil's source and head which had outlasted all its victims—who had created two children not only to destroy one another and his own line, but my line as well, yet I agreed to marry him. (12)

You want facts? There they are, a heap of them. It is as if Faulkner figured, let's show them how garish all this is, right at the outset, by giving them the bare bones: marriage forbidden, birthright repudiated, sweetheart murdered, victim agreeing to marry evil's source. It is a Gothic mess, larded with disasters that are begging for interpretation. *Why* did all of this happen?

For Rosa Coldfield, no mystery. Sutpen is little less than the devil incarnate. He is the reason "God let us lose the War." Sutpen is the ogre, the djinn, the demon, the monster who has stolen her sister and destroyed the lives of all: her family and his. Sutpen is Bluebeard who locks damsels up in his lair, he is the prince of darkness who has laid waste to her life. Rosa's feverish take on things has bemused Faulkner scholars—turning her into that well-known species, an unreliable narrator—but in our own heated-up geopolitical moment of paranoia and jihads and seeing the world in terms of God's friends and enemies, such vitriol seems oddly familiar. I also think Faulkner wants to graph the catastrophic impact humans sometimes have on one another, and Rosa is, to a very great degree, exactly what Sutpen has turned her into. Faulkner is interested in her as a window onto his story. After all, if you come upon a highway accident and want to know what happened, whom should you ask? The pilot in the plane flying overhead? The folks at the edge of the road who witnessed it? Or the bleeding person who just got pulled out of the vehicle? Rosa is the bleeding person of the story.

MR COMPSON'S PERSPECTIVE

But the tone changes when the narration moves from Rosa to Mr Compson. Like the Coldfields, the Compsons also are inscribed in the life and fortunes of Thomas Sutpen, especially through the figure of Grandfather Compson, who was to be the closest thing to a friend that Sutpen was to have. Hence, Quentin's father is possessed of much information concerning Sutpen and family, and he is free of the hellfire-and-brimstone logic subscribed to by Rosa Coldfield. And he has come a long way from the jaded figure of *The Sound and the Fury*; it is as if Faulkner discovered, in revisiting his people from the earlier novel, that all of them could be developed further, could be used in ways he'd never suspected while writing the first book. Hence, Mr Compson emerges as a storyteller of the first rank, a learned, urbane, reflective, and generous student of his culture and his family's past. You'd want him to be piecing together your own story if it were to be done after your death.

We watch, through his telling, the arduous process of Sutpen cementing his position in the community: the harassment suffered at his wedding (where people threw dirt and vegetable refuse), Ellen's tears and travails and eventual accommodation, the birth and maturation of the two Sutpen children, Henry and Judith, the closeted family life of little Rosa Coldfield, living alone with her widowed hermit-father, the coming of the war. All is not dark. With a light and keen touch, Mr Compson evokes these antebellum days, and we learn of Judith's love interests at the age of seventeen, her betrothal to one Charles Bon, dear (slightly older) friend of Henry's from the University of Mississippi, where both were students, Ellen's giddiness at planning the wedding, Sutpen's blooming affairs as "the biggest single landowner and cotton-planter in the county now" (56), yet always the rumbling of the coming war. Faulkner expresses the apparent disconnect between Sutpen flourishing and impending national calamity in a very memorable passage:

> Because the time now approached . . . when the destiny of Sutpen's family which for twenty years now had been like a lake welling from quiet springs into a quiet valley and spreading, rising almost imperceptibly and in which the four members of it floated in sunny suspension, felt the first subterranean movement toward the outlet, the gorge which would be the land's catastrophe too, and the four peaceful swimmers turning suddenly to face one another, not yet with alarm or distrust but just alert, feeling the dark set, none of them yet at that point where man looks about at his companions in disaster and thinks *When will I stop trying to save them and save only myself?* (58)

Supremely confident writing, conveyed through a deceptively pastoral swimming simile, evoking the power of history itself as it sweeps us up unawares, gathering energy and force, yoking ever more firmly and ineluctably the story of a family to the fate of a nation. It also tells us, in its very figures, that we do not stand on firm earth, but rather float in water, and that the tranquil lake is a mirage, for it conceals the catastrophic gorge into which we will plunge. To be sure, this simile does not contain the unheard-of raw traumatic power that we feel in seeing pictures of the twin towers falling, but I think it beautifully conveys the moment when our complacent sense of security and normalcy receives its very first jolts, its first seismic tremors, the moment when cataclysm whispers to us and alters us forever.

The war comes. Henry and Charles sign up. Sutpen is made colonel. And then the family catastrophe happens, like a bombshell going off inside Sutpen's Hundred, rearranging the givens, scattering the players; but what bombshell? Examined some half a century later, those Christmas events are sketchy and conjectural:

> . . . and so the tale came through the negroes: of how on the night before Christmas there had been a quarrel between, not Bon and Henry or Bon and Sutpen, but between the son and the father and that Henry had formally abjured his father and renounced his birthright and the roof under which he had been born and that he and Bon had ridden away in the night (62)

Here is the private rupture that somehow parallels the national divisions. Things darken further. The war continues. Rosa Coldfield's father (who abhors the war) shuts himself in his attic and starves himself to death. His daughter Rosa writes odes celebrating the valor of Confederate youth. People are beginning to go hungry. Ellen Coldfield dies (largely out of a collision with reality, Faulkner implies). Only Clytie (Sutpen's black daughter, named after Greek Clytemnestra, real mother unknown) and Wash Jones (poor white retainer) and Judith remain at Sutpen's Hundred. Chapter 3 ends with Jones riding up to the Coldfield gate shouting "Hello" at intervals until she comes to the door, at which point he says "Air you Rosie Coldfield?"

"Air you Rosie Coldfield?" Curious way to close a chapter, wouldn't you say? We must wait thirty-six pages until the final lines of chapter 4 to get the full account of Jones's tidings: " 'Air you Rosie Coldfield? Then you better come out yon. Henry has done shot that durn French feller. Kilt him dead as a beef' " (106). Who ever heard of breaking up a conversation in this fashion, making readers wait a whole chapter to hear how it finished? The central event of the novel—Henry Sutpen's murder of Charles Bon at the very gate of Sutpen's Hundred—is now out in the open, yet is no more comprehensible now than it was in Rosa's earlier notation of the brother flinging the bloody corpse of the sister's sweetheart at the hem of her wedding gown. What does this murder mean? How is it related to the exodus from the homestead?

Starting with Henry's abdication and abjuration, Mr Compson seeks to explain why it all happened. The book gathers ever more coherence. Yet, as you work through Mr Compson's genial efforts to make sense of these key events, it is good to ask yourself: How many decisive choices and fateful moves are there in your own history, choices and moves that had their clear logic then, but which may look like pure riddle now, in the eyes of someone trying to figure out exactly who you were? Quentin's father broods over the family crisis, probes more and more deeply into Henry's dilemma and Bon's character, tries to understand the peculiar role of Judith within this unmistakably libidinal triangle of brother-sister-friend. A twisted love story is beginning to come into view, thanks in great part to the probing generosity of Mr Compson, who is out to transform the scant facts into something humanly meaningful. We learn that Sutpen had suspected something concerning Bon, had even made a trip to New Orleans to investigate still further, had doubtless learned something damning and had then communicated it to Henry on Christmas Eve.

What it was we are not quite told, except that Mr Compson is certain that Henry knew, intuitively, that his father was telling the truth but repudiated his father nonetheless, remained loyal to his friend at the cost of his relation to his father. Why? Love has to be the answer. Henry loved Bon. Henry had to be loyal to the man he loved. The man he himself had selected as future husband for his sister. And Bon? He, too, as Mr Compson sees it, loved. He loved Henry, and indeed he loved Judith, too, Judith the Mississippi maiden all picked out for him.

I have put these matters baldly. Mr Compson puts them with both nuance and force, and he makes us see what an astonishing thing this love triangle actually is. To do this, he offers us two remarkable portraits: one of Henry Sutpen—Mississippian, Protestant, straightforward, country, angular, loyal, innocent, instinctive, passionate, violent—and one of Charles Bon—New Orleans, Catholic, sensual, sophisticated, elegant, mature, jaded, fatalistic, indolent, dashing, seductive. When you then factor in Judith as well—the country girl who remains an enigma, who agrees to marry Bon out of . . . love? . . . desire? . . . loyalty?—you end up with something explosive and not easily charted. The sexual displacements at hand are shocking and unmistakable, so that this projected marriage between Judith and Bon not only has an unavowed incestuous dimension, but also does something for *Henry* that cannot be done in any other way:

> In fact, perhaps this is the pure and perfect incest: the brother realising that the sister's virginity must be destroyed in order to have existed at all, taking that virginity in the person of the brother-in-law, the man whom he would be if he could become, metamorphose into, the lover, the husband; by whom he would be despoiled, choose for despoiler, if he could become, metamorphose into the sister, the mistress, the bride. (77)

It is an amazing passage, light-years more complex than the arrangements desired by Quentin Compson in *The Sound and the Fury*, wise about the substitutions that routinely and invisibly govern desire and behavior. And when you consider that it comes from the thoughts of a genial observer—for the principals would have died rather than say something so revealing—then we see how ripe and productive the Faulknerian imagination has become, how much projection (on our part) is required to make full sense, emotional sense, of the doings of others. I believe this passage does honor to the reality of human feeling, to the mixed and conflicted pulsions that underlie all our acts, but are rarely visible in the record we leave.

Incest, Faulkner says, but we are hardly likely to stop at this notion when we read this passage and this novel, because what also jumps out at us is the homoerotic current on show here, the inadmissible desire that Henry feels for Bon, so that the projected sexual union between Bon and Judith works doubly for Henry, gratifies at once his desire for his sister and for his friend, enables him subliminally to have intercourse with each of them. Especially, one feels, with Bon. For Charles Bon is the lightning rod of the novel, the erotically charged figure whom no one can resist. We know that Faulkner spent some time in New Orleans during his apprentice years as writer, with Sherwood Anderson as the supposed mentor, but I'd say that New Orleans is coming fully into its own here, in this novel, as a place of Old World culture, sensuality, languor, and wisdom, against which puritan Mississippi looks fierce and backward indeed.

It is in that New Orleans that Henry finally sees for himself, according at least to Mr Compson, the shocking truth about Charles Bon that Sutpen has presumably already learned, and communicated to his son that Christmas Eve: Bon is married, has a wife and a child. Now this damaging information would appear to scotch, definitively, any ideas about marriage with Judith.

But things are not this simple. Yes, Bon is married, but it is a morganatic union with an octoroon, a woman with one-eighth black blood who has been selected for her rare beauty and then nurtured and sheltered behind walls to serve the white man who has bought her and sworn to protect her. Bon and his fraternity of one thousand white men have played God, have saved from slavery perhaps one "in a thousand" of these octoroons, "creatures taken at childhood, culled and chosen and raised more carefully than any white girl, any nun, than any blooded mare even, by a person who gives them the unsleeping care and attention which no mother ever gives" (93). At this, Henry balks. This is betrayal. There can be no marriage. And now, Bon plays his trump card: " 'Have you forgot that this woman, this child, are niggers? You, Henry Sutpen of Sutpen's Hundred in Mississippi? You, talking of marriage, a wedding, here?' " (94).

A son repudiated his birthright and elected loyalty to his friend, the fiancé of his sister, rather than believe his own father. Four years later, the son kills his friend at the gates of his father's home in order to prevent him from marrying his sister. What could produce such extreme acts? The episode of the morganatic union with the octoroon whispers its racial venom to us; could race be the key? What is there about Bon that they either know or imagine, but that we ignore?

Later, we are presented with an actual datum, a real letter that Mr Compson has been holding in his hands the entire time, a letter that perhaps cannot bear too much light, but which is finally read. It is from Bon to Judith at war's end. It announces Bon's decision that they have waited long enough. It is written in stove polish on fine vellum, Yankee stove polish found (in gallons and gallons) where they (starving) had hoped to find food, Southern notepaper (from a gutted mansion) with French watermarks dated seventy years before, leading Bon to conclude:

> And since because within this sheet of paper you now hold the best of the old South which is dead, and the words you read were written upon it with the best (each box said, the very best) of the new North which has conquered and which therefore, whether it likes it or not, will have to

> survive, I now believe that you and I are, strangely enough, included among those who are doomed to live. (104–105)

It is vintage Faulkner. Here is the materiality of history: a resonant document whose mix of vellum and stove polish says perhaps more than any words could about the ravages of war. Judith and Clytie make the wedding dress. Charles and Henry finally arrive at the gate of Sutpen's Hundred. Henry shoots Charles. Wash Jones rides into town to the Coldfield house: " 'Air you Rosie Coldfield? Then you better come on out yon. Henry has done shot that durn French feller. Kilt him dead as a beef' " (106).

THE FABRIC OF HISTORY

Even though I myself have moved in a relatively linear path in discussing this novel, you cannot have missed what a chopped-up, convoluted, pieced-apart story this is. Faulkner is no sadist, he wants us to get our fill, but he will not hand us, as Margaret Mitchell did, a once-upon-a-time confection. Instead his question is: How do we get to know the past? And his answer is: We suffer it, we make it.

And even that is too simple. How do we make it? Take another look at the stationery with the stove polish: That is the past. A man's letter to his betrothed, saying they have waited long enough. An actual letter in the hands of Mr Compson (who got it from his mother, who got it from Judith, who got it from Bon) now being read by his son Quentin. Words written on a page, words written by real people who are now dead, words read by real people who have only those words, those markers on a page, and need to convert them into living reality. Here is the challenge: How do we access the genuine life of the past? Mr Compson, arguably the most urbane narrator of the novel, the man who seems to have gone furthest in actually imagining the feelings and motivations behind the events of the Sutpen story, knows that he has nonetheless come up short. We have a murder at a gate, and we cannot understand:

> It's just incredible. It just does not explain. Or perhaps that's it: they dont explain and we are not supposed to know. We have a few old mouth-to-mouth tales; we exhume from old trunks and boxes and draw-

> ers letters without salutation or signature, in which men and women who once lived and breathed are now merely initials or nicknames out of some now incomprehensible affection which sound to us like Sanskrit or Chocktaw; we see dimly people, the people in whose living blood and seed we ourselves lay dormant and waiting, in this shadowy attenuation of time possessing now heroic proportions, performing their acts of simple passion and simple violence, impervious to time and inexplicable—Yes, Judith, Bon, Henry, Sutpen: all of them. They are there, yet something is missing; they are like a chemical formula exhumed along with the letters from that forgotten chest, carefully, the paper old and faded and falling to pieces, the writing faded, almost indecipherable, yet meaningful, familiar in shape and sense, the name and presence of volatile and sentient forces; you bring them together in the proportions called for, but nothing happens; you re-read, tedious and intent, poring, making sure that you have forgotten nothing, made no miscalculation; you bring them together again and again nothing happens: just the words, the symbols, the shapes themselves, shadowy inscrutable and serene, against that turgid background of a horrible and bloody mischancing of human affairs. (80)

Nothing that Faulkner ever wrote surpasses this beautiful and wise utterance about the nature of both history and writing. History and writing: How little such things matter in *The Sound and the Fury*, where we are plunged into the interiors of Benjy, Quentin, and Jason, with no questions asked. The earlier book, breathtaking though it is, is innocent in comparison with this far more reflexive and—yes—ambitious undertaking. Because we can hardly fail to see that Faulkner has widened and deepened the stage enormously, so as to see the earlier Compson saga as an entry into the past, as a doorway onto Southern history and tragedy. And, no less profound, he has now tackled the single most pressing issue for any writer: To what end, words? How can the past, even if known, be told? How can it be told in such a way that the listener/reader lives it?

All these matters are especially acute when it comes to the writing and understanding of history. All we have from the past are a few documents, dead words, scribbled pages that, Faulkner says, "sound to us like Sanskrit or Chocktaw." And he goes on to dramatize our encounter with such documents, an encounter that routinely fails; like a careful scientist in his laboratory, we unfold the paper, put things together in the proportions called for, reread, try our utmost to make no miscalculation, and fail again. And again. Fail at what? Fail at bringing off the miracle whereby these documents—"familiar in shape and sense, the name and presence of volatile and sentient forces"—might disclose their secrets, might birth the life they conceal, might explode with presence.

I read Faulkner's words and think about my own (unavowed) fiascoes as history reader, how dead and inert the names and dates were in the history books I read, how stillborn it all was for me. And I revisit, in my mind, the sometimes dazed and glazed-over faces of generations of students who've come my way, to whom I have assigned endless works of literature, in hopes that the miracle would happen, the explosion of life via book. And I remember my own children going through their paces, reading the various assignments given them in school, finding some exciting, finding others dead, but rarely finding any of it as explosive and breathless as it used to be long ago, when my wife and I sat at their bedside and read to them; then, it was electric.

And then I think even darker thoughts: how our daily lives are dogged by this same routine failure. Not simply when we are in the library or archive or lecture hall, but when we are speaking and listening to people we know, people we love: And—even though no one dares admit it—it is all just dead words, meaningless sounds. Oh, yes, we know the dictionary meanings of the words we hear, but that larger miracle of communication, of hearts speaking to hearts, that is what fails over and over. And I write these words as someone who is reasonably articulate, who thinks of himself as a listener, who has spent his life writing and talking, and who nonetheless senses that the whole enterprise is all too often doomed from the outset, an affair of ships passing in the dark, emitting signals that no one hears or understands.

WHY NOT TELL IT STRAIGHT?

There can be little doubt that Mr Compson is taking his own pulse when he acknowledges the failure of his (heroic) interpretations to take the actual measure of the past, to move from words to flesh. Such passages advertise the self-awareness of *Absalom, Absalom!* Today's academy employs terms such as "metatextual" to denote the issues Faulkner raises here, and I myself called such writing "reflexive." Yet these words suggest, I think, all the wrong things: navel-gazing, writerly narcissism, art for art's sake, narrative high jinks. The truth goes the other way. Faulkner is getting down to basics, is rock-bottom in his inquiry, elemental in his purpose, dead-on in his project. Nothing gussied up or esoteric about *Absalom, Absalom!* at all, even if bewildered readers might be tempted to see it that way.

Yes, this novel looks awfully fractured. Yes, it looks as though readers are going to be kept in the dark for as long as Faulkner is able to keep them there. Yes, you might be tempted to throw up your hands and say: Just tell us what happened! But this book is written this way in order to make history come alive. Those old apocryphal stories about William Faulkner writing a straightforward tale and then taking the scissors to it, so as to piece it apart into jagged segments, served up as Modernist cocktail, well, such thinking is titillating but worthless. And misleading, for it implies that we all know what a story is, how it should be told. And we do know, don't we? We've read lots of traditional fictions that start at the beginning and stop at the ending, and are done in such a way that you don't get lost in the process, either. That is the way life moves, we say. So why shouldn't stories be written like that? What's not to like?

For starters, it's not true. Faulkner is suggesting that life does not move that way, that we process/invent our own story retrospectively, looking back, and that the coherence of our lives—if any—is something we arduously construct. Heaven knows that your CV or résumé is a constructed affair, one where you begin at your current level/phase and write backward; but, mind you, write backward in such a fashion that it reads nicely forward, that it looks logical, even inevitable, that your schooling and series of degrees and sequence of jobs and spate of experiences add up perfectly to the present moment, the present self. Just imagine yourself at six or twelve or eighteen or even twenty-five prophesying all the steps to come; what a lark! We know the cliché that behind every successful man stands a surprised woman. I'd also say that behind every evolved life lurks a host of earlier selves who couldn't have had a clue, who may have thought they were headed in all sorts of other directions, who'd be stunned to know how they ultimately were to turn out. So much for good old linear narrative.

And then there is this business of direct writing that does not dillydally or get lost and mired in its own devices. Just the facts, ma'am. Faulkner has the courage to say: What facts? *Absalom, Absalom!* suggests that traditional writing is a huge con game, a form of emperor's new clothes in which well-behaved sentences are trotted out in order to deliver their message. Faulkner says, what message? Faulkner says, words only deliver words. What counts is to—somehow—convert those words into something else, something like actual life. And that is not easy. One could say: That is not possible. I think Faulkner himself felt that it was inherently not possible, not doable, and that every novel he wrote was impossible, quixotic, in its way, was a form of tilting against windmills, trying to burst out of language, since he was out to make words do something they are not equipped to do: generate life. Remember, again, Benjy's "trying to say"; remember Reverend Shegog's sermon, a sermon that goes directly to the heart, connects it with other hearts, beyond the need for words. But there is no little black church in sight in this sweeping historical fiction. So where do you go to speak the human heart?

ROSA COLDFIELD: "A MIGHT-HAVE-BEEN WHICH IS MORE TRUE THAN TRUTH"

The middle chapter of *Absalom, Absalom!*, written entirely in italics, returns us to Rosa Coldfield, but she is now a different person from the pickled, mummy-like figure of the book's beginning. This Rosa is volcanic in her tidings, possessed of a fire that is to fuel the entire second half of the novel with its vision of love. Love. What can the vitriolic and seething Rosa Coldfield tell us of love? Well, the "little dream woman" (as Shreve fondly calls her) has some surprises for us. She starts with the familiar, the known and recorded data: "*So they will have told you doubtless already* . . ." (107) but soon enough we see this phrase change into its opposite: "*But they cannot tell you* . . ." (108) and this crucial shift is the "Open, Sesame" of both the chapter and the novel, leading us into the most overheated, often hallucinatory prose that Faulkner ever wrote. It is a dithyramb to what did not happen; it is an account of aborted love: that between Rosa and Bon, that between Rosa and Sutpen.

By now we are familiar with the notion of interior monologue conveying to the reader an entire inner landscape that would otherwise be unknown. Faulkner's portrayal of Rosa in the fifth chapter goes beyond even this, in order to speak of the things that never happened. I realize that my formulation seems paradoxical. But consider: History may indeed be the account of all that transpired, but what are we to say of all the rest, all the possibilities that were dormant, latent, perhaps believed in and yearned for, but never actualized? Rosa Coldfield actually dives into the wreck, goes deeply into the quarry, makes us understand how much pathos and feeling and outright life go into things that never succeed in happening, never come off.

And we begin to realize that this is ultimately the great untold story of any life, every life: all that we wanted, imagined, feared—and never got. The familiar cliché "tip of the iceberg" seems appropriate here, especially for denoting the sheer discrepancy in size and volume between the (paltry) record and the (enormous) possibilities. If for a moment we think about our own circumstances, about the immensity of dream and desire, of project and ambition, that bubble inside us at all times, and we then measure the actual outcomes, the actual results, then I think the cartography coming into view in this chapter makes sense. Here would be indeed the fuller weather of both mind and heart, all those might-have-beens that never make it into reality, hence never appear on any CV or résumé. Is this not the unrecognized carnage of real history, the routine decimations of life and love that take place on the inside, leaving no cadavers to count, no gravestones for markers?

Need I add that this evocation of what we desired and felt—as opposed to what we got—radically challenges any staid views we might have about "our story?" Perhaps the true parameters of a life have only a passing resemblance to the so-called facts and data, the measurable and the known. To put it in other terms, these muffled inner dramas are precisely the "books" that no one keeps, no one other than the buried scribe who is lodged permanently in our hearts, who never goes off duty, who tallies all our gains and losses, yet whose testimonial rarely makes it onto the record. Rosa's account of what she felt is like a depth charge that explodes *Absalom, Absalom!* right in the middle, opening up a new territory altogether.

HUMAN GARDEN, HUMAN SEED

The reader enters Rosa's chapter thinking that the story is being filled out, that Rosa's fateful trip out to Sutpen's Hundred (following Wash Jones's announcement of the murder of Charles by Henry) will add to our knowledge of actual events. But soon enough we encounter language of a different sort altogether, language virtually liberated from the ongoing plot, but focusing instead on Rosa's past, especially a certain moment in her past. The writing is thick, incandescent, lyrical, mythic:

> *Once there was (they cannot have told you this either) a summer of wistaria. It was a pervading everywhere of wistaria (I was fourteen then) as though of all springs yet to capitulate condensed into one spring, one summer: the spring and summertime which is every female's who breathed above dust, beholden of all betrayed springs held over from all irrevocable time, repercussed, bloomed again. It was a vintage year of wistaria: vintage year being that sweet conjunction of root bloom and urge and hour and weather; and I (I was fourteen)—I will not insist on bloom, at whom no man had yet to look—nor would ever—twice . . . Nor do I say leaf—warped bitter pale and crimped half-fledgling intimidate of any claim to green . . . But root and urge I do insist and claim, for had I not heired too from all the unsistered Eves since the Snake? Yes, urge I do: warped chrysalis of what blind perfect seed: for who shall say what gnarled forgotten root might not bloom yet . . . ?* (115–116)

The fifth chapter of *Absalom, Absalom!* wafts us into a writerly domain of extraordinary heat and density, conveyed in a poetic idiom that breaks every possible rule of traditional prose, eschews all clarity and verisimilitude in order to evoke a green world of garden and seed, of life's ever-present promise. There will be readers who find such writing indigestible, too purple for comfort, outright appalling. (I always tell my writing students: If you turn in something like this to a teacher or publisher, you'll be laughed at, and told to start over.) But you won't understand this novel unless you are willing to negotiate this charged, sensuous, dripping, poetic, even garish language of fertility and organic life. (And, by the way, who ever decreed that Hemingway and Raymond Carver and all the tight-lipped writers in their wake ever had a lock on what prose could or should be?)

If *The Sound and the Fury* moves us by its beautiful evocation of vulnerable childhood, this episode fiercely reconceives what it means to know—to have known—desire. Is there any living person who hasn't been there, even if long ago? Why not (when one, near the end, remembers back) invoke wistaria, spring, root, bloom, and urge? Why not see oneself inscribed (later, after life's disappointments and denials), even as "unsistered Eve," in nature's pageant? Why not do justice (later, when the body is withering) to the wild, incredible, aching wants of the flesh? Surely this organic discourse is as close to the mark, concerning what our bodies feel, as the more docile and abstract terms of psychological notation. Rosa is evoking her moment of puberty (I was fourteen, she repeats), the moment when she could make life, the moment of her entry into sexual possibility and the dance of the species. Yes, she also speaks of her dark, prison-like, and sterile childhood, "that unpaced corridor" where she seemed banished and cut off from the living, but we are to understand that such deprivation has only intensified her longing for life. And she exited this dungeon to find "*a world filled with living marriage*" (116). Puberty as the release from the prison, as the entry into the flow.

And it was exactly at that time that she almost met Charles Bon. Almost. Something quite wonderful here: Henry had brought Charles home with him that summer, had come to visit Rosa, had found her not there; yet this visit was productive, indeed seminal, nonetheless: "*There must have been some seed he left, to cause a child's vacant fairytale to come alive in that garden*" (117–118). All the motifs are now coming together: the prison, the fairy tale, the seed, the garden. Perhaps this is what love is: a child's vacant fairy tale that comes alive. Perhaps this is what our unwritten story might sound like, had we written it then. A seed was left; it came alive. How few facts are needed! How worthless a camera would have been, to catch this! The combustible engine is the human heart, and it requires so very little, for its invisible explosions, for its creation of life. Thus, Rosa, who never saw Bon, never heard his voice, still became, in the logic of this novel, inseminated, "*as though that casual pause at my door had left some seed, some minute virulence in this cellar earth of mine*" (117).

LET FLESH TOUCH WITH FLESH

Rosa Coldfield is the novel's love apostle, and she delivers her paean to love in the most extravagant language that Faulkner ever wrote: "*I who had learned nothing of love, not even parents' love—that fond dear constant violation of privacy, that stultification of the burgeoning and incorrigible* I *which is the meed and due of all mammalian meat, became not mistress, not beloved, but more than even love; I became all polymath love's androgynous advocate*" (117). Faulkner never surpassed this; could anyone? We see here a celebration of human connection that seems to transcend all the markers we are accustomed to: gender, psychology, self. The connective principle, in all its gaudy and mesmerizing splendor, is trumpeted as the ultimate truth in life. There is nothing easy about this: Love is understood as the rupture of privacy, as the hallowing of an elemental force that is as basic and impersonal as photosynthesis. The little lady dressed in black has the most carnal and fiery imagination of the novel, for it is she who knows that "*living is one constant and perpetual instant when the arras-veil before what-is-to-be hangs docile and even glad to the lightest naked thrust if we had dared, were brave enough (not wise enough, no wisdom needed here) to make the rending gash*" (114). Phallic perhaps, above all existential: Love means going through, entering.

Rosa rode out to Sutpen's Hundred and found decimation everywhere: Charles dead, Henry gone, Judith widowed before being married. Running into the house, she is stopped by Clytie, stopped physically by Clytie's (black) hand on her (white) flesh. This leads to the keenest, most prophetic and fateful insight of the book:

> *Because there is something in the touch of flesh with flesh which abrogates, cuts sharp and straight across the devious intricate channels of decorous ordering, which enemies as well as lovers know because it makes them both:—touch and touch of that which is the citadel of the central I-Am's private own: not spirit, soul; the liquorish and ungirdled mind is anyone's to take in any darkened hallway of this earthly tenement. But let flesh touch with flesh, and watch the fall of all the eggshell shibboleth of caste and color too.* (111–112)

Once again this novel explodes with a spellbinding vision of human connection as the ground zero of both sexual and political life. It is impossible to overstate the significance of this credo—for it is that—with regards to the central moral and ideological issues of Faulkner's book and his world. Often thought of as long-winded and rhetorical, Faulkner can also be taut, almost surgical in his phrasing, displaying the kind of strange economy that we find in "*which enemies as well as lovers know because it makes them both.*" Human touch is the most powerful explosive known to our species. In this very passage we watch it blow sky-high all the codes and categories that the antebellum South had to see as God-given: "*the eggshell shibboleth of caste and color too.*" (The bearing of this wisdom on *Absalom*'s plot is immeasurably important, as we shall see.)

But I want also to note the sheer philosophical oomph and reach of Rosa's claim: Touch alters/annihilates all pretensions of individual sovereignty and hegemony, cashiers any notion of an integral self, an atomic individual, busts wide open the closed doors of the "*central I-Am's private own.*" We cannot fail to see that American individualism itself is on the block here, and is in trouble, is exposed as a precarious construct—yes, the armored nuclear self is a construct—slated for destruction by the most elemental act in human (and political and racial and sexual) life: touch. Perhaps the most striking feature of this stupendous passage is the strange metaphor of mind versus body as path of knowledge. The mind, Faulkner says, is "*liquorish and ungirdled,*" is "*anyone's to take in any darkened hallway of this earthly tenement.*" What an amazing statement! The adjectives themselves are so perfect—liquorish and ungirdled—signifying not only the fluidity, but also the capriciousness, the uncontrollability, the promiscuity of thought itself.

I see a mind/body dyad that has been with us at least since Saint Paul—always and ever privileging mind over body, seeing mind as the repository of soul and self, whereas body is the doomed, mortal, inferior flesh (not to mention the ramifications of pride versus shame that go into this dyad)—and I see it being turned upside down, inside out. Faulkner is telling us we've had it wrong for centuries, that the body is our true inner sanctum, our holy of holies, and the language of the body is not verbal but corporeal: touch. One reason I love this passage is its marvelous send-up of all intellectual positions and loyalties: The mind is anyone's to take in this darkened hallway. This is a mugging scenario, and I cannot help thinking it is an apt figure for the intellectual traffic, the shifting and buying and selling of ideas, that characterizes high culture, especially the academy. Faulkner does not quite go this far, but his phrase suggests: Hey, we swap our ideas as easily as we change cereal brands; all it takes is to be hit by a new concept or be exposed to a potent speaker. And when I think of the actual character of intellectual exchange, I think he's right: Folks trade in their old beliefs and acquire new ones every few years, or months, or weeks.

But the body—which we've been trained to see as lesser, as malleable, as promiscuous—is the site of our deepest exchanges and of our only lasting knowledge. You touch my body, you alter me. Can it be accidental that the man who most ignores the sanctity of others' bodies and feelings, Thomas Sutpen, tells the man who's going to kill him, " '*Don't you touch me, Wash*' " and receives as answer: " '*I'm going to tech you, Kernel*' " (151)? We are dead center. Touch is a mode of passion, discovery, knowledge, transformation, and murder.

ROSA AS SUN

Rosa Coldfield is no longer a witness telling us about Sutpen; she is the novel's visionary. Her affirmation of love, first felt when she came to puberty and saw a "*world of living marriage*" and received some "*seed*" from Charles Bon, later tested when she came to Sutpen's Hundred after the murder at the gate and stayed on there with Judith and Clytie, has nothing whatsoever to do with psychology. Or even emotion. It is far more elemental. It is as basic as choosing life over death. That is why she accepts the marriage offer from Thomas Sutpen when he finally comes back, at war's end, to the ruined plantation. No histrionics, no falling in love at all. Simply a man (without much time left) looking at a woman in the garden with a hoe: "*He had seen me for twenty years, but now he was looking at me*" (131). This courtship differs entirely from the dalliance of Bon and Judith; it is about light and dark, sun and swamp, about a man standing in the path "*looking at me with something curious and strange in his face as if the barnlot, the path at the instant when he came in sight of me had been a swamp out of which he had emerged without having been forewarned that he was about to enter light*" (131). Rosa thinks of herself as nothing more or less than sun. Love is the raw vital force that lives in light, earth, and flesh: "*You see, I was that sun, or thought I was who did believe there was this spark, that crumb in madness which is divine*" (135). And again: "*I was that sun, who believed that he . . . was not oblivious of me but only unconscious and receptive like the swamp-freed pilgrim feeling earth and tasting sun and light again and aware of neither but only of darkness's and morass's lack—who did believe there was that magic in unkin blood which we call by the pallid name of love that could be, might be sun for him*" (135).

It is hard to imagine a more generic definition: the magic in un-kin blood that we call by the pallid name of love. Faulkner's novel deals with the threat of apocalypse, with the violent and bloody end of the antebellum South that still haunts him in 1936. Against the killing he posits the oldest, simplest virtue of all: love. Nothing to do with romance or happiness; no truck with name, face, psychology, or private wants. Love as continuation of the species, as life over death. That is why Sutpen is construed as a "*swamp-freed pilgrim,*" for this is a religious quest, a search for some force that might be stronger than destruction. That is what Rosa has learned: "*But love and faith at least above the murdering and the folly, to salvage at least from the humbled indicted dust something anyway of the old lost enchantment of the heart*" (120–121).

But Rosa's dream of seed and sun is not to be. Sutpen, worried he has very few shots left, proposes to try it and see; if it's a boy, they'll be married. This not only kills the dream, but is the coup de grâce that produces the embattled spinster who opens the novel forty-three years later. Yet Faulkner retains the haunting images of garden and seed in order to express her expulsion from life. She is seen, forever after, by the town itself as a woman without a garden: "*Because now the town—farmers passing, negro servants going to work in white kitchens—would see her after sunup gathering greens along garden fences, pulling them through the fence since she had no garden of her own, no seed to plant one with, no tools to work it with herself*" (138).

The fifth chapter casts the same radiance over this novel, both backward and forward, that the Easter sermon does in *The Sound and the Fury.* Rosa finishes her own life barren, but she seeds this book, just as Charles Bon had "*planted a seed*" in that "*cellar earth*" of hers. "A *vacant fairytale,*" she said; "*a might-have-been which is more true than truth.*" We will need to leave Mississippi and go to a Harvard dormitory for this vision to be actualized. It will be for Quentin and Shreve to make final sense of the Sutpen story—not just the murder at the gate, but the whole story: plantation, dynasty, war, and all—and Rosa Coldfield will be their guide.

FROM MISSISSIPPI TO MASSACHUSETTS: ENTER SHREVE

I have already noted the jagged nature of *Absalom, Absalom!*, its delayed disclosures and interrupted narrative flow. It is richly symbolic that the Sutpen story now travels from Mississippi to Massachusetts, from the memories of Southern "insiders" like Rosa and Mr Compson to the imaginings of two young people at Harvard, getting ready for bed. For this trajectory speaks for the mission of literature itself: how to capture the human story and make it live for others. And one can hardly fail to see, refracted if not reflected, the singular cultural and writerly position of William Faulkner himself, Southern writer displaying his wares for a wider audience, wondering whether the story of the South will make any sense in Cambridge, Massachusetts.

It ain't going to be easy. But then, if you've ever lived in a dormitory, if you've ever tried to explain the folklore that seems natural to you but weird to those around you, then you know that storytelling can be a complicated, even bellicose two-way street. Moreover, imagine Quentin Compson as a roommate. One can, I think, sympathize with Shreve McCannon, who is obliged to share his living space with this brooding and haunted Mississippian. Shreve is no easy listener; he puts up a fight; he has his own views.

In fact, this later Shreve is one satiric guy. First of all, you've got this place, the South. Please. It can't be real: *"Tell about the South. What's it like there. What do they do there. Why do they live there. Why do they live at all"* (142). Or, later: " 'Jesus, the South is fine, isn't it. It's better than the theater, isn't it. It's better than Ben Hur, isn't it. No wonder you have to come away now and then, isn't it' " (176). If Faulkner's early stint in New Orleans nourished the portrait of Charles Bon, we have to assume his trips up North convinced him that Shreve had been underutilized. (Perhaps being incomprehensible to Northerners is something that all Southerners learn sooner or later, if they venture northward; Faulkner must have had considerable experience here.)

Shreve is the book's joker, the fellow who delights in recasting Mr Compson's heroic Sutpen in his own spicy mock-heroic style. Likewise, when it comes to Rosa Coldfield and her dealings with Sutpen, Shreve goes berserk, seeing in her story of demons and ogres evidence of a larger absurdist comedy. Here is what he can sound like:

> "That this old dame that grew up in a household like an overpopulated mausoleum, with no call or claim on her time but the hating of her father and aunt and her sister's husband in peace and comfort and waiting for the day when they would prove not only to themselves but to everybody else that she had been right . . . and right about her brother-in-law [Sutpen] because if he hadn't been a demon his children wouldn't have needed protection from him and she wouldn't have had to go out there and be betrayed by the old meat and find instead of a

> widowed Agamemnon to her Cassandra an ancient stiff-jointed Pyramus to her eager though untried Thisbe who could approach her in this unbidden April's compounded demonry and suggest that they breed together for test and sample and if it was a boy they would marry . . ." (144)

This is how the reader learns of the mortal affront suffered by Rosa Coldfield forty-three years before. A Southern gentlewoman of Rosa's stripe was not equipped to take such an offer lightly, seriously, or forgivably. As I said, it pickled her.

And I think it is fair to say that Shreve himself is doing something comparable for this overheated novel as a whole, pickling it by his belly laughs. His recasting of this story as lunacy and joke, taking place in the asylum known as the South, shows just how aware Faulkner is of the extremist nature of his materials, his writing, and himself. But, putting the joker directly into the deck is, if I may put it this way, a form of insurance, a way of saying, "You think I don't know how extravagant all this is?" If anything, Shreve's view of the South as loony tunes liberates Faulkner, licenses him to go as far over the top as he pleases, since he can always rope in his textual policeman, Shreve, to point out the infraction, and then return to the party renewed.

There is a brilliant kind of narrative canniness in using Shreve the way Faulkner does. It establishes a dialogic energy that will become ever more important as the novel proceeds. And I cannot help thinking it expresses a vital speaker/listener relationship that lies at the core of much Faulknerian writing, that is perhaps as close as Faulkner can come to a counterweight against the violence and destruction he records in his novels. We see it with Gail Hightower and Byron Bunch in *Light in August*, with Ike McCaslin and his cousin Cass in *Go Down, Moses.* Yet I wonder if William Faulkner ever experienced it. I can still recall, from my graduate days at Harvard in the mid-1960s, hearing (from professors who had witnessed it much earlier) of Faulkner being seen in Cambridge, eating alone at the local cafeteria, unnoticed, not (yet) taken seriously by the Harvard English department. And what one knows of the biography certainly suggests a man who was dreadfully solitary, prey to his own demons, with few social or intellectual outlets in sight. It is against this likely experience of real-life isolation that the storytelling covenant between Quentin and Shreve emerging in *Absalom, Absalom!* is so poignant and profound.

TWO BOYS IN A DORMITORY: A MARRIAGE OF SPEAKING AND HEARING

The last half of the novel belongs to Quentin and Shreve—the next generation, the student/scribes, our surrogates—as they try their hand at unfolding and understanding those dark events of long ago. Quentin is, of course, the beneficiary of two prior accounts of Sutpen: Rosa's and that of his own father. A considerable amount of family history now enters the picture. In particular we learn about the strange Charles Etienne Saint-Valery Bon, whose tragic story is only now told. After Bon's death, Clytie went to New Orleans to bring both the octoroon wife and the little boy back with her to visit Sutpen's Hundred. The magnolia-faced woman and the thin, delicate child "with a smooth ivory sexless face," both evoked in terms of fin-de-siècle elegance and decadence identified with Aubrey Beardsley and Oscar Wilde, were hardly fit for the harsh conditions of postbellum Mississippi, and did not stay. The woman later died, and again Clytie went to New Orleans, to return with the dazed twelve-year-old boy whose calvary was now to begin. Displaced, undersized, speaking no English initially, finding himself ever more in a racial no-man's-land, brought up by Clytie and Judith as a displaced person, the child's life is evoked with great pathos, as in this passage about sleeping arrangements, where the two women who love him tenderly nonetheless consign him to his doom:

> You are not up here on this bed with me, where through no fault nor willing of your own you should be, and you are not on this pallet floor with me, where through no fault nor willing of your own you must and will be, not through any fault nor willing of our own who would not what we cannot just as we will and wait for what must be. (161)

This grand prose has a sonorousness and dignity that may seem marmoreal, but that cry out for our own critical intervention. All of these people are caught. Faulkner is probing the racial practices of the antebellum South, not to pronounce judgment but to depict the lives of those most coerced and destroyed by these conventions, victims white, black, and in between. The fragile orphan-child of Bon and the octoroon grows into his inevitable identity as racial misfit, as would-be "nigger," even though it is a term he could not even have heard of, in his New Orleans childhood, living in the "padden silken vacuum cell . . . where pigmentation had no more moral value than the silk walls and the scent and the rose-colored candle shades" (161). He will drain the cup: from pampered slight child to no less slight laborer working the soil, from desperate and confused youth to starter of racial brawls where he was invariably injured, from arranged departure to unannounced return, this time "with a coal black and ape-like woman and an authentic wedding licence" (166).

Critics have cried "foul!" at Faulkner's depiction of the abject creature ("the black gargoyle") now appearing as wife, but the portrait of Charles Etienne Saint-Valery Bon's life as a kind of ongoing, indeed lifelong racial hara-kiri has its undeniable dark logic. This grim story is completed by the young man's death by yellow fever, a fatal disease with consequences, since it will also kill Judith Sutpen, who nurses this "foster son" in his illness, and it will leave a further orphan, the idiot offspring produced with the black wife, Jim Bond. We have not seen the last of him. And we realize that Charles Bon may have been murdered at the gates, but that his story rolls on, moving into subsequent generations, taking on still different hues. When do things end?

SUTPEN'S PAST

But Sutpen himself remains an enigma. What did he tell his son about Charles Bon that could not be brooked, that fissured the family, that perhaps led to Bon's murder four years later? More massively still, who is this man? What drove him into Mississippi to create Sutpen's Hundred, just like the oldentime "Be Light"? Rosa Coldfield told us with no uncertainty that this man "came out of nowhere," and that the townspeople indeed saw him as enigmatic outsider crashing the gates.

Only now, late into the novel, does this monumental silhouette start to fill in. After all the groping efforts to get one's mind around this man, Quentin now shares with Shreve something on the order of an actual Sutpen autobiography, namely Sutpen's own account of his origins as narrated to his friend Grandfather Compson, thus passed on to his son Mr Compson to Quentin (to Shreve to me to you). One can scarcely avoid thinking: Wait a minute! Why didn't we get all this at the outset? Indeed, most novels would have started with this information, but our man Faulkner believes you've got to be ready for what he's going to tell you; or perhaps he believes his own delayed explanations should only come when they are ripe. Most of all, Faulkner is convinced that writing is not all that different from the child's game show-and-tell, in the sense that telling acquires a different heft and aura when it follows showing, when it is preceded by our own prior interpretive labor.

Of course we saw this same model in the delivery of *The Sound and the Fury*. And I have insisted that "effects before causes" is actually the way we live, the in-the-dark groping through life that experience is all about. Only novels start at the beginning or underline the important things. Life is always in the middle and in the murk. I have conceded that this type of narration can be rough going, and that readers may feel frustrated when tackling *Absalom, Absalom!* But that is only half the story. The other half (the bigger half) consists of the reward you get from such prose: It is the reward life itself offers us when key facts finally arrive—through labor, through happenstance—and shed precious light on much that has been in the dark. One doesn't quite say "Eureka," but these local moments of clarification—and perhaps there are only local moments, never definitive illuminations or revelations—go a long way toward sweetening our shadowy marathon. A final way to see this is, once again, to imagine your own story's fate: Decades after your death, others (perhaps grandchildren, now grown) are reminiscing, trying to make you out, and one of them says, wait a minute, I remember hearing from my father . . . And the curtain goes up at last.

Born in the West Virginia hills, the young Sutpen was forever marked by the long voyage down the mountain and into the South; this journey was, we realize, as momentous as the exit from the Garden of Eden, because it brought about the encounter between the Sutpen clan and "Culture," culture consisting of an entire series of hierarchies and gradations inflected by money, station, and race. To put it most bluntly, young Sutpen discovers that his family is (now recognizable as) white trash. This discovery is inseparable from another one: hatred for the black menials who work for the wealthy white landowners because they, the blacks, even though nominally the lowest of the low, nonetheless enjoy a position in the power scheme that Sutpens and their ilk will never have. It is no less than a crash course in ideology. How does it happen?

The boy Sutpen was sent by his father to the big house owned by a man who "spent most of the afternoon . . . in a barrel stave hammock between two trees, with his shoes off and a nigger who wore every day better clothes than he or his father and sisters had ever owned and ever expected to, who did nothing else but fan him and bring him drinks" (184). He had a message to deliver to the man from his pa. And he was excited because he was now going to see what wonders such a huge house might contain. Mind you, he was not envious in the least. He regarded the landowner's wealth and possessions as something that he, too, under propitious circumstances or with enough work, might also come to own one day. The boy goes up to the door. And the fateful initiation happens. It is now that he loses what the novel repeatedly calls "his innocence." Faulkner's way of narrating this is quite astonishing:

> . . . he told Grandfather how, before the monkey nigger who came to the door had finished saying what he did, he seemed to kind of dissolve and a part of him turn and rush back through the two years they had lived there like when you pass through a room fast and look at all the objects in it and you turn and go back through the room again and look at all the objects from the other side and you find out you had never seen them before, rushing back through those two years and seeing a dozen things that had happened and he hadn't even seen them before (186)

What are some of these things? The fact that the servants wear better clothes than his folks do, the hard looks on the faces of his family as they eyed the blacks, the desperate need for self-respect among the menfolk, the memory of a carriage driven in all haste by a black servant almost running down his sisters who refused to budge, and perhaps the most resonant image of all: his father coming home drunk one night, pleased that " 'We whupped one of Pettibone's niggers tonight,' " and he asking which one, and why, and his father saying, " 'Hell fire, that goddamn son of a bitch Pettibone's nigger' " (187), nothing more said, nothing more needed. The blacks are seen by the boy as a "balloon face," a smiling, jeering, taunting face that you could strike at, hammer at, but not defeat or remove. Two full pages of remembered images and incidents, all conveying a virulent sense of class desperation and rage, are noted. And here is how it closes: "And he never even remembered what the nigger said, how it was the nigger told him, even before he had had time to say what he came for, never to come to that front door again but to go around to the back" (188).

KEEPING YOUR STORY OPEN, MAKING YOUR WORDS REAL

This is signature Faulknerian narration. Remember how this began. The servant came to the door, but we do not know what he said: "Before the monkey nigger had finished saying what he did, he seemed to dissolve. . . ." Two pages crammed with drama and pith now come, as the boy at last learns who he is, ideologically. Only after those two pages can the episode come to an end, with its simple, tragic, hauntingly metaphorical denial: "never to come to that front door again but to go around to the back." I called it signature narration; it is also the signature event of Thomas Sutpen's life: standing in front of a closed door, being denied in his humanity. And Faulkner has written it with great cunning, holding off the final words and their life-defining image as long as he possibly can before bringing it to a close. He is obliging us, the readers, to negotiate his open-ended prose, his unfinished story; we are to travel his sentences, to absorb all the key data they pack in, to go through the room again ourselves, from the other side, before fully and finally learning what happened, what the servant actually said. Faulknerian writing is aligned with the way we actually learn things: by jolt, by surprise, by accident, by looking at things from the other side, by making our pilgrimage through the swamp life that is ours and then coming unexpectedly into light, into sun.

Is this not how the entire novel is written and constructed? Hence, Sutpen's story and the murder at the gate come to us initially as riddles, as incomplete sketchy outlines of a distant past. Yes, Sutpen is immediately seen as larger than life, but also as spectral, as opaque, needing to be filled in. Rosa claimed that he came from nowhere, that he "forbade that marriage without rhyme or reason" and she believes it, poor woman. But the novel is out to show that Sutpen's Hundred, Sutpen's design, has origins, is part of a causal chain. All of Faulkner's brilliance is invested in making the reader work, slowly and progressively, backward toward these origins, these explanations, this determining past. This is no mere aesthetic frill or sadistic technique (as it may appear), but is rather the way we go about our actual lives. The people we meet do not, again, have their stories written on their foreheads. The people we meet are, very often indeed, silhouettes, enigmatic, appearing out of nowhere. Just as, it seemed to Rosa and Quentin and the townspeople, Sutpen's Hundred itself had appeared, "the Be Sutpen's Hundred like the oldentime Be Light." Sutpen himself, Charles Bon, Charles Etienne Saint-Valery Bon, all seem (to the locals) to come from nowhere, to spring upon this community full-born, without warning or origin.

Folks, it's not true. The entire novel goes ultimately the other direction, fills its people in, shows us how coherent they really are, where they come from, why they were driven to do what they did. And this particular trio of men coming from nowhere: Well, that will turn out to be no less than the crucially concealed but explosive material of the family saga, the other branch of Sutpen's family tree, the death knell for his dynastic hopes.

SUTPEN'S DESIGN AND INNOCENCE

In the story of the boy being told to go around back, Faulkner has given us (finally) no less than the key to Sutpen. From this fundamental experience of exclusion and denial in front of a closed door is born Sutpen's design. His design comes from his hurt. He decides at this critical moment never again to suffer this rejection, this erasure. He will build his own plantation, own his own slaves, become the powerful man lying in the hammock. And that is what he does. This is the rags-to-riches story (not so different from Gatsby's meteoric career) he told to Grandfather Compson, the saga of his youthful adventures, his trip to the West Indies, his work at the sugar plantation, his uncommon courage and heroism during the revolt, the torture he received (and overcame) from the Haitians, culminating (once he had recovered from his wounds) with his marriage to the colonist's daughter, a marriage he later dissolved.

A marriage he later dissolved. Well, well. Not so different from those late-night conversations with acquaintances when, in the wee hours of the morning, perhaps aided by much lubrication, you learn that the person you thought you knew happens to have one or two other families: spouses, children, the works; and perhaps did a stint in the Far East to boot. What are we to make of Sutpen's exotic background?

This man of courage and volition has had, ever since the episode of the closed door, a design, a design so firmly etched in his mind that it served as a compass for all he later achieved, including his plantation in Mississippi. But things have not been going so well. Could the design be at fault? Yet, once his son has abjured him, he experiences tinges (nothing more than that) of doubt, and that puzzlement (nothing more than that) has led him to confide still further in Grandfather Compson, wondering where the problem could possibly lie:

> "You see, I had a design in mind. Whether it was a good or bad design is beside the point; the question is, Where did I make the mistake in it, what did I do or misdo in it, whom or what injure by it to the extent which this would indicate. I had a design. To accomplish it, I should require money, a house, a plantation, slaves, a family—incidentally of course, a wife." (212)

We gather that this last item—"incidentally of course, a wife"—has been the troublesome part. A misunderstanding occurred on the wife front. Some important facts were withheld. All this "rendered it impossible that this woman and child be incorporated in my design" (212). Sutpen actually says, at one point, " 'I found that she was not and could never be, through no fault of her own, adjunctive or incremental to the design I had in mind, so I provided for her and put her aside' " (194). It is the language of compensation and reparation you'd expect to hear in a courtroom, spoken by the attorney who is representing you in order to prove that you did not break the law. It is shockingly abstract, Latinate, and codified.

I think we are meant to perceive what is monstrous in this worldview, and meant to realize that this is what innocence means: to see other human beings as quantifiable units, as components of a design, as elements one is free to plug in or take out. Grandfather Compson's reaction goes to the core of the novel: " 'What kind of abysmal and purblind innocence could that have been which someone told you to call virginity? what conscience to trade with which would have warranted you in the belief that you could have bought immunity from her for no other coin but justice?' " (213). Hence, Quentin and Shreve need not be master sleuths to figure out that the key to the mystery doubtless lies here: the abandoned (albeit compensated) wife. And with this in mind, the mysterious key player, Charles Bon, assumes another identity altogether: He is Sutpen's son. This is what Sutpen must have told Henry that Christmas Eve. Things are heating up.

That may indeed be why the marriage was forbidden, but why was Bon there at all? Bon was abandoned by his father, yes. But—as Quentin and Shreve make it out—he was brought up and reared by his incurably injured mother—remember: "a marriage he later dissolved"—to be the tool of revenge that she has long sought. And now Shreve himself joins in the melee here, working with Quentin to imagine/invent a lawyer in charge of this vendetta, a lawyer who works out his own counterdesign: to send Charles Bon to the University of Mississippi so that he will be befriended by Henry Sutpen, all of which will lead to the most delicious punishment of all—Sutpen's own daughter will fall in love with the masquerading Charles Bon, her own half-brother. It is ingenious, it is a Faulknerian "mousetrap" of sorts. Sutpen will have been hoisted by his own petard.

SUTPEN'S TRAGIC FLAW

Ink has been spilled as to whether Sutpen qualifies as a classical tragic hero, and one point that is always made is: The man has no self-awareness. More damaging still, he has no real awareness of others as sentient beings. Indeed, if there is a tragic flaw, a clear moral transgression here, it is this: He reifies life, he instrumentalizes others, sees them only as abstract pawns in his design. This is the innocence that will lead to his downfall: "that innocence that believed that the ingredients of morality were like the ingredients of pie or cake and once you had measured them and balanced them and mixed them and put them into the oven it was all finished and nothing but pie or cake could come out" (211–212). The homely recipe simile unmistakably reminds us of Mr Compson's earlier admission of failure when trying to understand the human reality of the past; he spoke of a chemical formula, of bringing together things in the proportions called for, of making no miscalculation, and of failing nonetheless: "It just does not explain." An entire ethos of reasoning, measuring, and calculating is itself being weighed here, measured, and found horribly wanting. You do not understand the reality of others via scientific or legal logic. Recipes get you nowhere. Designs don't work.

Well, how do you understand things or people? It is a question Shreve himself asks, and then answers by referring precisely to Sutpen's opposite number, the little dream-woman Rosa Coldfield: "What was it the old dame, the Aunt Rosa, told you about how there are some things that just have to be whether they are or not, have to be a damn sight more than some other things that maybe are and it dont matter a damn whether they are or not?" (258). Laconic country talk maybe, but profound, even revolutionary nonetheless. Some things that just have to be whether they are or not: The truths that matter to us are the ones we have to have, the ones we create out of our own need, the ones that may be unprovable and outright illusory. Those home truths matter far more than tons of other (large and small) provable, documentable facts that have nothing to do with our lives and beliefs and needs.

It is an existential credo. It is also a recognition that proof itself is a lame virtue, good for some things but worthless in the arena of human values and choices. And it is, finally, a triumphant view of imagination as the cornerstone of reality, of human desire as the ultimate guarantor of truth itself. What if you apply this credo—things that just have to be—to those human lives you are trying to figure out? Might this be how we best understand others? How we ultimately gauge the coherence of our own choices and lives? Could you even refigure the Civil War along these lines, as a time of bloodletting and carnage that "had to be"? Why did it have to be?

THE HORRENDOUS LOGIC OF SUTPEN'S FALL

As Quentin and Shreve grapple with the issue of Sutpen's innocence, the pieces of the puzzle start to cohere ever more ominously. Sutpen's life now begins to acquire a hideous circularity. His own spectacular success as self-made man, as plantation owner, stems, as we have seen, from the crucial childhood baptism in front of a closed door; Quentin spells it out:

> "The design.—Getting richer and richer. It must have looked fine and clear ahead for him now: house finished, and even bigger and whiter than the one he had gone to the door of that day and the nigger came in his monkey clothes and told him to go to the back, and he with his own brand of niggers even . . . to cull one from and train him to go to the door when his turn came for a little boy without any shoes on and with his pap's cutdown pants for clothes to come and knock on it . . ." (209–210)

With the tautness of a sprung trap, with an economy and pattern worthy of Greek tragedy, the House of Sutpen implodes, for the entry of Charles Bon onto the scene and into the home is the direct equivalent of Orestes returning to avenge the misdeeds of the past. Henry introduces his father to his friend from the university, and even Sutpen begins to hear the whirring machinery, the gears going into motion, what Jean Cocteau called *la machine infernale:*

> . . . he stood there at his own door, just as he had imagined, planned, designed, and sure enough and after fifty years the forlorn nameless and homeless lost child came to knock at it and no monkey-dressed nigger anywhere under the sun to come to the door and order the child away; and Father said that even then, even though he knew that Bon and Judith had never laid eyes on one another, he must have felt and heard the design—house, position, posterity and all—come down like it had been built out of smoke. . . . (215)

I called this "Greek"; I could have said "biblical," since it reeks of the sins of the fathers, of long-overdue payments now being made for the transgressions of the past. One thinks of Ibsen and O'Neill as well as the Greeks and the Hebrews. It would seem that an angry god who keeps his books rules over the Sutpen destiny. You don't get away with anything. The wife and child you thought you put away are not put away at all; they've been plotting to get you for decades, and now they've done it.

And yet, despite the shimmering poetic logic of this turn of events, one is entitled to feel that this is almost too pat, too much of a determinist prison, a "tit for tat" mentality. It is also as if, somewhere offstage, the deck had been unfairly stacked against Sutpen, as if Faulkner had stooped to melodrama and coincidence in order to waylay his plantation owner. "You can't get away with it" may, as moral dictum, soothe our consciences (or unhinge them), but it won't take the fuller measure of Faulknerian fiction. That is why I want now to say that Faulkner's ultimate gambit goes beyond this boomerang scenario, this severe depiction of chickens coming home to roost. There is a boomerang, and the chicken does come home to roost, but the notion of a sprung trap, the notion of walls closing in on Sutpen is ultimately not only misleading but wrongheaded.

If the central motif in *Absalom, Absalom!* is closed doors, then the central action of the book consists of opening them. And that is what Quentin and Shreve do—and it earns them an understanding of what happened, and why it had to happen—and they do it by hallowing the logic of Rosa Coldfield. They turn their gaze increasingly on the man who is the key to the puzzle, Charles Bon, and they go a quantum leap beyond the revenge scenario in order to posit human love and recognition as the driving forces behind the entire tragedy. I say "they" because the story these two roommates tell is dialogic, interwoven, collective, "a marriage of speaking and hearing." For love can also be the motor force of narrative, the fuel for storytelling, the ultimate (and only) route into the heart and into the past. This is no desperate last effort to try it one more time, to get it right, by consulting the heart; on the contrary, it is the core wisdom of the novel; wisdom as the final residue that subsists after you've searched and combed the data, after you've sifted the clues and moved beyond the details; wisdom as the goal of human interrogation, what you ultimately strive for when looking at carnage. Here would be the larger vision toward which this baroque and convoluted novel has been moving all along: not so much punishment as illumination.

THE OVERPASS TO LOVE

In a novel that is so overrich, so larded with quotable phrases, that one sometimes feels almost surfeited by its eloquence, there is one speech, in my opinion, that rises above all the others and comes to stand for what is most elemental and most radical in Faulkner's scheme. The initial speaker is, significantly, Shreve, but soon enough we realize that it boots not to determine which of these youths is talking, since the subject here is love, love drawn from the ecstatic doctrine of Rosa Coldfield's "*I was all polymath love's androgynous advocate*" and now transformed further, made at once intimately interpersonal and also visionary, made into the life-giving energy that produces human connection and human story:

> "And now," Shreve said, "we're going to talk about love." But he didn't need to say that either, any more than he had needed to specify which he he meant by he, since neither of them had been thinking about anything else; all that had gone before just so much that had to be overpassed and none else present to overpass it but them, as someone always has to rake the leaves up before you can have the bonfire. That was why it did not matter to either of them which one did the talking, since it was not the talking alone which did it, performed and accomplished the overpassing, but some happy marriage of speaking and hearing wherein

> each before the demand, the requirement, forgave condoned and forgot the faulting of the other—faultings both in the creating of this shade whom they discussed (rather, existed in) and in the hearing and sifting and discarding the false and conserving what seemed true, or fit the preconceived—in order to overpass to love, where there might be paradox and inconsistency but nothing fault nor false. (253)

"Overpass to love" is a peculiar expression—reminding me, curiously, of the Jewish holy day Passover, with its severe account of the Angel of Death—and I think Faulkner wants to reverse the Old Testament story, to make us understand that love brings to life, that it is actually vehicular, a propulsion of sorts that lifts one beyond the existing obstacles and blind spots, beyond the closed doors and muddle, beyond logic and inconsistency, beyond even the words themselves in order to reach a kind of living truth. Not that this is easy; you cannot have the bonfire until you rake up the leaves. (Readers take note.) But that bonfire changes everything. It is hard to overstate the explanatory and generative power of "overpass to love" in this novel, for it will stamp all of the following: the forging of an intimate fusion between the narrators themselves, Quentin and Shreve, Southerner and Northerner (and the symbolic stakes of this harmony, this entente, are momentous); the forging of a no-less-intimate fusion between the twin narrators and their own quarry, the shades of the past (Sutpen and Henry and Charles) in particular, a fusion so intense that Faulkner claims they existed in the imagined and discussed figures; and finally, a new portrait altogether of Charles Bon, now infused with love as its primary motive. So much for the local, plot-related aspects of the overpass to love; we can hardly fail to see that it also announces an entire theory of both literature and history, a model for understanding the other and the past based on precisely love and intimate fusion. *Absalom, Absalom!* is the grandest and most self-reflexive of Faulkner's creations, his most Picasso-like opus, the one where he goes furthest in articulating—and then actualizing—his deepest beliefs about writing.

BECOMING CHARLES BON

The "new" Charles Bon that now emerges from the joint labor of Quentin and Shreve is a young man (very different from the jaded figure whom Mr Compson mused about) who keeps discovering he is even younger than he thought, who is tested and confused by the experience of being at Sutpen's Hundred: "Maybe he telling himself *I not only dont know what it is I want but apparently I am a good deal younger than I thought also*" (256). This Charles Bon is undecided, yet possessed of one great hunger: to be seen and recognized by his father. Not formally, not even in spoken words, perhaps, but at least by a sign:

> . . . thinking maybe how he would walk into the house and see the man who made him and then he would know; there would be that flash, that instant of indubitable recognition between them and he would know for sure and forever—thinking maybe *That's all I want. He need not even acknowledge me; I will let him understand just as quickly that he need not do that, that I do not expect that, will not be hurt by that, just as he will let me know that quickly that I am his son* (255)

We see the up-front tentative conjectural nature of this writing, the way that Quentin and Shreve are feeling their way into Bon ("thinking maybe"), imagining what he was going through, what he desired, what he found, at Sutpen's Hundred. As they see it, it wasn't enough, it wasn't anything at all, and that was worst of all: "and saw face to face the man who might be his father, and nothing happened—no shock, no hot communicated flesh that speech would have been too slow even to impede—nothing" (256). And nothing happened. Again we hear the echoes of Mr Compson's earlier formula about not understanding the past, about putting things together in the proportions called for, but nothing happens. What happens when you put two human beings together—a father and a son—and nothing happens?

Quentin and Shreve collaborate, almost lovingly (they are undressed, ready for bed, in a cold dormitory room), in a story about love, as if they had to experience human connection themselves in order to imagine its tragic denial in the fate of Charles Bon. The Bon that they make, a young man desperate for recognition, wanting only to be acknowledged by his father as a son, as a human being, is not only a heartbreaking figure, but also one who casts an unbearable light on the entire story. This Charles Bon, denied by his own father, repeats to perfection the original human denial that Sutpen experienced as a child in front of a closed door. Sutpen's entire dynastic dream came from this hurt, a dream of wealth and immunity at last, but this design is inhuman, treats others as pawns and objects, ultimately ends up replicating the exact denial of humanity that lay at its origin years ago. Sutpen repeats the very crime he suffered from as a child. And he repeats it upon his own child.

The two Harvard students insert love into the incomplete equations, and they thereby transform this story from one of doom and fate into one of inhumanity, coldness of heart, and failure of nerve. Love as missing ingredient not only makes Bon's situation into an emotional tragedy, but it also enables us to see precisely that "*might-have-been which is truer than truth*" that Rosa Coldfield clung to in her own embattled life. For it all might have been different. There did not need to be a murder at the gate. If Sutpen had recognized Bon, it would have turned out differently. That is how their Bon would have behaved: " 'He will not even have to ask me; I will just touch flesh with him and I will say it myself: You will not need to worry; she shall never see me again' " (278). "*Let flesh touch with flesh,*" Rosa Coldfield prophesied, and all the artificial codes that imprison and separate us will collapse. But flesh did not touch with flesh here. Yet if it had? If touch had prevailed? Love is a might have been that opens the closed past to show us how it all happened, why it happened, how it did not have to happen. The murder at the gate, the original enigma of this novel, may simply have been a stupid mistake, an unnecessary letting of blood, a failure of vision.

And now, of course, the follow-up question that this entire chapter has been leading to: Might we not regard the Civil War itself along exactly these lines, as an egregious mistake, a nationwide letting of blood, a colossal failure of vision? Is this not what Faulkner's larger aim has been all along: to tell a story of Thomas Sutpen and family in such a way as to illuminate the entire bloody history of the South? Now, that would be a bonfire: etching your story so profoundly, so searchingly, that it becomes radiant and incandescent, becomes a mirror in which one sees the fate of the land you live in.

FOUR BOYS ON TWO HORSES

Why, Faulkner is asking, was there this mistake, this failure of vision? Why the murder at the gate? Why could Sutpen not acknowledge his own son? The answer that Faulkner sketches here is threaded into the very fabric of this novel, inseparable from the questing and imaginative efforts of the two final narrators in the Harvard dormitory. We cannot know why Sutpen and Charles and Henry did what they did until we become Sutpen and Charles and Henry. Draconian, yes, but the only way, Faulkner is saying, that we come to an understanding of the other or of the past. That is the only way to recognize the full humanity of others: inhabit them, become them. And that is what Quentin and Shreve do—they fuse with the shades they are imagining:

> It did not matter to them [Quentin and Shreve] anyway, who could without moving, as free now of flesh as the father who decreed and forbade, the son who denied and repudiated, the lover who acquiesced, the beloved who was not bereaved, and with no tedious transition from hearth and garden . . . to saddle, be already clattering over the frozen ruts of that December night and that Christmas dawn, that day of peace and cheer, of holly and goodwill and logs on the hearth; not two of them there and then either but four of them riding the two horses through the iron darkness and that not mattering either: what faces and what names they called themselves and were called by so long as the blood coursed—the blood, the immortal brief recent intransient blood which could hold honor above slothy unregret and love above fat and easy shame. (237)

Here would be our truest commerce with the past: a magic entry, a leap into the unknown, a becoming other. Note how pungent and material the Christmas scene is, yet note also, by contrast, how ghostly and generic the players are: the father, the son, the lover, the beloved. Note, too, how ghostly and generic the Harvard students have had to become, forty-six years later, in order to negotiate what Faulkner offers as the only pathway to others and the past: blood. Blood: the most reactionary figure imaginable, responsible for so much of the world's carnage and hurt in the name of class and color, ethnicity and religion. And yet, blood is also the waterway of humankind, the flow that not only keeps the body in life, but also figures the quasi-cardiac medium of both love and imagination and fusion with others.

"Four boys on two horses" is the finest metaphor for reading, imagination, and fusion that I have ever seen. It announces the miraculous time travel and heart journey that we call "reading" and "understanding." It is a formula for showing what you actually have to do to make the longest voyage imaginable to humankind: from here to there, from now to then, from me to you, from words to life. You finally get the other's story when you merge your own with it. To go into the very heart of the labyrinth, to know finally why Sutpen forbade the marriage, why Charles came all the way back to the gate, why Henry murdered him, a trip is required, an overpass to love. Quentin and Shreve do it:

> He ceased again. It was just as well, since he had no listener. Perhaps he was aware of it. Then suddenly he had no talker either, though possibly he was not aware of this. Because now neither of them was there. They were both in Carolina and the time was forty-six years ago, and it was not even four now but compounded still further, since now both of them were Henry Sutpen and both of them were Bon, compounded each of both yet either neither, smelling the very smoke which had blown and faded away forty-six years ago from the bivouac fires burning in a pine grove, the gaunt and ragged men sitting or lying about them, talking not about the war yet all curiously enough . . . facing the South where further on in the darkness the pickets stood. . . . (289)

Much has been written about the use of italics in Faulkner's work, most especially in *The Sound and the Fury*, where it signals the crucial transitions between present and past in the minds of both Benjy and Quentin. Yet I don't think anything surpasses the simple beauty of this transition, this magic act of moving from Harvard to Carolina, from 1910 to 1864, from the persons of Quentin Compson and Shreve McCannon to those gaunt and ragged men sitting near the bivouac fires. Is this not the birth of fiction? The creation of history? At long last, we go "in," into the war itself, and Faulkner has his reasons for waiting this long to take us there; only now—after hundreds of pages of preparation, of negotiating this tortuous story—are we ready, primed, even schooled enough to understand the rock-bottom logic that caused this tragedy.

I said there is a simple beauty here, but there is also something menacing, on the order of a severe reckoning that goes with this "trip": a reckoning that we see in phrases such as "no listener," "no talker," "both . . . either neither," whispering to us that the singular "you" must disappear if this voyage is to happen. And this voyage must happen, for it is what the entire book has been leading to. This is what we signed on for, when we started *Absa-*

lom, Absalom! Faulkner's challenge is to convey this final outing in such a way that we feel the dreadful truths at hand, that we, too, ride on the two horses, travel the blood, enter the past, become the people.

In Carolina forty-six years earlier, we overhear the banter between Rebel and Yankee outposts, we see the message delivered to Henry that his father the colonel has sent for him, we follow Henry into his father's tent, see them embrace, then hear Sutpen's words about Charles Bon: "I have seen Charles Bon. . . . You are going to let him marry Judith, Henry. . . . He cannot marry her, Henry. . . . He must not marry her, Henry" (283). At each juncture, Henry protests, reaffirms his commitment to Charles, even in the face of incest, "Brother or not, I have decided. I will. I will" (283). At last comes Sutpen's trump card, the card we have been waiting for during the entire story: " 'He must not marry her, Henry. His mother's father told me that her mother had been a Spanish woman. I believed him; it was not until after he was born that I found out that his mother was part negro' " (283).

And we watch Henry make his way back to Charles. It is a scene that directly repeats the gestures of the two students late at night in that cold dormitory in Cambridge. Charles places a cloak on Henry's shoulders and a blanket on his own. It is dawn. Charles speaks: " 'So it's the miscegenation, not the incest, which you cant bear" (285). And again we hear that none of this had to happen, that a simple act of recognition on the father's part would have prevented it all:

> *And he sent me no word? He did not ask you to send me to him? No word to me, no word at all? That was all he had to do, now, today; four years ago or at any time during the four years. That was all. He would not have needed to ask it, require it, of me. I would have offered it. I would have said, I will never see her again before he could have asked it of me. He did not have to do this, Henry. He didn't need to tell you I am a nigger to stop me. He could have stopped me without that, Henry.* (285)

Final things are on show, in more ways than one. Now we realize that the racial transgression is what cuts deepest of all, that a drop or more of black blood suffices to expel you from the human family. Is that not what the institution of slavery was all about? Is this not why the war happened? All of us who read history have been told that the reasons for the Civil War are actually quite complex, having to do with political and economic matters well outside the slavery debate, and yet . . . we must realize that the supreme moral issue at the core of this paroxystic moment in American history is that of race: race as the element that obliterates your humanity in the eyes of the white Southern culture. Faulkner has elected to dramatize these matters in the most intimate fashion imaginable: the crisis of a house divided, the fratricidal war between white and black. Charles Bon has been waiting for four years for a recognition that never came. Now, at war's end, he will act, return to Sutpen's Hundred, carry out his own design: He will marry Judith. Henry begs him not to: "You are my brother" (286). Charles's answer carries all the venom of the novel: "No I'm not. I'm the nigger that's going to sleep with your sister" (286). Melodrama? Or rock-bottom picture of the racial arrangements of the antebellum South? Here is why things had to be what they were, why there was a murder at the gate and a four-year period of fratricidal war.

OVERPASS TO DEATH

One expects the novel to end with this spectacular revelation, but there is more to come. After all, we need to exit Carolina of forty-six years ago and make the return trip back to Harvard of 1910. We must leave the tale and return to the tellers. In that dormitory, Quentin finally recounts the strange postscriptum that seals the story and (I believe) seals his own life as well. He tells us of his actual trip out to Sutpen's Hundred with Rosa Coldfield. There is something quite astonishing here, because this trip was made in September, prior to his coming to Harvard; this trip was the reason Rosa invited Quentin over in the first place: to make him accompany her out to the still-standing house where Clytie still lives, where there were rumors of something strange going on. I call this astonishing because, according to traditional narrative rules, it should have been narrated in the first chapter of the novel. True as ever to his aesthetic of delayed disclosures, Faulkner has waited until now to air this material.

There is something poetically stunning going on here: Quentin's physical voyage to Sutpen's Hundred constitutes a real-life, real-time encounter between teller and tale. This actual voyage in a buggy to the old haunted house is the material version of the imaginative labor we have been witnessing for several hundred pages. Paydirt at last. It is the pure logic of Gothic tales and horror stories: You must go there, inside the haunted house, and encounter the ghosts. Goose bumps, shivering, hair standing on end, palpitating heart: Here is the gauge of understanding. (Cerebral notation counts for nothing here: Remember the touch of flesh with flesh.) Rosa is described repeatedly as "panting," "whimpering," "moaning," and Quentin at first thinks she is afraid, but then realizes it is something else entirely: It is the sexual climax of her life. They arrive at the old house, Rosa wants to go upstairs, a match is struck, Clytie appears, she tries to stop Rosa—this, too, a perfect repeat of past history—she fails, Rosa goes up and then, moments later, comes down, almost unrecognizable, "the eyes wide and unseeing like a sleepwalker's" (296), and goes back to the buggy.

Quentin, terrified, knows he should leave the premises but cannot do so: " 'But I must see too now. I will have to. Maybe I shall be sorry tomorrow, but I must see' " (296). The next sentence is vintage Faulkner: "So when he came back down the stairs . . ." (296). True to form, Faulkner bypasses the pièce de résistance, tracks Quentin's way to the buggy, gives us a fuller look at Jim Bond the idiot boy who lives out there with Clytie, describes the trip back home, follows Quentin right into bed, "naked, swabbing his body steadily with his discarded shirt, sweating still, panting" (298). Trapped in a state where there is no difference between sleeping and waking, Quentin now retraces, mentally, his steps in the haunted house: entering the bare, stale room upstairs, seeing "the bed, the yellow sheets and pillow, the wasted yellow face with closed, almost transparent eyelids on the pillow" (298), trapped in the vision: "Waking or sleeping it was the same and would be the same forever as long as he lived" (298).

And only now, with maximum and intolerable ripeness, the few scant echoing words come, the actual human exchange that took place at Sutpen's Hundred:

> *And you are—?*
> *Henry Sutpen.*
> *And you have been here—?*
> *Four years.*
> *And you came home—?*
> *To die. Yes.*
> *To die?*
> *Yes. To die.*
> *And you have been here—?*

Four years.
And you are—?
Henry Sutpen. (298)

We have moved from bonfire to crucible, from baroque narrative to chiseled poetry, a poetry that has distilled all the warm flesh and blood and passion into a residue as pure as ash or dry bones. In classical rhetoric, this would be called "chiasmus," writing that reverses itself midway in, using the same words in opposite order. We may also think of this as writing that literally goes into the looking glass, in order to bring past and present, tale and teller together. No adjectives, no psychology, no interpretation. Just the living/dead figure of Henry Sutpen come home to die, speaking across the gap of time and history to the boy who is telling his story. With perfect tact, this final exchange is almost wordless, even if suffocatingly intimate. Perhaps all true storytelling has a necrophiliac tinge to it, requires that the living narrator be brought into the very room where the "wasted yellow face" lies dying. This, one thinks, is how things end. In fact, they end a bit more spectacularly: Clytie sets fire—heaven knows the leaves have been raked—to the old mansion, in resistance to Rosa's return a few months later, finally destroying the house and its decaying occupants, all except for the "idiot negro," Jim Bond. Rosa Coldfield dies shortly thereafter.

Now that the Sutpen saga is finally told, the last of its players and ghosts laid to rest, the work of the two student narrators is over. Over as well, however, is the marriage of speaking and hearing. Shreve exits with some choice parting shots: He prophesies the eventual triumph of the Jim Bonds of the world—a dynastic outcome that blithely reverses all Sutpen strived for—and he then asks Quentin to tell him "just one thing more. Why do you hate the South?" (303). And Faulkner closes his novel with Quentin's agonized reply: " 'I dont hate it,' Quentin said quickly, at once, immediately; 'I dont hate it,' he said. I dont hate it he thought, panting in the cold air, the iron New England dark: I dont. I dont! I dont hate it! I dont hate it!" (303). It is, I believe, a perfect way to finish: It conveys something of the utter futility of judgment, especially futile when it comes to our deepest—hence most conflicted—beliefs and feelings. It reflects the helplessness and integrity not just of Quentin Compson, but of a writer who loves the culture he hates, and hates the culture he loves.

These matters bear still further reflection. At least for me, they do. As a

Southerner who left the South at college age to live both in the North and in Europe, I see in *Absalom, Absalom!* a magnificent and tragic reckoning with a world that no longer exists. Early on, I spoke of the difficulties, nay, the impossibility, of conveying Faulkner's demon-ridden South to students at Brown University, indeed to all the readers I address in my books and courses. And I called myself an "ombudsman," a kind of still-living link between that vanished culture and the modern scheme in which we find ourselves today. In all these senses, Faulkner's baroque, extremist novel about the curse of the South has a pathos for me that I can hardly expect others to share. I believe that Faulkner knew exactly that: The greatest challenge of all is to bring this tragic and perhaps crazy world—"it's better than Ben Hur," Shreve said—somehow over the great threshold separating language from life. His book is, at every turn, about how arduous it is to make the past and the other real. His solution—which I find sublime—is the overpass to love. Doubtless, no historian with self-respect will ever endorse love as the pathway to knowledge about the past—archival research! note-taking!—but that is the way Faulkner saw it; love alone gets us to the reality of the past.

But this is no happy ending. We have known all along that Quentin Compson is a condemned man, because we know the outcome of *The Sound and the Fury*. But this novel suggests that he is yet further doomed, that he carries a cultural inheritance that will kill him. Shreve ends his part in this "marriage" by a jeer, a taunt, to his Southern roommate. I see this as essentially an exit strategy, the sort of thing that Quentin Compson does not have, will never have. Shrevlin McCannon, Faulkner tells us in the "Genealogy" that he appended to this novel, is "Now a practising surgeon, Edmonton, Alta." (309). Quentin Compson dies in the Charles River. Faulkner is showing us, quite unconsciously, something profoundly unsettling about the things that will destroy us. It is not enough to say that the young man is doomed by his past. He is also undone by the epic adventure chronicled in this very novel. His death is testimony to the potentially lethal character of imagination.

Recall, once more, Faulkner's description of four boys on two horses; twice, he tells us it "did not matter . . . what faces and what names they called themselves and were called by so long as the blood coursed" (237). Yes, Quentin and Shreve enter into the past, become Henry and Charles; and we must realize they do so—one can only do so—namelessly and facelessly. That is what you give up in order to go there. It did not matter, the author says. But is that true? Can you slough off name and face with impunity? Become another and yet still remain yourself? At what point does the overpass to love become a death sentence? All true storytelling has a necrophiliac tinge to it, I wrote, referring to the corpse-like Henry Sutpen whom Quentin must finally encounter in the flesh. But we sense that Quentin, too, is under a death sentence, that storytelling itself may be a diseased activity, that it may—at its most extreme, at its most ecstatic, when the teller becomes the tale—be lethal. I said at the beginning of this chapter that Faulkner is the great death star of my book, and we now see what this means: not so much the deaths within his fictions, but the terrible view that recovering a story is death-inflected, is life-threatening, that even the overpass to love is a rendezvous, as Passover tells us, with the Angel of Death. Quentin Compson goes through this novel like a man with his edges being erased, a man en route to disappearing. There is, I believe, a great warning here: Imagination can kill.

I have spent my entire adult life preaching just the opposite: Imagination is what saves us, what alone gives us access to other lives, what makes the act of reading into an act of creation. And I still believe this. But Faulkner's work is as sinister as it is beautiful, and it calls the bluff on our soft terms such as "sympathy" and "empathy." He was a man beset by demons, and I think that his own commerce with the past (and the tumult within) was something fierce and unhinging, so powerful that the only two ways it could be withstood were via writing and drink. His difficult novels stretch our imaginations, force us out of our ruts and routines, make us try on other lives, like none other. But he understands the horror as well as the beauty of just these transactions. To overpass to the other is the only route out of the prison we inhabit. To exit ourselves can be a form of suicide. Both are true.

TONI MORRISON

SULA

and

BELOVED

TOXIC STORY

The great Modernists at the center of this book—Proust, Joyce, Woolf, and Faulkner—made their essential mark on Western literature over a scant decade, from the early 1920s to the mid-1930s. These four writers drastically altered the conventions of storytelling, and their work changed the way we see our own story. It seems both fair and necessary to ask: What continues to live through them in the literature of our day? It would be easy enough to invoke contemporary novelists who continue to make use of this heritage, since the great breakthroughs in the area of interior monologue and the depiction of consciousness are now a given, a taken-for-granted component of what fiction entails. One reason I have chosen to close this book with a look at the work of Toni Morrison—most especially her 1987 masterpiece, *Beloved*—is that she radically calls into question what they achieved: What if our "story" is something so toxic that it will not bear recovering? Will a literature of consciousness do justice to the life of the body? How can one record the inner story and yet depict the great historical nightmare of slavery? In short, there is a powerful ideological dimension to Morrison's writing, deriving largely from both her impassioned presentation of race and her creation of remarkable female characters, and this sets her apart.

The central premise in my earlier chapters is that a private story is buried in each of us, and that the great Modernist novels help us to see what it might look like. But what happens when there is no private sphere whatsoever? When your life has been so coerced that this inner realm has been locked shut forever? And how much do we unwittingly take for granted when we assume that our story can be retrieved? I'd say that we unthinkingly posit a fundamental kind of prior freedom, a freedom to ponder our actual contours and reaches, a freedom to go inside and recover what is lost or hidden, a freedom to shape ourselves anew. Reading literature may itself be thought of as the exercise of that freedom. But these freedoms presuppose a large array of privileges: political, material, and emotional. They presuppose a self with rights, indeed a propertied self who can at least take ownership of his or her own interior world. In Morrison's *Beloved,* we encounter a regime in which none of these operations can be carried out. We learn that one's story might just be a luxury item beyond reach, or—worse still—the door that opens onto the unbearable.

MORRISON UP-FRONT

Toni Morrison writes some half a century after my quartet of Modernists produced their greatest books. Sometimes regarded as a magical realist, she elects *love*—difficult love, lethal love—as her signature theme in book after book, and her focus on matters of race and ideology would seem to distinguish her sharply from Proust, Joyce, Woolf, and Faulkner. Yet she is their successor, and her magisterial reworking of the Modernist legacy shows us how art lives over time. Nonetheless, in her best work, the very basic assumptions of this study—the recovery of one's inner story via literature, the unprecedented rendition of human consciousness—are upended, shown as potentially lethal.

If *Beloved* (1987) is her dark masterpiece, then *Sula* (1973) is its luminous precursor. In this coming-of-age story between two black girls, Morrison makes spectacular use of magical realism's liberties: fantasy, folklore, reality of spirit(s). Above all, Sula herself is Morrison's most Nietzschean creation: a woman bent on self-enactment at all—all—costs, including the decimation of family and friends. We need to bear *Sula*'s proud individualism in mind when entering the death-haunted story of slavery *Beloved,* a book that may make use of spirits and folklore, but calls radically into question the untrammeled pursuit of freedom celebrated in the earlier novel. In its exploration of the psychic reality of slavery—an exploration that owes a great deal to the vision and achievement of Harriet Beecher Stowe—

Beloved makes surprising use of the Modernist legacy: the scope of one's inside story, the interplay of consciousness and event, the mother/daughter theme, the paralyzing burden of the past. But to this repertory she adds a crucial new element: the reality of ghosts.

One starts this novel by witnessing the damage that is still inflicted by a baby ghost, and Morrison (like Faulkner) is going to use every narrative device imaginable to make us understand what this seemingly supernatural event signifies. At the heart of this story lies a murder—Sethe's murder of her child, Beloved—and Morrison wants us to understand not only the ramifications of this event, but even more important, the *logic* of it, the kind of rationale that would mandate such an act. We also realize that every black family in this post–Civil War era has buried cadavers in its history. It is here that the central thesis of my book—recovering one's story—is most severely tested: None of Morrison's denizens can bear to dig into their pasts, to bring the repressed materials to light, because to do so would be unsurvivable. Her people all border on autistic; they spend their lives keeping the past at bay. Their hearts have become, to repeat a term that the male protagonist Paul D uses, "a rusted tobacco tin."

As we are brought ever deeper into the lives and secrets of these damaged people, we gauge ever more fully the depradations of slavery: its systematic piecing apart of the human family, its commoditizing and dismembering of the human body, its denial of all forms of *extension* to the human subject. Nowhere is the horror of this system more on show than in the paean to flesh that is mouthed by the novel's "natural preacher," Baby Suggs, the mother-in-law of Sethe, for she articulates the novel's powerful rival vision: a world of connectedness, an integral view of both body and family, a lyrical celebration of physical nurturance. Morrison is translating the discourse of slavery out of its familiar ideological form into a shocking somatic code, so that we see its true horrors. Morrison is asking the same question Stowe asked: Can you dismember the human family?

Much of the novel's beauty and mystery lies in the answer that is on show already on the first page: What are ghosts if not proof that the dead live, that murdered children return? And the book's plot hinges on just that: The dead child does return, not as a ghost but as a living creature, a young woman who walks out of the water, whose name is Beloved, who seems to be proof positive that spirit conquers flesh. This seems initially almost like a fairy tale, but soon enough we realize how complex and rich Morrison's meditation truly is, because the magic solutions solve nothing, because the human cost of slavery is unerasable. Thus, the novel moves in two directions at once: It unpeels layer after layer of the past, leading us inexorably to the scene of the crime, to the moment when Sethe murdered her daughter, and it simultaneously stages the uncanny entry and presence of Beloved into the life of this wrecked family, an entry and presence that provoke as much pain as pleasure, that open up wounds both old and new. Morrison's novel might be thought of as a whodunit, but perhaps one better assesses it along mythic lines, as a fable that takes both its people and its readers into the labyrinth so as to encounter the monster who lurks in its heart. All of us therefore go *in*, all of us are forced to come to terms with both the horrors of slavery and the no less terrifying rival vision—murder as an act of love, murder as salvation—that stamps Sethe's life. At stake are rich matters: the limits of self, the reality of connection, the authority of spirit, the evil of slavery, the purposes of art.

MORRISON AND THE MODERNIST LEGACY

Toni Morrison is unquestionably the great inheritor of the giant figures of the early twentieth century—Proust, Joyce, Woolf, and Faulkner; she is the proof that what they wrought is still going strong. Time, consciousness, history, the inside story: All this is at the heart of her fiction, even if it seems sea-changed. It is precisely because she reorients—reconceives—the central issues of the Modernists that she is the right figure for closing this book. Morrison's *Beloved* tests, as nothing else would, my claim that Proust, Joyce, Woolf, and Faulkner are of *our* moment as well as their own. The best way of freeing my great Modernists from the distant reaches of some kind of imaginary museum or walled-off eternal library is to show that they are surprisingly alive even in a body of work that seems sharply different from their own. Art lives in just this fashion: not via pious imitation, but via reworking, altering, even plundering and outright rejection. Here is one of the joys of much reading: to espy a living chain of ideas and forms, to see a family resemblance even when outward appearances are different. Above all: to discover that things live most vitally by being altered and reimagined. It is not so different from perceiving the living linkage between children and parents and grandparents.

Thus, it is immediately clear to all readers that Morrison's profound engagement with issues of race is going to be alien to Proust, Joyce, and Woolf, and that it will be virtually irreconcilable with the views presented by Faulkner. But we have everything to gain by yoking these performances together so that the black woman novelist not only now illuminates the blind spots of the white male Mississippian, but also *completes* his work in some strange fashion. Likewise, the Proustian concern with the past and inner story, the Joycean depiction of consciousness and the interplay between private and public, the Woolfian focus on mothers and daughters, on the dynamics of family: All this is wonderfully reconfigured in Morrison. I say "wonderfully" because it testifies to the lifeline of art, its unpredictable but real futurity, best understood as what Borges called a "forking path," rather than any measurable kind of cause and effect or conspicuous replay.

And I have not been fully fair to Morrison. By overly insisting on the racial dimension of her fiction, we lose sight, I think, of what her still deeper concerns might be. Morrison, in my view, has one and only one great overarching theme: love. No surprise that this is the title she used for her most recent book. One might object that the topic is scarcely new, that very few works of literature fail to say something about love; but Morrison is special. Her signature seems to be difficult love, tortured love, homicidal love. She can paint relations between men and women, but she seems most drawn to familial arrangements: parents and children, siblings, female friendships and rivalries that seem almost blood-driven, and, most especially, most profoundly, mothers and daughters. Moreover, it would seem that she sees the love theme most acutely as a narrative challenge, leading her to invent, ever more intricately in the more recent novels, disparate vantage points and perspectives of testimony. It is possible to feel that *Jazz*, *Paradise*, and *Love*, her latest works, are perhaps too layered and twisted in this respect, indeed too "Jamesian" in their use of *ficelles*, of sidelined, sometimes hidden narrators and storytellers trying to make out or unravel what they have witnessed or suspected. Such writing can frustrate, but it also pleases by its very narrative complexity, as if to say: Difficult love is everywhere around you—in the headlines and on the back pages, in your family and entourage, perhaps in the recesses of your own heart—but you haven't adjusted your sights, your angle of vision, enough to take it in.

It is, in my view, nonetheless true that her earlier books *Sula* and most especially *Beloved* are the most powerful, move us most by their frontal account of passional events, sometimes full-throttle, sometimes via delayed disclosures. But, even when at full throttle, Morrison is never simple; instead, she seems to have a kind of native genius for storytelling, for knowing how to get maximum impact out of her materials. One feels that she approaches her subject, love, first and foremost as artisan, as storyteller, asking: How can I devise ways to convey, to transfer palpably to the reader, the shocking richness of my materials? "Shocking richness" has nothing to do with mere shock. Morrison knows that some of her books could be seen as over the top, as extremist performances that are awash in violence and murder, including infanticide, and thus what matters is to package these stories in such a way that we find their terrors or virulence altogether natural, inevitable, almost sober in their dark logic. The Modernist legacy of representing consciousness will be among her central strategies, but oriented now toward wilder and murkier precincts, places unimaginable in the tidier arrangements of a Proust or Joyce or Woolf.

At her best, as in *Beloved*, where the plot embraces horrors of incomparable darkness, Morrison essentially reinvents narrative altogether: She manages to bring us into her tapestry, to bring us in so far that we assent to even the most extreme notations, for we have been led, step by step, into her labyrinth, and have at last met the monster at its heart. Such writing chastens its readers. When you finish *Beloved*, led magisterially through its many doors and vistas, you then know at last—and it is a terrible knowledge, one that straightforward narration could never convey—why a mother would kill her child. And when you know this, you begin—begin—to know what slavery means. And I am willing to state the stark corollary of this view: "Ordinary" prose, including the prose of historians and traditional novelists, the prose you and I use in letters or even literary criticism, falls short exactly here. It does *not* bring us inside, or, as the novel has it, "through the veil," to make us feel what these events actually meant and still mean.

SULA: MORRISON'S INDIVIDUALIST FANTASIA

To appreciate *Beloved*, however, one should first know *Sula*, her saucy, folkloric, brilliant, explosive earlier novel about female rites of passage and individual freedom. The claim that Morrison is to be understood as practitioner of the magical realism seen in the work of so many Latin American and South American novelists seems especially plausible with this prancing text about the inhabitants of the Bottom, a black community with some of the weirdest figures in American literature: Shadrack the wrecked survivor of the Great War haunts its edges; the remarkable females of the Peace family—Eva, Hannah, and Sula—assume center stage; loony bit players such as the three Deweys illuminate the sidelines. The novel focuses ostensibly on the story of the friendship between the sensitive but conventional Nel Wright and the fearless, untrammeled Sula Peace, but, in much the same way that Joe Christmas essentially hijacks Faulkner's *Light in August*, one is entitled to feel that Sula Peace—and the crazies who are her family and entourage—simply run away with the book, constitute an ongoing set of fireworks that makes this short novel the most pungent and exuberant fiction that Morrison has written.

For starters there is the shell-shocked, lewd, visionary Shadrack, the man whose body seems (to him) to explode due to the trauma he has experienced: His hands and fingers seem to grow monstrously, turning his perceptual world into a minefield, leading him to take refuge back in the Bottom, where he makes his fateful little contribution to the community—the annual ritual of National Suicide Day.

And then there is Eva Peace, the book's great matriarch. Abandoned by her husband, saddled with two children, dirt-poor, she has saved her boy Plum's life by taking their last scrap of lard and inserting it into his anus to pluck out the compacted dried turds that were racking him with pain, and she has altered her family's fortune by leaving (two-legged) and returning home (one-legged) with serious, mysterious money, enabling her to buy the big house. Morrison delights in portraying Eva's considerable powers: Men are still attracted to her, the missing leg is the subject of endless speculations (it is thought that she put it on a railway track, had it cut off by a train, and collected a huge insurance payout; the more level-headed wonder what kind of insurance would so richly compensate a single black leg), and she holds court in her house. She is assisted by her daughter Hannah, also competent and free-spirited and abandoned, mother of Sula, loving maleness the same way as Eva, but with more equanimity: "Her flirting was sweet, low and guileless. Without ever a pat of the hair, a rush to change clothes or a quick application of paint, with no gesture whatsoever, she rippled with sex" (42). There is a calm but steady parade of men into this house of strong women, and Hannah, who "would fuck practically anything" (43), gets her required ration of physical touching.

MURDEROUS LOVE, CREATURES OF FABLE

And yet this nature-driven, unrepressed, pagan woman world can turn on a dime. Eva's son Plum has not turned out well. Returned home, he, too, damaged by the war, he takes refuge in his bedroom, filling his needs out of the black bag he's brought with him, stealing occasionally from his family to maintain his habit, sleeping with the record player going, eating less and less, as sweet as ever. When Eva fully sizes up the condition and fate of her son, she acts. Nothing in Morrison's work quite matches the hallucinatory evocation of Eva's mission of love/murder. Coming down the stairs on her crutches, "swinging and swooping like a giant heron" (46), Eva makes her way into Plum's room, swings over to his bed, gathers her sleeping son into her arms. He partially awakens, chuckles at his mother's tenderness, as she holds him ever closer, rocking him back and forth, taking fuller cognizance of his terminal disarray, remembering his childhood. Again he wakes up, says " 'Mamma, you so purty. You so purty, Mamma' " (47). She reaches for his strawberry crush, discovers it is blood-tainted water, and throws it to the floor, causing him to assure her he's okay: " 'Hey, Mamma, whyn't you go on back to bed? I'm all right. Didn't I tell you? I'm all right. Go on, now' " (47).

Eva leaves, "swinging and swooping," drags herself to the kitchen, and the narration returns to Plum:

> Plum on the rim of a warm light sleep was still chuckling. Mamma. She sure was somethin'. He felt twilight. Now there seemed to be some kind of wet light traveling over his legs and stomach with a deeply attractive smell. It wound itself—this wet light—all about him, splashing and running into his skin. He opened his eyes and saw what he imagined was the great wing of an eagle pouring a wet lightness over him. Some kind of baptism, some kind of blessing, he thought. Everything is going to be all right, it said. Knowing that it was so he closed his eyes and sank back into the bright hole of sleep. (47)

The next paragraph describes Eva rolling a bit of newspaper into a stick, lighting it, and throwing it "onto the bed where the kerosene-soaked Plum lay in snug delight" (47). As the *whoosh* of flames envelops him, his mother makes her slow, painful way back to the top of the house. Faced a moment later by a desperate Hannah (screaming that Plum's room is on fire, that they cannot open the door), Eva looks her in the eye: "Is? My baby? Burning?" Both understand.

Do *we*? I see Morrison's signature in this fierce discourse of herons and eagles and baptism and flames. There is not a trace of psychological or moral notation. Instead, we are in a virtually heraldic universe, animated by exotic creatures and primitive forces reminiscent more perhaps of Bosch's strange paintings than of the magical realists. And there is more to come. With perfect biblical logic, the death-dealing birds return; on an impossibly hot and heavy day, with unusually powerful winds, Hannah bends to light the yard fire, and the next thing we know is Eva looking out the window, watching Hannah burn. More perhaps Brueghel than Bosch, Morrison seems to be a writer of illustrated proverbs (the chickens are coming home to roost):

> Eva knew there was time for nothing in this world other than the time it took to get there and cover her daughter's body with her own. She lifted her heavy frame up on her good leg, and with fists and arms smashed the windowpane. Using her stump as a support on the window sill, her good leg as a lever, she threw herself out of the window. Cut and bleeding, she clawed the air trying to aim her body toward the flaming, dancing figure. She missed and came crashing down some twelve feet from Hannah's smoke. Stunned but still conscious, Eva dragged herself toward her firstborn, but Hannah, her senses lost, went flying out of the yard gesturing and bobbing like a sprung jack-in-the-box. (75–76)

Here is a writerly direction Morrison might well have continued in. We see here an incandescent, legendary universe of fable in which human measures have no purchase, where careening, jack-in-the-box figures do their bizarre dance according to some immemorial scheme of animal deities and primal forces. One feels that the human form has been inserted into an explosive new force field.

NIETZSCHEAN SULA

It seems fair to say that the more fine-grained social and psychological features of the Nel story do not hold a candle to this baroque, fantastic art, and we understand why the Peace family takes over the book. What is especially stunning, I think, is Morrison's depiction of Sula as the progeny of eagles, herons, and dancing, burning figures. Stunning, because Morrison elects to move from the picturesque to the metaphysical, as if to translate this magical and fantastic background into an equally bold and shocking ethical portrait. Sula is the toughest creature Morrison ever penned. Early on, she cuts off a part of her own finger to show the neighborhood bullies she means business with the knife she's holding. A little later she sends Chicken Little to his death by dropping him (accidentally?) from a tall tree out over the water, mesmerized by his fall. Later still, grown up, she returns to Bottom and tells off her grandmother Eva quite royally. Advised to get married and settle down and make some babies, she replies: " 'I don't want to make somebody else. I want to make myself' " (92). This is the language of self-creation, and it quickly flexes its muscles, shrugging off all pieties. She tells her grandmother, straight-out, to shut up, and when Eva sputters that no one talks to her that way (" 'Don't nobody . . .' "), Sula explodes:

> "This body does. Just 'cause you was bad enough to cut off your own leg you think you got a right to kick everybody with the stump."
>
> "Who said I cut off my leg?"
>
> "Well, you stuck it under a train to collect insurance."
>
> "Hold on, you lyin' heifer!"
>
> "I aim to."
>
> "Bible say honor thy father and thy mother that thy days may be long upon the land thy God giveth thee."
>
> "Mamma must have skipped that part. Her days wasn't too long."
>
> "Pus mouth! God's going to strike you!"
>
> "Which God? The one watched you burn Plum?"
>
> "Don't talk to me about no burning. You watched your own mamma. You crazy roach! You the one should have been burnt!"
>
> "But I ain't. Got that? I ain't. Any more fires in this house, I'm lighting them!"

> "Hellfire don't need lighting and it's already burning in you . . ."
> "Whatever's burning in me is mine!" (92–93)

There is something outright mythic as well as fierce and extravagant in this battle between two strong women, as if they'd usurped the (traditionally) male roles of Vulcan, Lucifer, and Prometheus in their respective battles for fiery independence. Despite its appearance as a growing-up story about two black girls, *Sula* is ultimately a philosophical parable about self-invention, about exploding all the conventional barriers of belief and behavior. The acid test would seem to be: Can you kill someone? Can you throw them to their death or burn them alive or watch them burn? As we should expect, Sula is hardly going to turn out to be Nel's bosom buddy. On the contrary, she fornicates with Nel's husband, ruins Nel's life, and scarcely seems to bat an eye in the process. Morrison takes pains to define this kind of beyond-the-pale behavior as a principled position: "As willing to feel pain as to give pain, to feel pleasure as to give pleasure, hers was an experimental life" (118).

"Hers was an experimental life." This clarion call of revolt reminds me of Nietzsche, and even more of Rimbaud, who was among the first to systematize this kind of breakthrough: to craft oneself into something new and unheard-of, to destroy all the old binds and pieties, to arrive ultimately at a "*dérèglement de tous les sens*," ("a riot of all the senses"). The Christian tradition is sent packing: Nel asks why, why did Sula take her husband, since they were friends, " 'I was good to you, Sula, why don't that matter?' " (144); the answer contains much of this book's venom: " 'It matters, Nel, but only to you. Not to anybody else. Being good to somebody is just like being mean to somebody. Risky. You don't get nothing for it' " (144–145). Sula is the book's mad artist/scientist who is out to make herself anew via experiment. Just as Rimbaud claimed that "*l'amour est à réinventer*," so does Sula choose lovemaking as one of the arenas for self-invention: "When she left off cooperating with her body and began to assert herself in the act, particles of strength gathered in her like steel shavings drawn to a spacious magnetic center, forming a tight cluster that nothing, it seemed, could break" (122–123). Murder, sex, burning, or watching burn are just so many crucibles for self-spawning. Sula is the *Übermensch* of the novel, and even though she dies mysteriously at the end, she has effectively smashed every possible code around her (and several lives as well) into bits, except that of her own restless striving. Here is the book where Morrison goes furthest in charting the strength and vistas of human will, of desire. Sula goes right off the map. How's them apples? she seems to be saying. There cannot be, and will not be, a sequel.

REIMAGINING FREEDOM: *BELOVED*

I have wanted to delve into and map out Morrison's audacious performance in *Sula* so that we might have a deeper appreciation of what is achieved in the far darker and still more extreme *Beloved.* All those elements of fable and fantasy that expand the scene in *Sula,* that seem to herald its unstoppable drive for freedom at all costs, leave us with a feeling that the earlier book is somehow gravity-free, in a nowhere zone where pure creativity and self-invention reign. With *Beloved,* we are hurtled into a realm of horrendous gravity, a place where nothing, absolutely nothing, is ludic or for free or for you to invent. Hence, one feels that the earlier prancing story of an experimental life is now going to be turned inside out, to be weighed and measured and radically reconceived. The grand adventure of self, at the core of *Sula,* not only stands at the far side of things, perhaps even beyond death, in *Beloved,* but it may also be a mirage. And the splendid isolation of the earlier book may turn out to be something one suffers rather than celebrates.

Much seems, on the surface, familiar. *Sula* has shown Morrison the constrictions of a realist scheme, and the drastic story she wants to tell now requires a comparable liberty of expression. But the brightness and gaiety of the early text are gone for good, even if some of the staples remain. Once again there will be an infanticide, and it will even be cloaked in the language of birds, but Sethe's murder of her daughter drips with blood throughout the entire novel, and conceivably long afterward still in the minds of Morrison's readers. Not that there is no magic in *Beloved;* we find a different kind of folklore, one consisting of spirits and ghosts that roam the land and occupy everything: houses, bodies, minds. We won't see a one-legged Eva Peace, either, with her suitors and mystique, but rather an old woman named Baby Suggs, who hobbles because of injuries incurred during her six decades as slave, a woman with a calling and a spiritual mission of her own. No Shadrack, either, but he is replaced by a different kind of damaged man, Paul D, whose wounds are going to be explored and evoked with agonizing ferocity, yet who is someone bent on surviving and finding love, rather than signing on for a National Suicide Day. Finally, the high-flying Sula, champion of human daring and emancipation, disappears from the scene, and instead we have the unforgettable Sethe, low-profiled, close to the ground, engaged in the epic struggle of keeping herself and her loved ones alive, coping with injuries that are, literally, unspeakable and quite possibly unsurvivable, possessed of a belief system that defies our logic.

At the center of this magnificent novel lies the greatest moral transgression in American (and Western) history: slavery. I believe that Toni Morrison has given us the fullest account of the very logic and impact of slavery that we are likely to see. Moreover, this heinous regime of owning other people—a regime the reader probably assumes he or she knows all about—is used by Morrison in some sense as catalyst or springboard, changing all our notions of what is normal and what is not, what is tellable and what is not, what a life is and what it is not. It is all this that I have meant by my term "gravity"; against the backdrop of *Beloved,* all the flamboyant and delightful touches of *Sula* look weightless and frivolous, all the philosophical program of its beautiful protagonist—freedom at all costs, self-creation—looks inflated, capricious, unreal. With this book, not only does ethics (which Sula booted out of her life) come back into the picture, but it comes clothed in ways we have never before imagined. *Beloved* does nothing less than make us parse anew all the paradigms we are accustomed to. It remakes the world. Is this not what the greatest art is meant to do? To challenge, even to wreck some of our received ideas, to show us how privileged or complacent or constructed our arrangements are, to make us rethink drastic measures such as murder, and still other measures, too, such as "self" and "love," which we take for granted, as if they were guaranteed by the Constitution. *Beloved* is trouble, and this is why literature matters.

Yet, for all its novelty, *Beloved* has precursors. I will later signal Morrison's debt to Faulkner, but the most shining model for this book about slavery is Harriet Beecher Stowe's *Uncle Tom's Cabin.* That great novel is among the most influential fictions ever written in America, both at home and abroad—Lincoln is famously said to have greeted Stowe as "the little lady who made this big war"—and its current neglect among readers and even students is regrettable. In that nineteenth-century bestseller, Stowe brought news of American slavery to the world at large, but it is not so much through the Christlike figure of Uncle Tom as through the brilliant handling of the pieced-apart family that the book derives its great pathos. The supreme scandal of slavery, in Stowe's eyes, had to do with the reifying and merchandising of the black subject, resulting in the complete rupturing of all human bonds—mothers and children, husbands and wives, brothers and sisters—yielding a world of fissured bodies and souls. Even the title advertises familial connections, and Stowe repeatedly addresses her readers (especially her women readers, her mother-readers) directly, urging them to imagine such invasions and depredations in their own lives. Perhaps the boldest (even if most elemental) feature of *Uncle Tom's Cabin* is its belief in the priority as well as the sanctity of the human family, and I mean "priority" in every sense of the word: The infant begins life *in utero*, and the bondedness of human creatures cannot be severed, so that the separated are reunited—in dream, in fact, in death, in Heaven. And the crucial corollary here is: The seemingly atomistic and empowered individual—that creature so dear to American thinking and yearning—is a bit of a whimsical fiction, a mirage, made credible to us by the charade of weaning, by the illusion of a bounded and contoured body, but proven false by the deepest impulses of life and love. This is strong medicine. It will reappear in *Beloved*.

I believe that Stowe's book is still waiting for its proper reassessment. One reason it is hardly read by the general public today has to do with its preachiness and sentimentality. Scholars have pointed out that there was a powerful strain of the "jeremiad," the domestic, and religious effusion in mid-nineteenth-century America, and that Stowe is demonstrably of her moment. Yet the sad truth is that post-Hemingway readers have little patience with the longwindedness, didacticism, and religious artillery of Stowe's novel. Toni Morrison, supreme stylist, knows that. Hence, she has taken what is most profound and enduring in *Uncle Tom's Cabin*—the horrid dismantling of the human family—and has found astonishing ways to rewrite this dark chapter in our moral history. Her rewriting most commands our attention, I think, by its commitment to the psychic side of the story, as if to say: When you commoditize human beings, when you see them only as an assemblage of parts to be auctioned on the market, when you treat them as bodies you own, when you disallow all human connection between them, well, you have created a kind of psychic horror that almost defies understanding. Let me propose a sensationalist analogy to the transgression of slavery: The breaking of the armature of the family is akin to the breaking of the armature of the atom. By wrecking and rupturing this frame, you generate a dreadful kind of destructive power; you set all Hell loose. I do not think it exaggerated to say that Morrison sees slavery as a kind of taboo, an incursion into and annihilation of the oldest human forms: the body and the family. *Beloved* is a modern classic because Morrison has turned her genius for storytelling to this tragic material, and found a way to take its measure, to give its measure.

THE WALKING WOUNDED AND THE AMNESIACS

Indeed, *Beloved* thrusts you into a human landscape that seems post-nuclear. We are told of the routine decimations meted out to blacks both during and after the Civil War. When, for example, the strange Beloved appears out of nowhere, unable to say who she is, Paul D sees her as representative figure:

> During, before and after the War he had seen Negroes so stunned, or hungry, or tired and bereft it was a wonder they recalled or said anything. Who, like him, had hidden in caves and fought owls for food; who, like him, stole from pigs; who, like him, slept in trees in the day and walked by night; who, like him, had buried themselves in slop and jumped in wells to avoid regulators, raiders, paterollers, veterans, hill men, posses and merrymakers. Once he met a Negro about fourteen years old who lived by himself in the woods and said he couldn't remember living anywhere else. He saw a witless coloredwoman jailed and hanged for stealing ducks she believed were her own babies. (66)

These are the walking wounded, and Morrison wants us to realize that only so much damage is survivable, that beyond that, you crack. You think ducks are your babies; you "develop some permanent craziness . . . Like Aunt Phyllis, who slept with her eyes wide open. Like Jackson Till, who slept under the bed" (97). Another character, Stamp Paid, reflects on what appears to be business as usual in this great land: "Eighteen seventy-four and whitefolks were still on the loose. Whole towns wiped clean of Negroes; eighty-seven lynchings in one year alone in Kentucky; four colored schools burned to the ground; grown men whipped like children; children whipped like adults; black women raped by the crew; property taken, necks broken" (180). This novel is rough going for a white reader, for white readers are unaccustomed to seeing themselves portrayed as "on the loose," as a kind of scourge, as people who, in the mind of Baby Suggs (about to die), "could prowl at will, change from one mind to another, and even when they thought they were behaving, it was a far cry from what real humans did" (244).

There is simply no limit to the white atrocities—including scalpings—registered in this novel, but there is indeed a limit as to how much the blacks can endure before becoming unhinged. The *dérèglement de tous les sens* that Rimbaud postulated as the extreme condition of human freedom is now seen instead the as ultimate station of those who have been violated to the breaking point. This systematic violence and brutality will not bear thinking on. At a certain point, the abused and victimized simply go either mad or out of business: They become quasi-autistic, they blow a fuse, they grow amnesiac. Baby Suggs had eight children, four taken away, four chased, and all she can remember is how the firstborn "loved the burned bottom of bread" (5). Paul D's mind is such a chamber of horrors, including a stint in Alfred, Georgia, living in a cage and doing chain-gang labor, that "he had shut down a generous portion of his head" (41), placing all the worst memories "into the tobacco tin lodged in his chest," a tin that, by the time he arrives on the scene and enters Sethe's life again, "nothing in this world could pry . . . open" (113). As for Sethe, as we will see, the wounds of the past—having seen (as child) her mother hanged, being violated by white boys when six months pregnant, having her milk taken, her back opened up and turned into a chokecherry tree, and, topping the list, having murdered her own baby—constitute a body of psychic materials that is so toxic, so unbearable, that life is reduced to the here and now, to not looking back. One lives as best one can: hunkered down.

RECOVERING YOUR STORY?

For all these reasons, *Beloved* bids to annihilate the governing thesis of this book. Recovering your story—which I have presented as the great beauty and reward of Proust, Joyce, Woolf, and Faulkner, the best reason for reading them—is intolerable, is anathema in Morrison's novel. The untold, unknown, unshareable personal story that Proust ceaselessly illuminates and treasures has become, in *Beloved,* lethal. The bucolic Combray that

Marcel recovers through the madeleine dipped in tea appears to us, in light of Morrison's saga, obscenely sheltered and privileged. As for Joyce, the ghosts of the dead mother and the dead child that Stephen and Bloom carry within them and are visited by seem outright benign in comparison to the virulent baby ghost in *Beloved*, and one is hard put to construe their acts of remorse and guilt and hurt as having any parallels with the lesions that Sethe carries in both body and spirit. Woolf's entire social scheme of elegant, civilized gatherings belongs on a different planet, in contrast to Morrison; and her evocations of rituals such as parties and dinners, beautiful though they are, strike us as the prerogatives of class arrangements that are simply unimaginable to Morrison's denizens. Even Faulkner, whose view of the past is far from romantic, whose struggle with issues of race is often tragic, can seem almost whimsical when paired with Morrison; the grave problems of a Quentin Compson, tortured by his sister's love life, appear as peccadilloes when we think of Sethe or Paul D, and the horror of miscegenation that fuels the elaborate plot in *Absalom, Absalom!* looks awfully strained and self-serving when we consider the racial nightmares of *Beloved*. In short, Morrison's novel threatens to sink my entire fleet by exposing its taken-for-granted privileges, its preciousness and self-indulgence, its coddling concern with consciousness.

PROUST REDUX

It makes therefore good sense to return, even if briefly, to the commanding reasons why Morrison is the right way to complete our discussion of the Modernist giants, this time with a bit more specificity concerning just what Morrison owes these figures, and, in some slightly weird sense, what they owe her. The shadow of Proust looms large despite the radically different social carence of the Frenchman's work. He is the first major prose writer to zero in on the great untold story inside each of us that defies both conversation and realist description. True enough, there is in his work no historical circumstance on the order of slavery that would explain, along either societal or traumatic lines, why this story remains hidden, but I think his overarching view that we remain in the dark as to what most defines us is a view that Morrison shares. And she also shares his shrewd understanding of how society marginalizes or crucifies some of its members, and how these victimized groups create their own private discourse, their own forms of recognition and even love. Finally, the Proustian injunction to work toward what we'd have to call the "repossession" of our life speaks, I think, to the deepest thrust in *Beloved* as well, even though a term like "possession" has a ghastly different resonance in Morrison's scheme.

JOYCE REDUX

The ludic, playful wit and fireworks of Joyce are not to be found in *Beloved* (although one sees their trace in *Sula*). Yet Joyce's incomparable skill in not merely creating interior monologue and stream of consciousness as the private speech of human beings, but in then inserting this private performance onto the public stage, whether it be the streets and bars and brothels of Dublin or the bedroom on Eccles Street, testifies to a sense of conflict and drama and irony that Morrison reworks in her book. Morrison is as brilliant a listener to the inner musings of Sethe, Paul D, and Denver as Joyce is with Stephen, Bloom, and Molly, and she is as alert as he is to the tensions, loneliness, cacophony, and misfit that can result from this depiction of inner and outer. Finally, I think that Morrison shares Joyce's fascination with, humor about, and reverence for the human body, and even though she scarcely needed *Ulysses* to tap into this material, her book has a tragic somatic quality that is unparalleled in modern literature. The boisterous, often raunchy side of Joyce is quite at odds with the painful, tender wisdom Morrison evinces in *Beloved* concerning the body's needs, vulnerabilities, and pleasures, yet each book goes a long way to showing how body and mind must be written in tandem, and how traditional narrative discourse has scanted the realm of the flesh.

WOOLF REDUX

The Woolf-Morrison comparison seems especially crucial to me, given how outwardly different, indeed incompatible, these two fictional worlds appear to be. Yet take a second look and you find kinship everywhere: The well-known Woolfian imperative to "think back through our mothers if we are women" acquires an almost unbearable richness and dignity in the fissured slave world that Morrison is depicting. Moreover, Morrison understands this vital connection to be something far more urgent, difficult, and of-the-flesh than Woolf's "thinking back" implies; in Morrison, this project will result in the discovery of both a new language—a mother-language—and also a shocking view of human connection that has little that is cerebral, but is closer to a viscous form of human bonding that Morrison calls "thick love." For just these reasons, the beautiful tribute to the dead parents in *To the Lighthouse*, especially the unforgettable portrait of Mrs. Ramsay both alive and dead, becomes a mission of comparable pain and beauty in *Beloved*, even though the reign of death in the slave novel is crushingly wide and multidirectional, almost cubistic: Parents seek to remember their dead children, children recall their dead parents, and this incessant traffic takes on a narrative form of ghosts and outright "returnees" in Morrison's book that is unthinkable in Woolf. Finally, Woolf's portrait of the mother/daughter dyad in the figures of Mrs. Ramsay and Lily Briscoe, with its mix of need, tenderness, and irony, reappears unmistakably in the trio of Sethe, Beloved, and Denver in the later book; the tonality is much darker in Morrison, and we are not far from murder and cannibalism and a view of motherhood that is hardly different from slavery itself, but these two texts, taken together, offer us a fascinating cumulative perspective on a problematic—the meaning of motherhood, of female kinship and continuity—that is very much with us even today.

FAULKNER REDUX

And then there is Faulkner, Faulkner whom Morrison demonstrably knows inside out; knows especially, I think, inside out, because she sees at once all that is occulted and unresolved in his work, having written a master's thesis on his work. In Faulkner's last great book, *Go Down, Moses* (1942), he rather apocalyptically pronounces on the two great curses and transgressions that doom his native South: ownership of people and ownership of land. It is also in that book that Faulkner goes farthest in creating a black character with real subjectivity: Lucas Beauchamp. Yet the blind spots of this novel are no less eloquent: Faulkner can see—but cannot write—the devastated lives of those who were the truest victims of Southern racism, the black female slaves who were just so much sexual property in the patriarchal scheme. Likewise, we have had occasion to note that Dilsey and Caddy, the two beautiful figures of *The Sound and the Fury*, one white and one black, are each outside Faulkner's narrative reach; Caddy comes across as the tragically mourned sister who left, and Dilsey, untroubled Dilsey, is the bedrock that supports this dying white family. But Faulkner's narrative lenses are invariably those of the hurting and hungry males who usurp the stage. I rehearse this material because Morrison has gone where Faulkner could not, has told the inside story of the black slave women, both old and young, and she has endowed them—Sethe, Beloved, and Baby Suggs—with a consciousness we will not easily forget. But it is perhaps Faulkner's narrative genius in *Absalom, Absalom!*—the use of delayed disclosures to circle all horrors before finally evoking them, the notion of an overpass to love as the only bridge we have to the past (or, indeed, to the future)—that most shines in *Beloved* in the form of what I'd like to call "narrative redemption." As if to say: Art enables us to descend into the maelstrom, into the wreck, to see where we've been so that we know where we are and where we might go.

ENTER THE GHOST

With our overture now in place, we are prepared to go in, ourselves, to Morrison's *Beloved.* And the very first thing we meet is a spiteful baby ghost: "124 was spiteful. Full of a baby's venom" (3). Ghost stories may sometimes start with their ghost vedettes, but beginning with a baby ghost is unusual, to say the least, and causes readers at once to lose their bearings. Moreover, as we can already see, and will have ample opportunity to see ever more fully, Morrison's ghosts are creatures without any resemblance to the Gothic genre we may associate with writers as varied as Poe, Hawthorne, Wilkie Collins, Henry James, and so on up to Stephen King: Her creatures do not pop out of coffins or graves, and they are not clothed in white sheets. This baby ghost is indisputably a force to reckon with, a force requiring no special sensibilities or vision; on the contrary, it rules the roost, has been turning over slop jars, shattering mirrors, leaving handprints in cake, and creating general havoc for some eighteen years now, has caused the two older children, Howard and Buglar, to pack their bags and clear out, and is pretty much a regular in the household. No one has any doubt who it is: Sethe's dead baby who refuses to leave. Moreover, Baby Suggs suggests that there's nothing unusual here, that this ghost is pretty much par for the course for the black families she knows: " 'Not a house in the country ain't packed to its rafters with some dead Negro's grief. We lucky this ghost is a baby. My husband's spirit was to come back in here? or yours? You lucky . . .' " (5). Could ghosts be business as usual in the culture of slavery? Rethink your story in this light: You may be on a stage that is busier than you thought, for it could be brim-full of the dead who have refused to vacate the premises.

We learn at the outset that this baby ghost has some good reasons for spite: Its throat was cut. And very early as well, Morrison establishes a connection between the baby ghost's rage and the mother's feelings of love; Denver says, " 'For a baby she throws a powerful spell,' " and Sethe answers, " 'No more powerful than the way I loved her' " (4). You note how much I am emphasizing "outset" and "early," and Morrison resembles Faulkner especially in her talent for giving us information that we both can and cannot process. These basic facts—this ghost is Sethe's dead baby, its throat was cut, black folks all around the country have similar guests—are presented cleanly for our inspection on the opening pages of the novel. Not a world we are familiar with, but one we must negotiate, somewhat like an anthropologist making sense of a strange culture. And we have no inkling, at this juncture, just how much is hidden under what is said, how much more is to come: Why was this baby's throat cut? What role does the mother's love play? What is Denver's relation to the ghost? Lurking behind (or above) these local questions are still bigger issues that modern readers have to ponder: Do we believe in ghosts? Is this just a metaphor? Do the dead return? Can spirit cross over into flesh? Is there traffic (beyond our ken) between the living and the dead? By positing this ghost as live force (rather than as concept or projection or mind's game), she hits us, the secular readers, right where it hurts: This book isn't behaving right.

Not that her own people, the book's own denizens, are confused. They don't find it easy, but they know damn well it is real. Hence, Morrison adds to the opening gambit and gets the plot rolling by following the brief introduction of the house and its spiteful ghost with the arrival of a figure from Sethe's past, Paul D, one of the Sweet Home boys (i.e., from the same plantation Sethe lived on for many years, a place whose memories will soon begin to flood the text). Paul D recognizes at once that there's a problem in this house, because he walks through the door "into a pool of red and undulating light that locked him where he stood" (9). With great understatement, he asks, " 'You got company?' " " 'Off and on' " is Sethe's reply. Soon enough, he gets firsthand experience:

> It took him a while to realize that his legs were not shaking because of worry, but because the floorboards were and the grinding, shoving floor was only part of it. The house itself was pitching. Sethe slid to the floor and struggled to get back into her dress. While down on all fours, as though she were holding her house down on the ground, Denver burst from the keeping room, terror in her eyes, a vague smile on her lip.
>
> "God damn it! Hush up!" Paul D was shouting, falling, reaching for anchor. "Leave the place alone! Get the hell out!" A table rushed toward him and he grabbed its leg. Somehow he managed to stand at an angle and, holding the table by two legs, he bashed it about, wrecking everything, screaming back at the screaming house. "You want to fight, come on! God damn it! She got enough without you. She got enough!" (18)

I cite this passage in order to insist that there is nothing merely psychological or even visionary in play here, but rather a stark, in-your-face, physical fact of life. Moreover, I can hardly conceive of a better way for Morrison to assault, right at the outset, her readers' assumptions about reality: *The ghost is tearing the house apart.* That house is, in some sense, our house, our comfortable notions about the real and the unreal. These are the structures we are accustomed to, and they are being annihilated. In almost chivalric fashion, Paul D acts as our stunned surrogate, takes on the spiteful ghost, tries to unseat it, to vanquish it out of sheer physical strength and volition, so as to get it off the premises. And he seems to pull it off, although he almost wrecks the house in the process, necessitating several days of mending and patching up. But it is worth it, Paul D feels, now that he is reunited with this woman who was part of his past, who was married to his best friend; his traveling days, he tells Sethe a bit later, could at last be over: " 'Upstate, downstate, east, west; I been in territory that ain't got no name, never staying nowhere long. But when I got here and sat there on the porch waiting for you, well, I knew it wasn't the place I was heading toward; it was you. We can make a life, girl. A life' " (46). Why not? What is to prevent it? The ghost has been sent packing. True enough, Denver is hardly welcoming, but that can be worked on. Damaged though he is, he believes in the Dream: "We can make a life." It is all in front of you.

THE HEART: A CLOSED TOBACCO TIN

Except that it isn't. It is never in front of you. "Making a life" is among the most complex artisanal challenges known to our species, in part because the ground we stand on may be mined, in part because the maker may not be a free agent. "Moving ahead" sounds wonderful, but often enough, life travels, distressingly and paralyzingly, in the other direction. Paul D himself is a walking repository of past experiences, some shared with Sethe, some on his own, that are not faceable. Gradually this novel will circle back to them, unpack them, pirouette their horrors, display their pain and humiliation. Midway through the novel, we get a shorthand inventory: "It was some time before he could put Alfred, Georgia, Sixo, schoolteacher, Halle, his brothers, Sethe, Mister, the taste of iron, the sight of butter, the smell of hickory, notebook paper, one by one, into the tobacco tin lodged in his chest" (113). Had the novel started with this, it would just be what it is for you, my reader, if you haven't read *Beloved:* just words. What do they mean? Let me translate these dictionary terms into their horrible emotional content, their psychic reality as scar tissue. This procedure—to translate words into their emotional content—is the governing strategy of the novel, and it constitutes the fundamental challenge Morrison throws at us.

As for "Alfred, Georgia," that was the chain gang cage stint, the time when Paul D lived with other slaves in a hole in the ground, bound to each one, subject to systematic abuse (physical and sexual), and discovered that his whole body trembled in uncontrollable ways. (Remember Shadrack in *Sula;* this is worse.) "Sixo" is the wild, untamed free spirit of the bunch, the blue-black slave who was with them at Sweet Home, the philosopher of the group who refused to learn how to read or count in white man's terms, sensing that it (the language of the oppressor) would derail him, Sixo the suitor of the Thirty-mile woman (he walked thirty miles to see her for each rendezvous) whom he impregnates, so that his dying words can be "Seven-O." "Schoolteacher" is the Simon Legree of this novel, the villainous brother-in-law to the enlightened slave owner, Garner, who comes to Sweet Home after Garner's death to take over, and to begin his reign of terror. It is a cold, sadistic, intellectual terror, one that consists in treating his black slaves as a lower species, as animals, as so much measurable and controllable flesh, in contrast to Garner, who boasted, "my niggers are men," Schoolteacher who watched and took notes during the fateful scourging that Sethe received. "Mister" is the vicious rooster of Sweet Home, the cock of the walk whose virile power and male ease shames Paul D, for Mister's power is undiminished whereas Paul D has been horribly done unto and emptied of all self-assurance. "The taste of iron" is the iron bit that is routinely put in the mouths of troublesome slaves, creating a kind of creatural panic that is never forgotten, that gives them a smile that is not theirs, that stays in the eyes of those who've suffered this treatment. "The sight of butter" is what Paul D remembers when he last saw Halle (Sethe's husband) at Sweet Home, Halle who had, unbeknownst to Sethe, witnessed the exploit of Schoolteacher's nephews when they attacked the six-month pregnant woman and took her milk, Halle who went mad at this sight, rubbed butter all over his face, was never to be seen again. "The smell of hickory" is the smell of Sixo the incorrigible being burned alive by Schoolteacher, yet leaving his wonderful taunt, "Seven-O." "Notebook paper" is the prime weapon of Schoolteacher, the little book in which he carefully measures the animal versus the human characteristics of his black property, noting their behavior, inventorying their curious little habits, somewhat in the manner of a collector examining the features of a lesser species.

Borges once wrote a story, "The Aleph," about the discovery of a magic stone that was incredibly dense and heavy, that actually contained the entire world within it. In my view, Morrison's list of what is inside Paul D's tobacco tin works along similar lines, yielding an inventory that is intolerably dense and heavy, once you have understood it. Now you must imagine carrying this inside you, carefully shut, at all times. *This is the past.* How, exactly, do you plan to make a life? And how do you write your novel in such a way that that list attains its awful eloquence, so that your reader understands how much radioactive and explosive material is lurking inside these characters? If we are damaged enough, we try to do what they tried to do at Chernobyl: to seal off the deadly material, to wrap it in cement, to hope it never surfaces. Your story could kill you.

But, however you may try to close that tobacco tin, life has its strange ways of opening it up. Paul D and Sethe contain horrors, and, like polluted wells or gathering infections, the poison can't be contained: It seeps out. Sethe had no idea that Halle had witnessed the nephews' violation of her, but sooner or later, Paul D (who initially promised himself never to tell Sethe) lets it out, in order to defend Halle in the face of Sethe's severe judgment. Out come the horrors: Halle didn't come to Sethe's rescue, because the sight he witnessed "broke him"; Halle had butter all over his face; Paul D couldn't help because he had a bit in his mouth. Halle saw. Butter. Paul D. Bit. So much shorthand language for intolerable new facts, and doubtless more where those came from. At learning, many years later now, these gruesome events, Sethe wonders why it is that the brain doesn't simply shut down, simply say no:

> Why was there nothing it refused? No misery, no regret, no hateful picture too rotten to accept? Like a greedy child it snatched up everything. Just once, could it say, No thank you? I just ate and can't hold another bite? I am full God damn it of two boys with mossy teeth, one sucking on my breast the other holding me down, their book-reading teacher watching and writing it up. I am still full of that, God damn it, I can't go back and add more. Add my husband to it, watching, above me in the loft—hiding close by—the one place he thought no one would look for him, looking down . . . And not stopping them—looking and letting it happen. But my greedy brain says, Oh thanks, I'd love more—so I add more. And no sooner than I do, there is no stopping. There is also my husband squatting by the churn smearing butter as well as its clabber all over his face because the milk they took is on his mind. . . . And if Paul D saw him and could not save or comfort him because the iron bit was in his mouth, then there is still more that Paul D could tell me and my brain would go right ahead and take it and never say, No thank you. (70)

Think what we have already seen: Marcel's uncontrollable bouts of jealous mania as he tries to imagine Albertine's sexual crimes, Bloom's incessant (and ever-foiled) efforts to keep Molly's cuckolding of him out of his consciousness, Clarissa's and Peter's vivid, recurring, quicksilver memories of their stormy relationship, and of course the always/already lost and remembered Caddy, the one Faulkner himself called "my heart's darling," in the tortured minds of Benjy and Quentin. Proust, Joyce, Woolf, and Faulkner know something about the trapdoors and revolving doors of the mind, as well as the creatures that hide in the dark. Yet *Beloved* surpasses even these achievements. This warm book has nonetheless an almost clinical dimension in its unswerving focus, not merely on torture and damage, but on how much the human being can sustain before coming apart. As we noted at the beginning of this discussion, many did go mad, mistaking ducks for babies, sleeping with their eyes open or under the bed, or indeed covering their face in clabber. But in this passage Morrison posits the brain itself as voracious, insatiable, constitutionally unable to close its doors or refuse what is coming its way. The only therapy these people know is willed amnesia. Close up shop. Fence it off. Close up the tobacco tin. Let it rust. Don't ever go *inside*.

Can you see yourself in this severe light? I can only hope that none of my readers has memories remotely comparable to those of Sethe and Paul D, but no one is without injuries, scar tissue, and perhaps some wounds that don't heal, that won't bear scrutiny. How much does each of us rope off, inside, declaring it off-limits, unvisitable? This novel is wise about the toxic waste that life itself generates in us, and it is exquisitely attuned to our stratagems for keeping it buried, so that it does not bury us.

INSIDE: OFF-LIMITS

It thus makes sense when Paul D, after asking Sethe how things are going when he first encounters her, pushes then a little further with the truly dangerous question: " 'What about inside?' " The answer is not surprising: " 'I don't go inside' " (45–46). This gentle man's response is one of the loveliest lines in the novel: " 'Sethe, if I'm here with you, with Denver, you can go anywhere you want. Jump, if you want to, 'cause I'll catch you, girl. I'll catch you 'fore you fall. Go as far inside as you need to, I'll hold your ankles' " (46). Here is the topography of *Beloved.* It is comparable to a minefield, filled with unexploded bombs that you could run into, or to a cave with bottomless depths, which you dare not go in because horrors are housed there. One recalls Quentin Compson's set of damning memories, memories into which he increasingly falls as his grip on life diminishes. Yet this private hell is far more terrible, more stocked with atrocities, with things that were done to you that cannot be revisited much less processed. But can you keep the doors locked? Can you teach the greedy brain to stop receiving?

Morrison's depiction of Sethe is that of a woman at war with her past, working hard at keeping it at bay. At one point she is telling Denver about Sweet Home, retelling at least the material she has to some extent domesticated, when the machine simply stops: "The single slow blink of her eyes; the bottom lip sliding up slowly to cover the top; and then a nostril sigh, like the snuff of a candle flame—signs that Sethe had reached the point beyond which she would not go" (37). Likewise, when Paul D shares the terrible story about Halle, butter, and bit with her, Sethe puts her hand on his knee and rubs. Rubs. Morrison glides into each of their minds to depict how close to the breaking point they both are, how much repression is still necessary:

> Paul D had only begun, what he was telling her was only the beginning when her fingers on his knee, soft and reassuring, stopped him. Just as well. Just as well. Saying more might push them both to a place they couldn't get back from. He would keep the rest where it belonged: in that tobacco tin buried in his chest where a red heart used to be. Its lid rusted shut. He would not pry it loose now in front of this sweet sturdy woman, for if she got a whiff of its contents it would shame him. . . .
>
> Sethe rubbed and rubbed, pressing the work cloth and the stony curves that made up his knee. She hoped it calmed him as it did her. Like kneading bread in the half-light of the restaurant kitchen . . . Working dough. Working, working dough. Nothing better than that to start the day's serious work of beating back the past. (72–73)

THE BIRTH STORY

One way of beating back the past is to attempt to banish it altogether. Another, more accommodating strategy is to single out those morsels or episodes of it that can be put to use—the stories that soothe or affirm—and turn them into anthem, into lullaby. In some sense, this is what both Sethe and Denver have done regarding Denver's own birth. This fable about the exhausted, fleeing six-month pregnant slave girl trying to get away from Sweet Home and make it across the water to be reunited with her children is told many times in the novel. Denver rehearses it as a kind of founding narrative, a saga of blood, sweat, and tears that eventuates in her own birth. And in her naming. For the tale has two heroines: not merely Sethe, who miraculously "made it," but also the strange and improbable white girl

Amy Denver, who comes across the ready-to-die Sethe during her own pilgrimage out of Kentucky toward Boston, where she will be able to get herself some velvet. Utterly unsentimental and unvarnished—Amy Denver is not all that far from white trash, doesn't think much of blacks—this sequence is close to the moral heart of the book. It stages birthing as the central drama of human life—as eloquent contrast to killing, perhaps even as hint that some killings may actually be birthings—a drama that is preciously enabled by the sweet, firm, joint labor of two women. Joint labor: Amy Denver and Sethe birth this premature infant together, and this depiction of two capable women joined in a supreme physical effort—a form of intercourse in its own way, one pushing, one pulling, each attentive to the other's rhythms—is virtually all we know of Denver's origins. Mind you, we do understand that Denver was sired by Halle, but Morrison has demonstrably left that insemination scene in the shadows in order to cast her light on these intricate, harmonious, arduous efforts of the two women to bring it to fruition. It is a loving act of birth.

ANYTHING DEAD COMING BACK TO LIFE HURTS

As readers know, Amy Denver saves Sethe's life as well as the baby's. Sethe is in a bad way: exhausted, sour milk oozing on her, back so ripped apart by beating that it sports a "chokecherry tree," huge belly with its hurting "antelope" inside, bloody knees, chest "two cushions of pins," legs and feet swollen monstrously out of all recognition. Amy Denver, facing this, performs a simple yet profound act of human solidarity: "Then she did the magic: lifted Sethe's feet and legs until she cried salt tears. 'It's gonna hurt, now,' said Amy. 'Anything dead coming back to life hurts' " (35). It takes the reader a long time, I believe, to grasp the fuller reach of Amy Denver's elemental wisdom: *Anything dead coming back to life hurts.* The whole of the novel—its story of ghosts and damaged survivors, its cargo of unbearable memories, its view of the dread legacy of slavery, its vision of storytelling itself as a mode of retrieval, as a way of bringing back the dead—is adumbrated in that short, pithy phrase that seems merely to describe the hurting body. *Beloved* is written under the aegis of that phrase. Our reading of the book is governed by the logic and authority of that same perception. Why else would this book start with a spiteful baby ghost? The past is not dead: It lives, and it hurts. No amount of bread-kneading is going to prevent it from coming back to life.

Earlier, trying to shelter and warn her daughter of the terrors "out there," Sethe has signaled this same hard truth. Her past of torture and bondage cannot die or be put to death; worse still, her daughter could fall into it:

> "Where I was before I came here, that place is real. It's never going away. Even if the whole farm—every tree and grass blade of it dies. The picture is still there and what's more, if you go there—you who never was there—if you go there and stand in the place where it was, it will happen again; it will be there waiting for you. So, Denver, you can't never go there. Never. Because even though it's all over—over and done with—it's going to always be there waiting for you. That's how come I had to get all my children out. No matter what."
>
> Denver picked at her fingernails. "If it's still there, waiting, that must mean that nothing ever dies."
>
> Sethe looked right in Denver's face. "Nothing ever does," she said. (36)

How can you tell a story where nothing ever dies? Where would you start? What kind of sequence is even imaginable? What kind of logic would obtain here? Death as finality is the great boundary line—bottom line, finish line—that gives a shape to our existence and understanding. It is perhaps here that Morrison is most the disciple of Proust and Faulkner, but she is taking what they would have termed either "memory" or the "past," and endowing it with a presence such that those quaint terms no longer mean anything. Again, I ask: How could you *write* this vision of things? How could you convey to your reader what it must feel like to inhabit a world where nothing ever dies?

That is the bottom line with ghosts: They tell us that death is a fiction, that people do not disappear, however much we may think they do, even if we have put them into the ground ourselves, have held their bleeding body ourselves. And thus, when Paul D has his clashing encounter with that ghost at the beginning of the novel, when he violently does battle with it and sends it packing, we have to wonder: Is it gone? Can it go away? Can it be defeated? If it is a ghost, someone who was already killed once, how can Paul D conquer it? And if it goes away, where does it go? And if it is away, will it come back? These questions are the ones we should be formulating at the beginning of the novel, but of course we do not know enough, ourselves, to do so; we have not been sufficiently initiated into Morrison's spirit world, her world of ever-living dead things, to realize that something on the order of a spirit boomerang is about to come to pass, that a ghost chased out the door will return through the window. If it can survive having its head chopped off, then no amount of bashing on the part of Paul D is likely to be decisive. I'd want to say that all this is encoded in the book's opening line: "124 was spiteful. Full of a baby's venom." But it takes a complete reading of the novel to validate that line.

Beloved is a very savvy work of art, and although it hardly seems postmodern or self-regarding, nonetheless it is stamped by a magisterial sense of narrative delivery. Morrison tells us just enough about the baby's death to whet our appetite but not enough for us fully to grasp what happened. This is not coyness. She has kept it from us, much the way Faulkner withheld the miscegenation argument from us in *Absalom, Absalom!*, and for exactly the same reasons: to give it to us only when we are in a position to understand its true significance. This is the single hardest and most profound literary issue in *Beloved:* how to narrate certain things—in this instance, awful things—in such a way that they will seem inevitable. My phrase sounds banal, I realize, because every writer is of course concerned with doing just that. But think of it from your angle, the reader's angle. When is it best for you to get information? When can you make real sense of it? Real sense, not dictionary sense? I proclaimed this to be a difficult narrative issue, and it is. Writers worry incessantly about such matters.

Need I also say that it is one of the most diabolic issues in human life in general? *When* do we understand the words we hear or read? At first hearing? When experience has validated them? When the people who told us are long dead? Teachers and parents know something about this dynamic, because they sense how easily their words to the young fail to get in, are not understood, are understood only in a dictionary sense. How can we make our words carry their truths, their existential truths? (How can we hear these truths in the words others pronounce to us?) All of this is what Morrison has tackled. She, following in Faulkner's wake, is displaying a rare talent for delayed disclosures, for time-release narrative that would package its information in such a way as to maximize its impact. And thereby make it real.

One of the (unacknowledged) goals of literature is to present readers verbally with a reality they cannot afford to experience literally. And there is much we cannot afford to experience: madness, death, murder. Franz Kafka once said that art is the ax that chops through our frozen sea, and he meant: Art pulls us out of our torpor, dismantles our defenses, makes us taste life's ultimacies. While remaining, preciously, art. Morrison wants us to understand slavery in this same virtual, experiential fashion, and our route must be through infanticide. Bit by bit, the reader sees this infanticide gathering shape and form, acquiring definition. Its dictionary meaning has never been difficult—to kill one's child—but its moral significance is something else again. As we navigate this book and encounter more and more of the hidden secrets harbored by these damaged people, we feel that we are moving ever closer to a clarity that would be spiritual as well as factual.

SPIRIT BECOMES FLESH

But what on earth are we to make of the sentence that opens page 50: "A fully dressed woman walked out of the water"? Whoa. Who walks out of water? This is happening *now.* This cool, almost metaphysical utterance could have been penned by Borges. There is nothing remotely like it in Proust, Joyce, and company. With great flair Morrison upends her sleuthing story, brings a new figure onto the stage, and puts us on notice that the rules have just changed. And all at once, we begin to realize that the novel is bubbling over at *both* ends: Our progress into the concealed past continues apace, but now things are happening in real time, in front of our eyes. Maybe the past is involved, yet it is hardly some background to be examined, but rather something taking shape impudently, shockingly, and hurtling directly into us, without warning or preparation of any sort, in mysterious human form.

Morrison describes this creature as if it came from another world, indeed, were made of different materials from ordinary people: She sits down all day and all night, everything (especially her lungs) hurts her, her eyelids are too heavy and can be kept open scarcely two minutes or more, her skin seems like "new skin, lineless and smooth" (51), her hands seem "soft and new" (52), and we will be told over and over that her head seems too heavy for her slim neck, and even—later, as both Denver and Sethe become increasingly attentive to her markings—that she has a scar on her neck. And her body seems to want to mutiny: She fears that her appendages—tooth, arm, hand, toe—are going to drop off, that her legs will become unattached to her hips, that she will wake up and find herself in pieces. She had two dreams: "exploding and being swallowed" (133). She has virtually no memory; her name is Beloved.

Beloved walks into the book on page 50 and stays for the duration. In so doing, she lifts this novel right out of any realist precincts we might still be holding on to, and ushers us as readers into a new regime altogether. On the one hand, as all readers quickly suspect, this strange girl is the key to every wrecked life in 124. The ghost returns, this time in the flesh, at the same age she would be if she had not died. But there is still more: Beloved is, as it were, the book's vertical axis; she reinstates its emotional wiring, its choked circuits, its longitudinal reach. We sense this at once, by the sensations Sethe experiences when, returning with Paul D and Denver from the carnival, she first lays eyes on the bizarre young woman waiting for her at home:

> And, for some reason she could not immediately account for, the moment she got close enough to see the face, Sethe's bladder filled to capacity. She said, "Oh, excuse me," and ran around to the back of 124. Not since she was a baby girl, being cared for by the eight-year-old girl who pointed out her mother to her, had she had an emergency that unmanageable. She never made the outhouse. Right in front of its door she had to lift her skirts, and the water she voided was endless. Like a horse, she thought, but as it went on and on she thought, No, more like flooding the boat when Denver was born. So much water Amy said, "Hold on, Lu. You going to sink us you keep that up." But there was no stopping water from a breaking womb and there was no stopping now. (51)

UMBILICAL WORLD

Joyce's presentation of both Stephen and Bloom in *Ulysses*, and Faulkner's rendition of Benjy and Quentin in *The Sound and the Fury*, are each cued to the umbilical cord that links present event to past trauma, making visible an emotional network of sorts that broadcasts the inner wiring and past history of each of these characters. Virtually anything can touch off Stephen's guilt at his mother's death, Bloom's remembrance of the deaths of father and son, of his wife's impending infidelity, or the vibrant, loving, heartbreaking image of Caddy, whose loss is torture for her two brothers. Yet my term "umbilical cord" is of course a metaphor when it comes to Joyce and Faulkner; but in Morrison that term seems literally correct: What is being shown by the narrative is a real umbilical cord, a conduit of flesh that unites mother and child, a conduit that reality only *seems* to have cut, discarded, forgotten, or repressed. Hence, it is not only the past that flows in when Sethe sees Beloved, but it is a very special past: the maternal past, the primordial scene of mother-daughter connection. Mind you, Sethe barely knew her mother—such was the fissured, atomized slavery scheme that this bond meant nothing to the white owner—and has only the slightest memories of a mysterious marked woman pointed out to her by the eight-year-old girl. How does one measure the consequences of this ruptured connection, this severed link? It seems to me that Morrison, like Stowe, sees it as the very signature of slavery, a disabling, perhaps crippling legacy that deprives the child of any living connection with origin. This wound can be healed only by reestablishing the broken circuit, recovering the lost mother line. Morrison does not present this as some kind of meditative process, but rather as a kind of unexpected explosion, a somatic event, an encounter that bursts through the closed doors, liberates the blocked memories, reshapes your contours, your story.

Hence, the sight of Beloved leads Sethe inexorably, via the flowing waters of womb and bladder, to the other vital maternal memory: that of Denver's birth, midwifed by the white girl Amy, taking place in a boat with water rushing in. These images of flowing water, far from being incidental, convey what is most visceral and profound about the novel. There are no hard edges, no viable boundaries, no clear and defining limits. Events are not over. The sight of Beloved reinstates the umbilical cord through which blood flows from mother to child. It thus follows that mother and child are, in some sense, a single unit that is beyond rupturing. Your child is always just that: your child. Is this not what Sethe means when she categorically rejects Paul D's assertion that Denver is "grown up": " 'Grown don't mean nothing to a mother. A child is a child. They get bigger, older, but grown?

What's that supposed to mean? In my heart it don't mean a thing' " (45). At first this sounds like a truism; but, on reflection, it is a provocative insight into the workings of the human heart: Time and space are transcended, and even if, in this book's plot, a child's throat is severed, the cord cannot be cut.

Hence Beloved enters this house, this family, and this book as the unsevered, unseverable bloodline that restores the mother-daughter bond, thereby altering everything we ever heard, thought, or believed about what is alive and what is dead; or what the purpose of fiction might be. Beloved's hunger for Sethe is insatiable: "Sethe was licked, tasted, eaten by Beloved's eyes" (57). She likes Denver, but Sethe is the one she has to have; her longing is "bottomless." That early line about the baby ghost's rage being equal to its mother's love is being replayed here, and shown to be reciprocal. And this child without memory nonetheless remembers impossible things, things only Sethe's dead child could have known. She asks Sethe where her diamonds are, leading to Sethe's remembrance of the special earrings she'd been given by Mrs. Garner as a wedding present, earrings she sewed into her dress when escaping from Sweet Home, earrings the little baby girl had "reached for . . . over and over again" (94) when Sethe finally made it across to freedom, to Baby Suggs's, where the baby girl and her brothers were waiting. She asks Sethe, " 'Your woman she never fix up your hair?' " leading to still further maternal memories, opening up blocked or clogged passages, going deeper and deeper *in*, culminating in the aching story of Sethe's last encounter with her mother:

> "One thing she did do. She picked me up and carried me behind the smokehouse. Back there she opened up her dress front and lifted her breast and pointed to it. Right on her rib was a circle and a cross burnt right in the skin. She said, 'This is your ma'am. This,' and she pointed. 'I am the only one got this mark now. The rest dead. If something happens to me and you can't tell me by my face, you can know me by this mark.' "(61)

This mother material, this vital connective tissue, telling us that even mutilated and deformed the mother-daughter bond is intact, comes into the novel as response to Beloved's questions. And the memory troubles Sethe deeply because it opens the door still further, bringing still more repressed material into the open, on the order of a hemorrhage where the blood cannot be stanched, immersing her in ever more past, extending the parameters of who she is. Sethe now remembers Nan, the one-armed woman who cared for her and spoke a strange language, waving the stump of her missing arm in the air, speaking in a forgotten code, a code Sethe is obliged now to decipher in her mind, to pick meaning out of:

> "Telling you. I am telling you, small girl Sethe," and she did that. She told Sethe that her mother and Nan were together from the sea. Both were taken up many times by the crew. "She threw them all away but you. The one from the crew she threw away on the island. The others from more whites she also threw away. Without names, she threw them. You she gave the name of the black man. She put her arms around him. The others she did not put her arms around. Never. Never. Telling you. I am telling you, small girl Sethe." (62)

The mother-daughter connection is no less than a bridge to the past, a bridge that leads us to the very mechanics and dynamics of the slave trade, now seen in their inhuman material and psychic squalor: to the routinized horrors of the middle passage, evoking a life of sexual thralldom, of countless babies thrown away, without names; but of one alone that was different, a baby that came from a consented union with a black man, one single baby that was not thrown away, that was kept. Here are Sethe's origins, and much is grisly: The mother she never knew other than as a marked woman whose last words were about recognition, and then still further the almost unimaginable exploitation that had to have been her mother's life as slave coming from Africa to America; and yet there is something luminous and beautiful as well in this message to "small girl Sethe," for it speaks of a chosen embrace, it offers a grounding for a life, it places Sethe into a human continuum of love and feeling. This is what Sethe miraculously had, but we must understand that it is also what the slave culture routinely denied and destroyed, and it is not fanciful to see the traces of this legacy of fissure and rupture and ungroundedness even in the black community of today.

Morrison helps us to see the largeness of these matters. One would be forgiven for conceiving of memory and consciousness as private realms, and the prodigious work of the Modernists shows us how capacious and unmapped those inner worlds might be. But *Beloved* takes a graver and more tragic look at these issues, telling us that the loss of a past, the fissuring of all connective tissue between mother and child, the "islanding" of the human subject that results from such removal and destruction, all this constitutes a kind of permanent disabling wound meted out to an entire people, an entire race. One cannot be a functional "I" if there is no prior "we" matrix. Your story is not the bounded chronicle of unfurling events that started with your birth and continues by tracking your moves: It is a cumulative plural form anchored in history, part of an ecosystem moving toward a mysterious future. But without the fuller ingredients, without the fuller circulation, there is no movement at all.

RED HEART

Beloved triggers Sethe's memory of her own mother; Beloved unites Sethe with her dead child, for she is (must be) the baby ghost turned flesh. That is the restored circuitry of this book. Denver has known it from the first moment she saw Beloved: This is my sister returned. Sethe's exploding bladder has told her the same thing. Beloved's insatiable hunger for Sethe, her scar on her neck, her humming of songs that Sethe alone knew and sang to her children: Everything conspires to tell us what the first page put in front of our eyes (if we had had the wit to see it). The dead child is not dead, the mother-daughter connection is indestructible. Beloved is the novel's red heart, its restored blood flow, its principle of linkage. Her role is umbilical. And in one of the most audacious sequences in the book, she plays the same bonding role for Paul D. There would appear to be no love lost between Paul D and Beloved, since her arrival essentially supplants his role in the group, and yet he feels her strange presence and power, feels it initially as a force that *moves* him, makes it impossible for him to sleep in Sethe's bed, sends him downstairs to the armchair, finally banishes him to the keeping room. And there he is visited at night. He tries to send her away, but she pleads that she wants to be touched on the inside part. He urges her to go back in the house and to bed. She says she'll go if he'll touch her and call her by her name:

> "Beloved." He said it, but she did not go. She moved closer with a footfall he didn't hear and he didn't hear the whisper that the flakes of rust made either as they fell away from the seams of his tobacco tin. So when the lid gave he didn't know it. What he knew was that when he reached

> the inside part he was saying, "Red heart. Red heart," over and over again. Softly and then so loud it woke Denver, then Paul D himself. "Red heart. Red heart. Red heart." (117)

Why audacious? Because sex between Beloved and Paul D along any predictable moral or psychological lines has to be seen as betrayal, as damaging. And do not think they don't have sex, repeatedly; at book's end, Beloved is big with child, and it has to be Paul D's. And yet, it is as if this intercourse mattered most for Morrison as an opening of closed circuits and clogged channels, as a way of bringing Paul D to some form of fuller circulation, enabling him to open that rusted tobacco tin, to reclaim his red heart, to reclaim his life. And of course to reclaim hers as well, to move toward ownership by bringing together what was fissured, including flesh and name. A large project is coming into view.

DISMEMBERING, REMEMBERING

Once we understand Beloved's role as cardiac principle, as restored blood flow that enables these damaged human beings to retrieve their blocked memories, to put back together the bonds that slavery and fate have sundered, then we see the grandeur of Toni Morrison's design as well as the depth of her analysis. She has understood slavery itself as the systematic dismantling of human connections, the atomizing of the human subject, the piecing apart of the human family. Here is a crime that is almost immeasurable in its ramifications. It abolishes memory, relationship, and integrity. It annihilates the *proprietary* in every possible sense of the term. It drastically reifies and chops the black subject, denying him or her all reach. Morrison's characters in this novel—Sethe, Paul D, Denver, Beloved herself, Baby Suggs, Stamp Paid, Ella, all of them—are the most despoiled figures in Western literature, for their lives have been robbed of the density and breadth and web of human relations that we take for granted as the condition of life.

I don't quite know how to put this issue in such a way that it acquires its full resonance. All of us are born into a mesh of sorts, have an extended network—parents, siblings, community, society, country—that defines our outer boundaries, that gives a measure of our larger reach. Could you imagine being *only your body*? And love adds immeasurably to this original scheme, since marriage and love relations are precisely extensions of self, the creation of a composite form, a form where we invest our emotions and that redefines who we are, what our larger shape is. These linkages are also to be understood as temporal: We think back to our own pasts, to our parents and ancestors; and we think forward through our children and descendants. All of this is what slavery destroys, annihilates. It makes you a cipher. For the slave market, you are a fixed item, including those features of you that are hard to measure, as Paul D realizes: "The dollar value of his weight, his strength, his heart, his brain, his penis, and his future" (226).

I confess that I do not know how to present this point with the power and pathos it deserves. But Toni Morrison has done exactly that. What I have termed her "genius for storytelling" is essentially a brilliance in showing just what these truncated, severed, amputated, fissured lives are like. Human love is the first target and casualty. Paul D reenters Sethe's life, embraces her, cradles her breasts, and she experiences "this temptation to trust and remember" as a feeling of extreme danger, of risk: "Would it be all right? Would it be all right to go ahead and feel? Go ahead and *count on something?*" (38). Counting on something means a basic belief in stability and futurity, that the one you love today—husband, parent, child—will not be yanked away tomorrow. What is love if not a form of delicious freedom enabling you to cast your lot, your heart, with another person? Paul D has learned, the hard way, just how life-threatening such an investment would be:

> So you protected yourself and loved small. Picked the tiniest stars out of the sky to own; lay down with head twisted in order to see the loved one over the rim of the trench before you slept. Stole shy glances at her between the trees at chain-up. Grass blades, salamanders, spiders, woodpeckers, beetles, a kingdom of ants. Anything bigger wouldn't do. A woman, a child, a brother—a big love like that would split you wide open in Alfred, Georgia. He knew exactly what she meant: to get to a place where you could love anything you chose—not to need permission for desire—well now, *that* was freedom. (162)

It is an amazing passage, for it graphs the pitiful dimensions, the drastic emotional economics of slave life, the reduced scope of the heart, the way all beating hearts must become rusted tobacco tins within this dispensation.

(It illuminates, by contrast, an entire slew of invisible privileges that one takes for granted, as the unthreatened bounty of life.) Paul D is responding precisely to Sethe's declaration of how she felt once she crossed the waters and got to freedom. Her words were: "There wasn't nobody in the world I couldn't love if I wanted to. You know what I mean?" (162). He knew what she meant. The burden of the novel, the reason for its complex form and its savvy parceling out of information, is to ensure that we, too, know what she means.

THE HOLY BODY

Doubtless the most lyrical if wrenching description of the dismembered, ripped-apart, mutilated life within slavery is to be found in Baby Suggs's magnificent tribute to human flesh:

> "Here," she said, "in this place, we flesh; flesh that weeps, laughs; flesh that dances on bare feet in grass. Love it. Love it hard. Yonder they do not love your flesh. They despise it. They don't love your eyes; they'd just as soon pick em out. No more do they love the skin on your back. Yonder they flay it. And O my people they do not love your hands. Those they only use, tie, bind, chop off and leave empty. Love your hands! Love them. Raise them up and kiss them. Touch others with them, pat them together, stroke them on your face 'cause they don't love that either. *You* got to love it, *you!* And no, they ain't in love with your mouth. Yonder, out there, they will see it broken and break it again. What you say out of it they will not heed. What you scream from it they do not hear. What you put into it to nourish your body they will snatch away and give you leavins instead. No, they don't love your mouth. *You* got to love it. This is flesh I'm talking about here. Flesh that needs to be loved. Feet that need to rest and dance; backs that need support; shoulders that need arms, strong arms I'm telling you. And O my people, out yonder, hear me, they do not love your neck unnoosed and straight. So love your neck; put a hand on it, grace it, stroke it and hold it up. And all your inside parts that they'd just as soon slop for hogs, you got to love them. The dark, dark liver—love it, love it, and the beat and beating heart, love that too. More than eyes or feet. More than lungs

> that have yet to draw free air. More than your life-holding womb and your life-giving private parts, hear me now, love your heart. For this is the prize. (88–89)

It is probably the most glorious speech in this eloquent novel, and achieves a resonance that seems to leave even Morrison's own other work in the dust. Building on a masterful rhetoric in which the body's parts are at once evoked in their functional beauty—for nourishment, tenderness, utterance, love—and simultaneously exposed as targets of the slave owners—picking out eyes, flaying skin, binding and chopping off hands, breaking mouths, noosing necks—Morrison essentially grounds her entire novel by translating slavery out of all abstractions and into a deeply moving somatic register. In so doing, she exposes the horror of this system in its entirety, because nature's plan is inverted, and we see a kind of monstrous deformation and misuse at work here, a wreckage of natural potential and pleasure, an insult to God as well as man. For this book is a hymn to the body as divine: It celebrates the body's possibilities while inventorying the systematic manipulation of the body that is slavery's signature. And more still: It is a paean to human integrity, to wholeness, now understood as a consort—the complete body, the harmonious body, the loved body—that is at once spiritual and physical; that wholeness is what slavery seeks most to destroy.

Toni Morrison's signature resides, I think, in this bold act of translation from the abstract to the somatic. She seeks to display the scandal of slavery, its crime against nature, and she therefore threads into her severe and often violent book scenes of great tenderness, so that we can see the shimmering alternative to the butchery she is chronicling: Sethe and Halle's lovemaking in the cornfield on their wedding day, Paul D's caressing of Sethe's destroyed back, Amy Denver's massaging of Sethe's swollen feet and instrumental help in the delivery of Denver, Baby Suggs's ministering to Sethe's bloody wounds, even Stamp Paid's wrapping of the infant in his own nephew's clothes or his inserting the precious blackberries into the baby's mouth at party time. The body has a wisdom prior to that of the mind. We learn this when Sethe's waters are released at the sight of her returned dead baby; Paul D sees it in the strange shining of Beloved, who wants to be mated; Baby Suggs receives the premature infant and instructs the woman helping her "not to clean the eyes till she got the mother's urine" (92). The sanctity of the human body, the ethos of a *physical* kindness, the wisdom of a nurturing corporeal culture merge to yield a shocking (and utterly unsentimental) poetry. The whipped body creates flowers, roses of blood that blossom; the body speaks through the language of flowers, the dream-sucking of infants, the flow of its liquids.

Toni Morrison has always excelled at writing the body, at giving us a somatic world that seems both prior to and beyond the abstractions that too often parade as reality. One reads all her books, I think, with a kind of surprised assent, a rewarding sense that she has her fingers on the human pulse, that she knows which things are the first things. But the outright carnal wisdom of *Beloved* puts it in a class by itself. She is, in some sense, lifting the veil, restoring to us the physical immediacy and beauty of our own corporeal existence. And I believe we are in her debt for such illumination, because that fleshly regime—eyes, hands, arms, mouth, back, neck, lungs, and heart—may well be the bedrock of human life, but it is rarely front and center either in our literature or in our minds themselves. We have always known our bodies to be the site of both pleasure and pain, but we all too easily lose sight of this mix of flesh and blood when we conceptualize our moral or spiritual values. In this regard, Morrison adds something precious to our notion of story and self, because she understands them both to be, first and foremost, from beginning to end, *embodied.*

THE MILK OF HUMAN KINDNESS

Liquids. This is the most liquid novel I have ever read. Think, for a moment, of how most organized prose operates: in contoured units, blocks of information, logical development, conceptual design, extended argument. From school onward, we are taught to write and to think in this structured way. Yet one could argue that human life does not proceed along such lines, certainly not in any experiential sense, certainly not in terms of the testimony of consciousness and feeling. Morrison offers us something else entirely: The world flows through us, and we flow through the world. Memory, desire, sensation: All move in this fashion. Reality is fluid; reality is fluids. Hence, in *Beloved,* blood and urine and milk are shockingly highlighted as the central pathways and currents of human life and love. Perhaps milk is the most astonishing of all. What could better convey the connectedness of humankind, of mothers and their children, than the milk that infants suckle? No better way on earth to demonstrate the meaning of our poor words such as "nourishment" or "sustenance" than to focus on lactation itself, and on nursing, for they constitute the natural fluid connection that follows the exit of baby from womb, replacing the umbilical cord that served the same purpose in utero, linking body to body, heart to heart. For just this reason, how could you better illustrate the ravages and violations of slavery than by having two white boys assault the pregnant, lactating mother (six months pregnant with Denver, but lactating still for the new baby who is in safe keeping, whom she must reach) and taking her milk. Twice Sethe exclaims to Paul D, when they first meet and she relates her past travails, " 'And they took my milk' " (17). Does he really understand? Do we, the readers? Here is a taboo as transgressive as incest: the white invasion of the black body, the theft of its precious fluids, the sabotaging of nature's plan, the violation of the mother.

And yet even this does not stop this intrepid woman; she births her baby, crosses the waters, reaches her other infant and two young boys, and delivers her milk. She must think herself virtually ordained; it is as if Moses had entered the Promised Land. As she later puts it to Paul D, " 'I was big, Paul D, and deep and wide and when I stretched out my arms all my children could get in between. I was *that* wide' " (162). Deep and wide; a mother, a river, a continent: so many ways of expressing the sanctity and integrity and dimensionality of the human family. Knowing the mutilations that slavery consists of, that this novel's characters have suffered, we can perhaps understand both the pleasure Sethe experiences and the lengths to which she will go to safeguard this new life of freedom.

LETHAL LOVE

Our understanding matters, because all Morrison's art has been invested in bringing *us* into the interior, causing us to know and gauge the ravages both suffered and overcome. Initially in driblets, then in ever-larger chunks, as we have seen, the horrendous slave past emerges in this novel: emerges from the repressed depths of the characters' minds, emerges onto the page for the reader's comprehension. What exactly are we supposed to comprehend? The answer, at least in one regard, is shockingly simple: We are supposed to understand why a mother would murder her child. I believe this to be the deepest rationale for the narrative choices that Morrison has made. We are not only to understand, but in some frightening way to ratify, Sethe's violent deed.

It has been pointed out that *Beloved*'s infanticide plot bears some resemblance to the actions of Medea in Euripides' play. Each text centers on a crazed woman killing her child(ren). Yet it is as if Morrison had decided that Euripides did a poor job of grounding his terrible plot; so she unpacks this deed, sees it as logical rather than crazed, shows how you might end up in a situation where it is the inevitable act you perform, and ends up making it far more terrifying (because more cogent) than it is in the Greek play. Sethe kills her baby to save it.

I have already asserted that *difficult love* is Morrison's signature theme, and this novel is its supreme manifestation. But the issue is hardly that of mere psychology. Morrison has seen that the truest account of the slave system, the most accurate and adequate way of demonstrating what it really is, is to give a longitudinal account of what it produces in its victims. Longitudinal: By this, I mean the temporal curve that starts with what is done to us and finishes with what we do as result. There is no other way to understand the reality of trauma, indeed of all decisive influences on human behavior. Here is where art's picture of human behavior trumps other discourses, especially journalism and even most historical writing, inasmuch as all too often we read of deeds and events that come to us as *done*, but strangely flat and unmotivated, and hence easy to (mis)judge and then to dismiss. Morrison offers us findings of a different stamp.

Morrison wants to change our understanding of what life or death portends. Slavery would be the set of arrangements that is so terrible that death is preferable. Death for one's children. One thing, perhaps, to *say* something like this; but much harder for a mother to act out this preference. One has to wonder how many mothers have committed infanticide? Surely the numbers are in excess of any data we might have. And I submit that the logic behind such atrocities is almost always, in some ultimate sense, political, not psychological; that is, when circumstances are so dreadful that death is better than life. It is a hard lesson, but it is a lesson: We can learn from it (as from nothing else) just how dreadful circumstances really were. Morrison is a great teacher. *Teacher.* The text's most unforgettable villain is doubtless Schoolteacher with his notebook and measuring stick, his refusal of humanity to his slaves. But other forms of learning exist. Terrible acts instruct. The novel as a whole wants to teach us that love is the hallowing of human connection even at the cost of murder.

The black hole at the core of *Beloved* is the murder of the baby girl. Data, as I have said, is given—to us, to Paul D (for all the others know)—at the outset, but it is given cagily, sparingly, vaguely. To be sure, there is a baby ghost; and we know as well that Sethe and Denver are ostracized, that no one ever comes their way; and that Howard and Buglar did not so much leave as escape, out of fear that perhaps their mother might kill them, too; and Denver, having shared a jail experience with Sethe in the aftermath, has also experienced a stint of deafness when a schoolmate brought up the issue of mother-the-murderess; and Baby Suggs's belief in life and future is poisoned by this event, leading to her death. Yet all of these indices are still, in some important sense, nothing but aftereffects. What is missing, what must eventually be narrated when all parties are ready for it, is the event itself, the bloody event with its heinous internal logic.

And the author rises to the challenge. She opens the first crucial narration of the murder with these chilling words: "When the four horsemen came—schoolteacher, one nephew, one slave catcher and a sheriff—the house on Bluestone Road was so quiet they thought they were too late" (148). We are by now two-thirds of our way into the novel, primed to understand this fateful event, an event of such gravity that it warrants the unaccented allusion to the Four Horsemen of the Apocalypse. Then, amazingly enough in this novel that has so little interest in white folks as such, the narrative is entrusted precisely to these white horsemen whose expectations and responses are hideously and perfectly rendered. We start with the musings of the slave catcher, a wary man who has learned in his career that runaways are diabolically unpredictable in their behavior, that they will all of a sudden make a run for it or put up a fight when the odds are quite impossible for them, and "commence to do disbelievable things" (148). "Disbelievable": not a bad term for what is to follow.

Continuing to write from their alien and uncomprehending perspective, Morrison presents, in virtually cinematic fashion, a scene in which nothing makes sense:

> A crazy old nigger was standing in the woodpile with an ax. You could tell he was crazy right off because he was grunting—making low, catlike noises. About twelve yards beyond that nigger was another one—

> a woman with a flower in her hat. Crazy too, probably, because she too was standing stock-still—but fanning her hands as though pushing cobwebs out of her way. Both, however, were staring at the same place—a shed. Nephew walked over to the old nigger boy and took the ax from him. Then all four started toward the shed.
>
> Inside, two boys bled in the sawdust and dirt at the feet of a nigger woman holding a blood-soaked child to her chest with one hand and an infant by the heels in the other. She did not look at them; she simply swung the baby toward the wall planks, missed and tried to connect a second time, when out of nowhere—in the ticking time the men spent staring at what there was to stare at—the old nigger boy, still mewing, ran through the door behind them and snatched the baby from the arch of its mother's swing. (149)

Our gaze is led, almost in Hitchcock fashion, to the shed, the scene of the crime. One blood-soaked child and another swinging toward the wall: violence to the body on a scale equal to slavery itself, seemingly re-creating slavery's horrors, but meted out by mother to offspring. Morrison writes it as graphic notation, seen the way a camera—or a white man—would see it. Schoolteacher's response to the scene is spot-on in its grasp of this man's genuine racist beliefs: "There was nothing here to claim. The three (now four—because she'd had the one coming when she cut) pickaninnies they had hoped were alive and well enough to take back to Kentucky, take back and raise properly to do the work Sweet Home desperately needed, were not" (149). *Properly:* the God-given place of black slave children is on white farms. Moreover, he sees in Sethe's act a kind of pragmatic moral lesson: She was earlier whipped so fiercely by the nephew that she'd "gone wild," proving that one must think carefully about the consequences of whipping slaves, just as one considers such matters in disciplining hounds, because if you go too far, they just won't be reliable any longer. As for the nephew, he is genuinely undone by what he sees: He trembles uncontrollably, thinks over and over, "What she go and do that for?" (150). He remembers beatings he has received, but never could he have . . . "I mean no way he could have . . . What she go and do that for?" Morrison insistently stresses just how incoherent this is. Can it be understood? By whites or by blacks?

Paul D can't. Of course he was not there, but now, in the present, Stamp Paid shows him a photo of Sethe from the newspaper account eighteen years before, and he says it is not her. Not her. Not possible. Stamp chooses to keep to himself "how she flew, snatching up her children like a hawk on the wing, how her face beaked, how her hands worked like claws, how she collected them every which way: one on her shoulder, one under her arm, one by the hand, the other shouted forward into the woodshed . . ." (157). The images in Stamp's mind matter. One remembers the depiction of Eva Peace in *Sula* as huge bird, as swinging and swooping heron that burns up her son in his bed and leaps out the window to try to save her burning daughter. Perhaps there is no human scale imaginable here. Paul D, incredulous, confronts Sethe with Stamp's article and photo. He wants to know (as we want to know) what actually happened. She begins to spin, almost like a trapped animal, circling ever faster about the room, as if driven by unknown pulsions, telling her man how it felt to manage her escape, to give birth, at last to be free, reunited with all her children, "I was *that* wide." He still cannot understand.

And then, at long last, offering us the "narrative redemption" that finally turns fact into human truth, Morrison goes to the heart of the matter and tells us what Sethe herself saw, felt, and did:

> Simple: she was squatting in the garden and when she saw them coming and recognized schoolteacher's hat, she heard wings. Little hummingbirds stuck their needle beaks right through her headcloth into her hair and beat their wings. And if she thought anything, it was No. No. Nono. Nonono. Simple. She just flew. Collected every bit of life she had made, all the parts of her that were precious and fine and beautiful, and carried, pushed, dragged them through the veil, out, away, over there where no one could hurt them. Over there. Outside this place, where they would be safe. (163)

Again the birds are there: little hummingbirds, wings, beaks. World of fable. Birds, not people. It is distinctly possible to say this murder is off the charts, is not amenable to any form of human logic.

THROUGH THE VEIL

But everything I have tried to show in my account of *Beloved* goes entirely the other way; metaphor and fable are brought in to convey the deepest human truth that Morrison wants to tell: Sethe killed them to save them; she put them in another place altogether. Note how we move, in that passage, from birds to something else: collecting what is most precious and then carrying, pushing, and dragging them "through the veil, out, away, over there where no one could hurt them." Do not for a minute confuse this with some kind of primitive religious belief or naiveté on Sethe's part. We are talking about slavery and the human heart. Sethe's knowledge of the absolute evil of slavery is so total that it gives birth to its counterpart: another place, a beyond, a realm where the children will be safe, unhurt and free. Slavery dirties slaves so completely that murder cleanses. We are talking about slavery and the human heart. About the epistemology it creates, about the countertruth it can yield: transcendence, salvation, a space beyond the so-called real world. This "spiritual" world is not something Sethe is given, it is something Sethe makes. And it is made by the heart, the same heart that Baby Suggs prized above all else. The heart puts back together the pieced-apart world that slavery would destroy: the mutilated body, the fissured mind, the separated family, the lost and dead, the here and the beyond. Love, what Sethe is to call "thick love," overcomes time and space and, finally, death. It is a new cosmology, beyond anything Morrison ever imagined in the earlier books.

THE COSMOLOGY OF "THICK LOVE"

Paul D is understandably confused. Sethe is operating according to laws he cannot fathom: "This here Sethe talked about safety with a handsaw. This here new Sethe didn't know where the world stopped and she began" (164). It is a brave new world utterly unlike anything in Proust, Joyce, Woolf, or Faulkner. In this scheme, the old dispensations no longer hold sway. Paul D retorts that her love is "too thick," and the sublime answer is: " 'Too thick? . . . Love is or it ain't. Thin love ain't love at all' " (164). Paul D retorts again, " 'Yeah, it didn't work, did it? Did it work?' " And again the sublime answer is: " 'It worked.' " He retorts again: " 'How? Your boys gone you don't know where. One girl dead, the other won't leave the yard. How did it work?' " Once more the answer comes: " 'They ain't at Sweet Home. Schoolteacher ain't got 'em' " (164–165). *And the novel is on her side.* It has been on her side from the beginning. That is what we are finally supposed to understand. From the spiteful baby ghost to the woman who walks out of the water, from the stolen milk to the crossing of the waters, from the prison of Sweet Home to the wide, wide mother-world and its way station "over there" on the other side of the veil, *Beloved* is about the territorial reality of spirit and love. Those are the laws that govern this novel. And if you call this some form of magical realism, you have not understood the new ethos, the new metaphysic at hand.

Are we simply to assume that Morrison has opted to give us some kind of a fairy tale? (Strange fairy tale, this.) I think not. No, instead, she is reinventing narrative so as to take the measure of what slavery portends. No pedestrian code of realism will suffice. If the novel's great *hidden* story is the murder of the baby—a hidden story I have done my utmost to highlight—then its equally great unfurling story is the arrival of "the woman from the water" into this previously haunted house, taking her rightful place as the dead child brought back to life. No more excavating; time now for miracles. We watch, bewitched, as this strange young woman fills out her fated role, reenters the family, plays with Denver, hungers for Sethe, challenges all our assumptions of the living and the dead, about murder as end or beginning. We think: This cannot be possible, but it is beautiful beyond belief. We think: This is the true victory over slavery—to reconnect what was fissured. We think: Love does redraw the map, remake the world, redesign things according to its higher dictates.

THE MYSTERY OF BELOVED

Or do we? I am not a great fan of science fiction, and I have little fondness for anything smacking of New Age culture or beliefs. Even magical realism gives me pause. My assumptions about what is real and unreal are very close to those of the mystified Paul D. And I suspect that your views as well—you the reader—are scarcely in phase with the revealed laws of Morrison's book. And we wonder how this magic solution—if it is that—is going to play out. Will it lead to a utopian reunion in which all the players live together happily ever after? *If* the dead child returns alive to its mother, what then? What do they say to each other? How to explain what happened? These issues are going to loom large. Magic solutions create as many problems as they solve.

But are things so straightforward? Is it really the dead child? Early on, there are signs that Beloved may have origins unrelated to Sethe. She tells

Denver of living in an airless place, with no room to move in, surrounded by "heaps" of people, some of them dead, and having escaped in order "to see her [Sethe's] face." This sounds like a slave ship. But there are other indices as well, equally unsettling and destabilizing, concerning Beloved's possible past. Early on, while they are all trying to figure out who this bizarre half-amnesiac creature might be, we are told of a very different sort of putative origin for Beloved:

> She [Sethe] believed Beloved had been locked up by some whiteman for his own purposes, and never let out the door. That she must have escaped to a bridge or someplace and rinsed the rest out of her mind. Something like that had happened to Ella except it was two men—a father and son—and Ella remembered every bit of it. For more than a year, they kept her locked in a room for themselves. (119)

Stamp Paid, hearing of Beloved for the first time, thinks along the same lines: " 'Was a girl locked up in the house with a whiteman over by Deer Creek. Found him dead last summer and the girl gone. Maybe that's her. Folks say he had her in there since she was a pup' " (235). What are we to believe? How can these figures be the same? Why all these alternatives?

Yes, Beloved could be (a) Sethe's dead child brought back to life, (b) someone with a memory of an airless room and dead corpses, or (c) someone kept by a vicious white man in a cellar as sexual slave. And, at some poetic level, the reader may well feel that all these variants are true; one could say—and critics have said it—that the strange, dazed young woman appearing out of nowhere is a well-nigh perfect symbolic figure for *all* the children taken and despoiled by slavery. But this is a novel, not a myth. Sethe is not interested in these grand theories. And neither is Beloved herself. Nor is Denver. Multiple choice doesn't apply to emotions. Sethe and Denver are fierce literalists: For them, Beloved has come home. The family unit has been miraculously restored. The armature of the atom has been made intact again. It must remain forever inviolable.

THE REUNITED FAMILY: INSATIABLE NEEDS

And that is how the plot moves: Paul D, repulsed by the story of the murder, falls from grace and exits 124, leaving a community of three women behind. Sethe becomes ever more persuaded that this is how it was meant to be: a reunited family with no need for outsiders. With no need even for outside: "Whatever is going on outside my door ain't for me. The world is in this room. This here's all there is and all there needs to be" (183). Stamp Paid comes by twice and feels locked out each time, as though this were an enclave that could admit no newcomer whatsoever. Injured by the world, damaged survivors of evil, Sethe and her two daughters take permanent refuge *inside*. "When Sethe locked the door, the women inside were free at last to be what they liked, see whatever they saw and say whatever was on their minds" (199). These words connote the utopian, paradisal (even if claustrophobic) aura of this turn of events: At long last, Emancipation is at hand and freedom is real. What is there left to say?

The answer is: everything. Here is where Morrison shows her true colors. Yes, Sethe, Denver, and Beloved are now free to "say whatever was on their minds," but those minds are tragically unattuned to one another, for each is mired in its own awful history. If we have ever thought that *going in* resolves things, that one's inner story might be shared, Morrison dispels that illusion. Denver, who has seen it as her mission to protect Beloved at all costs, even against her own mother, comes to realize that things are getting terribly wrong, terribly skewed. Sethe now focuses obsessively on Beloved and her needs, gives her all the attention and love that the murder cut short, giving her the food off her plate and the clothes off her back, ingratiating herself, taking abuse from her, becoming virtually a slave to her daughter. Denver finds herself excluded, of no importance in this final reckoning. And the talking! Now that the dead baby is back, Sethe can at last make amends for what she did, explain what she did and why she did it, convince Beloved that she killed her to save her. (Imagine explaining this.) Killed her out of love. But Beloved has her own strange story to tell, her own raging hurt and hunger to assuage, and nothing Sethe says or does seems sufficient or, much worse, even relevant. This final reunion, this miraculous second go-around—cheating death of its reward, saying at last the love you felt, retrieving the past, undoing its horror, achieving connection—is going amok, is en route to being the ultimate torture:

> The best chair, the biggest piece, the prettiest plate, the brightest ribbon for her hair, and the more she [Beloved] took, the more Sethe began to talk, explain, describe how much she had suffered, been through, for

> her children, waving away flies in grape arbors, crawling on her knees to a lean-to. None of which made the impression it was supposed to. Beloved accused her of leaving her behind. Of not being nice to her, not smiling at her. She said they were the same, had the same face, how could she have left her? And Sethe cried, saying she never did, or meant to—that she had to get them out, away, that she had the milk all the time and had the money too for the stone but not enough. That her plan was always that they would all be together on the other side, forever. Beloved wasn't interested. She said when she cried there was no one. That dead men lay on top of her. That she had nothing to eat. Ghosts without skin stuck their fingers in her and said beloved in the dark and bitch in the light. Sethe pleaded for forgiveness, counting, listing again and again her reasons: that Beloved was more important, meant more to her than her own life. That she would trade places any day. Give up her own life, every minute and hour of it, to take back just one of Beloved's tears. Did she know it hurt her when the mosquitoes bit her baby? That to leave her on the ground to run into the big house drove her crazy. That before leaving Sweet Home Beloved slept every night on her chest or curled on her back? Beloved denied it. Sethe never came to her, never said a word to her, never smiled and worst of all never waved goodbye or even looked her way before running away from her. (241–242)

I have quoted this passage at length because there is something almost unbearable in this perfect cacophony, this exquisite mismatch, this litany of love offered and love denied, a singsong uttered with total sincerity by each player, a duet doomed to frustration and discord. All the repressed guilt and maternal love stored up during eighteen years in Sethe's ghostly heart is pouring out here, all the things she has never said are at last being expressed: her motherly tenderness, her painful past efforts to protect her baby, her unbearable remorse, a dirge of recalled devotion. And to no avail. Her pleas fall on deaf ears. But the same is true of Beloved: her rock-bottom certainty of abandonment and betrayal, of her mother leaving her without smiling after stealing her face, of some hard-to-specify stint of sexual defilement at the hands of white men, this inner torment is at last given full voice, turned into story, into reproach, and is equally unmet, ununderstood, even, I think, unheard.

WHY ALL THE BELOVEDS?

For years I read this passage (and others like it) as the final evidence that Beloved is *not* Sethe's dead child come back. For it is obvious that the two stories here do not mesh. This is stupendous: It signifies that the novel is less magical, less of a fable than one had thought. No poetic remaking of life. Instead, we have mistake, confusion, and misconception. It suggests a kind of almost Shakespearean deception and charade, a tragedy of errors, entailing the encounter of a childless mother and a motherless child, but a false encounter, a bogus fit—the wrong child, the wrong mother—and hence doomed to frustration, recrimination, endless beseeching and pleading, bitterness. But ask yourself: Why has Morrison written it this way? To stay honest in terms of real life where miracles do not usually happen? To suggest that her story of a "returnee" is a glorious illusion, doomed to finish badly? Then ask yourself further: But what about the baby ghost? What about the undeniable evidence that the dead infant continues to exist in some virulent form, even if the woman from the water is someone else altogether? Is it possible that Morrison is actually trying to have it both ways? To offer us both a poetic and a prosaic account of events? (Hawthorne did such things all the time, leaving it open, covering his bets, so to speak.)

I have been turning these issues around in my brain for close to two decades now, ever since I first read the novel when it appeared. My initial grasp of the book was simple: a beautiful (incredible?) fable of reunion past death. And I believe that is the reading the book inevitably gets, the first time. Then, later, thanks to the perspicuity of my wife, who pointed out that things are more complex, I realized the bizarre yet crucial misfit between Sethe and Beloved. So here is how I now see it. First of all, this is not a whodunit. Nor is it a story of mistaken identity in any ordinary sense. Morrison has put this turn of the screw into her book in order to extract the absolute maximum of suffering and pain out of it. For Sethe and Beloved are in an impossible bind: Each believes the other to be what she lost, the missing child or mother whose absence is the tragic event of her life. Yet they are destined to speak at cross-purposes, to be mistaken in their claim, and never to know it. It is a cruel twist, for there can be no reconciliation, no solution, no balm for the wounds life has inflicted. The story of the two women seeking from each other an impossible absolution is close to crucifixion.

But Morrison is not primarily interested in torture as such. I believe she has wanted to show just how deep the slave system goes, how monstrously it impacts the emotions and lives of those who survive it, how much its wounds cry out for healing, how impossible the hunger for love is that it leaves in its awful wake. Nothing can be made right. That is the legacy at its purest. And in this severe depiction of injury and impossible redress, Morrison moves perhaps beyond even slavery, and offers us a parable that might speak to the open wounds and unhealed injuries of our own later moment: the legacies of the Holocaust, of the disappeared in regimes that have practiced genocide, of the victims of ethnic cleansing of our own contemporary moment. *Beloved* seeks not only to comprehend injury and carnage on an unimaginable scale, but also to gauge the psychic wounds left in their wake, the arduousness (perhaps the outright impossibility) of understanding, the need to find forms of grieving and mourning that would somehow move the victims out of their Calvary and toward some kind of healing. These are large-souled matters, well beyond the ambitions of Morrison's other fictions, and arguably beyond the reach of any fiction. Moreover, Toni Morrison is not programmatic, does not have a specific agenda; she is a novelist. And she—as successor to Proust, Joyce, Woolf, and Faulkner—has elected to go *in*, to dive into the wreck that we call slavery so as to offer us a ravaged landscape unlike any we know, one of routinized mutilations so horrible that the red heart either dies or makes an alternate world of its own. This last, I think, is what Sethe has done: She took her baby through the veil to save her from slavery.

Is this possible? *Murderous love.* Can anything get past this? Morrison's ghosts and her fable of magic homecoming make everything harder, not easier. Opening one's heart and having one's say alleviate nothing, but darken things still further. As we have seen, peace and forgiveness are impossible because the wounded players are miscast. Moreover, energies of such vehemence and intensity have been let loose by this reunion plot that the figures now move full circle in their impossible dance: Like a ghastly allegory of inverted motherhood, of maternal power turned inside out, what we see is a frightening metamorphosis of mother and daughter, the one shrinking and the other growing, the one giving and the other taking. With this fateful turn, Morrison goes beyond anything Harriet Beecher Stowe ever imagined, and creates the ultimate nightmare. None of the "voyages in"—some radiant, some indicting—that we have seen earlier in Proust, Joyce, Woolf, and Faulkner is as twisted, bleak, and cannibalistic as this.

With vampirish logic, Morrison shows us how this mother/child drama of inexpiable guilt and insatiable hunger has to close: The avenging child bids to absorb, to swallow the mother altogether.

ENTER THE COMMUNITY, EXIT THE GHOST

Denver, reduced to the role of horrified spectator, acts to break the spell, and does so by heroically reentering the society from which she had hidden ever since the murder. She goes *out* of 124. We watch her pick up the social threads that had been cut, as she solicits gifts of food to feed her crazed mother and sister. Morrison now enlists for her out-of-control story (of devouring daughter and shrinking mother) the residual goodwill of a black community that was said to be partly responsible for the catastrophe in the first place by dint of its resentment of Baby Suggs and company, a resentment that prevented anyone from warning Sethe of the impending arrival of the four horsemen.

At the book's close, the community returns to save its pariah, to prevent the almost mad Sethe from a second murder (of the generous, genteel white owner of her house, en route to the house he had been born in but had not seen for thirty years). She sees a white man coming (again, again) into her space, and the infernal machine goes back into gear: wings, hummingbirds, needle beaks, no, nono, nonono. As if we were watching a Hitchcock film, we are frozen as we see her fly toward the intruder with an ice pick in her hands. But the community intervenes, prevents the catastrophe, and breaks the spell that has been building for some time now. In my view, these final pages of community support seem forced and maybe even a tad sentimental in their upbeat ambience, but I can see that Morrison wants very much to reorient her story before it's over, to find a way to reintegrate her exiled characters back into the human family, which means: to rupture the mesmerizing spell that holds Sethe and Beloved locked together in a dance of death. It is as if the unleashed forces of the slavery saga were so powerful, so unresolvable, that it became necessary to close up shop.

Denver, we now know, is launched into the world. Beloved, big-bellied, soon-to-be-mother herself, disappears from the scene, escapes into the woods, leaves the human realm, is later seen (by a little boy) naked with fish for hair. And Sethe is broken. The very last pages of the book stage Paul D's efforts to put some pieces back together, to salvage her and his life with her. With characteristic sweetness and gentleness, he caresses her, offers to rub her feet and soothe her tired body, tries to make her relinquish her crazed maternal mission and to believe in herself again. To her lament, " 'She left me. . . . She was my best thing' " (272), he finds the right words to bring this visionary book to an earthly close: " 'Sethe,' he says, 'me and you, we got more yesterday than anybody. We need some kind of tomorrow' " (273), then adding as he touches her face, " 'You your best thing, Sethe. You are' " (273). It is the right way to finish.

BEYOND SELF

But it is not the way I want to finish this discussion, because the power and beauty of this novel reside in its madness, not its sanity. That madness consists in a view of thick love that defies all of our received ideas about self and other, life and death, spirit and flesh. The baby ghost on the first page ushers us into an umbilical world of human connection that nothing can sever. Baby Suggs's plaint of the pieced-apart body posits love as the counterforce, the binding force that reconfigures the world, for *red heart* is the book's cardiac principle, yielding a pulsing waterway of blood, urine, and milk that knows only connection, only linkage, that strives for nurturance. "We flesh," Baby says, and the novel bears her out: Beyond anything written by the Modernist giants, *Beloved* is a story of bodies. Sometimes they are maimed bodies: Sethe's ripped-apart back, Paul D's bit-filled mouth, the torched body of Sixo, indeed the cut throat and oily blood of the baby girl whose murder is the book's great secret, whose murder writes large the atrocious price exacted by slavery. Sometimes they are bodies united in tenderness and pleasure: Amy's massaging of Sethe's legs and feet, Beloved's caressing of Sethe, Paul D's cradling of Sethe's breasts, even Beloved's intimate ritual of touch and tell with Paul D: "Touch me on the inside part and call me by my name."

The book's great power resides in its view of human connection, which is the supreme target of slavery. And the audacious fable at its heart is that of a dead girl—a baby murdered by its own mother so that it could be saved—come back to life and returned to her family. Ultimately it makes little difference whether this fable belongs in the realm of fact or fiction, because it is unquestionably the great narrative fact of the book: From title to plot, from ghost to woman from the water, Beloved is *present.* She is there not merely out of authorial fiat or whim; she is there because Toni Morrison, like Harriet Beecher Stowe, believes that connection precedes individuation, that our bonds with one another, especially the mother-child bond, are not destroyable. In the last analysis, *Beloved* is a strangely nostalgic book, a book that yearns for its native homeland of fleshly union, for which milk and love serve as precious conduits. I say "nostalgic" because I believe that Sethe's ultimate gesture of going through the veil speaks this book's deepest truth: to remove the veil of separate bodies and minds and souls so as to return to the originary condition of human linkage, a condition figured in the mysterious language of motherhood, a kind of utterance that precedes speech as we know it.

At its most luminous, this book articulates that language. We encounter it in the thirteen pages of dithyrambic notation toward the book's close, which express the deepest longings of Sethe, Denver, and Beloved. In these beautiful pages, Morrison shows us how the Modernist legacy can take consciousness into a new realm, yielding a poetry of human connection, expressing both the pith of self and union with the loved one. Sethe's portion begins, "Beloved, she my daughter. She mine" (200), and it goes on to chronicle at once the decimations and the miraculous reward at hand:

> I'll explain to her, even though I don't have to. Why I did it. How if I hadn't killed her she would have died and that is something I could not bear to happen to her. When I explain it she'll understand, because she understands everything already. I'll tend her as no mother ever tended a child, a daughter. Nobody will ever get my milk no more except my own children. . . . And when I tell you you mine, I also mean I'm yours. I wouldn't draw breath without my children. . . . My plan was to take us all to the other side where my own ma'am is. They stopped me from getting us there, but they didn't stop you from getting here. Ha ha. You came right on back like a good girl, like a daughter which is what I wanted to be and would have been if my ma'am had been able to get out of the rice field long enough before they hanged her and let me be one. (200–203)

One feels that Sethe's whole emotional life is on show here, the horrors and the joys, all in the service of family continuum, a continuum that death may parse but cannot stop. Who among us could say, I killed you so that you wouldn't die? And that "Ha ha" stops us in our tracks, for it is a voice from another world, sure of its overarching vista, no less sure of the accomplished return trip homeward from death. Here is a vantage point beyond realism and its rules, a spiritual vista that makes it possible truly to see into the beyond, to know that the mother-child compact is triumphant, because Beloved is back, because thick love is invincible.

Denver's dirge begins on the same note: "Beloved is my sister. I swallowed her blood right along with my mother's milk" (205), and it goes on to voice dreadful fears and nightmares where love and murder are inseparable:

> I thought she [Beloved] was trying to kill her [Sethe] that day in the Clearing. Kill her back. But then she kissed her neck and I have to warn her about that. Don't love her too much. Don't. Maybe it's still in her the thing that makes it all right to kill her children. I have to tell her. I have to protect her.
>
> She cut my head off every night. Buglar and Howard told me she would and she did. Her pretty eyes looking at me like I was a stranger. Not mean or anything, but like I was somebody she found and felt sorry for. Like she didn't want to do it but she had to and it wasn't going to hurt. . . . I know she'll be good at it, careful. That when she cuts it off it'll be done right; it won't hurt. (206)

We don't have a genre sufficiently terrible to fit these words into. Gothic, horror, nothing comes close to the (legitimate, acquired) fear of being killed (every night) by your mother out of love, an act Denver envisages with great clarity and precision, a fear that Denver has lived with all her life, that is not sayable but that cannot be silenced. We hear it now. Beloved brings it to utterance.

And then there is the densest piece of all: Beloved's own threnody of pain and hunger. It begins with the same proprietary language: "I am Beloved and she is mine" (210), and it goes on to give us the shards of an unspeakable life, a life of violation and abandonment, adorned with images that seem to hark back to a prior African past, perhaps a funeral, followed by the unforgettable crossing in the slave ship, with dead bodies everywhere, some on top of her, others sent out into the waters, with men without skin (white men) abusing her; and all these injuries seem to coalesce in the supreme wound of her life: the mother "with the face I want" who leaves, goes into the sea, "goes into the water with my face" (211–212). Here would be the origin of Beloved's unstillable hunger, her certainty of being abandoned. It is as if her own life ("my face") had been taken, stolen by the disappearing mother. And with this, we begin to realize that selfhood is what has been irredeemably violated, that the loss of the mother is a wound that is not survivable, just as the loss of the child marks Sethe forever. Morrison finds words for this saga of dismemberment, of being from then on nothing but hunger: "I am alone I want to be the two of us I want the join," an elemental desire that closes with the fixation on Sethe: "It is the face I lost she is my face smiling at me doing it at last a hot thing now we can join a hot thing" (213).

These pages distill all the poetry of this dark story in their haunted and hallucinatory images and cadences. Yet it is also luminous: These three suffering figures express here what is deepest and most unsayable in their hearts, recasting entirely what we customarily think of individual story, individual fate. "I want the join" is the language of the fissured subject that seeks reentry into the womb, into the sacred family. These sonorous figures have the austerity and mystery of a lost world, a world prior to slavery, indeed a world prior to birth itself, for we see here the lineaments of the umbilical world that precedes all else. At the very antipodes of Schoolteacher's sterile discourse of measurements between animal and human, Morrison's words, showing that there can be a language as well as an ethos of the body, possess the heft, resonance, and reach of thick love. If Proust, Joyce, Woolf, and Faulkner speak to us of the heart's secrets and the dimensions of the self, Toni Morrison dares to go still further inside, to a time and a place before we were individuated, to the red heart that fuels humankind and signals our connectedness to one another.

CONCLUSION

In closing this account of the great Modernist novels of Proust, Joyce, Woolf, and Faulkner with Toni Morrison's *Beloved,* I have wanted to show both continuity and change. Morrison's searing portrayal of the psychic legacy of slavery at once adapts and alters much of the Modernist repertory. That inner story of consciousness and memory that bursts upon the scene in *Remembrance of Things Past, Ulysses, Mrs. Dalloway, To the Lighthouse, The Sound and the Fury,* and *Absalom, Absalom!* is drastically reconceived in *Beloved,* reconceived as a site of such injury and pain that any effort to recover one's story appears virtually suicidal. And yet Morrison's book ultimately heeds the same injunction, and we see that the crucial role of the title character, Beloved—the returnee from death—is no less than to restore full circulation, to open up the closed tobacco tin of the damaged heart and amnesiac mind, so that wholeness and healing may be possible. *Beloved* also bids to explode the individualist scheme that has governed the earlier works—consciousness being the domain of *private* feeling and perception—by offering a view of human reality as inherently umbilical and connected, with the result that our customary view of living in a single body and mind is challenged by the relational and fluid world of Morrison's text.

I used the term "cardiac" when analyzing Morrison's book because her universe of pulsing blood and flowing milk is haunted by a view of life as connective tissue, of linkage as the primal reality. Is that not why the story is also haunted by ghosts? The return of the dead child tells us, as nothing else could, that not only severance, but also weaning and individual autonomy are a mirage. Morrison is concerned to depict the systemic transgressions of slavery—the rupturing of both the human family and the human body—but her project also illuminates the central issues in the other works as well, namely the traffic between self and other, a traffic that goes by many names: love, desire, anguish, horror. The literature of consciousness—and that is the literature we have been attending to—is surprisingly relational, even societal. The inside story is inevitably a story of complex interactions: wanted and unwanted.

Proust, the most assured egoist of our group, measures to perfection the hopelessness of getting from Marcel to Albertine, and thus elects finally a different grouping altogether: the society of self, the bringing into view of all the selves we have been, so that they can be, as it were, communalized into a final proprietary possession. Joyce enters Bloom's consciousness in order not only to tap into this little man's indigenous poetry, but also to point out the presence of visiting ghosts representing (like those who came to Scrooge) life past, present, and future: his dead father and dead son, the lost sexual heat of his marriage, the impending and looming sexual betrayal that cannot be repressed, that seems to punctuate whatever he does. Woolf goes perhaps further still in choreographing the vibrant presence of others within us: the mercurial and irrepressible memories that Peter and Clarissa have of their joint past; the generosity of spirit and heart that characterizes Mrs. Ramsay's gift of self; the aching longing that binds Lily Briscoe to Mrs. Ramsay. And everywhere in Woolf: the ethos of social bonds, seen in Clarissa's party, seen in Mrs. Ramsay's dinner, seen in the rituals and forms of friendship, marriage, and family. Faulkner's account of the Compson brothers may appear solipsistic, yet Caddy the lost sister lives forever in their minds, undying even if unpossessable. With *Absalom, Absalom!* we see just how elastic and connective the literature of perception can become, as Quentin and Shreve not only imagine the Sutpen saga in their Harvard dormitory, but ultimately fuse together with its doomed players—four boys on two horses—in what the author calls "an overpass to love," proffered as the only viable way of understanding the reality of the other. In Morrison, as I have suggested, the distance between selves is, in the final analysis, illusory; but this is true only in that fierce and awesome final analysis, because prior to that, in slave culture, in the fate that is theirs, separation and piecing apart are the basic givens.

In short, the literature of consciousness is not a solipsistic performance, even though it may convey with great pathos the loneliness of the human subject and the voraciousness of individual appetite. Living in one's own body-heart-mind may be a permanent jail sentence, but one finds soon enough that visitors and ghosts make their way in and out at will. One also finds that *inside* is far less controllable and domesticable than *outside* ever is, because it is the reality terrain where everything happens *to* you. At some level, all the novels under discussion reveal a story of invasion and takeover, for our thoughts and feelings seem to have a will of their own: Marcel's jealousy runs away with him, Stephen's dead mother invades him repeatedly, Lily finds that Mrs. Ramsay is as authoritative dead as alive, Quentin is bombarded by an outside world in cahoots with his unprocessed past, Sethe and Paul D are held hostage by the chamber of horrors inside them. These writers are taking their findings at a place where we have no defenses, where nothing can be held off or kept back. This is why one comes out of these books with an incomparable sense of what life actually feels like *on the receiving end:* love, hate, jealousy, fear, pain. We are there, on the roller coaster.

For the same reason, one exits these books with an increased reverence for human reflection and human dodging where it is possible: Marcel's bouts of theorizing about life, his commitment to art, his final retreat; Stephen's manic explosions of wit and learning, Bloom's wily, delicious, Odyssean musings and strategic gambits; the irresistible waywardness and flavor of the meandering, capricious mind in Clarissa and Peter, the Ramsays, Lily. In Faulkner's world, no such respite seems conceivable: Benjy and Quentin and Jason never go on holiday; Rosa is possessed; no sanctuary, no maneuvering room is the rule of the game. Morrison's model is the most daunting of all: To survive, you must simply close up shop altogether, and yet that proves impossible, because the brain is greedy and the ghosts are unstoppable, and you have elected living death.

Given these cheerful tidings, you may wonder how it is that I have proclaimed, whenever I have had a chance, that reading these novels is a worthwhile, even exhilarating experience. My answer is: These books, even at their darkest, give us light and life. To cite Kafka one more time, art is the ax that chops through our frozen sea. The paralysis and deadness of a frozen sea—which I take to be the complacency and torpor with which we customarily go through our lives; the routinized notions and received views and ready-made labels with which we tag experience—are they so desirable? The strangeness of these novels, I said, teaches us about our own strangeness, and that is a wake-up call, a form of discovery and renewal. Negotiating these rich books is not esoteric but intimate, because the depictions of consciousness that we find in them send us ineluctably into our own interiors, add to our own stock.

They alter us by making us realize: Yes, life does write *in* us, as Proust says it does, and our job (unremunerated, unscheduled) is to go inside to decode this script; yes, we go through life doodling and dawdling and processing events with the same weird zest and evasive tactics that Bloom does, and it is good to see, close up, how the mind (his, ours) is both caged and cagey; yes, if we are willing to unplug our ears and take the blinders off our eyes, then the wild, flamboyant, kaleidoscopic world rushes in on us, and we realize that the *circus is coming to town,* and in that circus that travels our neural circuits we will find, as Woolf's characters do, voices from the past and loved ones long gone; yes, each of us contains within him- or herself a chorus of voices and injunctions that makes us into a barracks of ghosts, just as Faulkner's Quentin is, but we also learn from the Mississippian something about why civil wars happen, about how race can cancel your humanity in the eyes of others, including your own blood kin; yes, Morrison wields an ax as mighty as Kafka's, and she chops into our frozen sea in order to assault us with the reality of what slavery actually was and did, showing us the psychic damage meted to those who were denied all human connection, thereby gifting her modern readers with a visceral and terrible understanding of a chapter in American history that we thought we knew.

We are lessoned by these books, but not lessened: On the contrary, they add to our own dimensions and vitalize our sense of what life and experience entail. By engaging us in their very texture, by obliging us to find our own way through their unmarked precincts, these novels transform the act of reading into a creative act that is worthy of its name. And they make life keener, richer, finer than it was before we read them. This, too, I ascribe to the very way they have been written. Each one of these novels is saying, indirectly but profoundly: *Normal writing fails.* Fails to cross the bridge from words to reality, fails to convey the pith and living pulse of those events and people and feelings that it names. Let me reference, here, a text I have not dealt with: Søren Kierkegaard's *Fear and Trembling.* The Danish philosopher is trying to tell a story that everyone knows but that no one understands: Abraham's willingness to sacrifice his son Isaac in obedience to God's demand. Kierkegaard tells this story from every possible angle, insisting on its horror and its incomprehensibility: How can God require murder? How can Abraham (be prepared to) kill what is most precious in the world to him? To make us understand this story we think we know, the author puts us at ground zero, makes us accompany Abraham (repeatedly) to Mount Moriah, hurls us into the impossible position of this father prepared to do the ultimate, thereby delivering to us the horror of this fable by putting us *in* it: We finally measure this act on the front side—that is *before* the outcome—rather than in the complacent light of history, of recorded event.

I have rehearsed Kierkegaard's story here because it deals with the central issue of my book: making the reader actually experience the story being told *as if it were happening to us.* And the austere, unstated corollary is: If it is not happening to you, you don't know what it is all about. That is why the story of consciousness is so riveting: It conveys to us what things feel like; we are there, on the inside. Kierkegaard has chosen a story from the Bible. Our authors are more secular, but have comparable aims: to bring us to a radical new understanding of things we think we know, things such as dipping a pastry into a teacup, learning the sexual preferences of your partner, sitting in a coach or at a table, trying not to think of being cuckolded, entering the marital bed and finding another's imprint, learning about a death in the midst of your party, serving a *boeuf en daube* at a dinner in a summer house, hearing someone say "here caddy," preparing for bed in a college dormitory while speaking of a war of long ago, getting past a life of slavery, murdering your child. I do not believe you will ever think of these things in the same way after reading these books. Each of my authors has plied all of his or her art to bring off the miracle: to shock us with the explosive living drama that lies under our stale notions, in our frozen sea.

Our frozen sea. The blankness on the inside. Ultimately great art is a question of enlivening what is dead. We know, thanks to the biologists and neurologists, that our cells die at a prodigious rate; whether our life has been filled with coercion and trauma (as in the stories of Faulkner and Morrison) or whether it has simply obeyed the law of time (as in Proust, Joyce, and Woolf), there is entropy, dying and disappearance going on inside. Life itself despoils the living, for who among us can summon his or her past in its plenitude and color and density? Whose childhood retains, via memory, the wonder it possessed when we lived it? Who among us can access—in any fleshed-out sense, replete with its sound and fury—his or her story?

These matters are existential, not aesthetic. Writing this book on the great Modernist novelists at a time when I approach the end of my career, and at a time marked by the death of my mother, has made these matters quite intimate for me. And I hope it will not be amiss to fold some personal final reflections into my conclusion.

As my mother sank further and further into senility during her last year of life, I frequently experienced a strange kind of double vision when I visited with her, for she spoke of me (and my twin brother) as both present and absent, as standing before her at once in the flesh (as grown, older men) and in her mind's eye (as the small children that we still were to her). I used to tease her gently, by saying, "Mother, but I'm right here, don't you see?" And she'd smile gently, not out of confusion, but rather out of certainty that the childlike figure in her mind was every bit as real as the man by her bed.

Every bit as real? Perhaps more real. For this is what I learned, to my great pain, the last time I saw her before her death. I had been in Memphis for several days, and we had had the type of exchanges to which I was accustomed: Her flitting into and out of coherence, with momentary glimpses of the here and now. But this final farewell was different: I was dressed in coat and tie, travel bag in my hands, airline tickets in my pockets, come to kiss her good-bye before returning to Providence. But she did not recognize me. In vain I reminded her who I was, but to no avail. For her, I had, as it were, already left. The man saying good-bye no longer had any connection whatsoever with the child in her mind, and only that child remained.

I was shaken, and it remains a dark memory that gnaws at me, because she died a month later, when I was on another continent; so I never saw her again. And yet, I realize now that the leave-taking had already taken place, during my final visit. She had let "me" go. But I do not believe that she ever let the small child go. It was as if she had to choose. It was a farewell before dying.

In writing these chapters on Proust, Joyce, Woolf, Faulkner, and Morrison, I have been further stirred by these memories, and I now see that this drama of nonrecognition speaks my story as much as hers. To construe her failure to recognize me as some form of dementia, or lack of oxygen in the brain or whatever material explanation the doctors would doubtless offer for such behavior, may make some narrow sense, but it essentially misses the picture. For there *was* a picture. And it was mine as much as hers. I now sense that my childhood existed for her in ways it never could for me, and that she was safeguarding it still. More brutally, I understand that *I* am now the one marooned, not her, for the child she remembered, the child she held on to so powerfully that she had to cut the long umbilical cord that tied him to Professor Arnold Weinstein who stood before her, that child died with her. With her death he, too, disappeared, and is gone from me forever.

Forever is a long time. Perhaps a cup of tea and a madeleine are out there somewhere, waiting for me.

Whatever may come my own way, however, in terms of recovering my personal story, I think these severe matters bear directly on this book, and on the reasons we read novels. I rehearse my story of a mother's death and a child's exit because I see in it a double loss, an increase of darkness and frozen sea. Still more deaths on the inside. And of course I know that literature will not restore my dead to me.

Nonetheless, these books have a double pulse, theirs and mine, and when *you* read them: theirs and yours. Proust, Joyce, Woolf, Faulkner, and Morrison—each uniquely voiced in portraying the quivering life of mind and body, of memory and desire, of mourning and renewal—are no less than beacons in the dark: beacons in *our* dark. Literature is a human-made sun that creates, as does photosynthesis, life. Against the sluggishness of our routinized notions and the erasures meted out by the years, these five authors—however somber their vision sometimes is—awaken us to a vibrancy and intensity that are life-renewing. As I said regarding Proust, they raid the peaceful cemetery. They counter the dulling work of habit and time. To read a page from any one of them is to be jolted out of inertia and torpor, because the space they are bent on illuminating and inventorying is *our* space. They restore us; they re-story us.

I have worked a lifetime in the academy, and I therefore know how suspicious, romantic, and perhaps specious these views might seem to many literary scholars today. The French critic Roland Barthes once wrote: "Literature does not express the inexpressible; it unexpresses the expressible." Barthes is seeking to call (what he perceives as) the huge bluff of Modernism, and perhaps of all literature: its claim to give us the inside picture, the portrayal of the inner reality, the hidden story. Or its claim to represent what Hamlet claimed he had inside himself: that which passes show. Barthes wants to demystify literature, to do away with this false promise. One of his points would be: Literature is only words. What I have been touting as the testimony of consciousness, the precious *story* that has gone unheard and unknown but is now retrievable, he would doubtless dismiss as pure fantasy, and then add: We want to *believe* this. We want to believe that art offers us a privileged and unique picture of life, of our own life. But how could we possibly prove it to be true? Is it not ultimately a yearned-for construct of both author and reader?

Barthes would go on to say that we should not personalize the books we read, not see them as an expression of the hidden truth, of soul. This, he thinks, is a lure, a con game. Moreover, if we see books as a kind of personal secret mirror, we may be blinded to the ideological arrangements they necessarily contain (and conceal). I do not think it exaggerated to say that an entire generation of professors has toed this particular line, in the wake of Barthes and most poststructuralist theory. They say: Deconstruct the books, historicize the books, see what is hidden by the books, uncover the veiled power arrangements that lurk behind these books. They also say: But do not make the mistake of *identifying* with the books, for then you lose all critical perspective and are set up for being duped. For then you have bought into a fantasy of recovery that is unwarranted and unprovable. For then you have simply wallowed amid your own ego projections. (Critics and professors can be pretty severe along these lines.)

My argument goes the other way: Open yourselves to these books. Endorse—and make your own—the human perspectives through which these stories are told and experienced. Heed the personal story that is emerging. See it as a mirror for yourself. Take every one of its nuggets of insight, its illuminated nooks and crannies about human sensation and behavior, and possess them as your own. Treat literature as the "walking mirror" that Stendhal claimed it was, and read every novel as an opportunity to see yourself anew. It is tolerably obvious that if Barthes is right, I am wrong, and this entire book of mine collapses like a house of cards. So how can I answer this charge? Therefore, let me admit the following: I can prove nothing. There is no scientific evidence to support my claim that the hidden inner story exists for real, or that language can convey it. Or, for that matter, that you and I have a soul. Or, when you come to think of it, a heart (in the nonsomatic sense). I cannot document any of this. And I understand why Barthes ultimately claims that the inside story is a *fiction*.

Here is where I take the offensive. I say: So be it. It is a wonderful fiction, a life-enhancing fiction, a fiction we believe in from cradle to grave, a fiction we need to believe in. It is the sustaining passion of every human life. Why? Not merely because we crave such blandishments (as Barthes would say). But rather because the notion of an inner story, of interiority itself, is a grand notion. It endows our world with dignity and scope. It does honor to human feeling by treating it as real. Seeking the life story (both in literature and in our own existence) is the ongoing, caretaking, endless artisanal labor that makes artists of every one of us. Through inwardness and the testimony of consciousness we possess our own form. We create our own form.

However, perhaps the finest recommendation for believing in the hidden life story, in the inner reaches of every human being, is counterintuitive and less obvious: Our belief in interiority and consciousness is an indispensable step for believing in the *reality of others*, the emotional and moral density of other people. This is no minor issue. I would claim that the great crimes of humanity committed over the ages stem from precisely this: a refusal to grant the humanity of others, an inability to see that others are conscious and sentient beings, possessed of hopes and desires and feelings just as we are. *Absalom, Absalom!* and *Beloved* are eloquent about the price we pay—the price that we have paid—for our failure to see others as fully human. But we hardly need consult the bloody historical record to discover such blindness; our own daily lives present, over and over the same challenge: Do we see those around us as silhouettes or as *storied* creatures? I ascribe this quotidian failure of imagination to the sheer complacency and self-involvement of creatures who know of their own depths while seeing only the surface of everyone else. Love is one exit from such isolation; literature is another. Every book in this study pays tribute to the living reality of others, even if this reality may produce paranoia and hatred as well as desire or tenderness or love.

My final conclusion is: The literature of consciousness schools us in just this fashion. It overwhelms us with the pulsating inner lives of its characters, and it thus helps us toward a more generous view of our species. This is a remarkable double gift: It makes our own days and nights keener and larger, but it also teaches us about the depths and integrity of others. I cannot prove that interiority is real, or that Modernist literature captures its secret. But I believe with all my heart that these novels both shock and educate us about the scope and intensity of human feeling. To read books that hurl us into the consciousness of figures such as Marcel, Bloom, Mrs. Ramsay, Quentin, and Sethe is to do something both precious and real: We humanize these figures as we vicariously share their lives. In short, we learn to endow others—not merely these characters, but the manifold other opaque, living human beings who cross our path in the world (outside books) that we inhabit—with consciousness. This is ultimately an ethical injunction, a requirement that quite complements the familiar "turn the other cheek," for it moves—in its grasp of others as sentient beings with their own depths—from self to world. Reading Proust, Joyce, Woolf, Faulkner, and Morrison does just that, it takes us across the single longest bridge in the universe: from me to you. Art, I said in my introduction, exists to help us recover our own story; this is precious ore. No less precious, however, is the second truth it urges upon us, literature's golden rule: Everyone has a story. Reading schools us for life.

ACKNOWLEDGMENTS

"Neither a borrower nor a lender be," says the fatuous Polonius to his son. Yet the passing of time makes us realize, ever more sharply, how much we are borrowers and lenders. Especially if we are teachers. In working out my lifelong engagement with Proust, Joyce, Woolf, and Faulkner—as well as my slightly briefer acquaintanceship with Morrison—I have massive debts, too numerous to name in any detail, given that the roster of brilliant minds that has discussed the work of this quintet is huge, and has been huge for close to three quarters of a century. (A glance at the Bibliography will confirm this.) I have been sampling that rich and multifaceted scholarly conversation ever since my days in college and graduate school, and continue to do so today. But my book is not a scholarly book, and there are no footnotes in it; still, the ghosts of many professors are there in the wings, unsignaled, yet present in my voice.

Nonetheless, I do want to signal the influence of one major critic, my twin brother, Philip Weinstein, who has been toiling in this same vineyard for as many years as I have, and whose ideas on Faulkner in particular (where I have shamelessly cribbed), but also on Joyce and Morrison, are so much a part of my own thinking, so interwoven with what I take to be "mine," that I realize the two of us have been happily borrowing and lending for more than forty years. His own study of Modernism—with a very different set of ideas from mine—will appear roughly at the same time as this book. Both of us, I think, are finishing a conversation that has been going on for a long time. *Recovering Your Story* suggests that all of us have a composite form that is larger than what the eye can see or the calendar can measure; such a view of life and literature, which may seem fanciful to some, is the flesh-and-blood reality of twinship that has governed our particular relationship since infancy, and which will live as long as we do. His presence in this book is pervasive and fertile, and it pleases me to acknowledge it.

My other debts are murkier but no less enabling. To my dead parents, my living children and grandchildren, I owe a sense of time's bounty (as well as its erosions), and in reflecting over the role of memory and the past in these authors, I have been sustained by what they—parents, children, grandchildren—have given to my life. To my wife, Ann, I owe—as I say in every book I've written—much more still; her canniness as reader—of books, of people—stands as a model for me, and her place in my own story is immeasurable. One of the motifs in my discussion of Proust concerns the "treasure" of our everyday lives, and this book has helped me to a keener sense of my own. I also want to thank her as well for putting up with the inevitable mental absenteeism that was occasioned by the writing of this book, as it was for other books I've written. As I approach the close of my career, I am ever more shocked by its selfish privilege: to spend countless hours reading and talking and writing about literature; to enjoy a life of borrowing and lending. I scarcely know who to thank for this, but I am grateful for the freedoms that have been mine, and I am still discovering just how special they are.

And I am indebted, once again, to Kate Medina at Random House. It was she who first suggested that I write, for the general public, a book on the modern authors who meant most to me, and she has lent her sharp eye to each of the drafts of these chapters, offering encouragement and helpful advice at every step of the way. I do not think she suspected that an opus of this length would be the result, but she has graciously played her midwifing role nonetheless in the making of this book. And, once again, her able colleagues at Random House have been unfailingly helpful: especially Danielle Posen, Robin Rolewicz, Abigail Plesser, and Vincent La Scala. On another front, in compiling the bibliography and in seeking permissions, I have also benefited from the unstinting aid offered to me by Teresa Villa-Ignacio, at Brown University, who has been something of a working partner in my recent courses and books. Finally, I want to thank two friends and mentors—Robert Fagles and Roger Shattuck—for taking the time to read this book and comment on it; their generosity speaks for what is best in the academy. It pleases me to see that lesson confirmed at this juncture of my life.

BIBLIOGRAPHY

PRIMARY TEXTS

Faulkner, William. *Absalom, Absalom!* New York: Random House (Vintage International), 1990.

——. *The Sound and the Fury.* New York: Random House (Vintage International), 1990.

Joyce, James. *Dubliners.* London: Penguin, 2000.

——. *A Portrait of the Artist as a Young Man.* New York: Penguin, 2003.

——. *Ulysses.* New York: Random House (Vintage), 1986.

Morrison, Toni. *Beloved.* New York: Penguin (Plume), 1988.

——. *Sula.* New York: Penguin (Plume), 1982.

Proust, Marcel. *Remembrance of Things Past.* Tr. Montcrieff, Kilmartin and Mayor. New York: Random House, 1981.

Woolf, Virginia. *Mrs. Dalloway.* New York: Harcourt, Brace, Jovanovich (Harvest), 1990.

——. *To the Lighthouse.* New York: Harcourt, Brace, Jovanovich (Harvest) nd (orig. copyright 1927).

MARCEL PROUST

Alter, Robert. *Partial Magic. The Novel as a Self-Conscious Genre.* Berkeley: University of California Press, 1975.

Auerbach, E. *Mimesis.* Princeton, N.J.: Princeton University Press, 1953.

Bales, Richard, ed. *The Cambridge Companion to Proust.* New York: Cambridge University Press, 2001.

Beckett, Samuel. *Proust.* New York: Grove Press, 1957.

Benjamin, Walter. "The Image of Proust." *Illuminations.* Tr. Harry Zohn. Ed. and introduction, Hannah Arendt. New York: Schocken Books, 1968, 201–15.

Bersani, Leo. *Marcel Proust: The Fictions of Life and Art.* London: Oxford University Press, 1965.

Brée, Germaine. *The World of Marcel Proust.* London: Chatto & Windus, 1967.

De Botton, Alain. *How Proust Can Change Your Life*. New York: Vintage, 1998.
Carter, William C. *Marcel Proust: A Life*. New Haven and London: Yale University Press, 2000.
Deleuze, Gilles. *Proust and Signs*. Tr. Richard Howard. London: Allen Lane, 1972.
Genette, Gérard. *Figures of Literary Discourse*. Tr. Alan Sheridan. Introduction, Marie-Rose Logan. New York: Columbia University Press, 1982.
Girard, René, ed. *Proust: A Collection of Critical Essays*. Englewood Cliffs, N.J.: Prentice-Hall, 1962.
Kristeva, Julia. *Time and Sense: Proust and the Experience of Literature*. Tr. Ross Guberman. New York: Columbia University Press, 1997.
Landy, Joshua. *Philosophy as Fiction: Self, Deception, and Knowledge in Proust*. Oxford: Oxford University Press, 2004.
Mortimer, Armine Kotin, and Katherine Kolb, eds. *Proust in Perspective: Visions and Revisions*. Urbana: University of Illinois Press, 2002.
Poulet, Georges. *Proustian Space*. Tr. Elliott Coleman. Baltimore: Johns Hopkins University Press, 1977.
Rose, Phyllis. *The Year of Reading Proust: A Memoir in Real Time*. Washington, D.C. : Counterpoint, 2000.
Shattuck, Roger. *Marcel Proust*. New York: Viking, 1974.
——. *Proust's Binoculars*. New York: Random House, 1963.
——. *Proust's Way: A Field Guide to* In Search of Lost Time. New York: Norton, 2000.
Stambolian, George. *Marcel Proust and the Creative Encounter*. University of Chicago Press, 1972.
Wassenaar, Ingrid. *Proustian Passions: The Uses of Self-Justification for "A la Recherche du temps perdu."* Oxford: Oxford University Press, 2000.
Weinstein, Arnold. *The Fiction of Relationship*. Princeton, N.J.: Princeton University Press, 1988.
——. *A Scream Goes Through the House: What Literature Teaches Us About Life*. New York: Random House, 2003.
Wimmers, Inge Crossman. *Proust and Emotion: The Importance of Affect in "A la recherche du temps perdu."* University of Toronto Press, 2003.

JAMES JOYCE

Adams, Robert M. *After Joyce: Studies in Fiction after Ulysses*. New York: Oxford University Press, 1977.
——. *James Joyce: Common Sense and Beyond*. New York: Random House, 1971.
Attridge, Derek. *Joyce Effects: On Language, Theory, and History*. Cambridge: Cambridge University Press, 2000.
Blamires, Harry. *The New Bloomsday Book: A Guide Through Ulysses*. Revised edition keyed to the corrected text. New York and London: Routledge, 1988.
Bloom, Harold, ed. *James Joyce's* Ulysses. New York: Chelsea House, 1987.
Bowen, Zack. Ulysses *as a Comic Novel*. Syracuse, N.Y.: Syracuse University Press, 1989.

Budgen, Frank. *James Joyce and the Making of* Ulysses. Bloomington: Indiana University Press, 1960.

Chace, William M., ed. *Joyce: A Collection of Critical Essays.* Englewood Cliffs, N.J.: Prenctice-Hall, 1974.

Cixous, Hélène. *The Exile of James Joyce.* Tr. Sally A. J. Purcell. New York: D. Lewis, 1972.

Ellmann, Richard. *James Joyce.* New York: Oxford University Press, 1959, 1982.

——. *Ulysses on the Liffey.* New York: Oxford University Press, 1972.

Friedman, Susan Stanford, ed. *Joyce: The Return of the Repressed.* Ithaca, N.Y., and London: Cornell University Press, 1993.

Hart, Clive. *James Joyce's* Ulysses. Sydney University Press, 1968.

Hart, Clive and David Hayman, eds. *James Joyce's* Ulysses: *Critical Essays.* Berkeley: University of California Press, 1974.

Hayman, David. *Ulysses, The Mechanics of Meaning.* Madison: University of Wisconsin Press, 1982.

Kenner, Hugh. *Dublin's Joyce.* London: Chatto & Windus, 1955.

——. *Joyce's Voices.* Berkeley: University of California Press, 1978.

——. *Ulysses.* rev. ed. Baltimore: Johns Hopkins University Press, 1987.

Levin, Harry. *James Joyce: A Critical Introduction.* Norfolk, Conn.: New Directions, 1960

Litz, Walton A. *James Joyce.* New York: Twayne Publishers, 1996.

McCarthy, Patrick A. Ulysses: *Portals of Discovery.* Boston: Twayne Publishers, 1990.

Senn, Fritz. *Joyce's Dislocutions: Essays on Reading as Translation.* Baltimore: Johns Hopkins University Press, 1984.

——. *Inductive Scrutinies: Focus on Joyce.* Baltimore: Johns Hopkins University Press, 1995.

Wollaeger, Mark A., Victor Luftig, and Robert Spoo, eds. *Joyce and the Subject of History.* Ann Arbor: University of Michigan Press, 1996.

VIRGINIA WOOLF

Bloom, Harold. *Virgina Woolf's "Mrs. Dalloway."* New York: Chelsea, 1988.

Bowlby, Rachel. *Virginia Woolf: Feminist Destinations.* New York: Blackwell, 1988.

Caramagno, Thomas C. *The Flight of the Mind: Virginia Woolf's Art and Manic-Depressive Illness.* Berkeley: University of California Press, 1992.

Caughie, Pamela L. *Virginia Woolf and Postmodernism: Literature in Quest and Question of Itself.* Urbana: University of Illinois Press, 1991.

Cunningham, Michael. *The Hours.* New York: Farrar, Straus & Giroux, 1998. (novel)

Dowling, David. *Mrs. Dalloway: Mapping Streams of Consciousness.* Boston: Hall, 1991.

Guiguet, Jean. *Virginia Woolf and Her Works.* Tr. Jean Stewart. London: Hogarth, 1965.

Haper, Howard. *Between Language and Silence: The Novels of Virginia Woolf.* Baton Rouge: Louisiana State University Press, 1982.

Homans, Margaret, ed. *Virginia Woolf: A Collection of Critical Essays.* Englewood Cliffs, N.J.: Prentice-Hall, 1993.

Hyman, Virginia R. *"To the Lighthouse" and Beyond: Transformations in the Narratives of Virginia Woolf.* New York: Lang, 1988.

Lee, Hermione. *The Novels of Virginia Woolf.* London: Methuen, 1977.

———. *Virginia Woolf.* New York: Vintage, 1999.

Majumdar, Robin, and Allen McLaurin, eds. *Virginia Woolf: The Critical Heritage.* London: Routledge, 1975.

Marcus, Jane, ed. *New Feminist Essays on Virginia Woolf.* Lincoln: University of Nebraska Press, 1981.

———, ed. *Virginia Woolf and Bloomsbury: A Centenary Celebration.* Bloomington: Indiana University Press, 1987.

McNichol, Stella. *Virginia Woolf and the Poetry of Fiction.* London: Routledge, 1990.

Miller, C. Ruth. *Virginia Woolf: The Frames of Art and Life.* New York: St. Martin's, 1988.

Naremore, James. *The World Without a Self: Virginia Woolf and the Novel.* New Haven, Conn.: Yale University Press, 1973.

Reed, Christopher. *Bloomsbury Rooms: Modernism, Subculture, and Domesticity.* New Haven, Conn.: Yale University Press, 2004.

Ronchetti, Ann. *The Artist, Society and Sexuality in Virginia Woolf's Novels.* New York: Routledge, 2004.

Ruotolo, Lucio P. *The Interrupted Moment: A View of Virginia Woolf's Novels.* Stanford, Calif.: Stanford University Press, 1986.

Ruddick, Lisa. *The Seen and the Unseen: Virginia Woolf's* To the Lighthouse. Cambridge, Mass: Harvard University Press, 1977.

Showalter, Elaine. *A Literature of Their Own: British Women Novelists from Brontë to Lessing.* Princeton, N.J.: Princeton University Press, 1999.

Snaith, Anna. *Virginia Woolf: Public and Private Negotiations.* New York: St. Martin's, 2000.

William Faulkner

Bleikasten, André. *The Most Splendid Failure: Faulkner's* The Sound and the Fury. Bloomington: Indiana University Press, 1976.

———. *The Ink of Melancholy: Faulkner's Novels from* The Sound and the Fury *to* Light in August. Bloomington: Indiana University Press, 1990.

Bloom, Harold, ed. *William Faulkner's* Absalom, Absalom! New York: Chelsea House, 1987.

———, ed. *William Faulkner's* The Sound and the Fury. New York: Chelsea House, 1988.

Brooks, Cleanth. *William Faulkner: The Yoknapatawpha Country.* New Haven, Conn.: Yale University Press, 1963, 1966.

Davis, Thadious M. *Faulkner's "Negro": Art and the Southern Context.* Baton Rouge: Louisiana State University Press, 1983.

Doyle, Don H. *Faulkner's County: The Historical Roots of Yoknapatawpha.* Chapel Hill: University of North Carolina Press, 2001.

Faulkner, William. *Faulkner in the University: Class Conferences at the University of Virginia, 1957–1958.* Frederick L. Gwynn and Joseph L. Blotner, eds. Charlottesville: University of Virginia Press, 1959.

Fowler, Doreen, and Ann J. Abadie, eds. *Faulkner and Women.* Faulkner and Yoknapatawpha Conference. Jackson: University Press of Mississippi, 1986.

Glissant, Édouard. *Faulkner, Mississipi.* Chicago: University of Chicago Press, 1999.

Hobson, Fred, ed. *William Faulkner's* Absalom, Absalom!: *A Casebook.* New York: Oxford University Press, 2003.

Howe, Irving. *William Faulkner: A Critical Study.* Chicago: University of Chicago Press, 1975.

Irwin, John. *Doubling and Incest/Repetition and Revenge: A Speculative Reading of Faulkner.* Baltimore: Johns Hopkins University Press, 1975.

Kartiganer, Donald M., and Ann J. Abadie, eds. *Faulkner and Ideology.* Faulkner and Yoknapatawpha Series. Jackson: University Press of Mississippi, 1995.

——, eds. *Faulkner and Psychology.* Faulkner and Yoknapatawpha Series. Jackson: University Press of Mississippi, 1994.

Kinney, Arthur F, ed. *Critical Essays on William Faulkner: The Sutpen Family.* New York: G. K. Hall, 1996.

Matthews, John T. *The Play of Faulkner's Language.* Ithaca, N.Y.: Cornell University Press, 1982.

Minter, David. *William Faulkner: His Life and Work.* Baltimore: Johns Hopkins University Press, 1980.

Parini, Jay. *One Matchless Time: A Life of William Faulkner.* New York: HarperCollins, 2004.

Singal, Daniel Joseph. *William Faulkner: The Making of a Modernist.* Chapel Hill: University of North Carolina Press, 1997.

Sundquist, Eric. *Faulkner: The House Divided.* Baltimore: Johns Hopkins University Press, 1983.

Wagner-Martin, Linda, ed. *William Faulkner: Four Decades of Criticism.* East Lansing: Michigan State University Press, 1973.

Warren, Robert Penn, ed. *Faulkner: A Collection of Critical Essays.* Twentieth Century Views Series. Englewood Cliffs, N.J.: Prentice-Hall, 1966.

Weinstein, Arnold. *Nobody's Home: Speech, Self, and Place in American Fiction from Hawthorne to DeLillo.* New York: Oxford University Press, 1993.

——. *Vision and Response in Modern Fiction.* Ithaca, N.Y.: Cornell University Press, 1974.

Weinstein, Philip M. ed. *The Cambridge Companion to William Faulkner.* Cambridge: Cambridge University Press, 1995.

——. *Faulkner's Subject: A Cosmos No One Owns.* Cambridge: Cambridge University Press, 1992.

Toni Morrison

Beaulieu, Elizabeth Ann, ed. *The Toni Morrison Encyclopedia.* Westport, Conn.: Greenwood Press, 2003.

Bloom, Harold, ed. *Toni Morrison.* New York: Chelsea House, 1990.

Butler-Evans, Elliott. *Race, Gender, and Desire: Narrative Strategies in the Fiction of Toni Cade Bambara, Toni Morrison, and Alice Walker.* Philadelphia: Temple University Press, 1989.

Grewal, Gurleen. *Circles of Sorrow, Lines of Struggle: The Novels of Toni Morrison.* Baton Rouge: Louisiana State University Press, 1998.

Gates, Henry Louis, Jr., and K. A. Appiah, eds. *Toni Morrison: Critical Perspectives Past and Present.* Amistad Literary Series. New York: Amistad, 1993.

Heinze, Denise. *The Dilemma of "Double-Consciousness": Toni Morrison's Novels.* Athens: University of Georgia Press, 1993.

McKay, Nellie Y., ed. *Critical Essays on Toni Morrison.* Boston: Hall, 1988.

Morrison, Toni. *Playing in the Dark: Whiteness and the Literary Imagination.* Cambridge, Mass.: Harvard University Press, 1992.

———. "An Interview with Toni Morrison." With Nellie McKay. Contemporary Literature 24 (1983), 413–29.

Page, Philip. *Dangerous Freedom: Fusion and Fragmentation in Toni Morrison's Novels.* Jackson: University of Mississippi Press, 1995.

Reyes-Conner, Marc Cameron, ed. *The Aesthetics of Toni Morrison: Speaking the Unspeakable.* Jackson: University of Mississippi Press, 2000.

Weinstein, Arnold. *Nobody's Home: Speech, Self, and Place in American Fiction from Hawthorne to DeLillo.* New York: Oxford University Press, 1993.

Weinstein, Philip M. *What Else But Love?: The Ordeal of Race in Faulkner and Morrison.* New York: Columbia University Press, 1996.

INDEX

L

M

ABOUT THE AUTHOR

ARNOLD WEINSTEIN is the Edna and Richard Salomon Distinguished Professor of Comparative Literature at Brown University. His books include *Vision and Response in Modern Fiction*, *Fictions of the Self: 1550–1800*, *The Fiction of Relationship*, *Nobody's Home: Speech, Self, and Place in American Fiction from Hawthorne to DeLillo*, and, most recently, *A Scream Goes Through the House: What Literature Teaches Us About Life*. He also gives a series of audio and video lectures on American literature and world literature for The Teaching Company. He divides his time among Providence, Block Island, Stockholm, and Brittany.

ABOUT THE TYPE

This book was set in Electra, a typeface designed for Linotype by W. A. Dwiggins, the renowned type designer (1880–1956). Electra is a fluid typeface, avoiding the contrasts of thick and thin strokes that are prevalent in most modern typefaces.

CHAPTER 1

Whitingham, Vermont

Birthplace of Brigham Young—Prophet, Colonizer, Statesman

Larry C. Porter
Professor of Church History and Doctrine
Brigham Young University

John Young (1763–1839), the father of Brigham Young, enlisted as a soldier in the Army of the Revolution in June 1780, at sixteen years of age. His enrollment in the military occurred in his home community of Hopkinton, Middlesex County, Massachusetts. Hopkinton was just twenty-five miles southwest of Boston, the leading spirit among communities in that area seeking autonomy for the united colonies. He was initially recruited into the 4th Massachusetts Brigade of Musketry, and he served two additional terms of enlistment during a period extending to 1783. John saw action in three campaigns in his native state and in one campaign in New Jersey.[1]

After the war, John returned to Hopkinton, and on 31 October 1785 he married nineteen-year-old Abigail Howe, nicknamed Nabby (1765–1815). Although Nabby had been born in Hopkinton, she was raised in Shrewsbury, Massachusetts, eleven miles to the northeast.

The Youngs settled in Hopkinton, where two daughters were born: Nancy in 1786 and Fanny in 1787. John then moved his family into the Platauva District of east-central New York, locating in what was then the township of Coxsackie, Albany County (where the village of Durham, Green County, now stands). Rhoda was born there on 10 September 1789.[2]

In this wilderness setting, John dispatched a large, wounded bear, which had attacked him and another man. John jammed a long, sharpened stick into the bear's mouth and throat, "which after a severe struggle brought the furious animal dead at his feet."

Nabby did not adjust well to these primitive surroundings. "Full of fear and cares, together with a delicate state of health," she wrote her family in Hopkinton, explaining her lonely situation. As soon as the "sleighing was pronounced good," her father, Phinehas Howe, "started two sleighs after his lost child and her family." All this was done much to the dismay of John Young, who thought their situation a promising one and resented the intrusion on his affairs. But, constrained by the entreaties of his wife and the teamsters sent by her father, he gave up his New York holdings and returned to Hopkinton at the end of 1789 or the beginning of 1790.[3]

Here their first son, John, Jr., was born in 1791.[4] Four more children were born in Hopkinton between 1793 and 1799: Nabby (1793), Susannah (1795), Joseph (1797), and Phinehas Howe (1799).

Phinehas Howe Young recorded an accident that occurred near the conclusion of the family's stay in Hopkinton, which marks the point of the family's departure for Vermont: "A short time before I was two years old, [Joseph] cut off my right hand, except a small portion of my little finger, with an ax, while we were at play; my mother doctored it and saved it. The same winter [1800–1801], or soon after this accident, my father moved to Whitingham, Windham Co., Vermont, where we lived three years."[5]

THE YOUNGS OF WHITINGHAM, VERMONT

John and Nabby's decision to leave their farming pursuits in Hopkinton and move to the wilderness area of Whitingham, Vermont, was obviously influenced by family ties. John's older sister, Susannah, had married Joseph Mosely, Sr. (also spelled Moseley and Mousley), an enterprising man of apparent substance. His business was dividing (or buying) and selling acreage in the township of Whitingham. Among those to whom he sold land were Samuel Moseley, Elisha Hale, David Eames, David Lamb, and Hezekiah Murdock.[6] Numerous land transactions that Joseph Mosely entered into can be traced for over a decade, up until 1806, when he disposed of his interests in the area. Arthur D. Wheeler, town clerk of Whitingham, commented, "Joseph Mosely was a realtor and working up something."[7]

On 18 November 1800, Joseph Mosely, yeoman, sold to his brother-in-law, John Young, yeoman, two parcels of adjoining land totalling 51½ acres (see aerial photograph, item no. 1). One parcel contained 50 acres, and the other contained 1½ acres, in Lot No. 21 of Fitches Grant, Whitingham, Windham County, Vermont. The indenture reads, ". . . beginning at the northwest corner of Lot No. 21. . . ." However, Arthur D. Wheeler cautioned, "John Young's property was not in the northwest corner of Lot No. 21. That would put it 1,000 feet too far north. The original description is wrong. It should read, 'southwest corner.'"[8]

Some histories have cited the cost of the transaction as being $50; however, an examination of the record clearly stipulates $100. John paid an equitable price for his land, approximately $2.00 per acre. This amount was appropriate to the times; the price of land in the area was from $1.00 to $3.00 per acre.[9]

It is doubtful that there were any buildings or improvements on John Young's acreage at the time of his purchase. It was probably pristine, covered with a growth of beech, birch, maple, spruce, hemlock, balsam, and oak trees—all indigenous to the area.[10]

Within two months of the transaction with Joseph Mosely, the Young family, minus eleven-year-old Rhoda, was on its way to Vermont. For unexplained reasons, Rhoda remained in Hopkinton with her maternal grandparents, Phinehas and Susannah Goddard Howe. Rhoda's brother Joseph said, "[She] did not join her father's family again until the year 1809. In September of that year she arrived at our humble home on Cold Brook [Smyrna, Chenango County, New York] in company with old Deacon Abner Morton, our mother's uncle."[11]

The Youngs made the move from Hopkinton, Massachusetts, to Whitingham, Vermont, eighty miles directly northwest, in January of 1801.[12] Typhus or typhoid fever was widespread in this region of Vermont in 1801. Forty adults died, despite the efforts of physicians to control the disease.[13] The John Young family would have been witness to this suffering. There is no known record of the effects of the sickness on the Youngs.

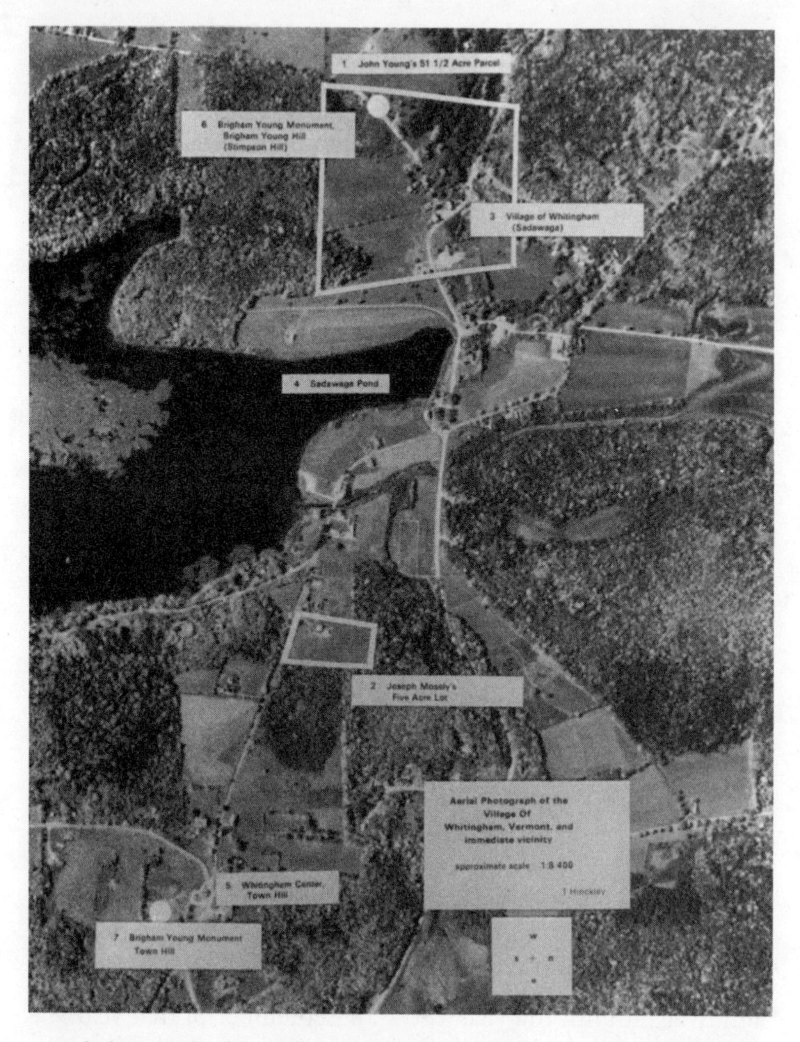

Aerial photograph of the village of Whitingham, Vermont, and vicinity, showing principal Brigham Young sites.

BIRTH AND EARLY LIFE OF BRIGHAM YOUNG

Unless John Young had previously constructed a cabin on the site, it is probable that the newcomers located temporarily with their in-laws, the Joseph Mosely family, or with friends from their same area in Massachusetts. The building of a cabin would have received first priority by the family, and that well in advance of the birth of their son Brigham the following June. Undoubtedly the log house on John's 51½ acres sheltered the birth of the future prophet.

Comparatively little is known relative to those attending Nabby during the birth of Brigham Young. Brigham's birth date, 1 June 1801, is accepted as authentic; however, there is some discussion concerning the origin of his given name. Susa Young Gates and Leah D. Widtsoe affirmed, "His name Brigham was the surname of his uncle, Phinehas Brigham, who married his mother's sister, Susanna."[14] Leonard J. Arrington, however, stated that Brigham was named "after the surname of Nabby's maternal grandparents," who were Sibil Brigham and Ebenezer Goddard.[15] Doris Kirkpatrick, local historian, averred that "substantial evidence points to the fact that John Young named his ninth child 'Brigham' out of respect for his friend and contemporary—John Brigham of Whitingham."[16] This latter assertion is open to question, because John Brigham reportedly did not arrive in Whitingham until 1808.[17]

Susa Young asserted that "Brigham and his brothers John and Lorenzo inherited the physical traits of the Howes, while . . . Joseph . . . very much resembled the Youngs, the father, John Young, being a small wiry man."[18] Commenting on Nabby Young's general physical condition, Susa reported, "Not robust in her constitution, she burned up her fires of youth in impetuous toil while constantly on the move with her pioneering husband. . . . The mother's health was poor for a long time, and it was family tradition that Fanny, the elder sister, 'raised' Brigham."[19] Joseph Young confirmed these circumstances. He recounted:

> In the spring of the year above named [1801], my father bought a cow of a man by the name of Caleb Murdock. It is worthy of note that the cow gave more milk than any one I have ever seen since that time. My Brother John has told me that she gave one bushel of milk a day during the season of feed on clover. One particular incident connected with this circumstance was that the animal would suffer no one to come near her except my sister Fanny and who with the infant Brigham in her arms performed this service twice each day during the summer time. This was in consequence of the sickness of my mother for the child had to be nursed

> from the bottle and no one could pacify him but his sister Fanny, who was passionately fond of him [and] if need be to have laid her life down for him every day.[20]

Fanny left the Young household in 1803; at the age of sixteen she married Robert Carr, who lived in Charleston, Montgomery County, New York.[21] Brigham Young's oldest sister, Nancy, also married that year; she married Daniel Kent on 13 January.[22] The Kents stayed in Whitingham and lived near the Youngs. Daniel's name is on the Grand List (which shows assessed value of properties) of 13 December 1803, with an assessed property value of $26.50.[23]

The members of the Young family were raised in a very orthodox religious environment. Lorenzo D. Young said of his father, John Young, "He was at first an Episcopal Methodist, but afterwards, in common with many others, became a Reformed Methodist [this latter affiliation occurred later in New York]."[24] The Whitingham Circuit of the Methodist Episcopal Church was one of the first three formed in the state of Vermont. The Methodist ministers who preached in Whitingham were, in 1801, Daniel Bromley; in 1802, Elijah Ward and Asa Kent; in 1803, Phinehas Peck and Caleb Dustin; and in 1804, John Tinkham.[25]

Susa Young Gates said of the Young family, "Father, mother, children, all of them loved and made music. The mother was a choir singer in the Methodist congregation, where she and her God-fearing husband worshipped. Parents and children read and studied the Scriptures and they were eager students of the primitive schools of their neighborhood during such periods as their almost nomadic life permitted."[26] Apparently the voices of the Youngs were among those heard in the congregation of the Methodists in early Whitingham.

ATTEMPTING TO PINPOINT BRIGHAM'S BIRTH SITE

Over a period of years, historians have attempted to pinpoint the exact location of the John Young cabin in an effort to better document the arrival of its famous occupant, Brigham Young. A notation appearing in Hamilton Child's *Gazetteer and Business*

Directory of Windham County, Vt., 1724–1884, contains the statement, "Brigham Young, the Mormon saint was born in Whitingham, on road 40 near the center of town. A part of the cellar walls of the old log house mark the place of his birth."[27]

Arthur Wheeler stated that he is sure that Hamilton Child arbitrarily numbered the various roads in the town of Whitingham in order to establish direction both for his descriptions of the area and to match the map that he appended to his Gazetteer. He further explained that what Hamilton Child identified as "road 40" for his own purposes is now Town Road 33 (Stimpson Hill Road). Town Road 33 runs by "Brigham Young Hill," or "Stimpson Hill," and the monument that has been placed there to honor Brigham Young (see aerial photograph, item no. 1).[28]

Clark Jillson spent many years in a minute study of Whitingham. In 1894 he published a history of the area, *Green Leaves from Whitingham, Vermont.* It was his opinion that Brigham Young was born on John's 51½ acre parcel. Doris Kirkpatrick, writer and historian, reiterated this claim when she observed, "Clark Jillson, local historian, repeatedly stated that Brigham Young was born on Stimpson Hill [also known as Brigham Young Hill]."[29] Clark Jillson also said that "Hezekiah Murdock [an early resident] repeatedly stated that Young was born on the hill [Brigham Young Hill or Stimpson Hill]."[30]

The exact site of the John Young cabin on this acreage is unknown today. At some point prior to the turn of the century, a stone memorial to Brigham Young was placed on the north side of Town Road 33 at the top of Brigham Young Hill or Stimpson Hill (see aerial photograph, item no. 6). This memorial is 0.2 mile up Brigham Young Hill, west of Brown's General Store and the U.S. Post Office, which are at the bottom of the hill on Vermont State Highway 100. The property on which the monument is located is presently owned by Raymond A. Purinton, who maintains a summer cabin just a few feet north of the monument.[31]

The inscription on the stone reads, "BRIGHAM YOUNG, BORN ON THIS SPOT 1801, A MAN OF MUCH COURAGE AND SUPERB EQUIPMENT" (see aerial photograph, item no. 6). It is not known locally who was responsible for the placement of this memorial. Arthur Wheeler explained, "The Brigham Young monument on Stimpson Hill was put up before the turn of the century. There were postcards of the monument around in 1900. I don't know by whom or exactly when it was placed there."[32]

John Young owned the property on Brigham Young Hill for a little over one year and ten months. On 24 September 1802, he sold back his 51½ acres to his brother-in-law, Joseph Mosely, for the original purchase price of $100. It is not known whether he needed the money in order for his family to subsist or for some other reason. Concerning the sale, Leonard J. Arrington poses two questions, "Did John arrange with Mosely to remain another year after his tentative decision to leave? Or did John simply sell the land back to Mosely early in order to get back $50 [$100], or whatever was the sale price, to live on?"[33] He may have done both. His name appears on the Grand List (showing assessed value of properties) for both 30 October 1802 ($26.50), and 13 December 1803 ($20), which is an indication that the property he was working (probably his own in 1802 and someone else's in 1803) was being assessed to him personally. His name is not on the 1804 Grand List, consistent with the family's move to New York early in that year.[34]

John apparently then rented from or worked for others; there are no records denoting personal ownership of new property. Whatever the circumstances, John Young remained in the vicinity. Brigham Young spoke of his father "opening new farms" in Whitingham, indicating more than one property was worked.[35] Arthur Wheeler suggested that John may have rented or worked land belonging to an absentee owner or owners, of which there were several in the area.[36] John's son, Joseph, commented: "*We changed places 4 times during our stay on Green Mountains.* Our last place of residence was over the pond in the Hemlock woods."[37] It is evident that John was on the move, living in several locations during his remaining time in Whitingham.

When asked about Joseph's description of residing "over the pond in the Hemlock woods," Mr. Wheeler made this observation, "Though there are a few natural ponds in the area, Sadawaga Pond is the most likely in this setting. Many of the settlers from

Massachusetts located together in the area of Sadawaga Pond. Now called Sadawaga Lake, it is up twelve feet from when the white men first came, because of the various dams that have been placed since. The lake covers a greater area than the original pond"[38] (see aerial photograph, item no. 4).

At the time the John Young family lived in the area (1801–1804), the emerging village of Whitingham Centre on Town Hill was only in its infancy; it did not see its primary development as such until after the departure of the Youngs for New York (see aerial photograph, item no. 5).

John Young's former property subsequently became central to the development of the village of Sadawaga (now Whitingham), immediately west of what was old Whitingham Centre. It was not until 23 February 1882 that Sadawaga became the community of Whitingham (see aerial photograph, item no. 1). It took its name from Nathan Whiting, one of the original grantees of the township.[39]

John Young's 51½ acres encompassed a most interesting section of realty in the modern-day village of Whitingham (see aerial photograph, items no. 1, 3, and 6). Within its boundaries are now the following: (1) a portion of Brigham Young Hill or Stimpson Hill, (2) the stone monument to Brigham Young on Brigham Young Hill or Stimpson Hill, (3) the Whitingham Historical Society's Green Mountain Hall, (4) the Whitingham Community Church, (5) Brown's General Store, and (6) the U.S. Post Office. However, the Whitingham town clerk's office is not within the boundaries of John Young's original property.[40]

In addition to John Young's 51½ acre holding, some local traditions also ascribe Brigham Young's birth site to a five-acre parcel of land in Fitches Grant, Lot 22 (see aerial photograph, item no. 2). The five acres is situated 0.7 mile east of the U.S. Post Office in Whitingham. It is on the left side of the Town Hill Road (Town Road 5). Currently (1995) Donald Boyd owns the five-acre parcel.[41] Clark Jillson, speaking at the Whitingham Centennial celebration on Town Hill, 18 August 1880, explored some of the local testimonies related to the five-acre lot:

> Now comes the more perplexing question; in what

> locality was he born? Henry Goodnow Esq., of this town, says . . . that Brigham was born in a house that stood on the five acres of land north of the road from his store, near a small bridge or culvert, before going down the last hill to Gate's and Morse's old tannery. He says that his mother, the wife of Joseph Goodnow, went to see the baby, Brigham Young, at this house when he was but a few days old, and after he was named Brigham. On the other hand it was stated that Brigham Young was born in a log house that stood north of the road on the hill near to and westerly from the village of Sadawaga [now Whitingham]. There seems to be but little doubt that he was carried from this place when his parents left town. *He might have been born at this other place [Brigham Young Hill or Stimpson Hill] and removed to and from the second* [five-acre lot]; but all the parties that personally know are dead. It is said that Hezekiah Murdock repeatedly stated that Young was born on the hill [Brigham Young Hill or Stimpson Hill], but before we allow this statement to crystalize into history and the statement of Mr. Goodnow declared to be a mistake, we must ascertain whether Mr. Murdock knew any more about it than Mrs. Goodnow, and also whether the facts have been reported correctly. These facts we shall never know, and we might as well be satisfied with saying that Brigham Young was born in Whitingham June 1, 1801. He was one of the most remarkable men of any age; and if his great ability had been employed in some rational pursuit he would have taken a prominent place among the great men of the world. His power as an organizer and a leader has seldom been surpassed.[42]

Mr. Jillson's suggestion that Brigham Young's birth may well have been on Brigham Young Hill or Stimpson Hill, and that the John Young family had simply moved to the five-acre lot during their tenure in Whitingham and then removed to New York from that place seems very plausible. Commenting on the Goodnow's recollections, Marjorie W. Graves, local historian, said, "Since the Goodnow family had lived on Town Hill so many years, you might think this was the real story of Brigham Young's birthplace. All that we really know is that most of the old stories place it somewhere on the slopes of Town Hill."[43]

Doris Kirkpatrick recorded some additional details of the Goodnow recollections:

> Mrs. Graves [Marjorie W. Graves] uncovered a statement by a Mrs. Joseph Goodnow who claimed that when John Young's newest child was born, the ninth, she went to visit mother and child in a small cabin at the far end of a five-acre lot north of the old culvert on the Town Hill road before one came to the Gates and Morse Tannery. The Tannery was located in the Shippee pasture south across the brook from the Whitingham Cemetery. The five acres known to old-timers as the Putnam or Stebbins lot could have been Brigham's birthplace. The cabin was on the north side of the lot probably near an old apple tree there.[44]

Joseph Mosely once owned this five-acre parcel. However, Arthur Wheeler stated, "The so-called five-acre 'Brigham Young Lot' went out of Joseph Mosely's hands in 1797 and apparently didn't come back into Mosely's ownership during the time that Brigham Young was in the area with his parents."[45]

Doris Kirkpatrick believed that the five-acre parcel had at one time belonged to John Young. She mistakenly recorded, "John Young also owned land on Town Hill. Arthur Wheeler, present-day town clerk and knowledgeable about town history, claims that town records show that John Young owned five acres on Town Hill."[46] I cited this quote to Mr. Wheeler and asked if indeed John Young had procured the five-acre lot mentioned. He responded, "*Doris has mistakenly quoted what I said. I have found only one deed for John Young, and that deed is for the 51½ acres on Stimpson Hill.* The five acres on Town Hill were never owned by John Young, but they did belong to Joseph Mosely, John Young's brother-in-law. At one time Joseph Mosely owned all of Lot 22 in which the five-acre parcel was located."[47]

Doris Kirkpatrick reported further evidence that the John Young family was living on the five-acre "Brigham Young Lot" when Brigham was born in 1801. She stated:

> Mrs. Graves talked with William D. Canedy, a long-time town clerk. He told her that when he was 19 he had discussed the question of Brigham's birthplace with John Sawyer, a local mill owner, at that time over 90 years old. Mr. Sawyer distinctly remembered being told by Alfred Green, son of Nathan, when Alfred himself was past 90, how as a young fellow of 19 he had assisted John Young in packing

> his covered wagon for the westward journey in the spring of 1804. One of his last acts of neighborliness was to hand little Brigham, then almost 3, up to his mother before they drove off. Both Alfred Green and Mrs. Goodnow thought the cabin [on the five-acre lot] had been Brigham's birthplace.[48]

It is possible that Alfred Green was present when the John Young family bid farewell to Whitingham and commenced their journey to New York in 1804. Perhaps they departed from Joseph Mosely's home, which could have been located either on the five acres or in the vicinity, as he owned some surrounding properties as well. The question remains: Was the purported point of departure also the birth site?

Even during Brigham Young's lifetime, there was interest in ascertaining the exact spot of his birth. Clark Jillson quoted President Young's response to a letter of inquiry that expressly asked the question of location:

> Salt Lake City, Utah, May 16, 1874
>
> Dr. Oramel Martin: Dear Sir,—
>
> In reply to your note of inquiry, May 6, at the request of President Brigham Young, I have to inform you that he was born in Whitingham, Vt., June 1, 1801. Dr. Humphrey Gould of Rowe, Franklin County, Mass., if I am rightly informed, can direct you to the spot in Whitingham where it was said the house stood in which President Young was born. President Young will be pleased to see you at any time it may suit you to visit this city.
>
> Very Respectfully, Albert Carrington. [49]

Unfortunately, President Young did not pinpoint the site of his birth in his answer, and I have been unable to determine what action may have been taken by Mr. Martin as a result of this correspondence.

Clark Jillson, Marjorie W. Graves, and Doris Kirkpatrick have rendered a valuable service in attempting to unravel the complexities of the contested birth sites of Brigham Young. After trying to balance the pros and cons of the varied claims, Mrs. Kirkpatrick mused, "Each summer visitors from many states pause on Town Hill and read the legend [inscription on the 1950 monument to

Brigham Young] commemorating Whitingham's most famous son—*birthplace more or less unknown.*"[50]

After an examination of related land deeds and a review of the historical elements of the Young family's presence in Whitingham, I asked Arthur Wheeler, Whitingham town clerk, if he had any assessments to make from the accumulated evidence. He replied, "It makes more sense to have Brigham born on the old property of John Young on Stimpson Hill than at the five-acre site. The land deeds don't justify the five acres as being the Brigham Young birthplace."[51]

My research persuades me to agree with Mr. Wheeler's judgment that the birthplace would logically have been the John Young cabin, somewhere on John Young's 51½ acre parcel on Brigham Young Hill (Stimpson Hill). For the modern inquirer, there is still much to be rediscovered concerning the obscurities of the Young family habitation "over the pond in the Hemlock woods" of Whitingham.

THE BRIGHAM YOUNG MONUMENT ON TOWN HILL

While the village of Whitingham has persisted, the older settlement of Whitingham Centre on Town Hill entered a period of steady decline during the 1880s and has now completely disappeared. Doris Kirkpatrick described the transformation in these terms:

> Town Hill was once a thriving village where stagecoaches pulled up in front of a commodious tavern; children learned their lessons in a school; a bell tolled from the church; a store offered merchandise; a militia trained in a field; a blacksmith shod horses and stray animals were rounded up in a pond [pound].
>
> Only a few grass-covered cellar holes remain as mute evidence that Town Hill was once a thriving village. Today it is a popular picnic spot where fieldstone fireplaces and rustic benches and tables provide for the comfort of the tourist.[52]

The former site of Whitingham Centre has become Town Hill Memorial Park. Here stand memorials to the dead of World War I, World War II, the Korean War, and the Vietnam War. To the south of these memorials stands a twelve-foot Brigham Young monument that was dedicated on Sunday, 28 May 1950 by President George Albert Smith (see aerial photograph, items no. 5 and 7). An estimated 1,000 persons, including descendants of Brigham Young, gathered to witness the unveiling and to view the memorial inscription:

BRIGHAM YOUNG

Church Leader—Colonizer—Statesman

> Born in the Town of Whitingham, Vermont, June 1, 1801. Leader of Mormon Pioneers from Nauvoo, Illinois to the Rocky Mountains, arriving in the Valley of the Great Salt Lake July 24, 1847. Second President of the Church of Jesus Christ of Latter-day Saints, serving from December 27, 1847 until his death at Salt Lake City, Utah, August 29, 1877.
>
> His statue occupies a place in Statuary Hall, National Capitol, Washington, D.C. This monument erected by Descendants of Brigham Young in cooperation with The Church of Jesus Christ of Latter-day Saints.[53]

REMOVAL TO NEW YORK

Unable to better his family's economic condition after three years and four moves in the Whitingham area, John Young sought new farming opportunities 135 miles to the southwest, in Sherburne, Chenango County, New York. The Daniel Kent family appears to have gone with them. In 1858, Brigham Young informed an inquirer from Canandaigua, New York, "My father and family removed to Smyrna [Sherburne at the time of the move], Chenango County, N.Y., when I was about eighteen months old."[54] For Brigham this would place the move in December 1802 or January 1803. However, it would appear that he was mistaken in this calculation. As previously mentioned, John Young, Sr.'s, name was still on the Grand (tax) List in Whitingham as late as 13 December 1803. And the marriages of Brigham's sisters, Fanny and Nancy, in Whitingham during 1803 identify the continued presence of the family in Vermont.

Brigham Young's older brother, Joseph, recorded, "We remained in this town [Whitingham] until the winter of 1804 when we moved to the State of New York, the town of Sherburn[e], Chenango County. The first place of our residence was on one of the hills of what was subsequently called Smyrna (Sherburn[e] was divided [1808]) at a farmhouse owned by a man by the name of Philip Truax."[55]

Joseph's reference to "the winter of 1804" seems to target the early part of 1804, rather than the latter part of that year, for their move. Further evidence is Louisa Young's being born to John and Nabby on 26 September 1804, at Sherburne, New York, and Nancy Young Kent's giving birth to Emily Kent on 2 October 1804 at "Smyrna" [then Sherburne], both in the fall of the year and not yet into a "winter" setting.[56]

In New York, the Young family was ideally situated to receive the restored gospel of Jesus Christ a quarter of a century later. In the interim period, Brigham Young found a wide variety of residences and formed a family of his own before his eventual conversion and baptism into the Church on 14 April 1831 at Mendon, Monroe County, New York.[57]

NOTES

1. M. Hamlin Cannon, "A Pension Office Note on Brigham Young's Father," *American Historical Review* 49 (October 1944): 82–90; "History of the Church," *Juvenile Instructor* 16 (1 March 1881): 52. For an extended discussion of John Young's age at enlistment and his Revolutionary War record, see also Gene Allred Sessions, *Latter-day Patriots: Nine Mormon Families and Their Revolutionary War Heritage* (Salt Lake City: Deseret Book Co., 1975), 24–28, 192–93.
2. "Manuscript History of Brigham Young," 1, Library-Archives, Historical Department of The Church of Jesus Christ of Latter-day Saints (hereafter cited as LDS Church Historical Archives). The township of Coxsackie had been created on 7 March 1788. See Thomas F. Gordon, *Gazetteer of the State of New York* (Philadelphia: T.K. and P.G. Collins, 1836), 472.
3. Fanny Young to Phineas Howe Young, 1 January 1845, 42–44; copy of original, microfilm 281261, Harold B. Lee Library, Brigham Young University.
4. S. Dilworth Young, *"Here Is Brigham": Brigham Young—the Years to 1844* (Salt Lake City: Bookcraft, 1964), 17–18.
5. "History of Brigham Young," *Deseret News* (Salt Lake City), 3 February 1858, 377.
6. Whitingham Town Record Book, 3: 72, 203. This record also shows that on 16 June 1795, Joseph Mosely, Sr., purchased 140½ acres of land in Lots 21

and 22 of Fitches Land Grant, Whitingham Township, Vermont, gaining in the process one-half ownership in a sawmill and corn mill on Sadawaga Brook. During October of that year, he acquired four more parcels of land in the north half of Lot 7, Fitches Grant, followed by 69¾ acres in Lot 22 of Fitches Grant. He then procured the south end of Lot 21, Fitches Grant, and the whole of Lot 9, Fitches Grant. This last lot totaled 250 acres.

7. Personal interview with Arthur D. Wheeler, 17 August 1987, Whitingham, Vermont. Mr. Wheeler served as Whitingham town clerk from 1954 to 1989; his knowledge of the records, physical location of properties, and history of the region was indispensable to the writer. Joseph Mosely sold his remaining holdings in Whitingham to Loveil Bullock on 2 June 1806. See Whitingham Town Record Book, 4: 233.
8. Whitingham Town Record Book, 3: 675; and personal interview with Arthur D. Wheeler, 17 August 1987.
9. Personal interview with Arthur D. Wheeler, 17 August 1987.
10. Clark Jillson, *Green Leaves from Whitingham, Vermont: A History of the Town* (Worcester, Mass.: Private Press of the Author, 1894), 51.
11. Joseph Young, Sr., Journal, 10–11, LDS Church Historical Archives.
12. "Manuscript History of Brigham Young," 1.
13. Extracts taken from the *Gazette and Courier* (Greenfield, Massachusetts), 23 August 1880, from the address of Hon. Clark Jillson at the centennial of Whitingham, 18 August 1880, on Town Hill; located in Marjorie W. Graves File, Whitingham town clerk's office.
14. Susa Young Gates and Leah D. Widtsoe, *The Life Story of Brigham Young* (New York: Macmillan Company, 1930), 3.
15. Leonard J. Arrington, *Brigham Young: American Moses* (New York: Alfred A. Knopf, 1985), 9.
16. Doris Kirkpatrick, "Where Was Brigham Young Born Anyway?" *Brattleboro Reformer* (Brattleboro, Vermont), 1 July 1983, 15.
17. Leonard Brown, Esq., *History of Whitingham from Its Organization to the Present Time* (Brattleboro, Vt.: Frank E. Housh, 1886), 169.
18. Susa Young Gates, "Mothers of the Latter-day Prophets: Abigail Howe Young," *The Juvenile Instructor* 59 (January 1924): 3.
19. Ibid., 4–5.
20. Joseph Young, Sr., Journal, 4–7.
21. "History of Brigham Young," *Deseret News,* 27 January 1858, 369.
22. Whitingham Town Record Book, 1: 77.
23. Grand List, 1802–1804, for 13 December 1803, Whitingham Town Record Book, vol. 1. Arthur D. Wheeler, town clerk, said that the Grand List is an assessed value of the property, not the tax that is actually assessed each person. The evaluation of the properties in the whole town would be totaled and a percentage then charged to the individual property holder, based on that evaluation. From personal interview, 18 August 1987.

24. James Amesy Little, "Brigham Young," 2, unpublished manuscript, LDS Church Historical Archives.
25. Leonard Brown, Esq., *History of Whitingham,* 99–100.
26. Gates and Widtsoe, 3.
27. Hamilton Child, *Gazetteer and Business Directory of Windham County, Vermont, 1724–1884* (Syracuse, N. Y.: Journal Office, 1884), 304. The "part of the cellar walls" is not discernable today.
28. Personal interview with Arthur D. Wheeler, 18 August 1987. Mr. Wheeler stated that the systematic numbering and posting of roads by civil authorities didn't occur until sometime after the turn of the century.
29. Doris Kirkpatrick, "Where Was Brigham Young Born Anyway?" 15; see also Doris Kirkpatrick, "Brigham Young Just Missed Being Born in Hopkinton," *Worcester Sunday Telegram* (Worcester, Massachusetts), 19 October 1958, sec. F, 7–8. (Doris Kirkpatrick is now deceased.)
30. Extracts taken from the *Gazette and Courier,* 23 August 1880, from the address of Hon. Clark Jillson at the Centennial of Whitingham, 18 August 1880, on Town Hill, located in Marjorie W. Graves File, Whitingham Town Clerk's Office.
31. Phone interview with Arthur D. Wheeler, 21 April 1995.
32. Ibid. Matthias F. Cowley said that the monument had been placed there by "non-Mormon residents," but did not specify who or when. See "My Acquaintance with President Brigham Young," *Millennial Star,* 100 (22 September 1938): 600.
33. Arrington, 435, n. 11.
34. Grand List, 1802–1804, Whitingham Town Record Book, vol. 1.
35. "Manuscript History of Brigham Young," 1.
36. Personal interview with Arthur D. Wheeler, 18 August 1987.
37. Joseph Young, Sr., Journal, 7, italics added.
38. Personal interview with Arthur D. Wheeler, 18 August 1987. Sadawaga Pond or Lake lies between Town Hill and the village of Whitingham. The large body of water to the west and northwest of the village of Whitingham is the Harriman Reservoir. The reservoir was made possible by an earth-fill dam completed in the spring of 1923.
39. Jillson, 227; see also Esther Munroe Swift, *Vermont Place-Names, Foot Prints of History* (Brattleboro, Vt.: Stephen Green Press, 1977), 512.
40. Personal interview with Arthur D. Wheeler, 18 August 1987.
41. Phone interview with Arthur D. Wheeler, 21 April 1995.
42. Phone interview with Arthur D. Wheeler, 21 April 1995; extracts taken from the *Gazette and Courier,* 23 August 1880, from the address of Hon. Clark Jillson at the Centennial of Whitingham, 18 August 1880, on Town Hill, and located in Marjorie W. Graves File, Whitingham Town Clerk's Office.
43. Marjorie W. Graves, "Stories of Whitingham" (n.p.: 1975), 97, copy located in Whitingham town clerk's office. (Marjorie Graves is now deceased.)

44. Doris Kirkpatrick, "Where Was Brigham Young Born Anyway?" 15.
45. Personal interview with Arthur D. Wheeler, 18 August 1987.
46. Doris Kirkpatrick, "Where Was Brigham Young Born Anyway?" 15.
47. Personal interview with Arthur D. Wheeler, 18 August 1987, italics added.
48. Doris Kirkpatrick, "Where Was Brigham Young Born Anyway?" 15. William D. Canedy served as Whitingham town clerk from 1917 to 1952. Marjorie Graves reported, "[Alfred Greene] remembered very well that their home [John Young's] was at the far end of the Stebbins lot." See Graves, 96–97.
49. Extracts taken from the *Gazette and Courier,* 23 August 1880.
50. Doris Kirkpatrick, "Where Was Brigham Young Born Anyway?" 35, italics added.
51. Personal interview with Arthur D. Wheeler, 18 August 1987. In a phone interview on 21 April 1995, Arthur again reiterated his original assessment that Brigham Young's birthplace was on John Young's 51½ acres.
52. Doris Kirkpatrick, "Where Was Brigham Young Born Anyway?" 15.
53. The monument, standing twelve feet high, is a polished shaft of light granite from Barre, Vermont. Following remarks by LDS Church officials and local civic leaders, the monument was unveiled by three granddaughters and two grandsons of Brigham Young: Leah Dunford Widtsoe (daughter of Susa Young), Gladys Young Orlos, Edith Young Booth, Don C. Young, and George S. Young; see "Commemorative Exercises, Unveiling of Monument at Birthplace of Brigham Young, Whitingham, Vermont, Sunday, May 28, 1950" (program); Clarence S. Barker, "Monument to Brigham Young Unveiled in Fitting Ceremonies at the Birthplace," *Deseret News,* 4 June 1950, Church section, 3, 16; Clarence S. Barker, "From the Green Hills to Statuary Hall," *Improvement Era* 53 (August 1950): 630–31.

    President George Albert Smith followed the ceremony with an address and a dedicatory prayer, petitioning that the Lord's Spirit might be enjoyed by those visiting the Town Hill memorial. He said:

    We are here now to present this monument of granite, the native granite of this great state, that which President Brigham Young himself undoubtedly would choose if he were here, and, Heavenly Father, we pray that thy Spirit may remain here that those who come to read the inscription on the monument may realize that thou art the Father of us all and that he whom we are gathered to honor was great enough to assume his responsibilities and carry a tremendous load during his long life (see President George Albert Smith, "Dedicatory Prayers at Unveiling Ceremonies," *Improvement Era,* 53 [September 1950]: 693).

    President George Albert Smith also gave a second dedicatory prayer the following Thursday in the rotunda of the Capitol Building, Washington, D.C., 1 June 1950, at the unveiling of the Brigham Young statue placed in Statuary Hall.
54. "A Letter from Brigham Young," *South County Journal* (Wakefield, Rhode Island), 25 September 1858, reprinted from *The Ontario Republican Times* (Canandaigua, New York).

55. Joseph Young, Sr., Journal, 7–8. Sherburne was divided and the town of Safford created on 25 March 1808. However, the name of the town of Safford was soon changed to Smyrna on 6 April 1808. See Hamilton Child, *Gazetteer and Business Directory, Chenango County, N.Y. for 1869–70* (Syracuse, N. Y.: The Journal Office, 1869), 132.
56. The births and birthplaces of Louisa Young and Emily Kent are found on the TIB cards located in the LDS Church Family History Department, Salt Lake City, Utah. Daniel Kent appears only in the Grand List for 13 December 1803 ($26.50). See Whitingham Town Record Book, vol. 1. It would seem that the Young and Kent families traveled together to Sherburne, New York, in 1804.
57. For an in-depth examination of Brigham Young and other family members in the state of New York, see Richard F. Palmer and Karl D. Butler, *Brigham Young: The New York Years* (Provo, Ut.: Charles Redd Center for Western Studies, 1982).

CHAPTER 2

Conversion and Transformation

Brigham Young's New York Roots and the Search for Bible Religion

Ronald K. Esplin

Director of the Joseph Fielding Smith Institute
Brigham Young University

Brigham Young's New England heritage and his youth and young adulthood in Western New York were the foundation for his later success as a powerful religious leader. Though his family left New England before Brigham was three years old, their Puritan mores vitally influenced his upbringing and character. The agrarian and frontier culture of Western New York, along with Brigham's own reactions to the fires of religious revival that seared the region, modified this Puritan heritage. Tracing his religious roots and his conversion to the restored gospel in New York allows us to see his profoundly religious nature and to understand that, despite having exceptional practical skills and successes, he was fundamentally a religious leader.[1]

Brigham Young's New England roots ran deep. He numbered among his ancestors several generations of New England Youngs, Brighams, Howes, and Goddards. His parents, John and Nabby Howe Young, were both natives of Massachusetts, he a poor orphan and she the daughter of an established and respected family.[2] After John and Nabby were married in 1785, they lived for a time near her family in Hopkinton. Though they were industrious and frugal, a large family soon outstripped their resources and forced them into several moves in an effort to improve their economic position.[3] One of these moves took the family briefly to Vermont, where Brigham Young, the ninth child, was born in Whitingham on 1 June 1801. Before Brigham's third birthday, the Youngs moved again, this time to the beautiful Finger Lakes country of Western New York, where Brigham grew to manhood.

John Young settled his family on new land in communities still without their first decent road or access to market. Laboring on and living off this land with his family, young Brigham was predictably influenced deeply. Rather than receiving formal schooling, Brigham received an education that consisted of clearing, planting, plowing, and learning to work with his hands. Speaking later of the background he shared with his New York friend Heber C. Kimball, he said:

> We never had the opportunity of letters in our youth, but we had the privilege of picking up brush, chopping down trees, rolling logs, and working amongst the roots, and of getting our shins, feet and toes bruised.[4]

"I have been a poor boy and a poor man, and my parents were poor," he said later. While that description fits most of Brigham Young's childhood, the hardest years came after the death of his mother soon after his own fourteenth birthday.[5] Without mother keeping house, the older children moved on, and the family was divided. Brigham and his younger brother Lorenzo accompanied their father, breaking land for a new farm and harvesting sugar maple on isolated acreage near the southern tip of Seneca Lake. During this difficult period they barely had enough to eat.[6]

Like most youth, Brigham Young enjoyed his times of fun and frolic, "running, jumping, wrestling" and "laying out [his] strength for naught." According to later memory, such frivolous pursuits stopped rather suddenly when John Young told his sixteen-year-old son, "You can now have your time; go and provide for yourself."[7]

Breaking with the farming of his youth, Brigham Young set out to become a builder and an artisan. As a young craftsman he developed patience with detail and a concern for honest, reliable work and quality workmanship. More than fifty years later, his response to the letter of an old New York friend stressed his lasting commitment to those qualities:

> I have believed all my life that that which was worth doing was worth doing well, and have considered it as much a part of my religion to do honest, reliable work, such as would

endure, for those who employed me, as to attend to the services of God's worship on the Sabbath.[8]

Young Brigham was conscious of his reputation and his standing in society. Although he recognized in himself "weakness, sin, darkness and ignorance," he sought to use appropriate language and to conduct himself in business and society "in a way to gain for myself the respect of the moral and good among my neighbors."[9] Those who knew him in Western New York later reported good of him. In contrast to Joseph Smith, who resided only a few miles away and who was ridiculed because of his youthful claims of visions, Brigham Young was thought of as upright and sober—until after he joined the Mormons at age thirty-one.

In 1857, one Canandaigua resident who had known the Youngs responded to the publication of an unflattering article about the later Brigham. Stressing that he defended not the Brigham Young of Utah "but Brigham Young as he was, while in Canandaigua, before he became a Mormon," the writer answered the charge that Brigham had been poor and indolent. "He was poor but had enough to be comfortable," insisted the writer. "He was not indolent, but was a hard working man, . . . very handy with tools"; and his neighbors thought him "a consistent Christian."[10]

By the time Brigham Young married on 8 October 1824 at age twenty-three, he was well prepared to provide for a family. He had supported himself for a half-dozen years as "painter, joiner, glazer," and was accepted as a responsible member of his community. His bride, Miriam Works, was five years his junior. A neighbor remembered Miriam as a "beautiful blond with blue eyes and wavy air; gentle and lovable," and Brigham as "vigorous, handsome and magnetic . . . as fine a specimen of young manhood as I have ever known."[11]

Caring for his family and toiling at his trade, however, were but part of his life. He yearned also for religious fulfillment and for answers to nagging questions about life and salvation.

As with his quest for economic independence, his quest for religious fulfillment was a journey of many years. Raised by parents of Puritan stock in the Western New York hotbed of religious enthusiasm, young Brigham grew up with religious and moral instruction. Though John and Nabby Young discarded the harsher Calvinist beliefs of their ancestors and had chosen Methodism, they were strict nonetheless—as Brigham Young put it, "some of the most strict religionists that lived upon the earth."

> When I was young, I was kept within very strict bounds, and was not allowed to walk more than half an hour on Sunday for exercise. The proper and necessary gambols of youth [were] denied me. . . . I had not a chance to dance when I was young, and never heard the enchanting tones of the violin, until I was eleven years of age; and then I thought I was on the high way to hell, if I suffered myself to linger and listen to it.[12]

His upbringing was so strict that if he exclaimed "Devil," he believed he had sworn "very wickedly." Any violation of family mores meant swift discipline from his father, whose practice was "a word and a blow . . . but the blow came first." Though his mother mellowed somewhat this stern, emotionally narrow approach, she generally sustained John's strict religious views.[13]

His parents' good example reinforced for Brigham the moral precepts they taught. For years he worked side by side with his father and saw his integrity firsthand, and of his mother he once said, "No better woman ever lived in the world than she was." No matter the provocation, neither would permit their children to wrong another. Brigham idealized his mother and long remembered her bedside pleas to "honour the name of the Father and the Son, and to reverence the holy Book. . . . Do everything that is good; do nothing that is evil; and if you see any persons in distress, administer to their wants."[14]

This strict moral training was effective. "I do not know that I ever wronged my neighbor, even to the value of a pin," he said, in reference to his parents' teachings. He said of himself on one occasion that from the days of his youth, he had tried to live a "pure and refined life. . . . I have not infringed upon any law, or trod upon the rights of my neighbors; but I have tried to walk in the paths of righteousness."[15] Though he sometimes yielded to anger, he had no memory of ever having "stole, lied, gambled, got drunk, or disobeyed my parents." Indeed, he abandoned his work as a painter when, in his words, "I had either to be dishonest or quit; and I quit."[16]

The strictness of Young's upbringing also showed itself in the control he maintained over feelings and emotions. Not until the sweeping changes in his life brought about by his conversion to Mormonism and his adoption of Joseph Smith as a model did many of his religious and personal feelings find expression, and throughout his life he remained reluctant to reveal deep emotion. No doubt this is one reason for the popular image of the later Young as a flinty and unfeeling leader. He once told the Saints that his heart was so full of tender emotions for them that he could easily weep like a child, "but I am careful to keep my tears to myself."[17]

In temperament Brigham Young was fiercely independent; the urge to be "free and untrammeled" was a vital part of his soul. "I am naturally opposed to being crowded," he once explained, adding that he instinctively opposed anyone who tried to force him. Although never attracted to drink, he stoutly refused to sign a temperance pledge when his father urged him to do so. "If I sign the temperance pledge," he told his father, "I feel that I am bound, and I wish to do just right, without being bound to do it; I want my liberty. My independence," he announced, "is sacred to me."[18] A son of the generation who fought the War for Independence, he saw himself as free before God, accepting all the rights and responsibilities that entailed.

Not surprisingly, this independence early manifested itself in matters of religion. Instead of accepting all of the strict Methodist views of his parents, Brigham developed independent ideas even as a youth. Of the existence of God he had no doubt; nothing else made sense. "I co[ul]d not get it into my mind that there was a sun moon & stars & nobody to make them—I never co[ul]d get it into my head 'heres a book, but there was no printer.'" He felt it "natural . . . to be reverential" toward God and His creation.

Nor did he have any difficulty following his mother's example of reverence for "the holy Book." At her urging, he read the Bible and tried to understand its precepts and apply them in his life.[19] Indeed, as with many who rejected the sectarian orthodoxies of that day, he parted with mainstream Protestantism partly because of his independent reading of the Bible and his inability to reconcile its teachings with the tumultuous world of religion around him. His stubborn independence encouraged him to chart a personal course as he pondered "these eternal things" amid the multiplicity of religious voices.[20]

Growing up in Western New York, he was early on exposed to contending creeds. "From my youth up," he remembered, "their cry was, 'Lo here is Christ, lo there is Christ,' . . . each claiming that it had the Savior, and that others were wrong." He decided to join none of them until he could judge for himself, and he often prayed, "if there is a God in heaven save me, that I may know all and not be fooled."[21] Brought up "amid . . . flaming, fiery revivals" in one of the greatest periods of religious turmoil ever, Young found it "all a mystery."

> I saw them get religion all around me—men were rolling and holloring and bawling and thumping but it had no effect on me—I wanted to know the truth that I might not be fooled—children and young men got religion, but I could not.[22]

The intensity of the religious climate affected his family as well. When Brigham Young was fifteen, his younger brother Lorenzo had a vivid dream. In this dream Lorenzo saw a brilliant gold carriage drawn rapidly by a beautiful pair of white horses:

> It was manifested to me that the Savior was in the carriage, and that it was driven by His servant. It stopped near me and the Savior inquired, "Where is your Brother Brigham?" After answering His question He inquired about my other brothers, and concerning my father. . . . He stated that He wanted us all, but especially my brother Brigham.[23]

The dream left such an impression that Lorenzo remained awake the rest of that night. Seeing no other interpretation, he felt that it portended some great evil about to befall his brother and perhaps the rest of the family. Though his father felt no such fears about it, such an experience could only have intensified Brigham's religious yearnings, perhaps suggesting that God was specifically aware of him.

Although the revivals did not move Brigham to a profession of religion, they did have an impact. They reminded him that he was "unchurched" and multiplied his religious concerns. He turned to his Bible and to family and friends who shared similar concerns. Unsatisfied by revivalist leaders, he concluded that he would gladly give all the gold and silver he ever could possess to meet "with one individual who could show me anything about God, heaven, or the plan of salvation." Though still a youth, he embarked on a serious quest for a satisfying religion and "the path that leads to the kingdom of heaven."[24]

Brigham Young actively inquired into the beliefs of the major denominations in his region, and of "almost every other religious ism" as well. Each time, the result was disappointing.[25] For one thing, it distressed him that the actions of professed Christians were not always in harmony with Christ's example or with his own strict upbringing. Too often, he thought, they oppressed the poor or cheated their neighbor.

Such hypocrisy was not his main objection, however. He parted company with all of them over doctrine. None preached doctrine that answered his personal yearnings and growing questions, or that harmonized with his own reading of the New Testament. Though morals, preaching, and intentions were satisfactory, none taught doctrines that suited him. All had truth, he was certain, but not one could he embrace without reservation. "As far as their teachings were in accordance with the Bible, I could believe them, but no further."[26]

Brigham wanted more than moral preaching and generalizations. He yearned for solid doctrine, for explicit teachings about God. He wanted concrete descriptions of the path to salvation which, he believed, required more than a mere profession of belief. In camp meetings, he observed men and women worked into a trance by religious excitement, motionless "from ten minutes to probably an hour without the least sign of life." When they awoke, he asked them what they had seen or learned. Always the answer was the same: "Nothing or nobody. Nothing at all."[27]

He went to hear the famed preacher Lorenzo Dow, hoping to learn "something about the Son of God, the will of God, what the ancients did and received, saw and heard pertaining to God and heaven." After an eloquent preachment, Brigham asked himself what he had learned. "Nothing, nothing but morals." Dow could talk about the Sabbath and tell the people not to lie, steal, or commit adultery, but when it came to teaching the "things of God," for Brigham he was "as dark as midnight."[28]

As Brigham Young grew older and bolder, he began to question the ministers directly: "I read so and so in the Bible, how do you understand it?" Not only did they fail to enlighten him ("they would always leave me where they found me, in the dark"), when he made known his own feelings, they often called him an infidel.[29] Neither their creeds nor their preaching gave him solace or taught him how to be saved.

We can best understand Brigham Young's religious longings and his reactions to sectarianism in the context of the widespread "seeker" and "Christian primitivist" movement of his day. Brigham Young grew to manhood in the time and place since known as "the burned-over district" because of the intense religious enthusiasm that swept it. Here waves of sectarian revivals provided fertile ground for religious discussion, dissention, and innovation.[30]

Exposed to competing religious claims from his youth on, Brigham developed his own religious philosophy partly in response to these. This philosophy led him, as it did other like-minded contemporaries, to become a "seeker" and a "primitivist." Dissatisfied with sectarian doctrines and practices—especially the unseemly division and rivalry—primitivists sought to return to New Testament patterns. Generally anticlerical, with limited formal training and a lay clergy, they remained aloof from existing denominations.

Although he may not have been even loosely associated with a "primitivist" or "seeker" group until his mid-twenties, he probably had acquaintances and associates who shared this religious orientation. His disappointments with the sects—and his expectations for religion rooted in the Bible—parallel the assumptions and conclusions of other primitivists too closely to be entirely coincidental.[31]

In general, primitivists were stirred by the revivals but reacted strongly against the sectarian conflict they fostered. Viewing the old-line churches as corrupt and apostate, they stressed the need for "a restoration" of the "primitive" faith. Some awaited a new prophet as the best answer to general apostasy. And, like Brigham Young, primitivists turned to the Bible—their own reading of the Bible—as the only authoritative guide. Brigham Young clearly did not stand alone in these principles. His reading of the Bible and his understanding of its message owed something to the primitivist movement that had gathered momentum since the turn of the century.[32]

Reading the Bible convinced Young that true religion was more than good morals and professions of belief, but that it needed also authority and structure:

> I understood from the Bible that when the Lord has a church upon the earth it was a system of ordinances, of laws and regulations to be obeyed, a society presided over and regulated by officers and ministers peculiar to itself to answer such and such purposes, and to bring to pass such and such results.

He challenged the ministers to tell him how the kingdom of God *should* be built up if the New Testament pattern was not the way. "My dear friend," they would answer, "these things are done away with." Ordinances? Mere matters of ceremony; belief was sufficient. He could not find a religious system that followed the scriptural pattern. For Brigham the conclusion was inescapable: "I knew that Jesus Christ had no true Church upon the earth."[33]

As Young understood the New Testament pattern, a people "built up and believing" according to its principles would have among them "all the gifts and graces of the Gospel," including Apostles "to rule, govern, control, dictate, and give counsel." Above all, he longed to associate with a man of God—not a preacher of morals alone, but a prophet with the knowledge and power of heaven. Later he remembered having felt

> that if I could see the face of a prophet, such as had lived on the earth in former times, a man that had revelations, to whom the heavens were opened, who knew God and his character, I would freely circumscribe the earth on my hands and knees.[34]

Although his convictions about biblical religion had not changed, in 1824, about the time of his marriage, Brigham Young formally associated with the Methodism of his parents. "I patiently waited until I was twenty-three years old," he said later, and then "to prevent my being any more pestered about it I joined."[35] Was he weary of being called an unbeliever? Did he respond to his wife's request? Did he seek formal religious association at the time of his marriage to further legitimize his position in the community? Or was this a response to revivals? According to one scholar, revivals reminded the unchurched that they must belong to a church, "a point about which they were already feeling guilty." Perhaps repeated revivals finally convinced Brigham that he ought to do what he could, even if it was not all he hoped for.

Clearly he remained concerned about salvation and viewed this as a proper time to "break off my sins and lead a better life." Perhaps a formal religious commitment would help. The Reformed Methodism that Brigham joined had rejected strict Calvinism and moved in some measure in the directions he sought. Though he did not agree with all of its teachings, he saw much good in it and no harm in joining. At his insistence, he was baptized by immersion by a society that held that the form of the ordinance was not important.[36]

Young's formal association with the Methodists was likely brief. Not long after his baptism he found employment in Oswego, New York, where he joined with other seekers in an informal society of prayer, song, and worship. Soon afterward, he moved to the Canandaigua-Mendon area, where the local Reformed Methodist organization had been dissolved.[37]

More than thirty years after he left Oswego, Brigham Young received a letter that opens a revealing window on his early religious quest. Hiram McKee (now a minister), having heard about "Brigham Young and the Mormons," feared that his old friend had lost the piety of his youth. "How sweet was our communion in old Oswego, how encouraging our prayers, and enlivening our songs," wrote McKee of the association they once shared:

> I have often thought of you as I have been engaged in trying to preach the gospel. . . . I have not forgotten your

> advise, counsel, prayers. My confidence was great in you, in view of your deep piety, and faith in God. You was one of my early spiritual friends, and guides, and I have often enquired in my mind, I wonder if Brigham enjoys as much piety now as then, or wheather ambitian, and love of power, and distinction did not hold some sway in that mind, that was once so humble, contrite and devoted.[38]

Brigham assured his friend that he, too, vividly remembered "the scenes, feelings and experience" of Oswego "when we were fellow seekers after the truths revealed from Heaven," adding that "so far as I am able to determine, I feel that I am and ever since have been as honest a seeker after truth as I was during our acquaintance in Oswego."[39]

Among acquaintances at this time, Brigham Young was known as honest, sober, and industrious, a "consistent Christian" who was interested in religion but not carried away by religious enthusiasms. When a Canandaigua newspaper reprinted many years later the charge that Brigham Young had been "very fanatical and consequently noisy in meetings, shouting, screaming and howling with all his energy," one who had known him well during this period replied. Young's older brother Phinehas, himself a preacher, may have been "noisy," conceded the respondent, "but it is not true of Brigham. . . . We never thought him fanatical until after he became a Mormon."[40]

Clearly, Brigham was a practical man, not visionary or fanatic. Yet he long remembered a remarkable "vision" that he and others saw in the fall of 1827. Later, in Nauvoo, he described the remarkable lights that for two hours on a moonless night formed marching armies across the sky. "I gazed at it with my Wife—the light was perfectly clear and remained several hours—it formed into men like as if there were great armies." Several miles away, Brigham's sister Fanny, father John Young, brother-in-law John P. Greene, and others witnessed the same display. Heber Kimball told the same Nauvoo audience that "President Young has given a short sketch of what has been. . . . I distinctly heard the guns crack and the swords clash."[41]

Joseph Young saw this as a sign of the coming of the Son of Man. No doubt Brigham and Miriam also saw it as a sign, but what it portended they did not know. For several years the experience remained for them a vivid memory without specific meaning.

It was probably soon after this experience that Brigham Young first heard of Joseph Smith's "Indian Bible":

> I suppose it was the first time that Joseph Smith gave to his Father the account of the finding of the records, that there was printed in the newspaper a short paragraph . . . that a young man had seen an angel and [the angel] had told him where to find an Indian Bible.[42]

Living only a few miles from the Smiths, the Youngs heard other stories about the young man and the book, generally negative stories that ridiculed his pretensions or exaggerated his foibles.[43] But not until several years later did Brigham learn that on 22 September 1827, the very night he and his wife observed the lights, the angel had delivered to Joseph Smith the gold plates. Brigham also did not know that the mysterious book would be part of his own long quest for personal religious integrity.

In 1829, Brigham and Miriam moved to Mendon and set up shop and home near Heber C. Kimball, a cousin soon to become Brigham's closest and lifelong friend. Father John Young was already in Mendon; and sisters Fanny Murray and Rhoda Greene, along with brothers Lorenzo and Phinehas, lived nearby. Like Brigham, some of his relatives and new associates in the Mendon area could be described as seekers. In the words of Heber Kimball, they shared the same principles, "for the truth was what we wanted and would have."[44] Others, like Phinehas and Joseph Young, associated with the churches and, as lay preachers, taught the religion they knew.

Here, only a few miles from Palmyra, they would all encounter the Book of Mormon and eventually accept it as new scripture. But that was yet to come. In 1829, when the local press reported that Martin Harris had been to Rochester to prepare for publication of the Golden Bible, the notice apparently aroused no great sense of anticipation.[45]

Far from anticipating great things in the future, Brigham Young at this time experienced gloominess, even despair. In part

Brigham Young and his four brothers, left to right, Lorenzo, Brigham, Phinehas, Joseph, and John, ca. 1871.

he was despondent over his failure to satisfy deep religious longings. Poverty and perhaps feelings of inferiority may also have contributed. Frequent moves suggest that he had not yet fulfilled his ambitions or found his niche in the world. Experience had also discouraged him about human nature in general. Already he had seen firsthand enough examples of how men treated one another to make him "sick, tired, and disgusted with the world." He felt like withdrawing from society and leaving behind its "vain, foolish, wicked, and unsatisfying customs and practices"—an impulse that helps us understand his later commitment to establishing a new society apart from the world.[46]

Brigham was not alone in feeling cast down. His friend Heber remembered feeling so gloomy during this period that he wished he were dead. Brigham's brothers Joseph and Phinehas sometimes expressed the same heaviness. According to Phinehas, both he and Brigham felt so disheartened in the fall of 1829 that they could not even pray with any enthusiasm. At the time Phinehas, echoing a common primitivist hope, tried to encourage his brother that surely things would soon change: "Hang on," he said, "for I know the Lord is agoing to do some thing for us."[47]

This, then, was the Brigham Young that Mormonism found. His manner of speech, his practical abilities, and his lack of formal training and refinement were common in the developing Western New York of his youth and young manhood. His vision of the good life, his closeness to the soil and to those who produced with their hands, his knowledge of human nature, were all rooted in the fertile soils of his homeland. A Puritan, disciplined and introspective, he found life less than fulfilling. He was pessimistic about his own future and the condition of mankind, and he found no solace in the philosophies of his day. Though a man of rough-hewn toughness, independence, and ability, Brigham had found no belief to unify mind and soul, no key to unlock his energies, no cause to prod him to the growth stoked by great efforts. Nearly thirty years old, he was liked and respected but not distinguished. He seemed likely to remain a craftsman, or certainly to become nothing more ambitious than a local politician.

The publication of the Book of Mormon set in motion the process that changed Brigham Young's life, eventually dispelling the gloom, satisfying his deep religious longings, and sending him in directions never anticipated. He later remembered an awareness of the Book of Mormon, both by news accounts and word of mouth, as soon as it was published in March 1830, only a few miles away.[48] Had he expected anything important in connection with it, no doubt he would have sought a copy instead of waiting until it came to him. But he did not.

Joseph Smith's brother Samuel Smith, an early missionary, left two copies of the book with members of the Young family—one purchased by Brigham's brother Phinehas, and another loaned to Brigham's sister Rhoda and her husband, John P. Greene.[49] Phinehas set aside all other labors, "read it twice through, and pronounced it true." He then lent the book to his father who, after reading it, said it was "the greatest work and the clearest of error of anything he had ever seen, the Bible not excepted." Phinehas's sister Fanny Murray got it next, read it "and declared it a revelation."[50] Soon Brigham Young read either Phinehas's or Greene's copy.[51]

Although Brigham apparently had access to the book within a month of its publication, he was slower than others of his family to pronounce the work divine.[52]

> "Hold on," says I. . . . "Wait a little while; what is the doctrine of the book, and of the revelations the Lord has given? Let me apply my heart to them"; and after I had done this, I considered it my right to know for myself. . . . I wished time sufficient to prove all things for myself.[53]

While intent on not being taken in by still another religious novelty, Brigham could not risk passing over something that might satisfy his long-felt desires. He sat down, alone, to ponder—and to test the book the only way he knew: slowly, carefully, methodically. As he approached the book, he felt no need for divine revelation about its authenticity. His "natural wisdom and judgment" had been sufficient, he thought, to comprehend the deficiencies and discrepancies in the creeds of the day, and he expected the same to be true with the Book of Mormon. Instead, he found something he could not fully comprehend, either to embrace or discard. As he later told his assembled kin in Nauvoo, "I could get to the bottom of all religions that I have any knowledge of, but this I reasoned on month after month. . . . This was out of my reach."[54]

For eighteen months, Brigham Young pondered the book and its message. He compared the book's teachings with the Bible and allowed its ideas to ripen in his mind.[55] Though he had long felt that traditions lay heavy upon the Christian world, blinding it to simple Biblical truths, he now struggled with his own traditions and presuppositions. Not until he had considered the book for more than a year did Brigham inform his brother Phinehas that he was "convinced that there was something in Mormonism." Phinehas replied that he had long been satisfied of that himself.[56]

As he began to be satisfied in his mind about the Book of Mormon, Brigham desired to meet those "who professed to believe it" and to judge in them the fruit of the doctrines. Ever practical, he wanted to see "whether good common sense was manifest; and if they had that, I wanted them to present it in accordance with the Scriptures."[57]

The first Mormon elders that he and his kin encountered were probably those from a small Mormon branch in Columbia, Bradford County, Pennsylvania, who several times passed through the Mendon area, traveling to or from Kirtland, Geauga County, Ohio. Heber Kimball may have listened to them before Brigham—likely in the spring of 1831, when the Mormon elders traveled to Kirtland for a conference to be held in June. Although Kimball first listened out of curiosity, their message that an angel had visited Joseph Smith with the fullness of the gospel, calling upon all men to repent, and their promise that the gifts of the Spirit would follow those that believed, immediately interested him. Said Kimball:

> As soon as I heard them I was convinced that they taught the truth, and that I had only received a part of the ordinances under the Baptist church. I also saw and heard the gifts of the spirit manifested by the elders, for they spoke in tongues and interpreted, which tended to strengthen my faith.[58]

Brigham and Heber both heard these elders preach in the fall of 1831 as they returned from Ohio. According to Kimball's account, he and Brigham were "constrained by the Spirit to bear testimony of the truth which we had heard, and when we did this, the power of God rested upon us and we had a testimony that the work was true." Young noted simply that they preached "the everlasting Gospel as revealed to Joseph Smith the Prophet, which I heard and believed."[59]

Brigham now pondered not only the Book of Mormon but also the message left by the elders and his feelings upon hearing them. Soon after, Heber Kimball accompanied Brigham, his brother Joseph, and his father to cut wood for Phinehas. As they labored, Heber related later, they reflected on the things the elders had told them, especially upon the gathering of the Saints. They felt the glory of God around them and saw in vision

> the gathering of the Saints to Zion, and the glory that would rest upon them; and many more things connected with that great event, such as the sufferings and persecutions which would come upon the people of God, and the calamities and judgments which would come upon the world.[60]

Heber interpreted this experience as a witness that the message of the Restoration was of God.

Although increasingly interested in Mormonism, they still had no opportunity to observe a Mormon meeting or worship with a Mormon family. Soon after the elders left Mendon, Heber proposed to Brigham and Phinehas that they use his horse and sleigh to visit the Pennsylvania members in their own homes.[61] Apparently Vilate Kimball remained behind to care for the children so the other wives could accompany their husbands. Miriam must have been as eager to visit the Pennsylvania Mormons as was Brigham; otherwise she, debilitated by consumption, would not have braved in winter the two hundred and fifty mile round-trip journey.[62] As Brigham later summarized,

> We stayed with the church the[re] about six days, attended their meetings, heard them speak in tongues, interpret and prophecy: these things truly caused us to rejoice and praise the Lord. We returned home being convinced of the truth of these things . . . and bore testimony to the truth of those things which we had seen and heard to our friends and neighbors.[63]

As soon as they returned from Pennsylvania, Brigham Young used the horse and sleigh to travel two hundred miles to discuss the gospel with his brother Joseph, then preaching Methodism in Canada. Although he had now largely satisfied his own mind about Mormonism, he wanted to share his feelings with his respected older brother and see if Joseph concurred. Young's minister brother-in-law, John Greene, traveling his own preaching circuit, accompanied him partway that February. As the two men discussed Mormonism, Brigham told Reverend Greene, "If you dont get snagged I'll treat."[64]

Brigham characterized his brother Joseph as a solemn man of sad heart, a "very spiritual man" who was always praying. Like Brigham, after seeking wisdom and solace from the Bible, he had concluded that there were no "Bible Christians" on the earth. That conclusion left him in despair; he neither laughed nor smiled. "I do not see any possible escape for the human family," he announced; "all must go to perdition." It was to this older and trusted brother that Brigham Young explained his feelings about the "folly and nonsense so prevalent in the Christian world" and about what he had found in Mormonism.[65] Joseph Young remembered Brigham reporting to him

> many things of interest concerning the signs and wonderful mericales being wraught through the believers in this new faith. I was ripe for receiving something that would feed my mental cravings, and this seemed to be the food I wanted—nothing could have been more acceptable to my poor famishing soul. I hailed it as my spiritual jubilee—a deliverance from a long night of darkness and bondage.[66]

Immensely interested, Joseph Young arranged to leave his Canadian ministry and return to Mendon with his brother. In March, shortly after the two arrived in Mendon, Joseph accompanied his father and his brother Phinehas to Pennsylvania, where the three were baptized. Brigham Young was notably absent. If he had found the message acceptable, why was he still hesitant to make the commitment?

Brigham recognized that Mormonism presented him with a momentous decision. He must be cautious lest he be deceived. Yet if it was what it professed to be, as he had progressively come to believe, he must carefully prepare himself for a lifetime commitment. The weight of such a decision intensified his usual caution. He would not act without "time sufficient to prove all things for myself."[67]

Was he weak and tentative, unable to make up his mind, unwilling to take a risk, awaiting a manifestation so that he could be *certain?* Some of his later statements suggest this. Or was he slowly and carefully preparing himself for a decision he understood to be crucial? It seems probable that his hesitancy resulted both from tentativeness and from a feeling of being inadequately prepared. There likely was, at the time, more tentativeness and unwillingness to be mistaken than is revealed in later statements that stressed careful preparation.

In addition to thoroughly examining the Book of Mormon, Brigham Young by this time had listened to the preaching of Mormon elders and had visited the Saints in their homes. All of this he discussed with family and friends. Gradually his cautious mind became satisfied. Even so, he went to Canada not only to share the tidings with his brother but also because he was unwilling to trust his own wisdom. He wanted reassurance. "I had more confidence in [Joseph's] judgement and discretion, and in the manifestations of God to him," he later acknowledged, "than I had in myself, though I then believed the Book of Mormon to be true." He wanted all his doubts removed; before he acted, he wanted to *feel* and *know* he was right. Had this not eventually occurred, he later insisted, "I never would have embraced it to this day."[68]

No matter how diligently Brigham applied himself, his rational, methodical approach to Mormonism was not sufficient. He had found the teachings of Mormonism reasonable as far as he could understand them, but he was full of questions. Some of the questions must have come from lingering doubts. He understood that the biblical pattern required Apostles, yet he had heard none preached. If the officers were incomplete, what about the ordinances of the New Testament church: Did Mormonism have all the ordinances and the authority to administer them? The Restoration message of a prophet on earth again, and of continuing revelation and new scripture, suggested possibilities for an expanding vista of knowledge that, in Young's words, "led the vision of my mind into eternity" and opened up possibilities beyond his ability to grasp. Neither his practical approach to Mormonism nor the example of family members who accepted baptism moved him to commitment. He was determined to pray "and feel right about it" in every respect before he could go ahead.[69]

Brigham also continued to sort out the implications and to test himself. If this were really the Bible religion he had long sought, then, as the Bible challenged, it must take precedence over all else. He wrestled within, testing his feelings, until he knew "in the vision of my mind" that he could, if required, even leave his family and "know no other family but the family of God gathered together, or about to be, in this my day."[70]

Later, when commitment to God and religion meant sacrifice, he did not hesitate. The decision had come long before. Because of this preparation, he later could truly say that his heart, soul, and affections had been with the kingdom of God since the day of his baptism.[71]

"I could not more honestly and earnestly have prepared myself to go into eternity than I did to come into this Church," he later affirmed.[72] Yet it was finally the plain testimony of a simple elder that firmly launched Brigham Young into Mormonism. His own "judgment, natural endowments, and education" bowed to the direct word of a man without eloquence who could only say "I know."

> The Holy Ghost proceeding from that individual illuminated my understanding, and light, glory, and immortality were before me. I was encircled by them, filled by them, and I knew for myself that the testimony of the man was true.

For Young, this testimony "was like fire in my bones. . . . It bore witness to my spirit, and that was enough for me."[73] The experience swept away his doubts and planted his feet in new directions. Thereafter he could say that when he encountered the Restoration, "I fathomed it as far as I could and then I embraced it for all the day long."[74]

Eleazer Miller, one of the Pennsylvania elders, baptized Brigham Young on a cold and snowy day, 14 April 1832. With the ordinance came "a humble, child like spirit," confirming in his mind that his sins were forgiven, even as the Savior had said. Then Miller astonished him by ordaining him an elder before his clothes were dry.[75] Three weeks later, Brigham's wife, Miriam, also was baptized. During this same period, in addition to Joseph, Phinehas, and John Young, Brigham also saw Lorenzo Young, the Kimballs, the Greenes, and other relatives and friends affirm their commitment to the Restoration.[76]

Baptism by immersion is a symbol of death and of a resurrection to new life. Seldom was the symbol more appropriate than in the case of Brigham Young. Instead of gloom and despair, he was filled with "good feelings, with joy rejoicing," until both man and nature took on new aspects in his eyes. Hope and purpose replaced discouragement, as if a curtain had been removed from the face of the sun. Instead of sorrow and grief, suddenly it became "Glory! Hallelujah! Praise God!"[77] Indeed, he later explained, from the day of his baptism forward, he had felt as if he were in another world: "I never look back upon the old world but it is like looking into Hell."[78]

Certain that the restored gospel had the power to revolutionize the world, Brigham Young felt from the time of his baptism an urge to share and to preach. He had thought society corrupt and foolish; now he felt he knew why: "The whole world . . . was vailed in darkness. . . . What they understood was nothing more than a faint glimmering of light." He wished to be an instrument to help lift the veil of darkness from others as it had been lifted from him. He would be a messenger not of the torment awaiting the wicked but of the hope and joy awaiting those who would repent.[79] Truth and the gospel of salvation became his text, he said, and the world his circuit.[80]

Realistically, Brigham's initial circuit was confined to his own region, where he was assisted by Joseph and Phinehas and Heber. As Brigham Young later summarized the labors of that first spring and summer, from Mendon they preached in every direction, and "seven months had scarce passed away when there was a dozen branches raised up." After that, he traveled twice to Canada to preach and twice to Kirtland, preaching along the way. The fire within would not let him rest.

> I wanted to thunder and roar out the Gospel to the nations. It burned in my bones like fire pent up. . . . Nothing would satisfy me but to cry abroad in the world, what the Lord was doing in the latter-days. . . . I had to go out and preach, lest my bones should consume within me.[81]

Because Brigham was a man of humble background and unpolished speech who had not often addressed the public, it is remarkable that he launched at once into preaching. Though he could express himself adequately in conversation, he was untrained and lacked the confidence to face an audience. Unlike his brothers, Brigham had no experience as a lay preacher; in public he felt self-conscious and hesitant. He later thought that only his excitement over the message of the Restoration and his conviction that the Lord could use even the weak things of the world could have persuaded him to become a public speaker.[82]

Young's initiation as a speaker came dramatically the week after his baptism. At a meeting with several experienced Mormon elders, to his surprise they insisted that, because they did not have the spirit to speak, he must.

> I was but a child, so far as public speaking and a knowledge of the world was concerned; but the Spirit of the Lord was upon me, and I felt as though my bones would consume within me unless I spoke to the people and told them . . . what I had experienced and rejoiced in.

He spoke for over an hour: "I opened my mouth and the Lord filled it."[83] On other occasions as well, it was the "fire" in his bones that motivated him to overcome his natural timidity. "I was obliged to do it, for I felt as though my bones would consume within me if I did not."[84]

While Young's speech had little in common with the eloquent and studied oratory of the schools, his conversational tone, with illustrations rooted in the experiences and idioms of the people, proved effective. Indeed, his style came to resemble that advocated by the prominent revivalist Charles Finney, who recommended even for learned preachers not "splendid exhibitions of rhetoric" but simple language, short sentences, and a colloquial manner, with frequent repetition and parables derived from the habits of the people. For Brigham this style came naturally.

His approach to speaking also resembled that urged by the seminarian Lyman Beecher. "Young men," said Beecher to his charges, "pump yourselves brim full of your subject until you can't hold another drop, and then knock out the bung and let nature caper."[85] In public or in private, in written or spoken language, the vigorous, colorful mode of discourse rooted in Western New York and developed as a Mormon traveling missionary remained always as part of Brigham Young's personality.[86]

Some of the changes following baptism were subtle and not immediately evident. Here began the process that eventually transformed Brigham Young—the carpenter and joiner who made fine furniture—into "President Young," committed to "making Saints," to working with people more than things. Here, too, began the process that eventually transformed an obscure and uneducated working man of upstate New York into a major religious leader and a widely acclaimed pioneer and colonizer of the West. For Brigham Young, baptism meant new directions, new priorities, and new opportunities. These released and channeled his energies, harnessed his abilities, and helped him develop new ones. From this time forward, Brigham Young's new religion assumed first importance in his life. Preaching and teaching this new religion became his first love, seeing its message spread and obeyed his chief satisfaction, and attending to its needs his principal concern.

In addition to new priorities, Brigham still had a family to care for. Miriam, ailing from the progressive disability of tuberculosis, needed assistance and special care, which he conscientiously provided. His daughter remembered him telling that when Miriam was nearly bedridden, he

> got breakfast for his wife, himself, and the little girls, dressed the children, cleaned up the house, carried his wife to the rocking chair by the fireplace and left her there until he could return in the evening. When he came home he cooked his own and the family's supper, put his wife back to bed and finished up the day's domestic labours.[87]

Years after Brigham Young left New York, a Canadaigua newspaper printed the charge that he had been indolent, neglected his family, and often left his wife without provisions. An acquaintance from this period responded, affirming his industry and labeling the charge that he was neglectful of his family

> the most unjust charge of all; there could scarcely be a more kind and affectionate husband and father than he was, and few men in his circumstances would have provided better for their families. Mrs. Young was sick, most of the time unable to do any kind of work, but she was a worthy woman, and an exemplary Christian; she was well deserving his care and attention, and she had it while she lived in Canadaigua.[88]

While his wife was still alive, Brigham limited his missions largely to his own region; this permitted him to assist Miriam and spend time with her. And Grandma Works, the Kimballs, and some of the Young family were near enough to assist Brigham's wife and children when he was away.

In September 1832, less than five months after their baptism, Miriam died, leaving Brigham alone with two young daughters. Though Miriam had departed, she and Brigham shared a conviction that they would meet again. Young later insisted that he did not mourn her passing, though he would have except for the gospel. He was certain that "because the Priesthood is here," the way was opened from earth to heaven "and my wife was going there."[89] Brigham and his daughters moved in with the Kimballs, and for the next eighteen months Vilate Kimball mothered her little namesake Vilate Young and Vilate's older sister Elizabeth.

Disestablishing his household after Miriam's death permitted Brigham Young to act on an impulse he had felt since baptism: he gave away many of his possessions and significantly decreased his business. From the time of his baptism he had felt not only a spirit of unity with all in the new faith but also a conviction that out of that faith and unity would come a new social and economic order. If they labored together to build up and beautify the earth, he was certain the Saints would produce more than enough, and that all would share in the plenty.

In the spring, he had commenced to "lay aside his ledgers." Once his daughters were in Vilate's care, he felt he could go further. He felt within himself the urge to be unencumbered with material things, free to preach the message of joy and peace until Christ should come, and he acted on it.[90]

Later, he would respond to a different agenda as he learned that the road to the new society would be long and difficult and would require more of him and the Saints than preaching alone. But in 1832, with fire in his bones and filled with the enthusiasm of a new convert, he closed his shop and set out Quixote-like to change the world.

NOTES

1. Though Latter-day Saint contemporaries recognized the depth of Brigham Young's faith and religious devotion, only the most astute outside observers saw beyond the "secular" successes to the religious motivations and power

behind them. One of these was the Frenchman Jules Remy, who, after visiting Brigham Young and the Mormons in 1855, commented both on his "remarkable talent and profound ability" and on the depth and sincerity of his religious belief. "We withdrew perfectly convinced of the sincerity of his faith," concluded Remy. See Jules Remy and Julius Brenchley, *A Journey to Great-Salt Lake City,* 2 vols. (London: W. Jeffs, 1861), 1: 303; see also 1: 201, 210.

2. For specifics about Young's New England background, see Rebecca Cornwall and Richard F. Palmer, "The Religious and Family Background of Brigham Young," *BYU Studies* 18 (Spring 1978): 286–310.
3. According to Gordon S. Wood, "Evangelical America and Early Mormonism," *New York History* 61 (October 1980): 359–86, Americans were on the move during this period like never before. Many families were uprooted several times. Wood suggests that these moves had profound social and psychological implications, influencing the reactions of those affected to the religious enthusiasms of the period. The Youngs, the Smiths, the Kimballs, and other prominent Mormon families were among those who experienced repeated uprootings.
4. Brigham Young, 2 August 1857, in *Journal of Discourses,* 5: 97. For an imaginative but nonetheless helpful reconstruction of Brigham's frontier education, see S. Dilworth Young, *"Here is Brigham . . ."—Brigham Young . . . the Years to 1844* (Salt Lake City: Bookcraft, 1964), 39.
5. Brigham Young, 6 April 1857, in *Journal of Discourses,* 4: 312; and Cornwall and Palmer, 308.
6. Lorenzo later remembered an occasion when their father left to take sugar to market. Before his return, the boys had exhausted all the food in the house. Brigham shot a robin and, with two spoonfuls of flour thumped out of an empty barrel, made robin stew, their only meal in two days. See James A. Little, "Biography of Lorenzo Dow Young," *Utah Historical Quarterly* 14 (1946): 130.
7. Brigham Young, 12 November 1864, in *Journal of Discourses,* 10: 360.
8. Brigham Young to George Hickox, 19 February 1876, Brigham Young Papers, Library-Archives, Historical Department of The Church of Jesus Christ of Latter-day Saints (hereafter cited as LDS Church Historical Archives). The indispensable reference for Brigham Young's residences, craftsmanship, and economic activity in New York is Richard F. Palmer and Karl D. Butler, *Brigham Young: The New York Years* (Provo, Utah: Charles Redd Center for Western Studies, 1982).
9. Brigham Young, 12 November 1864, in *Journal of Discourses,* 10: 360.
10. See letter of 7 September 1867, published in the *Republican Times* (Canandaigua), News Clippings Collections, LDS Church Historical Archives. Although Alonzo Beebe, the author of the first article, is identified, the respondent remained anonymous, perhaps because he was unwilling to be publicly known in 1857 as a defender of the then "notorious" Brigham Young.

11. As quoted in Mary Van Sickle Wait, *Brigham Young in Cayuga County, 1813–1829* (Ithaca: DeWitt Historical Society, 1964), 39.

12. Brigham Young, 15 August 1852, in *Journal of Discourses,* 6: 290; and 6 February 1853, in *Journal of Discourses,* 2: 94. Little, 28, adds that John Young also taught his boys never to play cards.

    As with many Mormon converts of this era, few contemporary documents detail Young's activities before he joined the Mormons. If he wrote early letters, they are not extant, and his first diary entry barely mentions his 1832 baptism before continuing as a record of his missionary labors. Of necessity, this reconstruction of his religious attitudes and experiences before and right after his baptism rests heavily on reminiscences.

13. Brigham Young, 15 August 1852, in *Journal of Discourses,* 6: 290; and 5 October 1856, in *Journal of Discourses,* 4: 112.

14. Brigham Young, 15 August 1852, in *Journal of Discourses,* 6: 290; and "History of Brigham Young," *Deseret News,* 10 February 1858, 385. See also Little, 25. Lorenzo, younger than Brigham, remembered his bedridden mother, dying of tuberculosis, frequently pulling him over and counseling him to be a good man.

15. Brigham Young, 15 August 1852, in *Journal of Discourses,* 6: 290; and 11 July 1852, in *Journal of Discourses,* 1: 41.

16. Brigham Young, 6 April 1860, in *Journal of Discourses,* 8: 37–38; and 7 April 1861, in *Journal of Discourses,* 9: 29. While he never enumerated his youthful foibles, he did acknowledge elsewhere that "like other young men, I was full of weakness, sin, darkness and ignorance." Brigham Young, 12 November 1864, in *Journal of Discourses,* 10: 360.

17. Brigham Young, 9 April 1852, in *Journal of Discourses,* 1: 49. See also minutes, 12 February 1849, Brigham Young Papers.

18. Brigham Young, 23 March 1862, in *Journal of Discourses,* 9: 248; 27 August 1871, in *Journal of Discourses,* 14: 225; and 21 May 1853, in *Journal of Discourses,* 10: 191. Brigham was probably in his mid-twenties—long accustomed to being on his own—when the temperance pledge incident occurred. The infant temperance movement that dated from his teens seldom required either a pledge or total abstinence; those developments characterized the vigorous movement of the mid-1820s. Young was not alone in thinking that those who bound themselves by pledge yielded their self-control, and that abstinence without a pledge was a morally superior position. See Alice Felt Tyler, *Freedom's Ferment: Phases of American Social History from the Colonial Period to the Outbreak of the Civil War* (New York: Harper and Row, 1962), 321–22, 335–36.

19. Minutes, 17 February 1860, Brigham Young Papers; and Brigham Young, 15 August 1852, in *Journal of Discourses,* 6: 290.

20. Gordon Wood, 374, 378, wrote that many of Young's generation came to believe that as in government, so in religion: "The people were their own theologians and could no longer rely on others to tell them what to believe." According to Wood, independent theology was a theme of the evangelical

movement from the early 1800s on. In this context he saw the appeal directly to the Bible as an understandable response to sectarian extremism. Earlier, Whitney R. Cross, *The Burned-Over District: The Social and Intellectual History of Enthusiastic Religion in Western New York, 1800–1850* (Ithaca: Cornell University Press, 1950), 81–82, 109, had noted that Yankee-bred New Yorkers had a stubborn introspection in the fashioning of personal beliefs, which recognized no authority this side of heaven. Though a minority, many laymen "thought seriously about religion and took pride in the ability to thresh out things for themselves."

21. Brigham Young, 7 May 1871, in *Journal of Discourses,* 14: 112–13; and minutes, 8 January 1845, Brigham Young papers. See also Brigham Young, 6 April 1860, in *Journal of Discourses,* 8: 38.
22. Minutes, 8 January 1845, Brigham Young Papers; Brigham Young, 6 April 1860, in *Journal of Discourses,* 8: 37; and 23 June 1874, in *Journal of Discourses,* 18: 247. According to Wood, 375, "Nowhere else in Christendom was religion so broken apart" as in areas like Young's, swept by revivals in the aftermath of America's Second Great Awakening. Cross, 29–31, 40, wrote of "a phenomenally intensive religious and moral awareness" in the region, of an "unremitting warfare of theologies," and of an "interdenominational strife of a bitterness scarcely to be paralleled."
23. Little, 26.
24. Brigham Young, 23 March 1862, in *Journal of Discourses,* 9: 248. No doubt Hill would include Young among those "casualities" of the "Protestant conversion process, of sectarianism, and especially of revivalism" who eventually accepted Mormonism. See Marvin S. Hill, "The Rise of Mormonism in the Burned-Over District: Another View," *New York History* 61 (October 1980): 425–26, and his analysis of the impact of revivals, 421–28, which seems to square with Young's experience.
25. Brigham Young, 6 April 1860, in *Journal of Discourses,* 8: 37; and 23 June 1874, in *Journal of Discourses,* 18: 247.
26. Brigham Young, 6 April 1860, in *Journal of Discourses,* 8: 38; and 23 June 1874, in *Journal of Discourses,* 18: 247. See also 9 October 1872, in *Journal of Discourses,* 15: 164–65.
27. Brigham Young, 9 April 1871, in *Journal of Discourses,* 14: 90; and 7 May 1871, in *Journal of Discourses,* 14: 113.
28. Brigham Young, 3 June 1871, in *Journal of Discourses,* 14: 197. This encounter with Dow may have occurred in the summer of 1827, when he preached only a few miles from Young's residence. See Marvin S. Hill, "The Role of Christian Primitivism in the Origin and Development of the Mormon Kingdom, 1830–1844" (Ph.D. diss., University of Chicago, 1968), 46. It should be noted that improving the morals of the people was one of the social purposes for revivals, and preaching morals was the order of the day. Young acknowledged in the discourse cited above, 198, that the preachers "can explain our duty as rational, moral beings, and that is good, excellent as far as it goes." Already blessed with a strict upbringing, he sought something more.

29. Brigham Young, 3 June 1871, in *Journal of Discourses,* 14: 197; and 26 July 1857, in *Journal of Discourses,* 5: 73. See also 7 May 1871, in *Journal of Discourses,* 14: 113. It was common for dissenters from the old-line denominations to face the charge of infidelity. Antisectarianism could lead to infidelity and, according to Hill, primitivists sometimes feared slipping away into total disbelief. See Marvin S. Hill, "The Shaping of the Mormon Mind in New England and New York," *BYU Studies* 9 (Spring 1969), 362; and Mario S. DePillis, "The Quest for Religious Authority and the Rise of Mormonism," *Dialogue: A Journal of Mormon Thought* 1 (Spring 1966), 75. As with Brigham Young, many of those who disagreed with the preachers and failed to make a profession of faith went to church regularly and looked for a future conversion experience. Though charged with being irreligious and destitute of the word of God, some responded that, in fact, they had too much of the word of God "to swallow the disgraceful absurdities" of the preachers. See Cross, 41, 45. Compare this with Brigham Young, 9 October 1872, in *Journal of Discourses,* 15: 164–65.
30. The classic study of the region by Whitney R. Cross appeared in 1950. Seeking an explanation for the unusual religious intensity and reform impulses that characterized the area, Cross investigated the waves of revivals that swept the region. In a more recent study of the region, Paul H. Johnson analyzed in detail the social, economic, and religious milieu of Rochester, less than twenty miles from where Young resided when he joined the Mormons. Johnson, moreover, focused on 1830–1831, years that coincide with Young's Mormon conversion. See Cross, *The Burned-Over District,* and Paul E. Johnson, *A Shopkeeper's Millennium: Society and Revivals in Rochester, New York, 1815–1837* (New York: Hill and Wang, 1978).

    Although Cross's generalizations and interpretations have been challenged, his book remains a useful sourcebook of important information helpful for understanding the experience of men like Young and Kimball. For critiques of Cross's work as it applies to Mormon origins, see Mario S. DePillis, "The Social Sources of Mormonism," *Church History* 37 (March 1968): 50–79; and Hill, "The Rise of Mormonism." See also James B. Allen and Leonard J. Arrington, "Mormon Origins in New York: An Introductory Analysis," *BYU Studies* 9 (Spring 1969): 241–74; Hill, "The Shaping of the Mormon Mind," and DePillis, "The Quest for Religious Authority."
31. Studies of this "primitive gospel" movement help us understand Young's experiences and lend credibility to his later memories of this period. The key study for the primitivist movement as it relates to Mormonism is Hill, "The Role of Christian Primitivism." Chapter 1 deals with the movement as a whole, and chapter 2 applies the analysis to the case of Joseph Smith and the rise of Mormonism. Hill's "Shaping of the Mormon Mind," 352–58, summarizes his argument on the primitivist context for the rise of Mormonism and the primitivist background of many of his converts. DePillis takes similar ground in his "Quest for Religious Authority," where he analyzes the appeal of Mormonism to those primitivists searching for an authoritative religion as an answer to sectarian confusion and competition. More recently, Gordon S.

Wood examined the religious setting for the rise of Mormonism, including the primitivist influence, in "Evangelical America."

Perhaps some of Young's reminiscences for this period tell more about what he had become than what he *was* in the 1820s. No doubt his view of these early years before his connection with Mormonism became colored by his later experiences. Still, complementary reminiscences, along with studies of his time and place, confirm that the memory of his experience is a credible one and that we can have confidence in the broad outlines of his story.

32. See Hill, "Role of Christian Primitivism," chapters 1 and 2. According to Hill, 23, as early as 1802 a number of Baptist ministers had concluded to reject every doctrine and practice not found in the New Testament. Compare this with Young's statements; see, for example, his discourse on 26 July 1857, in *Journal of Discourses,* 5: 72–73.
33. Brigham Young, 17 June 1855, in *Journal of Discourses,* 11: 254.
34. Brigham Young, 7 May 1871, in *Journal of Discourses,* 14: 122–23; and 28 September 1856, in *Journal of Discourses,* 4: 104.
35. Brigham Young, 6 April 1860, in *Journal of Discourses,* 8: 37; and minutes, 23 September 1849, Thomas Bullock Papers, LDS Church Historical Archives. On another occasion he said, "I joined the Methodists to get rid of them & all the Sects—same as the girl married the man to get rid of him" (Minutes, 8 January 1845, Brigham Young Papers).
36. Hill, "Rise of Mormonism," 422–24; Brigham Young, 3 June 1871, in *Journal of Discourses,* 14: 197; and 6 October 1870, in *Journal of Discourses,* 13: 267.
37. See letter to the *Republican Times* (Canandaigua), 7 September 1857, Newspaper Clippings Collection. The letter notes that Young had been a Reformed Methodist before arriving in the area, but the writer doubts that he united with any church while he lived there, "as the R.M. society was broken up, and its members scattered at that time."

    Questions remain about Young's location during the Canandaigua-Mendon years, 1829–1832. In reminiscences he spoke mainly of Mendon. There he built a house for his father, had his friend Heber Kimball nearby, and at least part of the time maintained a house and shop for himself on land owned by his father. Also, his wife Miriam was buried there. Most of the letters from New York acquaintances of this period come from the Canandaigua area, however, and he occasionally reminisced about "old number nine," referring to his Canandaigua residence. It seems likely, if the Canandaigua correspondent is correct, that Young moved first to Canandaigua and maintained at least a part-time residence there until his baptism. The New York census, listing Young in both communities, supports this possibility. The two locations are about ten miles apart.
38. Hiram McKee to Brigham Young, 4 April 1860, Brigham Young Papers.
39. Brigham Young to Hiram McKee, 3 May 1860, Brigham Young Papers.
40. See the charge of Alonzo Beebe in a letter to the *Republican Times* (Canandiagua), 27 August 1857, along with the 7 September reply to the same paper, News Clippings Collection.

41. Minutes, 8 January 1845, Brigham Young Papers; "Synopsis of the History of Heber Chase Kimball," *Deseret News,* 31 March–28 April 1858, 25.
42. Minutes, 8 January 1845, Brigham Young Papers.
43. See Brigham Young, 28 June 1876, in *Journal of Discourses,* 16: 67; and 19 July 1857, in *Journal of Discourses,* 5: 55.
44. "History of Heber Chase Kimball by his own Dictation," manuscript, Heber C. Kimball Papers, LDS Church Historical Archives. The several versions of this history, contained in two volumes, have been cited under various headings. The most used version, known in the past as "Journal 94–B" and sometimes cited as "The Journal and Record of Heber C. Kimball," is here given its original title.

    Kimball's experience had been much like Young's, though perhaps not as intense. He also "received many pressing invitations to unite with different sects" and "had been many times upon the anxious bench" without effect until eventually he joined the Baptists "to be a guard upon me, and to keep me from running into evils," though they believed things he did not. One of his principal complaints about the churches echoed one of Young's: they would tell him to believe in the Lord Jesus, "but never would tell me what to do [to] be saved, and thus left me almost in dispair."
45. This from *The Gem of Literature and Science* (Rochester, New York), 5 September 1829, 70, is an example of the kind of notice Brigham Young might have read.
46. Brigham Young, 15 November 1867, in *Journal of Discourses,* 6: 39. See also discourses on 17 May 1868, in *Journal of Discourses,* 12: 271, and 20 April 1856, in *Journal of Discourses,* 3: 320.
47. Heber Kimball, 8 January 1845, Brigham Young Papers; Phinehas Young to Brigham Young, 11 August 1845, Brigham Young Papers. No doubt in later remembering the conversation, Phinehas saw it as prophetic of the coming of Mormonism to them. However, the feeling that the world was in such a state that only God's intervention would save it, and that such intervention was imminent, was not uncommon at that time. See Wood, 376–77.
48. Brigham Young, 6 April 1855, in *Journal of Discourses,* 2: 249; and 6 April 1861, in *Journal of Discourses,* 9: 1–2.
49. For an account of the Greene volume, see *History of The Church of Jesus Christ of Latter-day Saints,* ed. B. H. Roberts, 7 vols., 2nd ed., rev. (Salt Lake City: Deseret Book Co., 1951), 7: 217–18. Phinehas tells in detail about his copy in "History of Brigham Young," 369.
50. Phinehas Young to Brigham Young, 11 August 1845, Brigham Young Papers; "History of Brigham Young," 377.
51. In preparing his history, Brigham Young merely noted that the first Book of Mormon he saw was Phinehas's copy; see "History of Brigham Young," 385. B. H. Roberts was sure that the one Brigham actually read was the Greene copy; see footnote in *History of the Church,* 7: 218. Preston Nibley, in *Brigham Young, The Man & His Work* (Salt Lake City: Deseret Book Co., 1970), 5, was just as sure it was Phinehas's book.

52. Brigham Young, 8 August 1852, in *Journal of Discourses,* 3: 91. "Upon the first opportunity I read the Book of Mormon," he said on another occasion. 6 April 1860, in *Journal of Discourses,* 3: 38.
53. Brigham Young, 8 August 1852, in *Journal of Discourses,* 3: 91.
54. Minutes, 8 January 1845, Brigham Young Papers; Brigham Young, 17 April 1853, in *Journal of Discourses,* 2: 123–24.

    For a consideration of the appeal of the Book of Mormon to someone like Young, see Wood, "Evangelical America," 380–83. See also Hill, "Role of Christian Primitivism," 100–104, 120–21.
55. Brigham Young, 8 August 1852, in *Journal of Discourses,* 3: 91. See also Brigham Young to David B. Smith, 1 June 1853, Brigham Young Papers.
56. "History of Brigham Young," 377. This would have been the fall of 1831. Lorenzo D. Young later said that Brigham, Heber Kimball, and Joseph Young brought him the Book of Mormon in February 1831. See Little, 33–34. If the date is correct, however, the circumstances are wrong, for Joseph Young was still in Canada; also, in spite of Lorenzo's allusion, we have no record of a visit to the Pennsylvania Saints until January 1832. Available evidence suggests that Brigham Young kept his meditations largely to himself in 1831 and that the religious transformation beginning to take place within him was still unknown—at least to most of his neighbors. One who knew him well during this period later wrote that two weeks after some Mormon visitors "used their influence to convert him," he and his wife were baptized. See letter to *Republican Times* (Canandaigua), 7 September 1851, Newspaper Clippings Collection.
57. Brigham Young, 6 April 1860, in *Journal of Discourses,* 8: 38.
58. "Synopsis of the History of Heber Chase Kimball," 25.
59. This appears in an early draft of his history, with the phrase *and believed* added in pencil. See "History of Brigham Young," manuscript no. 1, Historian's Office Papers; and Kimball, "History of Heber Chase Kimball," manuscript, Heber C. Kimball Papers.
60. "Synopsis of the History of Heber Chase Kimball," 25.
61. "History of Heber Chase Kimball," manuscript, Heber C. Kimball Papers. Phinehas later said that at the end of 1831 or the beginning of 1832, he and Brigham "both became more interested in the subject of Mormonism" and got Kimball to join them in traveling to Pennsylvania. In his history, published as a part of Brigham's, Phinehas says they left about 20 January 1832. See Phinehas Young to Brigham Young, 11 August 1845, Brigham Young Papers; and "History of Brigham Young," 369.

    This is another indication that Brigham Young had little to do with Mormons until after he had passed judgment on the Book of Mormon. Nor is there any evidence that Young ever met with any of the Smith family in the Palmyra area, even though they resided less than fifteen miles from Mendon for perhaps nine months after he first saw the Book of Mormon.
62. Minutes, 8 January 1845, Brigham Young Papers; and "History of Brigham Young," manuscript no. 2, Historian's Office Papers.

63. "History of Brigham Young," manuscript no. 1, Historian's Office Papers. In the published version, Young wrote that they left the Pennsylvania congregation "still more convinced of the truth of the work, and anxious to learn its principles and to learn more of Joseph Smith's mission." According to Phinehas, they "returned home rejoicing, preaching the Gospel by the way." "History of Brigham Young," 385, 369.
64. Minutes, 8 January 1845, Brigham Young Papers.
65. Brigham Young, 22 July 1860, in *Journal of Discourses,* 8: 129; and 6 April 1860, in *Journal of Discourses,* 8: 37. In the latter sermon, Young reminded his audience they had just heard his brother Joseph say that during this period he did not laugh for two years. "I did not know of his smiling during some four or five years," added Brigham.
66. Fragment of an autobiography of Joseph Young in Franklin Wheeler Young Papers, LDS Church Historical Archives; Brigham Young, 6 April 1860, in *Journal of Discourses,* 8: 38.
67. Brigham Young, 8 August 1852, in *Journal of Discourses,* 3: 91. Compare this with a discourse of 6 April 1860, in *Journal of Discourses,* 8: 38, where he said that "when I had ripened everything in my mind I drank it in, and not till then."
68. Brigham Young, 6 April 1860, in *Journal of Discourses,* 8: 37; and 8 August 1852, in *Journal of Discourses,* 3: 91.
69. Brigham Young, 6 April 1860, in *Journal of Discourses,* 8: 38.
70. Brigham Young, 15 March 1856, in *Journal of Discourses,* 4: 281–82. Years later he reiterated the same priorities and commitment: "If my Father, Mother, Brothers and Sisters rejects the gospel Farewell Father Mother Brothers and sisters. I am for the kingdom of Heaven." Minutes, 14 September 1849, Thomas Bullock Papers. Compare this with Matthew 10: 37; Luke 14: 26.
71. Minutes, 25 January 1873, General Minutes Collection.
72. Brigham Young, 6 April 1860, in *Journal of Discourses,* 8: 38.
73. Brigham Young, 13 June 1852, in *Journal of Discourses,* 1: 90; see also 28 July 1861, in *Journal of Discourses,* 9: 141.
74. Brigham Young, 31 August 1862, in *Journal of Discourses,* 9: 364; see also 5 March 1860, in *Journal of Discourses,* 8: 15–16; and minutes, 8 January 1845, Brigham Young Papers.
75. "History of Brigham Young," 385.
76. Brigham Young was but one of many seekers who found what they sought in Mormonism. He was, in fact, close to the "typical" Mormon convert of this time described by Marvin S. Hill, "Quest for Refuge: An Hypothesis as to the Social Origins and Nature of the Mormon Political Kingdom," *Journal of Mormon History* 2 (1975): 13: he was less than middle-class economically, had little formal education, was alienated from the sectarian world, thought old-line clergy corrupt, and saw the emerging social order as Babylon incarnate. For a description of the social changes that provided the context for this and the appeal of Mormonism for people in that society, see Wood,

"Evangelical America," 373–76, 379–86. For more on the appeal of Mormonism for people like Young, see DePillis, "The Quest for Religious Authority," 73ff; and Leonard J. Arrington and Davis Bitton, *The Mormon Experience: A History of the Latter-day Saints* (New York: Alfred A. Knopf, 1979), chapter 2. For other Mormon converts of this period who were much like Young and Kimball, see Hill, "Rise of Mormonism," 424–25.

77. Brigham Young, 20 April 1856, in *Journal of Discourses,* 3: 320–21; and 8 July 1860, in *Journal of Discourses,* 8: 119. In a discourse of 22 July 1860, in *Journal of Discourses,* 8: 129, he spoke of the gloom that had cast its pall over his feelings "from the earliest days of my childhood . . . until I heard the everlasting Gospel." See also discourses of 17 May 1868, in *Journal of Discourses,* 12: 217; and 4 March 1860, in *Journal of Discourses,* 8: 8.
78. Minutes, 7 April 1850, General Minutes Collection.
79. The quotation is from a discourse by Brigham Young, 26 July 1867, in *Journal of Discourses,* 5: 73. See also 16 January 1853, in *Journal of Discourses,* 1: 4–5; and 15 August 1862, in *Journal of Discourses,* 6: 291–97.
80. Brigham Young, 28 July 1861, in *Journal of Discourses,* 9: 137.
81. Brigham Young, 20 February 1863, in *Journal of Discourses,* 1: 313–14. Compare this with Kimball's description: "I received the Holy Ghost, as the disciples did in ancient days, which was like a consuming fire. . . . I continued in this way for many months, and it seemed as though my flesh would consume away." According to Kimball, the scriptures were then opened to his understanding by that same spirit ("Synopsis of the History of Heber Chase Kimball," 29).
82. See his comments in discourses on 17 November 1867, in *Journal of Discourses,* 12: 99; and 17 August 1856, in *Journal of Discourses,* 4: 20–21. It is likely that he had long expressed himself openly and forcefully in daily conversation. See for example his discourse of 29 July 1861, in *Journal of Discourses,* 9: 141, where he says that he could easily out-talk those who preached to him.
83. Brigham Young, 17 July 1870, in *Journal of Discourses,* 13: 211.
84. Brigham Young, 28 June 1873, in *Journal of Discourses,* 16: 69.
85. For Finney, see Cross, 173–74; for Beecher, Daniel J. Boorstin, *The Americans, The National Experience* (New York: Vintage Books, 1965), 320. Boorstin's whole section on "American Ways of Talking," 275–324, is useful in assessing Young's language. See also, Ronald W. Walker, "Raining Pitchforks: Brigham Young As Preacher," *Sunstone* 8 (May–June 1983): 4–9.

    Perhaps it was partly as a reaction to his overly strict upbringing that Brigham Young developed the colorful speaking style that consciously and effectively employed expressions forbidden to him as a young man. In the John Young home, such mild expressions as "darn it," "curse it," "the Devil," or "I vow" had merited punishment. See Brigham Young, 15 August 1862, in *Journal of Discourses,* 6: 290. Compare this with his own practice. On one occasion he apologized for using the devil's name, acknowledging that many considered such usage a sin. "I do not often use the old gentleman's name in vain," he explained, "and if I do it, it is always in the pulpit, where I do all my swearing," which was not strictly so. See Brigham Young, 31 July 1853, in *Journal of Discourses,* 1: 166. See also 2 August 1857, in *Journal of Discourses,* 5: 99–100, where he explained why he removed the "sharp words" before publishing his sermons; and 8 October 1868, in *Journal of Discourses,* 12: 298–99, and 2 March 1856, in *Journal of Discourses,* 3: 222–23, where he explained why he used them in the first place.

86. For descriptions of Young's style as a speaker after a quarter-century of experience, see Richard F. Burton, *The City of the Saints and Across the Rocky Mountains to California,* ed. Fawn M. Brodie (New York: Alfred A. Knopf, 1963), 264–65, 288; and Jules Remy and Julius Brenchley, 2: 496.

    Brigham Young's later success as a public speaker came only after much effort. Because of his lack of education, his speech was unsophisticated, and he long felt embarrassed and "destitute of language" before an audience. In spite of these recognized liabilities, he consciously concluded: "I have the grit in me, and I will do my duty anyhow" (Brigham Young, 2 August 1857, in *Journal of Discourses,* 5: 97). Here he also commented: "How I have had the headache, when I had ideas to lay before the people, and not words to express them; but I was so gritty that I always tried my best."

87. Susa Young Gates and Leah D. Widtsoe, *The Life Story of Brigham Young* (New York: The MacMillan Company, 1931), 5.

88. Letter in the *Republican Times* (Canandaigua), 7 September 1857, News Clippings Collection.

89. "History of Brigham Young," 385; and Brigham Young, 12 June 1859, in *Journal of Discourses,* 7: 175. See also Kimball, "History of Heber Chase Kimball." Miriam Works Young died 8 September 1832.

90. Brigham Young, 8 October 1876, in *Journal of Discourses,* 18: 260; 20 February 1853, in *Journal of Discourses,* 1: 314; and 28 June 1873, in *Journal of Discourses,* 16: 69. Young later said that by the time he arrived in Kirtland, "I had not a coat in the world, for previous to this I had given away everything I possessed, that I might be free to go forth and proclaim the plan of salvation" (discourse of 17 February 1853, in *Journal of Discourses,* 2: 128; see also a discourse of 3 February 1867, in *Journal of Discourses,* 11: 295, for another comment on his penury when he arrived in Kirtland).

CHAPTER 3

Brigham Young and the Transformation of the "First" Quorum of the Twelve

Ronald K. Esplin
Director of the Joseph Fielding Smith Institute
Brigham Young University

The Quorum of the Twelve Apostles was organized for the first time in this dispensation in February 1835.[1] Revelation and inspired counsel that very spring made clear their potential, but not until a half-dozen years later, and only after painful turmoil and tribulation,[2] were the relatively young and inexperienced Apostles fully prepared to shoulder the burdens of leadership. This, briefly, is the instructive story of the transformation of the Twelve from a sometimes petty and divided quorum to one of unity and power under Brigham Young. It is the story of how Brigham Young helped mold and transform a quorum, which at first had limited jurisdiction, until it was prepared to stand next to the First Presidency in overseeing the affairs of all the Church.

Initially, in 1835, members of the Quorum of the Twelve were not considered "General Authorities" in any modern sense. These "special witnesses" formed a "Traveling Presiding High Council," charged to carry the gospel abroad and preside where there were no stakes. But they were explicitly denied authority in the "stakes of Zion," where most of the Saints resided and where "standing high councils" served as their counterpart.[3]

Furthermore, despite scriptural models, the office of Apostle did not at first bring with it more prestige than membership on the standing high councils. On the contrary, the nature of their respective assignments assured that standing high councils had more local visibility and responsibility.

In retrospect, we can see this as an important period of testing and preparation for the Twelve before receiving greater responsibility. But the lack of status within organized stakes rankled some of the Twelve, including quorum president Thomas Marsh, and it contributed to misunderstandings and disharmony. The early quorum was also burdened by pettiness and strife within and, on occasion, conflict with other units. Notwithstanding the dictum in their charter revelation of March 1835 that quorum decisions must be unanimous in order to have power and validity,[4] they were often divided. Much must change before they would be prepared to fulfill their promise and stand with the First Presidency.

What follows is an overview of formative events involving the Quorum of the Twelve Apostles that transpired before Joseph Smith formally invited them in August 1841 to assist the First Presidency in governing the entire Church. For the Apostles, this was a period of struggling to define the scope of their office and to learn the meaning of the Apostleship. While the highlights of the period came in connection with important shared experiences in the Kirtland Temple, and later with missionary success in England, the early history was often characterized more by difficulties, disagreements, and division.

Brigham Young witnessed or participated in all of these experiences, and the negative may have influenced his later leadership as much as the positive. As quorum president after 1838, Brigham emphasized unity and duty—partly as a reaction against the disharmony and concern for status and authority that he had experienced earlier. It is only against the backdrop of this formative period that the decimation of the Twelve during the disaffections of 1837–1838 and Brigham Young's leadership of a revived quorum in 1839 can be adequately understood.

Just as Brigham Young helped set the tone for the quorum that emerged from this era, Thomas Marsh, first President of the Twelve, helped set the tone for the 1835 quorum.[5] President Marsh was among those most concerned that the Twelve were not more prominent. And because he was worried about his prerogatives as president and tended toward an overblown concern about appearances, his leadership of the quorum was often intrusive and officious. No doubt these characteristics contributed to the pettiness and self-concern that plagued the quorum.

Disharmony within the quorum cannot all be laid at the feet

of Marsh, however. Others, too, had visions of potential authority and prestige greater than the actual, creating tensions within and leading to anxiety about priority and position. Also, some of the difficulties clearly related to the newness of their office and their own relative youth and inexperience. Scripture and the Prophet's instructions provided guidelines; but unity and recognition of the precise bounds of their authority and methods of their work could be the product only of shared experience.

Finally, Joseph Smith ruffled the feelings of his sensitive Apostles as often as he soothed them. Whether this was a conscious ploy to teach that humility and service must precede authority, as Brigham Young came to believe, or simply a consequence of his own style, the results were the same. Anxious to be powerful men in the kingdom, some of the Apostles bristled and complained at every slight.

Brigham Young was not among the complainers. No doubt reverence for Joseph Smith's authority and a deep sense of duty contributed to his patience. Perhaps a sense of destiny also contributed—if not of personal destiny, at least a feeling that the fledgling quorum had an important future role and that this stage was a necessary preparation. Years later he related that when Marsh complained about the Prophet's treatment of the Twelve at this time, he told his president, "If we are faithful, we will see the day . . . that we will have all the power that we shall know how to wield before God."[6]

In Kirtland, Ohio, on Sunday, 8 February 1835, the Prophet invited Brigham and Joseph Young to his home to sing for him, as they often had done on Zion's Camp during the previous summer's arduous and dangerous expedition to Missouri to rescue the Saints expelled from Jackson County. There Joseph asked the brothers to invite all veterans of the camp to an extraordinary conference the following Saturday at which Oliver Cowdery, David Whitmer, and Martin Harris—the Three Witnesses—would select twelve Special Witnesses "to open the door of the gospel" in foreign lands, as foreseen by revelation nearly six years before.[7]

On Saturday, 14 February, Zion's Camp veterans and others

assembled. Explaining that he had seen in vision the calling and order of the Twelve and the Seventy, and that it was the will of God that those who went to Zion at the risk of their lives fulfill that vision, the Prophet separated the camp brethren from the rest. Then, after being blessed by the Presidency, the Witnesses named to the Apostleship Lyman E. Johnson, Brigham Young, Heber C. Kimball, Orson Hyde, David W. Patten, Luke S. Johnson, William E. McLellin, John F. Boynton, Orson Pratt, William Smith, Thomas B. Marsh, and Parley P. Pratt. All but three of those named—Boynton, McLellin, and Marsh—had been tested by the wrenching trials of Zion's Camp. Marsh, already in Missouri on the "receiving end" of the expedition, had had no opportunity to enlist.

Three of those to be ordained Apostles—the Pratt brothers and Thomas Marsh—were not yet in Kirtland. Marsh had left Missouri for Kirtland two weeks earlier, but he would not arrive nor learn of his call until late April—months after most of the quorum had been ordained, weeks after important instruction and revelation, and only days before the quorum would be fully organized and dispatched on its first mission. Thomas missed, for example, Oliver Cowdery's impressive charge to the new Apostles in February, which highlighted the need for brotherhood and unity within the Twelve and warned the Apostles to cultivate humility, beware of pride, and give all credit to God.[8] Rather than playing to natural strengths, such requirements would challenge Marsh where he was weakest.

As noted, the Apostles at first struggled to understand their proper role and to develop effective ways of working together as a quorum and with other leaders. As they prepared for their first mission—again, even before Thomas Marsh had arrived from Missouri—Joseph Smith instructed them by counsel and by revelation. In March 1835, feeling unprepared and unworthy, they petitioned the Prophet to "inquire of God for us, and obtain a revelation, (if consistent) that our hearts may be comforted."[9] The revelation "On Priesthood" (today Doctrine and Covenants 107) was the result. The Quorum of the Twelve "form a quorum equal in authority and power" to the Presidency of the Church, declared the revelation, but only when they are united and in harmony as a quorum. Similarly, the Seventy and the "standing high councils, at the stakes of Zion," are quorums equal in authority to the Twelve. The revelation suggested a hierarchy in which all were equal in authority but not in responsibilities or assignment: the Presidency directing the Twelve, the Twelve directing the Seventy. But the revelation left ambiguous the relationship between the standing high councils and the traveling high council, or Apostles.

Minutes kept by the Twelve that first season record the Prophet's additional emphasis on the authority they now held. It was "all important," he declared, that they understand their priesthood, for otherwise they could not fulfill their responsibilities. And because they now held the authority, it was their *duty* to unlock the kingdom of heaven to foreign nations, "for no man can do that thing but yourselves." Though their assignment differed from his, he concluded, "you each have the same authority in other nations that I have in this nation."[10]

Schooled in such precepts, it is no wonder that the Twelve soon had difficulty reconciling their treatment and actual status with the theology and potential of their office. Despite the reminder in the revelation on priesthood that relationships must be characterized by "lowliness of heart, meekness and long suffering, . . . temperance, patience, godliness, brotherly kindness and charity,"[11] these men, sensitive about priority and prestige, did not overlook supposed slights and soon felt aggrieved. Even additional clarification by the Prophet in the months ahead did not erase their concerns. Until experience taught them what it meant to be Apostles, understandably they would occasionally grope and stumble.

By 12 March 1835, the ten Apostles in Kirtland had already agreed on an itinerary and on an early May departure for their first mission, but not until late April did Thomas Marsh and Orson Pratt arrive to complete the quorum. After a meeting of the full Quorum of the Twelve on 28 April (at which the Prophet focused on the need for unity, forgiveness, and mutual love), Joseph Smith convened on 2 May a "grand council" of all Kirtland priesthood leaders. There he reaffirmed that the Twelve had no authority where existed a standing high council, nor had the standing high councils authority "abroad." The Prophet also told the Apostles that they should sit in council and preside *according to age*. By this rule Thomas Marsh, newly arrived and only weeks older than David W. Patten, took his place as President of the Quorum of the Twelve; Brigham Young and Heber C. Kimball were next in age or seniority.[12] Although this calling did not immediately offer the visibility and local honor he had enjoyed as a member of the high council in Missouri, President Marsh was determined that his quorum attain their potential as honored and effective leaders.

On Monday, 4 May, the new Apostles left Kirtland for their first and only mission under President Marsh as a full quorum. With pointed counsel and revelation vividly in mind, they labored conscientiously, and the result was good. Throughout New York and New England, the Apostles convened as a high council to regulate branches and conduct business, giving concrete meaning to their title of "traveling high council." Between appointed conferences they taught and preached. In five months they covered hundreds of miles by wagon, canal boat, river steamer, railroad, stage, and foot. Traveling without purse or scrip, they experienced both friendship and rejection. They felt the power of God, and they felt they "had done as the Lord had commanded."[13] This was a promising beginning.

But they returned home that fall not to accolades but to accusations, and these they did not handle well. What should have been minor difficulties arising from affronts or simple miscommunication aroused intense feelings, and soon the new Quorum of the Twelve found itself immersed in charges and countercharges with the First Presidency, concerns about position and precedence with the Kirtland High Council, even divisive complaints among its own members.[14] Under President Marsh, the quorum tended to meet such challenges in a manner that stressed rights, justice, and his (or his quorum's) prerogatives more than brotherhood or humble submission to counsel.

For the Apostles and other Church leaders in Kirtland, the fall of 1835 should have been a joyful season devoted to preparing hearts and spirits for long-awaited blessings in the nearly completed

Kirtland Temple. Instead, hurt feelings required council after council dedicated to airing complaints, soothing feelings, and generally working to reestablish brotherhood.[15] These efforts did bear fruit, however, and as far as records reveal, by November comparative harmony seemed to prevail. Then, without clarifying explanation, on 3 November the Prophet recorded in his diary the following:

> Thus came the word of the Lord unto me concerning the Twelve saying behold they are under condemnation, because they have not been sufficiently humble in my sight, and in consequence of their covetous desires, in that they have not dealt equally with each other.

The revelation named several as offenders and then concluded that "all must humble themselves before me, before they will be accounted worthy to receive an endowment."[16]

Understandably this caused a stir among the Apostles. The only other revelation addressing them directly had been the great revelation on priesthood, and now, only months later, this. Records do not preserve President Marsh's response to this chastisement, though we can surmise that he took it personally and was not pleased. But Joseph Smith did record that Elders Hyde and McLellin, two of those named, stopped by to express "some little dissatisfaction."

Brigham Young, on the other hand, "appeared perfectly satisfied" with the chastisement.[17] Perhaps he felt no need to take it personally or, if he did, he remembered the inspired counsel of the June 1833 revelation that taught: "Whom I love I also chasten that their sins may be forgiven, for with the chastisement I prepare a way for their deliverance in all things out of temptation."[18]

No doubt Brigham Young also recognized the justice of the rebuke. Not only had the Apostles clashed with other Church officials, they had also experienced jealousy and pettiness within their own quorum. Years later he characterized the Kirtland Twelve as "continually sparring at each other." To illustrate, he told of once being summoned to answer for having accepted an invitation to preach. By what authority, demanded his fellow Apostles, had he "presumed to appoint a meeting and preach" without consulting them? Under Thomas Marsh the Twelve met very often, Brigham continued, "and if no one of them needed cleaning, they had to clean' some one any how."[19] President Young contrasted his own later style as President, trying to be a father to all, with President Marsh's: "like a toad's hair comb[ing] up and down."[20]

Clearly, Thomas Marsh was impatient with criticism and tended to view a difference of opinion or even initiative by other Apostles as a challenge to his leadership. And he was impatient about the status of the Twelve. According to Brigham Young, he was among those who, when Joseph "snubbed" the Apostles, exclaimed, "We are Apostles[!] it's an insult for us to be treated so."[21]

Brigham, on the other hand, came to see the snubbing, the trials, in a way Thomas never did: as a necessary preparation and testing before they were ready for power. As he summarized in a quorum meeting three years after the Prophet's death, only when the Apostles "proved ourselves willing to be every bodys servant for Christs sake" were they "worthy of power." Those who think themselves great are not "fit for power," he deeply believed, and if the Prophet "snub[ed] them a bit it wo[ul]d be well for them."[22]

By January 1836 the Apostles had settled important differences and had come to enjoy both increased unity within their quorum and general harmony with other leaders.[23] Thus prepared, they shared with other Kirtland Saints the extraordinary blessings and manifestations associated with the Kirtland Temple in early 1836.

But for the Quorum of the Twelve, unity, harmony, and new spiritual strength did not last. They did not move as a quorum to Missouri once the temple was finished, as earlier contemplated. Joseph Smith announced that instead of another quorum mission, they were free to move or stay in Kirtland, as each chose; each was free to preach where he would. This postponed rather than changed their primary duty to take the gospel abroad. But Thomas Marsh and David Patten, the two senior Apostles, returned to Missouri, while most of the others continued to call Kirtland home. Within a year, the Twelve would be as divided spiritually as they were geographically.

In 1837 dissension and rebellion swept the Church, especially among the leadership. Most retained faith in the Book of Mormon and believed in the necessity of restored authority, but not everyone shared the Prophet's enthusiasm for the "ancient order of things." To some, a society modeled after ancient Israel, where prophetic authority directed all aspects of life (not just the religious), portended a reduction in cherished social and economic freedoms. It was too "Papist," they declared, too "un-American."

Those concerns underlay the discontent of many who ostensibly blamed Joseph for "meddling" in the Kirtland Bank, which ultimately failed, or who had other complaints against his conduct of economic or civic affairs.[24] While most members trusted the Prophet and remained loyal, even if they did not yet fully comprehend his vision, a rift developed between Joseph and many leaders, including some in the First Presidency and the Twelve who were certain they understood some things better than he.[25] Of the Apostles in Kirtland, only Brigham Young and Heber Kimball expressed unwavering support for Joseph Smith and his program throughout this difficult period.

When news of the rebellion reached President Marsh in Missouri, he was appalled. Word that several of his own quorum members were prominent among the dissenters especially humiliated him, because he had envisioned leading a united quorum abroad to introduce the gospel to Great Britain. It also distressed him to learn that an impatient Parley Pratt intended to leave on a foreign mission without him. Hurt, angry, and determined, Marsh hoped to "right-up" the Twelve and reestablish himself as an effective leader by holding a dramatic meeting with his quorum in Kirtland, where he would interject himself vigorously into the fray on the side of the Prophet. On 10 May, he and Elder Patten dispatched an urgent letter to Parley, advising him not to depart for England:

> The 12 must get together difficulties must be removed & love restored, we must have peace within before we can wage a successful war without. . . . Shall the 12 apostles of the Lambe be a disorganised body pulling different ways, Shall one [go] to his plough another to his merchandise, another to England &c. No! I even I Thomas will step in (if

> their is none other for it is my right in this case) and give council to you.

The letter appointed 24 July for an extraordinary council "to break through every obstacle" and prepare for their mission abroad.[26]

Since at least February 1837, the Apostles in Kirtland had discussed a summer mission to England; Parley Pratt was not alone in his intent. But amid dissension and the continuing absence of President Marsh, the mission appeared doubtful. Heber Kimball was thus shocked when the Prophet told him in early June that for the "salvation" of the Church the mission must go forth without delay, and that he must head it.[27] Though Heber pleaded for Brigham to accompany him, Joseph maintained that Brigham would be needed even more in Kirtland and therefore could not go. Joseph needed Brigham, Parley had now joined the others in rebellion, and the mission could not wait for Presidents Marsh and Patten. Therefore, Kimball was *the* man. Begging forgiveness, Orson Hyde sought reconciliation the very day Kimball was set apart for his mission and asked to join him. Thus it was that Elders Kimball and Hyde, not Marsh and Patten, left Kirtland 13 June to open the work abroad.[28]

A few days later, after Brigham Young tried but failed to reconcile Parley Pratt with Joseph, Pratt suddenly departed for Missouri. Providentially, he encountered Marsh and Patten en route, and they succeeded in turning him around.

As soon as they reached Kirtland, Brigham Young briefed Elders Marsh and Patten on the perplexing problems. Marsh then went directly to Joseph's home—his headquarters during his Kirtland stay—and set to work reconciling the disaffected. (David Patten, meanwhile, willing to face the worst, visited the dissenters next and, according to Brigham, "got his mind prejudiced" and then, presumably by reciting the charges he had heard, "insulted" Joseph. The Prophet reacted strongly to the affront which, in Young's view, "done David good" and quickly returned him to his senses.)[29] The Prophet arranged a special meeting at his home for several of the prominent malcontents, no doubt including Apostles. Marsh "moderated" and, he reported later, "a reconciliation was effected between all parties."[30]

Without question, President Marsh contributed to the healing and reconciliation in Kirtland that summer. He labored with the "merchant Apostles," Lyman Johnson and John Boynton, and with Apostle/constable Luke Johnson. Following their return, Apostles Orson Pratt and Parley Pratt, among others, made public confessions and expressions of support for Joseph Smith. While neither Marsh nor the Prophet swept away the basic differences in outlook that had sparked dissent, as President of the Twelve, Marsh was able to return a modicum of civility and unity to his quorum. An early departure for England seemed out of the question, however, and there is no evidence that Marsh convened the "extraordinary meeting" he had earlier proposed.

Despite modest success, President Marsh remained troubled—troubled that members of his quorum had rebelled, and troubled that missionary work was proceeding in England without him. Concerned about his own status, wondering if the Lord could still accept the Twelve, he visited with the Prophet on 23 July, the day before his extraordinary council would have been held. That evening Joseph Smith dictated as Thomas wrote "the word of the Lord unto Thomas B. Marsh concerning the twelve apostles of the Lamb."[31]

The revelation acknowledged Marsh's prayerful concern for his quorum and counseled him to continue to pray for them and, as needed, to admonish them sharply, for "after their temptations, and much tribulation, behold, I, the Lord, will feel after them, and if they harden not their hearts, . . . they shall be converted, and I will heal them." It reproved the Twelve—"Exalt not yourselves; rebel not against my servant Joseph"—and counseled Marsh to be more faithful and humble, reaffirming at the same time his position as President of the Twelve. It also comforted Marsh—and this is what really concerned him—that despite all the problems, he might yet "bear record of my name" and "send forth my word unto the ends of the earth."[32] Even though Elders Kimball and Hyde had departed for England, Thomas might yet have his day.[33]

Despite the best efforts of Joseph, Hyrum, Sidney, Thomas, David, and Brigham, the Church could not be saved in Kirtland.

Up to this point, the Prophet had patiently worked with dissenters, bringing back many. But when open rebellion broke out again in the fall of 1837, patience was no longer a virtue, and backsliders were cut off. Anger mounted, division deepened, apostates grew more bold, and by year's end Brigham Young, the most vigorous and outspoken among the Prophet's defenders, fled for his life. In early January, Joseph Smith and Sidney Rigdon followed, their families close behind, and by spring most of the faithful were on their way to Missouri.

The Saints in Far West, Missouri, could not have been impressed with the Quorum of the Twelve in the summer of 1838. The Apostles had yet to demonstrate much unity or power as a quorum, and worse, Joseph Smith had removed four of the Apostles in the aftermath of the Kirtland difficulties. At the conference on 7 April, David Patten had reviewed the status of each of the Twelve, including his concerns about William Smith and his unwillingness to recommend to the Saints Elders McLellin, Boynton, Johnson, and Johnson. Later that month the latter four Apostles, along with Oliver Cowdery and David Whitmer, were each formally tried and cut off.[34] After months of concern and labor with his quorum, Thomas Marsh's twelve now numbered only eight—and one of those could not be relied upon.

Pondering all this in July 1838, the Prophet prayed: "Show us thy will, O Lord, concerning the Twelve." The answer directed that the Twelve be reorganized with John Taylor, John E. Page, Wilford Woodruff, and Willard Richards replacing "those who have fallen." The revelation also promised that if the Apostles were humble and faithful, "an effectual door shall be opened for them, from henceforth." The Lord then charged the Twelve to depart on the following 26 April from the Far West Temple site and to go "over the great waters" to England.[35] Neither the Church nor the Apostles had yet seen the worst of their trials. Nonetheless, this revelation contained the seeds of renewal—and marks the beginning of the transformation of the Twelve.

The following day, the Apostles convened a formal quorum meeting for the first time in months. They agreed to notify immediately the four newly called Apostles, none of whom was in Far

West, and to prepare for their mission.[36] The anticipated ordination of new quorum members, the return from England later in the month of Elders Kimball and Hyde, and this renewal of their commission to carry the gospel to the nations seemed to portend a new day for Marsh's shattered quorum. The command had been given, and the date was known; finally President Marsh would lead his colleagues abroad.

But it was not to be. Before the anticipated mission, even before the existing vacancies could be filled, there would be two more vacancies—one caused by the death of David Patten during the violence that soon erupted in northern Missouri, and the other caused by the disaffection of President Marsh himself, a by-product of that same Missouri conflict.[37]

Marsh's disillusionment and decision to leave were the results of many factors. Pride, misunderstanding, hurt feelings, suspicion, and, in Marsh's own later words, stubbornness and a loss of the Spirit, were all involved.[38] Troubled, feeling himself wavering, he humbled himself before the Lord long enough to receive a revelation. Marsh later affirmed to Brigham and Heber outside his print shop that the Lord had told him to believe Joseph and sustain him. But then he promptly went out and did the opposite.

And once his face was set, the stubborn, inflexible Thomas was not a man who could be turned. By removing himself from the Saints when he did, he escaped the violence that soon decimated Far West and drove his co-religionists from Missouri, but at what cost? As he later acknowledged, his loss was the greater.[39]

The military confrontation in northern Missouri left the Church in disarray. Providentially, Brigham Young, who had not resided in Far West proper, and Heber Kimball, who had just returned from England, remained to fill the vacuum caused by the disaffection, death, or imprisonment of other key leaders. They faced a formidable challenge.

From Liberty Jail, Joseph Smith and his counselors, Sidney Rigdon and Hyrum Smith, addressed an important letter to "Bros H C Kimball and B Young." The 16 January 1839 letter began with an answer to an earlier query of Young and Kimball about leaving Missouri: "It is not wisdom for you to go out of Caldwell

[County] with your families yet." No doubt the Presidency hoped that they would soon be free and would be able to accompany them. But more vital, with the Presidency in prison, "the management of the affairs of the Church devolves on you that is the Twelve."[40] With the other leadership quorums in disarray and the Presidency disabled, suddenly everything came under the jurisdiction of the Twelve Apostles.

The Quorum of the Twelve Apostles hardly appeared equal to the exigency. Because of apostasy, death, and imprisonment, it was as disorganized as other quorums. The departure of the Johnson brothers, McLellin, and Boynton had left four vacancies in the quorum, and before those named to fill the vacancies had been ordained, the disaffections of Marsh and Hyde had created two more. Patten was dead, Parley Pratt was in prison, and William Smith could not be relied upon. Unless Orson Pratt had recently arrived in Far West from his New York assignment, only Brigham Young and Heber Kimball of the original Twelve could assist the Saints in the ravished Missouri settlements.

This same January letter from the First Presidency instructed Young and Kimball to implement the July revelation calling new men to the quorum. "Get the twelve together," they were told; ordain those who have not been ordained (none had), "or at least such of them as you can get" (some were not in Missouri). Then, as a quorum, "proceed to regulate the Elders as the Lord may give you wisdom." The letter also named George A. Smith and Lyman Sherman to fill the vacancies left by the departure of Marsh and Hyde.

How would the reviving quorum be organized? An important postscript said simply: "Appoint the oldest of the Twelve who were firs[t] appointed, to be the President of your Quorum." Heber Kimball and Brigham Young, both born in June 1801, had birthdays only a few days apart. By this postscript Brigham Young, not Heber Kimball, became President of the Quorum of the Twelve Apostles.

Although for now the Twelve must oversee the broader affairs of the Church, the January missive reminded them that their assignment of spreading the gospel throughout the world was not suspended—"but under wise management can go on more rapidly than ever." In spite of the disasters that had befallen the Saints, the July revelation appointing the Twelve to a foreign mission still stood. Even if Brigham and Heber moved their families to safety, the letter stressed, they must return to Missouri in order to depart for their foreign mission from the Far West temple site on 26 April, as the revelation had directed. "If we die for the testimony of Jesus we die, but whether we live or die let the work of God go on."

This January letter was not required for Young and Kimball to understand their responsibility. Consciously discarding the officious approach Marsh had taken, Young and Kimball set out to make the Twelve the servants of all. New Apostles were ordained, and for weeks they labored diligently to assist the Missouri Saints and to reestablish order within the Church. They bound the Saints by covenant to assist the poor and to take all, regardless of means, on the burdensome winter exodus from Missouri. Available records, though sparse, document the Twelve's involvement in every aspect of Church affairs in this troubled period.

In order to have a properly constituted council to conduct affairs for the Saints, the Apostles began by reorganizing the high council on 13 December.[41] During the following week, a council meeting presided over by Elders Young and Kimball voted that John E. Page and John Taylor be ordained according to the July revelation.[42] The two Apostles then ordained them, thus filling two vacancies in the Quorum of the Twelve.

In late January, soon after the letter arrived informing Young and Kimball of the appointments of George A. Smith and Lyman Sherman to the Twelve, Joseph and Hyrum, still in Liberty Jail, asked their brother Don Carlos to inform George A. of his call. When he did, George A. requested Don Carlos to tell no one else, because he felt unequal to the station. But learning that Brigham and Heber were leaving to visit the prisoners, George A. overcame his reticence and asked to join them, and the three mounted horses for the town of Liberty.

At the jail, the visitors spent the supper hour locked up with the prisoners. George A. later remembered that Joseph Smith spent the hour talking with Brigham and Heber, pausing only to ask him how he felt about his call. The young man replied that he was pleased and would do his best to honor it.[43] Soon after this, Lyman Sherman died of illness without learning that he had been named to the quorum.

By mid-March Brigham Young, Wilford Woodruff, and John Taylor had joined the Saints gathering near Quincy, Illinois, leaving only Heber Kimball to assist the few still in Missouri. Once in Illinois, the Apostles moved their families to Quincy, now temporary headquarters, and began meeting and operating as a quorum.[44]

In April 1839 the available Apostles—William Smith was not to be found, Parley Pratt was in prison, and Willard Richards was in England—boldly left Quincy to return to Missouri, whence they had so recently escaped, to fulfill the July 1838 revelation requiring them to depart 26 April from "the building-spot of my house" in Far West. Enemies had boasted that the revelation proved that Joseph Smith was a false prophet, since the prophecy could not be fulfilled. Some of the Saints urged that perhaps, under the circumstances, the Lord would "take the will for the deed." But Brigham Young and his associates were determined to succeed and not allow even supposed failure to stand as a witness against Joseph.

The enemies in Missouri were so certain that no one would attempt to return to the area that they did not even post a guard at the temple site. Thus, according to prophecy, in the pre-dawn hours of 26 April, Brigham Young and his associates and a small group of Saints sang hymns, ordained Wilford Woodruff and George A. Smith Apostles, laid a symbolic cornerstone, excommunicated dissidents, and departed before the first astonished anti-Mormon reached the site.[45]

From Far West, Missouri, the Apostles traveled to the newly designated city on the banks of the Mississippi, which would become Nauvoo, Illinois. There, in May, they were reunited with Joseph and Hyrum. Even as the Twelve had reentered Missouri, Joseph and Hyrum, finally free of their captors, were making their way out of the state. In the new gathering place, instead of keeping the Apostles at arm's length as he often had in Kirtland, Joseph Smith embraced them, instructed them, blessed them, and participated fully in their mission preparations.

No one, however, had the means to help the families of the Apostles. Destitute after the Missouri tragedy, without adequate shelter or provisions, everyone suffered—the more so when summer diseases befell them in the damp, sickly hollows along the river. Consequently, it was a great test of faith for the Apostles to leave their families in such circumstances. Essentially they left their families in the hands of God to embark on a mission that could not be postponed and that would eventually transform the Church.

The same revelation that had commanded their departure for England had also declared: "I, the Lord, give unto them a promise that I will provide for their families."[46] That promise, not the visible reality, was their comfort. The result of this obedience in difficult circumstances was perhaps the most successful mission in the history of the Church. As Elder Jeffrey R. Holland noted, following this mission "neither this group of men, the British Isles, nor the Church would ever be the same again."[47]

Because they were ill and without means, traveling from the Mississippi to New York and then crossing the Atlantic to Liverpool required several months. Brigham Young and the four Apostles with him—Heber Kimball, Parley and Orson Pratt, and George A. Smith—arrived in Great Britain in April 1840. Just as Kimball and Hyde had done when they opened the work in England nearly three years before, they first traveled to Preston. When Elders Woodruff and Taylor, who had preceded them by two months, joined them there, seven ordained Apostles and Willard Richards convened for what Woodruff called "The First Council of the Twelve among the Nations." After ordaining Richards, they formalized, for the first time since the apostasy of Thomas Marsh, the presidency of their senior member by setting Brigham Young apart as "the standing President of the Twelve." Eight of the Twelve now stood ready to fulfill their quorum mission and push forward the vital work in Great Britain.[48]

Expecting a great deal of himself and others, Brigham Young

Brigham Young
1801–1877

Heber C. Kimball
1801–1868

Parley P. Pratt
1807–1857

Orson Pratt
1811–1881

John Taylor
1808–1887

Wilford Woodruff
1807–1898

George A. Smith
1817–1875

Willard Richards
1804–1854

The eight Apostles in England, 1840–1841

could be firm and demanding. But rather than dictating to his peers or to the Saints, he consciously sought to promote the collegial fellowship that meant so much to him.[49] Instead of the abrasive leadership often exhibited by President Marsh, President Young treated his fellow Apostles more as associates than as subordinates.

If Brigham Young took the lead in emphasizing harmony within the quorum, he was not alone. Recognizing the need to conduct themselves differently than previously, others, too, made good feelings, mutual support, and cooperation high priorities.

One searches in vain for incidents of division or bad feelings. Instead one finds fellowship, concern for one another, communication, and commitment to shared responsibilities. That the records are silent about discord suggests that there was little to note. Records for the Kirtland period were not reticent about acknowledging difficulties within the Twelve; there had been severe problems earlier, and there would be tensions, at times, in the future. But the evidence suggests that this was a period when the Twelve were, as Elder Woodruff recorded, "well united & agree in all things & love one another."[50]

That April, after organizing their quorum and the mission, the Apostles parted for separate fields of labor within Great Britain. Brigham Young and Willard Richards accompanied Wilford Woodruff to Herefordshire and its environs to assist in ongoing work among a religious fellowship known as the United Brethren. Laboring in the region since March, Woodruff had already baptized perhaps 160, including more than three dozen lay preachers. Now, for a month, the three colleagues shared days packed with preaching, teaching, visiting, baptizing, confirming, ordaining, blessing, and counseling. By mid-May, nearly 400 people had accepted baptism. Working as a team, the Apostles formed the main body of United Brethren into Latter-day Saint branches.[51]

In the eyes of the Apostles and their new coreligionists, God's hand was evident in Herefordshire. For example, on 18 May, traditionally a feast day among the United Brethren, President Young, "clothed with the power of God," addressed the gathered Saints as a prelude to sharing a large banquet. It was apparently on this occasion that a "notable miracle was wrought by faith & the power of God." Writing two weeks later, Elder Woodruff recorded that the three Apostles had blessed Sister Mary Pitt, confined to bed for six years and unable to walk without crutches for eleven, "& her ancle bones received strength & she now walks without the aid of crutch or staff."[52]

It is hard to imagine better circumstances for developing confidence and leadership. Seldom had these young Apostles felt more needed; never had the results of their work been more dramatic. Without doubt the experience of transforming the United Brethren into Latter-day Saints helped transform and strengthen the Apostles as well. Though in scale the United Brethren conversions were extraordinary, Apostles in other fields experienced success and comparable challenges, which similarly spurred their development as leaders.

When the Twelve met with the Saints in July conference, 842 more members were represented than in April. The Apostles used this general mission conference to strengthen, counsel, and further regulate the Church. Ordinations, mission calls, interviews, and instruction occupied them for many hours. The Twelve also convened as a Traveling High Council to formally hear cases of alleged misconduct.[53] Throughout these proceedings, the Saints witnessed the Apostles giving counsel, expressing love and concern, and functioning with unity and effectiveness. As a quorum and individually, they were gaining an increased sense of authority and ability to perform.

The October conference marked the halfway point in their mission. It also marked a shift to a different managerial style. Joseph Smith had instructed them that, when united, they had authority as a quorum to conduct business without constant reference to a sustaining vote.[54] So far, however, they had chosen to present most matters to a conference representing all the British Saints. But as business and numbers multiplied (up 1,115 members since the last conference), it became less practical to convene a truly general conference, much less to entertain floor motions and discussion on every item of business. The conference accepted President Young's suggestion that the number of British general conferences be reduced and that ordinations, the regulation of officers, and other business be conducted by the Twelve as a quorum, or traveling high council.[55]

Administrative duties did not prevent Brigham Young from preaching or insulate him from the pressures and rewards of the front line. In this, too, he attempted to be an example. "Sence we have ben in Manchester," he wrote his wife Mary Ann, "We have don all that we posably could to spread this work. . . . We keepe Baptiseing every weak which causes much per[se]cution."[56]

In late October, Elders Young and Kimball, as part of a preaching circuit, traveled to the town of Hawarden, Wales.[57] There, Brigham Young noted in a letter to Mary Ann, their preaching elicited a singular response:

> We have hered from Wales whare Br Kimball and I went. . . . the report went out that we had the same power that the old apostles had, it is true we did lay hands on one young man that was quite low with a fevor, we rebuked his fevor and he got well we laid our hands on a woman that had verry bad eyes she emeditly recoverd, they have a gradel [great deal] to say about our preaching. they say that Elder Kimball has such sharp eys that he can look wright through them, and

Mary Ann Angell Young (1803–1882), ca. 1853. Mary Ann married Brigham Young on 18 February 1834 at Kirtland, Ohio

> Elder Young Preashes so that every Body that heres him must beleve he preaches so plane and powerful.[58]

Young's experiences illustrate the kinds of emotional and spiritual encounters that helped each of the Apostles gain while in Great Britain a sharper awareness of duty and authority.

Nearly a decade later, Brigham Young and Heber Kimball instructed newly called Apostles about their office. Distilling their own experiences, both compared the Apostleship to a harness that could not be set aside—not a light "carriage harness" either, insisted Kimball, but "an old Penn Wagon harness" suitable for heavy burdens. They would not know the weight of the harness, cautioned Elder Young, until they were in the traces under load. Then, especially, "look out how you walk or you will fall"; be one with the Twelve, for any variance of feeling "will cut."[59]

In Britain, Elders Young and Kimball and their associates learned to wear the harness and pull together. A deep sense of duty, reinforced by the enormous expectations of the Saints, kept them in the harness and at their task. Having left America in sickness, and then laboring in a far-away kingdom renowned for education and religion, these young, unsophisticated Americans were intensely challenged on this mission. Reaching beyond what they had done before, beyond even what they thought themselves capable of doing, they increased in confidence and ability.

On 1 April 1841, the Twelve assembled in Manchester for their final quorum meetings in England. With the addition of Orson Hyde, en route to Israel on a special assignment, nine Apostles attended, the most seated together since soon after the organization of the quorum in Kirtland six years earlier. These nine later served faithfully with Joseph Smith in Nauvoo, received temple ordinances at his hands, and, after his death, finished the temple and led the Saints west. This was their beginning as a close-knit quorum. "Perfect union & harmony prevailed in all the deliberations," wrote Wilford Woodruff of these first meetings of the nine in April 1841.[60]

The Apostles met with the Saints in conference on 6 April 1841, one year after their arrival in England. The accomplishments and changes of the intervening twelve months exceeded all expectations. "It hath truly been a miricle what God hath wrought by our hands . . . since we have been here," recorded Elder Woodruff, "& I am asstonished when I look at it."[61] Reports from branches throughout the kingdom showed an increase of nearly 2,200 since the last conference and well over 4,000 over the course of the year in Britain.[62] The influence of the quorum's mission on the lives of thousands of British Saints was profound. The influence on the Church as thousands of British emigrants began flowing to Nauvoo was likewise substantial and would continue.

The influence of the mission on Brigham Young and his colleagues was similarly enduring. Each of the three Nauvoo Apostles who was not in England in April 1841 was gone from the Church within a handful of years. Tempered by their shared British experience and bonded together as a quorum, the Apostles who served in Britain went on to provide the Church its top leadership for the remainder of the nineteenth century.[63]

On 15 April, the Twelve completed for publication "An Epistle of the Twelve" to the Saints throughout Great Britain—their last official act as a quorum in England. In it they expressed thanks for the diligence of the Saints in hearkening "to the council of those whom God has seen fit to send among them, and who hold the keys of this ministry." The result had been union and power. They urged the Saints to remember "that which we have ever taught . . . both by precept and example . . . to beware of an aspiring spirit."[64] A few days later, they set sail to return home.

A memorable event during the voyage home illustrates the sense the Twelve now firmly shared that the Lord oversaw their lives and labors. At midnight on 24 April, contrary winds that had blown since soon after their departure increased to gale strength and blew off the fore topsail. The next day the seas were "mountains high." Most aboard the pitching ship were sick. For days the gale continued, until there was fear that some of the children would die. In spite of the difficulty, Elder Woodruff judged the Twelve "generally well & vary patient well united & agree in all things & love one another." They prayed together and assisted the sick.

On 28 April, the storm worsened. Berths collapsed. Baggage broke loose, threatening to crush the emigrants. Facing disaster, the Apostles sought the Lord's intervention. The next day Elder Woodruff noted simply: "the Sun Shines plesent & we have a fair wind for the first time since we left Liverpool."

The following week, Brigham Young noted in his diary:

> When the winds ware contr[ar]y the 12 a gread to humble them selves before the Lord and ask him to calm the seas & give us a fair wind, we did so & the wind emeditly changed and from that time to this it has blone in our favor.[65]

The 1840–41 mission marked the beginning of the Twelve's functioning as a united and effective entity. In Britain, Brigham Young first presided over a quorum of Apostles unitedly engaged in a common labor. Far removed from Joseph Smith and other leaders, they relied on the Lord and on each other and together achieved a success unprecedented in the short history of the Church. The results reinforced confidence in the authority of their office, in the leadership of Brigham Young, and in each other. In Britain the Twelve not only proselyted successfully but also functioned for the first time as an effective agency of ecclesiastical administration. There, also for the first time, Brigham Young had the opportunity to shape the quorum into a different kind of council than had existed under Thomas Marsh. The Apostles grew individually—and collectively they nurtured a growing sense of fellowship and collegiality. In the words of Elder Woodruff, writing on the high seas: "I never enjoyed my self better with the Twelve. . . . . Union prevails among us & we dwell together in love."[66] For the Twelve, this shared mission set a pattern for relationships with one another, set a course for the quorum, and prepared them to receive new responsibilities soon afterward.

Nauvoo Saints, too, came to look upon the Apostles with more respect following their British labors. Extensive news of their ministry that circulated in Nauvoo increased their stature as leading elders. Without question, in 1841 many more Saints in America looked upon them as effective and trustworthy leaders than would have thought so previously. Nor did it hurt their reputation among Nauvoo Saints to have been preceded by several hundred British converts singing their praises.

The mission to Great Britain—especially leaving families sick and destitute—had been a test for the men. Wrote Wilford Woodruff, who lost a daughter to sickness while he served: "Never have I been called to make greater Sacrifices or enjoyed greater Blessings."[67] Undertaking the mission required greater dedication and faith than had their earlier assignments, yet eight of the Twelve responded to the call. If the thousand-mile march with Zion's Camp had been an important preparation for the calling of the original Apostles, as they believed, then the British experience of sacrifice, unity, success, and power was of crucial importance to the reconstituted Twelve. The one helped qualify men to be called as Apostles; the other helped prepare them to serve next to the Presidency as Apostles in deed.

The Quorum of the Twelve Apostles came of age at a time when Joseph Smith had pressing need for their talents and services. Within days of the return of Brigham Young and several of his associates to Nauvoo, Joseph Smith moved to put them permanently in the harness. On 10 August 1841, the Prophet, meeting with the Twelve, charged the Apostles to supervise "the business of the church in Nauvoo," marking a dramatic change from their Kirtland role.[68] This assignment substantially changed the earlier division of responsibility between standing high councils and the Twelve, or traveling high council. Now the Apostles would have churchwide responsibilities; under Joseph Smith they would administer in Nauvoo just as they had among the branches abroad.[69]

Unwilling to wait for general conference in October to explain this significant change to the Saints, the Prophet appointed a special conference for 16 August. With the dawn arrival of Willard Richards by riverboat, six of the Twelve assembled with the Saints for this extraordinary conference. Joseph Smith did not attend, due to the death of his youngest child, so Brigham Young called the meeting to order and was then voted to the chair. He stated that the Prophet had appointed the conference to transact business that should not wait until the October conference, specifically the calling of missionaries and providing for emigrants.

Conscious that the direction of these matters had not been associated previously with his office, President Young paused to explain that he and the Twelve had not stepped forward in this matter because of personal aspirations. "Nothing could be further from his wishes, and those of his Quorum," he assured his listeners, "than to interfere with church affairs at Zion and her stakes." So long had he been in the vineyard, he went on, that nothing could induce him to leave that field to attend to church affairs at home but the requirement of heaven or revelation "to which he would always submit, be the consequences what it might."[70] Young then read a list of prospective missionaries and another list of cities needing elders, and "by nomination" the conference began to designate who would go where.

At that point, Bishop Vinson Knight suggested, and the conference agreed, that to expedite the meeting, the Twelve should make the assignments and simply present them to the conference. That meant, in effect, that the Twelve would conduct the business "as a quorum" rather than by the voice of the conference—just as they had done in their last conference in England.

Present at the second session, Joseph Smith expanded on Elder Young's cautious remarks about the purpose of the conference. He explained directly

> that the twelve should be authorized to assist in managing the affairs of the Kingdom in this place [church headquarters]. which he said was the duties of their office &c. Motioned seconded and carried that the quorum of the twelve be authorized to act in accordance with the instructions given by president Joseph Smith in regulating and superintending the affairs of the Church.[71]

For publication, the brief minutes were fleshed out with additional explanations that seem consistent with the Prophet's intent in taking this action. According to the published account, he said that the time had come

> when the Twelve should be called upon to stand in their place next to the First Presidency, and attend to the settling of emigrants and the business of the church at the stakes, and assist to bear off the kingdom victorious to the nations.[72]

Authorized by Joseph Smith and the sustaining vote of the Saints in special conference, the Twelve now had the mandate to conduct Church affairs in the stakes of Zion as elsewhere. A motion that the conference accept the missionary assignments made by the Twelve allowed the Prophet to further clarify the implications of this mandate. According to a published account, he told the conference that as they had already sanctioned the doings of the Twelve, further vote was unnecessary, for transacting such business with the approval of the Presidency was a part of their office.

The manuscript version states without elaboration: "Resolved on Motion . . . that the Twelve be authorised to make the selection of elders independent of the conference and present them to President Joseph Smith for his approval."[73] The Twelve now had authority and responsibility to administer the affairs of the Church wherever and whenever Joseph Smith directed.

Willard Richards's terse diary entry adequately summed up the events of the conference: "Conference-Business of the Church given to the 12."[74] Following this significant realignment, the Twelve stood next to the Presidency in managing all Church affairs. The ambiguity between the high councils and the Twelve that had so vexed Thomas Marsh and the Kirtland Apostles was over. The Apostles had shown themselves servants of all—and the Prophet judged them, to use Brigham Young's phrase, "fit for power."

NOTES

1. Parts of this overview of the history of Brigham Young and the Quorum of the Twelve Apostles from 1835 to 1841 have been drawn from my dissertation, "The Emergence of Brigham Young and the Twelve to Mormon Leadership, 1830–1841" (Brigham Young University, 1981), and from in-depth treatment of portions of the story, which I published earlier in three essays: "Thomas B.

Marsh As President of the First Quorum of the Twelve, 1835–1838," in *Hearken, O Ye People, Discourses on the Doctrine and Covenants,* BYU 1984 Sidney B. Sperry Symposium (Sandy, Utah: Randall Book, 1984), 167–90; "The 1840–41 Mission to England and the Development of the Quorum of the Twelve," in *Mormons in Victorian England,* ed. Richard L. Jensen and Malcolm R. Thorp (Salt Lake City: University of Utah Press, 1989), 70–91; and "'Exalt Not Yourselves': The Revelations and Thomas Marsh, An Object Lesson for Our Day," in *The Heavens Are Open,* BYU 1992 Sidney B. Sperry Symposium on the Doctrine and Covenants and Church History (Salt Lake City: Deseret Book Co., 1993), 112–29.

See those sources for additional information, examples, and documentation on this period. Evidence and examples for the conclusions summarized at the beginning of this essay can be found in the dissertation, especially in chapters 4 and 5.

2. See D&C 112: 12–13.
3. See D&C 107: 23–24, 33, 35.
4. D&C 107: 27.
5. See Esplin, "Thomas B. Marsh As President."
6. Brigham Young, 7 October 1860, in *Journal of Discourses,* 8: 197. Brigham Young later said the Prophet's approach was: "snob [snub?] them a little & if they be true servants of all then they are to get the power." Minutes, 30 November 1847, Brigham Young Papers, Library-Archives, Historical Department of The Church of Jesus Christ of Latter-day Saints (hereafter cited as LDS Church Historical Archives).
7. The account here is based on a variety of sources. See Joseph Smith, *History of the Church of Jesus Christ of Latter-day Saints,* ed. B. H. Roberts, 7 vols., 2d ed., rev. (Salt Lake City: Deseret Book Co., 1971), 2: 180ff, for one detailed account; see Esplin, "Emergence of Brigham and the Twelve," 125–27, for additional sources. D&C 18: 26–37 (June 1829) foresaw the calling of the Twelve, charged to "go into all the world to preach my gospel unto every creature."
8. See *History of the Church,* 2: 194–98.
9. Minutes, 28 March 1835, Kirtland Record Book, 198, LDS Church Historical Archives.
10. Record of the Twelve, 27 February 1835, LDS Church Historical Archives. See also *History of the Church,* 2: 198–200.
11. D&C 107: 30.
12. "History of Brigham Young," *Deseret News,* 27 January to 24 March 1858, 386 (10 February 1858); see also *History of the Church,* 2: 219–20. The principle of seniority by age applied only to the members of this first quorum, all of whom were called on the same day. Thereafter, seniority would be established not by age but by date of entrance into the quorum. Records suggest the possibility that Thomas B. Marsh did not know his birthday—something not particularly rare in his day. According to vital statistics from his birthplace, he was born in 1800, making him younger than David Patten, instead of 1799 as Marsh himself believed. See *Vital Records of Acton,*

Massachusetts to the Year 1850 (Boston: New England Historical Genealogical Society, 1928), pp. 77–81, as cited in A. Gary Anderson, "Thomas B. Marsh: The Preparation and Conversion of the Emerging Apostle," *Regional Studies in Latter-day Saint Church History, New York,* ed. Larry C. Porter et al. (Provo, Ut.: Department of Church History and Doctrine, BYU, 1992), pp. 145, 148.

13. "History of Heber Chase Kimball," manuscript, LDS Church Historical Archives.
14. Instructed to raise funds both for "redeeming Zion" in Missouri and for constructing the Kirtland Temple, they were accused of focusing more on land and ignoring the priority of the temple. Two of the Apostles were charged with (and later admitted) making derogatory comments about President Rigdon, one of the First Presidency. Because these complaints were aired in meetings where the high council played a role, and because in subsequent conferences the high council was invited to vote ahead of the Twelve, issues of priority between the standing high council and the traveling high council exacerbated the problems. See Esplin, "Emergence of Brigham Young," 166–71.
15. For details, see ibid., chapter 4.
16. Joseph Smith Diary, 3 November 1835, in Joseph Smith, *The Papers of Joseph Smith, Volume 2: Journal, 1832–1842,* ed. Dean C. Jessee (Salt Lake City: Deseret Book Co., 1992), 63–64.
17. Joseph Smith Diary, 5 November 1835, in ibid., 65–66.
18. D&C 95: 1.
19. Historian's Office Journal, 16 February 1859, LDS Church Historical Archives.
20. Minutes, 12 February 1849, LDS Church Historical Archives.
21. Ibid., 30 November 1847. Young prefaced this by stating that Marsh's reaction to the Prophet's treatment of the Twelve was "the way T Marsh apostatized."
22. Ibid. Quotations here are drawn from two versions of the minutes.
23. The erratic behavior of William Smith, Joseph's volatile younger brother, was one source of difficulty. The problem was mainly between Joseph and William, but since William was a member of the Twelve, this also affected the quorum. The two were finally reconciled during an emotional New Year's Day meeting presided over by Father Smith. See Esplin, "Emergence of Brigham Young," 175–80.
24. For the Kirtland crisis, see ibid., chapters 5–7; and Milton V. Backman, Jr., *The Heavens Resound: A History of the Latter-day Saints in Ohio, 1830–1838* (Salt Lake City: Deseret Book Co., 1983), chapters 17–18; details not otherwise documented are from Esplin.
25. Brigham Young later said that the fact of "Joseph putting the 12 so far from him was the cause of many apostatizing." Minutes, 30 November 1847, LDS Church Historical Archives.
26. Thomas Marsh and David Patten to Parley P. Pratt, 10 May 1837, Joseph Smith Letterbook, Joseph Smith Papers, LDS Church Historical Archives.
27. *History of the Church,* 2: 489, and "History of Heber Chase Kimball."
28. Kimball's call and the Kimball-Hyde mission are described in James B. Allen, Ronald K. Esplin, and David J. Whittaker, *Men with a Mission: The Quorum of the Twelve in the British Isles, 1837–1841* (Salt Lake City: Deseret Book Co., 1992), 23–53.

29. Wilford Woodruff Journal, 25 June 1857, Wilford Woodruff Papers, LDS Church Historical Archives.
30. Marsh's autobiography was published in *Deseret News,* 24 March 1858.
31. See D&C 112.
32. See D&C 112: 1–17.
33. Unfortunately, instead of humbly accepting this as a renewed opportunity, Thomas immediately visited Vilate Kimball and, backed by this affirmation, told her that Heber could not open an "effectual door" in England because *he,* Thomas, held that responsibility and had not sent Heber! (See Esplin, "Exalt Not Yourselves," 121–22.)
34. Esplin, "Emergence of Brigham Young," 329–32.
35. D&C 118: 1–6.
36. Esplin, "Emergence of Brigham Young," 335.
37. Orson Hyde, ill since his return from England and strongly influenced by President Marsh's disaffection, followed his president away from the Quorum and out of the Church. However, he was reinstated the following year after a humble, deeply penitent letter of apology. See ibid., 342–43, 377–78.
38. Ibid., 339–43.
39. Heber C. Kimball, 12 July 1857, in *Journal of Discourses,* 5: 28–29: "God saw fit to give him a revelation to forewarn him of the course he would take," noted Kimball, "and still he took that course." For additional details, see Esplin, "Thomas B. Marsh As President," 183–86.
40. Sidney Rigdon, Joseph Smith, and Hyrum Smith to Heber Kimball and Brigham Young, 16 January 1839, Joseph Smith Papers, LDS Church Historical Archives.
41. Minutes, 13 December 1838, Far West Record, LDS Church Historical Archives.
42. Ibid., 19 December 1838. Woodruff and Richards, the other two named in the revelation, were still not available.
43. George A. Smith, "History of George Albert Smith," manuscript, George A. Smith Papers, LDS Church Historical Archives. Young George A noted: "I had felt very timid about conversing or making myself familiar with any of the Twelve, as Lyman E. Johnson, John Boynton and some of the others, who formerly belonged to the Quorum, had treated me rather aristocratically, which, added to the high respect I had for their calling, made me feel embarrassed in their Presence."
44. See Wilford Woodruff Journal, 17–18, 20 March 1839.
45. Esplin, "Emergence of Brigham Young," 380–83; see also *History of the Church,* 3: 322, 336–40.
46. D&C 118: 3.
47. Jeffrey R. Holland to Allen, Esplin, and Whittaker, 31 July 1992—this after reading *Men with a Mission.* See that book for the details of the powerful story only summarized here.
48. Wilford Woodruff, *Wilford Woodruff's Journal, 1833–1898, typescript,* ed. Scott

G. Kenney, 9 vols. (Midvale, Utah: Signature Books, 1983), 1: 435 [14 April 1840]; and Minutes, 14 April 1840, LDS Church Historical Archives. Though Orson Hyde passed through briefly on his way to Palestine, only eight Apostles served in England. William Smith and John E. Page failed to respond to the call, and the twelfth, Lyman Wight, was not named until just before the Apostles returned from England.

49. In 1833, Young copied into his diary an especially meaningful passage from a lengthy revelation called the "Olive Leaf," a charter for relationships between men involved in Kirtland's religious school and anticipated temple. That he copied this passage into a diary whose pages mostly record contacts and travels underscores his longing for such Christian bonds of fellowship. "Art thou a brother or brethren," reads the passage: "I salute you in the name of the Lord Jesus Christ, in token of the everlasting covenent; in which Covenant I receive you to fellowship in a determination that is fixed, immoveable and unchangeable to be your fri[e]nd and brother through the grace of God, in the bonds of love." Brigham Young Diary, undated entry at end of 1833, Brigham Young Papers, LDS Church Historical Archives; compare this with D&C 88: 133.
50. Woodruff, *Wilford Woodruff's Journal,* 2: 94 (27 April 1841).
51. See Allen, Esplin, and Whittaker, 147–55.
52. Woodruff, *Wilford Woodruff's Journal,* 1: 455 (3 June 1840).
53. See minutes in *History of the Church,* 4: 146–50; and Woodruff, *Wilford Woodruff's Journal,* 1: 480–82 (6–7 April 1840).
54. Instructions to Twelve and Seventy, 2 May 1835, in *History of the Church,* 2: 220; see also Esplin, "Emergence of Brigham Young," 451–52.
55. See minutes in *History of the Church,* 4: 214–18. This conference began by considering individual items of business, as had earlier ones. But mid-course, with time running out, it was agreed that the Twelve handle the remainder.
56. Brigham Young to Mary Ann Young, 16 October 1840, Blair Family Papers, LDS Church Historical Archives.
57. Nineteenth-century Mormon sources spell the town as Hardin or Harden. This was most likely Hawarden, a small town of northeast Wales a few miles west of Chester. Thanks to Peter C. Brown, England, for pointing this out.
58. Brigham Young to Mary Ann Young, 12 November 1840, Blair Family Papers, University of Utah Special Collections.
59. Council Minutes, 12 February 1849, LDS Church Historical Archives.
60. Woodruff, *Wilford Woodruff's Journal,* 2: 78 (5 April 1841); see also entries for 2–3 April.
61. Ibid., 2: 90 (15 April 1841). The entry continues: "during our Stay here we have esstablished churches in all the most noted cities & towns in the Kingdom have Baptized more then 5,000 souls Printed 5,000 Books of mormon 3000 Hymn Books 2,500 Volumes of the Millennial Star & about 50,000 tracts, & gatherd to the land of Joseph [America] 1,000 Souls & esstablished a great influence among those that trade in ships at sea & lacked for nothing to eat drink or ware. Truly the Lord hath been good."

62. With some excommunicated, hundreds emigrating, and some baptized before the first conference, the total converts for the period the Apostles were in England was 5,000–6,000.
63. Brigham Young, John Taylor, and Wilford Woodruff, Presidents of the Church from 1844 to 1898, were all in Great Britain as members of the Twelve in 1840–41. Lorenzo Snow, President from 1898 to 1901, served with them in Britain, but was not ordained an Apostle until 1849.
64. *Millennial Star* 1 (April 1841): 309–12. No doubt thinking of their own experiences in Kirtland and Missouri, they defined such a spirit as one "which introduces rebellion, confusion, misrule, and disunion, and would, if suffered to exist among us, destroy the union, spirit, and power which are associated with the priesthood and can only exist with the humble and meek."
65. Woodruff, *Wilford Woodruff's Journal,* 2: 93–96 (24–29 April 1841); and Brigham Young Diary, entries before and after 5 May 1841, Brigham Young Papers. See also preceding entry and George A. Smith's colorful diary account of 29 April 1841, George A. Smith Papers, LDS Church Historical Archives: "All the Beathren Were sick we Eat Nothing for th[r]ee Days vomiting Was the Principal Employment We had one Gale."
66. Woodruff, *Wilford Woodruff's Journal,* 2: 98 (6 May 1841). That he should write this after several weeks together in close quarters bespeaks genuine harmony and mutual affection.
67. Ibid., 1: 487 ("Close of the Year" entry for 1840).
68. "History of Brigham Young," 2 (10 March 1858); George A. Smith, "History of George Albert Smith."
69. Several of their new assignments can be seen as an extension of "traditional" ones. They were to call and appoint missionaries, for example, certainly related to their general charge to preach the message abroad. Similarly, since they had been responsible for teaching the gathering in the eastern United States and in Great Britain, it was merely an extension to have them also responsible for settling the gathered Saints once they arrived in Nauvoo. Nonetheless, by these new assignments, the Prophet significantly expanded the scope of their jurisdiction and responsibility.
70. *History of the Church,* 4: 402–4; "History of Brigham Young," 2 (10 March 1858).
71. Minutes, 16 August 1841, LDS Church Historical Archives.
72. "History of Brigham Young," 2 (10 March 1858). This version continues with the Prophet's explanation that the Twelve had been faithful, had born the burden in the heat of the day, and that it was right they be able to provide for their families in Nauvoo "and at the same time relieve him, so that he might attend to the business of translating."
73. Minutes, 16 August 1841, LDS Church Historical Archives.
74. Willard Richards Diary, 16 August 1841, Willard Richards Papers, LDS Church Historical Archives.

CHAPTER 4

Brigham Young and the Missionary Enterprise

David J. Whittaker
Archivist, Harold B. Lee Library
Brigham Young University

INTRODUCTION

We tend to remember Brigham Young primarily for his numerous temporal achievements—accomplishments ranging from his leadership in the pioneering and settling of the Great Basin of the American West to his many economic ventures. Fulfilling such diverse roles as territorial governor, *ex officio* superintendent of Indian Affairs, businessman, architect and builder, father and husband to a large family, and Apostle and President of the Church, Brigham Young almost defies the energy and ability of the modern student to survey and understand such a full and complex life.[1]

It is impossible to study the records of his life without seeing how central his testimony of the gospel of Jesus Christ was to everything he said and did. Such beliefs and revelations animated his whole being after his conversion and baptism into The Church of Jesus Christ of Latter-day Saints. His love for Joseph Smith and the founding revelations of the last dispensation directed his life and thought.

At the heart of this understanding was his desire to share the truths of the Restoration with all who would listen. As a missionary himself, he traveled without purse or scrip (see D&C 24: 18) on a variety of missions, and he helped lead the successful missionary efforts in the British Isles. As President of the Church, he continued to focus on missionary work as much as ever. While a full volume would be required to do justice to this topic, what follows is a survey, suggesting the role of the missionary enterprise in Brigham Young's life and thought.

BRIGHAM YOUNG AS A MISSIONARY

Following his own conversion and baptism in April 1832, Brigham Young served ten missions before the death of Joseph Smith in June 1844. Each experience broadened and deepened his love for the gospel, his loyalty to Joseph Smith, and his love for Church members. His obedience brought him increased Church responsibilities, and each mission helped shape his understanding of the missionary enterprise.[2]

His first mission (December 1832–February 1833) followed his initial meeting with Joseph Smith. With his brother Joseph Young, Brigham proselytized in Ontario, Canada. He returned to this area in April 1833, and in July led thirty converts to Kirtland, Ohio, then the headquarters of the Church.

In 1834, he marched from Ohio to western Missouri as part of Zion's Camp, a mission to redeem Zion and to take supplies to his fellow Saints who had recently been expelled from Jackson County. Following these experiences he was called to serve as a member of the first Quorum of the Twelve Apostles in February 1835, a call that only increased his missionary responsibilities.

From May to September 1835, he labored with his Brethren of the Twelve on missions to the eastern states. Following the dedication of the Kirtland Temple in March 1836, he returned to the East and labored in New England during the summer months. His sixth mission was on Church business in 1837 (March–June) with Willard Richards, again to the eastern states. A seventh mission to New York and Massachusetts lasted from June to August 1837.

His eighth mission, with his fellow Apostles, is his best known. This mission to Great Britain lasted from 14 September 1839 to 1 July 1841; during that time, on 14 April 1840, he became President of the Quorum of the Twelve Apostles. During this mission, his leadership abilities blossomed; in addition to his own personal development, he helped weld his quorum into a unified, powerful body that provided leadership for this foreign mission, including the beginnings of a massive emigration system and an important publishing program. Cut off from direct supervision from the Prophet Joseph by the Atlantic Ocean, President Young and his colleagues were required to make on their own a variety of decisions relating to all phases of Church government. Such responsibilities required prayer, group unity, hard work, and consecration. Brigham Young would often recall the lessons of his experiences in England as he later counseled members of his own family in private or taught Church members in public conferences.

On returning home to Nauvoo, Brigham Young and his quorum members were given increased responsibilities both in Church government and in running the affairs of the city. After proving his solid commitment to the kingdom, he was given a revelation through the Prophet Joseph Smith in July 1841 that counseled, "It is no more required at your hand to leave your family as in times past, for your offering is acceptable to me.

"I have seen your labor and toil in journeyings for my name.

"I therefore command you to send my work abroad, and take especial care of your family from this time, henceforth and forever" (D&C 126: 1–3).

Brigham Young did fulfill two more missions before Joseph's death brought him to the highest levels of Church leadership. From July to October 1843, he traveled in the eastern states to raise money for the building of the Nauvoo Temple and the Nauvoo House;[3] and in May 1844 he again went east to promote Joseph Smith's candidacy for president of the United States. Joseph's death in June terminated this mission.

During the subsequent months and years, Brigham Young focused much of his energies on the challenges of succession, schism, and the emigration west. His knowledge of the role of temple ordinances and the spiritual strength he could draw upon from these sacred rites were central to all the challenges that he would face. His missionary experiences in dealing with the issues of faith and loyalty, as well as the more practical matters of leadership, immigration, church finances, and publications, were critical assets in all of the challenges he faced from 1844 to 1847, when he was sustained as the second President of the Church.[4]

MISSIONARY WORK UNDER BRIGHAM YOUNG

Church membership in 1845 was 30,332; by 1877, the year of Brigham Young's death, the figure was placed at 115,065. (See Table A.) While a significant portion of this growth came from the missions in Great Britain and Scandinavia,[5] Brigham Young sent missionaries around the world during his presidency.

By today's standards the official missionary force was quite small. In no year before 1877 did the number exceed 222, and the average number was less than 80. (See Table B.) Excluding the informal missionary work performed by the members themselves (which has always been important), the formal missionary work during Brigham Young's administration was modest and must be seen as a function of the larger patterns of emigration to and colonization of the American West. Missionaries tended to be called at an older age than is now the case; this gave rise to the tendency

TABLE A
Church Membership Figures, 1845–1877

Year	Members	Year	Members
1845	30,332	1862	68,780
1846	33,993	1863	71,770
1847	34,694	1864	74,348
1848	40,477	1865	76,771
1849	48,160	1866	77,884
1850	51,839	1867	81,124
1851	52,165	1868	84,622
1852	52,640	1869	88,432
1853	64,154	1870	90,130
1854	68,429	1871	95,596
1855	63,974	1872	98,152
1856	63,881	1873	101,538
1857	55,236	1874	103,916
1858	55,755	1875	107,167
1859	57,038	1876	111,111
1860	61,082	1877	115,065
1861	66,211		

SOURCE: *Deseret News 1995–96 Church Almanac* (Salt Lake City: Deseret News, 1994), 418. The declining figures from 1855 to 1859 are explained by the retrenchment of the Mormon Reformation.

TABLE B

LDS Proselyting Missionary Distribution, 1845–1877

Year	*Number of Missionaries*	*Year*	*Number of Missionaries*
1845	72	1862	27
1846	25	1863	48
1847	26	1864	51
1848	48	1865	70
1849	49	1866	32
1850	50	1867	62
1851	40	1868	31
1852	159	1869	222
1853	33	1870	41
1854	145	1871	154
1855	124	1872	73
1856	144	1873	80
1857	96	1874	71
1858	[Utah War]	1875	202
1859	18	1876	200
1860	81	1877	43
1861	16	TOTAL:	2533

SOURCE: This information has been extracted from Gordon Irving, "Numerical Strength and Geographical Distribution of the LDS Missionary Force, 1830–1974," *Task Papers in LDS History,* no. 1 (Salt Lake City: Historical Department of The Church of Jesus Christ of Latter-day Saints, 1975), 9–13. Irving notes that exact figures are difficult to come by and that these numbers must be considered approximate.

for missionaries to be married. The length of the missionary call was also longer; for example, when Jesse Haven, the first president of the South African mission, was called, George A. Smith told him, "We are going to send you on a short mission, not to exceed 7 years."[6] Thus the statistics for formal missionary calls tell only part of the story.

Although the Church established a missionary fund during Brigham Young's presidency, it remained small. And, as is the case today, local ward assistance and family support of missionaries were an important aspect of Mormon community life.

Numerous missionary journals survive, as do collections of letters to and from missionaries. Such records are a rich source for

Mormon historical study, and they are the best windows into the lives and faith of those who carried the message of the Restoration throughout the world.

Special calls for a variety of assignments, sometimes announced at general conference or from a local pulpit, were common. This was true for preaching missions, and it was also true for other assignments. For example, as part of the program of "home missionaries" during the Reformation (1856–57), worthy men were called to reform and strengthen the faith of members at home.[7] Special assignments for emigration and colonization were also common during this period. It is clear that calls to settle in a specific place or to engage in a particular occupation demanded the same kind of obedience and consecrated labor as did the proselytizing missions.[8]

Building on earlier success in Britain, Brigham Young directed the expansion of LDS missions into Europe and, following the routes to and locations of the British Empire, to countries around the world. Before Joseph Smith's death in 1844, a few missionaries had been called to Australia (1840), India (1840), South America (1841), Germany (1841), Russia (1841), Jamaica (1841), and Tahiti (1843). Not all those called actually went, but an international flavor was evident in LDS missionary work from its earliest days.

President Young built on and then expanded these pioneering efforts. In 1849 the Italian, French, and Scandinavian missions were opened. In 1850 missionaries were in Switzerland and Hawaii.

Apostle Parley P. Pratt, assigned to the presidency of the Pacific Region, visited Chile in 1851, published the first Spanish language tract in 1852, and sent missionaries again to Australia in 1853. In 1852 additional missionaries were called to Gibraltar, South Africa, India, Ceylon, Burma, Siam (Thailand), and Hong Kong. In 1854 New Zealand was opened to missionary work, followed by Tonga in 1862 and Samoa in 1863. In 1865 Hungary and Austria were visited by Latter-day Saint missionaries, and Mexico received missionaries in 1875.

While most of these initial attempts had limited success, they do reveal that Brigham Young and his associates took very seriously the scriptural injunction to carry the gospel "unto the inhabitants of the earth" (D&C 1: 8; see also Matthew 28: 19–20). And during several of these missions, the foundation was laid that is still contributing to the growth and strength of the Church.

One can follow these missionary enterprises through the pages of the *Latter-day Saints' Millennial Star,* a major source for mission history in the nineteenth century. Established in May 1840 during Brigham Young's English mission, its pages record mission calls, letters to and from missionaries, minutes of mission conferences, published counsel from mission leaders, and a variety of other matters that reveal the larger story of Mormon missiology.

An important document—*Proclamation of the Twelve Apostles of the Church of Jesus Christ of Latter-day Saints. To all the kings of the world, to the president of the United States of America; to the governors of the several states, and to the rulers and people of all nations*—was composed by Parley P. Pratt and issued by the Twelve in 1845 in fulfillment of the revelation of 19 January 1841 (see D&C 124: 1–14).[9] Addressed to the kings and rulers of the earth, it announced: "You are not only required to repent and obey the gospel . . . but you are also hereby commanded, in the name of Jesus Christ, to put your silver and your gold, your ships and steam-vessels, your railroad trains and your horses, chariots, camels, mules and litters, into active use, for the fulfillment of these purposes." Such audacity has provided the grist for the Mormon missionary mill throughout the history of the Church.

The *Proclamation* provided a basic philosophy for those hardy missionaries who fanned out around the world carrying the essential messages of the Restoration in the nineteenth century. Its basic truths—inviting all to heed the message of the restored gospel and to contribute all to assist with the great work—remain central to the mission of the Church. Its warning of the consequences of rejection are also contemporary.

The Apostles who were assigned by President Young to lead the various missions published short accounts of their efforts. Lorenzo Snow's work is described in *The Italian Mission* (London:

Parley P. Pratt (1807–1857), ca. 1853. In March 1851 the First Presidency directed Elder Pratt to preside over a "General Mission to the Pacific." He established his headquarters in San Francisco and took a personal mission to Chile during 1851 and 1852.

Lorenzo Snow (1814–1901), ca. 1867–1868. At the October 1849 conference, he was called on a mission to Italy, to introduce the gospel in that land.

Erastus Snow (1818–1888), ca. 1853. Opened an effectual door to the gospel in Scandinavia.

Orson Spencer (1802–1855), ca. 1853. Visited the region of Prussia in northern Germany with the design of opening a mission.

W. Aubery, 1851); Erastus Snow's work is described in *One Year in Scandinavia; results of the gospel in Denmark and Sweden* (Liverpool: F. D. Richards, 1851); and Orson Spencer's work is recounted in *The Prussian Mission* (Liverpool: S. W. Richards, 1853). Parley P. Pratt's extensive missionary work is recounted in his *Autobiography,* first published in 1874.

Brigham Young kept Church membership informed of the missionary work in the "General Epistles" issued by the First Presidency from 1849 to 1856.[10] George A. Smith, Church Historian and Apostle, also provided a useful history of these missions in *The Rise, Progress, and Travels of the Church of Jesus Christ of Latter-day Saints* (Salt Lake City: Deseret News Office, 1869; 2nd ed., 1872).

One of the important consequences of these early missions was the translation of the Book of Mormon into non-English languages. Making the "keystone" of Mormonism available in other languages was a basic goal of President Young, and he rejoiced when these translations appeared in print.[11] It was during his administration that the first translations appeared: in Danish in 1851; in French, Welsh, German, and Italian in 1852; and in Hawaiian in 1855. Selections from the Book of Mormon appeared in Spanish in 1875, and an edition in Hindustani was prepared, but apparently not published, in 1855. The Doctrine and Covenants was translated and published in Welsh in 1851 and in Danish in 1852. The Pearl of Great Price, while not canonized as one of the standard works until 1880, was issued in a Welsh edition in 1852.[12]

Also important was the creation of the basic missionary literature of the Church. While the story of the emergence of Mormon missionary literature has been told elsewhere, it is clear that the basic texts and the doctrinal formulas that are used to define and defend the Mormon position were in place before Brigham Young's death.[13]

Another perspective on Brigham Young as a missionary can be seen in his relationship to Thomas L. Kane, a non-Mormon friend of the Latter-day Saints and a personal confidant of President Young. Kane became a defender of the Mormon cause

Thomas L. Kane as his wife, Elizabeth Dennistoun Wood Kane, photographed him (she was an amateur photographer) in 1870. Taken from the back of the Elizabeth Dennistoun Kane Journal, 1868–1870. Courtesy Brigham Young University Photo Archives.

following his personal visit during the sojourn at Winter Quarters in 1846. His friendship with President Young that began at Winter Quarters lasted throughout their lives. President Young realized that Kane's effectiveness in defending the Mormons before a national audience would be more compelling if Kane was not a member of the Church; but his desire to have his friend embrace the gospel led him to write a missionary letter to Kane during his visit to Salt Lake City during the Utah War.[14] Addressed to "My Dear and Tried Friend," it read:

> Though our acquaintance from its commencement, which now dates from many years past, has ever been marked by that frank interchange of views and feelings which should ever characterize the communications of those who have the welfare of mankind at heart, irrespective of sect or party, as I am well assured by a long and intimate acquaintance, is a feeling signally shared by yourself in common with your best friends; yet, so far as I can call to mind, I do not remember to have, either in correspondence, or in familiar conversation, except, by a casual and unpursed remark, alluded to matters of religious belief, as entertained by myself and others who are commonly called "Mormons", nor do I remember that you have ever overstepped the most guarded reserve on this subject in all your communications with me. So invariably and persistently has this peculiarity marked our friendly and free interchange of views, upon policy and general topics, that I have at times imagined, and still am prone to imagine, that you are more or less inclined to skepticism upon many points commonly received by the religious world.

> The faith embraced by the Latter Day Saints is so naturally philosophical, and so consistent with and enforcive of every valuable and true principle that should govern in every department of life, that I am strongly of the opinion that a plain, candid exposition of the faith of the everlasting gospel, which I have so much at heart, can not, probably, fail to at least interest a person of your reflective turn of mind. Such being by conviction, your permission to me to converse familiarly with you upon a subject of so much import, previous to your departure for your home, or to write to you upon your return to the society of your family and friends, will confer a highly esteemed favor upon, most truly
>
> Your Friend and the Friend of all good and honorable men.

BRIGHAM YOUNG ON MISSIONARY WORK

Having served as both missionary and mission leader, Brigham Young could draw on a wealth of personal and institutional experience. It is impossible to read through his over one thousand recorded public sermons and miss the central place missionary work held in his thoughts. We can only sample them here.[15]

For those who wished to withdraw from the world, Brigham retorted: "Some entertain the idea that we came here [to the Great Basin] to hide ourselves up from the world; but we have soon learned that our light had to be placed where the inhabitants of the earth could see."[16] Thus, "All the real business we have on hand is to promote our religion."[17] "The Kingdom of God is upward and onward, and will so continue until its power and influence extend to the relief of the honest of all nations."[18] Expressing sentiment that has been echoed by his successors: "We are to build up and establish Zion, gather the house of Israel, and redeem the nations of the earth. This people have this work to do, whether we live to see it or not."[19]

His own life was an example: "When I came into this Church, I started right out as a missionary, and took a text, and began to travel on a circuit. Truth is my text, the Gospel of salvation my subject, and the world my circuit."[20] Because he was the constant missionary, he could counsel: "We wish the brethren to understand the facts just as they are, that is, there is neither man or woman in this Church who is not on a mission. That mission will last as long as they live, and it is to do good, to promote righteousness, to teach the principles of truth, and to prevail upon themselves and everybody around them to live those principles that they may obtain eternal life. This is the mission of every Latter-day Saint."[21]

Brigham Young knew that at the heart of the missionary enterprise of teaching others was the issue of personal worthiness, and he knew just how transforming the experience would and ought to be. He knew that some would not go on missions because of their possessions;[22] but, reflecting on one of his missions, he recalled that "I would not exchange the knowledge I received this season for the whole of Geauga County; for property and mines of wealth are not to be compared to the worth of knowledge."[23]

To a group of departing missionaries, he counseled: "Go forth and preach the Gospel, gain an experience, learn wisdom, and walk humbly before your God, that you may receive the Holy Ghost to guide and direct you and teach you all things past, present, and to come."[24]

President Young wished the missionaries to go forth worthily. "If the Elders cannot go with clean hands and pure hearts, they had better stay here. Do not go thinking, when you arrive at the Missouri River, at the Mississippi, at the Ohio, or at the Atlantic, that then you will purify yourselves; but start from here with clean hands and pure hearts, and be pure from the crown of the head to the soles of your feet; then live so every hour. Go in that manner, and in that manner labor, and return again as clean as a piece of pure white paper. This is the way to go, and if you do not do that, your hearts will ache."[25]

Brigham Young knew that for each person the mission experience functioned on several levels: knowledge of God and eternal things; knowledge of self and the personal growth that came from the mission experience; and knowledge of the wider world, its people, and their cultures. Nowhere are these made clearer than in the letters he sent to his own missionary sons.[26]

To his sons Ernest and Arta, who were laboring in England, Brigham wrote:

> I have no doubt but that you appreciate the privileges you possess as ministers of salvation to the nations who sit in the shadow of the darkness of unbelief and of ignorance of the ways of the Lord. You have also had opened to you an inviting entrance to the living world of human thought and action. You are surrounded by influences from which you can learn lessons that will be of increasing influence in after years, and by comparing things as you meet them today with what they will be when the truth holds the sway, you will create within you a becoming respect for the dignity and honor of our sacred religion, and of the responsibilities of your holy calling. There is no position a man can occupy in this world, be he young or old, rich or poor, wise or simple, wherein he can learn so much of that which is truly valuable and worthy of acceptation as that of an elder in the Church of Jesus Christ in the active discharge of his calling. The present is the day of your opportunities, to mold your characters, to strengthen your faith, to develop your powers of mind and thought, and to acquire knowledge of men and manners that no books can teach or theoretical instruction impart. Stores of information surround you; you are in the midst of the world's activities. The discoveries of science and the masterpieces of inventive genius are within your reach and you have many bright opportunities of increasing your range of knowledge and widening your views of man and nature.[27]

Several months earlier, he had written Ernest some advice on resisting temptation while on his mission:

> I am much gratified, my son, that you are able to write: 'I feel good continually, and feel that I am blessed beyond expectation.' It is your privilege to feel thus as a laborer in the vineyard of the Lord; for the powers of the heavens are on your side, while you seek to walk in the path of your duty in trying to promote the interests of Zion. True, you must be tested in the great school of mortal experience. There are, as you properly state, 'many temptations, seen and unseen, to lead one astray, the tempter being always ready to take advantage where he can.' This is the common lot of man, but especially of the young and inexperienced. There is no exception. It was written of our Saviour, that he

'was in all points tempted like as we are.' But our duty is pointed out by him in the words, 'watch and pray that ye enter not into temptation.'

It should ever be borne in mind that sin does not consist of simply being tempted to do, to say, or to think wrong, but that the sin is in yielding to the temptation.

One strong safeguard against doing evil is to cultivate good thoughts, and when evil ones are presented, to *promptly* and manfully reject them, to dismiss them from the mind at once. This habit, together with never knowingly or heedlessly putting yourself in the way of temptation, will greatly aid in proving to you the truth of the scripture which saith, 'Resist the devil and he will flee from you.' And further, this course will assist in cultivating that high moral and religious tone which is indispensable to those who would wield the power of the holy priesthood.[28]

Having taught his sons well by precept and example, Brigham Young could write with confidence, as he did to his son Joseph, then serving in Manchester, England:

Joseph, this has been your privilege, to grow as the Church has grown; when it was in its infancy you were dandled on the knees of a tender mother and received the caresses of an affectionate father, and as you have grown to years of understanding you have had continually the instructions of one who has been appointed to stand at the head of God's kingdom on the earth, the front of the battle; you have seen his energy, observed his deportment both in private and public. Should not you therefore eventually prove yourself a skillful general, and even now able to wage war successfully with the powers of darkness, superstition, priestcraft, and ignorance, to overcome evil however it may present itself and preserve yourself a pure and holy tabernacle for the residence of the Holy Spirit. And by so doing you will never be led astray.[29]

When his son Willard wrote from West Point, where he was then studying, asking if he ought to attend a religious service of another faith as required by the military academy (no Latter-day Saint services being then available), Brigham again responded with the surety of a parent who had taught his children well:

With regard to your attending Protestant Episcopal service, I

> have no objections whatever. On the contrary, I would like to have you attend, and see what they can teach you about God and Godliness more than you have already been taught. When the Methodist big tent was here I advised old and young to attend their meetings for that very reason, but I was well satisfied it would not take our people long to learn what Methodists could teach them more than they had already been taught.[30]

As a loving parent, he watched the progress of his children, anxious for their success. Brigham wrote to his son Joseph:

> "Morning and evening do I call upon the Lord to bless you in your labors. Your course I watch with the eye of an affectionate and loving parent, whose anxiety for your welfare, I hope you will repay with a faithful and energetic performance of the duties assigned to you in the ministry. . . .
>
> I look upon this mission as a sort of probation—a kind of middle period between boyhood and manhood—a time which as you improve or neglect, will make or mar your future career.
>
> Therefore, my son, give heed to the instructions of those who are placed over you to counsel and direct you in the thorny and dangerous paths you now tread, and in no instance let me hear of your having neglected or disobeyed their injunctions.
>
> While you are absent from the Valley, I wish you to lose no opportunity of making yourself familiar with all that is useful and likely to benefit you, for to be able to combat with the world we must make ourselves acquainted with the ways of the world. This can only be done by keeping your mind constantly on the alert and when in society never allow anything to escape your notice. Listen attentively, and observe minutely the manners, customs, and remarks of all, for from the most humble of our fellow creatures an observing man can learn something that will be useful to him in after life. Such has been my course and, from daily and hourly experience of its benefits, I recommend you to pursue the same.[31]

To his son Oscar in Liverpool, Brigham wrote what could be considered his missionary manifesto:

> It gratifies me to see my sons manifest a desire to magnify the holy priesthood, for I know if they are faithful in the

> callings of that priesthood, their power and influence on the earth will increase and they will have the favor of God and His people. You are called in your youth to go forth and bear the message of life and salvation to the nations of the earth, and this is the most honorable and glorious calling that our Heavenly Father can bestow upon His children in this life. Since you left home you have no doubt seen considerable of the glory of this world. London is one of the greatest cities in Christendom; the wealth of ages has accumulated there, and human dignity receives the greatest honor that can be bestowed. But there is no king or queen, or potentate of any kind, whose honor can be compared to that which God bestows upon men when He gives to them the holy priesthood. Their glory fades away; it lasts only while life endures, but the holy priesthood when received and magnified by man is an eternal honor, which increases as years roll by, until, by faithfulness, man is brought back into the presence of his Maker, and is crowned with glory, immortality and eternal lives. By faithfully keeping the commandments of God and living humbly and faithfully before Him so as to partake of His power, while you are on your present mission, you will lay a foundation for future usefulness in the kingdom of God. If there be any difference in missions probably the first mission that a man takes has more influence on his future than any that he may take in the after life. On his first mission he lays the foundation and adopts the principles which are to guide him through his future career, and it has seldom been the case that a young man who has been dilatory and careless while upon his first mission has ever recovered the ground he then lost or obtained the confidence of his brethren to the extent that he would have enjoyed had he been more faithful. You now have opportunities of gaining experience in, and a knowledge of, your religion that you could not have obtained and to live so near to the Lord that you will have his holy Spirit to rest upon you to enable you to teach the people. This experience, if properly appreciated by you, will be of great benefit to you through your future life.[32]

What animated Brigham Young's missionary work was a deep and abiding faith in the ultimate power of God to establish his kingdom on the earth. Men were co-workers, but it was God's work. When Orson Pratt wrote to Brigham Young in 1853 of his depression and lack of success on the publishing mission he had been assigned, President Young wrote to him:

> It is true your reception at Washington was evil and forbidding, but we observe that your subscription list is increasing and you must be aware, without particularizing it, that Washington is the very place for you and your operations to hail from. . . . I am aware that the 'let alone' policy would tend to try the feelings of a person of your zeal and temperament when your appointments have no hearers, and your publications meet with so dull a sale, but never mind and do not be in a hurry, it is all right, and all will be well.[33]

When George Q. Cannon expressed similar concerns in 1859 during his special mission on the east coast, Brigham Young counseled him:

> Br. George, the casting your bread upon the waters, by way of your efforts in the states in our behalf, may at times appear to you a bootless labor, but it does not and at no time has so appeared to me. It is for us to labor, biding our time and resting events with Him who over-ruleth all things for good, caring only that we are lawfully striving for the right, which I have every reason to be assured that you are doing. The work in which we are engaged has to cope with a powerful array of opposition, and though our labors may at present seem puny, as they of themselves comparatively are, and the work may seem to progress slowly, yet *it is* visibly progressing and its progress will increase with astonishing ration, and the results of our faithful labors, feeble though they be, will rebound to the welfare of ourselves and all who love righteousness. All is well—be of good cheer.[34]

CONCLUSION

Many of Brigham Young's leadership and administrative talents were initially developed in a missionary setting. In 1860, Brigham Young provided a good summary of his philosophy of life and missionary work:

> Every sentiment and feeling should be to cleanse the earth from wickedness, purify the people, sanctify the nations, gather the nations of Israel home, redeem and build up Zion, redeem Jerusalem and gather the Jews there, and establish the reign and kingdom of God on the earth. Let

> that be the heart's desire and labour of every individual every moment.[35]

He gave his best to the work and encouraged all members to do likewise:

> If you give anything for the building up of the Kingdom of God, give the best you have. What is the best thing you have to devote to the Kingdom of God? It is the talents God has given you. How many of them? Every one of them. . . . Let us devote every qualification we are in possession of to the building up of God's kingdom, and you will accomplish the whole of it.[36]

Brigham Young's commitment to the gospel of Jesus Christ was focused and total. And, to him, the doctrine of the gathering was threefold:

First, he preached a doctrine of the spiritual gathering. This required a formal missionary enterprise that preached gospel principles to the honest in heart, followed by the performance of saving priesthood ordinances that spiritually gathered the righteous into Church membership.

Second, he preached a physical gathering of the converts to the Great Basin, where they could help build a latter-day Zion.

Finally, he stressed an educational gathering, a searching out of ideas and truths wherever they could be found. He wanted truth wherever it was and encouraged members to gather to themselves the best they could find throughout the world.

For missionaries or converted members, the requirements were the same. While the idea of a physical gathering to a central location was modified by President Joseph F. Smith after 1906, the core of the missionary enterprise remains at the heart of the Mormon approach to life. It remains one of the most important legacies of the Brigham Young era.

NOTES

1. The Brigham Young Collection is in the Library-Archives, Historical Department of The Church of Jesus Christ of Latter-day Saints, Salt Lake City, Utah (hereafter cited as LDS Church Historical Archives). It contains well over 100,000 pages of manuscript material ranging from diaries, minutes books, office journals, and speech files, to a voluminous correspondence collection.

In addition, it contains numerous records relating to all aspects of Brigham Young's life and the Church over which he presided. Many of the collections of the papers of his associates in the leadership of the Church are also located there. While he instructed the Church Historian's office to protect the privacy of his family, there are records that help the historian understand the history of the Young family. This essay has drawn on all these sources, but, where possible, cites the more accessible published versions.

The best biography is Leonard J. Arrington, *Brigham Young, American Moses* (New York: Knopf, 1985). It contains an extensive bibliography. Other essential works include Arrington, *Great Basin Kingdom, An Economic History of the Latter-day Saints, 1830–1900* (Cambridge: Harvard University Press, 1958); Eugene England, *Brother Brigham* (Salt Lake City: Bookcraft, 1980); Ronald K. Esplin, "From Rumors to the Records: Historians and the Sources for Brigham Young," *Brigham Young University Studies* 18 (Spring 1978): 453–65; Dean C. Jessee, "The Writings of Brigham Young," *Western Historical Quarterly* 4 (June 1973): 273–94; Ronald W. Walker, "Raining Pitchforks: Brigham Young As Preacher," *Sunstone* 8 (May/June 1983): 4–9; and Ronald W. Walker and Ronald K. Esplin, "Brigham Himself: An Autobiographical Recollection," *Journal of Mormon History* 4 (1977): 19–34.

2. For the sake of space, we only summarize these missions. More detailed information can be found in the following sources: Ronald K. Esplin, "Conversion and Transformation: Brigham Young's New York Roots and the Search for Bible Religion," in *Regional Studies in Latter-day Saint History: New York,* ed. Larry C. Porter, Milton V. Backman, Jr., and Susan Easton Black (Provo, Utah: Department of Church History and Doctrine, Brigham Young University, 1992); Eugene England, "Brigham Young As a Missionary," *New Era* 7 (November 1977): 30–37; Ronald K. Esplin, "Brigham Young in England," *Ensign* 17 (June 1987): 28–33; Esplin, "The Emergence of Brigham Young and the Twelve to Mormon Leadership, 1830–1841" (Ph.D. diss., BYU, 1981); and James B. Allen, Ronald K. Esplin, and David J. Whittaker, *Men with a Mission, The Quorum of the Twelve Apostles in the British Isles, 1837–1841* (Salt Lake City: Deseret Book Co., 1992). An excellent overview of the early Mormon missions is S. George Ellsworth, "A History of Mormon Missions in the United States and Canada, 1830–1860" (Ph.D. diss., University of California at Berkeley, 1951).

   Formal mission calls were not issued to women until 1898, but wives of missionaries occasionally accompanied their husbands into the mission field and were active in various aspects of missionary work. See, for example, Carol Cornwall Madsen, "Mormon Missionary Wives in Nineteenth Century Polynesia," *Journal of Mormon History* 13 (1986/87): 61–88; and Calvin S. Kunz, "A History of Female Missionary Activity in the Church of Jesus Christ of Latter-day Saints, 1830–1898" (master's thesis, BYU, 1976).

3. While on this mission, he wrote to his wife Mary Ann a letter that revealed his struggles with his health that plagued him throughout his life. The letter also revealed the religious focus of his life: "You and I must take som masurs to re [recover] cut our helth or we shall not last a grate meny years; and I want that we should live meny years yet and due much good on the earth." Brigham

Young to Mary Ann Young, 17 August–2 September 1843, Philadelphia. Original in uncatalogued manuscripts, Beinecke Rare Book and Manuscript Library, Yale University. Original spelling retained. The whole letter is printed in *Brigham Young University Studies* 32 (Summer 1992): 89–92. On Brigham Young's health history, see Lester Bush, Jr., "Brigham Young in Life and Death: A Medical Overview," *Journal of Mormon History* 5 (1978): 79–103.

4. Of course this was true for his whole administration, but it was especially critical during this period of challenges relating to his succession to Church leadership. Useful studies include Andrew F. Ehat, "Joseph Smith's Introduction of Temple Ordinances and the 1844 Mormon Succession Question" (master's thesis, BYU, 1982); Ronald K. Esplin, "Joseph, Brigham and the Twelve: A Succession of Continuity," *BYU Studies* 21 (Summer 1981): 301–41; and Esplin, "The Significance of Nauvoo for Latter-day Saints," *Journal of Mormon History* 16 (1990): 71–86.
5. In addition to the references already cited, the following publications are useful studies of the missions most productive of converts during Brigham Young's administration: P. A. M. Taylor, *Expectations Westward: The Mormons and the Emigration of Their British Converts in the Nineteenth Century* (Ithaca, New York: Cornell University Press, 1965); V. Ben Bloxham, James R. Moss, and Larry C. Porter, eds., *Truth Shall Prevail: The Rise of The Church of Jesus Christ of Latter-day Saints in the British Isles, 1837–1987* (Solihull, England: The Church of Jesus Christ of Latter-day Saints, 1987); Richard L. Jensen and Malcolm R. Thorp, eds., *Mormons in Early Victorian Britain* (Salt Lake City: University of Utah Press, 1989); William Mulder, *Homeward to Zion: The Mormon Migration from Scandinavia* (Minneapolis, Minnesota: University of Minnesota Press, 1957); and Andrew Jenson, *History of the Scandinavian Mission* (Salt Lake City: Deseret News Press, 1927). The extensive secondary literature on all the various missions is gathered in David J. Whittaker, "A Bibliography of LDS Missions and Missionary Work," *Mormon History Association Newsletter,* no. 69 (July 1988): 5–8; no. 70 (October 1988): 4–8; and no. 71 (January 1989): 3–4. Sources on the important Mormon Indian Missions are gathered in Whittaker, "Mormons and Native Americans: A Historical and Bibliographical Introduction," *Dialogue, A Journal of Mormon Thought* 18 (Winter 1985): 33–64.
6. Jesse Haven, Journal B, 20 March 1854, manuscript, LDS Church Historical Archives. The quote is in a letter to his family, copied into his journal.
7. See Paul H. Peterson, "The Mormon Reformation" (Ph.D. diss., BYU, 1981), 69–81; and A. Glen Humphries, "Missionaries to the Saints," *BYU Studies* 17 (Autumn 1976): 74–100.
8. While this topic is beyond the purpose of this essay, an overview is provided in Milton R. Hunter, *Brigham Young the Colonizer,* 4th ed. (Santa Barbara, California: Peregrine Smith, 1973). The larger literature is surveyed in Wayne L. Wahlquist, "A Review of Mormon Settlement Literature," *Utah Historical Quarterly* 45 (Winter 1977): 4–21. See also Dean L. May, "The Making of Saints: The Mormon Town As a Setting for the Study of Cultural Change," ibid., 75–92.

9. The authorship is made clear in the letter of Brigham Young to Parley P. Pratt, 26 May 1845, Nauvoo, Illinois, manuscript in Newell K. Whitney Collection, Special Collections and Manuscripts, Harold B. Lee Library, Brigham Young University, Provo, Utah. Unlike other Christian groups in the nineteenth century, Mormons did not undertake missionary work among the Jews. Brigham Young did not think they would be converted by mortal missionaries. Land would be dedicated for their latter-day gathering, but God himself would do the converting. For a discussion, with sources, see Hugh Nibley, *Brother Brigham Challenges the Saints,* vol. 13 of *The Collected Works of Hugh Nibley,* ed. Don E. Norton and Shirley S. Ricks (Salt Lake City: Deseret Book Co., and Provo: FARMS, 1994), 169–72. For the larger context, see Steven Epperson, *Mormons and the Jews, Early Mormon Theologies of Israel* (Salt Lake City: Signature Books, 1992); and Arnold H. Green, "Jews in LDS Thought: A Bibliographical Essay," *BYU Studies* 34, no. 4 (1994–95): 137–64. (Green unfortunately attributes the 1845 "Proclamation of the Twelve" to Wilford Woodruff rather than to its actual author, Parley P. Pratt.) See also the account of the dedication of Palestine for the return of the Jews—for the second time, but the first under Brigham Young's direction—in George A. Smith, *Correspondence of Palestine Tourists . . . in 1872 and 1873* (Salt Lake City: Deseret News Steam Printing Establishment, 1875).
10. The texts of the Twelve "General Epistles," plus other missionary-oriented statements issued by Brigham Young's First Presidency, are most conveniently found in James R. Clark, comp., *Messages of the First Presidency,* 6 volumes (Salt Lake City: Bookcraft, 1965–75), vols. 1 and 2.
11. See, for example, the correspondence between Brigham Young and George Q. Cannon during the time the Hawaiian edition of the Book of Mormon appeared in print. See especially the letters of President Young, 3 January 1856 and 3 April 1856, manuscripts in Brigham Young Letterbooks, box 13, folder 22, Brigham Young Collection, LDS Church Historical Archives.
12. Publishing information on these editions can by found in Chad J. Flake, *A Mormon Bibliography, 1830–1930* (Salt Lake City: University of Utah Press, 1978). See also L. R. Jacobs, *Mormon Non-English Scripture, Hymnals, and Periodicals, 1830–1986: A Historical Bibliography* (Ithaca, New York: By the author, 1986).
13. See Peter Crawley, "Parley P. Pratt: Father of Mormon Pamphleteering," *Dialogue, A Journal of Mormon Thought* 15 (Autumn 1982): 13–26; Crawley and David J. Whittaker, *Mormon Imprints in Great Britain and the Empire, 1836–1857* (Provo, Utah: Friends of the BYU Library, 1987); Whittaker, "Early Mormon Pamphleteering," *Journal of Mormon History* 4 (1977): 35–49; Whittaker, "Orson Pratt: Prolific Pamphleteer," *Dialogue* 15 (Autumn 1982): 27–41; and Whittaker, "Early Mormon Pamphleteering," (Ph.D. diss., BYU, 1982).
14. A copy of the letter, dated 8 May 1858, is in the Brigham Young Letterbooks, box 4, folder 6, Brigham Young Collection, LDS Church Historical Archives. This letter should end the speculation that Kane was secretly baptized by the

Mormons in 1846. Kane never did join the Church but remained a good friend until his death in 1883.

15. The most accessible source for Brigham Young's sermons is the *Journal of Discourses*, 26 vols. (Liverpool, 1854–1886). About 360 sermons are scattered throughout these volumes. Typescripts of the remaining talks have been assembled in chronological order, with references to those available in the *Journal of Discourses*, in Elden J. Watson, ed., *Brigham Young Addresses*, 6 vols. (Salt Lake City: By the compiler, 1979–1984).
16. Sermon, 8 October 1867, *Millennial Star* 29 (30 November 1867): 756–57.
17. Sermon, 14 June 1857, in *Journal of Discourses*, 4: 355.
18. Sermon, 6 April 1868, in *Journal of Discourses*, 12: 196.
19. Sermon, 3 June 1860, in *Journal of Discourses*, 8: 68.
20. Sermon, 28 July 1861, in *Journal of Discourses*, 9: 137.
21. Sermon, 7 April 1867, in *Journal of Discourses*, 12: 19. An excellent sampling of President Young's statements about missionary work is in *Discourses of Brigham Young*, John A. Widtsoe, comp. (Salt Lake City: Deseret Book Co., 1966), 319–37.
22. Sermon, 9 September 1860, in *Journal of Discourses*, 8: 179.
23. Sermon, 23 October 1853, in *Journal of Discourses*, 2: 10.
24. Sermon, 9 September 1860, in *Journal of Discourses*, 8: 176. See also sermon, 14 April 1867, in *Journal of Discourses*, 12: 34.
25. Sermon, 8 March 1867, in *Journal of Discourses*, 4: 264; sermon, 28 August 1852, in *Journal of Discourses*, 6: 273.
26. The following quotes are taken from *Letters of Brigham Young to His Sons*, ed. Dean C. Jessee (Salt Lake City: Deseret Book Co., in collaboration with the Historical Department of The Church of Jesus Christ of Latter-day Saints, 1974). Hereafter cited as Jessee.
27. Letter, 13 December 1875, Jessee, 158.
28. Letter, 4 February 1875, Jessee, 153.
29. Letter, 31 August 1854, Jessee, 7.
30. Letter, 25 July 1871, Jessee, 171.
31. Letter, 3 February 1855, Jessee, 13–14.
32. Letter, 16 March 1867, Jessee, 145–46.
33. Brigham Young to Orson Pratt, 13 December 1853, manuscript, Brigham Young Letterbooks, LDS Church Historical Archives.
34. Brigham Young to George Q. Cannon, 17 September 1859, Brigham Young Letterbooks, box 5, folder 6, LDS Church Historical Archives.
35. Sermon, 12 June 1860, in *Journal of Discourses*, 8: 294.
36. Sermon, 20 January 1861, in *Journal of Discourses*, 8: 346.

CHAPTER 5

"The Keys Are Right Here"

Succession in the Presidency

Milton V. Backman, Jr.
Director of Nauvoo Study Program
Professor Emeritus, Church History and Doctrine
Brigham Young University

While sitting in a railway station in Boston, Massachusetts, with Wilford Woodruff on 27 June 1844, Brigham Young became sorrowful and "felt a heavy depression of spirit." At the time, he did not understand the reason for his despondency; even on 9 July, nearly two weeks later, when he first heard that Joseph and Hyrum Smith had been killed, he dismissed the report, assuming that it was a just another vicious rumor. He did not comprehend the tragedy of Carthage until almost three weeks following the martyrdom, when he read a letter on 16 July that described in some detail the murder of the Prophet and the Patriarch.

The first thing he thought of was whether Joseph had taken the keys of the kingdom with him. But as he and his companion, Orson Pratt, leaned back on their chairs and pondered the loss of a dear prophet and friend, Brigham Young slapped his knee and said, "The keys of the kingdom are right here with the Church."[1] That recognition of authority and leadership was unitedly embraced by nine of the Twelve Apostles, the nine who had met as a quorum in Manchester, England, in April 1841.[2]

When Wilford Woodruff learned of the tragedy in Carthage, his immediate response was similar to Brigham Young's:

> He [Joseph Smith] told us that he was going away to leave us, going away to rest. Said he, "You have to round up your shoulders to bear up the kingdom. No matter what becomes of me. I have desired to see that Temple built, but I shall not live to see it. You will; you are called upon to bear . . . this kingdom." This language was plain enough, but we did not

> understand it any more than the disciples of Jesus when he told them he was going away, and that if he went not the Comforter would not come.[3]

PREPARING SUCCESSORS

One of the significant contributions the Prophet Joseph Smith made was to prepare successors, leaders who would continue the work he had established. Although Joseph Smith recognized that his life would not be taken until his work had been accomplished, he was prepared when he went to Carthage to seal his testimony with his blood.[4] Before the summer of 1844, he had conferred upon the Twelve the knowledge, authority, and keys necessary to continue the program of restoration.

For many years, Brigham Young was given the opportunities for service that trained him to become the leader of the Church. Following his travels with Zion's Camp, he commented that he would not have exchanged that experience for all the wealth of Geauga County.[5] When one-third of the General Authorities apostatized in Kirtland in 1837, Brigham remained a stalwart defender of the Prophet. Because of this loyalty, he also became a target for oppressors and had to flee Kirtland to save his life. After moving to the Missouri frontier, Brigham Young again supported the Prophet and refused to follow Thomas Marsh—his file leader and senior Apostle—as Marsh left the Church in apostasy. Marsh was replaced as senior Apostle by David Patten, but within a few days Elder Patten fell a victim of the Battle of Crooked River, leaving Brigham Young as leader of that quorum.[6]

Shortly after the death of Elder Patten, the Prophet gave Brigham Young new responsibilities. In late October 1838, when Governor Lilburn Boggs issued an order of expulsion from Missouri, Joseph Smith was imprisoned. In January 1839, during the exodus of the Saints from Missouri, the Prophet wrote to Brigham Young and Heber C. Kimball from prison, instructing them that "the management of the affairs of the Church devolves on you." Accepting this challenge, Brigham Young became one of the principal leaders in directing the exodus of Latter-day Saints from Missouri.[7]

THE EXPANDING ROLE OF THE TWELVE

The preparation of a successor continued during the sojourn of the Saints in Nauvoo. Under the leadership of Brigham Young, the Quorum of the Twelve gained increased unity while they were on their mission, directing the affairs of the rapidly growing Church in the British Isles. On 14 April 1840, during that mission, Brigham was chosen as standing President of the Twelve.[8] Following his return, he and other Apostles were given responsibilities both inside and outside the jurisdiction of the stakes of Zion, functioning immediately under the direction of the First Presidency.[9]

On 9 July 1841 (eight days after Brigham Young returned from England), Joseph Smith received a revelation in Brigham Young's home. In the revelation, the Lord told the President of the Twelve that he was not required to leave his family as (much as) in times past. Although he was to continue to spread the work abroad, he was to take special care of his family (see D&C 126: 1–3).

The Prophet Joseph Smith gave some clarification of the meaning of the July revelation on 10 August 1841, when he instructed the Twelve in a private council meeting to begin supervising "the business of the church in Nauvoo."[10] In order to explain to lay members this organizational realignment, the Prophet called a special conference on 16 August 1841. He explained that the Twelve would have the responsibilities of directing missionary work and the work of the gathering. "The time has come," Joseph Smith added, "when the Twelve should be called upon to stand in their place next to the First Presidency, and attend to the settling of emigrants and the business of the Church at the stakes, and assist to bear off the kingdom victoriously to the nations."[11]

The new responsibilities of the Twelve included managing the temporal affairs of the Church and assisting in the building of the Nauvoo Temple. While working closely with the Prophet on many assignments, Brigham Young and other Apostles met frequently with Joseph, receiving from him continual counsel and instruction, and, in return, assisting him with the burdens of administration. After this August conference, members of the Church in

Nauvoo and vicinity became accustomed to being led by both the Prophet and the Twelve.[12]

Brigham Young's leadership was visible on many occasions. On 8 November 1841, he participated in the dedication of the temple baptismal font. Describing that occasion, Joseph Smith said that Brigham Young was spokesman at that dedicatory meeting. Reuben McBride recalled that he was the first to be baptized, and added that he was baptized six times for the dead by Brigham Young.[13]

RESTORATION OF TEMPLE ORDINANCES

In December 1841, Joseph Smith assigned Brigham Young, as President of the Twelve Apostles, to "instruct the building committee in their duty."[14] In that same month, the Twelve wrote a letter (published in the *Times and Seasons*) instructing members regarding building the temple and the blessings they would receive in the House of the Lord. This letter included instructions on contributions of time and money, the relationship between proselyting missions and laboring on the temple, temporary housing in Nauvoo, and the need to keep the commandment to build the Temple of the Lord. The Twelve also warned the Saints that the Church would be "brought under condemnation and rejected with her dead" if they failed to build that house.[15]

Brigham Young was also among the first to receive an endowment and instructions that enabled him to continue the Prophet's program of restoration of temple ordinances. In 1836, he had received a partial endowment in the Kirtland Temple. He received a more complete endowment from the Prophet on 4 May 1842. Joseph asked Brigham Young and six other men to gather on the second floor of the Red Brick Store, where he taught them principles relating to the order of the priesthood. Then he administered to them the washings, anointings, and endowments.[16] Commenting on this experience, Brigham Young said that Joseph introduced to this group "the ancient order of things for the first time in these last days."[17]

When President Young later described the temple ordinance, he explained:

> Your endowment is, to receive all those ordinances in the House of the Lord, which are necessary for you, after you have departed this life, to enable you to walk back to the presence of the Father, passing the angels who stand as sentinels, being enabled to give them the key words, the signs and tokens, pertaining to the Holy Priesthood, and gain your eternal exaltation.[18]

This sacred ceremony included the story of man's eternal journey, instructions that enable participants to make this journey most meaningful, the making of covenants, and the receiving of blessings promised to the obedient.

One year later, beginning on 26 May 1843, the Prophet resumed bestowal of the endowment on others. Shortly thereafter, Brigham Young, Heber C. Kimball and Willard Richards assisted in introducing this temple rite to men and women, including other Apostles. During the summer and fall of 1843 and the winter of 1843–44, Joseph continued to meet with and teach a select group principles and practices relating to temple blessings.[19]

Some of the most important sessions of learning and bestowing of blessings relating to temple ordinances and worship occurred between December 1843 and early April 1844. Joseph Smith invited to these sacred sessions nine of the Twelve (the nine who had met in Manchester, England, in 1841), many of their wives, and a few others who had previously been endowed. In these sessions, he prepared them for additional ordinances relating to the temple. Sometimes this group met all day in the Brigham Young home or in the Red Brick Store, and in some instances they met at night.[20]

During the same winter months when the Apostles and many of their wives were receiving blessings and instructions relating to temple work, Joseph Smith bestowed on the nine Apostles all essential keys and authority that he had received from heavenly messengers, and he also gave them a charge to continue the work in which he had been engaged. This was the only quorum in the Church of which a majority of its members received the intense training, the keys, a fullness of temple blessings, and a charge of leadership.[21]

AFTER THE MARTYRDOM

Although Brigham Young and other Apostles had received from Joseph knowledge, authority, keys, and the charge "to bear the kingdom" before some of them left Nauvoo in early April 1844 to serve in the mission field, they undoubtedly did not realize the full significance of these blessings and responsibilities. They probably did not even imagine that within months the Prophet would be killed and they would be responsible to continue the program of the Prophet Joseph Smith.

Like many others, when Brigham Young learned of the tragedy at Carthage, he was temporarily overcome with grief. Yet this grief did not precipitate in him a period of inactivity; instead, he immediately accepted the responsibility of leadership. In his first talks to the Saints in Massachusetts, and again when he returned to Nauvoo and instructed the people on the principle of succession, Brigham uttered his claim that "the keys of the kingdom are right here" and that the kingdom would roll forth.[22]

When he arrived in Nauvoo on 6 August 1844, Brigham Young learned that Sidney Rigdon had already returned from Pittsburgh and was claiming that he should be the guardian of the Church. Sidney said that a guardian was needed because there would never be another like Joseph, that Joseph had died holding the keys of this kingdom, that Joseph still held them, and that he would continue to do so in eternity. Rigdon also predicted that the Saints would never complete the temple.[23]

The challenge of Sidney Rigdon to the leadership of the Twelve gave that quorum an opportunity to explain to the Saints in Nauvoo what they had learned from the Prophet Joseph Smith regarding succession in the Presidency. On 7 August 1844, the morning after Brigham Young had returned, he and the other Apostles met at the home of John Taylor, who was recovering from wounds received in Carthage Jail. After discussing the claims of Sidney Rigdon, the Twelve called a meeting of all high priests for that afternoon. During that gathering in the Seventies Hall, Brigham Young said:

> I have the keys and the means of obtaining the mind of God on the subject [of succession in the Presidency]. . . . Joseph

> conferred upon our heads [the Twelve] all the keys and powers belonging to the Apostleship which he himself held before he was taken away.

Citing a frequent instruction from the Prophet to the Twelve, Brigham Young continued, "I have laid the foundation and you must build thereon, for upon your shoulders the kingdom rests."[24]

The following day, 8 August 1844, the Saints gathered in the east grove at 10:00 A.M. in a special meeting called by William Marks, president of the Nauvoo Stake.[25] "That was a day never to be forgotten," Helen Mar Whitney remembered. "I was among the number that was obliged to stand, it being impossible for half of the congregation to be seated."[26] It was a cold, wet, rainy Sunday. Because the wind was blowing toward the stand, Sidney Rigdon left the stand and climbed on a wagon behind the congregation so the people could better hear his voice. The crowd of thousands turned around on their benches and faced the wagon. After Rigdon spoke for about an hour and a half, presenting his claim to the Presidency, Brigham Young spoke briefly, comforting the Saints.

Many Saints testified that as Brigham Young spoke, he was transfigured into the likeness of Joseph Smith. Benjamin F. Johnson, who attended that meeting, recalled that as soon as Brigham Young started to speak,

> I jumped upon my feet, for in every possible degree it was Joseph's voice, and his person, in look, attitude, dress and appearance was Joseph himself, personified; and I knew in a moment the spirit and mantle of Joseph was upon him. . . . I saw in the transfiguration of Brigham Young, the tall, straight and portly form of the Prophet Joseph Smith, clothed in a sheen of light, covering him to his feet; and I heard the real and perfect voice of the Prophet, even to the whistle, as in years past caused by the loss of a tooth said to have been broken out by the mob at Hyrum.[27]

Many others who gathered in the east grove on that occasion shared an experience similar to that of Benjamin F. Johnson. Nancy Tracy recalled that Brigham Young's "voice" and "gestures" were like Joseph's. "It seemed," she added, "that we had him again with us."[28] Mary Winters remembered that after the voice of

Brigham Young seemed to change so that it resembled that of Joseph Smith, people around her rose to their feet "to get a better chance to hear and see. I and my little companion of the day, Julia Felshaw, being small of stature, stood upon the benches that we, too might behold the wonderful transformation."[29]

And Helen Mar Whitney attested:

> I can bear witness with hundreds of others who stood that day under the sound of Brigham's voice, of the wonderful and startling effect that it had upon us. If Joseph had risen from the dead and stood before them, it could hardly have made a deeper or more lasting impression. It was the very voice of Joseph himself. This was repeatedly spoken of by the Latter-day Saints.[30]

For many Latter-day Saints, this experience resolved any questions they might have had regarding Brigham Young's divine calling.[31] After hearing the voice of Joseph as Brigham Young spoke, Zerah Pulsipher said that the people understood that "Brigham stood at the head of the twelve, therefore the church turned to him."[32] Helen Whitney explained, "Surely it was a most powerful and convincing testimony to them that he [Brigham Young] was the man, instead of Sidney Rigdon, that was destined to become the 'great leader,' and upon whose shoulders the mantle of Joseph had fallen."[33] John Welch, who also wrote an account of the mantle of Joseph falling on Brigham Young, concluded, "I was convinced then . . . that Brigham Young was the right man and the man chosen of God to lead the Church."[34]

In the afternoon meeting, Brigham Young spoke for about two hours on the subject of Church government and succession in the Presidency. One theme that he emphasized in that discussion was his unwavering loyalty to the Prophet Joseph Smith and his earnest desire to continue the program Joseph had restored. "Here is Brigham," he declared. "Have his knees ever faltered? Have his lips ever quivered?"[35] Then he succinctly explained the question of leadership when he said, "We have a head, and that head is the Apostleship, the spirit and power of Joseph, and we can now begin to see the necessity of Apostleship."[36]

THREE MAIN CONCEPTS REGARDING SUCCESSION

During that meeting in the east grove on 8 August 1844, and on many other occasions, Brigham Young and other members of the Twelve emphasized three main concepts regarding the order of succession of leadership.

First, Joseph Smith had conferred upon the Apostles (meaning a majority, and more specifically the eight who responded to the call to serve in the British Mission, and Orson Hyde, who continued to Palestine) a fullness of temple blessings and the keys of the priesthood, which included the sealing power restored by Elijah.[37] As Brigham explained, Joseph had bestowed upon the Twelve the "keys of the kingdom in all the world." "The Twelve," he added, "are appointed by the finger of God. . . . Here is Heber and the rest of the Twelve, an independent body who have the keys of the priesthood—keys of the kingdom of God to deliver to all the world: this is true."[38]

Orson Hyde wrote and published in the *Times and Seasons* in September 1844 another enunciation of the position of the Twelve regarding their possession of temple blessings and essential keys of the priesthood leadership:

> Before I went east on the 4th of April last [1844], we [Apostles] were in council with Brother Joseph almost every day for weeks, says Brother Joseph in one of these councils there is something going to happen; I don't know what it is, but the Lord bids me to hasten and give you your endowment before the temple is finished. He conducted us through every ordinance of the holy priesthood, and when he had gone through with all the ordinances he rejoiced very much, and says, now if they kill me you have got all the keys, and all the ordinances and you can confer them upon others, and the hosts of Satan will not be able to tear down the kingdom. . . . Now why did he say to the Twelve on *your* shoulders will this responsibility rest, why did he not mention Brother Hyrum? The spirit knew that Hyrum would be taken with him and hence he did not mention his name. Elder Rigdon's name was not mentioned, although he was here all the time, but he did not attend our councils.[39]

The second principle of succession emphasized by the Twelve on 8 August and at other times was that the Quorum of the Twelve Apostles "formed a quorum, equal in authority and power to the three presidents [First Presidency]." This principle was included in a revelation on priesthood that was recorded in Doctrine and Covenants 107: 24. "They [the Twelve]," Brigham Young explained, "stand next to Joseph, and are as the First Presidency of the Church."[40] According to Wilford Woodruff during the meeting of 8 August 1844, President Young "emphasized that the first presidency was dissolved with the death of the Prophet. . . . I say unto you," he added, "that the quorum of the Twelve have the keys of the kingdom of God in all the world and would have to ordain any man unto that appointment." Anyone appointed to that office, he insisted, would have to be ordained by the Twelve.[41]

And third, Brigham Young, in concert with other Apostles, affirmed that he acted in harmony with Joseph's charge to build the kingdom. In order to accomplish that objective, he declared that he would build the temple in which men and women would be endowed.[42]

ACKNOWLEDGING THE TWELVE AS PROPER SUCCESSORS

Following his and three other leaders' remarks in the afternoon meeting (all speaking in support of the leadership of the Twelve), Brigham Young asked the congregation to vote by "uplifted" hands on four questions.

The first question was, "Is it the will of this congregation that they will be tithed until the Temple is finished, as they have hitherto been?" The second question was, "Is it the mind of this congregation to loose the hands of the Twelve, and enable us to go and preach to all the world?" The third question was, "Will you leave it to the Twelve to dictate about the finances of the church?" And the fourth question was, "And will it be the mind of this people that the Twelve teach what will be the duties of the bishops in handling the affairs of the church?"

In all instances, a vast number of arms rose above a sea of

heads. Although a few present did not raise their hands in support of the motions by President Young, the clerks who recorded the minutes of this meeting were not aware of any dissenting votes and recorded in all instances that the voting was "unanimous" in the affirmative.[43]

Many who recalled the significance of that vote on 8 August recognized that they were acknowledging that the Twelve were proper successors to Joseph Smith, that they acted in the office of the First Presidency, and that Brigham Young was the leader of the Church in that he was the leader of the Twelve.

Although, with the death of Joseph Smith, President Young believed that there was a need to organize a First Presidency, he waited until after he led the pioneers to the Salt Lake Valley and returned to Winter Quarters to act on that reorganization. On 5 December 1847, the Twelve agreed to organize the First Presidency, and they ordained Brigham Young as President of the Church. Three weeks later, after he had selected Heber C. Kimball and Willard Richards as counselors, the First Presidency was sustained by a vote of the members who had gathered across the river from Winter Quarters at Kanesville, Iowa.[44]

The three basic themes that were reiterated during the meeting of 8 August 1844 were restated during the trial of Sidney Rigdon on 8 September 1844 (published in the *Times and Seasons*),[45] during a conference held in Nauvoo in October 1844,[46] and in a proclamation to the Saints abroad written by Parley P. Pratt and published in the *Millennial Star* in 1845.

In his "Proclamation," Elder Pratt asserted that before his death, Joseph Smith "from time to time" instructed the Twelve "in all things pertaining to the kingdom, ordinances and government of God." Elder Pratt added that the Prophet Joseph Smith was constrained to hasten the preparation of the Twelve and conferred upon them "all the ordinances, keys, covenants, endowments, and sealing ordinances of the priesthood, and so set before them a pattern in all things pertaining to the sanctuary and the endowment therein." During those gatherings, Elder Pratt testified, Joseph Smith conferred on Brigham Young, President of the Twelve, the keys of the sealing power as restored by Elijah. This last key pertained exclusively to the First Presidency, "without whose sanction and approval or authority, no sealing blessing" could be administered. Then, Elder Pratt continued, since Joseph often observed that he was "laying the foundation," he told us that the Twelve should "complete the building." This charge included doing "all things according to the pattern" he had restored. "Having done this," Joseph rejoiced exceedingly; for said he, "The Lord is about to . . . let me rest awhile." Therefore, Elder Pratt concluded, "the responsibility of bearing off the kingdom triumphantly now rests upon the Twelve."[47]

COMPLETING THE NAUVOO TEMPLE

In implementing the program of the Prophet Joseph Smith, President Young continued directing the building of the Nauvoo Temple. Latter-day Saints who acknowledged President Young's leadership rallied in support of this project. For about two weeks following the martyrdom, temple work had ceased as laborers devoted all their energies night and day toward guarding the temple. But work resumed on 8 July, and after the Saints had voiced their support of President Young's leadership one month later, President Young met regularly with the temple committee (Reynolds Cahoon and Alpheus Cutler) and architect William Weeks. He encouraged the women of the Relief Society to continue their penny program of raising money to purchase glass and nails. In August 1844, he sent an epistle to members of the Church, inviting "the brethren abroad, in obedience to the commandments of the Lord, to gather to Nauvoo, with their means to help build up the city, and complete the Temple." He noted also that the work was "going forward faster than it has at any time since it commenced."[48]

In another progress report on the temple sent to members of the Church in October, the Twelve announced that seven capitals had been set, the walls were ready to receive other capitals, and the workers were raising timbers and framing the interior of the building. "Let the saints," they solicited, "now send in their young men who are strong to labor, together with money, provisions, clothing, tools, teams, and every necessary means, such as they

Nauvoo Temple, ca. 1845–1846. Elders Orson Hyde and Wilford Woodruff conducted a private dedicatory service on the evening of 30 April 1846, after most of the Saints had left Nauvoo. The temple was dedicated publicly 1–3 May 1846.

know they will want when they arrive, for the purpose of forwarding this work."[49]

Construction of the temple continued rapidly in 1845. In May, the Twelve informed the membership that the walls had been completed and the roof was nearly finished. During that same month, President Young directed the architect to place a stone on the west end (front) of the temple with the inscription "Holiness to the Lord." In August, framing of the interior was finished, and in the fall, the steeple and tower had been completed. By October the building had been enclosed and the interior completed sufficiently for the first meeting to take place.

President Young presided during the October conference of 1845; in a dedicatory prayer, he declared that the portion of the temple that had been completed was a monument to the "saints' liberality, fidelity, and faith."[50]

Meanwhile, in the fall of 1845, partly because of renewed hostility against members of the faith in outlying areas and threats on Nauvoo, Church leaders announced that they were planning to abandon Nauvoo in the spring of 1846. Latter-day Saints needed time to prepare for the exodus and to complete the temple sufficiently so that they could receive temple blessings.

Under President Young's leadership, they finished the attic of the temple for ordinance work. They created a temporary garden room, using canvas walls for partitions and beautifying the room with plants; they furnished rooms in the attic with furniture, carpets, and pictures.[51] On 30 November, President Young "dedicated the attic story of the Temple," and beginning on 10 December, he directed the administration of temple ordinances. In two months, between 10 December 1845 and 7 February 1846, more than 5,500 Latter-day Saints received endowments in the temple.

Beginning 7 January 1846, the first marriages for time and all eternity were performed in the temple. "Such has been the anxiety manifested by the saints to receive the ordinances [of the Temple], and such the anxiety on our part to administer to them," President Young asserted under the date of 12 January, "that I have given myself up entirely to the work of the Lord in the Temple night and day, not taking more than four hours sleep, upon an average, per day, and going home but once a week." He also noted that Elder Heber C. Kimball "and the others of the Twelve Apostles were in constant attendance but in consequence of close application some of them had to leave the Temple to rest and recruit their health."[52]

On Sunday, 8 February, after the last endowments had been administered, President Young met with the Council of the Twelve in the southeast corner room of the attic of the Temple. "We knelt around the altar," he recalled,

> and dedicated the building to the Most High. We asked his blessing upon our intended move to the west; also asked him to enable us some day to finish the Temple and dedicate it to him, and we would leave it in his hands to do as he pleased; and to preserve the building as a monument to Joseph Smith. We asked the Lord to accept the labors of his servants in this land. We then left the Temple.[53]

DIRECTING THE WORK OF THE CHURCH

One week later, President Young crossed the Mississippi to direct the transplanting of the Nauvoo community to the Rocky Mountains. While President Young was supervising the building of the temple, he continued to direct and expand the Church's missionary work. In 1844, he told the Saints that elders who desired to preach and build up the kingdom should be ordained seventies.[54] During the October 1844 conference, President Young instructed high priests to prepare to go abroad and preside in the eastern states.

He also directed a major expansion of the seventies quorums. During this conference, the presidents of the seventies ordained approximately four hundred seventies. The calling and ordaining of seventies continued to a degree that had not previously occurred in the history of the restoration movement. Whereas only three quorums of seventies existed prior to the settlement of Nauvoo and only a few others had been constituted prior to the martyrdom of Joseph Smith, in October 1844, President Young called for a major expansion of this priesthood group. In December, because the seventies' numbers were increasing rapidly, the Twelve presided over the dedication of the Seventies Hall. By early 1846, thirty-four seventies quorums had been organized, and at that time three-fourths of Nauvoo's male residents were bearers of the priesthood, approximately 80 percent being seventies.[55]

The colonization of the West was another accomplishment of Brigham Young that fulfilled the charge of the Prophet to build up the kingdom. "I did not devise the great scheme of the Lord's opening the way to send this people to these mountains," President Brigham Young said. "Joseph contemplated the move for years before it took place."[56] Brigham told others that he sat for many hours with Joseph conversing about that country. Joseph said, "If I were only in the Rocky Mountains with a hundred faithful men, I would then be happy."[57] Joseph Smith had also predicted on 6 August 1842 "that the Saints would continue to suffer much affliction and would be driven to the Rocky Mountains, many would apostatize," he added, and "others would be put to death by our persecutors or lose their lives in consequence of exposure or disease, and some of you will live to go and assist in making settlements and build cities and see the Saints become a mighty people in the midst of the Rocky Mountains."[58]

Two years later, on 25 February 1844, Joseph Smith prophesied that within five years the Saints would be out of the power of their old enemies, whether they were apostates or of the world; and he told the brethren to record it, that when it came to pass they would not say they had forgotten the statement.[59]

As President Young envisioned a significant growth of the Church through increased missionary activity, he recognized a need to find a region where the Saints could gather and build temples and worship in peace. No such area was to be found in Illinois or east of that state with sufficient land for such a colonization movement. Serious planning by Church leaders to colonize western America was not revived until 1845.

In January 1845, under the direction of President Young, Church leaders renewed their discussion to send an expedition to California. On 9 September 1845, the Council of Fifty, a group organized in part to serve as a temporal arm of the Church, "resolved that a company of 1500 men be selected to go to the Great Salt Lake Valley and that a committee of five be appointed to gather information . . . in regard to the outfitting of families for emigration west of the mountains."

One month later, on 4 October, this committee submitted their report. They identified provisions needed for a family of five, which included food, seeds, cooking utensils, nails, and goods to trade with Indians. The committee also recommended "1 good strong wagon, well covered, 3 good yokes of oxen between the ages of four and ten, . . . and . . . sheep if they were available."[60]

The quest to gather information about the West intensified in December 1845. In that month, Church leaders "examined maps with reference to selecting a location for the Saints west of the Rocky Mountains" and read "various works written by travelers in those regions." Two of the works they studied carefully during that month included maps and writings of John C. Fremont and Lansford W. Hastings.[61]

Unusual courage was required to begin the long journey to the Great Basin. As Brigham Young and other leaders studied reports about Western America, they learned that the area of the Great Basin west of the Rockies was a land where there was a shortage of water and wood. Moreover, because of the harsh climate, many recognized that the growing season would be short. Many Americans believed that the Great Basin, which was part of the Great American desert, would not sustain a large population. Latter-day Saints also knew that they would encounter many unforeseen hardships, challenges manifest in the form of drought, crickets, grasshoppers, and a "cold, sterile climate."[62]

Although President Young knew that the Great Basin was primarily an uninviting desert, he and others recognized that the snow-capped mountains would provide settlers with water that could be diverted from the mountain streams to the valleys. He recognized that in that unfriendly environment, Latter-day Saints could live in peace.

Accepting the new challenge, Brigham Young became a modern Moses, leading his followers in one of the greatest migration and colonizing adventures in the history of this world.

NOTES

1. E. Watson, ed., *Manuscript History of Brigham Young, 1801–1844* (Salt Lake City: Smith Secretarial Service, 1968), 170–71.
2. James B. Allen, Ronald K. Esplin, and David J. Whittaker, *Men with a Mission 1837–1841: The Quorum of the Twelve Apostles in the British Isles* (Salt Lake City: Deseret Book Co., 1992), 300–302. The eight Apostles who served in England were Brigham Young, Heber C. Kimball, John Taylor, Wilford Woodruff,

Parley P. Pratt, Orson Pratt, George A. Smith, and Willard Richards. The ninth Apostle, Orson Hyde, attended the conference in Manchester, England, where he was blessed by the other Apostles, and then continued to Palestine to dedicate that land for the return of the Jews.

3. Wilford Woodruff, 12 December 1869, in *Journal of Discourses,* 13: 164. See also Wilford Woodruff, 16 September 1877, in *Journal of Discourses,* 19: 227–28.
4. See *History of the Church,* 6: 225, 546, and 555 for a few of many statements Joseph Smith made regarding his death.
5. Brigham Young, 23 October 1853, in *Journal of Discourses,* 2: 10. See also *History of the Church,* 2: 23.
6. Leonard J. Arrington, *Brigham Young: American Moses* (New York: Alfred A. Knopf, 1985), 60–63, 69.
7. Arrington, 69; Allen, Esplin, and Whittaker, 55.
8. Arrington, 81; Allen, Esplin, and Whittaker, 89, 134.
9. *Times and Seasons* 4 (1 May 1843): 182–83; Allen, Esplin, Whittaker, 314–17.
10. Watson, 106; Allen, Esplin, Whittaker, 314–15.
11. Watson, 108; *History of the Church,* 4: 403; *Times and Seasons* 2 (1 September 1841): 521–22.
12. Allen, Esplin, and Whittaker, 316--18.
13. *History of the Church,* 4: 446–47; letter of Reuben McBride to his sister, 1 November 1886, copy of typescript, Harold B. Lee Library, Brigham Young University.
14. *History of the Church,* 4: 470.
15. *Times and Seasons* 3 (15 December 1841): 625–27; *History of the Church,* 4: 473. In 1843, Joseph Smith told Brigham Young and other members of the Twelve that "they need not spend all their time abroad" but were to spend part of the time assisting in building the temple, collecting funds for the temple, and laboring for the support of their families. In order to magnify their callings, they were also instructed to receive contributions "to supply their wants" from others. See *Times and Seasons* 4 (1 May 1843): 182–83.
16. *History of the Church,* 5: 1. The seven men who received this endowment were Brigham Young, Heber C. Kimball, Willard Richards, Hyrum Smith, Bishops Newel K. Whitney and George Miller, and James Adams (of Springfield).
17. Ibid.
18. Brigham Young, 6 April 1853, in *Journal of Discourses,* 2: 31.
19. Ronald K. Esplin, "Joseph, Brigham and the Twelve: A Succession of Continuity," *BYU Studies* 21 (Summer 1981): 314–15.
20. See entries in Journal of Wilford Woodruff, December 1845 to March 1846; Esplin, 315.
21. Esplin, 318–33.

22. Wilford Woodruff, 12 December 1869, in *Journal of Discourses*, 13: 164. See also Wilford Woodruff, 16 September 1877, in *Journal of Discourses*, 19: 227–28.
23. *History of the Church*, 7: 229; Diary of Joseph Fielding, in "'They Might Have Known That He Was Not a Fallen Prophet'—The Nauvoo Journal of Joseph Fielding," transcribed and edited by Andrew F. Ehat, *BYU Studies* 19 (Winter 1979): 157.
24. *History of the Church*, 2: 415.
25. *History of the Church*, 7: 231. The east grove was located ¼ mile east of the temple on what is today Robinson Street, between Knight and Mulholland streets. Seven of the Apostles were present (a majority of the quorum). Of the absent ones, John Taylor was confined to his home, not yet recovered from his wounds obtained in the Carthage Jail. Orson Hyde, John E. Page, and William Smith had not yet arrived in Nauvoo, and Lyman Wight was still in the East.
26. Helen Whitney, "Scenes in Nauvoo," *Woman's Exponent* 11 (1882): 130.
27. Benjamin F. Johnson, *My Life's Review* (Independence, Missouri: Zion's Printing & Publishing Company, 1947), 103–4, 343. Benjamin F. Johnson, like many others, was not keeping a diary at that time and did not immediately record this experience. Later he explained one reason for his delay in this recording: "This view, or vision, although but for seconds, was to me as vivid and real as the glare of lightning or the voice of thunder from the heavens, and so deeply was I impressed with what I saw and heard in this transfiguration, that for years I dare not publicly tell what was given me of the Lord to see. But when in later years I did publicly bear this testimony, I found that others would testify to having seen and heard the same. But to what proportion of the congregation who were present I could never know. But I do know that this, my testimony is true" (343).
28. "Autobiography of Nancy Tracy," typescript, 31, Harold B. Lee Library.
29. "Autobiography of Mary Winters," typescript, Library-Archives, Historical Department of The Church of Jesus Christ of Latter-day Saints (hereafter cited as LDS Church Historical Archives), 13–14.
30. Whitney, 130.
31. "Autobiography of William Pace," typescript, 7, Harold B. Lee Library.
32. "Autobiography of Zerah Pulsipher," 20, Harold B. Lee Library.
33. Whitney, 130.
34. Deposition by John Welch regarding transfiguration of President Brigham Young, typescript, LDS Church Historical Archives.
35. *History of the Church*, 7: 233.
36. *History of the Church*, 7: 235.
37. These keys included those which had been conferred upon Joseph Smith and Oliver Cowdery in the Kirtland Temple in 1836 by Moses, Elias, and Elijah. The last journal entry in Joseph Smith's 1835–36 Diary was a description of this vision, now found in D&C 110. During that vision, Elijah restored the

keys of turning "the hearts of the fathers to the children, and the children to the fathers." After receiving these keys, the Prophet testified that Elijah declared, "The keys of this dispensation are committed into your hands" (D&C 110: 11–16).

38. *History of the Church,* 7: 233. Heber C. Kimball explained that Brother Joseph gave the Twelve endowments and keys and power. He further testified that Brother Brigham held the keys of this dispensation, which included all the priesthood and keys held during all previous dispensations (in *Journal of Discourses,* 19: 139–41; l: 206; 5: 7. See also *Journal of Discourses,* 3: 137, 315; 4: 275; 13: 164, 359).
39. "Trial of Elder Rigdon," *Times and Seasons* 5 (15 September 1844): 647–55; 660–66, italics added.
40. *History of the Church,* 7: 233.
41. Journal of Wilford Woodruff, 8 August 1844. See also *History of the Church,* 7: 232–41.
42. *History of the Church,* 7: 238–39.
43. *History of the Church,* 7: 241.
44. See references to those who witnessed the transfiguration of Brigham Young for responses to the significance of that event. See also Arrington, 153–54, for information on the organization of the First Presidency under the direction of Brigham Young.
45. *History of the Church,* 7: 268–69.
46. *History of the Church,* 7: 284–93.
47. Parley P. Pratt, "Proclamation to the Church of Jesus Christ of Latter-day Saints," *Millennial Star* 5 (March 1845): 149–53; dated New York, January 1, 1845. Other Apostles bore witness that the Prophet conferred upon them the keys of the priesthood and the responsibility of leadership following his death. For example, according to John Taylor, "Before the Prophet Joseph departed, he said, on one occasion, turning to the Twelve, 'I roll the burden of this kingdom on to you;' and, on another occasion, he said their place was next to that of the First Presidency." John Taylor, 14 October 1877, in *Journal of Discourses,* 19: 139–41; 1: 206; 5: 7. See also *Journal of Discourses,* 3: 137, 315; 4: 275; 13: 164, 359.
48. *Times and Seasons* 5 (15 August 1844): 638.
49. *Times and Seasons* 5 (1 October 1844): 668; *History of the Church,* 7: 281.
50. *Times and Seasons* 6 (1 November 1845): 1017–18; *History of the Church,* 7: 456.
51. J. H. Buckingham, "Letter from Nauvoo, July 1847," to the Boston *Courier;* "Illinois as Lincoln Knew It," Harry E. Pratt, ed., *Papers in Illinois History and Transactions for the Year 1937,* 171; Don F. Colvin, "A Historical Study of the Mormon Temple at Nauvoo, Illinois" (master's thesis, Brigham Young University, 1962), 100–104; Lisle G. Brown, "The Sacred Departments for Temple Work in Nauvoo: The Assembly Room and the Council Chamber," *BYU Studies* 19 (1979): 366–74.

52. *History of the Church,* 7: 567.
53. *History of the Church,* 7: 580.
54. *History of the Church,* 7: 307–8.
55. Beginning in late 1845, men were ordained to the Melchizedek Priesthood as a prerequisite to receiving their endowments and celestial marriage. See William G. Hartley, "Nauvoo Stake, Priesthood Quorums, and the Church's First Wards," *BYU Studies* 32 (Winter and Spring 1991): 71–76.
56. Brigham Young, 31 August 1856, in *Journal of Discourses,* 4: 41; Brigham Young, 11 December 1864, in *Journal of Discourses,* 11: 16.
57. *Journal of Discourses,* 11: 16.
58. *History of the Church,* 5: 85.
59. Journal of Wilford Woodruff, 25 February 1844; *History of the Church,* 6: 225. See also *History of the Church,* 5: 85–86. In addition to describing the area where the Saints would become a mighty people, Joseph Smith identified individuals who would build cities there, and he instructed others to prepare maps identifying the future course of Latter-day Saints. See "Autobiography of Mosiah Hancock," typescript, Harold B. Lee Library, 28–29. For additional references to Joseph Smith's Rocky Mountain prophecy, see the writings of Mary Maughn, John R. Young, George Washington Bean, Nathan Young, Edwin and Theodore Turley, and Oliver S. Olney, cited in Lewis Clark Christian, "A Study of Mormon Knowledge of the American Far West Prior to the Exodus" (master's thesis, BYU, 1972), 74–76.
60. *History of the Church,* 7: 438–39, 454–55.
61. *History of the Church,* 7: 548, 555, 558.
62. George Albert Smith, 8 October 1865, in *Journal of Discourses,* 2: 177.

CHAPTER 6

A PROPHET WHO FOLLOWED, FULFILLED, AND MAGNIFIED

Brigham Young in Iowa and Nebraska

GAIL GEO. HOLMES

President of Kanesville Restoration Inc.

In late May of 1846, the Latter-day Saints fleeing west across Iowa entered the Missouri River Valley. This was Indian country, and almost a century and a half of vigorous fur trade was drawing to a pitiful close. The Mormons' rustic covered wagons, drawn mostly by oxen, slowly but surely cut a permanent track where there had been none before.

Like putting a lariat on a wild stallion, the Saints cut a road and built bridges and ferries. By 1 July, they had crossed the loess-laden waters of the Middle Missouri River. After nearly a century and a half of Indian, French, Spanish, and early American river traffic, this area was now crossed by a new stream—on wheels. The Middle Missouri Valley would never again be the same.

There were about 2250 Pottawattamie/Ottawa/Chippewa Indians in at least five widely scattered villages of southwest Iowa. On the Nebraska side of the Missouri was a fortified Omaha tepee village of about 1300 Indians, three miles west of the American Fur Company trade post called Bellevue.

Former Methodist pastor John Miller, honored in post-American-Revolutionary style as Major Miller, was, in 1846, the United States Indian agent at Bellevue. His responsibility to the Indians and to the federal government extended over the Oto/Missouri, the Omaha, and the estimated 4500 Pawnee Indians in east-central Nebraska territory, which at that time was Indian country. Eight miles southwest of Bellevue's cluster of twelve log cabins was an Oto/Missouri village of about 450 poorly fed, poorly clothed, whiskey-plagued Indians in fire-damaged earth lodges.[1]

South across the shallow Nebraska or Platte River were three small, and perhaps more miserable, Oto/Missouri villages at about five-mile intervals, starting perhaps five miles west of the Missouri River. The total population of Oto/Missouri on both sides of the Platte numbered an estimated 930 in 1846.

East across the Missouri from Bellevue was a much larger French village. Its residents—Indian wives and children of French, Spanish, and American fur men working up the Missouri River, out along the Platte, or in the Rocky Mountains for a year or two at a time—called the town "Point aux poules." The name translates into English as "Prairie Chicken Point." Most river travelers called it "Traders Point." The Saints uniformly referred to it as "Trading Point," which it was, with three small trade houses, compared to only one on the Bellevue side. William Clayton said Point aux poules had blocks of houses, without giving descriptive detail.

This entire region on both sides of the Missouri River, for perhaps a 50-mile radius around the cluster of trade posts, was known as "Council Bluffs." The name was coined by fur traders and trappers coming down the Missouri River in 1804. They couldn't remember exactly where American Captains Lewis and Clark had told them the bluff site was of their historic meeting 3 August 1804 with the Oto/Missouri Indians. That district on both sides of the Missouri River would continue to be called "Council Bluffs" until the city of Kanesville, Iowa, was renamed "Council Bluffs" in 1853.

Federally aided Baptist and Presbyterian missionaries, government farmers, and government blacksmiths intermittently served the Indians west of the Missouri. Jesuit missionaries had given up in 1841 after three short years of work with the Pottawattamie/Ottawa/Chippewa in Iowa. The federal government also cut off assistant government farmer Davis Hardin in 1838 after one year of service. But he and his family continued to live in the area where the Mormons would plant their first Missouri Valley town, "Council Point," just west of the present-day Lake Manawa. Still maintained in Point aux poules, however, was the office of R. B. Mitchell, United States sub-agent to the Pottawattamie and their fragment of Ottawa/Chippewa allies.

The country had abundant grass and wild flowers and occasional groves of elm, oak, walnut, white ash, and cottonwood. There were nuts, berries, small game, and lots of birds and fish. A line of loess hills running gently northwest along the east side of the Missouri River rose intermittently to 200 or 250 feet above the alternately widening and narrowing flat floodplain of the river.

East of the line of bluffs were much smaller, more rounded hills and vales of rich grassland, with a few trees. Many creeks and some small rivers meandered southwest toward the bluffs, where they found low openings to rush through and empty into the Missouri River. Scattered over southwest Iowa were substantial groves of trees, which later would shelter or furnish wood for more than eighty Mormon villages.

Almost destitute by their five-month struggle to cross Iowa in a cold winter and wet spring, the refugee Mormons found the Indians also suffering from a lack of food and clothing—and from a clouded future.[2] Andrew Jackson's policy of pushing all Native Americans west of the Mississippi River threatened ruin to their ancient economy of hunting and gathering their needs from the bounties of nature.

Even small tribes required hundreds of square miles of virgin land to hunt wild game and gather nuts, berries, and roots. Each new tribe that was pushed west of the Mississippi by federal agents, as had been the Pottawattamie in 1835–37 from the Great Lakes area, reduced available lands for hunting. The influx of the Saints further taxed nature's resources.

The French and Canadians, commencing at least as early as 1714, had come up the Missouri River as traders. The Spanish, continuing the French tradition with mostly French river and fur men, also came as traders. The Americans changed that, coming both as traders and as trappers—poachers on Indian hunting lands.

The attractive trade goods of the whites could be had in exchange for furs. Native Americans soon forgot how to make useful implements, tools, weapons, and household items out of stone, bone, and wood. They became dependent on manufactured goods, for which they had to bring in furs—lots of furs.

When the Saints came rolling up to the Missouri River, telling of their woes in Illinois, the Indians felt great sympathy for them, as fellow sufferers. The Indians could not help but note, however, that the Mormon wagons were relatively full and that their herds of livestock were huge. All of that, and more, was needed for the migrating Saints. But it nonetheless must have caused doubt in the minds of many hungry Indians.

The Mormons intended to go on west to the Rocky Mountains in 1846, or at least as far as Grand Island in the Platte River of east-central Nebraska. The Indians welcomed the obviously well-armed Mormons as fellow sufferers and as a potential buffer between them and marauding bands of Dakota Sioux, living then primarily in what today is South Dakota. Pied Riche, "the great brave" and "interpreter of the nation," said in conference with the Saints:

> My Mormon Brethren,
>
> The Pottawattamie came sad and tired into this unhealthy Missouri Bottom, not many years back, when he was taken from his beautiful country beyond the Mississippi, which had abundant game and timber, and clear water every where. Now you are driven away, the same, from your lodges and lands there, and the graves of your people. So we have both suffered. We must help one another, and the Great Spirit will help us both. You are now free to cut and use all the wood you may wish. You can make all your improvements, and live on any part of our actual land not occupied by us. Because one suffers and does not deserve it, is no reason he shall suffer always: I say. We may live to see all right yet. However, if we do not, our children will.[3]

It was in this setting that Brigham Young followed the teachings, fulfilled prophecy, and magnified his calling as an Apostle and witness of the Lord, Jesus Christ. As senior member of the Quorum of the Twelve Apostles, he met many challenges in the Middle Missouri Valley. Indians were an immediate concern, as both the law and their proximity obliged him to pay special attention to their wishes, wants, and rights. Brigham had to be alert for real or only rumored treachery on the part of government. Past experiences had demonstrated that even rumors could not be ignored when it came to what government might offer or threaten.

Having spent more than five months coaxing the vanguard of the Mormon exodus across the frozen and then rain-drenched prairies of Iowa, Young found less physical challenge in seasonally blessed southwest Iowa. Nonetheless, the Saints had to build, on average, one bridge per day while moving through southwest Iowa; they also had to plan an express ferry over the swollen Missouri River.

Brigham's primary cares and concerns, of course, were the members of the Church—their health, their food, their security, and their willingness to follow counsel under exhausting, trying circumstances. Such cares and concerns were not only for those immediately around him, but also for those who were ill and impoverished, stalled or struggling along the Mormon Trail in south-central Iowa; the stragglers still in Nauvoo; members sailing around the tip of South America to California; leaders in England who were tempted by financial trust placed in their hands; and widely scattered members, some of whom were giving up their faith in the face of repeated adversity.

Brigham Young turned age 45 on 1 June 1846, not exactly the prime of life in the mid-1800s. Yet, here was a man who trusted the Lord so completely that he led thousands into a harrowing migration that better educated observers said would ruin the Church. Brigham calmly declared, "I just do the thing that I know to be right and the Lord blesses me."[4] It was that kind of burning testimony that kept most Church members together, in spite of bitter hardships.

THE MORMON SETTLEMENT IN COUNCIL BLUFFS

The first three wagon trains of the Mormon exodus from western Illinois and southeast Iowa reached the Missouri River on 14 June 1846. Helen Mar Whitney recorded, "We saw a number of Indians and half-breeds, who were riding about, accompanied by the agent, trading horses at the settlement [Point aux poules] below."[5] That suggests the three wagon trains camped at some distance from each other to keep their substantial herds of livestock separate.

Horace K. Whitney noted in his journal:

> The brethren met in council on the bank of the Missouri River to lay down certain rules for our observance while we remained here. They are as follows: Every 4th man is to assist in building the boat, one or two out of each Ten to herd cattle, while others are to go out in the country to trade for provisions. A committee of three, viz., Father (Bishop Whitney), Albert P. Rockwood and Bishop Geo. Miller to wait on the agents and ascertain the prices of things. Meanwhile, no man is permitted to have any traffic with the inhabitants or Indians without having permission so to do from the proper source.[6]

In the interests of security and good order, the wagon trains pulled back the next day, three miles east of the river, near present Iowa School for the Deaf, southeast of today's Council Bluffs.

Each group drew up its wagons in a great square on top of an adjacent bluff or hill. Tents were pitched between the wagons. Brigham Young's tent (in the vicinity of the 100 block East 29th Avenue in present Council Bluffs) was signified by a tall pole bearing an American flag. Not far distant was the Church Wagon Post Office. A large tent was pitched next to the post office, indicating an extended stay in the area. Members of the Church went there to inquire about mail or to read newspapers left in the tent for the benefit of all.

After a public meeting to consider building a ferry over the Missouri River, skilled volunteers were invited to step forward. One hundred men of designated skills did so, and plans were made to build a water-powered ferry. A dugway was cut into the Iowa bank of the Missouri, south of present South Omaha (Hwy 92) Bridge. Another dugway was cut into the bank on the Nebraska side, substantially downstream from the Iowa dugway. Reuben Allred set up a rope-walk by the Missouri River to make two huge ropes from local hemp. One rope was stretched from the Iowa dugway to the Nebraska dugway. The other was stretched from the Iowa dugway far upstream to the Nebraska bank.

The boat was built with lumber purchased at Pottawattamie Indian Mill on Mosquito Creek, about six miles northeast of the ferry site. When completed on 29 June, the boat was caulked and publicly launched. President Young directed Colonel Scott to "pass the ordnance over the river tonight." Then only General Authorities of the Church were invited to be at the river that night with Colonel Scott to test the boat. The test consisted of hauling arms, powder, and shot across the Missouri to Indian country.

The boat, filled with up to three loaded wagons, was pushed into the river and attached to the guide rope. The force of the river pushed it to the Nebraska dugway. When unloaded there, it was backed out of the Nebraska dugway and pulled and poled to the upper leg of the V-rope. There it was attached and pushed by the river back to the Iowa dugway for another load. The ferry commenced regular service on 1 July from Iowa to Nebraska.

Brigham suggested that the main body of the Church might winter east of the Missouri River, a small group might winter at Grand Island, and George Miller's wagon train might go over the mountains. He talked of sending a few elders to England and making arrangements for British Saints to go to Vancouver Island.

Brigham Young and a number of other leaders moved four miles west of the Missouri River to an advanced staging site called "Cold Spring Camp." About 65 families in 150 wagons had been sent on west with Bishop George Miller, both to advance the move to Grand Island or to the Rocky Mountains and to pick up and return about 90,000 pounds of buffalo hides to fur trader Peter Sarpy at Bellevue.

On the afternoon of 24 July 1846, Brigham Young, Dr. Willard Richards, and Bishop Newel K. Whitney rode in a carriage to a tall hill a mile northwest of Cold Spring Camp. There they were joined by Elders Ezra T. Benson, Orson Hyde, Heber C. Kimball, Amasa M. Lyman, Orson and Parley P. Pratt, George A. Smith, John Taylor, and Wilford Woodruff, all of the Quorum of the Twelve.

At the top of the hill, from which they could see the entire surrounding countryside, they pitched a tent and covered the ground with buffalo hides. In a meeting that started at about 2:00 P.M., Hyde asked what should be suggested to the British Parliament for Mormons settling Vancouver Island, off the southwest coast of what would become Canada. President Young said Parliament should be asked to grant each immigrant a certain number of acres of land. The Quorum of the Twelve voted to send Orson Spencer and Elias Smith to England as soon as possible to work there in Latter-day Saint printing and publishing.

At 4:00 P.M., the members of the Quorum of the Twelve put on their temple clothes and prayed. They laid hands on Orson Hyde, John Taylor, and Parley P. Pratt, setting them apart for missions to England. They also set apart Ezra T. Benson for a mission to the eastern states. President Young gave the brethren some instructions, and the council adjourned at 6:00 P.M. Most returned to Cold Spring Camp, but Elders Parley P. Pratt, John Taylor, and Wilford Woodruff crossed the Missouri River back to Grand Encampment.

The following day, Orson Hyde copied letters signed by Brigham Young, authorizing Elders Orson Hyde, Parley Pratt, and John Taylor to manage temporal and spiritual matters of the Church in Europe and throughout the British Empire.

About 1 August, the Quorum of the Twelve decided that all of the Saints should winter in the Missouri Valley. That day, word was sent west to Bishop George Miller and his party near the Loup Fork; they were stopped at a Pawnee village ravaged by Dakota Sioux, near the recently evacuated Presbyterian Mission. Instructions were to stop there or to return and winter by the Missouri River.

On 5 August, several parties scouted north to find a site for a winter quarters more removed from the Omaha and Oto/Missouri villages. Colonel Thomas L. Kane, who had received a message from President Young, returned from Grand Island and happened upon the Newel K. Whitney scouting party, probably about nine miles north of Cold Spring Camp.

Others streamed north on 6 and 7 August from Cold Spring Camp to the new location about three miles west of the Missouri River. It was named "Cutler's Park" in honor of Alpheus Cutler, who had found the location. Although short-lived, Cutler's Park was the first properly organized community in Nebraska.

President Young, Heber C. Kimball, Willard Richards, and Wilford Woodruff met with the Cutler's Park high council under the direction of Alpheus Cutler. Brigham said the council would act both as a city council and as a high council, and that it would decide matters of difference between members of the Church. He said some already had transgressed and should be brought to justice. He was not so much afraid of going into the wilderness alone, he said, as to let offenders go unpunished.[7]

President Young then asked the brethren to meet at 2:00 P.M. the following day to prepare hundreds of seats and a speaker's stand for public meetings. Some 300 seats were prepared the next day, and many more were prepared later. Leafy arbor work was raised over the meeting area.

Horace S. Eldredge was nominated and elected city marshal. It was decided to hire twenty-four police and fire guards to work equal shifts around the clock. Hosea Stout was chosen captain of the police and fire guards, to organize their shifts and to supervise. Personal property at Cutler's Park was assessed and taxed to pay the police. Young thought it best to have men working together

> because of the scarcity of tools which necessarily would leave many idle; and when the Saints could be united in all things, so that each will seek the interest and welfare of his brother, then the Lord would take up his abode with them.[8]

Young advised the camp to be numbered into hundreds, fifties, and tens, and the city council called for men from many companies to work on various projects.

By 13 August, the end of the first week at Cutler's Park, foremen reported 552 men and boys over age 10, 229 horses, 49 mules, 2005 oxen, 1273 cattle, 660 sheep, and 588 wagons.

Helen Mar Whitney recorded on 14 August:

> The brethren then went to cutting and drawing house logs and one or two commenced digging a well. In two days they had dug to the depth of 28 feet without finding water. They also commenced building a house for the purpose of storing any provisions and other things that they might have the use of the wagons to haul hay.[9]

President Young received a letter on 20 August from George Miller. Miller said he was leaving a few families at Loup Fork and taking most of his wagon train north to the mouth of the Niobrara

River where the Ponca Indians lived. He estimated the distance about 50 miles; it was, in fact, more than 90 miles. Miller said it was "almost on a direct course to Fort Laramie," but it was 90 miles and 90 degrees off course. The Cutler's Park high council felt Miller was deceived about the locality of the Ponca village and was "running wild" under the influence of James Emmett, who had wintered with a small Mormon group near there in 1845 and 1846 in what now is South Dakota.

Meanwhile, on the Iowa side of the Missouri River, wagon masters since early July had been scouting north, south, and east for access to more wood, water, and grass. Grand Encampment had grown to about 10,000 refugees, and it stretched east for nine miles. The heat of summer; the grazing of many thousands of oxen, cattle, horses, mules, and sheep; and the tidy split-rail fencing of the Mormons had stripped Grand Encampment of much of its wood, water, and grass. One wagon train after another pulled away from those nine miles, stretching from what today is Iowa School for the Deaf to near what now is Treynor, Iowa.

PREPARING FOR WINTER 1846–47

Parley P. Pratt wrote on 3 July:

> The lateness of the season, the poverty of the people, and, above all, the taking away of five hundred of our best men [in the Mormon Battalion], finally compelled us to abandon any further progress westward till the return of another spring. The camps, therefore, began to prepare for winter.[10]

His assessment was true for those who were still east of the Missouri River—who were the least prepared. It became true about 1 August for those on the west side, too. Limited farming began at scattered sites in Iowa at least as early as the first week of July. Turnips were planted in August at Cutler's Park.

More than 80 Latter-day Saint communities were organized in southwest Iowa (see adjacent map). More than 50 branches of the Church were organized to serve those communities.[11] Most prominent was the Blockhouse Branch, near what today is downtown Council Bluffs (East Pierce Street, between Grace and Union).

Bishop Henry W. Miller settled a part of his wagon train there when a member bought the blockhouse, adjacent buildings, and 40 acres of standing corn for $300. The blockhouse had been built by United States dragoons, mounted infantry from Fort Leavenworth, in northeast Kansas Territory in 1837. Those staging through this area enjoyed genuine hospitality shown by Indian youths:

> Their hospitality was sincere, almost delicate. Fanny Le Clerc, the spoiled child of the great brave, Pied Riche, interpreter of the nation, would have the pale face Miss Devine learn duets with her to the guitar; and the daughter of substantial Joseph La Framboise, the interpreter of the United States,—she died of the fever that summer,—welcomed all the nicest young Mormon Kitties and Lizzies, and Jennies and Susans, to a coffee feast at her father's house, which was probably the best cabin in the river village. They made the Mormons at home, there and elsewhere.[12]

After 5:00 P.M. on 27 August, the high council was notified that Omaha Chief Big Elk had arrived to confer with Church leaders. Horace K. Whitney recorded, however, that there were, in fact, six chiefs and about 150 braves (which may have been an overestimation) of both Omaha and Oto/Missouri wishing to talk with President Young about the Mormons wintering on Indian lands.

The Mormons agreed to meet with them the following morning. Hosea Stout said the Omaha were ordered to camp on the ridge east of Cutler's Park since there were so many of them. He said the Oto were afraid to camp outside "our square" for fear the Omaha would attack them.

Brigham Young and members of the Cutler's Park high council met at 9:30 A.M. in a big double tent with Chief Big Elk, his interpreter Logan Fontanelle, and some of the 80 Omaha braves. The Oto refused to meet the Mormons with the Omaha present. President Young told the Omaha Indians:

> We are on our journey to California [of which Utah then was considered a part]. . . . With your permission we would like to winter here. We can do you good. We will repair your guns, make a farm for you and aid you in any other way that our talents and circumstances will permit us. We would also

> like to get some of your honorable men to watch our cattle. . . . Have you any objections to our getting timber, building houses and staying here until spring, or longer? The government is willing if you are. . . . We are your friends and friends to all mankind. We wish to do you good and will give you food, if you need it. . . . We wish you to give us a writing, stating what you are willing to do, and if you wish, we will prepare to have schools kept among you.

Aged and almost blind, Chief Big Elk encouraged his people to speak. Finally, when he was assured no other Omaha wished to respond to President Young, the old chief said:

> I am an old man and will have to call you all sons. I am willing you should stop in my country, but I am afraid of my great father in Washington. I would like to know what the Ottoes say; if they claim this land, you can stay where you please; if they do not, I am willing you should stay. One half of the Ottoes [from south of the Platte River] are willing the Omahas should have these lands. . . . I hope you will not kill our game. I will notify my young men not to trouble your cattle. If you cut down all our trees, I will be the only tree left.
>
> We heard you were a good people; we are glad to have you come and keep a store where we can buy things cheap. You can stay with us while we hold these lands, but we expect to sell as our Grandfather will buy; we will likely remove northward.
>
> While you are among us as brethren, we will be brethren to you. I like, my son, what you have said very well; it could be said no better by anybody.[13]

After the Omaha retired from the big tent, the Oto Indians filed in. An equal offer was made to them as compensation for use of the land. The Oto wanted to know what the Mormons had offered the Omaha. When they learned it was the same, the Oto were outraged because they had hunted the area since about 1700 A.D. The Omaha had fled there from the Dakota Sioux in 1845. The Oto threatened to make war on the Omaha.

The Mormons tried a number of times to appease the Oto and prevent a fight between the tribes. But the Oto, especially those from north of the Platte River, would never accept. Finally, the Saints decided to move east about three miles to a high plateau overlooking the Missouri River, where the Omaha waterworks are today. That ended the threats of the Oto.

It seems the Indians considered the Missouri River and the land immediately adjacent as a public highway for all travelers, not open to contest. A cemetery site was selected on a bluff halfway between Cutler's Park and the new Winter Quarters. A sexton was assigned and a detailed record kept of deaths and burials from 15 September 1846. Crews were assigned to survey, define streets, plat lots, build cabins, and construct a bridge over Turkey or Willow Creek, later known as "Mill Creek."

At this busy time, men at Cutler's Park were routed out of bed on 21 September with a call at 10:00 P.M.: "All hands repair to the center of the camp!" At the gathering, Heber C. Kimball explained that American Fur Company trader Peter Sarpy had told Jedediah M. Grant that the United States marshal from Missouri was coming up "after the Twelve." Sarpy also claimed to have learned that the United States Secretary of War had instructed U.S. Indian subagent R. B. Mitchell at Point aux poules to have all Mormons removed off Pottawattamie land by 1 April.

Kimball said it was necessary that every man be properly armed and equipped and that a guard should be kept up nights to keep spies from entering and leaving camp. Men were asked to obey orders of their foremen. Then the meeting was dismissed. Only later did the Saints learn that unfounded rumor was Sarpy's stock-in-trade.

The men assembled again at 9:00 A.M. the next day to reorganize the Nauvoo Legion. Brigham Young asked if the men wanted to sustain their old officers or to elect new ones. The men voted unanimously in favor of their old Nauvoo Legion officers. Immediate organization was begun. At 11:00 A.M., Colonel Albert P. Rockwood reported:

> Col. John Scott's artillery company, 63 men; Capt. Henry Harriman's company, 25; Capt. Jedediah M. Grant's company, 25; Capt. Reddin A. Allred's company, 25; Capt. Levi Stewart's company, 25; Capt. Wm. M. Allred's company, 25; Capt. Welcome Chapman's company, 25; Capt. John S. Gleason's company, 25; Capt. James W. Cummings' company, 25; Capt.

> Thaddeus T. Cutler's company, 25; Capt. Charles Bird's company, 25; Capt. Lev E. Riter's company, 25.[14]

Young passed down the lines and nominated a first lieutenant for each company. The new officers were unanimously sustained. Stephen Markham and Hosea Stout were elected colonel and lieutenant colonel of the first battalion of infantry. Brigham wrote an order that all discharging of firearms, day or night, should cease, except by special permission.

The entire camp met and voted to move immediately to Winter Quarters "as affording us a better place for convenience and self defense." It was decided to begin the move the next day, 23 September. The Middle Mormon Ferry was moved north to Winter Quarters just north of today's Interstate Highway 680 bridge. A support town for the ferry was established on the Iowa side, called Ferryville. A road was soon developed between Winter Quarters and other Mormon communities on the Iowa side of the Missouri. A road ran directly east from Ferryville to the line of the bluffs, or loess hills, about five miles east of the river. There it intersected a wagon road running north and south, linking communities north, south, and east of that point.

The building of log cabins and dugouts in the hillsides of Winter Quarters was intensified. The return of cold weather and memories of the previous winter in tents and wagons stimulated the workmen. Heber C. Kimball's daughter noted in her journal on 8 November:

> We congratulate ourselves considerably upon being able to live in a house again, as we have got thoroughly tired of living in a tent. This, like the majority of houses, was covered with sod and the chimneys were built of the same. Each room had one door and a window with four panes of glass, but no floor. . . . Our floors we managed to cover with canvas or pieces of carpeting which had outlived the storms and the wear and tear while journeying from the States [Iowa did not become a state until 28 December 1846]. We made curtains serve as partitions to divide the bedrooms, repositories, etc. from the kitchen. Most of our furniture we had made to order, such as cupboards, and bedsteads, they being attached to the house; also tables, chairs and stools, and an occasional rocking chair, relics of other days graced our

> ingleside. . . . The larger houses were generally shingled and had brick chimneys and puncheon floors with a six-lighted window to each room. Father's largest house contained four good-sized rooms on the ground and two upstairs. My brother William and family lived in one room, my mother, her four little boys, three or four young men and two women, who had been adopted and two of father's wives occupied the rest. The women assisted in sewing and housekeeping.[15]

A census of Winter Quarters, 20 December 1846, reported 3483 residents in 538 log houses and 83 sod houses (probably dugouts). It also reported 814 wagons, 145 horses, 29 mules, 388 yoke of oxen, and 463 cows. Many of the cattle and oxen were then wintered at some distance along the Missouri River. President Young certainly was more concerned about the welfare of the migrating Saints than he was about his cattle.

The number of deaths at Winter Quarters has been greatly overstated. Far more died before the frosts of autumn than in the so-called "terrible winter of 1846/1847." Of the 365 recorded deaths at both Cutler's Park and Winter Quarters between September 1846 and June 1848, only 67 were recorded during the winter months of December 1846 to March 1847. Likely, the misleading figure of 600 deaths at Winter Quarters came from John Bernheisel, LDS territorial representative in Washington, D.C. A footnote in Thomas L. Kane's published version of his 1850 address to the Historical Society of Pennsylvania stated:

> This camp (Cutler's Park) was moved by the beginning of October to winter quarters on the river, where, also there was considerable sickness before the cold weather. I am furnished with something over 600 as the number of burials in the graveyard there.[16]

Without intending to blame Brigham Young and other leaders of the time, writers have further compressed the "over 600" deaths there as having been during the "terrible winter" of 1846/1847—which is not part of Kane's footnote. Nor were there 600 deaths. The sexton's handwritten records of burials at Winter Quarters included name, age, family ties, date of death, cause of death, place and date of birth, and grave number. The sexton's record also showed 14 burials for which there was no data, except a grave number. That suggests some were too poor to pay for burials of family members and performed the tragic duties themselves. In any event, Brigham Young, the Quorum of the Twelve, and the high council of Winter Quarters are to be commended, not pitied, for their efforts to shepherd the flock to safety.

Brigham Young received a revelation on 14 January 1847 on how the Camp of Israel was to be organized to go to the Great Basin—the Saints were to live by gospel standards, and they should sing, dance, pray, and learn wisdom. Members of the Quorum of the Twelve crossed the Missouri River and visited communities in Iowa to present the revelation on how to organize for the trek west. The ever-observant Hosea Stout noted on 25 January 1847:

> This was a dull dark cloudy day, trying to snow. A drove of some one or two hundred hogs came in today. I was around as usual and arranged the guard as before. In the evening I went to the meeting of Brighams Company [organizing for the trip to the Rocky Mountains] at the Council House.[17]

The Council House was directly east of where the new water-powered mill was being built. A few yards to the northwest of the Council House was Brigham Young's home.

Members called to 1847 migrating companies busied themselves in preparing for the 1000-mile trek to and through the mountains. But they also reserved time for pleasure. A ball sponsored by the police and fire guard was held on 2 March in the Winter Quarters Council House, which served as town hall, school, church hall, and community social center. Of the policemen's ball, Stout wrote:

> Was not at home until one o'clock and then went with my wife to the council house to our police party. It was an uncommonly beautiful clear warm and pleasant day.
>
> We had the Police, Twelve and Band present, and enjoyed ourselves uncommonly w[e]ll by dancing, talking, eating sweet cakes &c, and some little preaching.[18]

By March, Winter Quarters had reached a population of nearly 5000. There were about 700 houses on 820 lots in the city of 41 blocks. Members of the Church were organized into 22 wards in Winter Quarters. There were more than 50 branches of the Church among more than 80 small LDS communities in southwest Iowa.

Heber C. Kimball moved out from Winter Quarters to "the stacks" (probably abandoned Cutler's Park) on 4 April with six teams to form a nucleus around which the pioneer migration to Salt Lake Valley could gather. President Young and party moved to the Elkhorn River on 14 April. Before leaving, he counseled those who remained at Winter Quarters to halt their early farming activities and complete a picket fence around Winter Quarters for their security.

Brigham Young led a pioneer group of 148 west along the north side of the Platte River, crossing to the south side at Fort Laramie, and on to the Great Basin. Others followed, bringing the total 1847 migration west to nearly 2000.

Near sunset on 31 October, President Young and about half of the pioneer company that had gone to the Salt Lake Valley returned to Winter Quarters. There was great rejoicing on both sides of the Missouri River.

Brigham Young sent a letter on 25 November 1847 to Orson Spencer in England, saying in part:

> Say to the Saints in Great Britain: Come, for all things are ready, and let them flock in clouds [by contract ships] to New Orleans where they will meet some one of the Elders, duly authorized to counsel them in re-shipping to this vicinity [by steamboat].[19]

President Young, George A. Smith, Amasa Lyman, and Wilford Woodruff met on 3 December 1847 with the high council in Iowa at the blockhouse in Kane(sville), Iowa. Brigham suggested organizing a carrying company from Kane to the Great Basin to haul as many Saints and as much merchandise and supplies as needed. He also recommended the brethren build a 50-by-100-foot meetinghouse for a Church conference in Kane the following spring. President Young also asked the high council in Iowa to help bishops in Winter Quarters provide support each day for 300 needy Saints.

Brigham Young and other members of the Quorum of the Twelve conducted conference on 4 December at the blockhouse in Kane. So many Saints wished to attend that they crowded around the small, high windows outside the blockhouse. Brigham suggested that a much larger building be constructed in Kane and that the conference be adjourned until that was accomplished. Members voted that Henry W. Miller superintend construction of the log conference center, and the conference then adjourned until 24 December.

President Young and his companions traveled the next day nine miles southeast of Kane to the home of Orson Hyde, in the community of Hyde Park. There nine members of the Quorum of the Twelve assembled. Parley P. Pratt and John Taylor had remained in the fledgling Salt Lake City, and Lyman Wight was in Texas.

On the return trip from the Great Basin and again at Winter Quarters, members of the Twelve had discussed the need to reorganize the First Presidency. Brigham had been the acting President of the Church in his capacity as senior member of the Quorum of the Twelve since the death of the Prophet Joseph Smith on 27 June 1844.

After some discussion about reorganizating the First Presidency, Orson Hyde moved that Brigham Young be sustained as President and Prophet of The Church of Jesus Christ of Latter-day Saints, that he name two counselors, and that they form a new First Presidency. The motion was seconded by Wilford Woodruff. It carried unanimously.

Many years later, Orson Hyde testified in Salt Lake City:

> We were in prayer and council, communing together; and what took place on that occasion? The voice of God came from on high and spake to the Council. Every latent feeling was aroused, and every heart melted. What did it say to us? 'Let my servant Brigham step forth and receive the full power of the presiding Priesthood in my Church and Kingdom.' This was the voice of the Almighty unto us at Council Bluffs. . . .
>
> We said nothing about the matter in those times, but kept it still. . . . Men, women, and children came running

> together where we were, and asked us what was the matter. They said their houses shook, and the ground trembled, and they did not know but that there was an earthquake. We told them that there was nothing the matter—not to be alarmed; the Lord was only whispering to us a little, and that he was probably not very far off. We felt no shaking of the earth or of the house, but were filled with the exceeding power and goodness of God.[20]

After he was sustained by the Quorum of the Twelve, President Young nominated Heber C. Kimball and Willard Richards as counselors. They also were sustained by the quorum.

On the following day, the First Presidency and the Quorum of the Twelve met again in the home of Orson Hyde. The urgency of building a tabernacle in Kane and a temple in Salt Lake City was discussed. John Smith, brother of Joseph Smith, Sr., and known to all as Uncle John Smith, was named Patriarch to the Church.

Orson Hyde was assigned to go to the eastern states, and Amasa Lyman to the southern states to seek help for the migrating poor. Orson Pratt was asked to take charge of the Church in England. Luke S. Johnson, who had returned to the Church, was to be ordained an elder. Letters were written to carry out the assignments and to appeal for help for the poor.

President Young and others left Hyde Park and returned by way of the North Mormon Ferry to Winter Quarters. No public announcement was made of the new First Presidency prior to the vote of Church members later that month in Kane.

Henry W. Miller organized about 200 men to build the tabernacle near Indian Creek in Kane. Because of the size of the timber available, it was laid out with 40-by-60-foot inner dimensions, and with a 12-by-20-foot extension for a stand for a band and speakers. The log structure had 13-foot walls and puncheon floor. A sod roof peaked at 20 feet. The roof was held up by four poles in a square between the speakers' stand and the two four-foot doors, 14 feet apart, on the south. The 40-foot west wall was bevelled out six feet to accommodate a huge fireplace and a sod chimney that was lined with sticks and was held in place by fired clay.

Conference resumed in the new building on 24 December.

Brigham Young, ca. 1853. He was sustained as President of the Church on 27 December 1847 in the log tabernacle at Kanesville (Council Bluffs), Iowa.

Heber C. Kimball (1801–1868), ca. 1853. He was sustained as first counselor to President Brigham Young on 27 December 1847 by a congregation estimated at 1,000 persons.

Willard Richards (1804–1854), ca. 1853, was sustained as second counselor to President Brigham Young on 27 December 1847 at Kanesville, Iowa. In the fall of 1848 he returned to the Salt Lake Valley as captain of a large company of Saints.

Orson Hyde dedicated the building as a house of prayer and thanksgiving. Brigham Young presided over forenoon, afternoon, and evening sessions. Meetings continued from 24 through 27 December.

On the final day of the conference, the First Presidency and the new Patriarch were presented and sustained by about 1000 members in attendance. George A. Smith gave the benediction on the conference, and then the congregation shouted three times: "Hosanna, Hosanna, Hosanna to God and the Lamb, Amen, Amen, and Amen."

The next day the First Presidency returned to Winter Quarters. Brigham and Joseph Young went to Kane from Winter Quarters on 15 January 1848 for the beginning of a five-day Seventies Jubilee in the log tabernacle. William W. Phelps read a petition addressed to the new Iowa State Legislature asking for formation of a Pottawattamie County, to include all of southwest Iowa. The petition was approved, and Henry W. Miller and Andrew Perkins were elected delegates to present the petition to the legislature.

Joseph Young conducted the Monday sessions of the jubilee. W. W. Phelps, Isaac Morley, and Brigham Young preached in the forenoon. There were social activities and dancing in the afternoon and evening. That pattern was followed through Thursday, with dancing, singing, amusements, band performances, and solos by John M. Kay, a favorite singer in the Missouri Valley. A memorial and petition was drafted to send to the Postmaster General asking for establishment of a post office near the new tabernacle with semiweekly mail service.

President Young and others returned on 21 January to Winter Quarters. Brigham wrote to Thomas L. Kane on 9 February asking for help in getting a post office and including the memorial—and 1805 signatures—addressed to the Postmaster General. President Young also asked Kane to seek permission from the Superintendent of Indian Affairs for the Saints who could not go to the mountains to stay at Winter Quarters and on their farms on the Nebraska side of the Missouri River. Finally, Brigham asked Kane to draft a petition for a territorial government in the Salt Lake Valley and to "agitate the subject in the halls of Congress!"[21]

In late February, Brigham Young wrote a letter advising the members of the Church who were living distant from Iowa and who were not able to migrate west to the Great Basin in 1848 to come by steamboat as far as Council Bluffs. (They would land at

Council Point.) There, he said, was plenty of farmland where they could raise young cattle for teams and make their own wagons. Brigham said they could develop preemption rights to the land, which they could sell before continuing on to the Salt Lake Valley.

Evan M. Greene arrived from Winter Quarters to begin his appointment as postmaster near the tabernacle. The post office was to be called Kanesville in honor of Thomas L. Kane.[22]

An Iowa Whig Executive Committee wrote to Brigham Young to arrange a discussion of interests between the Saints and the Whig party. Sidney Roberts was sent to Winter Quarters to talk with President Young. Heber C. Kimball said he had about as much confidence in the Loco Focos as in the Whigs. Brigham said the Whigs were leaders in driving the Saints from Illinois. He said he would vote for good men, independent of party lines. However, those participating in the meeting with Roberts voted to attend a larger such gathering in Kanesville.

A political caucus was held in the log tabernacle on 27 March. George Q. Cannon capsulized the Whig memorial to the Saints in a letter, stating:

> The address reviewed, at length, persecutions heaped upon the Saints in Missouri, the martyrdom of Joseph and Hyrum Smith, their leaders, and their expulsion from the States of Missouri and Illinois. The address also dwelt feelingly upon the deception and treachery of the Democrats for asking favors so often from, and as often heaping neglect, abuse and persecution upon the Saints, depriving them from time to time of civil and religious liberty and the inalienable rights of freemen. . . . P. Lyon and Sidney Roberts to visit them (the LDS) and lay before them the national policy of the Whigs and solicit their co-operation; assuring them that their party was pledged to them and the country to 'a firm and unyielding protection. . . . Although it looked rather suspicious to the Saints that the Whigs of Iowa should at that particular time become deeply interested in their welfare.[23]

With repeated assurances from Roberts, the caucus agreed to support the Whig party of Iowa when legal county status should be extended to the thousands of residents in southwest Iowa.

The First Presidency and other leading men of the Church returned to the tabernacle on 6 April for general conference,

LDS (Mormon) Communities in Missouri Valley, 1846–1853

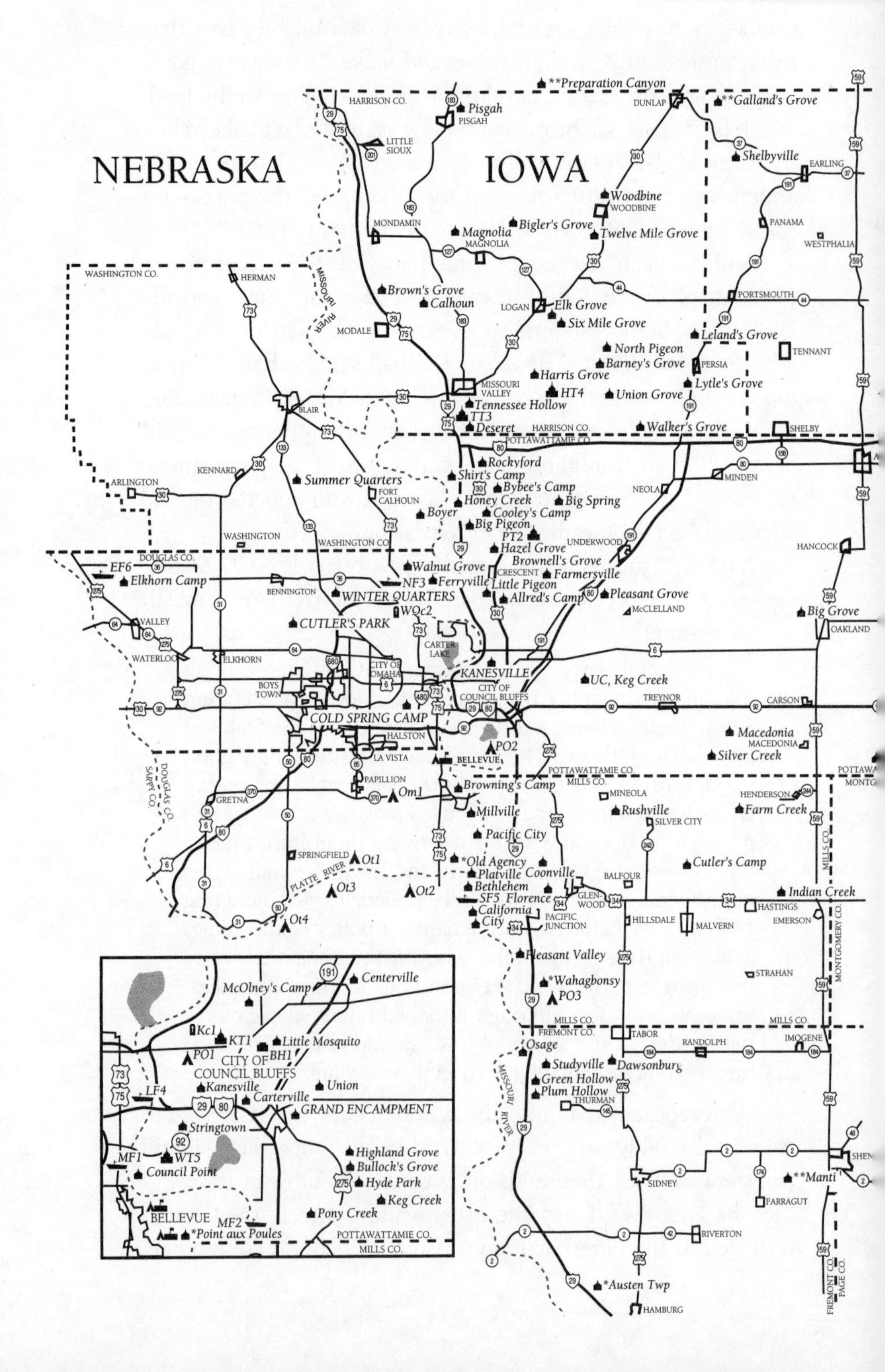

LDS Emigration to Utah

from 1847 through 1843*

1847	about	2000
1848	"	4000
1849	"	3000
1850	"	5000
1851	"	5000
1852	"	10,000
1853	"	2603
		31,603

* Compilation by Church Historian Andrew Jenson

"Many came with freight companies and for that reason were not listed with the regular emigrant trains."

—ANDREW JENSON

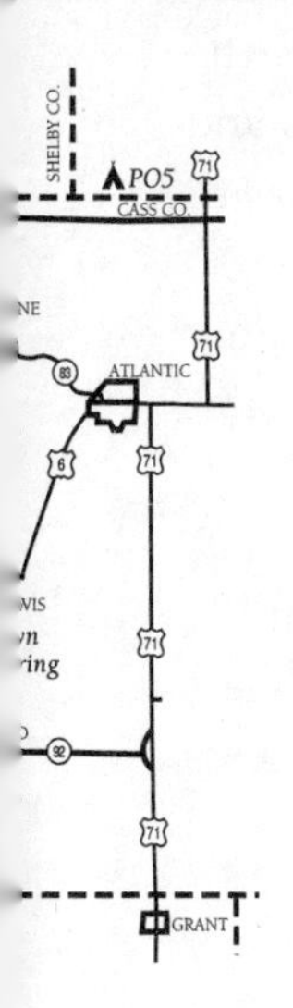

Based on studies funded by:
Iowa Humanities Board
Nebraska Humanities Committee
Charles Redd Center for Western Studies, Brigham Young University, Provo

Legend for Accompanying Map

LDS Mormon Communities:
* shared with non-LDS
**built by dissident LDS

Names of LDS Communities for which Locations Are Unknown:
Bertrand, Davis Camp, Kidd's Grove, McLellin's Camp, Nishnabotna, Perkin's Camp, Springville, Unionville, West Boyer.

LDS Tabernacles:
Conference and social centers of 1840s & 1850s: (KT1) Kanesville; (PT2) Pigeon Creek; (TT3) Tennessee Hollow; (HT4) Harris Grove; (WT5) Welsh Tabernacle.

Cemeteries [Kc1]:
1846–1863 Kanesville Cemetery at Lafayette & 2nd St. Council Bluffs, converted in 1863 to Fairview Cemetery and replatted. Look in high east end of cemetery for half-dozen surviving LDS burial sites. This is the largest LDS cemetery in Iowa or Nebraska. [Wqc2] 1846–1848 Cutler's Park/Winter Quarters Cemetery at State St & N Ridge Drive in NE Omaha (Florence). Sexton's handwritten record shows 365 burials, one body brought downriver from what later was Summer Quarters; 56 deaths were at Cutler's Park. Of 308 deaths exclusively at Winter Quarters, 14 burials were unknown or unreported to the sexton, likely poverty cases buried by family or friends. There probably were LDS cemeteries for virtually every LDS community shown on this map, plus many trailside burials.

Ferries [Mf1]:
July–Sept 1846 Middle Mormon Ferry 1 mile south of present South Omaha Bridge over Missouri; [MF2] summer 1846 Middle Ferry 2 (built either by LDS or by fur trader Peter Sarpy) between Point aux Poules (Traders Point) & Bellevue; [NF3] Sept 1846–spring 1850 (bought in 1850 from LDS by Peter Sarpy & partners) North Mormon Ferry just north of present I-680 bridge over Missouri & operated between Ferryville & Winter Quarters; [LF4] 1849–1853 Lone Tree Ferry established by Gold Rush dropout Wm D Brown about two blocks N of present I-480 bridge between downtown Omaha & Council Bluffs; [SF5] 1850–1853 South Mormon Ferry, over Missouri south of the Platte River, so migrating LDS could escape north-of-the-Platte Gold Rush crowd; [EF6] 1847–1850 Elkhorn Mormon Ferry near Elk City, NE; now less than half a mile east of Elkhorn because river was straightened in the 1890s.

Blockhouse Site [BH1]:
On E Pierce St. between Grace and Union Sts. Near downtown Council Bluffs; built 1837 to protect newly arrived Pottawattamie/Ottawa/Chippewa Indians; 1838–1841 St Joseph/St Mary Catholic Mission & Indian School; 1846–1853 Blockhouse Branch of The Church of Jesus Christ of Latter-day Saints, around which Miller's Hollow (1846)/Kanesville (1848)/Council Bluffs (1853–) grew up.

Indian Villages:
1837–1847 Pottawattamie/Ottawa/Chippewa [PO1] just NE of downtown Council Bluffs post office; [PO2] north of Point aux Poules, across Missouri from Bellevue; [PO3] S of Waubonsie Bible Church on Hwy 45 south of Glenwood, Mills Cty; [PO4] by Indian Creek 2 mi W of Lewis, in Cass Cty; [PO5] along East Nishnabotna River, 40 mi N of P4. Audubon Cty, IA; 1837–1854 Oto-Missouri lived both N & S of Platte River; [Ot1] 8 mi SW of Bellevue; [Ot2, 3 & 4] just south of Platte, at about 5 mi intervals, commencing about 5 mi W of the Missouri River; Omaha [Om1] lived 3 mi W of then Bellevue from 1845 till 1856.

U.S. Indian Agency & Sub-Agency:
Agent responsible for Oto-Missouri, Omaha, and Pawnee Indian Tribes was resident in Bellevue; sub-agent responsible for Pottawattamie/Ottawa/Chippewa was in Point aux Poules.

LDS Church Branches

1846–1853 in SW Iowa

(boundaries unknown)

llred Branch
mbrosia Branch
ertrand Branch
g Bend Branch
g Grove Branch
g Pigeon Branch
g Spring Branch
lockhouse Branch
uff Branch
oyer Branch
Carterville Branch
Centerville Branch
Cooley's Camp Branch
Coonville Branch
Council Point Branch
Davis Camp Branch
Ferryville Branch
Harris Grove Branch
High Prairie Branch
Highland Grove Branch
Honey Creek Branch
Hunt's Branch
Hyde Park Branch
Indian Creek Branch
Indian Mill Branch
Keg Creek Branch
Kidd's Grove Branch
Lake Branch
Long Creek Branch
Macedonia Branch
Martindale Branch
McOlney's Branch
Mill Branch
North Pigeon Branch
Old Agency Branch
Pigeon Creek Branch
Pigeon Grove Branch
Pleasant Grove Branch
Pleasant Valley Branch
Plum Hollow Branch
Point aux Poules Branch (Prairie Chicken Point)
Pony Creek Branch
Rushville Branch
Shirts's Branch
Silver Creek Branch
Springville Branch
Union Branch
Upper Keg Creek Branch

where priesthood assignments were given. Missionaries were named to visit all branches of the Church in southwest Iowa, preach the gospel, and instruct and encourage the Saints. On a motion by Orson Hyde, Kane was renamed Kanesville on 8 April, the final day of general conference.

On 29 May 1848, Heber C. Kimball led 662 members of the Church out of Winter Quarters toward the Salt Lake Valley. Brigham Young led 1220 west from the log cabin and dugout city on 6 June. A final party of 526 Saints departed Winter Quarters for the Salt Lake Valley on 3 July under the direction of Willard Richards. Those who remained were moved back across the Missouri River to spend another year assembling supplies and equipment they would need to cross the high plains and mountains to Salt Lake City.

Behind were left the graves of those who had died. Leading the way to a future in the West and dominating somber memories of the Missouri Valley was Brigham Young. Guided by the Spirit, President Young left behind him more than 80 Mormon communities that would prosper until their residents chose to abandon their substantial and flourishing farms, businesses, churches, tuition schools, and county governments for the spiritual blessings of being with the Brethren in the Great Basin.

NOTES

1. See Daniel Miller, United States Indian Agent Report, 16 September 1844, from Council Bluffs Agency (Bellevue, Nebraska Territory) to Superintendent of Indian Affairs D. D. Mitchell, St. Louis, Missouri, Harold B. Lee Library, Brigham Young University.
2. See Miller to Mitchell, 3 September 1842 and 18 August 1843, Harold B. Lee Library.
3. As quoted in Thomas L. Kane, "1850 Address to Historical Society of Pennsylvania," in Albert L. Zobell, Jr., *Sentinel in the East: A Biography of Thomas L. Kane* (Salt Lake City: Utah Printing Co., 1965).
4. As quoted in Thomas Bullock, notes, 8 March 1847, Leonard J. Arrington, *Brigham Young, American Moses,* 130, from typescript of minutes on file in LDS Church Historical Archives.
5. Andrew Jenson, *Compilation of Journals,* 14 June 1846, unpublished manuscript, Library-Archives, Historical Department of The Church of Jesus Christ of Latter-day Saints (hereafter cited as LDS Church Historical Archives).

6. As quoted in *Women's Exponent,* 12: 170.
7. See Jenson, *Compilation of Journals,* 7 August 1846.
8. Ibid., 13 August 1846.
9. Ibid., 14 August 1846.
10. Ibid., 3 July 1846.
11. See map.
12. Kane, "1850 Address."
13. As quoted in Jenson, *Compilation of Journals,* 28 August 1846.
14. Jenson, *Compilation of Journals,* 22 September 1846.
15. Andrew Jenson, *Manuscript History of Winter Quarters,* 8 November 1846, unpublished manuscript, LDS Church Historical Archives.
16. See Kane, "1850 Address."
17. Hosea Stout, *On the Mormon Frontier: The Diary of Hosea Stout, 1844–1861,* Juanita Brooks, ed. (Salt Lake City: University of Utah Press, 1982), 1: 230.
18. Ibid., 1: 239.
19. As quoted in Jenson, *Compilation of Journals,* 25 November 1847.
20. *Journal of Discourses,* 8: 234.
21. As quoted in Jenson, *Compilation of Journals,* 9 February 1848.
22. See ibid., 18 March 1848.
23. Ibid., 27 March 1848.

CHAPTER 7

THE MORMON BATTALION

Religious Authority Clashed with Military Leadership

SUSAN EASTON BLACK
Professor of Church History and Doctrine
Associate Dean of General Education and Honors
Brigham Young University

A comprehensive study of the Mormon Battalion reveals disagreement between the rank and file over religious authority and military leadership. Brigham Young asserted his authority early in the battalion's formation by recruiting and appointing religious military officers and ecclesiastical leaders to guide and "father" the enlistees. Government officials appointed military officers who viewed their leadership as superior to Young's. Conflict bordering on mutiny riddled the battalion march as religious authority clashed with military leadership in a verbal battle from Council Bluffs to California.

This article will show the influence and leadership of Young over the Latter-day Saint recruits. In addition, it will analyze the conflict over leadership by focusing on key individuals who fired the flames of continual strife by disregarding the orders and counsel of the recognized Mormon leader.

BRIGHAM YOUNG, RELIGIOUS LEADER OF THE BATTALION

Young's directive to Jesse C. Little, Little's journey to Washington, D.C., his meeting with U.S. President James K. Polk, and Polk's offer to aid the pioneers by permitting them to raise a battalion are well documented. Little's acceptance of Polk's offer committed a Mormon Battalion to join Colonel Stephen Watts Kearney, Commander of the Army of the West, to fight for the United States in the Mexican War.

Kearney's designated leader, Captain James Allen,[1] arrived at the Mount Pisgah encampment with three dragoons from the

United States Army on 26 June 1846. He was treated with suspicion because many believed the raising of a battalion to be a plot to trouble the migrating Saints.[2] By 1 July 1846, Allen had allayed fears by giving the pioneers permission to camp on United States lands if they raised the desired battalion.

Recruitment

Brigham Young recognized the enlistment as a government effort to aid the Mormons. He vigorously endorsed the recruitment of volunteers, saying, "Let the Mormons be the first to set their feet on the soil of California."[3] On 7 July 1846, Young wrote to Samuel Bent, "This thing is from above, for our good." He later declared, "Hundreds would eternally regret that they did not go, when they had the chance."[4]

Young not only publicly endorsed enlistment, but he also personally visited with potential recruits. For example, he asked Matthew Caldwell to volunteer. When Caldwell expressed hesitancy, Young's promised blessings encouraged him to enlist. Caldwell relates:

> I did not see how it would be possible to go as I had nothing to leave for my family. Whereupon President Young replied, "I will tell you in the name of the Lord, if you will go, you shall have health, and strength to perform the trip, and you shall not have occasion to fire at the enemy, and you shall not be shot at, you shall return and find your family in a better condition than when you left them.
>
> "With that promise, I'll go," I replied.[5]

When volunteers wished to renege on their commitment to military service, Young took a firm stand. He would not allow sixteen-year-old Matthew Fifield, who had enlisted to spite his father, to resign until his father enlisted in his place.[6] Owing primarily to Young's various recruitment efforts, approximately 543 men were mustered into the Mormon Battalion on 16 July 1846.

Selection of Officers

From among these recruits, Brigham Young, not Captain James Allen, selected the commissioned officers. His selection of

Jesse C. Little (1815–1893), ca. 1866–1867. As agent of the Church in the eastern states, Little was instrumental in the enlistment of the Mormon Battalion through U.S. President James K. Polk in 1846.

Captain Jefferson Hunt (1803–1879), ca. 1865–1875. Commander of Company A and senior Latter-day Saints officer in the Mormon Battalion.

Levi Ward Hancock (1803–1882), First Council of the Seventy. Musician (fifer), Company E, Mormon Battalion.

Lt. Col. Philip St. George Cooke (1809–1895), ca. 1851–1853, commanding officer of the Mormon Battalion from Santa Fe, New Mexico, to the Pacific coast.

officers was not in accord with Allen's directive from General Kearney. Nevertheless, Young believed himself capable of nominating men for officers, even though he himself had not enlisted. The enlistees voted unanimously that Young and his council should proceed as they thought proper.[7] His influence solidified as he handpicked the officers.

On 18 July 1846, commissioned and noncommissioned officers gathered to receive counsel and instructions from Young and other Church leaders. Officers were advised "to be as fathers to the privates, to remember their prayers, to see that the name of the Deity was revered, and that virtue and cleanliness were strictly observed." Young also cautioned the men to "manage their affairs by the power and influence of the Priesthood," with the realization that "a private soldier is as honorable as an officer, if he behaves as well."[8]

Young's Role on the March

It is reasonable to assume that Brigham's role diminished when the battalion, accompanied by approximately thirty-three women and fifty-one children, left Council Bluffs on 21 July 1846. But such was not the case. On 21 July 1846, word came from Young that he reserved authority over the Latter-day Saint officers. It appears that this authority was solicited and supported by Mormons and non-Mormons alike.

For example, word from Young was needed to settle the confusion of battalion leadership after Captain Allen's untimely death. A council of officers had agreed that the senior Mormon officer, Captain Jefferson Hunt,[9] should assume the command. A few days following this affirmation, Lieutenant A. J. Smith[10] claimed command by authority of the commandant at Fort Leavenworth. Given two viable candidates, the question of leadership could be solved only by Brigham Young, not the government.

Hunt wrote to Young and was informed that the battalion itself should settle the question of leadership. The non-Mormon Smith also wrote to Young: "If it is the wish of your people that I should take charge of the Battalion and conduct it to General

Kearney, I will do it with pleasure and feel proud of the command."[11] Young responded:

> Sir, on the subject of command we can only say, Col. Allen settled that matter at the organization of the Battalion; therefore, we must leave that point to the proper authorities, be the result what it may.[12]

Yet Young did not allow it to be "what it may." He wrote to Samuel Gully:

> You will all doubtless recollect that Colonel Allen repeatedly stated . . . if he fell . . . sick, . . . the command would devolve on the ranking officer, which would be the Captain of Company A, and B, and so on.
>
> . . . Consequently, the command must devolve on Captain Jefferson Hunt.[13]

John D. Lee, in an attempt to follow Young's instructions, was so overbearing in pressing the issue of Mormon leadership that he was threatened with being placed under guard. His manipulative efforts antagonized both Mormon and non-Mormon officers. Perhaps because of Lee's actions, the leadership of the battalion went to A. J. Smith rather than to Hunt. Concerned that Lee would distort events when he returned to the Camps of Israel, religious officers wrote Young to justify previous and current actions as supportive of their continual allegiance to his leadership.[14]

Young instructed his officers by correspondence throughout the march; for example, he wrote, "If you are sick, live by faith, and let the surgeon's medicine alone if you want to live, using only such herbs and mild foods as are at your disposal." In another letter, Young counseled, "Remember the ordinances in case of sickness."[15]

Most of Young's correspondence was addressed to the Latter-day Saint military leader, Captain Jefferson Hunt. It could be assumed that the men viewed Hunt as their religious leader. However, one reason that the enlistees did not view him as such is that they saw his actions as incongruent with those expected from a man of God. For example, one evening Captain Hunt was approached by Private Erastus Bingham, who requested an exchange of rations. Hunt exclaimed, "I'll give you your rations when I get ready." His remark so angered Erastus that the private retorted, "I'm not afraid of any Hunt that God ever made." Hunt immediately jumped through the campfire and hit Erastus. They exchanged punches until comrades calmed them. The bruised captain then stammered, "You may come and get your rations."[16]

The men's failure to recognize Hunt as their spiritual leader was due more to the presence of Levi W. Hancock,[17] one of the seven presidents of the Seventy, than to Hunt's sporadic fisticuffs. Apparently Hancock could advise Hunt in ecclesiastical matters. For example, on 20 August 1846, Hancock recorded, "I called upon Capt. Hunt and told him we ought to have some meetings and he then appointed me to take charge of the same."[18]

With two strong Mormon leaders emerging—one Young's designated military leader and the other his appointed religious spokesman—Young's influence continued to permeate the battalion during and after the march. Continual correspondence and directives served to increase his influence. For example, (1) the letter from Lorenzo Clark written on 14 May 1847 to Young sought instructions on what the battalion men should do while stationed in California;[19] (2) Young's correspondence to Captain James Brown, the senior military leader at Pueblo, and to A. Porter Dowdle, ecclesiastical leader at Pueblo, advised, "Throw all the Gentile officers out of the Battalion when you come up to it";[20] and (3) on 31 July 1847, "Brigham Young personally assumed command of the soldiers [in the Salt Lake Valley] and ordered them to gather brush for the bowery."[21]

As late as August 1847, Young sent James Brown and others to collect back pay for the sick detachment and to secure the soldiers' official discharges. In these directives, Young was representing himself, not General Kearney or any other officer recognized by the United States Army. Brigham Young, who never enlisted or marched with the battalion, was the actual leader of the battalion for the Latter-day Saint recruits.

AUTHORITY IN CONFLICT

Conflict over authority developed when leaders of the battalion went against the counsel and direction of Brigham Young. Obviously, military appointees did not concur with his dominant leadership role. Lieutenant A. J. Smith, Dr. George B. Sanderson, and Adjutant George P. Dykes best illustrate this conflict. These officers challenged Young's authority repeatedly from Kansas to Santa Fe.

Lieutenant Andrew Jackson Smith

As A. J. Smith took command, the transition in leadership proved difficult for battalion privates, who blamed their officers for not consulting them on Smith's military appointment. This cancer festered slowly at first as Smith, unaware of growing sentiment, wrote, "We are getting along very well so far."[22]

Daniel Tyler contrasted these sentiments by bitterly claiming that "foolish and unnecessary forced marches of Lieutenant Smith . . . utterly broke down both men and beasts, and was the prime cause of the greater part of the sickness and probably of many deaths."[23] Smith's policy of "punishing privates for the merest trifles, [while] officers could go where and do what they pleased, without any notice being taken of them"[24] mushroomed sentiment against Smith because such practice was contrary to Young's advice. Tyler penned, "I am satisfied that any other set of men but Latter-day Saints would have mutinied rather than submit to the oppressions and abuse thus heaped upon them."[25]

This growing division filtered through the ranks until many of the men used tactical efforts to cause Smith difficulty. For example, sentinel guard Thomas Howell imprisoned Smith for giving the wrong countersign. From the incident, Smith believed that Howell would just as soon kill him as look at him.

But Smith's cruelties toward the men did not cease. He pulled the sick from wagons when they neglected to report to the doctor. He shouted horrid oaths, threatened his soldiers, and on one occasion drew a sword and vowed to run Thomas S. Williams through if he allowed the sick to rest in his wagon without permission. He reduced the men to two-thirds rations and forced brackish water on the thirsty.

Smith was not the father figure Brigham Young had advised the officers to be. Perhaps William Follet's derogatory nickname for Smith, "Negro Driver," was not far from the truth. John D. Lee's reference to him as "little wolfish tyrant" reflected many men's feelings for this government leader who attempted to assert his authority above Young's.

Dr. George B. Sanderson

Doctor Sanderson, recognizing the important role of Brigham Young in the battalion, wrote to him, "I am in hopes, in fact I have no fears, . . . [that] your people will be taken care of."[26] Even though Young responded with "We doubt not your services to the Battalion will be duly appreciated," such was never the case.[27] Some might claim that Sanderson never received the proper respect due a surgeon because he was a Missourian and punctuated his speech with vulgar, profane innuendos. But though these were obvious reasons for his lack of proper appreciation, they were not the main cause.

The core issue was the conflict between Sanderson's medical treatments and Young's remedy of faith healing. Sanderson ignored pleas to discontinue medical treatment, and he employed antiquated prescriptions of arsenic and calomel for rheumatism, boils, lameness, and other unrelated diseases. The sick were compelled to take the medicine quietly, having it forced down them with a rusty spoon, or be left to perish on the plains. So adamant and confident was Sanderson of his generic remedy that he "threatened with an oath, to cut the throat of any man who would administer any medicine without his orders."[28]

The physical side effects of consuming the poison-laced prescriptions were debilitating during the march and also allegedly caused suffering long after the march. Abraham Day claimed that his teeth became loose and some even dropped out because of this medication.[29] Joseph Bates testified that Doctor Sanderson's treatment for an "inward rupture" resulted in his kidney disease.[30] Jonathan Callahan claimed that the doctor's treatment for a "displaced ankle bone" caused "lameness which afflicted him the rest of his life."[31] Amos Cox concluded his sentiments regarding the malpractice of Sanderson by lamenting, "I am an Invalid."[32]

Yet even worse than the incapacities and loss of health resulting from his malpractice were his threats of death. Private John Calvert recalled having typhoid on the march and being so ill that he could not move. He claimed that while in this weakened condition, he overheard Dr. Sanderson boast, "I've given this G— D— Mormon enough calomel to kill a horse but it looks like the stubborn cuss is still alive."[33]

Calvert did survive, unlike privates Alva Phelps and David Smith, who lost their lives following treatment. Phelps begged Doctor Sanderson not to give him any strong medicine; he needed only a little rest and then would return to duty. Relentlessly, the doctor forced the medication upon him until he died. The sentiment at the funeral was that "the doctor had killed him in premeditated murder." David Smith's condition worsened until two days before his death, when he became speechless. All attending him concurred that "his death was the result of medicine given him by Dr. Sanderson previous to the command leaving that post."[34]

Doctor Sanderson, aware of being nicknamed "Doctor Death" as early as 10 September 1846, was afraid to sleep near the men because he feared for his life.[35] This fear arose from the men's reaction to his consistent efforts to force medication on the sick, disregarding Young's remedy of faith healing.

Adjutant George P. Dykes

Adjutant Dykes proved to be the turncoat of the battalion.[36] He first demonstrated his break from Mormon leadership at a council meeting held on 3 October 1846. Dykes opposed Brigham Young's advice to keep the battalion together. He justified his stance by reasoning that Young did not know their present circumstances and thus should not have counseled the men against separating.

Although Latter-day Saint officers bickered among themselves, it was an unwritten rule that no one opposed the absentee leadership of Brigham Young. Faithful stalwarts noted Dykes's affronts to Young's prophetic leadership. Sergeant William Hyde wrote, "It was plainly manifest that Lieutenant Dykes sought to gain favor of and please the wicked rather than favor his brethren."[37] A fellow officer stated, "[Dykes's] conduct has rendered him odious to the whole Mormon Battalion."[38]

Dykes continued to undermine Young's counsel and to discredit his appointed leaders. His accusations earned him the nickname "accuser of the brethren" and led to the loss of rank for Sergeant Jones and Corporal Lewis and to the resignation of Samuel Gully. As government-appointed leaders welcomed Dykes into their inner circle, Dykes became boastful and pompous. When privates Philander Fletcher and Boyd Steward neglected to salute him, they were forced to march behind an ox wagon in unfavorable weather conditions.

Before long, government-appointed officers began to recognize Dykes's chameleon character. Colonel Cooke conceded, "Officers and men were abused and ill treated by a man called 'Talebearing Dykes.' . . . He has been a trouble-maker all the way. . . . He had to look to members of the Battalion for protection, he made so many enemies."[39]

The commonalities between Smith, Sanderson, and Dykes were their efforts to thwart the leadership of Brigham Young in the battalion. Their efforts instigated bickering and conflict, which grew until all three men were fearful of death from all ranks of the battalion.

THE CONFLICT DIMINISHES

The lessening of these conflicts began when the first division of the battalion approached Santa Fe, New Mexico, on 9 October 1846. In Santa Fe, Lieutenant Smith was relieved of his command by Lieutenant Colonel Philip St. George Cooke.[40] Cooke, aware of the rugged trail between Santa Fe and California, ordered most of the women and children to accompany the sick detachment to Fort Pueblo, Colorado. There, conflict and bickering continued. But without the key players, it lessened.

Colonel Philip St. George Cooke

The remaining soldiers, under the leadership of Cooke, left Santa Fe for California on 19 October 1846. During this leg of the march, Cooke's leadership was viewed by some as superior to that of Smith. Tyler penned, "We found the judgement of Colonel Cooke in travelling much better than that of Smith, in fact, it was first-class. He never crowded the men unnecessarily."[41]

Cooke's theory that officers should obey and set an example for privates was in accord with Young's counsel. For returning to Santa Fe without Cooke's permission, Captain Jesse D. Hunter was arrested on 21 October 1846 and was forced to march at the rear of his company. Such impartial treatment of an officer did not go unnoticed by the subordinate rank and file.

Nevertheless, the Mormon enlistees often questioned Cooke's sentiments toward them because of his strict discipline, stern appearance, and expressions of doubt regarding the battalion's capability. William Coray named him "old culprit."[42] James Pace wrote that Cooke "was abusive to officers & soldiers seaming to drive round as tho he was before a set of wild goat."[43] Elijah Elmer recorded, "The Colonel is as cross as hell all the time and crabbed and overbearing."[44] Levi Hancock concurred in a journal entry of 26 January 1847: "He is a miserable creature and often curses and damns the soldiers. He is as mean as I ever saw a man. Smith who led us is a gentleman to him—he is a small, low lived cuss."

Cooke countered these sentiments by writing, "[Mormons] exhibit great . . . ignorance and some obstinacy."[45] It was not until 17 December 1846 that "Cooke proudly proclaimed that at last he was convinced that the Mormons would fight for the United States Army."[46] On 30 January 1847, he praised the Mormon Battalion, writing, "History may be searched in vain for an equal march of infantry."[47]

MILITARY AUTHORITY DECLINES

Upon the battalion's arrival in California, the influence of military leaders declined. This decline was a direct result of the varied assignments that separated members of the battalion. Some members were assigned to garrison duty at San Diego, some at San Luis Rey, and some at Ciudad de los Angeles. Others were designated to accompany General Kearney back to Fort Leavenworth. With the dissipation of the battalion, the strict leadership and conflict lessened. Henry Standage noted the change:

> Our officers are becoming more and more like men, giving us as many privileges as they can conveniently. They have not been more than half as strict for a few days past. In fact, they seem to realize that their power as military commanders will soon be gone, and that their influence will be gone too. Inasmuch as they know that there are men in this battalion who stand as high and much higher in the Priesthood, therefore it seems as though they wished to restore the confidence in some measure which they well know that has departed during the last 12 months.[48]

As the military leadership waned, the authority of Levi Hancock and father-figure David Pettigrew[49] increased, even though little mention of this gradual change appears in journal entries. Latter-day Saint military officers often regarded Hancock's and Pettigrew's zeal and diligence as officious, and they entertained feelings of jealousy toward them. For example, Hancock's climb of five hundred feet to "Point of the Rocks," where he built an altar and prayed in the name of the God of Israel, seemed to some a showy pretense. Hancock's and Pettigrew's going from tent to tent and in a low voice counseling the men to pray to the Lord to influence the colonel's thinking was viewed as officious. Meetings that included the washing of feet (which excluded military leaders) were tolerated with suspicion. Hancock, aware of unfavorable comments of zeal, wrote to Brigham Young:

> A jealousy arose among us; some of the officers said that there was a secret conspiracy in the camp. I then called on all the brethren to bear testimony that I had taught nothing but against wickedness, and that I had a perfect right to do it wherever I was in any part of the earth.[50]

Yet despite jealousies, the privates increasingly turned to religious leaders for justification to oppose the military leaders.

RELIGIOUS LEADERSHIP TRIUMPHS

By April 1847, it was obvious that Hancock and Pettigrew had assumed leadership and were respected by the men. Their triumph is best illustrated by studying the attempt made to reenlist the men of the battalion for another term of duty. Colonel Stevenson arrived in Los Angeles on 28 June 1847 to reenlist the battalion. At a meeting that day, Captains Hunter, Hunt, and Davis and Lieutenants Canfield and Dykes, appointed by Brigham Young to be military leaders, also spoke strongly in favor of reenlistment.

However, the men resisted, as if waiting to hear from Musician Hancock and Private Pettigrew. Then David Pettigrew, the father-figure religious leader, countered the words of the officers:

> [It was] our duty to return and look after our outcast families; others could do as they thought best, but he believed that we had done all that we had set out to do, and that our offering was accepted and that our return would be sanctioned by the Church leaders.[51]

The meeting was then adjourned to avoid the heat of the day, with another meeting scheduled in the big tent at the fort.

This second meeting revealed that most of the men preferred to take the advice of Hancock and Pettigrew and other faithful priesthood holders. They viewed it as more religious to look forward to reuniting with their families than to reenlist. Suspicions that Hancock and Pettigrew were influencing the men against the wishes of officers were openly raised. Yet some of the officers bowed to ecclesiastical position as superior to their appointed military position. Sergeant William Hyde arose, stating that "he had but little to say, but what he should say would be at the risk of all hazard. This was that Levi Hancock was his file leader and that he would obey his counsel, let the circumstances be what they may."[52]

This clear transfer in leadership authority occurred because military leaders failed to act as fathers to their brethren as Young had advised. As a result, only eighty-one men chose to reenlist and to serve an additional eight months of military duty under Captain Daniel C. Davis in Company A of the Mormon Volunteers.

The clear majority followed the counsel of religious leaders and began migrating to the Salt Lake Valley, where they reunited with their pioneering families.

Such transfer of power to ecclesiastical position was noted by Colonel Stevenson, who wrote:

> My intercourse with the Mormons has satisfied me that the great mass of them are . . . entirely under the control of their leaders, and that in every community or association, there is some one man who is the controlling spirit, and that all are under the direction and control of some one Master Spirit. In the Battalion were two men, one of which was a private soldier—who were the chief men, and but for them, at least, three companies would have re-entered, but they opposed, and not a man would enter, and I do not believe we should have succeeded in getting one company, if they had not given it their countenance or at least made no formal objection.[53]

In a final effort to increase reenlistment, Stevenson appealed to the true leader of the battalion, Brigham Young, on 8 February 1848. "I therefore ask you,"[54] he wrote, expressing his hope for help from the Latter-day Saint leader.

CONCLUSION

The men of the Mormon Battalion are honored for their willingness to fight for the United States, for their march of some two thousand miles from Council Bluffs to California, for their participation in the early development of the West, and for making the first wagon road over the southern route from California to Utah in 1848.

Perhaps their greatest honor came from their religious leader, Brigham Young. Redick Allred recorded in his diary that, at a celebration held in the log tabernacle in Kanesville, Iowa, Young said to Heber C. Kimball and others, while pointing to the members of the Mormon Battalion, "These men were the salvation of this Church."[55]

In the Salt Lake Valley, Young called the men of the battalion together and blessed them in the name of the Lord for their fidelity to the kingdom of God. "It was to the praise of the

Battalion that they went as honorable men, doing honor to their calling and to the United States, and he was satisfied with all of them. If some had done wrong and transgressed and been out of the way," Young exhorted them to "refrain therefrom, turn to the Lord and build up His kingdom."[56]

This praise surpassed the honors of men, for it was given by their true leader—who had not marched with the battalion but who had never doubted his position nor varied from his stance as leader of the Latter-day Saints in the Mormon Battalion.

NOTES

1. Captain James Allen was born in 1806 in Ohio. After graduating from West Point Academy in 1829, he served as a lieutenant in the infantry. In 1833, he joined the 1st Dragoons and served the remainder of his career as a cavalryman. During most of his career, he was on the frontier at Fort Riley and Fort Leavenworth, where he was stationed with the 1st Dragoons. He died at 6:00 A.M. on Sunday, 23 August 1846, of congestive fever.
2. Wilford Woodruff wrote, "I had some reasons to believe them to be spies & that the president had no hand in it." Wilford Woodruff Journal, 27 June 1846, Library-Archives, Historical Department of The Church of Jesus Christ of Latter-day Saints (hereafter cited as LDS Church Historical Archives).
3. "Manuscript History of Brigham Young," 1 July 1846, LDS Church Historical Archives.
4. "Journal History," 7 July 1846 and 17 July 1846, microfilm, LDS Church Historical Archives.
5. Robert Lewis Woodward and Lucinda Uzella Caldwell Koch, "The Life Story of Matthew Caldwell: A Member of the Mormon Battalion Company E." (n.p., n.d.), 7–8.
6. Life Sketch of Joseph Fifield (n.p., n.d.), in author's possession.
7. The commissioned officers included Jefferson Hunt, captain of Company A; Jesse D. Hunter, captain of Company B; James Brown, captain of Company C; Nelson Higgins, captain of Company D; and Daniel C. Davis, captain of Company E. These officers were entrusted with religious leadership as well as military supervision of the men.
8. "Journal History," 18 July 1846.
9. Jefferson Hunt and two of his sons, Gilbert and Marshall, enlisted in the Mormon Battalion. His two wives and five additional children elected to accompany them on the march. At the time of Jefferson's enlistment, he was six feet tall, weighed 180 pounds, and had light complexion, dark hair, and blue eyes. Pension File of Jefferson Hunt, U.S. Library of Congress.
10. Andrew Jackson Smith was born 28 August 1815 in Pennsylvania. He graduated from West Point in 1838 and was the highest-ranking officer at Fort

Leavenworth following the death of Captain Allen. Prior to his military involvement with the battalion, he was a lieutenant of the 1st Dragoons in the West. During the Civil War he served as a cavalry commander.

11. Daniel Tyler, *A Concise History of the Mormon Battalion in the Mexican War, 1846–1847* (Chicago, Illinois: Rio Grande Press, Inc., 1964), 154.
12. Brigham Young to Andrew J. Smith, Camp of Israel, Omaha Nation, 27 August 1846, as cited in Tyler, 154.
13. John F. Yurtinus, "A Ram in the Thicket: The Mormon Battalion in the Mexican War" (Ph.D. diss., Brigham Young University, 1975), 113.
14. Ibid., 152.
15. Both letters are cited in Tyler, 146.
16. Cedenia Bingham Hale, "Biography of Erastus Bingham, Jr. 1847" (n.p., n.d.), in author's possession.
17. Levi Ward Hancock was born 7 April 1803 in Springfield, Hampden, Massachusetts. He was ordained a seventy on 28 February 1835 by Joseph Smith and was selected as a member of the first Quorum of the Seventy. Soon afterward he was chosen one of the seven presidents of that quorum. He functioned in that calling for forty-seven years. Levi was the only General Authority to enlist in the battalion. He died 10 June 1882 in Washington, Washington, Utah, at the age of 79.
18. Levi Hancock Journal, typescript, Harold B. Lee Library, Brigham Young University. However, it does appear that officers listened to and accepted Hunt's counsel on religious issues also. Sergeant William Coray wrote, "[Hunt] advised the Captains of the companies to get their men together frequently and pray for them and teach them the principals of virtue and be united with each other." William Coray Journal, LDS Church Historical Archives.
19. Kate Carter, *Our Pioneer Heritage,* 17 vols. (Salt Lake City: Daughters of the Utah Pioneers, 1968), 11: 357, 389.
20. Thomas Bullock Journal, 3 June 1847, LDS Church Historical Archives.
21. Norton Jacob, "The Life of Norton Jacob," typescript, 31 July 1847, Harold B. Lee Library; Joel Terrel, "The Journal of Joel Judkins Terrell, being a daily record of the Mormon Battalion from July 16th, 1846 to July 28, 1847," 31 July 1847, as cited in Yurtinus, 333.
22. A. J. Smith to Adjutant General Roger Jones, Camp near Council Grove, 2 September 1846 (Bancroft Library, Berkeley, California), as cited in Yurtinus, 122.
23. As cited in Tyler, 174.
24. Ibid., 177.
25. Ibid., 174.
26. Ibid., 153.
27. Ibid., 154.
28. Ibid., 146.

29. Grace Candland Jacobsen, "A Short History of the Life of Abraham Day" (n.p., February 1936), in author's possession.
30. Pension File of Joseph Bates, National Archives, Washington, D.C.
31. Pension File of Jonathan Callahan, National Archives, Washington, D.C.
32. Pension File of Amos Cox, National Archives, Washington, D.C.
33. Pension File of John Calvert, National Archives, Washington, D.C.
34. As cited in Tyler, 158.
35. William Coray Journal, 10 September 1846.
36. On the march, George P. Dykes served as an adjutant from 16 July 1846 to 15 October 1846. He resigned the adjutancy to assume command of the company on 1 November 1846.
37. As quoted in Tyler, 187.
38. Jefferson Hunt, Daniel C. Davis, Jesse D. Hunter, William W. Willis, to Brigham Young, Santa Fe, October 1846, Brigham Young Papers, LDS Church Historical Archives, as cited in Yurtinus, 186.
39. "Life Sketch of George Dykes" (n.p., n.d.), in author's possession.
40. Subsequently, Smith was appointed quartermaster. Philip St. George Cooke was born 13 June 1809 near Leesburg, Virginia. He graduated from West Point Academy in 1827. He was commissioned as a brevet 2nd Lieutenant of Infantry and also as a 1st Lieutenant in the 1st Dragoons.
41. As quoted in Tyler, 184–85.
42. William Coray Journal, 4 November 1846.
43. "Autobiography and Diary of James Pace, 1811–1888," 5 March 1847, in author's possession.
44. Elijah Elmer, "Journal of Elijah Elmer 1st Sergeant, Company 'C' Mormon Battalion 1846–47," 3 January 1847, San Diego Historical Society, San Diego, California.
45. Philip St. George Cooke, "Cooke's Journal of the March of the Mormon Battalion, 1846–1847," ed. Ralph P. Bieber and Averam B. Bender, in *Exploring Southwestern Trails 1846–1854,* vol. 7 of *The Southwest Historical Series* (Glendale, California: The Arthur C. Clark Company, 1938), 69.
46. "David Pettigrew Autobiography," 17 December 1846, as cited in Yurtinus, 412.
47. As cited in Tyler, 254–55.
48. Journal of Henry Standage, LDS Church Historical Archives.
49. David Pettigrew was born 29 July 1791 in Weathersfield, Windsor, Vermont. Baptized in 1832 by Isaac Higbee, he became a high priest in 1839 in Nauvoo. He died 31 December 1863 in Salt Lake City.
50. Levi Hancock, letter record in Journal History of the Mormon Battalion, 12 May 1847, LDS Church Historical Archives.
51. As quoted in Tyler, 295.
52. Journal of William Hyde, LDS Church Historical Archives.

53. J. D. Stevenson to R. B. Mason, 23 July 1847, Los Angeles, California (10 Military Department Letters: n.p.), as cited in Yurtinus, 601.
54. J. D. Stevenson to Brigham Young, as cited in Yurtinus, 605.
55. Redick Allred Diary, LDS Church Historical Archives.
56. As quoted in Tyler, 343–44.

CHAPTER 8

Colonizer of the West

DALE F. BEECHER

Registrar, Museum of Church History and Art
The Church of Jesus Christ of Latter-day Saints

Brigham Young has been called the "American Moses" and the "Colonizer." He might also be called history's greatest real-estate developer. Of the four official hats worn by Brother Brigham—Church President, governor, Indian agent, and community builder—the latter duty probably consumed more of his energy than the other three combined. Indeed, he did not generally separate them but thought of them as part of the same enterprise.

Spurred by his leadership, the extent of Latter-day Saint colonization is impressive. Some 400 cities, towns, and villages were settled during his lifetime, and 342 more after his death—planted in twelve western states in the United States and in three foreign countries. Although 113 of these settlements were subsequently abandoned, even by the Mormons, more than 600 still serve his intended purpose today.

The colonization movement of the Church began seventeen years before the founding of Salt Lake City. In 1830, the Lord instructed the Church "to bring to pass the gathering of mine elect; . . . they shall be gathered in unto one place upon the face of this land" (D&C 29: 7–8). Their new Zion was to be "a land of peace. . . . And it shall come to pass that the righteous shall be gathered out from among all nations, and shall come to Zion" (D&C 45: 66, 71).

Under the precept defined by these and other revelations, Joseph Smith supervised the founding of more than a dozen settlements in Missouri, Illinois, and eastern Iowa. After being expelled from those places, the refugee Saints, now under the leadership of Brigham Young, planted scores of temporary towns in western Iowa and a few in eastern Nebraska. These were all virtually evacuated by 1853 as the Church moved away from its enemies.

As Brigham Young made his way to the Great Basin, the scope of the colonization program became clear to him: the Saints must occupy an area large enough to accommodate an influx of tens of thousands of Church members. Its borders must reach out to mountains or deserts to provide a barrier that would keep "gentile" colonies away. The inhabitable areas must be populated as quickly and as densely as possible to lay a valid claim on this vast area. Social and economic systems must be put in place to ensure independence and isolation from the outside world.

The first step was to explore the region. Within four days of his arrival in the Salt Lake Valley, Young had led an exploration of the valley and the adjacent Tooele Valley, noting the fertility of the soil and availability of water. Before the end of the year, expeditions examined prospective settlements in Davis, Weber, Box Elder, and Cache Valleys to the north; Utah Valley to the south; Cedar Valley to the west; and along both northern and southern routes to California.

In 1849, a party explored the Sanpete Valley, and at Chief Wakara's invitation, settlers were sent there. Later that year, the largest expedition of all spent two winter months reconnoitering central and southwestern Utah. From then to the end of the settlement period, numerous small explorations, some sent by the Church and some by private initiative, surveyed most of western North America, seeking suitable sites for colonization.

The next step was to set up a system of land distribution. Utah was still nominally part of Mexico until March 1848. But with the Mexican War in progress, no one looked at that country's laws. Even after the land had been annexed to the United States, federal law did not govern the ownership of land in Utah Territory until 1869. Characteristically, Brigham Young stepped in to fill the void. He told the immigrants of 1848:

> No man can ever buy land here, for no one has any land to sell. But every man shall have his land measured out to him, which he must cultivate in order to keep it. Besides, there shall be no private ownership of the streams that come out of the canyons, nor the timber that grows on the hills. These belong to the people.[1]

Community leaders assigned town lots, fields for farming, and pasture lands. Some towns had a "big field," fenced in common, in which each family had a large garden plot. Since large-scale irrigation was necessary in the dry climate, the riparian water rights of common law were replaced by a system wherein

> . . . the county court shall have control of all timber, water privileges, or any water course or creek, to grant mill sites, and exercise such powers as in their judgment shall best preserve the timber and subserve the interest of the settlement in the distribution of water for irrigation or other purposes.[2]

When Congress finally caught up to the Mormons on these issues, it recognized the wisdom of their system and ratified it. Land assigned to individuals became their personal property. The idea (although not entirely new) of public timber control, with cutting by concession, became the basis of United States Forest Service policy. The system of water rights evolved into a body of law that is still used throughout the West.

At first the Church organization handled everything; there was no need for statutes or civil government. However, the colony soon needed some type of legal structure to deal with its rapid growth and with the outside world. The ultimate goal was to enter the Union as a state. Young called a constitutional convention in March 1849 that created the "state of Deseret."

The boundaries of this state circumscribed the entire Great Basin and the Colorado River drainage, with an extension to take in the Pacific coast from San Pedro, just south of Los Angeles, to the Mexican border. This area included nearly all of Utah and Nevada, most of Arizona, nearly a third of California, and parts of Oregon, Idaho, Wyoming, Colorado, and New Mexico. The state of Deseret's form of government, modeled after that of other states, included the executive, legislative, and judicial branches.

In 1850, the Church's First Presidency reported:

> The General Assembly of Deseret have held an adjourned session, at intervals, through the winter, and transacted much important business, such as dividing the different settlements into Weber, Great Salt Lake, Utah, Sanpete, Yoab, and Tuille counties, and establishing County Courts, with their Judges, Clerks and Sheriffs, and Justices and Constables in the sev-

> eral precincts; also a Supreme Court, to hold its annual sessions at Great Salt Lake City, attended by a State Marshall and Attorney, and instituting a general jurisprudence, so that every case, whether criminal or civil, may be attended to by officers of State, according to law, justice, and equity, without delay. They have also chartered a State University.[3]

This government functioned conjointly with the Church organization at all levels, most officials serving in dual capacities. It operated for a year and a half with no other authority than the consent of the residents. Meanwhile, Deseret petitioned to the Union for admission as a state.

But the population was not yet sufficiently large to qualify for statehood. In any case, Congress was not inclined to grant such a huge area—or the status of statehood—to the hated Mormons. Instead, Congress created the Territory of Utah, with much reduced boundaries and authority. However, President Fillmore did appoint Brigham Young to be governor and permitted the retention of local bishops as magistrates. This left the Church some official status, and it was free to continue its colonizing efforts in the region.

The federal appointment also made President Young an Indian agent for the territory. He had already assumed this responsibility, having met with Indian leaders. He had also sent a military campaign to punish a band of Utes that had attacked settlers moving onto their land. While he did not believe in racial equality any more than anyone else of that day, he insisted that relations be paternally friendly and peaceful. In an 1875 letter to leaders in northeastern Arizona, Young states: "We request that in all your conversations and associations with the Lamanites you treat them with kindness and present before them an example which they can imitate with propriety."[4]

A third step in Young's pioneering program was to build an economic system that would free Zion from the need to deal with outside suppliers. Self-sufficiency would help keep out worldly influences. His goal was not to achieve affluence, which he saw as dangerous to the soul and counter-productive to the community, but to develop unity and cooperation among the Saints; his system was designed to that end.[5]

Early elements of the colonial infrastructure were built according to this principle. Farmers paid for the use of their land with work on roads, bridges, dams, and canals. Tradesmen in town paid their "labor tithing" by working in public works factories or construction.

A key effort involved using local resources. Men with skills in mining and smelting were called to start specialized colonies in Iron County, Utah, and in Las Vegas, Nevada. These missionaries did not usually take their families along, and although Irontown and Lead Mission were intended to be permanent industrial towns, most residents stayed only a year or two and did not think to make their homes there. Others were called to take their families and settle permanently in Washington County, Utah, to grow cotton and other warm-weather crops.

In order to establish control over this vast area and to make governmental and economic systems viable, it was necessary to increase the population as fast as possible. A more densely populated Zion would also be better able to nurture a society of Saints. Missionary work greatly expanded in the 1850s, and converts joined the Church by the thousands, especially in Britain, Scandinavia, and Switzerland. Over the next half century, the First Presidency of the Church strongly urged immigration to the new Zion.[6]

They came. The 1880 census shows that two-thirds of Utah residents were born outside the United States. They were told to learn English, to become American citizens as quickly as they could, and to take an active role in civic affairs. They did. Although immigrants tended to settle in groups of their own nationality, holding Church meetings and publishing newspapers in their own languages, the Mormon colonies are among the best examples of the American ethnic and social melting pot.

Since the plan called for colonization, not urbanization, and because conventional wisdom held that hard work on the farm was better for the soul than soft work in town, newcomers were most often sent to the smaller settlements. They found that the new towns always included veteran farmers and stockmen who knew what to do. They usually included a bishop or town president who, with his two counselors, administered both civil and

President Brigham Young and company at the confluence of the Colorado and Virgin Rivers, Arizona, Friday, 18 March 1870. President Young is seated on a chair in the center, wearing a top hat, white shirt, and dark vest. This was the farthest point south that Brigham Young reached during his entire residence in the West.

ecclesiastical affairs. Of course, each group tried to take along a miller, a weaver, a carpenter, a blacksmith, a fiddler, an interesting orator, and possessers of all the other skills and talents that constitute a successful community.

Sometimes Church members were called by Church leaders to colonize, a few of them unaware of their calling until their names were read out in a meeting. More often, a few were called to lead a group and to recruit the rest of the group. On occasion these leaders were called as temporary missionaries and stayed in the new village only a year or two to get things started. Many times, groups would strike out for promising areas on their own, with no authorization from Church officials beyond a tacit blessing on their enterprise.

On arrival in a valley, the pioneers located a good townsite, nearly always where a large stream issued from the mountains. As other pioneers joined them, the village grew, and satellite hamlets sprang up nearby. Colonization thus spread out unevenly: new settlements were being established at the edge of the frontier, while the existing central settlements were expanding.

Mormons typically did not make their homes on farms or ranches away from town. The ideal shape of society had been outlined in Joseph Smith's plan for the "City of Zion," wherein all were to live together and work cooperatively. Brigham Young based his advice and land distribution policy on that ideal, encouraging the Saints to live in small towns and commute out to their farms.[7]

The rationale for this method of colonizing was reiterated by a later Church Presidency:

> In all cases in making new settlements the Saints should be advised to gather together in villages, as has been our custom from the time of our earliest settlement in these mountain valleys. . . . By this means the people can retain their ecclesiastical organizations, have regular meetings of the quorums of the Priesthood and establish and maintain day and Sunday schools, Improvement Associations and Relief Societies; they can also co-operate for the good of all in financial and secular matters, in making ditches, fencing fields, building bridges and other necessary improvements. Further than this they are a mutual protection and source of strength against horse and cattle thieves, land jumpers, etc., and against hostile Indians, should there be any, while their compact organizations give them many advantages of a social and civil character which might be lost, misapplied or frittered away by spreading out so thinly that intercommunication is difficult, dangerous, inconvenient or expensive.[8]

This grand colonization plan produced a result that corresponds closely to Young's vision. He could not keep the "world" out of Zion or prevent its influences from affecting the Saints; but Mormonism now occupied its own domain, where it developed its own characteristic society—a community so distinctive that it has been studied as an ethnic group.

Sending gifted people with leadership qualities and other skills out to the settlements might appear to be dispersing talent, reducing the effective pool. In fact, however, it appears that these people brought much more than good management to their scattered villages. Among frontier settlements, Mormons had higher than average educational and cultural activities. Thus, many of these small towns produced individuals who achieved promi-

"Company 6" of seven companies crossing Hams Fork not far from Kemmerer, Wyoming. The colonizers met at Hams Fork on 25 April 1900. The last company left Hams Fork on 3 May 1900 and reached the Big Horn Basin on 24 May 1900.

nence in various fields, including a much higher than average proportion of notable women.[9]

Fifty years of migratory "gathering to Zion" was sufficient to fulfill the purpose. As late as 1897, George Q. Cannon of the Church's First Presidency advised members to come to Utah. However, by this time the rural economy of the region was straining to support so many people who had growing expectations of a modern lifestyle. And the number of members outside the United States was increasing rapidly.

In 1898, President Cannon announced a new policy.[10] Henceforth, Zion would be defined as being wherever the pure in heart meet in the name of the Lord. Members outside the area were counseled to stay where they were and, after the pattern set in the Mormon colonies, build up the Church in their own lands. Immigration decreased thereafter, but hardy pioneers in the younger generation were still able to colonize new lands as they became available. At a declining pace, new Mormon colonizing continued for another thirty years.

THE COLONIES

Milton R. Hunter broke ground with his list of Mormon settlements in the 1930s,[11] but his resources were limited, and his period covered only Brigham Young's lifetime. Lynn Albert Rosenvall took the list up to 1900 in his thesis of 1972.[12] This writer, while doing research for the Museum of Church History and Art, found more nineteenth-century communities and others that were founded as Latter-day Saint colonies up to 1930. The inventory now stands at a total of 742 in the western United States, Canada, Mexico, and Polynesia. This figure may yet be incomplete, but nearly final.

TOWN	COUNTY	STATE/*NATION*	YEAR
New Hope	Stanislaus	CALIFORNIA	1846
Salt Lake City	Salt Lake	UTAH	1847
Bountiful	Davis	UTAH	1847
Farmington	Davis	UTAH	1847
Pleasant Green	Salt Lake	UTAH	1847
Snyderville	Summit	UTAH	1847
Big Cottonwood	Salt Lake	UTAH	1848
Centerville	Davis	UTAH	1848
East Millcreek	Salt Lake	UTAH	1848
Mound Fort	Weber	UTAH	1848
North Salt Lake	Davis	UTAH	1848
Natoma	Stanislaus	CALIFORNIA	1848
Ogden	Weber	UTAH	1848
South Cottonwood	Salt Lake	UTAH	1848
South Ogden	Weber	UTAH	1848
Sugar House	Salt Lake	UTAH	1848
Taylorsville	Salt Lake	UTAH	1848

West Jordan	Salt Lake	UTAH	1848
Woods Cross	Davis	UTAH	1848
Brighton	Salt Lake	UTAH	1849
Draper	Salt Lake	UTAH	1849
Genoa	Douglas	NEVADA	1849
Granger	Salt Lake	UTAH	1849
Kaysville	Davis	UTAH	1849
Lynne	Weber	UTAH	1849
Manti	Sanpete	UTAH	1849
Marriott	Weber	UTAH	1849
Mills Junction	Tooele	UTAH	1849
Northpoint	Salt Lake	UTAH	1849
Provo	Utah	UTAH	1849
Tooele	Tooele	UTAH	1849
Union	Salt Lake	UTAH	1849
Alpine	Utah	UTAH	1850
American Fork	Utah	UTAH	1850
Grantsville	Tooele	UTAH	1850
Harrisville	Weber	UTAH	1850
Irontown	Iron	UTAH	1850
Lakeview	Tooele	UTAH	1850
Layton	Davis	UTAH	1850
Lehi	Utah	UTAH	1850
Lindon	Utah	UTAH	1850
North Ogden	Weber	UTAH	1850
Parley's Park	Summit	UTAH	1850
Payson	Utah	UTAH	1850

Pleasant Grove	Utah	UTAH	1850
Pleasant View	Utah	UTAH	1850
Riverdale	Weber	UTAH	1850
Slaterville	Weber	UTAH	1850
Spanish Fork	Utah	UTAH	1850
Springville	Utah	UTAH	1850
Uintah	Weber	UTAH	1850
West Weber	Weber	UTAH	1850
Brigham City	Box Elder	UTAH	1851
Cedar City	Iron	UTAH	1851
Enoch	Iron	UTAH	1851
Farr West	Weber	UTAH	1851
Fillmore	Millard	UTAH	1851
Herriman	Salt Lake	UTAH	1851
Midvale	Salt Lake	UTAH	1851
Millcreek	Salt Lake	UTAH	1851
Mona	Juab	UTAH	1851
Nephi	Juab	UTAH	1851
Parowan	Iron	UTAH	1851
Pleasant View	Weber	UTAH	1851
Salem	Utah	UTAH	1851
San Bernardino	S. B.	CALIFORNIA	1851
Santaquin	Utah	UTAH	1851
South Weber	Davis	UTAH	1851
Taylor	Weber	UTAH	1851
Willard	Box Elder	UTAH	1851
Cedar Fort	Utah	UTAH	1852

Erda	Tooele	UTAH	1852
Hamilton's Fort	Iron	UTAH	1852
Harper	Box Elder	UTAH	1852
Mount Pleasant	Sanpete	UTAH	1852
New Harmony	Washington	UTAH	1852
Palmyra	Utah	UTAH	1852
[Panther Lake]	Kitsap	WASHINGTON	1852
Paragonah	Iron	UTAH	1852
Spring City	Sanpete	UTAH	1852
Fort Supply	Uinta	WYOMING	1853
Perry	Box Elder	UTAH	1853
West Warren	Weber	UTAH	1853
Wilson	Weber	UTAH	1853
Clover	Tooele	UTAH	1854
Crescent	Salt Lake	UTAH	1854
Ephraim	Sanpete	UTAH	1854
Ephraim, Lanai	Maui	HAWAII	1854
Fort Saint Luke	Utah	UTAH	1854
Hatton	Millard	UTAH	1854
Hooper	Weber	UTAH	1854
Lake Point	Tooele	UTAH	1854
Santa Clara	Washington	UTAH	1854
Wanship	Summit	UTAH	1854
College	Cache	UTAH	1855
Fairfield	Utah	UTAH	1855
Fort Lemhi	Lemhi	IDAHO	1855
Fort Bridger	Uinta	WYOMING	1855

Holden	Millard	UTAH	1855
Lakeview	Utah	UTAH	1855
Las Vegas	Clark	NEVADA	1855
Moab	Grand	UTAH	1855
Morgan	Morgan	UTAH	1855
Peterson	Morgan	UTAH	1855
Pine Valley	Washington	UTAH	1855
Portage	Box Elder	UTAH	1855
Beaver	Beaver	UTAH	1856
Frankton	Washoe	NEVADA	1856
Hamblin	Washington	UTAH	1856
Littleton	Morgan	UTAH	1856
Mapleton	Utah	UTAH	1856
Milton	Morgan	UTAH	1856
Pinto	Washington	UTAH	1856
Wellsville	Cache	UTAH	1856
Goshen	Utah	UTAH	1857
Grafton	Washington	UTAH	1857
Gunlock	Washington	UTAH	1857
Meadow	Millard	UTAH	1857
Mendon	Cache	UTAH	1857
Mountain Green	Morgan	UTAH	1857
Peoa	Summit	UTAH	1857
Supply City	Uinta	WYOMING	1857
Washington	Washington	UTAH	1857
Deseret	Millard	UTAH	1858
North Creek	Beaver	UTAH	1858

Price	Washington	UTAH	1858
Shivwits	Washington	UTAH	1858
Virgin	Washington	UTAH	1858
Charleston	Wasatch	UTAH	1859
Cluff	Summit	UTAH	1859
Coalville	Summit	UTAH	1859
East Porterville	Morgan	UTAH	1859
Eden	Weber	UTAH	1859
Fairview	Sanpete	UTAH	1859
Fountain Green	Sanpete	UTAH	1859
Gunnison	Sanpete	UTAH	1859
Harrisburg	Washington	UTAH	1859
Heber	Wasatch	UTAH	1859
Henefer	Summit	UTAH	1859
Hoytsville	Summit	UTAH	1859
Ibapah	Tooele	UTAH	1859
Kanosh	Millard	UTAH	1859
Logan	Cache	UTAH	1859
Manderfield	Beaver	UTAH	1859
Midway	Wasatch	UTAH	1859
Millville	Cache	UTAH	1859
Minersville	Beaver	UTAH	1859
Moroni	Sanpete	UTAH	1859
Mound City	Wasatch	UTAH	1859
Mounds	Emery	UTAH	1859
Plain City	Weber	UTAH	1859
Providence	Cache	UTAH	1859

Richmond	Cache	UTAH	1859
Smithfield	Cache	UTAH	1859
South Jordan	Salt Lake	UTAH	1859
Springlake	Utah	UTAH	1859
Summit	Iron	UTAH	1859
Tonaquint	Washington	UTAH	1859
Toquerville	Washington	UTAH	1859
Adventure	Washington	UTAH	1860
Avon	Cache	UTAH	1860
Benjamin	Utah	UTAH	1860
Center Creek	Wasatch	UTAH	1860
Cove Fort	Millard	UTAH	1860
Franklin	Franklin	IDAHO	1860
Greenville	Beaver	UTAH	1860
Huntsville	Weber	UTAH	1860
Hyde Park	Cache	UTAH	1860
Hyrum	Cache	UTAH	1860
Juab	Juab	UTAH	1860
Kamas	Summit	UTAH	1860
North Morgan	Morgan	UTAH	1860
Paradise	Cache	UTAH	1860
Porterville	Morgan	UTAH	1860
Richville	Morgan	UTAH	1860
Rockport	Summit	UTAH	1860
Scipio	Millard	UTAH	1860
Duncan's Retreat	Washington	UTAH	1861
Echo	Summit	UTAH	1861

Enterprise	Morgan	UTAH	1861
Enterprise	Washington	UTAH	1861
Fayette	Sanpete	UTAH	1861
Honeyville	Box Elder	UTAH	1861
Kanarraville	Iron	UTAH	1861
Mountain Dell	Salt Lake	UTAH	1861
Mountain Dell	Washington	UTAH	1861
Pintura	Washington	UTAH	1861
Rockville	Washington	UTAH	1861
St. George	Washington	UTAH	1861
Upton	Summit	UTAH	1861
Adamsville	Beaver	UTAH	1862
Croydon	Morgan	UTAH	1862
Hebron	Washington	UTAH	1862
Northrup	Washington	UTAH	1862
Shonesburg	Washington	UTAH	1862
Springdale	Washington	UTAH	1862
Vernon	Tooele	UTAH	1862
Wallsburg	Wasatch	UTAH	1862
Zion	Washington	UTAH	1862
Ajax	Tooele	UTAH	1863
Cheney's Ranch	Juab	UTAH	1863
Foster's Ranch	Washington	UTAH	1863
Mantua	Box Elder	UTAH	1863
Middleton	Washington	UTAH	1863
Monroe	Sevier	UTAH	1863
Nashville	Franklin	IDAHO	1863

Paris	Bear Lake	IDAHO	1863
Pipe Springs	Mohave	ARIZONA	1863
Salina	Sevier	UTAH	1863
Bennington	Bear Lake	IDAHO	1864
Bloomington	Bear Lake	IDAHO	1864
Call's Landing	Clark	NEVADA	1864
Circleville	Paiute	UTAH	1864
Clarkston	Cache	UTAH	1864
Clinton	Davis	UTAH	1864
Dalton	Washington	UTAH	1864
Deweyville	Box Elder	UTAH	1864
Eden	Jerome	IDAHO	1864
Fish Haven	Bear Lake	IDAHO	1864
Glendale	Kane	UTAH	1864
Glenwood	Sevier	UTAH	1864
Indianola	Sanpete	UTAH	1864
Joseph	Sevier	UTAH	1864
Kanab	Kane	UTAH	1864
Laketown	Rich	UTAH	1864
Liberty	Bear Lake	IDAHO	1864
Malad	Oneida	IDAHO	1864
Marsh Valley	Bannock	IDAHO	1864
Marysvale	Paiute	UTAH	1864
Moccasin	Mohave	ARIZONA	1864
Montpelier	Bear Lake	IDAHO	1864
Mount Carmel	Kane	UTAH	1864
Ovid	Bear Lake	IDAHO	1864

Oxford	Franklin	IDAHO	1864
Panaca	Lincoln	NEVADA	1864
Panguitch	Garfield	UTAH	1864
Richfield	Sevier	UTAH	1864
Round Valley	Rich	UTAH	1864
St. Charles	Bear Lake	IDAHO	1864
Walnut Grove	Yavapai	ARIZONA	1864
Alton	Kane	UTAH	1865
Bluffdale	Salt Lake	UTAH	1865
Cherry Creek	Oneida	IDAHO	1865
Eagle Valley	Lincoln	NEVADA	1865
Laie, Oahu	Honolulu	HAWAII	1865
Littlefield	Mohave	ARIZONA	1865
Logandale	Clark	NEVADA	1865
Milburn	Sanpete	UTAH	1865
Mill Point	Clark	NEVADA	1865
Mound Valley	Franklin	IDAHO	1865
Oak City	Millard	UTAH	1865
Paria	Kane	UTAH	1865
Saint Thomas	Clark	NEVADA	1865
Simonsville	Clark	NEVADA	1865
Spring Valley	Lincoln	NEVADA	1865
Wardboro	Bear Lake	IDAHO	1865
Weston	Franklin	IDAHO	1865
Woodruff	Oneida	IDAHO	1865
Bear River City	Box Elder	UTAH	1866
Beaver Dam	Box Elder	UTAH	1866

Fort Sanford	Garfield	UTAH	1866
Thatcher	Franklin	IDAHO	1866
Elephant	Wayne	UTAH	1867
Leeds	Washington	UTAH	1867
Petersboro	Cache	UTAH	1867
Saint John	Tooele	UTAH	1867
Sandy Town	Clark	NEVADA	1867
West Point	Davis	UTAH	1867
Dayton	Franklin	IDAHO	1868
Kanesville	Weber	UTAH	1868
Levan	Juab	UTAH	1868
Newton	Cache	UTAH	1868
Oakley	Summit	UTAH	1868
Ridgedale	Oneida	IDAHO	1868
Samaria	Oneida	IDAHO	1868
St. John	Oneida	IDAHO	1868
Treasureton	Franklin	IDAHO	1868
Cleveland	Franklin	IDAHO	1869
Clifton	Franklin	IDAHO	1869
Eureka	Juab	UTAH	1869
Fairview	Franklin	IDAHO	1869
Junction City	Clark	NEVADA	1869
Meadowville	Rich	UTAH	1869
Overton	Clark	NEVADA	1869
Park Valley	Box Elder	UTAH	1869
Plymouth	Box Elder	UTAH	1869
Skull Valley	Tooele	UTAH	1869

Wales	Sanpete	UTAH	1869
West Point	Clark	NEVADA	1869
Cambridge	Bannock	IDAHO	1870
Cannon	Salt Lake	UTAH	1870
Chester	Sanpete	UTAH	1870
Clover Valley	Lincoln	NEVADA	1870
Lewiston	Cache	UTAH	1870
Milford	Beaver	UTAH	1870
Randolph	Rich	UTAH	1870
Riverton	Salt Lake	UTAH	1870
Scutumpah	Kane	UTAH	1870
Trenton	Cache	UTAH	1870
Woodruff	Rich	UTAH	1870
Annabella	Sevier	UTAH	1871
Benson	Cache	UTAH	1871
Cove	Cache	UTAH	1871
Dingle	Bear Lake	IDAHO	1871
Freedom	Sanpete	UTAH	1871
Georgetown	Bear Lake	IDAHO	1871
Hillsdale	Garfield	UTAH	1871
Johnson	Kane	UTAH	1871
Leamington	Millard	UTAH	1871
Mayfield	Sanpete	UTAH	1871
Moencopi	Coconino	ARIZONA	1871
Pioche	Lincoln	NEVADA	1871
Sandy	Salt Lake	UTAH	1871
Snowville	Box Elder	UTAH	1871

Soda Springs	Caribou	IDAHO	1871
Vermilion	Sevier	UTAH	1871
Asay Town	Garfield	UTAH	1872
Ashley	Uintah	UTAH	1872
Central	Sevier	UTAH	1872
Hatch	Garfield	UTAH	1872
Lake Shore	Utah	UTAH	1872
Lee's Ferry	Coconino	ARIZONA	1872
Mink Creek	Franklin	IDAHO	1872
Preston	Franklin	IDAHO	1872
Riverdale	Franklin	IDAHO	1872
Sterling	Sanpete	UTAH	1872
Warren	Weber	UTAH	1872
Adairville	Kane	UTAH	1873
Antimony	Garfield	UTAH	1873
Bern	Bear Lake	IDAHO	1873
Burrville	Sevier	UTAH	1873
Elba	Cassia	IDAHO	1873
Prattville	Sevier	UTAH	1873
Tuba City	Coconino	ARIZONA	1873
Venice	Sevier	UTAH	1873
Whitney	Franklin	IDAHO	1873
Buysville	Wasatch	UTAH	1874
Cannonville	Garfield	UTAH	1874
Clinton	Utah	UTAH	1874
Crafton	Millard	UTAH	1874
Daniel	Wasatch	UTAH	1874

Elsinore	Sevier	UTAH	1874
Grass Valley	Washington	UTAH	1874
Greenwich	Paiute	UTAH	1874
Koosharem	Sevier	UTAH	1874
Mount Trumbull	Mohave	ARIZONA	1874
Orderville	Kane	UTAH	1874
Thatcher	Box Elder	UTAH	1874
Woodland	Summit	UTAH	1874
Albion	Cassia	IDAHO	1875
Argyle	Rich	UTAH	1875
Aurora	Sevier	UTAH	1875
Carterville	Utah	UTAH	1875
Chesterfield	Caribou	IDAHO	1875
Collinston	Box Elder	UTAH	1875
Escalante	Garfield	UTAH	1875
Kahana, Oahu	Honolulu	HAWAII	1875
Mapleton	Franklin	IDAHO	1875
Marion	Summit	UTAH	1875
Nounan	Bear Lake	IDAHO	1875
Redmond	Sevier	UTAH	1875
Washakie	Box Elder	UTAH	1875
Brigham City	Navajo	ARIZONA	1876
Clifton	Garfield	UTAH	1876
Fremont	Wayne	UTAH	1876
Grouse Creek	Box Elder	UTAH	1876
Hunter	Salt Lake	UTAH	1876
Joseph City	Navajo	ARIZONA	1876

Kingston	Paiute	UTAH	1876
Millville	Coconino	ARIZONA	1876
Obed	Navajo	ARIZONA	1876
Ramah	McKinley	NEW MEXICO	1876
Raymond	Bear Lake	IDAHO	1876
Seboyeta	Valencia	NEW MEXICO	1876
Sunset	Navajo	ARIZONA	1876
Tonto Basin	Gila	ARIZONA	1876
Widtsoe	Garfield	UTAH	1876
Woodruff	Navajo	ARIZONA	1876
Austin	Sevier	UTAH	1877
Bunkerville	Clark	NEVADA	1877
Castledale	Emery	UTAH	1877
Dover	Sanpete	UTAH	1877
Etna	Box Elder	UTAH	1877
Ferron	Emery	UTAH	1877
Garden Creek	Bannock	IDAHO	1877
Garden City	Rich	UTAH	1877
Granite	Salt Lake	UTAH	1877
Huntington	Emery	UTAH	1877
Jensen	Uintah	UTAH	1877
Lake Creek	Wasatch	UTAH	1877
Lanark	Bear Lake	IDAHO	1877
Loa	Wayne	UTAH	1877
Orangeville	Emery	UTAH	1877
Orem	Utah	UTAH	1877
Papago	Maricopa	ARIZONA	1877

Price	Carbon	UTAH	1877
Showlow	Navajo	ARIZONA	1877
St. David	Cochise	ARIZONA	1877
Syracuse	Davis	UTAH	1877
Wellington	Carbon	UTAH	1877
Almo	Cassia	IDAHO	1878
Basin	Cassia	IDAHO	1878
Conejos	Conejos	COLORADO	1878
Forest Dale	Navajo	ARIZONA	1878
Fort Moroni	Coconino	ARIZONA	1878
Fruitland	San Juan	NEW MEXICO	1878
Gooseberry	Sevier	UTAH	1878
Holbrook	Oneida	IDAHO	1878
Maeser	Uintah	UTAH	1878
Mazatzal	Yavapai	ARIZONA	1878
Mesa	Maricopa	ARIZONA	1878
Molen	Emery	UTAH	1878
Mountain Dell	Uintah	UTAH	1878
Naples	Uintah	UTAH	1878
Oasis	Millard	UTAH	1878
Pine	Gila	ARIZONA	1878
Pinedale	Navajo	ARIZONA	1878
Reidhead	Navajo	ARIZONA	1878
Snowflake	Navajo	ARIZONA	1878
Taylor (#1)	Navajo	ARIZONA	1878
Taylor (#2)	Navajo	ARIZONA	1878
Vernal	Uintah	UTAH	1878

Adair	Navajo	ARIZONA	1879
Alpine	Apache	ARIZONA	1879
Annis	Jefferson	IDAHO	1879
Auburn	Lincoln	WYOMING	1879
Bicknell	Wayne	UTAH	1879
Bloomington	Washington	UTAH	1879
Eager	Apache	ARIZONA	1879
Ephraim	Conejos	COLORADO	1879
Erastus	Apache	ARIZONA	1879
Freedom	Lincoln	WYOMING	1879
Greer	Apache	ARIZONA	1879
Hunt	Apache	ARIZONA	1879
Junction	Paiute	UTAH	1879
Lawrence	Emery	UTAH	1879
Linden	Navajo	ARIZONA	1879
Manassa	Conejos	COLORADO	1879
Meadows	Apache	ARIZONA	1879
Menan	Jefferson	IDAHO	1879
Nutrioso	Apache	ARIZONA	1879
Parker	Fremont	IDAHO	1879
Pima	Graham	ARIZONA	1879
Pleasant Valley	Carbon	UTAH	1879
Rockland	Power	IDAHO	1879
Scofield	Carbon	UTAH	1879
Shumway	Navajo	ARIZONA	1879
Spring Glen	Carbon	UTAH	1879
Springerville	Apache	ARIZONA	1879

St. Johns	Apache	ARIZONA	1879
Teasdale	Wayne	UTAH	1879
Alma	Maricopa	ARIZONA	1880
Bluff	San Juan	UTAH	1880
Carey	Blaine	IDAHO	1880
Edgemont	Utah	UTAH	1880
Egin	Fremont	IDAHO	1880
Glenbar	Graham	ARIZONA	1880
Glines	Uintah	UTAH	1880
Lorenzo	Jefferson	IDAHO	1880
Mancos	Montezuma	COLORADO	1880
Mesquite	Clark	NEVADA	1880
Montezuma	San Juan	UTAH	1880
Oakley	Cassia	IDAHO	1880
Richfield	Conejos	COLORADO	1880
Torrey	Wayne	UTAH	1880
Eden	Graham	ARIZONA	1881
Emery	Emery	UTAH	1881
Graham	Graham	ARIZONA	1881
Holbrook	Navajo	ARIZONA	1881
Marion	Cassia	IDAHO	1881
Neeley	Power	IDAHO	1881
Thatcher	Graham	ARIZONA	1881
Aldridgeville	Wayne	UTAH	1882
Centerfield	Sanpete	UTAH	1882
Central	Graham	ARIZONA	1882
Hatch	Caribou	IDAHO	1882

Lewisville	Jefferson	IDAHO	1882
Lyman	Madison	IDAHO	1882
Lynne	Box Elder	UTAH	1882
MacDonald	Cochise	ARIZONA	1882
Moulton	Cassia	IDAHO	1882
Pleasanton	Capron	NEW MEXICO	1882
Rexburg	Madison	IDAHO	1882
Richville	Apache	ARIZONA	1882
River Heights	Cache	UTAH	1882
Tempe	Maricopa	ARIZONA	1882
Alma	Capron	NEW MEXICO	1883
Archer	Madison	IDAHO	1883
Bryce	Graham	ARIZONA	1883
Caineville	Wayne	UTAH	1883
Giles	Wayne	UTAH	1883
Hanksville	Wayne	UTAH	1883
Heber	Navajo	ARIZONA	1883
Henrieville	Garfield	UTAH	1883
Hibbard	Madison	IDAHO	1883
Iona	Bonneville	IDAHO	1883
La Plata	San Juan	NEW MEXICO	1883
Layton	Graham	ARIZONA	1883
Luna	Capron	NEW MEXICO	1883
Pleasant View	Oneida	IDAHO	1883
Rigby	Jefferson	IDAHO	1883
Safford	Graham	ARIZONA	1883
Salem	Madison	IDAHO	1883

Teton	Fremont	IDAHO	1883
Ucon	Bonneville	IDAHO	1883
Wilford	Navajo	ARIZONA	1883
Wilford	Fremont	IDAHO	1883
Bothwell	Box Elder	UTAH	1884
Burton	Madison	IDAHO	1884
Jaroso	Costilla	COLORADO	1884
Labelle	Jefferson	IDAHO	1884
Ririe	Jefferson	IDAHO	1884
Afton	Lincoln	WYOMING	1885
Basalt	Bingham	IDAHO	1885
Cleveland	Emery	UTAH	1885
Colonia Juarez		CHIHUAHUA, *MEXICO*	1885
Colonia Díaz		CHIHUAHUA, *MEXICO*	1885
Deep Creek	Duchesne	UTAH	1885
Fairview	Lincoln	WYOMING	1885
Franklin	Graham	ARIZONA	1885
Grover	Lincoln	WYOMING	1885
Lakeside	Navajo	ARIZONA	1885
Morgan	Conejos	COLORADO	1885
Notom	Wayne	UTAH	1885
Poplar	Bonneville	IDAHO	1885
Riverside	Bingham	IDAHO	1885
Sanford	Conejos	COLORADO	1885
Shelley	Bingham	IDAHO	1885
Spry	Garfield	UTAH	1885

Taylor	Bonneville	IDAHO	1885
Victor	Emery	UTAH	1885
Ellwood	Box Elder	UTAH	1886
Georgetown	Kane	UTAH	1886
Mill Fork	Utah	UTAH	1886
Mountain View	Costilla	COLORADO	1886
Osmond	Lincoln	WYOMING	1886
Blanca	Costilla	COLORADO	1887
Cardston		ALBERTA, *CANADA*	1887
Cave Valley		CHIHUAHUA, *MEXICO*	1887
Colonia Pacheco		CHIHUAHUA, *MEXICO*	1887
Fox Creek	Conejos	COLORADO	1887
Fredonia	Coconino	ARIZONA	1887
Lehi	Maricopa	ARIZONA	1887
Monticello	San Juan	UTAH	1887
Nephi	Maricopa	ARIZONA	1887
Smoot	Lincoln	WYOMING	1887
Verdure	San Juan	UTAH	1887
Aetna		ALBERTA, *CANADA*	1888
Beulah	Rio Arriba	NEW MEXICO	1888
Cokeville	Lincoln	WYOMING	1888
Gandy	Millard	UTAH	1888
Chester	Fremont	IDAHO	1888
Geneva	Bear Lake	IDAHO	1888
Lago	Caribou	IDAHO	1888
Thayne	Lincoln	WYOMING	1888

Ammon	Bonneville	IDAHO	1889
Bates	Teton	IDAHO	1889
Boulder	Garfield	UTAH	1889
Bynum	Teton	MONTANA	1889
Colonia Dublán		CHIHUAHUA, *MEXICO*	1889
Eastdale	Costilla	COLORADO	1889
Grace	Caribou	IDAHO	1889
Iosepa	Tooele	UTAH	1889
Marysville	Fremont	IDAHO	1889
Tetonia	Teton	IDAHO	1889
Victor	Teton	IDAHO	1889
Abraham	Millard	UTAH	1890
Bedford	Lincoln	WYOMING	1890
Cascade	Cascade	MONTANA	1890
Central	Caribou	IDAHO	1890
Fielding	Box Elder	UTAH	1890
Garland	Box Elder	UTAH	1890
Malta	Cassia	IDAHO	1890
Manila	Utah	UTAH	1890
Mountain View		ALBERTA, *CANADA*	1890
North Logan	Cache	UTAH	1890
Turnerville	Lincoln	WYOMING	1890
Vernon	Apache	ARIZONA	1890
Beazer		ALBERTA, *CANADA*	1891
Hinckley	Millard	UTAH	1891
Pinetop	Navajo	ARIZONA	1891
Tropic	Garfield	UTAH	1891

Colonia Oaxaca		SONORA, *MEXICO*	1892
Fruita	Wayne	UTAH	1892
Liberty	Weber	UTAH	1892
Lund	Caribou	IDAHO	1892
Lyman	Uinta	WYOMING	1892
Romeo	Conejos	COLORADO	1892
Arbon	Power	IDAHO	1893
Burlington	Big Horn	WYOMING	1893
Byron	Big Horn	WYOMING	1893
Leavitt		ALBERTA, *CANADA*	1893
Lyman	Wayne	UTAH	1893
Bench	Caribou	IDAHO	1894
Bluewater	Valencia	NEW MEXICO	1894
Chuichupa		CHIHUAHUA, *MEXICO*	1894
Colonia García		CHIHUAHUA, *MEXICO*	1894
Driggs	Teton	IDAHO	1894
Moreland	Bingham	IDAHO	1894
Otto	Big Horn	WYOMING	1894
Riverside	Box Elder	UTAH	1894
Clawson	Emery	UTAH	1895
Galeana		CHIHUAHUA, *MEXICO*	1895
Meadow	Oneida	IDAHO	1895
Rich	Bingham	IDAHO	1895
Sigurd	Sevier	UTAH	1895
Buckhorn Springs	Iron	UTAH	1896

Hurricane	Washington	UTAH	1896
Kimball	Graham	ARIZONA	1896
Manila	Daggett	UTAH	1896
Moore	Emery	UTAH	1896
Bench Creek	Wasatch	UTAH	1897
Kimball		ALBERTA, *CANADA*	1897
Knightsville	Utah	UTAH	1897
Lund	White Pine	NEVADA	1897
Newcastle	Iron	UTAH	1897
Sharon	Bear Lake	IDAHO	1897
Turner	Caribou	IDAHO	1897
Caldwell		ALBERTA, *CANADA*	1898
Georgetown	White Pine	NEVADA	1898
Jackson	Teton	WYOMING	1898
La Verkin	Washington	UTAH	1898
Magrath		ALBERTA, *CANADA*	1898
Millburne	Uinta	WYOMING	1898
Mormon Row	Teton	WYOMING	1898
Mountain View	Uinta	WYOMING	1898
Preston	White Pine	NEVADA	1898
Standrod	Box Elder	UTAH	1898
Stirling		ALBERTA, *CANADA*	1898
Taylorville		ALBERTA, *CANADA*	1898
Thistle	Utah	UTAH	1898
Wilson	Teton	WYOMING	1898
Francis	Summit	UTAH	1899
Reed	Beaver	UTAH	1899

Roy	Weber	UTAH	1899
Vineyard	Utah	UTAH	1899
Algodon	Graham	ARIZONA	1900
Alpine	Lincoln	WYOMING	1900
Artesia	Graham	ARIZONA	1900
Basin	Big Horn	WYOMING	1900
Brooklyn	Sevier	UTAH	1900
Colonia Morelos		SONORA, *MEXICO*	1900
Cowley	Big Horn	WYOMING	1900
Kane	Big Horn	WYOMING	1900
Kirtland	San Juan	NEW MEXICO	1900
Leland	Utah	UTAH	1900
Lovell	Big Horn	WYOMING	1900
Nibley	Union	OREGON	1900
Niter	Caribou	IDAHO	1900
Welling		ALBERTA, *CANADA*	1900
Woolford		ALBERTA, *CANADA*	1900
Hammond	San Juan	NEW MEXICO	1901
Orton		ALBERTA, *CANADA*	1901
Raymond		ALBERTA, *CANADA*	1901
Frankburg		ALBERTA, *CANADA*	1902
Taber		ALBERTA, *CANADA*	1902
Mapusaga, Tutuila		*SAMOA*	1903
Sauniatu, Upolo		*SAMOA*	1903
Blanding	San Juan	UTAH	1904
Bancroft	Caribou	IDAHO	1905
Colonia San José		SONORA, *MEXICO*	1905

Duchesne	Duchesne	UTAH	1905
Heyburn	Minidoka	IDAHO	1905
Lapoint	Uintah	UTAH	1905
Midview	Duchesne	UTAH	1905
Randlett	Uintah	UTAH	1905
Strawberry	Duchesne	UTAH	1905
Tabiona	Duchesne	UTAH	1905
Talmage	Duchesne	UTAH	1905
Tridell	Uintah	UTAH	1905
Watson	Uintah	UTAH	1905
Ballard	Uintah	UTAH	1906
Bennett	Uintah	UTAH	1906
Boneta	Duchesne	UTAH	1906
Hayden	Uintah	UTAH	1906
Jackson	Cassia	IDAHO	1906
Kiz	Carbon	UTAH	1906
Monarch	Duchesne	UTAH	1906
Mount Emmons	Duchesne	UTAH	1906
Neola	Duchesne	UTAH	1906
Theodore	Duchesne	UTAH	1906
Utahn	Duchesne	UTAH	1906
Arcadia	Duchesne	UTAH	1907
Bluebell	Duchesne	UTAH	1907
Cedarview	Duchesne	UTAH	1907
Clearfield	Davis	UTAH	1907
Cornish	Cache	UTAH	1907
Delta	Millard	UTAH	1907

Hartford	Duchesne	UTAH	1907
Ioka	Duchesne	UTAH	1907
Malaeimi, Tutuila		*SAMOA*	1907
Roosevelt	Duchesne	UTAH	1907
Upalco	Duchesne	UTAH	1907
Glenwood		ALBERTA, *CANADA*	1908
Mountain Home	Duchesne	UTAH	1908
Buist	Oneida	IDAHO	1909
Carson	Taos	NEW MEXICO	1909
Crystal	Power	IDAHO	1909
Etna	Lincoln	WYOMING	1909
Summit	Oneida	IDAHO	1909
Hillspring		ALBERTA, *CANADA*	1910
Leeton	Uintah	UTAH	1910
Pauline	Power	IDAHO	1910
Rosette	Box Elder	UTAH	1910
Sharon	Utah	UTAH	1910
Trailton	Bingham	IDAHO	1910
Penrose	Box Elder	UTAH	1911
Sutherland	Millard	UTAH	1911
Altonah	Duchesne	UTAH	1912
Antelope	Duchesne	UTAH	1912
Axtell	Sanpete	UTAH	1912
Davis	Uintah	UTAH	1912
Elmo	Emery	UTAH	1912
Grover	Wayne	UTAH	1912
La Sal	San Juan	UTAH	1912

Virden	Hidalgo	NEW MEXICO	1912
Sugarville	Millard	UTAH	1913
Benmore	Tooele	UTAH	1914
Blue Creek	Box Elder	UTAH	1914
Bluemesa	Duchesne	UTAH	1916
Cedar Creek	Box Elder	UTAH	1916
Little Cottonwood	Salt Lake	UTAH	1916
Sevier	Sevier	UTAH	1916
Sunset	Davis	UTAH	1916
Deaver	Big Horn	WYOMING	1917
Emerson	Minidoka	IDAHO	1917
Leota	Uintah	UTAH	1917
Altera	Uintah	UTAH	1918
Amalga	Cache	UTAH	1918
Central	Washington	UTAH	1918
Gusher	Uintah	UTAH	1918
Stoddard	Morgan	UTAH	1918
Veyo	Washington	UTAH	1918
Genola	Utah	UTAH	1919
McCornick	Millard	UTAH	1919
Flowell	Millard	UTAH	1920
Nibley	Cache	UTAH	1920
Montwell	Duchesne	UTAH	1921
Greenwood	Millard	UTAH	1923
Ivins	Washington	UTAH	1926
Vaiola, Savai'i		*SAMOA*	1929
Gordon Creek	Carbon	UTAH	1930

NOTES

1. Ray Billington, *Westward Expansion: A History of the American Frontier,* 3rd ed. (New York: McMillan, 1967), 542.

2. Ibid., 544.

3. "Third General Epistle of the First Presidency," 12 April 1850, in James R. Clark, comp., *Messages of the First Presidency of The Church of Jesus Christ of Latter-day Saints,* 6 vols. (Salt Lake City: Bookcraft, 1965–75), 2: 45.

4. Brigham Young and Daniel H. Wells to Elders Smith, Ballinger, Allen, and the Brethren encamped on the Little Colorado, 15 July 1875, as quoted in Clark, 2: 274.

5. Leonard J. Arrington, *Great Basin Kingdom: An Economic History of the Latter-day Saints, 1830–1900* (Lincoln: University of Nebraska Press, 1966), 26–27.

6. Milton R. Hunter, *Brigham Young the Colonizer* (Salt Lake City: Deseret News Press, 1940), 13.

7. Eugene Campbell, *Establishing Zion: The Mormon Church in the American West* (Salt Lake City: Signature Books, 1988), 58.

8. As quoted in Clark, 2: 350–51.

9. From an informal conversation with Professors Leonard Arrington and Robert Bennion, 25 September 1994.

10. *Conference Reports of The Church of Jesus Christ of Latter-day Saints* (Salt Lake City: The Church of Jesus Christ of Latter-day Saints, April 1898), 8.

11. Hunter, 361–66.

12. Lynn Albert Rosenvall, "Mormon Settlement Patterns, 1830–1900" (Ph.D. diss., University of California, 1972).

CHAPTER 9

Brigham Young and the Gathering To Zion

Richard L. Jensen
Associate Research Professor of Church History and Doctrine
Associate Research Professor, Joseph Fielding Smith Institute
Brigham Young University

The call to flee from Babylon and gather to Zion had profound effects on the Latter-day Saint movement in the nineteenth century. No one shaped the gathering as much as Brigham Young. In turn, his role in this monumental task for four and a half decades was one of the major facets of his adult life. We can learn much about Brigham Young and about the dynamics of Mormon society from his approach to immigration and to the immigrants. Perhaps just as interesting is the feeling for the man and his times that can be gained from his correspondence and epistles.

Like most of the early converts to Mormonism, Brigham Young learned quickly what it meant to relocate one's family. His own experience as a Latter-day Saint emigrant from New York to Ohio, then to Missouri and to Illinois, provided background for his future leadership in the gathering process. He had major responsibilities for organizing emigration from Great Britain in 1840–41 during the mission of the Twelve to that kingdom. What he expected and required of European emigrants could not help but be influenced by his own experiences with a family and a people on the move, often under stress. Directing the migration of the Saints from Nauvoo to Winter Quarters and then to the Salt Lake Valley was, in its way, simply another phase in a process that continued with the gathering of European converts to Zion in the Rocky Mountains.

Church organization in Great Britain was already able to facilitate emigration to Deseret, but additional aid and encouragement were needed. Some of that came in the form of the Perpetual Emigrating Fund Company (PEF). That enterprise was organized

September 14. 1850. 10 a.m.

The General Assembly of the State of Deseret, met in the Bowery, in Great Salt Lake City; when was presented "An Ordinance incorporating the Perpetual Emigrating Company" which was discussed, amended and passed, as follows

Whereas in the fall of 1849, the Church of Jesus Christ of Latter Day Saints in this State, did by voluntary donation create a fund, for the laudable and benevolent purpose of facilitating the emigration of the poor to this State; and

Whereas there are many good and worthy people, who would gladly emigrate to this State, if they were provided with the means; and

Whereas labor, industry, and economy is wealth, and all kinds of Mechanics and laborers are requisite for building up and extending the benefits of civilized society, subduing the soil, and otherwise developing the resources of a new Country, and

Whereas we consider it a subject worthy of consideration and encouragement, fraught, as it is, with the best interest of society; not only by adding to the national wealth, and extending the area of civilization, but accomplishing the still more generous and benevolent purpose, of transplanting to a more genial soil to a place where labor and industry meet their due reward; where man's best nature and intelligence can arise and assert their supremacy: the poor and the oppressed, whose unremitting toil, owing to their location and associations with which they are surrounded, has been insufficient to procure even the most common necessaries of life, thereby dooming not only themselves, but their children in all future generations, to a precarious and bare subsistence, thereby binding the mind and the intelligence down to the unanswerable arguments of unrequited labor and want; therefore, to encourage and perpetuate this enterprize, **WE**, the General Assembly of the State of Deseret, do ordain and establish the following Ordinance to wit:

An Ordinance Incorporating the Perpetual Emigrating Company.

Sec. 1. Be it ordained by the General Assembly of the State of Deseret, that the General, or a Special Conference of the Church of Jesus Christ of Latter Day Saints, to be called

An ordinance passed by the General Assembly of the State of Deseret incorporating the Perpetual Emigrating [Fund] Company, 14 September 1850, Great Salt Lake City.

in 1849 to fulfill a covenant made in the Nauvoo Temple before the exodus to the effect that "to the extent of our property and influence, we never would cease our exertions, until all the Saints who desired, should be removed to a place of safety."[1]

While that might have seemed applicable only to refugees from Nauvoo, Brigham Young interpreted its intent broadly, designing the Perpetual Emigrating Fund "to increase until Israel is gathered from all nations, and the poor can sit under their own vine and inhabit their own house, and worship God in Zion."[2] President Young's efforts, along with assistance from the Fund and the Church, would help bring thousands of European emigrants to the Rocky Mountains.

The call to emigrate was particularly urgent in the 1850s and 1860s. As they sought to build a strong base of operations in the Mountain West and to provide converts with opportunities they lacked in Europe, the Latter-day Saints were actuated by a pervasive feeling that the second coming of the Savior was near at hand and that the millennial timetable called for swift action. The First Presidency directed in 1852:

> When a people, or individuals, hear the Gospel, obey its first principles, are baptized for the remission of their sins, and receive the Holy Ghost by the laying on of hands, it is time for them to gather, without delay, to Zion; unless their Presidency shall call on them to tarry and preach the Gospel to those who have not heard it; and generally, the longer they wait the more difficult it will be for them to come home; for he who has an oportunity to gather, and does not improve it, will be afflicted by the devil.[3]

Feelings of urgency were compounded by world events. The Crimean War in the mid-1850s and the American Civil War in the early 1860s saw Mormons emigrating in large numbers at times when other Europeans were less likely to leave their homes. Crises reinforced the call to flee to Zion. In 1863, George Q. Cannon reported that European Latter-day Saints felt they must emigrate that year because they were not sure when they would have another chance.[4]

The major immigration drive of 1868 also had overtones of

millennial urgency. Brigham Young wrote at the beginning of that year:

> The nation in which we dwell is surely ripening for destruction. . . . Not many years will roll away before the sceptre will pass into the hands of the righteous, and the people who possess this land be governed by the oracles of the Almighty.[5]

Encouraged by the number of donations being made to the PEF, President Young contended, "If the Saints who dwell in this Territory were to subscribe the means which they can well spare every honest person who has identified their interests with the Kingdom of God, might be emigrated next season."[6]

This was a persistent theme: it should be possible to help all the Saints emigrate from Europe who wished to do so. Indeed, the rumor spread that Brigham Young actually intended to help all the faithful Saints emigrate from Europe in 1868. But his optimism was tempered by the realization that his people as a whole would not tighten their belts enough to make such ambitious aid available to emigrants. In late 1867 he wrote:

> Donations for assisting the poor to emigrate from Europe another season are being pretty freely made by the brethren. If the saints would be prudent and not spend their means at the gentile stores, there would be no difficulty experienced in emigrating all who wish to come to Zion another season; but very stringent economy we cannot expect among the masses of people.[7]

President Young used his imagination in his never-ending crusade to encourage donations to help the poor Latter-day Saints to emigrate. In 1850, with the Perpetual Emigrating Fund Company only a year old, he tried a touch of humor: "Come on [you] tobacco chewers & put your 1000 [thousand dollars] into [the] Poor fund & I will give you liberty to chew anot[her]r year."[8]

Probably more effective was his own example. For the 1856 emigration season, with emigration funds depleted, he donated one of his homes, the White House, to be sold and the proceeds given to the PEF to help poor emigrants. In addition, he made available a flour mill and a house and farm in Sanpete County.[9] In 1862, he told a congregation:

> If any person or persons would purchase all my property at one half its cost and pay me the money, I would gladly sell all, devote the whole sum to gathering the poor, and begin anew to build and plant, and thus not only greatly bless thousands who are distressed, but also prove again, as I have already proved scores of times, that there is a giving that enriches.[10]

Expecting much of himself, Young also asked much of others, straightforwardly and with confidence. Characteristic was his written appeal to William H. Hooper in late 1867:

> If you are willing for me to draw on you for a thousand dollars to assist the poor to emigrate next season please signify as much in your next communication. I shall appropriate two thousand dollars for this purpose, and trust that you will find it convenient to donate the sum above mentioned.[11]

That same donation drive netted $1,000 from the Walker brothers. Though they were apostates, Brigham Young thanked them in a personal letter, with a note that he would be happy to apply the contribution to the names of any emigrants they might wish brought over.[12]

President Young called on Church members throughout the world to help in the emigration effort. In 1858, he wrote to England: "This we consider the duty of every Saint to help the poor Saints to gather home to Zion and use the means with which the Lord has blessed them to promote the cause of truth and righteousness upon the earth."[13]

If the Mormon people, with limited resources, were to effect the emigration of as many of their fellow believers as quickly as possible, priorities had to be set. The effort and expense involved in carrying extra luggage and more than minimal provisions would decrease the number of Saints who could be brought west in a given season. Brigham Young expected emigrants—particularly the poor who were being given aid—to make do without all the amenities one might appreciate on the overland trek. In 1850, the First Presidency instructed:

> The poor who can live in the States with little clothing, and little or no groceries, &c., can live equally as cheap on the road; and when once here, can procure the comforts of life

> by their industry. Souls are the articles for the Perpetual Fund to gather home, and that, too, as many as possible; and other things will be attended to in their time and place.[14]

Not only was unnecessary luggage to be eliminated, but immigrants were to plan to walk as much of the way as possible. In 1851, the First Presidency pointed out:

> Many of the English brethren and sisters think it a trifle to walk fifteen or twenty miles to hear preaching on the sabbath, and return home at evening, and then stand at their labor the remainder of the week; and can they not walk twenty miles per day for fifty days, for the sake of getting to their Father's house; to the home of the Saints in the Valley of the mountains?[15]

Those who received assistance were to

> . . . help themselves to the utmost of their ability; and not one bring stores of merchandize, to the expense of another's tarrying behind. . . . If those assisted by the Poor Fund expect to ride in carriages and wagons over the mountains, the number you can forward will be very small; but if they have faith to walk through, a few teams loaded with flour, will make a multitude comfortable, and many can be removed at little cost.[16]

President Young did not want to subject the Saints to unnecessary hazards. Although it might have raised the total cost of emigration by as much as $10 per person, in 1854 he called for all Mormon immigrants to land at ports in the northeastern United States, rather than at New Orleans, because the incidence of serious illness had been high on the Mississippi.[17]

On the other hand, President Young did not want to provide immigrants with too many opportunities to use illness as an excuse for special treatment. In 1856, during the first season of handcart immigration, he wrote,

> I will say that it is all right not to provide wagons for infirm persons to accompany the hand carts for it would encourage infirmity or rather laziness which is quite as bad. There would soon be but few able to walk if such arrangements were made.[18]

With a late start and with many aged and infirm in the last

companies, that year's handcart immigrants suffered tragic losses. Yet, overall, Brigham Young considered it an "eminently successful" experiment and hoped it would play a major role in future Mormon immigration.[19]

Minor changes would need to be made to avoid the recurrence of that year's pitfalls. He directed that a separate wagon train, rather than handcarts, be provided for those who were very aged or who had major disabilities, and that one team and wagon be provided for emergency hauling for every two hundred handcart immigrants.[20]

Brigham Young's fascination with the handcart scheme, despite its problems, suggests some interesting facets of his approach to immigration. For one thing, he seemed to have a certain urge to innovate—to explore new approaches. For another, he relished the feeling of equality which the handcarts inevitably brought. He pointed out that the immigrants, both with handcarts and with wagons, who came in late 1856 had to leave all their extra luggage on the plains, which meant that

> All the saints of the last companies came in on a principle of equality such as has not existed since saints began to migrate: they *all* had to be helped in. The Independent companies, and the hand cart saints of all grades and circumstances arrived here, having with them only the clothes they wore, these have cost us less trouble since their arrival and done more good for themselves, than any company that has preceded them, apparently under more favorable circumstances.[21]

Thus he suggested for the future:

> 1st. That all who can, will come by hand carts, & 2nd, that they bring nothing with them but what they wear, or may wear of necessity on the road, and can carry on their hand carts. Thus you will perceive the money usually spent in England for extra clothing, and unnecessary "fiddle-faddles"—for extra freight on the same, and for hauling this across the plains, can all be saved, and most assuredly, may be more profitably used on the arrival of the Saints here. Who will believe it? Who will act accordingly? Can we persuade men to do right? & to leave the Mo. River by 1st July.[22]

Brigham Young's hopes for handcart immigration were part of

a dream on which he and his people expended a great deal of effort, a dream that seemed on the verge of becoming a reality just before its hopes faded. Young's hope was that ultimately Mormon supply stations could be set up every fifty miles along the overland trail with provisions, feed for animals, and other necessities for immigrants. In early 1857, he wrote to England:

> We shall establish a few of such this year, thus you will perceive a man and his family with small means can walk from station to station, and have his supplies renewed at every such place, without encumbering himself with very heavy loads at the first; the time when he is least accustomed to such travel, nor so well able to endure as he afterwards can.[23]

These hopes were initially tied closely to the ambitious Brigham Young Express and Carrying Company, a scheme whereby the Mormons would solicit a federal contract to carry the mail as a base for a system of freighting, passenger transportation, and supply stations between the Missouri River and Salt Lake City. The mail contract was canceled in 1857, concurrent with preparations to send the U.S. Army to Utah. The idea of establishing supply stations and even wayside support settlements later surfaced now and again, and eventually flour was deposited for immigrants at a few locations along the route.[24]

Brigham Young continued to tinker with the handcart arrangements, although the number of people moved was not as great as he would have liked. Before the 1860 immigration season—the last with a wide use of handcarts—he wrote:

> The hand carts of last season suited me altogether better than those of any other season, for they are not only more reliable on the road but are also of value and real utility here. But I want those for this year so made that the wheels will track with the narrow track wagons, i.e. 4 feet and 8 inches from center to center of tire, with tire ½ inch *thick*, hubs 5½ inches in diameter beds 3 feet long, and the iron axle 1⅛ inch diameter at the shoulder.[25]

Yet at the same time, President Young was exploring a number of alternatives to cut the costs of immigration and freighting. A week after his handcart letter, he asked William H. Hooper to find a riverboat captain who would be willing to carry Mormon freight and immigrants up the middle stretches of the Missouri River, or even the Yellowstone. He hoped in this way to cut overland travel to a minimum of perhaps four hundred miles.[26] With a touch of humor, he acknowledged that it would be a challenge to navigate that far upriver: "They will perhaps require boats that can run where the ground is a little damp."[27]

Little came of that scheme, or of the later idea of shipping by way of the Colorado River. The most successful experiment was what became known in the years before the coming of the transcontinental railroad as the Church Trains system. In 1860, Brigham Young's nephew Joseph W. Young helped prove that oxen could leave the Salt Lake Valley in the spring, carry flour to be deposited for the use of immigrants, load freight and immigrants at the Missouri River, and return to the valley the same season in good time and full health.[28] This provided the basis for efficient, inexpensive emigration during the American Civil War, when millennial expectations and anxiety to emigrate were again at a high point.

Providing aid to poor immigrants and a support system for each season's overall Mormon immigration often sorely taxed Mormon resources. Brigham Young wrote in late 1861,

> The gathering of Israel is so important a part of the great work in which we are engaged that it occupies much of our thoughts, and we are ever anxious to afford it all just facilities and influence, even to the risk of infringing upon other requirements.[29]

That was, if anything, an understatement. Yet occasionally President Young stepped in to attend to other priorities. In 1864, during a heavy immigration season, he made the decision to focus Church resources the following year on the building of the Salt Lake Temple rather than sending teams and wagons to help immigrants across the plains.[30] Thus the 1865 immigrants came on a strictly private basis—in theory. Actually, delays, loss of cattle, and financial misfortunes for that year's immigrants necessitated a costly relief expedition; Brigham Young's own teams, wagons, and employees played an important role.[31]

Even a charitable enterprise, like relieving crippled immigrant companies, was a businesslike proposition under Brigham Young's leadership. Rather than relieving the disadvantaged immigrants of eventual responsibility for their own welfare, he had a strict accounting kept of the help they were given and expected them to reimburse their benefactors as soon as possible. He instructed captains of relief companies in 1854 that they were to charge the immigrants for the flour and provisions they used because the supplies were privately owned. If the immigrants were unable to pay cash, arrangements were to be made for later repayment. President Young suggested that the captains charge the going rate for flour in the Salt Lake market, six cents per pound, plus one and a half to two cents per pound for each hundred miles the flour was hauled before the relief wagons reached the immigrants.[32]

With characteristic attention to detail, the President directed further that tired animals must never be yoked with fresh ones, and that captains of the relief companies must appoint overseers to be responsible for all the animals they provided to relieve the immigrants.[33] The captain of each company receiving aid would be responsible to arrange reimbursement for all assistance his company received.

With the coming of the telegraph in 1861, President Young could keep abreast of the progress and problems of each immigrant company. Captains routinely sent him brief reports from telegraph stations en route, and more timely relief could be sent when it was required.[34]

Brigham Young's involvement in immigration arrangements showed not only his concern for details but also some of his homely insights into the idiosyncracies of his people. In 1866, he instructed supervisors of the overland immigrants that they should not caution the European Saints too much about their choice of drinking water along the way because the immigrants would not be in a position to make good judgments on the matter, regardless of such instructions.

> Though the river water will be apt to give them the diarrhea, until they become accustomed to it, yet it is much healthier than the wells and springs usually found in the neighbor-

> hood of the river, and it will be better to direct the people to use it.[35]

President Young and his agents felt that divine aid was a significant factor in the success of Mormon immigration efforts. At the end of a busy, challenging season in 1866, he paused to confide,

> The Lord has signally fulfilled his promises; and if the people would open their eyes, they could easily perceive that there has been a greater power than that of man exercised in their preservation in the midst of the varied vicissitudes through which they have passed.[36]

He noted that during the Civil War, Latter-day Saint immigrants came through unscathed, although "rebel cruisers roamed the Ocean almost unchecked, capturing Federal vessels at their pleasure."[37] Looking forward, he exclaimed, "When the great Work shall be fully consummated, and the victory be fully achieved, man will be compelled to giving the praise and glory unto the Lord for all that will have been done."[38]

After their arrival in Utah, immigrants sometimes needed practical advice to help them thrive in the new environment. While President Young was seldom the one to give such counsel directly, he sometimes made suggestions to those who had that responsibility. In 1866, he called Norwegian Canute Peterson and former Scandinavian mission president John Van Cott to serve as missionaries among the Scandinavian Saints of Sanpete and Sevier Counties and gave them these instructions:

> We wish them to be taught the necessity of taking care of themselves, their stock and all that is entrusted to them. They should learn to handle their guns to advantage, so as to be able to protect themselves and their families against the attacks and ravages of the Indians. Upon this point they have been generally remiss, and have not felt the necessity of taking those precautions which people in new Settlements exposed to Indian attack, should always be vigilant in attending to. They must wake up upon these points, and not allow covetousness to take such entire possession of them that their own true interests and the interests of the Kingdom, are neglected. They should be willing to assist the

> Indians who are friendly when they need help, and not be so stingy as to disgust them.
>
> You should urge them to seek for and recover the Spirit of the gospel which they received when they embraced this Work, and which, in many instances, has leaked away from them in crossing the Ocean and the Plains and since their arrival here. They should be in possesion of the Spirit of their religion and have the power of God resting down upon them; and if they enjoy these blessings, they will not be likely to apostatize.[39]

The need to implement these instructions was particularly urgent in that they were given during the Black Hawk War, which involved hostilities in Sanpete and Sevier counties and evacuation of some settlements.

Some immigrants had more difficulty adjusting to life in frontier Utah than others. A poignant illustration is the story of a British-born divorcee, converted in India, who immigrated in 1865. About fifty years old, she wrote that she was "not used to any out door or in door work, such being the matter we are brought up in India, not from choice but from custom of the country where there are many servants to work for us."[40] She hoped to be able to teach reading, writing, arithmetic, knitting, and sewing to the children of Brigham Young or another "well regulated family," and she assured the President that she could produce good recommendations. Bothered by rheumatism, unable to tolerate the cold Utah winters, she wrote,

> I cannot stir from the fireside much less do out door work, I do not wish to live upon the Church for my entire support but I shall do what I can to work a living for myself shall make myself generally useful in a family if I have time from my other duties but will be excused cooking & washing.[41]

Brigham Young was frankly perplexed. He wrote, "I really do not know what to do with you. It would not be convenient for me to take you into any of my families. My own folks have to work, carry water, wash, build their own fires, cook, &c., and mostly wait upon themselves."[42] Then he added some homely advice about frontier Mormon hospitality:

> The Saints who gather here we are glad to see, and we

> feel to do all that we can to aid, comfort and counsel them; but it is as absolutely necessary for every man, woman and child who embraces this work and gathers to Zion to do all that he or she can to forward the work of God to build up Zion, and to aid in the redemption thereof. We, all of us, have as much as we can do to discharge the duties which devolve upon us. Our zeal in this labor, and the earnestness with which we pursue it, causes us sometimes to appear, in the eyes of the inexperienced, indifferent to the situation of new-comers. Still, this has a tendency to develop energy and self-reliance in the Saints that they could not otherwise have, were they not to be thrown on their resources.
>
> I should advise you to get acquainted with the people around, and see if you can get situated to suit yourself; and then if you are not able to provide yourself as you need we will render you assistance.[43]

Mutual acquaintances tried to help, and President Young himself offered his aid, but the woman could not accommodate herself to the climate and the frontier way of life. She asked if she might have her endowment and have help to return to England, where she had friends who might help her back to India. Although the president advised her to stay in Utah and try to fit in, she apparently left the territory after more than three years of maladjustment.[44]

Some immigrants left the faith. Of some of these Brigham Young wrote,

> It is often the case that so soon as a man who never owned a cow or a pig nor any living animal gets here and begins to rise in regard to property that he forgets his God and all that has been done for him, and from thenceforth is not satisfied until he gets back into hell from whence he came. It is manifestly better for all such persons to remain and even die in the world without gathering at all so they die in the faith than come here only to apostatize and finally go to hell at last.[45]

In view of all the problems of acculturation of immigrants, President Young could be permitted a little tongue-in-cheek enthusiasm over an alternative method for swelling the population of Zion. In 1867—another year without official Church promotion of immigration—he wrote to England:

> Of late we have felt led to give considerable instruction to our young people respecting marriage—encouraging them to enter into the bonds of matrimony, and in the absence of a foreign emigration, endeavor to increase our home emigration, which we have, heretofore, found to be far the best, very few ever apostatizing and proving recreant to the truth.[46]

Actually, at the same time, he was putting together plans for a very heavy immigration season in 1868. Thus he was not abandoning the "foreign" emigration—far from it.

A major frustration for President Young for the last quarter-century of his life was the failure of many immigrants to repay promptly the aid they had received for the journey. More conscientious repayment could have enabled the Perpetual Emigrating Fund Company to extend help to many hundreds more than it did, but its effectiveness was constantly hampered by a lack of the resources to which it was entitled. In September 1855, Young sent PEF debtors an exhortation through their bishops and presidents:

> Will the Lord, Angels, and holy beings fellowship you if you longer neglect these matters, if you longer exhibit a careless indifference to this important subject? Will the church and the brethren sustain you in their faith and prayers, while the lamentations and cries of the worthy poor are filling the ears of the Almighty for release and deliverance?
>
> No they will not; and if you do not act, feel, and do different, the withering curse of the Almighty will be upon you to darken your minds, to lessen your faith, and cause a famine spiritual and temporal to consume you.[47]

President Young asked all bishops to find the PEF debtors in their wards, notify his office, assess the debtors' circumstances, and obtain repayment as expeditiously as possible. None should be unable to begin to pay something, but many might lack the skill or judgment to succeed financially. The bishops were to counsel with these and do everything possible to help them increase their earnings and repay the Fund.[48] Bishops were to allow no one still owing the Fund to leave their wards without first either repaying their loan or giving security for future payment.[49]

In 1859, a collector was appointed for PEF accounts and for other debts owed the Church. President Young instructed him to be energetic, thorough, and systematic. But he counseled that rather than to "oppress the poor," when the collector found someone too poor to pay, he should give the debtor additional time and ask for a promissory note.[50]

In an economy largely based on barter of perishable goods, repayment of PEF indebtedness sometimes became rather involved. Brigham Young advised the bishop of Moroni:

> We will receive an ox from Sister Martha Blackham to apply on her indebtedness to the P.E. Company for her immigration, at such price as it may be appraised at when it reaches here. Should the ox be incondition for beef and you *soon* meet a good chance for sending it before it *shrinks*, it may be well to forward it at once, otherwise sister Blackham had better winter it and forward in the Spring, for cattle, other than those fit for beef, are of no use to us until another season.[51]

In order to carry forward the gathering of the Latter-day Saints, Brigham Young expected much of his people, both of the immigrants and those who were already gathered. Spartan travel arrangements, strict expectations for repayment, and the requirement to do as much as possible for oneself were just as much hallmarks of the Mormon immigration process as were effective organization and mutual aid.

Yet when arrangements were found which could save lives or make more effective use of manpower, Brigham Young demonstrated that he had no fixation on rigor or economy for its own sake. Although the transcontinental railroad—and initially the steamship—brought higher costs in cash, they made important savings in time and lives, which he was quick to appreciate.

In 1868, with the railroad having eliminated about 650 miles of travel by foot or wagon, he reported enthusiastically to a missionary in Hawaii that the change "renders their journey far less tedious and wearisome than formerly, to which, the health and spirits of these laterly arrived amply testify."[52]

In 1877, shortly before President Young's death, a missionary suggested that a group of poor converts travel by handcart.

Although the handcart scheme had been a pet project of his, by now Brigham Young was far beyond that. He suggested that the money saved would be inconsequential in comparison to the time and exertions it would require. Rather than resorting to handcarts, he preferred to let the people work for the Church the number of days equivalent to the handcart journey in order to pay for their rail travel.[53]

If his correspondence is any indication, Brigham Young's day-to-day involvement with immigration matters tapered off after the coming of the transcontinental railroad. His resignation as president of the Perpetual Emigrating Fund Company in 1870 was part of this process, signaling a transition to a different style of management for the immigration effort. With cash, not manpower or oxen, being the key to passenger arrangements, and with fewer worries about immigrant companies encountering problems en route, Young could relax a bit more. Still, he continued to maintain a lively interest in the enterprise.

The extent of President Young's emotional involvement in the gathering process is evident in his 1869 response to a question posed by an Eastern periodical about the mission of Mormonism. As he discussed his people's accomplishments, he passed lightly over the proverbial conquering of the desert and their material achievements. His main emphasis was on their success in gathering together converts of diverse backgrounds to form a remarkably harmonious community. For Brigham Young, this was evidence of divine inspiration.[54]

NOTES

1. Minutes of Special Conference, 15 September 1850, Perpetual Emigrating Fund Company Records, Library-Archives, Historical Department of The Church of Jesus Christ of Latter-day Saints, Salt Lake City, Utah (hereafter referred to as LDS Church Historical Archives). The abbreviation PEF will hereafter be used to denote Perpetual Emigrating Fund Company. See also Second General Epistle, 12 October 1849, in James R. Clark, comp., *Messages of the First Presidency of The Church of Jesus Christ of Latter-day Saints*, 6 vols. (Salt Lake City: Bookcraft, 1965–75), 2: 34.
2. First Presidency (Brigham Young, Heber C. Kimball, Willard Richards) to Orson Hyde, 16 October 1849, in Clark, 2: 39.
3. Seventh General Epistle, 18 April 1852, in Clark, 2: 98.

4. Cannon to Young, 2 January 1863, European Mission Letterpress Copybooks (hereafter referred to as EM Letterbooks), LDS Church Historical Archives.
5. Brigham Young to John Brown, 1 January 1868, Brigham Young Letterbooks (hereafter referred to as Young Letterbooks), Brigham Young Papers, LDS Church Historical Archives.
6. Ibid.
7. Brigham Young to William H. Hooper, 20 December 1867, Young Letterbooks.
8. Conference, 7 [8] September 1850, 2:00 P.M., General Minutes, Brigham Young Papers, LDS Church Historical Archives.
9. List of property, 31 August 1855, Young Letterbooks.
10. Brigham Young to George Q. Cannon, 11 October 1862, Young Letterbooks.
11. Brigham Young to W. H. Hooper, 20 December 1867, Young Letterbooks.
12. Brigham Young to Walker Brothers, 7 January 1868, Young Letterbooks.
13. Brigham Young to Asa Calkin, 10 September 1858, Young Letterbooks.
14. Fourth General Epistle, 27 September 1850, in Clark, 2: 60.
15. Sixth General Epistle, 22 September 1851, in Clark, 2: 88.
16. Ibid., 89.
17. Brigham Young to Franklin D. Richards, 30 June and 2 August 1854, Young Letterbooks.
18. Brigham Young to John Taylor, 28 July 1856, Young Letterbooks.
19. Fourteenth General Epistle, 10 December 1856, in Clark, 2: 199–201.
20. Ibid., 200.
21. Brigham Young to Orson Pratt, 27 January 1857, Young Letterbooks.
22. Ibid.
23. Brigham Young to Orson Pratt, 1 March 1857, Young Letterbooks.
24. On the Brigham Young Express and Carrying Company, see Leonard J. Arrington, *Great Basin Kingdom: An Economic History of the Latter-day Saints 1830–1900* (Cambridge, Massachusetts: Harvard University Press, 1958), 162–70. On later consideration of way stations and support settlements, see Brigham Young to Joseph E. Johnson, Young Letterbook, 4: 449–50; to Joel H. Johnson, 17 October 1858; to Horace S. Eldredge, 20 October 1858 and 6 May 1859; to William H. Hooper, 30 January 1860; to J. E. Johnson, 19 April 1860; to William Pyper, 25 April 1860; to W. H. Hooper, 5 December 1865, Young Letterbooks.
25. Brigham Young to W. H. Hooper, 23 February 1860, Young Letterbooks.
26. Brigham Young to William H. Hooper, 23 February and 8 March 1860, Young Letterbooks. Brigham Young first proposed this scheme as early as November 1855. See Arrington, 163.
27. Brigham Young to W. H. Hooper, 8 March 1860, Young Letterbooks.
28. Brigham Young to Nathaniel V. Jones and Jacob Gates, 20 December 1860, Young Letterbooks.

29. Brigham Young to Amasa Lyman, 15 November 1861, Young Letterbooks.
30. Brigham Young to Joseph W. Young at Wyoming, Nebraska, 9 June 1864, Young Letterbooks.
31. Brigham Young to presiding officers and bishops, 26 October 1865; to Orson Arnold, 28 October 1865, Young Letterbooks.
32. Brigham Young to captains of relief companies, September 1854, Brigham Young Letterbook, 1: 665–66.
33. Ibid.
34. Incoming Telegrams, 1862–1866, Brigham Young Papers.
35. Brigham Young to Isaac Bullock and William W. Riter at Wyoming, Nebraska, 6 May 1866, Young Letterbooks.
36. Brigham Young to Orson Pratt, Sr., 29 October 1866, Young Letterbooks.
37. Ibid.
38. Ibid.
39. Brigham Young to Canute Peterson, 16 May 1866, Young Letterbooks.
40. Emilia McMahon to Brigham Young, 7 February 1866, Brigham Young Papers.
41. Ibid.
42. Brigham Young to Mrs. E. McMahon, 4 May 1866, Young Letterbooks.
43. Ibid.
44. Mrs. E. McMahon to Brigham Young, 8 April, 3 May 1866; to Young, undated letter received 5 August 1866, Brigham Young Papers; Brigham Young to Mrs. E. Mahon, 5–7 January 1869, Young Letterbook.
45. Brigham Young to Asa Calkin, 10 September 1858, Young Letterbooks.
46. Brigham Young to Franklin D. Richards, 25 September 1867, Young Letterbooks.
47. Circular to presidents and bishops in Utah, September 1855, in Clark, 2: 176.
48. Notice, 2 November 1854, in Clark, 2: 156.
49. Circular, September 1855, in Clark, 2: 174.
50. Brigham Young to Patrick Lynch, 8 March 1859, Brigham Young "Nauvoo Legion" Letterbook, LDS Church Historical Archives.
51. Brigham Young to Bishop George W. Bradley, 26 November 1861, Young Letterbooks.
52. Brigham Young to George Nebeker, 3 September 1868, Young Letterbooks.
53. Brigham Young to James A. Little, 31 May 1877, Young Letterbooks; and Letterbook 14: 946–48.
54. Brigham Young to Editor, *The Religio-Philosophical Journal*, 7 January 1869, Young Letterbooks.

CHAPTER 10

Brigham Young

Builder of Temples

Richard O. Cowan
Professor and Department Chair of Church History and Doctrine
Brigham Young University

On one occasion, Brigham Young made the interesting assertion that "we never began to build a Temple without the bells of hell beginning to ring." Then he fearlessly added, "I want to hear them ring."[1] During his lifetime, he repeatedly caused those bells to peal loud and clear.

When Brigham Young moved to Kirtland as a recent convert, the Saints were already planning to build a temple; Brigham would play a key role in that construction. As the temple neared completion, Brigham was appointed to direct the painting and finishing work. This consumed his energies to the point that he scarcely had time to support his family. "He possibly designed and quite certainly glazed the windows—both the dramatic Federal-style arched windows that framed the triple-tiered pulpits at each end of the temple, and the unusual Gothic but sectioned side windows with their intricate panes."[2]

Brigham Young was with the Twelve at one of the first meetings in the new temple when the Brethren were anointed with oil and spoke in tongues, and when "the heavens were opened, and angels ministered unto us."[3]

The dedication of the temple two months later climaxed this Pentecostal season. That evening Brigham Young attended an especially remarkable meeting at which some saw angels, heard the sound as of a mighty wind, and prophesied. "So spiritually exalted was the experience that for several hours the participants did not wish to leave."[4]

Unfortunately, these glorious days in Kirtland did not last. Early in 1838, Joseph Smith, Brigham Young, and hundreds of the faithful were forced to flee from persecutions in Ohio. Settling at Far West in northern Missouri, the Prophet received on 26 April a revelation directing that a temple be built there. Work was to begin that summer and then was to resume following the winter break one year from the date of the revelation (see D&C 115: 8–16). A subsequent revelation directed the Twelve to meet at the temple site in Far West on that same date the following April to fill vacancies in their quorum and then to depart for a mission overseas (see D&C 118).

In the fall of 1838, however, Governor Lilburn W. Boggs ordered that the Mormons be exterminated or driven from the state of Missouri. While Joseph Smith and other Church leaders were imprisoned in Liberty, Brigham Young took the lead in the Saints' exodus, and it appeared unlikely that the Twelve could meet their appointment in Far West the following spring. Apostates openly boasted that this failure would prove Joseph Smith to be a false prophet. It was obvious that the lives of the Twelve would be in peril if they were to attempt to return to Missouri. Nevertheless, Elder George Q. Cannon later testified, "The Spirit rested upon President Young and his brother Apostles, and they determined to go."[5]

The Apostles entered Missouri individually and traveled by different routes in order to avoid attracting attention. Shortly after midnight on the appointed day, they met at Far West, offered prayer, sang a hymn, ordained Wilford Woodruff and George A. Smith to the apostleship, symbolically moved a stone into place for the temple's foundation, and prepared to depart for their mission.

The Saints next turned their attention to building a temple in Nauvoo. Brigham Young realized that in Kirtland they had received only a "portion of their first endowments . . . or initiatory ordinances, preparatory to an endowment." Specifically, he pointed out, the Kirtland Temple "had no basement in it, nor a font, nor preparations to give endowments for the living or the dead."[6] At Nauvoo, he saw these deficiencies remedied.

A revelation that the Prophet Joseph Smith had received in January 1841 emphasized that sacred ordinances belong in the temple (see D&C 124: 29–30). In July of that year, William Weeks began preparing plans for a baptismal font to be located in the Nauvoo Temple basement. By November, the basement, with its wooden font, was enclosed by frame walls and covered by a temporary roof. Brigham Young was involved when the first baptisms were performed here. On Sunday, 21 November, a large congregation gathered at 4:00 P.M. to witness this event. Elder Young, together with Heber C. Kimball and John Taylor, baptized about forty persons in behalf of their ancestral dead.[7]

Brigham Young was impressed with the sacrifices made by those who labored to build the temple. Some had no shoes for their feet or shirt to cover their arms. An outstanding example of generosity was Joseph Toronto, a convert from Sicily, who contributed his entire life's savings. Brigham later remembered:

> It was difficult to get bread and other provisions for the workmen to eat. I counseled the committee who had charge of the temple funds to deal out all the flour they had, and God would give them more; and they did so; and it was but a short time before Brother Toronto came and brought me twenty-five hundred dollars in gold. . . . So I opened the mouth of the bag and took hold at the bottom end, and gave it a jerk towards the bishop, and strewed the gold across the room and said, now go and buy flour for the workmen on the temple and do not distrust the Lord any more; for we will have what we need.[8]

While the Saints were making such sacrifices, the Lord was revealing important temple-related blessings.[9] The endowment would be given in a place of privacy because it was sacred and would make known "things which have been kept hid from before the foundation of the world" (D&C 124: 41). Such a facility became available when Joseph Smith completed a twenty-five-by-forty-four-foot red brick building early in 1842. The Relief Society was organized in the large "assembly room" on the second floor on 17 March, and the first endowments were given seven weeks later.[10]

With the assistance of five or six workmen, the Prophet partitioned the assembly room to represent the various stages in man's eternal progress. These preparations were completed by 4 May, when the first endowments were given.[11]

Brigham Young was one of the original nine who received these blessings on this occasion. Afterward, the Prophet turned to him and remarked:

> Brother Brigham, this is not arranged perfectly; however, we have done the best we could under the circumstances in which we are placed. I wish you to take this matter in hand: organize and systematize all these ceremonies.[12]

Before his martyrdom in 1844, the Prophet conferred "the keys of the sealing power" upon Brigham Young, who was President of the Twelve, indicating that this was the "last key," the "most sacred of all," and that it pertained "exclusively to the first presidency."[13]

Following the Prophet's death, construction on the temple pushed forward under the Twelve's leadership. The building's capstone was formally put in place on 24 May 1845. The ceremony was conducted at 5:45 A.M. in order not to attract the attention of the Saints' enemies. "The last stone is now laid upon the temple," declared Brigham Young as he tapped the capstone into its proper position, "and I pray the Almighty in the name of Jesus to defend us in this place and sustain it until the temple is finished and we have all got our endowments." The congregation then shouted "Hosanna to God and the Lamb."[14]

Specific parts of the temple were completed and dedicated piecemeal so that ordinance work could begin as soon as possible. On 30 November 1845, for example, Brigham Young and twenty others who had received their endowments from Joseph Smith gathered to dedicate the attic for ordinance work. During the next ten days, Brigham Young, Heber C. Kimball, and others were busy preparing the attic's eighty-eight-by-twenty-nine-foot central hall for the presentation of the endowment. As had been done in the Red Brick Store, canvas partitions in the "council chamber" divided the temple into separate areas representing distinct stages in man's eternal progress.

Saints throughout the city contributed furnishings for these rooms. Potted plants were gathered for the area representing the

Garden of Eden. The room on the east had a large gothic window and was furnished with fine carpets and wall hangings; this most beautiful area represented the celestial kingdom.[15] Flanking each side of the central hall were six rooms, about fourteen feet square, which served as private offices for Church leaders or for the initiatory ordinances connected with the endowment. Some of these side rooms, including Brigham Young's, contained altars at which sacred sealing ordinances were performed. Endowments were given beginning 15 December. Despite threats of arrest and other forms of harassment from their enemies, Brigham Young and the Twelve came to the temple regularly in order to take an active lead in the ordinances. By the end of the month, over a thousand Saints had received their endowment blessings.

As the year 1846 dawned, pressure on the Saints to leave Illinois mounted. There were rumors that even federal troops might be used against them. Hence, Church leaders decided to commence the exodus early in February rather than wait until spring. This decision increased the Saints' eagerness to receive temple blessings before leaving Nauvoo, so the level of temple activity during January was even greater than during the previous month.

On 12 January, Brigham Young recorded:

> Such has been the anxiety manifested by the saints to receive the ordinances [of the Temple], and such the anxiety on our part to administer to them, that I have given myself up entirely to the work of the Lord in the Temple night and day, not taking more than four hours sleep, upon an average, per day, and going home but once a week.[16]

The day selected for the exodus to begin was 4 February. As this date drew closer, the pace in the temple became even more intense. On 3 February, Brigham Young recorded:

> Notwithstanding that I had announced that we would not attend to the administration of the ordinances, the House of the Lord was thronged all day, the anxiety being so great to receive, as if the brethren would have us stay here and continue the endowments until our way would be hedged up, and our enemies would intercept us. But I informed the brethren that this was not wise, and that we should build

> more Temples, and have further opportunities to receive the blessings of the Lord, as soon as the saints were prepared to receive them. In this Temple we have been abundantly rewarded, if we receive no more. I also informed the brethren that I was going to get my wagons started and be off. I walked some distance from the Temple supposing the crowd would disperse, but on returning I found the house filled to overflowing. Looking upon the multitude and knowing their anxiety, as they were thirsting and hungering for the word, we continued at work diligently in the House of the Lord.[17]

Nearly 300 persons received their endowment on that day alone. During the eight weeks before the exodus, approximately 5,500 were endowed, fulfilling the Prophet Joseph Smith's compelling desire to make these blessings available to the Saints in Nauvoo.

As the Latter-day Saints headed toward the Rockies, their interest in temple service did not diminish. At Winter Quarters, for example, President Brigham Young declared that when the Saints should reach their resting place in the mountains, his intention was to labor hard to build another temple.[18]

Within four days of President Young's arrival in the Salt Lake Valley, he designated the site for the future temple. On 28 July 1847, he and a few others were walking across the area that one day would be Temple Square. He stopped between the two forks of City Creek, struck the ground with his cane, and declared: "Here will be the Temple of our God." Wilford Woodruff placed a stake in the ground to mark the spot that would become the center of the future building. Many years later, President Woodruff would call the construction of the temple on the designated site "a monument to President Young's foresight and prophetic accuracy."[19]

Cornerstones were laid on 6 April 1853, the twenty-third anniversary of the organization of the Church. Large stones, measuring approximately two-by-three-by-five feet, were placed in convenient positions ahead of time. This was a beautiful spring day in the valley as general conference convened in the old adobe Tabernacle on the southwest corner of the temple block.

Dedication and ground-breaking ceremony of the site for the Salt Lake Temple, 14 February 1853. Heber C. Kimball "dedicated the ground unto God."

Accompanied by military honor guards and the music of three bands, a procession headed by Church leaders marched to the spot where the First Presidency and patriarch laid the southeast cornerstone. President Brigham Young then spoke, explaining that the temple had to be built in order that the Lord "may have a place where he can lay his head, and not only spend a night or a day, but find a place of peace."[20] The remaining three cornerstones were then laid by representatives of other priesthood groups. These proceedings lasted from 10:00 A.M. through 2:00 P.M., at which time President Young blessed the assembled congregation and prayed that God might protect them until the temple was finished and they had received their endowments.

After a one-hour break, the conference resumed in the Old Tabernacle. Concerning the future temple, President Young declared:

> I scarcely ever say much about revelations, or visions, but suffice it to say, five years ago last July [1847] I was here, and saw in the Spirit the Temple not ten feet from where we have laid the Chief Corner Stone. I have not inquired what kind

> of a Temple we should build. Why? Because it was represented before me. I have never looked upon that ground, but the vision of it was there. I see it as plainly as if it was in reality before me. Wait until it is done. I will say, however, that it will have six towers, to begin with, instead of one. Now do not any of you apostatize because it will have six towers, and Joseph only built one. It is easier for us to build sixteen, than it was for him to build one. The time will come when there will be one in the centre of Temples we shall build, and on the top, groves and fish ponds. But we shall not see them here, at present.[21]

Some temples built in the twentieth century would fulfill President Young's prophecy.

The great temple would not be completed for forty years. In the meantime, the Saints would need to have access to temple blessings, so temporary facilities had to be provided. During the pioneers' early years in the Salt Lake Valley, the endowment was given in a variety of places. In the fall of 1849, Elder Addison Pratt was appointed to a second mission in the South Pacific, and he received his endowment on Ensign Peak before his departure.[22] This action was consistent with the Prophet Joseph Smith's earlier instructions that under certain circumstances these sacred blessings could be received on mountaintops, as had been the case with Moses.[23] These blessings were also received in Brigham Young's office, or in the Council House.

Erection of the Endowment House, a two-story adobe structure located in the northwest corner of the temple block, got under way during the summer of 1854. It was dedicated in the spring of the following year. President Brigham Young declared that "the house was clean and named it 'The House of the Lord'" and explained that "the spirit of the Lord would be in it, for no one would be permitted to go into it to pollute it."[24] Over the years, this prophetic statement would be confirmed by repeated spiritual experiences in the Endowment House.

Meanwhile, the Saints maintained their interest in constructing the temple. In the spring of 1856, President Young sent architect Truman O. Angell on a special mission to Europe, where he was to make sketches of important architectural masterpieces in

Endowment House (1855–1889), northwest corner of the Salt Lake Temple Block. The structure was designed by Truman O. Angell, Church architect, and dedicated on 5 May 1855.

order to become better qualified to continue his work on the temple and other buildings.[25]

On 24 July 1857, as the Latter-day Saints were celebrating the tenth anniversary of their entrance into Salt Lake Valley, they received the disturbing word that a potentially hostile division of the United States Army was approaching Utah. Not knowing the army's intentions, President Young placed some important records in the temple foundation. He then directed that dirt be hauled in to fill the excavation. When the army arrived the following year, Temple Square looked like a freshly plowed field, with no visible evidence of the temple's construction.

As it turned out, the army marched through without harming any property and set up its camp some forty miles to the south near Utah Lake. By 1860, Church leaders concluded that the temple was safe and directed that the site be reexcavated. With the outbreak of the American Civil War in 1861, the army was needed elsewhere and left Utah in December of that year.

At this time, President Young examined the newly uncovered foundation and became aware that it was defective. He and his associates concluded that its small stones could not carry the massive weight of the temple. On 1 January 1862, he announced that the inadequate foundation would be removed and replaced by one made entirely of granite. The footings would be sixteen feet thick. "I want this Temple to stand through the Millennium," he said a few months later, "and I want it so built that it will be acceptable to the Lord."[26]

During these years, most looked forward to returning to Jackson County, Missouri, and anticipated the privilege of building the great temple there in the not-too-distant future. Once, while Brigham Young was walking through the Temple Block in Salt Lake City, his thoughts turned to Jackson County. He described what he thought the great temple might look like: Each building would have its own tower, and in the center of the "temple complex" there would be a "high tower" and a square beautified by "hanging gardens" where the people could meet.[27]

As the pioneers became more securely established in their mountain valleys, Brigham Young gave more emphasis to temple activity. In 1872 he declared:

> We are now baptizing for the dead, and we are sealing for the dead, and if we had a temple prepared we should be giving endowments for the dead—for our fathers, mothers, grandfathers, grandmothers, uncles, aunts, relatives, friends and old associates. . . . The Lord is stirring up the hearts of many . . . to trace their genealogies and it will continue and run on from father to father, father to father, until they get the genealogy of their forefathers as far as they possibly can.[28]

Nevertheless, "there are some of the sealing ordinances that cannot be administered in the house that we are now using," President Young had explained. "We can only administer in it some of the first ordinances of the Priesthood pertaining to the endowment. There are more advanced ordinances that cannot be administered there."[29] He also explained that ordinances designed

> to connect the chain of the Priesthood from father Adam until now, by sealing children to their parents, . . . they cannot be done without a Temple. . . . Neither will children be

sealed to their living parents in any other place than a Temple.

President Young also specified that "no one can receive endowments for another, until a Temple is prepared in which to administer them."[30] Therefore, in 1876, the First Presidency and the Twelve challenged the Saints to build three additional temples and called on ward bishops to provide donated labor for this task.[31]

The first of these temples was built in Utah's "Dixie." After ten years of struggle to gain a foothold in the desert, the population of St. George had reached only 1200. At a council meeting with local leaders on 31 January 1871, President Brigham Young proposed that a temple be built in the city. This announcement was received with "Glory! Hallelujah!" from Elder Erastus Snow of the Twelve, who had presided in Dixie. These feelings were shared by all present.[32]

With such a small population in the area, many wondered why a temple was to be built there. President John Taylor later pointed out that "it was found that our Temple in Salt Lake City would take such a long time to build, it was thought best" to erect another one in southern Utah. In the warmer climate, construction could proceed year-round. Furthermore, President Taylor continued, "there was a people living here who were more worthy than any others. . . . God inspired President Young to build a Temple here because of the fidelity and self-abnegation of the people."[33]

Brigham Young directed local Church leaders to consider possible sites where the temple might be built. Two hilltop locations were proposed, but the group could not agree on which to recommend. When President Young arrived, he "somewhat impatiently chided them, and at the same time asked them to get into their wagons, or whatever else they had, and with him find a location (site)." He had them drive to the lowest part of the valley, a swamp infested with marsh grass and cattails.

"But, Brother Young," protested the men, "this land is boggy. After a storm, and for several months of the year, no one can drive across the land without horses and wagons sinking way down.

St. George Temple during construction phase, ca. 1875. Ground was broken 9 November 1871 under the direction of President Brigham Young. The temple was officially dedicated on 6 April 1877, the dedicatory prayer being offered by President Daniel H. Wells, second counselor to President Young.

There is no place to build a foundation." President Young countered, "We will make a foundation."

Later on while plowing and scraping where the foundation was to be, a horse's leg broke through the ground into a spring of water. The brethren then wanted to move the foundation line twelve feet to the south, so that the spring of water would be on the outside of the temple.

"'Not so,'" insisted Brigham Young. "'We will wall it up and leave it here for some future use. But we cannot move the foundation. This spot was dedicated by the Nephites. They could not build it [the Temple], but we can and will build it for them.'"[34]

Because of the sparseness of the population and the lack of funds, many wondered how the temple could be built. "We do not need capital," President Young insisted. "We have raw material; we have labor; we have skill. We are better able to build a temple than the Saints were in Nauvoo."[35]

When ground was broken on 9 November 1871, music was provided by a Swiss brass band from nearby Santa Clara. "If the brethren undertake to do this work with one heart and mind," President Brigham Young promised, "we shall be blessed exceedingly, and prospered of the Lord in our earthly substance."

Placing his spade in the ground, President Young declared: "I now commence by moving this dirt in the name of Israel's God." All present responded with "Amen." Erastus Snow earnestly prayed "that our beloved President, Brigham, might live to officiate at [the temple's] dedication." The people again "gave a hearty Amen." After the congregation sang "The Spirit of God," President Young stood on a chair and led them in the Hosanna Shout. That very afternoon, plows and scrapers began excavating for the foundation.[36]

The baptismal font and oxen, constructed in Salt Lake City, were a personal gift of President Brigham Young. The font was shipped in sections and assembled in the partially completed temple.

The Southern Utah Saints eagerly pushed the temple's construction so that sacred ordinance work could begin as soon as possible. They gathered at the temple on New Year's Day of 1877 in order to dedicate the portions of the building sufficiently completed at that time. President Brigham Young was determined to attend the services, even though he was so ill that he had to be carried about in a large chair by four men. He had not expected to speak but during the service received enough strength that he was able to walk to the pulpit and address the congregation with great power:

> Now we have a Temple which will all be finished within a few days. . . . We enjoy privileges that are enjoyed by no one else on the face of the earth. Suppose we were awake to this thing, namely, the salvation of the human family, this house would be crowded, as we hope it will be, from Monday morning until Saturday night. . . . What do you suppose the fathers would say if they could speak from the dead? Would they not say, "We have lain here thousands of years, here in this prison house, waiting for this dispensation to come?" . . . When I think upon this subject, I want the tongues of

> seven thunders to wake up the people. Can the fathers be saved without us? No. Can we be saved without them? No.

One who was present recalled that as President Young spoke, he "brought his cane down very hard on the pulpit. He said, 'If I mar the pulpit some of these good workmen can fix it up again.' He did mar the pulpit but the people did not fix it up again. They left it for a mark to be carried through the years."[37]

Baptisms for the dead commenced in the temple 9 January 1877, with Elder Wilford Woodruff personally baptizing and confirming the first 141. President Brigham Young also assisted in the laying on of hands. Two days later, for the first time in this dispensation, the endowment was also given in behalf of the dead. Not long before, President Young had told some temple workers that he had just learned by revelation "that it takes as full and complete a set of ordinances for the dead as for the living."[38]

Up to this time, the endowment teachings had been communicated from one person to another in oral form only. President Brigham Young, however, as the lone survivor of the original group receiving the endowment from Joseph Smith in 1842, was concerned that this ordinance be preserved in a perfect form. He therefore spent much time during the early months of 1877 working with two members of the Twelve, who wrote these ceremonies from beginning to end and then taught them to the temple workers.[39] In the midst of these developments, the Church's annual general conference convened in the now completed St. George Temple, which was officially dedicated at this time.

On his way back to Salt Lake City from the St. George Temple dedication, President Brigham Young stopped in Manti to dedicate the site for another temple. A controversy had arisen concerning whether the temple should be located in Manti or the nearby larger town of Ephraim. He arrived 24 April 1877, and on that same afternoon personally supervised the work of William Folsom and Truman O. Angell, Jr., as they surveyed the Manti site and set stakes.

During a stake conference meeting the following morning, Brigham Young unexpectedly stood up and left. He asked Warren S. Snow to go with him to the temple hill. Snow recalled that they proceeded to the southeast corner of where the temple would stand. "Here is the spot where the Prophet Moroni stood and dedicated this piece of land for a Temple site," President Young affirmed, "and that is the reason why the location is made here, and we can't move it from this spot; and if you and I are the only persons that come here at high noon to-day, we will dedicate this ground."[40] Several hundred were present at the appointed hour.

Ground was broken for the Logan Temple the following month. President Young reminded the Saints that the temple would be constructed by volunteer labor; "wages are entirely out of the question." Nevertheless, the temple can be built "without any burden to ourselves," he insisted, "if our hearts are in the work, and we will be blessed abundantly in doing so. We will be better off in our temporal affairs when it is completed than when we commenced."[41]

The basic architectural concept for these new temples was worked out by Truman O. Angell, Jr., under the personal direction of the Prophet Brigham Young. Both the Manti and Logan Temples had similar dimensions, were built in the castellated style with local stone, and had two towers. Even though these temples were completed under the direction of John Taylor, their architects acknowledged that the concept for their design had originated with Brigham Young.[42]

Brigham Young did not live to see either of these last two temples completed. However, his involvement in temple work did not end with his death. Those speaking at later temple dedications often declared him to be among guests from the spirit world that were present. Without a doubt, Brigham Young's achievements and lingering influence have caused those "bells of hell" to ring!

NOTES

1. *Journal of Discourses,* 8: 355.
2. Leonard J. Arrington, *Brigham Young: American Moses* (New York: Alfred A. Knopf, 1985), 51.
3. *History of the Church,* 2: 383.
4. Arrington, 53. For additional information on the temple-related events in which Brigham Young participated, see Richard O. Cowan, *Temples to Dot the Earth* (Salt Lake City: Bookcraft, 1989), chapters 2–5.

5. *Journal of Discourses*, 14: 320; 24: 197.
6. *Journal of Discourses*, 2: 31; 18: 303.
7. *History of the Church*, 4: 454.
8. Brigham H. Roberts, *A Comprehensive History of the Church of Jesus Christ of Latter-day Saints* (Provo, Utah: BYU Press, 1965), 2: 472.
9. James E. Talmage, *The House of the Lord* (Salt Lake City: Bookcraft, 1962), 99–100.
10. Lyle G. Brown, "The Sacred Departments for Temple Work in Nauvoo: The Assembly Room and the Council Chamber," *BYU Studies* 19 (Spring 1979): 363.
11. Lucius N. Scovil letter in *Deseret News Semi Weekly*, 15 February 1884, 2, as quoted in *BYU Studies* 19 (Winter 1979): 159n.
12. Diary of L. John Nuttall, 7 February 1877, as quoted in *BYU Studies* 19 (Winter 1979): 159n.
13. *Millennial Star* 5 (March 1845): 151.
14. Heber Kimball Journal, in Helen Whitney, *Women's Exponent* 11, 1883, 169–70.
15. *History of the Church*, 7: 417–18.
16. *History of the Church*, 7: 567.
17. *History of the Church*, 7: 579.
18. Matthias F. Cowley, *Wilford Woodruff: History of His Life and Labors* (Salt Lake City: Deseret News, 1909), 255.
19. Ibid., 619–20.
20. *Journal of Discourses*, 2: 33; James H. Anderson, "The Salt Lake Temple," *The Contributor* 14 (April 1893): 252–59.
21. *Journal of Discourses*, 1: 132–33.
22. Roberts, 3: 86.
23. *History of the Church*, 4: 608.
24. Journal History of The Church of Jesus Christ of Latter-day Saints, 5 May 1855, 1–2, Library-Archives, Historical Department of The Church of Jesus Christ of Latter-day Saints (hereafter cited as LDS Church Historical Archives).
25. Marvin E. Smith, "The Builder," *Improvement Era* 45 (October 1942): 630.
26. Wilford Woodruff Historian's Private Journal, Ms F 348, No. 4, entry 22 August 1862, LDS Church Historical Archives; see also Wilford Woodruff's Journal, 23 August 1862, 6: 71.
27. Wilford Woodruff Historian's Private Journal, Ms F 348, No. 4, entry 7 July 1863.
28. *Journal of Discourses*, 15: 138.
29. *Journal of Discourses*, 10: 254.
30. *Journal of Discourses*, 16: 186–87; Wilford Woodruff's Journal, 13 July 1865, 6: 232.
31. James R. Clark, comp., *Messages of the First Presidency of The Church of Jesus*

Christ of Latter-day Saints, 6 vols. (Salt Lake City: Bookcraft, 1965–75), 2: 278–80.

32. Daniel Tyler, "Temples," *Juvenile Instructor* 15 (15 August 1880): 182.
33. *Journal of Discourses,* 23: 14.
34. Statement by David H. Cannon, Jr., 14 October 1942, quoted in Kirk M. Curtis, "History of the St. George Temple" (master's thesis, Brigham Young University, 1964), 24–25.
35. Juanita Brooks, "The St. George Temple," Juanita Brooks Papers, Utah State Historical Society, 3.
36. Tyler, 182; Janice Force DeMille, *The St. George Temple First 100 Years* (Hurricane, Utah: Homestead Publishers, 1977), 21–23.
37. Maggie Cragun interview, "The Dedication of the St. George Temple," Juanita Brooks papers, Utah State Historical Society; Brigham Young, 1 January 1877, in *Journal of Discourses,* 18: 304.
38. Brigham Jarvis to Susa Young Gates, 8 November 1926, Susa Young Gates papers, Utah State Historical Society.
39. Wilford Woodruff's Journal, 14 January, 12 February, and 21 March 1877, 7: 322, 327, and 340; see also "St. George Temple: One Hundred Years of Service," *Ensign* (March 1977): 94.
40. Moses F. Farnsworth (Manti Temple Recorder) to George Teasdale, 2 July 1888, as cited in *Millennial Star* 50 (13 August 1888): 521; Barbara Lee Hargis, "A Folk History of the Manti Temple: A Study of the Folklore and Traditions Connected with the Settlement of Manti, Utah, and the Building of the Temple" (master's thesis, Brigham Young University, 1968), 55–56.
41. *Journal of Discourses,* 19: 33.
42. Cowan, 83–84.

CHAPTER 11

Brigham Young and the Mormon Reformation

Paul H. Peterson
Associate Professor of Church History and Doctrine
Brigham Young University

The Mormon Reformation of 1856 and 1857 was the most fervent, emotionally laden reform movement in Church history. No other reform effort in the one hundred sixty-five years since the organization of the Church has been characterized by such earnestness, such ardor, such impetuosity, and even such extremes.

In recent years, this interesting and controversial era has received a fair bit of scholarly attention. Various books and essays have told us much about the origins and course of reform, as well as about some of the principal reform leaders, especially Jedediah Grant and Wilford Woodruff.[1] But little has been said regarding the role President Brigham Young played in the Mormon Reformation.

In this essay, I will attempt to address this deficiency. Naturally, in detailing Young's involvement it will be necessary to review some of the basic history of the reform movement.

THE ORIGINS OF REFORM

It was with high expectations that Brigham Young and the Mormon pioneers traveled westward to the Great Basin. Throughout their brief history, Latter-day Saints had been kicked about with some regularity; it happened with varying degrees of severity wherever they had located as a people—in New York, Ohio, Missouri, and Illinois.

Understandably, the Saints expected an end to gentile intrusion and harassment when they moved to the isolated region of the Rocky Mountains. Here, they reckoned, peace would finally prevail. As Brigham indicated in a speech given to assembled pioneers on the way westward, "they were going to look out [for] a home for the saints where they would be free from persecution by the gentiles, where we could dwell in peace and serve God according to the Holy Priesthood, where we could build up the kingdom, so that the nations would begin to flock to our standard."[2] The climax of this kingdom-building effort, the Saints anticipated, would come with the second coming of the Savior.

But no kingdom could be built, Brigham Young reasoned, without a unified and prepared people. Latter-day Saints "would have to keep the Celestial law." They would have to "keep the law of the gospel & obey his commandments undisturbed."[3] Not surprisingly, for almost all Saints, reaching such lofty standards required some modification in behavior, however great or small. Earlier, while sojourning at Winter Quarters, Brigham had intimated that certain actions that had been tolerated in the past would no longer be countenanced once they reached their Rocky Mountain haven. Regarding the comparatively lax approach that some Saints had assumed toward drinking and using tobacco, for example, Brigham told Saints outright that "when you go to a Stake of Zion you will have to quit it [using the forbidden articles]."[4]

But the Saints, good people as they were, could never quite reach a level of behavior that satisfied the idealistic expectations of Church leaders. In fact, it may be that in some aspects of gospel living, there had been some spiritual slippage along the way. Assessing the collective moral tone of any community without some hard data is always risky business, but it may be that B. H. Roberts was right when he observed that the Saints' decade of "camp life" existence following the exodus from Nauvoo in 1846 "made it difficult to establish regularity of life and to enforce discipline."[5] More recently, historian Thomas G. Alexander, in a perceptive article on Wilford Woodruff's role in the Reformation, suggested that Church leaders wanted to restore the collective spirituality that Saints had enjoyed earlier in the 1830s and 1840s.[6]

In practical terms, of course, whether there had been

progression or retrogression in keeping the commandments was hardly the point. In the minds of Church leaders, the present level of obedience was deemed insufficient. Thus, within a few years of the Saints' arrival in the Valley, reform sentiment could be detected. As early as 1851, Heber C. Kimball "noted that there is a reformation about to commence and my heart and soul is in it."[7] By 1854, reform became a recurrent theme.

Finally, in 1855, dissatisfied with the Saints' collective level of obedience, Brigham Young instigated a home missionary program. Young called the Pratt brothers, Orson and Parley, and Wilford Woodruff to supervise the program. The overall intent of the program, as Thomas Alexander noted, was to "reinfuse the temporal shell with spiritual substance."[8] In other words, it was an attempt to shake the Saints from their perceived spiritual lethargy and point them in a more righteous direction. "Many are stupid, careless, and unconcerned," remarked Brigham at the October 1855 general conference. "They are off their watch, neglect their prayers, forget their covenants and forsake their God, and the devil has power over them."[9] Later in that same address, the Mormon president urged the Saints to repent "that we be chastened no more."[10]

The chastening Young had reference to, at least in part, was a series of natural disasters that had, from 1855 on, brought hardship and heartache to the Latter-day Saint community. In April 1855, grasshoppers caused extensive damage to crops. Even worse, a severe drought accompanied the grasshopper invasion. Further damage to the community was brought about by canyon fires that destroyed valuable stands of timber. And finally, as though the Saints had not suffered sufficiently, the uncommonly harsh winter from the end of 1856 through the beginning of 1857 destroyed much of the Church cattle stock.[11]

The effect of such natural afflictions upon the Latter-day Saint community was devastating. Church members were short on foodstuffs, poverty was widespread, and, for some, begging and hoarding became habitual. Money was next to useless and could not buy flour or meal. Altogether, it was perhaps the most challenging crisis the Saints had yet faced during their short sojourn in Utah Territory.[12]

Throughout this difficult period, the response of Mormon leaders was both predictable and consistent. Like their Old Testament forebears, they reasoned that modern Israel's problems were rooted in disobedience and unrighteousness. In this context, then, the natural disasters were viewed as but one more evidence that God was displeased with the Saints and that a course of reform was in order.[13]

THE INSTIGATION OF THE MORMON REFORMATION

By late August or early September of 1856, it was apparent that Brigham Young felt that the home missionary movement he had instigated a year earlier had not produced sufficient results and that more potent measures were needed. On 7 September 1856, Brigham told Jedediah M. Grant, Wilford Woodruff, and Parley P. Pratt that he personally desired to accompany Grant (his second counselor in the First Presidency) and the Twelve on a preaching mission through the Territory. On this occasion, Brigham lamented that he spent "so much of my time in attending to temporal matters. I feel that with the assistance of my brethren," he declared, "that I could make a great wake by going through this Territory & preaching the gospel to the people."[14]

Judging by a comment Young made approximately one year later, he clearly felt that a "great wake" was necessary. In August 1857, some four months after the Reformation in Zion had run its course, President Young described how his concern and frustration with the spiritual condition of the Latter-day Saints a year earlier eventually culminated in a reformation in the fall of 1856:

> I thank my Father in heaven, yes my soul says glory, hallelujah, praise the name of Israel's God, for the blessings I enjoy at the present time. One year ago this very day, and previous to that time, my soul was pained within me. No tongue could tell, it could not be portrayed before the people, the feelings that I had; I could not tell them, and I did not know but that, if I should come out in the presence of the people and try to speak my feelings, they would call

> me crazy. However, I tried to make the people understand my feelings, but no tongue could tell them; and I actually believe that I would have lived but a little time in this existence, had not God waked up the people. I wanted to take up my valise and go throughout the Territory crying, is there a man in this Territory for God.
>
> If you want to know how I felt, I cannot tell you better than by describing my feelings in the way that I am now doing. One day I told a number of the brethren how I felt, as well, as I could, and br. Jedediah M. Grant partook of the Spirit that was in me and walked out like a man—like a giant—and like an angel—and he scattered the fire of the Almighty among the people. But what was the result, so far as he was concerned? He went beyond his strength, and it cost him his life.[15]

But if it was Brigham Young who conceived the idea of a reformation, it was his counselor Jedediah Grant, at least early on, who charted its course and molded its contours. It was Grant who, on assignment from Brigham Young, journeyed to Kaysville, Davis County, Utah, to conduct a four-day conference. During the course of that conference, Grant urged the Saints not only to stay true to their covenants but also to indicate their desire to do so by renewing them through rebaptism. Some five hundred Saints were immersed under Grant's direction; approximately eighty, including the bishop and his counselors, were baptized by Jedediah himself. Clearly, it was Jedediah Grant's decision to require rebaptism as an indication of covenant renewal. As Jedediah himself later observed, "when he got there he felt like baptizing and confirming them anew into the Church."[16]

It was also likely that Jedediah Grant conceived the idea of a catechism and actually formulated it. The catechism consisted of a number of questions to measure individual worthiness. Most often it was administered by home teachers to assigned families. It would appear that Jedediah devised the idea of catechism on his initial reformation journey to Davis County settlements in September 1856. On that occasion, Grant questioned bishops and counselors on such things as whether they prayed regularly and whether they bathed as often as they should. Obviously not satisfied with the answers to his queries, Brigham's forthright counselor supplemented

Jedediah M. Grant (1816–1856), ca. 1855. Second counselor to Brigham Young and a leading participant in the Mormon Reformation.

these early questions with later ones, and a twenty-seven-question catechism covering both temporal and spiritual realms was the end result.[17]

It is interesting, perhaps instructive, that Brigham Young allowed Grant so much leeway in directing reformative efforts. Leonard J. Arrington, Young's foremost biographer, noted that when Brigham was President of the Church, "he was so confident of his own abilities that he was loath to delegate responsibility or authority."[18] Assuming Arrington is correct, it may be, some might argue, that the Reformation provides a notable exception. Certainly, it would seem Brigham had no qualms about letting Jedediah set both the early tone and the pace. Clearly, up to mid-November 1856, the Reformation movement bore the stamp of Jedediah Grant's imprint. Indeed, it almost appears that Brigham made a calculated decision to let his fiery counselor hold rein over the Reformation while he himself, inconspicuously but deliberately, retreated into the background.

Jedediah once observed that President Young was "more merciful than I am. When he extends mercy to the people," Grant said, "he deals it out more lavishly than I would."[19] Perhaps the paternalistic and pragmatic Mormon prophet reasoned that given the Saints' lack of spiritual fiber, a fair dose of Grant's "merciless talk" was in order. It could well serve, he likely assumed, the propitious purpose of frightening them into conformity with gospel principles.

BRIGHAM YOUNG'S ROLE

What part then, it may fairly be asked, did Brigham Young play during the Reformation? What role or roles, if any, did he assume? Was he an absentee landlord, willing to allow Jedediah Grant to assume full responsibility? Hardly. A careful review of the sources indicates that Brigham, while not always a visible, front-stage performer, was a major player in reformative events.

It is quite true that Jedediah Grant set the early impassioned pace of reform and that after Jedediah's death, Wilford Woodruff introduced a moderate, merciful tone into reform efforts. But I believe that both Grant and Woodruff were operating with the tacit approval, if not actual marching orders, of Brigham Young. In the remainder of this essay, I have identified at least six contributions, some of which admittedly were no more than symbolic gestures, that Young made to the course of reform. All six were of fundamental importance in shaping the pattern of reform.

Brigham Young's first contribution, of course, was his instigation of the actual reformation. The evidence, while not overwhelming, suggests that it was Brigham who first recognized that the Saints needed to be roused from their spiritual slumber, and it was Brigham who sent Jedediah Grant to Davis County to preach reform.

Brigham's second contribution was providing prophetic sanction and support to the early fervent, revivalistic tone established by Jedediah Grant by delivering his own series of stinging addresses on successive Sundays at the reform's outset. In so doing, President Young was supported by loyal confidante and first counselor, Heber C. Kimball. On the same Sunday that Jedediah was telling Saints in Kaysville to live their religion, Brigham was rebuking Saints convened in Salt Lake City for "lying, stealing, swareing, commiting Adultery, quarelling with Husbands wives & Children & many other Evils." Wilford Woodruff recorded that "it was one of the strongest addresses . . . ever delivered to this church" and that Young's "voice & words were like the thundering of Mount Sinai."[20]

One week later, on 21 September, the entire First Presidency spoke to Saints assembled in Salt Lake City. On this occasion, Brigham Young gave two sermons—one in the morning and another in the afternoon. In the morning session, Brigham, along with counselors Kimball and Grant and others, "spoke by the power of the priesthood & the Holy Ghost." According to Woodruff, "they sent arrows into the harts of men & at the Close of the meeting President Young Called upon all the Congregation who were for God & who would covenant to keep his Commandments to rise upon their feet & evry person rose in the Congregation."

During the afternoon session, President Young "reproved & rebuked the sins of the people" and suggested that "for some sins no blood would be acceptable except the life & blood of the individual." Not surprising, Woodruff noted that this last observation caused "the Harts of many [to] tremble."[21]

On the third Sunday, 28 September, probably by design, Young again admonished Church members to repent. Woodruff recorded in his journal that evening that "I never heard as strong & powerful sermons ever delivered by the presidency of this Church as I have heard of preached from them of Late."[22]

All in all, the sermons Brigham Young preached in September 1856 were as bold and controversial as any he gave in his storied administration. It is clear that in some cases, and especially in the sermon on 21 September, Brigham resorted to hyperbole and incendiary images in an effort to frighten Saints into compliance with gospel principles. The ever-practical Mormon leader was never above resorting to rhetorical excess if it resulted in practical good—in this case, the enhancement of the collective moral tone of the community.

A review of Brigham Young's correspondence during these months makes it clear that Brigham hardly expected any Saint to shed his blood. Indeed, in private letters to Church leaders, Brigham instructed them to forgive Saints freely, even of serious sin, if they evidenced any desire to repent.[23] But some Church members, unaware of Brigham's penchant for calculated exaggeration, were undoubtedly concerned. Certainly his rhetoric caused excitement among some Latter-day Saints and contributed to the emotionally charged atmosphere that prevailed in Zion during the remainder of the year.

Brigham Young's third contribution had to do with setting a standard of behavior that ultimately became a Reformation fundamental—rebaptism. Grant had instigated rebaptism at the beginning conference of the Reformation in Kaysville, and the ordinance quickly became a test of fellowship for the Saints. Those who were unwilling to renew their gospel covenants through the waters of rebaptism were considered spiritually unfit.

On 2 October 1856, Brigham, Heber, Jedediah, Wilford, and other Church leaders knelt around the newly completed baptismal font just east of the temple site. Upon direction from Brigham Young, Heber dedicated the baptismal font to the Lord. "Now O Lord except of this dedication at our hands," Heber solemnly pleaded, "and as we go into this water may our sins be forgiven & not be remembered against us any more. May we feel the power of God and have power to work a great Reformation among this people."[24] President Young then rebaptized and reconfirmed counselors Kimball and Grant and various others. After Brigham had performed these ordinances, he himself was rebaptized and reconfirmed by Heber.[25] Three days later, after the Sunday worship session had concluded, Brigham, Heber, and other leaders retired to the baptismal font, where they rebaptized and reconfirmed their own families. Altogether, Brigham Young rebaptized seventy-five family members.[26]

Brigham's fourth and fifth contributions were closely related. The fourth, the withdrawal of the sacrament, had the effect of reminding the Saints that in their present state of unworthiness, they were unfit to partake of the holy emblems. The fifth, coming within hours of the fourth in almost an orchestrated manner, was a spirited declaration that the Reformation era was to be a singularly unique dispensation of mercy—a period when the Lord would forgive any and all sins.

It was around 9 November 1856 that the decision to withdraw the sacrament was announced to the Saints in the immediate area surrounding Church headquarters. Although there is no way of knowing if the denial of the sacrament was expressly Brigham Young's idea, it is inconceivable that such a course would have been taken without his consent or encouragement. It is clear that, early on, Brigham was concerned about Saints who would participate in the ordinance of rebaptism merely to satisfy current fashion. In a letter to Church member Welcome Chapman, Brigham

Young observed that "many will go into the waters of baptism . . . who are guilty of the most heinous crimes in the sight of both God and Man." "We want the guilty," asserted the Mormon leader, "to confess their sins, and repent of all their wickedness before they go into the waters of baptism."[27] In all probability, Brigham would have been equally concerned about those who partook of the sacrament as a matter of convention with little concern about their individual worthiness.

Heber C. Kimball, first counselor in the First Presidency, gave the primary sermon justifying sacrament withdrawal in the afternoon worship session on 9 November 1856. While bishops were preparing the sacramental emblems, Kimball forthrightly told assembled Saints, "I forbid all unworthy persons partaking of this sacrament; and if such do partake of it, they shall do it on their own responsibility, and not on mine."[28]

Jedediah M. Grant, second counselor, spoke immediately after Kimball and reinforced his fellow counselor's emphasis. "I therefore, want every person to leave the bread in the salvers, and the water in the cups, and not partake of the sacrament," Jedediah warned the Saints, "unless they are right."[29] It would appear that from mid-November 1856 until April 1857, a majority of Saints in the Salt Lake City area (and perhaps elsewhere) were denied the sacrament.

It would also appear that the restoration of the sacrament in April 1857 was the logical culmination of a series of important decisions that were coordinated by Church leaders. In early February 1857, Brigham returned to public life after an eight-week hiatus, an obvious indication that he was pleased with the reformative efforts of the Saints.[30] On 10 February, home missionaries reported that nearly all members in their assigned wards were worthy and ready for rebaptism.[31] In March, most Salt Lake area Church members were rebaptized as ward units on designated days.[32] And in April, the sacrament was finally restored.

Elder Thomas Jeremy likely represented the feelings of most Church members when he thanked God for his kindness in restoring the sacrament. "I pray . . . to my Heavenly Father," Jeremy wrote, "that He may bless me and my family that we may ever be worthy of partaking of this most holy ordinance acceptably."[33]

It was also on 9 November 1856, probably in the evening at a meeting of seventies, that Brigham Young first announced that the sins of the Latter-day Saints could be forgiven. Up to that point, Jedediah Grant's approach of "raining pitchforks" had characterized the course of reform. But, ultimately, the seemingly contrary elements of mercy and forgiveness that Young introduced and that Wilford Woodruff promulgated became a dominant reformation theme. Obviously some of this change was due to Grant's untimely death in early December, but it undoubtedly would have occurred sooner or later.[34] The notion that forbearance and forgiveness were dominant Reformation themes is one that has by and large eluded the analysis of many scholars who have studied this era, probably because it, at least on the surface, seems to run counter to the prevailing image of the Reformation as a time of sternness and unbending severity.

Brigham Young introduced the notion of mercy in a dramatic manner. He apparently entered the Seventies Hall on the evening of 9 November as Wilford Woodruff was in the middle of a spirited sermon. Three additional speakers addressed the congregation, whereupon Brigham strode to the platform and "promised the people in the name of Jesus Christ if they would repent & turn from their sins from that hour all their sins should be forgiven them & not remembered against them No more forever either on Earth or in Heaven." Understandably, Young's declaration was received with elation by many, some of whom likely felt they were beyond pardon. "O what Joy this should give the people," Wilford Woodruff wrote, "for they have nearly all signed [sinned] more or less. My soul was filled with Joy," Woodruff added, "at the teachings presented by President Young."[35]

Brigham Young's declaration that the Reformation was to be a time of mercy was quickly conveyed to ecclesiastical leaders throughout the Territory. Bishop Tarleton Lewis of Parowan was instructed to tell his congregation that "all manner of sin, save it be the sin against the Holy Ghost," was forgiven.[36] "I do not wish to know the names nor the errors of them who are called Saints,"

Brigham stressed in a letter to Bishop Philo Farnsworth. "Let it suffice that they [sinners] confess and forsake their sins, and live nearer to the Lord than they have hitherto done."[37]

While stressing that the Reformation was an almost unparalleled time of mercy, Church leaders also made it plain that this spiritual injunction was a temporary one. "Give them [the saints] to understand if . . . they commit sins hereafter they will be brought to judgment," Apostle Franklin D. Richards instructed home missionaries, "and it will be laid to the line and there will not be the mercy that is now shown."[38]

"Our sins are looked upon as the sins of ignorance," noted Lorenzo Brown, a member of the Church, "and the God of Heaven in His infinite goodness is pleased to pass by them without an atonement, but from this time forward all sins have to be atoned for."[39]

Brigham Young's sixth and final contribution to the course of reform amounted to a simple retirement from public worship services. Recognizing that many Church members feared that a removal of the sources of revelation would result in individual spiritual deprivation, Brigham and other Church leaders threatened to leave the Latter-day Saint community spiritually stranded, by death or otherwise, if the Saints didn't repent. Indeed, President Young indicated that unless the Saints speedily repented, there would be little option but to leave—the sins of the Saints had put inexorable burdens on Church leaders—burdens that could not be borne much longer. Jedediah Grant had sensed this, and in trying to share the weight of collective sin, died of fatigue.[40] Fortunately, the improvement in community morals and righteousness as a result of the Reformation had alleviated much of the burden.[41] Any future deviation, however, could result in the Saints being stripped of their leadership and priesthood.[42]

To give the Saints a taste of what could happen without presiding leaders, Brigham and Heber deliberately stayed away from weekly public worship services at the Tabernacle through December and January. Brigham's last public address was given on 4 December at Jedediah Grant's funeral. Later, while Apostles, such as Wilford Woodruff and Orson Hyde, sometimes spoke, Young and Kimball never even appeared on the stand. During this period, they did attend meetings with missionaries and bishops, legislative council sessions, and Sunday prayer circle meetings, but they never attended large public worship assemblies.

On 28 December 1856, Wilford Woodruff told assembled Saints at the Tabernacle that "the First Presidency . . . have retired from our midst because the people will not do as they are told—that is they withdrew themselves from the people for the present."[43] On this occasion, Woodruff gave the Saints two alternatives: Would they "Go to & get the power of God & sustain the Melchezedek Priesthood with the first Presidency & Twelve or would they reject it & have the Presidency & Twelve & Melchezedek [Priesthood] taken from them & ownly [possess] the Aaron[ic] Priesthood given them & a Law of Carnal Commandments." Observed Woodruff: "The people must do one or the other."[44]

On 1 February 1857, Presidents Young and Kimball returned to the Saints in striking fashion. Wilford Woodruff noted that, perhaps in anticipation of the return of their leaders, the "Tabernacle & the House was Filled to overflowing." As Church member A. Cordon, spoke, Heber came in and was soon followed by Brigham Young. According to Woodruff, "it created a great Sensation among the people." Apparently Cordon, sensitive to the long-awaited return of President Young, completed his address quickly, whereupon Brigham "arose and addressed the people" for about an hour an a half.[45]

THE REFORMATION LEGACY

The Reformation, at least in the area around Church headquarters, ended in the spring of 1857, when Salt Lake City ward members were rebaptized and the sacrament was restored. Many Saints noted that reform had led to a marked improvement in community morale. And even Brigham Young, it would seem, was pleased with the results of the Reformation, at least initially. "When Bro. Brigham comes to the stand there is no scourging and whipping as it used to be," noted Salt Lake Fifth Ward member David Fulmer, "but he is full of blessings for the people which is a manifestation that the Lord is pleased with us. I never saw such a time as the present since I came into the Church."[46]

But President Young was clearly humming a different tune some eighteen months later. In that intervening period, traumatic events took place that both deflated much of the good that had been achieved during the reform and altered President Young's own personal theological landscape. Johnston's army had marched through Salt Lake City in spite of Orson Hyde's assurance that it would be overthrown on the way.[47] Instead of defiantly challenging the forces of evil, as Church leaders initially declared, the Saints chose to retreat. Between the end of March and mid-May 1858, some thirty thousand Saints moved south to the area around Provo, Utah. On 30 June, two weeks after a peace agreement, Brigham told his bedraggled followers they could return home.

During the months immediately following the return of the Saints to their former homes, there was clearly a waning of Reformation zeal. Seemingly, the frustration of realizing that an army had not only reached the Valley but had actually set up shop in Utah Territory, and the tumult and turmoil occasioned by the Saints' move and their return, caused many Church members to lose their reform fervor.

Understandably, the fact that so many Saints squandered their spiritual gains so quickly caused Brigham Young some amount of pain. After all, he, Jedediah, Wilford, and others had invested more than a fair amount of time and energy into the reform effort. It was clearly a disappointed and possibly even a disenchanted leader who made the following assessment of the Reformation in November 1858:

> Do you think I feel like preaching to such a people? I have preached to them until they are almost preached to death, and I do not feel like preaching much more to them. You know how I felt some two or three years ago this fall or the latter part of the summer. I felt as tho' I could not live without taking my valise in my hand and walking through this Territory to find out if there was a man for God, for it seemed to me as tho' the whole people had gone astray. I related my feelings to a few, and they started out. Jedediah fell a victim to that spirit, he took it from me, and he labored until he went into his grave, to find among all the people who had forsaken their homes and their all in foreign countries to come to this place [who] were still for Christ and

> none else. We had a reformation, and what is the result? I will tell you by relating an anecdote. It was asked an Elder in one of the settlements if the reformation had reached them; "Yes," he replied, "and thank God it is all over." That is the almost universal feeling now. Unless some men are held by the collar, or by the hair of the head they will go to hell—they will not cleave to the Lord with all their hearts.[48]

But Reformation failure brought more than just suffering to Brigham Young's soul. Indeed, it may well be that the failure of the Reformation to take hold in any meaningful, long-term way in the Mormon community initiated a change in Brigham's preaching—both with regard to style and substance. To be sure, the change was a gradual one—extending from 1857 to the end of the Civil War in 1865. This was a process—not an event. But imperceptible as it might be to some, a close reading of Brigham's sermons lends support to such a conclusion.

In terms of style, Brigham's later speeches featured less overstatement and hyperbole, less bombast and militancy. Perhaps it was the failure of the Reformation to bring about lasting change that made Brigham Young first realize that he could not "drive a man or a woman to heaven." "People are not to be driven," Brigham told Saints in 1861, "and you can put into a gnat's eye all the souls of the children of men that are driven into heaven by preaching hell-fire." One could be much better served, he maintained, by "instruct[ing] people until they increase in knowledge and understanding, until their traditions pass away, and they will become of one heart and mind in the principles of godliness."[49]

The stylistic changes were but a manifestation of some substantive reflection. From late 1857 on, there was a good bit of theological reevaluation that ultimately led to community redirection. The notion of creating what sociologist Thomas O'Dea called a "near nation" needed to be weighed against pressing realities.[50] For Brigham Young, as historian Leonard J. Arrington observed, the 1850s had been a confidence shaker. There were the harsh natural disasters, the coming of an army and subsequently more gentiles to Utah Territory, and the failure of the Saints to maintain early Reformation levels of obedience and unity. On top of these concerns, the Civil War, which for a time rekindled nationalistic fires, did not bring about the cataclysmic societal upheaval that would result in the consummation of all things.[51]

But interestingly, there is little evidence that the unforeseen disruptions of the 1850s and early 1860s had much effect on Brigham Young's eternal scheme of things. He remained adamant that God's designs would never be canceled.[52] But the wise, astute Mormon leader probably did concede that they might need to be postponed. It just might be, he reasoned, that the Saints might not go to Missouri for a while. It just might be that gentiles were here to stay. It just might be that the United States will be intact for an extended period of time.

Such realizations, not surprisingly, led to a spirit of semi-conciliation and long-term planning. Brigham Young placed new emphasis on temple-building and temple work. The Relief Society was reorganized after a fifteen-year gap, and retrenchment societies were founded. The nationalistic fervor and feelings of immediacy that characterized the 1850s and that were brought to their apogee by Reformation fervor gradually gave way to compromise, conciliation, and conformity. In short, gradual and piecemeal as it may have been, it was the dawning of a new spirit and of a new era.[53]

NOTES

1. Standard studies on the Reformation era include Howard Claire Searle, "The Mormon Reformation of 1856–1857" (master's thesis, Brigham Young University, 1956); Gustive O. Larson, "The Mormon Reformation," *Utah Historical Quarterly* 26 (January 1958): 45–63; Michael Orme, "The Causes of the Mormon Reformation of 1856–1857," *Tangents* (Spring 1975): 15–40; and Paul H. Peterson, "The Mormon Reformation of 1856–1857: The Rhetoric and the Reality," *Journal of Mormon History* 15 (1989): 59–87. Helpful studies on important Reformation leaders include Gene Sessions' *Mormon Thunder: A Documentary History of Jedediah Morgan Grant* (Urbana: University of Illinois Press, 1982); and Thomas G. Alexander, "Wilford Woodruff and the Mormon Reformation of 1855–1857," *Dialogue* 25 (Summer 1992): 25–39.
2. George D. Smith, ed., *An Intimate Chronicle: The Journals of William Clayton* (Salt Lake City: Signature Books in association with Smith Research Associates, 1991), 325 (29 May 1847). See also *Wilford Woodruff's Journal: 1833–1898*, typescript, Scott Kenney, ed., 9 vols. (Midvale, Utah: Signature Books, 1983–1985), 3: 188–189 (29 May 1847).
3. *Wilford Woodruff's Journal*, 3: 188–89.

4. Minutes of Thomas Bullock, 26 March 1847, typescript, copy Joseph Fielding Smith Institute, Brigham Young University.
5. B. H. Roberts, *A Comprehensive History of The Church of Jesus Christ of Latter-day Saints,* 6 vols. (Provo, Utah: Brigham Young University Press, 1965), 4: 119.
6. Alexander, 28.
7. Martha Spence Heywood Diary, typescript, Library-Archives, Historical Department of The Church of Jesus Christ of Latter-day Saints (hereafter cited as LDS Church Historical Archives), 19 January 1851, 22–23.
8. Alexander, 26.
9. Brigham Young sermon, 8 October 1855, in *Journal of Discourses,* 26 vols. (Liverpool: Latter-day Saints' Book Depot, 1858), 3: 115–18.
10. Brigham Young sermon, 8 October 1855, in *Journal of Discourses,* 3: 117.
11. Peterson, 62–63; *Wilford Woodruff's Journal,* 4: 316, 398, 421; Brigham Young to John Taylor, 30 April 1855, Brigham Young Letterbooks, LDS Church Historical Archives.
12. Peterson, 63; minutes of Presiding Bishop's Meetings with Bishops, 1851–1862, 6 November 1855, 8 January and 12 February 1856, manuscript, LDS Church Historical Archives.
13. Two insightful analyses of the "LDS-Israel connection" are Melodie Moench, "Nineteenth-Century Mormons: The New Israel," *Dialogue* 12 (Spring 1979): 42–56, and Jan Shipps, *Mormonism: The Story of a New Religious Tradition* (Urbana: University of Illinois Press, 1985), 119–124.
14. *Wilford Woodruff's Journal,* 4: 448.
15. Brigham Young sermon, 30 August, 1857, in *Journal of Discourses,* 5: 167–68.
16. *Deseret News* (Salt Lake City, Utah), 1 October 1856.
17. Sessions, 218–21; Peterson, 69–70.
18. Leonard J. Arrington, *Brigham Young: American Moses* (New York: Alfred A. Knopf, 1985), 408.
19. Jedediah M. Grant sermon, 2 November 1856, in *Journal of Discourses,* 4: 86.
20. *Wilford Woodruff's Journal,* 4: 448.
21. *Wilford Woodruff's Journal,* 4: 451; Brigham Young sermon, 21 September 1856, in *Journal of Discourses,* 4: 52–57.
22. *Wilford Woodruff's Journal,* 4: 456.
23. Refer to correspondence listed under footnotes 36 and 37.
24. *Wilford Woodruff's Journal,* 4: 458–59.
25. Ibid., 4: 459–61.
26. Ibid., 4: 463.
27. Brigham Young to Welcome Chapman, 13 November 1856, Brigham Young Letterbooks.
28. Heber C. Kimball sermon, 9 November 1856, in *Journal of Discourses,* 4: 81.
29. Jedediah M. Grant sermon, 9 November 1856, in *Journal of Discourses,* 4: 84.

30. *Wilford Woodruff's Journal,* 5: 13.
31. Home Missionary Meeting Minutes, 10 February 1857, General Minutes Collection, manuscript in LDS Church Historical Archives.
32. I formed this conclusion from a variety of sources.
33. Thomas Evans Jeremy Diary, 5 April 1857, manuscript in LDS Church Historical Archives.
34. Grant's period of "ascendancy" was actually brief. He apparently gave his last public address on 9 November. Wilford Woodruff first mentioned his sickness on 14 November. Despite repeated administrations, Grant died on 1 December 1856.
35. *Wilford Woodruff's Journal,* 4: 489.
36. Brigham Young to Tarleton Lewis, 9 April 1857, Brigham Young Letterbooks.
37. Brigham Young to Philo Farnsworth, 4 April 1857, Brigham Young Letterbooks.
38. Manuscript History of the Church, 27 January 1857, LDS Church Historical Archives.
39. Lorenzo Brown Diary, 6 and 7 April 1857, typescript, LDS Church Historical Archives.
40. James Henry Martineau Journal, 30 December 1856, manuscript, LDS Church Historical Archives; William Gibson Journal, vol. 2, 8 December 1856, manuscript in LDS Church Historical Archives.
41. Martineau Journal, 30 December 1856.
42. Gibson Journal, 8 December 1856.
43. Richard Ballantyne Journal, 28 December 1856, manuscript in LDS Church Historical Archives.
44. *Wilford Woodruff's Journal,* 28 December 1856.
45. *Wilford Woodruff's Journal,* 5: 13.
46. Salt Lake Fifth Ward Fellowship Meeting Minutes, 28 June 1857, manuscript in LDS Church Historical Archives.
47. Orson Hyde sermon, 7 October 1857, in *Journal History,* 7 October 1857.
48. Brigham Young sermon, 13 November 1858, Unpublished Speech File, LDS Church Historical Archives.
49. Brigham Young sermon, 17 February 1861, in *Journal of Discourses,* 9: 125.
50. Thomas O'Dea, *The Mormons* (Chicago: University of Chicago Press, 1957), 115. See also Arrington, 300–301; Charles S. Peterson, *Utah: A History* (New York: W. W. Norton, 1977), 77–85.
51. Arrington, 301–2.
52. Arrington, 301, citing Brigham Young to Charles S. Kimball, 31 December 1864, Brigham Young Letterbooks.
53. Arrington, 300–1; Charles S. Peterson, 77–81.

CHAPTER 12

THE RAILROAD BUILDER

JOHN J STEWART
Professor of English
Utah State University

On Monday, 10 May 1869, at Promontory Summit in northern Utah, one of the most significant events of the nineteenth century occurred: completion of America's first transcontinental railroad, linking the nation from the Atlantic to the Pacific. The placing of a golden spike in a polished laurelwood railroad tie symbolized the culmination of a herculean project that many considered the greatest man-made wonder of the world.

In today's age of miracles—when we can fly from New York to San Francisco in four hours and enjoy instant electronic communication with any part of the globe—it is difficult to comprehend the impact of the construction of this iron trail across the vast continent. Perhaps only those who had walked the many weary miles across the American plains and mountains could fully appreciate and cherish this dream come true.

Although he did not participate in the Golden Spike celebration, no one was more appreciative of the railroad's completion than Brigham Young, who for twenty-two years had encouraged its construction—from the time he led the first pioneer company to the Salt Lake Valley in the summer of 1847. Placing the golden spike in 1869 brought to a climax an even half-century of dreaming of building a railroad to the Pacific coast, achieving the northwest passage that waterways had failed to provide. In 1819, Robert Mills, architect for the Bunker Hill and Washington monuments, urged Congress to consider a system of "steam-propelled carriages" to run from the Mississippi to the Columbia River Valley. From 1826, when the first U.S. railway was constructed, the idea gradually gained public interest.

Foremost of the early advocates was Asa Whitney, a wealthy

New York merchant, who had visited China and had seen in the Pacific railway a means for the U.S. to capture much of the European trade with China and other Far East countries. For a decade, Whitney devoted his time and fortune to trying to sell Congress and state legislatures on the worth of such a railroad. Although extensive trade with the Orient never materialized—due largely to the completion of the Suez Canal, also in 1869—the hope of such trade was a prime motive for construction of the railroad.

From the 1830s, railroads were being built throughout the eastern half of the United States, and Whitney's and others' efforts to get congressional action on a Pacific railroad might well have succeeded had it not been for the bitter sectional jealousy that gripped the country, culminating in the war between the northern and southern states.

In 1849, Senator Thomas Hart Benton of Missouri introduced a bill in Congress seeking federal financing of a railroad from St. Louis to San Francisco. Brigham Young and his associates also urged Congress to proceed with construction of a road from the Missouri to the Pacific. Early Mormon lobbyist efforts were summarized by George A. Smith, first counselor to President Young, in Salt Lake City in 1868 as the railroad fast approached the valley:

> We started from Nauvoo in February, 1846, to make a road to the Rocky Mountains. A portion of our work was to hunt a track for the railroad. We located a road to Council Bluffs, bridging the streams, and I believe it has been pretty nearly followed by the railroad. In April, 1847, President Young and one hundred and forty-three pioneers left Council Bluffs, and located and made the road to the site of this city. A portion of our labor was to seek out the way for a railroad across the continent, and every place we found that seemed difficult for laying the rails we searched out a way for the road to go around or through it. We had been here only a short time until we formed the provisional government of the State of Deseret, and among the subjects of legislation were measures to promote and establish a railroad across the continent. In a little while we were organized into a Territory and during the first session of the Legislature a memorial to

> Congress was adopted and approved, March 3rd, 1852 . . . of this railroad being necessary to develop the mineral and other resources of the continent and to bring the trade of China and the East Indies across the continent.[1]

In confirmation of President Smith's recollection, President Young commented,

> I do not suppose we traveled one day from the Missouri River here, but what we looked for a track where the rails could be laid with success, for a railroad through this Territory to go to the Pacific Ocean. This was long before the gold was found, when this Territory belonged to Mexico. We never went through the canyons or worked our way over the dividing ridges without asking where the rails could be laid; and I really did think that the railway would have been here long before this. . . .
>
> When we came here over the hills and plains in 1847 we made our calculations for a railroad across the country, and were satisfied that merchants in those eastern cities, or from Europe, instead of doubling Cape Horn for the west, would take the cars, and on arriving at San Francisco would take steamer and run to China or Japan and make their purchases, and with their goods could be back again in London and other European cities in eighty or eighty-five days. All these calculations we made on our way here, and if they had only favored us by letting us have a State government, as weak as we are we would have built railroads ourselves. . . .
>
> We want the benefits of this railroad for our emigrants, so that after they land in New York they may get on board the cars and never leave them again until they reach this city. And this they can do when the Missouri river is bridged.
>
> . . . When this work is done if the tariff is not too high, we shall see the people going east to see their friends, and they will come and see us, and when we are better known to the world, I trust we shall be better liked.[2]

Those values that Young and other Utahns foresaw in the construction of a railroad included eliminating the hazards, hardships, and several weeks of traveling by covered wagons or handcarts; facilitating missionary travel to distant parts of the world; enabling the import of furniture, machinery, and building materials, and the export of agricultural produce; enabling the construction of branch railroads connecting communities from north to south, including a branch line to Little Cottonwood Canyon to haul granite stone to speed the construction of the Salt Lake Temple; and providing cash employment for Utahns as railroad workers at a time when there was little cash in the Territory.

Despite strong Mormon support, it was rumored that Brigham Young and other leaders of the Church attempted, through sermons, newspaper articles, and their memorials to Congress to halt the coming of the railroad. In answer to the threats of anti-Mormons who smugly predicted the demise of the LDS Church when the railroad reached Utah, and to the fears voiced by some Mormons about the railroad's coming, President Young confidently declared that Mormonism "must indeed be a damned poor religion if it cannot stand one railroad!"[3]

In 1852, Utah's first territorial legislature, with Brigham Young as governor, sent a memorial to the U.S. Senate and House of Representatives. It stated, in part,

> Not less than five thousand American citizens have perished on the different routes [between the Missouri River and the Pacific Coast] within the last three years, for the want of proper means of transportation. . . . We know that no obstruction exists between this point [Salt Lake City] and San Diego, and that iron, coal, timber, stone and other materials exist in various places along the route; and that the settlements of this territory are so situated as amply to supply the builders of said road with material and provisions for a considerable portion of the route, and to carry on an extensive trade after the road is completed.[4]

FIVE POSSIBLE ROUTES CONSIDERED

How much influence this memorial had with Congress is unknown. Many others in the United States were also urging construction of a transcontinental railroad. In the following year, 1853, Congress passed, and President Millard Fillmore signed, a bill providing for army surveys of four possible railroad routes to the Pacific, including one that closely followed the Mormon Trail to Utah. Secretary of War Jefferson Davis took the liberty of having five routes surveyed rather than four. One was far north of the Mormon route, up through Montana; three were south of the

Mormon route, including one through southern Utah. Due to bitter sectional rivalry between North and South, largely over the issue of slavery, it was impossible to achieve congressional consensus for construction of a railroad on any route until after the South had seceded from the Union.

In 1856, Congress appropriated funds for improvement of the Oxbow, Santa Fe, and California-Mormon trails. Frederick Lander, a civil engineer and builder of some renown, was appointed chief engineer and field superintendent for improvement of the California-Mormon Trail—the road that in large part the Union Pacific later built upon. In 1858, shortly after the arrival of Johnston's army in the Salt Lake Valley, Lander wrote a report to Washington expressing his appreciation for the help he had received from the Mormons in the road improvement project. His report observed, in part,

> I was assured by ex-Governor Young, whom I visited while in Salt Lake City, that . . . he would be very glad to have his people employed by me, not only because the work was one of public utility, but because it aided the people in getting a little money. . . . I paid them a dollar a day for work, but the next season I shall probably have to pay them at higher rates. Ex-Governor Young told me that he would engage to find laborers and mechanics to build that portion of a Pacific railroad which should extend across the Territory of Utah.[5]

Californians were as eager as Utahns to have a railroad constructed. In October 1859, a California convention on the Pacific Railway appointed Theodore Dehone Judah its agent to carry a petition to Congress seeking federal financing. And in April 1861, as the nation became embroiled in a bloody Civil War, Judah, Leland Stanford, Collis Potter Huntington, Mark Hopkins, Charles Crocker, and others organized the Central Pacific Railroad Company, determined to raise funds sufficient to start building a railway eastward from Sacramento over a route that Judah had surveyed through the Sierra-Nevada mountains. Stanford was elected president; Huntington, vice president; Hopkins, secretary; and Judah, engineer. But it was nearly two years later, on 8 January 1863, that the Central Pacific broke ground at Sacramento to begin construction of its railroad.

Meanwhile, on 1 July 1862, while in the throes of Civil War, President Abraham Lincoln signed the Pacific Railway Act, passed by an all-northern Congress. Lincoln designated the Union Pacific Railroad to start at Council Bluffs, Iowa, and follow the Mormon Trail up the Platte River Valley. The act provided huge land grants to both Union Pacific and Central Pacific: "vacant lands with ten miles on either side of the lines for five alternate sections per mile, mineral lands excepted";[6] also, 30-year first mortgage federal loans at six percent interest to the contractors, not to exceed $50 million, to be allocated on the basis of $16,000 per mile to the base of the mountains, $32,000 per mile across the desert high plains of Nevada and Utah, and $48,000 per mile on 150 miles of mountain construction.

In May 1864, Congress revised the railroad act, shifting the federal loans from first to second mortgages, making it much easier for the two companies to interest private investors. The revised railroad act also doubled the land grants to ten sections per mile within twenty miles on each side of the tracks. This gave the railroad companies a total of 12,800 acres of land for each mile of track laid and ownership of all iron and coal deposits on the grant lands.

Union Pacific's ground-breaking ceremony was conducted on 3 December 1863 on the Missouri River bluffs two miles north of Omaha, Nebraska. But because the Civil War was still raging, a shortage of investors, private money, manpower, locomotives, iron for rails, and other materials kept Union Pacific and Central Pacific from making any real progress for another year and a half. With the close of the war in the spring of 1865, increased progress on the two roads began, but it was not until the spring of 1866 that a substantial amount of trackage was laid. Thousands of Civil War veterans, both Union and Confederate, were glad to get employment with Union Pacific. The Central Pacific solved most of its labor problem by recruiting and importing thousands of young Chinese, who proved to be excellent workers. It also employed some war veterans, along with other whites and Mexicans.

Although eastern and California bankers and other capitalists were reluctant to invest in the Union Pacific and Central Pacific under the terms of the first railroad act, Brigham Young showed no reluctance. He promptly bought five shares of Union Pacific stock at $1,000 per share. With passage of the revised act in 1864, and especially after the close of the war in 1865, other investors began pumping needed funds into the two roads.

Oliver Ames, a wealthy Boston shovel manufacturer, became president of Union Pacific on 23 November 1866. His brother and partner, Oakes Ames, as a U.S. congressman, gave considerable political—legislative and financial—support to Union Pacific. Although anti-Mormon politics at the Washington level had deprived Brigham Young of his position as governor of Utah Territory, it was obvious to the officials of the two railroads that as President of the Mormon Church, Brigham Young, rather than the territorial governor, was the real power in Utah.

Union Pacific and Central Pacific were eager to build as many miles as possible to get the lucrative land grants and federal monetary loans. Union Pacific hoped to build as far west as Reno, Nevada, and Central Pacific hoped to build as far east as Fort Bridger, Wyoming, or beyond. The revised railroad act had specified only that the two companies would build until they met, wherever that might be. So it became a great race between the two; and to do as well as possible in that race, each eventually sought the help of Brigham Young and the Mormon work force.

MORMONS CONTRACT WITH UNION PACIFIC

Union Pacific was first to solicit President Young's support. After preliminary discussions with General Grenville M. Dodge, Union Pacific chief engineer, on 21 May 1868, the Mormon leader signed a contract with Samuel B. Reed, Union Pacific superintendent of construction, to do road grading, tunneling, and bridging from the head of Echo Canyon, or approximately the Utah-Wyoming border, down to the Salt Lake Valley. Accounts of the terms of the contract vary, some claiming it was for $1 million worth of work, others reporting it specified 90 miles of work, or even 100 miles of work. The contract did specify that 80 percent of the contract price was to be paid monthly as the work progressed, and the other 20 percent would be paid when the project was completed.

Orson F. Whitney, who as a youngster worked on the Union Pacific portion of the road, gives one version of the contract:

> The principal sub-contractors under President Young—whose contract amounted to about two and a quarter millions of dollars—were Bishop John Sharp [Acting Superintendent of Public Works for Utah Territory, President Daniel H. Wells being the Superintendent as well as Brigham Young's second counselor in the Church's First Presidency] and Hon. Joseph A. Young, the President's eldest son. They employed between five and six hundred men, and the amount of their contract was about a million dollars. To them fell the heavy stone work of the bridge abutments and the cutting of the tunnels in Weber Canyon. Afterwards, in the "race" between the Union Pacific and Central Pacific constructing companies, Sharp and Young took another contract amounting to a hundred thousand dollars, upon which they employed from four to five hundred men. . . . President Young is said to have realized from his contract about eight hundred thousand dollars.[7]

George Q. Cannon, editor of the *Deseret News* and later a counselor to Brigham Young and then to his uncle John Taylor, heralded the railroad contract as a "great cause for thankfulness" because of what it could do for the labor situation and the general economy of Utah. He editorialized:

> Now no man need go East, or in any other direction in search of employment. There is enough for all at our very doors and in the completion of a project in which we are all interested. Coming as it does when there is such a scarcity of money and a consequent slackness of labor, it is most advantageous.
>
> With the cash that the Union Pacific would be paying them, the Mormons "who owe may pay their debts, and have the necessary funds to send for machinery and establish mercantile houses in the various settlements.[8]

Railroad workers were paid from two to three dollars per day, depending on their skills and assignments. Those with horse teams and scrapers were paid additional compensation. Physically fit men emigrating to Zion from England, Europe, or the eastern

Ezra T. Benson (1811–1869), ca. 1868–1869. Member of the Quorum of the Twelve Apostles and presiding elder in Cache Valley. Along with Lorin Farr and Chauncey West, he contracted with Central Pacific for grading and bridge work through Utah. He died suddenly on 3 September 1869.

John Sharp (1820–1892), n.d. A chief subcontractor under Brigham Young on the Union Pacific contract. He represented Brigham Young at the Golden Spike ceremony, Promontory Summit.

U.S. could ride on the train from Omaha to the end of the line free of charge if they agreed to work for the Union Pacific when they arrived at the line's end. Their children under fourteen years of age could ride at half price.

In a letter to Franklin D. Richards, agent in charge of emigration at Liverpool, England, President Young observed,

> For many reasons that will readily occur to you, this contract is viewed by the brethren of understanding as a Godsend. There is much indebtedness among the people, and the territory is drained of money, but labor here and [more laborers] coming we have in large amount, and this contract affords opportunity for turning that labor into money, with which those here can pay each other, and import needed machinery, and such useful articles as we cannot yet produce, and those coming can pay their indebtedness, and

Lorin Farr (1820–1909), n.d. Mayor of Ogden, Utah, the city destined to become the eastern and western terminus of the Central Pacific and Union Pacific Railroads, respectively.

Chauncey W. West (1827–1870), n.d. Presiding Bishop of Weber County and one of three chief contractors for grading the Central Pacific Railroad through Utah.

> have ready means with which to gather around them the comforts of life in their new homes.[9]

Unfortunately, while some 3,000 Mormons went diligently to work to complete the grading, tunneling, and bridge building in Echo and Weber Canyons, rejoicing in anticipation of the cash they were earning, Union Pacific officials were scheming to avoid as much of the payment due them as possible. It was not until October 1868, five months after Brigham Young and Samuel Reed had signed the contract, and more than four months after Mormon railroad gangs were hard at work, that Union Pacific's board of directors approved the contract—five months of deliberate stalling to avoid making payments due. This, of course, wreaked havoc with the Mormon subcontractors, the workmen, and the economy generally. Supplies had been purchased on credit in anticipation of the monthly payments from Union Pacific. With so many of the farmers working on the railroad, foodstuffs soon were in short supply, and inflation followed. Butter, for instance, was selling for $1.25 per pound, when in the opinion of President Daniel H. Wells it should not have been selling for more than 25 cents per pound.

Echo and Weber Canyons were the most difficult terrain through which Union Pacific had to build. Several tunnels were blasted and dug in these narrow canyons, and floods washed out both grading and bridges. Mormon workmen became experts in the use of nitroglycerin "blasting oil" and other explosives used to help tunnel through rock formations and to carve out roadbeds from steep, rocky hillsides. When work on the canyon tunnels did not seem to be going fast enough to please the anxious Union Pacific officials, they brought from Wyoming non-Mormon crews to take over the tunneling. A month later, however, they were ready to turn it back to the Mormons.

"The big tunnel which the [Union Pacific] company's men took off from our hands to complete in a hurry, has been proffered back again," wrote Brigham Young to his secretary Albert Carrington:

> They have not less than four men to our one constantly employed and, withal, have not been doing over two-thirds as much work. Superintendent Reed has solicited us to resume it again. We were well pleased to have the job off from our hands when it was, as it enabled us to complete our other work on the line; but now that it is so nearly complete, probably we shall finish the tunnel. Bishop Sharp and Joseph A. Young are using nitro-glycerine for blasting, and its superiority over powder, as well as the sobriety, steadiness and industry of our men, gives us a marked advantage.[10]

Edward Lennox Sloan, *Deseret News* assistant editor, whose stories have been praised by historian Robert West Howard as "the best panorama extant of the Great Iron Trail's gargantuan routine," visited the Echo and Weber Canyon work sites and reported,

> After the day's work was done, their animals turned out to herd and the supper over, a nice blending of voices in sweet singing proved that the materials exist among the men for a capital choir. . . . Soon after, the call for prayers was heard,

> when the men assembled and reverentially bowed before the Author of all blessings.[11]

Sloan reported that "in but one camp of less than one hundred men, out of between two and three thousand working in the two canyons, did I hear profanity; and it is not likely to be tolerated there long."[12] The *Deseret News* also published a song that Mormon graders at the head of Echo Canyon were singing as they worked:

> We surely live in a very fast age;
> We've traveled by oxteam, and then took the stage;
> But when such conveyance is all done away
> We'll travel in steam cars upon the railway!!
> Hurrah! Hurrah! for the railroad's begun!
> Three cheers for our contractor, his name's Brigham Young![13]

To Sloan, the approach of the Union Pacific non-Mormon camps seemed like an invasion of Zion by the drunken hordes of Babylon. In a visit to the once peaceful Mormon town of Echo City in the week before Christmas 1868, he found "saloons, doggeries, whiskey-holes, dram-barrels, gambling-hells," also "private dwellings," with "nymphs du grade," whence "femininity stalks out with brazen publicity." Sloan direfully warned his readers, "They are coming, coming, coming!" This "hell on wheels," which had plagued Union Pacific from day one, sometimes got so rank that the Casement brothers, Jack and Dan, the Union Pacific's construction foremen, organized vigilante teams among their work crews to hang or otherwise dispose of con men, pimps, and cutthroats.[14]

Colonel Charles R. Savage, a Mormon photographer in Salt Lake City (who became father-in-law of President J. Reuben Clark, Jr.), was employed by Union Pacific to supplement the work of its chief photographer, Andrew J. Russell. Savage recorded in his diary that upon a visit to one of the Casement brothers' camps he was

> creditably informed that 24 men had been killed in the several camps in the last 25 days. Certainly, a harder set of men were never before congregated together. . . . At Blue River the returning "Democrats," so-called, were being piled upon the cars in every stage of drunkenness. Every ranch or tent

has whiskey for sale. Verily, men earn their money like horses and spend it like asses.[15]

Collis P. Huntington, Central Pacific's vice president, spent most of his time in New York City and Washington, D.C., arranging for shipment of locomotives, rails, and other supplies by ship to California and lobbying congressmen for further financial help. When he learned that Union Pacific had signed a contract with Brigham Young for Mormon workmen, he telegraphed Leland Stanford, president of Central Pacific, to hasten to Salt Lake City and strike a similar deal with the Mormon leader to provide workers for Central Pacific. Traveling by train to rail's end in Nevada and then by buggy, Stanford reached Brigham Young as soon as he could.

MORMONS CONTRACT WITH CENTRAL PACIFIC

President Young had recently learned to his keen disappointment that Union Pacific was reneging on its promise to route its line through Salt Lake City and instead intended to go around the north end of the Great Salt Lake. He was also keenly chagrined that Union Pacific had not met its commitment on timely pay for his work crews. As a result, he was inclined to give favorable consideration to Stanford's request for Mormon workmen. Instead of taking a contract with Central Pacific himself, he arranged for Stanford to contract with Lorin Farr, LDS stake president and mayor of Ogden; Chauncey Walker West, presiding bishop in the Ogden area; and Elder Ezra Taft Benson of Logan. Early in September 1868, Stanford agreed to pay Mormon workmen from three to six dollars per day for manual and skilled labor and ten dollars per day for wagon men to grade the Central Pacific road from the Utah-Nevada border east through Ogden and to some point in Weber Canyon. At President Young's insistence, he also made a cash down payment in advance.

In his negotiations, Stanford carefully avoided telling President Young that Central Pacific had also decided that it was best to go around the north end of Great Salt Lake; he gave the impression that Central Pacific still planned to go around the south end and through Salt Lake City. General Dodge of Union

Pacific claims it was he who told President Young the truth of Central Pacific's intentions, hoping this would dissuade the Mormon leader from helping Central Pacific. When confronted with the truth, Stanford lamely alibied that Central Pacific was being forced to go north of the lake because of Union Pacific's decision.

Dodge, who as chief engineer of Union Pacific was largely responsible for the decision to go north of the lake, reported,

> We had only one controversy with the Mormons, who had been our friends and had given the full support of the Church from the time of our first reconnaissances until the final completion. It was our desire and the demand of the Mormons that we should build through Salt Lake City, but we bent all our energies to find a feasible line passing through that city and around the south end of the Great Salt Lake and across the desert to Humboldt Wells, a controlling point in the line. We found the line so superior on the north of the lake that we had to adopt that route with a view of building a branch to Salt Lake City, but Brigham Young would not have this, and appealed over my head to the board of directors, who referred the question to the government directors, who finally sustained me. Then Brigham Young gave his allegiance and aid to the Central Pacific, hoping to bring them around the south end of the lake and force us to connect with them there.[16]

When news of the Mormon contract with Central Pacific reached New York City, the Union Pacific board of directors suddenly found it expedient to approve the contract Sam Reed had made in Union Pacific's behalf with President Young the previous May. The fearful thought seems to have struck the Union Pacific officials that the Mormons might turn over to Central Pacific the road they had graded in Echo and Weber Canyons for Union Pacific, inasmuch as the latter had not met its financial obligations. Vice president Thomas C. Durant hurried to Salt Lake City with a partial payment of the money due, handed it to President Young with an apology, and begged him to rescind his decision to help Central Pacific. When Young refused, Durant vainly attempted to persuade Dr. Daniel W. Strong at Dutch Flat, California—a close friend of the late Theodore Judah, who disliked Central Pacific's "Big Four"—to contract for 2,000 Chinese laborers for Union Pacific. Getting no response to his telegram to Strong, Durant negotiated another contract with Young for further work.

So from September 1868 to 11 April 1869, when an agreement was reached on Promontory Summit as the junction point, Mormon crews were heavily involved on both sides in the hectic race for additional mileage. They were grading parallel roads clear across northern Utah, from east to west and from west to east, each company hoping its road would be the one to gain government approval, and thus the land grants and monetary loans. A few miles east of Promontory Summit, Union Pacific built one of its largest trestles, 400 feet long and 85 feet high—a frightening spectacle to cross. Right next to it, Central Pacific built a huge landfill, which still stands. Actual rails were laid by each company only as far as Promontory Summit, but the grading was done far beyond either side of that point.

Corinne and Promontory Station were the final permanent towns created by the construction of the Pacific Railroad. In its issue of 5 March 1869, the *Deseret News* reported:

> Five miles west of Brigham City is situated the new town of Corinne, built of canvas and board shanties. The place is fast becoming civilized, several men having been killed there already. The last one was found in the [Bear] river with four bullet holes through him and his head badly mangled. Work is being vigorously prosecuted on the U.P.R.R. and C.P.R.R., both lines running near each other and occasionally crossing.
>
> . . . From Corinne west thirty miles, the grading camps present the appearance of a mighty army. As far as the eye can reach are to be seen almost a continuous line of tents, wagons and men. . . . Sharp & Young's blasters are jarring the earth every few minutes with their glycerine and powder, lifting whole ledges of limestone rock from their long resting places, hurling them hundreds of feet in the air and scattering them around for a half mile in every direction. At Carlisle's works a few days ago four men were preparing a blast by filling a large crevice in a ledge with powder. After pouring in the powder they undertook to work it down with iron bars. The bars striking the rock caused an explosion;

> one of the men was blown two or three hundred feet in the air, breaking every bone in his body; the other three were terribly burnt and wounded with flying stones.[17]

Inasmuch as Ogden was a more logical place than either Promontory or Corinne for a permanent junction of the two roads, the government and the two companies decided that, after the joining of the rails at Promontory, the Union Pacific would sell to Central Pacific its trackage from Promontory to Ogden, which would become the permanent junction of the two roads.

Brigham Young did not attend the famous Golden Spike ceremony at Promontory Summit on Monday, 10 May 1869. According to Orson F. Whitney,

> President Young, President [Daniel H.] Wells, Apostles [Wilford] Woodruff, [George Q.] Cannon and other prominent churchmen who would also have been present on the occasion [of the Salt Lake City celebration, not the Promontory ceremony] had they been in the city, had started some time before [on April 25] on their customary annual tour through the southern settlements.[18]

It seems likely that President Young deliberately chose not to be present at either of the celebrations, probably because the railroad had not been built through Salt Lake City as he had requested and because the companies had not fully paid the Mormons for their work.

Utah and the Mormon Church nevertheless were well represented at both the Golden Spike program and the Salt Lake City celebration. Those at the Golden Spike included Bishop John Sharp, Charles R. Savage, William Jennings, and other dignitaries of Salt Lake City; Elder Franklin D. Richards, Mayor Lorin Farr, and Bishop Chauncey West of Ogden; Elder Ezra Taft Benson of Logan; Abraham Hunsaker of Honeyville; and many other Utahns. Some accounts claim that Bishop Sharp was designated as President Young's official representative; others say Mayor Farr had been designated. Perhaps neither one was, or maybe both were. There are so many conflicting reports of who did what on the program that it is impossible to know of a certainty today.

The only Utahn who possibly had any speaking part was

Bishop Sharp; some accounts say he was invited to offer a second prayer after the Reverend Dr. John Todd of Pittsfield, Massachusetts, offered a lengthy invocation. Most accounts do not mention it. Whether there were two prayers or not, the telegrapher sent the following message over the nationwide wire as the program proceeded: "We have got done praying! The spike is about to be driven!"

The Salt Lake City Tenth Ward Band did play some music on the program, as did the Army 21st Infantry Band. The director of the army band reported that his men played fairly well until they got too drunk. The abundance of liquor at the ceremony perhaps accounts for the numerous conflicting reports of who did what.

So far as the reports indicate, little if any mention was made of the Mormon contribution to the railroad construction. But noted historian Samuel Bowles speculated in his 1869 book *Our New West,*

> But for the pioneership of the Mormons, discovering the pathway, and feeding those who came out upon it, all this central region of our great West would now be many years behind its present development, and the railroad instead of being finished, would hardly be begun.[19]

As the concluding feature of a very noisy, poorly organized celebration, an official announcement was sent over the telegraph line:

> Promontory Summit, Utah, May 10th. The last rail is laid! The last spike is driven! The Pacific Railroad is completed! The point of junction is 1,086 miles west of the Missouri River [at Omaha, Nebraska], and 690 miles east of Sacramento City. [signed]: Leland Stanford, Central Pacific Railroad. T. C. Durant, Sidney Dillon, John Duff, Union Pacific Railroad.[20]

Millions of Americans in cities large and small all over the country engaged in local celebrations of the great event. Utah historian and Apostle Orson F. Whitney provides a vivid description of Salt Lake City's observance:

> The news of the driving of the last spike and the welding of the two great railways at Promontory reached Salt Lake City at thirty-two minutes past noon, being flashed

over the wires to Utah's capital, and to the various settlements along the line of the Deseret Telegraph, simultaneously with its transmission throughout the length and breadth of the Union. Instantly the stars and stripes were unfurled from public buildings and at other prominent places, brass and martial bands stationed expectantly at several points struck up lively airs, and artillery salutes were fired from Arsenal Hill [now known as Capitol Hill] and from the vicinity of the City Hall and the County Court House. The principal stores and manufactories, public and private offices were then closed and business was suspended for the rest of the day.

At 2 p.m., between six and seven thousand citizens had assembled at the Tabernacle. On the stand were his Excellency, [Utah Territory] Governor [Charles] Durkee, Hons. George A. Smith, John Taylor, William H. Hooper and John M. Bernhisel; Hon. John A. Clark, Surveyor-General of Utah; Bishop Edward Hunter, Aldermen S. W. Richards and A. H. Raleigh and General R. T. Burton. The last named three were a committee previously appointed by the City Council to arrange for the celebration now begun. . . .

Judge Elias Smith was elected president of the meeting, A. M. Musser, secretary, Messrs. G. D. Watt and D. W. Evans, reporters, and Colonel J. C. Little, chaplain. . . . Croxall's and Huntington's bands discoursed stirring and appropriate music, and speeches were made by Governor Durkee, Hons. John Taylor, George A. Smith and William H. Hooper. Three cheers were given for the Union Pacific and Central Pacific companies, "the heroes who have consummated the work", and three more for the national government.[21]

A committee appointed "to draft resolutions expressive of the sense of the meeting" declared, in part:

Resolved, That the people of Utah—the great pioneers of the Rocky Mountains—receive with acclamation the glad news of the completion of the mighty work to which as a people they have contributed their part; and hand in hand with the great circle of States and Territories now rejoicing in union over the event, do thank God for its accomplishment.[22]

After the resolutions were unanimously adopted,

Colonel David McKenzie then took the stand and read to the assembly the railroad memorial sent to Congress by the Utah

> Legislature during its first annual session, in March, 1852 [pleading for construction of the railroad and offering Utah's help]. Music, toasts and sentiments followed and the meeting then adjourned. In the evening the business portions of the city were beautifully illuminated, there was a huge bonfire on Arsenal Hill and displays of fireworks in various parts in honor of the great event at Promontory.[23]

MORMONS BUILD UTAH CENTRAL

Considering the keen disappointment that Brigham Young and other Utahns had expressed regarding the railroad companies' decision to not go through Salt Lake City, Union Pacific offered to build a connecting road from Ogden to Salt Lake City, according to Grenville Dodge. But in June 1868, President Young decided that the LDS Church would build such a road itself. At a mass meeting he said,

> If the company which first arrives [in the Salt Lake Valley] should deem it to their advantage to leave us [Salt Lake City] out in the cold, we will not be so far off but we can have a branch line for the advantage of this city.[24]

To build this thirty-seven-mile branch railroad, President Young initiated organization of the Utah Central Railroad Company, with himself as president, on 8 March 1869, the day Union Pacific tracks reached Ogden. Other organizers and stockholders were his three oldest sons, Joseph A., Brigham, Jr., and John W. Young; George Q. Cannon, Daniel H. Wells, George A. Smith, John Sharp, David P. Kimball, William Jennings, Feramorz Little, James T. Little, Bryant Stringham, David O. Calder, and Isaac Groo, all of Salt Lake City; and Christopher Layton of Kaysville. William Jennings became vice president; John W. Young, secretary; Daniel H. Wells, treasurer; Jesse W. Fox, chief engineer; Feramorz Little, Christopher Layton, and Brigham Young, Jr., directors. Joseph A. Young was named superintendent, and John Sharp assistant superintendent.

In May 1869, Utah Central Railway broke ground. "The point of beginning was near Weber River, just below the city of Ogden," reports Elder Whitney. "The weather was bright and beautiful, and a large concourse of people assembled, including the principal men of Weber County and many notable citizens of Salt Lake."[25] Included at the ground-breaking, besides the railroad officers, were Elder John Taylor of Salt Lake City; Elder Ezra Taft Benson of Logan; and Elder Franklin D. Richards, Mayor Lorin Farr, and Bishop Chauncey W. West of Ogden—all of whom had participated in construction of the transcontinental railroad.

> It was not quite 10 a.m. when President Young, after a few preliminary remarks, cut with a spade the first sod, observing as he did so that it was customary in breaking first ground to use a pick, but that he believed in using the tool best adapted to the soil. President George A. Smith offered prayer, dedicating the ground for a railroad and invoking heaven's blessing on the enterprise. President Young then removed the sod that he had cut, after which President Smith, President Wells, William Jennings and others cut sods. Three cheers were given for the president of the road, and after the band had played the assembly dispersed.[26]

When the transcontinental railroad was completed on 10 May, both the Union Pacific and Central Pacific were in arrears in their payments to the Mormons for their work, and neither was in any hurry to make further payments. Union Pacific owed them well over a million dollars. Before the end of May, Durant was voted out as Union Pacific's vice president and general manager. He had siphoned off most the profits into his Credit Mobilier Corporation, leaving Union Pacific near bankruptcy. President Young sent Elder John Taylor, Bishop John Sharp, and his son Joseph A. Young to New York and Boston to meet with President Oliver Ames and other Union Pacific officials in an effort to obtain payment due the Mormons. They had little success, but in lieu of cash they did receive promises of surplus rails and other equipment with which to begin construction of the Utah Central.

The company was organized with a capital stock of $1,500,000, comprised of 15,000 shares valued at $100 each. As with other Church-sponsored enterprises, construction of Utah Central was to be a cooperative effort. Land right-of-ways, timber for ties and trestles, labor, and other aspects of construction were assigned through bishops from Ogden to the Salt Lake City area.

All those owning the designated land were asked to surrender a right-of-way as part of their contribution to the project. Generally, the response was a generous contribution of time, labor, materials, and land.

It was estimated that the railroad could be completed in four months, perhaps by mid-September. Had Union Pacific kept its promise on delivery of rails, rolling stock, and other materials, that schedule could have been met. But Union Pacific was having to rebuild much of its hastily constructed railroad between Omaha and Ogden. Paying its debt to the Mormons and delivering the promised materials for Utah Central were low priorities.

In the 1 September 1869 issue of the *Deseret News,* under the heading "UP and CP Companies' Indebtedness to the People of Utah," editor George Q. Cannon made public the shabby treatment Utahns had suffered, one result of which was delay in construction of the Utah Central:

> Perhaps on no one point for many years have the people of Utah exhibited more of their characteristic patience and forbearance than in the case of the railroad contracts for grading which they have filled for the Union Pacific and Central Pacific Railroad Companies. Upward of fifteen months ago a contract was made by the Union Pacific Railroad Company, through its Superintendent of Construction and Engineer, S. B. Reed, Esq., with President B. Young for the grading of a large extent of its Line. . . .
>
> The non-fulfillment of this agreement on the part of the Company was a most serious loss to the contractor and his subcontractors. It was not only a loss at the time; but it was a cause of incalculable loss afterwards. Many who could have finished their jobs when the weather was favorable were thrown behind and had to complete them when the expense of grading was very much enhanced by the severity of the weather. The tools, also, which had been promised by the company, were not forthcoming by the time stipulated, and many of the sub-contractors were put to serious inconvenience and heavy expense to obtain the necessary implements to keep their teams and hands employed. . . .
>
> The people of this Territory may well be proud of their share of the grading of the great continental highway; for their work will bear the closest scrutiny, and their patience,

perseverance, sobriety, language and general demeanor while on the Line were such as to extort praise from all who were brought in contact with them. . . . The Union Pacific Railroad Company owes the people of this Territory upwards of a million of dollars for the grading of its roads. . . .

The situation of affairs here at the present time demands that there should be some plain talking on this subject. If the credit of the people is endangered, or if our business men fail to meet their engagements, ordinary justice requires that the cause of this should be known. A moment's reflection will convince every person that the withholding of a million and a quarter of dollars from a community no larger than ours must produce serious loss, embarrassment and distress. Had there been no hopes of pay held out, the consequences would not have been as serious as they are, for every man would then have known what to depend upon and would have arranged accordingly. But, as it is, there is not a business man in the country who is not affected, and some very seriously, by the failure of these companies to pay for their work, and hundreds of men are literally destitute of the necessaries of life for the want of the money which they worked hard to earn. . . . Its injustice is so apparent that it needs no comment.[27]

Two days after the editorial was published, Elder Ezra Taft Benson of Logan was in Ogden still trying to collect payment from Central Pacific so he could pay his workmen. Just after his arrival in "Junction City" in Ogden on 3 September, he died of a heart attack at the age of 58. Extreme anxiety over financial obligations incurred by the unpaid railroad work was believed to be the main cause of his death. Bishop Chauncey West of Ogden, one of the other two Mormon contractors with Central Pacific, died four months later, on 9 January 1870, at the age of 42, his death also likely induced by the financial anxiety. Joseph A. Young died at age 40.

Whether either Cannon's editorial or Benson's and West's untimely deaths had any influence on their decision or not, Central Pacific officials in September paid all but $200,000 of their debt to the Mormons. Union Pacific officials in September agreed to turn over to the Church $600,000 worth of iron and rolling stock immediately and to pay sometime later another

$200,000 in cash. This settlement was far short of the original agreement. By December 1869, the Mormons finally did get an estimated $500,000 worth of material from Union Pacific that was used in completion of the Utah Central. Unable to get the needed cash payment from Union Pacific, Brigham Young borrowed $125,000 from Union Pacific President Oliver Ames at 9 percent interest to help pay the Mormon graders on Union Pacific's line and to help finance completion of Utah Central.

UTAH CENTRAL COMPLETED

On 10 January 1870, some 15,000 people gathered in Salt Lake City for ceremonies marking completion of the Utah Central. That was about thirty times the number present at the Golden Spike ceremony eight months earlier. Elder Wilford Woodruff offered the dedicatory prayer. Brigham Young drove the last spike, on which was inscribed the emblem of a beehive, the initials "U.C.R.R." (Utah Central Railroad), and the words "Holiness to the Lord." The same engravings were on the mallet with which he drove the spike. Band music and fireworks were interspersed with several speeches, the main one being by President Young, who, because of the cold weather, had George Q. Cannon read it for him. He reviewed Mormon pioneer struggles and triumphs, declaring,

> Since the day that we first trod the soil of these valleys, have we received any assistance from our neighbors? No; we have not. We have built our homes, our cities, have made our farms, have dug our canals and water ditches, have subdued this barren country, have fed the strangers, have clothed the naked, have immigrated the poor from foreign lands, have placed them in a condition to make all comfortable and have made some rich. We have fed the Indians to the amount of thousands of dollars yearly, have clothed them in part, and have sustained several Indian wars, and now we have built thirty-seven miles of railroad.[28]

Brigham Young took particular pride in the fact that Utah Central had been built entirely with volunteer labor, without financial aid from either the federal government or other sources. Two Union Pacific officials, as guest speakers, commended the

Utah Central Railroad steam locomotive and tender attached to Union Pacific boxcar and other rolling stock. Brigham Young served as president of U.C.R.R. Company, organized 8 March 1868. Completion of the line was celebrated on 10 January 1870 in Salt Lake City.

Mormons on that same point. Colonel Carr said, "It has been built solely with money wrung from the soil which, a few years ago, we used to consider a desert, by the strong arms of men and women who stand before me."[29]

Despite the cold weather, the celebration continued into the night with fireworks throughout the city and a huge bonfire and a special pyrotechnic display on Arsenal [Capitol] Hill. "A grand ball and supper at the [Salt Lake] Theater, attended by leading Church officials, prominent merchants of the city—Mormon and gentile—officers from Camp [Fort] Douglas, and many prominent citizens," records Orson Whitney, "made a fitting finale for the day's memorable proceedings."[30]

In the *Deseret News,* editor Cannon expressed the belief that the advantages of having a railroad connection with the rest of the country would far outweigh any disadvantages that could possibly arise. "The days of isolation are now forever past. We thank God for it."[31]

Brigham Young had admired the private cars of Leland Stanford, Thomas Durant, and other Pacific Railroad officials.

Now with Utah Central, he would have a private car of his own. When he traveled, he would travel in style, as was becoming for a railroad president and the most prominent man in Utah Territory. One of the cars acquired from Union Pacific was especially decorated to his taste, including handsome ornamentation of scrolls and gilding, and angels and cherubim on the ceiling. Such a heavenly touch was well earned, considering the infernal torment he had been through. He also found pleasure in giving free passes to other officials of the Church, to missionaries, and to general conference attenders.

While successfully building the Utah Central, the Church met with disappointment in a second railroad project—construction of a narrow gauge (three-foot) railroad from Coalville to Echo, a distance of five miles. Its main purpose was to freight coal from the Coalville area to Echo, at which point it would be transferred to the Union Pacific line for shipment to Ogden, then to the Utah Central for shipment to Salt Lake City. Local residents completed the grading and prepared the ties. Iron and rolling stock were to be provided by the Church from Union Pacific supplies in settlement of its debt to Brigham Young. But Union Pacific failed to send the amount agreed, and there was only sufficient for the Utah Central. Union Pacific also increased its freight rate from Echo to Ogden to a prohibitive figure to quell the competition to its coal mines at Rock Springs, Wyoming, which were selling to the Ogden and Salt Lake markets.

UTAH SOUTHERN AND NORTHERN

Brigham Young's next railroad venture was the Utah Southern Railroad, extending railroad service from Salt Lake City to points south. Organized in January 1871, it broke ground on 1 May. Several of the same Utah Central officials were involved, such as Brigham Young, his son Joseph, William Jennings, and John Sharp. Feramorz Little was appointed superintendent. The road reached Sandy by September—thirteen miles. A year later it reached Lehi in Utah County. Fourteen months later it was to Provo. By 1 April 1875, it was in York, twenty-seven miles south of Provo.

The first lap of the road to Sandy had particular significance for Brigham Young and the Mormons. A narrow-gauge spur was built seven miles east to Little Cottonwood Canyon, where the Church was quarrying granite stones for the Salt Lake Temple. Upon completion of this spur in 1873, all granite stones for the temple were hauled by railroad cars, greatly facilitating temple construction. Mines in the Alta area were also served by this spur, and other branches were constructed along the line—such as out to Bingham—to facilitate freighting of ores. Passenger service between communities and freighting of agricultural products from Utah county and points south figured significantly in its business.

But financial difficulties soon beset both Utah Central and Utah Southern. Reluctantly, President Young invited Union Pacific to buy into both roads. Paying partly in cash and partly in rails and rolling stock, Union Pacific soon acquired control of Utah Central and Utah Southern. It eventually continued the line on to Los Angeles, changing its name to Utah Central Railway System in 1881.

Brigham Young and his associates initiated one other railroad—the Utah Northern, later known as the "Utah and Northern." It ran from Ogden north to Brigham City, paralleling the Pacific Railroad. But then, instead of turning west, it continued north to Collinston, then east into Cache Valley—first to Mendon, then to Logan, then north to Franklin, Idaho, making it the first railroad in Idaho. A four-mile branch ran west from Brigham City to Corinne in deference to Corinne's importance as a freight transfer point. But when the Utah Northern reached Franklin, it killed Corinne as a shipping point to the mines of western Montana. The plan was to extend the Utah Northern line up to Soda Springs, Idaho, and eventually to the Montana mining area.

The Utah Northern was organized 23 August 1871 with John W. Young, Brigham's third son, as president and superintendent; Bishop William B. Preston of Logan, vice president and assistant superintendent; and Moses Thatcher of Logan, secretary (he soon became superintendent and later an Apostle). Several Church leaders in Weber, Box Elder, and Cache Valley were named directors, along with two New York City investors, Joseph Richardson and LeGrand Lockwood, who, along with Joseph's brother Benjamin, supplied the capital for the rails and rolling stock. Because of limited financing, it was decided to make Utah Northern a narrow-gauge (three-foot wide) railroad, which could be built for one-third the cost of a standard gauge and could be operated at a lower expense. Locomotives and other rolling stock were much smaller and less expensive. The engines, known as "Little Fellers," weighed a mere 17 tons but were capable of achieving a maximum speed of 35 miles per hour.

Inasmuch as the Pacific Railroad already ran between Ogden and Brigham City on its way to Corinne and points west, it was decided to build the first stretch of the Utah Northern from Brigham City to Logan. Then, while the road was being continued on north from Logan toward Soda Springs, other crews could be building from Brigham City to Ogden, connecting it to its companion road, the Utah Central.

Ground-breaking for the Utah Northern was on a hot summer day in Brigham City, 26 August 1871. Brigham City resident Lorenzo Snow, who later became President of the Church, dedicated the project unto the Lord. The Brigham City band played, a chorus sang, bells rang, and the old Nauvoo Legion cannon fired a mighty salute. The road reached Cache Valley on 22 December 1872, Logan on 31 January 1873, and Franklin, Idaho, in May 1874.

Brigham Young, Elder Erastus Snow, and others were invited to Franklin as guests for the big celebration on 2 May; they gladly accepted the invitation. Unfortunately, their "Little Feller" engine jumped the tracks just north of Logan, and Brigham Young's group never arrived at the celebration. Still, it was satisfying to the Mormon leader to know that the road had been completed—114.5 track miles from Salt Lake City.

Although several miles of grading had been done, the Utah Northern did not build to Soda Springs as planned. An alternative route was decided on, and the road got as far as Battle Creek, north of Preston, near the Bear River. Then funds ran out. The

New York financiers were unable or unwilling to invest further in it, and the Church lacked the means to continue.

As a result, Brigham Young once again contacted Union Pacific about buying a Mormon-built railroad. Jay Gould, a wealthy financier who had become a major stockholder in and president of Union Pacific, bought the Utah Northern. In 1877, the year of Brigham Young's death, Gould reorganized it as the Utah and Northern and extended its line up to McCammon, Idaho, where he connected it to Union Pacific's Oregon Shortline, which ran to Helena, Montana, and Portland, Oregon. He changed it from a narrow gauge to a standard gauge.

Although Brigham Young suffered many frustrations and disappointments in his career as a railroad builder, he had the great satisfaction of seeing Utah connected by rail to the rest of the United States, east and west, and of having most of the Mormon communities in Utah and Idaho served by rail. He personally enjoyed a financial profit from his railroad enterprises, a profit he needed to help support his extensive family.

Perhaps the five greatest values realized from his railroad efforts were these: (1) aid to convert emigration; (2) aid to missionary travel; (3) aid in construction of the Salt Lake Temple through transportation of the huge granite blocks from Little Cottonwood Canyon; (4) greater cohesion among Mormon communities; and (5) improvement in living standards through transportation of machinery, furniture, and other commodities.

NOTES

1. As quoted in Orson F. Whitney, *History of Utah* (Salt Lake City: George Q. Cannon & Sons Co., 1893), 2: 239–40.
2. Ibid., 240–41.
3. As quoted in John J Stewart, *The Iron Trail to the Golden Spike* (Salt Lake City: Deseret Book Co., 1969), 185.
4. Ibid., 181–82.
5. Ibid., 179–80.
6. Robert West Howard, *The Great Iron Trail* (New York: G. P. Putnam's Sons, 1962), 120.
7. Whitney, 2: 244.
8. As quoted in Stewart, 189.

9. Ibid., 190.
10. Ibid., 192–93.
11. Ibid., 192.
12. Ibid.
13. *Deseret News,* 31 July 1868; Howard, 269.
14. Stewart, 193–94; Howard, 275–77.
15. As quoted in Howard, 33–34.
16. As quoted in Stewart, 195–96.
17. *Deseret News,* 5 March 1869.
18. Whitney, 2: 259.
19. Samuel Bowles, *Our New West* (Hartford, Connecticut: Hartford Publishing Co., 1869), 260.
20. As quoted in George Kraus, *High Road to Promontory* (Palo Alto, California: American West Publishing Co., 1969), 282.
21. Whitney, 2: 258–59.
22. Ibid.
23. Ibid., 260.
24. Ibid.
25. Ibid., 261–62.
26. Ibid.
27. *Deseret News,* 1 September 1869.
28. As quoted in Whitney, 2: 264.
29. Ibid., 266.
30. Ibid., 267.
31. Ibid., 268.

CHAPTER 13

Brigham Young and the Great Basin Economy[1]

Leonard J. Arrington
Professor Emeritus of History
Past Director of the Joseph Fielding Smith Institute
Brigham Young University

When Brigham Young joined the Church in 1832, he discontinued his business operations, laid aside his account books, and covenanted to spend the rest of his life promoting righteous principles and encouraging the Saints to be of one heart and mind. "I expected," he said, "we should be one family, each seeking to do his neighbor good, and all be engaged to do all the good possible."[2] His sermons and letters often repeated a plea for the Latter-day Saints to maintain a strong sense of community. He explained:

> After we believed in the Gospel we were baptized for the remission of our sins—and by the laying on of hands we received the Holy Spirit of Promise and felt that "we shall be one." I felt that I should no longer have need to keep a day book and ledger in which to keep my accounts, for we were about to consolidate and become one; that every man and every woman would assist by actually laboring with their hands in planting, building up and beautifying this earth to make it like the Garden of Eden. I should therefore have no farther occasion to keep accounts. I should certainly accumulate and earn more than I needed, and had not a single doubt but what my wants would be supplied. This was my experience, and this is the feeling of every one who received the Gospel in an honest heart and contrite spirit.[3]

The Prophet Joseph Smith had, of course, revealed the law of consecration and stewardship in 1831, and Brigham had witnessed its application and had been imbued with the rhetoric associated with it. He believed, with the early Saints, that members of the Church constituted a community or Church family.

They must work together, just as they worshiped together; they must share with each other to build up the kingdom of God—not as individuals but as a group; not by competition but by cooperation; not by individual aggrandizement but by community development; not by profit-seeking but by working selflessly to build the kingdom.[4]

In Nauvoo, where Brigham was business manager of the Church, in-migration of skilled workers and capitalists was encouraged, local factories and shops were erected, and extensive public works projects provided infrastructure and employment. Highly committed to "the Lord's law," the Saints consecrated their time, talents, and material resources to realizing the goal of building the kingdom. Impressed with the Mormon achievement of causing Nauvoo to emerge Phoenix-like out of a swamp on the edge of the Mississippi, D. H. Lawrence remarked, "It is probable that the Mormons are the forerunners of the coming real America."[5]

Shortly after he succeeded Joseph Smith as President of the Church in 1847, Brigham received a revelation in Winter Quarters that showed the organization of the kingdom of God as one great family. The revelation has not been incorporated into the Church's Doctrine and Covenants, but it was precious to Brigham, and he often referred to it in sermons.

After the Saints reached Utah, various attempts were made, under Brigham's direction, to apply all parts of the law of consecration. In 1854–56, for example, more than half of the seven thousand families in the territory deeded all their property to the Church in a gesture of goodwill.[6] None of the property was ever taken over by the Church, but one can hardly deny that during most of the 1850s and 1860s, Mormon farmers and craftsmen came close to giving all their surplus in the form of tithing and other donations, and that in responding to Brigham's admonitions on colonizing and establishing new industries, they treated their property as a stewardship. They approached the goal of living as a united community of Saints. Harmony and unity were achieved through improved organization—priesthood quorums, Relief Societies, and village cooperatives. People received their pay in what they produced, and funds were accumulated to purchase machinery and supplies from the States.

After the Saints reached the Valley of the Great Salt Lake, Brigham's goal was to provide the basis for life of all the Saints who had come from the Midwest, and of all those in England, Scandinavia, and elsewhere who wished to gather in Zion. A way needed to be found for the thousands of gathering Saints to raise their families, build homes, erect meetinghouses and recreation halls, and produce everything necessary for their sustenance.

In seeking to build the kingdom of God in the Mountain West as he had been commanded, President Young engaged in what political economists call "nation-building." He adopted whatever policies were necessary to build his "nation"—the "Great Basin Kingdom." These policies can be summarized under five headings:

1. In order to maintain a favorable balance of trade for the region, exports were encouraged and imports were discouraged.

2. Export industries were stimulated by bounties, subsidies, liberal church credit, and the maintenance of low wages.

3. Imports were discouraged by purposeful establishment of substitute local industries, by voluntary abstention from buying imported products, by campaigns to support home industry, and by Church assumption of the importing function.

4. Development of the natural resources of the kingdom was encouraged by colonization projects, the establishment of new industries, and the cooperative organization of labor and management.

5. The improvement of the human resources of the kingdom was sought by importing skilled artisans with tools and equipment and with intelligent, well-disciplined laborers. The Church would assure employment in the region for these laborers.

Lengthy discussions of these policies may be found in the *Journal of Discourses*. All of them were applied by the Church, by the Church-controlled legislature, and by the local Latter-day Saint communities. They represent a consistent, original, and sophisticated application of nation-building principles in developing the economy of a semiarid region.

Unlike some economic administrators in European history,

Brigham Young had no interest in acquiring gold bullion, either for himself or for the kingdom. He understood that in a resource economy, of which the "Great Basin Kingdom" was an example, the pursuit of gold would serve only to undermine economic development. Gold was good only for purchases in the American East. Purchases were imports, and importing and exporting would lead to an exchange economy—and to assimilation into the greater national economy. What the Latter-day Saint financier strove for was a relatively independent and self-sufficient regional economy:

> Can you not see that gold and silver rank among the things that we are the least in want of? We want an abundance of wheat and fine flour, of wine and oil, and of every choice fruit that will grow in our climate; we want silk, wool, cotton, flax and other textile substances of which cloth can be made; we want vegetables of various kinds to suit our constitutions and tastes; and the products of flocks and herds; we want the coal and the iron that are concealed in these ancient mountains, the lumber from our sawmills, and the rock from our quarries; these are some of the great staples to which kingdoms owe their existence, continuance, wealth, magnificence, splendor, glory and power; in which gold and silver serve as mere tinsel to give the finishing touch to all this greatness. The colossal wealth of the world is founded upon and sustained by the common staples of life.[7]

It has been customary for historians and writers to begin discussions of Utah's industrial history with the assertion that Brigham Young and the Church were opposed to mining. According to this interpretation, Brigham Young not only opposed the idea of Latter-day Saints taking the pick and shovel, but he was also opposed to the development of Utah's mineral resources by the gentiles. "Developing of mining in the early days," one reads in *Utah: A Guide to the State*, "was deliberately retarded by the Mormon Church."[8] If the Latter-day Saints had participated actively in the development of mining, it has been claimed, they would have owned most of the mines in the territory and received the profits derived from working them. By refusing to permit the

Latter-day Saints to mine, the theory goes, Brigham was consigning this lucrative industry over to the gentiles.

The historical evidence points the other way. Brigham Young and his associates at no time were opposed to mining *as such*. Under Brigham's leadership, the Church commissioned several official exploring expeditions, followed by Church-called "missions" to develop iron, coal, silver, and lead resources, particularly in the 1850s, but also later; the Church called a group of fifty young men to mine gold in California for the benefit of the Church and its members; the Church opposed the premature mining activities of Colonel Patrick Connor and his California Volunteers in the 1850s for social and economic reasons, not theological reasons—and these reasons do not include opposition to mining *per se;* the Church encouraged the development of Utah's mineral resources after 1869, attempting only to counter what it regarded as undesirable social consequences of the rush of gentile miners and merchants to Utah; and the Church strongly encouraged the development of new industries.

There is, of course, some superficial evidence in favor of the theory that the Saints were opposed to mining. It is well established that Church leaders, especially Brigham Young, vigorously opposed the "desertion" of the Latter-day Saints to the California gold fields in 1849 and thereafter. Repeated advice was given to the faithful to resist the temptation to join the gold rush. For example, at a special meeting of the Utah Saints in the Salt Lake Valley in 1849, President Young dwelt at length on Church policy and the reasons for it:

> Some have asked me about going. I have told them that God has appointed this place for the gathering of His Saints, and you will do better right here than you will by going to the gold mines. Some have thought they would go there and get fitted out and come back, but I told them to stop here and get fitted out. Those who stop here and are faithful to God and His people will make more money and get richer than you that run after the god of this world; and I promise you in the name of the lord that many of you that go, thinking you will get rich and come back, will wish you had never gone away from here, and will long to come back but will

> not be able to do so. Some of you will come back, but your friends who remain here will have to help you; and the rest of you who are spared to return will not make as much money as your brethren do who stay here and help build up the Church and kingdom of God; they will prosper and be able to buy you twice over. Here is the place God has appointed for his people.
>
> We have been kicked out of the frying-pan into the fire, out of the fire into the middle of the floor, and here we are and here we will stay. God has shown me that this is the spot to locate His people, and here is where they will prosper; He will temper the elements for the good of His Saints; He will rebuke the frost and the sterility of the soil, and the land shall become fruitful. Brethren, go to, now, and plant out your fruit seeds.[9]

The President then went on to tell the people that the time had not come for the Saints to dig gold. "It is our duty," he said, "first to develop the agricultural resources of this country. . . . As for gold and silver, and the rich minerals of the earth, . . . let them alone; let others seek them, and we will cultivate the soil."[10]

Brigham wanted to discourage his followers from going to California for three reasons:

1. He wanted to hold the Church together in order to build the kingdom. "When I see some of the brethren going away," he said, "I feel like a mother seeing her child in the midst of the ocean, or in the roaring flames. We are gathered here, not to scatter around and go off to the mines, or any other place, but to build up the Kingdom of God."[11]

2. He considered the atmosphere of the gold fields unsuitable for the Saints. "This [the Salt Lake Valley] is a good place to make Saints," he said, "and it is a good place for Saints to live; it is the place that the Lord has appointed, and we shall stay here, until He tells us to go somewhere else." "To talk of going away from this valley for anything is like vinegar to my eyes." Again: "If you Elders of Israel want to go to the gold mines, go and be damned."[12]

3. He thought that at the time the average person would be better off economically by remaining in the Great Basin. "He told those who wanted to go to the mines that he would remain here,

mind his own business, help to build up the Kingdom of God, and when they returned from the mines he would agree to count dollars with them." Again:

> "I will commence at the north and go to the south settlements, and pick out twenty-five of our inhabitants as they average, and another man may take fifty of the gold diggers, off hand, and they cannot buy out the twenty-five men who have tarried at home. Before I had been one year in this place, the wealthiest man who came from the mines, Father Rhodes, with $17,000, could he buy the possessions I had made in one year? It will not begin to do it; and I will take twenty-five men in the United States, who have stayed at home and paid attention to their own business, and they will weigh down fifty others from the same place, who went to the gold regions: and again, look at the widows that have been made, and see the bones that lie bleaching and scattered over the prairies."[13]

Moreover, and this was important in a deliberately self-sufficient society, gold did not constitute "true riches." "True wealth," Brigham Young said, "consists in the skill to produce conveniences and comforts from the elements. All the power and dignity that wealth can bestow is a mere shadow, the substance is found in the bone and sinew of the toiling millions. Well directed labor is the true power that supplies our wants."[14]

In the self-sufficient commonwealth of Deseret, gold would not be wealth except insofar as it facilitated exchange. Brigham wanted his people to husband their gold and pay tithing with it in order to help the Church pay its immigration expenses in the East and England.

Having established the basic policy that the Saints must not join the gold rush, he permitted members of the Mormon Battalion to remain in California to earn money, by prospecting or otherwise, before returning to Salt Lake; he allowed a few of the Saints to go to California; and to protect the interests of the Church in California, he called two of his trusted Apostles, Charles C. Rich and Amasa Lyman, to go to California to minister to the Saints who were there, to establish a colony in Southern

Charles C. Rich (1809–1883). Together with his fellow Apostle, Amasa M. Lyman, he purchased Rancho San Bernardino containing about 100,000 acres in September 1851, ca. 1865.

Colonel (later General) Patrick E. Connor (1820–1891), ca. 1865. He established Camp Douglas in 1862. Connor organized a mining company, framed laws for the government of mining districts, and encouraged his officers and enlisted men to prospect for precious metals.

California at San Bernardino, and to collect tithing and other offerings.

The most remarkable evidence that Church opposition to the "California fever" did not constitute opposition to mining as such is the official call in 1849 of fifty select young Latter-day Saints to go "on a mission" to California to mine gold for the Church and its members. The story of the Gold Mission offers undeniable and fascinating proof of the nature of Church policy with respect to mining. The young men were not particularly successful, however, and their experience merely proved Brigham Young's conclusion that the Saints could do better in Zion than in the California gold fields.[15]

If Brigham's first preoccupation was to establish and build up Zion's commonwealth in the Great Basin as a place to shelter and raise Latter-day Saints during the years of the gold rush, the second was to solve problems created by the completion of the transcontinental railroad in 1869. Protecting the industries and

Amasa M. Lyman (1813–1877), ca. 1866–1877. In 1851 he and Apostles Charles C. Rich were called to lead a company of settlers to California, which started from Payson, Utah 24 March 1851 and arrived at San Bernardino in the following June.

way of life of Deseret was a high priority. The mining of Utah's precious metals was now a possibility; outside financial interests, encouraged by anti-Mormon federal officers, threatened to take over Mormon land and convert the Saints' self-sufficient economy into a tributary of Babylon.

In 1862, the Third California Volunteers, under Colonel (later General) Patrick Edward Connor, were ordered to Utah by Abraham Lincoln to protect the mail and overland telegraph and to "keep an eye on the Mormons." Wishing to solve "the Mormon problem"—the Mormon desire for self-government and independence—Connor organized a mining company, framed laws for the government of mining districts, and encouraged his officers and enlisted men to prospect by granting indefinite furloughs and furnishing provisions and equipment. Connor himself discovered the first silver-bearing rock in Little Cottonwood Canyon and erected a smelting furnace, and he distributed exaggerated releases to the eastern press advertising "rich veins of gold, silver, copper and other minerals" in Utah.

Connor's policy, clearly stated in public and in private, was "to invite hither a large gentile" population, "sufficient by peaceful means and through the ballot-box to overwhelm the Mormons by mere force of numbers."[16] Many miners rushed to Utah, as did merchants and traders to supply them. Fortunately for the Saints, mining could not be profitably conducted until railroad connections were provided. Indeed, there was not a single instance of profitable exploration of Volunteer discoveries until the completion of the transcontinental railway in 1869.[17]

What Connor and his Volunteers did was to prospect enough to support the belief that deposits of gold, silver, and copper existed in paying quantities in Cottonwood Canyon in the Wasatch, Bingham Canyon in the Oquirrh range, Rush Valley in northwestern Utah, and perhaps elsewhere. Brigham Young's position was not unlike that of political and religious leaders of developing nations who objected to opportunistic, exploitative foreign investment. It was an obvious unfairness, said Brigham, for Connor to use government funds without specific authorization, to supply and subsidize the prospecting activities of the Volunteers to their private benefit, especially when the avowed ultimate intention was to subvert the Mormon commonwealth.

> Who feeds and clothes and defrays the expenses of hundreds of men who are engaged in patroling the mountains and kanyons all around us in search of gold? Who finds supplies for those who are sent here to protect the two great interests—the mail and telegraph lines across the continent—while they are employed ranging over these mountains in search of gold? And who has paid for the multitude of picks, shovels, spikes and other mining tools that they have brought with them? Were they really sent here to protect the mail and telegraph lines, or to discover, if possible, rich diggings in our immediate vicinity, with a view to flood the country with just such a population as they desire, to destroy, if possible, the identity of the "Mormon" community, and every truth and virtue that remains?

Sound development was one thing, subversion another.

> On the bare report that gold was discovered over in these West Mountains, men left their thrashing machines, and their horses at large to eat up and trample down and destroy the precious bounties of earth. They at once sacrificed all at the glittering shrine of this popular idol, declaring they were now going to be rich, and would raise wheat no more. Should this feeling become universal on the discovery of gold mines in our immediate vicinity, nakedness, starvation, utter destitution and annihilation would be the inevitable lot of this people. . . .
>
> The business of the Saints at present [added a Mormon editor], is not to hunt or dig for gold, but to cultivate the soil, to manufacture everything that is necessary for their

> use, to make their habitations beautiful and full of comfort, to raise up a generation of sons and daughters who will serve the Lord from their childhood, and to do all that lies in their power to build up a kingdom that shall be full of strength, virtue, peace, and glory, while the world hurries on to its doom.[18]

Brigham Young's administration sought to accomplish the simultaneous, cooperative development of the region's resources by local interests. The building of the kingdom was to be achieved by well-planned growth in which the improvement of agricultural production, the stimulation of local industry, and the orderly development of mineral resources for local use were the essential ingredients. Brigham was certain that the development of a highly specialized economy based on mining and other export industries would be detrimental to the best interests of the commonwealth.[19]

Recognizing that the railroad would bring problems, Brigham, statesman that he was, welcomed its completion. He invested in the Pacific Railroad Company to show Church goodwill. He knew the connection would soften the journey of the thousands of converts who came each year, and he welcomed the ease with which useful machinery and equipment could be brought to Zion. The railroad did, in fact, speed the exploitation of Utah's mineral resources, but Brigham's policies served to counter the unhealthy adjustments that otherwise would have occurred.

Beginning in 1868, as the railroad neared, seeking to minimize the influence of "the outside world" on the culture and well-being of the saintly mountain valleys, Brigham and his associates organized the School of the Prophets and the Women's Relief Society as the effective agents of what was called "Protection." With their help, he implemented a seven-point program.[20]

1. He contracted to build the Utah portion of the railroad in order to keep out "swarms of scalawags" that would be imported into the territory to do the road-building. This would augment the incomes of local workers and ensure that the money they earned would be spent to benefit locally owned establishments.

2. Locally owned general stores and shops were established in

every locality to ensure that needs could be met with Mormon-produced goods.

3. Interior branch railroads were built by the Saints to serve localities not touched by the transcontinental: the Utah Central Railroad, from Ogden to Salt Lake City; the Utah Southern, from Salt Lake City to Provo and points south; the Utah Northern, from Ogden to Montana; and the Utah Eastern, from Echo to Park City.

4. To the extent that imports were necessary and desirable, they were canalized through a Church-established wholesale trading concern, Zion's Cooperative Mercantile Institution (ZCMI).

5. The School of the Prophets conducted a campaign to get a federal land office in Salt Lake City and to acquire and confirm the titles to land the Saints had settled.

6. All local and general leaders took pledges to observe the Word of Wisdom, to economize on other consumption expenditures, and to use the income created by this retrenchment to bring poor converts from the East and from Europe.

7. Saints were encouraged to grow crops, produce manufacturers, build railroads, and work for wages for mining companies, but not to hunt for ore or try to work their own mines. In giving this advice, Brigham was almost certainly correct. All evidence seems to indicate that the *average* returns of the miners were less than the earnings of Utah's farmers. Deep-shaft mining was extremely expensive, requiring large amounts of outside capital. Even here, however, it would appear that the average return on all invested capital was less than that received in other forms of enterprise. It is true that certain individuals made fortunes, but the large number of failures are seldom remembered. As Adam Smith wrote:

> The . . . absurd presumption . . . which the greater part of men have . . . in their own good fortune . . . is an ancient evil . . . less taken notice of . . . by the philosophers and moralists. . . . The chance of gain is by every man more or less over-valued, and the chance of loss is by most men under-valued. . . . Mining, it seems, is . . . a lottery, in which the prizes do not compensate the blanks, though the greatness of some tempts many adventurers to throw away their fortunes in such unprosperous projects.[21]

Thus, the Church assisted in promoting and financing the transcontinental railroad, without which mining would have been unprofitable; the Church assisted in promoting and financing the construction of branch roads to the mines; and the Church encouraged its members, when practicable, to work in the mines, carry supplies to mining camps, and in other ways to participate in resource development.

Brigham's counselor, President George A. Smith, gave a report in an 1870 general conference:

> He advised the brethren to work for a reasonable remuneration, and to do all the labor that has to be done in this Territory, instead of making it necessary for those who want it done to import it, on account of the high price demanded for it. If the brethren go to mining, he would advise them to work for pay instead of taking up claims for, in most cases, those who invest in mining speculations fail, financially. If those who own mines want the brethren to work for them, do so and get money.[22]

A year later, at the time of the Ophir and Little Cottonwood discoveries, Brigham Young wrote,

> We hear from all quarters of the great excitement about Utah—her mineral wealth, etc., and it is probable that a large emigration and a consequent increase of business will be the direct result. There is a need of money to pay Government for our lands, to stock and improve our farms, etc., and if in the providences of the Almighty these mines should for three or four years create an active circulating medium and thus enable the brethren to secure and improve their homesteads, we shall have reason to be thankful.
>
> Truly the Saints have reason to praise the Lord for His goodness constantly manifested towards His people.[23]

The discoveries, Brigham reported, were evidences of "God's blessings," and he expected them to redound to "the welfare of Israel."[24]

At general conference in 1871, the President expressed more explicitly the Church's policy on mining:

> I have a short discourse to preach now to my friends who may be here to-day, who are engaged in, or who may

> contemplate commencing operations in, the mining business. . . .
>
> We say to the Latter-day Saints, work for these capitalists, and work honestly and faithfully, and they will pay you faithfully. I am acquainted with a good many of them, and as far as I know them, I do not know but every one is an honorable man. They are capitalists, they want to make money, and they want to make it honestly and according to the principles of honest dealing. If they have means and are determined to risk it in opening mines you work for them by the day. Haul their ores, build their furnaces, and take your pay for it, and enter your lands, build houses, improve your farms, buy your stock, and make yourselves better off. . . .
>
> I will say still further with regard to our rich country here. Suppose there was no railroad across this continent, could you do anything with these mines? Not the least in the world. All this galena would not bear transportation were it not for the railroad. And then, were it not for this little railroad from Ogden to this city [the Utah Central] these Cottonwood mines would not pay, for you could not cart the ore. Well, they want a little more help, and we want to build them a railroad direct to Cottonwood, so that they can make money.
>
> We want them to do it and to do it on business principles, so that they can keep it, and when you get it, make good use of it and we will help you. There is enough for all. We do not want any quarreling or contention.[25]

Brigham Young recognized that neither the Church nor any conceivable combination of its members had the capital or the technical know-how to develop the rich mountains of ore that had been and were being discovered. Their most profitable participation, Young was certain, lay in the construction of arterial railways and the furnishing of food, feed, supplies, and services. Those few who did endeavor "to get rich quick" by prospecting were objects of pity. As he said in general conference in 1873:

> "What have you been doing?" "Oh, I have been mining, and it takes all my time and labor to support my family. I have a splendid claim—I am just going to have a hundred thousand dollars for it."
>
> We have plenty of this class around, and whenever I see

> a man going along with an old mule that can hardly stand up, and a frying pan and an old quilt, I say, "There goes a millionaire in prospect!" . . . These millionaires are all over our country; they are in the mountains, on our highways, and in our streets. And they haven't a sixpence.[26]

Clearly, Brigham favored those measures that he felt would "build the kingdom." Among these were agriculture, mining, and manufacturing. The strong preference that the economy be developed by Latter-day Saints rather than by "outsiders" does not negate the overwhelming desire that development take place.

With successful execution of the Protection program during the next fourteen years (1868–82), Utah's more than 100,000 Latter-day Saints—in a vigorous, well-organized, socially minded, and theocratically directed program of economic action—managed to preserve their beloved Deseret from destruction by the energetic and financially powerful outside enterprisers whose activities might otherwise have threatened the morality and well-being of the community of Saints.

This is not to suggest that all the Saints agreed with Brigham's program. A small group of "liberal Mormons," as they were called, conducted a campaign for cooperation with the gentiles, elimination of social and economic insularity, and development of mining. In a lengthy editorial on "The True Development of the Territory," which appeared in the *Utah Magazine,* the Godbeites, as they came to be called (after their leader, William S. Godbe), claimed that Utah's prosperity would depend on the development of mineral resources:

> Common sense would seem to say, develop that first which will bring money from other Territories and States, and then these factories and home industries which supply ourselves will have something to lean upon. . . . Summed up in a few words—we live in a country destitute of the rich advantages of other lands—a country with few natural facilities beyond the great mass of minerals in its bowels. These are its main financial hopes. To this our future factories must look for their life, our farmers, our stock, wool, and cotton raisers for their sale, and our mechanics for suitable wages. Let these resources be developed, and we have a future before us as bright as any country beneath the sun, because we shall be

> working in harmony with the indications of Nature around us.[27]

The Godbeites, unable to marshal widespread support, did not succeed in derailing Brigham's program.

Near the end of his life, Brigham became preoccupied with building the kingdom as a community or family of Saints. Still remembering the revelation he had received in 1847, he described at length in 1872 an ideal community of Saints:

> I will tell you how I would arrange for a little family, say about a thousand persons. I would build houses expressly for their convenience in cooking, washing, and every department of their domestic arrangements. Instead of having every woman getting up in the morning and fussing around a cookstove or over the fire, cooking a little food for two or three or half a dozen persons, or a dozen, as the case may be, she would have nothing to do but to go to her work. Let me have my arrangement here, a hall in which I can seat five hundred persons to eat; and I have my cooking apparatus, ranges and ovens, all prepared. And suppose we had a hall a hundred feet long with our cooking room attached to this hall; and there is a person at the further end of the table and he should telegraph that he wanted a warm beefsteak; and this is conveyed to him by a little railway, perhaps under the table, and he or she may take her beefsteak. . . . No matter what they call for, it is conveyed to them and they take it, and we can seat five hundred at once, and serve them all in a few minutes. And when they have all eaten, the dishes are piled together, slipped under the table, and run back to the ones who wash them. . . . Under such a system the women would go to work making their bonnets, hats, and clothing, or in the factories. . . .
>
> What will we do throughout the day? Each one go to his work. Here are the herdsmen—here are those who look after the sheep—here are those who make the butter and the cheese, all at their work by themselves. Some for the Kanyon, perhaps, or for the plow or harvest, no difference what, each and every class is organized, and all labor and perform their part. . . .
>
> Work through the day, and when it comes evening . . . repair to our room, and have our historians, and our different teachers to teach classes of old and young, to read the

> Scriptures to them; to teach them history, arithmetic, reading, writing, and painting; and have the best teachers that can be got to teach our day-schools. Half the labor necessary to make people moderately comfortable now, would make them independently rich under such a system. . . .
>
> If we could see such a society organized as I have mentioned, you would see . . . people all attending to their business having the most improved machinery for making cloth, and doing every kind of housework, farming, all mechanical operations, in our factories, dairies, orchards and vineyards; and possessing every comfort and convenience of life. A society like this would never have to buy anything; they would make and raise all they would eat, drink, and wear, and always have something to sell and bring money, to help to increase their comfort and independence.[28]

During the winter of 1873–74, Brigham organized St. George as a cooperative community called the "United Order of the City of St. George." Each person was asked to contribute all his economic or productive property to the community United Order, in return for which he received capital stock. To accomplish spiritual as well as temporal union, the participants drew up a long list of rules: no lying, backbiting, or quarrelling; all were to live as good Latter-day Saints ought. They were to pray daily, not use liquor or tobacco, obey their leaders, be frugal and industrious, and cultivate "the simple grandeur of manners that belong to the pure in heart." In addition, each person was rebaptized and made new covenants. Among the latter was the following:

> We agree to be energetic, industrious, and faithful in the management of all business entrusted to us; and to abstain from all selfish motives and actions, as much as lies in our power. We desire to seek the interest and welfare of each other; and to promote the special good of the Order and the general welfare of all mankind.[29]

Similar United Orders were founded in each settlement, and ultimately about two hundred were so organized. Beginning in 1875, a communal United Order was established in Orderville, Utah. People contributed all their property to the community United Order, had no private farming or business property, shared more or less equally in their common product, and lived as a village family. This organization lasted for eleven years and was successful until authorities introduced a system of differential wages.

Similar communal organizations functioned in Kingston, Utah; Bunkerville, Nevada; and in twelve Arizona communities. There was almost complete self-sufficiency. All the land, implements, and livestock belonged to the Order. All ate at a common table. Labor was directed by a Board of Management—and a United Order bugler who signaled for the community members to rise, to eat, to attend to prayers, and to go to work. In each community, everyone wore clothes from the same bolt of cloth.

Some of the United Order organizations lasted into the 1890s, but most were relatively short-lived. Reasons for their discontinuance include grasshopper plague; prominent men being placed in jail during the anti-polygamy crusade; bickering; and lack of support of leaders.

In essence, the United Order movement was Brigham's attempt to preserve internal unity and harmony as the Mormon economy was threatened by the opening of mines after the 1869 completion of the transcontinental railroad. As non-Mormon miners, bankers, freighters, suppliers, lawyers, and political leaders descended onto Utah, the United Order maximized production, helped the Saints maintain self-sufficiency, and pooled assets and labor to form more efficient production units.

Despite the eventual discontinuance of the formally organized United Orders, the divine law that moved Brigham remained a goal of Mormon aspiration, a symbol of Christian perfection, a remembrance of the oneness of mind and heart that God has prescribed for his people. Brigham's influence was immeasurable.

Abundant source materials reveal much about Brigham Young, the man. He was sincere in trying to establish friendly relations with Indians; he had a reverence for animal life and for nature; and he constantly admonished settlers to develop wholesome and harmonious communities.

The words of advice and instruction he gave the first settlers of Cache and Weber valleys on 10 and 12 June 1860 reflect the qualities of this practical yet idealistic leader:

> Keep your valley pure, keep your towns as pure as possible, keep your hearts pure, and labor as hard as you can without injuring yourselves. . . . Build cities, adorn your habitations, make gardens, orchards, and vineyards, and render the earth so pleasant that when you look upon your labors you may do so with pleasure, and that angels may delight to come and visit your beautiful locations. . . . Your work is to beautify the face of the earth, until it shall become like the Garden of Eden.[30]

Brigham Young was a wise and inspiring leader in both spiritual and temporal affairs.

NOTES

1. Treatments of this topic include Leonard J. Arrington, *Great Basin Kingdom: An Economic History of the Latter-day Saints, 1830–1900,* 2d ed. (Salt Lake City: University of Utah Press,1993); Leonard J. Arrington, *Brigham Young: American Moses* (Urbana and Chicago: University of Illinois Press, 1986); and Leonard J. Arrington, Feramorz Y. Fox, and Dean L. May, *Building the City of God: Community and Cooperation Among the Mormons,* 2d ed. (Urbana and Chicago: University of Illinois Press, 1992).
2. Sermon of 20 February 1853, in *Journal of Discourses,* 1: 314.
3. Sermon of 8 October 1876, in *Journal of Discourses,* 18: 260.
4. See Moses 7: 18–19; and *The Evening and The Morning Star* (Independence, Missouri), July 1832, 1.
5. *Studies in Classical American Literature* (New York: Viking Press, 1923, 1961), 94.
6. Arrington, Fox, and May, 63–78.
7. Sermon of 25 October 1863, *Deseret News,* 18 November 1863.
8. Utah Works Progress Administration, *Utah: A Guide to the State* (New York: Hastings House, 1945), 120.
9. James S. Brown, *Giant of the Lord: Life of a Pioneer* (Salt Lake City: Bookcraft, 1960), 132.
10. Ibid., 133. This statement should be viewed in the light of the year and the situation. What more effective way to discourage a wholesale desertion to California than to tell the people that the reserves of gold and silver in their own land were the equal of others they might encounter, and "if the mines are opened first, we are a thousand miles from any base of supplies, and the people would rush in here in such great numbers that they would breed famine; and gold would not do us or them any good if there were no provisions in the land."
11. Journal History of The Church of Jesus Christ of Latter-day Saints (hereafter cited as Journal History), 8 April 1850, Library-Archives, Historical Department of The Church of Jesus Christ of Latter-day Saints (hereafter

cited as LDS Church Historical Archives); "Eleventh General Epistle of the Presidency," 10 April 1854, *Deseret News,* 13 April 1854.

12. As cited in Preston Nibley, *Brigham Young the Man and His Work* (Independence, Missouri: Zion's Printing and Publishing, 1936), 256; Journal History, 1 October 1848, 8 July 1849.
13. Journal History, 26 May, 6 September 1850.
14. *Journal of Discourses,* 8: 168; 10: 189.
15. See Eugene E. Campbell, "The Mormon Gold-Mining Mission of 1849," *Brigham Young University Studies* 1 and 2 (Autumn 1959–Winter 1960): 19: 31.
16. Patrick Edward Connor to R. C. Drum, Assistant Attorney General, U. S. Army, 21 July 1864, as cited in *Tullidge's Quarterly Magazine* 1 (January 1881): 185.
17. T. B. H. Stenhouse, *The Rocky Mountain Saints....* (New York: n.p., 1873), 714–19.
18. Sermon of 6 October 1863, in *Journal of Discourses,* 10: 254–55, 271; "Gold Mining," *Millennial Star* 29 (1867): 618.
19. The great economist Adam Smith would have supported Brigham's policy:

    "Of all those expensive and uncertain projects . . . which bring bankruptcy upon the greater part of the people who engage in them, there is none perhaps more perfectly ruinous than the search after new silver and gold mines. It is perhaps the most disadvantageous lottery in the world, or the one in which the gain of those who draw the prizes bears the least proportion to the loss of those who draw the blanks. . . . Projects of mining . . . are the projects, therefore, to which of all others a prudent law-giver, who desired to increase the capital of his nation, would least choose to give any extraordinary encouragement, or to turn towards them a greater share of that capital than what would go to them of its own accord." *An Enquiry into the Nature and Causes of the Wealth of Nations* (New York: Modern Library edition, 1940), 529–30.
20. Arrington, *Great Basin Kingdom,* 235–349.
21. *Wealth of Nations,* 107–8, 170.
22. *Deseret News,* 8, 9 October 1870.
23. Brigham Young to Horace S. Eldredge, Journal History, 16 February 1871.
24. Ibid.
25. Sermon of 9 April 1871, in *Journal of Discourses,* 14: 82, 85–86.
26. Sermon of 7 April 1873, in *Journal of Discourses,* 16: 22; Andrew Love Neff, *History of Utah, 1847–1869* (Salt Lake City: Deseret News Press, 1940), 643.
27. As cited in *Tullidge's Quarterly Magazine* 1 (1880): 24–28. The Godbeites were later excommunicated from the Church for apostasy, but their view on mining development seems not to have been a consideration. See "Mining, the 'Mormons' and the Government," *Deseret News,* 18 August 1880; Ronald W. Walker, "The Commencement of the Godbeite Protest," *Utah Historical Quarterly* 42 (Summer 1974), 216–44.

28. Sermon of 9 October 1872, in *Journal of Discourses,* 15: 158–67.
29. "St. George Stake Manuscript History," September 1875, LDS Church Historical Archives.
30. "Cache Valley Stake History, 1860," LDS Church Historical Archives; sermons of 10, 12 June 1860, in *Journal of Discourses,* 8: 77–84.

CHAPTER 14

Brigham Young and the Awakening of Mormon Women in the 1870s

Jill Mulvay Derr
Research Historian, Joseph Fielding Smith Institute
Brigham Young University

For more than a century, those who have written about Brigham Young have inevitably taken an interest in his relationships with women, at least within the connubial context. To his American contemporaries, Young became the personification of Latter-day Saint involvement in plural marriage, or polygamy. They portrayed him as a despot with a harem, a man who had "outraged decency and riven asunder the most sacred social and domestic ties."[1]

Horace Greeley, who visited the Mormons in 1859, criticized President Young for esteeming so lightly the opinions of his wives and other women. Greeley considered the apparent restriction of woman to the single office of childbearing and its accessories an inevitable consequence of polygamy.[2]

Catherine V. Waite, the wife of a federal judge appointed to Utah Territory in the early 1860s, agreed that polygamous marriages could only degrade women. "Instead of being a companion to man . . . she becomes, under this system, merely the minister to his passions and physical comfort." Waite characterized Young as foremost among the oppressors of women. "He declares that women have no souls—that they are not responsible beings, that they cannot save themselves, nor be saved except through man's intervention," she wrote.[3]

Some twentieth-century biographers of Brigham Young have looked at his attitudes toward women almost exclusively in terms of his practice and explanation of polygamy. M. R. Werner's *Brigham Young* (1925) devoted three of thirteen chapters to polygamy and made no mention of Young's involvement in reorganizing the Relief Society, the official Church organization for Latter-day Saint women. Stanley P. Hirshson's biography of Brigham Young, *Lion of the Lord* (1969), considered polygamy in three of the book's fifteen chapters and mentioned the Relief Society only briefly as the women's advocate for retrenchment and plural marriage.[4] These studies are both indicative of an assumption about Brigham Young that has persisted for more than a century—that he was an oppressor of women.

A more complex view of Brigham Young's dealings with women in familial and organizational settings is provided in Leonard J. Arrington's *Brigham Young: American Moses* (1985). Arrington, well versed in Mormon history, had the advantage of access not only to Brigham Young's letterbooks but also to a fifteen-year flowering of women's studies, and particularly Mormon women's history. He therefore discussed at some length the period when Latter-day Saint women emerged into public life.[5] Between 1867 and 1877, Young himself was in part responsible for the increasing sphere of activity of Mormon women. His own people were convinced of that. In fact, Mormon *Woman's Exponent* editor Louisa Lula Greene Richards heralded Young as the "most genuine, impartial and practical 'Woman's Rights Man' upon the American Continent."[6]

Views of Brigham Young as "oppressor" and advocate of women are both in a sense correct. Each represents certain aspects of Young's attitudes toward women, but neither represents the whole. Young's vision was one of ultimate human liberation, to which personal choice and responsibility were integral. But equally necessary for the freedom promised with a knowledge of the truth (see John 8: 32) were obedience and submission to the order of the kingdom of God, The Church of Jesus Christ of Latter-day Saints. This freedom-submission paradox pervaded Young's attitudes toward the Mormon women (and men) he addressed and with whom he worked in various contexts.

He spoke of individual women as daughters of God, free agents, beings with the same eternal possibilities as men. Yet, within the family context, he insisted that wives submit themselves to their husbands and chided mothers who pursued personal interests at the expense of their children. However, as the Mormon community increased in complexity, Young gave sisters the resources and encouragement to pursue roles outside their homes.

This mélange of prescriptive behavior for women has never significantly blurred the monolithic image of Young as an oppressor of women, though in recent years some Mormon women have celebrated Young's declarations in support of women's education and employment. A more careful appraisal of Brigham Young must not only acknowledge the apparent incongruities in his prescriptions for women but also assess to what extent he resolved them.

At least as often as he addressed men and women separately, Brigham Young addressed them jointly, speaking to "ladies and gentlemen," or more likely to "brethren and sisters." They were "sons and daughters, legitimately so, of our Father in Heaven."[7] These children of divine parents (Brigham Young, like Joseph Smith, acknowledged a Mother as well as a Father in Heaven[8]) came to earth endowed with assorted talents and abilities that were not necessarily sex-differentiated. Speaking in tongues, the interpretation of tongues, and healing were spiritual gifts practiced by both men and women with the approval of President Young.[9] He preached that women and men alike had access to the promptings of the Holy Ghost ("Let every man and woman, without exception, obtain that Spirit . . .") and that in the next life their exaltation to godhood, the ultimate promise for righteous Saints, was predicated upon their personal choices in this life. "Now those men, or those women," he emphasized,

> who know no more about the power of God, and the influences of the Holy Spirit, than to be led entirely by another person, suspending their own understanding, and pinning their faith upon another's sleeve, will never be capable of entering into the celestial glory, to be crowned as they anticipate; they will never be capable of becoming Gods.[10]

Not only were spiritual resources available to women and men alike, but both were capable of developing more temporal skills. Young indicated that some Mormon sisters, "if they had the privilege of studying, would make just as good mathematicians or accountants as any man; and we think they ought to have the privilege to study these branches of knowledge that they may develop the powers with which they are endowed."[11] Susa Young Gates, daughter of Brigham and journalist and suffragist of national renown, said her father was "always proud to recognize and acclaim the woman of gifts and encourage her to use them to the fullest extent for the establishment of righteousness on earth."[12]

Young's emphasis on individual freedom and development was offered within a context ever present in Mormondom: the kingdom of God was in fact a kingdom governed by "the Government of the Son of God," "a heavenly institution among men"—the priesthood.[13] The presence of the priesthood among the Latter-day Saints was what designated them as God's covenant people. For Young, it was the priesthood that "forms, fashions, makes, creates, produces, protects and holds in existence the inhabitants of the earth in a pure and holy form of government preparatory to their entering the kingdom of Heaven."[14]

According to Young, Saints who subjected themselves to be governed by the priesthood would "live strictly according to its pure system of laws and ordinances" until they were unified as one. He promised, "The man that honors his Priesthood, the woman that honors her Priesthood will receive an everlasting inheritance in the Kingdom of God." In order to receive that "everlasting inheritance," Saints would not only have to honor the "pure system of government" but also to sanctify themselves through holy temple ordinances wherein priesthood covenants and blessings are proffered women and men alike.[15]

From the time the priesthood was restored to Joseph Smith, its ecclesiastical offices were available only to males. Like their Puritan counterparts two centuries earlier, Mormon women found themselves at the bottom of a hierarchically ordered system. The Latter-day Saints' ecclesiastical order extended from the First Presidency, with the responsibility of governing the entire Church; through stake presidents and bishops, with governmental responsibility for specific geographic regions; to the individual father, whose priesthood responsibility was righteous government of his family. Women assumed the responsibility for governing children and for heading households in the absence of their husbands, a frequent occurrence in Mormon society. This divinely designated order did not necessarily imply that females were intellectually or spiritually inferior to males.[16] Brigham Young himself acknowledged "that many women are smarter than their husbands," though it was "not the privilege of a woman to dictate [to] her husband."[17]

The number of Young's sermons pointing to the gifts and responsibilities of men and women would seem to indicate that, for him, this governmental system did not necessarily detract from the individual worth and agency of women. Nevertheless, critics who accused Young of placing women in a secondary or inferior position, particularly within the marital relationship, were not without some justification. "The man is the head of the woman," Young declared, tying into a Christian tradition that dates back to Paul.[18] "Let our wives be the weaker vessels," he said, "and the men be men, and show the women by their superior ability that God gives husbands wisdom and ability to lead their wives into his presence."[19] According to Young, the father was to be "the head of the family, the master of his own household," and the wives and children were to "say amen to what he says, and be subject to his dictates, instead of their dictating the man, instead of their trying to govern him."[20]

Woman was under the obligation to follow her husband because of the order set forth by the first parents, Adam and Eve, in the Garden of Eden. "There is a curse upon the woman that is not upon the man," said Young, "namely, that 'her whole affections shall be towards her husband,' and what is the next? 'He shall rule over you.'"[21] This explanation for woman's secondary position within marriage was not only popularly held during the nineteenth century but also strongly attacked at woman's rights conventions. Indeed, Elizabeth Cady Stanton published *The Woman's Bible* in 1895, attempting to analyze and reinterpret this and other passages from the Old Testament that seemed degrading to women.[22]

Certainly President Young's statements regarding the dominant role of the husband were not radical for the time. Ironically, in 1866 one of his female critics tried to describe the ideal position of woman in contrast with what was prescribed by Young:

> The position of woman, and her duties in life, are well-defined in the New Testament Scriptures. If married, she is to direct her household affairs, raise up children, be subject unto her husband, and use all due benevolence toward him; but his duties are equally well defined.[23]

The lack of contrast is what is striking, especially since Brigham Young did take time to define the responsibilities of the Latter-day Saint husband. For example, while he taught that a man should place himself at the head of his family as the master of his household, he also counseled each man to treat his family "as an angel would treat them." "A man is not made to be worshiped by his family," said Young. A man was to be good and upright so he could earn the respect of his family. They were not obligated to follow him in unrighteousness.[24]

Like many of his contemporaries, Young was sensitive to woman's dependence on man. He remarked on several occasions that such dependence was not only hard on women but sometimes harmful. "I do not know what the Lord could have put upon women worse than he did upon Mother Eve, where he told her: 'Thy desire shall be to thy husband,'" said Young, noting that he "would be glad if it were otherwise."[25] He saw that the female sex had long been deceived and "trodden under foot of man" and that "it is in their nature to confide in and look to the sterner sex for guidance, and thus they are more likely to be led astray and ruined."[26] And he preached that the curse "never will be taken from the human family until the mission is fulfilled, and our Master and our Lord is perfectly satisfied with our work." One implication of this was that woman's essential, "uncursed" nature was not marked by dependence upon man.[27]

Whether the notion of the curse upon woman was vitally Mormon or simply reflected the traditions of the larger culture in which Brigham Young lived, it explained the timid and abused women he encountered, and it provided a biblical precedent for placing the man at the head of the family. This biblical precedent complemented the Latter-day Saint concept of priesthood government with males as officeholders.

Thus the patriarchal family became part of a larger family-community with Brigham Young—"the controller and master of affairs here, under Heaven's direction"—at its head. Male and female submitted to a graded and ranked system, a "beautiful order," where all worked "for the good of the whole more than for individual aggrandizement."[28] This was different from the larger nineteenth-century American society, where submissiveness was prescribed behavior for women but generally not for men.[29]

Though Brigham Young saw woman's dependence upon man as a possible problem, he could not conceive a solution outside of adherence to the order of the kingdom. Total independence was no more an option for women than it was for men who chose to be part of the system. So while Young allowed that women should develop their talents, seek their own inspiration from the Holy Spirit, and make their own choices, according to Young a "woman of faith and knowledge" would say, "It is a law that man shall rule over me; his word is my law, and I must obey him; he must rule over me; this is upon me and I will submit to it." Young emphasized that by *rule* he did "not mean with an iron hand, but merely to take the lead," "in kindness and with pleasant words."[30]

But Young's message was interpreted variously. Some inferred from his statements that the patriarchal order of God's community, particularly within the family, was not arbitrary (that is, as God had decreed it, without offering any explanations). Martha Spence Heywood, plural wife and schoolteacher in Nephi, Utah, confided to her diary her reaction after hearing Brigham Young discuss the matter:

> Before he spoke, supposing that he would, I prayed my Heavenly Father that I might get instruction that would suit my particular circumstances and I felt that I did and had the very thing pointed out that I needed . . . especially the principle that a woman be she ever so smart, she cannot know more than her husband if he magnifies his Priesthood. That God never in any, any age of the world endowed woman with knowledge above the man.[31]

Young may not have taught intellectual or spiritual inferiority, but some of his followers heard it. Wrote Fanny Stenhouse, a woman whose twenty years as a Mormon culminated in apostasy, "I thought that I might perhaps derive some consolation from the sermons in the Tabernacle—something that might shed a softer light upon my rugged pathway. But instead of obtaining consolation, I heard that which aroused every feeling of my soul to rebellion."[32]

If some female members of Young's community were troubled by what he had to say, it is not surprising that non-Mormons were appalled as they filtered his words through their own perceptions of Mormon polygamy, turning the household-heading husband into a tyrant and the submissive wife into a subjugated woman. The fact that as many as twenty percent of Young's listeners were living in polygamy did affect what he had to say to them. According to Mormon doctrine, woman could not be exalted without man. Neither could a man be exalted without a woman. All were exhorted to marry, and Mormons prided themselves upon their marriage system, which allowed "every virtuous woman" to have a "husband to whom she can look for guidance and protection."[33]

But plural marriage posed peculiar problems, and Young particularly was aware of them. "Where is the man who has wives, and all of them think he is doing just right to them?" Young asked. "I do not know such a man," he continued; "I know it is not your humble servant." He said he found "the whole subject of marriage relation . . . a hard matter to reach."[34]

Though he was committed to a pure union between husband and wife without any "alienation of affection," Young knew from experience that a polygamous husband could not meet all of a wife's needs for companionship. "I feel more lonely and more unreconciled to my lot than ever," one of Brigham's wives wrote him in 1853, "and as I am not essential to your comfort or your convenience I desire you will give me to some other good man who has less cares." This wife did not divorce or leave Young—though under the system of plural marriage, divorce was liberally extended as an option for dissatisfied women. Four of Brigham's wives did eventually leave or divorce him.[35]

Perhaps because even within his own family he could see no way of meeting expectations for intimacy, he advised women not to worry about it but to turn their attention elsewhere, especially toward their children. "Are you tormenting yourselves by thinking that your husbands do not love you?" Young once asked. "I would not care whether they loved a particle or not; but I would cry out, like one of old, in the joy of my heart, 'I have got a man from the Lord!'"[36]

Young's emphasis on woman's childbearing/child-rearing role received as much criticism as anything he taught, and yet in no other area were Young's teachings so nearly identical with the ideals of the larger society. "The mothers are the machinery that give zest to the whole man, and guide the destinies and lives of men upon the earth," proclaimed Young in 1877.[37] "She controls the destiny of every community," one Henry C. Wright had written in 1870 in *The Empire of the Mother over the Character and Destiny of the Race.* While *Godey's Lady's Book* described mothers as "those builders of the human temple who lay the foundation for an eternity of glory or of shame," Young counseled that "it is the mother's influence that is most effective in moulding the mind of the child for good or for evil."[38]

Young's admonitions to pregnant women and nursing mothers to be faithful and prayerful so that their infants might enjoy a happy influence could have appeared in any number of contemporary women's magazines and mothers' manuals. In antebellum America, motherhood was seen as woman's "one duty and function . . . that alone for which she was created."[39] Even nineteenth-century feminists came to use the importance of motherhood as a basis for their reforms in education and civil rights.

So, within the context of his time, Young was not anti-woman's rights when he stated that the woman who rose at the Resurrection to find that her duty as a wife and mother had been sacrificed in order to pursue any other duty would find that her "whole life had been a failure."[40]

Why then did contemporary critics find Young's emphasis on woman's role as mother so disgusting? Because the closer polygamy-practicing Mormons came to laying claim to the ideals of the American family, the more threatening seemed their "distortions." For example, the raising up of children—posterity—was put forth by Mormons as one of the major purposes of polygamy.

Women had the privilege of bringing into mortality God's spirit children, Young taught, "that God may have a royal priesthood, a royal people, on the earth. That is what plurality of wives is for."[41]

Young's critics may also have been disturbed that, in a culture that so lavishly and exclusively praised women for motherhood, posterity was not the glory of woman only but of the man as well. "The more women and children a man has, the more glory," one critic summarized.[42] From time to time, Young counseled fathers to take the responsibility for training the children who would bring them honor, but he told mothers that they bore the major responsibility for raising righteous children. On the other hand, Young frequently addressed men as "fathers who shall endure, and whose posterity shall never end," while rarely speaking to women of parallel promises.[43]

To whom did the glory of posterity belong? In a study of the accommodation of religion to women, Barbara Welter suggested that the projecting of the marital relationship into eternity, with parenthood as the highest mutual goal, gave Mormon women greater status in their role here and hereafter.[44] However, for nineteenth-century onlookers, polygamy and a patriarchal order hearkening back to the Old Testament could not be reconciled with the contemporary "empire of the mother."

Finally, Young's critics felt that he emphasized childbearing and child-rearing at the expense of the marital relationship. Stenhouse said that the Saints were told that "the greater object of marriage . . . was the increase of children," and that other aspects of marriage such as "the companionship of soul; the indissoluble union of two existences—were never presented."

Certainly Young made it clear that most women would be happier if they worried less about their husbands and more about their children. While he understood that a romantic and close relationship might exist between a husband and a plural wife, he was not willing to engender such expectations in women whose husbands were regularly called away from home for Church service. He continually admonished men to humor and "happify" their wives, but Stenhouse was not far from Young himself when she affirmed that woman's aspirations for intimacy "had nothing to do with the hard, cruel facts of their life in Polygamy."[45] Ironically, perhaps, independence for women was a common by-product of the marital system that left them so often on their own to manage family, farms, and businesses.

For Brigham Young, woman's place was with the family in the home—but it was also with the larger family-community in the kingdom. Women submitted to the well-ordered kingdom, but the kingdom in turn gave them new freedom, particularly during the last decade of Brigham Young's administration.

Between 1861, when the telegraph linked Utah to the rest of the United States, and 1869, when the transcontinental railroad forged the bond with steel ties, soldier-miners came to Utah as troops of the Third California Volunteers. Their commander was Colonel Patrick Connor, who promised to "invite hither a large Gentile and loyal population, sufficient by peaceful means and through the ballot-box to overwhelm the Mormons."[46] The coming of the gentiles was inevitable, but the disintegration of the kingdom was not.

"I do not know how long it will be before we call upon the brethren and sisters to enter upon business in an entirely different way from what they have done," Young postulated at April conference in 1867. The following December he announced, "We have sisters now engaged in several of our telegraph offices, and we wish them to learn not only to act as operators but to keep the books of our offices."[47] While ten years earlier the Mormons had taken to the surrounding mountains to stave off the Utah Expedition, they would now fight on an economic front, and the draft was to be without regard for sex. "Let us . . . no longer sit with hands folded, wasting time, for it is the duty of every man and of every woman to do all that is possible to promote the kingdom of God on the earth," said Young.[48]

Through this emphasis on cooperative building of the economic kingdom, Brigham Young extended to women significant opportunities for personal and collective growth and advancement—first, through allowing them spiritual and economic influence within the Church organization, and second, through

Eliza R. Snow (1804–1887), ca. 1868–1869, second president of the Relief Society.

encouraging women's education for and involvement in a variety of trades and professions.

The Relief Society of The Church of Jesus Christ of Latter-day Saints, organized "under the priesthood after a pattern of the priesthood" by the Prophet Joseph Smith in March 1842, had functioned much as other benevolent societies of the time. The labors of the Relief Society were "deferred" by Brigham Young following the 1844 death of Joseph Smith because Emma Smith, society president, refused to follow priesthood counsel.[49] In 1854, following Mormon women's grassroots efforts to organize themselves for charity work, Brigham Young officially reinstated local Relief Societies. Their impressive contribution was cut short in 1857 by the Utah War.[50] However, by December 1867, Young had decided united sisters were a resource the kingdom could not do without, and he then announced that women and their bishops should immediately organize societies in local wards. "We have many talented women among us," he said, "and we wish their help in this matter. . . . You will find that the sisters will be the mainspring of the movement."[51]

Young's statement was prophetic. As a domestic revolution swept the United States in the years following the Civil War (including the development of gas lighting, domestic plumbing, canning, improved stoves, washtubs, and sewing machines), American women would increasingly turn their energies toward women's clubs—while Mormon women would expand their spiritual and temporal labors through the Relief Society.

Young commissioned one of his wives, Eliza R. Snow, who had served as secretary to the Nauvoo society and whose willingness to obey the priesthood was unwavering, to instruct bishops in the format of the organization and to teach the women their responsibilities. Their first responsibility was, as indicated by their name, to provide relief to the poor. Young encouraged them in this endeavor, particularly in finding for those in need "something to do that will enable them to sustain themselves."[52]

He also challenged the women to sustain the self-sufficiency of the Mormon community through retrenchment. They could help fight the economic battle by making and wearing homemade hats and clothes rather than buying goods imported from the eastern states. They were to set their own fashions, be thrifty in their households, and find ways to do their own carding, spinning, weaving, and knitting. "What is there in these respects that the members of the Female Relief Society cannot accomplish?" asked Young.[53]

Young presented this need to adapt economically as a religious obligation, counseling both men and women to cease their extravagance. He praised those women who were willing to "help build up the Kingdom of God" by wisely attending to their household affairs. "Every woman in this Church can be useful to the Church if she has a mind to be," Young concluded.[54]

Women may not have found themselves feeling useful to the kingdom by merely donning homemade hats and dresses. Many of them steered clear of Young's suggested apparel, and his reproofs were frequent, though he freely acknowledged that he could not control even his own family's taste for finery. What did give women a new sense of usefulness was their involvement in cooperative home industry, an effort that gave them, for the first time, business and financial responsibility within the Church. With money they had raised from fairs and parties, women imported knitting machinery; raised silk; set up tailoring establishments; bought, stored, and sold grain; made everything from straw hats to shoes; and bought property and built their own cooperatives where they could sell their homemade goods on commission.[55]

By 1876, Eliza R. Snow reported that 110 branches of the Relief Society had disbursed $82,397 over a seven to eight year period—73 percent of which was to relieve and support the poor.

Emmeline B. Wells (1828–1921), ca. 1879, the woman commissioned by President Young to head the Relief Society grain storage program in 1876.

Sixteen percent was for building purposes, 7 percent was to help the poor emigrate, and the remainder was for other charities and missionary work.[56] Without question, a great deal of what the women did came as a direct result of President Young's prompting and prodding.

"President Young recommends silk culture as one very profitable branch for the sisters, and offers, free of charge, all the cuttings they wish, from the Mulberry orchard on his farm," Eliza R. Snow editorialized in the Mormon *Woman's Exponent* in 1875. Sericulture became a "mission" for the Relief Society sisters, and they carried it out for nearly a decade. Utah women maintained their involvement in the silk industry until it faded from the state after the turn of the century. They took pride in the tablecloths, scarves, and dresses that came from their countless hours of labor with mulberry leaves and cocoons.[57]

"At the suggestion of President Brigham Young we would call the attention of the women of this Territory to the subject of saving grain," wrote Emmeline B. Wells, the woman commissioned by Young to head up the grain storage program in 1876.[58] The program was Emmeline's project, not Brigham's, and over a period of forty-two years it resulted in the storage of several hundred thousand bushels of grain in Relief Society granaries scattered throughout the Church. The grain was sent to earthquake and famine victims in San Francisco and China, and the remaining two hundred thousand bushels were sold to the U. S. government at the close of World War I. For fifty years beyond that time, the Relief Society operated partly on interest from the sale of wheat.[59]

One final example of Young's prodding is the Relief Society

cooperative established in Salt Lake City to serve all the women of the territory. In 1876, when Relief Society women had just completed a summer-long display of their homemade goods in commemoration of the nation's centennial, Brigham Young addressed them:

> It would be very gratifying to us if you could form an association to start business in the capacity of disposing of Home-made Articles such as are manufactured among ourselves. . . . If you can not be satisfied with the selection of Sisters from among yourselves to take charge, we will render you assistance by furnishing a competent man for the transaction of the financial matters of this Establishment.[60]

The Relief Society Mercantile Association opened the Woman's Commission Store within a month and operated it by themselves, without the assistance of "a competent man."

That the women took these stewardships seriously as their own is shown in the spunk they manifested in doing business with Young himself. Fifteenth Ward Relief Society president Sarah M. Kimball read Young's suggestion for the storing of grain by women and immediately contacted him to head her ward's subscription list for funds. "The more I weigh it the more my faith increases in our [the women's] power to accomplish in this direction with your [the men's] assistance."[61] She often preached that brethren and sisters should sustain and support one another in their callings.

Eliza R. Snow, who took it upon herself to manage the Woman's Commission Store, wrote to Young to explain to him that he could not dictate the terms of commission on the goods from his woolen mill. "Although we are novices in the mercantile business, we are not green enough for that kind of management."[62]

Young knew that Mormon women were inexperienced in public affairs; they needed the guidance of assigned tasks, he felt, especially in these early years of their involvement outside the home. But he did not present them with detailed programs—and though he expected them to account for their stewardships, he did not oversee their work. The growth of the women as individuals was a critical part of building the kingdom of God.

"The females are capable of doing immense good if they will," he said, "but if you sit down and say 'husband, or father, do it for me' or 'brother, do it for me, for I am not going to do it' when life is through you will weep and wail, for you will be judged according to your works, and having done nothing you will receive nothing."[63] Statements such as "We wish to develop the powers of the ladies to the fullest extent, and to control them for the building of the Kingdom of God" and "If we can succeed in guiding their [the ladies'] ideas correctly it will be an advantage to the whole community" underscore the fact that Young's primary motive was ever the growth of the kingdom; they also reveal his faith that only as Saints built God's kingdom could God build Saints.[64]

"If I had my way I would have every man and woman employed in doing something to support themselves," Brigham Young told a group of St. George Saints. At approximately the time he began the reorganization of the Relief Society in 1867, Brigham Young began emphasizing vocational and professional education for women. In reference to business classes opening at the University of Deseret, Young announced in December 1867 that he hoped young and middle-aged students, male and female, could learn the art of bookkeeping and acquire a good mercantile education.[65] Young's general epistle to Church members for January-February 1868 applauded the admission of women to the school:

> In addition to a knowledge of the elementary branches of education and a thorough understanding of housewifery, we wish the sisters, so far as their inclinations and circumstances may permit, to learn bookkeeping, telegraphy, reporting, typesetting, clerking in stores and banks, and every branch of knowledge and kind of employment suited to their sex and according to their several tastes and capacities. . . . Thus trained, all without distinction of sex, will have an open field, without jostling and oppression, for acquiring all the knowledge and doing all the good their physical and mental capacities and surrounding circumstances will permit.[66]

For Young, a division of community labor among men and

Deseret Hospital Association Board of Directors, ca. 1882. Front row, left to right: Phoebe Woodruff, M. Isabella Horne, Eliza R. Snow, Zina D. H. Young, Marinda N. Hyde. Back row, left to right: Romania B. Pratt Penrose, M.D.; Bathsheba W. Smith; Elizabeth Howard; Jane S. Richards; Emmeline B. Wells.

women would enable the community to function more efficiently. He saw women particularly better suited than men to some trades. He had "seen women in the harvest field, ploughing, raking, and making hay." This he found unbecoming: "This hard laborious work belongs to men," he said. But he was sure that a woman could pick up type and make a book. "I know that many arguments are used against this," Young admitted, "and we are told that a woman cannot make a coat, vest or pair of pantaloons. I dispute this. . . . Tell me they can not pull a thread tight enough, and that they can not press hard enough to press a coat, it is all folly and nonsense." Young liked to see women involved in telegraphy and clerking because he could not abide "great big, fat lazy men" doing such light work. Besides, he observed, "a woman can write as well as a man, and spell as well as a man, and better."[67]

"Keep the ladies in their proper places," said Young, which he described as "selling tape and calico, setting type, working the

Romania Bunnell Pratt Penrose (1839–1932), n.d., graduated from the Woman's Medical College at Philadelphia, Pennsylvania. She became a resident surgeon of the Deseret Hospital.

telegraph, keeping books, &c."[68] In addition, Young actively encouraged the movement of women into some professional fields, especially medicine. In 1873, Bathsheba Smith reported that "the President had suggested to her that three women from each ward be chosen to form a class for studying physiology and obstetrics."[69] A few weeks later, Eliza R. Snow declared that "President Young is requiring the sisters to get students of Medicine. He wants a good many to get classical education, and then get a degree for Medicine. . . . If they cannot meet their own expenses, we have means for doing so."[70] For several years, Young had been teaching that women should attend to the health of their sex. With the influx of educated gentile doctors following the Civil War and the coming railroad, Young realized the Latter-day Saints would need professional doctors in order to remain self-sustaining.

Romania Bunnell Pratt, the first Mormon woman to get professional training under this program, returned to Utah from the Woman's Medical College in New York after her freshman year there. Her finances were depleted, and so she paid a visit to President Young. He instructed Eliza R. Snow to "see to it that the Relief Societies furnish Sister Pratt with the necessary money to complete her studies." This encouragement came in spite of the fact that Romania had to leave her young children with her own mother in order to complete the training. "We need her here," said Young, "and her talents will be of great use to this people."[71]

After graduating from the Woman's Medical College at Philadelphia, Dr. Pratt returned to Utah in 1877 and announced her intention to practice as well as teach courses in anatomy, physiology, and obstetrics. She later served as resident surgeon of the Deseret Hospital, a hospital founded by the Relief Society as a result of her commitment to the obstetrical care of women and the training of nurses and midwives.

Young also encouraged the movement of women into journalism. When Louisa Lula Greene approached him about commencing a newspaper for Mormon women, he gave her the requisite sanction, and the *Woman's Exponent,* a semimonthly tabloid, was born. Over a forty-two year period, the paper was an outlet for the journalistic and literary endeavors of Mormon women.[72]

Young showed an interest in involving women in higher education, appointing Martha Jane Knowlton Coray to a three-member board of directors for Brigham Young Academy when the school opened under his direction in 1875. Two years later, he named Ida Ione Cook as one of three trustees for the proposed Brigham Young College in Logan, Utah. Cook had just lost the position of Cache County Superintendent of Schools because territorial laws did not allow women to hold public office.[73]

Ever concerned with order, Young never stopped prescribing a sphere of activity for women. But over a period of years, the sphere he prescribed became wider and wider. During the last decade of his life, Young taught that home and family were not the only means whereby a woman could make a contribution to the kingdom. "We believe that women are useful, not only to sweep houses, wash dishes, make beds, and raise babies," he said,

> but that they should stand behind the counter, study law or physic, or become good bookkeepers and be able to do the business in any counting house, and all this to enlarge their sphere of usefulness for the benefit of society at large.[74]

The status of Mormon women decidedly improved during the administration of President Brigham Young. His reorganization of the Relief Society launched women into an era of public activity that involved them in business and gave them new economic status in a community that was itself concerned with economic identity. Within Mormonism's social order, where women had previously held no offices, they gained position and visibility as leaders in organizations for women and children. Though women were clearly not ordained to priesthood offices, they assumed a new place within Church government and exercised significant authority with regard to their sisters through disbursement of funds and counsel at general, stake, and ward levels.

It was during this same period that Utah women were granted the elective franchise, though the extent to which Young may have influenced the territorial legislature in passage of the February 1870 act is not clear. He never publicly acknowledged that with passage of the act women were receiving rights long since due to them.[75]

While some Mormon women celebrated Young's advocacy of women's rights, he did not, like Henry Ward Beecher, affiliate himself with the national campaign for women's rights. Most of its ideals were not in conflict with Mormonism, and Young did not discourage the involvement of prominent Relief Society women in the nineteenth-century movement for woman's advancement. Certainly he felt free to borrow ideas and rhetoric from the movement: women were capable of doing many things tradition had made the work of men; it was time to awaken women to their possibilities.

With Young's endorsement and prodding, Mormon women joined their American sisters in attending universities, providing medical care for women, running telegraph offices, and staffing a money-making organization that contributed to their church's needs. Yet while Mormon women, and sometimes their national contemporaries, celebrated these advances as victories for women, Brigham Young never did.

Young was, for his people, a prophet and seer, whose ever-present vision and motivation was the kingdom of God, a holy family-community in which individuals did not advance independently of one another. He proclaimed that the priesthood order had been restored to Latter-day Saints. This order prescribed a system of interdependence through which members, working for the common good, individually sacrificed and would ultimately be individually benefited. The system Young administered furnished women both constraints and opportunities, but, given the clarity of his larger vision, he felt no need to explicitly resolve apparent incongruities or ambiguities in his messages to women.

It would seem that Young's strong emphasis on male dominance within the family unit did not dramatically forward the advancement of Mormon women. It reiterated the importance of the traditional order within the nontraditional plural marriage system; while it provided some women with security, it offended and confused others.

Had order been Young's only concern, Mormon women would have been stifled. But Young clearly articulated the divine attributes and potential of women and men. Further, his predilection for ordering the family-community was offset, if not overshadowed, by his commitment to put the community to work to build Zion. He used available human resources by distributing responsibilities at every level of the governmental system.

Through the 1850s and '60s, Young called upon women to assume responsibility at the family level to use their personal resources in maintaining households and nurturing Zion's rising generation. But in the years following the Civil War, the Mormon family-community demanded additional resources to stave off the growing economic, social, and political influence of non-Mormons. Without deemphasizing the importance of motherhood, Young was quick to shift available female resources to organizational levels other than the family. Relief Societies were formed in every ward, and various programs for them, including home industry and commission-cooperatives, grain storage, and obstetrical training, were administered by women working at a general level.

In proportion to Young's increased use of women as vital resources, the kingdom grew and the women grew. Inherent in Mormonism's hierarchically ordered system of interdependence were paradoxical possibilities for women. Brigham Young and his sisters maximized such possibilities and left a remarkable legacy of awakening and achievement.

NOTES

An earlier version of this article was originally published as "Woman's Place in Brigham Young's World," *BYU Studies* 18 (Spring 1978): 377–95).

1. Mrs. T. B. H. [Fanny] Stenhouse, *Tell It All: The Story of Life's Experience in Mormonism* (Cincinnati: Queen City Publishing, 1874), 273.
2. Horace Greeley, "Two Hours with Brigham Young," *Daily Tribune* (New York), 20 August 1859, as quoted in William Mulder and A. Russell Mortensen, eds., *Among the Mormons: Historical Accounts by Contemporary Observers* (New York: Alfred A. Knopf, 1967), 327.
3. Mrs. C. V. Waite, *The Mormon Prophet and His Harem; or an Authentic History of Brigham Young and His Numerous Wives and Children* (Cambridge, Massachusetts: Riverside Press, 1866), 217–18.
4. M. R. Werner, *Brigham Young* (London: Jonathan Cape, Ltd., 1925); Stanley P. Hirshon, *The Lion of the Lord: A Biography of Brigham Young* (New York: Alfred A. Knopf, 1969).
5. Leonard J. Arrington pioneered the field with "The Economic Role of Pioneer Mormon Women," *Western Humanities Review* 9 (Spring 1955): 145–64. Two important bibliographies that survey the multitude of works that followed, particularly after 1970, are Carol Cornwall Madsen and David J. Whittaker, "History's Sequel: A Source Essay on Women in Mormon History," *Journal of Mormon History* 6 (1979): 123–45 and Patricia Lyn Scott and Maureen Ursenbach Beecher, comps., "Mormon Women: A Bibliography in Process, 1977–1985," *Journal of Mormon History* 12 (1985): 113–27. An insightful overview of the development of Mormon women's studies is Carol Cornwall Madsen, "'Feme Covert': Journey of a Metaphor," *Journal of Mormon History* 17 (1991): 43–61.
6. Louisa G. Richards, "Work for Women," *Woman's Exponent* 1, 15 April 1873, 172.
7. *Journal of Discourses,* 8: 93 (8 August 1852).
8. Brigham Young taught that men could become gods and women "Eves," or "queens of heaven." See Brigham Young, "A Few Words of Doctrine," 8 October 1861, Brigham Young Papers, Library-Archives, Historical Department of The Church of Jesus Christ of Latter-day Saints (hereafter cited as LDS Church Historical Archives); see also *Journal of Discourses,* 3: 365. The clearest statement of the Mother in Heaven concept—Eliza R. Snow's hymn "O My Father," or, as she titled it, "The Eternal Father and Mother"—was said to be Young's favorite hymn. See "Deseret Theological Institute," *Deseret News,* 27 June 1855, and Heber J. Grant, "Favorite Hymns," *Improvement Era* 17 (June 1914): 777.
9. *Journal of Discourses,* 3: 364 (22 June 1856); and 13: 155 (14 November 1869).
10. *Journal of Discourses,* 7: 160 (29 May 1859); and 1: 312 (20 February 1853).
11. *Journal of Discourses,* 13: 61 (18 July 1869).
12. Susa Young Gates and Leah D. Widtsoe, *The Life Story of Brigham Young* (New

York: Macmillan, 1930), 293, 296; see also *Journal of Discourses,* 9: 330 (3 August 1862).

13. *Journal of Discourses,* 10: 320 (31 July 1864); and 9: 330 (3 August 1862).
14. *Journal of Discourses,* 13: 281 (30 October 1870). Indeed, according to Young, the priesthood is also "the law of heaven that governs and controls the Gods and the angels." Ibid.
15. *Journal of Discourses* 11: 249 (17 June 1866); and 17: 119 (28 June 1874). See Boyd K. Packer, *The Holy Temple* (Salt Lake City: Bookcraft, 1980), 153–54; also Carol Cornwall Madsen, "Mormon Women and the Temple," in *Sisters in Spirit: Mormon Women in Historical and Cultural Perspective,* ed. Maureen Ursenbach Beecher and Lavina Fielding Anderson (Urbana and Chicago: University of Illinois Press, 1987), 80–110.
16. Feminist scholar Mary Ryan observed of the American Puritan community: "No individual of either sex, could presume to be one among equals in the seventeenth-century community. . . . Within the church, all parishioners were subservient to the minister and found their destined places somewhere within the hierarchy of elders, deacons, and the general congregation. . . . Within the household, the ranks descended from the patriarchal father to his wife, the mistress of the household, and on to children and then to servants and any other non-kinsmen who resided in the home. . . . Within this hierarchical *Weltanschauung* of the seventeenth century, inequality was not the peculiar stigma of womanhood, but rather a social expectation of both sexes." Mary Ryan, *Womanhood in America from Colonial Times to the Present* (New York: New Viewpoints, Franklin Watts, 1975), 40–41.
17. *Journal of Discourses,* 9: 39 (7 April 1861); and 17: 159 (9 August 1874).
18. *Journal of Discourses,* 11: 271 (19 August 1866). See Ephesians 5: 23.
19. *Journal of Discourses,* 9: 308 (15 June 1862). See also 1 Peter 3: 7.
20. *Journal of Discourses,* 4: 55 (21 September 1856).
21. *Journal of Discourses,* 4: 57 (21 September 1856).
22. See Eleanor Flexner, *Century of Struggle: The Woman's Rights Movement in the United States* (New York: Atheneum, 1973), 47, 220, and Donna A. Behnke, *Religious Issues in Ninteenth Century Feminism* (Troy, N. Y.: Whiston Publishing Company, 1982).
23. Waite, 223. This was in accordance with a whole set of behavioral norms for nineteenth-century women. See Barbara Welter, "The Cult of True Womanhood: 1820–1860," *American Quarterly* 18 (Summer 1966): 151–74.
24. *Journal of Discourses,* 4: 55 (21 September 1856); and 14: 106 (8 August 1869).
25. *Journal of Discourses,* 16: 167 (31 August 1873).
26. *Journal of Discourses,* 11: 271 (19 August 1866); and 12: 194 (6 April 1869).
27. *Journal of Discourses,* 15: 132 (18 August 1872). Earlier he said, "There is one thing she [woman] cannot [do] away with, at least not so far as I am concerned, and that is, 'and he shall rule over thee.'" *Journal of Discourses,* 9: 195 (9 February 1862). Eliza R. Snow and other Mormon women, seemingly

without objection from Young, taught that men and women were equal before the Fall and that ultimately full union and equality between men and women would be restored. See Jill C. Mulvay [Derr], "Eliza R. Snow and the Woman Question," *BYU Studies* 16 (Winter 1976): 261, 264. Latter-day Saint leaders, male and female, became increasingly silent on the matter of the curse toward the turn of the century.

28. *Journal of Discourses,* 1: 48 (9 April 1852); and 12: 153 (12 January 1868).
29. Piety, purity, submission, and domesticity were valued in women but not in men. See Welter, "The Cult of True Womanhood." In Mormonism, as in Puritanism, the first three were common values for men and women, though Young was prone to teach that women were of a more refined nature than men, a little purer and more pious. *Journal of Discourses,* 12: 194 (6 April 1868); 14: 120 (21 May 1871); and 18: 233 (15 August 1876).
30. *Journal of Discourses,* 16: 167 (31 August 1873); 9: 195 (9 February 1862); and 9: 39 (7 April 1861).
31. Martha Spence Heywood Journal, 27 April 1858, photocopy of typescript, LDS Church Historical Archives.
32. Stenhouse, 343.
33. *Journal of Discourses,* 11: 268 (19 August 1866).
34. *Journal of Discourses,* 17: 159–60 (9 August 1874); and 2: 90 (6 October 1854).
35. Emily D. Young to Brigham Young, 24 February 1853, Brigham Young Family Correspondence, LDS Church Historical Archives. Jeffrey O. Johnson's "The Wives of Brigham Young," photocopy of typescript, LDS Church Historical Archives, is an informative listing including wives' birth and death dates, date of marriage to Brigham Young, number of children born to each marriage, and wives' other husbands and children. Johnson, who based his listing on sealing records, includes fifty-five women as wives, though only about sixteen of these were connubial wives. On divorce, see Lawrence Foster, "A Little-Known Defense of Polygamy from the Mormon Press in 1842," *Dialogue: A Journal of Mormon Thought* 9 (Winter 1974): 30. Foster compares early ideas about divorce within the plural marriage system with some of Young's later statements on the matter. See also Carol Cornwall Madsen, "'At Their Peril': Utah Law and the Case of Plural Wives, 1859–1900," *Western Historical Quarterly* 21 (November 1990): 425–43. It should be noted that Brigham Young told women never to seal themselves to a man they did not want to be sealed to. *Journal of Discourses,* 6: 307 (8 April 1853).
36. *Journal of Discourses,* 9: 37 (7 April 1861).
37. *Journal of Discourses,* 19: 72 (19 July 1877).
38. Henry C. Wright and *Godey's Lady's Book* as quoted in Ryan, 147 and 165. *Journal of Discourses,* 18: 263 (8 October 1876).
39. Ryan, 164.
40. Susa Young Gates, "Editor's Department," *Young Woman's Journal* 5 (June 1894): 449.

41. *Journal of Discourses,* 9: 37 (7 April 1861).
42. Waite, 218.
43. *Journal of Discourses,* 1: 67–68 (8 April 1852); and 4: 198 (1 February 1857); see also 8: 63 (20 May 1860) and 10: 355 (6 November 1864).
44. Barbara Welter, "The Feminization of American Religion," ed. Mary S. Hartman and Lois W. Banner, *Clio's Consciousness Raised: New Perspectives on the History of Women* (New York: Harper and Row, 1974), 149–50.
45. Stenhouse, 343–44. Lawrence Foster, in *Religion and Sexuality: The Shakers, the Mormons and the Oneida Community* (New York/Oxford: Oxford University Press, 1981), confirms that "by partially breaking down exclusive bonds between husband and wife and by undercutting intense emotional involvement in family affairs in favor of Church business, polygamy may well have contributed significantly both to the success of the long-range centralized plans set in motion at this time and to the rapid and efficient establishment of religious and communal order."
46. Connor to R. C. Drum, Assistant Adjutant General, U.S. Army, 21 July 1864, as cited in Leonard J. Arrington, *Great Basin Kingdom* (Cambridge, Massachusetts: Harvard University Press, 1958), 473.
47. *Journal of Discourses,* 12: 32 (8 April 1867); 12: 116 (8 December 1867).
48. *Journal of Discourses,* 18: 77 (31 August 1875).
49. This was presumably due to the confusion of the time but also undoubtedly because Joseph Smith's wife Emma, who presided over the society and wielded tremendous influence over the women, did not follow Young to the West and had already used her position to further her antipolygamy sentiments. See John Taylor address to women's conference, 17 July 1880, *Woman's Exponent* 9, 1 September 1880, 55. The organization, disbanding, and reorganization of the Relief Society, as well as its operation during Brigham Young's presidency, are discussed in Jill Mulvay Derr, Janath Russell Cannon and Maureen Ursenbach Beecher, *Women of Covenant: The Story of Relief Society* (Salt Lake City: Deseret Book, 1992), chapters 1–3.
50. An excellent study of early Relief Societies is Richard L. Jensen, "Forgotten Relief Societies, 1844–67," *Dialogue: A Journal of Mormon Thought* 16 (Spring 1983): 105–25.
51. *Journal of Discourses,* 12: 115 (8 December 1867).
52. *Journal of Discourses,* 14: 107 (8 August 1869).
53. *Journal of Discourses,* 14: 104 (8 August 1869).
54. *Journal of Discourses,* 11: 352 (6 April 1867).
55. See Arrington, "The Economic Role of Pioneer Mormon Women."
56. Eliza R. Snow, "The Relief Society," 1876, holograph, Special Collections, Western Americana, Marriott Library, University of Utah, Salt Lake City, Utah.
57. Eliza R. Snow, "To Every Branch of the Relief Society in Zion," *Woman's Exponent* 3, 1 April 1875, 164. See Chris Rigby Arrington, "Mormon Women

and the Silk Industry in Early Utah," *Utah Historical Quarterly* 46 (Fall 1978): 376–96.

58. Emmeline B. Wells, "Sisters Be in Earnest," *Woman's Exponent* 5, 15 October 1876, 76.
59. The most complete study to date is Jessie L. Embry, "Relief Society Grain Storage Program, 1876–1940," master's thesis, Brigham Young University, 1974.
60. Brigham Young to the President and Members of the Relief Societies . . . , 4 October 1876, Brigham Young Letterbooks, volume 14, LDS Church Historical Archives.
61. S. M. Kimball to President Young, 26 October 1876, holograph, Brigham Young Correspondence, LDS Church Historical Archives.
62. Eliza R. Snow to Prest. B. Young, 10 February 1877, holograph, Brigham Young Correspondence, LDS Church Historical Archives.
63. Brigham Young sermon, 5 August 1869, in *Deseret News Weekly*, 11 August 1869.
64. Ibid.
65. Brigham Young Unpublished Sermons, ca. 1876–1877, St. George, manuscript, LDS Church Historical Archives; see *Journal of Discourses*, 12: 116 (8 December 1867).
66. General Epistle, January–February 1868, manuscript, 26, Brigham Young Circular Letters, LDS Church Historical Archives.
67. *Journal of Discourses*, 16: 16, 21 (7 April 1873).
68. Ibid., 21.
69. *Woman's Exponent* 2, 1 August 1873, 35.
70. "An Address by Miss Eliza R. Snow . . . , August 14, 1873," *Woman's Exponent* 2, 15 September 1873, 63.
71. "A Biographical Sketch of R. B. Pratt," *Young Woman's Journal* 2 (September 1891): 534.
72. See Sherilyn Cox Bennion, "The Woman's Exponent: Forty-Two Years of Speaking for Women," *Utah Historical Quarterly* 44 (Summer 1976): 222–39.
73. Jill C. Mulvay [Derr], "The Two Miss Cooks: Pioneer Professionals for Utah Schools," *Utah Historical Quarterly* 43 (Fall 1974): 396–409.
74. *Journal of Discourses*, 13: 61 (18 July 1869).
75. Beverly Beeton, in *Women Vote in the West: The Woman Suffrage Movement, 1869–1896* (New York: Garland Publishing, 1896), suggests that the motivation behind the granting of suffrage to Utah women was a pragmatic political consideration rather than a commitment to woman's inherent rights. Lola Van Wagenen, on the other hand, examines Mormon women's commitment to claiming their own political rights in "In Their Own Behalf: The Politicization of Mormon Women and the 1870 Franchise," *Dialogue* 24 (Winter 1991): 31–43.

CHAPTER 15

Brigham Young and Priesthood Work at the General and Local Levels

William G. Hartley
Associate Research Professor
Joseph Fielding Smith Institute
Brigham Young University

Like an admiral commanding a fleet of ships sailing on heavy seas, Brigham Young, during his years as President of the Church, stood at the helm and directed the various offices and officers in the priesthood for the general good of the kingdom of God on earth. And yet, oddly, although biographies of Brigham Young devote much attention to the move west—the gathering, colonization, missionary outreach, Indian relations, economics, politics, and theology—they rarely assess him carefully as a leader of the priesthood or explore in detail how stakes, wards, and quorums—the Church's fundamental organizational units—operated during his administration.[1]

For President Young, the holy priesthood was "a perfect system of laws and government," one that "rules and reigns in eternity."[2] With total certitude he believed that "we have the only true authority, upon the face of the whole earth, to administer in the ordinances of the Gospel."[3]

"The Holy Priesthood is not on the earth, unless the Latter-day Saints have it,"[4] he proclaimed. "There is no act of a Latter-day Saint—no duty required—no time given, exclusive and independent of the Priesthood," he explained in 1858; "Everything is subject to it, whether preaching, business, or any other act pertaining to the proper conduct of this life."[5]

"No man can lawfully officiate in any office in the Kingdom of God," President Young believed, "[that] he has not been called to, and the authority of which has not been bestowed upon him."[6]

"Have we reason to rejoice?" he asked in 1857, and then he answered his own question:

> We have. There is no other people on this earth under such deep obligation to their Creator, as are the Latter-day Saints. The Gospel has brought to us the holy Priesthood, which is again restored to the children of men. The keys of that Priesthood are here; we have them in our possession; we can unlock, and we can shut up. We can obtain salvation, and we can administer it. We have the power within our own hands, and this has been my deep mortification, one that I have frequently spoken of, to think that a people, having in their possession all the principles, keys, and powers of eternal life, should neglect so great a salvation. We have these blessings, they are with us.[7]

Wanting Church members to be able to receive all the priesthood blessings to which they were entitled, he labored constantly to help priesthood bearers at all levels understand and then carry out their duties. At times he redeployed priesthood assignments to best utilize the quorums and officers while advancing the entire fleet through changing and unpredictable currents, winds, and weather.

To be assessed in proper context, Brigham Young's handling of priesthood operations needs to be compared both with prevailing Church practices at the time he succeeded Joseph Smith and with current priesthood functions. President Young presided over the Church for thirty-three years, more than twice as long as Joseph Smith (fourteen years). He presided over a church whose membership grew to more than five times that of Joseph Smith's time, more than 104,000 compared to about 20,000. The Church had a dozen bishops and wards in Nauvoo, but at Brigham's death it had 241—a twenty-fold increase. Joseph's ordained followers numbered perhaps 4,000 maximum, but a priesthood census taken among stakes within a year of Brigham's death found 22,000. During the same period, the number of seventies quorums increased from three to about seventy-five. Joseph Smith died before all ordinances for the dead could be implemented, particularly the sealing of deceased couples together—something Brigham Young later authorized. Joseph never presided over a church filled with believing adults who had received temple endowments; Brigham Young did. During President Young's watch, explosive growth in Church membership produced situations demanding expansion and adaptation by priesthood quorums and governing units.

As we might expect when comparing Brigham Young's Church of 125 years ago with today's Church, a number of priesthood practices implemented then are different than in our day. During the early 1870s, for example, middle-aged LDS stalwart John H. Picknell, an ordained seventy, was a counselor in the Salt Lake Stake deacons quorum presidency. "I've Seventies', Priests', Teachers' & Deacons' meetings to attend, Teacher in two wards, a Priest in one," he once itemized; "I'm out almost every night in the month." At another stake deacons quorum meeting, acting deacon Matthias Cowley explained that "I was an Elder before I was a deacon" and added that "if we were all to stay away because we are Elders or Seventies, where would the Teachers and deacons' quorums be? Why! Here your [deacons] president is a high priest, & his counsellors, Seventies."[8]

While Brigham Young was President, half of the Apostles served at times concurrently as stake presidents. For many years, the seventies quorums, not subject to stake presidents but administered by the First Council of the Seventy, were more numerous than elders quorums. At times, the Salt Lake Stake was the "center stake of Zion," exercising authority over other Utah stakes. Both a ward bishop and a ward president presided in several settlements, a double leadership structure Brigham Young favored. Other priorities sometimes meant that ward bishops served for years without being ordained, and a few bishops had counselors who were not high priests. Although most young men were not ordained to the Aaronic Priesthood, youths as young as fourteen were encouraged to receive their temple endowments, thus receiving the Melchizedek Priesthood without prior ordination to the Aaronic Priesthood.

It is not surprising that priesthood operations in the past differ from those of today, when the dynamic and adaptive sweep of LDS priesthood history from 1829 to the present is examined.

Since the 1830s, change has touched most priesthood offices and quorums. For example, at times the First Presidency has included more than two counselors; members of the First and Second Quorums of the Seventy are now General Authorities; the two Quorums of the Seventy have shouldered some of the responsibilities once carried by the Quorum of the Twelve Apostles; Assistants to the Twelve once served a vital function and then were phased out; the Presiding Bishopric no longer is responsible for Aaronic Priesthood operations; the Presiding Patriarch's authority over stake patriarchs has been redefined; administrative positions between the general and the stake levels, such as area presidents and area authorities, have been created; the position of regional representative was created and later phased out; terms of service for bishops and stake presidents have shortened over time; stake high councils receive a myriad of assignments beyond their scripturally assigned disciplinary function; stake presidents, rather than General Authorities, now set apart missionaries; the majority of men serving full-time missions once were seventies but now are primarily elders; and home teaching has replaced ward teaching, to cite some of the better-known changes.[9]

All LDS Church Presidents have tried diligently to tailor priesthood instructions, as recorded in the Doctrine and Covenants, to fit the pressing needs of their day.[10] No prophet presided during a period when the seas of changing circumstances churned more than they did during President Young's administration. His biographical record should show that among numerous contributions he made to the shape and development of priesthood operations in the Church, the following twelve are the most important historically:

1. Reconstituting the First Presidency and establishing how succession in the Presidency should take place.

2. Clarifying and institutionalizing the Apostles' roles at home and abroad.

3. Transforming the seventies' office into a major non-General Authority level of priesthood.

4. Institutionalizing and clarifying the role of the Presiding Bishopric.

5. Establishing wards as the Church's primary units of governance and ward bishops as the key local ecclesiastical officer.

6. Institutionalizing stakes to be meaningful intermediate units of administration.

7. Requiring endowments prior to missions or marriage, which caused men to receive the Melchizedek Priesthood, thereby depleting the Aaronic Priesthood of mature males.

8. Requiring boys to serve in at least one Aaronic Priesthood office before reaching adulthood.

9. Establishing patriarchal priesthood ordinances and practices, including the law of adoption, family organizations, and plurality of wives.

10. Preserving, promoting, and refining temple ordinances and rituals for the living and for the dead while making temple blessings available in the Nauvoo Temple, the Salt Lake Endowment House, and the St. George Temple.

11. Directing civic and secular affairs semi-theocratically through priesthood officers.

12. Conducting a thorough priesthood reorganization in 1877, including the issuing of the first "handbook" regarding Church administration.

I deal with these developments below at appropriate places, weaving them into a tapestry designed to showcase individually how each of the Church's priesthood offices and units functioned during Brigham Young's presidency. Each of the presiding quorums is discussed, followed by stake, ward, and local quorum operations.

THE APOSTOLIC PRESIDENCY, 1844–1847

Brigham Young's leadership of the Church began while he was president of the Quorum of the Twelve, a body that collectively succeeded Joseph Smith from August 1844 to December 1847. During that period, he and the Twelve promoted four major priesthood-related ventures.

The first occurred during the October 1844 conference (where he was sustained as President of the Twelve) when the Twelve declared every United States congressional district to be a missionary district and then assigned to each a high priest to reside there and "have entire charge" under the Twelve "of all spiritual matters, superintending the labors of the elders, and the calling of conferences."[11] Seven dozen high priests were set apart to permanent assignments and instructed to take their families with them to those districts. However, unexpected pressures for the Church to leave Nauvoo canceled the assignments.

The second venture, apparently linked to the Twelve's districting of the United States, was President Young's orchestration of a mass-ordination of seventies, expanding the number of seventies quorums from three to thirty (see "The Seventies," below). Apparently Young and the Twelve anticipated a vast missionary push, designed to convert individuals in the United States districts that had just been announced. But, again, the uprooting from Nauvoo and the tremendous work needed to build settlements in Utah allowed Church leaders to send out only a fairly limited missionary force year by year.

As a third priesthood-related measure, President Young implemented the bestowal of the temple endowment upon all Nauvoo adults who were "faithful and worthy" Saints and who wanted to receive that blessing.[12] To be endowed, he taught, is to "possess the keys of the eternal priesthood."[13] Day and night, the Nauvoo Temple stayed open in late 1845 and early 1846, during which time 5,615 adults received the endowment.[14] The availability of the endowment led to the priesthood practice of expecting an LDS male to hold the Melchizedek Priesthood and be temple-endowed before going on a full-time proselyting mission or being sealed in eternal marriage. A byproduct of this expectation was that almost all active, practicing LDS adult males received Melchizedek Priesthood ordinations, thus removing them from the pool of manpower eligible to receive Aaronic Priesthood offices (see "Aaronic Priesthood Quorums and Labors," below).

Fourth, with Brigham Young's guidance, the principle of succession in the Presidency was clarified and implemented. An absolutely critical test for a new organization is whether or not it can survive the passing or loss of its founder. The failure rate is substantial. The Church faced that test when Joseph Smith was killed. It wobbled slightly and dealt with a crucial succession question not fully articulated by revelations, handbooks, or Joseph Smith's teachings. Joseph Smith's successor was the Twelve as a body, and they directed the Church in lieu of a First Presidency for three-and-a-half years. Not until 27 December 1847 did the Twelve organize a new First Presidency and obtain ratification from the Church's membership. The precedent established then is still followed: the Twelve as a body succeeds a deceased prophet and then selects the senior Apostle, with divine sanction, as the new President of the Church.

THE FIRST PRESIDENCY

During the Brigham Young years, the First Presidency became a powerful quorum with well-defined purposes and procedures.

Personnel. Only six men served as first and second counselors to President Young during his twenty-nine years as President. His first counselors were Heber C. Kimball until 1868, then George A. Smith until 1875, followed by John W. Young until 1877. His second counselors were Willard Richards to 1854, Jedediah M. Grant to 1857, and Daniel H. Wells until Brigham's death in 1877. In 1873, Young called five extra counselors, who, a year later, were designated "assistant counselors": John W. Young, George Q. Cannon, Lorenzo Snow, Brigham Young, Jr., and Albert Carrington. Joseph Smith had set the precedent for having more than two counselors by having Oliver Cowdery, Hyrum Smith, Joseph Smith, Sr., and John Smith simultaneously serve as counselors.

Responsibilities. The First Presidency was responsible for all spiritual and temporal Church matters. They wanted all people to receive the gospel ordinances and temple blessings at the hands of the priesthood and to be set to work building the kingdom of God. They ensured that the basic ordinances of blessing babies, baptizing, confirming, administering the sacrament, and ordaining to the priesthood were performed properly.

One of the First Presidency's priorities was temple building and the performance of temple ordinances. Brigham Young believed that only in a temple could people "receive the ordinances of the holy Priesthood."[15] Fulfilling the Twelve's mandate from Joseph Smith, Brigham Young energetically rushed the Nauvoo Temple to basic completion and arranged for washings, anointings, endowments, and marriage sealings to be administered there. After the exodus from Nauvoo, lacking a Utah temple, he arranged for the temporary Endowment House to be built and placed his counselor, Heber C. Kimball, in charge of it. Some baptisms for the dead took place. President Young, anxious to have a fully-functioning temple operational before he died, dedicated the St. George Temple and installed Apostle Wilford Woodruff as its president.

The First Presidency performed many marriage sealings, including plural marriages. President Young exercised the sealing powers he held by virtue of being President of the Church and holding all the keys of the priesthood. He sealed couples together in celestial marriage and delegated that authority to a few others. Whereas Joseph Smith introduced plural marriage quietly among selected associates, to Brigham Young fell the responsibility of publicly announcing the doctrine and of convincing Latter-day Saints to believe in and participate in polygamy. Through example, public discourse, and private counsel, he championed plural marriage. As a result of his leadership, aided by that of other General Authorities, up to 25 percent of LDS households participated in plural marriage at a given point in time.[16] About two out of five men in good Church standing took plural wives.[17] President Young successfully promoted the principle.

Another sealing ordinance involved sealing family units for eternity. In the context of this ordinance, President Young promoted the law of adoption. Through the law of adoption, Church members whose own parents were not priesthood bearers could become sealed in life and for eternity to General Authorities, thereby joining that authority's family by priesthood adoption. This practice continued until the 1890s.[18]

In terms of manpower and resources, missionary work sometimes took a back seat to settlement and colonizing labors. Nevertheless, President Young promoted missionary work by

The First Presidency and the Quorum of the Twelve Apostles, 1869. Front row, left to right: George A. Smith, Brigham Young, Daniel H. Wells. Back row: Orson Hyde, Orson Pratt, John Taylor, Wilford Woodruff, Ezra T. Benson, Charles C. Rich, Lorenzo Snow, Erastus Snow, Franklin D. Richards, George Q. Cannon, Brigham Young Jr., and Joseph F. Smith.

involving the Twelve deeply in its management and by sending missionaries throughout the world.

Of necessity, President Young's primary labors were devoted to establishing a home base for the Church, securing a Mormon homeland in the Great Basin. His concern was to help LDS converts reach Zion, to develop agricultural and mineral-production settlements, and to see that the Saints received the gospel ordinances and had ecclesiastical leaders and organizations to belong to. Up to 1877, when President Young reorganized Church units, the Church in gathered Zion had 13 stakes and 101 wards, albeit in varying states of health and functionality. Young's 1877 restructurings (see below) were monumental in the course of the historical development of priesthood work.

Council meetings with Church leaders. After the First Presidency was reconstituted in December 1847, they met almost daily with the Twelve at Winter Quarters. In Utah, the two presiding quorums met together often, although a majority of the Twelve rarely was present because of assignments away from Salt Lake City.

These meetings were small council meetings that some additional persons attended—usually the senior president of the First Council of the Seventy, the Presiding Bishop, and the president of the Salt Lake Stake (regarded as a "center stake" for the Church—see below). When four men were added to the Quorum of the Twelve in 1849, those attending the historic meeting were the First Presidency; three of the Twelve; Presiding Bishop Newel K. Whitney; high priests president John Young and his counselor, George B. Wallace; and Jedediah M. Grant of the First Council of the Seventy.[19]

It appears that President Young regarded the First Presidency not so much as a quorum apart from the Quorum of the Twelve but "as a kind of executive committee of the Twelve."[20] Minutes exist for sixteen meetings of the First Presidency and Twelve in the 1850s, fifteen in the 1860s, and five in the 1870s.[21] Wilford Woodruff's journal itemizes 217 meetings of the First Presidency and the Twelve between 1847 and 1853. Those of the Twelve who were "home" did consult regularly with the First Presidency. Woodruff's annual summaries in his diary show that by the mid-1850s and continuing to 1876, their conjoint meetings became prayer circle gatherings, from 17 to 66 times a year, that served at times as "spiritually oriented council meetings" in which members discussed scriptures, doctrine, history, and occasionally organizational and temporal matters.[22] A review of the minutes of Brigham's meetings with the Twelve "show Brigham Young not always telling them what to do, not often chastising them, but usually sincerely seeking their judgment—seeking to establish and maintain harmony and unity. Most of the meetings took the form of relaxed discussions among peers."[23]

Throughout Brigham Young's presidency, most decisions came from "the President-in-council"—the President, his counselors, available members of the Twelve, one or more of the Seventies' presidency, one or more of the Presiding Bishopric, and one or more from the Salt Lake Stake Presidency and the Salt Lake high priests quorum.[24]

General epistles. Important to Church policy, practice, and belief were the First Presidency's general epistles to the Saints throughout the world. In Nauvoo, President Young and the Twelve utilized this method of communication with the Church worldwide. Then, when the First Presidency was reconstituted, it issued many general instructions during Brigham Young's tenure as President.

The first known document of the apostolic presidency was written by Brigham Young to the Church membership from Boston on 16 July 1844. The Twelve issued a general epistle on 23 December 1847, followed soon after by the First General Epistle of the First Presidency, dated 1 August 1849. A Fourteenth General Epistle is dated 10 December 1856, ending the practice of numbering the general letters. Others followed, however, including two in 1869 and the vital Circular of the First Presidency of 11 July 1877, which ordered the reorganization of stakes and quorums. In addition, the First Presidency sent numerous letters addressed to the bishops.[25]

General conferences. During Brigham Young's presidency, the Church's annual and semiannual conferences became major forums for the First Presidency and the Twelve to address the Saints, and, unlike at Nauvoo, the conferences took place in suitable conference auditoriums—the original Salt Lake Tabernacle and then the "new" (and now famous) Tabernacle. President Young arranged for clerks to record conference discourses in shorthand so they could be published in the *Deseret News* and in LDS periodicals abroad. A sixteen-page semimonthly publication called *Journal of Discourses* was published in England, which became a monumental reference collection packed with leaders' counsel, including discussions of priesthood theory and practice. It contains 390 sermons by Brigham Young.[26]

Tours to distant settlements. The First Presidency adopted a role that was not practiced and probably not needed before the Utah gathering: making visits into the Mormon communities to consult firsthand with local priesthood officers.[27]

Secular leadership. Before, during, and after his terms as governor of Utah Territory, Young acted forcefully to ensure that priesthood leaders, not unbelieving outsiders or apostates, were the political and economic leaders of the Mormon people. As a result, General Authorities and local Church leaders served prominently in territorial executive, legislative, and judicial positions and as county and city officials.

GENERAL CONFERENCE SUSTAININGS

A look at general conference sustainings between 1849 and 1877, specifically the order in which officers were presented, reveals several variations in priesthood sustaining practices during the Brigham Young period:

1. In 1873, the Church sustained seven counselors in the First Presidency; from 1874 through 1877, the Presidency was readjusted to include two counselors plus five assistant counselors.

2. Up through 1859 and again between 1872 and 1877, President Young was sustained as President and Prophet, Seer, and Revelator, but from fall 1859 to spring 1872, the terms *prophet, seer,* and *revelator* were not used.

3. A Presiding Patriarch or "Patriarch to the Whole Church" was sustained at every conference, although the title varied slightly.

4. Members of the First Council of the Seventy, who were the seven senior presidents of all the seventies quorums, were sustained variously as "President of the Presidency of Seventies and Six Associates," "President of the Presiding Council of Seventies," "President of the First Seven Presidents of the Seventies," "Members of the First Seven Presidents of the Seventies," "President of all the Seventies and Six Counselors," and "Presidents of all the Quorums of Seventies."

5. Until 1860, the Presiding Bishop was sustained without counselors, except on one occasion. At four conferences, the Church sustained Assistant Presiding Bishops and Traveling Bishops.

6. The president and counselors in the Salt Lake Stake presidency were sustained at nearly every general conference, as were the stake's high council, the president and counselors of the high priests quorum, and president and counselors for the stake's priests, teachers, and deacons quorums.

The sustaining order sometimes changed slightly. In 1849 and

1850, the high priests quorum presidency, which was the only such quorum in existence and served as the general quorum (see below) for all high priests in Utah no matter where they lived, was sustained before the Senior Presidents of the Seventies, and at other times before the Salt Lake Stake presidency. The stake presidency was sustained ahead of the Presiding Bishop in 1849, 1850, and 1851, probably reflecting its earlier role as the presidency of the Church in Utah during the first year. The Presiding Patriarch was sustained after the First Presidency and before the Twelve; it was later positioned after the Twelve.

THE TWELVE APOSTLES

Before Joseph Smith died, he placed upon the Twelve the responsibilities for gathered Zion in addition to the foreign ministry. They had crossed the threshold, comparatively speaking, but suddenly had to step forthrightly into the room after the martyrdom. Under Brigham Young, the Twelve learned from hard experience where they fit in the Church's administrative structure.

Although the Apostles were subordinate to the First Presidency "in cases of doctrinal and other pronouncements made as revelation from the Lord," the First Presidency sought and considered their opinions and insights. Once decisions were made, after differences of opinion were aired during discussion stages, the Twelve gave public support "despite any private reservations." President Young felt strongly about securing unity among the General Authorities.[28]

Personnel. While Brigham Young was Church President, there were few changes in personnel among the Twelve, who were relatively young men when called. Only twelve new members were called. And, during that time, four were dropped from the quorum: William Smith (1845), John E. Page (1846), Lyman Wight (1848), and Amasa Lyman (1867).

When the First Presidency was reconstituted late in 1847, it drew three members from the quorum: Brigham Young, Heber C. Kimball, and Willard Richards. Near that same time, Elder Wight was excommunicated. With President Young's approval, the four vacancies were filled on 12 February 1849 by Charles C. Rich,

Lorenzo Snow, Erastus Snow, and Franklin D. Richards. The First Presidency ordained these men and continued to ordain all new Apostles.[29]

When the First Presidency and Twelve met together in October 1859 to choose a replacement for Parley P. Pratt, who had died in 1857, President Young asked members of the Twelve to nominate one or two men in writing rather than having the First Presidency nominate someone. Several names were discussed, as were the merits of proven experience versus inexperienced potential. Finally the Twelve deferred to President Young, who selected George Q. Cannon; the Twelve sustained him without dissent.

In 1866, President Young received a revelation to ordain Joseph F. Smith to the apostleship even though there was no vacancy in the quorum. The Twelve approved and helped President Young ordain the new Apostle. Thereafter, though the Twelve did not select new Apostles on their own, their suggestions and opinions were solicited before the calls were issued.[30]

Of four men called into the First Presidency as counselors to Brigham Young after Elders Kimball and Richards, only George A. Smith was from the Quorum of the Twelve.

As noted earlier, rarely was a majority of the Twelve together at one time in Salt Lake City. In fact, the first time the entire Quorum of Twelve was able to meet together in Utah was on 6 October 1868.[31]

Assignments. From 1848 to 1877, President Young constantly gave assignments to members of the Twelve, the two main ones being to preside over missions outside Utah and to establish and direct remote settlements of the Church. A summary of the Apostles' activities shows the following:

> Orson Hyde spent nineteen years presiding over Great Basin settlements between 1854 and 1877. Orson Pratt spent eleven years on missions. John Taylor spent six years on missions. Ezra T. Benson spent three years on missions and nine years presiding over settlements. Charles C. Rich spent twenty-three years presiding over settlements. Lorenzo Snow spent three years on a mission and twenty-four presiding over the Brigham City settlement. Erastus Snow spent eight years on missions and sixteen years presiding over settlements.

Franklin D. Richards spent seven years on missions and eight presiding over Weber Valley.[32]

Inherent in the work of presiding over missions was the labor of organizing, scheduling, and arranging finances for each year's emigration. In addition, whenever Apostles returned home from such missions, they helped supervise the LDS emigrants traveling with them, such as happened in 1856 when Elders John Taylor, Erastus Snow, and Franklin D. Richards directed much of the movement. In 1860, Elders Erastus Snow and Orson Pratt went to the eastern United States to supervise LDS emigration.

Another assignment given to various Apostles related to publications and public relations. In the late 1840s, Elder Orson Hyde was sent east to obtain a printing press and then to publish a newspaper at Kanesville, which was named the *Frontier Guardian*. After the Church publicly announced its belief in polygamy, the First Presidency sent Orson Pratt to Washington, D.C., on a public relations crusade. There he published a periodical called *The Seer* for eighteen months in which he defended in print LDS doctrines. Similarly, John Taylor published *The Mormon* in New York, and Erastus Snow published the *St. Louis Luminary*.

In the mid-1850s, the First Presidency appointed several Apostles to divide Utah settlements into districts and then do "home missionary" work among them, mainly by holding conferences and meetings. They helped promote the Mormon Reformation of 1856. Upon the Twelve's shoulders fell the major work of instituting the Priesthood Reorganization of 1877 (see below).

Seniority. Brigham Young made a major seniority adjustment among the Twelve that proved to be crucial in determining who became his successor. At the time the First Presidency was reconstituted on 27 December 1847, the Twelve, in order of seniority, were: Brigham Young, Heber C. Kimball, Orson Hyde, Parley P. Pratt, Orson Pratt, Lyman Wight, Willard Richards, Wilford Woodruff, John Taylor, George A. Smith, Amasa Lyman, and Ezra T. Benson. But during a meeting with the Twelve in 1875, Brigham ruled that because Elders Hyde and Orson Pratt had separated themselves briefly from the quorum in 1838 and 1842 respectively, they had lost their seniority standings to Elders Taylor, Woodruff, and George A. Smith. And because John Taylor had helped ordain Wilford Woodruff to be an Apostle, Woodruff's seniority over Taylor in the quorum was not proper, so the two exchanged seniority positions.

When Brigham Young selected five extra counselors in 1874, four of them were members of the Twelve. However, those four served in both capacities and were not replaced within the Quorum of the Twelve.

THE PRESIDING PATRIARCH

On 24 May 1845, soon after Brigham Young assumed Church leadership, Apostle William Smith, the Prophet's brother, was ordained patriarch by virtue of his lineage. Immediately he claimed to have independent presiding authority in the Church and even primacy over the Twelve. (D&C 124: 124 placed the patriarch position hierarchically before the First Presidency.) He was excommunicated that fall for apostasy. After that, the hereditary office of Patriarch to the Church was vacant for two years.

John Smith, popularly known as Uncle John Smith (Joseph Smith's uncle), succeeded William on 1 January 1849. In theory, John presided over a "quorum" containing all other Church patriarchs. He died 23 May 1854.

Brigham Young determined that the position was subordinate to the First Presidency and Twelve and defined the office as being patriarch *to* the Church, not *over* the Church. During Uncle John Smith's tenure, the Presiding Patriarch was sustained after the First Presidency and before the Twelve. But when young John Smith (son of Hyrum Smith) succeeded Uncle John, the position was sustained *after* the Twelve, showing to the Church its relative position in the hierarchy. The younger John Smith was ordained at age twenty-two under the hands of Brigham Young and seven of the Apostles on 18 February 1855. In that position, he bestowed thousands of blessings upon the heads of the Saints. Patriarchs were called at the local level, but, apparently, no "quorum" of patriarchs was actually organized wherein the Presiding Patriarch directed or instructed the other patriarchs.[33]

THE SEVENTIES

At the time of the martyrdom, the Church had three seventies quorums.[34] But, under the direction of Brigham Young and the Twelve, new seventies units were created on such a scale that by the time of the exodus some thirty were in operation. In August 1844, the First Quorum of Seventies was divided to provide ten sets of seven presidents, who became the presidents of seventies quorums number two through eleven, effectively disbanding the first quorum. The seven presidents of the first quorum became the senior presidency over all seventies units, serving as the First Council of Seventy—the Church's third quorum of General Authorities. That October the Twelve instructed that elders under age thirty-five be ordained as seventies. Over 400 were ordained, so that eleven quorums were filled. By January 1846, the number of quorums increased to thirty, and in 1861, senior president Joseph Young reported that the quorums in Utah then numbered sixty-two.[35]

Why the number of seventies was so dramatically expanded is not understood. Apparently Brigham Young and the Twelve wanted these seventies to become a massive missionary force in the near future. "Seventies were designed to be messengers to every land and kingdom under heaven," Apostle Amasa M. Lyman said during dedicatory services of Nauvoo's impressive Seventies Hall in December 1844.[36] Seventies quorums provided many, perhaps most, of the ordinance workers in the Nauvoo Temple when washing, anointings, and endowments were administered late in 1845 and early in 1846. During the exodus to the west, seventies were the largest priesthood body in the Church. At Winter Quarters, seventies helped erect a Council House, and general conferences of seventies from all quorums occurred weekly that first winter. Seventies held a five-day jubilee at the log tabernacle on the Iowa side of the river (present Council Bluffs).[37]

Seventies were the largest body of priesthood in Brigham Young's 1847 vanguard party, which included eight Apostles, four bishops, fifteen high priests, eight elders, and seventy-eight seventies.[38] More than one-third of the men serving in the Mormon Battalion (1846–1847) were seventies.[39] Drawn from many different quorums, these men expediently formed one "mass" seventies quorum in Los Angeles on 18 April 1847 by electing their own seven presidents under the direction of Levi W. Hancock of the First Council of the Seventy, the only General Authority in the battalion.

During the trek west and then the settlement and colonization of the Great Basin, seventies quorum members became scattered; this was a serious problem, because once a man was enrolled in a particular quorum, he remained a member of it as long as he was a seventy. During the 1850s, the *Deseret News* ran frequent notices of seventies quorums presidents looking for their missing members and occasional inquiries by quorums searching for their presidents.[40] Many dispersed seventies did what the Mormon Battalion had done and regrouped themselves into "mass" quorums (disapprovingly dubbed "muss" quorums by Brigham Young), consisting of all seventies living in a ward or stake, without regard to the particular quorum to which they officially belonged.

Under Brigham Young, the seventies became the backbone of the missionary force. Seventy percent of all missionaries called between 1860 and 1875 were seventies or were ordained such in order to go on missions. New seventies, after returning from missions, were assigned to memberships in existing quorums. Between 1846 and 1856, only six new quorums were organized; but between March and July of 1857, sixteen new quorums were organized, possibly a product of the Mormon Reformation just ending. By the 1860s, the seventies quorums numbered more than sixty.[41]

President Joseph Young, Brigham's brother, being the senior member of the First Council of the Seventy, was the Church's senior president of all seventies. The First Council kept in touch with seventies quorums, which were not under stake jurisdictions. The quorums each met for gospel discussion, held conferences and socials, and advanced various community projects.

During Brigham Young's administration, three confusions developed and lingered for decades concerning the seventies. First, by vastly expanding the number of seventies quorums, he created two levels of seventies: the seven presidents of the first quorum, or First Council, were General Authorities, but the other quorums and their presidents were not. So the Church had two types of seventies, a practice that continued until October 1986, when local seventies units were phased out and the First and Second Quorums of Seventy were revitalized as General Authority level quorums.

A second problem involved the authority which First Council members held in comparison to high priests. Seventies could not be high priests, and yet Brigham Young's generation referred to the First Council members as Seventy Apostles.[42] Controversy regarding who had higher authority, seventies or high priests, continued into the twentieth century.

A third problem was that seventies quorums were based on memberships and not on geography; as noted above, they became mixed up, and quorums were depleted when their members moved. Revelations in the 1880s solved this dilemma by putting seventies quorums on geographic footings.[43]

By the time Brigham Young died, the elders in Utah's stakes had come to outnumber seventies by two to one—9,084 compared to 4,477. The elders' number had risen because men were ordained elders in order to receive the endowment.

THE PRESIDING BISHOPRIC

The Presiding Bishop was the last General Authority-level office in the Church's hierarchy to be implemented. That office was authorized by revelation in 1841 (see D&C 124: 20–21, 141). However, from then until 1847, Bishop Newel K. Whitney and Bishop George Miller functioned jointly as General Bishops for the entire Church. After the Saints' departure from Nauvoo, Bishop Miller became disaffected from Brigham Young's leadership. So, on 6 April 1847, Bishop Whitney was sustained as Presiding Bishop of the Church.

For a time his counselors were President Brigham Young and First Presidency counselor Heber C. Kimball. Bishop Whitney's successor, Edward Hunter, served without counselors at first. In 1852, Presidents Young and Kimball were designated as Bishop

Newel K. Whitney (1795–1850), n.d., sustained as Presiding Bishop of the Church on 6 April 1847 at Winter Quarters.

Edward Hunter (1793–1883), ca. 1866. Bishop Hunter was chosen to succeed Newel K. Whitney as Presiding Bishop of the Church on 7 April 1851.

Hunter's counselors, but then Hunter served again without counselors until 1856. Finally, starting in 1856 and continuing since then, the Presiding Bishop has had counselors who together form the Presiding Bishopric.[44]

From 1849 onward, the Presiding Bishop served President Young and the Church by handling numerous temporal matters, including tithing, and through direct contacts with bishops.[45] Regarding Bishop Hunter's relationship to the First Presidency, Brigham Young stated in 1851 that the Presiding Bishop's duty was to preside over all bishops, and "it is the business of the First Presidency to correct him and from whom he receives his instructions."[46] President Young made it clear that he felt he had upon himself more or less "the responsibility of both priesthoods."[47] The First Presidency framed policy, the Presiding Bishop supervised it, and the local bishops implemented it.[48]

At biweekly meetings with Salt Lake Valley bishops and any others who were in town, the Presiding Bishop dealt with practical and spiritual matters, including the operations of the Aaronic Priesthood and, by association, the Melchizedek Priesthood.

Constantly, Bishop Hunter labored to see that the Aaronic Priesthood offices were filled and honored.

To help handle tithing, Bishop Hunter used "assistant presiding traveling bishops" as well as regional presiding bishops from 1851 to 1877. The use of regional bishops became widespread.[49]

STAKES AND STAKE OFFICERS

Early in 1849, to overcome disruptions caused by the exodus from Nauvoo, the First Presidency took several major steps to "regularize church government" in the Salt Lake Valley. They selected John Young, Brigham's oldest brother, to be president of the Church's only high priests quorum; Daniel Spencer to be stake president; a high council with Isaac Morley as president; and John Nebeker as elders quorum president. They appointed Presiding Bishop Newel K. Whitney to organize in Great Salt Lake Valley one quorum each of priests, teachers, and deacons. A committee, chaired by Bishop Whitney but including Brigham Young, divided Salt Lake Valley into nineteen wards and established other wards in nearby areas; each ward soon had its own bishop.[50]

At Brigham Young's death, stakes in the Mountain West numbered twenty, including seven created during the previous five months. During Brigham Young's presidency, the terms *stakes, branches,* and *settlements* were used imprecisely and interchangeably. Always the basic local Church governing unit was a stake. When one place was settled, it was considered a stake in embryo and started with a president. Then a bishop and a high council were added. High councils usually had their own president who was not the stake president. More bishops would be called if more wards were created in that area. Each stake was expected to have one quorum each of high priests, elders, priests, teachers, and deacons. When Sanpete Stake finally established Aaronic Priesthood quorums, Ephraim and Manti each contributed half the needed 48 priests, 24 teachers, and 12 deacons.

Salt Lake Stake was unusual because of its size and because it was the headquarters location of the Church. Even as late as 1877, one-fifth of Utah Mormons resided in the Salt Lake Stake. Stake sizes then varied from Salt Lake Stake's 19,798 members to tiny

Panguitch Stake's 859. The average stake membership, not counting Salt Lake Stake, was 4,421. Stakes averaged twelve wards each, but Salt Lake Stake had thirty-five. For years, Salt Lake Stake served as a type of superior "central stake." Its high council was considered a "general high council" that could be asked to settle problems other high councils could not solve.[51] As noted earlier, Salt Lake Stake officers, including quorum presidents, often were sustained at general conference.

HIGH PRIESTS AND ELDERS

As noted earlier, Brigham Young had in mind sending high priests throughout the United States to preside over branches of the Church to be created by a major missionary labor. When Utah was first settled, a high priests quorum was formed in Salt Lake City, which served for several years as a general quorum to which all high priests in Utah belonged. "The High Priests' Quorum is strictly but one quorum," President Young explained in 1861, "though many quorums of High Priests are made to accommodate members of that quorum living in different localities."[52] Kaysville high priests, for example, were enrolled in the general quorum and journeyed to Salt Lake City to attend its meetings.

Brigham Young instructed quorum president David Pettigrew in 1854 to organize high priests in the various settlements into "branch quorums" to make the meetings more accessible and regular.[53] Such branch units, however, did not catch fire very well. Reports at the general quorum during October 1856 general conference revealed that one unit could get only seven out of thirteen members to attend. Other reports from various settlements north and south caused quorum president John Young to call not for a reformation but for a resurrection. In 1862, a general quorum was organized for high priests living outside of Salt Lake County, including among others Davis, Utah, and Weber counties, but no record of its meetings has been found.[54]

"It was a common practice among many of the early bishoprics in Utah to choose counselors who were elders and seventies and who remained as such during their service," one priesthood historian has noted, a practice Brigham Young did not seem concerned about until the 1870s.[55]

Elders' units were formed in some communities and not in others. Meetings, as with high priests and seventies meetings, consisted primarily in the bearing of testimony and admonishings from the quorum leaders to live right, attend meetings, sustain the leaders, and bear their testimonies.[56]

AARONIC PRIESTHOOD QUORUMS AND LABORS

Before the endowment was introduced, which required men to hold the Melchizedek Priesthood before receiving it, adult males served in Aaronic or Melchizedek priesthood offices as they were needed. Church practice was to have adult deacons, teachers, and priests—men of experience and wisdom—visit the members to help solve their problems, ferret out iniquity, reconcile feuding parties, and teach members to pray and to do their duties.

After the endowment was available, few stalwart men lacking Melchizedek Priesthood could be found for Aaronic Priesthood ordination. As a result, Brigham Young instructed that Melchizedek Priesthood holders be called by bishops or by Aaronic Priesthood quorum officers to act in the lesser offices. During his administration, *acting* deacons, *acting* teachers, and *acting* priests did the Aaronic Priesthood work of caring for meetinghouses, administering the sacrament, assisting the needy, and doing watch-care activity that today is called home teaching. Stake deacons, teachers, and priests quorums, organized in a few stakes, held monthly meetings where presidencies instructed the men in their duties. Though the quorums were stake entities, the work of quorum members always was ward work directed by ward bishops.[57]

As was the case before the exodus to Utah, selected young men received Melchizedek and Aaronic priesthood ordinations. Their numbers were not large. But in accordance with the philosophy that "the strong take along the weak," sometimes young men served like apprentices with older men in priesthood callings. Most LDS young men, however, first received priesthood when they needed to receive temple endowments.

WARDS, WARD BISHOPS, AND WARD PRESIDENTS

One of Brigham Young's major contributions to priesthood work was making wards an effective local unit of Church administration. Wards with bishops first existed in Nauvoo, created so that the poor could be cared for and funds for Nauvoo needs could be collected.[58] However, no wards held Sunday worship services or had buildings to meet in. By contrast, ward meetings and buildings became a common and central feature in Brigham Young's Utah.

President Young wanted wards (or *branches* or *settlements*) to have both a president and a bishop—a dual leadership. He explained that "as soon as Elders have wisdom sufficient to magnify their calling and Priesthood, we will give to every Branch, no matter how small the Ward, both a Bishop and a President."[59] Several ward presidents were called and served. In 1858, for example, Brigham Young told one settlement leader to "select one of your number for a President, and one for Bishop."[60] Late in 1859, the First Presidency ordained Charles Hancock "to be the President and Bishop in Payson." On 12 June 1872, Brigham Young sent a letter regarding the Perpetual Emigrating Fund "to the Presidents and Bishops of the various Wards throughout the Territory."[61]

At times, President Young selected the bishops. When a Salt Lake City bishop resigned in 1859, Brigham Young informed ward member Andrew Cunningham that "you are hereby requested to fill the vacancy thus created, and commence to act in the office upon receipt of this notification."[62] It was not unusual for President Young to name a bishop for a ward who had to move there to take office. In 1861, he sent advice to Andrew Moffitt, who had been ordained to be the bishop of Manti, replacing Bishop Warren S. Snow, who was leaving on a mission. "Proceed to Manti, at your earliest convenience," Young counseled, "and take charge of all matters and things pertaining to the Bishopric in that place."[63] When Canute Peterson was selected to be Fort Ephraim's bishop, he had to be released as a counselor in the Lehi bishopric.[64] President Young appointed outsider Thomas Callister to move to Fillmore to be the bishop there and to act as "presiding bishop over all the other Wards or settlements in Millard County."[65]

In some cases, President Young allowed people to help select their bishop. In 1855, he counseled North Cottonwood Ward "brethren" to "select some young and vigorous man faithful and capable as your Bishop and I would recommend Bro John Hess as a capable person." But, whomever the ward's brethren selected, Young wanted him to come to the President's office as soon as possible to be ordained.[66]

Late in 1859, the First Presidency sent some of the Twelve to Cache Valley and authorized them to organize the area into a stake. "Upon your selections and elections," the First Presidency instructed the people, "they will set apart and ordain a President to preside over all your settlements, also twelve men to compose a High Council, and a Bishop for each settlement, a settlement, for the present, constituting one ward."[67] Also in 1859, President Young wrote to Apostle Lorenzo Snow in Box Elder County and instructed him to call together the people of Willow Creek Ward and "inform them that they are at liberty and we wish them to select *one* good man of their number to be their Bishop, and President," whom Elder Snow should then ordain. "If they have no such man, and wish one sent into their Ward to fill those offices," Young added, Elder Snow should attend to it.[68]

Bishops were expected to serve for life, if possible. They were the workhorses of the Church, often managing both religious and secular concerns in their settlements: resource managers, land distributors, public works directors, helpers of the poor and needy, Church court judges, militia advisers, baptizers, blessers of babies and the sick, preachers, funeral conductors, directors of the home teachers of that era, planners and conductors of religious meetings, and enforcers of Church rules. By the mid-1850s, they became involved in annual tithing settlements with their ward members, who previously were expected to settle tithing affairs with the Presiding Bishop.[69]

President Heber C. Kimball, in charge of the Endowment House in Salt Lake City, requested ward bishops to call and interview appropriate candidates and arrange for their presence with letters of recommendation and temple clothing at the Endowment House at the proper times.[70] A form for a bishop's letter of recommendation, created for use in connection with the opening of the St. George Temple early in 1877, states that the person named is recommended as a faithful member, one who has paid tithing and donations, and is worthy to receive what ordinances are written in the blank lines "if endorsed by President Young."[71]

Because of Brigham Young's development of and reliance on bishops, ward bishops have been the Church's workhorse officer in the priesthood, the crucial local leader who brings people and the Church programs, including priesthood operations and ordinances, into a working relationship together.

TEMPLES AND PRIESTHOOD

Construction work on the Salt Lake Temple started in 1853, but progress was slow due to demands in Mormondom's capital for many projects, coupled with the temple's massive construction specifications. President Young alone held the sealing keys for temple work. The responsibility weighed on him, and he felt urgency to share the full range of temple ordinances, particularly the sealing of deceased relatives to each other, in a House of the Lord.

Years before, Joseph Smith had taken Brigham and other Church leaders into a room above his Nauvoo store. There he divided off the room as best he could and carefully instructed them about the various temple ceremonies. "Brother Brigham," he said when he was finished, "this is not arranged right . . . and I want you to take this matter in hand and organize and systematize all these ceremonies."

President Young fulfilled that assignment by personally directing the completion of the Nauvoo Temple and administering ordinances there. In 1871, he dedicated the St. George Temple site and earmarked Church resources to pay for materials and workmen. Labor missionaries were sent from northern Utah settlements to help. "You cannot realize . . . how anxious he is to get this temple completed," George Q. Cannon said of Brigham Young in 1876; "he has keys he wants to give in the Temple."

From January to April 1877, President Young presided over dedications of the St. George Temple. In January, endowments for the dead were administered for the first time in this dispensation, some 3,208 by the end of March. He spent time from January to March developing a "perfect form of the endowments," which was read and taught to temple workers in late March. Final dedications took place in April, four months before his death, and Saints immediately engulfed the temple to receive temple ordinances for themselves and others.[72]

THE PRIESTHOOD REORGANIZATION OF 1877

After opening the St. George Temple, ailing Brigham Young was suddenly filled with new life. Back in 1842, Joseph Smith had taught that "the Church is not fully organized, in its proper order, and cannot be, until the Temple is completed, where places will be provided for the administration of the ordinances of the Priesthood."[73] With the temple connecting heaven to earth, President Young felt an urgency to refine priesthood operations and make the earthly priesthood better mirror the heavenly one.

Rapid growth and other factors had made stakes, wards, and quorums "somewhat loose," so he felt overwhelming obligations to reform those units' operations. To start the task, he personally presided over a thorough reorganization of the St. George Stake that April. Then, during the middle months of 1877, he engineered sweeping reorganizations of priesthood involving twenty stakes, nine of which he personally conducted.

Only highlights of the extensive reorganization can be mentioned here.[74] Six of the Twelve Apostles were released as stake presidents so they could work in "a larger field than a Stake of Zion." The reorganization created seven new stakes and reorganized the thirteen existing ones. In the twenty stakes, fifty-three of the sixty members of stake presidencies were newly called, including sixteen new stake presidents. Most stakes created new high councils. Elders quorums were created or revitalized. Quarterly stake conferences were instituted, and the Church's first uniform system for keeping statistical records was established. Stakes were asked to build meeting halls for stake priesthood assemblies and quarterly conferences—Temple Square's Assembly Hall was one result. Adding to the existing 101 wards, 140 new ones were created, and 185 of the Church's 241 bishops were newly ordained or set apart. All bishopric counselors had to be high priests. Seventies quorums were severely depleted when many of their members were called into the new bishoprics. Scores of Aaronic Priesthood quorums were created. Probably more than a thousand members received new ward or stake callings. A new policy asking that all young men be given some Aaronic Priesthood office before they reached adulthood produced several hundred youthful ordinations.

The 1877 reordering was the single most important redirecting of priesthood since priesthood authority was restored forty-eight years earlier. The First Presidency's 11 July 1877 letter, which explained what changes were being made and why, was the Church's first priesthood handbook of instructions since publication of the Doctrine and Covenants. The reorganization was a final testament by Brigham Young, who sought all his life to follow accurately Joseph Smith's teachings regarding how priesthood should operate in the Church.

"It is a great joy and comfort to know that he had the privilege of living to complete one Temple and to see it dedicated," Apostle Erastus Snow observed, "and that he superintended the setting in order of the priesthood and the ordinances for the redemption of the dead . . . something he greatly desired to see done before he should pass away."[75]

"The Church is more perfectly organized than ever before, perhaps with the exception of the general assembly at Kirtland," Apostle John Taylor observed that September; "but in some things now we are more stable and complete than we were even then."[76]

In some respects, the Assembly Hall on Temple Square, started in 1877 and completed in 1880, stands as a stately and inspiring memorial to President Young's final priesthood reorganization. It also stands as a tribute to his lengthy stewardship as Church President over the workings of priesthood offices, quorums, and powers from 1844 to 1877.

NOTES

1. A recent example, Leonard J. Arrington's monumental *Brigham Young: American Moses* (New York: Alfred A. Knopf, 1985) devotes a chapter to Brigham Young as "President of the Church" (chapter 12), but gives more attention to theology than to priesthood operations. The biography provides only a short, albeit excellent, summary of the priesthood reorganization of 1877, which was one of Young's most important achievements—a culmination of his lifelong labors in behalf of the gathering, of Church organizational refinement, and of temple and priesthood concerns.
2. Sermon, 8 April 1871, in *Journal of Discourses,* 14: 95; and *Teachings of President Brigham Young,* comp. and ed. Fred C. Collier (Salt Lake City, Utah: Collier Publishing Co., 1987), 3: 230 (sermon, 15 February 1854).
3. Sermon, 18 February 1855, in *Journal of Discourses,* 2: 177.
4. Sermon, 18 February 1855, in *Journal of Discourses,* 2: 180.
5. Sermon, 6 June 1858, in *Journal of Discourses,* 7: 66.
6. *Teachings of President Brigham Young,* 3: 351.
7. Sermon, 8 April 1871, in *Journal of Discourses,* 4: 299.
8. Salt Lake Stake Deacons Quorum Minutes, 27 January, 4 February, and 26 May 1877, and 14 December 1875, Library-Archives, Historical Department of The Church of Jesus Christ of Latter-day Saints (hereafter cited as LDS Church Historical Archives).
9. Prophets have believed what the Lord said in a revelation on 14 April 1883 to President John Taylor, that Saints should not be troubled "about the management and organization of my Church and Priesthood, and the accomplishment of my work" but should trust the appointed channels. See James R. Clark, comp., *Messages of the First Presidency of The Church of Jesus Christ of Latter-day Saints,* 6 vols. (Salt Lake City: Bookcraft, 1965–75), 2: 347–49, 354–55.
10. John Taylor taught that "it is not wise to have cast iron rules by which to fetter the Priesthood. The Priesthood is a living, intelligent principle, and must necessarily have freedom to act as circumstances may dictate or require." Meeting, 15 December 1886, First Council of the Seventy Minutes, 1878–1894, microfilm, LDS Church Historical Archives.
11. Brigham Young, "An Epistle of the Twelve," *Times and Seasons,* 5: 670.
12. *Times and Seasons* 6, 1 December 1845, 1050; and *Times and Seasons,* 6, 15 January 1846, 1096.
13. Sermon, 8 July 1855, in *Journal of Discourses,* 2: 315.
14. Russell C Rich, *Ensign to the Nations: A History of the LDS Church from 1846–1972* (Provo, Utah: Brigham Young University Publications, 1972), 3, 24.
15. Sermon, 25 April 1877, reported in *Millennial Star,* 39: 371.
16. *Encyclopedia of Mormonism,* ed. Daniel H. Ludlow (New York: Macmillan Publishing Company, 1992), s.v. "Plural Marriage," Danel Bachman, Ronald K. Esplin, 3: 1095.

17. Jessie L. Embry, *Mormon Polygamous Families: Life in the Principle* (Salt Lake City: University of Utah Press, 1987), 38, 51, 63.
18. Gordon Irving, "The Law of Adoption: One Phase of the Development of the Mormon Concept of Salvation, 1830–1900," *BYU Studies* 14 (Spring 1974): 291–314.
19. Leonard J. Arrington and Ronald K. Esplin, "The Role of the Council of the Twelve during Brigham Young's Presidency of The Church of Jesus Christ of Latter-day Saints," *Task Papers in LDS History, No. 31* (Salt Lake City: History Division of the Historical Department of the LDS Church, December 1979), 32.
20. Arrington and Esplin, 38.
21. Ibid., 42.
22. Ibid., 41.
23. Ibid., 58.
24. Ibid., 52.
25. These general epistles are reprinted in Clark, vols. 1 and 2.
26. *Encyclopedia of Mormonism,* s.v. "Journal of Discourses," Ronald G. Watt, 2: 769–70.
27. Gordon Irving, "Encouraging the Saints: Brigham Young's Annual Tours of the Mormon Settlements," *Utah Historical Quarterly* 45 (Summer 1977): 233–51.
28. Arrington and Esplin, 37.
29. Minutes of the Twelve, 12 February 1849, LDS Church Historical Archives.
30. Arrington and Esplin, 47–48.
31. Andrew Jenson, *Church Chronology,* 2nd ed., rev. (Salt Lake City: Deseret News, 1899).
32. Arrington and Esplin, 39–40.
33. Irene May Bates, "Transformation of Charisma in the Mormon Church: A History of the Office of Presiding Patriarch, 1833–1979" (Ph.D. diss., University of California at Los Angeles, 1991), 211–24; E. Gary Smith, "The Office of Presiding Patriarch: The Primacy Problem," *Journal of Mormon History* 14 (1988): 35–47. In 1942 the title *Presiding Patriarch* was replaced by the title *Patriarch to the Church.*
34. The standard history of seventies' work is James N. Baumgarten, "The Role and Function of the Seventies in L.D.S. Church History" (master's thesis, Brigham Young University, 1960). See also S. Dilworth Young, "The Seventies: A Historical Perspective," *Ensign* (July 1976): 14–21.
35. Account of April 1861 general conference in *Millennial Star* 23 (15 June 1861): 370.
36. Joseph Smith, *History of the Church of Jesus Christ of Latter-day Saints,* ed. B. H. Roberts, 7 vols., 2nd ed., rev. (Salt Lake City: Deseret Book Co., 1971), 7: 339.

37. Journal History of the Church, 20 January 1848, LDS Church Historical Archives.
38. Journal History, 29 May 1847.
39. Based on the author's comparison of names of seventies listed in the Minutes and Genealogy Book B, and his own compiled roster of the Mormon Battalion.
40. Journal History, 4 December 1851.
41. Orson Pratt said there were sixty quorums of seventies in 1859, in *Journal of Discourses,* 7: 186–87.
42. During 1877 reorganizations at Logan, Utah, Brigham Young delivered a lengthy discourse in which he explained many priesthood matters, including the seventies-high priests authority issue (see Journal History, 25 May 1877). He said seventies had authority equal to high priests. In practice, however, he insisted that any seventy called into a bishopric be ordained a high priest.
43. William G. Hartley, "The Seventies in the 1880s: Revelations and Reorganizings," *Dialogue: A Journal of Mormon Thought* 16 (Spring 1983): 62–63.
44. D. Michael Quinn, "The Evolution of the Presiding Quorums of the LDS Church," *Journal of Mormon History* 1 (1974): 33–38.
45. William G. Hartley, "Edward Hunter, Pioneer Presiding Bishop," in Donald Q. Cannon and David Whittaker, eds., *Supporting Saints* (Salt Lake City: Bookcraft, 1985), 275–304.
46. Meeting, 29 November 1851, Presiding Bishops Meetings with Bishops, 1849–1884, LDS Church Historical Archives.
47. Ibid., 11 February 1875.
48. Donald Gene Pace, "The LDS Presiding Bishopric, 1851–1888: An Administrative Study" (master's thesis, Brigham Young University, 1978), 118.
49. Donald Gene Pace, "Community Leadership on the Mormon Frontier: Mormon Bishops and the Political, Economic, and Social Development of Utah before Statehood" (Ph.D. diss., Ohio State University, 1983), 63. John Banks, Alfred Cordon, and Nathaniel H. Felt were traveling bishops in 1851. Serving in 1852 were David Fullmer, David Hoagland, David Pettigrew, Daniel Spencer, and Seth Taft. Regional presiding bishops included Jacob Bigler (1852–1861, Juab County), John Rowberry (1853+, Tooele County), and Chauncey West (Fall 1855+, Weber County).
50. Arrington and Esplin, 34–35.
51. For example, in February 1852, President Young instructed Bishop Benjamin Cross of Payson, Utah, to appear with several brethren from his "branch"—who had difficulties with each other at a meeting with the "High Council of Provo"—before the Great Salt Lake City High Council for a hearing to settle the problem. See Thomas Bullock to Benjamin Cross, Brigham Young Letterbook 1, 4 February 1852, LDS Church Historical Archives. An

attempted appeal from South Weber Settlement to the Salt Lake high council is in Brigham Young to President Daniel Spencer, Brigham Young Letterbook 8, 26 February 1866, LDS Church Historical Archives.

52. During April 1861 general conference, Brigham Young delivered a major address regarding the order of the priesthood quorums, including the order of seniority among the Twelve and the seventies. See *Deseret News,* 10 April 1861.
53. Meeting, 17 January 1856, Cottonwood High Priests Quorum Minutes, 1856–1876, LDS Church Historical Archives.
54. Noel R. Barton, "Kaysville: A Study of the Bishoprics and the Organization of the Melchizedek Priesthood Quorums, 1851–1877," typescript, March 1983, p. 9, LDS Church Historical Archives.
55. Ibid., 5.
56. Ibid., 18.
57. William G. Hartley, "Ordained and Acting Teachers in the Lesser Priesthood, 1851–1883," *BYU Studies* 16 (Spring 1976): 375–98.
58. William G. Hartley, "Nauvoo Stake, Priesthood Quorums, and the Church's First Wards," *BYU Studies* 32 (Winter and Spring 1991): 57–80.
59. Sermon, 8 April 1862, in *Journal of Discourses,* 10: 33.
60. Brigham Young to John Reese and others, 6 September 1858, Brigham Young Letterbook 4, LDS Church Historical Archives.
61. Clark, 2: 248–49.
62. First Presidency to Andrew Cunningham, 10 January 1859, Brigham Young Letterbook 5, LDS Church Historical Archives.
63. Brigham Young to Bishop Andrew Moffitt, 10 April 1861, Brigham Young Letterbook 5, LDS Church Historical Archives.
64. Brigham Young to Bishop David Evans, 18 February 1867, Brigham Young Letterbook 9, LDS Church Historical Archives.
65. Brigham Young to Bishop Thomas Callister, 10 April 1861, Brigham Young Letterbook 5, LDS Church Historical Archives.
66. Brigham Young to the Brethren Residing in North Cottonwood Ward, 31 March 1855, Brigham Young Letterbook 22, LDS Church Historical Archives.
67. First Presidency to Authorities and Members, Cache Valley, Utah, November 1859, Brigham Young Letterbook 5, LDS Church Historical Archives.
68. Brigham Young to Lorenzo Snow, 18 July 1859, Brigham Young Letterbook 5, LDS Church Historical Archives.
69. William G. Hartley, "Ward Bishops and the Localizing of LDS Tithing," in *New Views of Mormon History,* ed. Davis Bitton and Maureen Ursenbach Beecher (Salt Lake City: University of Utah Press, 1987), 96–114.
70. Stanley B. Kimball, *Heber C. Kimball: Mormon Patriarch and Pioneer* (Urbana: University of Illinois Press, 1986), 200.
71. Form Letter, Recommendation to Temple, Brigham Young Letterbook 16, LDS Church Historical Archives.

72. William G. Hartley, "St. George Temple: One Hundred Years of Service," *Ensign* (March 1977): 92–94.
73. *History of the Church,* 4: 603.
74. William G. Hartley, "The Priesthood Reorganization of 1877: Brigham Young's Last Achievement," *BYU Studies* 20 (Fall 1979): 3–36.
75. Brigham H. Roberts, *A Comprehensive History of the Church of Jesus Christ of Latter-day Saints,* 6 vols. (Provo, Utah: Brigham Young University Press, 1965), 5: 516–17.
76. Hartley, "Priesthood Reorganization of 1877," 36.

CHAPTER 16

Reflections on the Teachings of Brigham Young

John W. Welch
Professor of Law
Brigham Young University
Editor, BYU Studies

and John Wm. Maddox
Research Assistant and Graduate of J. Reuben Clark Law School
Former Seminary Teacher, Church Educational System

The pioneer prophet Brigham Young was as expansive and pragmatic in word and thought as he was in deed and action. He spoke frequently to the Saints, who gathered at the bowery or in the Tabernacle on Temple Square in Salt Lake City or at many other locations; sometimes he delivered three sermons a day. His explanations and exhortations inspired and motivated his people as they developed much of the previously unexplored Great Basin region into a life-sustaining land.

Many studies about Brigham Young and his colonization efforts chronicle and quantify what he did, where he went, how he organized people, and how they survived and flourished.[1] Few of these studies, however, devote much time to explaining what Brigham Young and his people believed and how their ultimate religious commitments supplied good and sufficient reasons for their sacrifices in this remote and arid region.[2] Outside of a few papers on Brigham Young's political philosophy,[3] cosmology,[4] or religious philosophy,[5] only occasional attention has been given to the teachings of Brigham Young.

This brief study attempts to fill part of the doctrinal void found in most books about Brigham Young. Our pages will discuss the approaches taken by the main writers who have dealt with Brigham Young's thought and will provide an overview of the many topics found in Brigham Young's doctrinal teachings as they are reflected in his published speeches and sermons.

During his lengthy service as President of The Church of Jesus Christ of Latter-day Saints, Brigham Young delivered hundreds, if not thousands, of messages of a religious nature. About 400 of these talks have been published in the *Journal of Discourses;* others were reported in the *Deseret News* or are contained in other publications or collections.[6] The total number of known speeches by Brigham Young exceeds one thousand. In addition to the speeches reported in the *Journal of Discourses,* Elden J. Watson's compilation includes data concerning 734 further discourses. Most of Brigham Young's talks appear to have been extemporaneous, which accounts for some of their idiosyncracies. They were taken down in shorthand and transcribed and edited (sometimes) for publication.

Much can be said about Brigham Young's doctrinal teaching style. His oratory was pragmatic, eclectic, and dynamic. His wisdom was aphoristic, proverbial, clear, and commonsensical. His sentences were short. His tone was candid, blunt, and forthright. His humor was witty. He wryly recognized the shortcomings of communication: "The English language is better adapted than any other in existence to the using of thousands of words without conveying an idea."[7]

His spirit was encouraging, self-effacing, courageous, and expansive: "There is nothing that is out of the pale of our faith. There is nothing, I may say, good or bad, light or darkness, truth or error, but what is to be controlled by intelligent beings."[8] He never lost sight of the immanence of God: "If God withdraws his sustaining hand, you sink."[9] His pleadings were often couched in conditional and promisorial language: "If you take this course you will relieve the wants of the poor."[10]

He commonly began his sentences with imperatives, but his injunctions were frequently softened by the words "let us" do such and such, or "let it be" done. He was prone to utilize inescapable rhetorical questions, such as this: "For why should not a lady be capable of taking charge of her husband's business affairs when he goest into the grave?"[11]

And his speeches often have a penetrating cadence to them. For example, his rhetoric makes very effective use of doublets, as in this 1867 speech, which features an uninterrupted sequence of powerfully paired assertions:

> But *it is not so* in the Kingdom of God; *it is not so* with the law nor with the Priesthood of the Son of God.
>
> *You can* believe in one God, or in three gods, or in a thousand gods; *you can* worship the sun or the moon, or a stick or a stone, or anything you please.
>
> Are not all mankind *the workmanship of the hands* of God? And does he not control *the workmanship of His hands?*
>
> *They* have the privilege of worshiping *as they please. They* can do *as they please,* so long as they do not infringe upon the rights of their fellow-beings.
>
> *If they do* well they will receive their reward, and *if they do* ill they will receive the results of their works.[12]

Lines such as these are vintage Brigham. Undoubtedly much of his success as a communicator can be attributed not only to what he said, but how he said it.

Brigham Young's talks typically range over several subjects, often unrelated to each other, moving as the Spirit directed and responding specifically to the needs or attentiveness of his immediate audience. In most cases, his objective was to spur people on to action, to infuse them with enthusiasm and confidence, and to inspire them with an understanding of the immediate urgency and the eternal profundity of their thoughts and conduct. His driving desires that impelled his thoughts, words, and actions are capsulized in the concluding comments at the end of many of his speeches. The following is typical:

> I wish us to profit by what we hear, to learn how to live, to make ourselves comfortable, to purify ourselves, and prepare ourselves to inherit this earth when it is glorified, and go back in the presence of the Father and the Son. God bless you. Amen.[13]

Themes such as these usher the listener down some of the main hallways of Brigham Young's sermons: (1) how to live or how to form a good and righteous society, (2) how to make ourselves comfortable or how to properly utilize the untapped resources and talents given to us by the Lord, (3) how to purify ourselves or how to become clean and sanctified through the powers of the gospel and the priesthood of God, (4) how to prepare for the Millennium or how to lead the way for the Lord's reign on this earth, and (5) how to return to the presence of God and Christ in the celestial kingdom. If Brigham Young were to give his own description or overview of his teachings, these themes would probably be foremost on his list of key topics.

Subsumed beneath each of his main subjects and concerns were hundreds of more specific topics. Brigham Young's scope of interest was encyclopedic, ranging over and beyond even the wide domain of interests embraced by religion and natural theology in the nineteenth century. Major themes addressed at one time or another in his various discourses span the full spectrum of contrasting alternatives: from the mundane to the sublime, from daily tasks to eternal life; from industry to entertainment, ancient history to the last days, affliction to happiness, free agency to obedience; from study to revelation, theology to politics, and local domestic affairs to major national crises.

No one should take it on anyone else's authority what Brigham Young thought or said. Nothing would be more contrary to Brigham Young's own desire that everyone should stand spiritually and intellectually on his or her own two feet. As Hugh Nibley has argued, if we are to appreciate the practical wisdom as well as the rational coherence of Brigham Young's exhortations, "we must let him speak for himself."[14]

Fortunately for readers today, many of Brigham Young's sermons are readily available in print and on CD-ROM. These talks can be searched and read with considerable ease. Almost every page of his discourses yields practical wisdom, much of which still makes good common sense in a postmodern world because of Brigham's perceptiveness into the fundamental characteristics of human nature. For the most part, he spoke his mind openly, clearly, and frankly. Rarely is the precise meaning or intended application of his practical instructions or religious ideas in doubt.

A corpus of speeches as expansive and diffuse as the Brigham Young collection, however, can only be butchered and somewhat misrepresented by any single article or volume or limited approach that attempts to summarize or depict its full contents or character. Even the numerous quotations offered by Hugh Nibley on a few of the topics often addressed by Brigham Young are admittedly "only a tantalizingly small fraction of the Prophet's inspired and resounding utterances on the subject."[15]

The intent of the present paper is not to add to the literature another incomplete depiction of the monumental intellectual and spiritual achievements of Brigham Young. Any partial collection of "representative" statements by Brigham Young is, by its very nature, unrepresentative. We lay no claim to having made a comprehensive examination of each doctrine ever taught by Brigham Young, and we are wary of attempts to systematize or rationalize the prodigious mind and spontaneous tongue of Brigham Young. We will offer here, instead, a few comments on three previous attempts to take stock of the intellectual mettle of the Lion of the Lord, and then we will draw a few insights from a new inventory of the topics that he treated.

Over the years, the teachings of Brigham Young have been portrayed and discussed to some extent by several writers. We will focus here on the main treatments by John A. Widtsoe, Eugene E. Campbell, and Hugh W. Nibley. These studies, useful as they may be for their own purposes, nevertheless reflect as much the conceptual frameworks of their compilers as they tell of the personality and intentions of President Young.

A RATIONAL REFLECTION

John A. Widtsoe collected hundreds of short statements or segments out of the various sermons of Brigham Young in the *Journal of Discourses* and published these selections in a volume entitled *Discourses of Brigham Young* in 1954.[16] Elder Widtsoe divided these snatches of Brigham Young's thoughts into forty-two chapters or general categories, thereby attempting to give some type of rational order or thematic structure to some of the words of Brigham Young. None of the discourses is printed *in toto.*

While it is useful to have selected sayings from Brigham Young gathered and disseminated in this way, a study of the manner in which he summarized some of his own discourses would show that Brigham Young would not likely have organized his materials along the same lines. Widtsoe, a scientist living in an era of theological rationalism in the Church, was intent upon imposing a rational order on the teachings of Brigham Young.

While Widtsoe's selection and organization of the teachings of Brigham Young certainly feature many of his most important themes, Widtsoe began where his own interest was strongest—with eternal law, truth, a rational view of the gospel embracing all truth, and a practical everyday religion (chapter 1). He then went on to collect statements by Brigham on the Godhead, revelation, the plan of salvation, the premortal existence, agency, the power of evil, the law of eternal progression, the destiny of man, the dispensations of the gospel, and the last days (chapters 2–10). This organization of the gospel under these headings overlaps considerably with that of the first nine chapters of Widtsoe's *A Rational Theology,*[17] and the underlying methodology and resulting structures are similar to those in Widtsoe's *The Message of the Doctrine and Covenants.*[18]

Widtsoe then presented quotations from Brigham Young on certain Church-related or ecclesiastical topics—scriptures, priesthood, the first principles, Sabbath, meetings, sacrament, tithing, united order, Word of Wisdom (chapters 11–16); then he moved into social topics—family, women's duties, obedience, gratitude, humility, devotion, liberality, honesty, happiness, social enjoyment, education, self-control, fellowmen, unity and cooperation, thrift and industry, and wealth (chapters 17–27).

The intersection between Church and society in Widtsoe's early twentieth-century experience evidently led him next to discuss missionary work and the role of visions and miracles in the conversion process (chapters 28–29), followed by comments on trials, persecutions, and political government (chapters 30–31). Next, Widtsoe selected a number of statements dealing with the afterlife—death, resurrection, spirit world, eternal judgment, universal salvation, degrees of salvation, and the celestial kingdom (chapters 32–35), and in this context Widtsoe turned next to temple building, temple ordinances, and salvation for the dead (chapter 36).

Finally, Widtsoe returned to conclude with several chapters on one of his favorite themes: truth and the testimony of Mormonism. He collected here statements by Brigham Young regarding the search for truth, the testimony of the truth, the Church and kingdom of God on earth, the effects of the gospel as fruits of the truth, and the testimony of Joseph Smith (chapters 37–41). Widtsoe included a final chapter about the settlement of the West (chapter 42) as a testimony that the Saints should trust in the hand of God and not of man.

Our intent here is not to diminish or criticize Elder Widtsoe's work. Without this anthology, thousands of important comments by Brigham Young would have remained unknown and largely inaccessible to several generations of Latter-day Saints. And no doubt, Widtsoe's schematic selection appealed comfortably to his generation of Latter-day Saints in the mid-twentieth century. But be that as it may, Widtsoe still presented a portrait of Brigham Young painted primarily with the colors of that generation and in the style of John A. Widtsoe. One needs to delve further to recover a fuller view of the panorama of Brigham Young's thought.

FEATURING PARADOX

Another effort to communicate the real Brigham Young has been made by Eugene E. Campbell and his publishers in the pretentiously entitled volume, *The Essential Brigham Young.*[19] While admitting that "Young's expansive thought escapes easy definition,"[20] this publication nevertheless remains confident that the volume includes the "essential" and "most frequently cited sermons,"[21] but no explanation is given of the basis on which these twenty-five speeches were identified, selected, and sometimes truncated.

The editorial introductions in this book tend to examine Brigham Young in light of the interests of late twentieth-century America. For example, Campbell speaks of Brigham Young giving counsel "from his own experience, powers of observation, and reservoir of common sense,"[22] as if a modernist needs to make no effort to understand Brigham's spiritual attributes or inspiration. Similarly, Campbell's main interests include the few areas where Brigham Young's ideas were in tension with themselves, particularly his attitudes toward the federal government, women, blacks, Indians, and certain paradoxical aspects of his private life. Voguish allegations of inconsistency in Brigham's Indian policies, of misappropriation of Church funds, and of suspicion of the U.S. government bordering on paranoia[23] are not tempered here by deeper reflection on the historical context, by the hardships and circumstances involved, or by Brigham's full comments on these subjects. Well can the late twentieth-century reader note that Brigham Young never considered women equal to men,[24] but one should not ignore the many ways in which Brigham encouraged and supported women beyond the norms of his day.

While good history should represent a person, warts and all, it should not get so caught up in drawing attention to the warts (actual or imagined) that it forgets to give a full picture. Nor should the warts be mistaken for the essence.

The talks included in this book do not appear to have been chosen randomly, and they fail to give a fully balanced view of Brigham Young's doctrinal teachings. In contrast to Widtsoe's selections, these talks place eager emphasis on such infrequently mentioned or controversial topics as the Adam/God theory, the curse of Cain and the denial in Brigham Young's day of the priesthood to his descendants, isolationism of the Saints, the rebellion of Emma Smith, plural marriage, and examples of superseded opinions on scientific theories. All of these doctrines are either obscure points that receive little or no emphasis today or details that tend to be more sensational than substantial.

While this selection of talks reflects certain important teachings on God the Father, priesthood keys, and resurrection, this book omits nearly any reference to numerous topics such as the atonement of Christ, support of the United States Constitution, the Book of Mormon, the role of adversity in progression, the blessings of God on the Saints, education, freedom of religion, building Zion, love of neighbor, missionary work, sacrifice, self-sufficiency, and the final judgment of the world. Brigham Young spoke in depth about these kinds of faith-promoting subjects on many occasions.

LIBERATING A LION

Hugh W. Nibley also has written extensively on the mind and wisdom of Brigham Young. Nibley reads Brigham liberally and generously. A stimulating abstract of Nibley's reflections can be found in his article on the teachings of Brigham Young in the *Encyclopedia of Mormonism.*[25] Here Nibley emphasizes Brigham Young's faith in Jesus Christ, his indebtedness to Joseph Smith, and his emphasis on progression, work, caring for the world, enjoyment, thrift, and building the kingdom of Zion. This overview, substantiated by Nibley's longer expositions, draws out of Brigham's mouth primarily those themes and propositions that are the most compelling and attractive to Nibley's own mind, namely, concerns about the nature of existence, the environment, the misuse of power and wealth, and the neglect of education. Although this also is a highly interpretative approach, reading Nibley frees Brigham from obscurity and from the binding of old books.

In general, Nibley is concerned not only to make Brigham Young's teachings relevant to the modern world but also to rescue him from the critics who have dismissed his teachings because they appear to contain internal contradictions. For Nibley, Brigham Young said one thing on one occasion and something different in another setting because he understood the nature of this life only in terms of the next.[26] Thus, what might appear in his discourses to be the confusing of earthly concerns and spiritual matters is not the result of inconsistent thinking: "The distinction is not between the practical and the impractical; they are both practical and both spiritual; there is not difference in spiritual and temporal labors."[27]

Indeed, Brigham Young saw direct continuity and immediate relevance between this world and the next, between life as we know it here and as it will continue beyond the veil of death. In Nibley's view, Brigham Young based all of his teachings and world view on "that third dimension which makes the gospel."[28] Whereas most people see the world in two dimensions, Brigham Young lived in a three-dimensional world. This allowed him to transcend the present situation and move with confidence toward the eternal objective. Thus, he was not inconsistent in the fact that he did not like regimentation yet ordered the pioneers into companies; that he liked variety and difference yet built unity; that he encouraged everyone to be themselves yet exhorted them continually to strive for the establishment of Zion.

In "Brigham Young on the Environment,"[29] written shortly after Earth Day and the rise of environmental concerns in the early 1970s, Nibley featured statements by Brigham Young that celebrate the joy of the pure air of the mountain west, warn about pollution, and encourage the building of heaven here on earth (for heaven was the prototype of this earth). Brigham Young repeatedly taught that this earth is and will be our eternal home, that all things here are for our benefit and comfort, and that mankind has been charged to improve the world, beautify and tend the earth, plant gardens, and cultivate taste. Knowing that all the earth belongs to the Lord, mankind should act with restraint, avoid greed, and recognize that it is a high moral principle to honor God's creation.

Brigham Young, like Nibley, was not impressed with modern inventions, denied the right to property if the owner declined to use it to do good, and encouraged people to not worry about counting the costs of doing right, for God will provide as long as we avoid waste. In this regard, all waste is sin, for man cannot create; only a limited amount of property exists in the world, and thus we must avoid forest fires, show reverence for everything, and treat all life as holy. Accordingly, even the crickets are "creatures of God" and should be respected. All this implies that we may not take more than we need or use resources to obtain control over others. Indeed, Babylon is nothing other than seizing and selling the treasures of the earth beyond one's needs, and Zion is striving to love the world as God loves it.

How much of this is Brigham Young and how much is Hugh Nibley? (How much is Plato and how much is Socrates?) The two are difficult to separate. But for a modern reader of Nibley to conclude that Brigham Young was a modern liberal is, again, to see only part of the complex world of Brigham Young, for he was also an energetic industrialist, expansive colonizer, and political leader—but even then not as most people would understand those terms.

In "Brigham Young as a Statesman,"[30] written in the 1960s, Nibley drew heavily on Brigham Young's ideas about righteous and effective leadership, a rare commodity in the modern world. Here the good leader is one who knows by personal experience, who leads by doing, and who maintains a deep sense of responsibility, aloofness from the world, opposition to petty factionalism, bigotry, and unrealistic demands. Brigham Young encouraged people to control themselves, to support local government, to be forgiving, to take people as they are, and to sustain the Constitution and the liberties it guarantees. He taught that the only way to overcome persecution is to have the Spirit of the Lord, live at peace, treat every man as your brother, mind your own business, leave the enemy alone (war is futile and is instigated by wickedness), and affirm the brotherhood and equality of all men. Ultimately, the true statesman recognizes that people are responsible for their own afflictions because of their own wickedness, and that the more knowledgeable people are, the more accountable they become.

Similarly, in "Brigham Young and the Enemy,"[31] Nibley argued that Brigham Young knew how to deal with enemies, mainly by putting his faith in God and going on his way, for God is in control and enemies are actually for our good. He urged the Saints to search their own hearts, where the enemy really is, since Satan's only powers are to tear down, contaminate, mix truth with falsehood, and encourage such feelings as covetousness and greed. He encouraged the Church to avoid anger, bitterness, war, and contention. He found nothing worse than a Saint turned bad, but he told the faithful that they must not harbor vindictiveness or self-righteousness but let the Lord judge, for our own weaknesses and ignorance make judging futile. While finding no place for coercion, he pronounced scathing denunciations of businessmen and merchants who gathered power through wealth, and he advocated only spiritual solutions to our problems.

In "Brigham Young as a Leader,"[32] Nibley focused on Brigham Young's character and teachings relevant to the qualities that made him effective in inspiring, unifying, and reassuring the people who flocked to follow him: he was benevolent, practical, even-keeled, tolerant, charitable, self-directed, and inner-directed; he got things done but explained to people why they were doing them; he spoke from experience, was candid about the rebellious nature of his people, was firm but without compulsion, did not flatter anyone, dealt with people as individuals, abhorred regimentation, encouraged variety in all spheres of life, avoided stereotypes, exhorted people to do the best they could but not unless they wanted to, asserted his rights, saw God firmly in control, believed in being gentle ("light knocks can split great blocks"[33]), never showed emotion, corrected his mistakes, avoided contention, told people not to hurry and not to try to run things, and eschewed ambition; he promoted self-discipline, inspiration, and revelation; and he could not be moved because he knew exactly where he stood—all things that Nibley deeply admires.

In "Educating the Saints,"[34] Nibley again draws on Brigham Young to decry such flaws prevalent in academia as the showing off of titles, the tyranny of curriculum, and sophomoric pride. Education is a matter of eternal development, not just what is in it for a person here and now. Brigham spoke his mind openly, bound only by the gospel of Jesus Christ, and was able to "master the things of the world because he would not let them master him."[35] Joseph Smith brought heaven down to earth; we shall never cease to learn; the news is all good; gather up all the truths in the world pertaining to life and salvation; "improvement of the mind always came first";[36] study every art and science; think for oneself; and rebuke senseless applause. For Brigham "all science is cosmology" and "all cosmology is eschatology";[37] secular learning is sanctified if it is approached with a certain spirit, for "the object of this existence is to learn."[38] The expanding mind stands in contrast to the contracting mind, one diminished by fashion, kitsch, and riches. The cure for contraction is to be sent out into the wilderness, where "God will keep us after school until we learn our lesson."[39]

Finally, "More Brigham Young on Education"[40] develops these themes further, taking contemporary social trends as specific targets, juxtaposing "the wonder and the glory of the gospel against the background of a lost and distracted world."[41] Brigham Young's whole concern was to learn, and outside of the true religion he found nothing but death. Eternity in this sense begins here and now, and the curriculum is unlimited, embracing all truth, every useful branch of education; "all business must be undertaken with an eye to the eternities"[42] and to do good. Intelligence is problem solving that begins with an admission of ignorance and minding one's own business. In the style of Brigham Young, Nibley then applies these views to critique modern public relations ploys, "success," superficiality, overconfidence, double-mindedness, and kitsch, and to challenge the Saints who process knowledge without discovering it to speak out and declare the principles of the gospel, to open their books, and to present gospel alternatives to the reigning philosophies.

STRONG REFLEXES

Obviously, a teacher as broad and as deep as Brigham Young will continue to evoke strong reactions and diverse reflections from various quarters such as those represented by Widtsoe, Campbell, and Nibley. Accordingly, our objective has not been to add simply another refraction off this source of light and knowledge. Better, it seemed to us, to make an attempt at comprehending the whole. Clearly aware of the limitations of any such effort, we determined to digest as much as we could of the speeches of Brigham Young. Our hope was to determine the three or four main themes in each speech (numerous smaller themes could also be identified). By producing a composite listing of those dominant concepts in the discourses of Brigham Young, we hoped to identify the strongest reflexes in his typical teachings. This will provide, hopefully, a guide to the most important teachings of Brigham Young—points he would likely emphasize if we could hear him speak today, not tangential or marginal notes but his dominant messages. From such data, readers might go on to fashion a clearer comprehension of Brigham himself, not an image fashioned too heavily in our own likenesses.

The "Subject Index of Discourses of Brigham Young," below, is the result of our gathering.[43] Unless we found the contemporaneous headnotes contained in the *Journal of Discourses* to be inadequate, we tended to follow them in creating our index entries.[44] The results were somewhat surprising to us. Based on general impressions conveyed about Brigham Young from secondary sources, we expected to find more emphasis on the pragmatic, exotic, or eccentric. Instead, his main themes are religious, spiritual, and basic to the restored gospel of Jesus Christ. The vast majority of his most frequent and dominant topics (15 or more entries) were far and away theological:

God, Godhead (42)
Joseph Smith (32)
Gospel (32)
Knowledge (31)
Kingdom of God (30)
Temples (30)
Revelation (26)
Priesthood (25)
Mission, Missionaries (24)
Government (23)
Spirits (22)
Plural Marriage (21)
Religion (21)
Jesus Christ, Savior (20)
Spirit of God, Spirit of the Lord (20)
Testimony (20)
Zion (20)
Persecution (19)
Education, learning and schools (18)
Saints (18)
Blessings (18)
Apostasy, Apostates (17)
Faith (17)
Gathering (17)
Obedience (17)
Adam and Eve (16)
Salvation (16)
Tithing (16)

His next most prominent subjects (9–13 entries):

U.S. Constitution (13)
Apostles, Apostleship (13)
Prayer (13)
Truth (13)
Judgment (12)
Resurrection (12)
Spirit World (12)
Trials (12)
Women (12)
Unity (12)
Indians, Lamanites (11)
Poor, Poverty (11)

- Preaching (11)
- Agency and Choice (10)
- Duty (10)
- Evil (10)
- Happiness (10)
- Holy Ghost (10)
- Army, federal (9)
- Bishops (9)
- Children (9)
- Christianity (9)
- Freedom (9)
- Intelligence (9)
- Riches (9)
- Sacrament (9)
- Wickedness (9)

His other common themes (5–8 entries), arranged alphabetically:

- Baptism (8)
- Bible (5)
- Chastisement (8)
- Church (7)
- Counsel (6)
- Covetousness (7)
- Death (5)
- Debt (7)
- Earth (7)
- Endowment (8)
- Enemies (5)
- Eternal life and progression (7)
- Exaltation (5)
- Family (5)
- Fashions (6)
- Handcarts (5)
- Immigrants (7)
- Israel (6)
- Labor (5)
- Law (8)
- Life (8)
- Light (5)
- Marriage (8)
- Millennium (7)
- Miracles (5)
- Mormonism (7)
- Mothers (7)
- Mysteries (5)
- Opposition (8)
- Perpetual Emigrating Fund (5)
- Power (6)
- Property (5)
- Repentance (7)
- Sabbath (7)
- Sacrifice (7)
- Sealing (6)
- Self-control (5)
- Sin (6)
- Temporal affairs (8)
- Traditions (6)
- Wealth (5)
- Wisdom (7)
- Work (5)

Although this profile is not scientifically precise, it conveys at a glance a fair representation of most usual burdens of Brigham Young's teachings. To be sure, most of these themes are mentioned by Widtsoe, Campbell, and Nibley, but not always to the same degree or in the same configuration.

CONCLUDING REFLECTIONS

For years to come, the teachings of Brigham Young will surely continue to teach all people whose minds and spirits are amenable to firm counsel and principled instruction. His discourses contain something for everyone. They teach people what to believe about God, Jesus Christ, and Joseph Smith; how to become clean through the doctrines of the gospel and the powers and ordinances of the priesthood; how to live; how to form the society of Zion; how to withstand persecutions and difficulties to prepare for God's reign on earth and in heaven.

Each reader and each generation inevitably takes and remembers from the past what it wants to. What will the next generation of Saints and scholars find in the words and works of Brigham Young? How will it reflect the religious spirit of his thoughts and teachings?

NOTES

1. The premier biography of Brigham Young, emphasizing the economic and political features of his career, is Leonard Arrington, *Brigham Young, American Moses* (New York: Knopf, 1985). Other biographies, arranged chronologically, include Newell G. Bringhurst, *Brigham Young and the Expanding American Frontier* (Boston: Little Brown, 1986); Francis M. Gibbons, *Brigham Young: Modern Moses/Prophet of God* (Salt Lake City: Deseret Book Co., 1981); Eugene England, *Brother Brigham* (Salt Lake City: Bookcraft, 1980); Milton R. Hunter, *Brigham Young the Colonizer* (Santa Barbara, California: Peregrine Smith, 1973); Stanley P. Hirschon, *The Lion of the Lord: A Biography of Brigham Young* (New York: Knopf, 1969); Truman G. Madsen, ed., *Seminar on Brigham Young* (Provo, Utah: BYU Extension Publications, 1963); Clarissa Y. Spencer, *Brigham Young at Home* (Salt Lake City: Deseret News Press, 1947); Ray B. West, *Kingdom of the Saints: The Story of Brigham Young and the Mormons* (New York: Viking, 1957); Olive W. Burt, *Brigham Young* (New York: Messner, 1956); Preston Nibley, *Brigham Young: The Man and His Work* (Salt Lake City: Deseret Book Co., 1936); Susa Young Gates, with Leah D. Widtsoe, *The Life Story of Brigham Young* (New York: Macmillan, 1930); Morris R. Werner, *Brigham Young* (New York: Harcourt, Brace, and Co., 1925); Edward H. Anderson, *The Life of Brigham Young* (Salt Lake City: George Q. Cannon and Sons, 1893); Edward W. Tullidge, *Life of Brigham Young: Or Utah and Her Founders* (New York: n.p., 1876). Few of these books deal with Brigham Young's thought.
2. Preston Nibley, *Brigham Young: The Man and His Work* (Salt Lake City: Deseret Book Co., 1936), incorporates into its historical narrative excerpts from about twenty of Brigham's speeches, listed on pages 550–51; but most of these deal with construction projects, pioneers, practical affairs, and politics. James B.

Allen, *The Man—Brigham Young* (Provo, Utah: Brigham Young University Press, 1963), 32–38, touches on his general attitude toward religion, truth, knowledge, marriage, and the Sabbath.

3. J. Keith Melville, "Brigham Young's Ideal Society: The Kingdom of God," *BYU Studies* 5 (1963): 3–18; and "The Reflections of Brigham Young on the Nature of Man and the State," *BYU Studies* 4 (1962): 255–67.

4. Robert Miller, "Understanding Brigham Young: The Role of His Cosmology," unpublished paper, History of Science Colloquium, Johns Hopkins University, 1 May 1981, focuses on his teachings of uncreated matter, uncreated time and space, uncreated laws, and uncreated intelligence (8–27), and argues that any explanation of Brigham Young is misleading without attention to his cosmology (28). See also Boyd Kirkland, "Of Gods, Mortals, and Devils: Eternal Progression and the Second Death in the Theology of Brigham Young," *Sunstone* 10, no. 12 (1986): 6–12.

5. Carl J. Furr, *The Religious Philosophy of Brigham Young*, private ed. (Chicago: University of Chicago Libraries, 1939), 8 pp., mentions briefly temporal salvation, conception of God, system of Church government, beings, good and evil, nature of man, death, free agency, and various aspects of his philosophy of life.

6. Elden J. Watson, comp., *Brigham Young Addresses*, 6 vols. (n.p., 1979), lists virtually all of the known speeches said to be delivered by Brigham Young. Some are reported only by a brief statement from a journal or newspaper entry; others are represented by a reasonably long summary.

7. *Journal of Discourses*, 5: 336.

8. Ibid., 6: 145.

9. Ibid., 6: 195.

10. Ibid., 12: 115.

11. Ibid., 12: 116.

12. Ibid., 12: 114.

13. Ibid., 12: 116.

14. Hugh W. Nibley, "Educating the Saints," in *Brother Brigham Challenges the Saints*, ed. Don E. Norton and Shirley S. Ricks, volume 13 in *The Collected Works of Hugh Nibley* (Salt Lake City: Deseret Book Co., and F.A.R.M.S., 1994), 308 (hereafter this volume will be cited as CWHN, 13).

15. CWHN, 13: 308.

16. John A. Widtsoe, ed., *Discourses of Brigham Young* (Salt Lake City: The Church of Jesus Christ of Latter-day Saints, 1954; reprinted by Deseret Book Co., 1978).

17. John A. Widtsoe, *A Rational Theology* (Salt Lake City: Deseret Book Co., 1915). This book begins with the fundamentals of eternity, truth, the law of development, God, man's premortal existence and free agency, and the plan of salvation.

18. John A. Widtsoe, *The Message of the Doctrine and Covenants* (Salt Lake City: Bookcraft, 1969). Several of the chapters in this book compare, probably

unconsciously, with the categories used in arranging topics from Brigham Young's discourses; see, for example, the emphasis on truth, last days, persecution, law and civil government, social and family relations, salvation, and temple work.

19. Brigham Young, *The Essential Brigham Young,* foreword by Eugene E. Campbell (Salt Lake City: Signature Books, 1992). The editors do not indicate who made the selections or how they determined which they considered to be Brigham's "most frequently cited sermons."
20. Ibid., xi.
21. Ibid., xvi.
22. Ibid., xxviii.
23. Ibid., xxi–xxiii.
24. Ibid., xxvi.
25. Hugh W. Nibley, "Teachings of Brigham Young," *Encyclopedia of Mormonism,* ed. Daniel H. Ludlow, 5 vols. (New York: Macmillan, 1992), 4: 1609–11.
26. CWHN, 13: 309.
27. Ibid., 13: 352.
28. Ibid., 13: 179.
29. Ibid., 13: 23–54.
30. Ibid., 13: 138–86.
31. Ibid., 13: 187–246.
32. Ibid., 13: 449–90.
33. Ibid., 13: 464.
34. Ibid., 13: 306–45.
35. Ibid., 13: 310.
36. Ibid., 13: 318.
37. Ibid., 13: 325.
38. Ibid., 13: 327.
39. Ibid., 13: 340.
40. Ibid., 13: 346–79.
41. Ibid., 13: 346.
42. Ibid., 13: 353.
43. We express appreciation to Daniel B. McKinlay for his help in indexing some of the speeches of Brigham Young found in the LDS Church Historical Archives and in the collections of Elden J. Watson; and to Marny Parkin, Angela Ashurst-McGee, and others at *BYU Studies,* Brigham Young University, for their editorial assistance in formatting and proofreading this index.
44. We tried to identify the two or three main themes in each speech by Brigham Young, not to create a comprehensive index.

SUBJECT INDEX OF DISCOURSES OF BRIGHAM YOUNG

Unless otherwise indicated, all references are to the *Journal of Discourses* (1853–1886).

Other references included in this index are the following:

DBY	*Discourses of Brigham Young*, sel. John A. Widtsoe (Salt Lake City: Deseret Book Co., 1978)
CHD	Church Historical Department, ms d1234, boxes 48 and 49
CHD pam	Church Historical Department Pamphlet, no title, March 21, 1858
DCLW	Diary of Charles Lowell Walker, Utah State Historical Society
DNW	*Deseret News Weekly* (1850–1898)
HC	*History of the Church of Jesus Christ of Latter-day Saints*, ed. B. H. Roberts, 7 vols., 2nd ed. (Salt Lake City: Deseret Book Co., 1963)
HCKJ	Heber C. Kimball Journal, LDS Church Historical Archives
IE	*Improvement Era* (1897–1970)
ISP	Inauguration of Salt Lake City School of the Prophets, 2 December 1867
MS	*Millennial Star* (1840–1970)
SRBB	Seventies Record Book B, LDS Church Historical Archives
T&S	*Times and Seasons* (1839–1846)
UGHM	*Utah Genealogical and Historical Magazine* (1910–1940)
UHQ	*Utah Historical Quarterly*
WCJ	William Clayton Journal, LDS Church Historical Archives
WWJ	Wilford Woodruff Journal, LDS Church Historical Archives
YWJ	*Young Woman's Journal* (1889–1929)

Brigham Young (1801–1877), ca. 1845, in the City of Joseph (Nauvoo).

(Left) Brigham Young, ca. 1847–1850

(Bottom) Brigham Young and wife Margaret Pierce Young, ca. 1851.

(Right) Brigham Young, ca. 1858.

(Left) Brigham Young, ca. 1861.

(Bottom left) Brigham Young, ca. 1865–1868.

(Bottom right) Brigham Young, ca. 1866–1867.

(Right) Brigham Young, ca. 1869–1871.

(Top) Brigham Young, 1 June 1876.

(Left) Brigham Young, ca. 1876–1877. Brigham Young's death occurred on 29 August 1877.

INDEX

Note: Page numbers in italic type indicate a photograph or illustration; page numbers in bold type indicate a table, chart, or map